Applied Introduction to Cryptography and Cybersecurity

Applied Introduction to Cryptography and Cybersecurity

Amir Herzberg
University of Connecticut, USA

World Scientific

NEW JERSEY • LONDON • SINGAPORE • GENEVA • BEIJING • SHANGHAI • TAIPEI • CHENNAI

Published by

World Scientific Publishing Co. Pte. Ltd.
5 Toh Tuck Link, Singapore 596224
USA office: 27 Warren Street, Suite 401-402, Hackensack, NJ 07601
UK office: 57 Shelton Street, Covent Garden, London WC2H 9HE

Library of Congress Control Number: 2026937821

British Library Cataloguing-in-Publication Data
A catalogue record for this book is available from the British Library.

APPLIED INTRODUCTION TO CRYPTOGRAPHY AND CYBERSECURITY

ISBN 978-981-12-9910-0 (hardcover)
ISBN 978-981-98-0077-3 (paperback)
ISBN 978-981-12-9911-7 (ebook for institutions)
ISBN 978-981-12-9912-4 (ebook for individuals)

For any available supplementary material, please visit
https://www.worldscientific.com/worldscibooks/10.1142/14014#t=suppl

Desk Editors: Kannan Krishnan/Amanda Yun

Typeset by Stallion Press
Email: enquiries@stallionpress.com

Printed in Singapore

Preface

Cybersecurity is an important and broad area, including many aspects, technical as well as legal, economics, social and others. The technical aspects include cryptography, network-security, software security, system security, privacy, secure human–computer interaction and more. This book focuses on *applied cryptography*, although we also discuss a few of the cryptography-related aspects of network security, secure human–computer interaction, software security and system security. We believe that this focus on cryptography is a good way to introduce cybersecurity, for three reasons:

- Applied cryptography is essential to many areas of cybersecurity. Hence, this book may provide a common basis for students interested in these different areas. Some students may continue by focusing mostly on cryptography; for these, our goal is to provide a good basis in the applied aspects of cryptography. Other students may continue by focusing on other technical aspects of cybersecurity, such as network security, secure systems, privacy and human-centered security. All of these areas apply cryptography, and our goal is that this book will provide the necessary background in cryptography.
- The study of cryptography develops *adversarial thinking*, which is critical for *every* cybersecurity expert. Modern cryptography is based on precise definitions of goals and assumptions, with analysis and proofs of security for given *adversary capabilities*, not assuming a specific *adversary strategy* or attack method. Other areas of cybersecurity often use intuitive goals, design and analysis, and

may even focus on specific adversary strategies. Such approaches may be unavoidable since precise definitions and proofs are sometimes infeasible; however, these approaches appear less helpful in developing adversarial thinking.

- Finally, there is the pragmatic consideration of *scheduling* and *prerequisites.* Modern cryptography is based on both mathematics and on the theory of computing; however, as we believe you will find, we found it possible to use only a limited amount of math and theory. We introduce this limited amount of background within this book, mostly in the appendix. As a result, the text can be used by readers who did not learn previous math or computer-science courses, beyond what is learned in many high-school programs. This is in contrast to other areas of cybersecurity, which require considerable background (e.g., in networking, operating systems or programming).

The need for security against attackers with arbitrary strategies, restricted only by their capabilities, motivates the use of *provable security*, as well as the use of *standard, well-studied designs*, whose security was confirmed by experts. Indeed, some of the worst failures of security systems, and especially of cryptographic systems, are due to attempts by non-experts to design schemes and protocols.

This book tries to combine *practice* with *theory*, *applicability* with *precision*, *breadth* with *depth.* These are ambitious goals, and we hope we are not completely off the mark. Feedback and suggestions for improvement are highly appreciated.

Organization and usage of this book

This book is designed for a yearly introductory course to cybersecurity and applied cryptography, with emphasis on practical aspects and applications; the course can proceed in the order of the chapters in this book. The first term may focus on basic cryptography (signatures, encryption, hashing, message authentication, public key and post-quantum cryptography). The second term may focus on cryptographic systems: authentication protocols, TLS, PKI and human-centered security.

Chapter 1 introduces cryptography, providing intuitive discussion of the main mechanisms we discuss, and introducing the challenge of defining security, by defining security of signature schemes. It also introduces notations used throughout this book and provides the most essential background information, referring to Appendix A for additional background. The introduction also provides a brief historical perspective, which we hope some readers may find of interest.

In the following three chapters, we present the basic cryptographic schemes of shared-key encryption (Chapter 2), hashing (Chapter 3) and message authentication (Chapter 4). In Chapter 3, we also discuss other integrity mechanisms which are based on hashing, including *blockchains* and *accumulators*, specifically *Merkle trees*. Most of Chapter 4 does not depend on Chapter 3 and, therefore, may be covered/read before Chapter 3.

Chapter 5 introduces applied shared-key cryptographic protocols. We cover few practical protocols and their vulnerabilities, most significantly, GSM, and discuss important networking considerations, such as delays, time-outs, retransmissions, synchronization, the client–server model and more. By focusing on shared-key protocols, we also provide a gentle introduction to the important subject of *resiliency to key-exposure*, which motivates public-key cryptography, the topic of the following chapter (Chapter 6).

Chapter 6 deals extensively with different public-key protocols and applications and shows the powerful ability to use public-key cryptography to ensure resiliency to, and recovery from, key exposure. We also discuss applications, such as public key certificates and secure boot.

Two chapters introduce cryptographic aspects of *network security*: the important TLS protocol in Chapter 7 and Public Key Infrastructure (PKI) in Chapter 8.

Chapter 9 covers the topic of *human-centered cryptography and cybersecurity*. Too often, this critical aspect is not sufficiently taken in account, and cryptography is circumvented by exploiting human behavior and psychology.

We conclude this book in Chapter 10, briefly discussing some advanced topics that are beyond this text. The main topic in Chapter 10 is a brief, insufficient discussion of the wide and important topic of *quantum computing* and its impact on the security of cryptographic schemes, including both *quantum cryptography*, i.e., attacks using quantum computers against cryptographic algorithms, and *post-quantum cryptography*, i.e., the design of cryptographic schemes that are expected to remain secure even when attackers can use powerful quantum computers. Much of this text was kindly provided by Prof. Walter Krawec, an expert in this area; any mistakes are probably due to my efforts to further expand his text.

The use of background such as math and theory in this book is limited to what appears to be essential or helpful for understanding, at least for a significant fraction of readers. Some of this background is covered in Appendix A.

Study of this book may be followed by study of other areas in cybersecurity or by in-depth study of cryptography. There are multiple excellent in-depth textbooks on cryptography or specific cryptographic topics; some of my favorites are Refs. [23, 209, 210, 253, 392, 456].

Programming labs

Programming is a great way to learn and better understand cryptographic designs, challenges and attacks. This book contains several programming labs, which provide such hands-on experience. A list of the labs is provided right after this preface.

These labs, and possibly additional labs related to the topics we cover, are available in https://github.com/CyberSec-labs/labs. Dustin Binalla, Justin Furuness and Damon James have provided huge help in preparing, testing and improving the labs.

You will find in https://github.com/CyberSec-labs/labs a file containing Python scripts for generating each lab and evaluating its results, allowing self-study as well as automated grading. The scripts also provide examples of how to use the cryptographic functions. The lab-generation script generates random challenges for each student (or team), as well as solutions which will be used by the grading script. Professors and other readers are welcome to modify these scripts for their particular needs, e.g., to support other programming languages or libraries.

On the use of gendered names and charged terms

I wish to apologize for possible offense that some readers may take in the use, throughout this book, of gendered names and charged terms.

The examples and figures sometimes use gendered characters such as Alice, Bob and Eve, with the corresponding pronouns she, he and they. The reason is that the use of a different pronoun makes it easier to identify the entity associated with a particular message or object. These names and the use of pronouns is common in cryptographic literature and dates back to the early papers, in particular [419].

Readers may also be offended by our use of several charged terms, including terms which the ACM has recommended to avoid (see https://www.acm.org/diversity-inclusion/words-matter). The terms include blacklist, whitelist and blackbox. This author believes that at the current time, these terms will be clearer to readers compared to the replacement terms recommended by the ACM, and therefore preferred to retain these terms. Language often retains terms, words and expressions long beyond the reason they were coined.

Acknowledgments

I received a lot of help in developing this book from friends, colleagues and students; I am very grateful. Specific thanks to the following:

- The students and my peers in the University of Connecticut, who have been very understanding and supportive.
- Sara Wrótniak, my Ph.D. student, who gave me incredible feedback when she studied using this book as an undergrad and later when I asked her to review the text further.
- Professors and researchers who provided valuable feedback, with or without teaching a course using the book, including the following: Ghada Almashaqbeh, Nimrod Aviram, Ahmed El-Yahyaoui, Peter Gutmann, John Heslen, Walter Krawec, Laurent Michel, David Pointcheval, Ivan Pryvalov, Zhiyun Qian, Amir and Luba Sapir, Jerry Shi, Haya Shulman, Ewa Syta and Ari Trachtenberg. I am especially indebted to Walter, who has also kindly contributed (the initial version of) the text on quantum cryptography in Chapter 10. Special thanks to my friends Hugo Krawczyk and Moti Yung, who have each reviewed the book and provided excellent comments and reviews.
- Instructors and teaching assistants who used the text and provided important feedback, including Ali Arastehfard, Justin Furuness,

Hemi Liebowiz, Sam Markelon and Anna Mendonca. I'm especially indebted to Anna for collecting excellent feedback from her students — and for introducing me to Sara.
- Dustin Binalla, Justin Furuness and Damon James have provided huge help in preparing and testing the labs (https://github.com/CyberSec-labs/labs).
- Other readers who helped with feedback, corrections and suggestions, including Pierre Abbat, Bar Meyuchas, Raha Motaqy, Yanjing Xu and Yike (Nicole) Zhang.
- The Latex and Tikz communities, who provided amazing resources and support. Special thanks to Nils Fleischhacker for the cool 'tikz people' package and to Shaanan Cohney who kindly sent me the LaTeX source code from Ref. [127], which I turned into Figure 2.38.

I probably forgot to mention some important contributors; accept my apologies and let me know. Indeed, in general, let me know of any omission or mistake in the text and accept my thanks in advance. Feedback is greatly appreciated, definitely including harsh criticism.

This work was partially based on support for my research from the National Science Foundation, including grants 2247810, 2410268 and 2149765, and by my endowment from Comcast.

Special thanks to my friend, PhD adviser and mentor, Prof. Oded Goldreich, who endured the challenge of trying to teach me both cryptography and proper writing. I surely cannot meet Oded's high standards, but I believe and hope that this book does help provide the necessary foundations of applied cryptography to practitioners of cybersecurity. Laying foundations is definitely a goal I definitely share with Oded. Let me quote Oded's father:

> It is possible to build a cabin with no foundations, but not a lasting building.
> *Eng. Isidor Goldreich*

Last but not least, I wish to thank the incredible support and understanding of my family throughout the years, especially my amazing parents, Ada and Michael, my lovely and supportive wife Tatiana Noa, and my wonderful and talented children, Raaz, Tamir, Omri and Karina.

Amir Herzberg
April 2026

About the Author

Amir Herzberg is the Comcast professor for Cybersecurity Innovation in the School of Computing at the University of Connecticut. His research areas include Internet security, applied cryptography, privacy and anonymity, human-centered security, security for cyber-physical systems, and social, economic and legal aspects of security.

Dr. Herzberg earned his Ph.D. in Computer Science in 1991 from the Technion in Israel. From 1991 to 1995, he worked at the IBM T.J. Watson Research Center, where he was a research staff member and the manager of the Network Security research group. From 1996 to 2000, Dr. Herzberg was a research group manager at the IBM Haifa Research Lab. From 2002 to 2017, he was a professor at Bar Ilan University (Israel). Since 2017, he has been a professor at the University of Connecticut.

Dr. Herzberg is the author of numerous papers and patents in different areas of cybersecurity and of the book *Applied Introduction to Cybersecurity and Cryptography.* Dr. Herzberg is an associate editor of ACM TOPS and serves on the steering board of CANS. Previously, he served as a program chair for IEEE CNS'19 and as an editor of PoPETS and ACM TISSEC. He delivered multiple keynotes and tutorials and served on the program committee of different conferences. Dr. Herzberg is a recipient of the Internet Society's Applied Networking Research award, 2017.

Contents

List of Labs

List of Labs

List of Figures

List of Tables

List of Principles

Chapter 1

Introducing Cybersecurity and Cryptography

Cybersecurity and cryptography are exciting topics, with rich history and with an extensive impact on the practical world, as well as fascinating challenges of engineering, theory and mathematics. The goal of this book is to introduce cybersecurity, focusing on the area of *applied cryptography*, which is essential to most or all areas of cybersecurity. We believe that this basic knowledge in applied cryptography is desirable for any student of computer science, but especially for students interested in cybersecurity or cryptography.

This chapter provides several sections with important foundations to the rest of this book. Section 1.1 is a very high-level introduction to cybersecurity and cryptography, with few basic concepts. Section 1.2 provides an informal introduction to three basic cryptographic mechanisms: *encryption*, *signatures* and *collision-resistant hash functions*. Section 1.3 introduces notations used throughout this book, including *sequence diagrams* which illustrate the operation of cryptographic protocols as well as attacks on cryptographic systems. Section 1.4 provides essential *background and notation*, used throughout the text; additional background is provided in Appendix A. In Section 1.5, we discuss the challenge of *defining security* of cryptographic schemes, focusing on the important definition of security for signature schemes. Finally, Section 1.6 provides a few gems from the fascinating history of *cryptography* and *cybersecurity*, which may provide an interesting perspective.

1.1 Cybersecurity and cryptography: few basic concepts

The high-level goal of cybersecurity is to protect 'good' parties, who use computing and communicating systems legitimately, from damages due to *misbehaving* entities, to whom we usually refer as *attackers* (or *adversaries*), who abuse the systems to harm the users and/or to obtain an unfair advantage or benefit. Attackers could be rogue authorized users, often referred to as *insiders*, or *outsiders*, who only have some access to the systems or the communication, and are not authorized users. Attackers may also control one or multiple devices. Such devices may be legitimately owned by the attacker, or be *corrupted*, i.e., controlled by the attacker in spite of not being legitimately owned by the attackers; corrupted devices are often referred to as being *pwned*[1] by the attacker.

Unfortunately, it is not so easy to turn this high-level goal into precise *definitions of security*, allowing evaluation of the security of different systems and defenses. It is also challenging to design schemes that satisfy these definitions and to *prove* their security. In this section, we discuss the main approaches to ensure and define security. But first, in Section 1.1.1, we introduce the three *cybersecurity defense pillars:* prevention, detection and deterrence.

1.1.1 The cybersecurity defense pillars: prevention, detection and deterrence

Figure 1.1 illustrates the *three cybersecurity defense pillars*, i.e., basic ways of protecting against attackers: *prevention*, *detection* and *deterrence*.

Prevention: By *prevention* we refer to mechanisms that *prevent* an attacker from causing damage or that reduce the amount of possible damage. *Encryption* is an example of a cryptographic prevention

[1]The verb 'pwn' means to control or 'own' a computing system illegitimately, by exploiting a vulnerability. The verb 'pwn' is taken from gamers slang, where it was originally used for a player which is completely dominated by an opponent; its origin may come from chess and combine the chess 'pawn' with the verb 'own'. See Ref. [393].

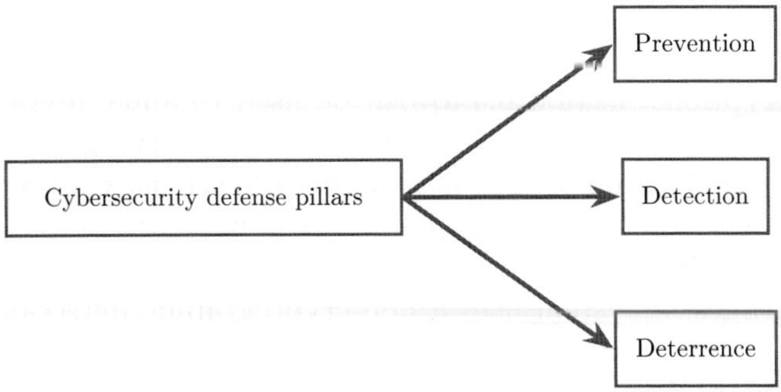

Figure 1.1. Cybersecurity defense pillars: prevention, detection and deterrence.

mechanism; it is usually used to *prevent* an attacker from disclosing sensitive information. When possible, prevention is obviously the best defense — 'an ounce of prevention is worth a pound of cure'. However, sometimes it is impossible to completely prevent an attack. For example, the TLS protocol (Chapter 7) relies on *public key certificates* issued and signed by a trusted party, called a certificate authority (CA); attacks due to a misbehaving CA cannot be completely prevented. Instead, such attacks are mitigated using detection mechanisms — and deterrence, with significant penalties for misbehaving CAs, as we discuss in Chapter 8. Even when a cryptographic mechanism seems to completely prevent an attack, e.g., when using encryption, it is still prudent to also deploy detection mechanisms since hidden, subtle vulnerabilities may exist even in thoroughly reviewed designs and systems.

Detection: By *detection* we refer to security mechanisms that *detect* an attack, usually while the attack is ongoing. Detection mechanisms are very important for ensuring security. First, detection is required to penalize attackers; *effective detection is necessary for effective deterrence.* Second, detection allows *reaction*, such as invoking additional defense mechanisms to foil attacks and performing operations to recover security and minimize damages. Therefore, security systems often invest a lot in *detection*, while attackers usually do their best to *avoid detection*, including refraining from attacks and actions that may result in detection.

Attack detection is a major component of widely deployed network-security and host-security defenses, such as an intrusion detection systems (IDS) and a honeypots [336, 341]. Detection systems sometimes make use of cryptography; for example, homomorphic encryption (Section 6.4.3) can be used to allow users to share information with the detection system while preserving the user's privacy; see also Section 9.4.5, where we discuss the use of cryptography to allow users to check if their passwords were compromised, without disclosing their passwords.

Sometimes, a system uses a non-cryptographic detection mechanism to distinguish between random errors and intentional attacks. In particular, message authentication code (MAC) schemes are often used to ensure the authenticity of messages, by detecting any modification to the message. By applying an error detection code (EDC) to the authenticated message, we can distinguish between an intentional modification (an attempt to circumvent the MAC scheme) and an unintentional modification (due to noise or error). We discuss MAC schemes in Chapter 4, and the combination of MAC and EDC in Section 4.5.5 (see illustration in Figure 4.4).

Deterrence: By *deterrence* we refer to mechanisms designed to discourage (deter) attackers from attacking. Deterrence is achieved either by the (visible) use of strong defenses, making it futile to attack, or by *penalizing* misbehaving entities. Penalizing requires *attribution* of the attack or misbehavior to the correct entity.

Signature schemes are of the most important cryptographic deterrence mechanisms. We discuss signature schemes later in this chapter (Section 1.2.4) and, in more details, in Chapters 4 and 6. A signature verified using the misbehaving party's well-known *public key*, over a given message, provides evidence that this party signed that message; we refer to such evidence of abuse as *Proof of Misbehavior*. The PoM can be used to punish or penalize the misbehaving party in different ways; this deters entities from abuse which could result in PoM and then a punishment or a penalty.

Deterrence is effective if the adversary is *rational* and would refrain from attacking if her expected profit (from attack) would be less than the expected penalty. In practice, most attackers *are* rational; hence, good deterrence is an effective defense. This introduces two challenges. First, some attackers are *not* rational and will not be deterred. Second, rational attackers will do their best to *avoid being detected*, in which case, they will not be penalized; for deterrence to be effective, it should be enforced by *effective detection* — and *sufficient penalties*.

1.1.2 Generic security goals

Different systems and schemes often have different security goals; however, some goals are *generic* and apply, possibly with some variations on details, to many systems and schemes. The generic goals, illustrated in Figure 1.2, include *confidentiality*, *integrity*, *availability*, *authentication* and *accountability*; we consider *non-repudiation* as a sub-goal of both authentication and accountability. Three of these goals, usually *confidentiality*, *integrity* and *availability*,[2] are referred to as the *CIA triad*, an easily memorable acronym.

Confidentiality: A system satisfies the *confidentiality* goal if it prevents an attacker from disclosing some information defined as *confidential*. The 'classical' confidentiality mechanism is *encryption*, illustrated in Figure 1.4, with two main variants: *shared key cryptosystems*, also referred to as symmetric encryption, and *public key cryptosystems*, also referred to as asymmetric encryption. We briefly discuss encryption in the following; we discuss encryption more extensively in Chapter 2 and the design of public key cryptosystem (PKCs) in Chapter 6.

Integrity: Ensuring integrity means prevention or detection of unauthorized operations, such as the modification of data. Integrity is applied to a wide range of situations, including the integrity of a computer system, information stored or transmitted, and more. We cover several cryptographic integrity mechanisms in Chapter 3, including *cryptographic hash functions*, *Merkle trees* and *blockchains*. See also Section 1.2.3, where we briefly introduce collision-resistant hash functions.

Authentication, accountability and non-repudiation: The goal of *authentication* is to verify that a particular information was originated from a specific entity (*message authentication*) or that a

[2]Sometimes, the *authentication* and/or *accountability* goals are included in the acronym, instead of or in addition to availability. *CIA* is a nice acronym; the longer versions (CIAA or CIAAA) are less popular. Maybe CIA^3 would do?

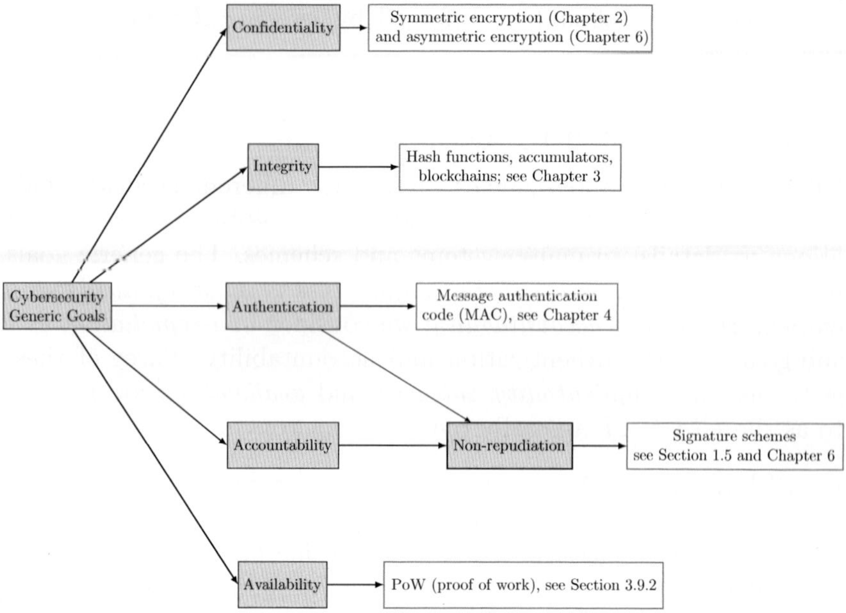

Figure 1.2. The generic security goals: *confidentiality, integrity, availability, accountability* and *authentication. Non-repudiation* is a sub-goal of both *accountability* and *authentication.* The *confidentiality, integrity* and *availability* goals are often referred to as the *CIA triad*; sometimes, *authentication* or *accountability* are used instead of, or in addition to, *availability.* For each goal, we list some of the corresponding cryptographic mechanisms covered in this book.

particular interaction involved a specific entity (*entity authentication*). The goal of *accountability* is to ensure that the entity responsible to an attack or other failure can be identified and made accountable, thereby ensuring *deterrence.* A sub-goal of both authentication and accountability is *non-repudiation*, which provides an *evidence* of the origin of information; such evidence can be presented, later, to a third party, to 'prove' the identity of the origin of the information (often, the accountable entity). The main cryptographic schemes to ensure authentication are *signature schemes*, which provides authentication, accountability and non-repudiation, and *message authentication code (MAC) schemes*, which only provide authentication. We discuss signature schemes later in this chapter and constructions of signature schemes in Chapters 3 and 6. See also Lab 1 where we discuss the important application of collision-resistant hash functions and signature schemes to ensure software integrity and authenticity, as a main defense against malware.

Availability: Availability mechanisms ensure that services can be provided efficiently, even if an attacker tries to disrupt services, in what is called a *Denial of Service (DoS) attack.* DoS attacks have become a major concern for network and service providers, and defenses against them are a major challenge of network security; DoS attacks, and defenses against them, are less relevant to cryptography.

Bespoke security goals: Most cybersecurity systems and cryptographic schemes have specific, bespoke security goals, often in addition to (variants of) the generic security goals. We see this in few definitions we present for the security requirements of different cryptographic schemes.

1.1.3 Attack model

Security goals should be defined and evaluated with respect to the *capabilities* of the attackers rather than by assuming a specific attacker *strategies.* This is an important principle of modern cryptology, which already appears in early publications, such as the seminal paper of Diffie and Hellman [155]: understand and define a clear model of the *attacker capabilities* (attack model) and then define the security goals — against attackers with the specified capabilities, regardless of the attacker's strategy (choices). This principle applies not only to cryptography, but also to security in general. Precise articulation of the *attack model* and of the *security requirements* is fundamental to the design and analysis of security. Let us re-state this important principle.

Principle 1 (Attack model principle: assume capabilities, not strategy). *Security should be analyzed with respect to a well-defined* attack model*, which specifies any restrictions of the* capabilities *of the attacker. The attack model should not restrict the attacker's* strategy*, only the attacker's* capabilities.

We discuss several attack models in this textbook and few of them already in this chapter. For example, we discuss several attack models for signature schemes, including the (weak) *key-only attack* (KOA) model and the (stronger) *chosen-message attack* (CMA) model. In the KOA model, the attacker is only given the public signature-verification key, while in the CMA model, the attacker can also receive signatures for arbitrary messages of its choosing. Note that both models only refer to the *capabilities* of the attacker and not to any specific attack strategy or to the security requirements. We discuss the security requirements of signature schemes separately, in Section 1.5.8, and we discuss attack strategies only when we discuss a specific attack.

The attack model principle applies also to areas of cybersecurity where it is harder to define a rigorous attack model. Even in such scenarios, it is important to limit our assumptions to the attacker capabilities rather than assuming a specific attacker strategy. However, where possible, a well-defined attack model, allowing *provable security*, is better — if this is done 'correctly', as we discuss in the following.

1.1.4 Provable security

In most areas of science and engineering, design and evaluation are based on experimental analysis, measuring the expected outcomes of the system under *typical* scenarios. In contrast, security should be ensured against an *adversary* (attacker) who is not bound to behave in some typical way; new attacks may be very different from past attacks. Observing the behavior of adversaries and designing defenses based solely on these behaviors may leave subtle or even gaping vulnerabilities that can be exploited by adversaries. That said, when a history of previous attacks is available and shows a clear pattern, it does make sense to evaluate defenses against the same type of attacks — *in addition* to evaluation against arbitrary attacker strategy, as per Principle 1.

It is challenging to ensure security against an arbitrary attacker strategy, only limiting the attacker's capabilities. There are many subtle ways in which intuition and imprecise arguments may fail, resulting in vulnerabilities. Cryptography and security are exceptions to the popular saying *'in theory there is no difference between theory and practice, while in practice there is'* [105]. In fact, in security, and especially in cryptography, precise definitions and proofs of security, or at least extensive, clear analysis, are highly desirable, to ensure that a system is secure against *arbitrary* attacker strategies. This approach is usually referred to as *provable security*.

That said, one has to be very careful *to understand the limitations and pitfalls of proofs*. This is discussed in a series of papers by Koblitz and Menezes, summarized in Ref. [298]. Proofs of security often involve simplifications and assumptions; in fact, analysis is often based on simplifying 'assumptions' *known to be incorrect*. An important example of such simplification is the *random oracle model* (ROM), discussed in Section 3.6. Using the ROM, a protocol using a specific cryptographic hash function, e.g., SHA-1, is analyzed as if the function used was selected at random. Clearly, this is not a correct assumption, yet, a proof using such assumption gives *some* indication of security or, at least, limits the possible types of attacks.

Simplifications can result in a system which has a proof of security — leading people to trust its security — however, in reality, this system is vulnerable and exploited. One reason this happens is that proofs are based on models of the attacker capabilities and of the system, which often do not fully capture reality; attackers often cleverly abuse and exploit exactly these aspects which were glossed-over and abstracted away. Furthermore, efforts to consider more realistic aspects tend to make analysis, proofs and provably secure designs, harder and more complicated. As a result, even for an expert, proofs may be challenging and require extensive effort — to write and to verify. Complex proofs may have subtle errors, which may remain undiscovered for years. *Proofs should be clean and enlightening, while reality is dirty and murky, and viruses, bugs, and vulnerabilities thrive in the dirt and the dark.*

Another challenge for provable security is to correctly identify and clearly, preferably rigorously, define the *security requirements (goals)*. This holds for cryptographic schemes and also to secure systems in general. Rigorous definitions of security requirements are often challenging — to define and to understand. However, clear definitions of security requirements are important, for several reasons:

1. A precise definition is necessary to allow precise analysis of security.

2. A precise definition allows researchers to investigate and publish attacks showing that requirements are *not* met. Even attacks whose practical significance may not be clear, have repeatedly proved beneficial in improving the designs and have often provided the basis for practical attacks.
3. A clear definition helps ensure correct use of the system or scheme, design secure applications using the system or scheme, avoiding vulnerabilities due to incorrect use of the scheme or assuming that the scheme ensures properties that it was not claimed to provide. Precise definitions are essential to analyze the security of applications which use the scheme.

The last item is worth extra attention; incorrect usage is a common reason for cryptography-related vulnerabilities, and the exploits are often devastating. In this book, we discuss several weaknesses in standards and in widely deployed products. We believe that one of the main reasons for these failures is the fact that the system designers were not sufficiently cognizant of the precise security definitions of the cryptographic schemes they used, including the requirements they ensure — and the prerequisites they assume. Our hope is that readers of this book will be able to use cryptographic schemes in systems they design, understanding the properties of the schemes and how to securely use them. On the other hand, we hope that the readers will learn when they should consult with an expert cryptographer, such as when the definitions are subtle. This will reduce the likelihood of usage errors.

The challenge of rigorously defining security requirements and proving security implies that protocols and mechanisms are sometimes used without a rigorous definition and/or a proof. It is sometimes necessary, for functionality, business or performance considerations, to take the risk of a subtle vulnerability, which could exist due to informal requirements or analysis. However, when feasible, there are important advantages to follow the provable security approach, with definitions (of requirements, models and assumptions) and proofs of security. The provable security approach helps avoid, or at least reduce, vulnerabilities and attacks. In particular, a proof of security rules out many possible vulnerabilities. In fact, vulnerabilities are often discovered, and circumvented, when researchers work toward a proof of security.

There are also several countermeasures which may help address the concerns about provable security:

1. The use of *computer-aided cryptography* [29], i.e., automated tools to aid in the generation of proofs and in the verification of the correctness of proofs.
2. The study of attacks, in particular of *cryptanalysis*, i.e., attacks against cryptographic mechanisms. Researchers studying attacks on systems would often 'think outside the box' and exploit subtle vulnerabilities, which may be hard to identify when we only consider the proofs of security.
3. Improved *understanding* of the value, as well as the limitations, of provable security, and better *intuition*, that help practitioners make use of provable security — while avoiding subtle pitfalls.

Note that while our discussion is focused on cryptographic definitions and proofs, these considerations apply to cybersecurity in general. However, rigorous definitions and proofs are less common in other areas of cybersecurity. The study of cryptography can help develop the 'adversarial thinking' which is essential in all areas of cybersecurity.

To sum up, a proof of security is a powerful tool, but, like other power tools, *should always be used carefully and correctly.* Namely, we must fully understand the definitions, assumptions and simplifications and never assume additional properties or applicability to scenarios where the assumptions do not hold. Therefore, cybersecurity experts must master both theory and practice. A fair amount of skepticism, paranoia and humility is also advisable.

1.1.5 Risk and costs–benefit analysis

The management of computation and communication systems involves multiple challenges, including security risks. Security managers have to consider the *costs* of deploying security mechanisms, against the *probability* of an attack and the expected *damages* from possible attacks, if the mechanisms are not deployed. *Risk analysis* is an attempt to estimate the probabilities of occurrence of different attacks and of the attacks being successful, and cost–benefit analysis uses these values, as well as the costs of deploying different security mechanisms, to decide which security mechanisms are worth deploying.

Risk and cost–benefit analysis are very important aspects of cybersecurity. However, we do not cover these topics in this book. The main reason is that the author is not aware of a sufficiently reliable and generally applicable methodology for such analysis. It seems to the author that practitioners often use approximations based on experience, common sense and industry-adopted estimates. Therefore, we focus on design and analysis of secure systems and on potential vulnerabilities and attacks; we mostly ignore the challenge of estimating the *risks* of different attacks and the *costs* of different defenses.

1.2 Basic cryptographic mechanisms: Encryption, signatures and hashing

In this section, we provide a birds-eye introduction to three basic cryptographic mechanisms, which are the ones most commonly used in practice: *cryptosystems*, *signature schemes* and *collision-resistant hash functions*. We also introduce *Kerckhoffs's principle*, a fundamental design principle for cryptosystems and other cryptographic schemes, applied also to other cybersecurity defenses.

1.2.1 Encryption: symmetric and asymmetric cryptosystems

Encryption schemes, also referred to as *cryptosystem* or *cipher*, are the oldest and most well-known cryptographic mechanism — and the main mechanism for ensuring *confidentiality*.

Encryption transforms sensitive information, referred to as *plaintext*, into a form called *ciphertext*, which allows the intended recipients to *decrypt* it back into the plaintext. The ciphertext should, ideally, not expose any information about the plaintext to an attacker. The focus on encryption and confidentiality is evident in the term *cryptography*, whose literal translation is 'secret writing'.

In all but some ancient (and completely insecure) cryptosystems, the encryption and decryption operations use a key. Figure 1.3 illustrates the basic concepts and typical use of encryption, including the use of a key for encryption and decryption. The most basic aspect of

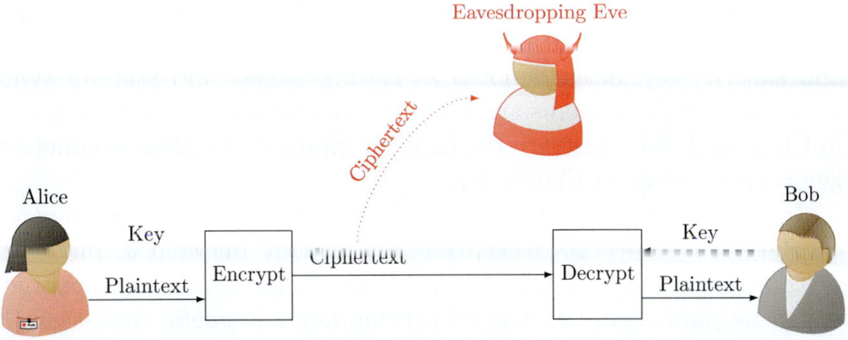

Figure 1.3. Encryption: terms and typical use. Alice uses a key to encrypt *plaintext* into *ciphertext* which it sends to Bob. Bob uses a key to decrypt the ciphertext and recover the plaintext, but Eavesdropping Eve does not have this key and cannot learn information on the plaintext.

cryptosystems is whether the two operations, encryption and decryption, use the same key (symmetric key cryptosystems) or use different keys, a public key for encryption and a private key for decryption (PKCs).

Figure 1.3 also introduces few 'characters' which we use throughout this book and are used in many papers and books on cryptography and cybersecurity. First, we have the pair of benign communicating entities, *Alice* and *Bob*. Then, we have the attacker; in this figure, as in much of this book (and many texts in cryptography), we focus on the *eavesdropping adversary*, i.e., an attacker who can (only) *eavesdrop* to the communication between the benign entities (Alice and Bob). We refer to the eavesdropping adversary by the mnemonic name *Eve*. In the figures, we illustrate Eve using an image of a red nun with horns; the horns and the color red symbolize that Eve is an attacker.

In some sections, we also discuss other attacker models. In particular, we often discuss *man-in-the-middle (MitM) attackers*. In figures, we use an image of a man-in-black for the MitM attacker, again with red horns.

We find it convenient to use different pronouns for each entity; so we use 'she' for Alice, 'he' for Bob and 'they' for the eavesdropping and MitM attackers. Note that we use the words 'attacker' and 'adversary' interchangeably.

In a *symmetric key cryptosystem*, also called *shared key cryptosystem*, the encryption and decryption operations use the same (secret and shared) key, often denoted k. Both stateless and stateful symmetric key cryptosystems are widely used, and we discuss both types in Chapter 2. We illustrate the (slightly simpler) stateless symmetric key cryptosystem in Figure 1.4.

In a *public key cryptosystem* (PKC), also called an *asymmetric cryptosystem*, only the decryption key, usually denoted d, must be *private (secret)*. The (related but different) encryption key, denoted e, can be published, i.e., the encryption key e is *public (non-secret)*. A state may be used for the encryption operation, but not for decryption, since typically, multiple parties should be able to decrypt, without sharing state. Therefore, usually, PKCs are stateless. A (stateless) PKC is illustrated in Figure 1.5. We study symmetric key cryptosystems in Chapter 2 and public key cryptosystems in Chapter 6.

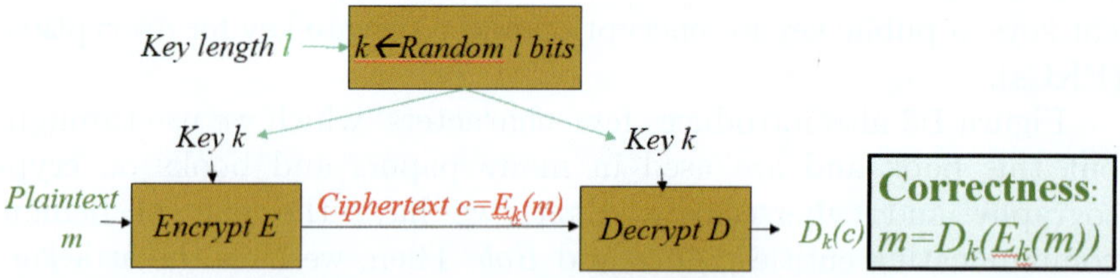

Figure 1.4. A (stateless) symmetric key cryptosystem, also called a shared key encryption scheme. Encryption and decryption use the *shared, secret key* k.

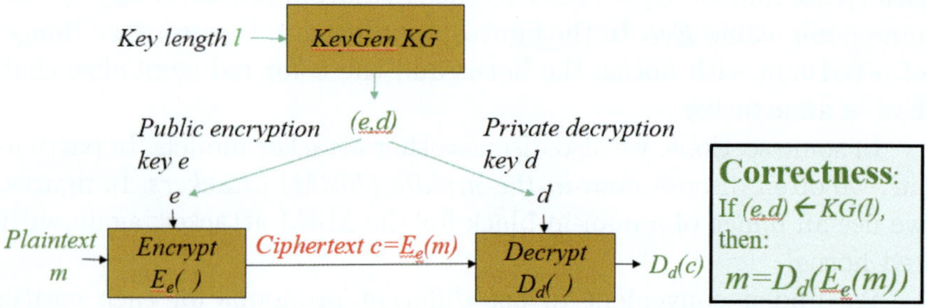

Figure 1.5. A (stateless) public key cryptosystem (PKC), also called an asymmetric encryption scheme. Encryption uses a *public* (not-secret) key e, and decryption uses the corresponding *private* (secret) key d.

Symmetric (shared-key) cryptosystems use the same key, e.g., k, for both encryption and decryption, as illustrated in Figure 1.4. The key k is usually chosen as a random bit-string. In the figure, the key length is variable, given as input (denoted l); in practice, many cryptosystems are designed for one or few specific key lengths. A symmetric cryptosystem must ensure *correctness*, i.e., $m = D_k(E_k(m))$, for every plaintext message m and every generated key k.

As illustrated in Figure 1.5, PKCs use a *pair* of two different, but related, keys: a *public encryption key* e for encryption, and a *private decryption key* d for decryption. The *keypair* (e, d) is produced by a *KG* algorithm, denoted KG, which is defined as part of the asymmetric cryptosystem. For public-key cryptosystems that support variable key length l, the length l is provided as input to the KG (as illustrated). PKCs should also satisfy *correctness*, namely, $m = D_d(E_e(m))$, for every keypair (e, d) generated by the *key generation* algorithm KG.

Note that a KG algorithm is rarely defined for symmetric key cryptosystems; instead, the shared key k is usually selected as a random string. However, for asymmetric cryptosystems, we cannot select randomly both the public key e and the private key d since the two keys must be related for decryption to recover the plaintext, i.e., for correctness to hold.

The basic security requirement from both symmetric key cryptosystems and PKCs is to ensure *confidentiality*, i.e., an adversary should not be able to learn, from the ciphertext, any information about the plaintext. A PKC should ensure confidentiality of the plaintext when the adversary is also given the public encryption key e. The definitions involve some subtle aspects, and therefore, we present them only in Chapter 2.

Designing a PKC which ensures correctness and confidentiality is a challenge. Even today, almost half a century since public key cryptosystems were first proposed, there is a limited number of candidate designs. In fact, while the *concept* of a PKC was proposed in a seminal paper by Whit Diffie and Martin Hellman from 1976 [155], the first *design*, RSA, was published only later, in 1978, in another seminal paper [418], by Rivest, Shamir and Adelman. We discuss these works and other results related to public key cryptography in Chapter 6.

1.2.2 Kerckhoffs's principle

In both symmetric and asymmetric cryptosystems, the key used for decryption must be kept secret. However, what about the *algorithms* used for encryption and decryption? Intuitively, it may seem that the algorithms should be kept secret since it is harder to attack a system without knowing how it works. Indeed, some ancient cryptosystems did not use a key at all and relied entirely on the secrecy of the algorithms; we give a few examples in Chapter 2. Even for keyed cryptosystems, it is harder to attack without knowing the design; see Exercise 2.18. This is often reflected using the expression *knowledge is power*. Indeed, traditionally, the design of cryptosystems, as well as of other cybersecurity systems, were kept secret, and this secrecy was considered as beneficial or even necessary for their security. This approach is called *security by obscurity*.

However, in 1883, Dutch cryptographer Auguste Kerckhoffs realized that 'security by obscurity' has serious disadvantages. In particular, if security relies on secrecy of design, then once an attacker obtains details of the design of the cryptosystem, the system cannot be considered secure. This motivated Kerckhoffs to publish the following principle [292], which is now considered the 'basic' rule in applied cryptography. We extended Kerckhoffs's principle to refer to arbitrary security mechanisms and not just to cryptosystems and other cryptographic systems.

Principle 2 (Kerckhoffs's principle). *When designing or evaluating the security of (cryptographic) systems, assume that the adversary knows the design, i.e., knows everything except the secret keys.*

Kerckhoffs's principle has additional advantages. One advantage is that the resulting design is likely to be more secure, as it was designed against a more powerful attacker — an attacker that knows the details of the design. An even more important advantage is the ability to *evaluate* the security of the design by experts which were not part of the design team, and challenging them to find vulnerabilities; it is often easier for an expert to find a vulnerability in a system designed by somebody else.

Kerckhoffs's principle does not *require* that the design be made public; it merely *allows* publication since it requires that the *goal* of the designers should be for security to hold even against an attacker than knows the design. In principle, we may follow Kerckhoffs's principle, yet keep the design private, thereby making it 'even harder' to find a vulnerability. Since security does not *assume* secrecy of the design, we can continue to use the system even if the confidentiality of the design is breached.

However, there are significant further advantages in using *public, standard* designs. First, published, standard designs have the advantage of improving the efficiency of production and use, by allowing interoperable implementations by arbitrary vendors. Second, when designers know that their design would be made public and evaluated by experts, this may further motivate them to produce a strong design.

The final advantage of a public design may be the most critical: it facilitates evaluation and cryptanalysis by many experts, motivating them to *find and publish vulnerabilities*. Public evaluation may take place during the design phase, with multiple proposals published and evaluated in the selection of the final design. However, public evaluation is also helpful after a system is deployed; if a vulnerability is found and published by researchers, then users can take different countermeasures, such as changing to a different system. Through evaluation of security by multiple, motivated experts is an excellent way to improve security. In fact, even 'provably-secure' designs were sometimes found to have vulnerabilities, when they were carefully reviewed by experts; such vulnerabilities in a proven-secure design may be due to a mistake in the proof or due to an unrealistic modeling or other assumption [298]. We see that Justice Brandeis' saying '*sunlight is the best disinfectant*' applies very well to cryptographic and cybersecurity systems.

The importance of Kerckhoffs's principle is demonstrated by two widely deployed cryptographic systems whose designs were kept confidential, both designed in the 1990s: the *GSM* mobile telephony network [249] and the *content scrambling system* (CSS) encryption for DVDs [35]. In both cases, it did not take very long for the algorithms to be leaked [106], and quite soon afterwards, they were found to be insecure and vulnerable to successful, practical attacks, e.g., Refs. [31,81]. The GSM case is particularly interesting and important, with several glaring vulnerabilities, some of which can be considered as design errors. The GSM designers did not plan a 'migration plan' for changing from the exposed ciphers and protocols to secure alternatives, which resulted in devices remaining vulnerable years after the vulnerabilities become known. We discuss some of the GSM vulnerabilities in Section 5.5.2 and in Example 2.7.

Sometimes, it is feasible to combine the security benefits of open design and of maintaining the secrecy of the design, by combining two candidate schemes. For example, one can combine a published, standard cryptosystems and another cryptosystem whose design was kept secret with the hope of making attacks harder. We use the term *robust combiner* for constructions which ensure security as long as *one* of the two schemes is not broken. Robust combiners are known for different cryptographic schemes; see Ref. [240] and Section 2.7.3.

1.2.3 Collision-resistant hash functions and malware

Let us now provide a high-level introduction to the important area of cryptographic hash functions, which is the main topic of Chapter 3. A hash function $h(\cdot)$ receives an arbitrary length input binary string, i.e., it is defined over the domain $\{0,1\}^*$, i.e., the set of all binary strings. The output of the hash function h applied to the message $m \in \{0,1\}^*$, i.e., $h(m)$, is called the *digest* of the message m. The digest is a fixed length, n-bits binary string; we refer to n as the *digest length*.

Since the input domain of a hash function h is infinite, and the range is the finite set of n-bits strings, there are more inputs than possible outputs, and therefore, for some inputs $m \neq m'$, the output is the same, i.e., $h(m) = h(m')$. We refer to such a pair of different inputs which result in identical outputs as a *collision*. Figure 1.6 illustrates a hash function with a collision.

Cryptographic hash functions are hash functions designed to satisfy different security requirements. In Chapter 3, we discuss several types of cryptographic hash functions; for now, we only provide a high-level introduction to the most important type of cryptographic hash function, namely, *collision-resistant hash function* (CRHF).

Basically, a hash function h is said to be a CRHF if, given the digest $h(m)$ of a string m, it is infeasible to find a different string $m' \neq m$, which has the same digest: $h(m') = h(m)$.

Collision-resistant hash functions are often used to ensure integrity. One common application is to distribute a (large) object m,

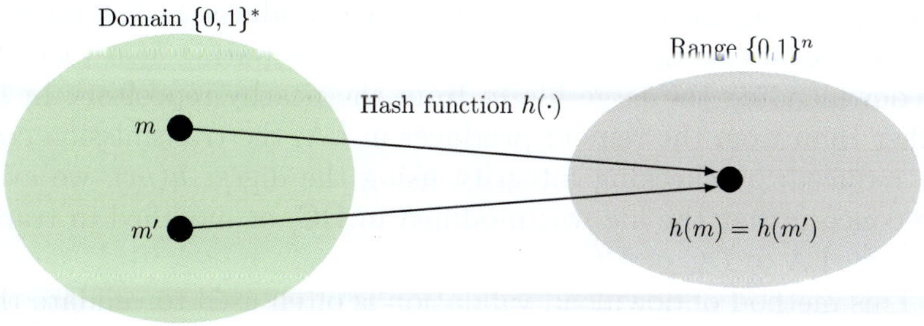

Figure 1.6. A (keyless) hash function $h : \{0,1\}^* \to \{0,1\}^n$ with a collision. The collision is a pair of input messages $m \neq m'$ s.t. $h(m) = h(m')$. Intuitively, we say that h is a (keyless) collision-resistant hash function (CRHF) if it is infeasible to find a collision, except with negligible probability in the digest length n.

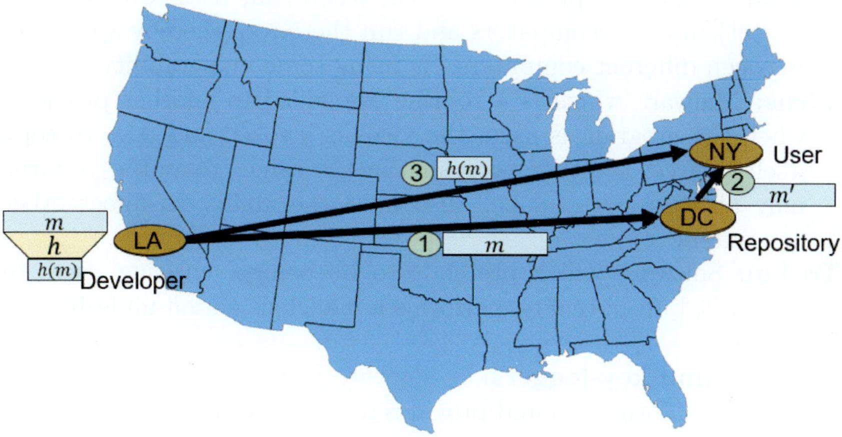

Figure 1.7. Use of a collision-resistant hash function h to validate integrity of file m downloaded by a user in NY, from an untrusted nearby repository in DC. To validate integrity, the user downloads the (short) digest directly from the remote website of the producer in LA. This reduces network overhead — and load on the producer's website — compared to downloading the entire file from the producer's website.

e.g., a file containing the executable code of a program. Suppose the file m is distributed from its producer in LA to a user or repository in Washington DC (step 1 in Figure 1.7). Next, a user in NY is downloading the file from the repository (or peer user) in DC (step 2), receiving m' (which should be the same as m, of course). To validate the integrity of the received file m', the user also downloads the digest $h(m)$ of the file, directly from the producer in LA (step 3), and then confirms that $h(m) = h(m')$ (by computing $h(m')$ locally). By downloading the large file m from the nearby repository in DC rather than from the remote producer in LA, the transmission costs are reduced; by checking integrity using the digest $h(m)$, we avoid the concern that the file was modified in DC, or modified in transit between LA to DC or DC to NY.

This method of download validation is often used to validate that a software download contains the legitimate, desired software and not a malicious software, i.e., *malware*. Malware is one of the major cybersecurity threats and plays a key part in many attacks; there are many different types of malware, including the following:

Worm: A malware program, which, when run, tries to copy itself (*infect*) to other computers and run there too, thereby spreading between different computers, by using some vulnerability.

Virus: Malware which is a routine appended to another program; when the program is used, the virus is invoked and tries to copy itself (*infect*) to other programs in the same computer. A virus may also be a worm, i.e., also have the ability to infect other computers.

Trojan: Software which pretends to be benign, enticing users to install it, but, in reality, performs a malicious action undesired by the user.

Spyware and key-loggers: A spyware is a malware that collects sensitive information and provides it to the attacker. A key-logger is a spyware that collects information typed by the user on the keyboard, often used to collect passwords or credit card information.

Learn more about malware and validation of the integrity of software in Lab 1.

A potential remaining concern is the modification of the digest $h(m)$ received directly from producer in LA, by a MitM attacker. This may be addressed in different ways, such as the use of a secure connection for retrieving $h(m)$, typically using HTTPS, i.e., a web (http) connection running over the TLS protocol; see Chapter 7. Other defenses include receiving the digest from multiple independent sources and receiving the digest with a *digital signature* by the trusted producer. This last method is basically the same as the

Hash-then-Sign method, which we discuss in Section 3.3.5. This motivates our high level introduction to digital signature schemes, in the following section.

1.2.4 Digital signature schemes

Let us now focus on *digital signature schemes*, whose goal is to ensure *authentication* and *non-repudiation* (Section 1.1.2). Signature schemes play a critical role in applied cryptography; for example, in Lab 1, we show the critical role of signature schemes in protecting against malware, and in Chapter 7, we show their critical role in the important TLS protocol (used to protect web and other client-server communication).

Digital signature schemes, like PKCs, were proposed as a concept in Ref. [155], but their first published design was in the RSA paper [418]. Later on, we discuss two constructions of signature schemes: the RSA design in Chapter 6, and a hash-based design which is limited to signing a single message, called a *one-time signature scheme*, in Chapter 3.

Handwritten signatures — goals and reality: Let us first consider *handwritten signatures.* Ideally, handwritten signatures should allow everyone to verify a signed document, by comparing the signature on the document to a sample signature, known to be of that signer. The purported security of handwritten signature is based on two (implicit) assumptions. The first assumption is that *only* the signer herself should be able to sign a document in a way which produces a signature matching her sample signature. The second assumption is that it is infeasible to *change* a signed document, without leaving marks that would invalidate the signature.

Reality is less ideal; handwritten signatures are forged and hand-signed documents are modified. Indeed, for these reasons, there are experts who are called upon to detect forged signatures and documents modified after signature. These experts may fail to make a correct determination — indeed, different experts may disagree. In particular, checks remain the payment method most subject to fraud, in spite of being signed [8]; in particular, paper checks are often stolen when sent to the payee and modified to allow the thief to deposit them.

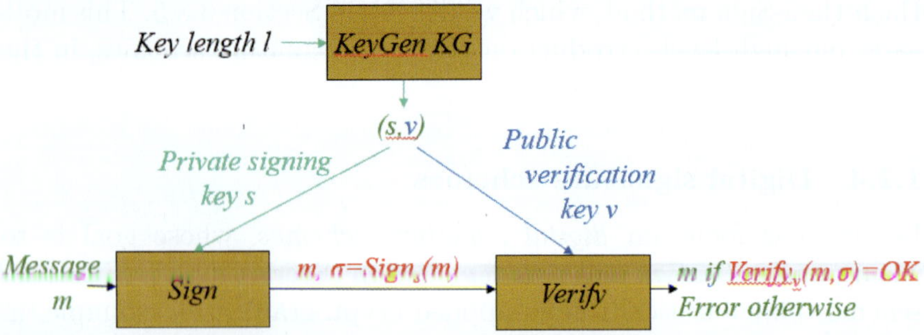

Figure 1.8. A digital signature scheme. To sign, use the private signing key s; to verify, use the public key v.

Digital signatures and their security: Let us now focus on digital signatures, illustrated in Figure 1.8, and their security properties. Basically, we argue that *digital signatures may provide the security that is desired, but not really provided, by handwritten signatures.*

There are some obvious differences between handwritten signatures and digital signatures. Obviously, the document and the signature are strings (files) rather than ink on paper, and the processes of signing and validating are done by applying appropriate efficient functions (or algorithms), as illustrated in Figure 1.8. The signing and verification functions require appropriate *keys*. The *private signing key*, s, replaces the unique personal characteristics of the signer, creating the personalized signature; the *public verification key*, v, replaces the sample signature necessary to verify signed documents. This keypair, (s, v), is produced together, using a *key generation* algorithm, KG.

A signature scheme $\mathcal{S}$, therefore, consists of these three algorithms: the *key generation* algorithm, KG, for producing the keys, the signing algorithm $\mathcal{S}ign$, for signing, and the verification algorithm, $\mathcal{V}erify$, for verifying signatures. These three algorithms are similar to these of a PKC (Figure 1.5), and, like there, the key generation algorithm, KG, may receive as input an indication of the required key-length l.

The KG algorithm outputs a pair of keys: a private signing key s, to be known only to the signer, and a corresponding public verification key v, which is used to verify signatures. The $\mathcal{S}ign$ algorithm is given the (private) signing key s and a message m; the output of the signature algorithm, which we denote in Figure 1.8 by σ, is usually referred to as the *signature* of the message m and computed as $\sigma = Sign_s(m)$.

Signature schemes *should* also ensure *unforgeability*. Intuitively, a signature scheme ensures unforgeability if attacker cannot *forge* messages. Namely, given the public verification key v, an attacker cannot obtain a signature σ such that $Verify_v(m, \sigma) = \text{TRUE}$, unless it was also given the private signing key s or the computed value of $\sigma = Sign_s(m)$.

We define signature schemes in Section 1.5.1 and their unforgeability requirements in Section 1.5.8, rather than here, since we need to first introduce required notations and background. The design of secure signature schemes is a challenge; we present two designs but only in later chapters. In Section 3.4.2, we present the one-time signature scheme, and in Chapter 6, we present the RSA signature scheme.

Considering that we present constructions of signature schemes only in later chapters, the reader may wonder why we define the security requirements of signature schemes already in this chapter. There are a few reasons:

- The security requirements of signature schemes are relatively simple and easy to define. By discussing the requirements and defining them, we demonstrate the tools of probability and computational complexity, which are later used to define other cryptographic schemes.
- Signatures are one of the most important and widely used cryptographic schemes, yet they are one of the least known and understood outside the cryptographic community.
- Signatures are the main *deterrence-based* cryptographic mechanism. Deterrence is not always sufficiently recognized for its potential to ensure security. Deterrence is based on the *non-repudiation* property of digital signature schemes, which we discuss next.

Non-repudiation: The public verification key v allows one to verify signatures but should not allow an attacker to generate valid signatures. Therefore, a digital signature can provide not only authentication but also *non-repudiation*: the signer cannot deny having signed the message. Non-repudiation is critical to some applications of public-key cryptography, such as providing *evidences*; see Section 1.2.5.

Warning — conflicting use of the term 'digital signature': To finish this high-level introduction to the cryptographic mechanism of digital signatures, we warn the reader about a conflicting use of the same term for a very different mechanism. Specifically, the term 'digital signature' is sometimes used in products and non-academic publications to refer to the inclusion, in a document, of a scan of a handwritten signature, of an image which somewhat resembles a handwritten signature, or even of writing the name or otherwise signaling agreement by interacting with a website. Such mechanisms, even when provided by third parties that perform some identification of the signer, are very different from digital signatures in the sense used by experts in cryptography and security, and their security depends on the third party rather than on cryptography.

1.2.5 Applying signatures: evidences, non-repudiation and certificates

Signatures are *asymmetric*: *signing* requires the private signing key, but *verification* of a signature only requires the corresponding public verification key. This property facilitates two applications which are critical to cybersecurity: provision of *non-repudiation* and facilitating public key certificates. Let us briefly discuss both of these applications.

Signatures facilitate non-repudiation and evidences: The recipient of a signed message 'knows' that once she validated a signature, using the verification key v, she would be able to *convince other parties* that the message was, in fact, signed by the use of the private key corresponding to v. We refer to this property as *non-repudiation*, since the owner of the private key cannot claim that the ability to verify messages allowed another party to forge a signature, i.e., to compute a seemingly valid signature of a message, without access to the private signing key.

The non-repudiation property allows a digitally signed document to provide an *evidence* for the agreement of the signer, much like the classical use of hand-written signatures. Indeed, the use of digital signatures to prove agreement has significant advantages compared to the use of hand-written signatures:

Security: Handwritten signatures are prone to forging of the signature itself, as well as to modification of the signed document. If the signature scheme is secure, then production of a valid signature over a document m practically requires the application of the private signing key to sign *exactly* m.

Convenience: Digital signatures can be sent over a network easily, and their verification only requires running of an algorithm. Admittedly, signature verification does involve some computational overhead, but this is incomparably easier — and more reliable — than the manual process and expertise required to confirm handwritten signatures. Later on, digital signatures may be easily archived, backed-up and so on.

Non-repudiation is essential for many important applications, such as signing an agreement or a payment order. Non-repudiation is also applied in different cryptographic systems and protocols, mainly, to identify a corrupt entity or device.

Legal interpretation of signatures and digitized handwritten signature: Digital signatures are covered by legislation in some jurisdictions; however, their legal definition and implications vary significantly between jurisdictions and often differs considerably from what you may expect based on the cryptographic definitions and properties. This subject is beyond our scope.

Signatures facilitate certificates: Most applied cryptographic systems rely on the use of *authentic public keys* for remote entities. Signature schemes provide a way to verify that a given public key is authentic, i.e., was not spoofed. Namely, a party receiving signed information from a remote peer can verify that information, using only the public signature-verification key of the signer. Furthermore, if the recipient does not have the public key of the sender, then the sender can attach a signature over their public key and their identity, signed by a *trusted third party*, whose public key is known to the recipient. The signature over the public key is called a *certificate*, and such trusted third parties that sign certificates are called *certificate authorities*. In Chapter 8, we discuss *Public Key Infrastructure*

(PKI), which is a set of mechanisms used to issue, verify and revoke certificates.

1.2.6 Attacker capabilities and the conservative design principle

If the adversaries are limited in their abilities to interfere with the communication between the parties, then it can be easier to guarantee the authenticity of the information received from a peer. In particular, some systems and protocols are designed to ensure security against a *passive adversary*, also called an *eavesdropping adversary*, i.e., an attacker who can only eavesdrop to messages but cannot modify messages. A protocol designed against an eavesdropping adversary can safely send the public key or other public value, knowing that the adversary cannot modify or inject (spoof) messages.

However, in many scenarios, the attacker may inject fake (spoofed) messages. In fact, sometimes an attacker can spoof messages but cannot eavesdrop on messages sent between benign parties. In this case, parties may easily authenticate a message from a peer, by previously sending a challenge to the peer, which the peer includes in the message. We refer to this kind of adversary capability as an *off-path adversary*. Off-path adversaries are mainly studied when focusing on non-cryptographic aspects of network security, e.g., see Ref. [205]. In particular, the Internet Protocol (IP) does not provide defenses against spoofing, while eavesdropping to Internet traffic requires direct access or complex attacks.

Some designs assume that the adversary is inactive or limited, e.g., passive or off-path, during an *initial* exchange, and use this exchange information such as keys between the two parties. The simplest case, where the attacker is inactive during the initial exchange, is called the *trust on first use* (TOFU) attack model; e.g., see Ref. [163].

Defenses that assume a weak adversary model may fail against a stronger attacker. In particular, systems that are secure under a weak adversary such as the eavesdropping attacker, the off-path attacker or the TOFU attack model, may fail against the stronger[3] MitM adversary. A MitM attacker can *modify, block and inject* messages

[3]The MitM attacker is sometimes referred to as the *monster-in-the-middle* or the *on-path attack model.*

as well as eavesdrop on messages. To ensure security against a MitM attacker, we must use strong, cryptographic authentication mechanisms.

There are many scenarios where attackers may obtain MitM capabilities. However, even when it may seem more likely that attackers will have more limited capabilities such as of the off-path attacker model or of the eavesdropping attacker model, it is always better to ensure security against more powerful attackers. This is a special case of the important *conservative design* principle, which basically says that security systems and, in particular, cryptographic mechanisms should be secure under minimal assumptions on the application scenarios, the underlying mechanisms and the attacker.

Principle 3 (Conservative design and usage). Cybersecurity mechanisms, *and in particular* cryptographic schemes, *should be specified and designed with minimal assumptions, strongest security requirements and maximal, well-defined attack model (attacker capabilities). On the other hand, when* using *an underlying cryptographic scheme, the design should assume the minimal* properties and requirements *from the scheme, and limit, as much as possible, the abilities of possible attackers.*

Both parts of the conservative design principle are very important. Many systems were vulnerable due to the use of mechanisms designed with subtle assumptions or restrictions, or ensuring insufficiently strong properties, e.g., assuming limited attacker capabilities. Other systems used cryptographic mechanisms in sub-optimal way, which unnecessarily gave the attacker ability to exploit later-discovered vulnerabilities of the cryptographic mechanisms.

Following the conservative design principle (Principle 3), we focus on attackers with MitM capabilities in most of this book.

1.3 Notations and sequence diagrams

Notations and figures are essential for precise, effective technical communication. However, it can be frustrating to read text which uses unfamiliar, forgotten or confusing notations and to see figures using unknown conventions. This could be a special challenge for these readers of this text who were not much exposed to some of the notations used in mathematics and theory of computer science. In particular, in most of the figures in this text, we use a specific style of *sequence diagrams*; readers not familiar with this convention may find it harder to make use of these figures.

Therefore, in this section, we introduce the notations and sequence diagrams conventions that we use in this text. Our choice of notations as well as of the use of sequence diagrams and their style is consistent, as much as possible, with common literature.

Table 1.1 presents notations which we use extensively. Refer to it whenever you see some unclear notation, and alert the author of any missing, incorrect or confusing notation.

Table 1.1. Notations used in this manuscript.

$S = \{a, b, c\}$, $X = (y, z)$	A set S with elements a, b and c, and a sequence x with elements y, z. Sets and sequences are denoted by a capital letter.
$\mathbb{Z}, \mathbb{Z}^+$ and $\mathbb{N}$:	Sets of integers. $\mathbb{Z}$: all integers; $\mathbb{Z}^+$: non-negative integers; $\mathbb{N}$: natural numbers (integers greater than zero).
$\mathbb{Z}_p$, $\mathbb{Z}_p^*$	The sets $\{0, \ldots, (p-1)\}$ and $\{1, \ldots, (p-1)\}$, respectively.
$\Pi_{x \in S} v_x$	Multiplication of the values v_x for every $x \in S$, e.g., $\Pi_{x \in \{a,b,c\}} V_x = V_a \cdot V_b \cdot V_c$. Similar to the use of $\Sigma_{x \in S}$ for addition.
$i!$	The factorial of i, defined as $i! \equiv \Pi_{j \in \{1,\ldots,i\}} j = 1 \cdot 2 \cdot \ldots \cdot i$.
$C \cup B$	Union of sets C and B.
$A \subseteq B$	Set A is a subset of set B, i.e., $a \in A \Rightarrow a \in B$.
$A \subsetneqq B$	Set A is a 'proper' subset of set B, i.e., $A \subseteq B$ but $A \neq B$. For example, $\mathbb{N} \subsetneqq \mathbb{Z}^+ \subsetneqq \mathbb{Z}$.
$A \times B$	Cross-product of sets A and B, i.e., the set $\{(a, b) \vert a \in A \text{ and } b \in B\}$.
$\{a, b\}^l$	The set of strings of length l over the alphabet $\{a, b\}$.
$\{a, b\}^*$	The set of strings of any length, over the alphabet $\{a, b\}$.
a^l (e.g., 1^l, 0^l)	String consisting of l concatenations of the letter/sequence a. For example, $0^4 = 0000, 1^3 = 111$, and $(01)^2 = 0101$. Also, 1^l is the number l in unary notation.
$\vert b \vert$	The length of string b; hence, $\vert a^n \vert = n \cdot \vert a \vert$ and $\vert 0^n \vert = n$.
$a[i]$	The ith most significant character of string a. For a binary string, the ith bit; for a byte-string, the ith byte. For example, if $a = 011$, then $a[1] = 0$ and $a[2] = 1$.
$a[i : j]$ or $a[i \ldots j]$	Substring containing $a[i] + \!\!\!+ \ldots + \!\!\!+ a[j]$.

Table 1.1. (*Continued*)

$+\!\!+$	Concatenation of strings; $abc +\!\!+ de = abcde$.
a^R	The 'reverse' of string a, e.g., $abcde^R = edcba$.
$a.b$	Dot notation: element b of tuple a (Section 1.3).
$x \wedge y$	x AND y; if x, y are binary strings, bitwise AND, e.g., $0111 \wedge 1010 = 0010$.
$x \vee y$	x OR y; if x, y are binary strings, bitwise OR, e.g., $0111 \vee 1010 = 1111$.
$x \oplus y$	x XOR y; if x, y are binary strings, bitwise XOR, e.g., $0111 \oplus 1010 = 1101$.
$\overline{x}$	The bit-wise inverse of binary string or bit x.
$x \xleftarrow{\$} X$	Select an element x from the finite set X with uniform distribution.
$\Pr_{x \xleftarrow{\$} X}(F(x))$	The probability of $F(x)$ to occur, when x is selected uniformly from set X.
$\mathcal{A}^{\mathcal{B}_k(\cdot)}$, $\mathcal{A}^{f_k(\cdot)}$	Algorithm $\mathcal{A}$ with *oracle access* to algorithm $\mathcal{B}$ or to function f, with key k. Namely, $\mathcal{A}$ can give input x and receive $\mathcal{B}_k(x)$ or $f_k(x)$. See Definition 1.3.
PPT	The set of *efficient*, aka *probabilistic polynomial time* (PPT), algorithms; see Definition A.1.
$NEGL(n)$	Set of 'negligible functions' in input $n \in \mathbb{N}$, see Definition 1.5.
$O(f(n))$	Big-O notation identifies the complexity of an algorithm; see Equation (A.1).
$⊠_k(\psi)$	String ψ protected ('enveloped') using key k, e.g., by the TLS record protocol (Chapter 7).

Unfortunately, the literature sometimes uses multiple notations for the same concept, or multiple conflicting interpretations for the same notation. We tried to choose the more widely used and least conflicting and confusing notations but that required some difficult tradeoffs.

1.3.1 The concatenation, dot, key and other notations

Let us now focus on three important conventions which we use extensively: the $+\!\!+$ notation, which denotes concatenation (of strings), the *dot notation*, which allows convenient referral to items within a tuple, and the *key notation*, which we use to specify the key provided as input to a cryptographic function.

The $+\!\!+$ notation for concatenation: Cryptographic protocols and designs often involve concatenation of strings. We use the symbol $+\!\!+$ to denote (string) concatenation, e.g., $00 +\!\!+ 111 = 00111$. This notation resembles but is different from the common notation for concatenation in publications in cryptography and the theory of computer science; the more common notation there for concatenation is $||$. The reason that in this book we denote concatenation using $+\!\!+$ rather than $||$ is to avoid confusing readers who are used to the symbol $||$ denoting the logical or operator, as used in few programming languages. The $+\!\!+$ symbol is an attempt to combine three notations for concatenation: the symbol $||$, which is used to denote concatenation in most publications in cryptography and the theory of computer science, and the symbols $+$ and $++$, which are used to denote concatenation in some programming languages.

The dot notation: The dot notation is a convenient way to refer to a value associated with a particular entity. For example, $Alice.s$ and $Alice.v$ denote the signing and verification keys, respectively, of Alice. Namely, the s and v after the dot represent specific values (keys) associated with Alice.

Another use of the dot notation is to avoid ambiguity when referring to the *different functions* comprising a specific cryptographic scheme. For example, consider a discussion which involves both a signature scheme $\mathcal{S} = (\mathcal{KG}, \mathcal{S}ign, \mathcal{V}erify)$ and a public key cryptosystem $\mathcal{PKC} = (\mathcal{KG}, \mathcal{E}, \mathcal{D})$. Both schemes have a key generation (KG) algorithm, and both denote it as KG. Using the dot notation, we refer to the KG algorithm of $\mathcal{S}$ as $\mathcal{S}.\mathcal{KG}$ and to the key generation algorithm of $\mathcal{PKC}$ by $\mathcal{PKC}.\mathcal{KG}$. For example, we have $(s, v) \xleftarrow{\$} \mathcal{S}.\mathcal{KG}(1^n)$ is the keypair returned by the KG algorithm of the signature scheme $\mathcal{S}$, consisting of the signing key s and the validation key v.

We also use dot notation to refer to *different outputs* of a function returning multiple values. For example, $\mathcal{S}.\mathcal{KG}.v(1^n)$ refers to the verification key returned by the KG algorithm $\mathcal{S}.\mathcal{KG}$.

The key notation: Cryptographic functions often use *keys*. While the key is, formally, an input to the function like any other input, it is often convenient, and customary, to place the key as *subscript*

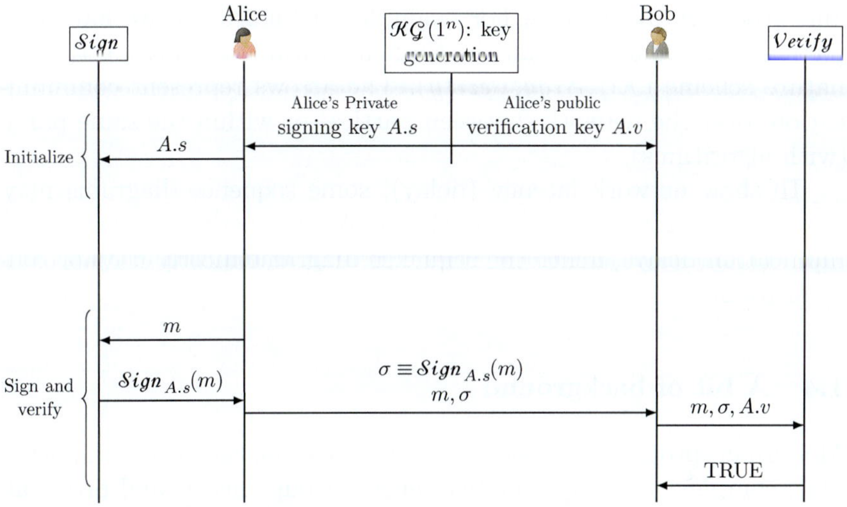

Figure 1.9. Sequence diagram for the initialization and use of a signature scheme. Alice *signs* message m with her private signing key $A.s$, resulting in $\sigma = Sign_{A.s}(m)$. Alice sends σ and m to Bob, who *verifies* the signature by computing $Verify_{A.v}(m, \sigma)$. Since in this example σ is a valid signature of m, the result is TRUE. If σ is not a valid signature of m, the result should be FALSE.

to the function name. For example, we use $Sign_s(m)$ to denote the signing algorithm $Sign$ applied to the message m, using the *signing key* s. We often use this notation together with the dot notation; e.g., in Figure 1.9, we write $Sign_{A.s}(m)$ to denote the result of applying signature algorithm $Sign$ to message m, using the signing key $A.s$ of Alice.

1.3.2 Sequence diagrams

Let us now present *sequence diagrams*, a widely used technique for illustrating the interactions between entities over time, which we use throughout this text, e.g., in Figure 1.9. Sequence diagrams are widely used in cybersecurity, communication protocols and other areas involving interactions between entities.

A sequence diagram illustrates the progression of events over time. In most figures in this book, the time proceeds from top to bottom; note that in some other schedule diagrams, time proceeds from left to right. The top of the diagram shows the different parties and processes/algorithms. For example, in Figure 1.9, we have two parties, Alice and Bob, and the three algorithms comprising the signature scheme $(\mathcal{KG}, \mathcal{Sign}, \mathcal{Verify})$. The arrows represent communication: over the network (between parties) or within the same party (with algorithms).

To show network latency (delay), some sequence diagrams may use slanted arrows. However, in this book, we mostly ignore the communication delays, hence the sequence diagrams mostly use horizontal arrows.

1.4 A bit of background

Modern cryptography makes extensive use of mathematics, in particular, complexity theory, number theory, group theory, and probability. These are large, important and interesting areas, which are often part of computer science curriculum. However, we believe that it is not essential to study these areas *before* studying this textbook; the textbook only requires limited use of basic concepts and results from these areas. Instead, we provide the necessary, limited background, for a reader who did not learn these areas so far, in Appendix A. In fact, studying this book before studying these topics may provide motivation and prepare the reader for in-depth study of these important and interesting areas.

In this section, we briefly introduce these topics, to allow readers to determine if they need to learn a bit from any of them, or if they know enough from prior studies. If readers find it necessary to learn a bit more about these topics, we provide the necessary background in Appendix A. Readers can read the appendixes in advance and/or 'as needed', i.e., when the text makes use of the relevant area.

1.4.1 A bit of computational complexity

Most cryptographic schemes assume restrictions on the computational capabilities of the adversary.[4] The focus on adversaries with

[4]There are also some definitions and constructions of *unconditionally secure* cryptographic schemes. We cover only one unconditionally secure scheme: the *one-time pad* cipher (OTP, Section 2.5).

restricted computational capabilities allows us to rule out some attacks which require absurd amount of resources, such as *exhaustive search* — trying out all possible keys (see Section 2.4.1).

However, how can we define a clear restriction on the adversary's computational abilities? This can be quite tricky. The theory of *computational complexity* provides an elegant solution. In this introductory book, we only need to understand some very basic notions and properties from the theory of complexity. Our discussion is quite restricted to the essential notions; we believe that readers should be able to follow the text even without learning computational complexity. We list in the following the main aspects of complexity theory that we use and explain them in Section A.1. For readers interested to learn more, we recommend one of the many excellent books on computational complexity, e.g., Refs. [134, 211], which provide a much more extensive introduction to this important and interesting subject.

The main aspects of computational complexity which we use in this book, and describe in Section A.1 include the following:

- The big-O notation and its use for specifying and comparing the asymptotic complexities (overhead) of algorithms. Asymptotic complexity focuses on the overhead of the algorithm as its input size grows toward infinity. This is convenient, since for smaller input size, the overhead may be dominated by fixed per-operation and startup factors, which become insignificant as the input size grows. The big-O notation basically ignores these fixed factors. For example, the big-O notation for linear functions is $O(n)$, for quadratic functions $O(n^2)$ and for exponential functions it is $O(a^n)$, where a is the exponent; see the illustration of specific linear, quadratic and exponential functions in Figure 1.10.
- The definition of *Probabilistic Polynomial Time* (PPT) algorithms, also referred to as *efficient* algorithms or *polytime* algorithms, and the corresponding notion for functions. Basically, an algorithm is efficient, or PPT, if its run time is bounded by any polynomial in its input length. Therefore, an algorithm is efficient (PPT) if its time complexity is linear, quadratic or any other polynomial in the input length n, e.g., $O(n^a)$ for any constant a. In contrast, an algorithm whose time complexity is exponential, e.g., $O(2^n)$, is considered inefficient. For motivation, see how in Figure 1.10 the

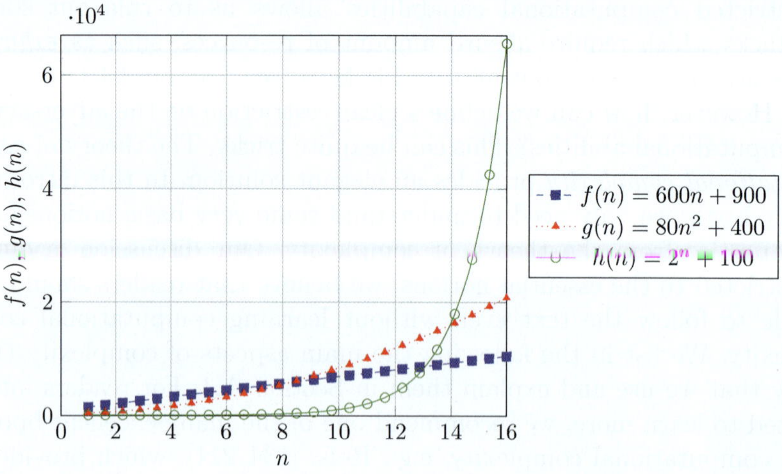

Figure 1.10. Comparing linear, quadratic and exponential complexities: comparing the linear function $f(n) = 600n + 900 = O(n)$, the quadratic function $g(n) = 80n^2+400 = O(n^2)$ and the exponential function $h(n) = 2^n+100 = O(2^n)$.

exponential function exceeds the linear and quadratic functions for sufficiently large input size n.

- The security parameter 1^n, which is a number encoded in unary (i.e., a string of l bits whose value is 1). The security parameter is often used as the input to the (randomized) KG algorithms. The reason for providing the security parameter and encoding it in unary is that the key-generation algorithm should be an efficient (PPT) algorithm; hence, its output (the key) must be bounded by a polynomial in its input (the security parameter).
- A *hard problem* is a computational problem that cannot be solved, with negligibly small error probability, by any efficient (PPT) algorithm.

In applied cryptography, and even in theory, we focus (almost) solely on efficient, PPT cryptographic schemes. Furthermore, the standard *attack model* is of an efficient, PPT algorithm. One exception is in works that consider an adversary who is efficient, i.e., runs in polynomial time, but using *quantum computing*, which provides capabilities stronger than that of standard computers modeled by a Turing machine; we discuss quantum computing in Section 10.1.

We provide a bit more background on computational complexity in Section A.1.

1.4.2 A bit of number theory and group theory

Number theory and group theory are often used in the design and analysis of cryptographic schemes. In this book, we use only a tiny subset that is necessary for our study of applied cryptography.

The subset of number theory that we need is mostly focused on *modular arithmetic*. Modular arithmetic studies operations over a set of integers defined by an integer called the *modulus*. If we denote the modulus by n, then the set of integers used by modular arithmetic is $\{0, 1, \ldots, n-1\}$ and denoted $\mathbb{Z}_n$.

To map an arbitrary integer a to $\mathbb{Z}_n$, we compute the reminder of a when divided by n; we refer to this as the *modulo operation* and denote the operation by mod. Namely, if $b = a \bmod n$, then there is some integer k such that $a - b = k \cdot m$.

When two numbers a, b have the same reminder when divided by n, i.e., $a \bmod n = b \bmod n$, then we say that a and b are *congruent* modulo n or that the *congruence relation modulo* n holds between a and b. We denote the congruence relation between a and b in a compact way by $a \equiv b \pmod{n}$. Namely,

$$a \equiv b \pmod{n} \text{ if and only if } a \bmod n = b \bmod n \tag{1.1}$$

Modular arithmetic shares many of the properties of regular arithmetic (over the integers and the real numbers); however, there are also important differences; a reader not familiar with these basic topics can learn this topic from one of the many good textbooks covering this topic or from the brief summary in Appendix A.2.

One example of a difference between modular arithmetic and regular arithmetic is the subject of *multiplicative inverse*, which we cover in Appendix A.2.2. The multiplicative inverse of a number x is denoted x^{-1} and is the number satisfying $x \cdot x^{-1} = 1$, where we may use modular multiplication or regular multiplication. Over the integers, only 1 has a multiplicative inverse (which is itself, i.e., also 1); other integers have no (integer) multiplicative inverse. Over the real numbers, in contrast, every number has a multiplicative inverse, except zero.

For modular arithmetic, the situation is a bit more complex: an integer a has multiplicative inverse modulo integer $m > 0$, if and only if a and m are *coprime*, namely, they do not have a common divisor except 1.

Computing the multiplicative inverse is widely believed to be *computationally hard*, i.e., it is believed that there is no efficient (PPT) algorithm to compute multiplicative inverses, for numbers which are hard to factor, in particular, numbers chosen as a multiplication of very large random primes. Finding the factors of such numbers is referred to as the *factoring problem*, and it is also considered to be *computationally hard* (Section A.1). When the factors are hard to compute, computing multiplicative inverses is also hard. In fact, this is crucial to the security of the well-known and important RSA PKC, which we discuss in Chapter 6. Specifically, in RSA, the private key is the multiplicative inverse of the public key, which means that if it is possible to efficiently compute multiplicative inverses, then RSA is insecure.

In Appendix A.2.3, we discuss two important and beautiful results of number theory, which are very important in cryptography: Fermat's and Euler's theorems. One application of these two theorems is an efficient algorithm to compute multiplicative inverses for numbers with known, or small, prime factors. These theorems can also allow one to reduce the complexity of modular exponentiation and are used in the design of the RSA PKC (see Chapter 6).

In Appendix A.2.4, we introduce basic notions from the domain of group theory, which are used widely in applied cryptography and a bit in this book. In particular, group theory is used to define the discrete logarithm problem, which is another important number-theoretic problem considered computationally hard. The discrete logarithm problem is used as the basis for several public-key schemes, including the important Diffie–Hellman key-exchange protocol (see Chapter 6).

1.4.3 A bit of probability

Probabilistic analysis and algorithms are very important for computer science in general and for cryptography in particular. Luckily, only the very basics are required for our study of applied cryptography. We present this minimal background on probability in

Section A.3; for more in-depth coverage, take a course and/or read one of the many excellent textbooks, e.g., Refs. [134, 210].

Probability deals with events which result in a value from some predefined set. For simplicity, we only consider a *finite* set of possible outcomes, and only *uniform distribution* and independent random variables.

We are often interested in the outcome of a *randomized (or probabilistic) algorithm* $\mathcal{A}$, i.e., an algorithm that can perform *bit flip* operations. We use the notation $\Pr(\pi(\mathcal{A}))$ to denote the probability that predicate π holds for the (randomized) output of $\mathcal{A}$ and the notation $y \stackrel{\$}{\leftarrow} \mathcal{A}(x)$ to denote that y is assigned the random outcome of a uniformly chosen run of $\mathcal{A}$ with input x.

In Section A.3, we present several useful and simple properties of probability, which we use in this book.

1.5 Defining security for cryptographic schemes: signatures as a case study

Ensuring security is challenging. It is tempting to identify a list of possible attacks and evaluate security against these, but that is often misleading, resulting in vulnerability to other, unforeseen attacks. Instead, modern cryptography is mostly based on *provable security*, whose goal is to *prove* that an attacker with given *capabilities* is unable or unlikely to 'break security' of a given system or cryptographic scheme.

Proving security requires to clearly and precisely define the cryptographic scheme and its interactions, the attacker capabilities, the security requirements and any additional assumptions. Only with precise definitions of the scheme, attacker capabilities, security requirements and assumptions, can we try to *prove* security. Vulnerabilities may be due to errors in the proof or due to 'incorrect' definitions for attacker capabilities, security requirements or assumptions.

In this section, we introduce the provable-security approach, by presenting the definition of *cryptographic signature schemes* (Section 1.5.1) and of the *security requirements* of signature schemes (Section 1.5.8). Our presentation follows the seminal paper of Goldwasser *et al.* [214], which is a highly recommended reading.

We first introduce several important concepts, which are essential to define security requirements of signature schemes. In Section 1.5.2, we introduce attack models relevant for signature schemes, including the *known-message attack (KMA) model* and the *CMA*. In Section 1.5.3, we discuss the different types of signature forgeries (universal forgery, selective forgery and existential forgery). In Section 1.5.4, we introduce the important notions of game-based security and the oracle notation. In Section 1.5.5, we introduce the *existential unforgeability CMA Game.* In Section 1.5.6, we present the *unforgeability advantage function.* In Section 1.5.7, we discuss *concrete security, asymptotic security and negligible functions.* Only then, in Section 1.5.8, we can use these concepts to finally present the EUF-CMA security requirement, i.e., defining signature schemes which ensure existential unforgeability under the chosen-message attack attack model.

Why signatures? Our choice of illustrating provable-security on signature schemes, rather than encryption, has multiple motivations. First, cryptographic signatures are fascinating and widely applied but are less known and understood by non-experts than cryptosystems. Second, the definition of security requirements of signature schemes is simpler and more intuitive than that of encryption schemes (see Section 2.9.3). Third, signatures allow us to define and compare multiple natural security requirements. Finally, these definitions are used in Chapter 3, which covers integrity and hash functions, including the *Hash-then-Sign* (HtS) paradigm and hash-based signature schemes, as well as in Chapter 4 which covers message authentication and in Chapter 6 which covers public key cryptography. Presenting them here allows the reader to chose the order of reading these chapters.

1.5.1 Definition of a signature scheme

A (digital/cryptographic) *signature scheme* $\mathcal{S}$ consists of three algorithms: $\mathcal{S} = (\mathcal{KG}, \mathcal{S}ign, \mathcal{V}erify)$. The $\mathcal{S}ign$ algorithm is used to sign messages, using a secret, private signing key s. The $\mathcal{V}erify$ algorithm is used to verify the purported signature over a message, using a known, public verification key v. Finally, the KG algorithm $\mathcal{KG}$ generates the *keypair* (s, v).

The definition, which follow, uses the concepts of efficient (PPT) algorithms and of security parameter, which we discuss in Appendix A. Intuitively, the security parameter indicates the desired tradeoff between security and performance; a longer security parameter implies more security and more overhead, e.g., longer keys. In most of the cryptographic literature, and specifically in this book, the *algorithms, including the adversaries, are efficient* (PPT). Namely, the run time of every algorithm is bounded by a polynomial in the length of its inputs, which usually includes the security parameter 1^n.

Usually, signature schemes can sign any binary string, i.e., any message in $\{0,1\}^*$. However, the definition requires signing only of messages from a given set M which can be the set of all binary strings ($M = \{0,1\}^*$) but can also be a subset of it, i.e., $M \subseteq \{0,1\}^*$. For example, M may be the set of binary strings of a specific length n, denoted $\{0,1\}^n$. When M is not explicitly mentioned, this implies the set of all binary strings, i.e., $M = \{0,1\}^*$.

Definition 1.1 (Signature scheme). A *signature scheme* is a tuple of three efficient (PPT) algorithms, $\mathcal{S} = (\mathcal{KG}, \mathcal{S}ign, \mathcal{V}erify)$, and a set $M \subseteq \{0,1\}^*$ of messages, such as follows:

$\mathcal{KG}$ is a randomized algorithm whose input is a unary string (security parameter 1^n) and whose output is a pair of binary strings (s, v), called the *private key* and the *public key*, respectively.

$\mathcal{S}ign$ is an algorithm that receives two binary strings as input, a signing key $s \in \{0,1\}^*$ and a message $m \in M$, and outputs another binary string $\sigma \in \{0,1\}^*$. We call σ the *signature* of m using signing key s.

$\mathcal{V}erify$ is an algorithm that receives three binary strings as input: a verification key v, a message $m \in M$, and σ, a purported signature over m, and whose output is TRUE or FALSE (i.e., a predicate). Intuitively, $\mathcal{V}erify$ should output TRUE if and only if σ is the signature of m using s, where s is the signature key corresponding to v (generated with v).

In practice, signature schemes often assume fixed input length n, i.e., $M = \{0,1\}^n$. To sign longer messages, the messages are *hashed* and *then* the output of the hash is *signed.* We refer to this as the *Hash-then-Sign* paradigm and discuss it in Section 3.3.5. The motivation is efficiency; the fixed-length signature schemes have high overhead (e.g., see Table 6.1), which further increase, super-linearly, as a function of the message size. Hashing longer messages, and then signing them, is much more efficient.

The definition allows the algorithms of the signature schemes to be *randomized*. This may look unnecessary, but, in fact, some important signing algorithms are randomized, e.g., using the *PSS* encoding [50, 364].

Signature scheme correctness requirement: The *correctness requirement* of a cryptographic scheme verifies that the scheme operates correctly under benign operating conditions, usually without allowing probability of error. For a signature scheme, this means that if the purported signature σ is indeed the output of the corresponding 'Sign' operation, then the verification will return TRUE, correctly indicating a valid signature. We next define this correctness requirement.

Definition 1.2 (Correctness of a signature scheme). We say that a signature scheme $(\mathcal{KG}, \mathcal{Sign}, \mathcal{Verify})$, with set M of messages, is *correct* if for every security parameter 1^n, every key-pair $(s, v) \overset{\$}{\leftarrow} \mathcal{KG}(1^n)$ and every message $m \in M$ holds:

$$\mathcal{Verify}_v(m, \mathcal{Sign}_s(m)) = \text{TRUE} \tag{1.2}$$

Signature scheme security requirements: Intuitively, the security goal of signature schemes is *unforgeability*, i.e., to prevent an attacker from obtaining a (meaningful) forgery, where a forgery is a valid signature for a message that was not signed by the owner of the private signing key s. However, this goal may be interpreted in several different ways. In the rest of this section, we discuss different aspects of the definition, including relevant attack models (Section 1.5.2) and types of signature forgeries (Section 1.5.3), as well as necessary notations and concepts, most significantly game-based security and the oracle notation (Section 1.5.4).

1.5.2 Signature attack models

Following the *attack model* principle (Principle 1), security should be defined and ensured with respect to *attacker capabilities*, i.e., *attack model*, rather than assuming a specific attack strategy. Let us discuss several attack models relevant to the security of signature schemes.

The key-only attack (KOA) model: The weakest attack model against a signature scheme is called the KOA model. In the KOA model, the adversary is given (only) the public verification key v. This attack model can be applied to most other cryptographic scheme; in the general case of an arbitrary scheme, the attacker is given (only) all the public keys and other public information.

However, the KOA model is usually considered too weak. In particular, for practical applications of signatures, the adversary would also be able to observe at least one signed message, in addition to the public key; this motivates the use of stronger attack models. Note that in all of these models, the adversary is assumed to be given, upon initialization, the public signature verification key v (like in the KOA model).

The known-message attack (KMA) model: In the KMA model, the attacker can receive (an arbitrary number of) pairs consisting each of a message and its signature. However, the attacker cannot control (choose) the messages. Variants of this model may require the attack to succeed for any given set of signed messages, possibly chosen by the attacker, or for a random set of messages (e.g., whose length is chosen by the attacker).

The KMA model is also usually considered too weak since in many applications and scenarios, the attacker may be able to lure the signer into signing *some* messages with specific format or content. For example, both parties are typically able to influence some of the text of a contract before it is signed.

The static and adaptive *chosen-message attack* (CMA) models: The static and adaptive CMA models allow the adversary to receive signatures over arbitrary messages, which we model by allowing the adversary to *choose* the messages to be signed.

We mostly focus on the adaptive CMA model, which allows the attacker to provide an arbitrary message and receive the signature of that message, and repeat this as many times as the attacker desires.

For the sake of brevity, we — and many texts in cryptography — usually simply refer to this attack model as CMA, i.e., do not include the word 'adaptive'.

In the (weaker) *static CMA* model, the attacker has to output the entire set of messages to be signed together, based only on the public key. Both attack models are stronger than the KMA and KOA

One may argue that the (adaptive) CMA model is 'unnecessarily strong'. In many applications, the adversary's ability to impact the contents of the signed message is very limited, and in some, the signer may phrase the contract, not allowing the adversary to have any (substantial) impact on it. It may seem that the KMA model may suffice; requiring security against the stronger models (static and adaptive chosen-message attack) may seem an unnecessary burden.

However, we want to avoid vulnerabilities in systems using cryptographic scheme, due to incorrect usage of the schemes, as well as due to an attacker which has capabilities not provided by the attack model adopted. It is difficult to predict the actual environment in which a cryptographic scheme would be used, and a subtle difference between the real attacker capabilities and the attack model we use may result in a vulnerability. Specifically, in Section 3.3.5, we show how an attacker who can receive signature over a document which is mostly benign, except for a short string selected by the attacker, is able to forge a signature over a very different document. This motivates a more *conservative* approach, e.g., the use of the stronger CMA or even adaptive chosen-message attack models, following the *conservative design and usage* principle (Principle 3). Therefore, in this book, and in most of the works in modern cryptography, we consider the adaptive chosen-message attack model against signature scheme.

1.5.3 Types of signature forgeries

Which forgery is considered as a successful attack? Clearly, the forgery must consist of a message which wasn't signed by the legitimate signer (owner of the private key) and a valid signature. However, *which* message is considered a *meaningful* forgery? We consider three types of forgeries:

Existential forgery: *Any* forgery is considered meaningful. Namely, the attacker is considered successful if it is able to obtain *any* pair of a message and a valid signature over it, where the message was not signed by the legitimate signer — even if the message is pure gibberish.

Selective forgery: The attacker selects some message $m \in M$ *before* it begins interacting with the system and then succeeds in generating a valid signature for m (without asking the signer to sign m, of course).

Universal forgery: The attacker can produce a valid signature to *any* message m given to it.

Attackers that can perform universal forgery can also perform selective forgery, and attackers that can perform selective forgery can also perform existential forgery.

For some application scenarios, it may suffice to prevent universal forgery or selective forgery, for example:

- Assume there are only two (or few) pre-defined messages to be signed, e.g., an inspector signing either 'valid' or 'invalid'. In this case, security against universal forgery suffices; the attacker cannot choose the message to be forged.
- Assume the application of signing a document, e.g., a contract. The attacker may have significant flexibility in which document it forges, but the forgery must be of a legible, meaningful contract. Existential forgery, where the attacker may only forge signature over some 'random' gibberish document, may not be a threat.

However, again following the *conservative design* principle (Principle 3), it is preferable to use signature schemes that prevent (even) existential forgery. Such schemes can be safely used, even in an application where the attacker may be able to exploit signatures over seemingly meaningless or benign messages.

Our discussion of signature schemes so far has been intuitive. In order to *prove* security, we need a precise definition of the security requirement from signature scheme; we present this later in this section (Definition 1.6). In order to present this definition, we need to first introduce and define several necessary concepts, beginning with *game-based security* and the *oracle notation*; we present these concepts in the following section.

1.5.4 Game-based security and the oracle notation

There are different methods of defining security requirements in general, and specifically, defining security for cryptographic schemes. This book, and many other works on applied provable security, follows the *game-based* approach; in particular, in the following section, we present the existential unforgeability CMA game, which is central to the definition of unforgeable signature schemes (Definition 1.6). But first, let us explain what we mean by a game.

Games: The term *game* refers to a well-defined algorithm that returns a binary outcome of one execution, where an adversary $\mathcal{A}$ attacks the scheme. The outcome is TRUE if the attack succeeded and FALSE if the attack failed. The game is often randomized; randomness may be used by the game itself, e.g., to define random challenges, by the adversary $\mathcal{A}$ and by the cryptographic scheme.

Game-based security definitions define a *game*, often using pseudocode, and then use the game to define the security requirements. A game is an algorithm which defines the outcome of an execution, involving a pair of efficient (PPT) algorithms, one for the adversary $\mathcal{A}$ and one for the scheme. The game usually provides adversary with *limited access* to the scheme; for example, the adversary may be able to request the scheme to sign some message using the private key, without the game providing the adversary with the private key itself. To explain how this is done, we introduce *oracles and the oracle notation.*

Oracles and the oracle notation: The attack model in many cryptographic games does not provide any of the secret or private keys to the adversary; the adversary would be given any non-secret keys, e.g., the public keys in a public–private key pair.

However, most attack models also allow the adversary to receive the result of specific, limited operations that *use* the private key. In particular, in the (adaptive) CMA model, which is the attack model usually used for analysis of signature schemes, the adversary can receive signatures of messages it chooses. The signatures are computed using the private signing key, which is not disclosed to the attacker.

Basically, the game provides the attacker with 'black box' or 'subroutine' access to a function that has access to the private key. Specifically, to allow a CMA, the attacker is given access to a function computing $\mathcal{S}ign_s(\cdot)$, where s is the private signing key (not given to the attacker $\mathcal{A}$).

We refer to the function $\mathcal{S}ign_s(\cdot)$ as an *oracle*; it allows the adversary to compute $\mathcal{S}ign_s(m)$ for any message $m \in M \subseteq \{0,1\}^*$ (typically, $M = \{0,1\}^*$) chosen by the adversary. Oracles are used extensively in cryptography and in complexity theory.

We use the *oracle notation* $\mathcal{A}^{\mathcal{S}.\mathcal{S}ign_s(\cdot)}$ to denote that the adversary $\mathcal{A}$ is given *oracle access* to $\mathcal{S}ign_s(\cdot)$, the signing functionality using the private signing key s, for attacker-chosen messages. This means that the attacker $\mathcal{A}$ can provide input $x \in M \subseteq \{0,1\}^*$ and receive $\mathcal{S}.\mathcal{S}ign_s(x)$, i.e., a signature of x using the secret key s. Note that $\mathcal{A}$ does not receive the private signing key s and does not learn additional information about the computation done by $\mathcal{S}.\mathcal{S}ign_s(\cdot)$, except for the outcome.

Definition 1.3 (Oracle notation). Let $\mathcal{A}$ be an algorithm, f be a function and $k \in \{0.1\}^*$ be a string (typically, a secret such as a private key). We use the notation $\mathcal{A}^{f_k(\cdot)}$ to denote that algorithm $\mathcal{A}$ can provide input x and receive $f_k(x)$. We refer to $f_k(\cdot)$ as the *oracle* of $\mathcal{A}^{f_k(\cdot)}$.

In the following section, we use the oracle notation to define the existential unforgeability CMA game.

1.5.5 The existential unforgeability CMA game

We now present a game for defining an *EUF-CMA* signature scheme $\mathcal{S}$, i.e., a signature scheme that is existentially unforgeability under the (adaptive) CMA model. We provide the algorithms of the attacker $\mathcal{A}$ and the signature scheme $\mathcal{S}$ as inputs to the game. The game defines the attack model, i.e., including the allows interactions between the attacker and the scheme. The game also defines the 'winning conditions', i.e., what we consider as a successful attack (e.g., for signature schemes, a successful forgery).

Algorithm 1 presents the pseudocode of the *existential unforgeability* CMA game, $EUF{-}CMA_{\mathcal{A},\mathcal{S}}(1^n)$. The game returns TRUE if the adversary 'wins', i.e., is able to output an arbitrary message m and a valid signature σ for the message m, without asking the oracle to sign m. Otherwise, the attack fails, and the game returns FALSE.

Algorithm 1 The existentially unforgeable (adaptive) chosen-message attack game $EUF{-}CMA_{\mathcal{A},\mathcal{S}}(1^n)$ between the signature scheme $\mathcal{S} = (\mathcal{KG}, \mathcal{S}ign, \mathcal{V}erify)$ and the adversary $\mathcal{A}$.

$(s, v) \xleftarrow{\$} \mathcal{S}.\mathcal{KG}(1^n)$
$(m, \sigma) \xleftarrow{\$} \mathcal{A}^{\mathcal{S}.\mathcal{S}ign_s(\cdot)}(v, 1^n)$
if m was given as input to $\mathcal{S}.\mathcal{S}ign_s(\cdot)$ **return** FALSE
return $\mathcal{S}.\mathcal{V}erify_v(m, \sigma)$

Explanation of the CMA existential unforgeability game: $EUF{-}CMA_{\mathcal{A},\mathcal{S}}(1^n)$ (Algorithm 1). The game receives as input the security parameter 1^n and has the following steps:

1. Use the KG algorithm of the signature scheme to generate the signing and verification keys: $(s, v) \xleftarrow{\$} \mathcal{S}.\mathcal{KG}(1^n)$. We use the $\xleftarrow{\$}$ symbol to emphasize that $\mathcal{S}.\mathcal{KG}$ is a randomized algorithm, i.e., it returns a randomly chosen key pair.
2. Receive a message m and a purported forged signature for it, σ, from the adversary $\mathcal{A}$. The adversary has oracle access to the signing algorithm, i.e., can receive the values $\mathcal{S}.\mathcal{S}ign_s(x)$ for any input x chosen by the adversary. Note that this step is also randomized since both the attacker $\mathcal{A}$ and the signature scheme may be probabilistic.
3. Check if the message m provided by the adversary is one of the messages x that $\mathcal{A}$ received their signatures from the oracles. If it is, then this is not a real forgery, and the attack fails, i.e., the game returns FALSE.
4. Finally, the game returns TRUE, i.e., the adversary 'wins', if σ is a valid signature on m (using the verification key v), and FALSE otherwise.

Intuitively, a CMA existentially unforgeable signature scheme $\mathcal{S}$ ensures that every efficient (PPT) adversary $\mathcal{A}$ would 'almost always' lose, i.e., $\Pr(EUF{-}CMA_{\mathcal{A},\mathcal{S}}(1^n) = \text{TRUE})$ would be tiny or negligible, provided that the security parameter 1^n is 'sufficiently large'. We define this requirement in the following, in Section 1.5.1, specifically, in Definition 1.6. However, Definition 1.6 uses another important concept which we must introduce first, called an *advantage function*. In Section 1.5.6, we introduce advantage functions and define the *existential unforgeability advantage function*.

Before we discuss the advantage function, let us present an exercise which explains why we must require $\mathcal{A}$ to be an efficient algorithm and why the definition of the signature scheme cannot be limited to a specific key size. Namely, the exercise shows that the adversary $\mathcal{A}$ can always 'win' the $EUF{-}CMA_{\mathcal{A},\mathcal{S}}(1^n)$ game against an arbitrary signature scheme $\mathcal{S}$, if either we allow $\mathcal{A}$ to be inefficient (i.e., not a *PPT* algorithm) or if the keys generated by $\mathcal{S}$ are of limited length. In both of these cases, there is an adversary $\mathcal{A}$ such that $EUF{-}CMA_{\mathcal{A},\mathcal{S}}(1^n)$ always returns TRUE.

Exercise 1.1 (Forgery if adversary is computationally unbounded or if key length is bounded). Let $\mathcal{S}$ be an arbitrary efficient (PPT) signature algorithm. Present an adversary $\mathcal{A}$ that is able to 'win' $EUF{-}CMA_{\mathcal{A},\mathcal{S}}(1^n)$ *every time* if we allow either of the following:

1. $\mathcal{A}$ does not have to be an efficient (PPT) algorithm.
2. $\mathcal{S}.\mathcal{KG}$ outputs bounded-length keys.

Sketch of solution to first item: Since $\mathcal{S}$ is efficient, there is some polynomial which bounds the running time of each of the three algorithms of $\mathcal{S}$ as function of their input length. In particular, this bounds the length of the private signing key s, generated by the KG algorithm, as a polynomial function of the length of the security parameter (which is the input to the KG). The adversary $\mathcal{A}$ tries all strings s' whose length is up to the bound on the length of s. Then, the adversary $\mathcal{A}$ applies the signature algorithm using each such potential signature key s'. Each time, $\mathcal{A}$ verifies the resulting purported signature using the public key v; eventually, the correct signing key is found.

Sketch of solution to the second item: Assume that the private signing key s is always of a specific length, e.g., 42. Then, $\mathcal{A}$ tries to sign using any of the 2^{42} possible keys, verifying the signatures using the (known) public key, until it finds the correct key. The number of keys is 2^{42}, which is a (large) constant but not a function of the security parameter; the adversary can test all 2^{42} possible keys. Note that any fixed number of bits in the key, even much larger than 42, will have the same impact. □

1.5.6 The unforgeability advantage function

The existentially unforgeable game (Algorithm 1) is a random process, which returns the outcome of a random run of the game, with the given adversary $\mathcal{A}$ and signature scheme $\mathcal{S}$. The outcome is TRUE in runs where the adversary 'wins', i.e., outputs a forgery, and FALSE in runs where the adversary 'loses', i.e., does not output a forgery.

The outcome of the game may depend on the (random) keys output by the (probabilistic) $\mathcal{KG}$ algorithm, as well as the outputs of the (randomized) adversary $\mathcal{A}$. The probability that the adversary wins usually depends on the security parameter 1^n. This probability is called the *existential unforgeability advantage* of $\mathcal{A}$ against $\mathcal{S}$.

Definition 1.4. The *CMA existential unforgeability advantage function* of adversary $\mathcal{A}$ against signature scheme $\mathcal{S}$ is defined as

$$\varepsilon^{EUF-CMA}_{\mathcal{S},\mathcal{A}}(1^n) \equiv \Pr\left(EUF-CMA_{\mathcal{A},\mathcal{S}}(1^n) = \text{TRUE}\right) \tag{1.3}$$

where the probability is taken over the random coin tosses of $\mathcal{A}$ and of $\mathcal{S}$ during the run of $EUF-CMA_{\mathcal{A},\mathcal{S}}(1^n)$ with input (security parameter) 1^n and $EUF-CMA_{\mathcal{A},\mathcal{S}}(1^n)$ is the game defined in Algorithm 1.

The advantage function gives us a measure of the security of the signature scheme; in particular, clearly, a scheme is secure only if for any efficient adversary $\mathcal{A}$, the advantage is small, or better yet, *negligible*.[5] Note, however, that for any fixed value of the security

[5]Unfortunately, no efficient signature scheme can ensure zero advantage; see Exercise 1.5.

parameter 1^n, there is an adversary $\mathcal{A}$ that *always wins*, i.e., such that $\varepsilon^{EUF-CMA}_{\mathcal{S},\mathcal{A}}(1^n) = 1$ (Exercise 1.1). Therefore, our definition of security cannot be bounded to a specific security parameter and must consider the advantage as a function.

Which advantage functions are sufficiently small (or negligible)? There are two main ways in which we can deal with this question: *asymptotic security* and *concrete security*. In this book, we adopt the asymptotic security approach, which we explain in the following, since it is a bit easier to use. However, let us first briefly explain the alternative approach of concrete security, which allows more detailed analysis of security — but is a bit harder to use.

1.5.7 Concrete security, asymptotic security and negligible functions

Concrete security: The concrete security approach uses the advantage function directly as the measure of security. Namely, in this approach, there is no explicit definition of a 'secure' scheme; each scheme is only associated with a specific advantage function. This allows the calculation of the advantage as a specific probability value — for any given, concrete values of the security parameter 1^n; this is also the reason for the term, *concrete security*. In fact, in this approach, often the advantage function is given additional parameters. For example, the advantage function for a signature scheme may include the number of messages signed during the execution. In general, inputs to the advantage function often include the number of (different kinds of) oracle calls.

Concrete security allows precise analysis of security for specific key lengths and other parameters, and the security impacts of different cryptographic constructions. This is a significant advantage of concrete security over asymptotic security (defined next). However, in this book we use the *asymptotic security* approach, described in the following, since it results in simpler security definitions, where a design is either secure or insecure, rather than providing a quantitative measure of the security of a design.

Asymptotic security and negligible functions: Asymptotic security requires the advantage function, e.g., $\varepsilon^{EUF-CMA}_{\mathcal{S},\mathcal{A}}(1^n)$, to be *negligible* in the security parameter n.

What does it mean when we say that a function $\varepsilon : \mathbb{N} \to \mathbb{R}$ is *negligible*? Clearly, we expect such a function to converge to zero for large input, i.e., $\lim_{n\to\infty} \varepsilon(n) = 0$. Moreover, a negligible function is a function that converges to zero *faster than any (non-zero) polynomial*; the definition follows.

Definition 1.5 (Negligible function). A function $\varepsilon : \mathbb{N} \to \mathbb{R}$ is *negligible* if for every polynomial $p(n)$ holds:

$$\lim_{n\to\infty} \varepsilon(n) \cdot p(n) = 0 \tag{1.4}$$

We use $NEGL(n)$ (or sometimes simple $NEGL$) to denote the set of all negligible functions (in input n).

Notes:

1. An equivalent condition is to say that $\varepsilon : \mathbb{N} \to \mathbb{R}$ is *negligible* if for every c holds $\lim_{n\to\infty} \varepsilon(n) \cdot n^c = 0$.
2. Any non-zero polynomial is not negligible (prove this!).
3. For any constant $x > 1$, the inverse exponential function $\varepsilon(n) = x^{-n}$, e.g., 2^{-n}, is negligible (prove this!).

Here is an exercise to make sure this important concept is well understood.

Exercise 1.2. Which of the following functions are negligible? Why? (a) $f_a(n) = 10^{-8} \cdot n^{-10}$, (b) $f_b(n) = 2^{-n/2}$, (c) $f_c(n) = \frac{1}{n!}$, (d) $f_d(n) = \frac{(-1)^n}{n}$, (e) $f_e(n) = 0.5^n$.

Working with negligible functions is a useful simplification; here is one convenient property, which shows that if an algorithm has negligible probability to 'succeed', then running it a polynomial number of times will not help — the probability to succeed will remain negligible.

Lemma 1.1. *Consider negligible function $\epsilon : \mathbb{N} \to \mathbb{R}$, i.e., $\epsilon(n) \in NEGL(n)$. Then, for any polynomial $p(n)$, the function $f(n) = p(n) \cdot \epsilon(n)$ is also negligible, i.e., $f(n) \in NEGL(n)$.*

1.5.8 Defining unforgeable signature schemes

We now use the definitions of a negligible function and of the CMA existential unforgeability advantage function to define the asymptotic notion of an *existentially unforgeable* signature scheme.

Definition 1.6 (Existential unforgeability under CMA). A signature scheme $\mathcal{S}$ is *existentially unforgeable under (adaptive) chosen-message attack (CMA)* if for all PPT algorithms $\mathcal{A}$, the *EUF-CMA advantage* of $\mathcal{A}$ over $\mathcal{S}$ is negligible, i.e., $\varepsilon_{\mathcal{S},\mathcal{A}}^{EUF-CMA}(1^n) \in NEGL(n)$, where $\varepsilon_{\mathcal{S},\mathcal{A}}^{EUF-CMA}(1^n)$ is defined in Definition 1.4.

Recall that $\varepsilon_{\mathcal{S},\mathcal{A}}^{EUF-CMA}(1^n) \equiv \Pr(EUF-CMA_{\mathcal{A},\mathcal{S}}(1^n) = \text{TRUE})$ is the probability that the adversary $\mathcal{A}$ succeeds to forge a message, in a random run of the existential unforgeability game, with adversary $\mathcal{A}$, signature scheme $\mathcal{S}$ and security parameter 1^n.

Multiple other security requirements and games can be defined for signature schemes, using other attack models, including key-only attack, KMA and static CMA, or other types of forgeries, including universal and selective forgeries.

One-Time Signatures: Our definitions above focused on the 'classical' definitions of signature schemes and their security. However, there are many other variations considered in the cryptographic literature; let us mention one of these variants: *one-time signature* schemes. These are signature schemes which allow only a single signature operation. A similar variant allows a limited number of signature operations (*limited-use signatures*).

One-time (and limited-use) signatures can be more computationally efficient than the 'classical', unlimited-use signatures; see Section 3.4.2. They may also be a convenient way to ensure security against attackers with quantum-computing capabilities, see Section 10.1. Adapting the definitions we presented above to support such variants is not difficult; see Exercise 1.3.

Exercise 1.3. 1. Based on the definitions in this chapter, define a one-time signature scheme.
2. Define the EUF-CMA game for a one-time signature scheme.
3. Define an existentially unforgeable one-time signature scheme.

1.6 A brief history of cryptography, computing and cybersecurity

Cryptography is one of the earliest sciences, and it played a large role in the early development of computing. On the other hand, the history of computing is closely linked to the history of cyberspace and cybersecurity.

We conclude this chapter with a brief review of the history of cryptography (Section 1.6.1) and then of the history of computing and cybersecurity (Section 1.6.2).

1.6.1 A brief history of cryptography

We now present a brief history of cryptography. We are only able to give few important highlights from the fascinating history of cryptography, and interested readers should consult some of the excellent manuscripts, such as Refs. [279, 447]. We identify three main eras of cryptography: the *ancient, heuristic cryptography era* (until 1883), the *Enigma era* (1883–1970s) and the *modern cryptography era*. We chose the year 1883 to separate between the heuristic era and the Enigma era since in that year Kerckhoffs published his seminal manuscript [292].

The ancient, heuristic cryptography era [until 1883]: The terms *cryptography* and *cryptology* are both from Greek. The literal meaning of cryptology is the 'science of secrets', while the literal meaning of cryptography is 'secret writing', but the two are used mostly as synonyms. Cryptography has been used to protect sensitive communication since ancient times, before any computing devices. For most of this time, cryptology focused on protecting secrecy, i.e., on *confidentiality*, which is mainly provided by *cryptosystems*.

One of the early evidences of encryption is from about 1500BC; it is an encryption of a formula for pottery glaze, which presumably was commercially valuable. For this and other details of ancient cryptography, read some of the excellent books such as Refs. [279, 330, 447]. We present a few ancient ciphers in Section 2.2.

Kerckhoffs's publication (1883): We consider Kerckhoffs's publication [292], in 1883, as the end of the ancient, heuristic cryptography era. Kerckhoffs's work may have been the first major published work in cryptography; until it, most works in cryptography, and designs of cryptosystems, were kept secret, following the *security by obscurity* approach (with few limited exceptions). Kerckhoffs realized that it is better to assume that the attacker may be able to capture encryption devices and reverse-engineer them to learn the algorithm, as we paraphrase in Kerckhoffs's principle (Principle 2), see Section 1.2.2.

Kerckhoffs's principle remains a basic principle of cryptography and is gradually being adopted into other areas of cybersecurity. With the increased use of cryptography, adoption of standards, software implementations and advanced reverse-engineering tools, Kerckhoffs's principle only became even more important.

Note that Kerckhoffs did not argue that cryptographic designs *should* be published. Indeed, for many years after Kerckhoffs's book was published, research and development in cryptography remained an area mostly dealt with by intelligence and defense organizations, and mostly in secret. This was definitely true until, and during, World War II.

The Enigma era [1883–1970s]: The most important advances in cryptography after Kerckhoffs's publication were made as part of the efforts of the Second World War (WWII) and in the period leading to it. Cryptography, and in particular cryptanalysis, i.e., 'breaking' the security of cryptographic schemes, played a key role during the Second World War; an important by-product was the development of the first computer.

During the war, both sides used multiple types of encryption devices. The most well known is the *Enigma* encryption device, used by the Germans. The early versions of the Enigma were in use already from 1924, and it was modified and improved over the years. Due to the importance of the Enigma, we use it as the name of the era.

Details of the design of the Enigma were kept secret; however, the designers clearly tried to follow Kerckhoffs's principle and ensure security even if the design would be known to the cryptanalysts. This fact, together with continuous improvements to Enigma, made the Germans believe that Enigma will not be broken.

Indeed, the Allies were very concerned about their lack of ability to decipher Enigma traffic; the cryptanalysis of Enigma was a major undertaking and a huge achievement. However, there may have been also a drawback to the German cryptographic effort: they were over-confident in the security of Enigma and continued using it long after it was broken. Possibly due to this overconfidence, they also used Enigma in ways which made it easier to break the cipher, in violation of the *conservative design and usage* principle (Principle 3).

For example, operators often sent the same message at fixed times or upon specific events, allowing the cryptanalysts to perform a known-plaintext attack (KPA), as discussed in Section 2.3, which is much more effective than attacks without known plaintext.

When the Enigma was eventually broken, the allies took extraordinary measure to prevent the Germans from realizing this so that the Germans will not change keys, change Enigma or take other precautions. Usually, this meant creating alternate explanations to the Allies response to the information in the plaintext, but sometimes, the difficult decision was made to avoid reaction to the information since the resulting risks to people and/or property was deemed less than the risks if the Germans realize that Enigma was broken. It has been estimated that the successful cryptanalysis of Enigma shortened the war by about two years and saved millions of lives.

While the Enigma was designed following Kerckhoffs's principle, i.e., to ensure security even if its design is known, the German also made extensive efforts to maintain the secrecy of the design. Indeed, the successful attacks on Enigma were based on leakage of some information about it. In 1932, the French intelligence were able to obtain the secret manual and the settings for the Enigma from a German officer and shared this information with the British intelligence and the Polish cryptanalysis unit, called the *cipher bureau.*

In the Polish cipher bureau, Captain Maksymilian Ciężki led team that used mathematics for cryptanalysis, consisting of three of his cryptography students: Rejewski, Zygalski and Różycki. Using the Engima's manual and setting, the team reverse-engineered the Enigma and built Enigma replicates. Furthermore, they developed special-purpose electromechanical devices called *Bombe* that allowed efficient testing of different Enigma keys against limited exposed information, such as known pairs of ciphertext and (likely) plaintext.

In 1939, Poland shared their Bombe devices and their cryptanalysis results with the British. Using plaintext/ciphertext pairs and the Bombe machines, the cryptanalysis center in Bletchley Park, led by Alan Turing, was able to decipher much of the intercepted Enigma traffic.

However, the Germans periodically improved the Enigma. Every change in the Enigma required extensive effort to design and create modified Bombe devices, and a period when traffic could not be deciphered.

Furthermore, the somewhat less known *Lorenz* encryption devices were introduced by the Germans later in the war, and no complete device was captured and available to cryptanalysts.

The challenges of adapting Bombe devices to changes in Enigma, and of breaking the Lorenz devices, motivated the construction of the *first electronic computer*, called the *Colossus*. Since Colossus was programmable, it was possible to test many possible attacks and to successfully cryptanalyze (different versions of) the Lorenz, Enigma and other cryptosystems. For more on the history of computing and cybersecurity, and its relationships to cryptography, see Section 1.6.2.

Modern cryptography: Until the 1970s, cryptography remained mainly a topic for intelligence and research organizations. In the 1970s, this changed, quite dramatically, with the beginning of what we now call *modern cryptology*, which involves extensive academic research, publication, products and standards, and has many important commercial applications.

Two important landmarks mark the beginning of modern cryptology. The first landmark is the development and publication of the *Data Encryption Standard* (DES) [377]. The publication of DES as an open standard marks that cryptography began to be widely deployed in commercial products; in particular, DES was key to the security of the emerging bank networks and to the security mechanisms of the emerging computer communication networks, which was dominated, for many years, by IBM's Systems Network Architecture (SNA).

The second landmark is the introduction of radical, innovative concept of *Public Key Cryptography*, where the key to encrypt messages may be *public*, allowing easy distribution of encryption keys. The first publication was of the seminal paper *New directions in cryptography* [155], by Diffie and Hellman; see Chapter 6.

It is notable that in Ref. [155], Diffie and Hellman did not yet present a design of a PKC. The first published PKC was RSA by Rivest, Shamir and Adelman in Ref. [418].

In fact, the same design as RSA was already discovered a few years earlier, by the GCHQ British intelligence organization. However, the GCHQ kept this achievement secret until 1997, long after the same design was re-discovered independently and published in Ref. [418].

See Ref. [330] for more details about the fascinating history of the discovery — and re-discovery — of public key cryptology.

These two discoveries of public-key cryptology, with very different impacts on society, illustrate the dramatic change between 'classical' cryptology, studied only in secrecy and with impact mostly limited to the intelligence and defense areas, and modern cryptology, with extensive published research and extensive impact on society and economy.

1.6.2 A brief history of computing and cybersecurity

Early computing — from Babbage to the Colossus: The first known design of a computing device was developed by Charles Babbage in 1822. Babbage's created two designs of mechanical computing devices: the *difference engine* and the *analytical engine*. The difference engine was a special-purpose machine, designed to tabulate logarithms and trigonometric functions; however, the analytical engine was a general purpose computer, which was designed to process input consisting of data and a program, both provided using punched cards.

Babbage was also interested in cryptography and designed the first known practical attack against the *Vigenère cipher* (which we discuss in Section 2.2). The attack was based on usage of letter frequencies, and one of the applications Babbage designed for the analytical engine was to compute letter frequencies and perform frequency analysis. We discuss frequency analysis in Section 2.2.4.

Babbage was not able to complete implementing either engine, but his designs were correct; they were implemented and tested, for historical purposes, from 1989 to 1991, i.e., more than a century after he died. However, Babbage did build some modules of the engines and has demonstrated and described their designs to peers.

The demonstration and description excited Ada Lovelace, one of the few female mathematicians at the time. Ada wrote a description of the sequence of operations for solving certain mathematical problems by the analytical engine. This sequence of operations is considered the first computer program; Ada was also the first to suggest that computers may be used to manipulate non-numeric data, such as text or music.

It took about a century from the initial design of the engines and until the first *working* computing device was implemented. This was a mechanical device designed and implemented in 1938, by the German inventor Konrad Zuse; Zuse named it the Z1.

The Z1 was unreliable and slow. As a result, it did not have any useful applications or use, except as proof of feasibility. In particular, special-purpose calculating devices were way better in performing applied calculations. In particular, this held for electromechanical designs including the Enigma cipher used for encryption, and the Bombe machines used in Bletchley park to break the Enigma; both were much more efficient and reliable than the Z1.

However, as we discussed above, there was a repeated struggle to adapt the Bombe devices to changes in Enigma, and the Bombe failed to break the newer Lorenz cryptosystem. This motivated the construction of the *first practical computer*, called *Colossus.*

Colossus was designed by Tommy Flowers as part of the Bletchley park WWII cryptanalysis effort. Colossus was the first fully electric computing device, i.e., did not involve mechanical components. The Colossus was also the first *computer*, i.e., the first computing device that could be *programmed* for arbitrary tasks, rather than only perform a predefined set of tasks or computations. This was in contrast to previous devices, including the Enigma and the Lorenz cryptosystems, which were electro-mechanical and also were limited to a predefined computation.

From Colossus to Modern Computers: One critical difference between the Colossus and more modern computers, as well as from Babbage's design of the analytical engine, is that *the Colossus did not read a program from storage.* Instead, setting up the program for the Colossus involved manual setting of switches and jack-panel connections.

This method of 'programming' the Colossus wasn't very convenient, but it was acceptable for the Colossus since there were only a few such machines and only a few, simple programs, and the simplicity of design and manufacture was more important than making it easier to change programs. Even this crude form of 'programming' was incomparably easier than changing the basic functionality of the machine, as required in special-purpose devices — including the

Enigma devices and the Bombe devices used for cryptanalysis of the Enigma traffic.

Designs of an electromechanical computer which supports a stored program were proposed already in 1936/1937 — by two independent efforts. The first was by Konrad Zuse, who mentioned such design in a patent on floating-point calculations published in 1936 [503]; the second was by *Alan Turing*, who defined and studied a formal model for stored-program computers. This *Turing machine model*, introduced in Turing's seminar paper 'On Computable Numbers' [459], is fundamental to the theory of computing.

However, practical implementations of stored-program computers appeared only *after* WWII. Stored-program computers were much easier to use and allowed larger and more sophisticated programs as well as the use of the same hardware for multiple purposes (and programs). Hence, stored-program computers quickly became the norm — to the extent that some people argue that earlier devices were not 'real computers'.

Stored-program computers also created a vast market for programs. It now became feasible for programs to be created in one location and then shipped to and installed in a remote computer. For many years, this was done by physically shipping the programs, stored in media such as tapes, discs and others. Now that computer networks are widely available, program distribution is usually done by sending the program over the network.

Easier distribution of software meant also that the same program could be used by many computers; indeed, today we have programs that run on billions of computing devices.

Computer Networks and Cyberspace: The ability to develop a program and have it applied in multiple computers caused the economic 'network effect' that made computers and programming much more useful. This effect dramatically increased when *computer networks* began to facilitate inter-computer communication.

The introduction of personal computers (1977–1982), and the subsequent introduction of the Internet, the web and the smartphone, caused further dramatic increases in the use and impact of computing and of computer networking.

There was also a growing interest in the potential social implications of computers and networks, and a growing number of science-fiction works focused on these aspects. One of these was the novel 'Burning Chrome', published by William Gibson in 1982. Actually, it seems that it was this novel that introduced the term *cyberspace*, to refer to this interconnected environment connecting networks, computers, devices and humans.

The *cyber* part of the term *cyberspace* is taken from the term *cybernetics*, introduced in Ref. [481] to describe the study of communication and control systems in machines, humans and animals.

By now, computing is used not only in 'traditional computers', but as a critical component of many other devices, from tiny sensors to vehicles — cyber-physical systems and Internet of Things (IoT) devices. The term *cyberspace* is now mostly used for the ubiquitous use of devices with different computing capabilities, communicating via networks and interacting with humans.

Cybersecurity and Hacking: With great power, comes great responsibility — and risks. With the growing importance and popularity of computers and programs came abuses, most significantly, attacks by malicious software, which we now refer to as *malware*. Similarly, with the increased importance and popularity of the Internet and cyberspace came increased risks of abuse and cyber-attacks. The awareness of these risks significantly increased as attacks on computer systems and networks became widespread, especially attacks exploiting software vulnerabilities, and/or involving malicious software, i.e., *malware*. This awareness resulted in the study, research and development of threats and corresponding security mechanisms, including *computer security, software security, network security* and *data/information security.*

The awareness of security risks also resulted in important works of fiction. One of these was the 1983 novel *cyberpunk*, by Bruce Bethke. Bethke coined this term for individuals which are socially inept yet technologically savvy. Originally a derogatory term, the term cyberpunk is now also used with a positive interpretation, e.g., see Ref. [294].

The reverse process happened with regard to the term *hacker*, which was originally used, already from the 1960s, to describe proficient programmers, thinking 'out of the box' and finding creative solutions and shortcuts ('hacks'), and more recently, to experts of computer security. However, from the 1980s, the term hacker is often applied with a negative connotation, to a person who tries to *break* into computer systems and to circumvent defenses. The terms *black-hat hacker* (or *cracker*) and *white-hat hacker* (or just hacker) are often used to distinguish between the 'attacking hacker' and the 'defending hacker', or between hackers operating illegally and hackers following legal, and hopefully also ethical, principles.

In works of fiction, cyberpunks and hackers are often presented as socially inept yet technology savvy, with incredible abilities to penetrate systems. These abilities are mostly presented in glamorous ways, e.g., saving human society from oppressive, corrupt regimes, governments, agencies and rogue artificial intelligence systems. The focus on decentralization and personal freedom is definitely a main part of the cyberpunk manifestos [294].

Much of the success of the Internet is due to its decentralized nature and to the use of cryptography to provide security to financial transactions and some level of privacy. Important privacy tools, such as the *Tor* anonymous communication system [156], are based on cryptography and inherently decentralized, which may be hoped to defend against potentially malicious governments. Tor's security is based on its usage of the TLS protocol (Chapter 7); note, however, that its (correct) use of TLS and encryption does not suffice to ensure anonymity against an attacker with sufficient eavesdropping capabilities.

Several of the cryptography and privacy mechanisms, such as the *PGP* encryption suite [197], were developed in spite of significant resistance by governments. Cryptography is also at the core of the extensive efforts to develop *blockchain* (see Section 3.9) and other decentralized financial tools and cryptocurrencies, including Bitcoin; see Section 3.9.2. In fact, many people use the term 'crypto' as a synonym for 'cryptocurrency'.

1.7 Lab: using cryptography to verify downloads

Lab 1 (Using cryptography to verify downloads). *Malware*, i.e., *malicious software*, is among the most common and harmful cybersecurity threats. In this lab, we explore the use of basic cryptographic mechanisms, specifically, collision-resistant hash functions and signature schemes, which we introduced in Section 1.2, to *verify* *software downloads* and thereby distinguish between malware and legitimate downloaded software.

The labs and installation instructions are available from https://github.com/CyberSec-labs/labs; see more details in the preface:

1. *Using hash for download integrity*: In this question, we use a CRHF to ensure the integrity of software downloads, i.e., to ensure download is of the intended, authentic software, and not of a malware impersonated as the desired software. Software is often made available via repositories, which may not be fully secure; to ensure the integrity, the publishers often provide the hash of the software. Namely, to protect the integrity of some software download, say encoded as a string m, the publisher provides in some secure channel the value of the hash $H_m \equiv h(m)$. The user then downloads the software from the (insecure) repository, obtaining the downloaded string m'. To confirm its integrity, i.e., confirm that $m' = m$, the user uses m' if $h(m') = H_m$, i.e., $h(m') = h(m)$. Based on the collision-resistance property of h, the fact that $h(m') = h(m)$ is believed to imply that $m = m'$. Note that other applications of hash functions may rely on other properties, for example, on the one-way property (Section 3.4).

   Input: A folder *Q1files* containing several files, and a file *Q1.hash*, containing the SHA-256 hash applied to one of the files. Note that the file contains the hash in binary bytes, not encoded as text.

   Goal: Identify the file in *Q1files* whose hash is given in *Q1.hash*.

   Submission: (1) The name of the matching file, to be submitted in file *solution_1.txt*, and (2) a program, *A1.py* that, given a hash file *Q1.hash* and a folder *Q1files*, outputs the name of the matching file (or a message if there is no matching file).

2. *Using signatures to authenticate downloads*: The hash mechanism has two disadvantages: First, an attacker which controls the value of the Digest can set it to be the digest of a malware; second, the digest must be updated for any software update. In this question, we show an alternative: *authenticating* the software using a *digital signature scheme* (Section 1.2.4).

   Practical cryptographic libraries such as PyCryptodome use the HtS paradigm (Section 3.3.5), i.e., they apply the signing function to the *hash* of the information to be signed. Hence, you will need to specify both a signature scheme (e.g., use RSA) and a hash function (e.g., use again the SHA-256 hash function). The reason for using the HtS paradigm is that it is absurdly inefficient to apply the public-key signature algorithm directly over a (usually) long message rather than over the (short) hash:

Input: The file *Q2pk.pem*, which contains the public verification key, which can be used to verify files purportedly signed by the legitimate software, and the directory *Q2files* which contains several files and the corresponding purported signatures. *Note*: The signature was created by the *LabGen.py* script, using RSA signature (with PKCS #1 v1.5 padding) and using the SHA-256 hash function.

Goal: Identify the file(s) in *Q2files* which are properly signed, as verified using the public key given in *Q2pk.pem*.

Submission: The properly signed file(s), and a program, *A2.py* that, given the public verification key file *Q2pk.pem* and a folder *Q2files*, outputs the name(s) of the matching file(s) (or a message if there is no matching file).

3. To get a feeling for the performance of public key signatures and of cryptographic hash functions, perform experiments and presents graphs showing:

   (a) The time required for hashing as a function of the input length, from 100,000 bytes to one million bytes.

   (b) The time required for generation of signing and verification public key pairs, for keys of lengths from 1000 bits to the maximal length you find feasible (say, up to five minutes).

   (c) The time required to sign inputs for inputs of length from 100,000 bytes to one million bits, using each of the private signing keys you generated in the previous item.

   (d) The time required to verify signatures for inputs of length from 100,000 bytes to one million bits, using each of the private signing keys you generated in the previous item.

   (e) Explain how the results received in the previous items make sense, the implications for the time required for hashing, signing, and validating, and the relations to the *HtS* paradigm (Section 3.3.5).

Notes:

(a) You may need to repeat some operations multiple times to be able to measure the times with reasonable precision.
(b) You may compare different implementation options, such as using standard Python, using PyPy, and using optimized and non-optimized compilers, e.g., for a language such as C, C++ or Rust.
(c) In the folder *Q3files/inputs*, you will find files containing from 100,000 bytes to one million bytes, named according to the number of bytes contained within the file.

1.8 Additional exercises

Exercise 1.4. Let $\mathcal{S}$ be a signature scheme, and let $\mathcal{A}^{\text{Key}}$ and $\mathcal{A}^{\sigma}$ be the following two simple adversaries:

$\mathcal{A}^{\text{Key}}(v)$ randomly guesses the signing key s. After guessing s, the adversary signs the desired message using s and 'wins' if the signature verifies correctly using verification key v.

$\mathcal{A}^{\sigma}(v)$ randomly guesses the signature σ for a message m chosen by the adversary and 'wins' if σ verifies correctly using verification key v.

Consider a single guess by both adversaries. Let l_s denote the length of the signing key s and l_σ denote the length of the signatures produces by the signing algorithm (assume all signatures has same length l_σ).

1. Compute the exact probability that each adversary wins, after a single guess.
2. Compute the exact probability that each adversary wins, after two guesses.
3. Consider adversaries $\mathcal{A}_E^{\text{Key}}$ and $\mathcal{A}_E^{\sigma}$ which operate similarly to $\mathcal{A}^{\text{Key}}$ and $\mathcal{A}^{\sigma}$, except that instead of guessing only one or two times, they test every possible value (of s or of σ) until winning. What is the maximal and average number of guesses required by each of $\mathcal{A}_E^{\text{Key}}$ and $\mathcal{A}_E^{\sigma}$?
Note: The names of both adversaries use subscript E since they are *exhaustive search attacks*; in Chapter 2, we discuss exhaustive search attacks on cryptosystems.

4. What is the advantage of algorithms $\mathcal{A}_E^{\text{Key}}$ and $\mathcal{A}_E^{\sigma}$ over $\mathcal{S}$? (Definition 1.4)
5. Do the replies to the previous item imply that $\mathcal{S}$ is not existentially unforgeable?

Exercise 1.5 (There is always some probability of forgery). Show that there is no signature scheme $\mathcal{S}$ such that every efficient adversary $\mathcal{A}$ has zero advantage against $\mathcal{S}$, i.e., such that $\varepsilon_{\mathcal{S},\mathcal{A}}^{EUF-CMA}(1^n) = 0$. Preferably, show this result holds for any value of 1^n.

Hint: Show a counterexample, i.e., an adversary $\mathcal{A}$ that achieves, against every $\mathcal{S}$, a tiny, negligible — but not zero — advantage. In fact, you can use an adversary which we presented in another exercise!

Chapter 2

Confidentiality: Cryptosystems and Pseudorandomness

In this chapter, we begin our study of applied cryptography by studying cryptosystems, as well as the important notion of *pseudorandomness*, which is extensively used in the study of cryptosystems and in cryptography in general. The goal of cryptosystems is to protect the confidentiality of sensitive information, which we refer to as *plaintext message* m, by *encrypting* it into *ciphertext* c. The ciphertext c should hide the contents of m from the adversary yet allow recovery of the original information by legitimate parties, using a decoding process called *decryption*.

We begin, in Section 2.1, by defining and defining stateless and stateful (symmetric key and public key) cryptosystems. In Section 2.2, we discuss some historical symmetric key cryptosystems. In Section 2.3, we introduce the main *attack models* used to evaluate the security of cryptosystems. In Section 2.4, we discuss *generic attacks*, i.e., attacks which are oblivious to the design of the cryptosystem, such as the *exhaustive search* attack, which tries out all possible keys. In Section 2.5, we discuss the *one-time pad* (OTP), a simple stream cipher which is unconditionally secure, i.e., secure even against an attacker with unlimited computational abilities; the drawback is that the OTP requires the communicating parties to share an random key (the 'pad') which is as long as the plaintext.

In Section 2.6, we begin our investigation of secure and practical cryptosystems, by introducing the important notions of *pseudorandomness* and *indistinguishability* and using these to define *pseudorandom generators* (PRGs), *pseudorandom functions* (PRFs) and their *asymptotic security.* In Section 2.8, we define *block ciphers* and *pseudorandom permutations* (PRPs), which are the building blocks often used to construct practical secure symmetric key cryptosystems. In Section 2.9, we finally define secure encryption and explain why a block cipher does not suffice, i.e., why a block cipher cannot meet our definition of secure encryption. In Section 2.10, we introduce *modes of operation*, focusing on constructions of secure symmetric key cryptosystem using a block cipher; we defer constructions of public key cryptosystems to Chapter 6. In Section 2.11, we discuss *plaintext padding*, a practical requirement for the use of block cipher modes of operation to encrypt arbitrary-length strings, and discuss attacks against padding schemes. In Section 2.12, we present a vulnerability study of the WEP standard, as an example of the pitfalls of incorrect use of cryptosystems. We conclude the chapter in Section 2.13.

2.1 Definitions of stateless and stateful cryptosystems

The most basic categorization of cryptosystems is based on their use of keys. Some (historical, insecure) encryption schemes do not use keys at all; we discuss a few of these in Section 2.2.1. Our focus is on cryptosystems where *decryption* always uses a secret key. These have two basic categories, depending on the key used for *encryption*, as we already discussed in Chapter 1. A *symmetric key cryptosystem*, also called a *shared key encryption* scheme, uses the same key for both encryption and decryption, as illustrated in Figure 1.4. In contrast, a *public key cryptosystem* (PKC), also called an *asymmetric encryption* scheme, uses separate keys for the two functions: a *public (non-secret)* key for encryption and a *private (secret)* key for decryption, as illustrated in Figure 1.5.

There are other categorizations of cryptosystems, beyond their use of (public or symmetric) keys. Cryptosystems can be deterministic or randomized, have Fixed Input Length (FIL) or Variable Input Length (VIL), and be stateless or stateful.

In the three subsections of this section, we define and discuss *stateless symmetric key cryptosystems, stateful symmetric key cryptosystem* and *(stateless) PKC.*[1] Each of these can be deterministic or randomized, and have FIL or VIL. Defining the security requirements for these schemes is more subtle; therefore, we only present these later, in Section 2.9.

Cryptosystems, block ciphers and stream ciphers: The terms 'encryption scheme' and 'cryptosystem' are basically synonyms and are used for both symmetric (shared key) and asymmetric (public key) cryptosystems. Cryptosystems, and especially symmetric key cryptosystems, are also sometimes referred to as *ciphers.* The term *cipher* is mainly used for two specific types of deterministic symmetric key cryptosystems: *block ciphers* and *stream ciphers.*

Block ciphers are *stateless*, deterministic symmetric key cryptosystems that encrypt and decrypt *fixed-length blocks* of bits, i.e., are inherently FIL ciphers. *Stream ciphers*, in contrast, are *stateful*, deterministic symmetric key cryptosystems, which, often (but not always), encrypt and decrypt *bit by bit.*

As we later explain, stateless deterministic cryptosystems do not satisfy the (strong) confidentiality requirements that we define in Section 2.9. Therefore, stateless deterministic cryptosystems — and in particular block ciphers — are usually[2] not used directly to encrypt sensitive data. Instead, block ciphers are often used as a building blocks, to *construct* more advanced cryptographic schemes, including stateful symmetric key cryptosystems, probabilistic symmetric key cryptosystems and probabilistic PKC. Such constructions, using block ciphers, are often referred to as *modes of operation.* Modes of operation also allow the use of the FIL block ciphers for VIL plaintexts. We discuss modes of operations in Section 2.10.

---

[1]As we explain in Section 2.1.3, there does not appear to be a sufficient motivation to define stateful public key cryptosystems.

[2]Stateless deterministic cryptosystems are used in some special scenarios, most notably, to allow search over the encrypted data, without decryption (searchable encryption [37, 96]).

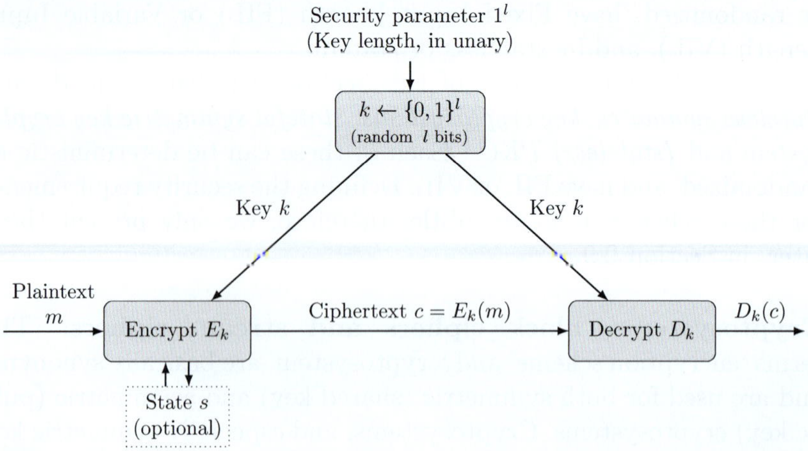

Figure 2.1. A stateless symmetric key cryptosystem, or symmetric key cryptosystem with stateless decryption.

2.1.1 Stateless symmetric key cryptosystem

Many symmetric key cryptosystems are stateless, or use stateless decryption; see Figure 2.1.

We next define a *stateless symmetric key cryptosystem* or, more precisely, a symmetric key cryptosystem with stateless decryption; the definition allows the encryption process to use state, although most designs are stateless. The definition allows for arbitrary sets of keys (K), plaintext messages (M) and ciphertexts (C), allowing both fixed and variable input length cryptosystems; in the common case, all of these sets consists are the set of all binary strings, although sometimes other sets are used, e.g., the set of binary strings of a given fixed length. The definition also allows the cryptosystem to be (optionally) randomized.

Definition 2.1 (Stateless symmetric key cryptosystems and their correctness). A *stateless symmetric key cryptosystem* consists of a pair of efficient (PPT) algorithms, $\langle E, D\rangle$, and sets K, M and C.

The encryption algorithm $E : M \times K \rightarrow C$ maps plaintexts and keys to ciphertexts; if encryption is stateful, then a state should be added to both input and output of encryption. The decryption algorithm $D : C \times K \rightarrow M \cup \{\perp\}$ maps ciphertexts and keys to plaintexts, or to the special symbol $\perp$ (representing decryption error, typically due to invalid ciphertext).

A stateless symmetric key cryptosystem ensures *correctness* if for every input key $k \in K$ and plaintext $m \in M$, the encryption of m using k returns ciphertext $c \in C$ that decrypts, using key k, back to m. Namely,

$$(\forall k \in K,\ m \in M)\ m = D_k(E_k(m)) \tag{2.1}$$

In a symmetric key cryptosystem with stateless decryption, the correctness requirement should hold for arbitrary input state, i.e., $(\forall k \in K,\ m \in M, s \in \{0,1\}^*\ m = D_k(E_k(m,s))$.

Note that the encryption process E may be randomized, and, in particular, $E_k(m)$ is a random variable, not necessarily a fixed value. As a result, in principle, $D_k(E_k(m))$ is also a random value. The correctness condition means that while $D_k(E_k(m))$ is computed by this (possibly probabilistic) process, then the result is always (with probability 1) equal to m. In fact, if we want to be really precise, we should write the correctness condition as $\Pr[m = D_k(E_k(m))] = 1$, where the probability is over the coin tosses by the encryption algorithm E. However, we use in Equation (2.1) and similar equations the simplified notation $m = D_k(E_k(m))$, which we believe is easier to understand (even if not 100% precise).

2.1.2 Stateful symmetric key cryptosystems

Many symmetric key cryptosystems use state, i.e., are *stateful*; typical uses for the state are to maintain a counter of the number of messages, bytes or bits encrypted (or decrypted), or to maintain a pseudorandom value. In any case, the state is used, and changed, in each encryption and decryption, and should be synchronized between encryption and decryption to ensure correctness. Note that when encryption can be done by multiple parties concurrently, such synchronization may not be feasible or convenient. We illustrate stateful symmetric key cryptosystems in Figure 2.2 and define them in Definition 2.2.

Definition 2.2 (Stateful symmetric key cryptosystem and their correctness). A *stateful symmetric key cryptosystem* consists

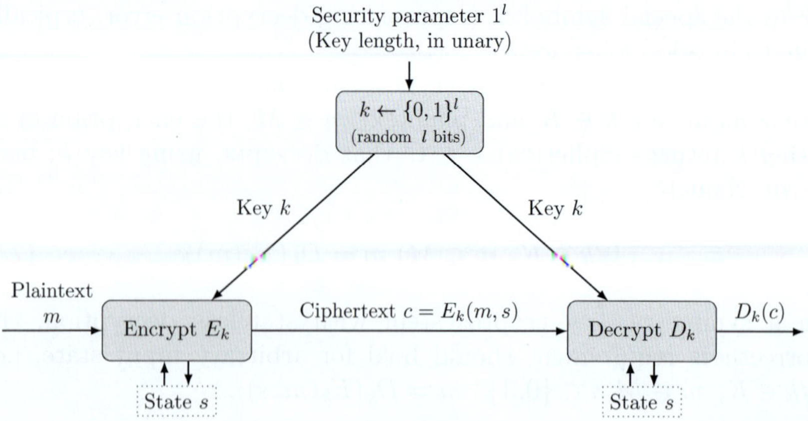

Figure 2.2. A stateful symmetric key cryptosystem.

of a pair of keyed efficient (PPT) algorithms, $\langle E, D\rangle$, and sets K, M, C and S, called the *key space, plaintext space, ciphertext space* and *state space*, respectively, such that E maps from plaintexts, state and keys to ciphertexts and a (new) state, and D maps from ciphertexts, state and keys to a plaintext or the special symbol $\perp$, and to a (new) state.

We use the dot notations to refer to the specific parts of the outputs of the stateful encryption E and stateful decryption D algorithms. Namely, $E_k(m, s) = (E_k.c(m, s), E_k.s(m, s))$, denoting the ciphertext and the new state, respectively, and similarly, $D_k(c, s) = (D_k.m(c, s), D_k.s(c, s))$, denoting the resulting plaintext message and the new state, respectively.

We say that a stateful symmetric key cryptosystem ensures *correctness* if for every input key $k \in K$, plaintext $m \in M$ and state $s \in S$, the encryption of $m \in M$ using $k \in K$ with state $s \in S$ returns ciphertext $c \in C$ and new state $s' \in S$, that decrypts, using the same key k and state s, back to the same plaintext m and the same new state s'. Namely,

$$(\forall k \in K,\ m \in M,\ s \in S)\ [(c, s') \leftarrow E_k(m, s)] \Rightarrow [(m, s') \leftarrow D_k(c, s)] \tag{2.2}$$

When it is clear from the context, we may abuse notation and use for a stateful symmetric key cryptosystems the same notations as of stateless symmetric key cryptosystem, i.e., denote the ciphertext output of the encryption simply as $E_k(m)$ or $E_k(m, s)$, omitting the dot notation and optionally also the state input, and similarly denote the decrypted plaintext simply as $D_k(c)$.

2.1.3 Public key cryptosystems (PKCs)

Public key cryptosystems (PKCs), also called asymmetric cryptosystems, use two different keys, a *public key* e for encryption and a *private key* d for decryption. We assume that the adversary knows the public encryption key e; in contrast, the private decryption key d should be hidden from the attacker.

The public encryption key e and the private decryption key d should be related for decryption to recover the plaintext from the (encrypted) ciphertext. Namely, we cannot simply generate the two keys by a uniform choice from some set K, as we do for symmetric key cryptosystems. Therefore, PKCs use a third algorithm, called the *key generation* algorithm and denoted KG, which receives the *security parameter*, typically as a unary number 1^n, and generates the keypair (e, d) of public encryption key e and corresponding private decryption key d. We focus on the typical case, where both the public key e and the private key d are binary strings.

A PKC is illustrated in Figure 2.3. In the figure and in our discussion, we assume that the *decryption* process is stateless; this is usually the case since public key encryption is usually used to support

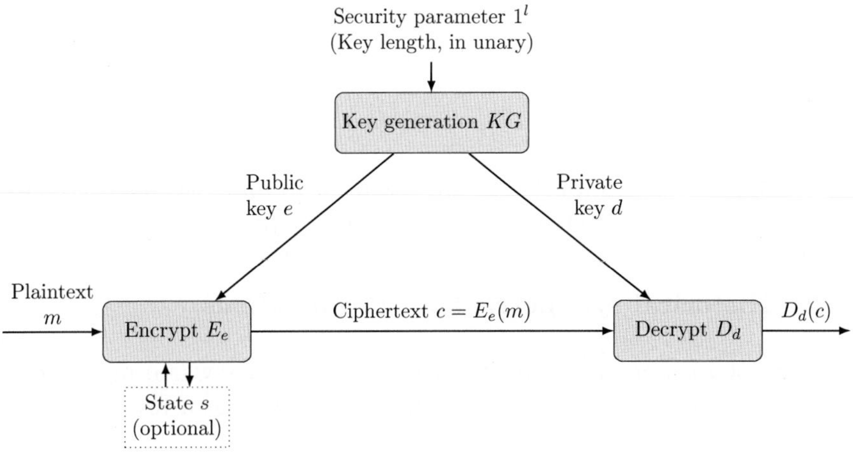

Figure 2.3. A PKC. Encryption process can optionally use state (but often does not).

multiple decrypting devices, and therefore, it is hard to maintain all of them synchronized.

In the definition we present, we allow the PKC encryption algorithm E to be stateful, i.e., use a state variable s.

Definition 2.3 (Public key cryptosystem and their correctness). A *PKC* is defined by a set of three efficient PPT algorithms, $\{KG, E, D\}$ and sets M, C (for plaintexts and ciphertexts) and, optionally, a set S of states for the encryption algorithm. The *key generation algorithm* (KG) is randomized, while the *encryption algorithm* E and the *decryption algorithm* D may be either deterministic or randomized; the encryption algorithm may also be stateful, i.e., use state s.

The KG receives a unary input and outputs a pair of a public encryption key e and a corresponding private decryption key d, where both keys are binary strings (i.e., in $\{0,1\}^*$). The decryption algorithm D maps a ciphertext and a private decryption key d to a plaintext message, or to the special symbol $\perp$ (representing decryption error, typically due to invalid ciphertext c). The encryption algorithm E can be stateful or stateless. Even if E is stateful, we often abuse notation and ignore the state output of E, i.e., use $E_e(m,s)$ to denote the ciphertext output of the encryption.

A PKC ensures *correctness* if for every generated keypair $(e,d) \stackrel{\$}{\leftarrow} KG(1^n)$, plaintext $m \in M$ and (optionally) state $s \in S$, the encryption of m using the public encryption key e and state s returns ciphertext $c \in C$ that decrypts, using the private decryption key d, back to m. Namely,

$$(\forall (e,d) \stackrel{\$}{\leftarrow} KG(1^n),\ m \in M)\ D_d(E_e(m,s)) = m \tag{2.3}$$

PKCs are very important, and essential to many scenarios, goals and scenarios; we discuss them mostly in Chapter 6.

2.2 Historical symmetric key cryptosystems

Cryptology is one of the most ancient sciences. To ‘warm up’ for our discussion of encryption schemes, let us first discuss a few historical ciphers, i.e., symmetric key cryptosystems which were in use from ancient times till the nineteenth century. These historical ciphers will help us to introduce some of the basic ideas and challenges of cryptography and cryptanalysis, and to provide some historical perspective, beyond the little we presented in Section 1.6. For more historical background, see Refs. [279, 447].

The *design* of many of these historical ciphers was mostly kept secret, believing that an attacker cannot break the cipher if it does not know its design; a (usually false) belief we refer to as ***security by obscurity***. In Section 1.2.2, we presented ***Kerckhoffs's principle***, which essentially says that the security of a cipher should not depend on the secrecy of its design, i.e., it is ill-advised to rely on 'security by obscurity'.

Clearly, Kerckhoffs's principle was not followed by many of the historical ciphers. In fact, these ciphers are often quite easy to break once the attacker is familiar with their design. Furthermore, some of the more ancient ciphers relied *only* on the secrecy of their design; they even did not use a secret key.

We discuss *keyless ciphers*, including ancient ciphers, in Section 2.2.1. The most well known of these keyless ciphers is the (ancient) Caesar cipher. In Section 2.2.2, we discuss the Keyed-Caesar cipher, which is a simple keyed version of the Caesar cipher — not much more secure.

Many historical ciphers, and in particular the ciphers we discuss in Sections 2.2.1 and 2.2.2, are *monoalphabetic substitution ciphers*. A monoalphabetic substitution cipher uses a fixed mapping from each plaintext character to a corresponding ciphertext character (or some other symbol). Namely, these ciphers are stateless and deterministic and defined by a permutation from the plaintext alphabet to a set of ciphertext characters or symbols.

In Section 2.2.3, we discuss a generalization of this type of cipher, which we call the *generalized monoalphabetic substitution cipher*. Then, in Section 2.2.4, we present the *frequency analysis attack*, which efficiently breaks *every* monoalphabetic substitution cipher, including the generalized monoalphabetic substitution cipher. We conclude this section with Section 2.2.5, where we discuss the Vigenère cipher and other historical polyalphabetic ciphers.

2.2.1 Ancient keyless ciphers

In this section, we discuss few ancient ciphers. These are all simple, *keyless* (no secret key) and *monoalphabetic substitution ciphers*. A cipher is monoalphabetic if it is defined by a single, fixed mapping from each plaintext letter to ciphertext letter or symbol.

The At-Bash cipher: The At-Bash cipher may be the earliest cipher whose use is documented in a historical document. Specifically, it is believed to be used, three times, in the Old Testament book of Jeremiah. The cipher maps each of the letters in the Hebrew alphabet to a different letter. Specifically, the letters are mapped in 'reverse order': first letter to the last letter, second letter to the second-to-last letter, and so on; this mapping is reflected in the name 'At-Bash'.[3]

The At-Bash cipher is illustrated in Figure 2.4. Even if you are not familiar with the letters of the Hebrew alphabet, the mapping may still be identified by the visual appearance. If you find it hard to match, that's Ok; we next describe an adaptation of the At-Bash cipher to the Latin alphabet.

To properly define ciphers as well as more complex cryptographic scheme, we use pseudocode or a formula. For monoalphabetic ciphers, a formula usually suffices. We define the cipher as a function mapping a plaintext (input) letter to the corresponding ciphertext (output) letter. Each letter is represented by its distance from the beginning of the alphabet.

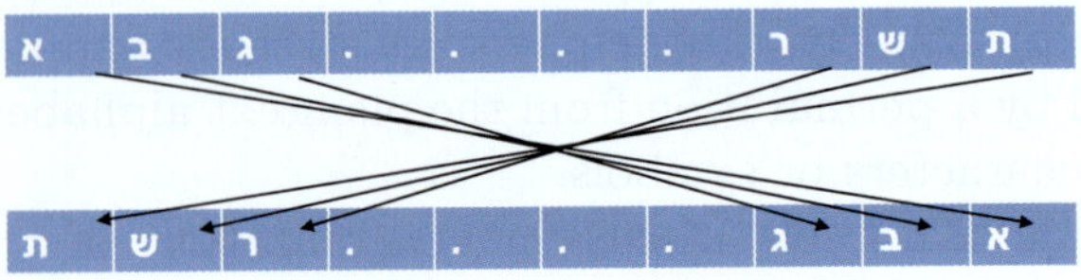

Figure 2.4. The At-Bash cipher.

[3]The name 'At-Bash', sometimes written as Atbash, reflects the 'reverse mapping' of the Hebrew alphabet. The 'At' refers to the mapping of the first letter ('Aleph', א) to the last letter ('Taf', ת) and of the second letter ('Beth', ב) to the second-to-last letter ('Shin', ש).

In the Hebrew alphabet, there are 22 letters. Therefore, we encode these letters by the numbers from 0, representing the first letter in the Hebrew alphabet, Alef (א), to 21, representing the last letter in the Hebrew alphabet, Taf (ת). Note that we find it a bit more convenient to use 0, rather than 1, as the index of the first letter in each alphabet.

Let p be a *plaintext* message consisting of l Hebrew letters, where $p[i]$, for $i = 0, \ldots, (l-1)$, is the encoding of the corresponding letter ($p[i] \in \{0, 1, \ldots, 21\}$). We use c to denote the corresponding l-letters *ciphertext*, i.e., the encryption of p using the At-Bash cipher: $c = E_{At\text{-}Bash}(p)$. We compute the c using the following formula, for $i = 0, \ldots, (l-1)$:

$$(\forall i = 0, \ldots, (l-1))\ c[i] = 21 - p[i] \tag{2.4}$$

It is convenient to denote the alphabet size by n, i.e., in Hebrew, $n = 22$. With this convention, we can rewrite the formula in Equation (2.4) as $c[i] = (n-1) - p[i]$.

The Az-By cipher: The Az-By cipher is the same as the At-Bash cipher, except using the Latin alphabet, which has $n = 26$ letters (from A to Z), instead of the Hebrew alphabet (with $n = 22$).

We illustrate the Az-By cipher in the top part of Figure 2.5; below it, we present two other keyless ciphers, which we discuss next — the *Caesar cipher* and the *ROT13* ciphers.

Let p be a *plaintext* message consisting of the encoding of l Latin letters, where $p[i] \in \{0, 1, \ldots, 25\}$, i.e., $p[i] \in \{0, 1, \ldots, (n-1)\}$. The corresponding ciphertext, $c = E_{Az-By}(p)$, is given by

$$(\forall i = 0, \ldots, (l-1))\ c[i] = 25 - p[i] = (n-1) - p[i] \tag{2.5}$$

Obviously, this formula is the same as of the At-Bash cipher (Equation (2.4)), except for adjusting for the fact that the Latin alpha has $n = 26$ letters, while the Hebrew alphabet has only 22.

The Caesar cipher: We next present the Caesar cipher, which may be the most well known of the ancient ciphers. The Caesar cipher has been used, as the name implies, by Julius Caesar. Like the At-Bash cipher and the Az-By cipher, the Caesar cipher is also a

AzBy	A	B	C	D	E	F	G	H	I	J	K	L	M
	Z	Y	X	W	V	U	T	S	R	Q	P	O	N
	N	O	P	Q	R	S	T	U	V	W	X	Y	Z
	M	L	K	J	I	H	G	F	E	D	C	B	A
Caesar	A	B	C	D	E	F	G	H	I	J	K	L	M
	D	E	F	G	H	I	J	K	L	M	N	O	P
	N	O	P	Q	R	S	T	U	V	W	X	Y	Z
	Q	R	S	T	U	V	W	X	Y	Z	A	B	C
ROT 13	A	B	C	D	E	F	G	H	I	J	K	L	M
	N	O	P	Q	R	S	T	U	V	W	X	Y	Z
	N	O	P	Q	R	S	T	U	V	W	X	Y	Z
	A	B	C	D	E	F	G	H	I	J	K	L	M

Figure 2.5. The Az-By, Caesar and ROT13 ciphers.

monoalphabetic cipher. We describe a variant of it,[4] which operates on the set of the $n = 26$ letters in the modern Latin alphabet, from A to Z.

In the Caesar cipher, each plaintext letter is replaced by the letter appearing in the alphabet three places after the plaintext letter. To map the last three letters in the alphabet (X, Y and Z), we repeat the three first letters (A, B and C), i.e., X is mapped to A, Y to B and Z mapped to C. See the middle row of Figure 2.5.

As with the Az-By cipher, we represent each letter by its distance from the beginning of the Latin alphabet; i.e., we represent the letter 'A' by the number 0, and so on; 'Z' is represented by 25.

Let p be a *plaintext* message consisting of the encoding of l Latin letters, where $p[i] \in \{0, 1, \ldots, 25\}$, and let c denote the l-lettered corresponding ciphertext $c = E_{\text{Caesar}}(p)$. Then, c is given by

$$(\forall i = 0, \ldots, (l-1))\ c[i] = p[i] + 3 \bmod 26 \tag{2.6}$$

For example, consider encryption of plaintext word 'axe', whose encoding is $p[0] = 0$, $p[1] = 23$ and $p[2] = 4$. This gives $c[0] = 3$, $c[1] = 0$, $c[2] = 7$, i.e., the ciphertext string 'dah'. Simple!

---

[4]In Caesar's time, the Latin alphabet contained only 23 characters; for simplicity, we describe a variant of it which is applied to the current Latin alphabet of 26 characters.

Exercise 2.1. Let p and c be a plaintext string and the corresponding ciphertext produced by the Caesar cipher, as above. Show the process for *decrypting* a given ciphertext c, i.e., computing the corresponding plaintext p. Use an equation similar to Equation (2.6).

The ROT13 cipher: ROT13 is a popular variant of the Caesar cipher, with the minor difference that ROT13 'rotates' the letters by 13 positions, while Caesar rotates by 3 positions.

Let p be a *plaintext* message consisting of the encoding of l Latin letters, where $p[i] \in \{0, 1, \ldots, 25\}$, and let c denote the l-lettered corresponding ROT13 ciphertext $c = E_{\mathrm{ROT13}}(p)$. Then, c is given by

$$(\forall i = 0, \ldots, l-1) \; c[i] = p[i] + 13 \bmod 26 \tag{2.7}$$

The ROT13 cipher is illustrated by the bottom row in Figure 2.5.

We are not aware of usage of ROT13 to obtain secrecy; it is normally used only to prevent inadvertent exposure to the plaintext, such as to hide potentially offensive jokes or to obscure an answer to a puzzle or other spoiler. Since ROT13 does not provide secrecy against attackers, the term ROT13 is often used to refer to other weak encryption schemes (e.g., 'this cryptosystem is as secure as ROT13').

A convenient feature of ROT13 is that it is an *involution* (self-inverse function), i.e., decryption is exactly the same process as encryption.

Exercise 2.2. Show that ROT13 is an involution. Namely, show that for every plaintext message p holds: $p = E_{\mathrm{ROT13}}(E_{\mathrm{ROT13}}(p))$. Can you identify additional ancient ciphers which are involutions?

The Masonic cipher: A final example of a historic, keyless, monoalphabetic cipher is the *Masonic cipher*. The Masonic cipher is from the 18th century and is illustrated in Figure 2.6. This cipher uses a 'key' to map from plaintext to ciphertext and back, but the key is only meant to assist in the mapping since it has a regular structure and is considered part of the cipher.

The Masonic cipher is an example of a cipher that uses a special alphabet for the ciphertext. In the Masonic cipher, the *ciphertext alphabet* consists of simple symbols consisting of few lines and, sometimes, a dot, which correspond to the location of the corresponding plaintext letter in the 'key' of the Masonic cipher, as shown in

Figure 2.6. The Masonic cipher, mapping the Latin alphabet to a set of symbols called the *Masonic alphabet*.

Figure 2.6. Note that we refer to this set of symbols as an alphabet although they are only used for that purpose by the Masonic cipher.

2.2.2 Keyed-Caesar cipher

Keyless ciphers must, by necessity, violate Kerckhoffs's principle; the design of the cipher is a critical secret, whose exposure completely breaks security. Indeed, every modern cipher and many historical ciphers rely for their security on the use of secret keys.

Readers who are interested in these (keyed) historical ciphers should consult manuscripts on the history of cryptology, e.g., Refs. [279, 447]. We only discuss, briefly, few simple and well-known keyed historical ciphers in Section 2.2.5.

In this section, we present a very simple, and trivially vulnerable, keyed cipher: the *Keyed-Caesar cipher*, also referred to as the shift cipher. The Keyed-Caesar cipher is a simple keyed variant of the Caesar cipher. The Keyed-Caesar cipher helps us explain the Vigenère cipher (in Section 2.2.5) and illustrates the fact that using a key — even a long key — is not sufficient for security.

Recall that the Caesar cipher is defined by $c[i] = p[i] + 3 \mod n$, where $p[i] \in \{0, 1, \ldots, n-1\}$ is a single letter (with $n = 26$ for Latin). The Keyed-Caesar cipher is defined with an additional parameter: a key $k \in \{0, 1, \ldots, n-1\}$.

Given an input plaintext string p consisting of l 'letters', $p[0], \ldots, p[l-1]$, the ciphertext string $c[0], \ldots, c[l-1]$ is computed as

$$(\forall i = 0, \ldots, l-1)\ c[i] = p[i] + k \mod n \tag{2.8}$$

When using $n = 26$, the Keyed-Caesar cipher encrypts a single Latin character at a time, just like the Caesar cipher; it simply uses an arbitrary rotation k rather than the fixed rotation as done in the original Caesar cipher ($k = 3$) and in the ROT13 cipher ($k = 13$).

Obviously, with only $n = 26$ keys, the Keyed-Caesar cipher is also insecure; the attacker only needs to try the 26 possible key values. This attack, where the attacker tries all possible keys, is called *exhaustive search* and can be used against any cipher.

To foil exhaustive search, we can use longer keys and blocks of plaintext. For example, if we extend our character set to include the 16-bit UCS-2 character set, then $n = 2^{16}$, making exhaustive search much harder. By using even longer keys and blocks, say, five UCS-2 characters (80 bits), we have $n = 2^{80}$ keys, making exhaustive search impractical.

However, even with very large n, the Keyed-Caesar cipher is still insecure. In particular, even with huge n, Keyed-Caesar cipher can still be easily broken by an attacker who has access to a single pair consisting of a plaintext letter and the corresponding ciphertext letter. For example, say that we know the first letter $p[0]$ of the plaintext and the first letter $c[0]$ of the ciphertext. Then, we can easily recover the key k:

$$k = c[i] - p[i] \bmod n \tag{2.9}$$

This is a very weak form of the known-plaintext attack (KPA) model, which we discuss, along with other other attack models, in Section 2.3.

2.2.3 The Generalized Monoalphabetic Substitution Cipher

Monoalphabetic substitution ciphers are deterministic, stateless permutations from the *plaintext alphabet* to the *ciphertext alphabet.* In the Masonic cipher, the plaintext alphabet was Latin and the ciphertext alphabet was the simple geometric symbols, as shown in Figure 2.6. In the other monoalphabetic substitution ciphers we discussed, the plaintext alphabet and the ciphertext alphabet are identical, i.e., the Hebrew alphabet for the At-Bash cipher and the Latin alphabet for the other ciphers. While the use of a special ciphertext alphabet, as in the Masonic cipher, may appear more secure, in reality, there is no significant impact on security compared with other monoalphabetic substitution ciphers that use the same alphabets for plaintext and for ciphertext.

We have seen that monoalphabetic substitution ciphers can either be keyed or keyless. The Mason cipher, the At-Bash cipher, the Az-By cipher and the Caesar cipher are all keyless monoalphabetic substitution ciphers, i.e., are defined by a specific permutation. For example, the Caesar cipher is the rotate-by-three permutation. The Keyed-Caesar cipher is a simple keyed cipher, which uses the rotate-by-k permutation, where k is the key.

The generalized monoalphabetic substitution cipher is a keyed monoalphabetic substitution cipher obtained by applying an *arbitrary invertible permutation* (mapping) from letters of the plaintext alphabet to letters of the ciphertext alphabet. *The key k is the permutation.* Namely, given an plaintext $p = p[0], \ldots, p[l-1]$ and a key (permutation) k, the ciphertext consists of the l letters $c[0], \ldots, c[l-1]$ from the ciphertext alphabet, computed as

$$(\forall i = 0, \ldots, l-1)\ c[i] = k(p[i]) \tag{2.10}$$

For example, Caesar cipher is the same as generalized monoalphabetic substitution cipher with the key (permutation) $k(p) = p + 3 \bmod 26$, and the Keyed-Caesar cipher, with key k, is the same as generalized monoalphabetic substitution cipher with the key (permutation) $k'(p) = p + k \bmod 26$.

The key of the generalized monoalphabetic substitution cipher is often written as a table with two rows: the first containing the plaintext letters and the other containing the corresponding ciphertext letters; for example, see Figure 2.5. Some readers may recall having used sometime, maybe long ago, such 'key tables' to create a monoalphabetic substitution cipher; many kids do.

In the Latin alphabet, there are $n = 26$ letters; each could be chosen for A, then any of the remaining 25 could be used for B, and so on. Namely, the total number of permutations (i.e., keys) is 26!, the *factorial*[5] of 26. The factorial grows very fast as a function of n; for example, $26! > 2^{88}$, i.e., there are over 2^{88} permutations (keys) for 26-letters generalized monoalphabetic substitution cipher.

---

[5] $26! \equiv 26 \cdot 25 \cdot \ldots 2 \cdot 1$.

Namely, the Latin alphabet, with $n = 26$ characters, suffices to make exhaustive search infeasible for generalized monoalphabetic substitution cipher. This improves significantly compare to the Keyed-Caesar cipher, where to obtain the same number of keys, we need a huge alphabet of $n = 26! > 2^{88}$ letters.

However, when using a small alphabet such as of Latin, any monoalphabetic substitution cipher, including the generalized monoalphabetic substitution cipher, is vulnerable to the *frequency analysis* attack, a simple attack that we describe in the following.

2.2.4 Frequency analysis attacks on monoalphabetic ciphers

Plaintext messages are rarely completely random strings; some messages, or part of messages, are more common than others. A *frequency analysis* attack exploits knowledge about the *plaintext distribution*, to facilitate cryptanalysis. Frequency analysis attacks often succeeded against historical ciphers, using *only* this knowledge about the plaintext distribution, and a collection of ciphertext messages. The frequency analysis attack is effective against any monoalphabetic cipher, including generalized monoalphabetic substitution cipher. The only exceptions, where frequency analysis may fail, are when using extremely large alphabets, and/or in applications where the plaintext has uniform ('random') distribution, e.g., if the plaintext is the result of compression rather than being directly a text in human language.

Classical monoalphabetic ciphers map each letter in the alphabet of a specific natural (human) language, to a fixed letter (or symbol) in the ciphertext alphabet (often the same as the plaintext alphabet). In the typical case where the plaintext is a message in a natural, human language, e.g., English, then the alphabet is not very large, e.g., the Latin alphabet, which has 26 characters. Also, the distribution of different letters in the plaintext is not uniformly distributed. In fact, some letters are significantly more common than others. Furthermore, some pairs of letters (*bigrams*) and some strings of several letters (*ngrams*) are significantly more common than others. See Figure 2.7.

The frequency analysis attack requires (only) knowledge about the language, such as knowledge of the distributions of letters,

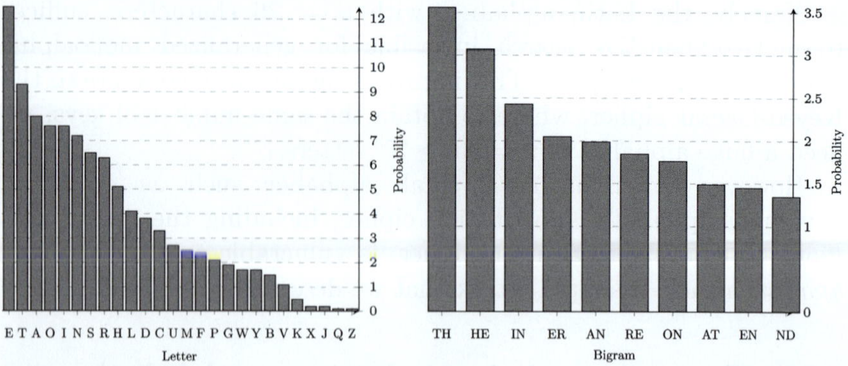

Figure 2.7. Frequencies of letters and of the most common bigrams in English. Probabilities are given as percent.

Source: Based on Ref. [383].

bigrams and ngrams. This information is not part of the secret, randomly chosen key; therefore, following Kerckhoffs's principle, we assume that this knowledge is available to the attacker. Frequency analysis attacks work exceedingly well against classical monoalphabetic ciphers, given encryption of text in a known language. Indeed, some deductions, and often complete decryption, may be done manually; for example, in texts in English, the most common letter is almost always E (12.49%). Identification of T and H is also quite easy; T is the second-most-common (9.28%), and TH and HE are the most common bigrams (3.56% and 3.07%, respectively). Similarly, since we identified E, it is now easy to identify R too since ER and RE are of the most common bigrams (2.02% and 1.85%). These easy deductions suffice to decrypt about about a third of the letters in the ciphertext, given a rather short ciphertext message. The reader can surely find few other easy deductions. Of course, no reason to work manually; it is easy to write a program to efficiently cryptanalyze any monoalphabetic cipher, including the generalized monoalphabetic substitution cipher.

Exercise 2.3. Write and test two programs: one that implements generalized monoalphabetic substitution cipher encryption and decryption, and another that cryptanalyzes the resulting ciphertexts (without being given the key). Your cryptanalysis program should assume that the encrypted plaintext is typical text in English.

By experimenting with the cryptanalysis program of Exercise 2.3, you will find that it may fail if given short ciphertext. However, given sufficiently long ciphertext, the cryptanalysis will succeed and be correct. This phenomenon exists for other attacks too; cryptanalysis often requires a significant amount of ciphertext encrypted using the same encryption key. This motivates *refreshing (changing) the key*, thereby limiting the use of each key to a limited amount of plaintext (and ciphertext). Frequent key refresh make cryptanalysis harder or, ideally, infeasible. Note that in a PKC, whenever we change the private decryption key, we will also need to change the corresponding encryption key.

Principle 4 (Limit usage of each key). *Systems deploying ciphers/cryptosystems should limit the amount of usage of each key, changing keys as necessary, to foil cryptanalysis attacks.*

An extreme example of this is the OTP cipher, which we discuss in Section 2.5. The OTP essentially maps each bit in the plaintext to a corresponding bit in the ciphertext using a one-bit substitution cipher, using independently, randomly chosen substitutions for each bit. Namely, using the OTP is equivalent to using a one-bit substitution cipher, while changing the key after encrypting *every bit*. This extremely frequent change of keys turns the insecure substitution cipher into a *provably unconditionally secure* cipher!

Another way to defend against letter frequency attacks is to use a larger alphabet. For example, instead of mapping each plaintext character into a ciphertext character, the cipher may map a *block* consisting of a sequence of multiple plaintext characters (or bytes), into a block consisting of a sequence of (the same number of) ciphertext characters (or bytes). Such a cipher, which maps an entire block of plaintext characters/bytes to an entire block of ciphertext characters/bytes, is called a *block cipher*.

Encryption by applying a block cipher to each block of plaintext is, essentially, a monoalphabetic substitution cipher with a large alphabet, which reduces the effectiveness of frequency analysis attacks. Let us consider the case where the 'block' consists of only two characters (two bytes). This already prevents a frequency analysis attack using the letter-frequency table. With this relatively small block size, an attacker can still take advantage of the bigram distribution; however, adding even just one more character to the block would prevent this threat as well.

In principle, we could implement a block cipher by generating and storing a table randomly mapping each plaintext block to the corresponding ciphertext block. However, such table would have 2^l entries, where l is the number of bits in the block, which is exponential in the block size. Therefore, practical implementations of block ciphers use an algorithm to compute the mappings between plaintexts and ciphertexts.

In Section 2.8, we present *block ciphers*, which are basically efficient monoalphabetic substitution ciphers which use a large 'alphabet', e.g., 64 bits for *DES* or 128 bits for *AES*. Such block ciphers use much shorter keys compared to the generalized monoalphabetic substitution cipher for the same alphabet size; however, their keys and blocks should be sufficiently large to foil exhaustive search and other generic attacks, as well as frequency analysis and other non-generic cryptanalysis attacks. For example, AES supports keys with 128, 192 or 256 bits; DES keys are only 56 bits long, which is one of the main weaknesses causing DES to be considered insecure.

2.2.5 The Vigenère ciphers and the One Time Pad (OTP)

We conclude our discussion of historical ciphers, by discussing *polyalphabetic ciphers*, and in particular, two variants of the *Vigenère cipher*. We first describe the simpler (and weaker) *(repeating-key) Vigenère cipher* published, in 1553, by Giovan Battista Bellaso.[6] We then describe the stronger *Autokey cipher*, published in 1586 by Blaise de Vigenère. We refer to these two ciphers as the Vigenère ciphers.

[6]The (repeating-key) Vigenère cipher is usually referred to simply as the Vigenère cipher. We add the qualifier *(repeating key)* to avoid confusion with the Autokey cipher, which is the stronger cipher published, later, by Vigenère. The Vigenère cipher was published first by Bellaso, so its name is anyway misleading.

Both Vigenère ciphers are ***polyalphabetic ciphers***, namely, they use multiple mappings from plaintext characters to ciphertext characters. The motivation to use multiple mappings is to defeat *frequency analysis* attacks, and different variants of the Vigenère cipher were used until the twenty century; in fact, even the Enigma (Section 1.6) is a polyalphabetic cipher and essentially similar to application of a cascade of few Vigenère ciphers.

The (repeating-key) Vigenère cipher: The (repeating-key) Vigenère cipher extends the Keyed-Caesar cipher, by using a string of few characters as the key, rather than a single character as in the Keyed-Caesar cipher. The (repeating-key) Vigenère cipher simply applies the letters of the key, one by one, repeating the key after using its last character.

Namely, given an input plaintext string p consisting of l characters $p[0], \ldots, p[l-1]$, from the alphabet mapped to the integers $\{0, 1, \ldots, n-1\}$, and a key k consisting of λ characters, $k[0], \ldots, k[\lambda]$, the ciphertext string consists of the l characters $c[0], \ldots, c[l-1]$ computed as

$$(\forall i = 1, \ldots, l)\ c[i] = p[i] + k[i \bmod \lambda] \bmod n \qquad (2.11)$$

Example 2.1. Consider encryption of the string $p =$'ABCDEFG', whose encoding is $(i = 0, \ldots, 6) p[i] = i$, using the key $k =$'BED', whose encoding is $k[0] = 1$, $k[1] = 4$ and $k[2] = 3$. The resulting ciphertext c is the string $c =$ 'BFFEIIH'.

Attacking the (repeating-key) Vigenère cipher: Since polyalphabetic cipher such as the Vigenère cipher use different keys (offsets) for different characters, direct application of frequency analysis would fail. The first attack against the (repeating-key) Vigenère cipher was published by Kasiski in 1863.[7] This attack proceeds in two steps: finding the length λ of the key k and then finding the key itself $(k[0], \ldots, k[\lambda - 1])$.

[7]This attack was known earlier but not published; in particular, it was found in personal notes written by Babbage in 1846.

Once the key length λ is found, we can apply frequency analysis separately to each of the λ *sequences* s_i $(i = 0, \ldots, \lambda - 1)$ of ciphertext characters generated by the different key letters:

$$\begin{aligned} s_0 &\equiv (c[0], c[\lambda], \ldots) \\ s_1 &\equiv (c[1], c[\lambda+1], \ldots) \\ &\ldots \\ s_{\lambda-1} &\equiv (c[\lambda-1], c[2\lambda-1], \ldots) \end{aligned}$$

To find λ, Kasiski looked for repeating sequences of characters (ngrams) in the ciphertext. For example, assume that for some m, m' hold $c[m : m+3] = c[m' : m'+3]$. By substituting $c[m : m+3]$ and $c[m' : m'+3]$ from Equation (2.11), we have

$$\begin{aligned} (\forall i = 0, \ldots, 3)\ p[m+i] + k[m+i \bmod \lambda] \bmod\ n \\ = p[m'+i] + k[m'+i \bmod \lambda] \bmod\ n \end{aligned} \tag{2.12}$$

Very often, the plaintext contains some repeating words or strings, ranging from relatively common words or ngrams to terms which are specific to that plaintext. This would be the most common reason for repeating strings in the ciphertext. Namely, when we find such m, m', it is likely that $p[m : m+3] = p[m' : m'+3]$. Hence, from Equation (2.12), holds:

$$(\forall i = 0, \ldots, 3)\ k[m+i \bmod \lambda] \bmod\ n = k[m'+i \bmod \lambda] \bmod\ n \tag{2.13}$$

Usually, when Equation (2.13) holds, then $m = m' \bmod \lambda$, i.e., $m - m'$ is either λ or a multiple of λ. The attack usually proceed by finding few such repeating sequences, e.g., $m_1 = m'_1 \bmod \lambda$ and $m_2 = m'_2 \bmod \lambda$, and λ is the common divisor of $m_1 - m'_1$ and of $m_2 - m'_2$, or one of the (few) common divisors. We then apply frequency analysis to find each of the λ characters of the key, $k[0], \ldots, k[\lambda-1]$.

The one-time pad: An important scenario is when we use the Vigenère cipher with a key which is (at least) as long as the plaintext. Namely, each character of the key is used to hide only one character of the plaintext. In this case, Equation (2.11) simplifies to $c[i] = p[i] + k[i] \bmod n$, and in the special case of $n = 2$, we have $c[i] = p[i] \oplus k[i]$.

When the key k is chosen randomly, and especially when $n = 2$, this cipher is referred to as the one-time pad (OTP); we discuss it in details in Section 2.5. The OTP is *unconditionally secure*, i.e., the attacker cannot learn from the ciphertext anything about the plaintext, except its length, regardless of the attacker's computational capabilities (for any $n > 1$).

The Autokey cipher: We now describe the *Autokey cipher*, which is the cipher that Vigenère actually designed; it is an enhancement or variant of the (repeating-key) Vigenère cipher. Both Vigenère ciphers operate in the same way, until exhausting the characters of the key, but then they differ. Recall that the repeating-key Vigenère cipher reuses the same key string. Instead, the Autokey cipher uses the *plaintext*.

Suppose we are given an input plaintext string p consisting of l characters, $p[0], \ldots, p[l-1]$, and a key k consisting of λ characters, $k[0], \ldots, k[\lambda - 1]$. We compute the ciphertext string $c = E_k^{\text{Autokey}}(p)$ as follows:

$$\begin{aligned} &(\forall i = 1, \ldots, l)\ c[i] = p[i] + k'[i] \bmod n \\ &\text{where } k' \equiv k \mathbin{+\!\!+} p \end{aligned} \tag{2.14}$$

Typically, $\lambda < n$, i.e., the Autokey cipher 'extends' the key k into the *extended key* k', by concatenating the plaintext message. The extended key would contain $\lambda + n$ characters, i.e., *more* than the n characters required to encrypt the entire plaintext without repeating. Let us give an example.

Example 2.2. Consider encryption of the string $p =$ 'ABCDEFG', whose encoding is $(i = 0, \ldots, 6) p[i] = i$, using the key $k =$ 'BED', whose encoding is $k[0] = 1$, $k[1] = 4$ and $k[2] = 3$. The extended key would be $k' =$ 'BEDABCDEFG', and the resulting ciphertext c is the string $c =$ 'BFFDFHJ'.

Attacking the Autokey cipher: In Section 2.3, we discuss several attack models used to evaluate the security of cryptosystems. We illustrate two of these attack models, the KPA model and the ciphertext-only attack (COA) model, by presenting simple attacks against the Autokey cipher.

2.3 The COA, KPA, CPA and CCA attack models

As stated in Principle 1, security should be defined and analyzed with respect to a clear, well-defined model of the attacker capabilities, which we refer to as the *attack model*. In particular, cryptanalysis attack models define the capabilities of attackers trying to 'break' an encryption scheme. Note that different attack models are often required for different schemes, for example, compare the attack models we discuss here to the attack models for signature schemes (Section 1.5).

In this section, we introduce the four basic *cryptanalysis attack models: COA, KPA, CPA and CCA*. Table 2.1 summarizes these four basic cryptanalysis attack models, as well as the padding oracle attack model presented in Section 2.11. Following Kerckhoffs's principle, in all of these attack models, the design of the cryptosystems are known to the attacker; defense is only provided via the secret keys,[8] which are selected or generated randomly.

Table 2.1. Cryptanalysis attack models against cryptosystems. In *all* attack types, the cryptanalyst knows the design of the cryptosystem (as per Kerckhoffs's principle).

Attack Model	Cryptanalyst Knowledge, Capabilities	Sections	Figure
Ciphertext-only attack (COA)	Some knowledge of the distribution of plaintext messages.	2.3	2.8
Known-plaintext attack (KPA)	A set of (ciphertext, plaintext) pairs.	2.3	2.9
Chosen-plaintext attack (CPA)	Ciphertexts for arbitrary plaintext messages chosen by the attacker.	2.3	2.10
Chosen-ciphertext attack (CCA)	Plaintext for arbitrary ciphertext chosen by the attacker.	2.3	2.11
Padding oracle attack	An indication whether an attacker-provided ciphertext is properly padded.	2.11, 6.5.7	2.37

[8]Private keys for public key cryptosystems.

2.3.1 The ciphertext-only attack (COA) model

Based on Kerckhoffs's principle, we always assume that the attacker knows the design of the system. We usually also assume that the attacker knows some probability distribution for the plaintext messages. In practice, such knowledge is typically implied by the specific application or scenario. For example, when it is known that the message is in English, then the attacker can apply known statistics such as the letter and bigram distribution in English, as in Figure 2.7. In other scenarios, the attacker may know that the plaintext messages are given in a fixed format or syntax, e.g., following a standard such as HTTP, or that the plaintext includes an error detection code (EDC) or an error correction code (ECC).

In the COA model, this is the *only* knowledge provided to assist the attacker in cryptanalysis of ciphertext messages; see Figure 2.8. The limited information provided to the attacker in the COA model suffices to attack many (weak) cryptosystems. We have seen a few examples already; let us present a slightly more involved example — a COA attack against the Autokey cipher.

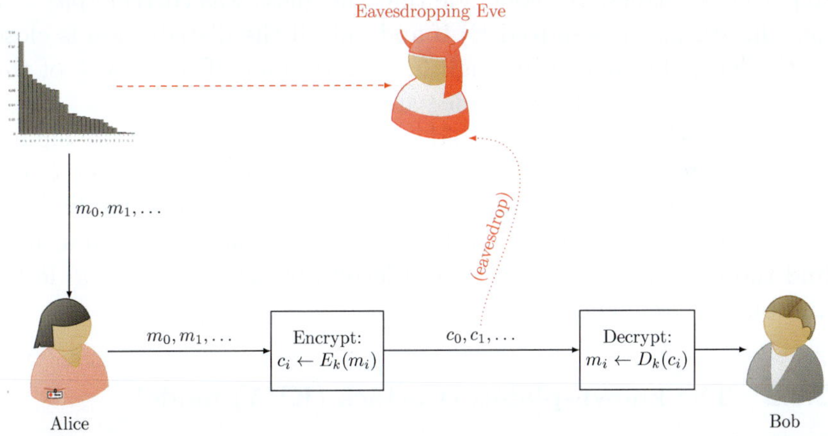

Figure 2.8. The ciphertext-only attack (COA) model. Note the small image representing the *plaintext distribution*, which is a tiny-version of the letter-distribution graph of Figure 2.7; this is used to sample the plaintext, for both the plaintext messages $m_0, m_1, \ldots$ and for sample ciphertext messages given to the attacker, designated by the dashed red line.

Example 2.3 (A ciphertext-only attack (COA) against the Autokey cipher). In spite of its name, the *COA* provides the attacker some knowledge to assist in the cryptanalysis of the ciphertext, specifically *some* knowledge about the distribution of the plaintext messages. For example, assume that the plaintext is known to be in English, allowing us to use frequency analysis (as in Section 2.2.4).

For simplicity, assume that the attacker knows the number of characters in the key, λ. Namely, $c[i + \lambda] = p[i + \lambda] + p[i] \bmod n$; hence, once the attacker finds $p[i]$, then the attacker can also find $p[i + \lambda] = c[i + \lambda] - p[i]$. Now that $p[i + \lambda]$ is known, the attacker can similarly find $p[i + 2\lambda]$, and so on. Namely, given a guess for $p[i]$, the attacker can find $p[j]$ for every $j = i \bmod \lambda$.

This allows the attacker to decrypt the ciphertext, by using frequency analysis; let us sketch how. Since the letter E is very common (more than $\frac{1}{8}$ of the letters!), the attacker tries different indexes i, testing if $p[i] = 4$ (indicating the letter E). To test if this is the case, the attacker uses the above process to find what would be the letters $p[j]$ for every $j = i \bmod \lambda$ and checks the distribution of the resulting sequence of letters. We conclude that the guess was correct ($p[i] = 4$, i.e., the *ith* letter is indeed E) if and only if the distribution is close to the letter frequency in English, in particular, if roughly $\frac{1}{8}$ of the plaintext letters in this sequence are E.

Usually, this technique would suffice to decrypt the entire ciphertext since for most $j \in \{0, \ldots, \lambda - 1\}$, and for each integer l, the probability that $p[j + l \cdot \lambda] = 4$ (plaintext letter E) is roughly $\frac{1}{8}$. In the (unlikely) case that this technique fails for some j, we can usually find the mapping of one (or more) letters by using additional letter and bigram frequencies.

2.3.2 The known-plaintext attack (KPA) model

In the KPA model, the attacker receives one or multiple pairs of *plaintext* and the corresponding *ciphertext*. However, the attacker cannot choose the plaintext; we model this by assuming that the plaintext is chosen randomly, according to a known plaintext distribution. See Figure 2.9.

In the historical attacks on cryptographic systems, known-plaintext attacks were sometimes possible, such as when some text

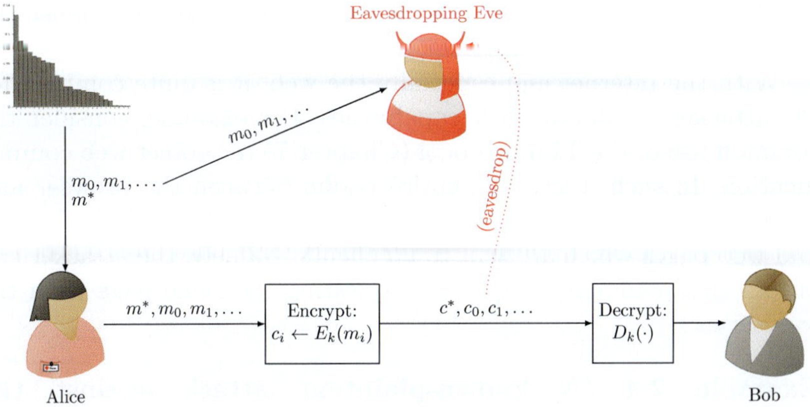

Figure 2.9. The known-plaintext attack model (KPA). As in the COA model, all plaintext messages, m^* and $m_0, m_1, \ldots$, are chosen from a known *plaintext distribution*, and the eavesdropping adversary receives their encryptions, c^* and $c_0, c_1, \ldots$, and tried to learn m^* — or something about m^*. In the KPA model, the adversary receives, in addition, the plaintext messages $m_0, m_1, \ldots$, except for the 'challenge message' m^*. The plaintext messages $m_0, m_1, \ldots$ are *not* given to the COA attacker.

was available both in plaintext and in ciphertext. One interesting example is the 'deciphering' of the Rosetta stone, which contained the same inscription, engraved in three different ways: one in Greek and two in Egyptian, once using hieroglyphic script and once using Demotic script. This is how archaeologists learned to read hieroglyphic. Previous attempts to decipher hieroglyphic, using only ciphertext, i.e., without known plaintext, were in vain.

Another example of historical KPA was the cryptanalysis of the *Enigma* cipher by the Allies during WW II (Section 1.6). The Germans were often sending encryptions of plaintext which would either be known or could be guessed with reasonable probability. Sometimes, the same message was sent to some recipients encrypted and to others in plaintext, and often the message began with a predictable greeting or otherwise contained some predictable content. The (plaintext m, ciphertext $E_k(m)$) pairs were fed to the *Bombe* devices, which tried all possible keys, until finding the correct key (*exhaustive search*, discussed in Section 2.4.1). Note that this was an incorrect use of Enigma; following the *conservative design* principle, the exposure of (plaintext, ciphertext) pairs should have been avoided, although the goal of Enigma was to be secure against the KPA.

With the Internet and especially the web, it is quite common for the attacker to obtain KPA capabilities. For example, consider the common use of the TLS protocol (Chapter 7) to protect web communication. In such usage, the entire traffic between the browser and the web server is encrypted by TLS. Typically, this includes images and web pages which are sent to *all* clients. Namely, the attacker can obtain this plaintext, simply by requesting the same page from the web server.

Example 2.4 (A known-plaintext attack against the Autokey cipher). Assume that the attacker captures ciphertext c and knows that the plaintext is of the form $p = p_{\text{Known}} + p_{\text{Secret}}$; for example, $p_{\text{Known}} =$ 'The password is:'.

The attacker can find the key k and the plaintext p_{Secret} as follows, assuming that the key k is not longer than p_{Known}. Let λ denote the number of characters in the key k, i.e., $k = k[0 : \lambda]$. Hence, for $i = 0, \ldots, \lambda$ holds, (1) $k'[i] = k[i]$ (by definition of the extended key k'), (2) $p[i] = p_{\text{Known}}[i]$ and (3) $c[i] = p[i] + k'[i]$ (Equation (2.14)). The attacker can, therefore, find the key k since for $i = 0, \ldots, \lambda$ holds, $k[i] = k'[i] = c[i] - p_{\text{Known}}[i]$.

In the (less likely) case that k is longer than p_{Known}, this attack will expose the first $|p_{\text{Known}}|$ characters of k. This will allow exposure of the first $|p_{\text{Known}}|$ characters of the plaintext of other messages encrypted using k. To expose additional characters, we will need to use a different attack, such as the CPA attack which we describe in the following.

2.3.3 The chosen-plaintext attack (CPA) model

In the *chosen-plaintext attack (CPA) model*, the attacker can *choose* plaintext messages $m_0, m_1, \ldots$ and receive the corresponding ciphertexts $c_0 = E_k(m_0), c_1 = E_k(m_1), \ldots$. This is in addition to knowing the distribution from which m^* is sampled and the design of the cryptosystem, information available also under the ciphertext-only attack (COA) model. The CPA model is illustrated in Figure 2.10.

Security against CPA has been studied extensively in modern cryptography but was rarely considered in historical cryptanalysis.

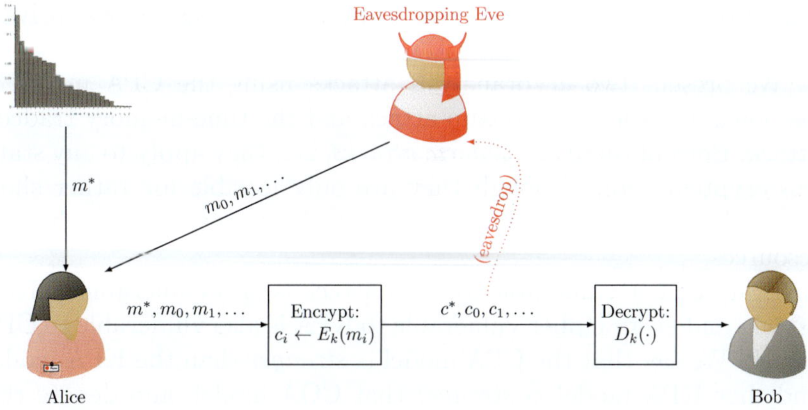

Figure 2.10. The *chosen-plaintext attack* (CPA) model. In the CPA model, the attacker can *choose* the plaintext messages $m_0, m_1, \ldots$, in addition to knowing the distribution from which m^* is sampled.

For example, in the Second World War, cryptanalysts in Bletchley Park made extensive use of known plaintexts, i.e., used KPA; however, they did not have control over the plaintext, as in the chosen-plaintext attack model.

However, attackers against the Internet, and in particular against web users and servers, often are able to control the contents of messages, at least partially, i.e., they often have (complete or partial) CPA capabilities. For example, consider, as for KPA, the common use of the TLS protocol (Chapter 7) to protect web communication. When the browser visits a website controlled by an attacker, the website can instruct the browser to send requests to other web (victim) web servers; this allows the attacker's website to launch different *cross-site attacks* against the victim website and the user using the browser. In particular, since the attacker controls much of the content of the request that the browser sends to the victim website, this allows a CPA on the TLS connection between browser and victim website. Successful cryptanalysis of this connection may expose sensitive information sent by the browser to the victim server, such as an authenticating cookie[9] or a password, as well as sensitive information

[9]Modern browsers support the *SameSite* cookie attribute which can restrict or prevent sending of the cookie over such cross-site requests; see Ref. [75].

sent from the website to the browser, such as user's private data.

We present two cryptanalysis attacks using the CPA model in Section 2.4.2: the table lookup attack and the time-memory tradeoff attack. Both of these are *generic attacks*, i.e., they apply to any stateless cryptosystem, although they are only feasible for rather short keys; when using longer keys, these attacks require excessively high resources.

Every cipher vulnerable to COA attack is also vulnerable to KPA attack, and every cipher vulnerable to KPA is also vulnerable to CPA attack. We say that the CPA model is *stronger* than the KPA model, and that KPA model is *stronger* that COA model, and denote this by $CPA > KPA > COA$.

2.3.4 The Chosen-Ciphertext Attack (CCA) model

The last attack model we study in this section is also the most powerful one: the *CCA model* illustrated in Figure 2.11. In the CCA model, the attacker has the ability to receive the decryption of arbitrary ciphertexts, chosen by the attacker. This attack model may seem absurd; if the attacker can receive decryption of arbitrary ciphertexts, then the encryption does not protect confidentiality even without cryptanalysis, no? However, there are situations where the attacker may obtain partial knowledge from decryption, which makes the chosen-ciphertext attack model useful since a cryptosystem secure against chosen-ciphertext attack would surely also be secure against attackers who can only obtain such partial knowledge. Indeed, in practice, it is common that the attacker can obtain partial information such as about the validity of the plaintext, often due to the application of padding and/or error detection/correction schemes applied to the plaintext (before encryption). We discuss such attacks in Sections 2.11 and 6.5.7; both exploit a weaker form of the chosen-ciphertext attack model, which we refer to as the *padding oracle attack* model.

There are a few variants to the CCA model. One set of variants combines the CCA model with the COA, KPA or CPA models, i.e., allows the adversary also the ability to receive *encryptions* of

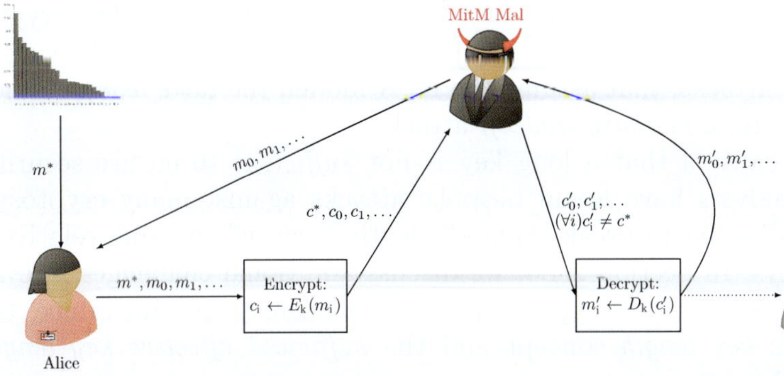

Figure 2.11. The *chosen-ciphertext attack* (CCA) model. In the CCA model, the adversary can select *ciphertext messages* $c'_0, c'_1, \ldots$, all different from the 'challenge ciphertext' c^*, and receive their decryptions $m'_i = D_k(c'_i)$.

random plaintext from a known distribution, known plaintexts or chosen plaintexts, respectively. We adopt the common definition, where CCA attackers are also allowed to perform CPA, i.e., the attacker can obtain the encryptions of attacker-chosen plaintext messages. With this definition, we have $CCA > CPA > KPA > COA$.

Another set of variants concern the *timing* of the choice of ciphertext messages to be decrypted; some CCA models require the adversary to choose these ciphertexts *before* receiving the challenge ciphertext c^*, and other CCA models allow the adversary to select these ciphertexts *after* receiving c^*, of course, forbidding the use of c^* as one of these ciphertexts to be decrypted.

2.4 Generic attacks and sufficient key length

We discussed ancient keyless ciphers in Section 2.2.1 and mentioned that they are inherently insecure since they do not use a key. In this section, we discuss several *generic attacks*, which are effective against *any stateless cryptosystem* which uses a short key. Namely, these attacks show that a sufficiently long key is *required* for security.

We first present, in Section 2.4.1, the *exhaustive search* attack. This is a COA which essentially tries out all the keys until finding the right one. Exhaustive search works against *most* stateless cryptosystems and in most scenarios. In Section 2.4.2, we discuss two other generic attacks, that assume the KPA model: the *table lookup* attack and the *time-memory tradeoff* attack.

We caution that a long key is not *sufficient* to ensure security; cryptanalysts have found bespoke attacks against many cryptosystems, allowing to break them efficiently, even when using relatively long keys. In Section 2.4.3, we discuss additional challenges in evaluating security of cryptographic mechanisms, and introduce the *effective key length* concept and the *sufficient effective key length* principle.

2.4.1 The exhaustive key search attack

Recall that in the COA attack model, the attacker has some knowledge about the distribution of plaintexts. In this section, we discuss the *generic exhaustive search attack*, also called sometimes the *brute-force* attack, where attackers use their knowledge of the plaintext distribution to cryptanalyze a generic cryptosystem, i.e., without dependency on the design of the specific cryptosystem.

To simplify, we assume that valid plaintexts are an easily identifiable and small subset of the set of all possible strings. Namely, we assume an efficient deterministic predicate $Valid(p)$ that validates if a given string p is a valid plaintext. Namely, $Valid(p)$ returns TRUE if p is a valid plaintext, and for most strings, p', holds that $valid(p') = $ FALSE — and p' is not a valid plaintext. Note that we allow $valid(p')$ to be true for some invalid plaintexts, as long as it is FALSE for most (invalid) plaintexts.

This assumption actually holds in many scenarios; let us list three such scenarios. First, the assumption holds when the plaintext is in a natural language with high redundancy, e.g., using the distribution of letters in English (Figure 2.7). Second, the assumption hold when the plaintext is generated by a program, whose output has a specific structure or format. Finally, the assumption holds for the *Encode-then-Encrypt* design, where encryption is applied to the plaintext $m + EDC(m)$, where EDC is an error detection code (or an error correction code).

Algorithm 2 Exhaustive search algorithm using predicate $Valid(\cdot)$, for stateless decryption algorithm D.

Set K of possible (symmetric or decryption) keys, initially contains all possible keys.
Set C of observed ciphertexts.
Predicate $Valid(p)$: returns TRUE if p is valid plaintext, FALSE for most strings
for all c in C **do**
  for all k in K **do**
    if $Valid(D_k(c)) =$ FALSE **then** Remove k from K
  if $|K| \leq 1$ **then** Return K and terminate
Return K and terminate

We present the generic exhaustive search attack in Algorithm 2. The algorithm works for cryptosystems where the decryption process is stateless, since otherwise, decryption of the same ciphertext may return different results depending on the state. The algorithm assumes a known $Valid$ function that identifies valid plaintext, as discussed above. We also assume that if c is an invalid ciphertext, i.e., $D_k(c)$ returns an error, than $Valid(D_k(c)) =$ FALSE. The algorithm applies to both symmetric key cryptosystems and public key cryptosystems; we use the symbol k for the key (shared key for symmetric key cryptosystem and decryption key for PKC).

Decryption of a ciphertext c with an incorrect key k returns, with high probability, an invalid plaintext — or a decryption error. In both cases, $Valid(D_k(c)) =$ FALSE. Therefore, a single ciphertext suffices to eliminate most keys. Usually, we only need to repeat the process once or twice to find the correct decryption key. Incorrect keys are discarded quickly, after testing them against a small number of ciphertexts.

Feasibility of Exhaustive Search: Exhaustive search is sometimes infeasible, since the attacker cannot identify legitimate plaintext, i.e., no $valid(\cdot)$ function. A modified algorithm can be used if all plaintexts are *possible* but some have very low probability. Exhaustive search is infeasible if the plaintext space is uniformly random, i.e., any string is equally likely to be used as plaintext.

Often, however, what makes exhaustive search infeasible is simply the *high computational costs*, duc to the use of a sufficiently long keys. Assume that the key is chosen as a random binary string of given length l, i.e., there are 2^l keys ($|K| = 2^l$). Namely, the attack succeeds after decrypting one or few valid ciphertexts, for each of the 2^l possible keys. The attack is therefore feasible, when 2^l is not too large, i.e., when using insufficiently long keys. Surprisingly, designers sometimes underestimate the risk of exhaustive search and used ciphers with insufficiently long keys, i.e., insufficiently large key spaces. Let us elaborate.

Let T_S be the *sensitivity period*, i.e., the duration required for maintaining secrecy, and T_D be the time it takes to test each potential key, by performing one or more decryptions, assuming the fastest hardware which may be available to the attacker over the sensitivity period. Hence, the attacker can test T_S/T_D keys out of the key space containing 2^l keys. If $T_S/T_D > 2^l$, then the attacker can test all keys, and find the key for certain (with probability 1); otherwise, the attacker succeeds with probability $\frac{T_S}{T_D \cdot 2^l}$. By selecting a sufficient key length, we can ensure that the success probability is as low as desired.

For example, assume the attacker can test a billion keys per second, i.e., $T_D = 10^{-9}$ seconds, and requiring the security for three thousand years, i.e., $T_S = 10^{11}$ seconds, with probability of attack succeeding at most 0.1%. We find that to ensure security with these parameters against brute-force attack, we need keys of length $l \geq \log_2\left(\frac{T_S}{T_D}\right) = \log_2(10^{20}) < 74$ bits.

The above calculation assumed a minimal time to test each key. Of course, attackers will often be able to test many keys in parallel, by using multiple computers and/or parallel processing, possibly with hardware acceleration. Such methods were used during 1994–1999 in multiple demonstrations of the vulnerability of the *Data Encryption Standard* (DES) to different attacks. The final demonstration was exhaustive search completing in 22 hours, testing many keys in parallel using a $250,000 dedicated-hardware machine ('deep crack') together with *distributed.net*, a network of computers contributing their idle time.

However, the impact of such parallel testing, as well as improvements in processing time, is easily addressed by reasonable extension of key length. Assume that an attacker is able to test 100 million keys in parallel during the same 10^{-9} second, i.e., $T_D = 10^{-17}$. With the same goals and calculation as above, we find that we need keys of length $l \geq \log_2\left(\frac{T_S}{T_D}\right) = \log_2(10^{26}) < 100$. This is far below even the minimal key length of 128 bits supported by the *Advanced Encryption Standard* (AES). Therefore, exhaustive search is not a viable attack against AES or other well-designed cryptosystems with over 100 bits.

In principle, exhaustive search can also be applicable to public key cryptosystems (KG, E, D), where the public and private keys are generated by the randomized key-generation algorithm, i.e., $(e, d) \xleftarrow{\$} KG(1^n)$. However, this is usually impractical, for two reasons: First, all known PKCs have orders of magnitude more overhead than shared key cryptosystems, which makes testing all keys impractical. Second, known public key cryptosystems are all vulnerable to attacks which are significantly more efficient than exhaustive search and therefore are used with significantly longer keys, which make exhaustive search attacks infeasible. See details in Chapter 6 and in particular in Table 6.1.

Exhaustive search for stateful cryptosystems: Exhaustive search may be harder against stateful ciphers since decryption depends on the current state of the cryptosystem. The natural adaptation of the exhaustive search attack of Algorithm 2 requires to consider the state as a part of the key, which makes the attack harder.

2.4.2 The table lookup and tradeoff attacks

Exhaustive search is very computation-intensive; it finds the key, on the average, after testing half of the keyspace. On the other hand, its storage requirements are very modest and (almost[10]) independent of the key space.

In contrast, the *table lookup attack*, which we explain in the following, uses $O(2^l)$ memory, where l is the key length, but only table-lookup time. However, this requires ciphertext of some pre-defined plaintext message, which we denote p^*. This can be

[10]Exhaustive search needs storage for the key guesses.

achieved by an attacker with CPA capabilities or whenever the attacker can obtain encryptions of some well known message p^*. Many communication protocols use predictable, well-known messages at specific times, often upon connection initialization, which provides the attacker with encryptions of this *predictable* known plaintext message p^* — and suffice for this attack. Note also that the table lookup attack is only applicable to deterministic, stateless encryption; it cannot be applied for cryptosystems which are probabilistic or stateful and, hence, may return multiple different ciphertext values when applied to the the same plaintext.

In the table lookup attack, the attacker first *precomputes* the table $C(k) = E_k(p^*)$, i.e., for every key k, the entry $C(k)$ is the encryption of the pre-defined plaintext p^* using key k. The attacker then uses $C(\cdot)$ to create the reverse table $K(c) = \{k \text{ s.t. } c = E_k(p^*)\}$, i.e., $K(c)$ contains the set of all keys k such that the encryption of the pre-defined plaintext p^*, using key k, gives ciphertext c. We call such keys *matching keys* and $K(\cdot)$ the *matching keys table.* Note that an entry in $K(\cdot)$ may contain multiple matching keys, e.g., k and k'; this occurs when $E_k(p^*) = E_{k'}(p^*)$, which is possible, although not common.

Later, the attacker asks the CPA oracle to encrypt the same plaintext p^*, using the unknown secret key, which we denote k^*; let $c^* = E_{k^*}(p^*)$ denote the received ciphertext. The attacker now identifies the key as one of the matching keys in $K(c^*)$. If $K(c^*)$ contains more than one matching key, e.g., $K(c^*) = \{k, k'\}$, then the attacker encrypts another string, say p', by each of the matching keys (e.g., k and k') and compares to the result of the encryption of p' by the oracle. Since the number of matching keys of c^* is small, this step is efficient — in fact, often there will only by one matching key.

The table lookup attack requires $O(2^l)$ storage to ensure $O(1)$ computation, while the exhaustive search attack uses $O(1)$ storage and $O(2^l)$ computations. Several more advanced generic attacks allow different *tradeoffs* between the computing time and the amount of storage (memory) required for the attack. The first and most well-known *time-memory tradeoff* attack was presented by Martin Hellman [237]. Later works presented other tradeoff attacks, such as the *time/memory/data tradeoff* of Ref. [80] and the *rainbow tables* technique of Ref. [384]. We describe the rainbow table attack in

Section 9.4.2.2, where we focus on its main practical application, which is to find passwords from exposed files containing hashed passwords.

2.4.3 Sufficient effective key length

Cryptanalysis, i.e., developing attacks on cryptographic mechanisms, is a large part of the research in applied cryptography; it includes generic attacks such as these presented earlier in this section, as well as numerous attacks which are tailored to a specific cryptographic mechanism. This may look surprising; why publish attacks? Surely the goal is not to help attacks against cryptographic systems?

Cryptanalysis facilitates two critical decisions facing designers of security systems which use cryptography: *which cryptographic mechanism* to use, and *which key length* to use.

All too often, when cryptographic products and protocols are mentioned in the popular press, the key length in use is mentioned as an indicator of their security. Furthermore, this is sometimes used to argue for the security of the cryptographic mechanism, typically by presenting the number of different key values possible with a given key length. The number of different keys is the time required for the exhaustive search attack and has direct impact on the resources required by the other generic attacks we discussed. Hence, clearly, *keys must be sufficiently long* to ensure security. But how long?

It can be *incorrect* to compare the security of two different cryptographic systems, which use different cryptographic mechanisms (e.g., ciphers), by simply comparing the key length used in the two systems. Let us give two examples:

1. We saw that the generalized monoalphabetic substitution cipher (Section 2.2.3) is insecure, even when using a large key space.
2. The keys used by symmetric cryptosystems are typically much shorter than the keys used with comparably secure public key cryptosystems; see Table 6.1.

It is useful to compare the security of different cryptosystems, when each is used with a specific key length, e.g., with comparable efficiency. As explained above, using the key length alone would be misleading. One convenient, widely used measure for the security of a given cryptosystem, used with a specific key length, is called the *effective key length*; essentially, this uses exhaustive search as a measure to compare against.

We say that a cryptosystem using k-bit keys has *effective key length* l if the most effective attack known against it takes about 2^l operations, where $k \geq l$. We expect the effective key length of good symmetric key cryptosystems to be close to their real key length, i.e., l should not be 'much smaller' compared to k. For important symmetric key cryptosystems, any attack which increases the gap between k and l would be of great interest, and as the gap grows, there will be increasing concern with using the cryptosystem. The use of key lengths which are 128 bits or more leaves a 'safety margin' against potential better future attacks and gives time to change to a new cipher when a stronger, more effective attack is found.

As shown in Table 6.1, for asymmetric cryptosystems, there is often a large gap between the real key length l and the effective key length k. This is considered acceptable since the design of asymmetric cryptosystems is challenging, and it seems reasonable to expect attacks with performance much better than exhaustive search. In particular, in public key systems, the private keys are not chosen as a random binary string.

The evaluation of the effective key length depends on the *attack model*; there are often attackers with much smaller effective-key length, when assuming a stronger attack model, e.g., CPA compared to KPA or COA. One should therefore also take into account the expected attack model.

Normally, we select sufficient key length to ensure security against any conceivable adversary, e.g., leaving a reasonable margin above an effective key length of say 100 bits; a larger margin is required when the *sensitivity period* of the plaintext is longer. The cost of using longer keys is often justified, considering the damages of loss of security and of having to change in a hurry to a cipher with longer effective key length.

In some scenarios, however, the use of longer keys may have significant costs; for example, doubling the key length in the RSA cryptosystem increases the computational costs by about six. We therefore may also consider the risk from exposure, as well as the resources that a (rational) attacker may deploy to break the system. This is summarized by the following principle.

Principle 5 (Sufficient effective key length). *Deployed cryptosystems should use keys which are long enough to ensure a sufficient effective key length to foil feasible attacks, considering the maximal expected adversary resources, as well as cryptanalysis and computational resource improvements expected over the sensitivity period of the plaintext.*

Experts, as well as standardization and security organizations, publish estimates of the required key length of different cryptosystems (and other cryptographic schemes); we present a few estimates in Table 6.1.

2.5 The One-Time Pad (OTP) cipher

The exhaustive search and table lookup attacks are generic — they do not depend on the specific design of the cryptosystem: their complexity is merely a function of the key length. This raises the natural question: is every cryptosystem breakable, given enough resources? Or, can a cryptosystem be secure *unconditionally* — even against an attacker with unbounded resources, i.e., unlimited time, computation speed and storage capabilities?

We next present such an unconditionally secure stream cipher: The one-time pad (OTP). The OTP is often attributed to a 1919 patent by Gilbert Vernam [469], although this seems to be imprecise.[11]

The OTP is not just unconditionally secure — it is also an exceedingly simple and computationally efficient. Specifically:

Encryption: To encrypt a message, compute its bitwise XOR with the key. Namely, the encryption of each plaintext bit, say $m[i]$, is one ciphertext bit, $c[i]$, computed as $c[i] = m[i] \oplus k[i]$, where $k[i]$ is the ith bit of the key.

Decryption: Decryption simply reverses the encryption, i.e., the ith decrypted bit would be $c[i] \oplus k[i]$.

[11] Some of the critical aspects of the OTP design seem to have been due to Mauborgne, and the basic idea was already proposed by Miller in 1882; see Refs. [55, 56, 279, 447].

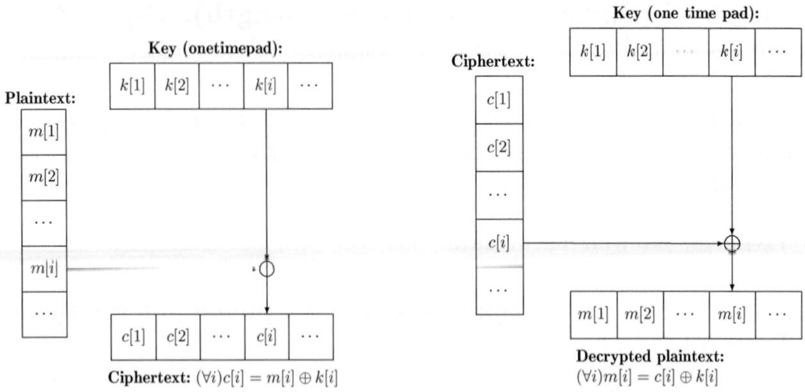

(a) One-time pad encryption (b) One-time pad decryption

Figure 2.12. One-time pad (OTP) encryption and decryption.

Key: The key bits $k = \{k[1], k[2], \ldots\}$ should consist of independently drawn fair coins, and the key length must be at least as long as that of the plaintext. Note that this long key should be — somehow — shared between the parties, which is a challenge in many scenarios.

See illustration in Figure 2.12.

The correctness of OTP, i.e., the fact that decryption recovers the plaintext correctly, follows from the properties of exclusive OR. Namely, given $c[i] = m[i] \oplus k[i]$, the corresponding decrypted bit would be $m[i]$, as required, since

$$\begin{aligned} c[i] \oplus k[i] &= (m[i] \oplus k[i]) \oplus k[i] \\ &= m[i] \oplus (k[i] \oplus k[i]) \\ &= m[i] \end{aligned} \tag{2.15}$$

The unconditional security of OTP follows from the properties of the XOR operator. We only explain intuitively why the OTP provides unconditional security, i.e., prevents exposure of the plaintext, even if the attacker has unbounded computational resources. First, OTP handles each bit completely independent of others, so we can focus on the security of a particular bit $m[i]$, encrypted as $c[i] = m[i] \oplus k[i]$. Recall that each key bit $k[i]$ is selected randomly, and suppose, for simplicity, that the message bit $m[i]$ was also selected randomly. Namely, both bits can be either 0 or 1 with probability half. Given $c[i]$, there are two equally likely explanations: either $k[i] = 0$ and therefore $m[i] = c[i]$, or $k[i] = 1$ and therefore $m[i] = 1 - c[i]$. Namely, seeing $c[i]$ does not change our knowledge about $m[i]$, simply since $k[i]$ is a random bit. The precise argument avoids the assumption that the message bit is fair, i.e., allows the attacker to know the distribution of the input bit.

The unconditional secrecy of OTP was recognized early on and established rigorously in a seminal paper published in 1949 by Claude Shannon [437]. In that paper, Shannon also proved the more challenging fact that *every unconditionally secure cipher must have keys as long as the plaintext*; namely, as long as unconditional secrecy is required, this aspect cannot be improved.

The fact that OTP requires a key as long as the total number of plaintext bits to be encrypted makes the use of OTP rarely practical. Therefore, we next show a *computationally secure variant* of OTP, where the key can be much smaller than the plaintext; such variants are often used in practical systems. Note, however, that this variant, as well as any other encryption scheme where the key is shorter than the total set of plaintexts, is — at best — secure only against computationally bounded attackers.

Note that OTP handles multiple plaintext messages as part of one long plaintext string, i.e., it uses $m[i]$ for the ith plaintext bit, and similarly for ciphertext and key bits; basically, one could say that the OTP encrypts its input as one long plaintext message, which it encrypts one bit at a time. Some other stream ciphers encrypt multiple bits at a time.

Changing the OTP to use a bounded key, by simply reusing key bits, is *insecure*. Consider a stream cipher which uses a limited-length key $k[0], k[1], \ldots, k[l]$ and encrypts plaintext bit $m[i]$ by $c[i] = m[i] \oplus k[i \bmod l]$. Then, an attacker knowing one known plaintext, e.g., $m[i]$ and $c[i]$, and eavesdropping on $c[i + l]$, can find $m[i + l]$. Specifically, in this case, $m[i + l] = c[i + l] \oplus (m[i] \oplus c[i])$.

In the following section, we introduce PRG, which can be used to implement a stream cipher with bounded key length, which would be secure against computationally bounded (efficient) attackers.

2.6 Indistinguishability tests and PRGs

The OTP is rarely applicable since it requires the parties to share a random secret key, which is as long as all the plaintext to be encrypted. We discussed that naive adaptations of the OTP to use bounded-length keys, e.g., using the key $k[0], k[1], \ldots, k[l]$ by encrypting bit i as $c[i] = m[i] \oplus k[i \bmod l]$, are trivially insecure and could be 'broken' even by computationally bounded attackers.

In this section, we introduce the concept of a PRG, a cryptographic function which, when given as input a random string shorter than the plaintext, produces a longer *pseudorandom* string. We can use a pseudorandom string as long as the plaintext as the key to the OTP and encrypt the plaintext. This combination of the PRG and the OTP is a *stream cipher with a bounded-length key*, which is secure against *computationally bounded adversaries.*

In slightly more details, a PRG is a cryptographic function $f_{PRG} : \{0,1\}^n \rightarrow \{0,1\}^m$ that maps an n-bits binary string, into a longer output string, consisting of $m > n$ bits.[12] Intuitively, we require that, given a random input $x \stackrel{\$}{\leftarrow} \{0,1\}^n$, the output $f_{PRG}(x)$ of the PRG would be *pseudorandom*, i.e., that a polynomial-time adversary will not be able to *distinguish* between the output of the PRG and a truly random n-bits string, $r \stackrel{\$}{\leftarrow} \{0,1\}^m$. If this holds, then we say that the output of the PRG is *indistinguishable from random*, or simply, that the PRG is *secure.*

In this section, we first present, in Section 2.6.1, the *Turing indistinguishability test.* The goal of the *Turing indistinguishability test* is not cryptographic at all; Turing presented it as a test for *machine/artificial intelligence.* However, in cryptography, we use similar indistinguishability tests for different cryptographic mechanisms, including indistinguishability tests for pseudorandom generators and cryptosystems. Specifically, in Section 2.6.2, we define the

[12]Formally, the domain of the PRG should include arbitrarily long input lengths n.

PRG indistinguishability test and use it to define a *secure pseudo-random generator*.

Later on, we define several additional indistinguishability tests. In the following section (Section 2.7), we present PRF, together with the corresponding indistinguishability games; in Section 2.8.1, we discuss PRP and the corresponding indistinguishability games, and in Section 2.9, we define indistinguishability tests for symmetric key cryptosystems and PKCs.

2.6.1 The Turing indistinguishability test

In order to precisely define a PRG, we first present the ingenious concept of *indistinguishability test*, which is key to the notion of pseudorandomness — and to many definitions in cryptography. This concept was introduced by Alan Turing, in a seminal paper [460] that Turing published at 1950, as a method to define artificial intelligence or, as Turing called it, an *intelligent machine.* Turing referred to this test as the *imitation test*, but it is currently called the *Turing test.*

The design of the Turing indistinguishability test is quite simple. A machine is considered *intelligent*, or at least to have passed the test, if it appears that no judge is able to distinguish between the machine and a human. Namely, the judge interacts, by asking questions and receiving responses, with both the machine and a person, and yet, the judge fails to identify which of the two is the machine and which is the person, i.e., fails to identify the machine correctly in significantly more than 50% of the attempts, i.e., not better than a random guess.

In order to focus the distinguishing ability on the intelligence of the machine rather than on other aspects such as its appearance, both machine and human are hidden from view of the judge, who can only interact them them by printed questions and answers. See Figure 2.13.

Many cryptographic mechanisms are defined using indistinguishability tests, whose basic concept is similar to the Turing indistinguishability test. We next present the first such test: the PRG *indistinguishability test.*

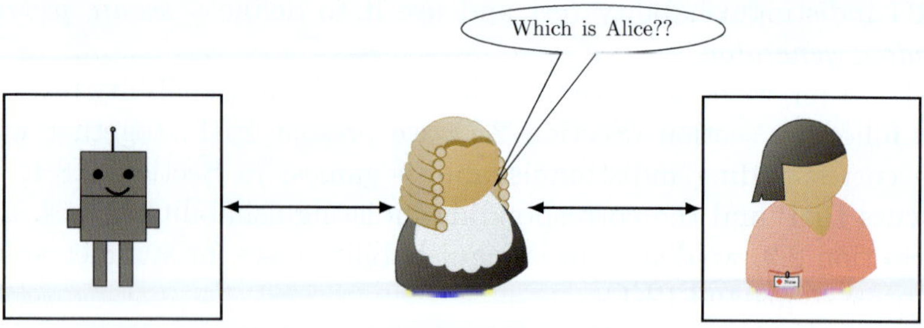

Figure 2.13. The Turing indistinguishability test. A machine is considered *intelligent* if a *distinguisher* (judge) cannot determine in which box is the machine and in which is the human. The judge can only exchange textual messages with the two boxes.

2.6.2 Pseudorandom generators (PRGs)

A Pseudorandom generator (PRG) is a function $f_{\text{PRG}} : \{0,1\}^n \to \{0,1\}^m$ that maps a (short) n-bits binary string into a longer $m > n$ output string, which *should* be pseudorandom, i.e., indistinguishable from a truly random string of the same length. We *expect* a PRG to ensure that its output is *pseudorandom*, i.e., *indistinguishable from random.*

In this section, we define this indistinguishability requirement which is expected from well-designed PRGs.

What does it mean for the output to be indistinguishable from a random string? This is defined by the *PRG indistinguishability test*, which we define in the following. In concept, this test resembles the Turing indistinguishability test, although the details are quite different. The similarity can be seen from comparing the illustration of the PRG indistinguishability test, in Figure 2.14, to the illustration of the Turing test, in Figure 2.13.

The *PRG indistinguishability test* is similar in structure to the Turing indistinguishability test of Figure 2.13, in the sense that a distinguisher is asked to identify which is the box containing the 'original' object and which is the box containing the 'imitation' object. In the Turing test, the original object is the person and the imitation object is the machine programmed to try to impersonate as a person. Similarly, in the PRG indistinguishability test, the imitation object is $f_{\text{PRG}}(x)$ for $x \xleftarrow{\$} \{0,1\}^n$, and the original object is a random

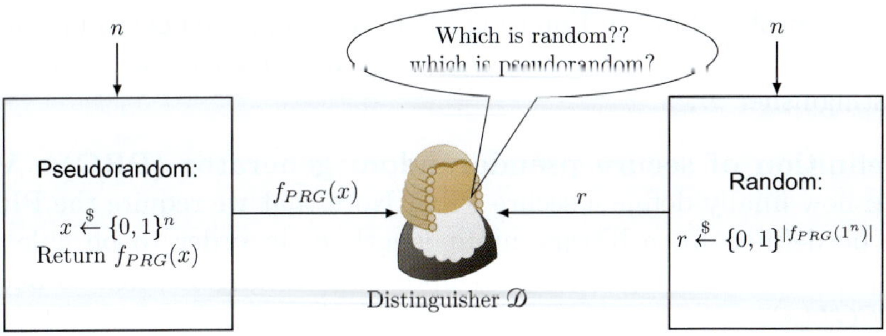

Figure 2.14. The pseudorandom generator (PRG) indistinguishability test. We say that f_{PRG} is a secure PRG, if no efficient PRG distinguisher $\mathcal{D}$ can distinguish, with non-negligible advantage, between (a) $f_{\text{PRG}}(x)$, for a random input $x \xleftarrow{\$} \{0,1]^n$, and (b) a random string of the same length ($|f_{\text{PRG}}(x)|$).

string of the same length, $r \xleftarrow{\$} \{0,1\}^{|f_{\text{PRG}}(1^n)}$. The length n is a parameter of the test. The PRG indistinguishability test is illustrated in Figure 2.14.

Let us turn this intuition into a definition, by defining the *capabilities* of the PRG distinguisher $\mathcal{D}$ and the *criteria* for the outcome of the experiment, i.e., when we would say that f_{PRG} is a secure *PRG*.

Distinguisher capabilities: We model the distinguisher $\mathcal{D}$ as an efficient algorithm which receives a binary string and outputs 'R' (for *random*) or 'P' (for *Pseudorandom*). For the definition of efficient algorithms, see Section A.1.

The advantage of a PRG distinguisher: The *advantage* $\varepsilon^{PRG}_{\mathcal{D},f_{\text{PRG}}}(n)$ of PRG distinguisher $\mathcal{D}$ for PRG function f_{PRG} is the probability that $\mathcal{D}$ outputs 'R' (for *random*) when given input r *minus* the probability that it outputs 'R' (incorrectly) when given input $f_{\text{PRG}}(x)$, where $x \xleftarrow{\$} \{0,1\}^n$ and $r \xleftarrow{\$} \{0,1\}^{|f_{\text{PRG}}(1^n)|}$, i.e., both are random bit strings, x with n bits and r with $f_{\text{PRG}}(1^n)$ bits. Namely,

$$\varepsilon^{PRG}_{\mathcal{D},f_{\text{PRG}}}(n) \equiv \begin{bmatrix} \Pr(\mathcal{D}(r) = \text{'R'}) - \Pr(\mathcal{D}(f_{\text{PRG}}(x)) = \text{'R'}), \\ \text{where } r \xleftarrow{\$} \{0,1\}^{|f_{\text{PRG}}(1^n)|},\ x \xleftarrow{\$} \{0,1\}^n \end{bmatrix} \tag{2.16}$$

The probabilities in Equation (2.16) are computed over uniformly random strings x and r and uniformly random coin tosses of the distinguisher $\mathcal{D}$.

Definition of secure pseudorandom generator (PRG): We can now finally define a secure PRG. Note that we require the PRG to be defined for arbitrary input length n, in order to be able to require the advantage to be asymptotically negligible, i.e., to be in $NEGL(n)$.

Definition 2.4 (Secure pseudorandom generator (PRG)). *An efficient function* $f_{\text{PRG}} : \{0,1\}^* \to \{0,1\}^*$, *s.t.* $(\forall x \in \{0,1\}^n)$ $|f(x)| > |x|$, *is a* secure PRG, *if for every efficient algorithm* $\mathcal{D} \in PPT$ *(the* distinguisher*), the advantage of* $\mathcal{D}$ *for* f *is negligible, i.e.,* $\varepsilon^{PRG}_{\mathcal{D},f}(n) \in NEGL(n)$, *where* $\varepsilon^{PRG}_{D,f}(n)$ *is defined as in Equation* (2.16).

The term 'secure' is often omitted when discussing a secure PRG, i.e., when we say that function f_{PRG} is a PRG, it usually means that f_{PRG} is assumed or required to be a secure PRG.

To understand the definition better, in the following exercise, we present few functions which can be, quite easily, shown to *not* be a secure PRG.

Exercise 2.4 (Examples of functions which are not PRGs). Let $x \in \{0,1\}^n$. Using the value of x as a number encoded in binary. Show that *none* of the following functions is a secure PRG:

(a) $f_a(x) = 3x \bmod 2^{n+2}$ encoded as an $n+2$ bits string.
(b) $f_b(x) = 2x \bmod 2^{n+1}$ encoded as an $n+1$ bits string.
(c) $f_c(x) = 3x \bmod 2^{n+1}$ encoded as an $n+1$ bits string.
(d) $f_d(x) = x + \text{parity}(x)$, where $\text{parity}(x)$ returns 1 if the number of 1 bits in x is odd and 0 if it is even.
(e) $f_e(x) = x + g(x)$, where $g(\cdot)$ *is* a secure PRG.

Present, for each item, a distinguisher which efficiently and with significant advantage distinguishes between the output of the function and a random string of the same length.

Solution for part (a): Let y be an $(n+2)$-bit string which can be either truly random or the result of $f_a(x)$ for a random n-bits string x. One distinguisher for f_a simply identifies a function as pseudorandom (returns 'P') if the most significant bit of the output is zero, and otherwise identifies the function as random (returns 'R'). This distinguisher is very simple, and, although it is not always correct, it has non-negligible advantage, which suffices to show that f_a is *not* a secure PRG. Specifically, this distinguisher, which we denote D_a, has advantage of at least $\frac{1}{6}$.

To see this, consider a random n-bits string x. We have

$$\Pr_{x \xleftarrow{\$} \{0,1\}^n} (MSb(f_a(x)) = 0) = \Pr_{x \xleftarrow{\$} \{0,1\}^n} \left(3x < 2^{n+1}\right)$$
$$= \Pr_{x \xleftarrow{\$} \{0,1\}^n} \left(x < \frac{2}{3} \cdot 2^n\right) > \frac{2}{3}$$

Namely, with probability over $\frac{2}{3}$, $D_a(f_a(x))$ returns 'R' (correctly). On the other hand,

$$\Pr_{r \xleftarrow{\$} \{0,1\}^{n+2}} (D_a(r) = 1) = \Pr_{r \xleftarrow{\$} \{0,1\}^{n+2}} (MSb(r) = 0) = 0.5$$

Hence, $D_a(r)$ returns both 'P' and 'R' with probability half. □

Solution for part (d): Given an $n + 1$-bits string y, define

$$D_d(y) \equiv \{\text{'P' if } parity(y) = 0, \text{ else 'R'}\}$$

Obviously, if y is a random $(n + 1)$-bit string, then its parity is a random bit; hence, $\Pr(D_d(y) = \text{'R'}) = \Pr(D_d(y) = \text{'P'}) = \frac{1}{2}$. On the other hand, for *any* n-bit string, x holds $D_d(f_d(x)) = D_d(x + parity(x))$, which always returns 'R', since the parity of a string x concatenated to the parity of x is always zero. It follows that D_d has advantage of one half, which is surely not negligible. □

2.7 Random and pseudorandom functions

One drawback of stream ciphers is the fact that they require *state* to remember how many bits (or bytes) were already output.

What happens if the state is lost? Can we recover from loss of state? Or, even better: can we eliminate or reduce the need to preserve state, especially when encryption is not used, e.g., between one message and the next?

In Section 2.7.2, we introduce another pseudorandom cryptographic mechanism, called a PRF. PRFs have many applications in cryptography — including *stateless, randomized symmetric key cryptosystems.* However, first, in Section 2.7.1, we introduce the more basic concept of *random functions.*

2.7.1 Random functions and their applications

Before we introduce PRFs, we dedicate this section to discuss 'truly' *random functions and their usage.*

Intuitively, a random function from domain D to range R is a mapping of each value in the domain to a uniformly randomly selected corresponding value in the range. Namely, for each $x \in D$, we randomly select a value $f(x) \stackrel{\$}{\leftarrow} R$.

This description is only intuitive, since we cannot select a value with uniform probability from an infinite range R. We deal with this by adopting the common simplification, where the range of the PRF is always *finite*, allowing to pick values uniformly.

Often, both D and R are sets of of binary strings, with R being a finite set of strings, often, the set of all strings of a specific length, e.g., $\{0,1\}^n$. The domain can be an arbitrary set and is often either the set of all strings or the set of strings of a specific length; in fact, often D and R are the *same* set containing the strings of some length n, i.e., $D = R = \{0,1\}^n$.

Selecting a random function: How can we *select* a random function from the set of functions from the finite domain D to the finite range R? One way is as follows: for each input $x \in D$, select, uniformly at random, an element in R to be $f(x)$, namely,

$$(\forall x \in D) f(x) \stackrel{\$}{\leftarrow} R \tag{2.17}$$

This process can be done manually for small domain and range, by randomly choosing the mapping and writing it in a table, e.g., as in Exercise 2.5. We focus on the typical case where both D and R are sets of binary strings of specific length. For given integers n, m, we have $D = \{0,1\}^n,\ R = \{0,1\}^m$.

Exercise 2.5. Select randomly the following functions, e.g., by flipping a coin; count your coin flips.

1. Select a random function $f_{n,m} : \{0,1\}^n \leftarrow \{0,1\}^m$, for $n = 2$ and for m between 1 and 3, by flipping a coin. Count your coin flips.
2. Repeat, for m fixed at 2 and n between 1 and 3.
3. How many coin flips would be needed for $n = 2$ and m between 4 and 8? Plot the number of coin flips (for $m = 1$ to 8).
4. How many coin flips would be needed for $m = 2$ and n between 4 and 8? Plot the number of coin flips (for $n = 1$ to 8).
5. Let $F_{n,m}$ denote the set of all functions from $\{0,1\}^n$ to $\{0,1\}^m$, as in Equation (2.18). Compute and plot the number of such functions, i.e., $|F_{n,m}|$, for $n = 2$ and for m between 1 and 6.
6. Repeat, for $m = 2$ and n between 1 and 6.

As you can experience from the exercise, the number of coin flips required both to *choose*, *store* and *communicate* the random function $f_{n,m} : \{0,1\}^n \leftarrow \{0,1\}^m$ is $2^n \cdot m$, i.e., is exponential in the number of bits in the domain (n).

The total number of functions grows even more rapidly. Let $F_{n,m}$ denote the set of all functions from $\{0,1\}^n$ to $\{0,1\}^m$, namely,

$$F_{n,m} \equiv \{f_{n,m} : \{0,1\}^n \leftarrow \{0,1\}^m\} \tag{2.18}$$

Each function $f_{n,m} \in F_{n,m}$ maps each element in the domain $D_n = \{0,1\}^n$ to an element in the range $R_m = \{0,1\}^m$. Hence, we can map each string in D_n to any of the values in R_m. The number of elements in D_n is $|D_n| = 2^n$ and the number of elements in R_m is $|R_m| = 2^m$. Therefore, the total number of functions in $F_{n,m}$ is $|F_{n,m}| = (2^m)^{2^n}$ (or, in general, $|R|^{|D|}$). Each function is selected with probability $(2^m)^{-2^n}$.

We see that selecting and storing a function from a large domain (and to a large range) would be difficult, as would be *sending* it — which is required if we want multiple parties to use the same random function. This is a pity; a shared random function can be very useful for cryptographic applications; we discuss some of these in the following. In practice, instead of using a random function for these applications, we use, instead, a PRFs, which we discuss in the following section.

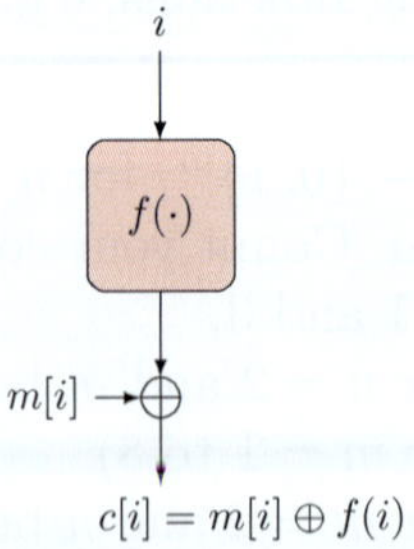

(a) A stream cipher for stateful bit-by-bit encryption, using limited storage (for a counter). Communication-optimal, i.e., |ciphertext| = |plaintext|.

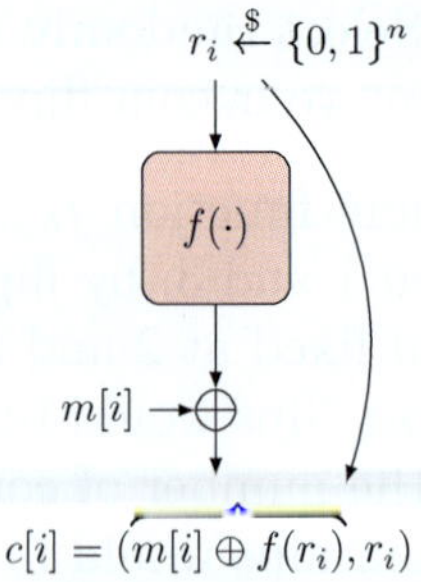

(b) Stateless, randomized bit-by-bit encryption. Notice the high communication overhead: $n+1$ ciphertext bits per one plaintext bit.

Figure 2.15. Bitwise encryption using a random function $f(\cdot) \in \{0,1\}$: (a) stream cipher, i.e., stateful encryption and (b) randomized, stateless encryption.

Stream cipher using a random function: Figure 2.15(a) presents the design of a (stateful) stream cipher using a randomly chosen function f with a single bit output, which is shared by the two parties and kept secret.

One drawback of the use of stream ciphers is the need to maintain *synchronized state* between sender and recipient. This refers to the (typical) case where the input is broken into multiple messages, each provided in a separate call to the encryption device. To encrypt all of these messages using a stream cipher, the two parties must maintain the number of encryptions i (of bits or messages of fixed length). To avoid this requirement, and have a stateless design, we can use *randomized encryption*, as we explain in the following.

Stateless, randomized encryption using a random function f: An even more interesting application of random functions, is to avoid the need for the two parties to maintain state (of the message/bit counter i). To do this, we use the random function to construct *randomized encryption*, as shown in Figure 2.15(b).

Here, again, we use a random function f which outputs a single bit. To encrypt each plaintext bit $m[i]$, we choose a string r_i of n random bits, i.e., $r_i \xleftarrow{\$} \{0,1\}^n$. The ciphertext $c[i]$ corresponding to plaintext bit $m[i]$ is the pair $(m[i] \oplus f(r_i), r_i)$.

This solution is indeed stateless, but it has high communication overhead: for every plaintext bit, we must send n bits of randomness. We explain below how to reduce this overhead; but let us first discuss security. This is in contrast to the stateful block cipher, which does not have any overhead in the number of bits sent, i.e., the size of the ciphertext is equal to the size of the plaintext. We say that the stateful stream cipher is *communication optimal.*

Security: Are the designs in Figure 2.15 secure? In this case, we assume that the two parties share a random function f which is unknown to the adversary; basically, the function is considered as a shared secret 'key'.

Intuitively, the design of Figure 2.15(a) is secure if we never reuse the same counter value, since then each plaintext bit, e.g., $m[i]$, is encrypted with an independently chosen pad bit $f(i)$, just like in the OTP.

The design of Figure 2.15(b) can be secure, but only *provided* that we use a sufficient number of random bits n; let us explain why it is secure. An obvious concern is that an attacker may try to predict the value of $f(r_i)$ used to encrypt a message (or bit) $m[i]$, from previously observed ciphertexts $\{c[j]\}_{j<i}$. Assume that r_i is selected (randomly) as the same as one of the previously used random values, i.e., $r_i = r_j$ for some $j < i$. In this case, the attacker may have already observed $c[j]$. If the attacker knows $m[j]$, then the attacker can expose $m[i]$, by computing:

$$m[i] = c[i] \oplus f(r_i) = c[i] \oplus f(r_j) = c[i] \oplus (m[j] \oplus c[j]) \qquad (2.19)$$

We can control this risk by selecting sufficiently long random strings r_i and r_j, making it very unlikely that we will repeat the same value.

Note that exposure of the value of the random function for other inputs, i.e., $f(r)$ for $r \neq r_i$, would not expose any information about $f(r_i)$. To see this, reconsider the process of selecting a random function, as in Exercise 2.5. What we did was to select the entire table — mapping from every element in the domain to a random element in the range — *before* we applied the random function. However, note that it does not matter if, instead, we choose the mapping for each element $r_i \in D$ in the domain *only on the first time we need to compute* $f(r_i)$.

This means that if $r_i \notin \{r_j\}_{j<i}$, then the attacker *does not learn anything about* $f(r_i)$, even if the attacker is given all of the 'previous' $\{f(r_j)\}_{j<i}$ values. Until we select (randomly) the value of $f(r_i)$, the attacker cannot know anything about it. Therefore, the only concern we have is with the case that $r_i \in \{r_j\}_{j<i}$.

What is the probability of repeating the same random value, i.e., of $r_i \in \{r_j\}_{j<i}$? Since each mapping is selected randomly, this probability is $\frac{i-1}{|D|}$. Focusing on the typical case where the input domain is $\{0,1\}^n$, this is $\frac{i-1}{2^n}$.

Therefore, if n is 'sufficiently large', then $\frac{i-1}{2^n}$ would be negligible, i.e., the maximal number $i-1$ of observations by the attacker would be negligible compared to 2^n.

Communication efficiency of stateless, randomized encryption: We have argued that the stateless, randomized scheme of Figure 2.15(b) is secure — provided n is 'sufficiently large'. However, the design has high communication overhead: sending $n+1$ ciphertext bits for each plain text bit.

The efficiency can be improved by changing from a stream cipher to a block cipher, as shown in Figure 2.16. In this case, both input messages $m[i]$ and the output of the random function could be strings of some length, e.g., n. Each invocation of the random function will produce n pad bits, which we can XOR against with n bits of the plaintext to produce n ciphertext bits.

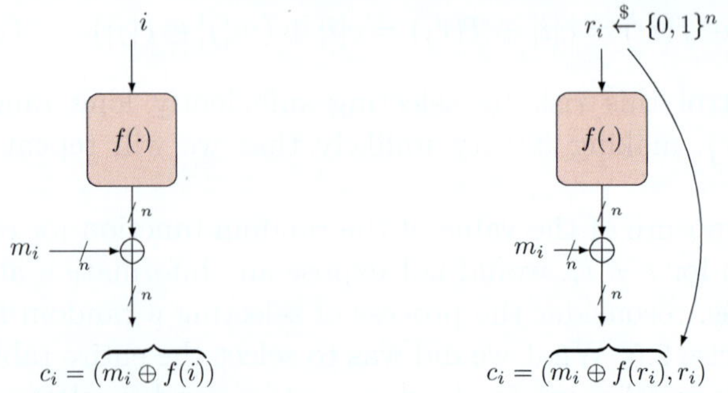

(a) Stateful block encryption with a random function $f(\cdot)$.

(b) Stateless, randomized block encryption with a random function $f(\cdot)$.

Figure 2.16. Block (n-bits) encryption using a random function $f(\cdot)$. Use only one function application for n plaintext bits.

We still need to send also the n randomly chosen bits, and the ciphertext remains significantly longer than the plaintext; however, the overhead is much reduced since we use the same random bits to encrypt multiple plaintext bits. When the number of random bits is the same as the number of plaintext bits encrypted each time, e.g., n in Figure 2.16(b), then the length of the ciphertext would be twice the length of the plaintext.

Figure 2.16 also shows a stateful block cipher which also uses a random function with n bits outputs, which reduces the number of function lookup operation compared to the single-bit design of Figure 2.15(a).

It is possible to further reduce the communication overhead by using a random function whose range is larger than its domain, or by using $f(r_i)$ as seed of a Pseudorandom generator (PRG). The PRG can 'expand' $f(r_i)$ into as many bits as required to bit-wise XOR with the plaintext, or to encrypt a large block of $m > n$ plaintext bits. In this way, the n bits of r allow encryption of $m > n$ plaintext bits. This is essentially what is done by the *Output Feedback (OFB) mode of operation*, which we see later on, except that the OFB mode also *implements the PRG* using the PRF, instead of using two separate functions (a PRF and a PRG).

Efficiency of storing and sharing the random function: Finally, we recall the main problem with the schemes of this section: their reliance on a 'truly' random function. To implement both schemes, both entities need to compute the same random function f. Namely, we need to select and exchange all of f before we begin sending ciphertexts. This requires us to flip and (securely) share a large number of bits. For the stateful scheme, we need at least one bit for each plaintext bit — the same as the requirements of the OTP. For the stateless scheme, we need at least 2^n bits where n is sufficiently large to make it unlikely that we will reuse the same input and output for f, which would require an excessive amount of storage and communication.

We next present an alternative, efficient solution: instead of using a random function, we can use a PRF, providing an efficient solution which is still secure, albeit only against computationally limited adversaries.

2.7.2 Pseudorandom functions (PRFs)

A PRF is an efficient substitute to the use of a random function, which ensures similar properties, while requiring the generation and sharing of only a short key. The main limitation is that PRFs are secure only against computationally bounded adversaries.

A PRF scheme is an efficient *deterministic* algorithm with two inputs: a *secret key* k, whose length is often denoted n, and a 'message' $m \in \{0, 1\}^*$. The output of the PRF is a fixed-length binary string, which may also contain n bits, or some other number of bits (even just one bit). We typically denote a PRF as a function, e.g., f, with the key k as a subscript and the message m as a parameter, e.g., $f_k(m)$.

2.7.2.1 *The PRF indistinguishability test and definition of security*

Intuitively, for a fixed key k, the PRF $f_k(\cdot)$ should be *indistinguishable* from a truly random function. Namely, an efficient adversary should be unable to tell if it is interacting with the pseudorandom function $f_k(\cdot)$, with secret key k, domain D and range R, or with a random function f^R over the same domain D and range R. The adversary can provide inputs, e.g., x, to either functions, and receive the result of applying the function, e.g., $f_k(x)$ or $f^R(x)$.

Figure 2.17 illustrates the PRF indistinguishability test. In this illustration, the adversary/distinguisher receives blackbox access to two functions: the PRF $f_k(\cdot)$, using a secret key k, and the function $f^R(\cdot)$, which was selected randomly from the set of all functions from the domain D to the range R. The adversary can, repeatedly, provide an input x to a specific blackbox and receive the output of the corresponding function, i.e., if the input x is provided to the blackbox containing the PRF $f_k(\cdot)$, the adversary receives $f_k(x)$, and if the input x is provided to the blackbox containing the PRF $f^R(\cdot)$, the adversary receives $f^R(x)$. The adversary should identify which blackbox contains which of the two functions.

We define a *(secure)* PRF in Definition 2.5. The *PRF advantage* of an adversary $\mathcal{A}$ for (purported PRF) function f (Equation (2.20)) is the probability that $\mathcal{A}$ outputs TRUE ('correctly') when given

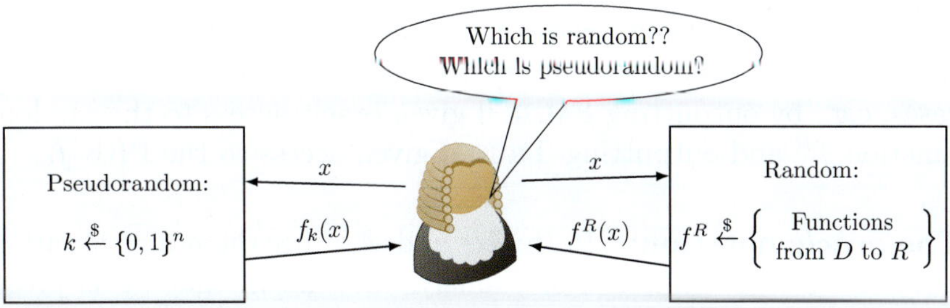

Figure 2.17. The pseudorandom function (PRF) indistinguishability test. We say that function $f_k(x) : \{0,1\}^* \times D \to R$ is a (secure) PRF, if no distinguisher D can efficiently obtain a non-negligible advantage in distinguishing between $f_k(\cdot)$ and a random function f^R from the same domain D to the same range R, when the key k is a randomly chosen n bits long binary string.

oracle access to the pseudorandom function f_k, minus the probability that $\mathcal{A}$ outputs TRUE ('incorrectly') when given oracle access to the random function f^R. Both functions are over the same domain D and range R. We say that $f_k(\cdot)$ is a (secure) PRF if every efficient adversary $\mathcal{A}$ can only obtain negligible advantage for f, i.e., the advantage of $\mathcal{A}$ for f is bounded by a polynomial in the length of the key k, often referred to as the *security parameter*.

Definition 2.5. A (secure) *PRF* from set D to set R is a polynomial-time computable function $f_k(x) : \{0,1\}^* \times D \to R$ s.t. for all efficient algorithms $\mathcal{A}$ holds that $\varepsilon^{PRF}_{\mathcal{A},f}(n) \in NEGL(n)$, i.e., the *advantage* $\varepsilon^{PRF}_{\mathcal{A},f}(n)$ of f against adversary $\mathcal{A}$ is negligible, where the advantage $\varepsilon^{PRF}_{\mathcal{A},f}(n)$ is defined as:

$$\varepsilon^{PRF}_{\mathcal{A},f}(n) \equiv \Pr_{k \xleftarrow{\$} \{0,1\}^n} \left[\mathcal{A}^{f_k}(1^n)\right] - \Pr_{f^R \xleftarrow{\$} \{D \to R\}} \left[\mathcal{A}^{f^R}(1^n)\right] \qquad (2.20)$$

The probabilities are taken over random coin tosses of $\mathcal{A}$, and random choices of the key $k \xleftarrow{\$} \{0,1\}^n$ and of the function $f^R \xleftarrow{\$} \{D \to R\}$. The notation $f^R \xleftarrow{\$} \{D \to R\}$ means that f^R is a random function from the domain D to the range R.

In Definition 2.5, the adversary $\mathcal{A}$ has *oracle access* to one of two functions: a random function from domain D to range R, i.e., $f^R \xleftarrow{\$} \{D \to R\}$, or the PRF f_k, keyed with a random n-bit key

$k \xleftarrow{\$} \{0,1\}^n$. We denote these two cases by $\mathcal{A}^{f^R}$ and $\mathcal{A}^{f_k}$, respectively. The adversary should try to distinguish between these two cases, e.g., by outputting FALSE if given oracle access to the random function f^R and outputting TRUE if given access to the PRF f_k.

The *oracle* notation: Both $\mathcal{A}^{f_k}$ and $\mathcal{A}^{f^R}$ use the *oracle* notation introduced in Definition 1.3. Namely, they mean that $\mathcal{A}$ is given 'oracle' access to the respective function ($f_k(\cdot)$ and $f^R(\cdot)$). Oracle access means that the adversary can give any input x and get back that function applied to x, i.e., $f_k(x)$ or $f^R(x)$, respectively

Why allow arbitrary key length (security parameter)? The definition allows arbitrarily long keys, although in practice, cryptographic standards often have a fixed key length, or only a few options. The reason that the definition allows arbitrary length is that we present an asymptotic security definition, i.e., we require the success probability to be negligible — smaller than any positive, non-zero polynomial in the key length — which is meaningless if the key length is bounded.

Why is 1^n given as input to the adversary? A subtle, yet important, aspect of the definition is the fact that in the two calls to the adversary $\mathcal{A}$, we provide the adversary with the value 1^n as input, where n is the key length (security parameter). The value 1^n simply signifies a string of n consecutive bits whose value is 1, i.e., it is the value of n encoded in *unary*. But why provide 1^n as input? It makes sense that the adversary should be informed of the key length n, but why use unary encoding? Why not provide n using the 'standard' binary encoding?

To understand the reason, first recall that we focus on *efficient* algorithms; namely, the running time of both the pseudorandom function F and the adversary $\mathcal{A}$ is bounded by a polynomial in the *size of their inputs.* The inputs to the PRF include the key and, hence, consist of at least n bits; hence, the running time of the PRF is (at least) polynomial in n. It is therefore 'only fair' that the running time of the adversary $\mathcal{A}$ is also allowed to be polynomial in n; to ensure this, we provide to it 1^n as input, similarly to our provision of the security parameter 1^n to other algorithms. See Section A.1.

2.7.2.2 *Constructions of secure and insecure PRFs*

To clarify Definition 2.5, and to demonstrate how to show if a given function is a PRF or not, we present two exercises. The first exercise shows two insecure PRF designs; the following exercise proves that a given construction is a secure PRF. We present solutions, however, we encourage readers to first look for their own solutions and only then read our solution.

Exercise 2.6. *Examples of an insecure PRF constructions:*

1. Show that $F_k(m) = k \oplus m$ is not a secure PRF.
2. Let p be an n-bits prime number, and $F_k(m) \equiv k \cdot (m + k) \bmod p$. Show that F is not a secure PRF (to the domain $\{0, \ldots, p-1\}$).
3. Show that $F_k(m) \equiv k \vee (m^k + k^{m+k} \bmod 2^n)$ is not a secure PRF.
4. Assume that secure PRF functions exist. Given a function $F_k(m)$, define $\hat{F}_k(m) \equiv F_m(k)$, i.e., $\hat{F}$ switches between the key and the input of F. Show that even if we know that F is a secure PRF, it is possible that $\hat{F}$ is not a secure PRF.

Solutions:

1. The adversary $\mathcal{A}^g$ is given an oracle to a function g and needs to output TRUE if $g(\cdot) = F_k(\cdot)$ for a random key k and FALSE if $g(\cdot)$ is random function. A simple way to do this is for $\mathcal{A}^g$ first to make a query for $g(0)$; if $g(\cdot) = F_k(\cdot)$, then $\mathcal{A}^g$ receives back $g(0^n) = F_k(0^n) = k \oplus 0^n = k$. So, in this case, $(g(\cdot) = F_k(\cdot))$, adversary $\mathcal{A}^g$ 'learns' k; it can check if indeed $g(\cdot) = F_k(\cdot)$ (or g is a random function) by giving any other input $m \neq 0^n$. If $g(m) = k \oplus m$, then (with very high probability) the function is indeed $g(\cdot) = F_k(\cdot)$, i.e., not a random function, and $\mathcal{A}$ returns TRUE; if $g(m) \neq k \oplus m$, then the function g is definitely *not* $g(\cdot) = F_k(\cdot)$, which means, in this case, it must be a random function, and $\mathcal{A}$ returns FALSE.
2. The adversary $\mathcal{A}^g$ is given an oracle to a function g and needs to output TRUE if $g(\cdot) = F_k(\cdot)$ for a random key k and FALSE if $g(\cdot)$ is random function. Similarly to the previous item, the adversary first gives to the oracle the input 0. If the oracle is to $F_k(m) \equiv k \cdot (m + k) \bmod p$, then the adversary receives $k^2 \bmod p$. A number whose value is $k^2 \bmod p$ for some integer k is called a *quadratic residue*. We discuss quadratic residues in Section 6.1.8.3,

in particular, explaining that there is an efficient algorithm to determine if a number is quadratic residue or not (Fact 6.3). The adversary may use this test, and if the oracle returns a quadratic residue, the adversary assumes that the oracle is to $F_k(m) \equiv k \cdot (m + k) \bmod p$ and returns TRUE since, with high probability, a random function would not return a quadratic residue.

Let us see another solution that does not require testing the output for being a quadratic residue. Observe that $m + k$ is even, if and only if either both m and k are even, or both m and k are odd. This motivates the following distinguishing adversary $\mathcal{A}^g(m)$, that outputs 'True', with high probability, if $g(m) = F_k(m)$, and with low probability, if g is a random function. The adversary asks the oracle to compute *both* $g(0)$ and $g(2)$. If the two results, $g(0)$ and $g(2)$, have the same parity (either are both even, or are both odd), then the adversary concludes that g is more likely to be pseudorandom and outputs TRUE. Otherwise, if one of $\{g(0), g(2)\}$ is even and the other is odd, then g *cannot* be $F_k(m) \equiv k \cdot (m + k) \bmod p$ and hence must be a random function, and $\mathcal{A}$ outputs FALSE.

Note that when this adversary outputs TRUE, it would be wrong in the cases where the oracle function g was selected at random but happens to return an even number for both inputs (zero and 2). However, since g was selected at random, the values $g(0)$ and $g(2)$ were also selected at random, and the probability of both $g(0)$ and $g(2)$ being even would be only $\frac{1}{4}$. Hence, while the adversary could be wrong, it still has a significant (non-negligible) advantage.

3. We present a specific adversary $\mathcal{A}^g$ that is given an oracle to a function g; the adversary outputs TRUE with probability at least $1/2$ if g is pseudorandom, i.e., $g(\cdot) = F_k(\cdot)$ for a random n-bit key k, and outputs TRUE with probability much smaller than $1/2$ if $g(\cdot)$ is random function, thereby achieving significant advantage as required. For simplicity, let us focus on the case that n is even. Specifically, $\mathcal{A}^g$ returns TRUE if $popcount(g(0^n) \wedge g(1^n)) \geq n/2$, and FALSE otherwise, where $popcount(x)$ returns the number of bits turned on (i.e., with value 1) in the binary string x.

   Let us explain why $\mathcal{A}^g$ has a significant advantage against F_k. We first show that A^g outputs TRUE with probability at least $1/2$ if g is pseudorandom, i.e., $g(\cdot) = F_k(\cdot)$ for a random n-bit key k. Observe that for a random n-bit, key k, for even n, holds $popcount(k) \geq n/2$ with probability (at least) $1/2$. Now, $F_k(m) = k \vee (m^k + k^{m+k} \mod 2^n)$; therefore, every bit which is turned on in the key k is also turned on in any output of $F_k(m)$, and in particular, in $F_k(0^n)$ and in $F_k(1^n)$. Therefore, with probability at least $1/2$ holds $popcount(F_k(0^n) \wedge F_k(1^n)) \geq n/2$. Since A^g returns TRUE in this case, we conclude that when $g(\cdot) = F_k(\cdot)$, then A^g returns TRUE with probability at least half, as claimed.

It remains to show that if g is a random function, then A^g outputs TRUE with probability much smaller than $1/2$. If g is a random function, then for any two given, different n-bits strings $x \neq y$, the values of $g(x)$ and $g(y)$ are two independent random n-bits string. Namely, for any given bit position i, $g(x)[i] = 1$ with probability half, and $g(y)[i] = 1$, independently, also with probability half. Therefore, the probability that *both* $g(x)[i] = 1$ and $g(y)[i] = 1$ is a quarter. In particular, this holds for the specific values $x = 0^n$ and $y = 1^n$. The probability that $popcount(g(0^n) \wedge g(1^n)) \geq n/2$ is very small, definitely much smaller than half. In particular, from *Hoeffding's inequality* follows that this probability is bounded by $e^{-n/8}$, i.e., for any $n \geq 8$, the probability is less than $1/e$, i.e., significantly less than half, as claimed.

4. Let F' be a secure PRF; define

$$F_k(m) \equiv \left\{F'_k(m) \text{ if } k \neq 0^n, \text{ otherwise } (k = 0^n)\text{: } 0^n\right\} \qquad (2.21)$$

As long as the key chosen is not the special all-zeros key, F is the same as F'; hence, F is also a PRF since keys are selected randomly, so $k = 0^n$ is selected only with probability 2^{-n}. It remains to show that with this F function, $\hat{F}$ is not a secure PRF.

However, an adversary given an oracle to either $\hat{F}$ or a random oracle can simply give the input 0^n. If the oracle is to $\hat{F}$, then this returns $\hat{F}_k(0^n) = F_{0^n}(k)$. However, by definition (Equation (2.21)), $\hat{F}_k(0^n) = F_{0^n}(k) = 0^n$. Hence, an adversary can easily distinguish between $\hat{F}_k(m)$ and a random function. □

Exercise 2.7 (Proving security (of PRF) by reduction). Let $\mathbb{B}^n \equiv \{0,1\}^n$ denote the set of n-bits binary strings. Assume that $F_k(m) : \mathbb{B}^n \times \mathbb{B}^n \to \mathbb{B}^n$ is a secure PRF. Prove that $\hat{F}_k(m)$ is also a secure PRF, where

$$\hat{F}_k(m) \equiv F_k(m \oplus (0^{n-1} + 1)). \qquad (2.22)$$

Solution: The solution uses the main technique in proofs of security of a construction in cryptography, which is called *proof by reduction*, which works as follows. We assume, *to the contrary*, that the construction is insecure. In this exercise, this means that we assume that $\hat{F}$ is not a PRF. Namely, from Definition 2.5, there exists an efficient adversary $\hat{\mathcal{A}}^{\hat{f}}$, with an oracle denoted $\hat{f}$, such that $\hat{\mathcal{A}}^{\hat{f}}$ has a significant (non-negligible) probability of distinguishing between the following two cases:

Case 1 — oracle $\hat{f}$ is a random function: The oracle $\hat{f}$ is selected at random from the set of functions from n bits to n bits, i.e., $\hat{f} \xleftarrow{\$} \{f : \mathbb{B}^n \rightarrow \mathbb{B}^n\}$.

Case 2 — oracle $\hat{f}$ is the PRF with a random key: The oracle $\hat{f}$ is to the function $\hat{F}_k(\cdot)$, where k is a random n-bits key. Namely, $\hat{f} \leftarrow \hat{F}_k(\cdot)$ where $k \xleftarrow{\$} \mathbb{B}^n$.

In other words, we assume, to the contrary, that the efficient adversary $\hat{\mathcal{A}}$ has a significant advantage in the PRF indistinguishability test (Figure 2.17) against the constructed PRF $\hat{F}$, i.e.,

$$\varepsilon^{PRF}_{\hat{\mathcal{A}},\hat{F}}(n) \equiv \Pr_{k \xleftarrow{\$} \mathbb{B}^n}\left[\hat{\mathcal{A}}^{\hat{F}_k(\cdot)}(1^n)\right] - \Pr_{\hat{f} \xleftarrow{\$} \{\mathbb{B}^n \rightarrow \mathbb{B}^n\}}\left[\hat{\mathcal{A}}^{\hat{f}(\cdot)}(1^n)\right] \notin NEGL(n) \tag{2.23}$$

In the left-hand expression, the oracle is $\hat{F}_k(\cdot)$, for a random key k, while in the right-hand expression, the oracle $\hat{f}(\cdot)$ is a random functions from n-bits to n-bits.

We then present another efficient adversary $\mathcal{A}^f$ which we show, under this assumption, to have a significant advantage in the PRF indistinguishability test (Figure 2.17) against F, i.e.,

$$\varepsilon^{PRF}_{\hat{\mathcal{A}},\hat{F}}(n) \equiv \Pr_{k \xleftarrow{\$} \mathbb{B}^n}\left[\hat{\mathcal{A}}^{F_k(\cdot)}(1^n)\right] - \Pr_{f \xleftarrow{\$} \{\mathbb{B}^n \rightarrow \mathbb{B}^n\}}\left[\hat{\mathcal{A}}^{f(\cdot)}(1^n)\right] \notin NEGL(n) \tag{2.24}$$

Namely, we show that if $\hat{F}$ is not a secure PRF (Equation (2.23)), then F cannot be a secure PRF (Equation (2.24)), which is a contradiction since we were given that F *is* a secure PRF.

Given $\hat{\mathcal{A}}^{\hat{f}}$, we define adversary $\mathcal{A}^f$ as follows:

$$\mathcal{A}^{f(\cdot)}(1^n) \equiv \left\{\text{Return } \hat{\mathcal{A}}^{\hat{f}(\cdot)}(1^n) \text{ where } \hat{f}(m) \equiv f(m \oplus (0^{n-1} + 1))\right\} \tag{2.25}$$

Namely, we implement the adversary $\mathcal{A}^f$ against F, using the adversary $\hat{\mathcal{A}}^{\hat{f}}$ against $\hat{F}$, where we compute the value of $\hat{f}$ on a given input m using the oracle we have for f, i.e., by computing $\hat{f}(m) = f(m \oplus (0^{n-1} +\!\!+ 1))$.

To complete the proof, we show that $\varepsilon^{PRF}_{\hat{\mathcal{A}},\hat{F}}(n) = \varepsilon^{PRF}_{\mathcal{A},F}(n)$, or more specifically, that the following two equations hold:

$$\Pr_{k \xleftarrow{\$} \mathbb{B}^n} \left[\mathcal{A}^{F_k}(1^n)\right] = \Pr_{k \xleftarrow{\$} \mathbb{B}^n} \left[\hat{\mathcal{A}}^{\hat{F}_k}(1^n)\right] \tag{2.26}$$

$$\Pr_{f \xleftarrow{\$} \{\mathbb{B}^n \to \mathbb{B}^n\}} \left[\mathcal{A}^{f}(1^n)\right] = \Pr_{\hat{f} \xleftarrow{\$} \{\mathbb{B}^n \to \mathbb{B}^n\}} \left[\hat{\mathcal{A}}^{\hat{f}}(1^n)\right] \tag{2.27}$$

Equation (2.26) follows from substituting Equation (2.25) and then the definition of $\hat{F}_k$ (Equation (2.22). To prove Equation (2.27), we observe that

Let us show that the following also holds:

$$\Pr_{f \xleftarrow{\$} \{\mathbb{B}^n \to \mathbb{B}^n\}} \left[\mathcal{A}^{f}(1^n)\right] = \Pr_{f \xleftarrow{\$} \{\mathbb{B}^n \to \mathbb{B}^n\}} \left[\hat{\mathcal{A}}^{\hat{f}}(1^n)|_{\hat{f}(m) \equiv f(m \oplus (0^{n-1} +\!\!+ 1))})\right] \tag{2.28}$$

Now, if $\hat{f}(m) \equiv f(m \oplus (0^{n-1} +\!\!+ 1))$, then $f(m) \equiv \hat{f}(m \oplus (0^{n-1} +\!\!+ 1))$; namely, the probability of picking uniformly f is the same as the probability of picking $\hat{f}$ — in fact, both are equal to 2^{-2n}. Hence,

$$\Pr_{f \xleftarrow{\$} \{\mathbb{B}^n \to \mathbb{B}^n\}} \left[\hat{\mathcal{A}}^{\hat{f}}(1^n)|_{\hat{f}(m) \equiv f(m \oplus (0^{n-1} +\!\!+ 1))}\right] = \Pr_{\hat{f} \xleftarrow{\$} \{\mathbb{B}^n \to \mathbb{B}^n\}} \left[\hat{\mathcal{A}}^{\hat{f}}(1^n)\right]$$

This completes the proof. □

2.7.2.3 *Applications of PRFs and the random function design method*

PRFs can be used in many applications, providing an efficient, easily deployable alternative to the impractical truly random functions. In particular, PRFs can be used to construct symmetric key cryptosystems, as illustrated in Figure 2.18. The figure presents two designs of a cryptosystem from a PRF: a stateful encryption, as a stream cipher, in Figure 2.18(a), and a stateless randomized encryption, in Figure 2.18(b).

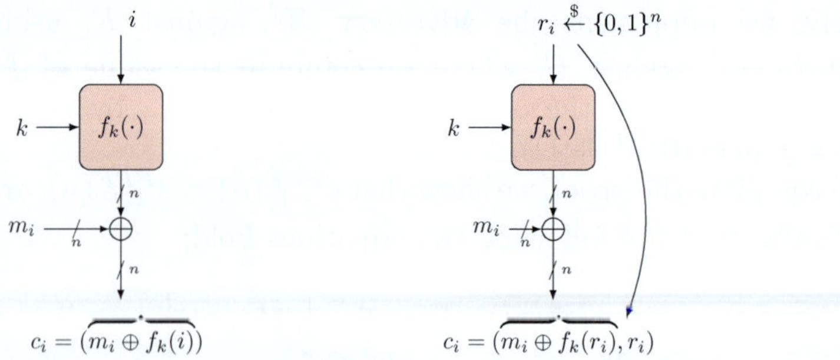

(a) Stateful block encryption with a PRF $f_k(\cdot)$.

(b) Stateless, randomized block encryption using a PRF $f_k(\cdot)$.

Figure 2.18. Secure encryption using a pseudorandom function (PRF) $f_k(\cdot)$. Use only one PRF application for n plaintext bits.

Both designs use a PRF instead of a random function which is used in the corresponding designs in Figure 2.15. The security of the PRF designs follows from the security of the corresponding random-function-based designs — and from the indistinguishability of a PRF and a random function. Indeed, this is one case of a very useful technique, which we refer to as the *random function design principle.*

Principle 6 (Random function design method). *Design cryptographic protocols and mechanisms using a random function, to make the security analysis easier. Once secure, implement using a pseudorandom function; security would follow since a PRF is indistinguishable from a random function.*

Note that the random function design method requires the parties to share the random key k of the PRF f_k. The key k should not only be shared, but also be kept secret.

Deriving independent keys and other applications of PRFs: PRFs have many additional applications; we see few of them later in this chapter and in other chapters of this book. For example, in Chapter 4, we show that a PRF may be used for message authentication.

Let us say a few words about one application, which is particularly important and interesting: the use of a PRF to derive *independently random keys or values.* In many scenarios, two or more parties share a secret key k but need to use multiple independently random secret shared keys. For example, the two keys may be used for different purposes, e.g., one key may be used for authentication and another for encryption.

This can be achieved using a PRF f, as follows. Let $g_1, g_2, \ldots$ be distinct identifiers, one of each required shared secret key value. We can derive the keys as $k_1 = f_k(g_1), k_2 = f_k(g_2)$, and so on. As a concrete example, to derive separate keys for each day d from the same k, we can use $k_d = f_k(d)$; the exposure of k_2 and k_4 will not expose any other key, e.g., k_3. We elaborate on this application in Section 2.7.4.

2.7.3 PRF: constructions and robust combiners

The concept of PRFs was proposed in a seminal paper by Goldreich, Goldwasser and Micali [212]; the paper also presents a provably secure construction of PRF, given a PRG. That is, if there is a successful attack on the constructed PRF, this attack can be used as a 'subroutine' to construct a successful attack on the underlying PRG. However, the construction of Ref. [212] is inefficient: it requires many applications of the PRG for a single application of the PRF. Therefore, this construction is not applied in practice. The construction, while elegant, is also too complex for us to describe and analyze in this book. Instead, the following exercise presents a simple construction that *uses* a PRF to construct a PRG (basically, the 'reverse direction').

Exercise 2.8. Let f be a secure PRF over $\{0,1\}^n$ bits, and let $k, r \in \{0,1\}^n$. Prove that $f'(k) = (f_k(1) + f_k(2))$ is a secure PRG.

Practical systems mostly implement PRFs using a standard *block cipher* (Section 2.8) or a cryptographic hash function (Chapter 3). One could also construct candidate PRFs *directly*, without assuming and using any other 'secure' cryptographic function, basing their security on failure to 'break' them using known techniques and efforts by expert cryptanalysts. In fact, pseudorandom functions are among the cryptographic functions that seem good candidates for such *ad hoc* constructions; it is relatively easy to come up with a reasonable candidate PRF, which will not be trivial to attack.

Finally, it is not difficult to *combine* two *candidate PRFs* F', F'', over the same domain and range, into a combined PRF F which is secure as long as either F' or F'' is a secure PRF. We refer to such a construction as a *robust combiner*. Constructions of robust combiners are known for many cryptographic primitives; see simple robust combiners in Ref. [240]. The following lemma, from Ref. [240], presents a trivial yet efficient robust combiner for PRFs.

Lemma 2.1 (Robust combiner for PRFs). *Let $F', F'' : \{0,1\}^* \times D \to R$ be two polynomial-time computable functions, and let*

$$F_{(k',k'')}(x) \equiv F'_{k'}(x) \oplus F''_{k''}(x) \tag{2.29}$$

If either F' or F'' is a PRF, then F is a PRF. Namely, this construction is a robust combiner for PRFs.

Proof. See Ref. [240]. □

The study of robust combiners often helps us to better understand the properties of cryptographic schemes; for example, we use it in Exercise 2.9, to introduce and motivate the key separation principle.

2.7.4 The key separation principle

In the PRF robust combiner (Equation (2.29)), we used *separate* keys for the two candidate-PRF functions F', F''. In fact, this is *necessary*, as the following exercise shows.

Exercise 2.9 (Independent keys are required for PRF robust combiners). Let $F', F'' : \{0,1\}^* \times D \to \{0,1\}^*$ be two polynomial-time computable functions, and let $F_k(x) = F'_k(x) \oplus F''_k(x)$. Demonstrate that the fact that one of F', F'' is a PRF may not suffice to ensure that F would be a PRF.

Solution: Suppose $F' = F''$. Then for every k, x holds: $F_k(x) = F'_k(x) \oplus F''_k(x) = F'_k(x) \oplus F'_k(x) = 0^{|F'_k(x)|}$. Namely, for any input x and any key k the output of $F_k(x)$ is an all-zeros string ($F_k(x) \in 0^*$). Hence, F is clearly not a PRF. □

In general, we should use different secret keys for different cryptographic schemes; while each scheme may properly use its keys and prevent their disclosure, there may be some incompatibility between the use of the key in different systems which will cause key exposure or other vulnerability. A system may use multiple different cryptographic functions or schemes, combining them for improved security (as above) or using them for different goals, e.g., encryption vs. authentication. In any case, security may fail if the same or related keys are used for multiple different functions. Similarly, if a system supports different versions of a cryptographic protocol or scheme, then we should use different keys when using different versions, to prevent exposure of the key its use by a vulnerable scheme/protocol from exposing the key used by the secure scheme/protocol.

There are two additional motivations for using multiple independent secret keys:

Limit information for cryptanalysis: By using separate, independently pseudorandom keys, we reduce the ability of the attacker to attack each key. For example, we reduce the amount of ciphertext available to attacker, and/or the number of known/ chosen plaintext-ciphertext pairs that the attacker can obtain.

Limit the impact of key exposure: By using separate keys, we ensure that exposure of some of the keys will not jeopardize the use of the other keys. See Example 2.5.

We summarize this discussion in the *key separation* principle.

Principle 7 (Key separation). *Use separate, independently chosen, uniformly random or pseudorandom keys for (1) different cryptographic schemes and functions, (2) different types and/or different sources of plaintext, (3) different periods and (4) different versions of the protocol or scheme.*

One important application of PRFs is *derivation of multiple separate keys* from a single shared secret key k. Namely, a PRF, say f, is handy whenever two parties share one secret key k and need to derive multiple *separate, independently pseudorandom* keys $k_1, k_2, \ldots$ from k. A common way to achieve this is for the two parties to use some set of identifiers $\gamma_1, \gamma_2, \ldots$, a distinct identifier for each derived key, and compute each key k_i as $k_i = f_k(\gamma_i)$.

As another example, system designers often want to limit the impact of key exposure due to cryptanalysis or to system attacks. One way to reduce the damage from key exposures is to change the keys periodically, e.g., use key k_d for day number d:

Example 2.5 (Using a PRF for independent per-period keys). Assume that Alice and Bob share one *master key* k_M. They may derive a shared secret key for day d as $k_d = PRF_{k_M}(d)$. Even if all the daily keys are exposed, except the key for one day $\hat{d}$, the key for day $\hat{d}$ remains secure as long as k_M is kept secret.

By changing the encryption key daily, we ensure that even if the attacker manages to find out the key of some days, by cryptanalysis or otherwise, this will not expose plaintexts encrypted during other days.

2.8 Block ciphers and PRPs

Modern symmetric encryption schemes are built in modular fashion, using a basic building block — the *block cipher*. A block cipher is defined by a pair of keyed functions, E_k, D_k, such that the domain and the range of both E_k and D_k are $\{0,1\}^n$, i.e., binary strings of fixed length n; for simplicity, we (mostly) use n for the length of both keys and blocks, as well as the security parameter, although in some ciphers, these are different numbers.

Block ciphers should satisfy the *correctness* requirement $m = D_k(E_k(m))$ for every $k, m \in \{0,1\}^n$. Note that the correctness requirement should hold *always*, i.e., not only with high probability. This is in contrast to security requirements, which are typically defined to hold only against efficient adversaries — and allow a negligible failure probability, i.e., the adversary may win with negligible probability. But there seems to be no reason to allow probability for incorrect decryption.

Block ciphers are in wide use in many practical systems and constructions, and two of them were standardized by NIST: the *Data Encryption Standard* (DES) (1977–2001) [377], the first standardized cryptographic scheme, and its successor, the *Advanced Encryption Standard* (AES) (2002–present) [140] (Figure 2.19). DES was replaced, since it was no longer considered secure; the main reason was simply that improvements in hardware made exhaustive search feasible, due to the relatively short, 56-bit key. Another reason for reduced confidence in DES — even in longer-key variants — was the presentation of *differential cryptanalysis* and *linear cryptanalysis*,

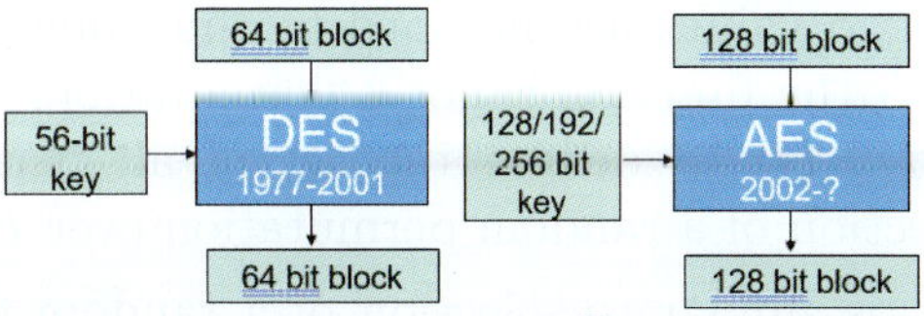

Figure 2.19. High-level view of a block cipher, such as the NIST standards, AES block cipher (current) and DES block cipher (obsolete).

two strong cryptanalysis attacks, which were developed to cryptanalyze DES and are effective against many cryptographic designs as well [73,349]. AES was designed for resiliency against these and other known attacks, and so far, no published attack against AES appears to justify concerns.

We encourage interested readers to follow up in the extensive literature on cryptanalysis in general and on these attacks, e.g., Refs. [164,274,297].

While the definition of correctness for block ciphers (above) is simple and widely accepted, there is not yet universal agreement on the security requirements. We adopt the common approach, which requires a block cipher to be a pseudorandom permutation (PRP). In the following section, we define pseudorandom permutations; then, in Section 2.8.2, we extend the definition of pseudorandom permutations, to define block ciphers and their security.

2.8.1 Random and pseudorandom permutations

After discussing random functions and PRFs, we now introduce two related concepts: a *random permutation* and a PRP.

Random permutations: A *permutation* is a function $\pi : D \rightarrow D$ mapping a domain D onto itself, where every element is mapped to a distinct element, namely,

$$(\pi : D \rightarrow D) \text{ is a permutation } \iff (\forall x, x' \in D)\,\big(\pi(x) \neq \pi(x')\big) \tag{2.30}$$

Note that a permutation may map an element onto itself, i.e., $\pi(x) = x$ is perfectly legitimate. Also, note that a function $f : D \rightarrow D$, which has identical domain and range (both D), could be a permutation or not; whenever two values are mapped to the same output, $f(x) = f(x')$, for $x \neq x'$, the function is not a permutation.

We use $Perm(D)$ to denote the set of all permutations over domain D. Selection of a random permutation over D, i.e., selecting $\rho \xleftarrow{\$} Perm(D)$, is similar to selection of a random function (Equation (2.17)) — except for the need to avoid *collisions.* A collision is a pair of elements $(x \neq x')$, both mapped to the same element: $y = \rho(x) = \rho(x')$.

One natural way to think about this selection is as being done *incrementally,* mapping one input at a time. Let $D' \subseteq D$ be the set of elements we didn't map yet, and $R \subseteq D$ be the set of elements to which we didn't map any element yet; initially, $R = D' = D$. Given any 'new' element $x \in D'$, select $\rho(x) \xleftarrow{\$} R$, and then remove x from D' and $\rho(x)$ from R.

Using this process, for a small domain, e.g., $D = \{0, 1\}^n$ for small n, the selection of a random permutation ρ can be done manually — similarly to the process for selecting a random function (over small domain and range). However, as for random functions, the generation, transmission and storage of a random permutations are too inefficient for this to be used in practice. Instead, let us consider pseudorandom permutations.

Pseudorandom permutation (PRP): Similarly to a pseudorandom function, a *PRP* over domain D, denoted $E_k(\cdot)$, is an efficient algorithm which cannot be distinguished efficiently from a randomly selected permutation ρ over the set D, i.e., $\rho \xleftarrow{\$} Perm(D)$, provided that the key k provided is 'sufficiently long' and chosen randomly.

In the definition, the adversary $\mathcal{A}$ has *oracle access* to one of two functions: either $E_k(\cdot)$, keyed with a random n-bit key k, or a random permutation over domain D, i.e., $\rho \xleftarrow{\$} Perm(D)$. We denote these two cases by $\mathcal{A}^{E_k(\cdot)}$ and $\mathcal{A}^{\rho(\cdot)}$, respectively. The adversary should try to distinguish between these two cases, by outputting FALSE if given access to the random permutation $\rho(\cdot)$ and outputting TRUE if given access to the PRP $E_k(\cdot)$. We refer to this process as the PRP indistinguishability test and illustrate it in Figure 2.20.

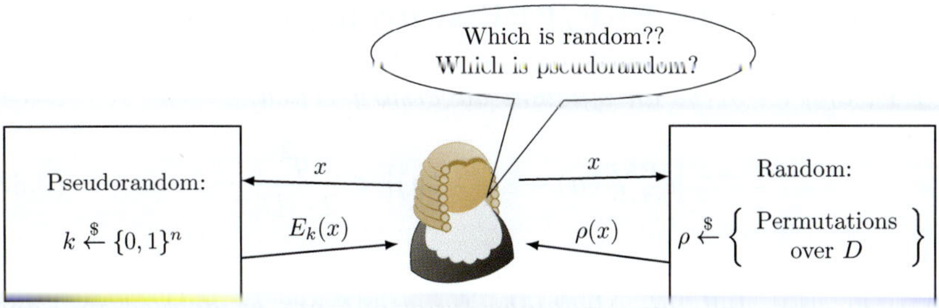

Figure 2.20. The PRP indistinguishability test. Intuitively, a function $E_k(x) : \{0,1\}^* \times D \rightarrow D$ is a *(secure)* PRP, if no distinguisher D can efficiently, and with significant advantage, distinguish between $E_k(\cdot)$ and a random permutation ρ over domain D, where the key k is a randomly chosen sufficiently-long binary string.

We next present the definition. Note that the definition requires the PRP to allow arbitrary length (n) of the key since indistinguishability is only defined asymptotically.

Definition 2.6. A *PRP* for domain D is a polynomial-time computable function $E_k(x) : \{0,1\}^* \times D \rightarrow D \in PPT$ s.t. for all efficient algorithms $\mathcal{A}$ holds $\varepsilon^{PRP}_{\mathcal{A},E}(n) \in NEGL(n)$, i.e., the distinguishing-advantage of $\mathcal{A}$ for E is negligible in n, where the *advantage* $\varepsilon^{PRP}_{\mathcal{A},E}(n)$ of $\mathcal{A}$ for E is defined as:

$$\varepsilon^{PRP}_{\mathcal{A},E}(n) \equiv \Pr_{k \stackrel{\$}{\leftarrow} \{0,1\}^n} \left[\mathcal{A}^{E_k}(1^n)\right] - \Pr_{\rho \stackrel{\$}{\leftarrow} Perm(D)} \left[\mathcal{A}^{\rho}(1^n)\right] \tag{2.31}$$

The probabilities are taken over random coin tosses of $\mathcal{A}$, a random choice of the key $k \stackrel{\$}{\leftarrow} \{0,1\}^n$ and a random choice of the permutation $\rho \stackrel{\$}{\leftarrow} Perm(D)$.

One natural — and important — question is the relation between a PRP over domain D and a PRF whose domain *and range* are both D. Recall that there are functions whose domain is also their range but are not a permutation. However, somewhat surprisingly, it turns out that *a PRP over D is indistinguishable from a PRF over D*. This important result is called the *PRP/PRF switching lemma* and has multiple proofs; we recommend the proof in Ref. [448]. Note that the lemma provides a relation between the advantage functions; this is an example of *concrete security*.

Lemma 2.2 (The PRP/PRF switching lemma). *Let E be a polynomial-time computable function $E_k(x) : \{0,1\}^* \times D \rightarrow D \in PPT$, and let $\mathcal{A}$ be an efficient adversary. Then,*

$$\left|\varepsilon^{PRF}_{\mathcal{A},E}(n) - \varepsilon^{PRP}_{\mathcal{A},E}(n)\right| < \frac{q^2}{2 \cdot |D|} \tag{2.32}$$

where q is the maximal number of oracle queries performed by $\mathcal{A}$ in each run, and the advantage functions are as defined in Equations (2.20) *and* (2.31).

In particular, if the size of the domain D is exponential in the security parameter n (the length of key and of the input to $\mathcal{A}$), e.g., $D = \{0,1\}^n$, then $\varepsilon^{PRF}_{\mathcal{A},E}(n) - \varepsilon^{PRP}_{\mathcal{A},E}(n) \in NEGL(n)$. In this case, E is a pseudorandom permutation over D, if and only if it is a pseudorandom function over D.

Proof sketch. In a polynomial set of queries of a random function, there is negligible probability of having two values which will map to the same value. Hence, it is impossible to efficiently distinguish between a random function and a random permutation. The proof follows since a PRF (PRP) is indistinguishable from a random function (resp., permutation). □

The PRP/PRF switching lemma is somewhat counter-intuitive since, for large D, there are many more functions than permutations. Focusing on $D = \{0,1\}^n$ for convenience, there are $(2^n)^{2^n} = 2^{n \cdot 2^n}$ functions over D, and 'only' $2^n!$, i.e., the factorial[13] of 2^n, permutations.

When considering only asymptotic security, the PRP/PRF switching lemma may be interpreted to imply that we can use a PRP (or a block cipher, which we discuss in the following) for applications designed to use a PRF, and vice versa, use a PRF in applications designed to use a PRP. However, when we consider also the concrete security part of the lemma, we see that such usage can involve a significant loss in security, i.e., significant increase in the attacker's advantage. This motivated design of other constructions, mainly of a PRF from a PRP (or block cipher). These constructions are efficient and simple yet avoid this loss in security; see Refs. [45, 230].

[13]For every integer i, the *factorial* of i is denoted $i!$ and defined as $i! \equiv 1 \cdot 2 \cdot \ldots (i-1) \cdot i$.

2.8.2 Block ciphers

A *block cipher* is one of the most important cryptographic mechanisms, with multiple applications and implementations, often used as a 'building block' to construct other mechanisms. The symbols (E, D) are often used for the functions of the block cipher since one basic application of a block cipher is as an encryption scheme; intuitively, E is 'encryption' and D is 'decryption'. However, as we see, a block cipher does *not* meet the (strong) definition of secure encryption.

Intuitively, a block cipher is an *invertible PRP*; this is the reason that we often use the letter E to denote a PRP. The definition, which follows, is an extension of Definition 2.6.

Definition 2.7. Let D be a finite domain. Given a permutation $\rho : D \to D$ over domain D, define the *inverse* of ρ, denoted $\rho^{-1} : D \to D$, as the permutation over D such that $(\forall x \in D)\ x = \rho^{-1}(\rho(x))$.

A (secure) *block cipher* over domain D is a *pair* of keyed polynomial-time computable functions, (E_k, D_k) over domain D, which satisfies the following:

Correctness: For every $x \in D$ and every key $k \in \{0,1\}^*$ holds $x = D_k(E_k(k(x)))$.

Indistinguishability: The pair (E, D) is indistinguishable from the pair (ρ, ρ^{-1}) where ρ is a *random permutation* over domain D and ρ^{-1} is the inverse of ρ. Namely, for every efficient algorithm $\mathcal{A}$, the advantage of $\mathcal{A}$ for (E, D), denoted $\varepsilon_{\mathcal{A},(E,D)}(n)$ and defined as follows, is a negligible function of n, i.e., $\varepsilon_{\mathcal{A},(E,D)}(n) \in NEGL(n)$, where

$$\varepsilon_{\mathcal{A},(E,D)}(n) \equiv \Pr_{k \xleftarrow{\$} \{0,1\}^n} \left[\mathcal{A}^{E_k, D_k}(1^n)\right] - \Pr_{\rho \xleftarrow{\$} Perm(D)} \left[\mathcal{A}^{\rho,\rho^{-1}}(1^n)\right] \tag{2.33}$$

Note: $\mathcal{A}^{f,g}(1^n)$ is the *oracle notation* (Definition 1.3), where algorithm $\mathcal{A}$ runs with input 1^n and has oracle access to both function f and function g.

Let us give an example.

Example 2.6. Let $E_k(m) = m \oplus k$ and $E'_k(m) = m + k \bmod 2^n$. Show the corresponding D, D' functions such that both (E, D) and (E', D') satisfy the correctness requirement, and show that neither of them satisfy the security requirement, i.e., neither are secure block ciphers.

Solution: $D_k(c) = c \oplus k$, $D'_k(c) = c - k \bmod 2^n$. Correctness follows from the arithmetic properties.

It remains to show that (E, D) and (E', D') are not secure block ciphers. Let us first show that (E, D) is not a secure block cipher. Recall that we need to provide an efficient adversary $\mathcal{A}$, s.t. $\varepsilon^{PRP}_{E,\mathcal{A}}$ is not negligible. We present a simple adversary $\mathcal{A}$ that only makes two queries, both of them to the oracle for the 'encryption' operation (E_k or ρ), and whose advantage is almost 1. The first query of $\mathcal{A}$ will be for input 0^n; if we denote the oracle response by $f(\cdot)$, then $\mathcal{A}$ receives $f(0^n)$. If the oracle is for E, $\mathcal{A}$ receives $E_k(0^n) = 0^n \oplus k = k$, i.e., the key k. Intuitively, this clearly 'breaks' the system; let us show exactly how. Note that from this point, our solution holds for the general case where the adversary found k.

Our second query can be for any other value (not 0^n), e.g., let's make the query 1^n, so we now receive $f(1^n)$, where, again, f is either E_k or a random permutation ρ. Adversary $\mathcal{A}$ checks if $f(1^n)$ (which it received from the oracle) is the same as $E_{f(0^n)}(1^n)$, using the value $f(0^n)$ that it received earlier as the key; recall that if the oracle is to E_k, then $f(0^n) = E_k(0^n) = k$, namely, $E_{f(0^n)}(1^n) = E_k(1^n) = f(1^n)$. Hence, if the value returned $(f(1^n))$ is the same as $E_{f(0^n)}(1^n)$, then, with very high probability, $f(\cdot) = E_k(\cdot)$, i.e., $\mathcal{A}$ returns TRUE (block cipher). Otherwise, i.e., if $f(1^n) \neq E_{f(0^n)}(1^n)$, then f cannot be E_k and must therefore be a random permutation, and $\mathcal{A}$ returns FALSE. So, the advantage of $\mathcal{A}$ is almost 1, specifically,

$$\varepsilon_{\mathcal{A},E}(n) = \Pr_{k \xleftarrow{\$} [0,1]^n} \left(\mathcal{A}^{E_k,D_k}\right) - \Pr_{\rho \xleftarrow{\$} Perm(\{0,1\}^n)} \left(A^{\rho,\rho^{-1}}\right) \tag{2.34}$$

$$= \Pr_{k \xleftarrow{\$} [0,1]^n} \left(\mathcal{A}^{E_k,D_k}\right) - \Pr_{\rho \xleftarrow{\$} Perm(\{0,1\}^n)} \left(E_{\rho(0^n)}(1^n) = \rho(1^n)\right) \tag{2.35}$$

$$= \Pr_{k \xleftarrow{\$} [0,1]^n} \left(E_{E_k(0^n)}(1^n) = E_k(1^n)\right) - 2^{-n} \tag{2.36}$$

$$= \Pr_{k \xleftarrow{\$} [0,1]^n} \left(E_k(1^n) = E_k(1^n)\right) - 2^{-n} \tag{2.37}$$

$$= 1 - 2^{-n} \tag{2.38}$$

The changes from Equations (2.34) to (2.35) and from Equations (2.35) to (2.36) are due to the operation of $\mathcal{A}$ as described above and to the fact that when ρ is a random permutation, therefore, $\rho(1^n)$ is a random n bit string independent of $E_{\rho(0^n)}(1^n)$. The change from Equations (2.36) to (2.37) is due to the definition of E, i.e., the fact that $E_k(0^n) = k$.

The *same adversary* $\mathcal{A}$ also distinguishes E'. We leave to the reader to substitute the values as necessary; after the point where $\mathcal{A}$ 'finds' k, the solution becomes essentially identical. □

See Table 2.2 for a summary and comparison of pseudorandom generators (PRG), PRF, pseudorandom permutations (PRP) and block ciphers.

Robust combiner for block ciphers: Let (E', D') and (E'', D'') be two block ciphers that satisfy correctness, and define their *cascade* as $E_{k',k''}(x) \equiv E'_{k'}(E''_{k''}(x))$, $D_{k',k''}(x) \equiv D''_{k''}(D'_{k'}(x))$. If one (or both) of (E', D') and (E'', D'') also satisfy security, i.e., is a secure

Table 2.2. Pseudorandom generator (PRG), pseudorandom function (PRF), pseudorandom permutation (PRP) and block cipher.

Function	Property
Pseudorandom generator (PRG) $f(seed)$	if *seed* is random, then $f(seed)$ is indistinguishable from random
Pseudorandom function (PRF) $f_k(\cdot)$	if k is random, then $f_k(\cdot)$ is indistinguishable from a random function
Pseudorandom permutation (PRP) $f_k(\cdot)$	if k is random, then $f_k(\cdot)$ is indistinguishable from a random permutation
Block cipher (E_k, D_k)	if k is random, then the pair $(E_k(\cdot), D_k(\cdot))$ are indistinguishable from the pair (ρ, ρ^{-1}) where ρ is a random permutation and ρ^{-1} is its inverse

block cipher, then (E, D) is a secure block cipher. Namely, the cascade construction is a robust combiner for block ciphers.

A similar property holds for PRP but *not* for all PRFs. The reader may prove these statements or see Ref. [240].

2.8.3 The Feistel construction: a block cipher from a PRF

It is not too difficult to design a candidate PRF from basic operations, although, often a weakness could be found allowing distinguishing between the candidate PRF and a truly random function, i.e., the candidate would not be secure. However, designing a candidate PRP directly from basic operations seems harder since in addition to the indistinguishability requirement, we need to also ensure that the result is a permutation, i.e., every input is mapped to a distinct output. Directly constructing a block cipher seems even harder since, in addition to the indistinguishability and the permutation properties, we need to also find the inverse permutation. This motivates a two phase design: first design a PRF, then use a construction of a block cipher from a PRF.

Note that the PRP/PRF switching lemma (Lemma 2.2) shows that every PRF can also be used as a pseudorandom permutation. Namely, a PRF over a domain D is indistinguishable from a PRP over D, and vice verse: no efficient adversary is likely to distinguish between a PRP and a PRF (over domain D). So, it seems that we can just use a PRF instead of a PRP — albeit, with a significant loss in (concrete) security.

However, this does not directly allow us to use a PRF as a block cipher. A block cipher requires *two* functions (E_k, D_k), s.t. $m = D_k(E_k(m))$; finding the inverse function can be challenging. In fact, a PRF is allowed, and even likely, to have *collisions*, i.e., values $x \neq x' \in D$ such that $E_k(x) = E_k(x')$, for the same key k, in which case, there is no inverse function (i.e., no way to 'decrypt'). Collisions do not exist for (random or not) permutations, and contradict the correctness requirement of block ciphers.

In this section, we study the Feistel construction of a block cipher from a PRF. The construction ensures the correctness of the block cipher and the indistinguishability of the block cipher, assuming the indistinguishability of the PRF. Furthermore, the Feistel construction is simple and efficient; it only requires three applications of the PRF. Finally, when given a PRF with inputs and outputs of n bits, the Feistel construction produces a block cipher of $2n$ bits, which is usually an advantage.

The Feistel construction is simple — but ingenious. The following two exercises may help the reader appreciate it.

Exercise 2.10. Let f be a PRF from n-bit strings to n-bit strings, and define $g_{k_L,k_R}(m_L +\!\!+\, m_R) \equiv f_{k_L}(m_L) +\!\!+\, f_{k_R}(m_R)$. Show that g is *neither* a PRF nor a PRP (over $2n$-bit strings).

Hint: Given a black box containing g or a random permutation over $2n$-bit strings, design a distinguishing adversary $\mathcal{A}$ as follows. $\mathcal{A}$ makes two queries: one with input $x = 0^{2n}$ and the other with input $x' = 0^n +\!\!+\, 1^n$. Denote the corresponding outputs by $y = y[0 : 2n-1]$ and $y' = y'[0 : 2n-1]$. If the box contained g, then $y_{0,\ldots,n-1} = y'_{0,\ldots,n-1}$. In contrast, if the box contained a random function, then the probability that $y[0 : n-1] = y'[0 : n-1]$ is very small — only 2^{-n}. The probability is about as small as if the box contained a PRP. The argument for the PRP can also be made using the PRP/PRF switching lemma. □

The following exercise presents a slightly more elaborate scheme, which is essentially a reduced version of the Feistel construction (presented in the following). The solution is a bit harder and left as a challenge to the readers.

Exercise 2.11. Let f be a PRF from n-bit strings to n-bit strings. Show that $g_{k_L,k_R}(m_L +\!\!+\, m_R) = m_l \oplus f_{k_R}(m_R) +\!\!+\, m_R \oplus f_{k_L}(m_L)$ is *not* a PRP (over $2n$-bit strings).

Finally, we present the Feistel construction, the most well known and probably the simplest construction of a block cipher from a PRF. As shown in Figure 2.21, the Feistel construction transforms an n-bit PRF into a $2n$-bit block cipher.

Formally, given a function $y = F_k(x)$ with n-bit keys, inputs and outputs, the three-rounds Feistel construction $g_k(m)$ is defined by the following three equations, each corresponding to one 'round' of

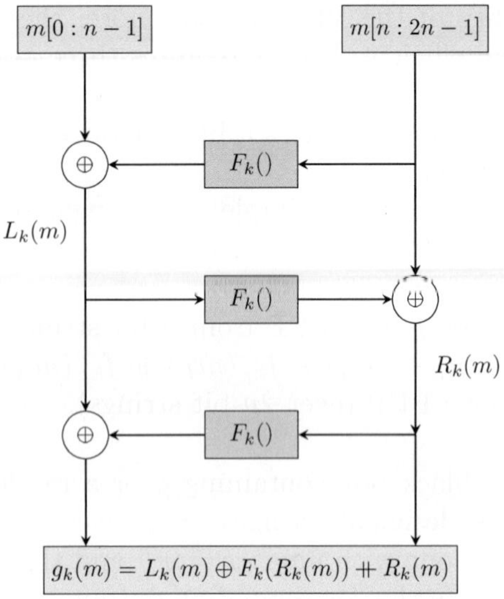

Figure 2.21. Three 'rounds' of the Feistel construction, constructing a block cipher from a PRF $F_k(\cdot)$. The Feistel construction is used in DES (but not in AES). *Note*: Many publications present the Feistel construction a bit differently, by 'switching sides' in each round.

the construction (and one invocation of the PRF):

$$L_k(m) = m[0 : n-1] \oplus F_k(m[n : 2n-1])$$
$$R_k(m) = F_k(L_k(m)) \oplus m[n : 2n-1]$$
$$g_k(m) = L_k(m) \oplus F_k(R_k(m)) + R_k(m)$$

The Feistel construction as presented above has only a 'three rounds' and uses the same underlying function F_k in all three rounds. Neither aspect is mandatory; in particular, the variants of the Feistel construction used in the design of DES and several other block ciphers use more rounds (e.g., 16 in DES). DES, and most block ciphers using variants of the Feistel construction, also use different functions at different rounds. The goal of these additional rounds and of the use of different functions is to further improve security, i.e., ensure the indistinguishability of the resulting block cipher even if the underlying functions are not truly indistinguishable PRF functions.

Luby and Rackoff [337] proved that a Feistel construction of three or more 'rounds', using a PRF as $F_k(\cdot)$, is a block cipher.

An advantage of using the Feistel construction is that it allows the designer to focus on the pseudorandomness requirements when designing the PRF, without having simultaneously to make sure that the design is also an invertible permutation. As a result, the Feistel construction is part of the design of many block ciphers, but not all; in particular, AES does not use the Feistel construction. Readers are encouraged to try to find a significantly different construction of a PRP from a secure PRF, where the resulting PRP is invertible and seems to possibly satisfy indistinguishability. You may find it harder than it looks!

2.9 Defining security requirements for cryptosystems

So far, we discussed several cryptographic schemes involving pseudorandomness: the PRG, the PRF, the PRP and finally the block cipher. These are important mechanisms related to encryption but not yet a full cryptosystem (encryption scheme). In this section, we finally make the next step and define secure encryption — and explain why it requires more than the block cipher.

The definition of secure encryption is quite subtle. In fact, people have been designing — and attacking — cryptosystems for millennia, without a precise definition of the security goals of encryption schemes. This changed with the seminal paper of Goldwasser and Micali [213], which presented the first precise definition of secure encryption, along with a design which was proven secure (under reasonable assumptions); this paper is one of cornerstones of modern cryptography.

It may be surprising that defining secure encryption is so challenging; we encourage the readers to try to define secure encryption on their own, before reading the rest of this section, and later compare their results with the definition we present.

2.9.1 Attack model

Security definitions require a precise *attack model*, defining the maximal expected capabilities of the attacker. We discussed already some of these capabilities for adversaries against cryptosystems. In particular, we already discussed the *computational limitations* of the attacker: in Section 2.5, we discussed the *unconditional security* model, where attackers have unbounded computational resources, and from Section 2.6.1, we focus on *efficient, probabilistic polynomial time* (PPT) adversaries, whose computation time is bounded by some polynomial in their input size.

Another important aspect of the attacker model is the interactions with the attacked scheme and the environment. In Section 2.3, we introduced the COA, KPA, CPA and CCA attack models. Specifically, in a chosen-plaintext attack (CPA), the adversary can choose plaintext and receive the corresponding ciphertext (encryption of that plaintext), and in the *chosen-ciphertext attack* (CCA), the adversary can choose *ciphertext* and receive the corresponding plaintext (its decryption), or an error message if the ciphertext does not correspond to well-encrypted plaintext.

It is desirable to allow for attackers with maximal capabilities. Therefore, when we evaluate cryptosystems, we are interested in their resistance to all types of attacks, and especially the stronger ones — CCA and CPA. On the other hand, when we design systems using a cryptosystem, we try to limit the attacker's capabilities. For example, one approach to foil CCA attacks is to apply a *padding function* to add redundancy to the plaintext before encryption; the padding function may be as simple as appending a fixed string. For example, given message m, key k, encryption scheme (E, D) and a simple padding function, e.g., $pad(m) = m + 0^l$, i.e., concatenate l zeros, we now encrypt by computing $c = E_k(pad(m)) = E_k(m + 0^l)$. This allows the decryption process to identify *invalid ciphertexts*. Namely, given $c = E_k(pad(m)) = E_k(m + 0^l)$, then $D_k(c) = m + 0^l$, and we output m as usual; but if the output of D_k does not contain l trailing zeros, then we identify a faulty ciphertext and output an error. This approach often helps to make it hard or infeasible for the attacker to apply a chosen-ciphertext attack; in particular, a random ciphertext would almost always be detected as faulty.

Note, however, that adding redundancy to the plaintext may make it *easier* to perform a ciphertext-only attack (COA); see Principle 10. In particular, if the plaintext contains known redundancy, then an attacker can launch an exhaustive search attack, by excluding keys that result in incorrect padding (see Section 2.4.1).

2.9.2 Toward definition of secure encryption

Intuitively, the security goal of encryption is *confidentiality*. Namely, encryption should encrypt plaintext into ciphertext in such way that will allow specific parties ('recipients') — and only them — to perform decryption, transforming the ciphertext back to the original plaintext. However, the goal as stated may be interpreted to only forbid recovery of the exact, complete plaintext. What about recovery of partial plaintext?

For example, suppose an eavesdropper can decipher half of the characters from the plaintext — is this secure? We believe most readers would agree it is not. What if the attacker can decipher less, say only one character? Only a specific character, e.g., the first? In some applications, this may be acceptable; in others, even exposure of one character may have significant consequences. The encryption should be appropriate for *any* application, including one in which there are only two possible plaintext messages, known to the attacker — who 'just' needs to know which of them was encrypted. For example, consider an application where the messages are either 'attack' or 'retreat', or either 'sell' or 'buy'. Exposing just one letter would suffice for the attacker.

We require that an adversary cannot learn *anything* given the ciphertext. This may be viewed as extreme; for example, in many applications, the plaintext includes known fields, and their exposure may not be a concern. However, it is best to minimize assumptions and use definitions and schemes which are secure for a wide range of applications. This is part of the *conservative design principle* (Principle 3).

How do we define the requirement that the attacker cannot learn anything? This is not so easy. The seminar paper by Goldwasser and Micali [213] presented two definitions for the security of cryptosystems and showed them to be equivalent. These definitions are *semantic security* and *indistinguishability*. The semantic security definition captures directly the intuition that the attacker cannot 'learn anything'; however, it is more complex and less convenient to use.

Therefore, we focus on the simpler and easier to use indistinguishability definition. The indistinguishability requirement for cryptosystems resembles the indistinguishability tests we discussed for PRGs,

PRFs, PRP and block ciphers, as well as the Turing indistinguishability test. Intuitively, an encryption scheme ensures indistinguishability if an attacker cannot distinguish between encryption of any two given messages.

Indistinguishability of cryptosystems is reminiscent of disguises; let us consider the properties we can hope to find in an 'ideal disguise service':

Any two disguised persons are indistinguishable: We cannot distinguish between *any* two well-disguised persons. Even Rachel from Leah.[14]

Except, the two persons should have the 'same size': Assuming that a disguise is of 'reasonable size' (overhead), a giant can't be disguised to be indistinguishable from a dwarf.

Re-disguises should be different: We see Rachel in disguise; then she goes to another room. Out comes a person with a different disguise. Is this disguised person Rachel, in a new disguise, or is it Leah? We should not be able to tell. This means that the disguising process must be randomized or stateful; if the process is deterministic and stateless, then the disguised Rachel will always look exactly the same.

We present the corresponding properties for indistinguishable encryption:

The ciphertexts of any two plaintext messages are indistinguishable: To allow arbitrary applications, we allow the attacker to choose the two plaintext messages $m[0], m[1]$.

Except, the two messages should have the same length: We expect that the encryption of a short message would result in short ciphertext, while the encryption of a long message would necessarily result in long ciphertext (or decryption cannot recover the plaintext). To simplify, we simply require the two messages to have exactly the same length, i.e., $|m[0]| = |m[1]|$.

Re-encryptions should be different: The attacker should not be able to distinguish encryptions based on previous encryptions of the same messages. This means that encryption must be randomized or stateful so that two encryptions of same message

[14]See Genesis 29:23, King James Bible.

will be different. (A weaker notion of 'deterministic encryption' allows detection of re-encryption of a message and is sometimes used for scenarios where state and randomization are to be avoided.)

2.9.3 Indistinguishability of stateless symmetric key cryptosystems

Let us now describe the indistinguishability tests for stateless symmetric key cryptosystems. We later discuss the slightly more involved cases of stateful symmetric key cryptosystems (Section 2.9.4) and of public key cryptosystems (PKCs).

We illustrate the IND-CPA and IND-CCA indistinguishability tests for stateless symmetric key cryptosystems in Figure 2.22.

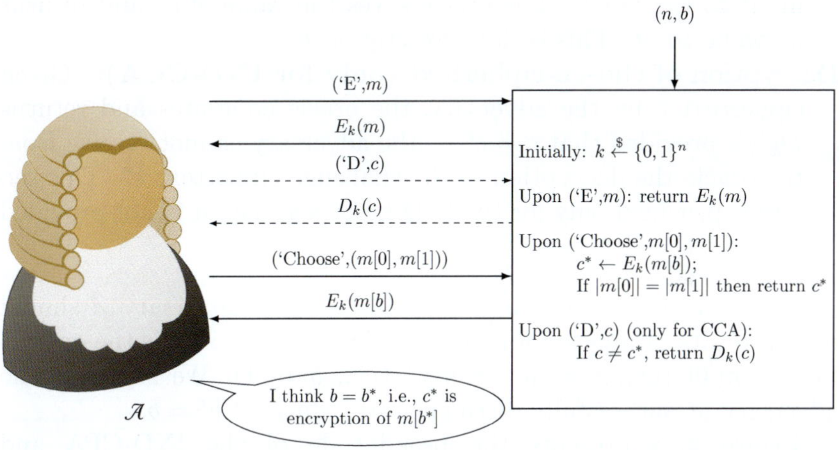

Figure 2.22. The CPA and CCA indistinguishability tests (IND-CPA and IND-CCA) for stateless symmetric key cryptosystems, $T^{IND\text{-}CPA}_{\mathcal{A},\langle E,D\rangle}(b, n)$ and $T^{IND\text{-}CPA}_{\mathcal{A},\langle E,D\rangle}(b, n)$. Both tests receive as input the security parameter n and a bit b. Throughout the test, the adversary $\mathcal{A}$ may ask for encryption of one or more plaintext messages (denoted m). At some point, $\mathcal{A}$ chooses and sends two *same length challenge messages*, $m[0]$ and $m[1]$ (s.t. $|m[0]| = |m[1]|$), and receives the encryption of $m[b]$, which we denote c^* i.e., $c^* \equiv E_k(m[b])$. In the IND-CCA test, the adversary can also ask for decryptions of chosen ciphertexts, denoted c, provided that $c \neq c^*$; these interactions are marked by dashed arrows since they are not included in IND-CPA. Finally, $\mathcal{A}$ outputs its guess b^* for the input bit b; the adversary 'wins' if $b = b^*$.

In both tests, the adversary $\mathcal{A}$ is given oracle access to the symmetric key cryptosystem. The oracle is configured with two inputs: n, the security parameter, which, in symmetric key cryptosystems, is used as the key length; and b, a bit which the adversary $\mathcal{A}$ should try to identify by sending requests to the oracle and receiving the oracle's responses.

As Figure 2.22 illustrates, the oracle initially generates the n-bits shared key, $k \xleftarrow{\$} \{0,1\}^*$. It then offers the following services to the distinguisher (adversary) $\mathcal{A}$:

Encryption of chosen-plaintext: Given plaintext m by the adversary $\mathcal{A}$, the oracle computes and returns $E_k(m)$.

Encryption of a pair of chosen plaintexts: In this service, the adversary $\mathcal{A}$ gives a pair of plaintexts $(m[0], m[1])$ to the oracle. If the two plaintexts are of the same length, i.e., $|m[0]| = |m[1]|$, then the oracle computes $c^* \equiv E_k(m[b])$, where b is the bit provided as input to the oracle. The oracle saves the value of c^* and returns its value to $\mathcal{A}$. This is done exactly once.

Decryption of chosen-ciphertext (only for IND-CCA): Given ciphertext c by the adversary, the oracle computes and returns $D_k(c)$, provided that $c \neq c^*$ — the adversary cannot receive from the oracle the decryption of the challenge ciphertext c^*. This service is provided only for the IND-CCA test, i.e., it is not provided by the IND-CPA test.

At the end of the indistinguishability test, the adversary $\mathcal{A}$ should output b^*, its estimation for the bit b, i.e., identify if c^* is the encryption of $m[0]$ (i.e., $b = 0$) or $m[1]$ (i.e., $b = 1$). We say that the adversary $\mathcal{A}$ successfully distinguished ('wins') if $b^* = b$.

Figure 2.23 presents the pseudocode of the IND-CPA and IND-CCA tests for stateless symmetric key cryptosystems. Note that in the computations involving possibly random bits, specifically, of the adversary $\mathcal{A}$ and of the encryption function $E_k(\cdot)$, we use the notation $\xleftarrow{\$}$ for the assignment, to emphasize that the outcome is the result of a probabilistic process, done with uniformly chosen random coin tosses.

The pseudocode uses the *oracle* notation defined in Definition 1.3. In the IND-CPA test, the adversary has an oracle only to the encryption function $E_k(\cdot)$, i.e., $\mathcal{A}^{E_k(\cdot)}$.

$T^{IND-CPA}_{\mathcal{A},\langle E,D\rangle}(b,n)$

$k \xleftarrow{\$} \{0,1\}^n, c^* \leftarrow \bot$
$(m[0], m[1]) \xleftarrow{\$} \mathcal{A}^{E_k}(\text{'Choose'}, 1^n)$
If $|m[0]| = |m[1]|$ then $c^* \xleftarrow{\$} E_k(m[b])$
$b^* \xleftarrow{\$} \mathcal{A}^{E_k}(\text{'Guess'}, c^*)$
Return b^*

(a) The IND-CPA indistinguishability test for a stateless symmetric key cryptosystem.

$T^{IND-CCA}_{\mathcal{A},\langle E,D\rangle}(b,n)$

$k \xleftarrow{\$} \{0,1\}^n, c^* \leftarrow \bot$
$(m[0], m[1], s_{\mathcal{A}}) \xleftarrow{\$} \mathcal{A}^{E_k(\cdot), Dec_k(\cdot,c^*)}(\text{'Choose'}, 1^n)$
If $|m[0]| = |m[1]|$ then $c^* \xleftarrow{\$} E_k(m[b])$
$b^* \xleftarrow{\$} \mathcal{A}^{E_k(\cdot), Dec_k(\cdot,c^*)}(\text{'Guess'}, c^*, s_{\mathcal{A}})$
Return b^*

Oracle $Dec_k(c, c^*)$:

If $c \neq c^*$ then $m \leftarrow D_k(c)$
Return m

(b) The IND-CCA indistinguishability test for a stateless symmetric key cryptosystem.

Figure 2.23. The IND-CPA and IND-CCA tests for stateless symmetric key cryptosystem (E, D), as illustrated in Figure 2.22.

In the IND-CCA test, the adversary has an oracle to the encryption function $E_k(\cdot)$, like in the IND-CPA test. However, in the IND-CCA test, the adversary has an *additional oracle*, $Dec_k(\cdot, c^*)$. The $Dec_k(\cdot, c^*)$ oracle allows the adversary to decrypt arbitrary ciphertext — with the exception of the 'challenge ciphertext' c^*. To ensure that the ciphertext decrypted is not c^*, the oracle is to a function $Dec_k(\cdot, c^*)$, which verifies that its input, denoted c, is not the same as c^*, before applying the decryption function $D_k(\cdot)$ of the symmetric key cryptosystem to the ciphertext c, i.e., returning $D_k(c)$.

Note that in both the IND-CPA and the IND-CCA tests, the attacker outputs an 'adversary state' variable $s_{\mathcal{A}}$ from the 'Choose' call, which is given as input to the 'Guess' call. Namely, although here we discuss a stateless symmetric key cryptosystem, the *adversary* can still be stateful.

We next discuss the minor variations in the indistinguishability tests required for a *stateful* symmetric key cryptosystem.

2.9.4 Indistinguishability of stateful symmetric key cryptosystems

Let us now describe the indistinguishability tests for *stateful* symmetric key cryptosystems; see the illustration of a stateful symmetric key cryptosystems (Figure 2.2). These tests are a minor extension of the

$T^{IND-CPA}_{\mathcal{A},\langle E,D\rangle}(b,n)$

$k \xleftarrow{\$} \{0,1\}^n, c^* \leftarrow \bot$
$(m[0], m[1], s_{\mathcal{A}}) \xleftarrow{\$} \mathcal{A}^{Enc_k}(\text{'Choose'}, 1^n)$
If $|m[0]| = |m[1]|$ then $c^* \xleftarrow{\$} Enc_k(m[b])$
$b^* \xleftarrow{\$} \mathcal{A}^{Enc_k}(\text{'Guess'}, c^*, s_{\mathcal{A}})$
Return b^*

Oracle $Enc_k(m)$:

Initially: $s_E \leftarrow \bot$
$(c, s_E) \leftarrow E_k(m, s_E)$
Return c

(a) The IND-CPA test for a stateful symmetric key cryptosystem.

$T^{IND-CCA}_{\mathcal{A},\langle E,D\rangle}(b,n)$

$k \xleftarrow{\$} \{0,1\}^n, c^* \leftarrow \bot$
$(m[0], m[1], s_{\mathcal{A}}) \xleftarrow{\$} \mathcal{A}^{Enc_k(\cdot), Dec_k(\cdot, c^*)}(\text{'Choose'}, 1^n)$
If $|m[0]| = |m[1]|$ then $c^* \xleftarrow{\$} Enc_k(m[b])$
$b^* \xleftarrow{\$} \mathcal{A}^{Enc_k(\cdot), Dec_k(\cdot, c^*)}(\text{'Guess'}, c^*, s_{\mathcal{A}})$
Return b^*

Oracle $Enc_k(m)$:

Initially: $s_E \leftarrow \bot$
$(c, s_E) \leftarrow E_k(m, s_E)$
Return c

Oracle $Dec_k(c, c^*)$:

Initially: $s_D \leftarrow \bot$
If $c \neq c^*$ then $(m, s_D) \leftarrow D_k(c, s_D)$
Return m

(b) The IND-CCA test for a stateful symmetric key cryptosystem.

Figure 2.24. The IND-CPA and IND-CCA tests for stateful symmetric key cryptosystem (E, D).

tests for stateless PKCs; the only difference is that the encryption and decryption oracles should maintain state.

Since this is just a minor extensions, we directly present, in Figure 2.24, the pseudocode for the IND-CPA and IND-CCA tests, without presenting an illustration.

Note that the pseudocode shows the two oracles — $Enc_k(m)$ for encryption and $Dec_k(c, c^*)$ for decryption — as stateful functions. The encryption oracle $Enc_k(m)$ and the decryption oracle $Dec_k(c, c^*)$ each keep their own state variable, denoted, respectively, s_E and s_D. The test needs to maintain two separate state variables since, although the encryption and decryption operations *should* be synchronized for decryption to work correctly, the adversary $\mathcal{A}$ *could* use them without synchronization; we always restrict only the attacker's capabilities, not the attacker's strategy.

2.9.5 IND-CPA and IND-CCA symmetric key cryptosystems

We are finally ready to formally present an indistinguishability-based definitions for secure symmetric key cryptosystems, similarly to how we defined PRGs, PRFs, pseudorandom permutations and block ciphers. The definition is basically the same for stateless and stateful symmetric key cryptosystems; the difference is only in the definitions of the indistinguishability tests, i.e., using the stateless definitions (Figure 2.23) for a stateless symmetric key cryptosystem and using the stateful definitions (Figure 2.24 for a stateful symmetric key cryptosystem.

Definition 2.8 (IND-CPA and IND-CCA symmetric key cryptosystems). Let $\langle E, D\rangle$ be a (stateless or stateful) symmetric key cryptosystem. Define $T^{IND\text{-}CPA}_{\mathcal{A},\langle E,D\rangle}$ and $T^{IND-CCA}_{\mathcal{A},\langle E,D\rangle}$ as in Figure 2.23 if $\langle E, D\rangle$ is stateless and as in Figure 2.24 if $\langle E, D\rangle$ is stateful.

We say that $\langle E, D\rangle$ ensures *IND-CPA*, if every efficient adversary $\mathcal{A} \in PPT$ has negligible advantage $\varepsilon^{IND\text{-}CPA}_{\langle E,D\rangle,\mathcal{A}}(n) \in NEGL(n)$, where:

$$\varepsilon^{IND\text{-}CPA}_{\langle E,D\rangle,\mathcal{A}}(n) \equiv \Pr\left[T^{IND\text{-}CPA}_{\mathcal{A},\langle E,D\rangle}(1,n) = 1\right] - \Pr\left[T^{IND\text{-}CPA}_{\mathcal{A},\langle E,D\rangle}(0,n) = 1\right] \tag{2.39}$$

Similarly, we say that $\langle E, D\rangle$ ensures *IND-CCA*, if every efficient adversary $\mathcal{A} \in PPT$ has negligible advantage $\varepsilon^{IND-CCA}_{\langle E,D\rangle,\mathcal{A}}(n) \in NEGL(n)$, where:

$$\varepsilon^{IND-CCA}_{\langle E,D\rangle,\mathcal{A}}(n) \equiv \Pr\left[T^{IND-CCA}_{\mathcal{A},\langle E,D\rangle}(1,n) = 1\right] - \Pr\left[T^{IND-CCA}_{\mathcal{A},\langle E,D\rangle}(0,n) = 1\right] \tag{2.40}$$

For both IND-CPA and IND-CCA, the probability is over uniformly random coin tosses by $\mathcal{A}$ and E.

Note that we define the advantage of the adversary as the difference between the probability that the adversary outputs '1', in two different scenarios:

Case 1: The test is given the bit '1' as input. In this case, the adversary 'should' indeed have output '1', i.e., the adversary 'wins'.

Case 2 (or 0): The test is given the input bit '0'. In this case, the adversary 'should' have output '0'; since, in fact, it has output '1', then the adversary 'lost'.

This is similar to our previous indistinguishability definitions, where we compared the probabilities of the adversary outputting TRUE 'correctly' and 'incorrectly'.

The following exercise shows how two variants of the advantage functions would allow the adversary to 'win' without justification, against *any* symmetric key cryptosystem.

Exercise 2.12. Consider the two following alternative definitions for the IND-CPA advantage function, $\tilde{\varepsilon}^{IND\text{-}CPA}$ and $\hat{\varepsilon}^{IND\text{-}CPA}$:

$$\begin{aligned}
\tilde{\varepsilon}^{IND\text{-}CPA}_{\langle E,D\rangle,\mathcal{A}}(n) \equiv \Pr\left[T^{IND\text{-}CPA}_{\mathcal{A},\langle E,D\rangle}(1,n)=1\right] \\
- \Pr\left[T^{IND\text{-}CPA}_{\mathcal{A},\langle E,D\rangle}(1,n)=0\right] \\
\hat{\varepsilon}^{IND\text{-}CPA}_{\langle E,D\rangle,\mathcal{A}}(n) \equiv \Pr\left[T^{IND\text{-}CPA}_{\mathcal{A},\langle E,D\rangle}(1,n)=1\right] \\
- \Pr\left[T^{IND\text{-}CPA}_{\mathcal{A},\langle E,D\rangle}(0,n)=0\right]
\end{aligned}$$

Show that both $\tilde{\varepsilon}$ and $\hat{\varepsilon}$ are not reasonable definitions for the advantage function, by presenting (simple) adversaries which achieve significant advantage for *any* cryptosystem, including cryptosystems which satisfies indistinguishability, i.e., where any efficient adversary will have negligible advantage.

What, if any, would change in your answer for IND-CCA?

Indistinguishability for the COA and KPA attack models: Modifying the indistinguishability test for COA and KPA attack models is a bit more challenging. For KPA, the obvious question is *which* plaintext-ciphertext messages are known; this may be solved by using random plaintext messages; however, in reality, the known plaintexts are often taken from a specific, non-uniform distribution.

It is similarly challenging to modify the definition so it covers the COA model, where the attacker must know *some* information about the plaintext distribution. In some applications, this information may be related to the distribution of plaintexts; for example, this is the case when the plaintext is in some natural language, e.g., English.

In other cases, information about the plaintext distribution may be derived from system design. One example is text encoded using a code with some built-in error-detection capability, e.g., the ASCII encoding [121], where one of the bits in every character is the parity of the other bits.

An even more extreme example can be seen in the design of encryption in the GSM standards. In GSM, the plaintext is the result of the application of an error correcting code (ECC), providing significant redundancy which even allows an effective COA attack on GSM's A5/1 and A5/2 ciphers, as shown in Ref. [31]. In such a case, the redundancy in the plaintext can be compared to the redundancy provided by a known-plaintext attack (KPA) attack. We consider the attack to be a COA, as long as the attacker does not need to know (all or much) of the plaintext corresponding to the given ciphertext messages.

Some systems, including GSM, allow the attacker to guess all or much of the plaintext for *some* of the ciphertext messages, e.g., when sending a predictable message at a specific time; this often suffices for the attacker to use a KPA. Such systems violate the Conservative Design Principle (Principle 3) since a KPA vulnerability of the cipher renders the system vulnerable. A better system design could limit the adversary's knowledge about the distribution of plaintexts, requiring a COA vulnerability to attack the system.

Finally, note that the COA and known-plaintext attack models are not relevant for PKCs since PKCs use a *public* encryption key e, i.e., e is known to the attacker. Therefore, the attacker can encrypt arbitrary chosen plaintexts.

2.9.6 Indistinguishability of public key cryptosystems (PKCs)

As illustrated in Figure 1.5 and defined in Definition 2.3, public key cryptosystems generate a pair of related keys: a public encryption key e and a matching private decryption key d. Public key cryptosystems are required to ensure confidentiality assuming that the public encryption key e is known to the attacker.

Figure 2.25 presents the IND-CPA and IND-CCA indistinguishability tests for a stateless PKC (KG, E, D); it is rather similar to the corresponding tests for a stateless symmetric key cryptosystem (E, D) (Figure 2.23). The tests share a lot in common, with only few small — yet essential — differences. Let us identify and explain the these differences:

$T^{IND-CPA}_{\mathcal{A},\langle KG,E,D\rangle}(b, n)$
{
$(e, d) \xleftarrow{\$} KG(1^n), c^* \leftarrow \perp$
$(m[0], m[1], s_{\mathcal{A}}) \xleftarrow{\$} \mathcal{A}(\text{'Choose'}, e, 1^n)$
If $|m[0]| = |m[1]|$ then $c^* \xleftarrow{\$} E_e(m[b])$
$b^* \xleftarrow{\$} \mathcal{A}(\text{'Guess'}, e, c^*, s_{\mathcal{A}})$
Return b^*
}

(a) The IND-CPA test for a stateless PKC.

$T^{IND-CCA}_{\mathcal{A},\langle KG,E,D\rangle}(b, n)$
{
$(e, d) \xleftarrow{\$} KG(1^n), c^* \leftarrow \perp$
$(m[0], m[1], s_{\mathcal{A}}) \xleftarrow{\$} \mathcal{A}^{Dec_d(\cdot,c^*)}(\text{'Choose'}, e, 1^n)$
If $|m[0]| = |m[1]|$ then $c^* \xleftarrow{\$} E_e(m[b])$
$b^* \xleftarrow{\$} \mathcal{A}^{Dec_k(\cdot,c^*)}(\text{'Guess'}, e, c^*, s_{\mathcal{A}})$
Return b^*
}
Oracle $Dec_d(c, c^*)$:
{
If $c \neq c^*$ then $m \leftarrow D_d(c)$
Return m
}

(b) The IND-CCA test for a stateless PKC.

Figure 2.25. The IND-CPA and IND-CCA tests for a PKC (KG, E, D).

Key generation: PKCs include an explicit key generation algorithm KG, while symmetric key cryptosystems generate the secret key as a random bit string.

No encryption oracle for public key cryptosystems: The indistinguishability tests for PKCs do not provide the attacker with an oracle to the encryption algorithm; instead, the attacker is given the public encryption key e as input. The attacker can use e to encrypt arbitrary, chosen plaintexts without an oracle. Note that, following Kerckhoffs's principle, we assume that attackers know the algorithms.

Stateless decryption: As explained and defined in Section 2.1.3, PKCs may use state for encryption but not for decryption. Stateless PKCs are not widely used, and we do not include the corresponding indistinguishability tests, which require quite minor changes from these presented.

Finally, let us define IND-CPA and IND-CCA public key cryptosystems. This definition is essentially the same as the corresponding definition for symmetric key cryptosystems (Definition 2.8); the difference is only that PKCs also include a key generation algorithm KG.

Definition 2.9 (IND-CPA and IND-CCA public key cryptosystem). Let $\langle KG, E, D\rangle$ be a (stateless) PKC. Define $T^{IND-CPA}_{\mathcal{A},\langle KG,E,D\rangle}$ and $T^{IND-CCA}_{\mathcal{A},\langle KG,E,D\rangle}$ as in Figure 2.25. We say that $\langle KG, E, D\rangle$ ensures

IND-CPA, if every efficient adversary $\mathcal{A} \in PPT$ has negligible advantage $\varepsilon^{IND\text{-}CPA}_{\langle KG,E,D\rangle,\mathcal{A}}(n) \in NEGL(n)$, where:

$$\varepsilon^{IND\text{-}CPA}_{\langle KG,E,D\rangle,\mathcal{A}}(n) \equiv \Pr\left[T^{IND\text{-}CPA}_{\mathcal{A},\langle KG,E,D\rangle}(1,n) = 1\right] - \Pr\left[T^{IND\text{-}CPA}_{\mathcal{A},\langle KG,E,D\rangle}(0,n) = 1\right] \quad (2.41)$$

Similarly, we say that $\langle KG, E, D\rangle$ ensures *IND-CCA*, if every efficient adversary $\mathcal{A} \in PPT$ has negligible advantage $\varepsilon^{IND-CCA}_{\langle KG,E,D\rangle,\mathcal{A}}(n) \in NEGL(n)$, where:

$$\varepsilon^{IND-CCA}_{\langle KG,E,D\rangle,\mathcal{A}}(n) \equiv \Pr\left[T^{IND-CCA}_{\mathcal{A},\langle KG,E,D\rangle}(1,n) = 1\right] - \Pr\left[T^{IND-CCA}_{\mathcal{A},\langle KG,E,D\rangle}(0,n) = 1\right] \quad (2.42)$$

For both IND-CPA and IND-CCA, the probability is over uniformly random coin tosses by $\mathcal{A}$ and E.

We further discuss PKCs in Chapter 6.

2.10 Constructing secure symmetric key cryptosystems from a block cipher

In this section, we first present the *cryptographic building blocks principle* and specifically motivate the use of a block cipher to construct symmetric key cryptosystems; the usual term for such constructions is a *mode of operation* or simple a *mode.* We then present an overview of modes of operation (Section 2.10.2), and discuss well known modes of operation, including the ECB, CTR, OFB, CFB and CBC modes.

2.10.1 The Cryptographic Building Blocks principle

The Cryptographic Building Blocks principle: The cryptographic building blocks principle is a basic principle to the specification and design of secure cryptographic schemes, including symmetric key cryptosystems.

Before introducing the principle, let us discuss the three basic approaches to establish the security of cryptographic schemes:

Unconditional proof of security: Few schemes, e.g., the one-time pad (OTP), can be proven secure, without relying on unproven or simplifying assumptions, such as the assumption from the theory of complexity that $P \neq NP$ (Section A.1). However, such schemes often have special requirements, e.g., the one-time pad (OTP) requires a shared key as long as all plaintext to be encrypted, making it impractical in many scenarios. This requirement, of a key as long as the plaintext, is necessary for *every* cryptosystem unconditionally secure against computationally unbounded adversaries. Even if we limit ourselves to efficient adversaries, an unconditional proof that a cryptosystem ensures indistinguishability, with key length smaller than the plaintext length, would provide a way to *prove* that $P \neq NP$, which is unlikely (see Section A.1).

Establish security by failed cryptanalysis: Once we give up on unconditional proof of security, we have to rely on the fact that some cryptographic schemes have successfully resisted extensive efforts to cryptanalyze them, i.e., to prove that they do not satisfy their security requirements. For example, for symmetric key cryptosystems, this will mean that extensive efforts by cryptanalysts failed to show an algorithm that achieves significant (non-negligible) advantage against the cryptosystem.

Provable security reduction: Suppose that we have established the security of cryptographic scheme $\mathcal{S}$ by the above method, i.e., failure of extensive efforts to cryptanalyze. We now want to establish the security of another scheme $\mathcal{S}'$. One way to do that is by *proving* that any attack that successfully cryptanalyzes $\mathcal{S}'$ can be abused to cryptanalyze $\mathcal{S}$. This makes finding a successful attack against $\mathcal{S}'$ to be as challenging as finding a successful attack against $\mathcal{S}$. Note that $\mathcal{S}'$ does not have meet the same goals as these of $\mathcal{S}$.

An attacker with unbounded computational resources would be able to 'break' any symmetric key cryptosystems whose key is shorter than the plaintext. Therefore, the security of practical symmetric key cryptosystems can only be established based on the computational limitations of the adversary. We can establish such security either by failed efforts to cryptanalyze the symmetric key cryptosystems or by a provable security reduction, typically, showing that any attack on the symmetric key cryptosystems implies an attack on an another cryptographic scheme $\mathcal{S}$, whose security is well established.

It may seem that the importance of symmetric key cryptosystems should motivate us to establish the security of a symmetric key cryptosystem by relying on failed efforts to cryptanalyze that symmetric key cryptosystem. Surely this was the approach taken in the past.

However, symmetric key cryptosystems are quite complex schemes. It is better to base the security of complex schemes, and in particular of symmetric key cryptosystems, on provably secure reduction from the security of a simpler cryptographic schemes, such as a *block cipher*. Usually, this is achieved by constructing the complex scheme, e.g., a symmetric key cryptosystems, using the simpler scheme, e.g., a block cipher. We refer to this as the *cryptographic building blocks principle*. Let us first present the principle and then provide additional motivation.

Principle 8 (Cryptographic building blocks). *The security of cryptographic systems should only depend on the security of a few basic building blocks. These blocks should be* simple *and with* well-defined and easy to test *security properties. More complex schemes should be proven secure by reduction to the security of the underlying blocks.*

The advantages of following the cryptographic building blocks principle include the following:

Efficient cryptanalysis: By focusing cryptanalysis effort on few schemes, we obtain much better validation of their security. The fact that the building blocks are simple and are selected to be easy to test makes cryptanalysis even more effective.

Replacement and upgrade: By using simple, well-defined modules, we can replace them for improved efficiency — or to improve security, in particular after being broken or when doubts arise.

Flexibility and variations: Complex systems and schemes naturally involve many options, tradeoffs and variants; it is better to build all such variants using the same basic building blocks.

Robust combiners: There are known, efficient robust-combiner designs for the basic cryptographic building blocks [240]. If desired, we can use these as the basic blocks for improved security.

The cryptographic building blocks principle is key to both applied and theoretical modern cryptography. From the theoretical perspective, it is important to understand which schemes can be implemented given another scheme. There are many results exploring such relationships between different cryptographic schemes and functions, with many positive results (constructions), few negative results (proofs that efficient constructions are impossible or improbable) and few challenging open questions.

From the perspective of applied cryptography, the principle implies the need to define and standardize a small number of basic building blocks, which would be very efficient, simple functions — and convenient for many applications. The security of these building blocks would be established by extensive (yet unsuccessful) cryptanalysis efforts — instead of relying on provably secure reductions from other cryptographic mechanisms.

Block ciphers as cryptographic building blocks: *Block ciphers* are one of the most widely used cryptographic building blocks; the other widely used building block is *cryptographic hash functions*, which we discuss in Chapter 3. In particular, block ciphers satisfy well the requirements of the cryptographic building blocks principle. They are simple, deterministic functions with Finite Input Length (FIL), which is identical to their output length. This should be contrasted with 'full fledged encryption schemes', which involve multiple functions, each of which can be randomized or stateful, have Variable Input Length (VIL), and whose output is often longer than their input.

The obvious next step is to use a block cipher to build a secure symmetric key cryptosystem, i.e., ensure indistinguishable encryption. But how?

At first sight, it may appear that we can simply use a block cipher as a symmetric key cryptosystem. In fact, block ciphers, in particular DES and AES, are often referred to as encryption schemes and typically use the notation (E, D) for their keyed functions. However, block ciphers do not satisfy the requirements of most definitions of encryption, e.g., the IND-CPA test of Definition 2.8.

Exercise 2.13. Explain why a block cipher fails the IND-CPA test (Definition 2.8).

Solution: Consider $E_k(m)$, which is the 'encryption' operation of a block cipher (i.e., a pair (E, D) of a PRP E and its reverse $D = E^{-1}$). Then, $E_k(m)$ is a function; whenever we apply it to the same message m, with the same key k, we will receive the same output $(E_k(m))$. The attacker $\mathcal{A}$ would choose any two different messages as $(m[0], m[1])$, confirm that $c[0] = E_k(m[0]) \neq c[1] = E_k(m[1])$ and then use $(m[0], m[1])$ as the pair of challenge plaintext messages. When $\mathcal{A}$ receives $c^* = E_k(m[b])$, it checks if, for $b^* \in \{0, 1\}$, $c[b^*] = c^*$ holds. If so, then $\mathcal{A}$ outputs b^*. □

We see that a block cipher does not ensure indistinguishability when used for encryption 'as is'. However, as we discuss in the next section, there are multiple, simple constructions of secure encryption schemes *from* block ciphers. Such constructions are often referred to as *modes of operation*. The modes of operation we present were thoroughly analyzed, and most of them were proven secure by a reduction to the security of the underlying block cipher.

Don't roll your own cryptography! As we discussed above, cryptographic schemes should be carefully analyzed. Only very few, basic cryptographic building blocks can be sufficiently well evaluated by cryptanalysis efforts; the rest should be proven by reduction to one or more of these basic cryptographic building blocks.

In this book, we discuss several examples where designers did not follow this approach. Instead, they relied on their intuition, and on limited cryptanalysis efforts, to establish the security of their designs. In many cases, probably most cases, the result was a vulnerable, exploitable design. The design of new cryptographic schemes should be very rare and done only when well motivated — and by expert cryptographers, who learned much more than what we cover in this book.

This is especially true when it comes to complex cryptographic protocols, such as the shared-key protocols we discuss in Chapter 5 and the TLS protocol we discuss in Chapter 7.

There can be subtle yet critical vulnerabilities in the implementations of (well-designed) cryptographic schemes and protocols. A particularly critical concern is the prevention of different side channels and other implementation vulnerabilities that can cause a system to be exploitable — even when using well-designed, secure cryptographic schemes.

Our strong recommendation is, therefore, to use established cryptographic schemes, protocols and implementations. When a new scheme, protocol or implementation is needed, the development team should include expert, experienced cryptographers.

Principle 9 (Don't roll your own cryptography). *Use well-established and evaluated cryptographic schemes, protocols and implementations. If new schemes, protocols or implementations are absolutely necessary, their development should be done by expert, experienced cryptographers.*

2.10.2 Modes of operation

In the rest of this section, we present several constructions of symmetric key cryptosystems from a block cipher, following the cryptographic building blocks principle. Most of these constructions were defined originally in the DES specifications [377], where they were referred to by the term *modes of operation*, which is still the widely used term for different cryptographic schemes from block ciphers. We also present the Counter mode (CTR) mode of operation, defined in the AES specifications [167], with minor simplifications. In this section, we discuss modes of operation for symmetric key cryptosystems, and in Chapter 4, we discuss modes of operation for authentication, authenticated encryption and more.

For didactic purposes, we also describe a simple, non-standard and inefficient mode of operation, which we call the *Per-Block Random* (PBR) mode.

Table 2.3 summarizes the modes of operation we present in this section. For each mode, we list the encryption process; these processes are simple enough that it should not be too difficult for the reader to figure out the corresponding decryption process.

The third column of Table 2.3 lists the impact on the decrypted plaintext, due to a change ('flipping') of the value of a specific bit, $c_i[j]$, in the ciphertext, where $c_i[j]$ is the jth bit of the ith block of the ciphertext. The impact of bit flipping is significant for two reasons.

Table 2.3. Encryption modes of operation using n-bit block cipher. The plaintext is given as a sequence consisting of blocks $m_1 + m_2 + \cdots$, where each block has n bits, i.e., $m_i \in \{0,1\}^n$. Similarly, the ciphertext is produced as a sequence of n-bits blocks $\{c_i \in \{0,1\}^n\}$, where i begins in 0 or 1, depending on the mode, except for PBR, where $c_i \in \{0,1\}^{2n}$. We use $m_i[j]$ ($c_i[j]$) to denote the jth bit of the ith plaintext (respectively, ciphertext) block.

Mode	Encryption	Flip bit $c_i[j] \Rightarrow$	Properties
Electronic code book (ECB)	$c_i = E_k(m_i)$	Corrupt m_i	Insecure (not IND-CPA)
Per-Block Random (PBR)	$r_i \xleftarrow{\$} \{0,1\}^n$, $c_i = (r_i, m_i \oplus E_k(r_i))$	$j \leq n \Rightarrow$ corrupt m_i $n < j \Rightarrow$ flip $m_i[j-n]$	Inefficient, non-standard
Counter (CTR) [simplified]	$c_i = m_i \oplus E_k(s)$ $s \leftarrow s+1$ (stateful)	Flip $m_i[j]$ (no integrity)	Stateful, parallelizable, preprocessing
Output Feedback (OFB)	$r_0 \xleftarrow{\$} \{0,1\}^n$, $r_i = E_k(r_{i-1})$, $c_0 \leftarrow r_0$, $c_i \leftarrow r_i \oplus m_i$	Flip $m_i[j]$ (no integrity)	Parallelizable, preprocessing
Cipher Feedback (CFB)	$c_0 \xleftarrow{\$} \{0,1\}^n$, $c_i \leftarrow m_i \oplus E_k(c_{i-1})$	Flip $m_i[j]$; if $i < n \Rightarrow$ corrupt m_{i+1}	Parallel decryption
Cipher Block Chaining (CBC)	$c_0 \xleftarrow{\$} \{0,1\}^n$, $c_i \leftarrow E_k(m_i \oplus c_{i-1})$	Flip $m_{i+1}[j]$ and corrupt m_i	Parallel decryption

First, to ensure that systems using encryption can ensure reliable, efficient communication in spite of (unintentional) bit errors; second, *intentional bit flipping* has been abused in multiple attacks.

The fourth column of Table 2.3 lists few other important properties, related to security and efficiency. The modes we discuss ensure IND-CPA, except ECB, which is insecure, and they are all reasonably efficient, with PBR being the only one which is quite inefficient, resulting in ciphertext which is twice as long as the plaintext. Therefore, only four of the modes in the table — CTR, OFB, CFB and CBC — are both secure (ensure IND-CPA) and efficient. Of these,

CTR and OFB allow both encryption and decryption to be done in parallel, and also allow preprocessing, i.e., performing the computationally intensive operations before receiving the plaintext, while the CFB and CBC modes only allow decryption to be done in parallel.

The modes of operation in Table 2.3 are designed to turn block ciphers into IND-CPA symmetric key cryptosystems, handling goals such as the following:

Randomization and/or state: Block ciphers are deterministic and stateless. However, for a symmetric key cryptosystem to ensure IND-CPA (and IND-CCA), the encryption must be randomized, stateful or both. The reason is that the adversary is allowed to make encryption queries for arbitrary messages — including the chosen challenge plaintexts $m[0], m[1]$. If the encryption scheme is both deterministic and stateless, then all encryptions of a message, e.g., $m[0]$, will return a fixed ciphertext, e.g., c_0. This will allow the attacker to trivially 'win' in the IND-CPA and IND-CCA experiments. Therefore, most modes (PBR, OFB, CFB and CBC) are randomized, and the CTR mode is stateful, allowing them to ensure that in every invocation of the block cipher, there would be unique inputs, which allows them to ensure IND-CPA (but not IND-CCA). The Electronic Code Book (ECB) mode is the only mode of operation that is both deterministic and stateless — and, as a result, ECB is, indeed, insecure (not IND-CPA).

Variable Input Length (VIL) and padding: We allow encryption of arbitrary, VIL messages. All modes of operation are defined for input whose length, in bits, is a multiple of the block length n, i.e., their input is an integral number of blocks. If the plaintext may not be an integral number of blocks, then it should be *padded* to an integral number of blocks before being given as input to the encryption defined by the different modes of operation. The padding can be quite simple; however, surprisingly, incorrect padding can result in serious vulnerabilities; see Section 2.11.

PRF: Most modes of operation (PBR, OFB, CFB and CTR) use only the encryption function E — even for decryption. This has an important implication: they may be implemented using a PRF instead of a block cipher. This may make them harder to attack, esp. when the same key is used for an extensive number of messages, due to providing a smaller advantage to an attacker, depending on the PRF used. See Refs. [45, 230].

Efficiency: Efficiency is important — and multi-faceted. All of the modes we present use one block cipher operation per each block of plaintext, and allow parallel decryption, as well as 'random access' decryption, i.e., decryption of only specific blocks from the plaintext. The OFB, CTR and PBR modes of operation also allow parallel encryption. Another efficiency consideration is *offline pre-computation*; in the CTR, OFB and PBR modes of operation, we may conduct all the block cipher computations offline, i.e., before receiving the corresponding plaintext or ciphertext. After receiving the plaintext/ciphertext, we only need a single exclusive OR (XOR) operation to process each block.

Integrity/authentication: Using the CBC mode of operation, any change in ciphertext block c_i causes decryption to return 'garbled' plaintext for that block, i.e., instead of the correct plaintext block m_i, decryption returns some 'garbled' value (pseudorandom for the attacker). The OFB mode has a similar property: a change in c_i causes decryption to return 'garbled' value for m_{i+1}; however this is relevant only if the plaintext contains at least $i+1$ blocks, i.e., $i < n$. These properties can provide weak protection of integrity, if the plaintext is augmented with an appropriate error detecting code (EDC), which is validated upon decryption. In Chapter 4 we discuss this integrity protection and modes of operation that ensure strong integrity and authentication, preventing an attacker from modifying intercepted messages to mislead the recipient, or from forging messages as if they were sent by a trusted sender. Some modes of operation ensure authenticity and integrity in addition to confidentiality, others ensure *only* authenticity.

Error localization: In the OFB and CTR modes of operation, the corruption (flipping) of one or more ciphertext bits results in corruption (flipping) of only the corresponding plaintext bits. This may help to recover from some corruptions of bits during communication, since no additional bits are lost. However, this minor fault-tolerance benefit is rarely significant. Often, it is much more significant that an attacker may 'flip' plaintext bits by 'flipping' the corresponding ciphertext bits. We discuss the error localization further in Section 2.10.4. Later, we discuss the error localization property when we discuss each mode of operation.

We now describe each of the modes of operation in more details.

2.10.3 The Electronic Code Book (ECB) mode

ECB is a naïve mode of operation. In fact, it is not a true mode of operation: using the ECB mode simply means applying the block cipher separately to each block of the plaintext. Namely, to encrypt the plaintext string $m = m_1 + m_2 + \cdots$, where each m_i is a block (i.e., $|m_i| = n$), we simply compute $c_i = E_k(m_i)$. Decryption is equally trivial: $m_i = D_k(c_i)$, and correctness of encryption, i.e., $m = D_k(E_k(m))$ for every $k, m \in \{0,1\}^*$, follows immediately from the correctness of the block cipher $E_k(\cdot)$. See Figures 2.26 and 2.27.

In principle, ECB is a monoalphabetic substitution cipher and, therefore, similar to the other monoalphabetic substitution ciphers discussed in Section 2.2.3. However, the 'alphabet' of the ECB mode of operation is very large: each 'letter' is a whole n-bit block. For typical block ciphers, the block size is significant, e.g., $n_{DES} = 64$ bits and $n_{AES} = 128$ bits. The use of such large alphabet improves security compared to the monoalphabetic substitution ciphers of Section 2.2.3, in particular, the use of frequency analysis becomes impractical.

However, obviously, ECB maps each plaintext block ('letter') to a fixed ciphertext block ('letter'). This may expose some information about the plaintext, in particular, encryptions of the same plaintext block will result in the same ciphertext block, which may allow the

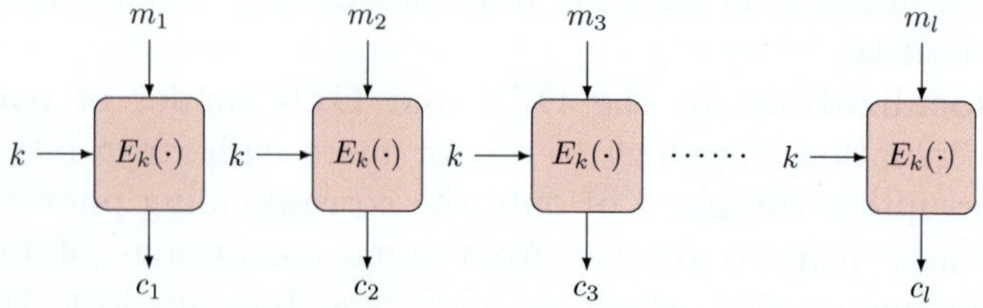

Figure 2.26. Electronic Code Book (ECB) mode encryption of plaintext message m consisting of l blocks, $m = m_1, \ldots, m_l$.

Source: Adapted from Ref. [268].

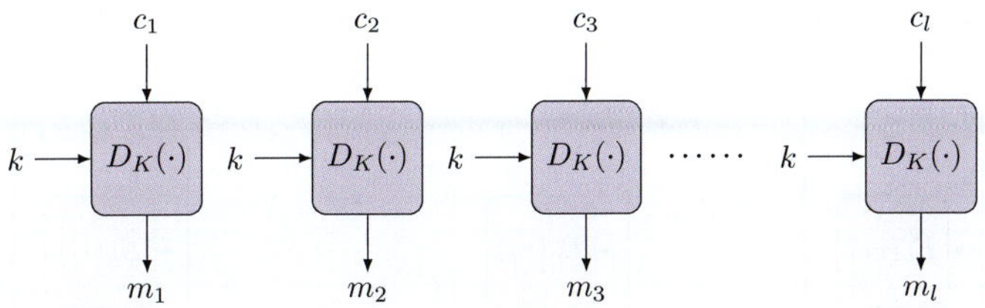

Figure 2.27. Electronic Code Book (ECB) mode decryption of ciphertext message c consisting of l blocks, $c = c_1, \ldots, c_l$.

Source: Adapted from Ref. [268].

Figure 2.28. The Linux penguin visualization comparing the ECB and CBC modes of operation [178, 483]. From left: the plaintext Linux penguin image, in bitmap format; the ECB encryption of the image; and finally, the CBC encryption of the same image.

attacker to recognize encryptions of the same plaintext message. Even with relatively long blocks of 64 or 128 bits, such repeating blocks are quite likely in practical applications and scenarios since *inputs are not random strings*. Essentially, this is a generalization of the frequency analysis attack of Section 2.2.3 (see Figure 2.7). This weakness of ECB is often visualized by the example shown in Figure 2.28, using the *Linux penguin* image [178, 483].

2.10.4 The Per-Block Random (PBR) mode

We next present the *Per-Block Random* (PBR) mode of operation. This mode of operation is simple but inefficient, which may be the reason that it has not been proposed in the DES specifications or otherwise. We present the PBR mode of operation for didactic purposes, namely, since it provide a simple way to construct an indistinguishable symmetric key cryptosystem from a block cipher (or from a PRF). The PBR mode of operation is also similar to the

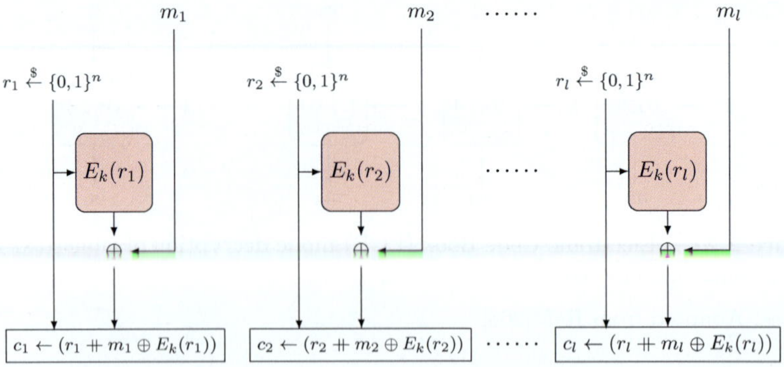

Figure 2.29. The per-block randomization (PBR) mode of operation.

stateful, deterministic CTR mode, and to the randomized, stateless OFB mode.

The PBR mode is illustrated in Figure 2.29. Let us first describe the PBR mode of operation and then discuss its correctness, security and efficiency.

Let $m = m_1 + m_2 + \cdots + m_l$ be a plaintext message, where each m_i is one n-bits block, i.e., $m_i \in \{0,1\}^n$. Let E denote a block cipher for n-bit blocks, and let k denote a key for E. For each plaintext block m_i, containing n bits, we generate a corresponding block r_i of n random bits. We then compute the ciphertext block c_i as the pair of r_i and the exclusive OR (XOR) of m_i with the result of applying the block cipher to r_i, i.e., $E_k(r_i)$. Namely, we compute the *PBR-mode encryption* of m using block cipher E and key k, denoted $PBR.E_k^E(m)$, as follows:

$$PBR.E_k^E(m) \equiv (r_1 + [m_1 \oplus E_k(r_1)]) + \cdots (r_l + [m_l \oplus E_k(r_l)]) \tag{2.43}$$

Each ciphertext block c_i is computed as $c_i = (r_i + [m_i \oplus E_k(r_i)])$ and is a string of $2n$ bits.

PBR decryption performs the dual operation. Namely, given key k and ciphertext $c = (r_1 + c_1) + \cdots + (r_l + c_l)$, where each r_i and c_i are one block (n bits), we compute the *PBR-mode decryption* of c, denoted $PBR.D_k^E(c)$, as follows:

$$\begin{aligned}(r_1 \mathbin{+\!\!+} c_1) \mathbin{+\!\!+} \cdots \mathbin{+\!\!+} (r_l \mathbin{+\!\!+} c_l) &\leftarrow c;\\ (\forall i \in \{1, \ldots, l\})\ m_i &\leftarrow c_i \oplus E_k(r_i);\\ PBR.D_k^E(c) &\leftarrow m_1 \mathbin{+\!\!+} \cdots \mathbin{+\!\!+} m_l\end{aligned} \tag{2.44}$$

It is not difficult to show that PBR mode ensures correctness.

Exercise 2.14. Show that PBR mode ensures *correctness*, i.e., that for every plaintext message m holds $m = PBR.D_k^E(PBR.E_k^E(m))$.

The PBR mode does not use the 'decryption' function D of the underlying block cipher. Therefore, the PBR mode of operation can be instantiated using a PRF instead of using a block cipher.

PBR is *not* a standard mode, and we do not recommend its use since it is wasteful: it requires the use of one block of random bits per each block of the plaintext, and all these random blocks also become part of the ciphertext and are used for decryption, i.e., the length of the ciphertext is double the length of the plaintext. However, PBR is convenient as a simple example of a mode of operation which constructs a IND-CPA symmetric key cryptosystem from a secure block cipher (or PRF). The reader may want to recall the IND-CPA test for stateless symmetric key cryptosystems (Figure 2.23(a)).

Theorem 2.1. *Let (E, D) be a secure block cipher. Then $(PBR.E^E, PBR.D^E)$ ensures IND-CPA.*

Proof. We begin with the main part of the proof, in which we show that, for a ('truly') *random function* f over $\{0,1\}^n$, the PBR construction ensures IND-CPA. Namely, $(PBR.E^f, PBR.D^f)$, where f is random function, ensures IND-CPA.

During the IND-CPA test, the adversary $\mathcal{A}$ provides a sequence of input messages to be encrypted by $PBR.E^f$, either by using the oracle or when providing the pair $m[0], m[1]$ of challenge plaintext messages to be distinguished (in the 'Choose' operation). Each of these messages may consist of a number of blocks. Let L denote the *total* number of input blocks provided by $\mathcal{A}$ in *all* of these input messages.

The runtime of the adversary $\mathcal{A}$ is bounded by some polynomial in the length of its input, i.e., to a polynomial in the security parameter n. Therefore, L, the total number of plaintext blocks that $\mathcal{A}$ provides in these messages, is bounded by a polynomial in n. Let $\pi_1, \ldots, \pi_L$ denote the sequence of the L blocks provided in all messages provided by the adversary. To encrypt each block π_i, PBR selects a n-bits random string, which we denote ρ_i, and outputs a $2n$-bits ciphertext string, which we denote γ_i, where $\gamma_i \leftarrow \rho_i +\!\!+ \pi_i \oplus E_k(\rho_i)$.

Since L is polynomial in n, and there are 2^n binary strings of length n, *the probability of selecting the same random string ρ_i twice is negligible*, i.e., $\Pr(\rho_i = \rho_j | i \neq j) \in NEGL(n)$. Therefore, with overwhelming probability, we can assume for for every $i \neq j$ holds $\rho_i \neq \rho_j$.

Since the outputs of the random function f are each chosen as a random n-bit string, knowing $f(\rho_i)$ does not give any information about $f(\rho_j)$ where $\rho_i \neq \rho_j$ - it is still a uniformly random n-bit string. Since we assume that for every $i \neq j$ holds $\rho_i \neq \rho_j$, then for every $i \neq j$ holds that $f(\rho_j)$ is a uniformly random n-bit string, even when $f(\rho_i)$ is fixed and known.

Consider the challenge ciphertext c^* which the adversary $\mathcal{A}$ receives in the the IND-CPA test of $(PBR.E^f, PBR.D^f)$. Recall that we focus on the case where the length of all plaintexts is a multiple of n and that in the IND-CPA the adversary selects two 'challenge plaintexts' $m[0], m[1]$ of the same length, say l blocks, i.e., $|m[0]| = |m[1]| = l \cdot n$. Therefore, the length of the resulting ciphertext c^* would be $2l$ blocks, i.e., $2ln$ bits, regardless of the choice of the bit b, i.e., regardless of whether c^* is encryption of $m[0]$ or of $m[1]$. Furthermore, for every $2n$-bit 'block' of c^*, with high probability, we use a different n-bit random string ρ_i, and therefore $f(\rho_i)$ is a uniformly random n-bit string. Therefore, c^*_i, the ith block of c^*, is equally likely to be the result of the ith block of $m[0]$ and of the ith block of $m[1]$.

Therefore, under the assumption that all random blocks ρ_i are different ($\rho_i \neq \rho_j$ for $i \neq j$), the probability that $\mathcal{A}$ outputs $b^* = 1$ when c^* is indeed the encryption of $m[1]$ (i.e., $b = 1$) is *identical* to the probability that $\mathcal{A}$ outputs $b^* = 1$ when c^* is the encryption of $m[0]$ (i.e., $b = 0$). Namely, under the assumption that all random blocks ρ_i are different, the adversary $\mathcal{A}$ *gains no advantage*. Of course, this assumption does not always hold, but since it holds with overwhelming probability, it follows that the advantage of $\mathcal{A}$ against $(PBR.E^f, PBR.D^f)$ is negligible. Namely, we have shown that $(PBR.E^f, PBR.D^f)$, where f is random function, ensures IND-CPA.

If remains to show that $(PBR.E^{E_k}, PBR.D^{E_k})$ is IND-CPA when E is the encryption function of a secure block cipher (E, D), i.e., E is a PRP. By definition, the adversary cannot distinguish between a random function f (over $\{0,1\}^n$) and a secure PRF F_k (over $\{0,1\}^n$), except with negligible probability. Hence, $(PBR.E^{F_k}, PBR.D^{F_k})$ is IND-CPA when F is a secure PRF. The claim follows by the PRP/PRF switching lemma (Lemma 2.2). □

PBR does not protect integrity: Some modes of operation protect the *integrity* of the decrypted plaintext message, at least to some degree. For example, in the ECB mode, the attacker cannot 'flip' a specific bit in the decrypted plaintext since any change in the corresponding ciphertext block will modify the entire decrypted plaintext block. What about the PBR mode of operation?

The PBR mode encrypts the plaintext by bitwise XOR, i.e., $c_i = (r_i + m_i \oplus E_k(r_i))$. This allows an attacker to 'flip' a bit in the decrypted plaintext, by 'flipping' a corresponding bit in the ciphertext.

Let us explain how the attacker can flip specific bits in the decrypted plaintext by flipping bits in the ciphertext. Let $m = m_1, \ldots, m_l$ be a plaintext message, and let $c = (r_1 + \gamma_1) + \cdots + (r_l + \gamma_l)$ denote the corresponding PBR ciphertext. Let $c' = (r_1 + \gamma'_1) + \cdots + (r_l + \gamma'_l)$ denote the ciphertext with bits in some of the $\gamma_i = m_i \oplus E_k(r_i)$ strings flipped but without changing the r_i (random) stings. This will cause flipping of the corresponding bits in the decryption of c', which we denote m'.

For example, if we flip the last bit in some ciphertext block γ_i, i.e., $\gamma'_i = \gamma_i \oplus \left(0^{n-1} + 1\right)$, and do not modify other blocks, i.e., $(\forall j \neq i)\gamma'_i = \gamma_i$, then this will only flip the corresponding bit in the decrypted plaintext m'. Namely,

$$m' = m \oplus \left(0^{(i-1)\cdot n} + \left(0^{n-1} + 1\right) + 0^{(l-i)\cdot n}\right)$$

Therefore, the PBR mode of operation does not provide defense of *integrity*; given the ciphertext of a some plaintext message, the attacker can flip the values of arbitrary bits in the decrypted plaintext, by intentionally flipping the corresponding bits in the ciphertext.

The attacker can also modify the decrypted plaintext in other ways. For example, consider $c'' = (r_l + \gamma_l) + \cdots + (r_1 + \gamma_1)$, i.e., reversing the order of the ciphertext blocks. The decryption of c'' would be $m_l + \cdots m_1$, i.e., reversing the order of the plaintext blocks. Essentially, the PBR mode provides no protection for the integrity of the recovered plaintext.

PBR error localization: Another property of some modes of operation is *error localization*. Namely, which bits of the decrypted plaintext are modified by an (intentional or unintentional) change in some ciphertext bits?

In both the ECB and PBR modes of operation, a change in the ith block c_i results in changes in the ith decrypted plaintext block m'_i but not in other blocks of the decrypted plaintext; namely, at most, n bits are corrupted. We say that the PBR and ECB modes of operation ensure *n-bits error localization* since an error in one ciphertext block corrupts at most n plaintext bits upon decryption.

In general, we say that a cryptosystem *ensures η-bits error localization* if an error in one ciphertext bit corrupts at most η bits in the decrypted plaintext. All the modes of operation we discuss ensure η-bits error localization, with η being n for the PBR mode, 1 for the CTR and OFB modes, and $n + 1$ for CFB and CBC modes.

PBR does not ensure IND-CCA: Of possibly larger concern is the fact that PBR, and every cryptosystem that ensures error localization, including all of the modes we discuss in this chapter, do not ensure IND-CCA, as we show in the following exercise.

Exercise 2.15 (A symmetric key cryptosystem cannot ensure both error localization and IND-CCA). Prove the following claims:

1. PBR does not ensure IND-CCA.
2. *Any* symmetric key cryptosystem (E, D) that ensures correctness and η-bits error localization does not ensure IND-CCA.

Solution of part 1: The adversary gives to the test two different challenge plaintext, $m[0] \neq m[1]$, both consisting of a single block. The adversary receives the encryption $c^* = PBR.E_k^E(m[b])$. From Equation (2.43), $c^* = r^* + \gamma^*$, where r^* is a random string ($r^* \xleftarrow{\$} \{0,1\}^n$) and $\gamma^* \leftarrow m[b] \oplus E_k(r^*)$.

The adversary then asks the decryption oracle to decrypt the ciphertext $c' = r^* + (1^n \oplus \gamma^*)$. Since $c' \neq c^*$, the decryption oracle returns

$$\begin{aligned} PBR.D_k^E(c') &= (1^n \oplus \gamma^*) \oplus E_k(r^*) \\ &= 1^n \oplus m[b] \oplus E_k(r^*) \oplus E_k(r^*) = 1^n \oplus m[b] \end{aligned}$$

Namely, if $PBR.D_k^E(c') = 1^n \oplus m[1]$, then the adversary returns $b^* = 1$, else the adversary returns $b^* = 0$. Trivially, the adversary always correctly finds the correct bit, i.e., it achieves the maximal advantage (1), i.e., the PBR mode of operation does not ensure IND-CCA. □

Solution of part 2: The adversary operates quite similarly, except that the two input plaintext messages, $m[0] \neq m[1]$, consist each of 3η identical bits; for example, $m[0] = 0^{3 \cdot \eta}$ and $m[1] = 1^{3 \cdot \eta}$.

Upon receiving the ciphertext c^*, the adversary requests decryption of a value c' defined as follows. The value c' is identical to c^* except for a change in the value of *one* bit, say the first bit of c^*.

Clearly, $c' \neq c^*$. Therefore, the decryption oracle returns a decrypted plaintext which we denote m', where $m' \leftarrow D_k(c')$. Since (E, D) ensures error localization and c' is identical to c^* except for one bit, then at most η bits of m' may differ from the corresponding bits of $D_k(c^*)$. Since (E, D) ensures correctness, $E_k(c^*) = b^{3\eta}$. Hence, at least 2η of the bits of m' would have the value b, i.e., the same value as of the bits of $E_k(c*)$. □

2.10.5 The Counter mode (CTR) mode

We present a slight simplification of the *Counter mode* (CTR), a standard mode of operation, defined in Ref. [167]. As the name implies, the Counter mode (CTR) mode maintains a counter of the number of blocks encrypted/decrypted so far, which is incremented whenever encrypting/decrypting a new block. The counter is used as input

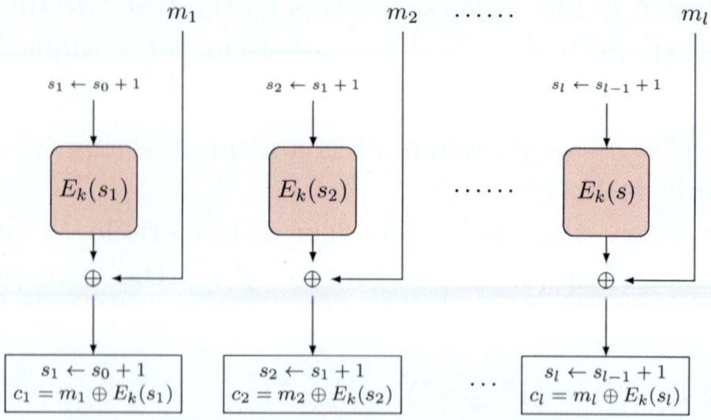

Figure 2.30. Counter (CTR) mode encryption of plaintext message m consisting of l blocks, $m = m_1, \ldots, m_l$, with initial state s_0 and final state $s_l = s_0 + l$. The *state* is a counter of the number of blocks encrypted so far, i.e., its value is incremented whenever encrypting a new block.

to the underlying block cipher, ensuring that a different input is provided at each invocation of the PRF. Therefore, the *output* of the block cipher is pseudorandom, and encryption is done by exclusive OR (XOR) between each plaintext block and the pseudorandom output of the block cipher. This operation is illustrated in Figure 2.30, where we denote the initial state by s_0 and denote the final state (after encrypting l blocks) by $s_l = s_0 + l$. Note the similarity to the PBR mode of operation; the difference between CTR and PBR is just in how we ensure different inputs to the block cipher at every invocation: using a counter (CTR mode) or using random input bits (PBR mode).

The CTR mode preserves the value of the counter between different invocations, i.e., it is *stateful* — in fact, the only stateful mode of operation we discuss. The use of the pseudorandomness of the output of the block cipher suffices to allow the CTR mode to ensure IND-CPA, without requiring the input of true random bits.

By using state, the CTR mode avoids the need to generate and send a new random block for each plaintext block as done in the PBR mode. Therefore, when we can reliably use state, the CTR mode offers efficiency. Senders and recipients can pre-compute the block cipher operations even before they receive the plaintext or ciphertext, requiring only block-wise XOR when the data (plaintext or ciphertext) arrives. Also, all operations could be done in parallel on different blocks, allowing significant speed-up (if using appropriate hardware).

2.10.6 The Output Feedback (OFB) mode

We now proceed to discuss the three stateless modes of operation which are both efficient and ensure IND-CPA: OFB, CFB and CBC. We begin, in this section, with the Output Feedback (OFB) mode of operation.

The OFB mode is simple; OFB encryption is illustrated in Figure 2.31 and OFB decryption is illustrated in Figure 2.32. The OFB mode ensures IND-CPA and is efficient, requiring the generation and exchange of only a *single block of random bits* to encrypt multiple-block plaintexts. This improves upon the PBR mode, which requires one block of random bits per each plaintext block.

OFB is a variant on the PRF-based stream cipher discussed in Section 2.6.2 and illustrated in Figure 2.18 and, like it, operates on input which consists of l blocks of n bits each. The difference is that OFB uses a block cipher E_k instead of the PRF PRF_k.

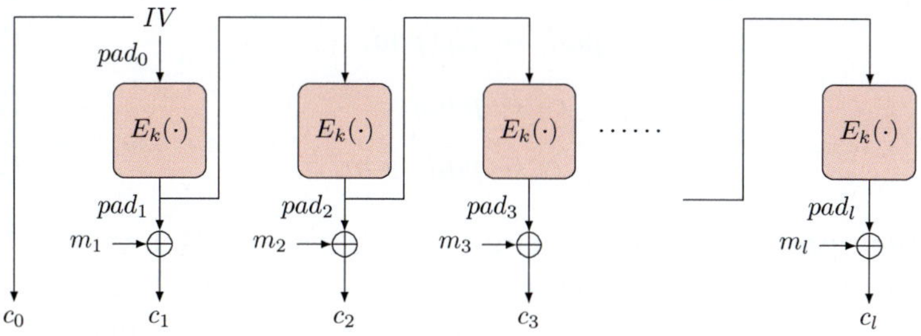

Figure 2.31. Output Feedback (OFB) mode encryption.

Source: Adapted from Ref. [268].

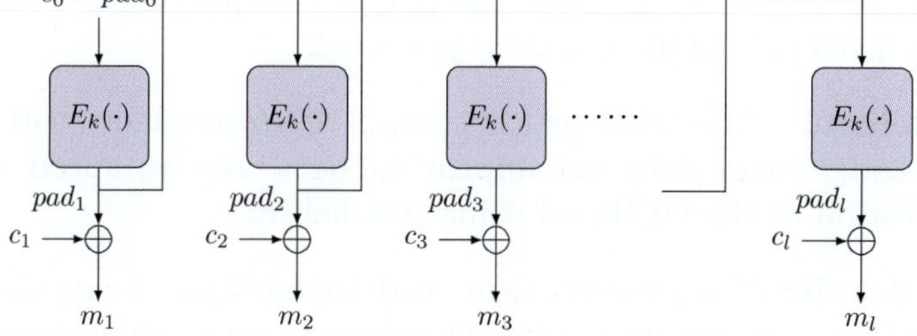

Figure 2.32. Output Feedback (OFB) mode decryption.

Source: Adapted from Ref. [268].

The OFB mode uses a random n-bits string, called an *initialization vector (IV)*, as a 'seed' to generate a long sequence of pseudo-random n-bit *pad blocks*, $pad_1, \ldots, pad_l$, to encrypt plaintext blocks $m_1, \ldots, m_l$. We next compute the bitwise XOR of the pad blocks $pad_1, \ldots, pad_l$, with the corresponding plaintext blocks $m_1, \ldots, m_l$, resulting in the ciphertext. The ciphertext consists of the random initialization vector (IV), which we send as c_0, and the results of the XOR operation, which we denote $c_1 = m_1 \oplus pad_1$, $c_2 = m_2 \oplus pad_2, \ldots$.

Let us now define $OFB.E_k^E(m)$, the OFB mode for a given block cipher (E, D). For simplicity, we define $OFB.E_k^E(m)$ for messages m which consist of some number l of n-bit blocks, i.e., $m = m_1 + \cdots + m_l$, where $(\forall i \leq l)|m_i| = n$. Then, $OFB.E_k^E(m)$ is defined as

$$OFB.E_k^E(m_1 + \cdots + m_l) = (c_0 + c_1 + \cdots + c_l) \tag{2.45}$$

where

$$pad_0 \xleftarrow{\$} \{0,1\}^n \tag{2.46}$$

$$pad_i \leftarrow E_k(pad_{i-1}) \tag{2.47}$$

$$c_0 \leftarrow pad_0 \tag{2.48}$$

$$c_i \leftarrow pad_i \oplus m_i \tag{2.49}$$

Offline pad precomputation: Both the OFB and the CTR modes allow both the encryption process and the decryption process to precompute the pad, 'offline' — i.e., before the plaintext and ciphertext, respectively, are available. Offline pad precomputation is possible since the pad does not depend on the plaintext (or ciphertext). This can be important, e.g., when a CPU with limited computation speed needs to support a limited number of 'short bursts', without adding latency. Once the plaintext/ciphertext is available, we only need one XOR operation per block.

Parallelism: The OFB pad is computed sequentially. Unlike the CTR mode, there does not appear to be a way to speed up the computation of the OFB pad using parallelism.

Error localization, correction and integrity: Since the OFB and CTR modes operate as a bit-wise stream cipher, then they ensure 1-bit error localization: a change in any ciphertext bit causes a change to the corresponding decrypted plaintext bit — and only to that bit, i.e., to no other decrypted plaintext bit.

The 1-bit error localization property implies that an *error correction and/or detection code* can be equally effective when applied to the ciphertext (after encryption) or to the plaintext (before encryption). Without localization, a single bit error in the ciphertext could translate to many bit errors in the plaintext. This implies that error correction, and, to lesser degree, detection, should be applied to the ciphertext, as it may be ineffective if applied before encryption.

2.10.7 Encode-then-Encrypt considered harmful and the minimize plaintext redundancy principle

There are two natural ways to apply error correction/detection codes to encrypted data: *Encode-then-Encrypt* and *Encrypt-then-Encode*. *Encode-then-Encrypt* applies error correction/detection to the plaintext and then encrypts the concatenation of the plaintext with the resulting error detecting code (EDC). This allows error detection/correction to work, if the encryption ensures 1-bit error localization, as for the PBR, CTR and OFB modes of operation; in a such case, a single bit flip in the ciphertext causes only a single bit flip in the decrypted plaintext. This motivated the use of OFB or a similar XOR-based stream cipher, allowing application of EDC or ECC (error correcting code) on the plaintext; we refer to this as the *Encode-then-Encrypt* design. We now explain why this design could cause vulnerability (hence 'considered harmful').

Our discussion of Encode-the-Encrypt applies to both EDC and ECC codes; let us focus on ECC codes. Error correction codes have two functions: $encode(\cdot)$ and $decode(\cdot)$; the input domain to *encode*, denoted Dom, may be fixed-length strings (in *block codes*) or variable-length strings (in *convolution codes*). All error correction codes must satisfy the basic correctness property, which is that for every input string $m \in Dom$ holds $m = decode(encode(m))$.

An ECC should ensure *noise correction* property, i.e., it should ensure recovery from some set of possible errors in encoded messages; often, an ECC also allows detection of some additional errors. For example, one classical noise model focuses on bit-flip errors, which are usually referred to as Hamming errors. The *Hamming distance* is a useful measure for categorization of Hamming errors. The Hamming distance $H(x,y)$ between two equal-length binary strings ($|x| = |y|$ and $x, y \in \{0,1\}^*$) is the number of different bits, i.e.,

$$\left(\forall l \in \mathbb{N},\ x, y \in \{0,1\}^l\right)\ H(x,y) \equiv |\{i\ :\ x[i] \neq y[i]\}| \qquad (2.50)$$

We say that an ECC *ensures correction of t_c-bit-flip errors*, namely, corrects errors up to Hamming distance t_c, if for every message $m \in Dom$ and every binary string $y \in \{0,1\}^*$:

$$H(y, code(m)) \leq t_c \Rightarrow m = decode(y) \qquad (2.51)$$

Similarly, an ECC (or EDC) *ensures detection of t_d-bit-flip errors*, or detects errors up to Hamming distance t_d, if for every message $m \in Dom$ and every binary string $y \in \{0,1\}^*$:

$$H(y, code(m)) \leq t_d \Rightarrow (decode(y) \in \{m, \text{FALSE}\}) \qquad (2.52)$$

For example, the *Hamming code* allows correction of a single bit-flip error and detection of two bit-flip errors, i.e., $t_c = 1$ and $t_d = 2$.

The use of ECC and EDC is important to ensure reliable communication over noisy channels. However, applying error correction or detection codes on the plaintext, and relying on perfect bit error localization to allow error detection/ correctness of the ciphertext, is not recommended. One reason is that such codes create structured redundancy in the plaintext, which may *facilitate ciphertext-only attacks (COA)*. Let us give an example.

Example 2.7 (COA on GSM). The A5/1 and A5/2 stream ciphers were the (only) stream ciphers defined as part of the GSM cellular communication standard and were intentionally kept secret (in the vain hope of ensuring security by obscurity); they were published first, informally, by reverse-engineering, in Ref. [106]. Initial attacks, e.g., Ref. [81], against A5/1 seemed to require KPA, and were therefore claimed to be impractical. However, the GSM protocols apply an extensive ECC to the input message before encryption, creating extensive, known relationship between plaintext bits. This redundancy suffices for an efficient and practical COA; see Ref. [31]. As a result of this attack, the use of the (weaker) A5/2 was completely discontinued, and the use of new ciphers was recommended (over using A5/1). However, the GSM protocol still applies Encode-then-Encrypt, providing extensive plaintext redundancy which can facilitate new ciphertext-only attacks.

One may wonder, why would designers prefer to apply error correction to the plaintext rather than to the ciphertext? One motivation may be the hope that this may make cryptanalysis harder, e.g., corrupt some plaintext statistics such as letter frequencies. This may hold for some codes and some (weak) symmetric key cryptosystems. However, the recommended way is to design such defenses explicitly into the cryptosystem and not rely on such fuzzy properties of encoding.

Another motivation may be the hope that applying error correction/detection to the plaintext may provide integrity. Note that due to the perfect bit error localization of OFB, an attacker can easily flip a specific plaintext bit — by flipping the corresponding ciphertext bit. If we applied error detection to the plaintext, then corruption of a single bit will corrupt the entire plaintext. However, since the attacker can flip multiple ciphertext bits, thereby flipping the corresponding plaintext bits, there are cases where the attacker can modify the ciphertext in such a way as to flip specific bits in the plaintext while also 'fixing' the error detection/correction code, to make the message appear correct.

We conclude the following principle.

Principle 10 (Minimize plaintext redundancy). *Plaintext should preferably have minimal redundancy. In particular, plaintext should preferably not contain an ECC or an EDC. To handle errors in transmission and storage, apply an ECC or an EDC to the ciphertext, not to the plaintext. Namely, use* Encrypt-then-Encode *rather than* Encode-then-Encrypt.

Applying error correction to the plaintext is a bad idea — certainly when using stream cipher design such as OFB. This raises the obvious question: can an encryption mode of a block cipher also protect the *integrity* of the decrypted plaintext? Both of the following modes, CFB and CBC, provide a limited defense of integrity — by *ensuring that errors do propagate to an entire block.* Namely, flipping of one or few bits — as part of an attack or due to noise — will result in corruption of at least one block of the decrypted plaintext, which practically ensures detection of the error.

2.10.8 The Cipher Feedback (CFB) mode

We now present the Cipher Feedback (CFB) mode of operation. The CFB mode, like OFB, uses a random first block which is referred to as the *initialization vector* (IV), which becomes the first block of the ciphertext ($c_0 = IV$). Then, iteratively, each ciphertext block c_i is used to generate the following pseudorandom pad block $pad_{i+1} = E_k(c_i)$; note that there is no pad_0 (as c_0 is simply the IV). Finally, the next ciphertext block, c_{i+1}, is computed by bitwise XOR between the corresponding pseudorandom pad block pad_{i+1} and the corresponding plaintext block m_{i+1}.

We define $CFB.E_k^E(m)$, the CFB mode of operation for a given block cipher (E, D), as follows. As for other modes, we simplify by defining $CFB.E_k^E(m)$ for messages m which consist of an integral number l of n-bit blocks, i.e., $m = m_1 + \cdots + m_l$, where $(\forall i \leq l)|m_i| = n$. The ciphertext $CFB.E_k^E(m)$ consists of $l + 1$ blocks $c_0 + c_1 + \cdots + c_l$, defined by:

$$
\begin{aligned}
CFB.E_k^E(m) &\equiv c_0 + c_1 + \cdots + c_l, \text{ where:} \\
c_0 &= IV \xleftarrow{\$} \{0,1\}^n \qquad (2.53) \\
c_i &= m_i \oplus E_k(c_{i-1}) \ \ (\text{ for } i \in \{1, \ldots, l\})
\end{aligned}
$$

Note that the difference between CFB and OFB is in the 'feedback' mechanism, namely, the computation of the pads pad_i (for $i > 1$). In the CFB mode, this is done using the ciphertext rather than the previous pad. See Figure 2.33 (CFB encryption) and Figure 2.34 (CFB decryption).

Optimizing implementations — parallel decryption, but no precomputation: Unlike the OFB mode, the CFB mode of operation does not support offline precomputation of the pad since the pad depends on the ciphertext (of the previous block). Furthermore, the encryption process seems to require sequential calculation of the block cipher since each pad, e.g., pad_i, is computed by applying the block cipher to the previous ciphertext block c_{i-1}. Namely, the encryption process does not seem amenable to parallelization.

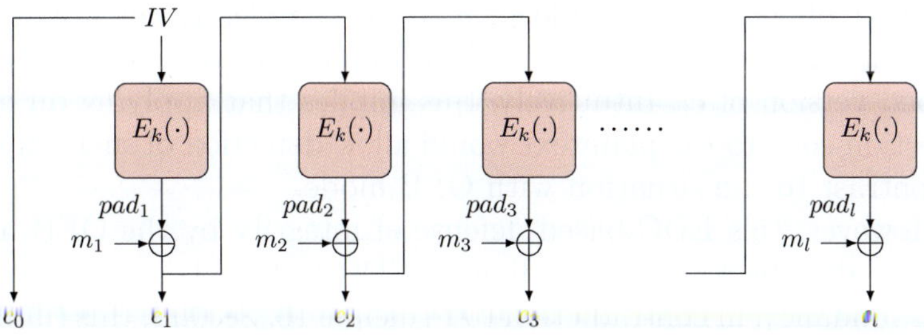

Figure 2.33. Cipher Feedback (CFB) mode of operation encryption.
Source: Adapted from Ref. [268].

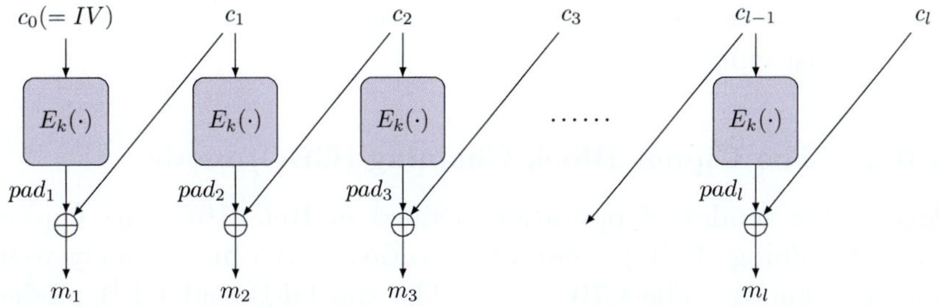

Figure 2.34. Cipher Feedback (CFB) mode of operation decryption.
Source: Adapted from Ref. [268].

One possible optimization is to parallelize the *decryption* operation. Namely, decryption may be performed for all blocks in parallel since the decryption m_i of block i is $m_i = c_i \oplus p_i = c_i \oplus E_k(c_{i-1})$, i.e., can be computed based on the ciphertexts of this block and of the previous block.

Error localization and integrity: Error localization in the CFB mode of operation is not perfect; a single bit error in one ciphertext block completely corrupts the following block of the decrypted plaintext, in addition to corrupting the corresponding bit (in the current block). Namely, the CFB mode ensures $n + 1$-bits error localization.

As we discussed for OFB, this reduction in error localization may be viewed as an advantage in ensuring integrity. Like OFB mode, the CFB mode of operation allows the attacker to flip specific bits in the decrypted plaintext, by flipping corresponding bits in the ciphertext. However, as a result of such bit flipping, say in block i, the decrypted plaintext of the following block, m_{i+1}, is completely corrupted, due to applying the block cipher's 'decryption' function D_k to the bit-flipped version of c_i. Intuitively, this implies that applying an error-detection code to the plaintext would allow detection of such changes, in contrast to the situation with OFB mode.

However, this EDC-based defense of integrity by the OFB mode has two drawbacks. First, adding an EDC to the plaintext increases its redundancy, in contradiction to Principle 10. Second, this (limited) integrity protection does not apply when the bit flipping is done to the last ciphertext block c_l.

We next present the CBC mode, which provides a similar-yet-different defense for integrity. The CBC defense has similar properties to that of CFB, and avoids the limitation of the CFB integrity to the non-last ciphertext block.

2.10.9 The Cipher Block Chaining (CBC) mode

Among the modes of operation defined in Ref. [167], the Cipher Block Chaining (CBC) mode of operation is the most widely used and well known. The CBC mode, like the OFB and CFB modes, uses a random initialization vector (IV) as the first block of the ciphertext, $c_0 \xleftarrow{\$} \{0,1\}^n$. However, in contrast to OFB and CFB, to encrypt the ith plaintext block m_i, CBC XORes m_i with the previous *ciphertext* block c_{i-1}, and *then* applies the block cipher. Namely, $c_i = E_k(c_{i-1} \oplus m_i)$. We illustrate CBC encryption in Figure 2.35 and CBC decryption in Figure 2.36.

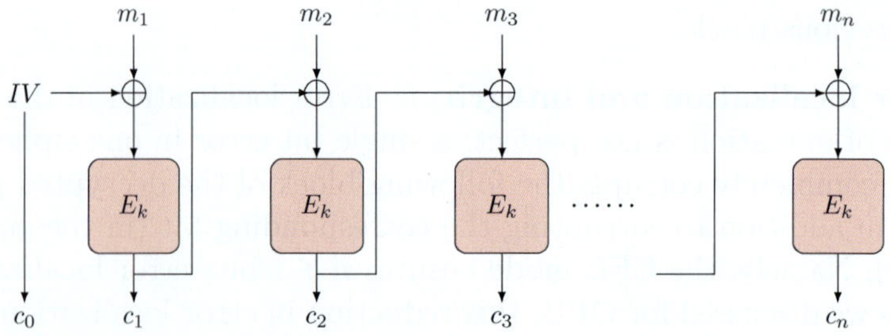

Figure 2.35. Cipher Block Chaining (CBC) mode encryption.
Source: Adapted from Ref. [268].

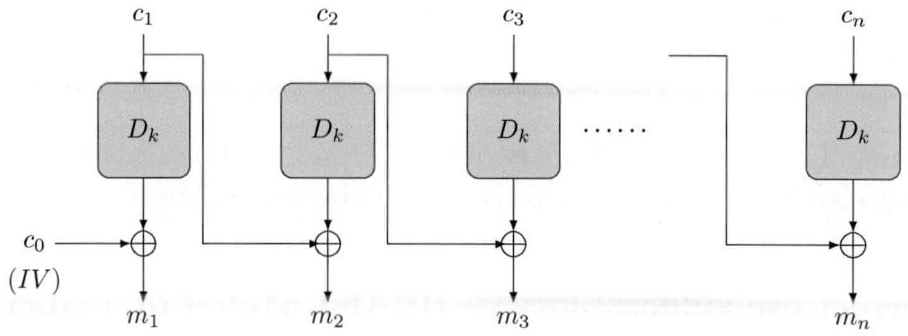

Figure 2.36. Cipher Block Chaining (CBC) mode decryption.

Source: Adapted from Ref. [268].

More precisely, let (E, D) be a block cipher with l bits blocks, and let $m = m_1 +\!\!+ \cdots +\!\!+ m_n$ be a message (broken into n blocks, each containing l-bits). The CBC encryption of m using key k and an (l-bits) initialization vector IV, selected randomly ($IV \stackrel{\$}{\leftarrow} \{0,1\}^l$), is defined as:

$$CBC.E_k^E(m_1 +\!\!+ \cdots +\!\!+ m_l; IV) = (IV +\!\!+ c_1 +\!\!+ \cdots +\!\!+ c_l) \tag{2.54}$$

where:

$$c_0 \leftarrow IV \tag{2.55}$$

$$(\forall i \in \{1, \ldots, l\})\ c_i \leftarrow E_k\left(c_{i-1} \oplus m_i\right) \tag{2.56}$$

We may also simply write the CBC encryption of m as $CBC.E_k^E(m_1 +\!\!+ \cdots +\!\!+ m_l)$, i.e., omitting the IV, with the understanding that the encryption is using a uniformly chosen random l-bits string as the IV, which is also output as the first block c_0 of $CBC.E_k^E(m_1 +\!\!+ \cdots +\!\!+ m_l)$.

We leave it to the reader to write the corresponding equations for CBC decryption (illustrated in Figure 2.36). The reader should also find it easy to confirm that the CBC mode, like the CFB mode, allows parallel decryption but not offline pad precomputation or parallel encryption.

The CBC mode, like the other modes (except ECB), ensures IND-CPA, i.e., security against CPA, provided that the underlying block cipher is secure, i.e., ensures indistinguishability. However, like all of the other modes of operation we present in this chapter, the CBC mode is vulnerable to CCA.

Exercise 2.16. Demonstrate that *CBC* mode does ***not*** ensure security against CCA attacks, i.e., is not IND-CCA.

Hint: The direct solution is quite similar to that of the first part of Exercise 2.15. Another way is to use the second part. □

Incorrect use vulnerability — BEAST exploit of predictable IV: While CBC mode ensures IND-CPA, this is only true if CBC is used correctly; in particular, the IV (also used as c_0) must be random. The SSL protocol, as well as version 1.0 of TLS, uses CBC encryption in the following incorrect way. They select the IV randomly only for the first message $m[0]$ in a connection; for subsequent messages, say $m[i]$, the IV is simply the last ciphertext block of the previous message. This creates a vulnerability exploited, e.g., by the BEAST attack. For details, see Section 7.2.4 and Exercise 7.5, or Refs. [30, 165].

Error propagation and integrity: Any change in the CBC ciphertext, even of one bit, results in unpredictable output from the block cipher's 'decryption' operation, and hence unpredictable decryption, of the corresponding block. Namely, flipping a bit in the ciphertext block i 'corrupts' block i of the decrypted plaintext rather than flipping the corresponding bit in the decrypted plaintext block, as it did in the OFB and CFB modes.

However, the flipping of a bit in the ciphertext block c_{i-1}, without change to block c_i, results in the flipping of the corresponding bit in the ith decrypted plaintext block. Namely, bit-flipping is still possible in CBC, it is just a bit different — and in order to flip a bit in the decrypted-plaintext block i, the adversary has to flip the corresponding bit in the *previous* block $(i-1)$, which results in corruption of the decryption of block $i-1$. Indeed, this kind of tampering is used in several attacks on systems deploying CBC, such as the Poodle attack [362], which we discuss in Section 7.2.3. Note also that bit flipping in the first decrypted-plaintext block only requires flipping of the corresponding IV block — and hence does not corrupt any plaintext block.

2.10.10 Ensuring CCA security

We already observed, in Exercise 2.15, that any cryptosystem (and mode) that ensures error localization cannot be IND-CCA secure. This implies that none of the modes we discussed is IND-CCA secure.

In fact, these schemes are not even proven secure for the much weaker — and quite common — case where the attacker does not receive the decrypted plaintext but only an indication of whether the plaintext was 'valid' or not, often facilitated by plaintext redundancy due to padding and/or to error detection/correction schemes applied to the plaintext, motivating the minimization of plaintext redundancy, as per Principle 10.

One intuitive defense is to avoid giving any feedback on invalid-plaintext failures. However, this is harder than it may seem. In particular, many systems respond with different messages, and often after different delays, to messages which are incorrectly padded, messages which fail error detection/correction, messages which are otherwise non-conformant with the protocol and messages which conform with the protocol. By observing if a response is sent, which response is sent, and the timing of the response, an attacker may obtain feedback on the attack. Such unintentional indications are referred to as *side channels*; for example, when the feedback is based on the time the response is sent, this is a *timing side channel.* We discuss in the following attacks exploiting such indications of padding errors (Section 2.11); we also discuss side channel attacks in the later chapters, in particular, see the Bleichenbacher attack against padded RSA in Section 6.5.7.

A better approach may be to *prevent response to chosen ciphertext queries*, **without** decrypting them; this prevents chosen-ciphertext attacks, not only attacks exploiting (only) feedback on whether plaintext is valid or not. One simple way to prevent response to chosen ciphertext queries is to *authenticate the ciphertext*, typically by appending to the ciphertext an *authentication tag*, which allows secure detection of any modification in the ciphertext. Several of the more modern, widely used modes of operation, e.g., GCM [168, 426], combine authentication of the ciphertext with encryption of the plaintext, thereby protecting against chosen-ciphertext attacks. Authentication is the subject of Chapter 4.

2.11 Padding schemes and the padding oracle attack model

All modes of operation are defined for input whose length is an integral number l of blocks. In many applications, the input is not always an integral number of blocks; instead, the input is a string containing an arbitrary number of bits or, more commonly, of bytes; we focus on this common case, where the input always consists of whole bytes. In such cases, we need to apply a *padding scheme*.

Standard padding schemes: The operation of padding schemes is quite simple. Before encryption, the plaintext is *padded* to an integral number of blocks, by appending a *pad* string to the message, which is removed (*unpadded*) after decryption. The length of the pad is between one byte and a whole block (l bytes) and it is chosen to ensure that the padded message (message plus pad) fits in an integral number of blocks.

Padding schemes mainly differ in the *contents* of the pad string and in the validation of the pad after decryption. Some of the commonly used padding schemes applied to plaintext before encryption by a symmetric key cryptosystem include the following:

X9.23/SSL padding: In *X9.23 padding* [17], the last byte of the pad contains the length of the pad in bytes (including this last byte); the other bytes of the pad may contain arbitrary values and are ignored. The length of the pad is restricted to the block length l; hence, the value of the last byte must be a number between one and l. If the results of decryption does not end with a byte whose value is between one and l, then the ciphertext is considered to have invalid padding. SSL padding, used by the SSL protocol (Chapter 7), is similar, except that the last byte contains the pad length minus one, allowing the last byte to have values from zero (for a pad consisting only of this byte) till $l - 1$ (for a pad consisting of an entire block, i.e., l bytes, including the last byte, which contains the pad length minus one).

PKCS #7, PKCS #5 and TLS padding: In CMS padding [255], also referred to as PKCS #7 padding [281], all pad bytes should contain the length of the pad. TLS padding, used by the TLS protocol (Chapter 7), is similar, except that all bytes should contain the length of the pad minus one. PKCS #5 padding has the last byte contain the length of the pad, and the other pad bytes contain zero (0×00). These padding schemes are *deterministic*, i.e., all of their bytes must have specific values.

With all of these padding schemes, the decrypted plaintext should end with a valid pad, which should be (efficiently) verified and removed by the recipient. We say that ciphertext c has *invalid pad*, and expect the protocol to return a padding error, if the decrypted plaintext has invalid pad.

Consider an l-bytes block m, or a multi-block message whose last l-bytes block is m. Let $m[i]$, for $i = 1, \ldots, l$, denote the ith most-significant byte of m. Block m has *valid X9.23 padding* if $m[l] < l$. For example, for blocks of $l = 16$ bytes, the four most-significant bits of the last byte must be all zeroes, i.e., the last byte must be of the form $0x0\phi$ in hexadecimal notation. In this case, ϕ can be any hexadecimal digit, from 0 to F, representing the corresponding four bits in binary.

Similarly, plaintext block m has *valid PKCS #7 padding* if the value of the last byte of m is also the value of preceding x bytes of m, i.e., if the last x bytes of m contain the same value x, which is considered the pad. These x bytes (all containing x) are removed in the *unpad* operation, performed after decryption. Let l denote the length of m (i.e., $l \equiv |m|$), and let x denote the value of the last byte of m, i.e., $x \equiv m[l]$. Then, the block m has valid PKCS #7 padding if $(\forall i \text{ s.t. } l - x \leq i \leq l)\ m[i] = x$.

The reader may wonder why we bother describing these simple and very similar schemes. The reason is that *padding error indications* can be exploited by attackers. The *padding-error oracle attack model* allows the attacker to provide one or more ciphertexts and receive the padding error indicator corresponding to each ciphertext. Note that the padding oracle attack model is much weaker than the chosen-ciphertext attack (CCA), where the attacker receives the *decryption* of each of the ciphertexts provided by the attacker.

In this section, we describe the *padding-error oracle attack model* and present a simple padding oracle attack against the ECB and CBC modes of operation using X9.23 padding, extended in Exercise 2.17 to an attack against CBC mode of operation using PKCS #7 padding. In Chapter 7, we discuss additional padding oracle attacks against symmetric key cryptosystem based on block ciphers, specifically, exploiting the SSL padding, used by SSL, and exploiting the TLS padding, used by TLS. In Chapter 6, we present a padding-error oracle attack against the RSA PKCs, when implemented using the PKCS #1 version 1.5 padding scheme.

Note that all padding schemes introduce a significant amount of *plaintext redundancy*, violating Principle 10. Therefore, in addition to the padding oracle attacks, the redundancy also facilitates exhaustive search ciphertext-only attack (COA). This is especially true for CMS/PKCS #7 padding, TLS padding and PKCS #5 padding, which are completely deterministic, i.e., all pad bytes are determined by the pad length. It is unlikely for such sequences to occur randomly in non-padded messages; if the plaintext is random, such a sequence of l bytes occurs with the small probability of $2^{-8 \cdot l}$. This may have motivated allowing these bytes to have arbitrary values as in SSL padding and X9.17 padding; however, these schemes often make padding-error oracle attacks easier. Typically, the keys are sufficiently long to make exhaustive search impractical, and a padding-error oracle attack is usually much more practical.

The padding-error oracle attack model: In many systems, an attacker may be able to detect when a message with invalid padding is received, by observing an explicit 'invalid pad' error message, or otherwise, e.g., by detecting the different behavior of the recipient due to invalid pad, such as different timing of a response; the later is a special case of a *timing side channel.* In any case, we refer to this ability to detect the validity of the padding of the (decrypted) plaintext, for a given ciphertext, as a *padding oracle.*

We illustrate the basic padding-error oracle attack model in Figure 2.37; this is basically a COA with the addition of the padding oracle capability. Note that, following Kerckhoffs's principle (Principle 2), we assume that the attacker knows the details of the padding scheme in use, as well as other aspects of the system, e.g., the encryption algorithm.

Side-channel attacks: In the attack models we discussed in Section 1.1, the adversary either received the entire output of an operation of the cryptosystem (e.g., decryption of chosen ciphertext,

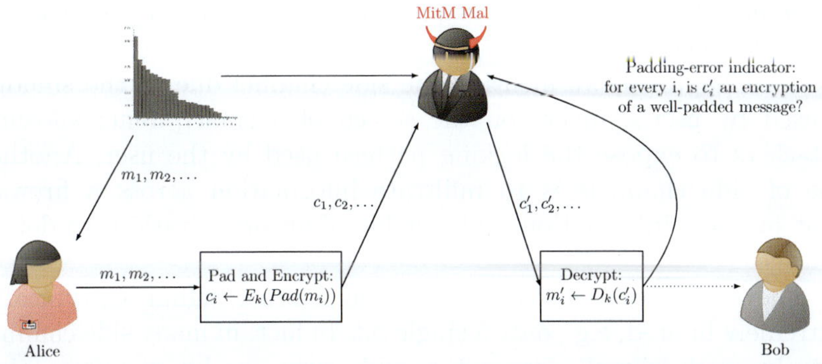

Figure 2.37. The padding-error oracle attack model. Note that the ciphertexts $c'_1, c'_2, \ldots$ provided by the attacker to the oracle do not necessarily correspond to the eavesdropped ciphertexts $c_1, c_2, \ldots$; typically, the attacker will provide many more ciphertexts than the eavesdropped ciphertexts.

in the chosen-ciphertext attack) or did not receive any indication regarding the operation or its output. For example, in the chosen-plaintext attack model (CPA), the attacker receives the encryption of the chosen plaintext; other information is excluded, e.g., no information is provided regarding the decryption of ciphertexts.

In contrast, the padding-error oracle attack provides only partial indication regarding the output of the decryption operation, specifically, the bit indicating if the resulting plaintext was correctly padded or not. This information is not an output of an operation of the cryptosystem.

Attacks of this kind, where the attacker uses information which is not an intentional output of the cryptosystem, are called *side channel attacks*. In a side channel attack, the attacker receives some limited information regarding the cryptographic operation (often, decryption) and its outcome. Often, side channel attacks exploit indications which were not considered, or not sufficiently considered, when evaluating the security of the system. Such a channel is due to some 'side-effect' of the operation of the system.

The padding-error oracle attack is a specific side channel attack, which exploits the *error indication* side channel. Other side channels, exploited in different attacks, include the timing of events, power consumption, electromagnetic radiation, audio signals, and more.

Some side channels may be quite surprising, and they are used to attack both cryptographic and non-cryptographic systems. For example, in Chapter 9, we mention the side channel due to the smudge caused by user's fingers on the screen of a smartphone, allowing attackers to expose the locking pattern used by the user. Another use of side channels is to infiltrate information across a firewall that inspects information sent outside of an organization, to detect leakage.

The information leaked in each side channel 'signal' is, typically, extremely limited, e.g., only a single bit. In fact, in many side channel attacks, each 'signal' does not provide even one bit of information since the side channel signal is obscured by random noise. In spite of that, there have been many successful side channel attacks on cryptographic systems and other security systems.

Padding oracle attacks on X.23: Let us present simple padding oracle attacks against the ECB and CBC modes of operation, when using X9.23 padding. Assume, for example, that we use blocks of 16 bytes. Hence, the length of the pad is between 1 and 16, and the encoded value in the last byte should be $0x0\phi$ in hexadecimal notation (where ϕ is one hexadecimal digit). Typical encryption schemes use shorter blocks (8 bytes for DES and 12 bytes for AES), which requires a tiny change in the attack and slightly increases the exposure due to the attack.

Padding-Oracle attack on X9.23 padding using ECB mode. Consider plaintext message $m = m_1 + \cdots + m_n$, containing $n-1$ full blocks and one empty or non-full block m_n. In ECB mode, each non-final plaintext block m_i (i.e., $i < n$) is encrypted directly as $c_i = E_k(m_i)$. The final plaintext block m_n is padded before encryption, i.e., encrypted as $c_n = E_k(pad(m_n))$, where $pad(\cdot)$ is the X9.23 padding function.

The attack can be applied to any block of the ciphertext, *except* the last block; let us focus on some block c_i where $i < n$. Instead of sending c_i as an intermediate block of a longer ciphertext message, the attacker sends c_i as if it is the *last* block of a ciphertext message, e.g., the ciphertext consist only of this single block c_i. If the protocol expects the ciphertext to have at least (or exactly) some number l of blocks, the attacker can prepend arbitrary $l-1$ blocks before c_i, e.g., $l-1$ blocks containing c_i, or any other values. The attack only requires c_i to be the last block of the ciphertext.

Following the padding-error oracle attack model, the attacker receives an indication whether the decryption of c_i, i.e., $m_i = D_k(c_i)$, has valid padding or has invalid padding. If m_i has valid padding, then the value of its last byte must be less than the block length, $l = 16$; namely, the last byte of m must be of the form $0x0\phi$ (in hexadecimal notation), i.e., its four most significant bits must be zeros. This is an exposure of (limited) information about these four bits of the plaintext, i.e., an indication if these four bits are all zeros or not. A limited exposure — but still, definitely an exposure.

Padding-Oracle attack on X9.23 padding using CBC mode. This attack, like the one on ECB mode, is applicable to every non-last ciphertext block c_i. Again, the basic idea is to send c_i as the *last* block of ciphertext messages to the recipient and learn information about the value of few bits of plaintext m_i, using the response of the padding oracle.

Specifically, let $m_i[j]$ denote the jth *bit* of m_i. Let l denote the number of bits in each block, i.e., $m_i = m_i[1] + \cdots + m_i[l]$. We show how, when using X9.23 padding, the attack finds the four plaintext bits $m_i[j]$ for $j = l-7, l-6, l-5$ and $l-4$. This requires only access to c_i and to the padding oracle for CBC mode. Exercise 2.17 extends the attack to PKCS #7 padding, where the attack finds the entire last byte of m_i.

Recall that in CBC mode, the ciphertext block c_i is computed as $c_i = E_k(c_{i-1} \oplus m_i)$. The attacker now sends ciphertext c' containing i blocks, where $c'_i = c_i$, and using different previous ciphertext blocks c'_{i-1}. The value of c'_{i-1} may be different from the value of c_{i-1}, the original previous ciphertext block. (The other blocks of c' do not have any impact on the attack and can even be eliminated, but to simplify notations, assume c' contains at least i blocks.)

Let m'_i denote the last decrypted plaintext block; since we use CBC, it is computed as follows:

$$m'_i = D_k(c_i) \oplus c'_{i-1} = (m_i \oplus c_{i-1}) \oplus c'_{i-1} \tag{2.57}$$

The attacker has (only) access to the padding oracle, which indicates if the last block of the decrypted message, m'_i, has correct padding or not. This depends only on the value of the last byte of m'_i; correct padding requires that last byte of m'_i be of the form $0x0\phi$, i.e., its four most significant bits should be all zeros. In other words, $m'_i[l-7:l-4] = 0000$ (in binary).

Recall that $m'_i = D_k(c_i) \oplus c'_{i-1}$; therefore, the attacker can try the 16 different values of 4 most significant bits of the last byte of c'_{i-1}, until it finds a value c'_{i-1} that has correct padding, i.e., resulting in plaintext m'_i whose last byte is of the form $0x0\phi$, i.e., $m'_i[l-7:l-4] = 0000$. Hence, from Equation (2.57), we have:

$$m_i[l-7:l-4] = c_{i-1}[l-7:l-4] \oplus c'_{i-1}[l-7:l-4] \qquad (2.58)$$

The reader may have noted that the attack exploits the fact that X9.23 padding limits the pad length to one block. PKCS #7 padding does not make this restriction, which may seem to make it secure against such padding oracle attack. However, in fact, Exercise 2.17 extends the attack for the case of PKCS #7 padding. The extended attack requires more padding-oracle queries, but is also more rewarding, as it allows *recovery of the entire plaintext.*

Exercise 2.17. Present a padding attack, assuming the availability of a padding oracle and the use PKCS #7 padding. The attack should find the *entire* non-last plaintext block m_i, given only the corresponding ciphertext block c_i and previous ciphertext block c_{i-1}, and access to the padding oracle.

Hint: A random plaintext block would have valid padding if its last byte contains $0x00$, i.e., the entire pad is this single last byte; other random plaintext blocks are unlikely to have valid padding (why?). Use this to find the last byte of m_i. Once this byte is found, we repeat a similar logic to find the preceding byte of m_i, using the fact that a valid random plaintext whose last byte contains $0x01$, would also have $0x01$ in the preceding byte. We then proceed similarly to find all plaintext bytes of m_i. □

The reader also find the solution to this exercise by reading Ref. [467]. Additional padding oracle attacks are presented for RSA in Section 6.5.7 and for TLS in Section 7.2.3.

2.12 Vulnerability study: The WEP standard

We conclude this chapter by discussing a case study: vulnerabilities of the WEP protocol [130]. WEP stands for *Wired Equivalency Privacy*;

it was developed as part of the IEEE 802.11b standard, to provide some protection of data over wireless local area networks (also known as WiFi networks). As the name implies, the original goals aimed at a limited level of privacy (meaning confidentiality), which was deemed 'equivalent' to the (physically limited) security offered by a wired connection.

The critical vulnerabilities presented here were discovered long ago, mostly in Ref. [94], relatively soon after the standard was published, yet, products and networks supporting WEP still exist. This is an example of the fact that once a standard is published and adopted, it is often very difficult to fix security. Hence, it is important to carefully evaluate security in advance, in an open process that encourages researchers to find vulnerabilities, and, where possible, with proofs of security. To address these vulnerabilities, WEP was replaced with a new standard, the *Wi-Fi Protected AccessWPA (Wi-Fi Protected Access)* (WPA), which so far has three versions (WPA1, WPA2, WPA3). Vulnerabilities were also found in these, e.g., see Refs. [465, 466], but these are more subtle and harder to exploit.

Confidentiality in WEP is protected using the RC4 stream cipher. RC4 is a widely deployed, efficient stream cipher; its design was also kept initially secret but was unofficially disclosed [487]. Later, RC4 was adopted by several standards, including the WEP and *WPA* wireless-LAN standards, as well as by TLS (Chapter 7). In WEP, RC4 is normally used with a very short key of 40 bits long; this short key size was chosen intentionally, due to restrictions existing at that time on export of products providing encryption with longer keys. Many WEP implementations also support longer, 104-bit keys for RC4. There are known attacks showing that even with 104-bit keys, RC4 may still be vulnerable, see Section 7.2.5 and Refs. [13,295,346]. However, for now, let us discuss weaknesses which are more related to *how* WEP is using RC4, than to weaknesses of RC4 itself.

WEP assumes a symmetric key between the mobile device and an *access point*; this symmetric key is used as the key (seed) for the RC4 cipher. WEP networks share the same key with all mobiles; this means that *each device which has the key can eavesdrop on all communication*; this vulnerability exists also for the common use of more advanced WiFi security protocols, such as WPA (versions 1–3). We discuss specific additional vulnerabilities which are specific to

WEP and make it insecure even against an attacker that is not given the key to connect to the network.

The WEP PRG is initiated with a 24-bit per-packet random *initialization vector (IV)*. We use $RC4_{IV,k}$ to denote the string output by RC4 when initialized using a given (IV, k) pair. More specifically, we use $RC4_{IV,k}[l]$ to denote the first l bits in $RC4_{IV,k}$, i.e., in the output by RC4 when initialized using given IV, k pair.

WEP packets use the *CRC-32* error detection code (EDC), computed over the plaintext message m. CRC-32 [301] is one of the standard variants of the *CRC cyclic redundancy check* codes. CRC codes are popular error detection codes (EDC); they are simple to implement and efficiently detect errors in data, caused by random noise corruptions. Namely, if m' is the result of such random corruption of m, then, with high probability, m and m' will have different CRC codes, i.e., $\text{CRC}(m) \neq \text{CRC}(m')$, allowing detection of the corruption by comparing their CRC codes. Note that, for simplicity, and since we do not discuss other CRC codes, we use $\text{CRC}(m)$ to denote the CRC-32 code computed over message m.

CRC codes, and in particular CRC-32, are *linear*, in the sense that for any two strings $m, m' \in \{0,1\}^*$ of equal length ($|m| = |m'|$), the following holds:

$$\text{CRC}(m \oplus m') = \text{CRC}(m) \oplus \text{CRC}(m') \text{ (if } |m| = |m'|) \tag{2.59}$$

WEP uses CRC as follows. To send a message m using secret key k, WEP implementations select a random 24-bit IV and transmit the IV together with $WEP_k(m, IV)$, defined as:

$$WEP_k(m, IV) \equiv RC4_{IV,k}[32 + |m|] \oplus (m + \text{CRC}(m)) \tag{2.60}$$

The length of the WEP transmission is, therefore, the length of the message m, plus 56 bits: 24 bits for the IV and 32 bits for the CRC-32 code.

CRC-then-XOR does not ensure integrity: CRC-32 is a quite good EDC. By encrypting the output of CRC-32, specifically by XORing it with the pseudorandom pad generated by RC4, the WEP designers hoped to protect message integrity, i.e., to not only detect random, unintentional corruptions but also prevent intentional modification or forgery of messages.

However, error-detection codes are designed to detect random, unintontional, corruptions; i.e., for reliability, not for security. In particular, it is easy to find a *collision* for CRC-32, i.e., messages m and m' such that $m \neq m'$ yet $\text{CRC}(m) = \text{CRC}(m')$. Furthermore, we show in the following how the linearity of the CRC (Equation (2.59)) allows an attacker to change the message m sent in a WEP packet, by flipping any desired bits and appropriately adjusting the CRC field.

Specifically, let Δ represent the string of length $|m|$ containing 1 for bit locations that the attacker wishes to flip. Having eavesdropped and obtained $WEP_k(m, IV)$, the attacker can compute a *valid* $WEP_k(m \oplus \Delta, IV)$ as follows:

$$
\begin{aligned}
&WEP_k(m \oplus \Delta, IV) \\
&\quad = RC4_{IV,k}\left[32 + |m \oplus \Delta|\right] \oplus ([m \oplus \Delta] + \text{CRC}(m \oplus \Delta)) \\
&\quad = RC4_{IV,k}\left[32 + |m|\right] \oplus ([m \oplus \Delta] + [\text{CRC}(m) \oplus \text{CRC}(\Delta)]) \\
&\quad = RC4_{IV,k}\left[32 + |m|\right] \oplus (m + \text{CRC}(m)) \oplus (\Delta + \text{CRC}(\Delta)) \\
&\quad = WEP_k(m, IV) \oplus (\Delta + \text{CRC}(\Delta))
\end{aligned}
$$

We conclude that the CRC mechanism, XOR-encrypted, *does not provide any meaningful integrity protection.* Since WEP is using XOR encryption, using the RC4 stream cipher, we see that an attacker can easily flip bits in a WEP message, and yet this message would be properly received, i.e., without detection of the bit-flipping.

WEP confidentiality vulnerability due to WEP authentication: We have just seen that WEP failed to provide integrity; however, as we now show, *WEP also fails to ensure confidentiality.* Interestingly, the most devastating vulnerability, which is the one we show, takes advantage of WEP's *shared-key authentication* mode. In fact, this specific attack will not work when WEP uses a mode called *open-system authentication*, which simply means that there is no authentication; this mode is therefore not vulnerable to the specific attack we show. However, note that also when using open-system authentication, i.e., giving up on authentication, WEP is still vulnerable to other cryptanalysis attacks exploiting RC4 weaknesses, e.g., see Ref. [346].

However, we focus on the vulnerability of WEP when using the *shared-key authentication* mode. The authentication in this mode works very simply: the access point sends a random challenge R, and the mobile sends back $\text{WEP}_k(R, IV)$, i.e., a proper WEP packet containing the 'message' R.

First, note that this authentication mechanism provides a trivial way for the attacker to obtain pairs of known plaintext and the corresponding ciphertext ('cribs'), allowing the attacker to deploy a known-plaintext attack (KPA) against the cipher. Of course, encryption systems *should* be protected against KPAs; however, following the *conservative design principle* (Principle 3), system designers should try to make it difficult for attackers to obtain such pairs, allowing the attacker to use a KPA against the cipher. In the common, standard case of 40-bit WEP implementations, such a pair ('crib') is deadly — an attacker can now do a exhaustive search and find the key.

Even when using longer keys (104 bits), the shared-key authentication exposes WEP to a simple cryptanalysis attack. Specifically, since R is known, the attacker learns $RC4_{IV,k}$ for a given, random IV. Since the length of the IV is only 24 bits, it is feasible to obtain a collection of most IV values and the corresponding $RC4_{IV,k}$ pads, allowing decryption of most messages.

As a result of these concerns, most WEP systems use only open-system authentication mode, i.e., do not provide any authentication.

2.13 Encryption: final words

Confidentiality, as provided by encryption, is the oldest goal of cryptography and is critical to cybersecurity. Encryption has been studied for millennia, but for many years, the design of cryptosystems was kept secret, in the hope of improving security. More recently, however, Kerckhoffs's principle (Principle 2) has been widely adopted, allowing cryptography to be widely studied, improved and deployed.

Cryptography was further revolutionized by the introduction of precise definitions and proofs of security by reduction, based on the theory of complexity. In particular, modern study of applied cryptography makes extensive use of provable security, especially *computational security*, i.e., ensuring security properties with high probability, against efficient adversaries. We have seen a small taste of such definitions and proofs in this chapter.

In this chapter, we focused mostly on symmetric key cryptosystems; we discuss RSA and other public key cryptosystems (PKCs) in Chapter 6. We have also introduced the important concepts of pseudorandomness and indistinguishability tests, and introduced important related cryptographic schemes, including pseudorandom generators, PRFs, PRPs and block ciphers.

2.14 Lab: Ransomware and Encryption

Lab 2 (Ransomware and Encryption). *In this lab, we explore the* abuse *of cryptography by ransomware. Ransomware encrypts the user files and requires the user to pay 'ransom', with the promise of sending back the decryption key or program.*

The labs and installation instructions are available from https://github.com/CyberSec-labs/labs; see more details in the preface.

The lab has three parts:

1. In this part, you are given a ransomware program, *R1.py*, and your task is to reverse-engineer and break it, i.e., decrypt the files without paying ransom. You will be able to do it since *R1.py* is a simple Python program *using a symmetric key cryptosystem*, specifically, the AES block cipher in CBC mode; see Section 2.8.

   When run, the ransomware *R1.py* will take a file path as an input. It will then encrypt the data within that file and output a new file, {*file path*}*.Token*, containing a token to be sent with the ransom payment, and an encrypted version of the file, {*file path*}*.encrypted*. The token is needed since *R1.py* selects a different random shared key to encrypt each file, e.g., encrypting *example.txt* into *example.txt.encrypted*. The attacker uses *example.txt.Token* to find the decryption key.

   Input: The 'weak ransomware program', given conveniently (and unrealistically) as a Python script, *R1.py*; the encrypted file, *Solution_1.txt.encrypted*; and the token, *Solution_1.txt.Token*. You are also given a decryption file template, *D1.py*, for you to fill in with the necessary code.

Goal: Reverse-engineer *R1.py* and then, using the token *Solution_1.txt.Token*, recover the original (decrypted) file, *Solution_1.txt*.

Submission: The recovered *Solution_1.txt* file and your program, *D1.py*. Your program may be based on the template version of this file.

Note: Before encryption, the plaintext (*Solution_1.txt*) was *padded* so that its length would be a multiple number of 'blocks'. The padding has to be removed after applying the block-cipher's decryption function.

2. To try and prevent reverse-engineering, *obfuscation* can be used to make it harder to understand what is happening in the program. If someone cannot understand the steps taken or the order in which they were taken, they will not be able to trace them back in order to undo them. In this part, the ransomware program *R2.py* has been obfuscated to make it more difficult to find the key and recover the original file.

   Using *R2.py*, *Solution_2.txt.Token*, *D2.py* and *Solution_2.txt.encrypted*, your task is once again to reverse-engineer the ransomware program *R2.py* and recover the contents of *Solution_2.txt*, which you will submit along with *D2.py*.

3. In this part, the ransomware program *R3.py* uses a public key cryptosystem rather than using a symmetric key cryptosystem. Therefore, the code of *R3.py* contains only the public key and does not allow you to find the private key necessary for decryption. However, you will be able to decrypt the encrypted files since the ransomware, insecurely, uses a weak PRG. Specifically, *R3.py* uses a PRG with a seed of only 16 bits, making it feasible to exhaustively search the seed values. *R3.ply* uses this weak PRG both to generate the key pair for the public key cryptosystem and to generate a new key for the symmetric key cryptosystem whenever encrypting a file. This allows you two ways to decrypt files by finding either the private decryption key (allowing decryption of all files) or the symmetric key used to decrypt a particular file.

   Using *R3.py*, *Solution_3.txt.Token*, *D3.py* and *Solution_3.txt.encrypted*, use either method to recover the contents of

Solution_3.txt, which you will submit along with *D3.py*. Explain your choice of attack method.

2.15 Additional exercises

Exercise 2.18. Table 2.4 shows eight ciphertexts, all using one of the four simple substitution ciphers identified in the top four rows. Decipher the ciphertexts, measuring the time it took you to decipher each of them. Fill in the blanks in the table: the plaintexts, the time it took you to decipher each message, and the ciphers and key (when relevant). Did the knowledge of the cipher significantly ease the cryptanalysis process? Did the key?

Exercise 2.19. ConCrypt Inc. announces a new symmetric key cryptosystem, CES. ConCrypt announces that CES can use keys from 256-bits to 512-bits and is therefore much more secure than AES; furthermore, their announcement says that ConCrypt is 'the first practical cipher to be secure against computationally-unbounded attackers'. ConCrypt is also five times faster than AES. Can you evaluate the correctness of any or all of these claims? How? Would you recommend to use ConCrypt to specific (or all) applications?

Table 2.4. Ciphertexts for Exercise 2.18. All plaintexts are pairs of two simple five to six letter words. The four upper examples have the cipher spelled out, the four lower examples hide it ('obscurity'). It does not make them secure, but decryption may take a bit longer.

Identifier	Cipher	Ciphertext	Plaintext and Key	Time
A	Caesar	JUHDW SDUWB		
B	AzBy	ILFMW GZYOV		
C	ROT13	NYBAR NTNVA		
D	Keyed Caesar	XRORT SQUIQH		
E		BLFMT OLEVI		
F		LGTIE JXKYY		
E		FZNEG UBHFR		
F		EUHDN UXOHV		

Exercise 2.20. Alice is communicating using the GSM cellular standard, which encrypts all calls between her phone and the access tower. Identify the attacker model corresponding to each of the following cryptanalysis attack scenarios, against communication between Alice and Bob:

1. Assume that Alice and the tower use a different shared key for each call and that Eve knows that specific, known message is sent from Bob to Alice at given times.
2. Assume that Alice and the tower use a different shared key for each call. The attacker does not know any of the messages sent between Alice and Bob.
3. Assume all calls are encrypted using a (fixed) secret key k_A shared between Alice's phone and the tower and that Eve knows that specific, known control messages are sent, encrypted, at given times.

Exercise 2.21. Consider use of AES with key length of 256 bits and block length of 128 bit, for two different 128-bit messages, A and B (i.e., one block each). Compute, approximate or bound (the best you can), the probability that the encryption of A will be identical to the encryption of B, in each of the following scenarios:

1. Both messages are encrypted with the same randomly chosen key, using ECB mode.
2. Each message is encrypted with a key chosen randomly and independently, using ECB mode.
3. Both messages are encrypted with the same randomly chosen key, using CBC mode.
4. Each message is encrypted with a key chosen randomly and independently, using CBC mode.
5. The messages are *identical* ($A = B$) and encrypted using the same key and using CBC mode.
6. The messages are *identical* ($A = B$) and are encrypted using two randomly and independently chosen keys.

Exercise 2.22. Present a very efficient CPA attack on the mono-alphabetic substitution cipher for the Latin alphabet, which allows complete recovery of arbitrary messages, using the encryption of a single, preferably short, plaintext string.

Exercise 2.23 (PRG constructions). Let $G : \{0,1\}^n \to \{0,1\}^{n+1}$ be a secure PRG. Is G', as defined in each of the following sections, a secure PRG? Prove.

1. $G'(s) = G(s^R)$, where s^R means the reverse of s.
2. $G'(s) = G(s \oplus G(s)_{1\ldots n})$, where $G(s)_{1\ldots n}$ are the n most-significant bits of $G(s)$.
3. $G'(r \parallel s) = r \parallel G(s)$, where $r, s \in \{0,1\}^n$.
4. $G'(s) = G(\pi(s))$, where π is a (fixed) permutation.
5. $G'(s) = G(s + 1)$.
6. (harder!) $G'(s) = G(s \oplus s^R)$.

A. Solution to $G'(r \mathbin{+\!\!+} s) = r \mathbin{+\!\!+} G(s)$

B. Solution to $G'(s) = G(s \oplus G(s)_{1\ldots n})$: May not be a PRG. For example, let g be a PRG from any number m bits to $m+1$ bits, i.e., output is pseudorandom string just one bit longer than the input. Assume even n; for every $x \in \{0,1\}^{n/2}$ and $y \in \{0,1\}^{n/2} \cup \{0,1\}^{1+n/2}$, let $G(x \mathbin{+\!\!+} y) = x \mathbin{+\!\!+} g(y)$. If g is a PRG, then G is also a PRG (why?). However, when used in the above construction,

$$\begin{aligned} G'(x \mathbin{+\!\!+} y) &= G\left[(x \mathbin{+\!\!+} y) \oplus G(x \mathbin{+\!\!+} y)\right] \\ &= G\left[(x \mathbin{+\!\!+} y) \oplus (x \mathbin{+\!\!+} g(y))\right] \\ &= G\left[(x \oplus x) \mathbin{+\!\!+} (y \oplus g(y))\right] \\ &= G\left[0^{n/2} \mathbin{+\!\!+} y) \oplus (x \mathbin{+\!\!+} g(y))\right] \\ &= 0^{n/2} \mathbin{+\!\!+} y \oplus g(y) \end{aligned}$$

As this output begins with $n/2$ zero bits, it can be trivially distinguished from random. Hence, G' is clearly not a PRG. □

Exercise 2.24. Let $G_1, G_2 : \{0,1\}^n \to \{0,1\}^{2n}$ be two different candidate PRGs (over the same domain and range). Consider the function G defined in each of the following sections. Is it a secure PRG — assuming *both* G_1 and G_2 are secure PRGs, or assuming only that one of them is a secure PRG? Prove:

1. $G(s) = G_1(s) \oplus G_2(s)$.
2. $G(s) = G_1(s) \oplus G_2(s \oplus 1^{|s|})$.
3. $G(s) = G_1(s) \oplus G_2(0^{|s|})$.

Exercise 2.25. Let $G : \{0,1\}^n \rightarrow \{0,1\}^m$ be a secure PRG, where $m > n$:

1. Let $m = n + 1$. Use G to construct a secure PRG $G' : \{0,1\}^n \rightarrow \{0,1\}^{2n}$.
2. Let $m = 2n$. Use G to construct a secure PRG $G' : \{0,1\}^n \rightarrow \{0,1\}^{4 \cdot n}$.
3. Let $m = 4n$. Use G to construct a secure PRG $\hat{G} : \{0,1\}^n \rightarrow \{0,1\}^{64 \cdot n}$.

Exercise 2.26. Let $G : \{0,1\}^n \rightarrow \{0,1\}^m$ be a secure PRG, where $m = 2n$, and consider $G'(x) = G(x) +\!\!\!+ G(x+1)$. Is G' a secure PRG? Prove.

Solution: Not necessarily. Assume we are given a PRG $f(\cdot)$ from $n-1$ bits to m bits. Next, define $G(x) = f(x[0 : n-2])$, i.e., $G(x)$ returns the value of $f()$ when applied to the string which is the same as x except for the removal of the least significant bit (LSb) of x, which we denote $LSb(x)$. Since f is a PRG, then G is also a PRG, although a less efficient one. However, for a random x, with probability half, $LSb(x) = 0$ holds and hence $G(x) = G(x+1)$. Therefore, $G'(x) = G(x)||G(x+1)$ is surely not a secure PRG. □

Exercise 2.27. Let f be a function from n bit binary strings to n' bit binary strings, i.e., $f : \{0,1\}^n \rightarrow \{0,1\}^{n'}$:

1. Let $m_1 \neq m_2 \in \{0,1\}^n$ be two different random n bit strings. Present the best upper and lower bounds you can, for the probability that $f(m_1) = f(m_2)$, assuming $n > n'$:

$$\_\_\_\_\_\_\_\_\_\_ \leq \Pr_{m_1 \neq m_2 \leftarrow \{0,1\}^n} (f(m_1) = f(m_2)) \leq \_\_\_\_\_\_\_\_\_\_$$

   Justify your answer.
2. Repeat, when f is a *random* function from $\{0,1\}^n$ to $\{0,1\}^{n'}$:

$$\_\_\_\_\_\_\_\_\_\_ \leq \Pr_{m_1 \neq m_2 \leftarrow \{0,1\}^n} (f(m_1) = f(m_2)) \leq \_\_\_\_\_\_\_\_\_\_$$

3. Repeat items 1 and 2 for the case $n = n'$.
4. Repeat items 1 and 2 for the case $n' > n$.
5. Let f' be another arbitrary function from n bit binary strings to n' bit binary strings. Repeat items 1 and 2, for the probability that $f(m_1) = f'(m_2)$. In item 2, only f is chosen randomly.

Exercise 2.28. Let f_k be a (secure) PRF from n bit binary strings to n' bit binary strings, i.e., $f : \{0,1\}^* \times \{0,1\}^n \rightarrow \{0,1\}^{n'}$. Assume that the key k is chosen randomly as a string of length l; the key length l is specified so you can reference it in your responses, but do so only if you find it relevant; otherwise, you may ignore it. Assume that l is sufficiently large for the PRF to be secure:

1. Is it possible that $n < n'$? Is it possible that $n' < n$? Explain.
2. Let $m_1 \neq m_2 \in \{0,1\}^n$ be two different random n bit strings. Present the best upper and lower bounds you can, for the probability that $f_k(m_1) = f_k(m_2)$, assuming $n < n'$:

   $$\_\_\_\_\_\_\_\_\_\_ \leq \Pr_{m_1 \neq m_2 \leftarrow \{0,1\}^n} (f_k(m_1) = f_k(m_2)) \leq \_\_\_\_\_\_\_\_\_\_$$

   Justify your answer.
3. Repeat for the case $n = n'$.
4. Repeat for the case $n > n'$.

Exercise 2.29 (*Ad Hoc* PRF competition project). In this exercise, you will experiment in trying to build directly a cryptographic scheme — in this case, a PRF — as well as in trying to 'break' (cryptanalyze) it. This exercise is best done by multiple groups, with each group consisting of one or few persons:

1. In the first phase, each group will design a PRF, whose input, key and output are all 64 bits long. The PRF should be written in Python (or some other agreed programming language), and only use the basic mathematical operations: table lookup, modular addition/subtraction/multiplication/division/remainder, XOR, max, min, and rotations. You may also use comparisons and conditional code. The length of your program should not exceed 400 characters, and it must be readable. You will also provide (separate) documentation.
2. All groups will be given the documentation and code of the PRFs of all other groups, and try to design programs to distinguish these PRFs from a random function (over same input and output domains). A distinguisher is considered successful if it is able to distinguish in more than 1% of the runs.

Exercise 2.30. Let f be a secure PRF with n bit keys, domain and range, and let k be a secret, random n bit key. Derive from k, using

f, two pseudorandom keys k_1, k_2, e.g., one for encryption and one for authentication. Each of the derived keys k_1, k_2 should be $2n$-bits long, i.e., twice the length of k.

Note: The two keys should be *independent*, i.e., each of them (e.g., k_1) should be pseudorandom, even if the adversary is given the other (e.g., k_2).

1. $k_1 =$ ____________
2. $k_2 =$ ____________

Exercise 2.31 (PRF constructions). Let $F_k(m) : \{0,1\}^n \times \{0,1\}^n \rightarrow \{0,1\}^n$ be a secure PRF. Is $\hat{F}$, as defined in each of the following parts, a secure PRF? Justify your answers. Where the function is *not* a secure PRF, present the adversary that can distinguish between the function and a random function (as in Exercise 2.6). Where the function *is* a PRF, a precise proof as in Exercise 2.7 is best, but a good intuitive argument will also do:

1. $\hat{F}_k(m) = F_k(m^R)$, where m^R means the reverse of m.
2. $\hat{F}_k(m_L \mathbin{+\!\!+} m_R) = F_k(m_L) \mathbin{+\!\!+} F_k(m_R)$.
3. $\hat{F}_k(m_L \mathbin{+\!\!+} m_R) = (m_L \oplus F_k(m_R)) \mathbin{+\!\!+} (F_k(m_L) \oplus m_R)$.
4. $\hat{F}_k(m) = LSb(F_k(m))$, where LSb returns the least-significant bit of the input.

Exercise 2.32 (Key dependent message security). Recall that in many cryptographic definitions, the attacker has access to one or more oracle function, e.g., the chosen-plaintext oracle for encryption $E_k(\cdot)$ using secret key k. In a *key dependent message attack*, the attacker has similar access to the oracle function, but instead of specifying directly the value of the input to the oracle, the attacker specifies a function f and the oracle is applied to $f(k)$ where k is the key the relevant cryptographic function. For example, for chosen-plaintext oracle for encryption using a shared key k, the attacker receives $E_k(f(k))$. See, e.g., Ref. [82]:

1. Extend the definition of secure pseudo-random function, to define a PRF scheme secure against key-dependent message attacks.
2. Repeat, for a block cipher.

3. Repeat, for an IND-CPA-ensuring symmetric key cryptosystem.
4. Show that every PRF secure against key-dependent message attack is also a secure PRF under the standard definition.
5. Suppose that F is secure PRF. Show a ('weird') function F' which is also a secure PRF under the standard definition but *not* secure against key-dependent message attacks.

Exercise 2.33 (Stateful PRG, ANSI X9.31 and the DUHK attack). The ANSI X9.31 is a well-known design of a stateful PRG design built using a block cipher E, illustrated in Figure 2.38. In this exercise, we investigate a weakness in it, presented in Ref. [290]; it was later shown to be relevant for some devices using this standard, in the so-called *DUHK attack* [127]. Our presentation is a slight simplification of the X9.31 design but retains the important aspects of the attack.

The stateful PRG is used in 'rounds', with the state of round i being output from round $i-1$. Specifically, the X9.31 PRG works as follows, given the current state s_{i-1}, with s_0 selected randomly, and some 'timestamp' T_i. First, compute an 'internal' value, $x_i = E_k(T_i)$. Then, output the values $r_i = E_k(x_i \oplus s_{i-1})$ and $s_i = E_k(r_i \oplus x_i)$. See Figure 2.38. The specification does not restrict the choice of k, and several implementations use constant k as part of their code; assume, therefore, that k is known:

1. Assume T_i, k and s_{i-1} are known. Show how the attacker can find r_i and s_i.
2. Assume that the values $\{T_j\}$ are known for all j, and that k, r_i are known (for specific i). Show how an attacker can compute $\{s_j, r_j\}$ for every j.

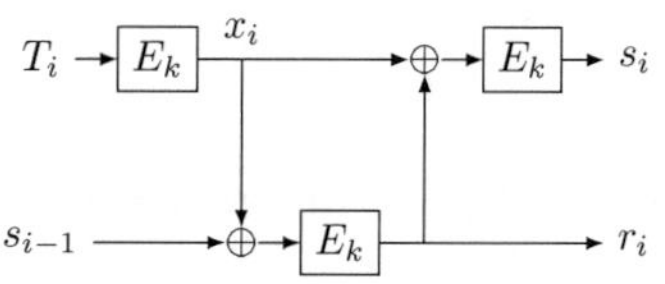

Figure 2.38. A single round of the ANSI X9.31 stateful pseudorandom generator (PRG), using block cipher $E_k(x)$, e.g., AES.

Source: This figure was adapted from Ref. [127].

Exercise 2.34 (Cascade is not a robust combiner for PRFs). Let $F', F'' : \{0,1\}^* \times D \to D$ be two polynomial-time computable functions, and let their *cascade*, denoted $F \equiv F' \circ F''$ be defined as:

$$F_{(k',k'')}(x) \equiv F'_{k'} \circ F''_{k''}(x) \equiv F'_{k'}\left(F''_{k''}(x)\right) \tag{2.61}$$

Give an example of F', F'' s.t. *one* of them is a PRF, yet their cascade $F \equiv F' \circ F''$ is *not* a PRF. This shows that cascade is not a robust combiner for PRFs.

Exercise 2.35. A message m of length 256 bits is encrypted using a 128-bit block cipher, resulting in ciphertext c; no padding is used. During transmission, the 200th bit was flipped due to noise. Let c' denote c with the 200th bit flipped and m' denote the result of decryption of c':

1. Which bits in m' would be identical to the bits in m, assuming the use of each of the following modes of operation: (1) ECB, (2) CBC, (3) OFB and (4) CFB? Explain (with a diagram).
2. For each of the modes, specify which bits is predictable as a function of the bits of m and the known fact that the 200th bit flipped.

Exercise 2.36. Consider a scenario where randomness is scarce, motivating attempts to design encryption schemes that use less randomization. Specifically, consider the following two variants of the CBC mode of operation, both using, per message, only 20 random bits rather than n random bits (block size) in standard CBC. Both variants are identical to CBC mode, except for the choice of c_0 (the *initialization vector* or IV), which is as specified below; both use a 20-bits random string $r \stackrel{\$}{\leftarrow} \{0,1\}^{20}$. Show that neither variant suffices to ensure IND-CPA.

Append zeros: $c_0 = r||0^{n-20}$.
Pseudorandomly: $c_0 = E_k(r)$.

Note: Your solution may require up to few million queries.

Exercise 2.37 (Modes of operation: decryption and correctness). Table 2.3 specifies only the encryption process for each mode of operation. Write the decryption process for each mode and show that correctness is satisfied.

Exercise 2.38. Hackme Bank protects money-transfer orders digitally sent between branches, by encrypting them using a block cipher. Money transfer orders have the following structure: $m = f \# r \# t \# x \# y \# p$, where f, r are each 20-bits representing the payer (from) and the payee (recipient), t is a 32-bit field encoding the time, x is a 24-bit field representing the amount, y is a 128-bit comment field defined by the payer and p is 32-bit parity fields, computed as the bitwise-XOR of the preceding 32-bit words. Orders with incorrect parity, outdated or repeating time field, or unknown payer/payee are ignored.

Mal captures ciphertext message x containing money-transfer order of 1$ from Alice to his account. You may assume that Mal can 'trick' Alice into including a comment field y selected by Mal. Assume 64-bit block cipher. Can Mal cause transfer of larger amount to his account, and how, assuming use of the following modes of operation:

1. ECB
2. CBC
3. OFB
4. CFB

Solution: The first block contains f, r (10 bits each), and top 24 bits of the time t, the second block contains 8 more bits of the time, x (24 bits) and 32 bits of the comment; block three contains 64 bits of comments, and block four contains 32 bits of comment and 32 bits of parity. Denote these four plaintext blocks by $m_1 \# m_2 \# m_3 \# m_4$.

Denote the ciphertext blocks captured by Mal as $c_0 \# c_1 \# c_2 \# c_3 \# c_4$, where c_0 is the IV (except for ECB):

1. ECB: The attacker selects the third block (completely comment) to be identical to the second block, except for containing the maximal value in the 24 bits from bit 8 to bit 31. The attacker then switches between the third and fourth block before giving to the bank. Parity bits do not change.
2. CBC: Attacker chooses y s.t. $m_3 = m_2$. Then, the attacker sends to the bank the manipulated message $z_0 \# c_3 \# c_3 \# c_3 \# c_4$, where $z_0 = m_1 \oplus m_3 \oplus c_2$. As a result, decryption of the first block retrieves m_1 correctly (as $m_1 = z_0 \oplus m_3 \oplus c_2$) and decryption of the last block similarly retrieves m_4 correctly (no change in c_3, c_4).

However, both the second and the third block, decrypt to the value $(c_3 \oplus c_2 \oplus m_3)$. Hence, the 32 bit XOR of the message does not change. The decryption of the second block (to $c_3 \oplus c_2 \oplus m_3$) is likely to leave the time value valid — and to increase the amount considerably.

3. OFB: The solution is trivial since Mal can flip arbitrary bits in the decrypted plaintext (by flipping corresponding bits in the ciphertext).
4. CFB: As in CBC, attacker chooses y s.t. $m_3 = m_2$. Attacker sends to the bank the manipulated message $c_0 + c_1 + c_1 + c_1 + z_4$ where $z_4 = p_4 \oplus c_2 \oplus p_2$.

Exercise 2.39 (Affine block cipher). Hackme Inc. proposes the following highly-efficient block cipher, using two 64-bit keys k_1, k_2, for 64-bit blocks: $E_{k_1,k_2}(m) = (m \oplus k_1) + k_2 (mod\ 2^{64})$:

1. Show that E_{k_1,k_2} is an invertible permutation (for any k_1, k_2) and the inverse permutation D_{k_1,k_2}.
2. Show that (E, D) is not a secure block cipher.
3. Show that encryption using (E, D) is not CPA-IND, when used in the following modes: (1) ECB, (2) CBC, (3) OFB, (4) CFB.

Exercise 2.40 (How *not* to build PRP from PRF). Suppose F is a secure PRF with input, output and keyspace all of length n bits. For $x_L, x_R \in \{0,1\}^n$, let $F'_k(x_L + x_R) = F_k(x_L) + F_k(x_R)$ and $F''_k(x_L + x_R) = F_k(x_L \oplus x_R) + F_k(x_L \oplus F_k(x_L \oplus x_R))$. Prove that neither F'_k nor F''_k are a PRP.

Exercise 2.41 (Building PRP from a PRF). Suppose you are given a secure PRF F, with input, output and keyspace all of length n bits. Show how to use F in a cryptographic protocol designed for:

1. a PRP, with input and output length $2n$ bit and key length n bits,
2. a PRP, with input, output and key all of length n bits.

Exercise 2.42. Show that the simple padding function $pad(m) = m + 0^l$ *fails* to prevent CCA attacks against most of the modes of operation we discussed (Figure 2.3), when $l \leq n$. The attacker may perform CPA and CCA queries, and the plaintext contains multiple blocks.

Exercise 2.43 (Indistinguishability definition). Let (E, D) be a stateless shared key encryption scheme, and let p_1, p_2 be two plaintexts. Let x be 1 if the most significant bits of p_1, p_2 are identical and 0 otherwise, i.e., $x = \{1 \text{ if } MSb(p_1) = MSb(p_2), \text{ else } 0\}$. Assume that there exists an efficient algorithm X that computes x given the ciphertexts, i.e., $x = X(E_k(p_1), E_k(p_2))$. Show that this implies that (E, D) is not IND-CPA secure, i.e., there is an efficient algorithm ADV which achieves significant advantage in the IND-CPA experiment. Present the implementation of ADV by filling in the missing code in the following:

$ADV^{E_k}(\text{'Choose'}, 1^n) : \{$ ______________________________ $\}$
$ADV^{E_k}(\text{'Guess'}, s, c^*) : \{$ ______________________________ $\}$

Exercise 2.44 (Robust combiner for PRG). 1. Given two candidate PRGs, say G_1 and G_2, design a *robust combiner*, i.e., a 'combined' function G which is a secure pseudorandom generator if either G_1 or G_2 is a secure PRG.

2. In the design of the SSL protocol, there were two candidate PRGs: one (say G_1) based on the MD5 hash function and the other (say G_2) based on the SHA-1 hash function. The TLS working group decided to combine the two; a simplified version of the combined PRG is $G(s) = G_2(s +\!\!+ G_1(s))$. Is this a robust combiner, i.e., a secure PRG provided that either G_1 or G_2 is a secure PRG?

Hint: Compare to Lemma 2.1. You may read on hash functions in Chapter 3, but the exercise does not require any knowledge of that; you should simply consider the construction $G(s) = G_2(s +\!\!+ G_1(s))$ for arbitrary functions G_1, G_2. □

Exercise 2.45 (Using PRG for independent keys). In Example 2.5, we saw how to use a PRF to derive multiple pseudo-random keys from a single pseudo-random key, using a PRF:

1. Show how to derive two pseudo-random keys, using a PRG, say a PRG from n bits to $2n$ bits.
2. Show how to extend your design to derive four keys from the same PRG, or any fixed number of pseudo-random keys.

Exercise 2.46. Let (E, D) be a block cipher which operates on 20 byte blocks; suppose that each computation of E or D takes 10^{-6} seconds (one microsecond), on given chips. Using (E, D), you are asked to implement a secure high-speed encrypting/decrypting gateway. The gateway receives packets at line speed of 10^8 bytes/second but with maximum of 10^4 bytes received at any given second. The goal is to have minimal latency, using minimal number of chips. Present an appropriate design, argue why it achieves the minimal latency and why it is secure.

Exercise 2.47. Consider the AES block cipher, with 256-bit key and 128-bit blocks, and two random one-block (128 bit) messages, m_1 and m_2, and two random (256-bit) keys, k_1 and k_2. Calculate (or approximate/bound) the probability that $E_{k_1}(m_1) = E_{k_2}(m_2)$.

Exercise 2.48 (PRF→PRG). Present a simple and secure construction of a PRG, given a secure PRF.

Exercise 2.49 (Independent PRGs). Often, a designer has one random or pseudo-random 'seed/key' binary string $k \in \{0,1\}^*$, from which it needs to generate two or more independently pseudorandom strings $k_0, k_1 \in \{0,1\}^*$; i.e., each of these is pseudorandom, even if the other is given to the (PPT) adversary. Let *PRG* be a pseudorandom generator, which on input of arbitrary length l bits, produces $4l$ output pseudorandom bits. For each of the following designs, prove its security (if secure) or its insecurity (is insecure):

1. For $b \in \{0,1\}$, let $k_b = \text{PRG}(b + k)$.
2. For $b \in \{0,1\}$, let $k_b = \text{PRG}(k)[(b \cdot 2 \cdot |k|) \ldots ((b+1) \cdot 2 \cdot |k| - 1)]$.

Solution:

1. Insecure, since it is possible for a secure PRG to ignore the first bit, i.e., $\text{PRG}(b + s) = \text{PRG}(\overline{b} + s)$, resulting in $k_0 = \text{PRG}(0 + k) = \text{PRG}(1 + k) = k_1$. We skip the (simple) proof that such a PRG may be secure.
2. Secure, since each of these is a (non-overlapping) subset of the output of the PRG.

Exercise 2.50 (Indistinguishability hides partial information). In this exercise, we provide an example to the fact that a cryptosystem that ensures indistinguishability (IND-CPA) is guaranteed not to leak partial information about plaintext, including relationships between the plaintext corresponding to different ciphertexts.

Let (E, D) be an encryption scheme, which leaks some information about the plaintexts; specifically, we assume that there exists an efficient adversary A s.t. for two ciphertexts c_1, c_2 of E, $A(c_1, c_2) = 1$ holds if and only if the plaintexts share a common prefix, e.g., $c_1 = E_k(ID + m_1)$ and $c_2 = E_k(ID + m_2)$ (same perfix, ID). Show that this implies that (E, D) is not IND-CPA secure.

Chapter 3

Integrity and Hashing

Integrity has multiple meanings; we focus on the ability to check if an object was modified, using a concise *digest* of the (original) object. In this chapter, we discuss three important cryptographic integrity mechanisms: *hash functions*, *blockchains* and *accumulators*, most notably, the *Merkle tree accumulator*. We also briefly discuss some additional properties and applications of hash functions (beyond hashing).

Integrity mechanisms, including different variants of hash functions, blockchains and accumulators, mainly the Merkle tree accumulator, have been extensively studied and widely deployed in practice. Their correct, secure use requires good understanding of their properties; designs based on intuitive understanding have often proved vulnerable, and we see some examples. Therefore, it is important to understand their correct definitions, properties and use. This is the goal of this chapter.

Much of this chapter deals with cryptographic *hash functions*, used to compute the digest of a binary string. Cryptographic hash functions are among the most widely used cryptographic schemes and have many diverse properties, uses, and applications. In Section 3.1, we introduce cryptographic hash functions, their properties and variants. In Sections 3.2 and 3.3, respectively, we discuss the two main *integrity* properties of hash functions, collision-resistant hash functions (CRHF) and *second-preimage-resistant* (SPR) hash functions. In Section 3.4, we discuss *one-way functions* (OWF), which is another property often expected from cryptographic hash functions, and used for different purposes. In Section 3.5, we discuss one final important property often expected from cryptographic hash functions: *randomness extraction*; and in Section 3.6, we introduce the random oracle model, an important paradigm often used to provide a simplified security analysis of protocols and schemes using cryptographic hash functions. Later, in Chapter 4, we discuss the *use* of cryptographic hash functions for *authentication*, in message authentication code (MAC) and signature schemes.

In Section 3.7, we introduce (cryptographic) *accumulators*. Accumulators provide integrity to a *sequence of strings* rather than to a single string as provided by hash functions. Accumulators typically ensure additional, sequence-related properties and functions, such as *Proof of Inclusion* (PoI). We focus on the keyless *Merkle tree* ($\mathcal{MT}^h$), a simple, widely used accumulator, which is used in blockchains such as Bitcoin (Section 3.9.2) as well as by the Certificate Transparency (CT) Public Key Infrastructure (PKI), which we cover in Section 8.5.

In Section 3.8, we present the *Merkle–Damgård* construction for constructing cryptographic hash functions from their fixed-input-length variant, called *compression functions*.

Finally, in Section 3.9, we discuss *blockchains*, in particular the *Bitcoin* blockchain, and the *proof of work* (PoW) mechanism, which is central to the design of Bitcoin.

3.1 Introducing cryptographic hash functions, their properties and variants

Hash functions map variable input length (VIL) binary strings to n-bit strings, referred to as the *digest* of the input. Since the input may be arbitrarily long, and the output is always n bits, the basic property of hash functions is that the digest (output) is normally shorter than the input, a property often referred to as *compression*.[1]

The compression property, on its own, may be achieved trivially, e.g., by truncating the input; however, hash functions are expected, intuitively, to map their inputs to seemingly random

[1]Do not be confused with *compression functions*, which, similarly to hash functions, compress their input into a shorter output (digest), but their input is of fixed length m. Namely, compression functions compress from m bits strings to $n < m$ bits strings.

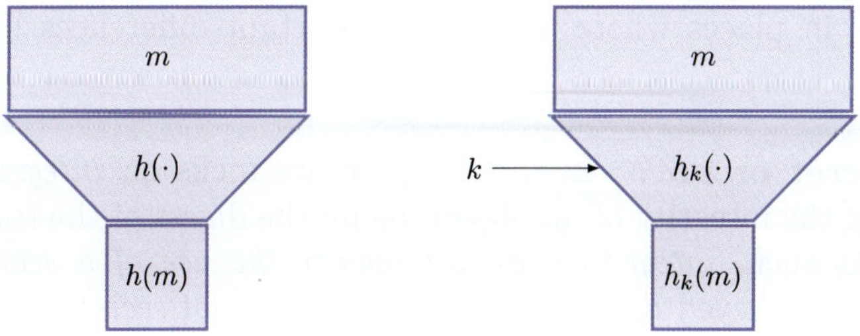

(a) Keyless hash function
$h(\cdot) : \{0,1\}^* \to \{0,1\}^n$.

(b) Keyed hash function
$h_k(\cdot) : \{0,1\}^* \times \{0,1\}^* \to \{0,1\}^n$.

Figure 3.1. Keyless and keyed hash functions: mapping from a variable-length input to n-bits output (digest).

outputs. We discuss *cryptographic hash functions*, for which we present precise requirements that capture different security requirements from this seemingly random mapping of inputs to outputs, e.g., collision resistance. Of course, hash functions are also used extensively for non-cryptographic applications, such as efficient data structures and load balancing, where the designers may simply assume that the inputs are mapped 'randomly' to outputs; the random oracle model (ROM) is a similar simplification which is often used to analyze cryptographic protocols using hash functions, which we discuss in Section 3.6.

As illustrated in Figure 3.1, hash functions may be keyed ($h_k(\cdot) : \{0,1\}^* \times \{0,1\}^* \to \{0,1\}^n$) or keyless ($h(\cdot) : \{0,1\}^* \to \{0,1\}^n$).

To key or not to key? As we see in Section 3.3.2, keyless hash function *cannot* ensure important security requirements, most notably, *collision resistance.* This motivates using keyed hash functions, and, indeed, theoretical works on cryptographic hash functions mostly refer to keyed functions. However, the well-known standard cryptographic hash functions, e.g., SHA Section 3.1.4, are keyless. Many of the definitions and applications of hash functions could be presented using either keyed or keyless functions; using keyed hash is slightly more involved since they involve this additional input. In practice, applications mostly use keyless hash functions.

For simplicity, in this book, we mostly use and discuss keyless hash functions. We mention the keyed versions mainly in this chapter, and especially in places where there are important differences between the two.

Key: secret or not? In this chapter, we focus on *integrity*, i.e., validating the integrity of an object, using the digest of the (original) object. As such, *integrity does not require the use of a secret key*; even if we use keyed hash functions, *the key is not secret*, i.e., we let the adversary know the key.

There are several construction of cryptographic functions which combine a keyless cryptographic hash function with a secret key, typically, by combining the key with other data to produce the input to the keyless hash. The resulting functions are often referred to as *keyed hashs* function; we avoid this term, as we consider it somewhat confusing since the constructed functions rely on the secrecy of the key to ensure properties beyond the integrity and pseudo-random mapping which are expected from hash functions. Such constructions which combine a keyless hash function with a secret key are used for MAC (see Chapter 4), PRF (see Section 2.7.2), KDF (see Section 3.5.3) and more. We discuss one such construction, the well-known, standardized HMAC construction (Section 4.4.5).

Specifying the digest length n: Much of the literature on cryptographic hash functions does not specify the digest length n as an input of the hash function. In fact, existing standard cryptographic hash functions are designed for specific digest lengths. For example, the SHA-1 standard cryptographic hash function Section 3.1.4 uses $n = 160$, i.e., the output (digest) length is 160 bits. The improved SHA-2 and SHA-3 standards each define a few functions, each with its own output length, which is encoded in their names, e.g., SHA-256 and SHA-512 (defined in the SHA-2 specifications [406]) and SHA-3-256 and SHA-3-512 (defined in the SHA-3 specifications [146]).

However, to properly define security, we must consider hash functions as supporting different digest length since the advantage of the adversary is a function of the digest length n; in a secure hash function, the advantage should be negligible in n. For keyed hash functions, we adopt a simple convention: the key length is also the digest length. However, a different solution is needed for keyless hash functions.

We solve this by defining a *keyless hash function h* as a *family of functions* $h[n] : \{0,1\}^* \rightarrow \{0,1\}^n$. Namely, formally, the digest length n is another input to the hash function h. However, for simplicity, we use this explicit notation $h[n](\cdot)$ only when necessary, mainly for definitions; in other places, we simply use the simple keyless notation of $h(\cdot)$. For example, we did not write n as input in Figure 3.1. The digest length n should be considered as a parameter even where omitted for simplicity.

3.1.1 Warm-up: hashing for load balancing

Before we focus on cryptographic hash functions and their definitions, we first discuss, intuitively, the use of hash functions for randomly mapping data, as used for load-balancing and data structures. Let us focus on load balancing.

In load balancing, we may use a hash function to map the inputs into the possible digests values ('bins') in a 'random' manner, i.e., with a roughly equal probability of assignment to each bin (digest value). For the typical case of n-bit digest values, there would be 2^n bins. This is illustrated in Figure 3.2. Here, a hash function h maps from the set of names (given as unbounded-length strings) to a smaller set, say the set of n-bit binary strings. The goal is to roughly balance the number of entries (names) assigned to each bin.

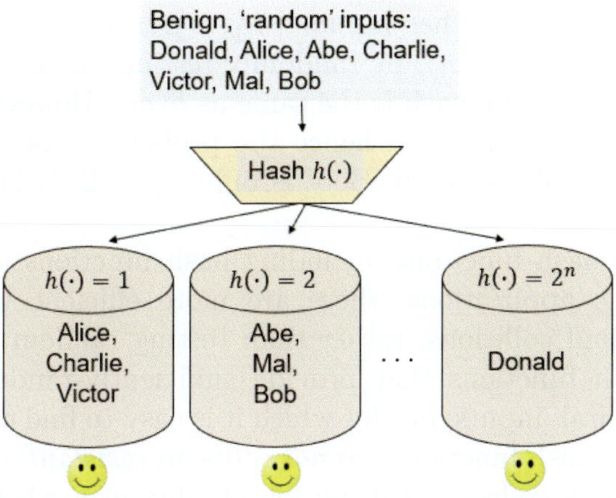

Figure 3.2. Load-balancing with (keyless) hash function $h(\cdot)$.

For example, this may be used to split, efficiently and fairly, the load of requests coming from many users to a set of web servers.

Of course, in cryptography, and cybersecurity in general, we mainly consider adversarial settings. In the context of load-balancing applications, as shown in Figure 3.2, this refers to an adversary who can manipulate some of the input names, and whose goal may be to cause imbalanced allocation of names to bins, i.e., many collisions. This can cause bad performance, potentially even a *Denial of Service* (DoS), i.e., a disruption or degradation of the service provided.

Consider an attacker whose goal is to degrade the performance of a web service for request coming from a particular benign user, say Bob, as part of a DoS attack. The attacker may provide to the system requests from a long list of names $m_1, m_2, \ldots$, deviously selected such that all of them are mapped to the same bin as Bob. We refer to a pair of different inputs $m_1 \neq m_2$ that have the same digest, i.e., $h(m_2) = h(m_1)$, as a *collision*; see illustration of a collision in Figure 1.6.

The attacker's goal, therefore, is to find multiple collisions $\{m_i\}$, which all collide with the string 'Bob', i.e., for all i holds $h(\text{'Bob'}) = h(m_i)$. This will cause the bin (list) in which 'Bob' is placed to become very long. In the case of load balancing between web servers, this will cause the web server to which Bob is assigned, to also handle all these DoS requests, resulting in poor performance, as illustrated in Figure 3.3.

Note that for *any* hash function h and input m (e.g., $m =$'Bob'), it is possible to find other inputs $\{m'_1, m'_2, \ldots\}$ which collide with m, i.e., $(\forall i) h(m'_i) = h(m)$, by randomly testing different inputs and collecting these whose hash is the same as $h(m)$. However, for digest length n, there are 2^n bins, hence the probability of such random guess to be a collision with 'Bob' is only $\frac{1}{2^n} = 2^{-n}$, i.e., negligible in n.

For some hash functions, including hash functions used for non-cryptographic applications, there are more efficient ways for the attacker to find collisions, rather than testing random inputs. This includes hash functions that provide sufficiently-randomized mapping for 'natural' inputs, but for which it is easy to find collisions. We say that such hash functions are *not collision resistant*, i.e., these are functions where collisions can be found efficiently when the inputs are selected by an attacker.

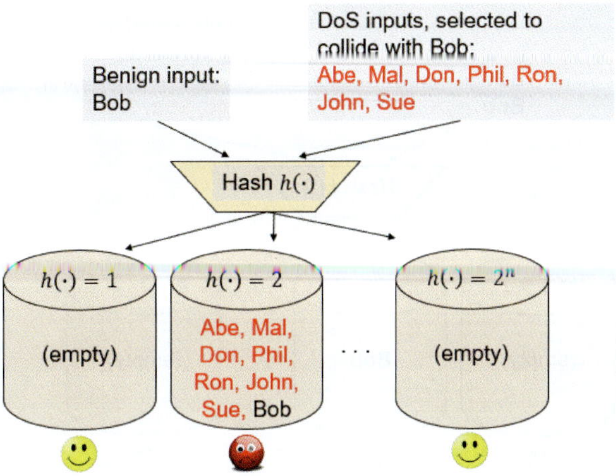

Figure 3.3. Algorithmic complexity Denial of Service (DoS) attack exploiting an insecure hash function h to cause many collisions.

It isn't surprising that collisions can be found efficiently for a hash function not designed to ensure collision resistance. However, this indicates the importance of defining and evaluating the collision resistance requirement and other security requirements from cryptographic hash functions, as per the *attack model principle* (Principle 1). In Section 3.3, we define *collision-resistant hash functions* (CRHFs); intuitively, in such functions, an attacker cannot efficiently find a collision. This should foil the algorithmic complexity Denial of Service attack of Figure 3.3, provided we use a sufficiently long digest length n (i.e., 2^n bins). See Figure 3.4.

3.1.2 Properties of cryptographic hash functions

Cryptographic hash functions are used for many different applications, often assuming different security properties. Roughly, these properties fall into three broad goals: *integrity, confidentiality* and *randomness.* Intuitively, *integrity* ensures the uniqueness of the message, given the digest; *confidentiality* ensures the digest does not 'expose' the message, and *randomness* ensures that the digest is pseudorandom, provided that the input 'contains sufficient randomness'.

We define four security requirements: *collision resistance*, *second-preimage-resistant*, *one-way function* (OWF) (also referred to as

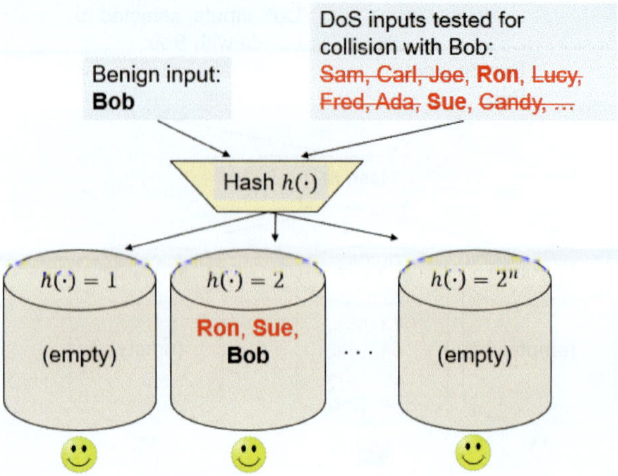

Figure 3.4. Load balancing with a *collision-resistant hash function* (CRHF) with n bits digest, i.e., using 2^n bins. The probability of a random name to collide with 'Bob' is only 2^{-n}; furthermore, the probability of collision is negligible for guesses by all efficient algorithms.

Table 3.1. Goals and requirements for keyless cryptographic hash functions, presented for the hash function $h : \{0,1\}^* \to \{0,1\}^n$.

Goal	Requirement	Abridged Description
Integrity	second-preimage-resistant (SPR; Definition 3.1)	Can't find collision to a random m: $m' \neq m$ yet $h(m) = h(m')$.
Integrity	Collision resistance (CRHF; Definition 3.2)	Can't find collision (m, m'), i.e., $m \neq m'$ yet $h(m) = h(m')$.
Confidentiality	One-way function (OWF; Definition 3.7	Given $h(m)$ for random m, can't find preimage (m' s.t. $h(m) = h(m')$).
Randomness	Randomness extractor (Section 3.5)	If input is sufficiently random, then output is pseudorandom.

preimage resistance) and *randomness extraction*. Table 3.1 maps these requirements to the three goals and gives an abridged descriptions of these properties, for keyless hash functions.

Assuming that a given hash function has these security properties makes it possible to use the hash function for different applications, ensuring security as long as the hash function indeed satisfies the properties assumed. We should only assume properties which the hash function was designed and tested to ensure. Even seemingly minor differences between the security requirements for which the hash function was designed and tested, and the security properties required for the application, may result in a vulnerability. For example, Table 3.1 presents two integrity requirements, CRHF and SPR; we later show applications which are secure using a cryptographic hash function which satisfies the CRHF requirement but may be vulnerable assuming 'only' the SPR requirement. Namely, even if the definitions may appear similar, it is still important to use the correct definition; the differences can be meaningful and even critical.

Here is an exercise which may strengthen your intuitive understanding of the different security requirements in Table 3.1.

Exercise 3.1 (Examples of (insecure, simple) hash functions). Let $h(x) = x \bmod 2^n$ and $h'_k(x) = k + x \bmod 2^n$. The functions are computed by considering their inputs as integers in binary representation. Note that h' is keyed, while h is keyless:

1. Show that $h(x) = x \bmod 2^n$ is *not* a CRHF, SPR, OWF or randomness extractor, based on the abridged descriptions in Table 3.1.
2. Repeat for $h'_k(x) = k + x \bmod 2^n$, assuming that k is chosen randomly between 1 and a million.

Solution of the first part:

1. **SPR and CRHF:** We show that h is not a CRHF or an SPR hash function, by showing a collision for any given input x. Specifically, let $x' = x + 2^n$. Clearly, $x' \neq x$, and yet $h(x') = (x + 2^n) \bmod 2^n = x \bmod 2^n = h(x)$, namely, x' is a collision (second preimage) with x.
2. **OWF:** We next show that h is not a OWF. Specifically, given $h(x)$ for any preimage x, let $x' = h(x)$; clearly,

$$\begin{aligned} h(x') = x' \bmod 2^n &= h(x) \bmod 2^n \\ &= (x \bmod 2^n) \bmod 2^n = x \bmod 2^n = h(x) \end{aligned}$$

   Namely, x' is a preimage of $h(x)$, and hence h is not a OWF.
3. Finally, we show that h is not a *randomness extractor* hash function. Specifically, let $r \xleftarrow{\$} \{0,1\}^n$ be a random n bit string, and let $x = r +\!\!+ 0$, i.e., let x be an $n+1$-bits binary string, whose least

significant bit is zero and the other bits selected randomly. The value of $h(x) = x \bmod 2^n$ is the same as the n least-significant bits of n, and in particular, the least significant bit of $h(x)$ is zero. Hence, $h(x)$ is easily distiniguishable from a random n bit string.

□

3.1.3 Applications of cryptographic hash functions

Cryptographic hash functions are used in many systems and for an extensive variety of applications. These different applications and systems rely on different security requirements. As in any security system, it is important to identify the exact security requirements and assumptions; however, published designs, and even standards, do not always define the requirements precisely. Important applications of cryptographic hash functions include the following:

Integrity of a message, file or set: The hash $h(m)$ is a short *digest* of a typically much longer string m. The integrity properties of the hash function allows us to use the (short) digest $h(m)$ to validate the integrity of the (longer) message m. The term 'message' here should be interpreted broadly, e.g., it may include a whole file; one typical application is to ensure the integrity of files being downloaded, one of the defenses against malware (see Section 1.2.3). Hash functions are also used in the construction of *accumulator schemes*, in particular, in the *Merkle tree*, to produce a digest of a set of strings rather than of a single string.

Signatures: Another use of the integrity property of hash functions is to implement a signature scheme. We discuss two ways in which this is done: First, there are some constructions of a signature scheme from hash functions. We discuss simple designs in Section 3.4.2; in Chapter 10, and we also mention more elaborate designs which facilitates the post-quantum signature schemes.

Second, practical signature schemes usually use the *Hash-then-Sign* paradigm, where they first apply an cryptographic hash function to the input and then sign the digest using a Fixed Input Length signature scheme. This is done for efficiency; hash functions are efficient, and signature schemes are computationally heavy. See Section 3.3.5.

Improved login mechanisms: Hash functions are used to improve the security of password-based login authentication, in several ways. The most widely deployed method is using a *hashed password file*, which makes exposure of the server's password file less risky — since it contains only the hashed passwords. Another approach is to use a hash-based *one-time password* (OTPw), which is a random number allowing the server to authenticate the user, with drawbacks of single use and having to remember or have this random number; see Section 3.4.1, and a more extensive discussion of different login mechanisms in Chapter 9.

Proof of Work: Cryptographic hash functions are often used to provide PoW, i.e., to prove that an entity performed a considerable amount of computation. This is used by Bitcoin and other cryptocurrencies, and for other applications. See Section 3.9.2.

Key derivation and randomness extraction: Hash functions are used to extract pseudorandom bits, given input with 'sufficient randomness'; we refer to such hash functions as *randomness extractor hash functions*. Cryptographic hash functions are also used to construct *Key Derivation Function* (KDF) schemes, which can derive multiple independently pseudorandom keys from the same 'sufficiently random' input. See Section 3.5.

3.1.4 Standard cryptographic hash functions

Due to their efficiency, simplicity and wide applicability, cryptographic hash functions are probably the most commonly used cryptographic building blocks. The cryptographic building blocks principle (Principle 8) motivates defining and adopting standard cryptographic hash functions, which can be widely evaluated for security — mainly by cryptanalysis.

There have been multiple proposals for (keyless) cryptographic hash functions. Some of the most well-known cryptographic hash functions include the MD5 function proposed by RSA Inc., the SHA-1, SHA-2 and SHA-3 standards[2] [146, 406]), SHAKE [33] and more. Several of these, however, were already 'broken', i.e., shown to

[2]SHA-1 has digest length of 160 bits. Both SHA-2 and SHA-3 are defined for digest lengths of 224, 256, 384 or 512 bits.

fail some of the security requirements. In particular, *collisions* were found for both MD5 and SHA-1 [328, 451, 452, 474], as well as for other hash functions. Some attacks can be exploited, e.g., to forge signatures; see Section 3.3.6.

3.2 Second-preimage-resistant (SPR) hash functions

In this section, we consider the SPR requirement from cryptographic hash functions. The SPR property is weaker — and simpler — than the CRHF property that we discuss in the following section.

While SPR can be defined for keyed hash functions, it is usually presented only for keyless hash functions, and that is also what we will do here. Intuitively, a SPR hash function h accepts one input, an arbitrary-length binary string $m \in \{0,1\}^*$, and outputs an n-bit long binary string $h(m) \in \{0,1\}^n$, and satisfies the SPR *property*.

Intuitively, the SPR property requires that an efficient adversary $\mathcal{A}$ has negligible probability, when given a random binary string x, to find a *collision* to x, i.e., a different string $x' \neq x$ which has the same hash: $h(x') = h(x)$. We refer to x' as the *second preimage* and to x as the random (first) preimage since they are both preimages of $h(x') = h(x)$.

We illustrate the SPR property in Figure 3.5. The reader will note that the property as illustrated (and defined in the following) is a bit more complex than the description above: we let the adversary *select the length* l of the random (and first) preimage x. The reason that we cannot select a random preimage from the set of *all* strings, $x \xleftarrow{\$} \{0,1\}^*$, is that $\{0,1\}^*$ is an infinite set; we can only select an element uniformly from a finite set. The set $\{0,1\}^l$ is a natural choice of a finite set since it contains all binary strings of length l; we can select a random string by flipping l fair coins — giving probability $\frac{1}{2^l}$ to each of the 2^l strings in the set $\{0,1\}^l$. Letting the adversary select the length l seems prudent — why limit the adversary to find a second preimage to a random first preimage of specific length?

There are two subtle points on the specification of l by the adversary: First, we require $l \geq n$. We require this since if l could be

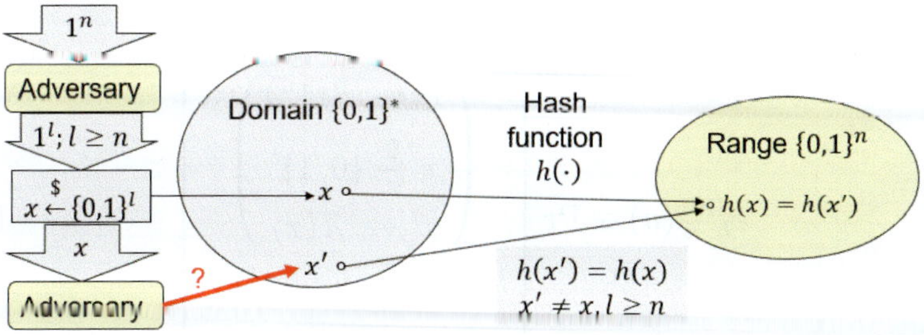

Figure 3.5. Second-preimage resistance (SPR): given keyless hash function $h : \{0,1\}^* \to \{0,1\}^n$, the adversary select bit-length $l \geq n$ and is given a random l-bits *first preimage* $x \xleftarrow{\$} \{0,1\}^l$. The adversary should output a colliding *second preimage* x', namely, $x' \neq x$ s.t. $h(x) = h(x')$.

(significantly) shorter, then the number of strings in $\{0,1\}^l$ may be small enough, to allow an adversary to maintain a table of preimages for each $x \in \{0,1\}^l$, much like the argument presented later for non-existence of keyless CRHF (Lemma 3.1). Second, the adversary must specify l in *unary*, i.e., as a string 1^l rather than by specifying l in binary. This prevents the adversary from specifying l to be very long, in particular, preventing l from being exponential in the length of the digest n. This is required since if l is exponential in n, and considering that the adversary receives as input a string x of length l, then the adversary can run time exponential in n, allowing it to find collisions for most such x values. For example, the adversary would be able to compute $h(x')$ for all values of $x' \in \{0,1\}^{n+1}$, which would often contain a collision, i.e., a value x' s.t. $h(x') = h(x)$. The reader should be able to show that such relaxations of the requirement would make it impossible to satisfy the requirement; see Exercise 3.10. The definition follows.

Definition 3.1 (Second-preimage resistance (SPR) Hash Function). Let $h[n] : \{0,1\}^* \to \{0,1\}^n$ be a family of keyless hash functions. We say that h is (SPR) if for every efficient algorithm $\mathcal{A}$, the *advantage function* $\varepsilon^{\mathrm{SPR}}_{h,\mathcal{A}}(n)$ is *negligible* in n, i.e., smaller than any positive polynomial for sufficiently large n (as $n \to \infty$), where:

$$\varepsilon^{\text{SPR}}_{h,\mathcal{A}}(n) \equiv \Pr\left[\begin{array}{c}\left(\begin{array}{c}1^l \leftarrow \mathcal{A}(1^n)\\ x \xleftarrow{\$} \{0,1\}^l\\ x' \leftarrow \mathcal{A}(x)\end{array}\right)\\ h[n](x) = h[n](x') \wedge\\ \wedge\, x \neq x' \,\wedge\, l \geq n\end{array}\right] \tag{3.1}$$

where the probability is taken over the choice of x and the random coin tosses of $\mathcal{A}$.

SPR is sometimes referred to as *weak collision resistance* since an SPR hash is only required to prevent the attacker from finding collision with a message selected randomly. This is weaker than a CRHF, which is required to prevent the attacker from finding any pair of colliding messages. Therefore, every CRHF is also an SPR hash function. However, the reverse is not necessarily true; in fact, if an SPR exists, then there also exists an SPR which is *not* a CRHF. The reader should be able to prove both of these statements; see Exercise 3.15.

In practice, quite a few proposed hash functions, including the SHA-1 and MD5 standard hash functions, were shown to fail the CRHF requirement but not (yet?) shown to fail the (weaker) SPR requirement. Namely, attacks were able to find collisions but not collisions to randomly chosen messages, i.e., *not second-preimage attacks.* Note, however, that some of these attacks, including against SHA-1 and MD5, allowed the attacker to find collisions to large families of inputs, facilitating practical attacks against applications of hash functions, attacks which would not be possible with only some arbitrary collision; see Section 3.3.6.

Therefore, whenever possible, protocols and systems should require only an SPR hash function rather than a CRHF. However, ensuring security when the hash function is only required to be SPR can be challenging since SPR hash functions are only expected to prevent collisions to *randomly selected messages.*

Let us consider one application which is often proposed for SPR hash functions: validating the integrity of downloaded files.

This application was discussed in Section 1.2.3 and illustrated in Figure 1.7, but there we discussed the solution using a CRHF h. The goal of this process is to allow the producer of a very large file m to place it in an untrusted repository yet allow a user to validate a download m' received from the untrusted repository, using only a small *fingerprint* f (where $|f| << |m|$), received securely from the producer.

In the process described in Section 1.2.3, the fingerprint of m, denoted $f(m)$, is computed simply as $f(m) = h(m)$. The user validates the download m' from the repository against the securely received fingerprint $f(m)$, by computing $h(m')$ and validating that $h(m') = f(m)$. If h is a CRHF, then a rogue repository would not be able to (efficiently) find such a collision, i.e., a file m' such that $m' \neq m$ yet $h(m') = f(m) = h(m)$.

Note that in this application, the attacker (rogue repository) should find a collision to the original file m, i.e., a collision to a specific preimage of h. Suppose that the attacker finds a collision for a different preimage of h, say x, x' s.t. $h(x) = h(x')$ and $m \notin \{x, x'\}$. It does not seem to be possible to use this collision (x, x') to find a collision $m' \neq m$ s.t. $h(m') = h(m)$. Therefore, SPR hash functions are sometimes said to suffice to secure this application.

However, downloaded files are not likely to contain randomly generated contents. In fact, many downloaded files have specific headers and other types of redundancy. Exercise 3.11 shows that if the files are not selected randomly, the attacker may be able to find a collision $m' \neq m$ s.t. $h(m') = h(m)$, even if h is a SPR hash function.

Let us give, therefore, an example of an application for which we can use a SPR hash function with confidence, i.e., where security provably follows from the requirements of the SPR. This example would be *proof of ability to foretell.* The example is illustrated in Figure 3.6; let us explain.

Cassandra had the ability to predict the future, but nobody believes her. She decides to prove her abilities to Bob. To do this, she predicts the sequence of the outcomes of the coin tosses that Bob will make; let us denote her prediction by $m = \{m_1, \ldots, m_M\}$. Cassandra could send m to Bob, but, instead, she sends $h(m)$, where h is an SPR hash. One motivation to send $h(m)$ instead of sending m could be efficiency, e.g., if m is very long.

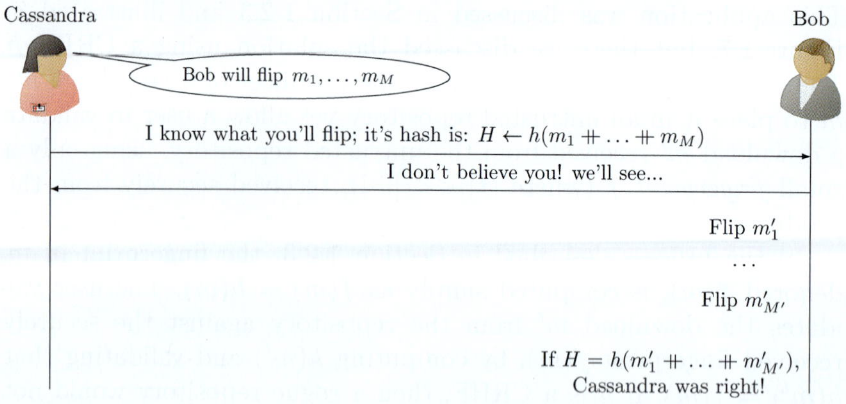

Figure 3.6. The Cassandra protocol, an application of a SPR hash to prove ability to predict coin flips.

Bob then begins flipping coins, until he is satisfied. Let the sequence of coin tosses by Bob be $m' = \{m'_1, \ldots, m'_{M'}\}$. To see if Cassandra can really predict the future, Bob now can simply compare $h(m')$ to the value $h(m)$ sent by Cassandra.

A few notes about this solution. *First*, note that Cassandra should be able to predict not just the values of Bob's coin flips but also the number of coin flips that Bob will do before he decides to check, but, for Cassandra, predicting the number of coin tosses is clearly hardly a challenge. *Second*, the fact that h is a SPR does not prevent Bob from possibly learning something about m from $h(m)$; the protocol was not designed for a self-deceiving Bob. *Third*, the author can foretell, but not prove, that not many soothsayers will adopt this protocol.

We conclude when we want to use a hash function to ensure integrity, we should use a hash believed to be a CRHF, and not a hash function only believed to be a SPR. In particular, both MD5 and SHA-1 should be avoided since collisions for them were found, although finding a second preimage is still considered hard for these hash functions.

3.3 Collision-resistant hash function (CRHF) schemes

In this section, we discuss CRHFs. Section 1.2.3 already presented a high-level description of CRHFs and their application to validate the integrity of downloaded software. In this section, we define a *keyless* CRHF, as well as two variants of keyed CRHFs: *Target-Collision-Resistant* (TCR) hash function and *Any-Collision-Resistant* (ACR), also called simply keyed CRHF.

3.3.1 Keyless collision-resistant hash function (keyless CRHF)

The input domain of a hash function is the (infinite) set of all binary strings, and, for any given digest length n, the range is finite ($\{0,1\}^n$). Hence, there are infinitely many *collisions*, i.e., messages $m \neq m'$ s.t. $h(m) = h(m')$, as illustrated in Figure 1.6. Indeed, even if we limit ourselves to the input set of messages $m \in \{0,1\}^{n+1}$, the number of messages is 2^{n+1} and the number of digests is 'only' 2^n, so clearly at least half (2^n) of the inputs must result in a collision. Namely, *collisions are common* — in *every* hash function.

However, for a sufficiently large digest length n, it is *conceivable* that *finding* a collision may be hard. Intuitively, we say that a hash function is *collision resistant*, if it is hard to find *any* collision. The definition follows.

Definition 3.2 (Keyless Collision-resistant hash function (CRHF)). Let $h[n] : \{0,1\}^* \to \{0,1\}^n$ be a family of keyless hash functions. We say that h is a CRHF if for every efficient algorithm $\mathcal{A}$, the *advantage function* $\varepsilon^{\text{CRHF}}_{h,\mathcal{A}}(n)$ is *negligible* in n, i.e., smaller than any positive polynomial for sufficiently large n (as $n \to \infty$), where:

$$\varepsilon^{\text{CRHF}}_{h,\mathcal{A}}(n) \equiv \Pr\left[(m,m') \leftarrow \mathcal{A}(1^n) \text{ s.t. } (m \neq m') \wedge \big(h[n](m) = h[n](m')\big)\right] \tag{3.2}$$

where the probability is taken over the random coin tosses of $\mathcal{A}$.

3.3.2 There are no keyless CRHFs

We now show that there is *no* keyless hash functions which satisfies Definition 3.2, i.e., there are *no keyless* CRHFs. Let us first present and prove this, and then discuss the implications.

The reader is right to be suspicious of a 'trick' here — after all, we just explained that all *standard* cryptographic hash functions are keyless! Indeed, the proof uses a 'trick': we show that for every keyless hash function h, there *exists* an efficient adversarial algorithm $\mathcal{A}_h$ that outputs a collision for h (for any given digest length n), and we show the 'structure' of a simple A_h, but A_h uses a set of collisions of h, which we only show exists but do not show how to find.

Lemma 3.1 (Keyless CRHFs do not exist). *There is no family of functions $h[n] : \{0,1\}^* \to \{0,1\}^n$ which is a collision-resistant hash function* (CRHF).

Proof. Given an arbitrary keyless hash function $h[n]$, we prove that there exists an efficient adversary algorithm $\mathcal{A}_h(1^n)$ that *always outputs a collision*, for every digest length 1^n (in unary). Namely, for every n holds $\varepsilon^{\text{CRHF}}_{h,\mathcal{A}}(n) = 1$; this clearly shows that $h[n](\cdot)$ does not satisfy the definition of a keyless CRHF.

For any given digest length n, the range of $h[n](\cdot)$ is the finite set $\{0,1\}^n$. On the other hand, the domain of all $h[n](\cdot)$ functions is the set of all binary strings, $\{0,1\}^*$. Since the (infinite) domain of $h[n](\cdot)$ is (much) larger than its range, it follows that there are (infinite number of) messages with the same digest.

For every digest length n, let $m_n \neq \hat{m_n}$ denote a pair of messages s.t. $h[n](m_n) = h[n](\hat{m_n})$, i.e., a collision for $h[n](\cdot)$. The adversary $\mathcal{A}_h(1^n)$ simply outputs the collision $(m_n, \hat{m_n})$. $\mathcal{A}_h$ is efficient, as it only needs to look up $(m_n, \hat{m_n})$, and *always* outputs a collision. Therefore, $h[n](\cdot)$ is not a keyless CRHF (as defined in Definition 3.2). □

Lemma 3.1 shows that *there is no keyless* CRHF as defined in Definition 3.2. Of course, there may be some other reasonable notion for collision resistance for keyless hash, for which the lemma does not apply. Indeed, SPR (Section 3.2) is basically a weaker collision-resistance property, which appears to be feasible; in particular, SPR hash functions can be constructed from cryptographic schemes which appear significantly weaker, such as one-way function (OWF), which we discuss in Section 3.4).

In spite of this result, many of the constructions we discuss later in this book use keyless hash functions, often assumed to be collision resistant. The main justification is that the use of keyless hash is much more common in practice, including in cryptographic standards; in particular, existing standards designs of hash functions are keyless, e.g., SHA.

Another justification is that if the system using the keyless hash h is insecure, then we should be able to use the attack to find a collision in h, and, so far, significant cryptanalysis efforts failed to find such collisions (for the standard keyless hash considered secure). In fact, many cryptographic designs and texts use an even stronger simplification — the *random oracle model* (ROM), which we discuss in Section 3.6.

Finally, it is usually easy to modify a construction using a keyless CRHF, into a construction that uses a keyed hash function satisfying a collision requirement. Which is a good point for us to discuss collision resistance for keyed hash functions.

3.3.3 Keyed collision resistance: ACR and TCR hash functions

We next discuss *keyed* CRHFs $h_k(m)$. Notice that we always reserve the term keyed hash functions to the use of a *non-secret* key, i.e., security requirements always assume that the key is known to the attacker. The fact that the key isn't secret is quite important to allow the use of keyed hash functions for integrity applications, e.g., integrity of downloaded files (Section 1.2.3) and as part of the Hash-then-Sign construction of efficient signature schemes (Section 3.3.5). The entity verifying the integrity of the file or verifying the signature will need to use the hashing key; therefore, it should not be secret.

Note that some places use the term 'keyed hash function' differently, in applications where the key should be secret. This use is often applied for constructions of PRFs or MAC functions which involve a combination of a keyless hash function with a secret key, often, the HMAC construction, see Section 4.4.5.

Keyed CRHFs are quite similar to keyless CRHFs, but the probability is also taken over the random choice of the key, which is provided as input to the adversary (since it is not secret). For simplicity, we focus on the case that the length of the key is the same as the length of the digest length, i.e., for every message $m \in \{0,1\}^*$ holds $|k| = |h_k(m)|$; this allows us to eliminate the (clumsy) provision of the digest length n as 'another' input, in brackets, given to the keyless hash function (as in $h[n](\cdot)$). However, we still denote the digest length — which is now also the key length — as n, i.e., $n \equiv |k| = |h_k(m)|$.

As for keyless CRHFs, a collision is any pair of different messages that hash to the same digest, now, using the randomly selected key. However, Bellare and Rogaway observed that the *order* between the choice of the key and the choice of the messages — or at least of one of the two messages — is significant, and defined (in Ref. [51]) two notions of keyed collision resistance: ACR and TCR. We present both notions.

Any-Collision-Resistant (ACR) hash functions: We first define ACR hash functions; this notion was defined early on by Damgård, using the term *keyed* CRHF, in Ref. [143]. However, we try to consistently use the term ACR, introduced later by Bellare and Rogaway (in Ref. [51]). The reason to prefer the term ACR is to emphasize the difference from the term TCR, defined in the following.

Intuitively, a keyed hash function $h_k(\cdot)$ is ACR if, with high probability, it is infeasible for an attacker to find efficiently a pair of colliding inputs for the hash function, using a randomly chosen key known to the attacker. We illustrate ACR hash functions in Figure 3.7; the definition follows.

Definition 3.3 (Any-Collision-Resistant (ACR) hash function, aka keyed CRHF). Consider a keyed hash function $h_k(\cdot) : \{0,1\}^n \times \{0,1\}^* \to \{0,1\}^n$, defined for any digest length $n \in \mathbb{N}$. We say that h is ACR if for every efficient algorithm $\mathcal{A}$, the *advantage*

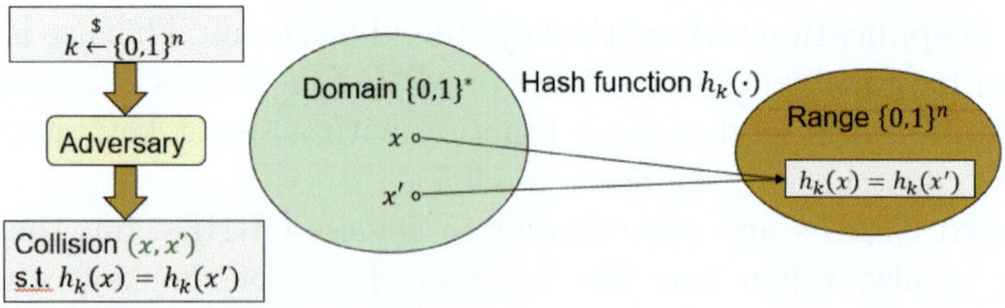

Figure 3.7. The test for an Any-Collision-Resistant (ACR) hash function, also called keyed CRHF. Given a random n-bits key k, it should be hard to find any collision for h_k, i.e., a pair of inputs $x, x' \in \{0,1\}^*$ s.t. $h_k(x) = h_k(x')$. Compare to TCR hash (Figure 3.8).

function $\varepsilon^{\text{ACR}}_{h,\mathcal{A}}(n)$ is *negligible* in n, i.e., $\varepsilon^{\text{ACR}}_{h,\mathcal{A}}(n) \in \text{NEGL}(n)$, where:

$$\varepsilon^{\text{ACR}}_{h,\mathcal{A}}(n) \equiv \Pr_{k \leftarrow \{0,1\}^n} \left[(x, x') \leftarrow \mathcal{A}(k) \text{ s.t. } (x \neq x') \wedge ((h_k(x) = h_k(x'))\right] \tag{3.3}$$

where the probability is taken over the random coin tosses of the adversary $\mathcal{A}$ and the random choice of k.

We note that the hashing key is needed to use a keyed hash function to validate integrity, e.g., to validate downloaded files (Section 1.2.3) or signatures (Section 3.3.5). When using ACR hash functions, this is relatively easy since the same hashing key can be used repeatedly, as we assume it is known to the attacker who is looking for a collision; in particular, for signatures, the hashing key can be treated and distributed just like the public key of the scheme or simply become a part of the public key. We next present TCR hash functions, which do not have this advantage and may require a separate hashing key each time we compute the digest of a message or file.

Target-Collision-Resistant (TCR) hash functions: The ACR requirement allows the adversary to select both colliding messages *after* the random key is chosen and becomes known to the attacker. In Ref. [51], Bellare and Rogaway suggested the term TCR for a weaker notion of collision resistance for keyed hash functions, where the adversary has to select the first of the two colliding messages *before* it knows the key; the adversary is still allowed to know the key before selecting the colliding (second) message. This notion was introduced earlier by Naor and Yung in Ref. [376], where they referred to it as *universal one-way hash functions (UOWHF)*; both terms are still used in the literature, and we use TCR.

The use of TCR requires the selection of a separate hashing key for each message being hashed[3] and integrity-protected distribution

[3] To be more precise, we need a separate hashing key each time we use-up a key by potentially exposing it to the attacker.

of that key, e.g., together with the digest. This is less convenient than ACR hash, where the hashing key can be made public *before* hashing, and reused for hashing many messages. This is a disadvantage for TCR hash, although the size of the hashing key is small, i.e., the communication and storage overhead is small. On the other hand, TCR hash functions may be easier to design, and the TCR property may be harder to break, exactly since it is a weaker requirement. These advantages motivate the use of TCR hashing, following the conservative design principle (Principle 3).

In a successful attack against a TCR hash function, the attacker *first selects the target* x_T, i.e., one of the two colliding strings. Only *then* would the attacker receive the (random) key k. Finally, after the attacker is given the random key k, the attacker has to output the colliding string $x_C \neq x_T$ s.t. $h_k(x_C) = h_k(x_T)$. Indeed, in many applications, the attacker *may* have some influence over the choice of the legitimately integrity-protected 'target' x_T, but since the key k is selected only later, the attacker is prevented from selecting a target x_T for which the attacker can find a collision x_C for k.

The definition follows and is illustrated in Figure 3.8.

Definition 3.4 (Target-Collision-Resistant (TCR) hash). A keyed hash function $h_k(\cdot) : \{0,1\}^* \times \{0,1\}^* \to \{0,1\}^*$ is called a TCR hash, if for every efficient algorithm $\mathcal{A}$, the *advantage function* $\varepsilon^{TCR}_{h,\mathcal{A}}(n)$ is *negligible* in n, i.e., smaller than any positive polynomial

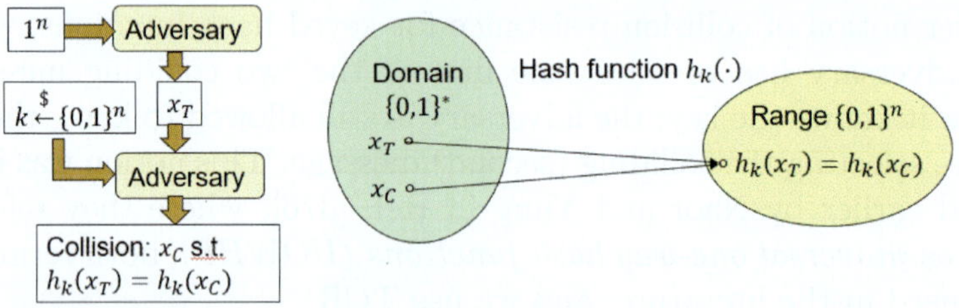

Figure 3.8. The test for a Target-Collision-Resistant (TCR) hash function, also called a universal one-way hash function (UOWHF). An adversary, given only the security parameter 1^n, should not be able to efficiently find a collision $x_C \neq x_T$ s.t. $h(x_C) = h(x_T)$, for a specific *target* preimage x_T, where x_T was chosen before the random key k is known. Compare to ACR hash, as illustrated in Figure 3.7.

for sufficiently large n (as $n \to \infty$), where:

$$\varepsilon_{h,\mathcal{A}}^{\text{TCR}}(n) \equiv \Pr_{k \leftarrow \{0,1\}^n} \left[\left\{ \begin{array}{c} x_T \leftarrow \mathcal{A}(1^n); \\ x_C \leftarrow \mathcal{A}(x_T, k) \end{array} \right\} \begin{array}{c} \text{s.t. } (x_C \neq x_T) \wedge \\ (h_k(x_C) = h_k(x_T)) \end{array} \right] \quad (3.4)$$

where the probability is taken over the random coin tosses of $\mathcal{A}$ and the random choice of k.

Note that in Equation (3.4) the hashing key k is chosen randomly *before* the adversary is selects the target message x_T. However, k is only *given* to the adversary *after* the adversary selected X_T; it doesn't matter if the selection occurred earlier or later, it only matters when the adversary *knows* the target x_T. Choosing the key earlier is simply a bit more convenient for the layout of the equation.

Let h be a keyed hash. Suppose h is not TCR, i.e., there is some adversary $\mathcal{A}$ and target x_T such that, given k, the adversary can find efficiently a collision $x_C \neq x_T$ (s.t. $h(x_T) = h(x_C)$). Therefore, $\mathcal{A}$ can surely output this collision (x_C, x_T) after being given k, i.e., h is also not ACR. Namely, if a hash function h' is ACR, then it must also be TCR.

The reverse appears unlikely; Exercise 3.28 which shows that if TCR hash functions exist, then there exists a TCR hash which is not an ACR hash, and specific examples of a hash which is not ACR (but could be TCR) and a hash which is neither ACR not TCR.

Following the conservative design principle (Principle 3), when we design a keyed hash function, our goal should, therefore, be for it to be an ACR hash so that it would be secure for applications requiring either ACR or TCR hash. On the other hand, designs of applications, protocols and schemes, should use, where possible, a TCR hash rather than an ACR hash since then they will be secure even if the hash function in use turns out to be 'only' TCR.

Another important motivation for designs to use a TCR hash rather than an ACR hash is that ACR hash functions are subject to the *birthday attack*, which we discuss in the following section. TCR hash functions are not subject to the birthday attack; therefore, a TCR hash can use significantly shorter keys and digests.

3.3.4 Birthday and exhaustive attacks on CRHFs

In Exercise 3.30, we discuss that for every hash function h, an attacker can find collisions, with significant probability of success, but only *inefficiently*, using $O(2^n)$ computations; this includes collisions for keyless hash, as well as both any-collision or target-collision for keyed hash.

However, in this section we show that finding collisions in a keyless hash function, or finding any-collision for a keyed hash, requires only $O(2^{n/2}) = O\left(\sqrt{2^n}\right)$ expected number of hash-computations, rather than $O(2^n)$.

This attack is called the *birthday attack* since it is due to the so-called *birthday paradox* [134,219,358]. Consider a room containing 23 persons. What is the probability of a *collision*, i.e., two people having birthday on the same day of the year? Many people expect this probability to be quite small, but in reality, the probability is about half. To understand why this is true, note that when a person is added to a room currently containing i persons (with no collisions), the probability of a collision with *some* person in the room is $\frac{i}{356}$, not $\frac{1}{356}$.

More precisely, the expected number q of messages $\{m_1, m_2, \ldots, m_q\}$ which should be hashed before finding a collision $h(m_i) = h(m_j)$ is approximately:

$$q \lessapprox 2^{n/2} \cdot \sqrt{\frac{\pi}{2}} \lessapprox 1.254 \cdot 2^{n/2} \tag{3.5}$$

Hence, to ensure collision-resistance against adversary who can do 2^q computations, e.g., $q = 80$ hash calculations, we need the digest length n to be roughly twice that size, e.g., 160 bits. Namely, the *effective key length* of a CRHF is only $q = n/2$. This motivates the fact that hash functions often have digest length larger than the key length of symmetric key cryptosystems used in the same system, even twice the size of the key length of the symmetric key cryptosystems. Using longer digest length and/or longer key length does not harm security, but may have performance implications. The impact is similar — possibly a bit smaller — when considering attackers with quantum-computing capabilities, see Section 10.2.

Note that the birthday attack applies to both ACR hash functions and *keyless* CRHFs. However, it does *not* apply to *TCR* hash functions. Can you see why? Carefully compare Definition 3.3 vs.

Definition 3.4, and you will see. This provides another important advantage to designing cryptographic protocols and schemes by using TCR hash functions rather than using ACR hash functions (or keyless hash functions).

3.3.5 The Hash-then-Sign (HtS) paradigm

Collision resistance is a powerful property; in particular, it facilitates one of the most important applications of cryptographic hash functions: the *Hash-then-Sign* (HtS) *paradigm*. The HtS paradigm is essential for efficient deployment of public-key digital signatures, which we introduced in Section 1.5.1. We present constructions for signature schemes based on public key cryptosystems in Section 6.6, and in Section 3.4.2 we discuss *one-time signatures* and present their constructions, based on one-way functions. However, both approaches result in signatures for *limited-length inputs*; furthermore, extending the input length would significantly further increase the already high overhead of signature computation and validation (see Table 6.1). Therefore, practical applications *always* use a more efficient solution: the HtS design, which we discuss in this section.

The HtS design can be applied using either keyed or keyless hash functions. We first discuss the keyless-hash variant (or 'keyless HtS') and then discuss two variants for keyed hash functions, one for ACR hash and one for TCR hash.

Hash-then-Sign using keyless hash: The keyless Hash-then-Sign construction applies a keyless hash function $h(\cdot)$ to the 'long' message m, and signs the (short) output $h(m)$. Namely, given a signature scheme $\mathcal{S}$ defined for domain $\{0,1\}^n$ and a hash function h with domain $\{0,1\}^*$ and range $\{0,1\}^n$ (i.e., $h : \{0,1\}^* \rightarrow \{0,1\}^n$), we define the HtS scheme $\mathcal{S}^h_{\text{HtS}}$ as follows:

$$\mathcal{S}^h_{\text{HtS}}.\mathcal{KG}(1^n) \equiv \mathcal{S}.\mathcal{KG}(1^n) \tag{3.6}$$

$$\mathcal{S}^h_{\text{HtS}}.\mathcal{S}ign_s(m) \equiv \mathcal{S}.\mathcal{S}ign_s(h(m)) \tag{3.7}$$

$$\mathcal{S}^h_{\text{HtS}}.\mathcal{V}erify_v(m,\sigma) \equiv \mathcal{S}.\mathcal{V}erify_v(h(m),\sigma) \tag{3.8}$$

The HtS scheme $\mathcal{S}^h_{\text{HtS}}$ may be applied to any binary string, i.e., its domain is $\{0,1\}^*$. The reader may confirm that it is a correct signature scheme over $\{0,1\}^*$ (Exercise 3.19).

However, is it a secure signature scheme, i.e., prevents forgeries? Obviously, if the attacker can find a collision for h, i.e., $x \neq x'$ s.t. $h(x) = h(x')$, then a signature over x is also a valid signature over x', i.e., the attacker can produce a forged signature.

Intuitively, if $h : \{0,1\}^* \rightarrow \{0,1\}^n$ is a CRHF, as in Definition 3.2, and $\mathcal{S}$ is an existentially unforgeable *signature scheme* over $\{0,1\}^n$, then the HtS scheme $\mathcal{S}^h_{\text{HtS}}$ is an existentially unforgeable *signature scheme* over $\{0,1\}^*$. Note that Lemma 3.1 showed that keyless CRHFs do not exist at all, which reduces the motivation to present a formal of security.

The HtS for ACR hash functions: We now present a simple HtS construction, presented by Damgård [143], which uses a (keyed) ACR hash function. The ACR-HtS construction is identical to the keyless HtS construction, except for the use of a keyed hash $h_k(\cdot) : \{0,1\}^n \times \{0,1\}^* \rightarrow \{0,1\}^n$, defined for arbitrary key and digest length $n \in \mathbb{N}$. The hash key is selected *once*, during the key-generation process, and becomes part of the public verification key of the composed signature scheme, as well as a part of the private signing key (since it is also used for signing). We define the ACR-HtS construction $\mathcal{S}^h_{\text{HtS}}$ as follows.

Definition 3.5 (The ACR-HtS construction). Given a signature scheme $\mathcal{S}$ with domain $\{0,1\}^n$ and a keyed hash (CRHF) $h_k(\cdot) : \{0,1\}^* \times \{0,1\}^* \rightarrow \{0,1\}^*$, the ACR-HtS signature using signature $\mathcal{S}$ and keyed-hash h is defined as follows:

$$\mathcal{S}^h_{\text{HtS}}.\mathcal{KG}(1^n) \equiv \begin{bmatrix} (s,v) \xleftarrow{\$} \mathcal{S}.\mathcal{KG}(1^n) \; ; \\ k \xleftarrow{\$} \{0,1\}^n \; ; \\ \text{return } ((s,k),(v,k)) \end{bmatrix} \tag{3.9}$$

$$\mathcal{S}^h_{\text{HtS}}.\mathcal{Sign}_{(s,k)}(m) \equiv \mathcal{S}.\mathcal{Sign}_s(h_k(m)) \tag{3.10}$$

$$\mathcal{S}^h_{\text{HtS}}.\mathcal{Verify}_{(v,k)}(m,\sigma) \equiv \mathcal{S}.\mathcal{Verify}_v(h_k(m),\sigma) \tag{3.11}$$

The ACR-HtS construction requires the underlying keyed hash function to satisfy a relatively-strong requirement, namely, to make it infeasible to find *any* collision (what we referred to as keyed-CRHF or ACR hash).

The HtS for TCR hash functions: Bellare and Rogaway show, in Ref. [51], a HtS construction which uses the TCR hash functions; we refer to this construction as TCR-HtS. TCR-HtS is similar to ACR-HtS but with a critical difference: instead of using a fixed hashing key k and considering it part of the public key, we select a new random hashing key k whenever a message is signed, and sign it together with the message. We define the TCR-HtS construction $\mathcal{S}^h_{\text{TCR-HtS}}$ as follows.

Definition 3.6 (The TCR-HtS construction). Given a signature scheme $\mathcal{S}$ with domain $\{0,1\}^n$, defined for any integer n, and a keyed hash $h_k(\cdot) : \{0,1\}^n \times \{0,1\}^* \rightarrow \{0,1\}^n$, the TCR-HtS signature using signature $\mathcal{S}$ and keyed-hash h is defined as follows:

$$\mathcal{S}^h_{\text{TCR-HtS}}.\mathcal{KG}(1^n) \equiv \mathcal{S}.\mathcal{KG}(1^n) \tag{3.12}$$

$$\mathcal{S}^h_{\text{TCR-HtS}}.\mathcal{S}ign_s(m) \equiv \begin{bmatrix} k \xleftarrow{\$} \{0,1\}^n \; ; \\ \sigma \leftarrow \mathcal{S}.\mathcal{S}ign_s(k + h_k(m)) \\ \text{return } (k,\sigma) \end{bmatrix} \tag{3.13}$$

$$\mathcal{S}^h_{\text{TCR-HtS}}.\mathcal{V}erify_v(m,(k,\sigma)) \equiv \mathcal{S}.\mathcal{V}erify_v(k + h_k(m),\sigma) \tag{3.14}$$

There are two important advantages to using a TCR hash rather than an ACR hash. The first advantage is that the TCR requirement is *weaker*. Namely, a keyed hash function may meet the TCR requirement even if it fails to meet the ACR (keyed CRHF) requirement (see Section 3.3.3). By ensuring security of the signature while relying on a weaker property of the hash function, the construction may remain secure even if the hash function in use will eventually be found to fail the (stronger) ACR requirement. This follows the conservative design principle (Principle 3).

The second advantage is that the ACR property is subject to the generic *birthday attack*, while the TCR property is not. As a result, a significantly shorter hash length may suffice for a design requiring TCR hash, compared to design requiring ACR hash.

Challenges and solutions for deploying keyed HtS: Unfortunately, both of the keyed HtS constructions (using ACR or TCR hash) involve challenges for deployment by modification of existing systems, which are designed for HtS using keyless hash functions. The ACR-HtS construction requires the distribution of a longer public key since the random hash key becomes part of the public key, and the TCR-HtS construction requires a longer *signature* (k, σ), i.e., the signature has to include also the random key chosen for the hash function. Several papers propose alternative HtS constructions with provable security properties but without such deployment challenges, some of them also based on keyless hash functions; for example, see Ref. [397].

3.3.6 Identical-prefix and chosen-prefix collisions attacks

Practical systems often use keyless cryptographic hash functions assuming they are collision-resistant, e.g., for the HtS construction. This is in spite of the fact that there is no keyless CRHF, in fact, every hash function *must* have an infinite number of collisions.

Suppose that an attack is found that allows the attacker to find collisions, but only of very specific content, with only limited ability of the attacker to control the colliding values. Such collisions could be hard to exploit, and practitioners may not consider them as a sufficient reason to change to a different hash function. Changing deployed systems and standards is hard; it is easier to motivate the community and industry to adopt a change, once we have a convincing proof of vulnerability.

This situation happened with collision attacks against cryptographic hash functions, in particular, attacks against MD5 and SHA-1. The first attacks against both hashes were of a type named *identical-prefix collision attacks.* Given a prefix p, we say that a collision for h is a *p-prefix collision* if p is a prefix to both colliding preimages. An attacker $\mathcal{A}$ *can find identical-prefix collisions* for h, if for *any* prefix p, $\mathcal{A}$ can (efficiently) output a p-prefix collision for h.

The first identical prefix attacks were published in 2005 against MD5 (by Wang and Yu [474][4]), and in 2017 against SHA-1 (by

[4]This paper and a companion paper [473] show related attacks against other well-known stateless hash function including MD4, RIPEMD and HAVAL.

Stevens *et al.* [451]). We discuss below exploits of identical-prefix collisions; however, it is arguable whether these exploits can be exploited for actual attacks against deployed systems. This question does not exist for a stronger type of attack, named *chosen-prefix collision attacks.* An attacker $\mathcal{A}$ *can find chosen-prefix collisions* for h, if for *any pair of same-length prefixes* p_1, p_2 (s.t. $|p_1| = |p_2|$), $\mathcal{A}$ can (efficiently) output a pair of *collision strings* $c_1 \neq c_2$ such that $h(p_1 + c_1) = h(p_2 + c_2)$.

The first chosen-prefix collision attacks against MD5 were published already in 2005 by Lenstra and De Weger [326], with significantly improved attacks in Refs. [452–454]. The first chosen-prefix collision attack against SHA-1 was published by Leurent and Peyrin in 2020 [328].

We note that both MD5 and SHA-1 use the Merkle–Damgård construction (Section 3.8), which hashes long messages iteratively, block by block. Hash functions using this construction allow length-extensions to collisions, i.e., if $x_1 \neq x_2$ is a collision ($h(x_1) = h(x_2)$), then for every suffix s holds $h(x_1 + s) = h(x_2 + s)$. Namely, appending any suffix s to two colliding preimages will result in a pair of (longer) colliding preimages. This property is extensively used by the published exploits for identical-prefix and chosen-prefix collisions.

Let us now briefly describe a few exploits of chosen-prefix and identical-prefix collision attacks. All exploits are for applications using the HtS design, used to sign Variable Input Length messages by hashing them into a fixed-length digest, and then sign the digest using a Fixed Input Length signature scheme (e.g., RSA). The attacker uses the chosen-prefix vulnerability of the hash function, to find two colliding preimages for the hash function, a seemingly benign preimage and an 'attack preimage' (that would not be signed intentionally). The attacker tricks a victim to sign the seemingly benign preimage. The resulting signature would also be a valid signature over the attack preimage. The attack differ in how the attacker constructs the colliding preimages, gets the seemingly benign preimage signed and exploits the signature.

We begin by discussing the (easier) case of exploiting chosen-prefix collisions and then discuss exploits of identical-prefix collisions.

3.3.6.1 *Exploiting chosen-prefix collision attacks*

It is relatively easy to exploit a hash function h which is vulnerable to chosen-prefix collision attacks. We present two such exploits: in the following, and in Figure 3.9, a simple exploit, which seems impractical; and in Section 8.2.5, a very practical exploit, which allows forgery of a public-key certificate.

The exploit of Figure 3.9 involves a small bit of social engineering, mainly, Mal convinces Alice to donate \$1 to the World Wildlife Fund (WWF), for some cause, e.g., feeding the apes. To donate, Alice should sign a *donation e-check* whose contents are kindly provided by Mal and which *seems* to be such a contribution. (We discuss other social-engineering attacks and defenses against them in Chapter 9.)

The donation e-check was actually carefully engineered by Mal, to allow Mal to abuse Alice's signature on the donation e-check, to deposit a (very different) *fake e-check*, where Alice instructs her bank to pay \$1000 to Mal. Specifically, Mal carefully prepares two equal-length messages, p_1 and p_2 (s.t. $|p_1| = |p_2|$), such that p_1 is

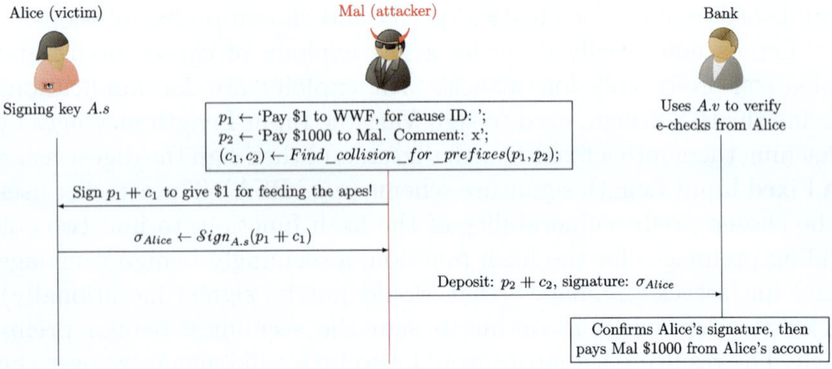

Figure 3.9. Attacker exploiting a chosen-prefix collision of h to forge a deposit from Alice. The attacker asks Alice for a \$1 contribution to the World Wildlife Fund (WWF), claiming this will be used to feed apes. The message includes a string which is supposed to be a 'cause identifier' but, in reality, will contain a collision string c_1. Alice signs, not knowing that the message collides with an e-check where she pays \$1000 to Mal; the e-check contains a string which is supposed to be a comment but is really the second collision string c_2.

an e-check for Alice to donate \$1 to the WWF for a specific cause and p_2 is an e-check where Alice pays \$1000 to Mal (with some comment). Mal then exploits the vulnerability of the hash function h to compute a collision (c_1, c_2) for this pair of prefixes, i.e., $(c_1, c_2) \leftarrow Find\_collision\_for\_prefixes(p_1, p_2)$.

Next, Mal convinces Alice to donate \$1 for feeding the apes, by signing the e-check $p_1 + c_1 =$ 'Pay \$1 to WWF, for cause ID:' $+ c_1$. Note that Mal used the 'cause ID:' field to concatenate the collision string c_1 to be part of the preimage, ensuring the collision with the fake e-check, when concatenated with the other collision c_2. Similarly, ended the fake e-check with the string 'Comment: x' followed by the other collision string c_2 so that the bank will not suspect the e-check due to the inclusion of this arbitrary string of characters. Note that the comment begins with the letter 'x' simply to make sure that the two prefixes are of the same length.

We denote Alice's signature on this e-check by σ_{Alice}. Remember that Alice's signature is the result of the signature operation of a FIL signature scheme, e.g., RSA, applied to the hash of the message being signed. Since $h(p_1 + c_1) = h(p_2 + c_2)$, then σ_{Alice} is also a valid signature for the fake e-check $p_2 + c_2 =$ 'Pay \$1000 to Mal. Comment: x'$+ c_2$. Therefore, all that remains is for Mal to deposit the fake e-check in the bank, with Alice's signature σ_{Alice}. Since the two e-checks have the same digest (using the vulnerable hash h), then σ_{Alice} is a valid signature also for the fake e-check, and the bank pays \$1000 to Mal from Alice's account. Alice should be grateful that the amount was only \$1000 (which we used to simplify the example a bit). Or maybe that's all Alice had in her account; attackers may use social engineering also to trick Alice into disclosing her balance.

3.3.6.2 *Exploiting Identical-prefix collisions*

Figure 3.10 illustrates an exploit of the identical-prefix collision vulnerability of hash function h. Namely, for any given prefix p, the attacker can efficiently find a *collision*, i.e., a pair of different strings $c \neq c'$ such that for any suffix t holds that the two resulting messages, $bait \equiv p + c + t$ and $fake \equiv p + c' + t$ would be a collision for h, i.e., $h(bait) = h(fake)$.

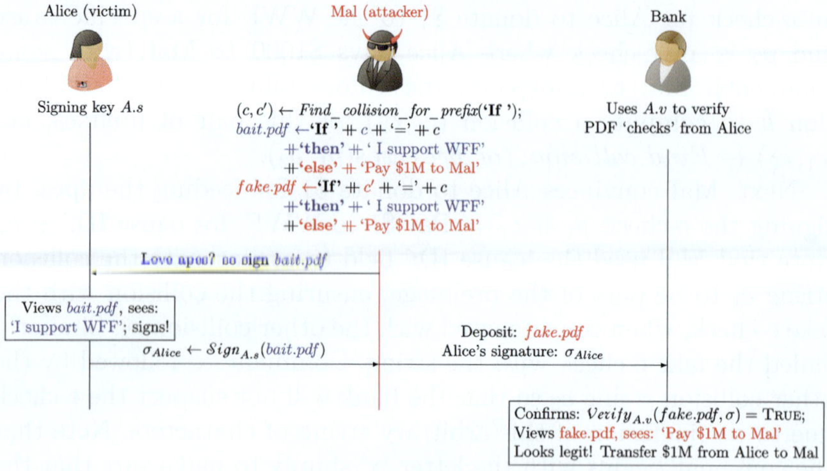

Figure 3.10. Attacker exploiting identical-prefix collision of h to forge Alice's signature over a PDF version of an e-check, fake.pdf, which transfers \$1M from Alice to Mal. The PDF file that Alice received and signed, bait.pdf, displays a message or petition that Alice is willing to sign, e.g., support for the World Wildlife Fund (WWF). The two files have been doctored by Mal to have the same hash value — and hence, the same signature too. The contents of both PDF files have been simplified for readability; for the complete details, see Ref. [198].

Exploiting the identical-prefix collisions vulnerability can be challenging since the two colliding messages, *bait* and *fake*, begin with a common prefix p which is not controlled by the attacker. In fact, this vulnerability can be exploited only in a limited set of applications and scenarios. Figure 3.10 illustrates the exploit as applied to PDF documents (*bait.pdf* and *fake.pdf*); this is a simplification of the original demonstration of the exploit, also for PDF documents, presented in Ref. [198].

Let us briefly explain the attack. A bank allows a customer, e.g., Mal (the attacker), to deposit a PDF check signed by another customer, e.g., Alice. In the attack, Mal deposits a check signed by Alice for \$1M (one million dollars), without Alice ever signing such a check. In fact, Alice only signs an innocent-looking PDF document provided by Mal, stating that she (Alice) supports the World Wildlife Fund (WWF); we call this innocent-looking file *bait.pdf*. However, as illustrated in Figure 3.10, Mal has carefully constructed the file *bait.pdf* so that its hash will be the same as the hash of another file, $fake.pdf$, instructing the bank to transfer \$1M from Alice to Mal. Namely, $h(bait.pdf) = h(fake.pdf)$. Therefore, Mal can deposit fake.pdf together with Alice's signature on bait.pdf since:

$$Sign_{A.s}(bait.pdf) = Sign_{A.s}(fake.pdf)$$

To create these two colliding PDF documents, the attacker exploits the fact that PDF documents support *conditional formatting*, such as an 'if-then-else' statement, where depending on the 'if' condition, the PDF viewer displays either the 'then' text or the 'else' text. Figure 3.10 illustrates the exploit, with a simplification of the PDF file content focusing on a (simplified) 'if-then-else' statement.

3.4 One-Way Functions (OWFs)

In this section, we discuss *one-way functions* (OWFs), another basic form of keyless cryptographic functions. Intuitively, a function h is a OWF, if, given $h(x)$ for a (sufficiently long) random preimage x, it is infeasible to find either x or any other preimage x' of h, s.t. $h(x') = h(x)$. This is illustrated in Figure 3.11.

As shown in Figure 3.11, we focus on one-way functions which are also hash functions, i.e., they map from arbitrary binary strings to outputs (digests) of fixed length n. Such OWFs are sometimes referred to as *preimage-resistant hash functions*; however, we prefer the term OWF to the term *preimage-resistant hash function* since the term 'one-way function' is more widely used and emphasizes the

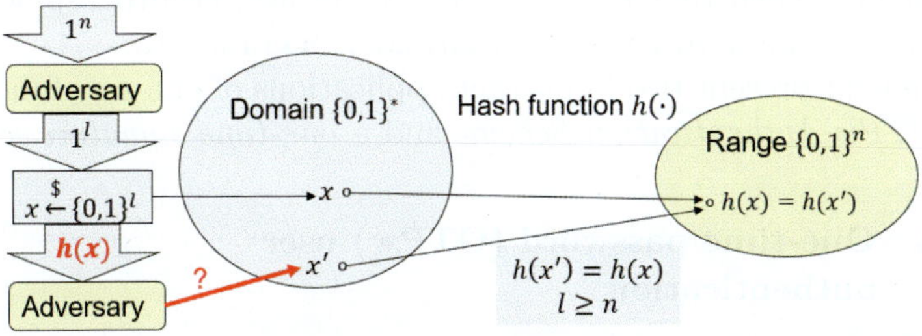

Figure 3.11. Intuition of the one-way function (OWF) property, aka *preimage-resistant hash* function: given $h(x)$ for a (sufficiently long) random preimage x, it is infeasible to find x, or any other preimage x' of h, i.e., s.t. $h(x') = h(x)$. Details in Definition 3.7.

'one-way' property: computing $h(x)$ is easy, but 'inverting' it to find x, or a colliding preimage x' s.t. $h(x') = h(x)$, is hard.

The definition follows; for simplicity, we focus on the of a one-way hash function, i.e., the inputs can be any binary strings. Note that the input x is selected as a random $l \geq n$ bits string, where l is selected by the adversary (in unary). This selection process is similar to the one used in the definition of second-preimage resistant (SPR) hash and for the same reasons: to ensure that the adversary is limited to runtime polynomial in n and to allow random choice of x (from a finite domain); we can't choose a random value from an infinite set with uniform (non-zero) probability.

Definition 3.7 (One-Way Function (OWF)). An efficient function h, with domain $\{0,1\}^*$ and range $\{0,1\}^n$, is called a OWF, if for every efficient algorithm $\mathcal{A} \in PPT$, the *advantage function* $\varepsilon^{\text{OWF}}_{h,\mathcal{A}}(n)$ is *negligible* in n, i.e., smaller than any positive polynomial for sufficiently large n (as $n \to \infty$), where:

$$\varepsilon^{\text{OWF}}_{h,\mathcal{A}}(n) \equiv \Pr\left[\begin{array}{c}\left(1^l \xleftarrow{\$} \mathcal{A}(1^n)\ ;\ x \xleftarrow{\$} \{0,1\}^l\right) \\ h\left(\mathcal{A}(h(x))\right) = h(x) \wedge l \geq n\end{array}\right] \tag{3.15}$$

where the probability is taken over the random coin tosses of $\mathcal{A}$ and over the choice of $x \xleftarrow{\$} \{0,1\}^l$.

The definition of a OWF *requires* the input x to be selected as a *random* l bits string. If x is selected from a different set or not uniformly, then an attacker given $h(x)$ may be possible to find a preimage x' such that $h(x') = h(x)$. As always, cryptographic functions should be used correctly, to avoid vulnerabilities.

We next present two important applications of one-way functions: the *OTPw Authentication Scheme* and a *one-time signature* scheme.

3.4.1 One-time password (OTPw) user authentication

Passwords are the most well-known and widely used method for user authentication, in spite of significant security concerns. We discuss these concerns, and alternative or complementary methods for user authentication, in Chapter 9. One concern is that a password may be exposed when used, e.g., by an observer who can see the user typing the password (a *shoulder surfing* attack). In Chapter 9, we also discuss several OTPw[5] user authentication methods, which address this concern by requiring the user to provide a different 'one-time password' at every login.

We describe here a OTPw scheme that uses a OWF, as an example of an application of a OWF. This design was proposed in one of the earliest publications in the theory of cryptography, published as early as 1974 [177]. In addition to using each password only once, this design also provides some security against exposure of the server's password file, which is another concern with password-based user authentication. In Chapter 9, we discuss designs which build on this basic design but extend it to allow multiple authentications, including the hash chain, S/Key and T/Key designs.

Each user, say Alice (denoted by A), selects, or is assigned, one or more one-time passwords. In reality, user's choice of passwords is far from uniform; therefore, implementations often assign random OTPw rather than unrealistically assume that users choose uniformly random one-time passwords; of course, this means that users usually save the one-time passwords to ensure their availability.

Let us denote a specific OTPw by PW_A; preferably, PW_A would be a random string containing at least n bits, e.g., $\mathrm{PW}_A \stackrel{\$}{\leftarrow} \{0,1\}^n$. Alice then computes $\mathrm{HPW}_A \leftarrow h(\mathrm{PW}_A)$, where $h : \{0,1\}^* \rightarrow \{0,1\}^n$ is a OWF. Alice sends HPW_A, over secure communication, to the server. The server saves HPW_A to be used to authenticate Alice.

To authenticate herself, Alice sends the OTPw PW_A to the server; the server computes $h(\mathrm{PW}_A)$ and verifies that it is the same as the stored value HPW_A.

If h is a OWF and the password PW_A is random then, from Definition 3.7, an efficient adversary cannot find a random preimage

[5]We use the abbreviation OTPw rather than the acronym OTP, to avoid confusion with one-time pad (OTP), introduced in Section 2.5.

PW_A, even if given the validation token HPW_A. Hence, the OTPw scheme is secure: if Bob finds that $HPA_A = h(PW_A)$, this should mean that PW_A is the correct OTPw. If Alice kept PW_A securely and only disclosed PW_A to authenticate herself to Bob, then Bob knows this also means that Alice has initiated the authentication (by disclosing PW_A). Of course, an attacker who obtains the OTPw PW_A could try to abuse it; therefore, Bob should only accept the one-time password PW_A once, i.e., 'one time'.

The OTPw scheme requires the transmission of the password to be done over a secure (encrypted) channel; if an attacker can eavesdrop to the password, then security is trivially broken. A secure connection is also required if the user wishes to replace the password (after authenticating successfully). Also, remember that the security of the scheme depends on the use of random passwords; if the password is selected by the user, then it is likely to be non-random. In fact, many users often select passwords from a limited sized set, referred to as a *dictionary*, allowing the attacker may find the password PW_A from HPW_A by hashing the different passwords in the dictionary — an *offline dictionary attack* (Section 9.3.5).

In the following section, we move to a different — albeit related — application of one-way functions: the *one-time signature scheme*.

3.4.2 One-time signature scheme

We next show how to use a OWF to implement a public key signature scheme. In the simple forms that we present in this chapter, the resulting signature scheme can only be used once, i.e., to sign only a single message. We call such a scheme a *one-time signature scheme*. More elaborate hash-based signatures were designed, most notably, the SPHINCS signature scheme [63] and the (improved) SPHINCS+ signature schemes [64]. SPHINCS+ was adopted as the *stateless hash based Digital Signature Algorithm*, published in FIPS 205 and named (SLH-DSA) [388], one of the standards for post-quantum signature schemes; see Section 10.2.

Note that our definition of signature schemes (Section 1.5.1) did not allow a restriction on the number of applications of the signature scheme; therefore, one-time signature schemes are not within the scope of Section 1.5.1. However, it is not hard to extend the definitions in Section 1.5.1 so that they support limited number of applications.

In spite of their obvious limitations, one-time signatures have important advantages in *security* and *performance*, making them a good choice for many applications. These advantages are in comparison to the widely used public-key signatures schemes such as RSA and DSA, whose security is based on the hardness of factoring (RSA) or of computing discrete logarithms (DSA); we discuss RSA, factoring and discrete-log in Chapter 6. Let us discuss these advantages of one-time signatures.

Possibly the most significant *security advantage* of one-time signatures is that they are not (too) vulnerable to the potential availability to an attacker of a *quantum computing* device. This is in contrast to factoring, discrete-logarithms and many other computational problems, which may be efficiently solved (broken) using an appropriate quantum computer; we briefly discuss the impact of quantum computing in Section 10.1. Known quantum algorithms provide only a very limited advantage against cryptographic hash functions, compared to their dramatic ability to solve the factoring and discrete logarithm problems.

Signature schemes based on computational assumptions (factoring, discrete logarithm) are also subject to other possible improvements in the algorithms to solve these problems. One-time signature schemes are also subject to vulnerabilities of the underlying hash function, but changing to another function/scheme, as well as using a significant margin (longer digests), would be easier for signature schemes based on hash functions, compared to signature schemes based on specific computational assumptions.

The *efficiency advantage* of one-time signatures is their low computational overhead compared to regular signature schemes. This advantage can be further increased, if longer key size are used for the public key signatures, to ensure security against a future quantum computer and against algorithmic advances in solving the underlying 'hard' problem.

Note, however, that one-time signatures require rather long public keys and signatures. Of course, the overhead depends on the scheme used. We present a simple scheme; some other schemes require shorter public keys and signatures.

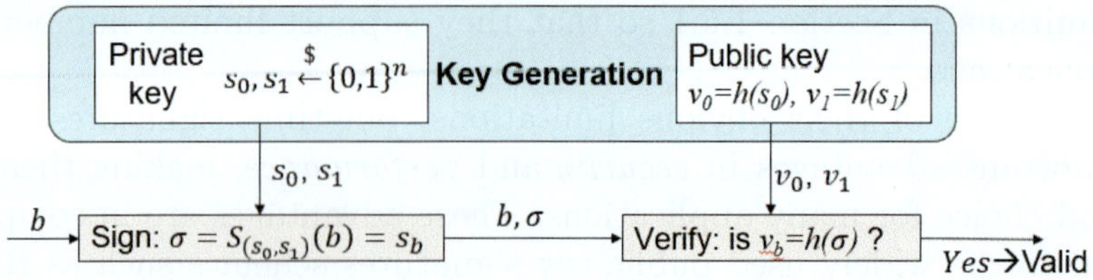

Figure 3.12. A very simple one-time signature scheme, limited to signing only a single bit b, using a OWF h. The private key is a random pair of n bits preimages $s_0, s_1 \overset{\$}{\leftarrow} \{0,1\}^n$; the public key is the corresponding pair $(b \in \{0,1\}) v_i \leftarrow h(s_i)$.

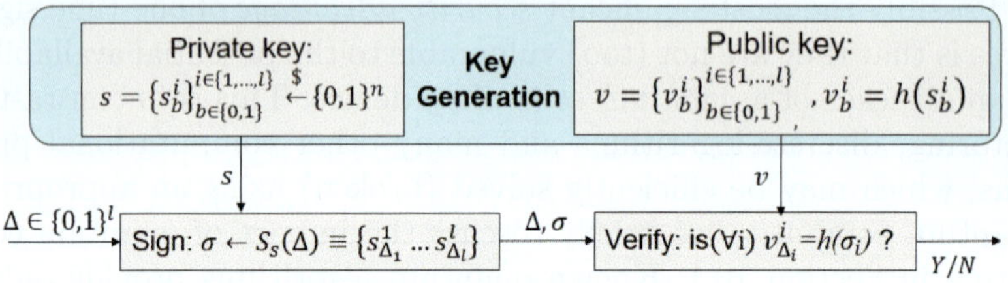

Figure 3.13. A one-time signature scheme for signing l-bit strings (digest) $\Delta \in \{0,1\}^l$.

We present the construction in three steps, gradually improving performance.

One-time signature for a single bit: Figure 3.12 presents a one-time signature scheme which is defined only for the case of a single-bit message.

The private key s consists of a pair of two random n-bits strings $s_0, s_1 \leftarrow \{0,1\}^n$, while the public key consists of the hashes of these strings: $v_0 = h(s_0), v_1 = h(s_1)$. To sign a bit b, we simply send $\sigma = s_b$; to validate incoming the bit b and its purported signature σ, we validate that $v_b = h(\sigma)$. Note that the pair of values $v = (v_0, v_1)$ is the *public* key, and not secret; only the pair $s = (s_0, s_1)$ is secret, and we disclose s_b upon signing bit b.

One-time signature for an l-bit string: We next extend the scheme, to allow one-time signature of an l-bit string, as illustrated in Figure 3.13. We use the symbol Δ for the string which is signed since we extend this scheme in the next step, where we use Δ for the *digest* of a longer message. To allow signing of l bit strings, this scheme basically amounts to l applications of the one-bit one-time signature scheme, illustrated in Figure 3.12.

The private signing key of this scheme consists of a set of l pairs of random strings, denoted $\{(s^i_0, s^i_1)\}^l_{i=1}$, and the public validation key is the corresponding set of l pairs of strings denoted $\{(v^i_0, v^i_1)\}^l_{i=1}$, computed as $(\forall i \in \{1,\ldots,l\}$ and $b \in \{0,1\})$ $v^i_b = h(s^i_b)$.

The signature over the binary string $\Delta = \Delta_1 \mathbin{+\!\!+} \cdots \mathbin{+\!\!+} \Delta_l$ is the set $\{s^1_{\Delta_1},\ldots,s^l_{\Delta_l}\}$. To validate that $\sigma = \sigma_1 \| \cdots \| \sigma_l$ is a valid signature of the l-bit string $\Delta = \Delta_1 \mathbin{+\!\!+} \cdots \mathbin{+\!\!+} \Delta_l$, confirm that for every i between 1 and l holds: $v^i_{\Delta_i} = h(s^i_{\Delta_i})$.

One-time signature allowing Variable Input Length (VIL) using Hash-then-Sign (HtS): Finally, we extend the one-time signature scheme further, to efficiently sign an arbitrary-length input string m. This extension, illustrated in Figure 3.14, uses the *Hash-then-Sign* paradigm (Section 3.3.5). Namely, we first compute the l-bit digest Δ of the message, as $\Delta = h'(m)$, where h' denotes a CRHF. Note that we present the design using two hash functions — h, which is required to be a OWF, and h', which is required to be a CRHF; of course, if h is assumed to be both a OWF and a CRHF, we can use it for both purposes.

After computing the digest $\Delta = h'(m)$, we apply the one-time signature scheme of Figure 3.13. Note that we described the scheme for a keyless CRHF h'. We leave it to the reader to modify the design to allow replacing the keyless CRHF h' by an appropriate keyed hash function — a keyed CRHF (aka an ACR hash), or TCR hash function. Note that the TCR construction requires sending a random hash key

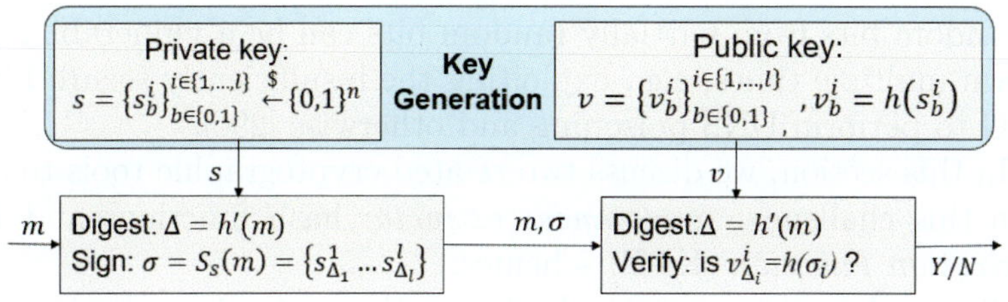

Figure 3.14. A one-time signature scheme, for variable-length message m, using (HtS).

as part of each signature; in spite of this, the use of TCR hash may allow significantly *shorter* signatures and keys (why?).

3.5 Randomness extraction and key derivation functions

Cryptographic protocols use randomness for multiple purposes, including encryption, key-generation and challenge-response authentication. For example, the TLS protocol (Chapter 7) uses random bits for multiple keys (authentication/encryption, client to server and server to client), for random bits sent in the protocol, and for randomized encryption (e.g., as an initialization vector (IV) for block-cipher modes of operation); and different independently random bits should be used in different connections.

Obtaining so many truly random bits can be a challenge since computers do not normally have a built-in source of randomness. A source of true, perfect randomness is usually unavailable. Instead, the computer can obtain some *partially random, sampled bits*; let x denote such a sample. The bits of x may be sampled from different imperfect sources of randomness, for example, timing and other parameters of events such as mouse movements by the user, delays of disk movements, time of initialization and messages received over the network. The hope is that some of these events are not fully visible to the attacker.

Note that the sampled bits x are partially random, i.e., not fully predictable, but are *not pseudorandom*, i.e., it may be possible, even easy, to distinguish between x and a truly random string of the same length. Therefore, we cannot use x directly for applications which require random bits, e.g., for secret shared keys. In fact, derivation of random bits from partially random bits can be a vulnerability, as shown multiple times, e.g., exploiting the insufficiently secure Linux PRG to perform DNS poisoning and otherwise [296].

In this section, we discuss two related cryptographic tools to deal with this challenge: *randomness extractor* hash functions and *Key Derivation Function* (KDF) schemes.

An randomness extractor hash function *extracts* a short, n-bits pseudorandom string from the partially random bits x. We can use either a keyless randomness extractor hash ($h(x)$) or a keyed randomness extractor hash ($h_s(x)$). A *keyed randomness extractor hash function* $h_s(x)$ has an additional input s, which is referred to as a *salt* or a key; s is selected randomly from the *salt-set* S and then made public, i.e., known to the attacker; for this reason, we use the term 'salt' rather than 'key'. The salt s does not need to be secret, but s should be independent of x and vice versa.

Intuitively, a *keyless randomness extractor hash function* is a hash function h, whose output $h(x)$ is pseudorandom.[6] Both types require that the sampled, partially random input x has 'sufficient randomness', i.e., satisfies a specified *randomness assumption*.

We say that h is a keyed randomness extractor hash function for salt-set S if, for salt randomly chosen from S ($s \stackrel{\$}{\leftarrow} S$) and for x sampled with 'sufficient randomness', the output $h_s(x)$ is indistinguishable from random, by an efficient attacker $\mathcal{A}$ which is given the salt s. A keyless randomness extractor hash function is a special case of a keyed randomness extractor hash function, where the salt-set S contains only one element, e.g., $S = \{0\}$.

The randomness extraction property is more subtle and harder to define than the the collision resistance, SPR and one-way properties, and not always listed as one of the goals of (standard) cryptographic hash functions. In particular, the definition of 'sufficiently random' is beyond our scope; we limit our discussion to two relatively-simple notions of keyless extractor hash functions.

In Section 3.5.1, we discuss the simple, keyless *biased-coin extractor* proposed by von Neumann, which ensures uniformly random output, provided that its input is a sequence of independently sampled bits from some (possibly biased) distribution. Then, in Section 3.5.2, we present a simple model of a *computational randomness extractor*, the *bitwise randomness extractor*, which ensures pseudorandom output, provided that its input contains a sufficient number of random bits.

[6]We focus on extraction of pseudorandom bits rather than true random bits; such extractors are often referred to as *computational extractors*, e.g., in Ref. [305]. Extractors whose output is random regardless of the adversary's computational abilities are often referred to as *statistical extractors*.

Randomness extractor hash functions, like other hash functions, have short, n-bits output (digest). To use a randomness extractor hash function h to generate multiple, independently pseudorandom strings, e.g., for multiple secret keys, we will need to apply h many times, to inputs which are independent (even if only partially random). In Section 3.5.3, we introduce and discuss *Key Derivation Function* (KDF) schemes; KDF schemes allow us to generate multiple independently pseudorandom strings, each of arbitrary length, that can be used for different applications. We also present there the *extract-then-expand* paradigm, for constructing a KDF from a randomness extractor hash and a PRF.

3.5.1 Von Neumann's biased-coin extractor

We first discuss a classical *biased-coin extractor* model, proposed, already in 1951 by von Neumann [470], one of the pioneers of computer science. In the von Neumann model, each of the input bits is the result of an independent toss of a coin with fixed bias. Namely, for every bit generated, the value 1 is generated with probability $0 < p < 1$ and the value 0 is generated with probability $1-p$ — with no relation to the value of other bits. We refer to this as the *von Neumann assumption.*

von Neumann proposed the following method to extract perfect randomness from these biased bits. First, arrange these sampled bits in pairs $\{(x_i, y_i)\}$. Then, remove pairs where both bits are identical, i.e., leave only pairs of the form $\{(x_i, 1 - x_i)\}$. Finally, output the sequence $\{x_i\}$. This simple algorithm, is called the *von Neumann extractor.* We leave it to the reader to show that if the input satisfies the von Neumann assumption, then the output is a string of *uniformly random bits.* The von Neumann extractor does not make the optimal use of the input bits, i.e., it is possible to extract more random bits under the same model (how?).

Exercise 3.2 (von Neumann extractor). Show that, if the input of the von Neumann extractor satisfies the von Neumann assumption (above), then its output is uniformly random, i.e., each bit x_i is 1 with probability exactly half — independently of all other bits.

The von Neumann extractor is simple, and the output is proven uniform based only on the von Neumann assumption, without requiring any computational assumption. However, the von Neumann assumption is hard to justify for many typical security applications of randomness extraction. In particular, consider the goal of *key derivation*, where we use some large input x which is 'fairly random' but not truly random, such as many measurements (of time, movements, etc.). We cannot use x directly as a key, so we apply a hash and use $h(x)$. However, can we be certain the von Neumann assumption holds? The following simple exercise shows this assumption may not hold — even when every second bit in the input is random!

Exercise 3.3. Consider the following random process for producing bit sequences $\{b_1, b_2, \ldots\}$:

$$b_i = \left\{ \begin{array}{cc} b_i \leftarrow 0 & \text{if } i = 1 \bmod 2 \\ b_i \xleftarrow{\$} \{0,1\} & \text{otherwise} \end{array} \right\} \tag{3.16}$$

Show that this sequence does not satisfy the von Neumann assumption and, in fact, that applying the von Neumann extractor will not result in random output string.

3.5.2 The bitwise randomness extractor

We now present another model for randomness extraction, which we call the *bitwise randomness extractor* (BRE) model. We present the BRE model as a simple way to provide readers with an understanding of randomness-extracting hash functions; you will find more advanced and stronger models in the literature, but these are beyond our scope. We focus on the definition for keyless hash, but the definition for keyed hash is similar.

Intuitively, a hash function h is a BRE if its output $h(x)$ is pseudorandom, even if the adversary can *select the input x, except for a 'sufficient' number of bits* of the input; these bits are selected randomly. This intuition is illustrated in Figure 3.15, which defines a 'game' where an adversarial algorithm $\mathcal{A}$ tries to defeat the randomness extraction — by selecting some input message x, except for at

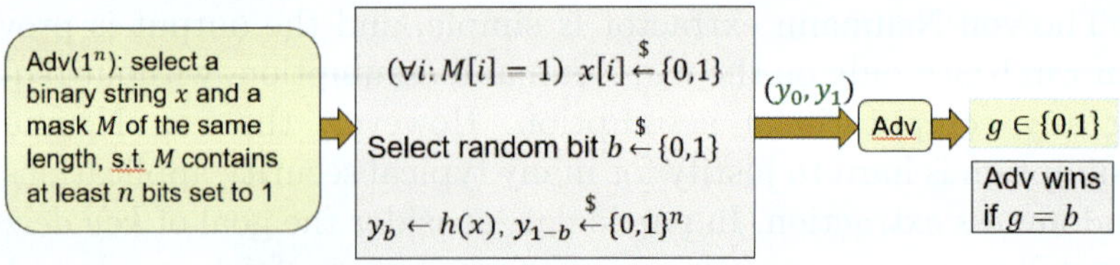

Figure 3.15. Bitwise randomness extractor (BRE) keyless hash function (simplified).

least n bits of x which are randomized,[7] and then distinguishing between $h(x)$ and a random n-bit string.

In order to properly define a BRE hash function, let us first define the *bitwise randomness extraction indistinguishability test* IND-BRE$_{\mathcal{A},h}(b, n)$ (Algorithm 3). The test allows the adversary to select the input message x given to h, except for at least n random bits.

We let the adversary select the length l of x, as well as two l-bits strings, x' and M. The test confirms that both x' and M are l-bits binary string; if this doesn't hold, the game immediately aborts and returns $\perp$ (adversary fails). The test also confirms that M contains at least n bits set to 1; this is done by validating that $\sum_{i=1}^{l} M(i) \geq n$.

We refer to M as a *mask*; it defines (n or more) bit positions of x which will be set to a random bit value. To do this, the test selects a random l-bits string $r \overset{\$}{\leftarrow} \{0,1\}^l$ and computes x as $x \leftarrow x' \oplus (r \wedge M)$. Namely, the string x is the same as x', which was completely chosen by the attacker, except for the positions i s.t. $M(i) = 1$, which are set to a random bit value.

Once x is chosen, the test selects a random bit b and computes the two challenges: $y_b \leftarrow h(x)$ and $y_{1-b} \overset{\$}{\leftarrow} \{0,1\}^n$. Since at least n bits in x are random, then $y_b = h(x)$ *should* be pseudorandom, i.e., indistinguishable from the random string y_{1-b}.

The test completes by giving the adversary $\mathcal{A}$ the strings y_0 and y_1. If $\mathcal{A}$ can distinguish between a random n-bits string and the output of h, even though the input to h contains (at least n) random bits, then $\mathcal{A}$ can learn b from seeing y_0 and y_1.

[7]The choice of requiring at least n random bits in the input is quite arbitrary — we could have required a larger number of input random bits; we chose n for simplicity.

Algorithm 3 Bitwise randomness extraction indistinguishability test IND-BRE$_{\mathcal{A},h}(b,n)$.

$(l, x', M) \leftarrow \mathcal{A}(1^n)$
If $x' \notin \{0,1\}^l$ or $M \notin \{0,1\}^l$ or $\sum_{i=1}^{l} M(i) < n$ **return** $\perp$
$r \overset{\$}{\leftarrow} \{0,1\}^l$
$x \leftarrow x' \oplus (r \wedge M)$
$y_b \leftarrow h(x)$
$y_{1-b} \overset{\$}{\leftarrow} \{0,1\}^n$
return $\mathcal{A}(y_0, y_1)$

We say that h is a BRE if there is no efficient adversary $\mathcal{A}$ that can 'win' in the bitwise randomness extraction indistinguishability test IND-BRE$_{\mathcal{A},h}(b,n)$.

Definition 3.8 (Bitwise randomness extractor (BRE) keyless hash function). An efficient keyless hash function $h : \{0,1\}^* \to \{0,1\}^n$ is called BRE if for every efficient algorithm $\mathcal{A} \in PPT$, the *advantage function* $\varepsilon^{\text{BRE}}_{h,\mathcal{A}}(n)$ is *negligible* in n, i.e., smaller than any positive polynomial for sufficiently large n (as $n \to \infty$), where:

$$\varepsilon^{\text{BRE}}_{h,\mathcal{A}}(n) \equiv \Pr\left[\text{IND-BRE}_{\mathcal{A},h}(1,n) = 1\right] - \Pr\left[\text{IND-BRE}_{\mathcal{A},h}(0,n) = 1\right] \quad (3.17)$$

where IND-BRE$_{\mathcal{A},h}(\cdot,\cdot)$ is defined in Algorithm 3 and the probability is taken over the random coin tosses of $\mathcal{A}$ and of IND-BRE$_{\mathcal{A},h}(\cdot,\cdot)$.

The reader can extend the definition for the case of keyed BRE hash function.

Exercise 3.8 gives a simple example of a hash function which is *not* a BRE.

3.5.3 Key derivation functions and the extract-then-expand paradigm

The output $h(x)$ is pseudorandom, provided the input x is a sufficiently random. However, $h(x)$ contains only n bits; applications usually need many more bits. Furthermore, we often need many independently pseudorandom bits for different *contexts*, e.g., different connections and different purposes (such as keys vs. random challenges, or authentication keys vs. encryption keys). Requiring separate inputs $x_1, x_2, \ldots$ and extracting only n bits each time ($\{h(x_1), h(x_2), \ldots\}$) would be inefficient and inconvenient; we would need to split the resulting pseudorandom bits into the separate strings for each application, and many times, the number of bits required by an application would not be n or even a multiple of n. It would not be so difficult to split them, but it would be a hassle.

A KDF, defined by Krawczyk in Ref. [305], provide an efficient and convenient solution. A KDF is a function $\text{KDF}(s, x, c, l)$, with four inputs:

- A salt s, which, like the salt of a keyed randomness extractor hash, is a non-secret value which should be selected randomly from a *salt set* S, which may even be simply a single value $S = \{0\}$.
- The partially random sample x. The input x should be 'sufficiently random', where different KDF schemes may require different minimal randomness requirements. For example, a KDF may require x to contain at least some number $l \geq n$ of (truly) random bits, similar to the requirement for a BRE hash function.
- The *context* c, given as an alphabetical string, and optionally empty. The context c allows the KDF to be used, with the same partially random input x, to generate multiple independently pseudorandom strings, e.g., to generate an encryption key, an authentication key and an IV, all from the same x.
- The required output length l, i.e., $l = |\text{KDF}(s, x, c, l)|$.

Krawczyk [305] also presented the *extract-then-expand* paradigm, which provides a modular and elegant design of a KDF. This KDF constructs a KDF from two more basic cryptographic functions: a randomness extractor hash function h and a PRF f. In the extract-then-expand process, we first use h to *extract* a limited-length pseudorandom key $k \leftarrow h_s(x)$ from the partially random input x and then 'expand' k into the required l-bits output $KDF(s, x, c, l)$ by using k as a key to the PRF f. This design was adopted by the IETF as RFC 5869 [306] and is deployed in TLS 1.3 (Section 7.6).

The *extract-then-expand* paradigm constructs the KDF in two steps. In the first step, *extract*, we use the keyed randomness extractor hash function to extract a pseudorandom key k from the partially random input x, and then *expand*, which uses k to efficiently generate the desired pseudorandom keys.

Let us provide the details, for a slightly simplified variant of the design of Ref. [305] and of the standardized version of that design published by the IETF as RFC 5869 [306]. For simplicity, assume that the PRF f has key length and output length of n bits, like the digest size (size of output of h). We compute $\text{KDF}(s, x, c, l)$ using the extract step and then the expand step, as follows.

Extract: Compute $k \leftarrow h_s(x)$. We can use here a keyed randomness extractor hash or, by restricting the set of salts to the single value $S = \{0\}$, a keyless randomness extractor hash. If the partially random input x is sufficiently random, then k would be a pseudorandom string, i.e., indistinguishable from a random string.

Expand: First, compute $T(i)$ for $i = 1, \ldots, \lceil \frac{l}{n} \rceil$, as $T(i) \leftarrow f_k(c+\!\!+ i)$. Then, concatenate all of these values, i.e., let $T' \leftarrow T(1) \ldots T(\lceil \frac{l}{n} \rceil)$. Finally, output $\text{KDF}(s, x, c, l) \leftarrow T'[1 : l]$, i.e., the first l bits of T'.

RFC 5869 [306] also proposes the use of the well-known *HMAC* construction to compute the PRF and possibly also the randomness extractor hash function. The HMAC design transforms a keyless hash function $\hat{h}$ into a keyed function $h_k(x)$, defined as

$$h_k(x) = \hat{h}(k \oplus OPAD +\!\!+ \hat{h}(k \oplus IPAD +\!\!+ x)) \tag{3.18}$$

The values $OPAD$ and $IPAD$ in Equation (3.18) are fixed strings defined in Ref. [306]. The keyed function h_k resulting from this construction, is used, in Ref. [306] and otherwise, both as a keyed randomness extractor hash and as a PRF, e.g., for the KDF construction. HMAC was originally designed as a MAC; we discuss it more extensively in Section 4.4.5.

Table 3.2 compares the three relevant types of functions: KDF, PRF and randomness extractor hash functions.

Exercise 3.4 shows that the keyed randomness extractor hash and PRF definitions are 'incomparable': a function can be a PRF but not a keyed extractor hash function, and vice versa, focusing on the special case of a keyed BRE hash. Try to solve Exercise 3.4 first and only then read the solution since if you directly read the solution, it may appear obvious.

Table 3.2. Comparison: PRF, KDF and randomness extractor hash functions. For all functions, outputs should be pseudorandom.

	PRF $f_k(x)$	KDF $KDF(s, x, c, l)$	Extractor (keyed) $h_k(x)$
Key	Secret k	Public salt s	Public k
Input x	Arbitrary	Sufficiently random	(e.g., some n random bits)
Output length	Fixed (n)	l bits	Fixed (n)

Exercise 3.4 (PRF vs. keyed BRE). Let f be a (secure) PRF and h be a (secure) keyed BRE hash function. For both functions, the output and the key contain n bits:

1. Use f and/or h to construct a (secure) PRF f', such that f' is *not* a secure keyed BRE hash.
2. Use f and/or h to construct a (secure) keyed BRE hash h', such that h' is *not* a secure PRF.

Solution:

$$f'_k(x) = \begin{cases} 0^n & \text{if } k = x \bmod 2^n \\ f_k(x) & \text{otherwise} \end{cases}$$

$$h'_k(x) = \begin{cases} k & \text{if } 0^n = x \bmod 2^n \\ h_k(x) & \text{otherwise} \end{cases}$$

Complete the solution by explaining or demonstrating why f' is a secure PRF but not a secure keyed BRE hash, and why h' is a secure keyed BRE hash but not a secure PRF. And find other solutions! □

3.6 The random oracle model

As we discussed in the earlier sections, many designs of cryptographic protocols and schemes use a keyless cryptographic hash function h. Most of these designs would not be secure if we only assume that h is a OWF or a SPR, or another reasonable assumption for a keyless hash function.

Some of these constructions were found to be insecure; however, other constructions have been published and applied for many years, and, so far, no practical vulnerability was published to their use with standard hash functions, in spite of considerable efforts. We discussed one of the most important examples: the use of a keyless hash function h in the HtS construction. This design is secure based on the assumption that h is a collision-resistant hash function; but this is not a reasonable assumption, since we know that a keyless hash cannot be a secure CRHF.

Furthermore, often, when a vulnerability is found in a system deploying a keyless hash function h, it usually — almost always — turns out that the attack techniques deployed are *generic*, i.e., do not exploit a weakness of the specific hash function h. In other words, these systems are vulnerable to an efficient generic attack, i.e., an attack which works when the system is implemented with any keyless hash function.

It is obviously desirable to identify designs using keyless hash functions which are vulnerable to a generic attack. We definitely want to avoid such a design! In other words, it is preferable to use designs which can be proven to be secure against any generic attack; such designs may still be vulnerable when using any given specific hash function, but they are not subject to a generic attack which works for any hash. Any vulnerability of the design can be attributed to a property[8] of the specific hash function used.

The *Random Oracle Model* (ROM),[9] proposed by Bellare and Rogaway [48], offers such a method.

Intuitively, *ROM* constructions and protocols are secure in the (impractical) case that the parties select the hash function $h(\cdot)$ *randomly* from the set of all functions from the set of all binary strings $\{0,1\}^*$ to a given domain. Of course, when the construction is deployed, it must use a concrete, specific hash function $h(\cdot)$ rather than a random function.

[8]Note we say 'a property' rather than 'a vulnerability'. Why?

[9]Often people use the term 'random oracle methodology' or instead of 'random oracle model'. Arguably, this would be more appropriate, but we use 'random oracle model' since it is more common.

We use $\mathcal{A}$ and $\mathcal{S}$ to denote efficient algorithms for the adversary and the scheme, respectively, which use, as a black box (oracle), a hash function h; we use $\mathcal{A}^h$ and $\mathcal{S}^h$ to denote their instantiations with the particular hash function h. Namely, $\mathcal{A}^h$ can provide an arbitrary input x to h and receive back $h(x)$. We define ROM security by requiring negligible advantage, as defined by an advantage function ε, which depends on the adversary $\mathcal{A}$, the scheme $\mathcal{S}$, the specific hash h and the security parameter 1^n. The advantage function would typically be defined as the probability of $\mathcal{A}$ to 'win' a game or a test where it has oracle access to h, interacts with $\mathcal{S}$ (which also uses h) and has input of at least n bits, e.g., the security parameter 1^n.

Definition 3.9 (ROM security). Let H_n be the set of all (hash) functions from $\{0,1\}^*$ to $\{0,1\}^n$, for integer (length) n. Let $\mathcal{A}$ and $\mathcal{S}$ be efficient algorithms (for the adversary and a cryptographic scheme, respectively), which use a hash function as a black box; and let $\mathcal{A}_n^h$ and $\mathcal{S}_n^h$ denote their instantiation with the hash function $h \in H_n$. Let $\varepsilon^h_{\mathcal{S},\mathcal{A}}(n) \rightarrow [0,1]$ be a function mapping an integer n (the security parameter) to a probability, defined for a given hash function $h \in H_n$, scheme $\mathcal{S}$ and adversary $\mathcal{A}$. We call ε the advantage function.

We say that $\mathcal{S}$ *ensures negligible* ε*-advantage under the ROM*, or ε*-secure under the ROM*, if the advantage of any efficient adversary $\mathcal{A}$, for a random hash function $h \xleftarrow{\$} H_n$, is negligible in n, i.e.,

$$\Pr_{h \xleftarrow{\$} H_n} \varepsilon^h_{\mathcal{S},\mathcal{A}}(n) \in \text{NEGL}(n) \tag{3.19}$$

Cryptographic schemes and protocols are so often proven secure under the ROM that schemes proven without the ROM are often explicitly said to be proven *under the standard model*, to emphasize the fact that their security proof does not require the ROM simplification. Whenever a cryptographic scheme is shown to be secure under the ROM, cryptographers will be looking for ways to prove the security of the same scheme, or of a modified, similar scheme, under the standard model, i.e., without using the ROM. For example, when the parties can share a secret, random key, then design which is proven under the ROM using a keyless hash function h, and usually be modified into a provably secure design (under the standard model) where the use of h is replaced by the use of a pseudorandom function (PRF) with a secret shared key. We refer to the technique of designing protocols using a random function (i.e., under the ROM) and then replacing them by a PRF with a shared secret key as the *random function design method*, see Principle 6.

Advanced: about the choice of h: The careful reader may have noted that it is not well defined how to select an element from an infinite set with uniform probability; hence, $h \xleftarrow{\$} H_n$ is not well defined. This choice should be interpreted as follows. For any $l > n$, let H_n^l be the set of all functions from $\{0,1\}^l$ to $\{0,1\}^n$, i.e., functions from l-bit binary strings to n-bit binary strings: $H_n^l = \{h : \{0,1\}^l \rightarrow \{0,1\}^n\}$. The set H_n^l *is* finite, hence we can define random sampling from it: $h_n^l \xleftarrow{\$} H_n^l$. When we write $h \xleftarrow{\$} H_n$, it should be interpreted as choosing $h_n^l \xleftarrow{\$} H_n^l$ for every integer l; and, for any input string $m \in \{0,1\}^*$, let $h(m) = h^{|m|}(m)$.

To prove that a protocol using a keyless hash function h is secure under the ROM, we analyze the protocol assuming that h is chosen randomly at the beginning of the execution. Once chosen, all parties will have 'black-box' (oracle) access to h. This includes the adversary as well as parties running the protocol.

ROM security does not necessarily imply that the design is 'really' secure, when implemented with any specific hash function; once the hash function is fixed, there may be an adversary that breaks the system. Still, ROM security is definitely a good *indication* of security since a vulnerability has to use some property of the specific keyless hash function. Indeed, there are widely deployed designs which are only proven to be ROM-secure.

3.7 Accumulator schemes and the Merkle tree

A CRHF h provides integrity for a binary string x, by computing the digest $h(x)$ (or $h_k(x)$, for keyed hash). However, often, we need to ensure integrity for a set or *sequence of strings*, $X = (x_0, x_1, \ldots, x_{l-1})$, where each string x_i can be of fixed length or of variable length. Can we compute a digest for this entire sequence X?

A naïve solution is to encode the set of strings X as a single string and then apply the hash function h. Namely, we compute $h(encode(X))$, where *encode* is a one-to-one encoding of multiple strings to one string, e.g., separating between strings using a special character not included in any of the strings. However, this design has a significant disadvantage: validation requires receiving *all* strings in X and computing the hash over their concatenation, even if we only need to validate that a single string, say x_i, is included in X.

In this section, we discuss *cryptographic accumulators*, which are schemes designed to efficiently compute the digest of a sequence X of strings and to efficiently validate that a particular string x_i is included in the sequence X. An accumulator produces a *collision-resistant digest* for the sequence of strings X, which we denote by Δ, and an efficient PoI for each string $x \in X$. We first introduce accumulators and their security properties (Section 3.7.1). Then, in Section 3.7.2, we focus on the *Merkle tree* accumulator $\mathcal{MT}^h$, which is an accumulator constructed from a CRHF h. The *Merkle tree* is widely deployed, e.g., in blockchains (Section 3.9), in particular Bitcoin, as well as in the CT PKI scheme (Section 8.5). Merkle trees are of the simplest accumulators and well known — in fact, you may encounter more mentions of Merkle trees than of accumulators. We conclude this section by briefly discussing, in Section 3.7.3, some extensions of our definitions of accumulators and their properties.

3.7.1 Accumulators and their security requirements

An *accumulator* α consists of two algorithms, which we denote α.Accum and α.VERPOI. When the relevant accumulator is clear from context, we simply write Accum and VERPOI.

The Accum algorithm accumulates a sequence (ordered set) of binary strings X into an n-bits digest Δ (where n is an implicit parameter of the accumulator). It also produces, for every input string $x_i \in X$, a corresponding POI. In principle, the POI is allowed to be of arbitrary length; however, typically, proofs of inclusion are quite short. For example, when using the Merkle tree to accumulate l strings, then each POI contains about $\log_2(l)$ hash digests, i.e., $n \log_2(l)$ bits (where n is the length of the hash digests).

The VERPOI algorithm is a predicate, i.e., returns FALSE or TRUE; it uses a POI to verify the inclusion of an input string x in a sequence with a given digest Δ.

Keyed and keyless accumulators: Accumulators, like hash functions, can be either *keyed* or *keyless*. A keyless accumulator can ensure collision-resistance only under the ROM (Section 3.6) — much like the case for collision resistant hash functions. For simplicity, we focus mostly on keyless accumulators, and in particular on the keyless Merkle tree design. The construction can be modified into a keyed accumulator, using a keyed CRHF instead of a keyless CRHF.

Specifying the digest length n: Similarly to the case for hash functions, we do not specify the digest length n as an explicit input parameter of the (keyless) accumulators. Although not explicitly included, the digest length n should still be considered as an input parameter, since the advantage of the adversary is a function of the digest length n, and the advantage should be negligible (in n), for an adversary whose runtime is polynomial (in n).

Definition 3.10 (A (keyless) accumulator). A (keyless) accumulator α is a pair of efficient deterministic algorithms, $\alpha.\mathsf{Accum}$ and α.VERPOI, where:

$\alpha.\mathsf{Accum}(X) \rightarrow (\Delta, \mathbf{PoI})$ accumulates a sequence of binary strings $X = (x_i)_{i=0}^{l-1}$. The accumulator produces a digest $\Delta \in \{0,1\}^n$ and a corresponding sequence $(\text{POI}[i])_{i=0}^{l-1}$, where POI$[i]$ is a binary string called is the POI for x_i. We may also allow the output to be a special 'error value' $\perp \notin \{0,1\}^*$, to designate that the input is not an allowed sequence (e.g., it contains a non-binary string). We use $\alpha.\mathsf{Accum}.\Delta(X)$ to refer to the digest output; when the relevant accumulator α is clear from the context, we often use the shorthand notation $\Delta(X)$. Similarly, we use $\alpha.\mathsf{Accum}.\text{POI}[i](X)$, or the short hand notation POI$[i](X)$, to refer to the POI for the *ith* input string, x_i.

$\alpha.$**VERPOI**$(\Delta, x, \pi) \rightarrow \{\textbf{TRUE}, \textbf{FALSE}\}$ is a predicate that returns TRUE if Δ is the digest output of an Accum operation, where x was one of the input strings and π was the POI output corresponding to x, i.e., $(\exists i)\pi = \text{POI}[i](X)$.

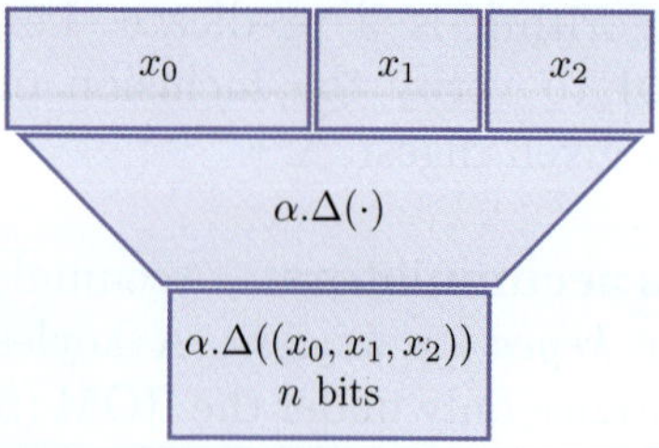

Figure 3.16. The digest $\alpha.\Delta(X)$ of a keyless accumulator α, on input sequence $X = (x_0, x_1, x_2)$.

We illustrate the digest function Accum.Δ of a keyless accumulator in Figure 3.16.

3.7.1.1 *Collision-resistant accumulators*

To define a *collision-resistant accumulator*, we first extend the notion of a *collision* to the sequences of strings which are provided as input to the accumulator. For example, consider two sequences of strings $X \equiv (x_0, \ldots, x_{l-1})$ and $X' \equiv (x'_0, \ldots, x'_{l'-1})$. We say that the pair of sequences (X, X') *is a collision for accumulator* α if $X \neq X'$ yet $\alpha.\mathsf{Accum}.\Delta(X) = \alpha.\mathsf{Accum}.\Delta(X') \neq \perp$. The definition follows.

Definition 3.11 (collision-resistant accumulator). Let α be a keyless accumulator scheme, with a parameter (n) for the digest length. We say that α is a collision-resistant accumulator if for any PPT adversary $\mathcal{A}$ there is negligible probability for $\mathcal{A}$ to output a collision. Namely,

$$\text{Prob}\begin{bmatrix} \alpha.\mathsf{Accum}.\Delta(X) = \alpha.\mathsf{Accum}.\Delta(X') \neq \perp, \\ \text{where } (X, X') \leftarrow \mathcal{A}(n) \text{ s.t. } X \neq X' \end{bmatrix} \in \text{NEGL}(n) \quad (3.20)$$

Other notions of collisions may be natural for accumulator schemes. For example, an *unordered collision* would consider input sequences X and X' as a collision, only if $\Delta(X) = \Delta(X')$, yet the two sequences, viewed as (unordered) sets, contain *different elements*, i.e., $\exists x$ s.t. $(x \in X \cup X') \wedge (x \notin X \cap X')$. Another natural notion would consider X and X' as a collision only if the concatenation of the bits in the two sequences differ. See Exercise 3.17.

The reader should be able to define similar notions for keyed accumulators, including ACR and TCR keyed accumulators, as well as an SPR notion for keyless accumulators (see Exercise 3.18). In fact, these notions are important, as it is infeasible to construct a provably secure collision-resistant accumulator under the standard model, i.e., a keyless collision-resistant accumulator is only feasible when we adopt the simplifying ROM.

3.7.1.2 *The Proof of Inclusion (PoI) requirements*

Many applications use accumulators to verify the inclusion of a specific input x_i in the input to the accumulator, namely, verify that $x_i \in X$, where X was the input given to the accumulator resulting in the given digest. Such verification of a specific input x_i may be done using the VerPoI operation, which uses the corresponding *Proof of Inclusion* output, PoI$[i](X)$, produced when applying the Accum operation to X. To verify the integrity of only one input string x_i, or of only few input strings, the use of VerPoI can be more efficient than relying on the collision-resistance of the accumulator by applying the Accum operation to the entire sequence of input strings X.

Verifying the integrity by using VerPoI has two additional advantages: First, validation only requires the value of the purported input string x_i and of the PoI, not the entire purported input sequence X, as required to verify integrity by applying Accum; the entire sequence X may be unavailable, and even if X may be obtained or maintained, this may involve overhead. Second, the use of VerPoI may also provide some *privacy* since a party may verify a particular input string x_i without having access to other input strings in X. This follows the 'need to know' principle of restricting access to sensitive information. Note, however, that to properly protect the privacy of the other inputs, the accumulator should also satisfy appropriate confidentiality/privacy requirements; we leave the definition of such requirements as an exercise (Exercise 3.23).

Verification of the PoI involves two complementing requirements: *correctness* and *unforgeability*. Intuitively:

PoI Correctness requires that if the inputs are 'correct', then VerPoI will return True. Namely, let X be a sequence and x be one of the strings in X, say $x = X[i]$, and let $(\Delta, \text{PoI}) \leftarrow \mathsf{Accum}(X)$. Then, $\text{VerPoI}(\Delta, x, \text{PoI}[i]) = \text{True}$.

PoI Unforgeability requires that if $\text{VerPoI}(\Delta, x, \pi) = \text{True}$, then there exists a sequence X and an index i s.t. $x = X[i]$, $\Delta = \Delta(X)$ and $\pi = \text{PoI}[i](X)$.

Let us define these intuitively described requirements.

Definition 3.12 (PoI Correctness and Unforgeability). Let α be an accumulator scheme, with digest length n given (implicitly) as a parameter. We define the following two properties.

PoI correctness: We say that accumulator α ensures *Proof of Inclusion (*PoI*) Correctness* if for every input sequence X containing l elements and $(\Delta, \text{PoI}) \leftarrow \alpha.\mathsf{Accum}(X)$, holds $(\forall i < l)\alpha.\text{VerPoI}(\Delta, X[i], \text{PoI}[i]) = \text{True}$.

PoI unforgeability: We say that accumulator α ensures PoI *Unforgeability under the ROM* if for every efficient adversary $\mathcal{A}^h$ interacting with accumulator α^h, where both $\mathcal{A}^h$ and α^h use a hash function h from binary strings to n-bit strings, holds:

$$\text{Prob}\left[\begin{array}{c}\alpha.\text{VerPoI}(\Delta, x, \pi) \wedge x \notin X, \\ \text{where } \Delta, X, x, \text{ and } \pi \text{ were generated by:} \\ \left\{\begin{array}{l} X \leftarrow \mathcal{A}(1^n)\ ; \\ (\Delta, \text{PoI}) \leftarrow \alpha.\mathsf{Accum}(X)\ ; \\ (x, \pi) \leftarrow \mathcal{A}(\Delta, \text{PoI}) \end{array}\right\}\end{array}\right] \in \text{NEGL}(n) \tag{3.21}$$

Note that the unforgeability requirement allows $\mathcal{A}$ to provide any PoI π, not necessarily the output of the accumulator. Also, we require that x would not be any string in X, not necessarily in a specific position.

3.7.2 The Merkle tree ($\mathcal{MT}^h$) accumulator

The Merkle tree accumulator was first presented by Merkle [353]. Variants of this design are deployed in different systems and used in different standards, papers and proposals.

Most variants of the Merkle tree are *keyless* and are built using a keyless hash function h. We focus on a specific keyless design of the Merkle tree, which we denote $\mathcal{MT}^h$. This is essentially the design used by Bitcoin (Section 3.9.2) and by the CT PKI standard [320] (Section 8.5). Essentially the same design, but with different notations, was analyzed in Ref. [159].

The reader should be able to modify the $\mathcal{MT}^h$ design into a *keyed Merkle tree* (and a keyed accumulator), using a keyed hash function — either an ACR hash or using a TCR hash (Section 3.3.3).

We first discuss the digest function $\mathcal{MT}^h.\mathsf{Accum}.\Delta$ and then the PoI and the VerPoI functions.

3.7.2.1 *The Merkle tree digest function* $\mathcal{MT}^h.\mathsf{Accum}.\Delta$.

Figure 3.17 illustrates the digest function $\mathcal{MT}^h.\mathsf{Accum}.\Delta$ of the Merkle tree ($\mathcal{MT}^h$) accumulator, applied to the sequence $(x_i)_{i=0}^{l-1}$, using the 'shorthand notation' $\Delta_{i,j} \equiv \mathcal{MT}^h.\mathsf{Accum}.\Delta((x_i, \ldots, x_j))$. Note that in this notation, we do not explicitly identify the hash function h, but we will only use it when h is clear from context.

As illustrated in Figure 3.17, the Merkle tree ($\mathcal{MT}^h$) accumulator constructs a (full or partial) binary tree whose leafs are the accumulated input strings $x_0, \ldots, x_{l-1}$.

We define the tree recursively, as follows. We first define the $\mathcal{MT}^h$ digest of a sequence containing a single string x_i from the sequence $(x_i)_{i=0}^{l-1}$. We denote this by $\Delta_{i,i}$ and compute it as

$$\Delta_{i,i} \equiv \mathcal{MT}^h.\mathsf{Accum}.\Delta((x_i)) = h(0x00 \mathbin{+\!\!+} x_i) \tag{3.22}$$

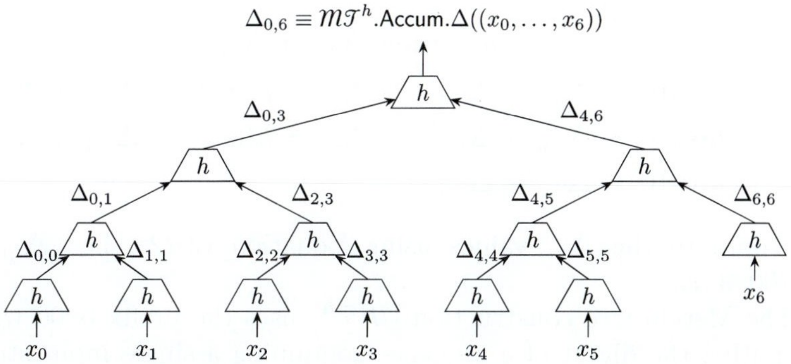

Figure 3.17. The Merkle tree construction using keyless hash function h. The figure illustrate computation of the digest $\Delta_{0,6} \equiv \mathcal{MT}^h.\Delta((x_0, \ldots, x_6))$, using the notation $\Delta_{i,j} \equiv \mathcal{MT}^h.\mathsf{Accum}.\Delta((x_i, \ldots, x_j))$.

Table 3.3. The Merkle tree lP_2 function: $lP_2(d) \equiv 2^{\lfloor \log_2(d) \rfloor}$.

d	1	2–3	4–7	8–15	16–31	32–63	64–127	128–255
$lP_2\ (d)$	1	2	4	8	16	32	64	128

Next, consider the sub-sequence $(x_i, \ldots, x_j)$ for $j > i$, which contains $(j+1) - i > 1$ elements. We compute the $\mathcal{MT}^h$ digest of $(x_i, \ldots, x_j)$, where $j > i$, denoted $\Delta_{i,j}$, using the following recursive equation together with Equation (3.22):

$$\begin{aligned} \Delta_{i,j} &\equiv \mathcal{MT}^h.\mathsf{Accum}.\Delta((x_i, \ldots, x_j)) \\ &= h(0x01 +\!\!+ \Delta_{i,i+lP_2(j-i)-1} +\!\!+ \Delta_{i+lP_2(j-i),j}) \end{aligned} \tag{3.23}$$

where $lP_2(d)$ is the *largest power of two* which is less than or equal to d, i.e.,

$$lP_2(d) \equiv 2^{\lfloor \log_2(d) \rfloor} \tag{3.24}$$

Note that if $d \geq 1$ is a power of two, then $lP_2(d) = d$; otherwise, $\frac{d}{2} < lP_2(d) < d$. Also, if $d > 1$ is a power of two, then $lP_2(d-1) = \frac{d}{2}$; otherwise, $lP_2(d-1) = lP_2(d)$. The $lP_2(\cdot)$ function is convenient for the design and analysis of the Merkle tree; Table 3.3 lists a few values of its values.

Let us compute $\Delta_{0,6} \equiv \mathcal{MT}^h.\mathsf{Accum}.\Delta((x_0, \ldots, x_6))$ for the example of Figure 3.17. We apply Equation (3.23) iteratively, computing

$$\Delta_{0,6} = h(0x01 +\!\!+ \Delta_{0,3} +\!\!+ \Delta_{4,6})$$

$$\begin{aligned} \Delta_{0,3} &= h(0x01 +\!\!+ \Delta_{0,1} +\!\!+ \Delta_{2,3}) & \Delta_{4,6} &= h(0x01 +\!\!+ \Delta_{4,5} +\!\!+ \Delta_{6,6}) \\ \Delta_{0,1} &= h(0x01 +\!\!+ \Delta_{0,0} +\!\!+ \Delta_{1,1}) & \Delta_{4,5} &= h(0x01 +\!\!+ \Delta_{4,4} +\!\!+ \Delta_{5,5}) \\ \Delta_{2,3} &= h(0x01 +\!\!+ \Delta_{2,2} +\!\!+ \Delta_{3,3}) \end{aligned}$$

We compute the $\Delta_{i,i}$ values using Equation (3.22), i.e., $\Delta_{i,i} = h(0x00 +\!\!+ x_i)$.

The Merkle tree construction ($\mathcal{MT}^h$) uses the prefix $0x00$ when computing the digest of a sequence containing a single input string (x_i), as in Equation (3.22), and a different prefix, $0x01$, when computing the digest of a sequence containing multiple strings $(x_i, \ldots, x_j)$, for $j > i$, as in Equation (3.23). In the following exercise, we show that a simplified design that does not include these prefixes is *not* collision resistant. A similar result holds when using the same prefix for a single string and for a sequence of strings.

Exercise 3.5 (Collisions for a simplified Merkle tree). Let $\widehat{\mathcal{MT}^h}$ be a simplified Merkle tree, where the digest function does not use the one-byte prefixes when hashing, i.e., omitting the $0x00$ or $0x01$ prefixes used by $\mathcal{MT}^h$ (in Equations (3.22) and (3.23)). Let:

$$\widehat{\Delta}_{i,i} \equiv \widehat{\mathcal{MT}^h}.\mathsf{Accum}.\Delta((x_i)) \equiv h(x_i)$$

$$\widehat{\Delta}_{i,j} \equiv \widehat{\mathcal{MT}^h}.\mathsf{Accum}.\Delta((x_i, \ldots, x_j))$$
$$\equiv h(\widehat{\Delta}_{i,i+lP_2(j-i)-1} + \widehat{\Delta}_{i+lP_2(j-i),j})$$

Show that $\widehat{\mathcal{MT}^h}$ would have collisions even when using a random hash function (i.e., under the ROM), or assuming that the hash function h is a CRHF.

Solution (sketch): Consider an arbitrary sequence $X \equiv (x_0, \ldots, x_3)$ and define the sequence $X' \equiv (h(x_0) + h(x_1), h(x_2) + h(x_3))$. Obviously, $X \neq X'$, yet $\widehat{\Delta}(X) = \widehat{\Delta}(X')$. □

Let us show that the digest function of Merkle tree ($\mathcal{MT}^h$) ensures collision resistance, when h is chosen randomly, following the random oracle model (ROM,[10] see Section 3.6).

Lemma 3.2. *Assume that h is a randomly chosen function from binary strings to n-bits strings. Then, the Merkle tree using hash function h, denoted $\mathcal{MT}^h$, is a collision-resistant accumulator.*

Proof. Suppose, to the contrary, that for a randomly chosen hash function h, the Merkle tree ($\mathcal{MT}^h$) has a collision with high probability, i.e., two different sequences of strings $X \neq X'$ s.t. $\mathcal{MT}^h.\mathsf{Accum}.\Delta(X) = \mathcal{MT}^h.\mathsf{Accum}.\Delta(X')$. Let $l \equiv |X|$ and $l' \equiv |X'|$. Denote the elements of X by x_i (for $i = 0, \ldots, (l-1)$) and the elements of X' by x'_i (for $i = 0, \ldots, (l'-1)$). Assume, without loss of generality, that $l' \geq l \geq 1$.

[10]Requiring the ROM is necessary since h and Merkle tree ($\mathcal{MT}^h$) are keyless, so they cannot be a CRHF without simplifications such as the ROM,

If $l = l' = 1$, then $X \neq X'$ simply means $x_0 \neq x'_0$, and we have:

$$\Delta(X) = \Delta((x_0)) = h(0x00 + x_0) \tag{3.25}$$
$$\Delta(X') = \Delta((x'_0)) = h(0x00 + x'_0) \tag{3.26}$$

And since we also have that $\Delta(X) = \Delta(X')$, then we obtain $h(0x00 + x_0) = h(0x00 + x'_0)$, i.e., we found a collision to h, which is infeasible to find efficiently if given a random function h.

Consider now the case that $l' > 1$. Denote:

$$\Delta_{i,j} \equiv \mathcal{MT}^h.\mathsf{Accum}.\Delta((x_i, \ldots, x_j))$$
$$\widehat{\Delta}_{i,j} \equiv \mathcal{MT}^h.\mathsf{Accum}.\Delta((x'_i, \ldots, x'_j))$$

If $l = 1$, then we have, from Equations (3.22) and (3.23),

$$h(0x00 + x_0) = h\left(0x01 + \widehat{\Delta}_{0,lP_2(l')-1} + \widehat{\Delta}_{lP_2(l'),l'-1}\right)$$

This is a collision for h since the first bytes of the two hashed strings are different, and collisions are infeasible to find efficiently for a random function h.

Finally, consider $l' \geq l > 1$; WLOG, consider the smallest such l'. From Equation (3.23), we have:

$$h(0x01 + \widehat{\Delta}_{0,lP_2(l')-1} + \widehat{\Delta}_{lP_2(l'),l'-1})$$
$$= h(0x01 + \Delta_{0,lP_2(l)-1} + \Delta_{lP_2(l),l-1})$$

If the inputs to h differ, then we have a collision (i.e., a contradiction). Therefore, assume that the inputs are identical. Since the digests of the Merkle tree are always of the same length (which is the length of a single hash output), then we have $\widehat{\Delta}_{0,lP_2(l')-1} = \Delta_{0,lP_2(l)-1}$ and $\widehat{\Delta}_{lP_2(l'),l'-1} = \Delta_{lP_2(l),l-1}$, i.e., $\Delta(X'[0 : lP_2(l')-1]) = \Delta(X[0 : lP_2(l)-1])$ and $\Delta(X'[lP_2(l') : l']) = \Delta(X[lP_2(l) : l])$. Since the sequences X and X' differ, then either $X'[0 : lP_2(l') - 1]) \neq X[0 : lP_2(l) - 1]$ or $X'[lP_2(l') : l']) \neq X[lP_2(l) : l]$ (or both). However, this gives one (or two) collisions with shorter inputs, contradicting our choice of the collision with the shortest l'. □

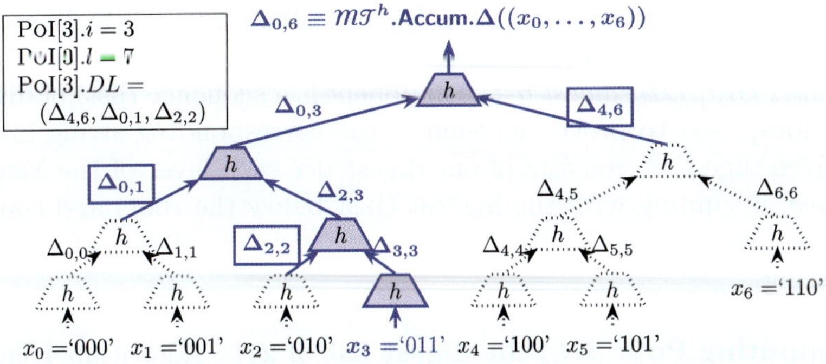

Figure 3.18. The Merkle tree Proof of Inclusion function PoI$[i](X) \equiv \mathcal{MT}^h$.Accum.PoI$[i](X)$, shown for $i = 3$, i.e., the PoI showing that x_3 = '011' is included in the sequence whose digest is Δ('000','001','010','011','100','101','110'). The PoI has three components: the string identifier $\mathcal{MT}^h$.PoI[3].$i = 3$, the list length $\mathcal{MT}^h$.PoI[3].$l = 7$ and the *digest list* $\mathcal{MT}^h$.PoI[3].$DL = (\Delta_{4,6}, \Delta_{0,1}, \Delta_{2,2})$. The digest list is in the order of the layers in the tree (from top to bottom). The other bold, blue hash values, over thick lines, are used for PoI verification. The dotted inputs and hash operations are not used for the verification of the PoI of x_3.

3.7.2.2 *The Merkle tree PoI*

To complete the definition of the Merkle tree accumulator $\mathcal{MT}^h$, we present its PoI and VERPOI functions, $\mathcal{MT}^h$.Accum.PoI and $\mathcal{MT}^h$.VERPOI. We then prove that $\mathcal{MT}^h$ ensures PoI correctness and unforgeability. Note that there are several options for the design, with similar performance; we describe a variant that we find convenient.

Figure 3.18 illustrates the computation of the PoI for the input string x_3, which is part of the sequence $(x_i)_{i=0}^{6}$ given as input to $\mathcal{MT}^h$ (the same sequence as in Figure 3.17), using the 'shorthand notation' PoI$[i] \equiv \mathcal{MT}^h$.Accum.PoI$[i]$. As the figure illustrates, each Proof of Inclusion, e.g., PoI$[i]$, has three components: PoI$[i].i$, PoI$[i].l$ and PoI$[i].DL$. Let us explain these components:

- The PoI$[i].i$ component is the index of the corresponding string, i.e., PoI$[i].i = i$, e.g., PoI[3].$i = 3$. The index is used to verify the PoI.
- The PoI$[i].l$ component is the number of strings in the accumulated sequence; this component is the same in all PoIs produced

in the same operation, e.g., in Figure 3.18, it is 7 for all PoIs, i.e., $(\forall i : 0 \leq i < l)$ PoI$[i].l = 7$.

- The PoI$[i].DL$ (*digest list*) component is a sequence (list) of digest values, used to prove inclusion of the corresponding string in the given digest. It consists of one digest per each layer of the Merkle tree, beginning with the highest (just below the root) and continuing down until the lowest layer, which is the digest of a single string.

Computing PoI$[i].DL$, the digest list of x_i: Algorithm 4 shows the algorithm for computing the digest list $\mathcal{MT}^h$.Accum.PoI$[i].DL(X)$ for the input sequence of strings $X = (x_0, \ldots, x_j)$. For brevity, we use the 'shorthand notation' PoI$[i].DL(x) \equiv \mathcal{MT}^h$.Accum.PoI$[i].DL(X)$. Let us explain this algorithm.

Consider first the base case, where the input sequence X contains a single element, i.e., $X = (x_0)$. In this case, no PoI would be needed for verification; therefore, the PoI is simply the empty list $\emptyset$, i.e., PoI$[0].DL((x_0)) = \emptyset$. We also return PoI$[i].DL((x_0, \ldots, x_j)) = \emptyset$ if $j < i$ or if $i < 0$, two cases where the PoI isn't defined.

Algorithm 4 Algorithm PoI$[i].DL((x_0, \ldots, x_j))$: returns the digest list (DL) component of the PoI of x_i; for brevity, we denote PoI$[i].DL(x) \equiv \mathcal{MT}^h$.Accum.PoI$[i].DL(X)$. The algorithm uses the notation $lP_2(d) \equiv 2^{\lfloor \log_2(d) \rfloor}$ (Equation (3.24)).

1: **if** $(j \leq 0) \vee (i < 0) \vee (j < i)$ **return** $\emptyset$
2: $X_L \leftarrow (x_0, \ldots, x_{lP_2(j)-1})$; $X_R \leftarrow (x_{lP_2(j)}, \ldots, x_j)$;
3: **if** $i < lP_2(j)$ **then**
4:     **return** $\Delta(X_R) + PoI.DL(i, X_L)$
5: **else**
6:     **return** $\Delta(X_L) + PoI.DL(i - lP_2(j), X_R)$

Consider now the main case, where the input list has more than one element, i.e., $(x_0, \ldots, x_j)$ with $0 < j$, and we compute the PoI$[i]$ for $0 \leq i \leq j$, i.e., for element x_i in the list. We compute the digest list by recursion, by applying the PoI and Δ functions, where the input to both functions is a shorter sequence.

Specifically, we split the input list X into two shorter lists, X_L and X_R, such that $X = (x_0, \ldots, x_j) = X_L + X_R$, where X_L contains the first $lP_2(j)th$ elements of X, i.e., $X_L \leftarrow (x_0, \ldots, x_{lP_2(j)-1})$, and X_R contains the rest of the elements, i.e., $X_R \leftarrow (x_{lP_2(j)}, \ldots, x_j)$.

Recall that $lP_2(j) \equiv 2^{\lfloor \log_2(j) \rfloor}$, i.e., the largest power of two which is not larger than j. Therefore, in the example of Figure 3.18, $j = 6$, $lP_2(j) = 4$ and we will have $X_L = (x_0, \ldots, x_3)$ and $X_R = (x_4, x_5, x_6)$. Note that for any inputs i and X, both X_L and X_R contain less than $j + 1$ elements, i.e., are shorter than the input sequence X.

If $lP_2(j) \leq i$, then $x_i \in X_R$. In this case, the PoI's digest list consists of $\Delta(X_L) = \Delta_{0,lP_2(j)-1}$, followed by the PoI of x_i in X_R, i.e., PoI$[i - lP_2(j)].DL(X_R)$. Otherwise, if $i < lP_2(j)$, then $x_i \in X_L$, and the digest list consists of $\Delta(X_R) = \Delta_{lP_2(j),j}$ followed by the PoI of x_i in X_L, i.e., PoI$[i].DL(X_L)$.

As an example, let us use Algorithm 4 to compute the digest list (DL) component of the PoI for x_3 ='011', as illustrated in Figure 3.18. Namely, we invoke

$$\text{PoI}.DL(3, (\text{'000'},\text{'001'},\text{'010'},\text{'011'},\text{'100'},\text{'101'},\text{'110'}))$$

As a result, the PoI algorithm calls itself recursively three times. Let us review the operation of each of these four invocations of the algorithm:

1. The initial call is PoI.$DL(3, (\text{'000'}, \text{'001'}, \text{'010'}, \text{'011'}, \text{'100'}, \text{'101'}, \text{'110'}))$, i.e., $i = 3$, $j = 6$, and the input sequence is ('000','001','010','011','100','101','110'). Therefore, $lP_2(j) = lP_2(6) = 4$, $X_L \leftarrow$ ('000','001','010','011'), $X_R \leftarrow$ ('100','101', '110'). Finally, we return the concatenated list $\Delta((\text{'100'}, \text{'101'},\text{'110'}))$ + PoI.$DL(3, (\text{'000'},\text{'001'},\text{'010'},\text{'011'}))$. Note that $\Delta((\text{'100'},\text{'101'},\text{'110'}))$ is denoted as $\Delta_{4,6}$ in Figure 3.18.
2. The first recursive call is PoI.$DL(3, (\text{'000'},\text{'001'},\text{'010'},\text{'011'}))$, i.e., $i = 3$, $j = 3$, and the input sequence is ('000','001','010', '011'). Therefore, $lP_2(j) = lP_2(3) = 2$, $X_L \leftarrow$ ('000','001'), $X_R \leftarrow$ ('010','011') and we return $\Delta((\text{'000'},\text{'001'}))$ + PoI.DL $(1, (\text{'010'},\text{'011'}))$. Note that $\Delta((\text{'000'},\text{'001'}))$ is denoted as $\Delta_{0,1}$ in Figure 3.18.

3. The second recursive call is $\text{PoI}.DL(1, (\text{'010'},\text{'011'}))$, i.e., $i = j = 1$ and the input sequence is ('010','011'). Therefore, $lP_2(j) = lP_2(1) = 1$, $X_L \leftarrow (\text{'010'})$, $X_R \leftarrow (\text{'011'})$ and we return $\Delta((\text{'010'})) + \text{PoI}.DL(0, (\text{'011'}))$. Note that $\Delta((\text{'010'}))$ is denoted as $\Delta_{2,2}$ in Figure 3.18.
4. The last recursive call is $\text{PoI}.DL(0, (\text{'011'}))$, i.e., $i = j = 0$, therefore, it returns the empty sequence $\emptyset$.
5. After the layers of recursion complete, the initial call returns the concatenated result: $(\Delta_{4,6}, \Delta_{0,1}, \Delta_{2,2})$, as required.

$\mathcal{MT}^h$.VerPoI — verifying proofs of inclusion: Algorithm 5 presents the $\mathcal{MT}^h$.VerPoI algorithm, which verifies PoIs. VerPoI has three inputs: a digest Δ, a string x, and a PoI, denoted π. Its output should be True if x is a part of a sequence whose digest is Δ, and False otherwise.

The Merkle tree PoI, in turn, has the three components discussed earlier: $\pi.i$, the index of the corresponding string within the accumulated sequence; $\pi.l$, the number of strings in the accumulated sequence; and $\pi.DL$, the ***digest list***, which is a sequence (list) of digest values. The digest list $\pi.DL$ is used by VerPoI for verification that x is included in a sequence X whose digest is Δ. The digest list $\pi.DL$ consists of one digest per each layer of the Merkle tree, beginning with the highest (just below the root) and continuing down until the lowest layer, which is the digest of a single string.

Most of the algorithm (lines 3–15) is the recursive function DigPoI, which receives a string x and the purported PoI π, and returns the digest of the Merkle tree corresponding to x and π. The VerPoI function simply returns True if DigPoI, when applied to the inputs x and π given to the VerPoI, returns the digest Δ given as input to VerPoI; otherwise, VerPoI returns False.

Let us explain the function DigPoI, and how it returns Δ if π and Δ were indeed the outputs of $\mathcal{MT}^h$.Accum when given a sequence containing the string x (correctness), as well as why it is infeasible to find another string $x' \neq x$ and a (fake) PoI π' for which DigPoI will return Δ (unforgeability).

Algorithm 5 The $\mathcal{MT}^h$.VERPOI(Δ, x, π) algorithm: using Proof of Inclusion π, verify that string x is included in a sequence whose digest is Δ.

function VERPOI(Δ, x, π)
  return $(\Delta =$ DIGPOI$(x, \pi))$
function DIGPOI(x, π) ▷ Compute digest from x, π
  if $\pi.l \leq 1$ **then return** $h(0x00 + x)$ ▷ Digest of one string.
  if $|\pi.DL| = 0$ **then return** $\perp$ ▷ Some digest(s) must exist in $\pi.DL$.
  $\Delta' \leftarrow \pi.DL[0]$ ▷ Extract first digest from the list $\pi.DL$
  $\pi'.DL \leftarrow \pi.DL[1:]$ ▷ $\pi'.DL \leftarrow$ rest of digest list
  $m \leftarrow lP_2(\pi.l - 1)$ ▷ Length of the left subsequence
  if $\pi.i < m$ **then** ▷ PoI is for a string in the left subsequence
    $\pi'.l \leftarrow m;\ \pi'.i \leftarrow \pi.i;$
    return $h(0x01 + $ DIGPOI$(x, \pi') + \Delta')$
  else ▷ PoI is for a string in the right subsequence
    $\pi'.l \leftarrow \pi.l - m;\ \pi'.i \leftarrow \pi.i - m$
    return $h(0x01 + \Delta' + $ DIGPOI$(x, \pi'))$

Consider first the base case, where $\pi.DL$ is empty ($\pi.DL = \emptyset$). This should hold only if Δ is the digest of the sequence (x) which consists of a single string x. In this case, we should have $\pi.l = 1$, and the digest should be $h(0x00 + x)$. Indeed, this is what DIGPOI returns, directly due to the first line; therefore, for this case, we already see that $\mathcal{MT}^h$ ensures POI correctness. POI unforgeability for this case follows directly from the unforgeability of h.

Let us now consider the operation of DIGPOI when $\pi.DL$ is not empty. In this case, we should have $\pi.l > 1$, and the conditions of the two 'if' statements at the beginning of DIGPOI should both fail. DIGPOI extracts Δ', the first digest in $\pi.DL$, and computes $m \leftarrow lP_2(\pi.l - 1)$. Note that m is the largest power of two which is *strictly smaller* than $\pi.l$, i.e., $m < \pi.l$. The value of m would be the first index in the right-hand branch of the Merkle tree, e.g., in the example of Figure 3.18, we'll have $m = 4$.

DIGPOI now checks if the string x is supposed to be in the left-hand branch or the right-hand branch of the Merkle tree, i.e., if $\pi.i < m$ or $\pi.i \geq m$, respectively. In either case, DIGPOI first computes the 'remaining POI' π', whose digest list contains the remainder of $\pi.DL$ ($\pi'.DL \leftarrow \pi.DL[1:]$). If x belongs in the left-hand branch ($\pi.i < m$), then $\pi'.l \leftarrow m$ and $\pi'.i \leftarrow \pi.i$; otherwise, $\pi'.l \leftarrow \pi.l - m$ and $\pi'.i \leftarrow \pi.i - m$.

Finally, DIGPOI returns the digest corresponding to string x and POI π, which is the hash digest of the concatenation of the fixed prefix $0x01$, the digest Δ' of the branch not containing x, and the digest corresponding to x and POI π', computed by recursively calling itself (DIGPOI(x, π')).

To illustrate the operation of $\mathcal{MT}^h$.VERPOI, let us track the validation of x_3 using the Proof of Inclusion POI[3] and the digest $\Delta_{0,6}$ computed by $\mathcal{MT}^h$.Accum, in the example illustrated in Figure 3.18:

1. $\mathcal{MT}^h$.VERPOI invokes DIGPOI(x_3, POI[3]), with POI[3]$.i = 3$, POI[3]$.l = 7$ and POI[3]$.DL = (\Delta_{4,6}, \Delta_{0,1}, \Delta_{2,2})$. Namely, DIGPOI is invoked with $x \leftarrow x_3$ and $\pi \leftarrow$ POI[3].
2. The conditions of the 'if' statements in lines 4 and 5 do not hold.
3. We have $\Delta' \leftarrow \Delta_{4,6}$, $m \leftarrow 4$ and $\pi'.DL \leftarrow (\Delta_{0,1}, \Delta_{2,2})$.
4. Since $\pi.i = 3 < m = 4$, we set $\pi'.l \leftarrow m = 4$, $\pi'.i \leftarrow 3$ and return $h(h(0x01 + \text{DIGPOI}(x_3, \pi') + \Delta_{4,6})$. Namely, we next invoke DIGPOI(x_3, π').
5. In this invocation, we'll get $\Delta' \leftarrow \Delta_{0,1}$, $m \leftarrow 2$, and $\pi'.DL \leftarrow (\Delta_{2,2})$.
6. This time, $\pi.i = 3 > m = 2$, therefore we set $\pi'.l$ to 2 and $\pi'.i$ to 1, and return $h(h(0x01 + \Delta_{0,1} + \text{DIGPOI}(x_3, \pi'))$.
7. In this invocation, we'll have $\pi.i = 1$, $\pi.l = 2, \Delta' \leftarrow \pi.DL[0] = \Delta_{2,2}$, $m \leftarrow 1$, and $\pi'.DL \leftarrow \emptyset$.
8. Now, $\pi.i = m = 1$, therefore we set $\pi'.l \leftarrow 1$, $\pi'.i \leftarrow 0$ and return $h(h(0x01 + \Delta_{2,2} + \text{DIGPOI}(x_3, \pi'))$.
9. This time, $\pi.l = 1$, therefore we return $h(0x00 + x_3) = \Delta_{3,3}$.
10. Upon receiving this, the calling invocation returns $\Delta_{2,3} = h(0x01 + \Delta_{2,2} + \Delta_{3,3})$.
11. Similarly, the calling invocation returns $\Delta_{0,3}$ and the top-level DIGPOI invocation returns $\Delta_{0,6}$.

12. The digest input to VERPOI should also be $\Delta_{0,6}$, therefore, it returns TRUE, as required.

Finally, in the following lemma, we state the correctness and the unforgeability of the $\mathcal{MT}^h$ accumulator.

Lemma 3.3. *Using the ROM, let h be a randomly chosen function from binary strings to* $\{0,1\}^n$*. Then,* $\mathcal{MT}^h$ *accumulator, using hash function h, is an accumulator that ensures PoI correctness and unforgeability.*

Proof. Correctness follows directly by induction, similar to the discussion above; we omit the details and focus on the proof of POI unforgeability.

Suppose, to the contrary, that some efficient adversary $\mathcal{A}$ produces, with significant probability, a *PoI forgery*, i.e., a sequence X, a string $x \notin X$ and a POI π s.t. VERPOI$(\Delta, x, \pi) =$ TRUE, where $\Delta \equiv \mathcal{MT}^h.\mathsf{Accum}.\Delta(X)$. Without loss of generality, assume that this is the PoI forgery with shortest digest list $\pi.DL$.

Let us first show that $|X| > 1$. Suppose $|X| = 1$, i.e., $X = (x_0)$, i.e., $\Delta = h(0x00 + x_0)$. We know that $x \notin X$, which in this case means that $x \neq x_0$. If $\pi.l = 1$, then DIGPOI$(x, \pi) = h(0x00 + x)$, but this gives a collision for h since $x \neq x_0$ yet $h(0x00 + x) = h(0x00 + x_0)$. Similarly, if $\pi.l > 1$, then DIGPOI(x, PoI) is computed as DIGPOI$(x, \pi) = h(0x01 + \overline{\Delta}_L + \overline{\Delta}_R)$ for some (digests) $\overline{\Delta}_L, \overline{\Delta}_R \in \{0,1\}^n$, by either line 11 or line 14. This gives a collision for h since now we have $h(0x01 + \overline{\Delta}_L + \overline{\Delta}_R) = h(0x00 + x_0)$.

We conclude that $|X| > 1$. Therefore, directly from Equation (3.23), we have $\Delta = \mathcal{MT}^h.\mathsf{Accum}.\Delta(X) = h(0x01 + \Delta_L + \Delta_R)$, for some $\Delta_L, \Delta_R \in \{0,1\}^n$. Furthermore, there are two corresponding sequences X_L, X_R s.t. $X = X_L + X_R$, where $\Delta_L = \mathcal{MT}^h.\mathsf{Accum}.\Delta(X_L)$ and $\Delta_R = \mathcal{MT}^h.\mathsf{Accum}.\Delta(X_R)$. Note that since $x \notin X$, then $x \notin X_L$ and $x \notin X_R$.

Consider the computation of DIGPOI(x, π). If $\pi.l \leq 1$, we have a collision for h (as above); therefore, assume that $\pi.l > 1$. Also assume that $|\pi.DL| > 0$, otherwise DIGPOI would return $\perp$, again resulting in a collision. Therefore, we continue with lines 6–14 of Algorithm 5.

In lines 6 and 7, we set Δ' to be the first digest in $\pi.DL$, and $\pi'.DL$ to be the reminder of $\pi.DL$, i.e., $\pi.DL[1:]$.

In line 8, we set $m \leftarrow lP_2(\pi.l - 1)$; since $\pi.l > 1$, we will have $\frac{\pi.l}{2} \leq m < \text{PoI}.l$.

The 'if' statement at line 9 compares $\pi.i$ to m. Let us continue with the case $\pi.i < m$ (lines 10 and 11); we omit discussion of the other case ($\text{PoI}.i \geq m$, lines 13 and 14) since it is very similar. Hence, we set $\pi'.l \leftarrow m < \pi.l$, and then DIGPOI returns $h(0x01 \mathbin{+\!\!+} \text{DIGPOI}(x, \pi') \mathbin{+\!\!+} \Delta')$. Since VERPOI returns TRUE, this must be equal to Δ, i.e., $\Delta = h(0x01 \mathbin{+\!\!+} \text{DIGPOI}(x, \pi') \mathbin{+\!\!+} \Delta')$.

Recall that $\Delta = \mathcal{MT}^h.\mathsf{Accum}.\Delta(X) = h(0x01 \mathbin{+\!\!+} \Delta_L \mathbin{+\!\!+} \Delta_R)$. Therefore, we either obtain a collision for h — which contradicts the assumption that h is chosen randomly — or the preimages are also identical, and in particular $\text{DIGPOI}(x, \pi') = \Delta_L$. Recall that Δ_L is the digest of X_L and that $x \notin X_L$. But this means that (X_L, x, π') is also a PoI forgery. Since $\pi'.DL$ contains one less digest than $\pi.DL$, we have a contradiction to our assumption that (X, x, π) is the shortest PoI forgery. □

3.7.3 Other definitions of accumulators and security properties

In the previous two sections, we presented the basic definitions of cryptographic accumulators and discussed the basic Merkle tree construction. This is only a small sample of the extensive research on cryptographic accumulators, which began when accumulators were first defined and constructed by Benaloh and de Mare in 1993 [58]. There were many works following Ref. [58], presenting different definitions of accumulators, often with additional operations and properties, as well as different constructions, extensions and applications. Let us briefly mention a few of the important extensions.

Dynamic accumulators, proposed by Camenisch and Lysyanskaya in 2002 [111], support incremental accumulation of multiple input sequences of strings. Namely, a dynamic accumulator can accumulate new strings in addition to already-accumulated strings; some definitions also allow removal of strings.

To allow accumulation of multiple input sequences, dynamic accumulators have to be *stateful*. Furthermore, whenever accumulating an additional block, a dynamic accumulator outputs, in addition to the new digest and the PoI for each of the newly accumulated strings, also an *update value*. The update value will be used as input to an *update* function of the dynamic accumulator, to update existing digests and PoI values. This allows recipients to maintain and update the digest and PoI values for specific or all strings.

In some accumulators, the update operation also provides a *Proof of Consistency* (PoC). The PoC allows an entity receiving a new digest to confirm that this new digest is *consistent* with a previously received digest, i.e., that it is the result of accumulating additional (sequences of) strings. Accumulators ensuring consistency were proposed in Ref. [110], where they are referred to as *strong accumulators*. In particular, a dynamic variant of the Merkle tree accumulator is used by the CT PKI, as discussed in Section 8.5; this design provides a PoC for updates.

Another property defined and supported by the constructions in Ref. [110] is *Proof of Non-Inclusion (PoNI)*, i.e., the ability to show that a specific string is *not* one of these accumulated into the digest. Accumulators supporting this property are often called *universal accumulators*. See Exercise 3.26.

Most of the literature focuses on integrity properties of accumulators. However, some applications of accumulators also require confidentiality for the inputs. Such applications should use accumulators which ensure confidentiality requirements; for example, see Ref. [203] for such definitions and constructions.

3.8 The Merkle–Damgård construction

The Merkle–Damgård construction $\mathcal{MD}^h$ uses a cryptographic function which we denote h as its 'building block'. The function h is typically a *compression function*, i.e., a function whose domains are binary strings of length n' and whose ranges are shorter binary strings, of length $n < n'$, i.e., $h : \{0,1\}^{n'} \to \{0,1\}^n$. However, the construction also works when the domain of h is the set of all binary strings, $h : \{0,1\}^* \to \{0,1\}^n$.

We first show that $\mathcal{MD}^h$ is an accumulator. We then show how to use $\mathcal{MD}^h$ to transform a compression function $h : \{0,1\}^{n'} \to \{0,1\}^n$

into a hash function $h^{MD} : \{0,1\}^* \rightarrow \{0,1\}^n$. If h is a collision-resistant compression function, then h^{MD} would be a collision-resistant hash function.

Since in most of the discussion the specific function h is irrelevant, we usually abuse notation and simply write $\mathcal{MD}$ rather than writing explicitly $\mathcal{MD}^h$.

3.8.1 The Merkle–Damgård accumulator $\mathcal{MD}$

The Merkle–Damgård accumulator, $\mathcal{MD}^h$, is a simple accumulator, built using a CRHF h; we usually omit h and write simply $\mathcal{MD}$. We only define and use the accumulator's digest function, $\mathcal{MD}.\Delta(\{x_0, \ldots, x_{l-1}\})$, computed over a sequence which consists of binary strings, where each string may have arbitrary length, i.e., $x_i \in \{0,1\}^*$. A corresponding PoI function can be easily defined; however, it is inefficient, trivial and not useful, so we do not present it.

The Merkle–Damgård digest function $\mathcal{MD}.\Delta$ produces the digest resulting from accumulating the sequence of strings $\{x_0, \ldots, x_{l-1}\}$.

We compute the digest $\mathcal{MD}.\Delta(\{x_0, \ldots, x_{l-1}\})$ as follows:

$$\mathcal{MD}.\Delta\left(\{x_i\}_{i=0}^{l-1}\right) \equiv \begin{cases} \text{For } l > 1 : h\left(\mathcal{MD}.\Delta\left(\{x_i\}_{i=0}^{l-2}\right) + 1 + x_{l-1}\right) \\ \text{For } l = 1 : \qquad h(0^{n+1} + x_0) \end{cases} \tag{3.27}$$

Figure 3.19 illustrates the computation of $\mathcal{MD}.\Delta$ for the case of four input strings, $\{x_0, \ldots, x_3\}$, and Example 3.1 is a simple example for the computation of $\mathcal{MD}.\Delta$.

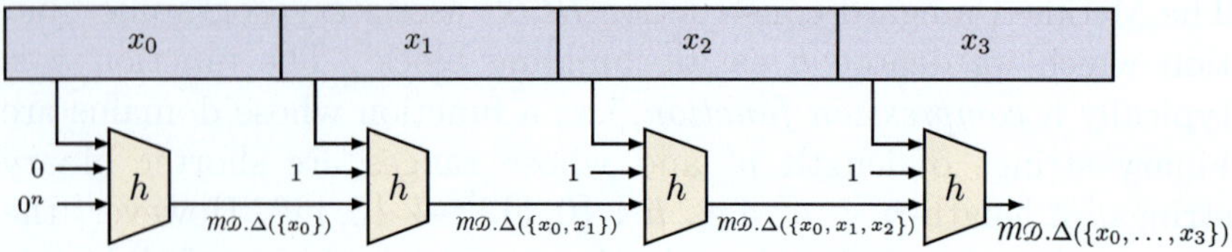

Figure 3.19. The digest function of the Merkle–Damgård accumulator $\mathcal{MD}$, applied to the input sequence $\{x_0, \ldots, x_3\}$.

Example 3.1. Let $X = \{\text{‘1’}, \text{‘10’}, \text{‘011’}\}$ be sequence of three binary strings. We compute the Merkle–Damgård digest of X, using underlying hash h, by:

$$\begin{aligned} \mathcal{MD}.\Delta\left(\{\text{‘1’}, \text{‘10’}, \text{‘011’}\}\right) &= h(\mathcal{MD}.\Delta(\{\text{‘1’}, \text{‘10’}\}) + 1 + \text{‘011’}) \\ &= h\left(h\left(\mathcal{MD}.\Delta(\{\text{‘1’}\}) + 1 + \text{‘10’}\right) + \text{‘1011’}\right) \\ &= h\left(h\left(h(0^{n+1} \parallel 1) + \text{‘110’}\right) + \text{‘1011’}\right) \end{aligned} \tag{3.28}$$

□

3.8.1.1 *The Merkle–Damgård accumulator ensures collision resistance*

We next show that $\mathcal{MD}$ ensures collision-resistance under the random oracle model (ROM).

Lemma 3.4. *Under the ROM, i.e., if h is selected randomly, then $\mathcal{MD}$ is a collision-resistant accumulator.*

Proof. Assume, to the contrary, that adversary $\mathcal{A}^{MD} \in PPT$ has non-negligible probability to output a collision. We use $\mathcal{A}^{MD}$ to construct adversary $\mathcal{A}^h$ which has non-negligible advantage to find a collision for h, which is infeasible for randomly chosen h. Specifically, $\mathcal{A}^h$ runs $\mathcal{A}^{MD}$, and whenever $\mathcal{A}^{MD}$ outputs a collision for $\mathcal{MD}.\Delta$, then $\mathcal{A}^h$ outputs a collision for h, which gives the contradiction. Let us explain how $\mathcal{A}^h$ outputs a collision for h.

Denote the collision for $\mathcal{MD}$ by (X, X'). Namely, $X \neq X'$ are different sequences of binary strings which have the same $\mathcal{MD}$ digest, i.e.,

$$\mathcal{MD}.\Delta(X) = \mathcal{MD}.\Delta(X') \tag{3.29}$$

Denote the number of messages in X by l and the number of messages in X' by l', i.e., $X = \{x_0, \ldots, x_{l-1}\}$ and $X' = \{x'_0, \ldots, x'_{l'-1}\}$.

First, consider the special case $l = l' = 1$. From Equation (3.27), we have:

$$\text{If } l = 1 : \mathcal{MD}.\Delta\,(X) = \mathcal{MD}.\Delta\,(\{x_0\}) = h(0^{n+1} + x_0) \tag{3.30}$$

$$\text{If } l' = 1 : \mathcal{MD}.\Delta\,(X') = \mathcal{MD}.\Delta\,(\{x'_0\}) = h(0^{n+1} + x'_0) \tag{3.31}$$

Since $X = \{x_0\} \neq X' = \{x'_0\}$, it follows that $x_0 \neq x'_0$. Let $y_0 = 0^{n+1} + x_0$, $y'_0 = 0^{n+1} + x'_0$; hence, $y_0 \neq y'_0$. Therefore, (y_0, y'_0) is a collision for h. Namely, $\mathcal{A}^h$ output a collision for h, which, as claimed, is a contradiction to the fact that h is a collision-resistant hash function.

Without loss of generality, assume $l' \geq l$. Consider first the case that $l' > l = 1$. Again from Equation (3.27), we have Equation (3.30) as before, but for X', we now have:

$$\begin{aligned} \text{If } l' > 1 : &\ \mathcal{MD}.\Delta\left(\{x'_0, \ldots, x'_{l'-1}\}\right) \\ &= h(\mathcal{MD}.\Delta(x'_0, \ldots, x'_{l'-2}) + 1 + x'_{l'-1}) \end{aligned} \tag{3.32}$$

Since the two digests are identical (Equation (3.29)), we have $h(0^{n+1} + x_l) = h(\mathcal{MD}.\Delta(x'_0, \ldots, x'_{l'-2}) + 1 + x'_{l'-1})$. However, the $(n+1)^{th}$ bit of the preimage of h on the right-hand side (RHS) is zero, and the corresponding bit of the preimage on the left-hand side (LHS) is one; hence, we again have a collision in h, which contradicts the fact that h is a CRHF.

It remains to consider the case where $l' \geq l > 1$. We again use Equation (3.32) for X', and now also have a similar equation for X, namely,

$$\text{If } l > 1 : \mathcal{MD}.\Delta\,(\{x_0, \ldots, x_{l-1}\}) = h(\mathcal{MD}.\Delta(x_0, \ldots, x_{l-2}) + 1 + x_{l-1}) \tag{3.33}$$

Without loss of generality, assume (or redefine) $l' \geq l > 1$ to be the minimal lengths such that the two sequences collide, i.e., the smallest values for which:

$$\begin{aligned} &(\mathcal{MD}.\Delta\,(\{x_0, \ldots, x_{l-1}\}) = \mathcal{MD}.\Delta\left(\{x'_0, \ldots, x'_{l'-1}\}\right)) \\ &\wedge\ (\{x_0, \ldots, x_{l-1}\} \neq \{x'_0, \ldots, x'_{l'-1}\}) \end{aligned} \tag{3.34}$$

Combining the first line of Equation (3.34) with Equations (3.32) and (3.33), we have:

$$\begin{aligned} &h(\mathcal{MD}.\Delta(x_0, \ldots, x_{l-2}) + 1 + x_{l-1}) \\ &\quad = h(\mathcal{MD}.\Delta(x'_0, \ldots, x'_{l'-2}) + 1 + x'_{l'-1}) \end{aligned} \tag{3.35}$$

If the preimages of h in the LHS and RHS of Equation (3.35) are different, then we have a collision for h, which is a contradiction to the fact that h is a CRHF.

Assume, therefore, that the preimages are equal. In particular, we have that $x_{l-1} = x'_{l'-1}$; since we know that $X \neq X'$, i.e., $\{x_0, \ldots, x_{l-1}\} \neq \{x'_0, \ldots, x'_{l'-1}\}$, we can remove the last elements from the two sequences since they are equal and conclude that:

$$\{x_0, \ldots, x_{l-2}\} \neq \{x'_0, \ldots, x'_{l'-2}\} \tag{3.36}$$

On the other hand, since the preimages of Equation (3.35) are equal, we can also conclude that:

$$\mathcal{MD}.\Delta(x_0, \ldots, x_{l-2}) = \mathcal{MD}.\Delta(x'_0, \ldots, x'_{l'-2}) \tag{3.37}$$

However, the combination of Equations (3.36) and (3.37) gives another collision for $\mathcal{MD}$, where the two colliding sequences are shorter than l' and l, contradicting our assumption above. □

3.8.1.2 *Collisions for 'slightly modified' Merkle–Damgård accumulator*

The design of the Merkle–Damgård accumulator may appear arbitrary, and some minor modifications, simplifying the design or improving performance, may appear harmless. However, changes to well-studied cryptographic mechanisms are dangerous; we demonstrate this by considering two subtle issues of the design.

First, let us consider the string of 0^n bits that we append to the first message x_1 in Equation (3.27), which is often referred to as an *Initialization Vector (IV)*, similarly to the term used for 'modes of operation' of block cipher (Section 2.10). One obvious question is whether the value of the IV must be 0^n rather than, say, 1^n or any other n-bit string. Here, in fact, the answer is that the choice of 0^n is completely arbitrary; any n-bit string could be used, as long as it is a *fixed* string.

But why must the IV be fixed? This seems wasteful. In particular, suppose that $|x_1| = n$. Can we then save one hash operation, by using x_1 as the n-bits input used to hash x_2? Unfortunately, this seemingly minor change would allow collisions, as the following exercise shows.

Exercise 3.6. Assume that $|x_1| = n$, and consider a variant on the MD construction where we change Equation (3.27) so that for $l = 1$, we have $\mathcal{MD}.\Delta(\{x_1\}) \equiv x_1$. This variant 'saves' a hash operation; however, show that it is not collision resistant.

Another possibly puzzling aspect of the construction is the fact that the input to the compression function includes one special bit, which is not taken from the input strings x_i and also not from the IV or from the previous digest. This bit is needed to allow for the case that an attacker may know a preimage of the IV string, with a particular property, and an attacker may know such preimage even if h is collision-resistant. See the following exercise.

Exercise 3.7. Show that collisions may be possible for a variant of the construction where Equation (3.27) is replaced by:

$$\overline{\mathcal{MD}}.\Delta\left(\{x_i\}_{i=1}^{l}\right) \equiv \begin{cases} \text{For } l > 1: h\left(\overline{\mathcal{MD}}.\Delta(\{x_i\}_{i=1}^{l-1}) + x_l\right) \\ \\ \text{For } l = 1: \qquad h(0^n + x_1) \end{cases}$$

Hint: Let h be a hash function with a known preimage of 0^n, i.e., where we know a value z such that $h(z) = 0^n$. Show a collision for $\overline{\mathcal{MD}}$. Then, show that such CRHF h may exist, by assuming some CRHF h', and using it, show that there exist a CRHF h with known preimage. The proof of Lemma 3.4 may be helpful. □

3.8.2 The Merkle–Damgård hash function h^{MD}

In this section, we present h^{MD}, the Merkle–Damgård construction of a hash function h^{MD}; this construction is used in the design of multiple hash functions, including the MD5, SHA-1 and SHA-2 hash functions.[11] The construction was proposed independently by Merkle [354] and Damgård [144]; I personally find Damgård's text easier to follow. Our presentation is different from the presentation in both papers since we present the Merkle–Damgård Hash Function

[11]The SHA-2 standard defines multiple hash functions using similar design but different sizes, including SHA-256, SHA-512 and others. SHA-3 uses a different design.

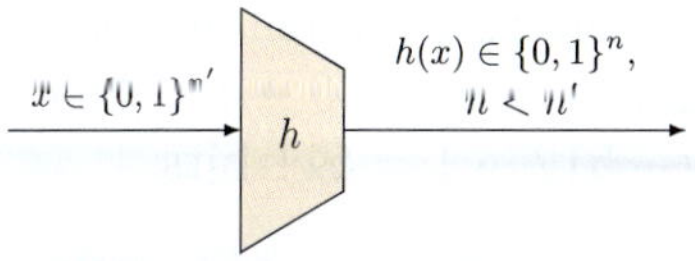

Hash	n'	n
MD5	512	128
SHA-1	512	160
SHA-256	512	256
SHA-512	1024	512

Figure 3.20. A compression function h: n'-bit input to n-bit output, $n < n'$, and the values of n' and n used by the compression functions of the $\mathcal{MD}$, SHA-1, SHA-256 and SHA-512 hash functions. Note that not all hash functions use the Merkle–Damgård construction or are based on a compression function.

construction using the Merkle–Damgård accumulator, presented in the previous section.

The Merkle–Damgård construction builds the hash function h^{MD} from a *compression function*[12] h. The compression function h is a special hash function that maps binary strings of a specific length n' into shorter strings of a specific shorter length $n < n'$. This is in contrast to most hash functions, including h^{MD}, which allow input strings of arbitrary length. See Figure 3.20.

One motivation to build a cryptographic hash function from a compression function is the cryptographic building blocks principle (Principle 8). Cryptographic hash functions are often viewed as a building block of applied cryptography, due to their simplicity and wide range of applications. However, compression functions are even simpler since their input is restricted to FIL strings. Furthermore, it is surely easier to test compression functions for collisions. Indeed, in cryptanalytical investigations of well-known hash functions, often success in finding collisions to the hash function followed from success in finding collisions to the compression function.

Let us proceed to explain the the Merkle–Damgård hash function construction h^{MD}. We begin with a simplified version, where the input messages consist of an integral number of *blocks*. As we see, for the h^{MD} construction, a *block* is a string of $(n' - n - 1)$-bits; for

[12]The term *compression function* may not be the best choice; it may have been clearer to refer to such functions, with Fixed-Input-Length (FIL), as FIL-hash functions. However, the use of 'compression functions' is entrenched in the literature; hence, it seems best to use it. Also, note that we denote the compression function by h, although it is not mnemonic, since we build h^{MD} from h using the $\mathcal{MD}$ accumulator, which we defined for a hash/compression function h.

convenience, we denote the block length by b, i.e., $b \equiv n' - n - 1$. For example, for SHA-256, we have $b = 512 - 256 - 1 = 255$ bits, while for SHA-512, we have $b = 1024 - 512 - 1 = 511$ bits.

The simplified Merkle–Damgård hash h^{simpMD}: We first describe a simplified Merkle–Damgård construction, denoted h^{simpMD}. To simplify, h^{simpMD} is defined only for input (binary) strings which contain an integer number, which we denote by l, of blocks of b bits; namely, $|x| = l \cdot b$.

Given a collision-resistant compression function h, we define the CRHF h^{simpMD}, restricted to input x which contains l blocks of b bits, i.e., $|x| = l \cdot b$, as follows. First, let x_i denote the ith block of x, namely,

$$x_i \equiv x\left[i \cdot b : (i+1) \cdot b - 1\right]$$

Now, we can define h^{simpMD}:

$$h^{simpMD}(x) \equiv \mathcal{MD}^h.\Delta\left(\{x_i\}_{i=0}^{l}\right) \tag{3.38}$$

The first step of h^{simpMD} is to split the input l into l strings, $\{x_i\}_{i=0}^{(l-1)}$, each containing b-bits. Then, we compute the $\mathcal{MD}$ digest of the sequence $\{x_i\}_{i=0}^{(l-1)}$, as in Figure 3.19. We illustrate h^{simpMD} in Figure 3.21; in the figure, we use $x[i : j]$ to denote the substring of x, from the ith bit to the jth bit.

From Lemma 3.4, if h is a collision-resistant compression function, then h^{simpMD} would be collision-resistant, for input x such that $|x| = 0 \bmod b$.

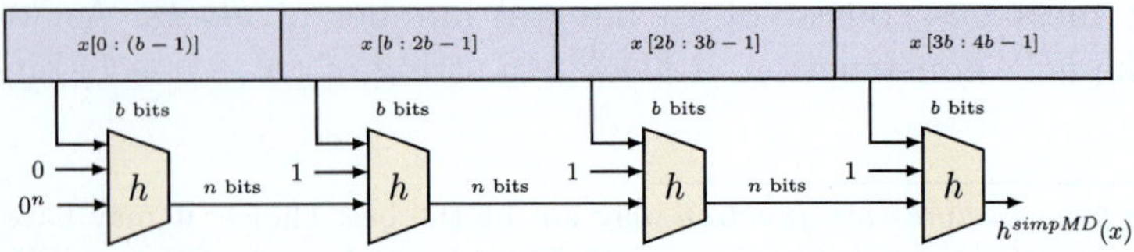

Figure 3.21. The simplified Merkle–Damgård hash $h^{simpMD}(x)$, defined for inputs x whose length is an integral number of 'blocks', each containing b bits, i.e., $|x| = 0 \bmod b$.

The Merkle–Damgård hash construction with MD-strengthening. The 'full' Merkle–Damgård hash function construction, h^{MD}, includes an additional preprocessing step, usually referred to as *MD-strengthening.* MD-strengthening avoids the restriction that the input x is an integral number of blocks, i.e., the assumption that $|x| \equiv 0 \bmod b$, required by h^{simpMD} (from Equation (3.38)). Namely, the MD-Strengthening step allows us to handle inputs which are binary strings of arbitrary length.

MD-strengthening pads the message x with additional bits before hashing it with h^{simpMD}. The padding should satisfy the following requirements:

- The padded message should consist of an integral number l of blocks, i.e., the padded message should consist of $l \cdot b$ bits.
- It should be easy to add the padding bits and to correctly remove them, recovering the pre-padding message.
- Padding should allow to send messages with any reasonable length, and the length of the padding should not cause excessive overhead.

To ensure easy and correct recovery of the original message, all padding bits are appended at the end of the padded message, and the length of the original message x is encoded at the very end of the padding, as an L-bits binary number, which we denote $bin_L(|x|)$. A typical value for L is 64, which allows padding of very long messages if needed but is still shorter than the block size, which is typically at least 255 bits (see Figure 3.20). The rest of the padding consists of a positive number z of *zero bits*, plus one bit whose value is 1, which is placed at the very beginning of the pad. Therefore, the total length of the pad is $L + z + 1$.

It remains to determine the number z of zero bits in the pad (not including the last L bits, which contains $bin_L(|x|)$). To make sure that the padded message consists of an integral number of blocks, $|x|+L+z+1 \equiv 0 \pmod b$. Hence, we select z to be $z \equiv b-(|x|+L+1) \bmod b$. Using this value of z and the simplified Merkle–Damgård hash function h^{simpMD} (Equation (3.38)), we construct the *Merkle–Damgård hash* h^{MD} as

$$h^{MD}(x) \equiv h^{simpMD}\left(x + 1 + 0^z + bin_L(|x|)\right) \tag{3.39}$$

Given a collision-resistant compression function h, the Merkle–Damgård hash construction produces a collision-resistant hash function (CRHF). This follows from Lemma 3.4.

3.9 Blockchains, Proofs of Work (PoW) and Bitcoin

In this section, we briefly introduce the large area of *blockchains*, a complex family of cryptographic protocols with extensive and important applications. Section 3.9.2 briefly introduces *cryptocurrencies*, the first and most well-known application of blockchains, and specifically Bitcoin, the first and most well-known cryptocurrency.

The basic goal of blockchains is to ensure integrity properties for a *ledger*, which is basically an ordered set of objects called *blocks*, each containing a set of *transactions*. A transaction is a *dictionary*, i.e., a mapping of multiple field names to values, e.g., date and amount. Different transactions in the ledger, and even in the same block, may be originated from different participants.

Blockchains allow multiple participants to securely add transactions and blocks to the same blockchain, under blockchain-specific constraints. Roughly speaking, blockchains should ensure that all benign entities should see a consistent ledger, i.e., the same sequence of blocks and the same transactions in each block.

To efficiently ensure integrity of the ledger, blockchains use cryptographic integrity and authentication mechanisms, such as accumulators, signature schemes and CRHFs. Blockchains also use *consensus (agreement)* protocols, to ensure benign participants all maintain consistent copies of the ledger. Blockchains use Proofs of Consistency that allow benign participants to verify that a new blockchain digest is consistent with a previous digest, i.e., the new digest represent accumulation of additional blocks and transactions. Once a block is added to the ledger, it becomes *immutable*, i.e., never changed or removed.

Blockchains produce *collision-resistant digests* of blocks and of the entire ledger, ensuring that it is infeasible to find two ledgers which produce the same digest. This allows the use of the digest to (efficiently) validate the integrity and *consistency* of the ledger.

In Bitcoin and (most) other cryptocurrencies, each transaction represents a payment and the ledger is the complete list of transactions, establishing the ownership of each Bitcoin. There are also other applications of blockchains where the term 'transaction' is relevant to financial transactions between entities. For the same reason, we refer to the entire sequence of transactions accumulated by the blockchain as a *ledger*. We discuss the Bitcoin cryptocurrency.

Blockchains support Proofs of Inclusion (PoIs), allowing participants to prove that specific transactions are included in the ledger. Blockchains ensure the unforgeability of PoIs, i.e., if there is a PoI for a specific transactions x, then this transaction must have been added to the ledger (and would remain on the ledger due to its immutability).

Blockchain ensure integrity under assumptions (models). For example, Bitcoin assumes that a majority of the computing power is controlled by benign participants; other blockchains may use other assumptions about the capabilities of the benign entities. Blockchains may also assume different cryptographic assumptions as well as system and communication assumptions, e.g., reliable communication with bounded delay and bounded clock drift. Rigorous definitions of these requirements, models and requirements are complex, and beyond our scope.

Consistency: The ledgers kept by different participants are required to be *consistent*. Consistency is defined with respect the the sequence of digests of blocks in the ledger kept by each participant, which, similarly to the digests of CRHFs and of accumulators, ensure consistency of the transactions in each block.

Let $\Delta_p(i)[t]$ be the digest for block i that participant p has at time t. Consistency boils down to a few basic requirements on the copies of the ledger as seen by different benign participants, p and p':

- The ledger kept by every benign participant p is a consecutively ordered set of blocks, without omissions. Namely,

$$(\forall t, i \leq j)\ \Delta_p(i)[t] = \perp \Rightarrow \Delta_p(j)[t] = \perp \qquad (3.40)$$

- Once a block is added to the ledger kept by a benign user, it becomes *immutable*, i.e., it is never removed. Namely,

$$(\forall i,\ t \leq t')\ \Delta_p(i)[t] \neq \perp \Rightarrow \Delta_p(i)[t'] = \Delta_p(i)[t] \qquad (3.41)$$

- The blocks kept by different participants are consistent. Namely,

$$(\forall i, t, t') \ \left(\Delta_p(i)[t] \neq \bot, \Delta_{p'}(i)[t'] \neq \bot\right) \Rightarrow \Delta_p(i)[t] = \Delta_{p'}(i)[t'] \tag{3.42}$$

- If one benign participant p adds a block, eventually other benign participants p' will also add that block, maintaining their order. Namely,

$$(\forall i, t) \ \Delta_p(i)[t] \neq \bot \rightarrow (\exists t')\Delta_p(j)[t'] = \Delta_p(i)[t] \tag{3.43}$$

  Typically, blockchains support an even stronger version of this property, which bounds the time when the block would be added by all benign participants by some value T, i.e., ensure further that $t' \leq t + T$.

Consistency ensures that the ledger can only grow, i.e., the ledger is *immutable*, and is *shared* among all participants. For example, a blockchain may be used to keep track of the *ownership* of objects belonging to some participants; a participant p who owns an object X at time t, may sign a transaction x which transfers ownership of X to participant p'. Once the transaction x is added to the blockchain, i.e., included in a block added to the blockchain, then the participants consider object X as belonging to p'. Consistency is key to such applications, as the ownership of an item must always be well defined.

Bounded delay and other requirements for transactions: Blockchains often also ensure a bound T on the maximal time (delay) for adding a transaction to the ledger. Namely, suppose that at time t a benign participant tries to add a new transaction to the ledger. Then, the new transaction should be included in a block which will be included in the ledger by time $t + T$ (or earlier).

Particular blockchain applications may require transactions to satisfy additional requirements in order to be considered 'valid'. For example, a Bitcoin transaction specifying payment of a Bitcoin is ignored, unless it is properly signed by the entity whom, according to the ledger, currently owns that Bitcoin.

3.9.1 Blockchain design: permissioned and permissionless blockchains

Blockchain schemes have many diverse designs and use different mechanisms to accumulate transactions into blocks which are added to the ledger and to ensure the blockchain requirements above, e.g., consistency and chain-growth, as well as other requirements. Blockchain schemes mostly belong to one of two categories: *permissioned blockchains* and *permissionless blockchains.*

Permissioned blockchains: In permissioned blockchains, only specific, authorized participants can add a block to the blockchain. In a typical permissioned blockchain scheme, the digest should be signed by at least one authorized (permissioned) participant; some schemes require multiple authorized parties to sign every new digest.

Specifically, if $A.s$ is an authorized (private) signing key, then the ith digest, denoted Δ_i, is sent together with a signature $\sigma_i \equiv Sign_{A.s}(\Delta_i)$. Note that this requires all participants to know the corresponding public validation key, $A.v$.

Permissionless blockchains: Permissionless blockchains are egalitarian: *every* participant may try to add a block to the blockchain, by following a process called *mining.* The participant to succeed in mining a given block should be selected by a fair process, e.g., randomly, with the probability of a participant to win proportional to the resources it allocates to the mining. To motivate participants to participate and to allocate resources to mining, permissionless blockchains provide a *reward* to a participant that mines a block. In permissionless blockchain cryptocurrencies such as Bitcoin, the reward is given in the cryptocurrency, e.g., as a number of Bitcoin. In fact, in Bitcoin, the mining rewards are the only mechanism which increases the amount of Bitcoin in circulation. This is the reason that this process is referred to as mining; mining Bitcoin, like mining gold, is a randomized process where the chance of success depends on the amount of allocated resources. We discuss Bitcoin in the following section.

3.9.2 The Bitcoin blockchain and cryptocurrency

Bitcoin is the first and the most well-known cryptocurrency, and also the first and most well-known application of blockchains. In Bitcoin, the ledger defines which Bitcoin is currently valid, and who the owner of each Bitcoin is. The owner is identified only using the owner's public key, which allows owners to transfer a number of Bitcoin to other participants, by signing an appropriate transaction using the public key 'owning' these Bitcoin. Bitcoin can be fragmented, allowing payments and ownership to be specified in fractions, as a multiple of the minimal denomination of 10^{-6} bitcoins.

Specifically, given a valid Bitcoin number c and a ledger X, the Bitcoin function *owner* returns the public validation key $v \equiv owner(c, X)$ which is said to *own* coin c. If $owner(c, X) = \bot$, then we say that c is not a valid coin number according to ledger X.

A Bitcoin *transaction* x specified a transfer of a number of Bitcoin from one owner to one or more new owners, identified by the corresponding public key(s). Transactions can specify rules for validity, including when and how the funds (Bitcoin) should be transferred; these rules are specified in the *Bitcoin Script* language.

Consider a simplified transaction $(x.coins, x.v, x.\sigma)$, where $x.coins$ is a list of Bitcoin numbers, $x.v$ is the public key to which the transaction transfers ownership of the Bitcoin in $x.coins$ and $x.\sigma$ is a digital signature. We say that x is a *valid transaction* for ledger X, if there is some public key v such that $(\forall c \in x.coins) v = owner(c, X)$ and $Verify_v((x.coins, x.v), x.\sigma) = \text{TRUE}$, i.e., $x.\sigma$ is a valid signature over $(x.coins, x.v)$ using the public key v. If X' is the ledger after adding a new block which includes transaction x, then the ownership over $x.coins$ will be passed to $x.v$, i.e., $(\forall c \in x.coins) x.v = owner(c, X')$.

Pseudonymity, Anonymity and Privacy in Bitcoin: Bitcoin provides *pseudonymity*, since transactions specify only the public validation key, and do not specify any identifier of the payer or recipient. The same person or organization may use different signature keys for different Bitcoin (of fractions of Bitcoin). For example, Charlie, whose (validation, signing) key pair is $(C.v, C.s)$, may transfer ownership of Bitcoin number c to Don, whose key pair is $(D.v, D.s)$, by using $C.s$ to sign the transaction $(c, D.v)$. There is however no need to know *who* is the payer or the payee.

This property is sometimes misunderstood to imply that Bitcoin ensures anonymity and privacy, which motivates the use of Bitcoin by people concerned about being associated with their transactions, including criminals. In particular, ransom payments, to ransomware or otherwise, and other payments for illegal products and services, are often made in Bitcoin. However, while Bitcoin transactions use pseudonyms rather than names, this does not provide real anonymity. In fact, since all Bitcoin transactions are documented on the public ledger, this makes it easy to trace the movement of Bitcoin between different owning public keys. This fact is often used by researchers and law enforcement agencies to track the flow of Bitcoin, which may allow identification of the persons involved in transactions, i.e., deanonymization.

The Bitcoin proof of work (PoW): In Bitcoin, mining a new block requires a solution to a difficult computational problem, namely, a PoW. There are other applications of PoW in cybersecurity, e.g., in defenses against some Denial of Service attacks, and there are also other approaches for mining in permissionless blockchains, e.g., *proof of stake*, where the mining probability is proportional to the amount of cryptocurrency held by each participant. We first discuss the general concept of PoW schemes and then focus on the Bitcoin PoW and block-mining operation.

Intuitively, a PoW scheme allows one party, the *worker*, to *solve* a *challenge*, with an *approximately known amount of computational resources*, resulting in a *proof* of this success, which can be efficiently verified by anyone.

PoW schemes belong in this chapter of hash functions, both due to their use in permissionless blockchains and in particular Bitcoin, but also since their most well known implementation, which is the one used in Bitcoin, is based on a hash function. Below, we explain this (simple) PoW, used by Bitcoin.

Notice that we used the general term 'computational resources' and not a more specific term such as computational power, i.e., number of computations per second, which is the resource used by the Bitcoin PoW. Indeed, some PoW proposals focus on other resources, e.g., storage, or on a combination of resources, e.g., time and storage. However, from this point, let us focus on PoW based on computational power, as used by Bitcoin. We will give only a simplified, intuitive 'definition' of PoW.

Definition 3.13 (Proof of Work (PoW) — intuitive 'definition'). A PoW scheme PoW consists of two efficient algorithms: *PoW.solve* and *PoW.validate*:

PoW.solve: The *PoW.solve* algorithm receives three inputs — a *challenge* $c \in \{0,1\}^*$, a (random) *nonce* value $r \in \{0,1\}^n$ and a *work-amount* w, where typically $w \in [1, 2^n]$. The *PoW.solve* function outputs an n-bit binary string, to which we refer as the *solution*.

PoW.Validate: The *PoW.Validate* algorithm has four inputs — the challenge c, the nonce r, the required work $w_r \in [1, 2^n]$ and a *purported solution* $\pi \in \{0,1\}^*$. The *PoW.Validate* algorithm returns TRUE or FALSE. The runtime of *PoW.solve* should be distributed randomly with average proportional to $\frac{2^\lambda}{w_r}$ computations of a given required work amount w_r. Typically, $\frac{2^\lambda}{w_r}$ computations of a given hash function h.

A PoW scheme is *secure* if it is infeasible to find a solution significantly more efficiently than by running the *PoW.solve* algorithm. The PoW is *correct* if

$$(\forall c, r, w) PoW.Validate(c, r, w, PoW.solve(c, r, w)) = \text{TRUE} \quad (3.44)$$

PoW mechanisms are often implemented using a cryptographic hash function. A typical implementation, which is a minor simplification of the one used in Bitcoin, is the PoW scheme PoW^B, which is constructed using a cryptographic hash function h, as follows:

PoW^B*.Validate*: On input (c, r, w, π), return TRUE if $h(c +\!\!+ r +\!\!+ \pi) \leq w$. Otherwise, return FALSE.

PoW^B*.solve*: On input (c, r, w), repeatedly compute $x \equiv h(c +\!\!+ r +\!\!+ \pi)$ for different $\pi \xleftarrow{\$} \{0,1\}^n$, aborting and returning π when $x \leq w$.

The Bitcoin blockchain: We illustrate the Bitcoin blockchain in Figure 3.22.

The transactions of block i, where $i \geq 1$, are accumulated using a keyless Merkle tree ($\mathcal{MT}^h$) scheme. We use Δ_i' to denote the digest of the transactions in block i, from which we later compute the digest Δ_i of the blockchain with i blocks. To compute Δ_i, we apply a hash function h to Δ_i' and two other values: the previous digest Δ_{i-1} and

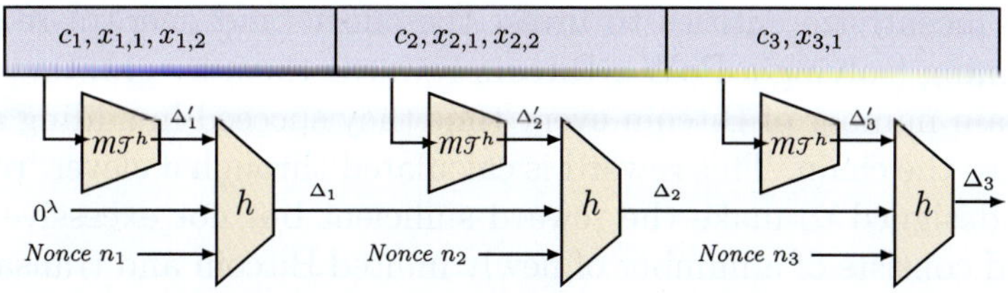

Figure 3.22. The (simplified) Bitcoin blockchain, illustrated for three blocks. Each block begins with the *coinbase* transaction (c_i), followed by regular transactions (two for blocks 1 and 2, one for block 3). The Merkle-tree digest of the transactions of block i is hashed with the digest of block $i-1$ (or with 0^λ for the genesis block) and with a *nonce* n_i. The value of the nonce should ensure that the resulting digest Δ_i is not higher than the current threshold.

a nonce value n_i, namely, $\Delta_i \equiv h(\Delta'_i + \Delta_{i-1} + n_i)$. The value of the nonce n_i is chosen randomly by the miner, until they find a nonce value n_i which ensures that $\Delta_i \leq w$, where w is the current work amount, following the Bitcoin PoW mechanism as described above.

Bitcoin operations and concerns — costs of PoW, rewards and adjustable work-amount w: Solving the Bitcoin proof of work requires considerable computational resources; this is intentional, to ensure that all entities have a fair chance to add new blocks, specifically, the probability of a specific miner to succeed in being the first to solve the PoW and to add the next block, is roughly the fraction of the number of hash computations by this miner, from the total number of hash computations done by all miners (for adding the block to the current blockchain). This prevents an attacker from adding most or all of the blocks, which would have allowed the attacker to abuse the system, e.g., by excluding specific transactions.

However, this means that adding blocks requires the use of significant amounts of energy. Most of this energy does not even result in a new block since only one miner can succeed in adding the new block. This wasteful use of large amounts of energy is one of the criticisms against Bitcoin and motivates the use of blockchains which are more energy-efficient. There are several alternative designs which avoid this waste of energy, including permissioned blockchains and blockchains using other mining mechanisms, e.g., *proof of stake*.

To incentivize entities to invest the effort (and energy) required for mining (solving a PoW), Bitcoin rewards them by granting them a certain number of Bitcoin every time they succeed in adding a new block to the chain. This reward is calculated through a clever 'reward rule', designed to make the reward sufficient but not excessive. The reward consists of a number of newly minted Bitcoin and transaction fees paid by the payers of transactions in the block. The rewards (new coins and fees) are allocated to the public key that the miner includes in a special transaction called the *coinbase transaction* which is included in every Bitcoin block, as illustrated in Figure 3.22.

The number of new Bitcoin rewarded upon mining is cut in half once per 210,000 blocks mined and would eventually become zero; this is estimated to happen around the year 2100. For Bitcoin to remain a viable system after that point, transactions fees should provide sufficient incentive to motivate miners. So far, transaction fees were only a small fraction of the incentive, typically, less than 5%.

The fee is indicated by the payer in each transaction, and this amount is moved from the payer to the miner of the block in the chain which includes this transaction; this is in addition to the amount of Bitcoin transferred to the payee. Different transactions offer different fees, and miners may prefer transactions with higher fees; each block has limited size, so miners may not be able to include all available transactions in their blocks.

The work-amount parameter w of the PoW is adjusted automatically by a feedback mechanism in Bitcoin, whose goal is to ensure that new blocks will be added at a *reasonable*, but not excessive, rate. Namely, if blocks are added more quickly, then the work amount is increased — making it harder to mine new blocks, i.e., slowing down the rate of adding blocks. This should maintain a stable rate of mining new blocks, and therefore, balancing between the overhead of block creation, and the delay until a new transaction appears on the chain. The mining rates can be impacted by multiple factors, including the energy costs of mining and the value of the award and fees obtained by a lucky miner, the likelihood of mining a block added to the chain (which depends on competition) and the costs and efficiency of mining hardware.

3.10 Lab: Checksum and CRC Collisions

Lab 3 (Checksum and CRC Collisions). In this lab, we experiment with attacks against a system using an insecure hash function, specifically, the *Internet Checksum* [99] error detection code (EDC); we denote this function as h. Namely, to hash input x, we compute $h(x)$, where h is the Internet Checksum function. In the lab files, you will find the file *Internet_Checksum.py* that computes h.

The labs and installation instructions are available from https://github.com/CyberSec-labs/labs; see more details in the preface:

1. Write a program to compute the Internet checksum, which we denote in this lab by h, of a given file. To allow you to test your program, you will find, in the *lab/q1* folder, the file *h1a.txt*, which is the result of applying h to another given file, *f1a.txt*. Once your program computes h correctly, use it to compute the Internet checksum h of the file *f1b.txt*, also in the *lab/q1* folder. Submit the result as the file *h1b.txt* in your submissions folder.
2. In the *lab/q2* folder, you will find the files, *f2a.txt, f2b.txt* and *h2.txt* which is the Internet checksum (h) of *f2a.txt*. In this question, you will want to find a *collision* for h, by changing *f2b.txt* so that the resulting file will also have the Internet checksum h in *h2.txt*, i.e., the same checksum as of *f2a.txt*. Submit *f2b.txt*, which must be different from *f2a.txt*, yet have the same Internet scheck-sum h, given in *h2.txt*. This shows that the Internet checksum h is not a CRHF.
3. In the *lab/q3* folder, you will find the file *f3a.txt*. File *f3a.txt* is made up of three lines; you will change the second line and put there a string of your choice. Create and submit a new file *f3b.txt* which will have the same Internet checksum h as of *f3a.txt* but have a different second line. This is a *partially chosen collision*, i.e., a collision between the Internet checksum over two files (documents) which differ only in a predefined location. Note that this implies universal forgery of signatures computed using the Hash-then-Sign construction using the Internet checksum h as the hash function.

4. In the *lab/q4* folder, you will find an HTML file, *f4a.html*. Open it in a browser; you will see a simple webpage with some text on it. Create and submit another HTML file, *f4b.html*, which will have the same Internet checksum as *f4a.html* but, when viewed via a browser, will display a webpage with a dramatically different message.
Hint: Within *f4a.html*, you will find an *if* statement. When the browser displays *f4a.html*, the *if* statement will evaluate to *true*. You can create *f4b.html* by changing the inputs to the *if* statement so that it will evaluate to *false*. Be sure to check that your changes will result in a collision despite the edits. As a result, when you open *f4b.html*, the browser will present a different message as required.

3.11 Additional exercises

Exercise 3.8 (XOR-hash). Consider the following hash function, defined for input messages consisting of a number l of n bits 'blocks', i.e., total of $l \cdot n$ bits, where n is the length of the digest, i.e., $n = |h(m)|$). Given such message m containing $l \cdot n$ bits, denote the ith block (of n bits) by m_i, i.e., $m = m_1 + \!\!\!+ m_2 + \!\!\!+ \cdots m_l$ and $(\forall i)|m_i| = n$. Define a hash function h for such $l \cdot n$ bit messages, as: $h(m_1 \ldots m_l) = \bigoplus_{i=1}^{l} m_i$.

Show that h does *not* have each of the following properties, or present a convincing argument why it does:

1. Second-preimage resistance (SPR), see Section 3.2.
2. Collision-resistance (CRHF), see Section 3.3.
3. Preimage resistance, i.e., h is not a OWF, see Section 3.4.
4. Bitwise randomness extraction (BRE), see Section 3.5.2.

Solution to part 4 (Bitwise randomness extraction): For simplicity, we present the solution for even n, i.e., $n = 2\mu$ where μ is an integer. Adversary $\mathcal{A}$ selects input message $m = 0^{2n}$ and mask $M = 0^{\mu} + \!\!\!+ 1^{\mu} + \!\!\!+ 0^{\mu} + \!\!\!+ 1^{\mu}$. Let y_b and y_{1-b} be the values computed by $\text{BRE}_{A,h}(b, n)$; the reader can confirm that y_{1-b} is random, while y_b is of the form $0^{\mu} + \!\!\!+ r$, where r is a random string of μ bits. On input (y_0, y_1, m, M), the adversary $\mathcal{A}$ returns:

$$\mathcal{A}(y_0, y_1, m, M) = \begin{cases} 0 \text{ if } m \bmod 2^{\mu} \neq 0^{\mu} \\ 1 \qquad \text{otherwise} \end{cases} \tag{3.45}$$

The reader should confirm that the adversary is correct with overwhelming probability. Hence, h is not a BRE. □

Exercise 3.9 (Insecure construction of a hash from a compression function). Let h be a compression function whose output (digest) is of length n and whose input is of length $l > n$. Let h' extend h to inputs x whose length is a multiple of l, e.g., $m \cdot l$, as follows: $h'(x) = \bigoplus_{i=1}^{m} h(x[(i-1) \cdot l : i \cdot l - 1])$. For each of the following properties, assume h has the property and show that h' may not have the same property. Or, if you believe h' does retain the property, argue why it does. The properties are:

1. collision-resistance,
2. second-preimage resistance,
3. one-wayness (preimage resistance),
4. bitwise randomness extraction.

Exercise 3.10 (Relaxed SPR definitions). Consider the following relaxed notions for a SPR hash function (Definition 3.1). Define the corresponding relaxed versions of the SPR advantage function, and show that no keyless hash function can satisfy these definitions. In fact, show that for these relaxed SPR definitions, and for any given hash function h, there is an efficient adversary $\mathcal{A}^h$ that achieves advantage of 1 using the corresponding relaxed SPR advantage function:

1. The adversary is allowed to pick arbitrary length l (not necessarily of length $l \geq n$).
2. Instead of outputting 1^l, the adversary outputs l (in binary).
3. Instead of outputting 1^l, the adversary outputs a set L such that $|L| \geq n$, and the preimage is selected uniformly from this set.

Exercise 3.11 (A hash which is SPR but insecure for file integrity). When using a hash function to protect integrity, the input is often not distributed randomly; different types of files often have specific structure and often other properties, including non-uniform distribution of byte values, similar to the letter distributions exploited in frequency analysis attacks (Figure 2.7). In this exercise, you show that this may be exploited by attacks against the use of SPR hash functions to ensure integrity. Assume, for simplicity, that the attacker's goal is to find a collision to a specific given file F.

Let h be an SPR hash function. Use h to construct another hash function, h', which is also SPR, but such that the adversary can efficiently find an *infinite* number of files F' that collide with F, i.e., such that $h'(F) = h'(F')$. Prove that h' is an SPR hash function and that the adversary can efficiently find any desired number of collisions to F when hashing using h'.

Exercise 3.12 (Cascade combining of hash). It is proposed to combine two hash functions by cascade, i.e., given hash functions h_1, h_2, we define $h_{12}(m) \equiv h_1(h_2(m))$. For each of the following, prove or present a counterexample:

1. The construction, $h_{12}(\cdot)$, is a robust combiner for collision-resistant hash functions, i.e., it suffices for either h_1 or h_2 to be a CRHF, for h_{12} to be a CRHF.
2. The construction, $h_{12}(\cdot)$, is a robust combiner for one-way functions, i.e., it suffices for either h_1 or h_2 to be a OWF, for h_{12} to be a OWF.
3. If *both* h_1 and h_2 are SPR hash functions, then h_{12} is also a SPR hash function.
4. If *both* h_1 and h_2 are BRE hash functions, then h_{12} is also a BRE hash function.

Exercise 3.13 (Insecure committee-designed combined hash). Recently, weaknesses were found in few cryptographic hash functions such as h_{MD5} and h_{SHA-1}, and as a result, there were many proposals for new functions. Dr. Simpleton suggests to combine the two into a new function whose output length is 160 bits: $h_c(m) = h_{SHA-1}(h_{MD5}(m) + h_{SHA-1}(m))$. Prof. Deville objects; she argued that hash functions should have longer outputs and suggested a complex function, h_{666}, whose output size is 666 bits. A committee is asked to evaluate these two proposals, and it comes up with a third design, which combines these two functions using XOR: $h_X(m) = [0^{506} +\!\!+ h_c(m)] \oplus h_{666}(m)$;

1. Present counterexamples showing that each of these may not be a CRHF.
2. Repeat, for one-way functions.
3. Repeat, for BRE hash functions.
4. Present a simp design where we can be sure that finding a collision is definitely *not* easier than finding a collision in h_{SHA-1} and in h_c, i.e., a robust combiner for CRHFs. *Hint*: The digest may be longer.

Exercise 3.14. Consider the hash function $h(x_1 +\!\!+ x_2 +\!\!+ \cdots +\!\!+ x_l) = \sum_{i=1}^{l} x_i \bmod p$, where each x_i is 64 bits and p is a 64-bit prime:

1. Is $h(\cdot)$ an SPR hash function? A CRHF?
2. Present an efficient algorithm that finds an identical-prefix collision for h.
3. Present an efficient algorithm that finds a chosen-prefix collision for h.
4. Create two html files $L.html, R.html$ which will be a collision ($h(L.html) = h(R.html)$) yet look exactly the same when viewed by a web browser.

Exercise 3.15. Let $h(\cdot)$ be a CRHF hash function. Use $h(\cdot)$ to construct another hash function, h', which you will show to be (1) an SPR but (2) *not* a CRHF.

Exercise 3.16. 1. Suppose that h is an SPR hash function. Use h to construct another hash function, h', which you will show to also be an SPR but to be vulnerable to *identical-prefix collisions*.
2. Repeat, for *chosen-prefix collisions*.

Exercise 3.17 (Unordered collision resistance). An *unordered accumulator collision* for accumulator schemes is a pair of sequences X and X' such that $\Delta(X) = \Delta(X')$ yet the two sequences contain *different elements*, i.e., $\exists x$ s.t. $(x \in X \cup X') \wedge (x \notin X \cap X')$:

1. Is every (ordered) collision also an unordered collision? Is every unordered collision also an ordered collision? Prove or present counterexample.

2. Define *unordered collision-resistant accumulator.*
3. Is the Merkle tree an *unordered collision-resistant accumulator*? Prove or present a counterexample.
4. Define a *concatenated collision* as a pair of sequences $X = \{x_1, \ldots, x_l\}$ and $X' = \{x'_1, \ldots, x'_{l'}\}$ such that $\Delta(X) = \Delta(X')$ yet the concatenation of all strings in X differ from the concatenation of strings in X'. Repeat items 1–3 for a concatenated collision.

Exercise 3.18 (SPR accumulator). 1. Define second-preimage-resistant (SPR) accumulators.
2. Show that every (keyless) collision-resistant accumulator is also an SPR accumulator.
3. Let α be a (keyless) collision-resistant accumulator. Use α to construct another accumulator α', which will be SPR but not collision resistant.

Exercise 3.19. Let $\mathcal{S}$ be a correct signature scheme over domain $\{0,1\}^n$, and let $h : \{0,1\}^* \to \{0,1\}^n$ be a hash function whose output is n bits long. Prove that the HtS construction $\mathcal{S}^h_{\text{HtS}}$, defined as in Equation (3.7), ensures correctness.

Exercise 3.20. Let $\mathcal{S}$ be an *existentially unforgeable signature* scheme over domain $\{0,1\}^n$, and let $h(x + y) = x \oplus y$ be a hash function whose input is $2n$ bits long, and whose output is the n-bit string resulting from the bit-wise exclusive-OR of the most-significant n input bits with the least significant n input bits. Prove that the HtS construction $\mathcal{S}^h_{\text{HtS}}$, defined as in Equation (3.7), is *not* an existentially unforgeable signature scheme.

Exercise 3.21 (Collisions for a variant of the Merkle tree). Let $\widehat{\mathcal{MT}^h}$ be a simplified Merkle tree, where the digest function always uses the same prefix $0x00$ when hashing, instead of using the $0x00$ or $0x01$ prefixes as used by $\mathcal{MT}^h$ (in Equation (3.22) and (3.23)). Namely, let

$$\widehat{\Delta}_{i,i} \equiv \widehat{\mathcal{MT}^h}.\mathsf{Accum}.\Delta(\{x_i\}) \equiv h(0x00 + x_i)$$

$$\widehat{\Delta}_{i,j}(j > i) \equiv h(0x00 + \widehat{\Delta}_{i,i+M(i,j)-1} + \widehat{\Delta}_{i+M(i,j),j})$$

Show that $\widehat{\mathcal{MT}^h}$ would have collisions even when using a hash function h which is a CRHF.

Hint: See Exercise 3.5 □

Exercise 3.22 (Signing an accumulator or a Merkle Tree). Let (KG, S, V) be an unforgeable (FIL) signature scheme and let α be a collision-resistant accumulator. Define $S_s^\alpha(X) \equiv S_s(\alpha.\Delta(X))$:

- Define the corresponding V^α algorithm and show that (KG, S^α, V^α) is an unforgeable signature scheme over sequences of strings.
- Would $(KG, S^{\mathcal{MT}^h}, V^{\mathcal{MT}^h})$ be also an unforgeable signature scheme over sequences of strings, where $\mathcal{MT}^h$ is defined in Equations (3.22) and (3.23)? Present a proof, under the random oracle model, or a counterexample.
- Would $(KG, S^{\widehat{\mathcal{MT}^h}}, V^{\widehat{\mathcal{MT}^h}})$ be also an unforgeable signature scheme over sequences of strings, where $\widehat{\mathcal{MT}^h}$ is defined as in Exercise 3.21? Present a proof or a counterexample.
- Explain how the PoI property of the accumulator can provide additional features to the signature scheme $(KG, S^{\mathcal{MT}^h}, V^{\mathcal{MT}^h})$, beyond these defined for all signature schemes.

Exercise 3.23 (Accumulator privacy). Intuitively, one of the advantages of the PoI mechanism of accumulator schemes over hashing of an encoding of the sequence of strings is that a PoI allows us to prove inclusion and integrity of one of the strings — without exposing the other strings:

1. Show why this property does *not* follow from the unforgeability and PoI properties defined in the text for accumulator schemes. Namely, let α be an accumulator that satisfies these properties; use α to define another accumulator, denoted α', that will also satisfy the same properties but will trivially expose some information about at least one of the other strings accumulated. Note: α' is designed especially to provide this counterexample; it does not have to be a sensible accumulator.

2. Present a simple yet conservative, reasonable definition of such a privacy (confidentiality) property, as a variant of the indistinguishability definition of encryption schemes.
3. Show that the Merkle tree construction does *not* satisfy the privacy property, even when using the ROM.
4. Present a small modification to the Merkle tree construction which has very similar performance properties but which also ensures the privacy property, assuming the ROM.

Exercise 3.24 (HMAC simplification). Consider the following slight simplification of the popular HMAC construction: $h'_k(m) = h(k + h(k + m))$, where $h : \{0,1\}^* \rightarrow \{0,1\}^n$ is a hash function, k is a random, public n-bit key and $m \in \{0,1\}^*$ is a message:

1. Assume h is a keyless CRHF. Is h'_k a keyed CRHF?
   ☐ Yes. Suppose h'_k is not a CRHF, i.e., there is some adversary $\mathcal{A}'$ that finds a collision (m'_1, m'_2) for h', i.e., $h'_k(m'_1) = h'_k(m'_2)$. Then, at least one of the following pairs of messages $(m_{1,1}, m_{2,1})$, $(m_{1,2}, m_{2,2})$ is a collision for h, i.e., either $h(m_{1,1}) = h(m_{2,1})$ or $h(m_{1,2}) = h(m_{2,2})$ (or both). The strings are as follows: $m_{1,1} =$________________, $m_{1,2} =$________________, $m_{2,1} =$________________, $m_{2,2} =$________________.
   ☐ No. Let $\hat{h}$ be some CRHF, and define $h(m) =$________________. Note that h is also a CRHF (you do not have to prove this, just to design h, so this would be true and easy to see). Yet, h'_k is not a CRHF. Specifically, the following two messages $m'_1 =$________________, $m'_2 =$________________ are a collision for h'_k, i.e., $h'_k(m_1) = h'_k(m_2)$.
2. Assume h is an SPR hash function. Is h'_k, for a fixed random (non-secret) key k, also a SPR?
   ☐ Yes. Suppose h'_k is not SPR, i.e., for some l, there is some algorithm $\mathcal{A}'$ which, given a (random, sufficiently long) message m', outputs a collision, i.e., $m'_1 \neq m'$ s.t. $h'_k(m') = h'_k(m'_1)$. Then, we define algorithm $\mathcal{A}$ which, given a (random, sufficiently long)

message m, outputs a collision, i.e., $m_1 \neq m$ s.t. $h_k(m) = h_k(m_1)$. The algorithm $\mathcal{A}$ is:

Algorithm $\mathcal{A}(m)$:
{
Let $m' =$______________
Let $m'_1 = \mathcal{A}'(m')$
Output ______________
}

☐ No. Let $\hat{h}$ be some SPR, and define $h(m) =$______________. Note that h is also an SPR (you do not have to prove this, just to design h so this would be true and easy to see). Yet, h'_k is not an SPR. Specifically, given a random message m', then $m'_1 =$______________ is a collision, i.e., $m' \neq m'_1$ yet $h'_k(m'_1) = h'_k(m'_2)$.

3. Assume h is a OWF. Is h'_k, for a fixed random (non-secret) key k, also a OWF?

☐ Yes. Suppose h'_k is not a OWF, i.e., for some l, there is some algorithm $\mathcal{A}'$ which, given $h'_k(m')$ for a (random, sufficiently long) message m', outputs a preimage, i.e., $m'_1 \neq m'$ s.t. $h'_k(m') = h'_k(m'_1)$. Then, we define algorithm $\mathcal{A}$ which, given $h(m)$ for a (random, sufficiently long) message m, outputs a preimage, i.e., m_1 s.t. $h_k(m) = h_k(m_1)$. The algorithm $\mathcal{A}$ is as follows:

Algorithm $\mathcal{A}(m)$:
{
Let $m' =$______________
Let $m'_1 = \mathcal{A}'(m')$
Output ______________
}

☐ No. Let $\hat{h}$ be some OWF, and define $h(m) =$______________. Note that h is also a OWF (you do not have to prove this, just to design h, so this would be true and easy to see). Yet, h'_k is not a OWF. Specifically, given a random message m', then $m'_1 =$______________ is a collision, i.e., $m' \neq m'_1$ yet $h'_k(m'_1) = h'_k(m')$.

Exercise 3.25 (HMAC is secure PRF and KDF under ROM). Show that the HMAC construction is secure under the random oracle model (ROM), when used as a PRF or a KDF.

Exercise 3.26 (HMAC using a CRHF is insecure PRF and KDF). Show counterexamples showing that even if the underlying hash function h is collision-resistant, its simplified HMAC construction $hmac_k(x) = h(k + h(k + m))$ is *insecure* when used as a PRF or a KDF.

Exercise 3.27 (Hash-tree with efficient Proof of Non-Inclusion (PoNI)). The Merkle tree allows efficient PoI of a leaf (data item) in the tree. Present a variant of this tree which allows efficient proof of either inclusion or non-inclusion of an item with given 'key' value. In this tree, each item consists of two strings, a key and data. Assume all data items are given together, sorted by their key values; no need to build the tree dynamically or extend it. Your solution may 'expose' one or two additional data items beyond the one queried. Note: Try to provide solution which is efficient in number of hash operations required for verification (the number should be about one more than in the regular Merkle tree).

Hint: You can see an example of Proof of Non-Inclusion (PoNI) and its application in the NSEC3 record of DNSSEC (RFC 5155 [321]).

Exercise 3.28 (A TCR but not ACR hash). Consider two keyed hash functions h, h', where for each of them, we know the following property:

$$h_k(k + x) = h_k(x)$$

$$h'_k(k + k) = h_k(k)$$

1. Show that *one* of the functions (h or h') is *not* an ACR hash.
2. Show that *neither* h nor h' is a TCR hash function.
3. (Harder) Assume that $\hat{h}$ is a TCR hash function. Prove that there exists a hash function h or h' which (1) has the corresponding property above, (2) is an ACR hash and (3) is not an TCR hash.

Exercise 3.29 (Universal collision resistance). 1. Define a new type of keyed CRHF, a *universal-collision-resistant* hash, whose property is that it should be infeasible for an efficient attacker to find a pair of preimages $x \neq x'$ which collide, with non-negligible probability, for a randomly chosen key k.

2. (hard) Prove that there is no universal-collision-resistant hash function.

Exercise 3.30 (Finding collisions inefficiently). Our definitions of collision-resistance (for both keyless and keyed hash) are limited to *efficient attackers*, and require the attacker to find collisions with *non-negligible probability*. In this exercise, we show that these restrictions are necessary:

1. Show that for every keyless hash function h, there is an efficient attacker that finds collisions for h with probability greater than zero.
2. Repeat for target-collision resistance. Namely, show that for any keyed hash h and length n of key and digest, an efficient attacker can find a target preimage x_T such that when given a random n-bits key k, the attacker can find, with probability greater than zero, a collision $x_C \neq x_T$ s.t. $h_k(x_C) = h_k(x_T)$.
3. (Harder) Repeat for any-collision resistance. Namely, show that for any keyed hash h, given a random key k, an efficient attacker can find a target preimage x_T such that when given a random n-bits key k, the attacker can find, with probability greater than zero, a collision $x \neq x'$ s.t. $h_k(x) = h_k(x')$.
4. Repeat the above items for non-negligible success probability (instead of non-zero probability), when the attacker computation time is $O(2^n)$ (where a hash computation is counted as a single operation).

Chapter 4

Symmetric-Key Message Authentication

Authentication is one of the main goals of cybersecurity and cryptography. There are two broad authentication goals: *entity authentication* and *message authentication.* Alice may use *entity authentication* to validate that she communicate with Bob and *message authentication* to validate that a specific message was sent or approved by Bob.

We discuss entity authentication in Chapters 5, 7 and 9. In Chapter 5, we discuss entity authentication protocols using symmetric-key cryptography; in Chapter 7, we discuss the TLS protocol, which uses public keys to provide entity authentication of servers (and optionally clients); and in Chapter 9, we discuss ceremonies for authentication of human users.

In this chapter, we focus on *message authentication* and mostly on *symmetric (shared key)* authentication schemes, called *message authentication code (MAC)* schemes. MAC schemes are among the most efficient cryptographic schemes. In particular, MAC schemes are significantly more efficient than comparably secure signature schemes, which use public keys to ensure message authentication but also ensure non-repudiation; we briefly introduced signature schemes in Section 1.5.1.

Contents of this chapter: We begin, in Section 4.1, by showing that message authentication cannot be achieved as a side product of encryption. Section 4.2 introduces the concept of *message authentication code (MAC) schemes*. Section 4.3 defines MAC schemes and discusses their correct (and incorrect) use. In Section 4.4, we discuss the construction of MAC schemes from other (cryptographic) schemes — pseudorandom functions, block ciphers and cryptographic hash functions. Finally, in Section 4.5, we discuss how to combine authentication with encryption and other functions, and schemes which provide such secure combinations, most notably, *Authenticated Encryption (AE)* schemes and *Authenticated Encryption with Associated Data (AEAD)* schemes.

4.1 Encryption for authentication?

Encryption schemes ensure *confidentiality*, i.e., an attacker observing an encrypted message (ciphertext) cannot learn anything about the plaintext (except its length). Sometimes, people expect encryption to also ensure *authentication*. In this section, we show that this can lead to vulnerabilities.

Note that some encryption schemes do have some integrity/authentication properties. For example, *non-malleable encryption* schemes, intuitively, prevents the attacker from *modifying* the decrypted plaintext message in a 'meaningful way'; see definition and secure constructions of non-malleable encryption schemes in Refs. [53, 157].

However, many cryptosystems are *malleable*; often, an attacker can easily modify the encryption of a message m using a secret key k, i.e., the ciphertext $c = E_k(m)$, to another ciphertext $c' \neq c$ s.t. the decryption of c' returns a message $m' \neq m$ (without an error indication).

Furthermore, often the attacker can ensure useful relations between m' and m. An obvious example is when using the (unconditionally secure) one-time pad (OTP), as well as using output feedback (OFB) mode of operation of a block cipher. For a more extensive example, see the following exercise.

Exercise 4.1. *Mal is a man-in-the-middle, able to intercept and modify ciphertext messages from Alice to her bank, encrypted using a key shared between Alice and the bank. In this question, we explore the ability of Mal to modify an encrypted payment order which Alice* *sends to her bank, instructing the bank to pay $10 to Bob. Mal's goal is to change the ciphertext so that the bank will transfer the largest possible amount from Alice to Mal; assume that Alice's account is not limited, allowing Mal to go for the highest amount and that Mal knows the contents of the original payment order.*

Alice's message is composed of the following fields, in the given order; first, the following four bytes fields: operation, account type, date, amount *and* payee's account, *and then an eight bytes* comment *field. When* operation= 1 *and* account type= 1, *and if the date is correct, then the bank transfers* amount, *specified as a dollar amount in binary, from the payer's account to the payee's account. The comment field can contain an arbitrary string; it is only logged by the bank and used for the payer's purposes. Assume account identifiers* 1 *for Alice,* 2 *for Bob and* 3 *for Mal:*

1. *Suppose the parties use one-time pad (OTP) encryption, and Mal intercept the ciphertext c sent from Alice to her bank, which is the encryption of a request to transfer $* 10 *to Bob. Explain how Mal can modify the ciphertext, causing the bank to transfer, instead, a much larger amount from Alice to Mal. Assume Mal knows all the details (amount, payee, etc.).*
2. *How would your response change when using, instead of OTP, the following modes of operation of DES, with a block size of* 64 *bits (*8 *bytes): (a) OFB, (b) CFB, (c) CBC, (d) CTR, (e) ECB and (f) PBR. Note: You may not be able to find a successful attack for some of the modes — but don't give up too easily!*

We conclude that encryption schemes may not suffice to ensure authentication. This motivates us to introduce, in the following section, another symmetric-key cryptographic scheme, which is designed explicitly to ensure authentication and integrity: the *MAC scheme.* Later, in Section 4.5, we also discuss how to achieve confidentiality together with authenticity.

4.2 Introducing message authentication code (MAC) schemes

Message authentication code (MAC) schemes are symmetric key cryptographic functions, designed to verify the authenticity and integrity of information (messages), namely, to detect that a message was not sent by the designated sender (or one of a group of designated senders), as well as to detect if a message was modified after it was sent. A MAC function $\text{MAC}_k(m)$ has two inputs: a (secret) n-bit *secret (symmetric) key* k and a message m.

As illustrated in Figure 4.1, MAC schemes consist of the single keyed function $\text{MAC}_k(m)$ and use the same function and the same key k to *generate* the *authenticator (tag)*, typically attaching it to the message m when sending it, and to *validate* the authenticator (tag), typically, upon receiving m and the authenticator. Upon receiving a message m with a purported authenticator σ, the recipient computes $\sigma' \leftarrow \text{MAC}_k(m)$ and verifies m by confirming that $\sigma = \sigma'$. Note that this assumes that MAC schemes, and authenticators, are *deterministic*.

Intuitively, given $m, \text{MAC}_k(m)$ for a secret, random key k, it should be infeasible for a (computationally bounded) attacker, who

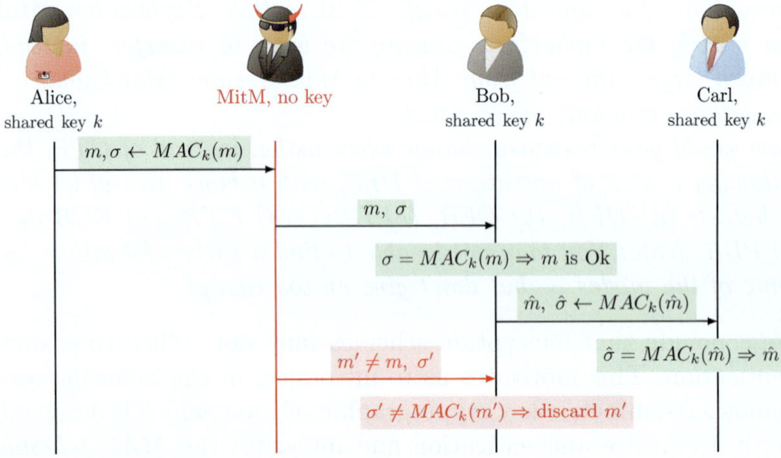

Figure 4.1. Using a MAC scheme, and a shared key k, to authenticate messages. The man-in-the-middle (MitM) adversary can observe message m and its authenticator $\sigma = \text{MAC}_k(m)$ but cannot *forge* the MAC, i.e., generate a pair m', σ' such that $\sigma' = \text{MAC}_k(m')$, for $m' \neq m$. Note, however, that if a key k is shared among more than two entities, e.g., Alice, Bob and Carl, then each entity can authenticate messages using k; e.g., when Carl receives $\hat{m}$, he cannot know if $\hat{m}$ was sent by Alice or Bob (or even by Carl himself), except by using some indication within m, e.g., if m includes sender identification. Due to this property, we say that MAC schemes allow *repudiation*; for *non-repudiation*, use a signature scheme instead of a MAC scheme.

is not given k, to find another message $m' \neq m$ together with the value of $\text{MAC}_k(m')$.

In a typical use, the key k is shared only between two parties, say Alice and Bob. One party, say Alice, sends a message m to Bob, authenticating m by computing and attaching the tag $T = \text{MAC}_k(m)$. Bob confirms that $T = \text{MAC}_k(m)$, thereby validating that Alice sent the message since he shares k only with Alice, and he knows that he didn't compute earlier $\text{MAC}_k(m)$. The parties may combine the message with a timestamp or a counter to prevent replay attacks or reordering attacks, i.e., an attacker re-sending the same messages from Alice multiple times or delivering messages in a different order from the one in which they were sent. The parties may also combine the message with an identifier, to prevent redirection attacks, i.e., an attacker sending to a party, say Alice, a message which Alice sent to another party, e.g., Bob. Such shared-key protocols, authenticating the communication between parties, are discussed in Chapter 5.

As shown in Figure 4.1, the same secret, symmetric MAC key k could also be shared between *multiple* trusted parties, e.g., Alice, Bob and Carl. Each party can use the key to authenticate a message m, by computing an *authentication tag* $\sigma \leftarrow \text{MAC}_k(m)$. Given a message m together with a previously computed tag σ, a party verifies the authenticity of the message m by re-computing $\text{MAC}_k(m)$ and comparing the result to the tag σ; if equal, the message is valid, i.e., the tag must have been previously computed using the same secret key k, i.e., by one of the parties sharing the key. As explained above, messages may be combined with a counter or timestamp, as well as with an identifier, to prevent replay, redirection and reordering attacks.

MAC schemes vs. signature schemes — non-repudiation, deniability, efficiency and key-distribution: We introduced signature schemes in Section 1.5.1, and, like MAC schemes, they are used to authenticate messages. However, there is a critical difference: a valid MAC can be computed by *any* entity that knows the shared key. Consider the scenario in Figure 4.1; even after Carl successfully validates $\hat{m}$ using $\hat{\sigma}$, he cannot know if $\hat{m}$ was sent by Alice or Bob. Of course, the sender identity may be indicated as part of the message m; however, there is nothing preventing an entity knowing the shared key k, e.g., Bob, from putting a different identity in the message and computing the MAC. This is in contrast to signature schemes, where the private signing key $A.s$ must be used to produce a valid signature σ for a given message m, namely, knowing the public validation key $A.v$ does not allow forgery of a message as if it was signed using $A.s$. This property of signature schemes is what facilitates their use for *non-repudiation*, as it prevents the sender of a (signed) message from repudiating (denying) having sent it.

In some situations, e.g., for a whistle-blower, we may have the opposite goal, i.e., of *preventing* the recipient from proving the identity of the sender to a third person; this goal is usually referred to as *deniability*.

MAC schemes are also much more efficient than signature schemes; on the other hand, authentication using MAC scheme requires a shared secret key, while authentication of a signed message only requires the use of the correct public validation key.

In summary, we should use a signature scheme when we need to ensure non-repudiation, i.e., to ensure that after validating a message with the key associated with Alice, we should know that Alice, or somebody knowing Alice's private signing key, has signed the message and that any party knowing Alice's public validation key can validate that Alice signed the message. We would also use a signature scheme when we need to validate the message using only Alice's public validation key and do not share a secret key with Alice. In other scenarios, when we need to validate a message authenticated by Alice but do not require non-repudiation, and when we share a secret key with Alice, it would be better to use a MAC scheme rather than a signature scheme. If Alice needs the ability to *deny* having signed the message, but we still need the ability to validate the authenticity of the message, then we *should* use a MAC rather than a signature scheme.

Note that we usually use the terms *authenticator* or *tag* to refer to the output $\text{MAC}_k(m)$ of the MAC function, i.e., if $\sigma = \text{MAC}_k(m)$, then σ is the *authenticator* of m using shared key k. There are many publications which refer to the authenticator/tag by the term *signature*; we think that the term 'signature' may cause confusion between MAC schemes and signature schemes, and therefore, we prefer *authenticator* or *tag*.

4.3 Defining and Applying MAC schemes

We define a MAC scheme as a function $f_k^{MAC}(m)$, whose inputs are an n-bit key $k \in \{0,1\}^n$ and a message m from domain D, and whose output is a string of some fixed length, which we denote l. Namely, $f_k^{MAC}(m) \in \{0,1\}^l$. Often, D is the set of all binary messages $D = \{0,1\}^*$.

MAC schemes should ensure an *unforgeability* property, which is quite similar to that of signature schemes. Specifically, an attacker, who is not given the key k of the computed value of $f_k^{MAC}(m)$ for some specific message m, is unable to find the value of $f_k^{MAC}(m)$, with better chance than a random guess. We allow the attacker to receive the MAC values of other messages, i.e., the attacker is given an oracle that computes $f_k^{MAC}(\cdot)$, and can use it to compute the MAC of any message except m.

Definition 4.1 (MAC). *For any given integer l and domain D, a function $f^{MAC} : \{0,1\}^* \times D \rightarrow \{0,1\}^l$ is called a* (secure) MAC *if for all efficient algorithms $\mathcal{A}$, the* advantage function $\varepsilon^{MAC}_{f^{MAC},\mathcal{A}}(n)$ *is* negligible *in n ($\varepsilon^{MAC}_{f^{MAC},\mathcal{A}}(n) \in$ NEGL(n)), i.e., smaller than any positive polynomial for sufficiently large n (as $n \rightarrow \infty$), where:*

$$\varepsilon^{MAC}_{f^{MAC},\mathcal{A}}(n) \equiv \Pr_{k \xleftarrow{\$} \{0,1\}^n}\left[(m, f_k^{MAC}(m)) \leftarrow \mathcal{A}^{f_k^{MAC}(\cdot|\text{except } m)}(1^n)\right] - \frac{1}{2^l} \tag{4.1}$$

The probability is taken over the uniformly random choice of an n bit key, $k \xleftarrow{\$} \{0,1\}^n$, as well as over the coin tosses of $\mathcal{A}$.

The definition has a lot in common with the definition of existential unforgeability of signature schemes (Section 1.5.1). One obvious difference is that the adversary does *not* receive the public signature verification key v. A more subtle change is that the advantage is computed relative to 2^{-l}, where l is the size of the output of the MAC. Signature schemes usually have sufficiently long outputs so that the probability of the attacker to win is negligible; many MAC schemes, for efficiency, have rather short l-bits output, therefore the advantage is computed with respect to a random guess of an l-bits, i.e., 2^{-l}.

Note that the definition does not require the 'forged' message to be 'meaningful'; this means that it isn't always trivial to *exploit* a vulnerable MAC. Following the 'conservative design' principle (Principle 3), the definition does not attempt to predict which forgeries will be meaningful, instead forbidding *any* forgery.

Oracle notation: The definition uses the oracle notation $\mathcal{A}^{f_k^{MAC}(\cdot|\text{except } m)}$ (Definition 1.3) to imply that the adversary can give arbitrary inputs $m' \neq m$ and receive the corresponding value $f_k^{MAC}(m')$. Note the exclusion of the message m, i.e., the adversary cannot receive directly $f_k^{MAC}(m)$ since this would have made the attack trivial (and prevented any secure MAC). We say that the adversary $\mathcal{A}$ has an *oracle* to the MAC function $f_k^{MAC}(\cdot)$ (excluding the message m).

The advantage function $\varepsilon^{MAC}_{f^{MAC},\mathcal{A}}(n)$ and key length n: The definition is for l-bit MAC, i.e., the output is always a binary string of length l. Hence, a random guess at the MAC of any input message m would be correct with probability 2^{-l}. Therefore, we defined the *advantage function* $\varepsilon^{MAC}_{f^{MAC},\mathcal{A}}(n)$ as the probability that the adversary finds a correct MAC value for a message m (not input to the oracle), *minus* the 'base success probability' of 2^{-l}. The function f^{MAC} is a (secure) MAC, if this advantage $\varepsilon^{MAC}_{f^{MAC},\mathcal{A}}(n)$ is negligible.

The key length is denoted n and, in the definition, should not be bounded. The reason that the key cannot be bounded is that the advantage of the adversary over random guess should be *negligible* in n, i.e., converge to zero as n grows, faster than any (strictly positive) polynomial in n. In practice, MAC functions are used with a specific key length, which is believed to be 'long enough' to foil attacks (by attackers with reasonable resources and time).

Input domain: Note that the definition allows an arbitrary input domain D to the MAC function. The two most commonly used domains are $D = \{0,1\}^*$, i.e., the set of all binary string (of unbounded length), and $D = \{0,1\}^{l_{in}}$, i.e., the set of all binary strings of some fixed length l_{in}. Of course, l_{in} may also be the same as l. A MAC function whose input is the set of binary strings of fixed length is called *FIL-MAC*, i.e., *Fixed Input Length MAC*. In contrast, a MAC function whose input is the set of all binary strings is called *VIL-MAC*, i.e., *Variable Input Length MAC.*

Examples of insecure MAC functions: To 'warm up', let us show two examples of *insecure* MAC design. Our examples follow the definition, i.e., the attacker is allowed to ask for the MAC for some messages and then has to come up with a *different* message and a correct MAC for that message.

Our first example is a very simple FIL-MAC construction which we denote $f^{\oplus E}$; the construction is defined for a given n-bit block cipher E. The $f^{\oplus E}$ construction is defined for inputs which are exactly *two blocks*, i.e., contain $2n$ bits. Its output is a single block, which is the result of XORing the 'encryption' of each block. Namely, for given key k,

$$f_k^{\oplus E}(m) \equiv E_k(m[0:n-1]) \oplus E_k(m[n:2n-1])$$

where $m[i:j]$ is the subsequence of m from bit i to bit j, i.e., $m = m[0:2n-1]$.

Exercise 4.2. *Show that $f^{\oplus E}$ is not a secure MAC.*

Solution: Observe that:

$$\begin{aligned} f_k^{\oplus E}(m) &= E_k(m[0:n-1]) \oplus E_k(m[n:2n-1]) \\ &= E_k(m[n:2n-1]) \oplus E_k(m[0:n-1]) \\ &= f_k^{\oplus E}\left(m[n:2n-1] + m[0:n-1]\right) \end{aligned}$$

Therefore, for every $2n$-bits input message m, we have $f_k^{\oplus E}(m) = f_k^{\oplus E}(\bar{m})$, where $\bar{m}$ is simply the message with the two blocks switched, $\bar{m} \equiv m[n:2n-1] + m[0:n-1]$.

Intuitively, this shows that $f^{\oplus E}$ is not a secure MAC. However, let us present a complete proof, i.e., present an efficient adversary $\mathcal{A}$ that 'breaks' $f^{\oplus E}$, i.e., $\varepsilon^{MAC}_{f^{\oplus E},\mathcal{A}}(n)$ is not negligible — in fact, it is $1-2^{-l}$.

First, $\mathcal{A}$ asks for the MAC of $m_{01} = 0^n + 1^n$ (a block of zeros followed by a block of 1's); we could have used any $2n-$bit message where the first n bits differ from the last n bits, but m_{01} is especially convenient.

As per the definition, $\mathcal{A}$ receives the MAC of m_{01}, i.e., $f_k^{\oplus E}(m_{01}) = E_k(0^n) \oplus E_k(1^n)$. Then, $\mathcal{A}$ returns the pair $\left(m_{10}, f_k^{\oplus E}(m_{01})\right)$, where $m_{10} = 1^n \mathbin{+\!\!+} 0^n$. This is a successful forgery since

$$f_k^{\oplus E}(m_{10}) = E_k(1^n) \oplus E_k(0^n) = E_k(0^n) \oplus E_k(1^n) = f_k^{\oplus E}(m_{01})$$

From Equation (4.1), $\varepsilon^{MAC}_{f^{\oplus E},\mathcal{A}}(n) = 1 - 2^{-l}$. □

Our second example is of a 'hairy' modular-polynomial function $f_k^{(p)}$, defined 'from scratch', i.e., *not* using an underlying block cipher. Such 'hairy' designs may appear to be good candidates for MAC — but all too often, they are vulnerable. Showing the vulnerability can be tricky, which motivates (1) the use of a strong definition and (2) the use of standard, secure constructions from basic building blocks, following the 'building blocks principle' (Principle 8). Specifically, given an integer p, define:

$$f_k^{(p)}(m) \equiv \left(k^3 \cdot m + k^2 \cdot m^2 + k \cdot m^3\right) \bmod p$$

Exercise 4.3. *Prove that $f_k^{(p)}$ is not a (secure) MAC scheme.*

Solution: The crux of the solution is simple. From the basic properties of modular arithmetic (Section A.2) follows that $f_k^{(p)}(m) = f_k^{(p)}(m + i \cdot p)$, for any integer i. In particular, $f_k^{(p)}(m) = f_k^{(p)}(m + p)$. (If this isn't clear, try to substitute some small integers for m, k and p, and/or read Section A.2).

Let us complete the details of the solution, by presenting an adversary $\mathcal{A}$ s.t. $\varepsilon^{MAC}_{f^{(p)},\mathcal{A}}(n)$ is non-negligible; in fact, we'll show that $\varepsilon^{MAC}_{f^{(p)},\mathcal{A}}(n) = 1 - 2^{-l}$, for every n. Note that although we show an advantage of (almost) 1, it suffices to show any non-negligible advantage.

The adversary $\mathcal{A}$ is the following simple algorithm:

1. Let m' be some arbitrary value, e.g., p, or 1, or 0, or whatever you like.
2. Let $x \leftarrow f_k^{(p)}(m')$, i.e., call the oracle on m'.
3. Let $m = m' + p$.
4. Output (m, x).

Let us explain why $\varepsilon^{MAC}_{f^{(p)},\mathcal{A}}(n) = 1 - 2^{-l}$. Given oracle access to $f^{(p)}_k(\cdot)$ (for some random k), the adversary gave some input m' and received $x \equiv f^{(p)}_k(m')$, i.e., in our case, $x = \left(k^3 \cdot m' + k^2 \cdot m'^2 + k \cdot m'^3\right) \bmod p$. Then, the adversary outputs (m, x), where $m = m' + p$. Obviously, $m \neq m'$, so the condition of the use of the oracle is satisfied; on the other hand, $x = f^{(p)}_k(m') = f^{(p)}_k(m + p) = f^{(p)}_k(m)$. Therefore, the expression is true for any k and we have: $\Pr_{k \xleftarrow{\$} \{0,1\}^n}[(m, f^{(p)}_k(m)) \leftarrow \mathcal{A}^{f^{(p)}_k(\cdot|\text{except } m)}(1^n)] = 1$, proving that $\varepsilon^{MAC}_{f^{(p)},\mathcal{A}}(n) = 1 - 2^{-l}$. □

4.3.1 Pitfalls in the application of MAC schemes

A MAC function is a simple cryptographic mechanism, which is quite easy to use; however, it should be applied correctly — with an understanding of its properties and without expecting it to provide other properties. We now discuss a few aspects of the usage of MAC schemes and give a few examples of common mistakes.

Confidentiality: A MAC function is a great tool to ensure integrity and authenticity; however, MAC *may not ensure confidentiality.* Namely, $\text{MAC}_k(m)$ may expose information about the message m. This is sometimes overlooked by system designers; for example, early versions of the *Secure Shell* SSH *protocol* used the *Authenticate-and-Encrypt* method, where to protect message m, the system sent $E_k(m) + \text{MAC}_k(m)$. One problem with this design is that $\text{MAC}_k(m)$ *may expose information about* m.

While obviously confidentiality is not a goal of MAC schemes, one may hope that $\text{MAC}_k(m)$ will not expose information about m. This can be true for some specific MAC schemes, but there can be secure MAC schemes for which this is not true. To see this, we construct a counterexample — a useful technique to prove that claims about cryptographic schemes are incorrect. The counter-examples to wrong claims about cryptographic schemes are often very simple — and often involve 'stupid' or 'strange' designs, which are specially designed to meet the requirements of the cryptographic definitions — while demonstrating the falseness of the false assumptions. Here is an example showing that (secure) MAC schemes may expose information about the input message.

Exercise 4.4 (MAC schemes do not ensure confidentiality). *Let f^{MAC} be an arbitrary secure MAC scheme (which may or may not ensure confidentiality). Use f^{MAC} to construct another MAC function, f^{ncM} (where ncM stands for 'non-confidential MAC'), and prove that f^{ncM} is a secure MAC but exposes information about its input.*

Solution: Define the non-confidential MAC function f^{ncM} as follows:

$$f_k^{ncM}(m) \equiv f_k^{MAC}(m) + LSb(m)$$

where $LSb(m)$ is the least-significant bit of m. Surely, f^{ncM} does not ensure confidentiality, since it exposes a bit of the message. Note that we could have obviously exposed more bits — even all bits.

On the other hand, we now show that f^{ncM} is a secure MAC. Assume, to the contrary, that there is some adversary $\mathcal{A}^{ncM}$ that succeeds (with significant probability) against f^{ncM}. We use $\mathcal{A}^{ncM}$ to construct an attacker $\mathcal{A}$ that succeeds with the same probability against f^{MAC}. Attacker $\mathcal{A}$ works as follows:

1. When $\mathcal{A}^{ncM}$ makes a query q to f^{ncM}, then $\mathcal{A}$ makes the same query to f^{MAC}, receiving $f_k^{MAC}(q)$; it then returns $f_k^{ncM}(q) = f_k^{MAC}(q) + LSb(q)$, as expected by $\mathcal{A}^{ncM}$.
2. When $\mathcal{A}^{ncM}$ outputs its guess m, T, where T is its guess x for $f_k^{ncM}(m) = f_k^{MAC}(m) + LSb(m)$ and m was not used in any of $\mathcal{A}^{ncM}$'s queries, then $\mathcal{A}$ outputs x except for its least-significant bit; namely, if $x = f_k^{ncM}(m) = f_k^{MAC}(m) + LSb(m)$, then $\mathcal{A}$ outputs $f_k^{ncM}(m) = f_k^{MAC}(m)$.

It follows that f^{ncM} is a secure MAC if and only if f^{MAC} is a secure MAC. □

We show, later on (Section 4.4.2), that every PRF is a MAC. The following exercise shows that the reverse is not true: a MAC is not necessarily a PRF. This exercise is similar to the example above.

Exercise 4.5 (Non-PRF MAC). *Show that a MAC function is not necessarily a pseudorandom function* (PRF).

Solution: Let f^{MAC} be an arbitrary secure MAC scheme that outputs n-bit tags. Construct a MAC scheme f', which outputs $2n$-bit tags, as follows:

$$f'_k(m) = f_k^{MAC}(m) + 0^n$$

Clearly, f' is not a PRF because $\mathcal{A}$ has a significant chance of distinguishing between an output of f' and a random $2n$-bit string (since the second half of the output of f' is all zeros). Yet, you can show that f' is a secure MAC if and only if f^{MAC} is a secure MAC, using a similar method to the one in Example 4.4. Therefore, a MAC function is not necessarily a PRF. □

Key separation: Another problem with the SSH Authenticate-and-Encrypt design, $E_k(m) + \text{MAC}_k(m)$, is the fact that it uses the same key for both encryption and authentication (MAC), violating the key separation principle (Principle 7). As we show in the following exercise, this results in a vulnerability; this vulnerability would hold even if using MAC and symmetric key cryptosystem for which the authenticate-and-encrypt design is secure if only using a separate key for each of the two functions.

Exercise 4.6 (Separate keys for separate functions). *Show that the use of the same key for encryption and MAC in $E_k(m) + f_k^{MAC}(m)$ can allow an attacker to succeed in forgery of messages — in addition to the potential loss of confidentiality shown above — even when E and f^{MAC} are secure (encryption and MAC, respectively).*

Solution: Let E', f' be secure encryption and MAC functions, respectively. Define $E_{k_E,k_M}(m) = E'_{k_E}(m) + k_M$ and $f^{MAC}_{k_E,k_M}(m) = k_E + f'_{k_M}(m)$. Obviously, the use of $E_{k_E,k_M}(m) + f^{MAC}_{k_E,k_M}(m)$ exposes both keys and is therefore insecure. However, using the method of Example 4.4, we can show that E and f^{MAC} are also secure encryption and MAC functions, respectively. See also Exercise 4.21. □

Another motivation to separate between the keys used by a given cryptographic function/scheme is to reduce the quantity of plaintexts and ciphertexts available to the cryptanalyst, especially the amount of known and chosen plaintexts.

4.4 Constructing MAC schemes

In this section, we discuss constructions of a MAC function.

We begin, in Section 4.4.1, by discussing how *not* to build a MAC, with some examples of failed efforts to build a MAC directly from non-cryptographic functions, such as error detection codes.

We then observe, in Section 4.4.2, that *every PRF is also a MAC*, i.e., given a PRF, we can use it directly as a MAC scheme. There is a caveat: the input domain of the MAC is the same as that of the PRF; additional steps are required to build a MAC allowing variable input length (as typically required), from a PRF supporting only fixed input length (as is often available in cryptographic libraries, e.g., using a block cipher).

In Section 4.4.3, we present the CBC-MAC construction, which constructs a $l \cdot n$-bit PRF from an n-bit PRF, for a given constant number of blocks l. This allows efficient and secure use of n-bit-input PRF (or block cipher), to encrypt a longer fixed-length message, containing $l \cdot n$ bits.

In Section 4.4.4, we show how to extend these constructions to result in a MAC whose input can be messages of *arbitrary length*.

Finally, in Section 4.4.5, we discuss constructions of a MAC from a cryptographic hash function, most notably, the HMAC construction.

4.4.1 How *not* to construct a MAC (from an EDC)

One can try to design a candidate MAC function from non-cryptographic functions, i.e., without a reduction to the security of some cryptographic scheme; such constructions of candidate cryptographic schemes from non-cryptographic schemes are said to be *from scratch*. The security of such constructions would be based on the failure of significant cryptanalysis efforts against the scheme, in our case, the MAC function.

Building 'from scratch' used to be the main method of design of new cryptographic mechanisms. However, following the cryptographic building block principle (Principle 8), the 'building from scratch' approach is now rarely used. In particular, MAC functions are rarely designed 'from scratch' since there are simple and efficient constructions from either block ciphers or cryptographic hash functions, as we discuss in the following sections.

However, let us give two examples of a (failed) attempt to construct MAC 'from scratch' since this can help understand the challenges, and provide examples of how to show that a certain construction is insecure. Both constructions use a (non-cryptographic) *error detection code* (EDC).

Error detection codes are designed to ensure *integrity*, i.e., to detect corruptions in data; however, they are designed only against *unintentional (random) errors*, and may fail to detect *intentional modifications*. We have seen already, in Section 2.12, that the *WEP* protocol failed to ensure integrity against attack, in spite of its use of the CRC-32 *Cyclic Redundancy Check* (*CRC*) EDC before encryption. Let us consider two other simple constructions of a MAC from an EDC, which do not involve encryption, and show that they, too, are not secure MAC schemes, when using the CRC code as the error detection code (EDC). The two constructions are $f'_k(m) = \text{EDC}(k + m)$ and $f''_k(m) = \text{EDC}(m + k)$.

Exercise 4.7 (Insecure CRC-based MACs). *Show that both of the following are insecure:*
(a) $f'_k(m) = \text{CRC}(k + m)$ *and (b)* $f''_k(m) = \text{CRC}(m + k)$.

Solution: We only solve (a) and leave (b) as an (easy) exercise to the reader. In fact, we show how an attacker that receives only the MAC $f'_k(m) = \text{CRC}(k + m)$ of any known message m can compute the MAC for any other message $m' \neq m$ of the same length, i.e., compute $f'_k(m') = \text{CRC}(k + m')$.

Recall that the CRC function is linear, namely, for any two strings of the same length, $|x| = |x'$, holds: $\text{CRC}(x \oplus x') = \text{CRC}(x) \oplus \text{CRC}(x')$ (Equation (2.59)). Hence,

$$\begin{aligned} f'_k(m') &= \text{CRC}(k + m') \\ &= \text{CRC}\left((0^{|k|} + m' \oplus m) \oplus (k + m)\right) \\ &= \text{CRC}(0^{|k|} + m' \oplus m) \oplus \text{CRC}(k + m) \\ &= f'_{0^{|k|}}(m' \oplus m) \oplus f'_k(m) \end{aligned} \tag{4.2}$$

The adversary computes $|k| = |f'_k(m')| - |\text{CRC}(m')|$, and can therefore compute $f'_{0^{|k|}}(m' \oplus m)$. By plugging this into Equation (4.2), the adversary find $f'_k(m')$. □

We conclude that f' is indeed insecure. The same seems to hold for other EDC-based constructions of a MAC function.

4.4.2 Every PRF is a MAC

In this section, we take the first step toward the CBC-MAC construction. This step is the observation that *every PRF whose range is* $\{0,1\}^l$ *is also an l-bit MAC*, with the same input and output domains. This is formalized in the following lemma.

Lemma 4.1 (A PRF is a MAC). *Let f be a* PRF *from input domain D to the range $\{0,1\}^l$. Then, f is also an l-bit MAC, with input domain D and output domain $\{0,1\}^l$.*

Proof. Assume that f is not a MAC (for same domain D and range $\{0,1\}^l$). Namely, assume that there exists some adversary $\mathcal{A}_{MAC}$ s.t. $\varepsilon^{MAC}_{\mathcal{A}_{MAC},f}(n)$ is non-negligible in n (as defined in Equation (4.1)). We use $\mathcal{A}_{MAC}$ to construct another adversary, $\mathcal{A}_{PRF}$, s.t. $\varepsilon^{PRF}_{\mathcal{A}_{PRF},f}(n)$ is non-negligible in n (as defined in Equation (2.20)); this shows that f is (also) not a PRF, which proves the claim.

Let us now define $\mathcal{A}_{PRF}$. First, recall that in Equation (2.20), adversary A_{PRF} is given an oracle *either* to a random function $f \overset{\$}{\leftarrow} \{D \to \{0,1\}^l\}$ *or* to the pseudorandom function $f_k : D \to \{0,1\}^l$ for some random n-bit key $k \overset{\$}{\leftarrow} \{0,1\}^n$. Adversary $\mathcal{A}_{PRF}$ runs $\mathcal{A}_{MAC}$, letting it use the same oracle. Namely, whenever $\mathcal{A}_{MAC}$ asks its oracle with input $x \in D$, adversary $\mathcal{A}_{PRF}$ calls its oracle with the same input x; and when it receives a result ξ, it returns that result to $\mathcal{A}_{MAC}$.

When $\mathcal{A}_{MAC}$ terminates, it should return some pair, which we denote by (m, σ). Upon receiving (m, σ), adversary $\mathcal{A}_{PRF}$ provides m as input to its oracle; denote the output by σ'. If $\sigma \neq \sigma'$, then $\mathcal{A}_{PRF}$ returns 'Rand'; otherwise, i.e., if $\sigma = \sigma'$, then $\mathcal{A}_{PRF}$ returns 'Pseudo'. Essentially, $\mathcal{A}_{PRF}$ outputs 'Rand' (i.e., guess it was given a random function), when A_{MAC} *fails* to predict correctly the output of the oracle for the input m.

Let us consider what happens if $\mathcal{A}_{PRF}$ is given an oracle to a random function $f \overset{\$}{\leftarrow} \{D \to R\}$. In this case, when running $\mathcal{A}_{MAC}$, the values returned from the oracle were for that random function f;

clearly, $\mathcal{A}_{MAC}$ cannot be expected to perform as well as when given an oracle to the function $f_k(\cdot)$. In fact, $\mathcal{A}_{MAC}$ has to return a pair (m, σ), *without* giving input m to the oracle. But if the oracle is to a random function f, then $f(m)$ is chosen independently of $f(x)$ for any other input $x \neq m$; learning other outputs cannot help you guess the output when the input is m! Hence, the probability of a match is (only) 2^{-l} — the probability of a random match between two random l bit strings. Namely, $\Pr_{f \xleftarrow{\$} \{D \rightarrow R\}} \left[\mathcal{A}^f(1^n) = \text{'Rand'}\right] = 2^{-l}$.

Now, consider what happens if $\mathcal{A}_{PRF}$ is given an oracle to a pseudorandom function $f_k(\cdot)$. The claim is that f is also a MAC, but we assumed, to the contrary, that it is *not*, so A_{MAC} *is* able to return a pair $(m, f_k(m))$ — with probability *significantly larger* than 2^{-l}. In these cases, $\mathcal{A}_{PRF}$ will return 'PR'. Namely, $\Pr_{k \xleftarrow{\$} \{0,1\}^n} \left[\mathcal{A}^{f_k}(1^n) = \text{'Rand'}\right] = 2^{-l} + p(n)$, where $p(n)$ is a *significant* (not negligible) function.

It follows that $\varepsilon^{PRF}_{\mathcal{A},f}(n)$ is not negligible, and hence, f is *not* a PRF. □

4.4.3 CBC-MAC: Extending a PRF into a MAC for longer fixed-length inputs

Lemma 4.1 shows that every n-bit PRF is also an n-bit MAC. But how can we deal with longer messages? In this section, we present the *CBC-MAC* construction, which produces an $l \cdot n$-bit PRF, using a given n-bit PRF. Since every PRF is a MAC, this gives also an $l \cdot n$-bit MAC. The CBC-MAC construction is a standard from 1989 [263], i.e., prior to the publication of Lemma 4.1 in Ref. [43]; this is probably the reason that it is usually presented as a construction of a MAC from a block cipher, rather than as a construction of an $l \cdot n$-bit PRF from an n-bit PRF.

Before we present the CBC-MAC construction, let us discuss two *insecure* constructions. First, consider performing MAC to each block independently, similar to the ECB-mode (Section 2.10). One drawback is that this would result in a long MAC. An even worse drawback is that this is *insecure*; an attacker may obtain a MAC for a different message, which contains re-ordered and/or duplicated blocks. The reader may want to write down the details of this simple counterexample.

Next, consider adding a counter to the input, to which we refer as *CTR-MAC*. This prevents the trivial attack — but not a variant. This variant is not very hard to find, so we leave it as the following exercise. For simplicity, the exercise is given for $l = 2n$.

Exercise 4.8 (CTR-MAC is insecure). *Let E be a secure $(n+1)-$bit block cipher and define the following $2n-$bit domain function: $f_k(m_0 + m_1) = E_k(0 + m_0) + E_k(1 + m_1)$ (CTR-MAC). Present a counterexample showing that f is* not *a secure $2n-$bit MAC.*

The CBC-MAC construction. Finally, we present the *CBC-MAC construction*, also known as the CBC-MAC mode of operation. This is a widely used, standard construction of an $(l \cdot n)$-bit MAC from an n-bit block cipher. The CBC-MAC mode, illustrated in Figure 4.2, is a variant of the CBC mode of operation used for encryption (Section 2.10). Given a block cipher or PRF E, we define $CBC\text{-}MAC^E$ as in Equation (4.3), for an l-block input message (i.e., of length $l \cdot n$ bits), $m = m_1 + m_2 + \cdots + m_l$:

$$CBC\text{-}MAC_k^E(m) = \left\{ \begin{array}{l} c_0 \leftarrow 0^n; (i = 1 \ldots l) \\ c_i = E_k(m_i \oplus c_{i-1}); \text{output } c_l \end{array} \right\}$$

See Figure 4.2.

When the relevant block cipher function E is obvious from the context, we may simply write $CBC\text{-}MAC_k(\cdot)$.

CBC-MAC is a widely used construction of a MAC from a block cipher (or PRF). There are other constructions of secure MAC schemes from PRFs and block ciphers, including more efficient constructions, e.g., avoiding the need to know the input length in advance (CMAC [169]) or allowing parallel computation and verification (e.g., XOR-MAC [42]). However, we focus on CBC-MAC,

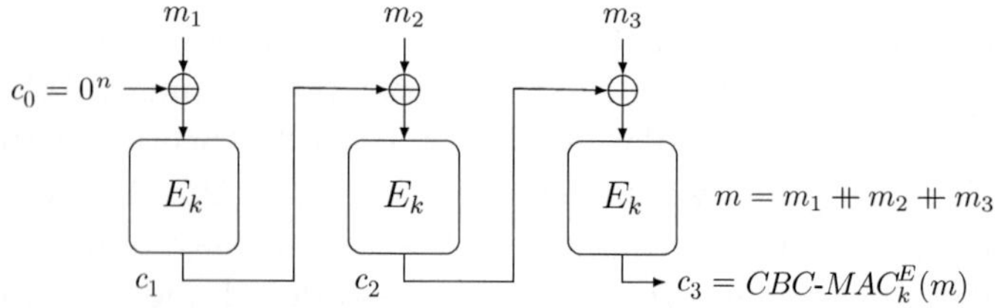

Figure 4.2. The CBC-MAC construction of an $l \cdot n$-bit PRF (and MAC), from an n-bit PRF or block cipher E.

which is not only widely used, but also one of the most simple constructions.

We next present Lemma 4.2 which shows that CBC-MAC constructs a secure $l \cdot n$-bits PRF (and hence also MAC), provided that the underlying function E is an PRF over $\{0,1\}^n$, i.e., an n-bits PRF.

Lemma 4.2. *If E is an n-bits PRF or block cipher, then CBC-MAC$_k^E(\cdot)$ is a secure $l \cdot n$-bit PRF and MAC, for any constant integer $l > 0$.*

Proof. See Ref. [43]. The fact that the proof also holds when E is a block cipher follows from the PRP/PRF switching lemma (Lemma 2.2). □

CBC-MAC does not support input of arbitrary length: The CBC-MAC construction is defined for input which is an integral number of blocks, i.e., $n \cdot l$ bits. Can we extend it to support input of strings of arbitrary length, i.e., a *Variable Input Length (VIL) PRF* (and MAC), with the input domain domain $\{0,1\}^*$?

One obvious problem is that an arbitrary binary string may not consist of an integral number of blocks, while CBC-MAC is defined only for inputs which are of length $n \cdot l$, i.e., integral number of blocks. However, let us ignore that problem for now, and focus on the *complete-block inputs*, i.e., inputs whose length is an *integer number of blocks*. Namely, here, the input *is* an integral number of blocks; we *can* apply the CBC-MAC construction. However, the input is still of variable length — and this suffices for the CBC-MAC construction to be *insecure*, as we show.

Let us first define the *complete-block inputs* domain, as: $\left\{m \in \{0,1\}^{n \cdot l} | l \in \mathbb{Z}^+\right\}$.

In the following exercise, we show that CBC-MAC is not a PRF, or a MAC, for the complete-block inputs domain, and, hence, surely not a VIL-MAC.

Exercise 4.9 (CBC-MAC is not a secure MAC for complete-block inputs). *Show that CBC-MAC is not a secure MAC or PRF for complete-block inputs and hence is definitely not a VIL-MAC or a VIL PRF.*

Solution: Let $f_k(\cdot) = $ *CBC-MAC*$_k^E(\cdot)$ be the CBC-MAC using an underlying n-bit block cipher E_k. Namely, for a single-block message

$a \in \{0,1\}^n$, we have $f_k(a) = E_k(a)$, and for a two block message $a \mathbin{+\!\!+} b$, where $a, b \in \{0,1\}^n$, we have $f_k(a \mathbin{+\!\!+} b) = E_k(b \oplus E_k(a))$.

We present a simple adversary $\mathcal{A}^{f_k}$, with oracle access to f_k, i.e., $\mathcal{A}$ is able to make arbitrary query $x \in \{0,1\}^*$ to f_k and receive the result $f_k(x)$. Let X denote all the queries made by $\mathcal{A}$ during its run. We show that $\mathcal{A}^{f_k}$ generates a pair $x, f_k(x)$, where $x \notin X$, which shows that f_k (i.e., CBC-MAC) is not a secure MAC for complete-block inputs (and hence also not a secure VIL-MAC).

Specifically, the adversary $\mathcal{A}$ first makes an arbitrary single-block query, for arbitrary $a \in \{0,1\}^n$. Let c denote the result, i.e., $c = f_k(a) = E_k(a)$. Then, $\mathcal{A}$ computes $b = a \oplus c$ and outputs the pair of message $a \mathbin{+\!\!+} b$ and tag c.

Note that $c = f_k(a \mathbin{+\!\!+} b)$, since $f_k(a \mathbin{+\!\!+} b) = E_k(b \oplus E_k(a)) = E_k((a \oplus c) \oplus c) = E_k(a) = c$. Namely, c is indeed the correct tag for $a \mathbin{+\!\!+} b$. Obviously, $\mathcal{A}$ did not make a query to receive $f_k(a \mathbin{+\!\!+} b)$. Hence, $\mathcal{A}$ achieves the (perfect) advantage of 1 against CBC-MAC. □

However, as we next explain, by merely *prepending the length to the input*, we can create a secure VIL-MAC from the CBC-MAC.

4.4.4 Extending a CBC-MAC into a VIL-MAC

Lemma 4.2 shows that CBC-MAC is a secure ln-bit FIL PRF (and MAC); however, Exercise 4.9 shows that it is *not* a secure VIL-MAC (and hence surely not a secure VIL PRF). The crux of the example was that we used the CBC-MAC of a one-block string, and presented it as the MAC of a 2-block string. This motivates a minor change to the construction, where we *prepend the block-encoded length* $L(m)$ of the input m to the input before applying CBC-MAC. We define $L(m)$ as an n-bit binary string (i.e., a block), whose binary value is the length $|m|$ of the input m. Lemma 4.3 shows that this construction is indeed a secure VIL-MAC. We refer to this variant as *length-prepending CBC-MAC*.

Lemma 4.3 (Length-prepending CBC-MAC is a VIL PRF). *Let* $f_k(m) = CBC\text{-}MAC_k^E(L(m) \mathbin{+\!\!+} m)$, *where* $L(m)$ *is the block-encoded length of* m *(as defined above). Then,* $f_k(\cdot)$ *is a PRF over the set of all binary strings (and MAC).*

Proof. See Ref. [43]. □

Note that the block-encoded length $L(m)$, can only support messages up to the maximal length encoded by n bits — i.e., $|m| < 2^n$. In practice, this isn't an issue — and it is not difficult to extend the construction to avoid this limitation, if you really want to. It is hard to imagine a practical scenario in which you will *have* to do this, though.

4.4.5 HMAC and other constructions of a MAC from a cryptographic hash function

Let us now discuss the widely used constructions of MAC functions from cryptographic hash functions, most notably the HMAC construction. Cryptographic *hash functions*, such as block ciphers, are defined in multiple standards; therefore, their use to construct a MAC function (and other schemes) follows the *cryptographic building blocks principle* (Section 2.10.1). Furthermore, since both MAC and hash functions support Variable Input Length (VIL), the constructions of MAC from hash functions are simpler than the constructions from block ciphers (Section 4.4.3). Furthermore, some cryptographic hash functions are extremely efficient, and this efficiency can be mostly inherited by HMAC.

In fact, the use of hash functions to construct a MAC is so common that many people use the term 'keyed hash' to refer to the resulting MAC functions. The meaning is that the hash function uses a *secret* key k. This *differs from our use of the term 'keyed hash function'*, as in Section 3.3.3, which is also the usage in most works in cryptography, where the key k is *not secret* (i.e., the key k is known to the adversary).

An additional problem with the term 'keyed hash' for the use of hash with a secret key to construct MAC is that it may be interpreted to imply that it is safe to use *any* keyed cryptographic hash function, e.g., a keyed CRHF, as a MAC, simply by keeping its key secret instead of publishing it. There *may* be a keyed cryptographic hash function h to be both a keyed CRHF (using a non-secret random key) and a secure MAC (using a secret key); however, it is also possible for h to be a keyed CRHF yet *not* to be a secure MAC (using a secret key), as we show in the following exercise. See also Exercises 4.24 and 4.25.

Exercise 4.10. *Let $h_k(m)$ be a keyed CRHF. Show a keyed hash function $h'_k(m)$ which is (1) a CRHF but (2)* not *a secure MAC.*

Solution: Let $h'_k(m) = k||h_k(m)$. Clearly, h' exposes its key, so it cannot be a secure MAC. However, h' is still a CRHF since any collision of h' is also a collision for h. □

We see that a function may be a keyed CRHF but not a secure MAC; can we, instead, *construct* a MAC from a cryptographic hash function? Ideally, we would want to construct the MAC from a *keyless* cryptographic hash function, since existing standard cryptographic hash functions are keyless (Section 3.1.4).

In the reminder of this section, we discuss four such constructions, whose goal is to create a MAC from keyless hash functions. We begin with three designs studied in the 1990s by Tsudik [458] and then describe HMAC [38], a somewhat more recent construction, which is widely deployed and defined as an IETF standard [39].

Tsudik's constructions of a MAC from a hash function — prepend key, append key and message-in-the-middle: Several heuristic proposals for the construction of a MAC from a cryptographic hash function were made, mostly constructing the MAC from a keyless hash function. Three of the most well-known heuristics were presented and compared by Tsudik [458]. Given keyless hash function h, key k and message m, these are as follows:

Prepend Key: $KM^h_k(m) = h(k + m)$

Append Key: $MK^h_k(m) = h(m + k)$

Message-in-the-Middle: $KMK^h_k(m) = h(k + m + k)$

An obvious question is whether these schemes are secure — assuming that the cryptographic hash function h satisfies some assumption. Let us first observe that *all* three constructions are *secure under the ROM* (Section 3.6).

Exercise 4.11. *Prove that (a) KM^h, (b) MK^h and (c) KMK^h are secure under the* random oracle model *(ROM).*

Proof sketch: Assume adversary outputs m, σ for a message m which it did not give as input to the 'oracle' for h. Then, the output of the corresponding h function, was never computed yet, i.e., it is still random. For example, for $KM^h_k(m) = h(k+m)$, the value of $h(k+m)$, for this m, was not computed yet. In fact, we need to pick it only to check the adversary's guess σ; at that point, we choose it randomly from the set $\{0,1\}^n$. The probability that our choice will be the same as σ is only 2^{-n}, i.e., negligible. Hence, $KM^h_k(m) = h(k \mathbin{+\!\!+} m)$ is secure under the ROM. This shows (a); essentially, the same argument holds for (b) MK^h and (c) KMK^h. □

To avoid the possible impression that every construction is secure under the ROM, let us give an example of construction which is *insecure even under the ROM.* Specifically, consider $KMKM^h_k(m) = h(k \mathbin{+\!\!+} m) \mathbin{+\!\!+} h(k \mathbin{+\!\!+} m \oplus 1^{|m|})$. Namely, $KMKM^h$ was made 'more complex' — maybe with the futile hope that this will make it more secure — by concatenating *two* hash values: one of $k \mathbin{+\!\!+} m$ and the other of $k \mathbin{+\!\!+} m \oplus 1^{|m|}$. Note that $m \oplus 1^{|m|}$ is just a weird way for writing the negation of m.

Exercise 4.12. *Show that $KMKM^h$ is insecure, (even) under the ROM.*

Solution: Adversary asks to receive $KMKM^h_k$ for the message $m = 0^l$ (for any length l); let the value returned be denoted $\sigma_L \mathbin{+\!\!+} \sigma_R$, where $|\sigma_L| = |\sigma_R| = n$. Then, the adversary returns the 'guess' $(1^l, \sigma_R \mathbin{+\!\!+} \sigma_L)$. Verify that this is the correct pair. □

We recommend the readers to follow carefully the arguments in Exercise 4.11 and find out why they do not hold for $KMKM^h_k(m)$. It is not trivial — and may help understand these important concepts.

We next observe that these three constructions, which *are* secure under the ROM, can be *insecure* using a hash function which satisfies standard requirements such as collision resistance and preimage resistance (one-way function), as in the following exercise. This illustrates the fact that security under the ROM does not imply security under standard assumptions.

Exercise 4.13. *Present a keyless hash function h such that:*

1. *h is a CRHF, yet (a) KM^h, (b) MK^h and (c) KMK^h are not secure MAC,*
2. *h is a SPR, yet (a) KM^h, (b) MK^h and (c) KMK^h are not secure MAC,*
3. *h is a OWF-hash, yet (a) KM^h, (b) MK^h and (c) KMK^h are not secure MAC,*

4. *h is a BRE, yet (a) KM^h, (b) MK^h and (c) KMK^h are not secure MAC,*
5. *h is CRHF, OWF and BRE, yet (a) KM^h, (b) MK^h and (c) KMK^h are not secure MAC.*

The examples may assume a hash function h' which has the corresponding property (CRHF, SPR, OWF, BRE or their combination).

Partial solution: Let h' be a hash function h' which is CRHF, SPR and OWF. We define $h(x)$ to return the n most significant bits of x if $|x| = 2n$ and the n least significant bits are all zero, and to return $h'(x)$ otherwise. We leave it to the reader to prove that h' is a secure CRHF, SPR and OWF, yet KM^h is not a secure MAC. Changing this construction to also cover BRE is not very difficult, as is modifying the constructions to show corresponding results for MK^h and KMK^h. □

While the examples in the solutions to Exercise 4.13 would be 'artificial' and irrelevant to any 'real' candidate hash function, some weaknesses of these constructions can apply to realistic hash functions. In particular, many hash functions have the following *extend property*: given $h(x)$, one can compute $h(x+\!\!+y)$, even *without* knowing anything about x. This property holds for any hash function using the (widely used) Merkle–Damgård construction, which is used by many hash functions; see Section 3.8.

In the following exercise, you are asked to show that if h has the *extend property*, then KM^h is not a secure MAC. This was shown by Tsudik in Ref. [458].

Exercise 4.14. *Show that KM^h is insecure, for* any *hash function h that has the extend property.*

HMAC: HMAC [38,39] is the most widely used construction of a MAC from a keyless hash function. HMAC is defined as:

$$HMAC_k(m) = h(k \oplus OPAD +\!\!+ h(k \oplus IPAD +\!\!+ m)) \qquad (4.3)$$

where OPAD and IPAD are fixed constant strings.

It is not difficult to see that HMAC is secure under the ROM (see Exercise 3.26). However, while the ROM is useful, and security under this model indicates that some attacks are infeasible, it would surely be much better if we could show that HMAC is secure under some 'reasonable' cryptographic assumption. In fact, this was done, in Ref. [38]. It would have been great if the assumption was one of the standard hash-function assumptions, e.g., second preimage resistant (SPR); however, the assumption in Ref. [38], while arguably reasonable, is somewhat more complex than these standard hash function assumptions. See the details in Ref. [38].

Note that HMAC construction may *not* be a secure MAC if we only assume that the underlying hash function h is collision-resistant hash, i.e., collision resistance is not a sufficient requirement from the hash function. See Exercise 3.27, where you were asked to construct a CRHF $h(\cdot)$, for which *HMAC is not a secure MAC*. To ensure that h is a CRHF, the construction uses a given CRHF, $h'(\cdot)$.

Due to the importance and wide use of HMAC, confidence in its security grew over the years, with several additional results establishing its security under 'even more reasonable' assumptions (compared to Ref. [38]). The confidence in the security of HMAC also grew due to the fact that such an important standard has not been 'broken' by cryptanalysis during this time. In fact, over time, HMAC is also often used for additional goals, such as a *pseudorandom function* (*PRF*) and as a *Key Derivation Function* (*KDF*); see Section 3.5.

4.4.6 Robust combiners for MAC

A *robust combiner* for MAC combines two (or more) candidate MAC functions to create a new composite function, which is proven to be a secure MAC provided that one (or a sufficient number) of the underlying functions is a secure MAC. There is a very simple robust combiner for MAC schemes: *concatenation* (denoted $+\!\!+$), as we show in the following exercise. Concatenation is also efficient, except for resulting in a longer authenticator (the concatenation of the authenticators produced by the different schemes).

Exercise 4.15. *Show that concatenation is a robust combiner for MAC functions.*

Solution (from Ref. [240]): Let f', f'' be two candidate MAC schemes, and define $f_{k',k''}(m) = f'_{k'}(m) +\!\!+ f''_{k''}(m)$. We should show that it suffices that *either* f' *or* f'' is a secure MAC, for f to be a secure MAC scheme as well. Without loss of generality, assume f' is secure, and assume, to the contrary, that f is not a secure MAC. Namely, assume an attacker $\mathcal{A}^{f_{k',k''}(\mu)|\mu\neq m}$ that can output a pair $m, f_{k',k''}(m)$, given access to an oracle that computes $f_{k',k''}$ on any value except m. We use $\mathcal{A}$ to construct an adversary $\mathcal{A}'$ which succeeds against f'.

Adversary $\mathcal{A}'$ operates by running $\mathcal{A}$, as well as selecting a key k'' and running $f''_{k''}(\cdot)$; this is needed to allow $\mathcal{A}'$ to provide the oracle service to $\mathcal{A}^{f_{k',k''}(\mu)|\mu\neq m}$, computing $f_{k',k''}(\mu)$ for any given input μ. Whenever $\mathcal{A}$ makes a query q, then $\mathcal{A}'$ makes the same query to the $f'_{k'}(\cdot)$ oracle, to receive $f'_{k'}(q)$. Then, $\mathcal{A}'$ computes by itself $f''_{k''}(q)$, and combines it with $f'_{k'}(q)$ to produce the required response $(f'_{k'}(q), f''_{k''}(q))$.

When $\mathcal{A}$ finally returns the pair $(m, f_{k',k''}(m)) = (m, f'_{k'}(m) \mathbin{+\!\!+} f''_{k''}(m))$, then $\mathcal{A}'$ simply returns the pair $(m, f'_{k'}(m))$, i.e., omitting the second part of the MAC that $\mathcal{A}$ returned. □

As noted above, concatenation is efficient to compute but results in a longer authenticator — the concatenation of the authenticators of the component-purported MAC functions. The following exercise shows that exclusive-or is also a robust combiner for MAC- and since the output length is the same as that of the component MAC schemes, it is efficient.

Exercise 4.16. *Show that exclusive-or is a robust combiner for MAC functions. Namely, that* $\text{MAC}_{(k',k'')}(x) = MAC'_{k'}(x) \oplus MAC''_{k''}(x)$ *is a secure MAC if one or both of* $\{MAC', MAC''\}$ *are secure MAC.*

Guidance: Similar to the solution of Example 4.15. □

4.5 Combining authentication with encryption and other functions

Message authentication combines authentication (sender identification) and integrity (detection of modification). However, when transmitting messages, we often have additional goals. These include security goals, such as confidentiality, as well as fault-tolerance goals, such as error-detection/correction, and even efficiency goals, such as compression.

In the first four sections, we focus on the combination of the two basic security goals: *encryption* and *authentication*. Finally, in

Section 4.5.5, we discuss the complete *secure session transmission protocol*, which addresses additional goals involving security, reliability and efficiency, for a session (connection) between two parties. We return to these issues in Section 7.2, where we discuss the SSL and TLS protocols, including their record protocol. There are several vulnerabilities of the SSL and TLS protocols which are due to their use of the (less-preferred, often vulnerable) combinations of authentication, confidentiality and other functions. The record protocol of TLS 1.3 was modified to a better design, to foils such attacks; see Section 7.6.

There are two main options for ensuring the confidentiality and authentication/integrity requirements together: (1) by correctly combining an encryption scheme with a MAC scheme, or (2) by using a scheme which combines the encryption and authentication functionalities. In the first section, we discuss *Authenticated Encryption (AE)* schemes and *Authenticated Encryption with Associated Data (AEAD)* schemes, which combine encryption (for confidentiality) and authentication. In the following sections, we discuss specific generic constructions, combining a MAC scheme and a symmetric key cryptosystem.

4.5.1 Authenticated Encryption (AE) and Authenticated Encryption with Associated Data (AEAD) schemes

Authenticated Encryption (AE) schemes: The combination of confidentiality and authenticity is often required, but we have seen that incorrect combinations may lead to vulnerabilities. This motivates the design of schemes which combine the authentication and the confidentiality functions. We use the term *Authenticated Encryption (AE)* for such schemes [422].

An AE scheme is defined by three algorithms:

Encode $c \leftarrow E_k(m)$, which *encrypts and authenticates* the input message $m \in \{0,1\}^*$, using the symmetric key k, and outputs ciphertext c.

Decode $m' \leftarrow D_k(c)$, which *decrypts and verifies* the ciphertext c, using the symmetric key k. Decode outputs either a message $m' \in$

$\{0,1\}^*$ or a failure indicator $m' = \bot$, which indicates that the ciphertext is not valid.

Key generation $k \xleftarrow{\$} KG(1^n)$**,** which generates the symmetric key k (given the security parameters 1^n). Many AE schemes do not use an explicit key generation algorithm, and simply use $k \xleftarrow{\$} \{0,1\}^n$, i.e., the key is just a random string of n bits. For simplicity, we focus on this kind of AE schemes, and ignore the key generation algorithm.

AE schemes should ensure *correctness*, *authentication* and *confidentiality*:

Correctness: for every message m and key k holds $m = D_k(E_k(m))$.

Authentication: Let $c^* \leftarrow \mathcal{A}^{E_k(\cdot),D_k(\cdot)}$ be the output of an efficient adversary which has oracle access to E_k and D_k, and let C be the set of outputs of the $E_k(\cdot)$ oracle. Then, the probability that $(D_k(c^*) \neq \bot \wedge c^* \notin C)$ is negligible. Namely, the adversary cannot produce a valid ciphertext which is not an output of the E_k oracle.

Confidentiality: AE schemes should not only ensure confidentiality but also ensure it in the strong sense of IND-CCA, as defined in Definition 2.8. Namely, every efficient adversary $\mathcal{A} \in PPT$ has negligible advantage $\varepsilon^{IND-CCA}_{\langle E,D\rangle,\mathcal{A}}(n) \in \text{NEGL}(n)$, as defined in Equation (2.40), where E and D are the encode and decode algorithms, respectively, of the AE scheme.

Note that the authentication property requires that the adversary would be unable to provide valid *ciphertext*, except ciphertext provided by the encode oracle. From the correctness property follows that for every valid ciphertext, the resulting plaintext must have also been input to the encode algorithm; therefore, this property implies also authentication of the resulting plaintext. However, by requiring validity of the ciphertext, we prevent the adversary from attacking confidentiality by providing the decode oracle inputs which were not received from the encode oracle. This helps ensure security against *chosen-ciphertext attacks*.

The use of an AE scheme allows simpler, less error-prone implementations compared to the use of a separate encryption scheme and authentication scheme, and possibly also better performance.

Many constructions of AE are *generic*, i.e., built by combining arbitrary implementation of cryptographic schemes, following the cryptographic building blocks principle. In Section 4.5.3, we discuss such generic constructions of AE schemes, which are different combinations of a symmetric key cryptosystem with a MAC scheme.

Other constructions of AE are *ad hoc*, i.e., they are designed using specific functions. Such *ad hoc* constructions may have better performance than generic constructions: however, that may come at the cost of requiring more complex or less well-tested security assumptions or proofs.

Authenticated Encryption with Associated Data (AEAD): In many applications, e.g., TLS (Chapter 7), *some* of the data to be authenticated should *not* be encrypted. Typically, this would be data that is used also by agents who do not have the secret (decryption) key; for example, the identity of the destination. Such data is often referred to as *associated data*; AE schemes supporting associated data are referred to as *AEAD* (*Authenticated Encryption with Associated Data*) schemes [421]. In particular, the AEAD scheme is used by the record protocol of TLS 1.3, see Chapter 7.

AEAD schemes have the same three functions (key-generation, encode and decode) as (AE) schemes. However, AEAD schemes have two additional inputs: an *associated data* input and a *nonce* input.

The *associated data* input is protected for integrity but not for confidentiality and typically sent 'in the clear' together with the ciphertext and therefore observable to the adversary. The associated data field allows the use of the AEAD scheme to authenticate messages which contain one or more elements which should be visible to all. These visible elements can contain 'control information' which is used to process the ciphertext by the recipient, or that is used by a router, firewall, intrusion detection system or other middlebox. See the use of AEAD in this way by the TLS record protocol (Section 7.2).

The *nonce* input is a generalization of the initialization vector (IV) used by different modes of operation; it can be implemented by a counter by as used by stateful modes, or as a random string (IV) by other modes. Instead of requiring the encryption process to be either stateful or randomized, it is simply required to have a nonce input, and to ensure security as long as the adversary cannot use the same nonce in more than one query to the encryption oracle (and also to the decryption oracle, for chosen-plaintext attack security). Some works, e.g., Ref. [421], define a nonce input also for symmetric key cryptosystems and AE.

Comparing cryptographic authentication schemes: Together with AE and AEAD schemes, we now have four different cryptographic authentication schemes. In Table 4.1, we sum up these four schemes; for each scheme, we list its intuitive goal, along with a metaphor to it. Like all metaphors, these should not be taken too seriously; hopefully, readers would find them helpful and not confusing and realize where the metaphors are imprecise.

The table includes another (fifth) authentication scheme: *SignCryption*. SignCryption combines the functions of public key cryptosystems and signature schemes. SignCryption schemes are beyond our scope; for their definitions and constructions; see Refs. [16, 28].

4.5.2 The EDC-then-Encrypt construction and its vulnerability

Several practical secure communication systems first apply an *error detection code* (*EDC*) to the message, and then encrypt it, i.e., $c = E_k(m + EDC(m))$. One motivation for this design is the hope that it would ensure authentication as well as confidentiality, i.e., the designers were (intuitively) trying to develop an AE scheme. Unfortunately, such designs are often insecure; in fact, the application of EDC/ECC before encryption may *facilitate attacks* on the confidentiality of the design. We saw one example, for the WEP protocol, in Section 2.12. Another example of such vulnerability is in the design of GSM, which employs not just an error detection code but even an error correction code (ECC), with very high redundancy. In both WEP and GSM, the encryption was performed by XORing the plaintext (after EDC/ECC) with the keystream (the output of a PRG).

EDC-then-Encrypt schemes are also often vulnerable when using other encryption schemes. For example, the following exercise shows such a vulnerability against the authentication property, when encrypting using the CBC mode of operation.

Table 4.1. Authentication schemes: Message authentication code (MAC), Authenticated Encryption (AE), Authenticated Encryption with Associated Data (AEAD), signature and SignCryption schemes [16, 28].

Schemes	Type	Goals	Metaphor
Message authentication code (MAC)	Symmetric	Authenticity	Document on a hard-to-duplicate paper available only to the communicating parties.
Authenticated Encryption (AE)	Symmetric	Authenticity and confidentiality	Document placed in a sealed envelope which is tamper proof and hard to duplicate, available only to the communicating parties.
Authenticated Encryption with Associated Data (AEAD)	Symmetric	Authenticity, and confidentiality for *part* of the document	Document placed in a sealed envelope which is tamper proof and hard to duplicate, available only to the communicating parties, with a window (e.g., showing the recipient address).
Signature	Asymmetric	Authenticity and non-repudiation	Signed document.
SignCryption	Asymmetric	Authenticity, non-repudiation and confidentiality	Signed document in a sealed envelope.

Exercise 4.17 (EDC-then-CBC does not ensure authentication). *Let E be a secure block cipher and let $CBC_k^E(m; IV)$ be the CBC-mode encryption of plaintext message m, using underlying block cipher E, key k and initialization vector IV, as in Equation (2.54). Furthermore, define the encoding function $EDCtCBC_k^E(m; IV) = (IV, CBC_k^E(m + h(m); IV))$, where h is a function outputting one block (which we consider here as an error detection code), and the corresponding decoding function $EDCtCBC_k^D(c)$. Show that*

($EDCtCBC^E, EDCtCBC^D$) is not a secure Authenticated Encryption (AE) scheme.

Hint: Attacker asks for $EDCtCBC^E$ encoding of the message $m' = m + h(m)$; let the output be $c' \leftarrow EDCtCBC_k^E(m; IV) = (IV, CBC_k^E(m + h(m) + h(m + h(m)); IV))$. The attacker can manipulate c' to obtain another ciphertext string c'' which is a valid encoding of m, i.e., such that $m = EDCtCBC_k^D(c'')$. This shows that ($EDCtCBC^E, EDCtCBC^D$) does not meet the authentication requirement. □

4.5.3 Generic AE and AEAD constructions

In this section, we discuss several 'generic' constructions of AE and AEAD schemes. These constructions combine an arbitrary secure MAC scheme and an arbitrary secure symmetric key cryptosystem to produce an AE or AEAD scheme, i.e., a scheme that (should) ensures both confidentiality and authenticity of the input. There are several 'natural' ways to combine the MAC scheme and the symmetric key cryptosystem, but some of them could be insecure — at least for some pairs of symmetric key cryptosystem and MAC.

In Section 4.5.3.1, we present three 'classical' designs for ensuring both authentication and confidentiality by combining a MAC scheme and a symmetric key cryptosystem: A&E, AtE and EtA. In Section 4.5.3.2, we show that two of these designs are insecure — i.e., the resulting AE scheme could be insecure, for specific *secure* MAC and symmetric key cryptosystem. In Section 4.5.3.3 we show that the third 'classical' design, EtA, *is* secure, i.e., the resulting AE scheme ensures both confidentiality and authentication, provided that the underlying symmetric key cryptosystem and MAC are secure. Finally, in Section 4.5.3.4, we present a generic AEAD construction.

4.5.3.1 *Classical generic constructions of authenticated encryption*

In this section, we present three 'classical' generic constructions of AE from a symmetric key cryptosystem (Enc, Dec) and a MAC scheme (denoted MAC). These three constructions were applied to important, standard applications. For each of the three designs, we present, informally, the process of authenticating and encrypting a message m, using two keys: k' used for encryption, and k'' used for authentication. We discuss the use of a single key rather than two keys in Section 4.5.4.

Authenticate-and-Encrypt (A&E), e.g., used in early versions of the SSH protocol [497, 498]: $C = Enc_{k'}(m),\ A = \text{MAC}_{k''}(m)$; send (C, A).

Authenticate-then-Encrypt (AtE), e.g., used in the SSL protocol and in versions 1.0 to 1.2 of the TLS protocols (Chapter 7): $A = \text{MAC}_{k''}(m),\ C = Enc_{k'}(m, A)$; send C.

Encrypt-then-Authenticate (EtA), e.g., used by the IPsec standard [189]: $C = Enc_{k'}(m),\ A = \text{MAC}_{k''}(C)$; send (C, A).

The description above is informal and did not describe the decryption process. The following exercise completes these aspects, as well as showing correctness.

Exercise 4.18 (Generic AE schemes). *Write explicitly, for each of the three generic constructions above, the implementation for the encode ('encrypt-and-authenticate') and the decode ('decrypt-and-verify') functions. Then, prove that these three constructions ensure* correctness *(provided that the underlying MAC and symmetric key cryptosystem ensure correctness, of course).*

Solution (only) for the A&E construction: The AE functions are:

$$A\&E.E_{(k',k'')}(m) \leftarrow (Enc_{k'}(m), \text{MAC}_{k''}(m))$$

$$A\&E.D_{(k',k'')}(c, a) \leftarrow \left\{\begin{array}{l} m \leftarrow Dec_{k'}(c); \\ \text{If } a = \text{MAC}_{k''}(m),\ \text{return } m; \\ \text{Otherwise, return } \bot.; \end{array}\right\}$$

Correctness follows from the correction of the symmetric key cryptosystem (Enc, Dec) and of the MAC scheme, i.e., for every message m holds, $m = Dec_{k'}(Enc_{k'}(m))$ and, therefore, $\text{MAC}_{k''}(m) = \text{MAC}_{k''}(Dec_{k'}(Enc_{k'}(m))$. Therefore, for every m, we have $A\&E.D_{(k',k'')}(Enc_{k'}(m), \text{MAC}_{k''}(m)) = m$, as required. □

While all the three generic constructions ensure correctness, two of them do not always ensure security (authentication and confidentiality), as we show in the following section. Namely, there are some secure symmetric key cryptosystems and MAC schemes that, when combined using two of the three generic constructions, result in an insecure AE, i.e., a scheme which does not guarantee authentication and/or confidentiality. Can you identify — or guess — which are these two weaker constructions?

4.5.3.2 *A&E and AtE do not ensure security*

Above, we presented three 'classical' generic constructions of AE from a symmetric key cryptosystem (Enc, Dec) and a MAC scheme (MAC). We now show that two of these constructions are insecure for particular pairs of (secure) symmetric key cryptosystem and MAC functions. This was shown by two beautiful papers [46, 303]: the first by Bellare and Namprempre and the second by Krawczyk.

Exercise 4.19 shows an example of secure encryption and secure MAC such that A&E is insecure. This is quite straightforward, and readers are encouraged to try to solve it by themselves before reading the solution.

Exercise 4.19 (Authenticate-and-Encrypt (A&E) is insecure). *Show that a pair of secure encryption scheme Enc and secure MAC scheme MAC may be both secure, yet their combination using the A&E construction would be insecure.*

Solution: Given any secure MAC scheme MAC, let:

$$MAC'_{k''}(m) = \text{MAC}_{k''}(m) + m[1]$$

where $m[1]$ is the first bit of m.

If MAC is a secure MAC, then MAC' is also a secure MAC. However, MAC' exposes a bit of its input; hence, its use in *A&E* would allow the adversary to distinguish between encryptions of two messages, i.e., the resulting, combined scheme is not IND-CPA secure — even when the underlying encryption scheme E is secure. □

Exercise 4.20 shows that AtE is also insecure. The argument is more elaborate than the A&E argument from Exercise 4.19, and it may not be completely necessary to understand it for a first reading; however, it is a nice example of a cryptographic counterexample, so it may be worth investing the effort. Readers may also consult Refs. [46, 303] for more details.

Exercise 4.20 (Authenticate-then-Encrypt (AtE) can be insecure). *Show that a pair of secure encryption scheme Enc and secure MAC scheme MAC may be both secure, yet their combination using the AtE construction would be insecure.*

Solution: Consider the following simplified version of the Per-Block Random (PBR) mode presented in Section 2.10.4, defined for single block messages: $Enc_k(m;r) = m \oplus E_k(r) \parallel r$, where E is a block cipher; notice that this is also essentially OFB and CFB mode encryptions, applied to single block messages. When the random bits are not relevant, i.e., simply selected uniformly, then we do not explicitly write them and use the simplified notation $Enc_k(m)$.

As shown in Theorem 2.1, if E is a secure block cipher (or even merely a PRF or PRP), then Enc is an IND-CPA secure encryption scheme. Denote the block length by $4n$, i.e., assume it is a multiple of 4. Hence, the output of Enc is $8n$-bits long.

We next define a randomized transform $Split : \{0,1\} \rightarrow \{0,1\}^2$, i.e., from one bit to a pair of bits. The transform always maps 0 to 00 and randomly transforms 1 to $\{01, 10, 11\}$ with the corresponding probabilities $\{49.9\%, 50\%, 0.1\%\}$. We extend the definition of $Split$ to $2b$-bit long strings, by applying $Split$ to each input block, i.e., given $2n$-bit input message $m = m_1 \mathbin{+\!\!+} \cdots \mathbin{+\!\!+} m_{2n}$, where each m_i is a bit, let $Split(m)$ be the $4n$ string $Split(m) = Split(m_1) \mathbin{+\!\!+} \cdots \mathbin{+\!\!+} Split(m_{2n})$.

We use $Split$ to define a 'weird' variant of Enc, which we denote Enc', defined as: $Enc'_k(m) = Enc_k(Split(m))$. The reader should confirm that, assuming E is a secure block cipher, then Enc' is also an IND-CPA secure symmetric key cryptosystem (for $2n$-bit-long plaintexts).

Consider now $AtE_{k,k'}(m) \equiv Enc'_k(m \mathbin{+\!\!+} \text{MAC}_{k'}(m)) = Enc_k(Split(m \mathbin{+\!\!+} \text{MAC}_{k'}(m)))$, where m is an n-bits long string and where MAC has input and outputs of n-bits long strings. Hence, the input to Enc' is $2n$-bits long, and hence, the input to Enc is $4n$-bits long — as we defined above.

However, AtE is *not* a secure authenticated-encryption scheme. In fact, given $c = AtE_{k,k'}(m)$, we can decipher m, using merely feedback-only CCA queries.

Let us demonstrate how we find the first bit m_1 of m. Denote the $8n$ bits of c as $c = c_1 \mathbin{+\!\!+} \cdots \mathbin{+\!\!+} c_{8n}$. Perform the query $c' = \bar{c_1} \mathbin{+\!\!+} \bar{c_2} \mathbin{+\!\!+} c_3 \mathbin{+\!\!+} c_4 \mathbin{+\!\!+} c_5 \mathbin{+\!\!+} \cdots \mathbin{+\!\!+} c_{8n}$, i.e., inverting the first two bits of c. Recall that $c = AtE_{k,k'}(m) = Enc_k(Split(m + \! + \text{MAC}_{k'}(m)))$ and that $Enc_k(m;r) = m \oplus E_k(r) + \! + r$. Hence, by inverting c_1, c_2, we invert the two bits of $Split(m_1)$ upon decryption.

The impact depends on the value of m_1. If $m_1 = 0$, then $Split(m_1) = 00$; by inverting them, we get 11, whose 'unsplit' transform returns 1 instead of 0, causing the MAC validation to fail, providing the attacker with an 'ERROR' feedback. However, if $m_1 = 1$, then $Split(m_1)$ is either 01 or 10 (with probability 99.9%), and inverting both bits does not impact the 'unsplit' result, so that the MAC validation does not fail. This allows the attacker to determine the first bit m_1, with very small (0.1%) probability of error (in the rare case where $Split(m_1)$ returned 11).

Both AtE and A&E *can* be secure: As we explained above, and shown in more details in Refs. [44, 303], both the Authenticate-and-Encrypt (A&E) and the Authenticate-then-Encrypt (AtE) constructions are insecure, when implemented using certain secure symmetric key cryptosystem and MAC scheme. However, in Ref. [303], Krawczyk shows that *AtE is secure*, if using a secure MAC scheme, and when the encryption scheme is one of the following implementations: the CBC mode of operation, or a secure stream cipher (such as exclusive-or with a random or pseudo-random string). Most applications of AtE in SSL and TLS use such schemes.

Similarly, in Ref. [44], Bellare *et al.* show that the A&E implementation in (early versions of the) SSH protocol is not subject to the weaknesses found in the generic A&E design.

However, both A&E and AtE are not a secure generic construction, since there exist *some* secure (IND-CPA) symmetric key cryptosystems and secure MAC schemes for which they are insecure. The security of these designs can also fail due to small variations. For example, in Chapter 7, we show padding-error oracle attacks against (versions 1.0 to 1.2 of) the TLS record protocol, when using AtE with *padded* versions of CBC.

Namely, Encrypt-then-Authenticate (EtA) is the only remaining candidate for a generic AE construction. Fortunately, we next show that *EtA is a secure generic construction*, i.e., it is secure using any secure (IND-CPA) symmetric key cryptosystem and secure MAC scheme.

4.5.3.3 *EtA is a secure construction of AE*

We now show that the generic EtA construction is secure. Namely, if the underlying symmetric key cryptosystem and MAC schemes are secure, than their combination using the EtA construction would also be secure, ensuring both authentication and confidentiality. In fact, if the MAC scheme ensures authentication, then it suffices for the underlying encryption scheme to be IND-CPA, for the AE scheme produced by the EtA construction to ensure the *stronger* confidentiality property of IND-CCA.

Intuitively, this holds since by validating the ciphertext before decrypting it, EtA schemes prevent chosen-ciphertext attacks against the underlying encryption scheme. Recall that in CCA attacks, the attacker provides specially crafted ciphertext messages and receives the corresponding plaintext, or a failure indication (if the ciphertext was not valid encryption). The attacker can use the resulting plaintext and/or failure indication to attack the underlying encryption scheme. If the attacker is creating such crafted ciphertext $c_{\mathcal{A}}$ and sending it to the decode oracle of the EtA scheme, then $c_{\mathcal{A}}$ *should* fail the MAC validation (since the attacker should not be able to forge the MAC), and, therefore, $c_{\mathcal{A}}$ would not even be input to the decryption process. Therefore, as long as the attacker cannot forge legitimate MAC authenticators, the attacker can only attack the MAC component of the EtA, and the encryption scheme is protected from this threat. Note that the attacker does receive indication whether the chosen ciphertext is valid or not, but this is only related to the validation by the MAC function and, therefore, should provide no information regarding the plaintext.

The following lemma summarizes and proves the security of the generic EtA construction.

Lemma 4.4 (EtA is secure [303]). *Given an IND-CPA encryption scheme Enc and a secure MAC scheme MAC, their EtA construction is a secure AE scheme, i.e., it ensures IND-CPA as well as IND-CCA, and is a secure MAC scheme.*

Proof sketch. We first show that the IND-CPA property holds. Suppose, on the contrary, that there is an efficient adversary $\mathcal{A}$ that 'wins' against EtA in the IND-CPA game, with significant probability. We construct adversary $\mathcal{A}'$ that 'wins' in the IND-CPA game against the encryption scheme Enc, employed as part of the EtA scheme. Specifically, $\mathcal{A}'$ generates a key k'' for the MAC function and runs $\mathcal{A}$. Whenever $\mathcal{A}$ chooses the two challenge messages m_0, m_1, and should be provided with the authenticated encryption of m_b, then $\mathcal{A}'$ chooses the same two messages and receives $c^* = Enc_{k'}(m_b)$. Then, $\mathcal{A}'$ uses the key k'' it generated to compute $a^* = \text{MAC}_{k''}(c^*)$ and return the pair (c^*, a^*) which would be the AE of m_b, as required.

Similarly, whenever $\mathcal{A}$ asks for encryption of a message m, then $\mathcal{A}'$ uses its oracle to compute $c = Enc_{k'}(m)$, and k'' to compute $a = \text{MAC}_{k''}(c)$. $\mathcal{A}'$ then returns the pair (c, a) to $\mathcal{A}$, which is exactly the required $EtA.E_{k',k''}(m)$.

Finally, when $\mathcal{A}$ guesses a bit b, then $\mathcal{A}'$ guesses the same bit. If $\mathcal{A}$ 'wins', i.e., correctly guesses, then $\mathcal{A}'$ also 'wins'. It follows that there is no efficient adversary $\mathcal{A}$ that 'wins' against EtA in the IND-CPA game.

We next show that EtA also ensures security against forgery, as in Definition 4.1, adjusted for AE schemes. Suppose there is an efficient adversary $\mathcal{A}$ that succeeds in forgery of the EtA scheme, with significant probability. Namely, $\mathcal{A}$ produces a message c and tag a s.t. $m = EtA.D_{k',k''}(c, a)$, for some message m, without making a query to $EtA.E_{k',k''}(m)$. By construction, this implies that $a = \text{MAC}_{k''}(c)$.

However, from the definition of encryption (Definition 2.1), specifically the correctness property, there is no other message $m' \neq m$ whose encryption would result in same ciphertext c. Hence, $\mathcal{A}$ did not make a query to $EtA.E_{k',k''}$ that returned $\text{MAC}_{k''}(c)$ as the tag — yet $\mathcal{A}$ obtained $\text{MAC}_{k''}(c)$ somehow — in contradiction to the assumed security of MAC.

The IND-CCA property follows from the combination of the other two properties; details omitted. □

Additional properties of EtA — efficiency and ability to foil DoS: Not only is EtA secure given any secure encryption and MAC scheme, but it also has two additional desirable properties:

Efficiency: Any corruption of the ciphertext, intentional or benign, is detected immediately by the verification process (comparing the received tag to the MAC of the ciphertext). And the validation (computation) of the MAC function, is much more efficient then the decryption operation.

Foil DoS: This improved efficiency implies that it is much harder, and rarely feasible, to exhaust the resources of the recipient by sending corrupted messages (ciphertext).

4.5.3.4 *Authenticated encryption with associated data (AEAD)*

Authenticated encryption with associated data (AEAD) schemes combine the encryption functionality with authentication, with support for *associated data* (which is authenticated but sent 'in the clear') and a *nonce*. An AEAD scheme has three functions: key generation, encode (encrypt-and-authenticate) and decode-and-verify. The encode operation has four inputs: the message m, the additional-data (AD), the nonce N, and the symmetric key k. The decode-and-verify operation has also four inputs: c, the ciphertext (which should be the output of the encode operation), the additional-data AD, the nonce N and the key k.

Figure 4.3 illustrates the encode (encrypt-and-authenticate) operation of the generic EtA AEAD construction, presented by Rogaway in Ref. [421]. As shown, the encode operation combines the symmetric key cryptosystem encryption $E^N_{k'}$, using the shared key k' and nonce N, with the MAC scheme $\text{MAC}_{k''}$, using the shared key k'', and the set-encoding operation $\langle \cdots \rangle$. The corresponding decode (decrypt-and-verify) operation uses the symmetric key cryptosystem decryption operation $D^N_{k'}$, the MAC scheme $\text{MAC}_{k''}$ and the corresponding set-decoding operation.

Let us explain two subtle issues of this construction: the set encoding and decoding operations, and the symmetric key cryptosystem with a nonce.

Set-encoding and set-decoding: As illustrated in Figure 4.3, the encrypt-and-authenticate process of the AEAD construction applies, twice, the *set-encoding operator*, denoted as $\langle \cdots \rangle$. We use this operator to encode a set of elements into a string.

In the first invocation, the input set consists of three values: the *associated data* AD, the *nonce* N and the ciphertext $E^N_{k'}(m)$. The construction uses a MAC scheme MAC, with key k'', to compute an authenticating tag that allows to verify these three values. We use the set-encoding operation $\langle \cdots \rangle$ to encode these three values into a string; this is needed since the input to a MAC scheme is a string, not a set of three values.

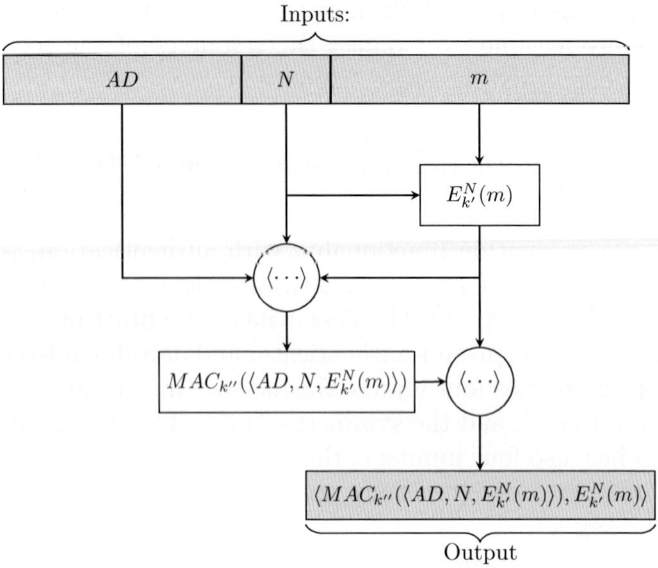

Figure 4.3. The encode (encrypt-and-authenticate) process of the generic AEAD construction.

In the second invocation, there are two inputs: the ciphertext $E^N_{k'}(m)$ and the authenticating tag $\text{MAC}_{k''}(\langle AD, N, E^N_{k'}(m)\rangle)$. We apply the set-encoding operation to these two values, since the output of AEAD consists of a single string, rather than a pair of strings.

The corresponding decrypt-and-verify function (not shown) applies, twice, the set-decoding operation, which receives a string and returns the corresponding set of elements.

Symmetric key cryptosystem with a nonce: The encode (encrypt-and-authenticate) function of an AEAD scheme uses a shared key, which is often a pair of keys (k', k''), and three other inputs: a message m, the *associated data* AD and a *nonce* N. The nonce takes the role of the initialization vector (IV) used in randomized modes of operation, e.g., the CBC mode, or of the counter used in stateful modes, e.g., the CTR mode. Namely, every times a benign party, say Alice, encodes a message using the same key k, Alice should use a unique nonce N, i.e., a nonce not used to encode previous messages, and the same nonce should be used to decode the resulting ciphertext. See Refs. [350, 421]

As can be seen in Figure 4.3, the encryption function used by the generic AEAD construction should also support a nonce, with similar properties. When using a mode of operation that uses a counter, the nonce would be the (monotonically increasing) counter; when using a mode that uses an IV, the nonce would be the random value used for the IV. The (newer) Galois/Counter Mode (GCM) already supports a nonce directly, with the same requirements as of the AEAD nonce.

4.5.4 Using a single key for AE and AEAD

The generic AE and AEAD constructions of the previous section required *two* separate keys: one key, k', for encryption, and another key, k'', for authentication. Sharing two separate keys may be harder than sharing a single key. Can we use a single key k for both the encryption and the MAC functions used in the generic AE constructions (or, specifically, in the EtA construction, since it is always secure)?

The following exercise shows that such 'key reuse' is insecure. Note that the exercise refers to the use of the same key k for *generic* symmetric key cryptosystems and MAC schemes; this use could be secure for specific schemes, e.g., using a 'double-length' key, split into an encryption key and a MAC key.

Exercise 4.21 (Key reuse is insecure). *Let E', MAC' be secure encryption and MAC schemes. Show (contrived) examples of encryption and MAC schemes, built using E', MAC', demonstrating vulnerabilities for each of the three generic constructions (authenticate-then-encrypt, encrypt-then-authenticate and authenticate and encrypt), which are each secure when using separate, independently chosen keys but insecure when using the same key for authentication and for encryption.*

Hint: Use the same or similar constructions to these of Exercise 4.6.

□

Since we know that we cannot reuse the same key for both encryption and MAC, the next question as follows: How can we securely derive two separate keys, k', k'', from a single key k? We leave this as a (not too difficult) exercise.

Exercise 4.22 (Generating two keys from one key). *Given a secure n-bit-key shared-key encryption scheme (E, D), a secure n-bit-key MAC scheme MAC, and a single random, secret n-bit key k, show how we can derive two keys (k', k'') from k, s.t. the EtA construction is secure, when using k' for encryption and k'' for MAC, given:*

1. *a secure PRF $f : \{0,1\}^n \times \{0,1\}^* \rightarrow \{0,1\}^n$ (with n-bits key and output),*
2. *a secure block cipher $(\hat{E}, \hat{D})$ with $n-$ bits key and $n/2-$bits input and output,*
3. *a secure PRG from n bits to $2n$ bits.*

4.5.5 Authentication, encryption, compression and error detection/correction codes

Data is often encoded for additional, non-security goals, including the following:

Reliability, via error detection and/or correction, typically using error detection code (EDC), such as Checksum, or error correction code (ECC), such as Reed–Solomon codes [479]. These mechanisms are designed against *random* errors, and may be insecure against intentional, malicious modifications. Note that secure message authentication, such as using a secure MAC scheme, also ensures error detection, which may appear to make the use of both MAC and EDC unnecessary. However, as we explain in the following, it is often *desirable* to use *both* a secure MAC and an (insecure) error detection code.

Compression for efficiency: Compression may improve efficiency by reducing message length. As we explain in the following, this requirement may conflict with the confidentiality requirement.

In this section, we discuss how to correctly and securely combine the security goals of encryption and authentication, with these additional goals of reliability and compression (for efficiency). Figure 4.4 presents the recommended process for combining all of these functions. Let us explain this recommendation:

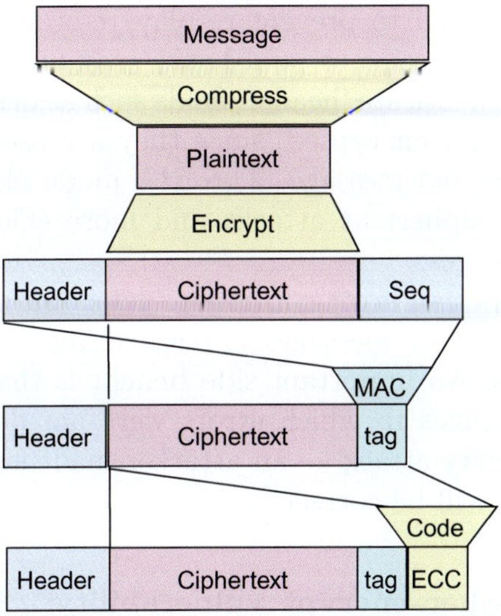

Figure 4.4. Combining security (encryption, authentication) with reliability (EDC/ECC) and compression. As the figure shows, compression must be the first function applied since compression of ciphertext would be ineffective; however, this use of compression can still expose information about the plaintext and, therefore, is best avoided for sensitive applications (see text). The application of EDC/ECC *after* the MAC allows recipients to discard messages corrupted by noise, without computing the MAC function; this saves overhead, and allows the recipient to detect attacks on the authentication.

- Compression is only effective when applied to data with significant redundancy; plaintext is often redundant, in which case, applying compression to it could be effective. In contrast, ciphertext would normally not have redundancy. Hence, if compression is used, it must be applied before encryption. Note, however, that this may conflict with the confidentiality requirement, as we explain in the following; for better confidentiality, avoid compression completely, or take appropriate measures to limit the possible exposure.
- Encryption is applied next, before authentication (MAC), following the Encrypt-then-Authenticate (EtA) construction. Alternatively, we may use an Authenticated Encryption (AE) or an Authenticated Encryption with Associated Data (AEAD) scheme to combine the encryption and authentication functions. Note that by applying authentication after encryption or using an AEAD scheme, we also facilitate authentication of a sequence number

or similar field used to prevent re-play/re-order/omission, which is often known to recipient, and hence may not be sent explicitly. We can also authenticate 'header' fields such as destination address, which are also not encrypted, since they are used to process and route the encrypted message. The EtA mode also allows prevention of chosen ciphertext attacks and more efficient handling of corrupted messages.
- Finally, we apply an error correction/detection code. This allows efficient handling of messages corrupted due to noise or other benign reasons. An important side benefit is that authentication failures of messages to which errors were not detected imply an intentional forgery attack — an attacker made sure that the error detection code will be correct.

The compress-then-encrypt vulnerability: There is a subtle vulnerability in applying compression before encryption. The reason is that encryption does not hide the length of the plaintext, while the length of compressed messages depends on the contents. In particular, a message containing randomly generated strings typically does not compress well (length after compression is roughly as long as before compression), while messages containing lots of redundancy, e.g., strings composed of only one character, compress well (length after compression is much shorter). This allows an attacker to distinguish between the encryptions of two compressed messages, based on the redundancy of the plaintexts.

This well-known vulnerability is not trivial to exploit; however, it was exploited by few attacks. We believe the first exploit was presented in Ref. [289]. The vulnerability was later exploited in several additional works and attacks, including attacks on the record protocol of SSL and of (versions 1.0 to 1.2 of) TLS; see Section 7.2.6 and Exercise 7.4.

4.6 Additional exercises

Exercise 4.23. *Mal intercepts a message sent from Alice to her bank and instructs the bank to transfer 10$ to Bob. Assume that the communication is protected by one-time pad (OTP) encryption,* *using a random key shared between Alice and her bank, and by including Alice's password as part of the plaintext, validated by the bank. Assume Mal knows that the message consists of the ASCII encoding of the exact string shown below:*

$$\textit{Transfer \$10 to Bob. From: Alice, PW: } \mathbin{+\!\!+} PW_A$$

where Alice's password (unknown to Mal) is also encoded in ASCII. Show how Mal can change the message so that upon receiving it, the bank will, instead, transfer 99\$ to Mal. Obviously, the modified message must have the same password and format.

Exercise 4.24 (A TCR hash is not necessarily a MAC). *Let $h_k(m)$ be a Target-Collision-Resistant (TCR) hash function (Section* 3.3.3*). Show a keyed hash function $h'_k(m)$ which is (1) also a TCR hash function but (2)* not *a secure MAC.*

Exercise 4.25 (A MAC is not necessarily a CRHF or a TCR). *Let* $\text{MAC}_k(m)$ *be a secure MAC function. Show a keyed hash function $h_k(m)$ which is (1) a secure MAC yet (2) not a (keyed) or a TCR hash function.*

Exercise 4.26. *Hackme Inc. proposes the following highly-efficient MAC, using two 64-bit keys k_1, k_2 for 64-bit blocks:* $\text{MAC}_{k_1,k_2}(m) = [(m \oplus k_1) + k_2] \pmod{2^{64}}$*. Show that this is not a secure MAC.*

Hint: Compare with Exercise 2.39.

Exercise 4.27. *Let $F : \{0,1\}^n \to \{0,1\}^l$ be a secure PRF, from n bit strings to $l < n$ bit strings. Define $F' : \{0,1\}^n \to \{0,1\}^l$ as $F'_k(m) = F_k(m) \mathbin{+\!\!+} F_k(\overline{m})$, i.e., concatenate the results of F_k applied to m and to the inverse of m. Present an efficient algorithm $ADV^{F'_k}$ which demonstrates that F'* is not *a secure MAC, i.e., outputs tuple (x, t) s.t. $x \in \{0,1\}^n$ and $t = F'_k(x)$. Algorithm $ADV^{F'_k}$ may provide input $m \in \{0,1\}^n$ and receive $F'_k(m)$, as long as $x \neq m$. You can present $ADV^{F'_k}$ by 'filling in the blanks' in the following 'template', modifying and/or extending the template if desired, or simply write your own code if you like:*

$ADV^{F'_k} : \{t' = F'_k($________________________________$);$

Return (________________________________); }

Exercise 4.28. *Consider CFB-MAC, defined in the following, similarly to the definition of CBC-MAC (Equation (4.3)):*

$$\textit{CFB-MAC}_k^E(m_1 \mathbin{+\!\!+} m_2 \mathbin{+\!\!+} \cdots \mathbin{+\!\!+} m_\eta)$$
$$\equiv \left\{ \begin{array}{c} c_0 \leftarrow 0^l; \\ (i = 1 \ldots \eta) c_i = m_i \oplus E_k(c_{i-1}); \\ \textit{output } c_\eta \end{array} \right\}$$

1. *Show an attack demonstrating that CFB-MAC$_k^E$ is* not *a secure $l \cdot \eta$-bit MAC, even when E is a secure l-bit block cipher (PRP). Your attack should consist of the following:*
   (a) *Up to three 'queries', i.e., messages m, m' and m'', each of one or more blocks, to which the attacker receives CFB-MAC$_k^E(m)$, CFB-MAC$_k^E(m')$ and CFB-MAC$_k^E(m'')$. Note: One query suffices, although you may use up to three:*
      - $m =$________________
      - $m' =$________________
      - $m'' =$________________

   (b) *A forgery, i.e., a pair of a message m^F*________________ *and its authenticator $a =$*________________ *such that $m^F \notin \{m, m', m''\}$ and $a =$ CFB-MAC$_k^E(m^F)$.*

2. *Would your attack also work against the (improved?) variant ICFB-MAC$_k^E(m) \equiv E_K($CFB-MAC$_k^E(m))$? If yes, prove or (at least) provide a convincing argument. If not, present an attack against ICFB-MAC$_k^E(m)$:*
   (a) $m =$________________
   (b) $m' =$________________
   (c) $m'' =$________________
   (d) m^F________________
   (e) $a =$________________

Exercise 4.29. *1. Alice sends to Bob the 16-byte message 'I love you Bobby', where each character is encoded using one-byte (8 bits) ASCII encoding. Assume that the message is encrypted using the (64-bit) DES block cipher, using the Output Feedback (OFB) mode of operation. Show how an attacker can modify the ciphertext message to result with the encryption of 'I hate you Bobby'.*

2. *Can you repeat for the Cipher Feedback (CFB) mode of operation? Show or explain why not.*
3. *Can you repeat for the Cipher Block Chaining (CBC) mode of operation? Show or explain why not.*
4. *Repeat previous items, if we append to the message its Cyclic Redundancy Check (CRC), and verify the CRC upon decryption.*

Exercise 4.30. *Consider a variant of CBC-MAC, where the value of the IV is not a constant, but instead the value of the last plaintext block, i.e.:*

$$CBC - MAC_k^E(m_1 + m_2 + \cdots + m_\eta)$$
$$= \left\{ \begin{array}{c} c_0 \leftarrow m_\eta; \\ (i = 1 \ldots \eta) c_i = E_k(m_i \oplus c_{i-1}); \\ output c_\eta \end{array} \right\}$$

Is this a secure MAC? Prove or present convincing argument.

Exercise 4.31. *Let E be a secure PRF. Show that the following are not secure MAC schemes:*

1. *ECB-encryption of the message,*
2. *the XOR of the output blocks of ECB-encryption of the message.*

Exercise 4.32. *This question discusses a (slightly simplified) vulnerability in a proposal made to a new standard. The goal of the proposal was to allow a server S to verify that a given input message was 'approved' by a series of* filters, $F_1, F_2, \ldots, F_f$ *(each filter validates certain aspects of the message). The server S shares a secret k_i with each filter F_i. To facilitate this verification, each message m is attached with a tag. The initial value of the tag is denoted T_0 and each filter F_i receives the pair (m, T_{i-1}). If filter F_i approves of the message m, then F_i outputs the next tag T_i. The server s will receive the final pair (m, T_f) and use T_f to validate that the message was approved by all filters (in the given order).*

A proposed implementation is as follows. The length of the tag would be the same as of the message m, which is assumed to be short (n bits). This is also the length of all secrets k_i and would be the length of each tag T_i. The initial tag T_0 is set to the message m. Each filter F_i signals approval by setting $T_i = T_{i-1} \oplus k_i$. To validate, *the server receives* (m, T_f) *and computes* $m' = T_f \oplus k_1 \oplus k_2 \oplus \ldots \oplus k_f$. *The message is considered valid if* $m' = m$.

1. *Show that in the proposed implementation, if the tag* T_f *is computed as planned (i.e., as described above), then the message is considered valid if and only if all filters approved of it.*
2. *Show that the proposed implementation is insecure.*
3. *Present a simple, secure alternative design, as efficient as you can. You may assume, as in the original design, that the message* m *is short (*n *bits).*
4. *Present an improvement to your method, which is appropriate for use for arbitrarily-long messages* m.

Note: You may combine the solutions to the two last items, but separating the two is recommended, to avoid errors and minimize the impact of errors.

Exercise 4.33 (Single-block authenticated encryption?). *Let* E *be a block cipher (or a PRP or a PRF), for input domain* $\{0,1\}^l$, *and let* $l' < l$. *For input domain* $m \in \{0,1\}^{l-l'}$, *let* $f_k(m) = E_k(m + \!\!\!+ 0^{l'})$:

1. *Prove or present counterexample:* f *is a secure MAC scheme.*
2. *Prove or present counterexample:* f *is an IND-CPA symmetric encryption scheme.*

Exercise 4.34. *Let* $f : \{0,1\}^\kappa \times \{0,1\}^{l+1} \to \{0,1\}^{l+1}$ *be a secure PRF, where* κ *is the key length, and both inputs and outputs are* $l+1$ *bits long. Let* $f' : \{0,1\}^\kappa \times \{0,1\}^{2l} \to \{0,1\}^{2l+2}$ *be defined as* $f'_k(m_0 + \!\!\!+ m_1) = f_k(0 + \!\!\!+ m_0) + \!\!\!+ f_k(1 + \!\!\!+ m_1)$, *where* $|m_0| = |m_1| = l$. *Present an adversary and/or counter-example, showing that* f' *is not a secure* $2l$*-bit MAC.*

Exercise 4.35. *Let* (Enc, Dec) *be an IND-CPA secure encryption scheme, and let* $Enc'_k(m) = Enc_k(Compress(m))$, *where* $Compress$ *is a compression function. Show that* Enc' *is not IND-CPA secure.*

Exercise 4.36 (AEAD). *In this exercise, we investigate possible designs for the encode function* $(\langle \cdot \cdot \cdot \rangle)$ *of the generic AEAD construction, illustrated in Figure 4.3:*

1. *Show why the trivial implementation of the encode function as concatenation should not be used.*
2. *Propose an implementation for the encode and decode functions, and prove that, with this implementation, the construction ensures correctness.*
3. *Design an alternative generic AEAD construction, following the authenticate-then-encrypt approach, and prove its correctness (using the same encode and decode functions).*

Exercise 4.37. *Figure* 4.4 *shows the typical sequence of operations when sending a message, with confidentiality (encryption), authentication (MAC), error detection/correction code and (optional) compression. Show the corresponding sequence of operations when* receiving *such a message, in a figure and/or in pseudo-code. Your solution should include the appropriate reactions if the MAC and/or EDC/ECC validation fails.*

Exercise 4.38 (Insecure prepend-key MAC). Consider the following construction: $h'_k(m) = h(k \mathbin{+\!\!+} m)$, where $h : \{0,1\}^* \to \{0,1\}^n$ is a hash function, k is a secret n-bit key and $m \in \{0,1\}^*$ is a message. Assume you are given some SPR hash function $\hat{h} : \{0,1\}^* \to \{0,1\}^{\hat{n}}$; you can use $\hat{n}$ which is smaller than n. Using $\hat{h}$, construct hash function h so that (1) it is 'obvious' that h is also SPR (no need to prove), yet (2) $h'_k(m) = h(k \mathbin{+\!\!+} m)$ is (trivially) *not* a secure MAC. Hint: Design h s.t. it becomes trivial to find k from $h'_k(m)$ (for any m):

1. $h(x) =$________________.
2. (Justification) h is an SPR, since ____________________________.
3. (Justification) $h'_k(m) = h(k \mathbin{+\!\!+} m)$ is *not* a secure MAC, since ______.

Chapter 5

Shared-Key Protocols

In the previous chapters, we discussed cryptographic schemes which consist of one or more functions. Cryptographic hash functions, message authentication code, pseudorandom function and pseudorandom generator schemes each consist of a single function, while cryptosystems and signature schemes consist of two to three functions (for public key cryptosystems: encryption, decryption and key generation). All of these cryptographic cryptographic schemes are often used as a part of a *protocol* involving two or more parties (entities).

In this chapter, we discuss a few basic shared-key protocols used for securing the communication between two parties, including the following:

Session/record protocols secure the communication of a session between two parties, which typically includes exchange of multiple messages, using a key shared between the two parties. See Section 5.1.

Entity-authentication protocols validate the identity of a peer involved in the communication, using a key shared between the peers. We discuss the vulnerable SNA protocol, and its replacement, the 2PP protocol, in Section 5.2.

Secure request-response protocols ensure the authentication and/or confidentiality of a *request-response protocol*, i.e., the exchange of a request, and a response to the request, between two parties. We discuss secure request response protocols in Section 5.3.

Key exchange protocols are run between the two parties, to establish shared keys to encrypt and authenticate communication. In Section 5.4, we discus *shared-key key exchange protocols*, which use an already shared key between the parties, to establish keys for encryption and authentication; these protocols ensure improved security compared to direct use of the shared key for these functions.

Key distribution protocols establish shared keys between two parties, with the help of a *Trusted Third Party* (TTP), often referred to as the *Key Distribution Center* (KDC). We discuss key distribution protocols in Section 5.5; much of our discussion is dedicated to studying the key distribution protocol defined in the GSM specifications, and its vulnerabilities.

Resilient key exchange protocols are key exchange protocols with mechanisms to reduce exposure due to key exposure. These include forward secrecy, perfect forward secrecy (PFS) and recover security key exchange protocols. See Section 5.6.

This chapter is mostly informal. In particular, we do not present rigorous definitions of security as we did in the previous chapters. This is since precise definitions of the execution of protocols and of the corresponding requirements and models seem to be unavoidably too complex for this book. We hope that the informal discussion will clarify the main issues and empower readers to properly use cryptographic protocols and avoid pitfalls. Hopefully, the discussion will also prepare readers interested in design and analysis of cryptographic protocols to study more advanced texts which address these challenges. Some of the many relevant texts include Refs. [52, 112, 210, 242, 443].

5.1 Cryptographic protocols

We begin our discussion informally explaining what we mean by a *cryptographic protocol*. We use the term 'cryptographic protocols' to refer to cryptographic algorithms that *involve interactions between two or more distinct entities,*[1] including *benign entities* and an *adversary.*

In this chapter, we mostly[2] focus on protocols involving only two benign parties, often called *Alice (A) and Bob (B)*, and one man-in-the-middle (MitM) adversary. Benign entities run the same protocol $\mathcal{P}$, which is an efficient algorithm; to model parties with different roles, e.g., client vs. server, the 'role' is provided as part of their initial state or input. The adversary also runs an efficient algorithm.

Entities interact via *interfaces*, typically, at least two: one interface, *APP,* for interacting with the *application* which uses the protocol, and one interface, NET, for interacting with other entities, typically via a communication network. Often, protocols use additional interfaces, such as an interface *SYS* that provides the protocol with system service, such as a clock. These three interfaces are illustrated, for record/session protocols, in Figure 5.1.

5.1.1 The session/record protocol

We illustrate the concept of a cryptographic protocol by focusing on the simple yet important *session/record protocol.* A session/record protocol uses a key shared between the two parties, to authenticate and/or encrypt the messages or *records* sent in a *session* or connection between them. In Chapter 7, we present a practical session/record protocol; this is the *TLS record protocol*, which is part of the TLS protocol.

Session/record protocols are among the simplest practical protocols, in particular, simpler than the other protocols we discuss, and therefore a good example.

Let us first describe the APP, SYS and NET interfaces of the session/record protocol, and the operations in each of them, as illustrated in Figure 5.1.

---

[1]In some works, the term 'cryptographic protocol' is used in a different way, mostly to mean what we refer to as a 'cryptographic scheme', i.e., not necessarily involving interactions between entities; e.g., you may see mention of 'encryption protocol'.

[2]An exception is Section 5.5, where we discuss protocols involving a third party, the Key Distribution Center (KDC).

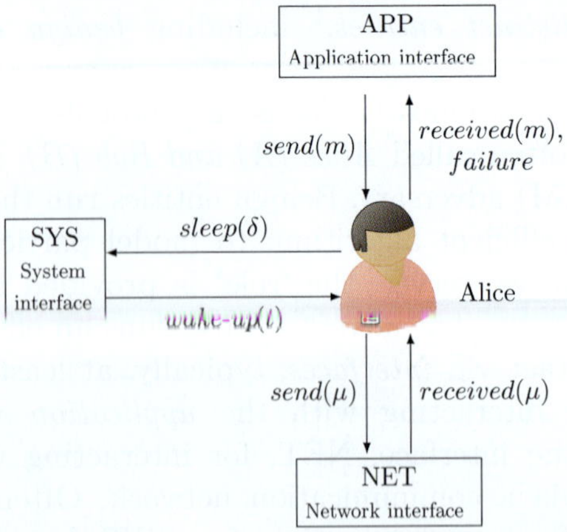

Figure 5.1. Interactions for the record/session protocols, illustrated for Alice; Bob has the same interfaces. Note that while we use the labels *send* and *received* for both the APP and NET layers, the semantics and the messages sent (m and μ) are very different. Typically, μ will contain an encoding of m, possibly encrypted and/or authenticated, and a header that identifies sender, recipient and key; see text for details. Other protocols we study use the same SYS and NET events but different APP events.

Application (APP): An interface for input/output interactions between a benign party and the *application* which uses it, to whom we sometimes refer as the *user* of the protocol. These interactions provide the inputs from the application or user to the protocol running on the (benign) party, and allow the protocol to provide outputs to the application/user. For the session/record protocol, the only input interaction in the APP interface is transmission of a message m from the application to be sent to the peer in a $send(m)$ interaction. There are two output interactions: the receipt of a message m from the peer in a $received(m)$ event and an indication that the protocol cannot send information due to a communication failure, in a $failure$ interaction. Here, *send*, *received* and $failure$ are labels and m is a value.

Network (NET): An interface for the communication between benign parties, allowing the parties to exchange information with each other, subject to manipulations by the adversary. We usually use the term a *packet*, and use the symbol μ, for a unit of information sent over the network, reserving the term *message*, and the symbol m, for the information received from the application or delivered to the application. To send a packet μ to the peer, the protocol uses the $send(\mu)$ output event on the NET interface; *send* is the label and μ is the value. We use the symbol μ for the messages in the NET interface, to separate them from the symbol m which we use for messages in the APP interface. Typically, a packet μ consists of two parts: *header*, identifying the sender, recipient and key(s) used, and *payload*, which may contain an encoding of a message m, possibly encrypted and/or authenticated. In a $received(\mu)$ input event on the NET interface, the protocol receives a packet μ, which typically contains a header which contains, among other things, two identifiers: an identifier for the peer who sent the packet and an identifier for the key(s) to be used, as needed, to decrypt and/or authenticate the packet.

System (SYS): An interface to other interactions of the protocol, typically to 'local' services, such as clock, sensors and relays/actuators. In this book, we only use clock service, with two interactions. Specifically, the protocol may invoke $sleep(\delta)$ to request a 'wake-up call' after δ time units (e.g., seconds); upon that time, the protocol should receive an incoming *wake-up*(t) event, with t indicating the current time. This interface allows both 'wake-up' service as well as a 'clock lookup' service (using $sleep(0)$).

The APP interface events are specific to each type of protocols, e.g., differ between session/record protocols and between entity-authentication and other protocols. However, all the protocols we study use the same SYS and NET events, as described above.

Adversary capabilities and security requirements: Our description of the interactions focused on their *intended* actions; however, obviously, the adversary can significantly interfere with the interactions in different ways. Following the *attack model principle* (Principle 1), we only limit the adversary's *capabilities* rather than assuming a specific attacker *strategy*. The adversary's capabilities include both *computational capabilities* and *access capabilities*.

In most works in cryptography, the *computational capabilities* of the adversary and the protocol are limited to be efficient (PPT) algorithms (see Section A.1), i.e., their run time must be bounded by a polynomial in the length of their inputs. To ensure that neither the protocol nor the adversary has an unfair advantage in computational capabilities, both the adversary and the protocol receive a special input called the *security parameter*, which we denote 1^n. The security parameter is a string of 1 bits, i.e., 1^n (or an integer n encoded in unary), which should be at least as long as the other inputs.

The *access capabilities* define the ability of the adversary to observe the outputs and control the inputs of the benign parties. Like most works in cryptography, we focus on the *man-in-the-middle (MitM) adversary*, which observes all the outputs and determines all the inputs of the benign parties, including any packets sent between the parties. Note that some security requirements restrict the adversary's capabilities; in particular, in Section 6.1.3, we study the *key agreement* problem, which assumes an *eavesdropping adversary*, who can observe packets but cannot modify, inject or drop packets.

Following the *conservative design principle* (Principle 3), we allow the adversary complete control and observation capabilities over the application interface. In the case of the session/record protocol, this means that the adversary determines when a *send*(m) request from the application occurs and what is the message m, except for *indistinguishability games* where the adversary can provide two equally long inputs, one of which will be used as input, and the adversary has to try to guess which input was used.

The ability to control the input message m corresponds to the *chosen-plaintext attack* (CPA) model for encryption and the *chosen-message attack* (CMA) for signatures, and to the other attack models defined in Chapter 2 for encryption and in Section 1.5.2 for signatures.

Informal requirements of session/record protocols: We focus on two basic properties of session/record protocols: *confidentiality* and *authentication*. Intuitively, these are as follows:

Confidentiality: The attacker cannot learn anything about the messages sent by the application layer of the parties, except possibly their length.

Authentication: At any time during the execution, the sequence of message received by the application at one peer, say Bob, should be a prefix of the sequence of message sent by the application at the other peer, Alice.

There may be additional goals, e.g., *bounded delay* Δ, i.e., a message sent at time t should be received before time $t + \Delta$, and *fault detection*, i.e., detection when packets are not transmitted correctly by the network between the entities.

5.1.2 *sEtA*: a simple EtA session/record protocol

We now present the *simple EtA session/record protocol* (sEtA). This is a very simple session/record protocol; in Chapter 7, we discuss the more elaborate TLS record protocols. The *sEtA* protocol uses the *Encrypt-then-Authenticate* (EtA) design which we discussed in Section 4.5. The EtA design is also used by the (much more elaborate) IPsec ESP protocol, standardized by the IETF in Ref. [189], but not by the TLS and SSL record protocols, discussed in Chapter 7, which use the Authenticate-then-Encrypt (AtE) design, or, in TLS 1.3, the Authenticated Encryption with Associated Data (AEAD) design.

We describe the protocol for two specific parties $\{A, B\}$, although, it can be easily extended to support arbitrary pairs or sets of parties. We also make several other simplifications, as listed below.

Simplifications of *sEtA*: The *sEtA* protocol makes the following simplifications:

***sEtA* assumes a reliable network (connection):** To ensure that the protocol *can* deliver messages, we require that the adversary, controlling the network, will typically, without attack, deliver packets correctly, i.e., every packet sent by one party to its peer, over the network (NET interface), is delivered *reliably* and in a timely fashion. Reliable delivery means that the sequence of packets is delivered exactly as sent: no forgery, reordering, modification, duplication or loss of packets; the one exception is that the most recently sent packets may still be in transit up to some maximal delay from the moment they were sent.

***sEtA* does not ensure bounded delay:** The protocol ensures that messages received *have* been sent by a peer but does not bound the delay or guarantee delivery. We may receive 'stale' messages sent unlimited time ago, i.e., *sEtA* does not ensure *freshness*.

No compression, padding or fragmentation: The protocol sends messages of unbounded size 'as-is', without applying compression and without fragmenting excessively long messages into multiple bounded length fragments, as done, e.g., by the TLS record protocol. Furthermore, the protocol assumes that the MAC and encryption functions can receive arbitrary-length messages, i.e., the protocol does not perform any padding before applying MAC and encryption.

Assumes initialization of *two* shared keys: The protocol assumes initialization of a shared encryption key k_E, as well as a shared authentication key k_{MAC}.

Explanation of the simple secure session/record protocol *sEtA*: The *sEtA* protocol uses a *symmetric key cryptosystem* (E, D), using a (shared) key k_E, together with a *message authentication code* (MAC) scheme MAC, using another (shared) key k_{MAC}. The description is simplified by ignoring the key-generation of both the cryptosystem and the MAC scheme; we assume that the two keys, k_E and k_{MAC}, are generated and shared securely securely with the two parties before the protocol begins.

Let us now explain how the *sEtA* protocol sends and receives messages, as illustrated in Figure 5.2.

Sending message m (received from the application): Assume that a party, say Alice, receives message m from the application, to be sent to Bob; namely, Alice has a *send*(m) event on the APP interface. The protocol should send the incoming message m, properly encrypted and authenticated. The protocol follows the (recommended) *Encrypt-then-Authenticate* (EtA) approach (Section 4.5.5).

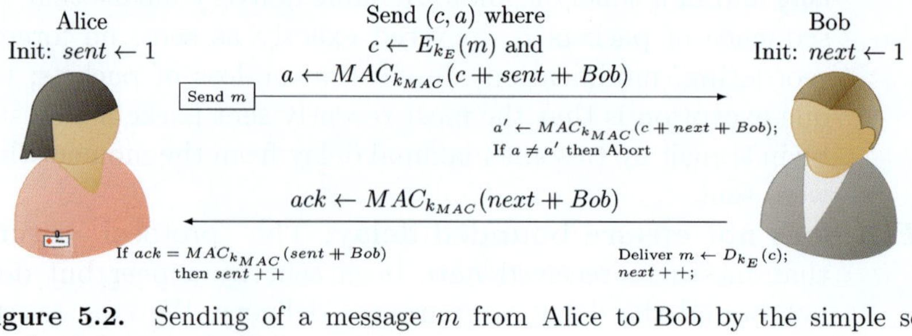

Figure 5.2. Sending of a message m from Alice to Bob by the simple session/record protocol *sEtA*.

Namely, the protocol first encrypts the message m, i.e., computes the ciphertext $c \xleftarrow{\$} E_{k_E}(m)$. Then, the protocol computes the authenticator: $a \leftarrow \text{MAC}_{k_{\text{MAC}}}(c + sent + Bob)$, where *sent* is the sequence number of the messages sent. The input to the MAC includes the sequence number *sent* of this message-send event and the recipient identification (Bob); this prevents manipulation by a MitM adversary. Finally, the protocol requests the network to send the *packet* (c, a) to the peer, by a *send* request in the NET interface. Note that we use the term *packet* for the information sent by the protocol, to distinguish between it and the *message* which is sent by the application using the protocol. The packet does not send the counter *sent* or the sender identification p; sending these is not required since the underlying networking service is assumed to ensure reliable delivery, namely, the packets sent should be received in the order sent. Therefore, the recipient can count the received packets and should have exactly the same inputs to the MAC. The TLS record protocol also does not include a counter since TLS sends the information over the TCP protocol, which ensures reliable delivery; see Chapter 7.

Receiving a message: Messages are received in incoming *packets*, via the NET (network) interface. Since we assumed a reliable network service (before attack), the incoming packet μ should be the next packet sent by the peer. The protocol parses the incoming packet μ as a pair (c, a). It verifies that the authenticator is valid; for example, when Bob receives a packet (c, a) from Alice, then the protocol running at Bob verifies that $a = \text{MAC}_{k_{\text{MAC}}}(c + next + Bob)$, where *next* is the sequence number of the next expected message. If the authenticator a is valid, then the protocol delivers to the application the plaintext message $m \leftarrow D_{k_E}(c)$, i.e., the decryption of the ciphertext part c. If validation fails, the protocol drops the packet, possibly providing an indication of the failure to the application.

Acknowledgments: Upon successful receipt of a new message, the recipient, e.g., Bob, sends an *acknowledgment packet ack* back to the sender (Alice), as a packet containing only the MAC of the message number and the recipient's identity. Namely, if Bob receives the *ith* message correctly (and delivers it to the application), then Bob will also compute and send to Alice $p_{\text{Ack}} \leftarrow MAC_{k_{\text{MAC}}}(i + Bob)$.

Alice may wait for the acknowledgment before ending the next message to Bob and possibly resend the message if the acknowledgment is not received in time.

5.2 Shared-key entity authentication protocols

In this section, we discuss shared-key protocols for authenticating an interaction between a pair of parties (entities). Entity authentication protocols are among the simplest and oldest cryptographic protocols and were in extensive use for years, although later they were mostly replaced by *authenticated key exchange protocols*, which combine entity authentication with exchange of a *session key*, later used by a session/record protocol to protect the communication between the parties; we discuss key exchange protocols in the following sections.

We focus on the common case of *mutual entity authentication*, i.e., both parties authenticate each other; however, our discussion mostly applies also to the simpler case where only one party authenticates its peer.

To refer to the party that initiates the handshake, we use the term *initiator* and similarly the term *responder* for the party that responds. For convenience, in our examples, we usually have Alice as the initiator (i.e., Alice initiates the handshake) and Bob as the responder; however, the roles could be reversed, i.e., Bob can be the initiator and Alice can be the responder.

5.2.1 Interactions and requirements of entity authentication protocols

Basically, the goal of an entity authentication protocol is to validate interaction with the (correct) peer. In mutual entity authentication protocols, both peers should authenticate each other, which requires, at least, one exchange of messages between the two parties, e.g., a message from Alice to Bob and a response from Bob to Alice. *Mutual* authentication means that both parties validate they interacted successfully with their peer.

We refer to the entire set of messages involved with a single run of the authentication protocol as the *handshake*. Mutual authentication requires at least two message flows (e.g., Alice to Bob and response from Bob to Alice). Some protocols require three or more flows, e.g., also a response from Alice to Bob.

Interactions of entity authentication protocols: An entity authentication protocol has the interactions illustrated in Figure 5.3. The interactions in the SYS and NET interfaces are the same as presented in Figure 5.1; let us explain the APP interface interactions, i.e., the interactions between the entity authentication protocol and the application using it.

A handshake begins at an initiator, say Alice, upon $Init(i)$ input interaction (request) from the user or application (APP interface). In the responder, say Bob, the handshake begins with a $Resp(i)$ output interaction, i.e., a notification by the protocol of a new handshake initiated by the peer (e.g., Alice). The identifier i is called the *session identifier*; identifiers are required to be distinct for different handshakes in each party.

Note that each handshake is assigned a unique identifier at each party, e.g., i_I at the initiator and i_R at the responder. The two identifiers may be assigned independently at each party; they only need to be unique for that party. One simple implementation would be as a counter maintained at each party, incremented by the application

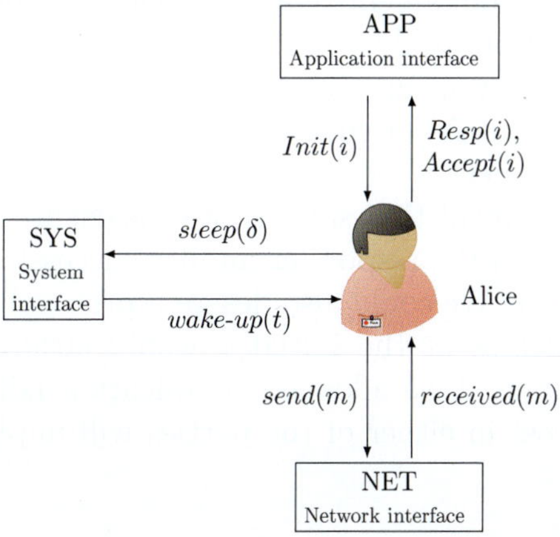

Figure 5.3. Interactions for entity authentication protocols, illustrated for Alice; Bob has the same interfaces. The *handshake identifier* i allows association of the different APP interactions related to the same handshake in each party, as explained in the text.

when it issues a new $Init(i_I)$ request and by the protocol when it notifies of a new handshake with a new $Resp(i_R)$ interaction.

A handshake *terminates* at a party, e.g., Alice, when she *Accepts*, i.e., validates successfully the interaction with the peer (Bob); this is done by the protocol returning *Accept* to the application (i.e., on the APP interface). If the validation fails, e.g., Bob never responds, the handshake may never terminate or terminate with a failure indication.[3]

To summarize, the interactions of the APP interface are as follows:

$Init(i)$ is an *input* interaction, i.e., a request from the application to initiate a new connection (with a distinct identifier i). *Init* is the only input interaction.

$Resp(i)$ is an *output* interaction, where the protocol informs that it is responding to a new session, and assigns this new session an identifier value i. This session identifier must differ from other session identifiers used by this party (in *Init* or *Resp* interactions).

$Accept(i)$ is an *output* interaction, where the protocol informs the applications that session i has successfully completed.

Security of entity-authentication protocols: Intuitively, the basic requirement from an entity-authenticating protocol is that successful authentication would imply a 'fresh' interaction with the peer. The term 'fresh' may mean either simply 'within the recent Δ seconds' (for some small Δ) or that there was overlap in the handshake periods in the two peers.

Another requirement that some protocols ensure is that a successful authentication in the responder implies successful authentication also in the initiator. We could also design a protocol with the reverse property, i.e., success at the initiator would ensure success at the responder. However, if we allow communication failures, we cannot ensure that success in either of the parties will imply success in the other party.

---

[3]The failure indicator is used to ensure that handshakes terminate within bounded time; for simplicity, we do not discuss this requirement or utilize it in the protocols and requirements that we cover.

Sequential vs. Concurrent Authentication: It is easier to ensure mutual authentication if handshakes must be done *sequentially*, i.e., no *concurrent handshakes*. However, concurrent sessions are required in many scenarios; e.g., web communication often uses concurrent connections (sessions) between browser and server, to improve performance.

Concurrent handshakes are also necessary to prevent 'lock-out' due to synchronization errors (e.g., lost state by Initiator) or an intentional 'lock-out' by a malicious attacker, as part of a *Denial of Service attack*. In any case, there is no strong motivation to allow only consecutive handshakes; protocols that support concurrent handshakes are as efficient, and not significantly more complex, than protocols that only allow sequential authentications. Therefore, following the conservative design principle (Principle 3), we focus on the case where concurrent handshakes are allowed.

We next discuss a vulnerable mutual entity authentication protocol. As we see, vulnerabilities are often due to failure to handle correctly concurrent handshakes.

5.2.2 Vulnerability study: the SNA mutual-authentication protocol

As a simple example of an (insecure) two-party, shared key mutual entity authentication protocol consider the *SNA mutual entity authentication protocol*. IBM's Systems Network Architecture (SNA) was the primary networking technology from 1974 till the 1990s.

We first describe the original, insecure version of the SNA mutual entity authentication protocol, which was in use until the late 1980s, and then we describe its replacement: the 2PP mutual entity authentication protocol. Both protocols use a shared secret key k, to authenticate two parties to each other, without deriving a session key; we later describe extensions which also establish a session key to protect communication, i.e., provide key exchange.

The SNA protocol, illustrated in Figure 5.4, operates in three simple flows. The protocol uses a block cipher E. The initiator, say Alice, sends to her peer, say Bob, her identifier, which we denote A, and N_A, a random n-bit binary string which serves as a challenge; such a random challenge is often called a *nonce*. Here, n is the size of the inputs and outputs to a block cipher E used by the protocol.

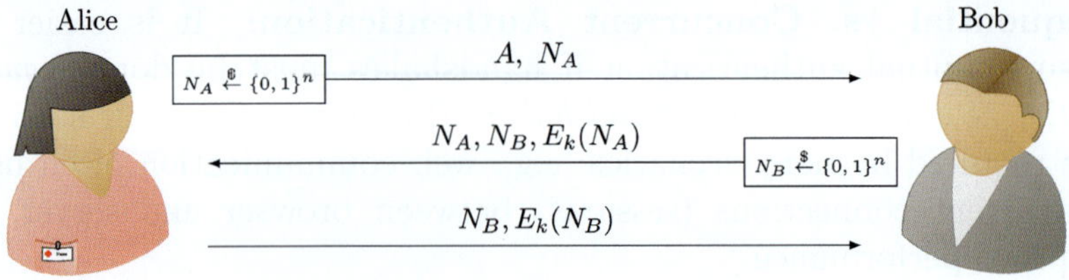

Figure 5.4. The (vulnerable) SNA mutual authentication protocol.

The responder, say Bob, replies with a *proof of participation* $E_k(N_A)$, i.e., encryption, using the shared key k, of the nonce N_A received. Bob also sends his own random n-bit challenge (*nonce*) N_B. To help Alice match this response with the correct handshake, as necessary to support concurrent handshakes, Alice also sends an identifier with her handshake message, which Bob returns with his response. Or, as we show in Figure 5.4, Alice only includes her nonce N_A, and Bob simply attaches Alice's nonce N_A with his handshake message (second flow).

Upon receiving Bob's response, Alice validates that the response contains the correct proof of participation $E_k(N_A)$, i.e., encryption, using the shared key k, of the nonce that she previously selected and sent. If so, Alice concludes that she communicates indeed with Bob. Alice then completes the mutual entity authentication by sending her own proof of participation, $E_k(N_B)$. Alice may also includes N_B with her response, to help Bob match the response with the correct handshake, similarly to the inclusion of N_A by Bob.

Finally, Bob similarly validates that he received the expected proof of participation, $E_k(N_B)$, i.e., encryption using the shared key k, of its randomly selected nonce N_B. If this holds, Bob concludes that this mutual entity authentication was initiated, and successfully completed, by Alice.

Upon receiving the expected responses, both parties, Alice and Bob, signal to their applications that the mutual entity authentication has completed successfully.

SNA mutual entity authentication ensures (only) *sequential* mutual authentication, and only for certain encryption schemes E: The simple SNA mutual entity authentication of Figure 5.4 does ensure mutual authentication, when E is a block cipher rather than a (arbitrary) symmetric key cryptosystem, and only if restricted to sequential mutual entity authentication; note that while the SNA design referred to E as encryption, it was implemented as a block cipher (specifically, DES). The protocol can be vulnerable when using an arbitrary symmetric key cryptosystem, including some standard modes of operation (see Exercise 5.10), or when allowing concurrent mutual entity authentication, as illustrated in Figure 5.5 (and explained in the following).

Let us first explain, intuitively, why the protocol ensures mutual authentication, when restricted to *sequential handshakes*, and if E is simply a block cipher. Suppose, first, that Alice completes the protocol successfully. Namely, Alice received the expected second flow, $E_k(N_A)$. Assume that this happened *without* Bob previously receiving N_A as the first flow from Alice (and sending $E_k(N_A)$ back). Due to the sequential restriction, Alice surely did not *receive* N_A as a challenge in the time since Alice sent N_A and hence did not compute and send $E_k(N_A)$. Since Alice selected N_A randomly, from a sufficiently large set (i.e., N_A is sufficiently long), it is unlikely that either Alice or Bob has received N_A before Alice completed the protocol. Hence, the adversary must have computed $E_k(N_A)$ rather than intercepted it. However, if the adversary can compute $E_k(N_A)$, then the adversary can distinguish between E_k and a random permutation,

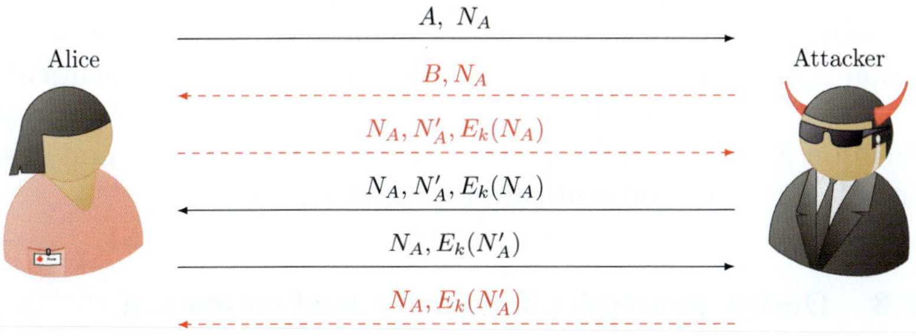

Figure 5.5. Attack on SNA mutual entity authentication with Alice initiating one session with Bob, which is actually intercepted by an Attacker; flows related to this session are marked in black and 'regular' arrows. In the attack, the Attacker, impersonating as Bob, initiates another session with Alice; flows related to this (second) session are marked in red and with dashed arrows. Both sessions terminate correctly, i.e., Alice would believe that she has successfully interacted with Bob in both sessions, while in reality, Bob was never involved. Note that this attack requires that Alice would agree to act both as an initiator and as a responder of sessions.

contradicting the PRP assumption for E. Note that an eavesdropping attacker may collect such pairs $(N_A, E_k(N_A)$ or $N_B, E_k(N_B))$: however, since N_A, N_B are random n-bit strings, with n selected to be sufficiently long, the probability of such reuse of the same N_A or N_B is negligible.

Next, let us explain why the SNA mutual entity authentication protocol *fails* to ensure *concurrent* mutual authentication. Namely, if the parties are willing to run two concurrent handshakes, then an attacker can cause a party to complete the protocol 'successfully', i.e., thinking it has communicated with its peer, while in reality the peer did not receive any message. Figure 5.5 illustrates an attack where Alice initiates one session with Bob, which is actually intercepted by an attacker. The attacker, impersonating as Bob, initiates another session with Alice. Both sessions terminate correctly, i.e., in both, Alice is tricked into believing that she has successfully interacted with Bob; however, in reality, Bob was never involved.

Note that the attack of Figure 5.5 requires that Alice would agree to act both as an initiator of a session and as a responder of a session. One may hope that SNA may be secure for concurrent mutual entity authentication, if each party is only willing to act in one role (initiator or responder). However, this is not the case; see Exercise 5.8.

In practice, SNA does allow concurrent mutual entity authentication handshakes since these are important for performance and to ensure synchronization, as we discussed toward the end of Section 5.2.1. To ensure security, the mutual entity authentication protocol of SNA was changed into the 2PP protocol, which we present in Section 5.2.4. Before we present 2PP, let us discuss several design principle for entity authentication protocols.

5.2.3 Design principles for entity authentication protocols

From the multiple attacks presented against the SNA mutual entity authentication protocol, we can derive several *design principles* for entity authentication protocols; these principle are mostly applicable to other protocols, in particular, to message authentication protocols.

Identify sender and recipient: The SNA protocol allowed *redirection*: giving to *Bob* a value from a message which was originally sent — in this case, by Bob himself — to a different entity (Alice). This motivates the following design principle: in each message, *identify the sender, the recipient or, best, both of them.* Authentication is usually easy and efficient, e.g., by adding an appropriate identifier(s) to the information being authenticated. Another solution may be to use independent pseudorandom keys for sending messages by the two parties.

Authenticate flow number and initiator/responder bit: The attacker sent in the third protocol flow (second message from the initiator), the authenticator received from the second protocol flow (first message from the responder). This motivate us to *authenticate the flow number (e.g., second vs. third) and a bit indicating if authenticator is sent by the initiator or the responder.*

Authenticate using AEAD or MAC: The SNA mutual entity authentication protocol uses a shared key but only for the symmetric key cryptosystem (or block cipher) function E. Encryption provides confidentiality but not authentication. In practically every application, it is be better to use, instead of encryption, an *Authenticated Encryption with Associated Data (AEAD)* scheme (Section 4.5.1). An AEAD scheme has the same shared-key requirement as symmetric key cryptosystem, but it ensures *authentication* in addition to confidentiality. In applications where part of the input should be authenticated but also be left visible to entities that are not trusted with the shared key, this data could be placed in the *associated data* input field of the AEAD. If *all* of the data should be visible yet authenticated, then we could also simply use a MAC scheme to authenticate the data. Note that SNA used a block cipher to implement E; from the PRP/PRF switching lemma (Lemma 2.2), a block cipher is also a PRF, and from Lemma 4.1, every PRF is also a MAC; therefore, the block cipher in SNA authenticates the nonces (N_A and N_B).

No free oracle: The SNA protocol applied the block cipher to inputs — the nonces — received entirely from the network, i.e., fully controlled by a MitM adversary, and sends back the result of applying the block cipher to this input. This provides the adversary with a 'free oracle' to the cryptographic function — in this case, the ability to receive the result of applying $E_k(\cdot)$ to input selected by the adversary. Such 'oracle' capability can often be abused by the attacker. A simple defense to avoid providing a 'free oracle' is to include some random input(s) before applying the cryptographic function, in addition to the adversary-provided inputs. This defense works in many scenarios, including mutual entity authentication protocols.

Adopting these design principles (or even just some of them) would foil the attack of Figure 5.5. The 2PP protocol, described in the following, is essentially the result of applying these principle to address the vulnerabilities of the SNA protocol.

5.2.4 The 2PP mutual entity authentication protocol

In this section, we present 2PP, a secure two party shared-key mutual entity authentication protocol. The name 2PP simply stands for *two party protocol*. The 2PP protocol, presented in Ref. [76], was a replacement to the insecure SNA mutual entity authentication protocol.

The flows of the 2PP mutual entity authentication protocol are presented in Figure 5.6. As in the SNA mutual entity authentication protocol, the values N_A and N_B are n-bit nonces, where n is the security parameter — typically, the length of the shared key k. The nonces N_A, N_B are selected randomly, by Alice (initiator) and Bob (responder), respectively.

The protocol, at both parties, outputs *Accept*(i) once it authenticates correctly the last flow from the peer for handshake i (second flow for the initiator, third flow for the responder). By validating this last flow, 2PP ensures mutual authentication.

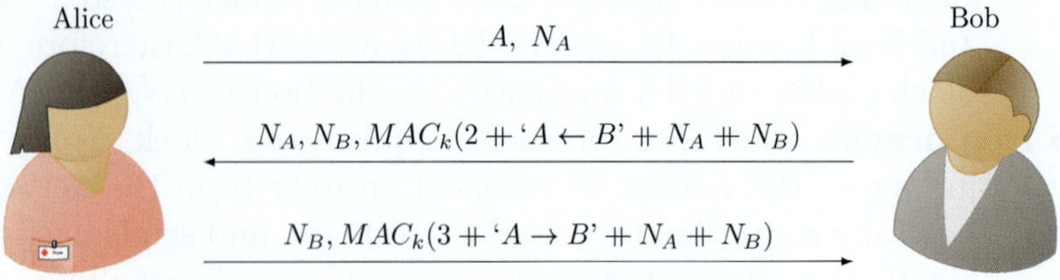

Figure 5.6. The 2PP mutual entity authentication protocol.

We will not *prove* the security of 2PP, but let us give an intuitive argument as to why it ensures mutual authentication, i.e., authentication of both responder and initiator. Note that the security of 2PP requires the MAC scheme to be secure and requires that the key k and the nonces are 'sufficiently long', i.e., at least as long as the security parameter 1^n.

Security of 2PP — responder authentication: Consider an execution in which the initiator (Alice in Figure 5.6) 'accepts', although Bob is not responding. In 2PP, Alice 'accepts' (only) upon receiving $\alpha \equiv \text{MAC}_k(2 + \text{'}A \leftarrow B\text{'} + N_A + N_B)$. Furthermore, a party computes the MAC over a message beginning with 2 only when sending a response, and according to the identifiers, Alice would never send α. If Bob sent α after Alice began this handshake, then responder authentication holds. If Bob computed α *before* Alice began this handshake, then Alice randomly selected the same N_A as previously received by Bob, which would occur with negligible probability, since N_A and N_B are random n-bits long strings.

There remains the possibility that Bob also did not compute α. In this case, the adversary somehow found α 'on its own', i.e., neither Alice nor Bob computed α. Such an adversary can produce a valid MAC on a message that was never MAC-ed by an 'oracle' knowing the MAC key; this contradicts the assumption that the MAC scheme used is secure, i.e., in the complete proof, this allows us to construct an adversary that forges a valid MAC authenticator. We conclude that 2PP ensures responder authentication.

Security of 2PP — sender authentication: The argument for sender authentication is very similar; we leave it to the reader to work it out.

5.3 Authenticated request-response (RR) protocols

Authenticated request-response protocols extend mutual authentication protocols such as 2PP: not only do they authenticate the *entities*, but they also further authenticate the exchange of a *request* and corresponding *response* messages between the two parties. More precisely, they ensure the following properties:

Request authentication: Every request received by a party was sent by its peer.

Response authentication: Every response received by a party, was sent by its peer, in response to a request sent by the party.

No Replay: Every request-response is received by a party, at most the number of times it was sent by the peer.

Let us first describe the interactions of authenticated request-response protocols, over the different interfaces (APP, NET and SYS). These are illustrated in Figure 5.7. Note that the interactions on the NET and SYS interfaces are exactly the same as in Figures 5.1 and 5.3. It only remains to explain the interactions on the APP interface, which are as follows:

send-req(r, i)**:** The application instructs the protocol to send request r to the peer, using the identifier i to identify the response (if and when it arrives). The identifier should be unique, i.e., different from previous identifiers used by the application in *send-req*(r, i) interactions. Unique identifiers can be implemented using a counter, e.g., a sequential number of this *send-req* interaction in this entity, or using randomness (avoiding the need to maintain state for the counter).

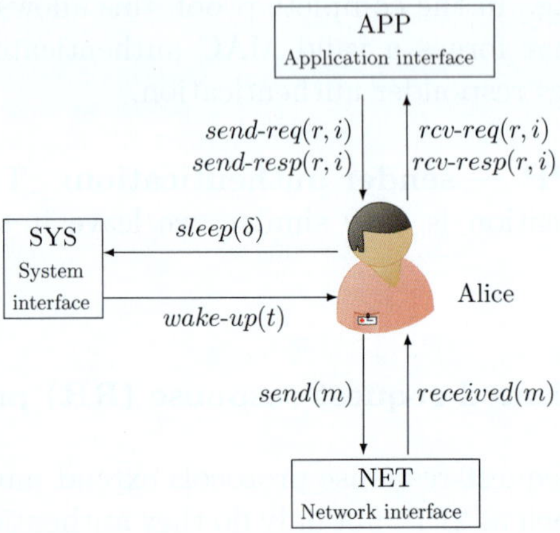

Figure 5.7. Interactions for authenticated request-response protocols, illustrated for Alice; Bob has the same interfaces. Each party may send either a request or a response (to a previously received request).

rcv-req(r, i)**:** The protocol delivers an incoming request r from the peer, specifying identifier i to be used by the application if and when it provides the corresponding response. The identifier i should be unique, i.e., different from previous identifiers used by the protocol in *rcv-req*(r, i) events. Note that this identifier does not have to be related to the identifiers used in *send-req*(r, i) interactions.

send-resp(r, i)**:** The application instructs the protocol to send to the peer a response, r. The response r is to a previously received request, which was identified by i; a *send-resp*(r, i) may occur only if a *rcv-req*(r', i) occurred earlier. The previous *rcv-req*(r', i) must have the same identifier i, but the request r' is usually different from the response, i.e., usually, $r' \neq r$.

rcv-resp(r, i)**:** The protocol delivers a response r from the peer, specifying identifier i; this must be the same identifier as in a previous *send-req*(r', i) interaction in this entity. Note that the value r of the response is typically different from the value r' of the corresponding request.

5.3.1 Overview of request-response (RR) protocols

We discuss four authenticated request-response (RR) protocols:

2PP-RR: This protocol extends 2PP by also authenticating a request message from the responder (e.g., Bob) and the corresponding response message from the initiator (e.g., Alice). Note the 'reverse' role of the parties: the 'initiator' is the party sending the response, while the 'responder' is the party sending the request. This is a bit confusing, and, more significantly, it implied that the responding party must periodically initiate the protocol to check if the other party has a query. Furthermore, a party wishing to make a querty must wait for the next check message from the peer, which may add considerable delay.

2RT-RR: This request-response protocol is initiated by the party making the request (like 2PP). However, the protocol requires *two round-trips* (hence the name, 2RT-RR).

Counter-based-RR: This protocol authenticates a session rather than just request-response and requires only one flow per each message. However, it requires both entities to maintain persistent state (counter).

Time-based-RR: This protocol requires the two parties to have *synchronized clocks*. It then uses the time within the request, allowing it to authenticates a request message and the corresponding response message, using only the minimal two flows: one for the request and one for the response. The protocol can handle (bounded) latency and clock drift, but this requires the responder to maintain a persistent state for the sum of the maximal latency and the maximal clock drift.

We compare these four types of authenticated request-response protocols in Table 5.1. We note that one of the most important differences among these protocols is the number of flows, which implies the number of *Round Trip Times* required by the protocol. This number of Round Trip Times is an important consideration in many practical scenarios; let us explain why.

Overall delay is dominated by the number of round-trips: The number of round-trips is one of the most important attributes of request-response protocols and is usually the dominant factor impacting the overall delay. As shown in Table 5.1, the Time-based-RR and the counter-based-RR require a single round trip (two flows) to receive the response; in contrast, the 2RT-2PP-RR requires two round trips. The 2PP-RR is an exception, as it requires 'role reversal': the protocol is initiated by the entity producing the response,

Table 5.1. Authenticated request-response (RR) protocols. The counter-based and time-based RR protocols require only one round trip (two flows), and the counter-based protocol does not ensure freshness. The 2PP-RR protocol requires periodic check messages from the responder, resulting in additional delay and possibly additional flows (for periodic checks not needed for a query).

Protocol	Figure	Section	Flows	Requirements/Drawbacks
2PP-RR	5.8	5.3.2	≥ 3	Periodical check.
2RT-2PP-RR	5.9	5.3.3	4	Two round-trips.
Counter-based-RR	5.10	5.3.4	2	Synchronized state; no freshness.
Time-based-RR	5.11	5.3.5	2	Synchronization.

but how would this entity know when to initiate the protocol? This seems to require this entity to initiate the protocol periodically (synchronously), which makes it inappropriate to many applications, where the request should be sent asynchronously, as needed, rather than periodically. It would also result in delay, since the requester has to wait for the periodical check message to arrive, and in additional flows (communication), for periodic check messages not used for a request.

The reason for focusing on the number of round trips is that in many applications and scenarios, *the number of round trips is the dominant factor impacting overall delay.* This is since often, the *Round Trip Time* (RTT) is the largest factor contributing to the delay. To emphasize this, let us state it as Fact 5.1 and briefly explain it.

Fact 5.1 (Round trip time (RTT) values are dominant). *Typical Round Trip Times, i.e., the delay (latency) from sending a short packet over the Internet and until receiving a response, can be quite significant and is usually the dominant element of the overall delay/latency. For example, Ref. [361] reports RTT values which are* mostly *below 200 ms. However, in some scenarios, e.g., under* bandwidth Denial of Service *(BW-DoS) attack, it can be it can be as high as one second and even more. In particular, when using geostationary satellite communication, typical delay is around 500 ms. These values are independent of the bandwidth, i.e., hold also when using high bandwidth connections (fast transmission rates). While network bandwidth has dramatically increased over the years, the Round Trip Time values did not reduce that much.*

To illustrate the importance of minimizing round-trips, Table 5.2 compares the overall delays in typical request-response scenarios when using protocols requiring one vs. two round trips, and when using lower bandwidth of 1 MB/s vs. higher bandwidth of 100 MB/s. Clearly, the transmission time is negligible compared to the Round Trip Time; the delay is dominated by the number of round trips and the Round Trip Time.

Indeed, TLS 1.3, the updated version of the TLS protocol, has a significantly modified design which allows it to minimize the number of round trips and therefore of the Round Trip Times; see Section 7.6.

Table 5.2. Comparing the delay of different request-response (RR) protocols, using different bandwidth. The comparison assumes the typical Round Trip Time (RTT) of 100 ms, and a typical response size of 50 KByte.

Round trips	Protocol(s)	Bandwidth	Delay
1	Time-based RR	1 MB/s (8 Mb/s)	150 ms
1	Time-based RR	100 MB/s (800 Mb/s)	100.5 ms
2	2RT-2PP-RR	1 MB/s (8 Mb/s)	250 ms
2	2RT-2PP-RR	100 MB/s (800 Mb/s)	200.5 ms

Note that Fact 5.1 may be a bit obscured in most of the sequence diagrams in this text since, for simplicity, compactness and clarity, we use horizontal arrows for transmissions, i.e., the diagrams do not indicate the network latency of messages. We also usually do not show other delays. Most sequence diagrams in the literature use the same style.

5.3.2 The 2PP-RR authenticated request-response protocol

We first discuss 2PP-RR, a three flow nonce-based authenticated request-response protocol, which is a minor extension to 2PP. The 2PP-RR protocol is illustrated in Figure 5.8. In fact, the only change compared to the 2PP protocol (Figure 5.6) is the addition of the request (req) from responder to initiator and of the response ($resp$) from initiator to responder, to the second and third flows, respectively.

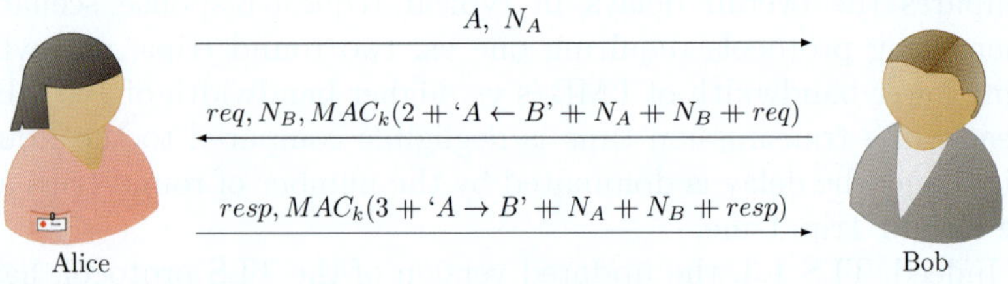

Figure 5.8. The 2PP-RR authenticated request-response protocol: a three flow nonce-based authenticated request-response protocol, based on 2PP.

The 2PP-RR protocol is simple and not too difficult to prove secure, by a reduction to the security of the underlying MAC function. Namely, suppose that we know an efficient algorithm (adversary) $\mathcal{A}$ which shows that 2PP-RR does not meet the definition of a secure authenticated request-response protocol. The reduction shows how, given such attacker algorithm $\mathcal{A}$, we can efficiently compute the value of the MAC function on some input, without knowing the key. This contradicts the assumption that we use a secure MAC. Namely, if we use a secure MAC, then 2PP-RR is secure.

The 2PP-RR protocol has, however, a significant drawback, which makes it ill-suited for many applications. Specifically, in this protocol, the request is sent by the *responder*, and the initiator sends the response. In most applications, it makes sense for a party to initiate the protocol when it needs to make some request rather than to wait for the initiator to contact it and only then, as a responder, send the response. Waiting for the periodical message from the responder, as in 2PP-RR, also involves delay and overhead and requires the requesting party to maintain state (see Table 5.1).

The next protocol, 2RT-2PP-RR, is a different adaptation of 2PP which avoids this drawback — but requires four flows, i.e., two full round-trips.

5.3.3 2RT-2PP-RR authenticated request-response protocol

In Figure 5.9, we present 2RT-2PP-RR, another authenticated request-response protocol based on 2PP. As the name implies, the 2RT-2PP-RR protocol requires *four flows*, i.e., *two round-trips*; this is a significant drawback. However, 2RT-2PP-RR improves upon 2PP-RR in that it authenticates a request from the initiator and the corresponding response to it from the responder.

The 2RT-2PP-RR protocol involves two simple extensions of the basic 2PP protocol. The first extension is the transmission and authentication of the request and response, similarly to their addition in 2PP-RR. The second extension is an additional (fourth) flow, from the responder back to the initiator, which carries the response of the responder to the request from the initiator. In a sense, the 2RT-2PP-RR protocol 'splits' the contents of the second flow of the 2PP-RR. In 2RT-2PP, these contents are split between the second

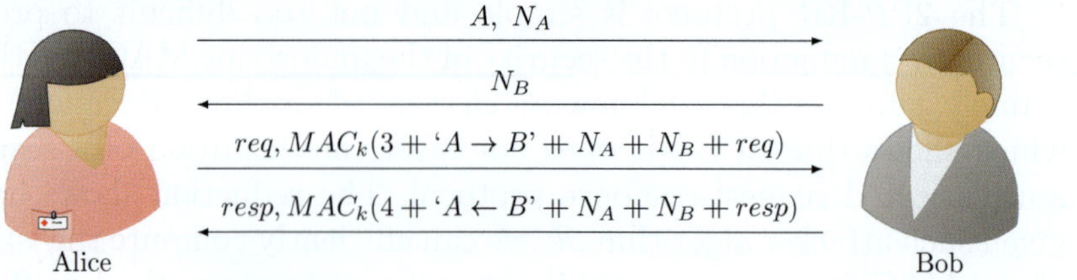

Figure 5.9. 2RT-2PP-RR: a two-round-trips authenticated request-response protocol.

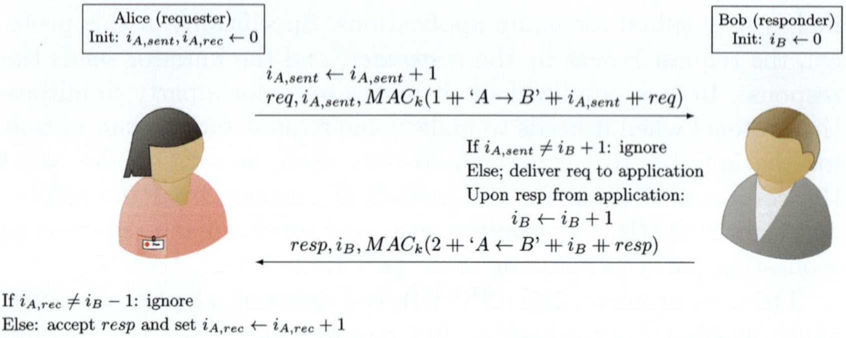

Figure 5.10. The counter-based RR authenticated request-response protocol.

flow (providing the nonce N_B) and the fourth flow (providing the authenticated response).

5.3.4 The counter-based RR authenticated request-response protocol

In Figure 5.10, we present the *counter-based authenticated request-response (RR) protocol.* This protocol requires only *one round-trip* — sending the (authenticated) request and receiving the (authenticated) response. However, to prevent replay of previously sent requests, in only one round-trip, this protocol requires *both parties to maintain a synchronized counters*, i.e., synchronized state.

The counter-based RR protocol includes a counter in the authenticated request and response. The requester, e.g., Alice (A), maintains two counters, both initialized to zero: $i_{A,sent}$, counting the requests it sent, and $i_{A,rec}$, counting the valid responses it received. The responder, e.g., Bob (B), maintains just one counter, i_B, which counts the valid requests it has received so far. All three counters are initialized to zero.

The protocol maintains these counters synchronized. Namely, if requests and responses are delivered in the order sent and without duplications or omissions, then the received counter values will match the values expected by the recipient.

The counter allows both parties to prevent replay or reordering of the request/response. In particular, the responder validates that the request is not a *replay* of a request already received in the past. The protocol allows multiple concurrent requests, each with a separate counter; the incrementing counter values would prevent *reordering*, i.e., if requests 2, 3 and 4 are sent concurrently, an attacker cannot provide request 4 before requests 2 or 3. The protocol similarly prevents replay and reordering of responses. The design could be slightly simplified if there is no need to support concurrent transmission of requests.

The protocol does not provide retransmissions or any other mechanisms to handle message losses or corruptions; with the current design, any such loss or corruption is likely to prevent any further query or response. This is reasonable in the common case where the protocol is run on top of a reliable transport mechanism, such as the TCP protocol, which ensures that packets are received in the order sent, without duplications or omissions, unless manipulated by a MitM attacker; and, indeed, the same assumption is done by the TLS record protocol (Chapter 7). However, it is not difficult to modify the protocol, so it would could be used over an unreliable transport, such as over the IP or UDP protocols; this is done by the secure record/session protocols of IPsec [158, 189] and DTLS [417].

Exercise 5.1. Extend the counter-based RR protocol of Figure 5.10, to allow it to run over an unreliable transport protocol, where some packets may arrive out of order or be corrupted in transit.

5.3.5 Time-based RR authenticated request-response protocol

Figure 5.11 presents another alternative single-round authenticated request-response protocol; this variant allows the Initiator

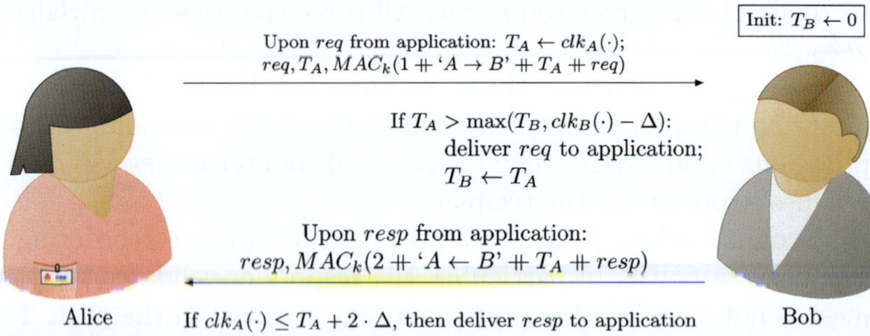

Figure 5.11. Time-based authenticated request-response protocol, using a bound Δ on the maximal delay plus maximal clock bias. We use $clk_A(\cdot)$ to denote the time according to the local clock of Alice upon sending *req*, and $clk_B(\cdot)$ for Bob's clock upon receiving *req*. Alice sets $T_A \leftarrow clk_A(\cdot)$ when she sends the request and authenticates it with the request. Bob uses T_A to validate that the request is *fresh*, using the bound Δ, and ensuring T_A is larger than previously received T_A values.

(e.g., Alice) to be stateless and also limits the time that the responder (e.g., Bob) must keep state.

The time-based RR protocol, such as the 2PP-RR and 2RT-2PP-RR protocols, allows the responder to ensure *freshness* of the request, i.e., discard requests which arrive 'too late', i.e., an unreasonable amount of time after they were sent. Note that freshness is *not* ensured by the counter-based RR protocol of Figure 5.10.

Instead of relying on counters maintained, in synchronized way, by the two parties, the protocol of Figure 5.11 relies on the use of *time* and on two *synchronization assumptions*, specifically, *bounded delay* and *bounded clock skew*. The protocol also requires, however, the responder to maintain state in a limited way.

Bounded delay assumption: Let $\Delta_{\text{delay}} \geq 0$ denote a bound on the *maximal delay*. Namely, if one party sends a message at time t, then this message is received by the destination at $t + \Delta_{\text{delay}}$ or earlier.

Bounded clock skew: Let $\Delta_{\text{skew}} \geq 0$ denote a bound on the *maximal clock skew*, i.e., the maximal difference between the values of the clocks of two entities at any given time. Let $clk_A(t)$ ($clk_B(t)$) denote the value of the clock at Alice (respectively, Bob) at time t;

then we have

$$clk_A(t) - \Delta_{\text{skew}} \leq clk_B(t) \leq clk_A(t) + \Delta_{\text{skew}} \tag{5.1}$$

The protocol is illustrated in Figure 5.11, with Alice sending the request and Bob responding. For simplicity, we use a combined bound: $\Delta \equiv \Delta_{\text{skew}} + \Delta_{\text{delay}}$, and the notation $clk_A(\cdot)$, $clk_B(\cdot)$ for the value of clk_A (respectively, clk_B) at the time Alice sends (Bob receives) the req message. Note also that we use T_A to denote the *timestamp* which Alice includes with the request and which Bob copies to his response.

The protocol at Bob confirms the received request req is valid, as follows:

No modification: Compare the received MAC value to the MAC computed with the correct inputs.

req **is a request from Alice to Bob:** The fact that the input to the MAC begins with $1 + 'A \rightarrow B'$ ensures this is a request (first flow) from Alice to Bob.

Freshness (acceptable delay): Bob validates that the timestamp T_A received within the request req is within Δ from his own clock $clk_B(\cdot)$ at the time the request req is received.

No replay: Bob validates that the received value of T_A is larger than the largest previously received value of T_A.

When Alice receives the response $resp$, she similarly confirms it is valid, as follows:

No modification: Alice compares the received MAC value to the MAC computed with the correct inputs.

$resp$ **is a response from Bob to Alice:** The fact that the input to the MAC begins with $2 + 'A \leftarrow B'$ ensures this is a response (second flow) from Bob to Alice.

$resp$ **is a response to request** req **and not a replay:** The value of the timestamp T_A included with the request (and echoed in the response) increments whenever Alice sends a new request, and therefore Alice sent only one request with this value of T_A. Furthermore, this cannot be a replay of previous response from Bob since no previous response would use this T_A.

Freshness (acceptable delay): Alice validates that the response is received within at most $2 \cdot \Delta_{\text{delay}}$ from the time in which the request was sent.

Note that both Alice and Bob may discard their state (the $s_A.T_A$ and $s_B.T_B$ variables) after some time, which the reader may compute.

Exercise 5.2. Modify the protocol to limit the amount of time where Bob must remember the last (largest) value received of T_A received. Explain why the modified protocol retains the security properties of the time-based-RR protocol as presented.

We presented the time-based protocol allowing only one query response at any given time and assuming reliable communication. However, it is not too difficult to extend it to allow multiple concurrent requests and responses, and handle unreliable communication.

Exercise 5.3. Extend the protocol of Figure 5.11, to allow Alice to send up to three concurrent requests to Bob; allow for receiving requests and responses out-of-order. Explain why the modified protocol is secure.

5.4 Shared-key key exchange protocols

Not all communication follows the request-response pattern, and even when it does, many times we may prefer to secure the communication using a *session/record protocol*, which secures arbitrary interactions, using a shared key, such as the simplified protocol in Section 5.1.2, or the TLS record protocol in Chapter 7.

In principle, the parties could simply use the same shared secret keys for all sessions between them. However, following Principle 4, it is desirable to limit the use of the secret keys used in each session, which we refer to as *session keys*.

In this section, we discuss shared-key key exchange protocols for two parties, which use a fixed shared *master key* to establish a *session key* for each session between the two parties. In Chapter 7, we study the widely used SSL and TLS protocols, which use public-key cryptography to establish a shared master key and also use shared-key key exchange to derive session keys from the master key.

Shared-key key exchange protocols are an extension to mutual entity authentication protocols, with the same functions, inputs and outputs, except for also outputting a session key k_i^S. This key is provided to the session/record protocol running in the peers.

A shared-key key exchange protocol should ensure a separate *session key* k_i^S for each session i so that exposure of one session key will not expose other session keys. The use of a separate session key k_i^S for each session, securely derived from the master key k, has multiple security benefits:

1. By changing the session keys periodically, we reduce the number of ciphertext messages encrypted using the same key, which may be available to the cryptanalyst. This usually makes cryptanalysis harder, and possibly infeasible, compared to the use of a fixed key to encrypt all messages, which would have allowed the adversary to collect plenty of ciphertext messages.
2. Periodically changing the session key reduces the damage from each session key exposure event, and the expected value to the attacker, and hence the incentive to expose a key. This consideration is relevant both for key exposure via cryptanalysis and to key exposure by other means, such as hacking. Note that this benefit requires that each of the session keys remains secret (pseudo-random) even if other session keys are exposed; in particular, this benefit depends on the master key remaining secret, which motivates using extra defenses against exposure of the master key. One way to achieve this is when the master key is kept offline, or confined to a separate *Hardware Security Module (HSM)*, protecting it even when the computer storage — except the internal storage of the HSM — is exposed.
3. Finally, most session/record protocols, including the one in Section 5.1.2 and the TLS record protocol in Chapter 7, rely on persistent counters kept by the peers. By changing the session keys, each session can use independent counters, removing the need to maintain persistent, synchronized counters for multiple sessions.

We say that a two-party shared-key key exchange protocol *ensures secure key-setup* if it ensures the following two requirements:

Key agreement: If both parties complete successfully, then they *both output the same shared key* k_i^S.

Key secrecy: Each session key k_i^S is secret, or more precisely, pseudo-random, i.e., indistinguishable from a random string of same length, even if the adversary is given all the other session keys. This implies that the master key k must remain secret, even if multiple (or all) session keys $\{k_i^S\}$ are exposed by the adversary.

5.4.1 The 2PP key exchange protocol

Our first key exchange protocol is a simple extension to the 2PP protocol, which suffices to ensure secure key-setup using a master key k^M. This can be achieved by outputting the session key k_i^S as

$$k_i^S = PRF_{k^M}(N_{A,i} + N_{B,i}) \tag{5.2}$$

In Equation (5.2), $N_{A,i}$ and $N_{B,i}$ are the nonces exchanged in the ith session of the protocol, and k_i^S is the derived ith session key. We use k^M to denote the master (long-term) shared secret key, provided to both parties during initialization. The protocol is illustrated in Figure 5.12.

Since both parties compute the session key k_i^S in the same way from $N_{A,i} + N_{B,i}$ and the master key k_i^M, it follows that they will receive the same key, i.e., the key exchange 2PP extension ensures key agreement. Since the session keys are computed using a pseudo-random function, $k_i^S = PRF_{k^M}(N_{A,i} + N_{B,i})$, it follows that the key of each session is pseudo-random, even given all other session keys. Namely, *the key exchange 2PP extension ensures secure key setup.*

Note that there is another, seemingly unrelated change between the mutual entity authentication 2PP (Figure 5.6) and the key exchange 2PP (Figure 5.12) protocols, namely, the use of PRF instead of MAC to authenticate the messages in the protocol. This

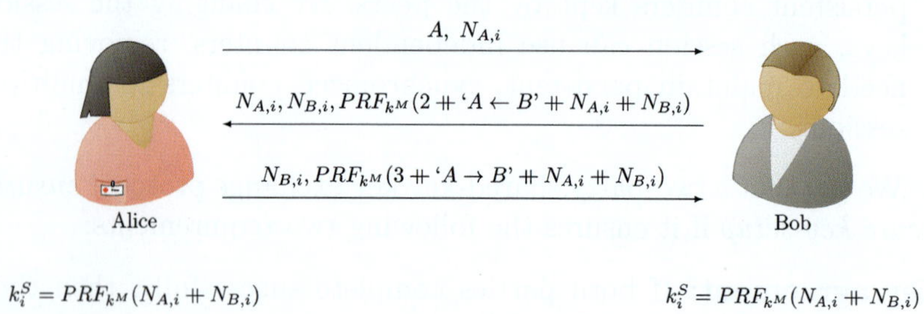

Figure 5.12. The 2PP key exchange protocol, shown generating ith session key, k_i^S, from the master key k^M.

change is needed to avoid using the same key in two different cryptographic schemes (MAC and PRF), which could, at least in some 'absurd' scenarios, be insecure (see Section 4.5.4). The change is also allowed since every PRF is also a MAC (Lemma 4.1).

5.4.2 Deriving per-goal keys

Following the *key separation principle* (Principle 7), session protocols often use two separate keyed cryptographic functions, one for encryption and one for authentication (MAC); the key used for each of the two goals should be pseudo-random, even given the key to the other goal. We refer to such keys as *per-goal keys.*

To further improve the security of the session/record protocol, we may use *two separate pairs of per-goal keys*, depending on the direction: one pair $(k_{E,i}^{A\to B}, k_{A,i}^{A\to B})$ for (encryption, authentication) of messages from Alice to Bob and another pair $(k_{E,i}^{B\to A}, k_{A,i}^{B\to A})$ for (encryption, authentication) of messages from Bob to Alice.

Exercise 5.4. 1. Show how to securely derive the four per-goal keys $(k_{E,i}^{A\to B}, k_{A,i}^{A\to B}, k_{E,i}^{B\to A}$ and $k_{A,i}^{B\to A})$ from the same session key k_i^S.
2. Show a (small) modification of the key exchange 2PP extension, which securely derives all four per-goal session keys 'directly' from the master key k^M, rather than by deriving them from k_i^S.

Hint: See Section 4.5.4. □

5.5 Key Distribution Center (KDC) protocols

In this section, we expand beyond our focus on two party protocols and discuss *three-party* protocols. Specifically, we study protocols for establishing a shared secret key between two parties, Alice and Bob, with the help of a *Trusted Third Party* (TTP), often referred to as the *Key Distribution Center* (KDC). The use of the term KDC is so common that these protocols are often referred to as KDC protocols.

There are different types of KDC protocols. We present two important and very different protocols, both simplified versions of practical protocols. In Section 5.5.1, we discuss the *Kerberos* protocol [380], which is the most widely known and widely used KDC protocol for computer networks. In Sections 5.5.2–5.5.5, we discuss the GSM protocol [31, 249], used to establish secure communication between a mobile device and the cellular network it visits (the *visited network*). GSM is the first widely deployed cellular communication protocol, still supported by most mobile devices and networks.

The Kerberos and GSM protocols are very different. They even differ in their assumptions. In Kerberos, a single KDC shares a key with each of two parties: k_A with Alice and k_B with Bob. In GSM, each mobile shares a secret key only with its home network, which provides the session key to the visited network.

Another important difference is that the Kerberos protocol is secure, while the GSM protocol is *notoriously insecure*. We study some of the vulnerabilities of the GSM protocol, using them as examples to introduce important attack techniques. These GSM vulnerabilities have been exploited in practice; in fact, there are even *products* that use these and other vulnerabilities to attack GSM, and extensions of the attacks (and products) for some of the more modern cellular communication protocols.

5.5.1 The Kerberos key distribution protocol

Kerberos [380] is a widely deployed shared-key system for authorization and authentication, used by Windows and other distributed systems.

Kerberos is mainly designed and used for systems using the *client–server model*, where communication is typically in the form of *request-response*, where a client sends a request to a server and receives a response, without requiring the server to maintain state for a longer interaction with the client, as in a session. The client–server model makes it easier to provide a unified service using multiple servers, e.g., for load balancing, since there is no need to coordinate the state of the client's session across the different servers or to ensure that the same server communicates with the client throughout the session.

In this section, we present a simplified version of the Kerberos [380] Key Distribution Center protocol. The use of the client–server model has some impact on the design of the Key Distribution Center protocol of Kerberos since the server should only respond to the client, namely, the server cannot directly interact with the KDC. Note that servers may maintain long-term state for client; in particular, in Kerberos, the KDC itself is a server, yet it shares a long term (master) key with each party, e.g., key k_A for Alice (which we use as the client), as key k_B for the Bob (which we use as the server).

Using the long-term keys, k_A for Alice (the client) and k_B for the server (Bob), the KDC establishes a shared symmetric key k_{AB} between Alice and Bob. For simplicity, we describe the protocol assuming that each party has *two* long-term keys shared with the KDC, one for encryption and one for authentication (MAC): k_A^E and k_A^{MAC} shared with Alice and k_B^E and k_B^{MAC} shared with Bob. The (simplified) protocol is illustrated in Figure 5.13; let us explain the details.

The Kerberos KDC protocol consists, essentially, of two key exchanges: first between the client (Alice) and the KDC, and then between Alice and the server (Bob). Both exchanges resemble

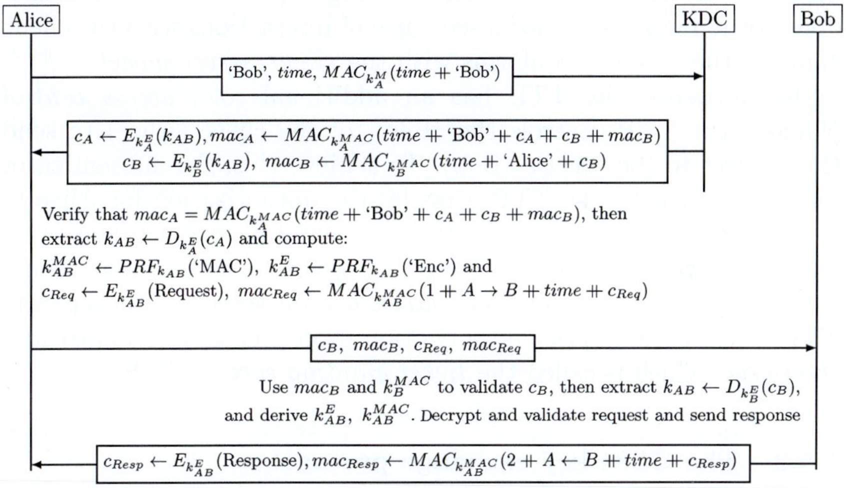

Figure 5.13. The Kerberos Key Distribution Center protocol (simplified). As a simplification, we present the protocol as if the KDC shares with each party two master keys, one for encryption and one for authentication (MAC): k_A^E and k_A^{MAC} shared with Alice and k_B^E and k_B^{MAC} shared with Bob. The KDC selects a shared session key k_{AB} to be used by Alice and Bob for one or multiple request-response interactions. Alice and Bob use k_{AB} and a pseudorandom function PRF to derive two shared keys, $k_{AB}^E = PRF_{k_{AB}}(\text{'Enc'})$ (for encryption) and $k_{AB}^{MAC} = PRF_{k_{AB}}(\text{'MAC'})$ (for authentication, i.e., MAC). All parties validate contents of MAC fields before decrypting authenticated ciphertexts.

the exchange of the time-based authenticated request-response (Figure 5.11).

The first exchange is between Alice (the client) and the KDC. In this exchange, the KDC sends to Alice the key k_{AB} that will be shared between Alice and Bob, encrypted (c_A) and authenticated (mac_A). In addition, Alice receives the pair c_B and mac_B, which also provide encryption and authentication of k_{AB}, but this time, using the keys shared between the KDC and Bob. Alice would next relay c_B and mac_B to Bob. Note that the authenticator mac_A that the KDC sends to Alice also authenticates the pair of c_B and mac_B.

In the second exchange, Alice sends her request to Bob, encrypted and authenticated using k_{AB}. Alice also sends the pair c_B and mac_B, which Bob uses to securely retrieve k_{AB}. Alice and Bob both derive, from k_{AB}, the shared encryption and authentication (MAC) keys k^E_{AB} and k^{MAC}_{AB}, respectively.

Note that in the above protocol, the KDC never initiates communication, but only *responds* to an incoming request, and, in particular, does not maintain state for a sequence of interactions with the client. Namely, the protocol conforms with the *client–server model*.

In Kerberos, the TTP has an additional role: *access control*. Namely, the TTP controls the ability of the client (Alice) to send the request to the service (Bob). To achieve this, the authenticator mac_B provided by the TTP provides the authorization for Alice to send the request; Kerberos uses the term *ticket* for such authenticator. Kerberos separates between the KDC, which provides the authentication and is referred to as the *authentication server*, and a separate TTP which performs the authorization (access control) and provides the ticket, which is called the *ticket granting server* (TGS).

5.5.2 The GSM key exchange protocol

We next discuss the *GSM key exchange protocol*, an important-yet-vulnerable shared-key key exchange protocol. This protocol is performed at the beginning of each connection between a *mobile* device belonging to a user, e.g., cellular phone, and a *visited network* (VN); the protocol involves also the user's *home network*. The mobile is only connected via the visited network, i.e., any communication between the mobile and the home network must be via the visited network.

The GSM protocol is based on a shared master key k_i, shared between the home network and the user's mobile device, which is associated with mobile user identifier i. The identifier, which we denote simply i, is called the *International Mobile Subscriber Identity* (IMSI).

The visited network is not fully trusted by the user and by the home network and, therefore, is not provided with the shared master key k_i, which should remain secret from it. The GSM design assumes secure communication between the visited network and the home network; in particular, information sent by the home network to the visited network is not exposed to any other party. This may be ensured by running the TLS protocol (Chapter 7) or another secure communication protocol between these two parties.

The basic idea of the GSM key exchange protocol is for the home network to provide the visited network with a *triplet* (r, K_c, s) for every session of the mobile, where:

K_c is the *session key*. This key is used by the visited network and the client to encrypt the connection between them.

s **(or** $SRES$**)** is a *secret authenticator/result*; the mobile device authenticates itself to the visited network by sending to it the same value of s, as the visited network received in the triplet (r, K_c, s) from the home network.

r **(or** *Rand***)** is a *random* 128-bits string selected by the home network and used, together with the client's key k_i, as input to an algorithm called $A38$,[4] to compute the pair $(K_c, s) \leftarrow A38(k_i, r)$. The home network operator is free to select the $A38$ algorithm; the GSM specifications only specify that $A38$ should be a one-way function. Since (K_c, s) are derived from k_i and r, it suffices for the visited network to send to the mobile device only r, and the mobile can compute the same values (K_c, s) which were computed by the home network and sent to the visited network.

[4]Actually, the GSM specifications define two separate functions, $A3$ and $A8$, to compute each parameter: $s \leftarrow A3(k_i, r)$, $K_c \leftarrow A8(k_i, r)$. But since they are always computed together and are expected to have similar cryptographic properties, they are usually considered and implemented by a single algorithm, which we denote $A38$; you may also see it denoted $A3A8$.

The GSM key exchange protocol, and two messages m_1, m_2 illustrating how GSM protects data transfer with the session key K_c, are illustrated in Figure 5.14. The design uses two 'cryptographic functions', $A38$, introduced above, and $A5$. In the specifications, $A38$ is described as a *one-way function* (OWF), and $A5$ is referred to as *encryption*; however, from their use in the protocol, both functions should really be *pseudorandom functions* (PRFs). The standard

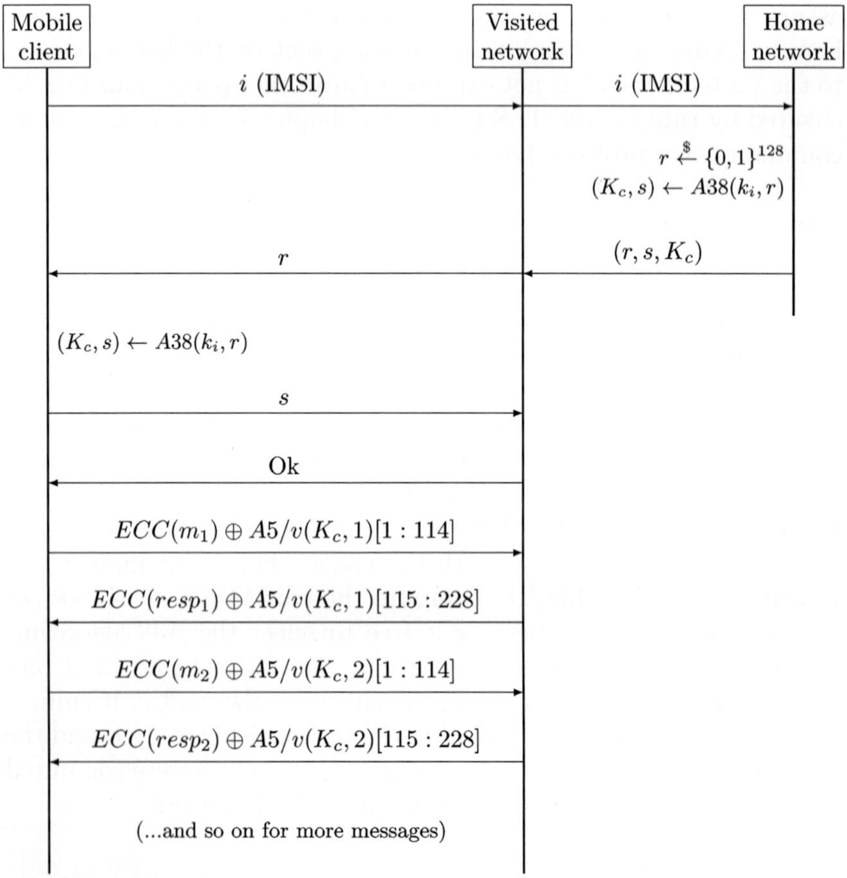

Figure 5.14. The GSM key exchange protocol; the standard defines 'cryptographic functions' $A38$ (defined in the specifications as a OWF, but actually used as a PRF) and $A5$ (referred in the specifications as encryption, but actually also used as a PRF). The standard defines three variants of $A5$ denoted $A5/v$ for $v \in \{0,1,2,3\}$, where $A5/0$ denotes no encryption. The GSM standard also specifies the *error correction code* function $ECC(\cdot)$.

defines three variants of $A5$, denoted $A5/v$ for $v \in \{1, 2, 3\}$, and uses $A5/0$ to denote no encryption.

The GSM specification allows some flexibility as to the specific functions. In fact, the operator of the home network is free to select the $A38$ function. A common choice is an algorithm called COMP128 which was defined by the GSM consortium and shared under non-disclosure agreement.

The $A5/i$ 'encryption' functions, however, must be supported by both mobile and the visited network. The GSM specifications included two implementations of $A5$, denoted $A5/1$ and $A5/2$; the $A5/2$ algorithm is an intentionally weaker variant of $A5/1$, included to allow export of GSM system for network operators in countries to which it was, at the time, not allowed to export 'strong security' encryption products. Similarly to COMP128, both $A5/1$ and $A5/2$ were shared under non-disclosure agreement, i.e., were supposed to be kept 'secret', for security by obscurity; however, it did not take long until they were disclosed after reverse-engineering [106]. Later, another option was added — the $A5/3$ algorithm, based on the *KASUMI* block cipher.

As can be seen in the bottom (last) messages of Figure 5.14, the $A5/i$ functions output 228 bits. Half of them, bits 1 to 114, are used to encrypt messages from the mobile client to the visited network; the other half, say from bit 115 to bit 228, is used to encrypt 'responses', i.e., messages from the visited network to the mobile client.

Note that the input to the $A5/i$ functions is always the key K_c and a non-secret number — for simplicity, we show it as a sequential counter.[5] These values should be normally synchronized between mobile client and visited network; the synchronization is due to the underlying communication protocol (TDMA).

Overview of the GSM key exchange: The key exchange begins with the mobile sending its identifier International Mobile Subscriber Identity (*IMSI*) to the visited network; we denote this as simply i. The visited network forwards i to the home network.

The home network uses i to retrieve the key k_i of the mobile client. Then, the home network selects a random 128-bit binary string r

[5]The actual numbers used in GSM are a bit more complex but still non-secret.

and uses k_i and r to compute: $(K_c, s) \leftarrow A38(k_i, r)$, using the $A38$ algorithm. The home network sends the resulting *GSM authentication triplet* (r, s, K_c) to the visited network.

Figure 5.14 also shows an example of two messages m_1, m_2 sent from mobile client to the visited network, and two corresponding 'responses', $resp_1, resp_2$, sent from the visited network to the mobile client. Note that these do not have to be really responses to the messages; the visited network would send in the same way any other message to the mobile client, e.g., from some remote communicating client — we just used 'resp' (for 'response') since it seems a bit clearer, avoiding confusion with messages from the mobile client. Of course, in typical real use, the mobile and the visited network exchange more than two messages and responses.

All the messages, including responses, that are exchanged between the mobile client and the visited network (VN) are encrypted using the connection's key K_c. The encryption uses the $A5$ algorithm chosen by the client, e.g., $A5/1$. More correctly, the messages (and responses) are encrypted by *bitwise-XOR* to the output of the $A5$ function. This implies that the $A5$ algorithms is expected to be a pseudorandom function (PRF), as we explained above.

GSM use of ECC and Encode-then-Encrypt: Before XORing the messages (and responses) with the output of $A5$, the protocol first applies an error correction code (ECC) to the message/response, to allow recovery from bit errors — common in wireless communication. In fact, GSM uses quite strong error correction codes, e.g., with input of 184 (non-encoded) bits and output of 456 (encoded) bits.[6] Note that since every flow applies exclusive-OR to the message/response with only 114 bits from the output of $A5$, this means that every 'real' GSM message, would actually be transmitted using multiple of these 114-bit flows; what we show for the messages and responses in Figure 5.14 is only a simplification.

The use of error-correction *before* encryption may have been designed as a heuristic attempt to provide *authentication as a by-product of encryption*. However, as discussed in Section 4.5.2, this

[6]This is a simplification; in reality, different lengths are used for different types of messages.

approach is *not advisable*. First, it may fail to prevent message modification. Second, it foils the use of authentication and then applying error-detection/correction code, as a way to detect corrupted ciphertext and the abuse of corrupted ciphertext in chosen-ciphertext attacks and to waste recipient computation time (for Denial of Service). Finally, and critically in the case of GSM, the plaintext will have a lot of redundancy due to the ECC, which facilitates ciphertext-only attack. See Ref. [31] for an effective ciphertext-only attack (COA) attacks on GSM encryption using $A5/1$ or $A5/2$ encryption. The attacks exploit the fact that the plaintext has huge redundancy due to the use of ECC before encryption.

Attacks against the GSM key exchange and their feasibility: In the following Sections, we present several attacks against the GSM key exchange protocol: the VN-impersonation replay attack in Section 5.5.3 and few MitM *downgrade attacks* in Section 5.5.5. The downgrade attacks take advantage of the GSM cipher suite negotiation mechanism, which we introduce in Section 5.5.4.

All of these attacks require the attacker to intercept traffic from the mobile and impersonate as a visited network (VN); the MitM downgrade attacks also require the attacker to relay traffic to a benign visited network, i.e., act as a man-in-the-middle between the mobile and the VN.

After these attacks were published (in Ref. [31]), some of the responses argued that building a device that will intercept the traffic from the mobile, and especially a device that will allow MitM between a mobile and a benign VN, is too complex and impractical. However, devices allowing GSM-MitM attacks have been constructed — by academic researchers, students and companies which made such products available.

5.5.3 Vulnerability study: VN-impersonation Replay attack on GSM

In this section, we discuss the *VN-impersonation replay attack* against the GSM key exchange protocol. This attack involves a *fake visited network* (VN), i.e., the attacker is impersonating as a legitimate VN. The attack assumes two significant capabilities for the attacker: First, the attacker needs the ability to *eavesdrop* on an execution of the GSM key exchange between the mobile and a benign VN; second, the attacker should be able to cryptanalyze the ciphertext from that connection, and eventually find the corresponding session key K_c, although this process may require more time than the maximal time allowed for the completion of the GSM key exchange. This assumption is justified for the $A5/1$ and $A5/2$ algorithms since there are reasonably efficient attacks against both of them.

The VN-impersonation attack has three phases, as illustrated in Figure 5.15.

Eavesdrop: In the first phase, the attacker eavesdrops on a legitimate connection between the mobile client and a legitimate visited network (VN). The key exchange between the client and the home network is exactly like in Figure 5.14, except that, for simplicity, Figure 5.15 does not show the home network and the messages exchanged between the visited network and the home network.

Cryptanalysis: In the second phase, the attacker cryptanalyzes the ciphertexts collected during the eavesdrop phase. Assume that the attacker is successful in finding the session key K_c shared between client and visited network; this is reasonable since multiple effective attacks are known on the GSM ciphers $A5/1$ and $A5/2$. Note that the time required for the cryptanalysis may be longer than the maximal time allowed for the handshake; this is Ok since the next phase of the attack is in a new handshake, not as part of the current handshake.

Impersonate: Finally, once cryptanalysis has exposed the session key K_c, the attacker impersonates as a legitimate visited network and *replays the same random challenge* r sent by the legitimate visited network in the eavesdrop phase. Since the connection key K_c is derived in a deterministic way from r, by $(K_c, s) \leftarrow A38(r)$, then the client would reuse the same connection key K_c as in the eavesdropped-to connection — the one exposed by the attacker during the cryptanalysis phase. The attacker now uses K_c to communicate correctly with the client; in particular, this allows the adversary to decrypt any messages $m'_1, \ldots, m'_{n'}$ encrypted and sent by the client in this new connection.

Is the VN-impersonation attack a real threat? The VN-impersonation allows the attacker to impersonate as a

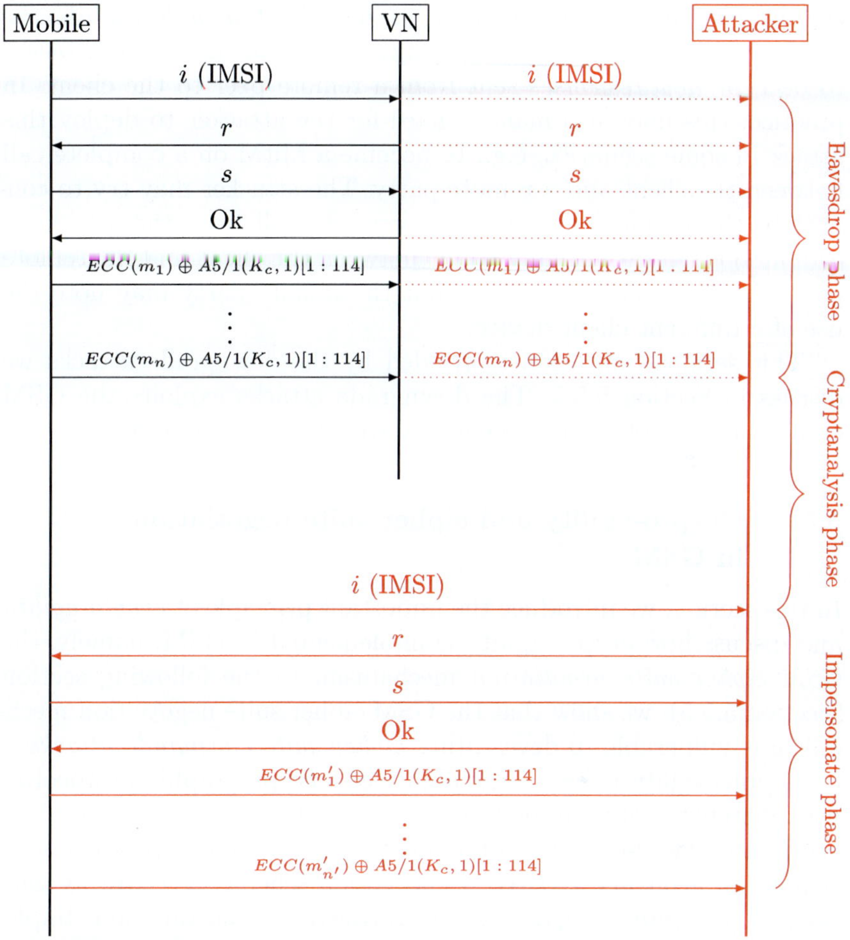

Figure 5.15. The VN-impersonation attack by a MitM attacker on the GSM key exchange, shown when using the $A5/1$ cipher, which can be broken by a chosen-ciphertext attack or known-plaintext attack in reasonable time (but in more time than the maximal allowed handshake time); the attack can also be applied against the $A5/2$ cipher. We omit the key exchange between the visited network and the home network (shown in Figure 5.14) and the cipher-negotiation details (shown in Figure 5.16).

visited network and cause the mobile client to send (new) messages encrypted with the (old) key, which the attacker can now decrypt. The attacker may also respond with fake messages, of course, to continue the dialog. However, this attack has one significant drawback:

the attacker cannot *impersonate as the client to a legitimate visited network*. In particular, the attack does not allow the attacker to decrypt *new responses* sent from a remote peer to the client. In practice, this may also make it hard for the attacker to deploy this attack in some scenarios, e.g., to become a MitM on a complete call between the client and a remote party. The attacker may try to connect to the remote party using a separate call from the attacker's own mobile device, relaying traffic between the client and the remote party via the client's device — but the remote party may note the use of a different client device.

This serious limitation is avoided by the downgrade attacks we discuss in Section 5.5.5. The downgrade attacks exploits the GSM cipher suite negotiation mechanism, which we discuss next.

5.5.4 Crypto-agility and cipher suite negotiation in GSM

In this section, we introduce the important principle of *crypto-agility*, and discuss how crypto-agility is implemented in GSM, namely, the *GSM cipher suite negotiation* mechanism. In the following section (Section 5.5.5), we show that the GSM cipher suite negotiation mechanism is vulnerable to devastating *cipher suite downgrade attacks*.

Crypto-agility refers to the ability of a cryptographic protocol to use different cryptographic functions and schemes, as long as each of them satisfy well-defined requirements. For example, a protocol may require an arbitrary *IND-CPA* encryption scheme, a secure *pseudo-random generator* and/or a collision-resistant hash function. Implementations and standards may limit the choices to a specific set of corresponding functions/schemes, which we refer to as a *cipher suite*. For example, GSM can use an arbitrary stream cipher, and the standard defines three specific stream ciphers to be supported: $A5/1$, $A5/2$ and $A5/3$.

Crypto-agility requires a modular design, where the design of the protocol does not depend on the specific components (cipher suite) used, only on their required security properties. This has several important benefits:

1. Crypto-agility allows replacing a cryptographic scheme/function which is found or suspected to be vulnerable, while continuing to use the same protocol.

2. Crypto-agility allows different users to use the same protocol, but using different schemes, due to different trust assumptions, different efficiency/security tradeoffs and considerations, or other reasons, such as licensing, availability and legal restrictions. In particular, some countries restrict the export of some cryptographic mechanisms; specifically, until about 2000, the USA restricted export of cryptographic systems using symmetric encryption with keys longer than 40 bits, and some restrictions are still enforced.
3. The security of a crypto-agile protocol can be established based on the well-defined requirements from the cipher suite, which makes it easier to design, evaluate, understand and prove security of the protocol, compared to a design which uses specific functions and schemes but without specifying the specific requirements. This is especially relevant for protocols using a crytographic hash function, which may be required to satisfy one of several different requirements.
4. By requiring cryptographic functions and schemes satisfying specific properties, designers are more likely to use a small number of *cryptographic building blocks*, following Principle 8.

Let us restate the need to support crypt-agility as one of the cybersecurity principles.

Principle 11 (Crypto-agility). *Cryptographic protocols should be designed using abstract 'building block' cryptographic functions and schemes, required to satisfy well-defined requirements; the set of functions and schemes is called a* cipher suite. *Protocols should allow* cipher suite negotiation, *i.e., allow the parties to determine the specific cipher suite to be used in a particular run of the protocol among multiple options. Protocols should further support a secure* cipher suite negotiation mechanism *that allows the parties to choose the 'best' cipher suite supported by both (or all) of them.*

Note the requirement that cipher suite negotiation should be done securely. Cipher suite negotiation is secure if the negotiated cipher suite is *never inferior* to another cipher suite that is supported by both/all parties involved in the protocol. In contrast, cipher suite negotiation is *vulnerable* if an attacker — usually, a MitM attacker — can manipulate the parties to use a cipher suite CS_1, which is less secure than some other cipher suite CS_2, although both (or all) parties support and prefer CS_2.

A vulnerable cipher suite negotiation may allow *downgrade attacks*, which allow an attacker to trick the parties into using a vulnerable cipher suite chosen by the attacker. These attacks usually involve a man-in-the-middle (MitM) attacker. In Section 5.5.5, we show downgrade attacks against GSM; later, in Chapter 7, we see downgrade attacks against SSL and TLS. But first, let's discuss the GSM cipher suite negotiation mechanism.

The GSM cipher suite negotiation process: GSM supports *crypto-agility*, in the sense that the protocol is defined for any stream cipher, with two stream ciphers ($A5/1$ and $A5/2$) standardized from the very first version of GSM; additional stream ciphers, e.g., $A5/3$, either proprietary or standard, are also in use. Basically, the choice of the stream cipher is the cipher suite in GSM; other mechanisms are fixed.

GSM has the following simple process for negotiating the stream cipher (cipher suite) to be used: the client sends the list of supported stream ciphers, and the visited network indicates which of them it prefers. This negotiation is essential to allow interoperability between mobiles and visited networks.

All clients are expected to support (at least) the $A5/1$ and $A5/2$ stream ciphers. The cipher suite negotiation mechanism allows mobiles to communicate using $A5/1$ with a visited network that supports $A5/1$, using $A5/2$ with a visited network that only supports the (exportable and weak) $A5/2$ stream cipher, and using another stream cipher, e.g., $A5/3$, if both mobile and visited network support that stream cipher, and the visited network prefers it over $A5/1$ and $A5/2$.

Figure 5.16 presents the GSM key exchange protocol, with details of the cipher suite negotiation process, which were omitted, to avoid clutter, in Figure 5.14.

In the first flow of the key exchange, containing the mobile client's identity (IMSI), the mobile also lists the supported stream ciphers. For example, in Figure 5.16, the mobile supports $A5/1, A5/2$ and $A5/3$. Note that *all mobiles should support the* $A5/1$ *stream cipher*; therefore, the visited network (VN) would abort the connection if $A5/1$ is not included in the list of supported stream ciphers.

The second and third flows of the key exchange do not involve cipher suite negotiation, i.e., are identical in Figures 5.14 and 5.16:

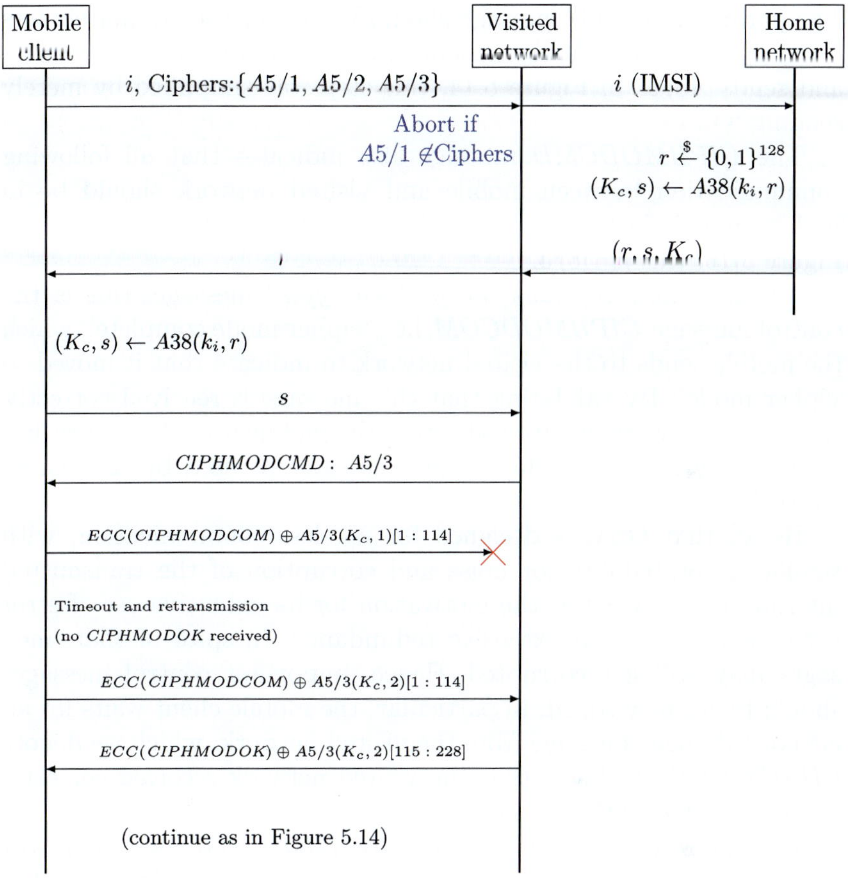

Figure 5.16. The GSM key exchange protocol, including details of cipher suite negotiation, i.e., the *CIPHMODCMD*, *CIPHMODCOM* and *CIPHMODOK* control messages (omitted in Figure 5.14); see details in the text. In the example shown, the mobile supports three stream ciphers, $A5/1$, $A5/2$ and $A5/3$, and the visited network prefers and chooses $A5/3$. The VN aborts if the ciphers offered by the client do not include $A5/1$.

the visited network sends the random challenge r (second flow), and the mobile computes and replies with the authenticator s (third flow).

After the visited network receives the (correct) authenticator s from the mobile, in the third flow, it only remains to complete the cipher suite negotiation and begin the communication. In the fourth flow, the visited network indicates the chosen cipher suite; this is done in the control message *CIPHMODCMD* ('cipher mode command').

The parameter of this message should be one of the stream ciphers listed by the mobile in the first flow; in Figure 5.16, the VN prefers and sends $A5/3$. In Figure 5.14, this step was simplified by merely sending 'Ok'.

The *CIPHMODCMD* message also indicates that all following communication between mobile and visited network should be in 'cipher mode', i.e., encrypted using the chosen stream cipher; in Figure 5.16, this is $A5/3$.

The fifth flow contains *the first encrypted* message; this is the control message *CIPHMODCOM*, i.e., 'cipher mode complete', which the mobile sends to the visited network to indicate that it moved to 'cipher mode'. By validating that this message is received correctly, the visited network confirms also that the mobile uses the correct key K_c and stream cipher ($A5/3$), i.e., the same as used by the visited network.

Recall that GSM is designed for wireless communication, with significant probability for noise and corruption of the transmitted information — which is the motivation for its extensive use of error correction code, with extensive redundancy. In spite of that, messages may still get corrupted. Hence, important control messages should be acknowledged; in particular, the mobile client waits for an acknowledgment message from the visited network, which we denote *CIPHMODOK*, to know that the visited network received correctly the *CIPHMODCOM* message.

If, as shown in Figure 5.16, the *CIPHMODCOM* message is lost in transit, or if the response from the visited network is lost, then the mobile would not receive *CIPHMODOK* in time, i.e., it would *times-out* (after a few milliseconds). In this case, the mobile retransmits the *CIPHMODCOM* to the visited network. In Figure 5.16, we show the case where the first retransmission is successful. As shown, each retransmission uses a distinct sequence number (e.g., numbers 1 and 2 for the first and second transmission of *CIPHMODCOM* in the figure).

The following fact summarizes important properties of the handshake, which are significant for the design of the downgrade attacks.

Fact 5.2 (*CIPHMODCOM* message and its retransmission). *After a mobile receives the CIPHMODCMD ('cipher mode command') control message, instructing the mobile to use a specific* *cipher mode, the mobile encrypts and sends CIPHMODCOM ('cipher mode completed') control message to the VN; this message contains* 456 *bits (including the ECC). The mobile then waits for an acknowledgment — a CIPHMODOK ('cipher mode OK') control message from the VN. If the CIPHMODOK isn't received after time-out of few milliseconds, then the mobile re-transmits the CIPHMODCOM message, with a new counter value.*

A failure may also occur in the reverse direction, i.e., the visited network (VN) may time-out while waiting for the *CIPHMODCOM* ('cipher mode completed') from the client. In this case, the visited network *aborts* the key exchange. Again, this happens after a timeout of few milliseconds. Similarly, a failure may occur also in the earlier phases of the key exchange, i.e., between sending i and receiving r, or between sending r and receiving s. However, GSM allows for much larger delays in these early phases — up to 12 seconds! This fact is also significant.

Fact 5.3 (GSM key exchange allows about 12 **seconds delays till *CIPHMODCMD*).** *The Mobile and the VN abort the key exchange if they do not receive the expected responses, after timeout of about* 12 *seconds; this holds for the messages until the CIPHMODCMD is sent (and received), from which point, responses are expected to be almost instantaneous (few milliseconds). If responses are not accepted after about* 12 *seconds, the key exchange is aborted.*

5.5.5 Downgrade attacks on GSM

The *GSM cipher suite negotiation is not well protected* against downgrade attacks; in this section, we show this by presenting few downgrade attacks by a MitM adversary against GSM. These attacks allow an attacker to manipulate a pair of a GSM mobile and a GSM visited network into using a weak stream cipher, even when both the mobile and the VN support and prefer a stronger cipher.

In Section 5.5.5.1, we present a simple downgrade attack, which manipulates the connection between a mobile and a visited network to use $A5/1$, even if both mobile and visited network support (and prefer) a stronger stream cipher, e.g., $A5/3$.

However, why downgrade to $A5/1$ if you can downgrade to the much weaker $A5/2$? In Section 5.5.5.2, we present a stronger downgrade attack, which allows the attacker to obtain the key and be a MitM to a connection between a mobile and a visited network that both support (and prefer) a strong stream cipher, e.g., $A5/3$ (or $A5/1$), requiring the attacker only to break the weak $A5/2$ cipher, a much easier task. However, as we explain, this attack should still fail in practice, due to some of the restrictions of the GSM key exchange protocol.

Finally, in Section 5.5.5.3, we present an improved version of the attack. This downgrade attack achieves the same goal, and does work in practice, since it circumvents the aforementioned restrictions of GSM.

5.5.5.1 *GSM downgrade attack to A5/1*

GSM visited networks do not downgrade to $A5/2$: A critical property of the GSM negotiation mechanism is that *all clients should support the A5/1 protocol.* Based on this, GSM specifies that *visited networks that support A5/1, as most do, should refuse to use A5/2*, i.e., abort a connection when the $A5/2$ is the only stream cipher supported by the visited network and offered by the mobile. This is an important fact which has significant impact on GSM downgrade attacks; therefore, let us state it again clearly:

Fact 5.4 (GSM visited networks refuse to downgrade to $A5/2$). *A GSM visited network that supports A5/1 will abort a connection if the cipher suites offered by the mobile do not include A5/1.*

The reason for the policy of Fact 5.4 is that the $A5/2$ cipher is known to have been designed intentionally to be vulnerable. Support for a vulnerable cipher (i.e., $A5/2$) was necessary to gain government permission to export GSM equipment. Specifically, the US and several other countries restricted export of GSM network operator equipment supporting strong encryption, allowing unlimited export only of equipment which supports only the (weak, exportable) $A5/2$ stream cipher. These restrictions were relaxed, but not entirely removed, by the early 2000s. Note, however, that *all GSM mobiles* are expected to support the (stronger) $A5/1$ stream cipher, i.e., any GSM mobile is expected to offer $A5/1$ as a possible stream cipher, allowing the communication with any visited network that supports $A5/1$ and possibly other strong stream ciphers, to be protected using a 'strong' stream cipher such as $A5/1$, namely, a stream cipher which is stronger than $A5/2$.

Without the policy of Fact 5.4, a MitM attacker could simply remove $A5/1$ (and any other 'strong' cipher) from the list of ciphers sent by the mobile, and as a result, communication would use the vulnerable $A5/2$.

Downgrading to $A5/1$: While $A5/1$ is stronger than $A5/2$, it is still not a very strong stream cipher, and attacks against it are known see, e.g., Ref. [31].

The policy of Fact 5.4 does not prevent *downgrade from $A5/3$ (or another secure stream cipher) to $A5/1$*. For example, if the set of stream ciphers that a mobile supports is $\{A5/1, A5/2, A5/3\}$, then a MitM attacker can remove the $A5/3$ option from the list sent by the mobile client and thereby cause the visited network and mobile client to use the (weaker) $A5/1$ protocol.

This attack is conceptually very simple. Implementing it is not as trivial since the attacker needs to construct a device that will capture the traffic from the mobile and yet be able to communicate with the visited network, impersonating as the mobile. This is not trivial but definitely can be done (and is done by GSM eavesdropping products). The attacker also needs to cryptanalyze the $A5/1$ traffic; since this takes considerable time, the adversary is unlikely to be able to modify or forge messages while the connection is active and would only be able to later decipher ciphertexts obtained by eavesdropping.

5.5.5.2 *A simplified downgrade to $A5/2$ attack*

$A5/2$ is an absurdly vulnerable algorithm since it was intentionally designed to be weak in order to obtain permission to export GSM network equipment. In fact, cryptanalysis of $A5/2$ can be done quickly enough, to allow the attacker to do it during the connection establishment, allowing the attacker to be a MitM during the connection, and not just to decipher ciphertexts which the attacker eavesdropped to during the connection (as for $A5/1$).

However, due to Fact 5.4, it is not as simple to downgrade GSM to $A5/2$ as it is to downgrade to $A5/1$; the downgrade attack to $A5/2$ is a non-trivial attack, involving practical network constraints and manipulations. Therefore, in this section, we present only a simplified variant of the attack that is unlikely to work in practice. In Section 5.5.5.3, we present the 'real', practical downgrade to $A5/2$ attack. Both attacks are based on the GSM key-reuse vulnerability, which we describe in the following.

GSM key-reuse vulnerability: GSM has an *unusual additional vulnerability*, making downgrade attacks much worse than with most systems/protocols. This vulnerability is due to the following fact:

Fact 5.5 (GSM key-reuse vulnerability). *The GSM key exchange establishes* the same key K_c, *regardless of the cipher used (e.g.,* $A5/1, A5/2$ *or* $A5/3$*). Namely, GSM protocol uses the same key* K_c *for all ciphers.*

Note that this vulnerability is due to the fact that the GSM designers did not follow the key separation principle (Section 2.7.4).

Fact 5.5 allows an attacker to find a key used with one (weak) scheme and use it to decipher communication protected with a different (stronger) cipher. This is indeed deployed by the GSM downgrade attacks we present. Another fact used by the attack is that $A5/2$ is absurdly vulnerable, i.e., extremely effective and efficient attacks against $A5/2$ are known.

Fact 5.6 (CTO attack on $A5/2$ requires 900 ciphertext bits and 1 seconds). *The ciphertext-only attack (COA) of Ref.* [31] *finds the connection encryption key* K_c, *given* 900 *bits or more of ciphertext which is the encryption of ECC-encoded messages; the attack takes less than one second (using standard computing capabilities).*

Simplified, unrealistic downgrade attack: We first present a simplified, unrealistic downgrade attack against GSM in Figure 5.17. In this attack, the client supports $A5/1$ and $A5/2$, but the MitM attacker 'removes' $A5/1$ and only offers $A5/2$ to the visited network. As a result, the entire session between visited network and client is only protected using the (extremely vulnerable) $A5/2$ cipher.

5.5.5.3 *Practical downgrade to A5/2 attack*

The downgrade attack of Figure 5.17 would usually fail in practice, for the following two reasons:

1. As per Fact 5.3, the visited network would time-out when it does not receive the *CIPHMODCOM* message within few milliseconds — while the fastest ciphertext-only cryptanalysis process of $A5/2$, from Ref. [31], takes about a second (Fact 5.6).
2. The length of the *CIPHMODCOM* message is only 456 bits (including the ECC), while the cryptanalysis attack of Ref. [31] requires 900 bits. Hence, the attack will not succeed to find the key at all.

The 'real' GSM downgrade attack (to $A5/2$), illustrated in Figure 5.18, overcomes these challenges as follows:

1. As per Fact 5.3, GSM allows delays of about 12 seconds *until* the visited network sends *CIPHMODCMD*. The attack delays the

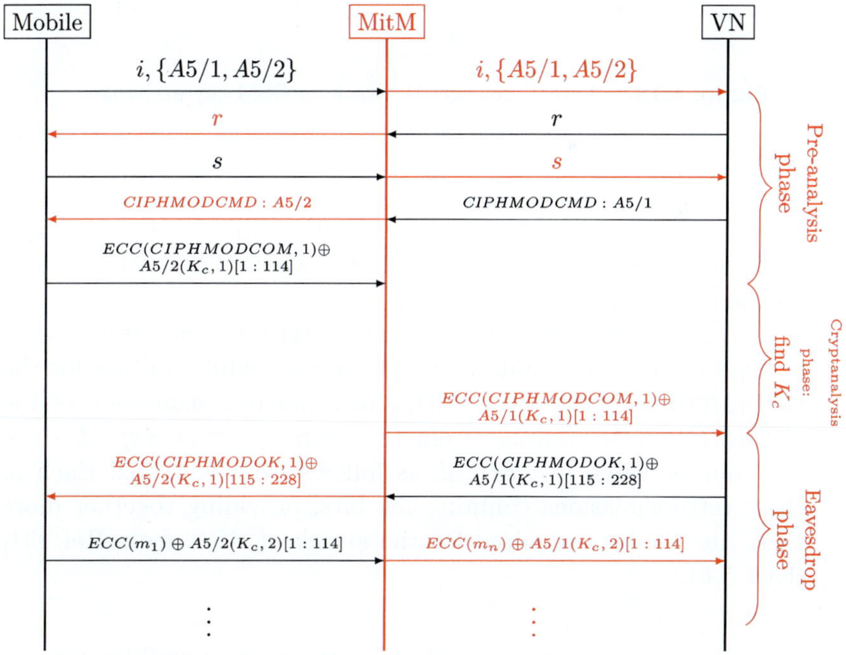

Figure 5.17. Simplified downgrade attack on GSM key exchange.

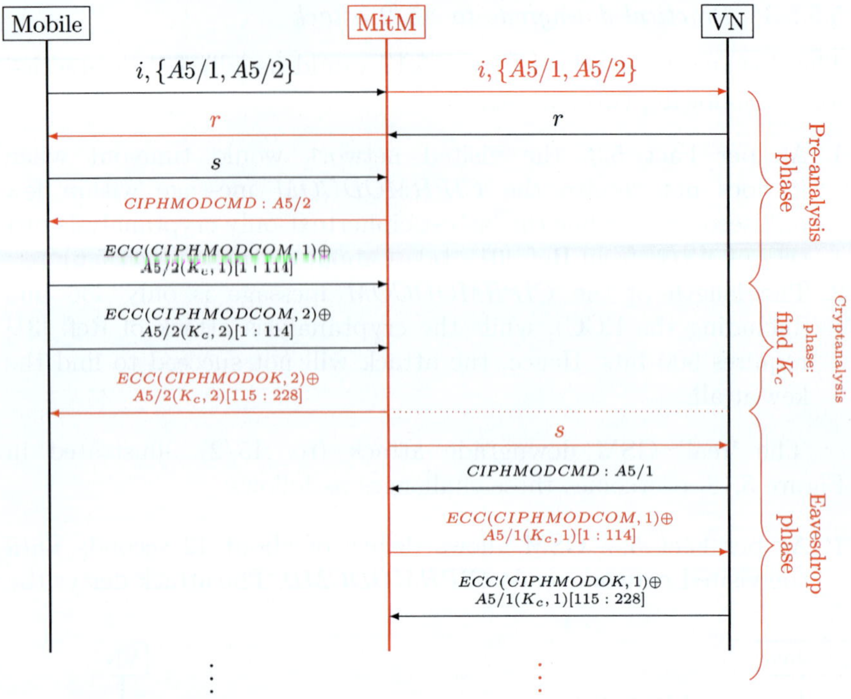

Figure 5.18. A 'real' downgrade attack on GSM key exchange.

s response from the client — this gives the MitM attacker 12 seconds, much more than enough for the ciphertext-only cryptanalysis process of $A5/2$ from Ref. [31], which takes only about a second (Fact 5.6).

2. To obtain a sufficient number of ciphertext bits, the attack *intentionally causes* the mobile client to time-out while waiting for the *CIPHMODOK* message, resulting in rapid retransmission of the *CIPHMODCOM* message from the client — *re-encrypted*, since the counter value is *modified*, as follows from Fact 5.2. Each of these retransmissions contains 456 bits, providing together more than the 900 bits required for the attack of $A5/2$ from Ref. [31] (Fact 5.6).

Several additional variants of this attack are possible; see, for example, the following exercise.

Exercise 5.5 (GSM combined replay and downgrade attack). Consider an attacker who eavesdrops and records the entire communication between mobile and visited network during a connection which is encrypted using a 'strong' cipher, say $A5/3$. Present a sequence diagram, like Figure 5.15, showing a 'combined replay and downgrade attack', allowing this attacker to decrypt all of that ciphertext communication by *later* impersonating as a visited network, and performing a downgrade attack.

Hint: The attacker will resend the value of r from the eavesdropped-upon communication (encrypted using a 'strong' cipher) to cause the mobile to reuse the same key — but with a weak cipher, allowing the attacker to expose the key. □

5.6 Resiliency to key exposure: forward secrecy and recover security

One of the goals of deriving pseudorandom keys for each session was to reduce the damage due to exposure of one or some of the session keys. A natural question is as follows: *can we improve the resiliency to exposure*? In particular, can a key exchange protocol provide some security, even when an adversary may sometimes expose also the master key, or, more generally, *the entire state* of the parties? Note that with all the key exchange protocols we studied, exposure of the master key, at any time, allows an adversary to easily expose *all* (past and future) session keys.

One approach to this problem is to place the master key κ within a *Hardware Security Module (HSM)*. As a result, the key is assumed *not* to be part of the state exposed to the attacker.

However, an HSM is not always a feasible or sufficient solution. It is often unrealistic to require every party to use an HSM; the system design may be restricted to the hardware available to the parties. Even when an HSM is available, an attacker may be able to circumvent it. One way that the attacker may circumvent the HSM is by manipulating the HSM to allow the attack to succeed without direct access to the master key, e.g., to compute past and future session keys; this threat should be prevented by careful design of the HSM and the protocol using it. Furthermore, cryptographic keys may be exposed even when using an HSM — by cryptanalysis or by some weakness of the HSM, such as *side channels* allowing (immediate or gradual/partial) exposure of keys.

In this section, we discuss a different approach to provide security with resiliency to key exposures. This approach is to design the key exchange protocol to ensure *some* security, even after the adversary obtains the master key (or the contents of the entire storage). We mostly focus on two notions of resiliency to key exposure: *forward secrecy* and *recover security*. We explain these two notions and present key exchange protocols satisfying them. Both of these notions can be achieved using shared-key only.

We also briefly discuss additional, even stronger notions of resiliency to key exposures, mainly, an extension for each of the two notions: *perfect forward secrecy* (PFS) and *perfect recover security* (PRS). For these stronger notions of resiliency, it seems necessary to use public key cryptography, which we introduce in Chapter 6. We present PFS and PRS protocols in Section 6.3; later, in Chapter 7, we discuss how PFS is provided by the TLS protocol.

Terms for resilient security: Our use of *perfect forward secrecy* is consistent with most of the literature. However, the term *forward secrecy* is not always used as we define it; e.g., often it is used to refer to the stronger notion, that is, we refer to as *perfect forward secrecy*. Furthermore, the terms *recover security* and *perfect recover security* are not widely used in the literature; indeed, these notions are not widely discussed.

5.6.1 Forward secrecy 2PP key exchange

We use the term *forward secrecy* to refer to key exchange protocols where exposure of the entire storage of the communicating party in some future time period, including every (master and session) key kept at that future time, would not expose the keys used in previous time periods or the plaintext encrypted (and sent) during these previous periods. This should hold although all previous communication could have been intercepted and recorded by the attacker.

To ensure forward secrecy, each period i would use a *separate master key* k_i^M. For simplicity, we map sessions to time periods, i.e., run the key exchange protocol once at the beginning of every period.

At the beginning of period/session i, we must erase any previous master key (e.g., k^M_{i-1}). Definition follows.

Definition 5.1 (Key exchange with forward secrecy). A key exchange protocol $\mathcal{P}$ ensures *forward secrecy* if once session i terminated, exposure of the state of the entity will not compromise the confidentiality of information sent by the entity or sent to the entity in session i.

Some authors use the term *weak forward secrecy* to what we define and refer to as forward secrecy, to emphasize the distinction from the stronger notion of *perfect forward secrecy* (which we present later).

We next discuss the *forward secrecy 2PP key exchange*, a forward secrecy variant of the key exchange 2PP protocol, which we discussed and presented in Section 5.4.1. The difference is that instead of using a single master key k, received during initialization, the forward secrecy key exchange uses a *sequence of master keys* $k^M_0, k^M_1, \ldots$; for simplicity, assume that each master key k^M_i is used only for the ith key exchange, with k^M_0 received during initialization.

The key to achieving the forward secrecy property is to allow easy derivation of pseudorandom future master keys $k^M_{i+1}, \ldots$ from the current pseudorandom master key k^M_i but prevent the reverse, i.e., maintain the previous master keys $k^M_{i-1}, k^M_{i-2}, \ldots, k^M_0$ pseudorandom, even for an adversary who knows $k^M_i, k^M_{i+1}, \ldots$. Namely, the derivation of the master key should be a 'one-way' operation. However, this should be done carefully, e.g., deriving future master keys using a one-way function (OWF) may not be secure.

Exercise 5.6. Consider the following OWF-based derivation of master keys: $k^M_i = h(k^M_{i-1})$. Show that this design may not be secure for some one-way functions.

Hint: Assume a given secure OWF h', and use it to construct an intentionally weak OWF such that the design is insecure, yet h still satisfies the definition of a OWF. In particular, note that the output of a OWF is not required to be uniformly random. □

However, it is not difficult to design a secure process for deriving the master keys by using an appropriate cryptographic scheme such as a PRF (or a block cipher). In particular, consider the following design using a secure PRF denoted simply $PRF_k(\cdot)$:

$$k_i^M = PRF_{k_{i-1}^M}(0) \tag{5.3}$$

The session key k_i^S for the ith session can also be easily derived using the same PRF and master key. One way to derive the session keys is using the corresponding minor change to Equation (5.2), namely,

$$k_i^S = PRF_{k_i^M}(N_{A,i} + N_{B,i}) \tag{5.4}$$

The resulting forward secrecy 2PP key exchange protocol is illustrated in Figure 5.19.

The Forward-Secure 2PP key exchange protocol ensures that the communication in any period that completed before any key exposure remains secure regardless of key exposures in later periods. See Figure 5.20.

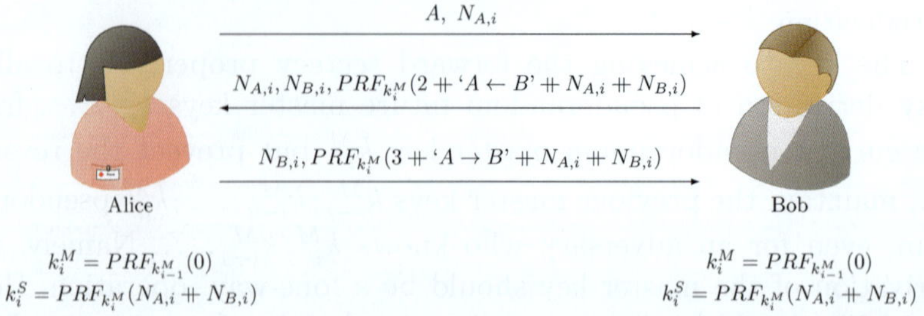

Figure 5.19. The forward secrecy 2PP key exchange protocol. This protocol is similar to the 2PP key exchange protocol (Figure 5.12). The main difference is that this protocol uses a different master key k_i^M for each period i; the initial master key, shared by the two parties, is k_0^M.

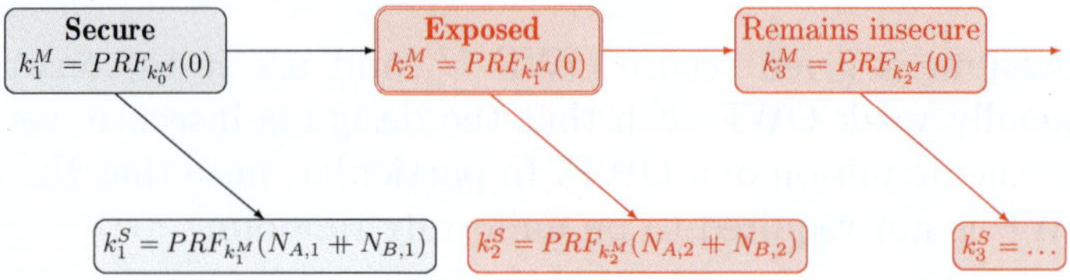

Figure 5.20. Result of running the forward secrecy 2PP key exchange for three periods, with the keys exposed in the second period. Periods prior to the exposure (in this example, only the first period) remain secure even after the period where keys are exposed. Periods from the exposure onward are insecure.

5.6.2 Recover security key exchange protocols

We use the term *recover security* to refer to key setup protocols where a single session *without eavesdropping or other attacks* suffices to recover security from previous key exposures. Definition follows.

Definition 5.2 (Recover security key exchange). A key exchange protocol *recovers security* if session i is secure, i.e., k_i^M, the master key of session i, is pseudorandom, when either of the following holds:

No attack during session: During session i, there was no exposure of the master key k_i^M, and all of the key exchange messages were delivered correctly, without eavesdropping, injection or modification.

Preserve security from previous session: During session i, there was no exposure of the master key k_i^M, and the previous session $(i-1)$ was secure, i.e., k_{i-1}^M is pseudorandom.

The forward-secure 2PP key exchange protocol (Figure 5.19) ensures *forward secrecy* — but not *recover security.* This is since the attacker can use one exposed master key, say k_j^M, to derive all of the following master keys, including k_i^M for $i > j$, using Equation (5.3); in particular, $k_{j+1}^M = PRF_{k_j^M}(0)$.

However, a simple extension suffices to ensure recover security, *as well as* forward secrecy. One way to extend the protocol to ensure also recover security is to use the random values exchanged in each session, i.e., $N_{A,i}, N_{B,i}$, in the derivation of the next master key, e.g., as follows:

$$k_i^M = PRF_{k_{i-1}^M}(N_{A,i} \oplus N_{B,i}) \tag{5.5}$$

We refer to this protocol as the *recover security 2PP key exchange protocol* and illustrate its operation in Figure 5.21.

By computing the new master key using the nonces (and the previous master key), the new master key would be secret provided that at least *one* of the nonces or the previous key is secret. Since the recover security requirement assumes at least one session where the attacker does not eavesdrop or otherwise interfere with the communication, then both $N_{A,i}$ and $N_{B,i}$ are secret; hence, the new master

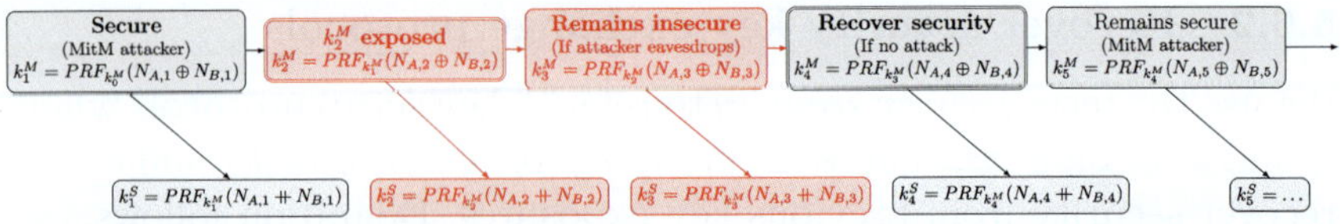

Figure 5.21. Running the *recover security 2PP key exchange* protocol for five periods. The master key and the session key are exposed in the second period; security is recovered after at the fourth period since there is no exposure of the master key and no network attack (not even eavesdropping). Periods prior to the exposure (in this example, only the first period) remain secure even after the period where the keys are exposed. Periods after exposure, e.g., period 3, remain insecure, until a 'recovery period' (in this example, period 4) where there is no attack. Following recovery period, security is maintained until the next exposure.

key k_i^M is secret. Indeed, we could have used just one of $N_{A,i}$ and $N_{B,i}$; by XOR-ing with both of them, we ensure secrecy of the master key even if the attacker is able to capture one of the two flows, i.e., even stronger security.

Two notes are in order. The first note is that, as described, the protocol is *fragile*, in the sense that an attacker who sends corrupted nonce value to one (or both) parties in a given period can prevent recovery of (secure) communication in future rounds. This can be improved with some additional protocol complexity; we leave it as a challenge to the interested reader.

The second note is that the protocol requires the parties to have a source of *true randomness*, i.e., a source which produces random bits even if the party is broken-into, ensuring indistinguishability even against a computationally unbounded adversary. In reality, many systems only rely on *pseudorandom generators* (PRGs), or *pseudorandom functions* (PRFs), whose future values are computable using a past value and/or using an exposed key, as well as to a computationally unbounded adversary. In such case, it becomes critical to use also the input from the peer ($N_{A,i}$ or $N_{B,i}$), and these values should be also used to re-initialize the PRG so that new nonces ($N_{A,i}, N_{B,i}$) are pseudorandom (or truly random) and not predictable. Truly random bit generators require an appropriate hardware device and relying on physical properties, such as thermal noise and quantum phenomena [445].

5.6.3 Stronger notions of resiliency to exposure

Forward secrecy and recover security significantly improve the resiliency against key exposure. There are additional and even stronger notions of resiliency to key exposure, which are provided by more advanced key exchange protocols; we only cover a few of these in this book — specifically, the ones in Table 5.3.

All known protocols that achieve more advanced notions of resiliency use public key cryptography, and in particular, key-exchange protocols such as the Diffie–Hellman protocol. Indeed, it seems plausible that public-key cryptography is necessary for many of these notions. This includes the important notions of *perfect forward secrecy* (PFS) and *perfect recover security* (PRS), which, as the names imply, are stronger variants of forward and recover security, respectively. We now briefly discuss PFS and PRS, to understand their advantages and why they require more than the protocols we have seen in this chapter; we discuss these notions further, with implementations, in Section 6.3.

Table 5.3. Notions of resiliency to key exposures of key exchange protocols. See implementations of forward secrecy and recover security in Sections 5.6.1 and 5.6.2, respectively, and for the corresponding 'perfect' notions (PFS and PRS) in Sections 6.3.1 and 6.3.2, respectively.

Notion	*Session i is secure, if no key exposure during it and:*	Crypto
Secure key-setup	Attacker is given *session* keys of other sessions, but *master* key is never exposed.	Shared key
Forward secrecy	Attacker is given *all keys*, but only of sessions $j > i$, i.e., sessions *after* session i.	Shared key
Perfect forward secrecy (PFS)	No MitM attack during session i, or master keys of session i and previous sessions not exposed before end of session i.	Public key
Recover security	No network (eavesdropping or MitM) attack during session i, or session $i-1$ is secure and no key exposure during session i.	Shared key
Perfect recover security (PRS)	No MitM attack during session i, or session $i-1$ is secure, and the master keys of sessions $i-1$ and i are not exposed before the end of session i.	Public key

Perfect forward secrecy (PFS): PFS, like forward secrecy, also requires resiliency to exposures of state, including keys, occurring in the future. However, on top of that, PFS also requires *resiliency to exposure of the previous* state, again including keys, as long as this exposure occurs only *after* the session ends. We next define this notion. The term *perfect forward secrecy* (PFS) was apparently first coined by Gunther [223]; unfortunately, the term is not always used with a consistent meaning and definition, but the following definition seems to capture the meaning usually used by experts.

Definition 5.3 (Perfect forward secrecy (PFS) key exchange). A key exchange protocol $\mathcal{P}$ ensures *perfect forward secrecy* (PFS) if data sent during session i is confidential (indistinguishable), provided that either (1) there is no MitM attack during session i or (2) the master key of session i and of any previous session is not given to the adversary or given to the adversary only after session i terminates.

We discuss some PFS key exchange protocols in the following chapter, which deals with asymmetric cryptography (also called public-key cryptography, PKC). All known PFS protocols are based on PKC. In particular, see the following exercise.

Exercise 5.7 (Forward secrecy vs. Perfect forward secrecy (PFS)). Present a sequence diagram, showing that the forward secrecy 2PP key exchange protocol presented in Section 5.6.1 does *not* ensure perfect forward secrecy (PFS).

Perfect recover security (PRS). We introduce the term *perfect forward secrecy* to refer to key exchange protocols where a single session without exposure or MitM attacks suffices to recover security from previous key exposures. Definition follows.

Definition 5.4 (Perfect recover security (PRS) key exchange). A key exchange protocol ensures *perfect recover security (PRS)*, if security (confidentiality and authentication) is ensured for messages exchanged during session i, provided that there is no key exposure during session i and that either (1) there is no MitM attack during session i (session i is a *recovery session*) or (2) session $i-1$ is secure and the master keys of sessions $i-1$ and i are not exposed or only exposed after the end of session i.

Note the similarity between perfect forward secrecy (PFS) and perfect recover security (PRS). Both definitions ensure that session i is secure if there is no MitM attack or direct key exposure during session i. Furthermore, both definitions ensure that session i is secure if there is no exposure of master keys of session i or previous sessions before session i completes. However, perfect recover secrecy also ensures that session i is secure if session $i-1$ is secure, as long as there was no key exposure during session i; this can occur even after the keys of some previous sessions, including master keys, were exposed. In this sense, security is *recovered.* Security is preserved until the master key is exposed again, i.e., for all sessions $i < j$, where session j is the first session after i where the master key is exposed.

We discuss perfect recover security key exchange protocols in the following chapter, which deals with asymmetric cryptography (PKC).

Comparison of the notions of resiliency: We compare the four notions of resiliency (forward secrecy, PFS, recover security and PRS) in Table 5.3, along with 'regular' secure key exchange protocols.

Additional notions of resiliency: The research in cryptographic protocols includes additional notions of resiliency to key and state exposures, which we do not cover in this book. These include *threshold security* [150], which ensures that the entire system remains secure even if (up to some threshold of) its modules are exposed or corrupted, *proactive security* [113], which deals with recovery of security of some modules after exposures, and *leakage-resiliency* [171], which ensures resiliency to gradual leakage of parts of the storage.

5.7 Additional exercises

Exercise 5.8 (Attack against SNA with 'fixed roles'). Show that the SNA handshake protocol does not ensure concurrent mutual authentication, also for a scenario where each party is only willing to act in one role, i.e., either as an initiator or as a responder but not as both.

Hint: As in Figure 5.5, the attack will involve two sessions, but you are not required that both sessions will terminate correctly — one of them may fail. □

Exercise 5.9. Some applications require only one party (e.g., a door) to authenticate the other party (e.g., Alice); this allows a somewhat simpler protocol. Consider the following simple, stateless and efficient protocol for this task. The protocol uses a key k shared between the door and Alice and a secure symmetric key cryptosystem (E, D). In this protocol, the door selects and sends a nonce N_D; Alice computes and sends back $E_k(N_D)$. The door decrypts and opens if the decrypted value is the correct value of the nonce N_D:

1. Show that for at least some IND-CPA symmetric key cryptosystems (E, D), this protocol is vulnerable.
2. Show that this vulnerability holds for some of the secure modes of operation presented in Section 2.10, even when using a secure block cipher.
3. Propose a secure protocol for the same task, which will also be simple, stateless and efficient.
   Hint: Your solution may require both door and Alice to be able to generate random bits.
4. Propose another secure protocol for the same task, which will also be simple and efficient but should not require the door to generate random bits; this solution may be stateful.

Exercise 5.10. As explained in Section 5.2.2, the SNA mutual entity authentication (Figure 5.4) ensures sequential mutual entity authentication if E is a block cipher. Identify one (or more) of the standard modes of operation for which the protocol fails to ensure sequential mutual entity authentication, and present the attack with a sequence diagram.

Exercise 5.11. Consider the following mutual-authentication protocol, using shared key k and a (secure) block cipher (E, D):

1. Alice sends N_A to Bob.
2. Bob replies with N_B, $E_k(N_A)$.
3. Alice completes the handshake by sending $E_k(N_B \oplus E_k(N_A))$.

Show an attack against this protocol, and identify the design principles which were violated by the protocol and which, if followed, should have prevented such attacks.

Exercise 5.12 (GSM). In this exercise, we study some of the weaknesses of the GSM handshake protocol, as described in Section 5.5.2.

We ignore the existence of multiple cipher suites (in the case of GSM, multiple stream ciphers).

1. Present functions $A3, A8$ such that the protocol is insecure when using them, against an eavesdropping-only adversary, even if using a secure symmetric key cryptosystem for encryption of the messages.
2. Present functions $A3, A8$ and a symmetric key cryptosystem that will ensure security against MitM adversary, assuming an indistinguishable pseudorandom function (PRF).
3. Let $r[j]$ denote the random value (r) selected by the home network in the jth connection of a particular customer, say the customer with identifier i, to a particular visited network. Let $K_c[j]$ denote the corresponding key K_c, derived from K_i, which is derived by the home network and used between the mobile and the visited network. Assume that *after* connection j terminates, the attacker exposes this key $K_c[j]$. Furthermore, assume that now the attacker can perform a MitM attack on a new connection that the mobile tries to setup with (the same or other) visited network. Explain, with sequence diagram, how this allows this MitM attacker to expose the messages sent during the new connection.
4. Present a possible fix to the protocol, as simple and efficient as possible, to prevent the vulnerability discussed in the previous item. The fix should only require changes only to the mobile and the visited network, not to the home network, and ensure that the exposure of $K_c[j]$ would not allow exposure of messages sent by the client in later connections.

Exercise 5.13 (Downgrade to A5/1 attack on GSM). Consider a mobile client and a visited network that both support $A5/3$ (or some other strong stream cipher). Present a sequence diagram showing how a MitM attacker can cause them to use the (weaker) $A5/1$ protocol.

Exercise 5.14. Consider the following protocol for server-assisted group-shared-key setup. Every client, say A, shares a key k_A with the server. Let G be a group of users; user $A \in G$ can send, at any time, a request to the server for the (fixed) group key k_G; the request consists of the list of users in G, the time t (in seconds) according to the clock of user A and an authenticator $\text{MAC}_{k_A}(G, t)$. If the value of

t is within one minute from its own clock value, the server responds by sending to i the encrypted key: $x_G(t) = k_G + \Pi_{x \in G} PRF_{k_x}(t)$, where $\Pi_{x \in G} PRF_{k_x}(t)$ is multiplication of the values $PRF_{k_x}(t)$ for every user x in G, including $x = A$. User A then computes $k_{A,G}(t) = x_G \mod PRF_{k_A}(t)$:

1. Draw a sequence diagram showing the operation of the protocol.
2. Let A, B be two users in group G, i.e., $A, B \in G$. Suppose user A sends a request at time t_A and user B sends request at time t_B. Explain the conditions for them to receive the same key k_G.
3. Present an attack allowing a malicious user $M \notin G$ to learn the key k_G for a group that M does not belong to. User M may eavesdrop to all messages, and request the key $k_{G'}$ for any set of users G' s.t. $M \in G'$.

Exercise 5.15. In the GSM protocol, the home sends to the visited network one or more *authentication triplets* (r, K_c, s). The visited network and the mobile are to use each triplet only for a single handshake; this is somewhat wasteful, as often the mobile has multiple connections (and handshakes) while visiting the same visited network:

1. Suppose a visited network decides to re-use the same triplet (r, K_c, s) in multiple handshakes, for efficiency (less requests to home). Present message sequence diagram showing that this may allow an attacker to impersonate as a mobile of some benign client. Namely, show that mobile authentication fails.
2. Suggest an improvement to the messages sent between the mobile and the visited network, which will allow the visited network to reuse the (r, K_c, s) triplet received from visited network, for multiple secure handshakes with the mobile. Your improvement should consist of a single additional challenge r_B which the visited network selects randomly and sends to the mobile, together with the challenge r received in the triplet from the home; and a single new response s_B which the mobile returns to the server, *instead* of sending the response s as in the original protocol. Show the computation of s_B by mobile and visited network: $s_B =$________________.
   Your solution may use an arbitrary pseudorandom function.
3. Suppose, again, that a visited network decides to re-use the same triplet (r, K_c, s) in multiple handshakes. A mobile has two connections to the visited network, sending message m_1 in the first

connection and message m_2 in the second connection. Assume that the visited network re-uses the same triplet (r, K_c, s) in both connections and that the attacker knows the contents of m_1. Show how the attacker can find m_2, even if using a secure stream cipher (not $A5/1$ or $A5/2$).

Note: The improvement suggested in the previous item (r_B, s_B) does not have significant impact on this item — you can solve with it or without it.

4. To prevent the threat presented in the previous item, the mobile and visited network can use a different key $K_c' =$________________ (instead of using K_c).
5. Design a *visited network-only forward secrecy* improvement. Namely, even if attacker is given access to the entire memory of the visited network after the jth handshake using the same r, the attacker would still not be able to decipher information exchanged in past connections. Your design may send the value of j together with r from visited network to mobile and may change the stored value of s at the end of every handshake; let s_j denote the value of s at the jth handshake, where the initial value is s received from the home (i.e., $s_1 = s$). Your solution consists of defining the value of s_j given s_{j-1}, namely, $s_j =$________________.

Exercise 5.16. Consider the following key establishment protocol between two users with an assistance of a server S, where each user, e.g., A, shares a secret key, e.g., K_A, with a central server S;

$$A \to B : (A, N_A)$$
$$B \to S : (A, N_A, B, N_B, \mathcal{E}_{K_B}(A + N_A))$$
$$S \to A : (A, N_A, B, N_B, \mathcal{E}_{K_A}(N_A + sk), \mathcal{E}_{K_B}(A + sk), N_B)$$
$$A \to B : (A, N_A, B, N_B, \mathcal{E}_{K_B}(A + sk))$$

Assume that $\mathcal{E}$ is an authenticated encryption. Show an attack which allows a man-in-the-middle attacker to impersonate one of the parties (A or B) to the other, and expose the secret key sk.

Exercise 5.17 (Hashing vs. Forward Secrecy). We discussed in Section 5.6.1 the use of PRG or PRF to derive future keys, ensuring forward secrecy. Could a cryptographic hash function be securely used for the same purpose, as in $\kappa_i = h(\kappa_{i-1})$? Evaluate if such a design is guaranteed to be secure, when h is a (1) collision-resistant hash function (CRHF), (2) one-way function (OWF), (3) bitwise randomness extractor (BRE) and (4) under the random oracle model (ROM).

Exercise 5.18 (PFS definitions). Following are informal definitions for forward secrecy and PFS. Compare them to our definitions; are they 'weaker' — a protocol may satisfy them yet not satisfy (both or one) of the notions we defined? Are they 'stronger' (the other way around)? Equivalent? Or are they incomparable (not equivalent, and neither of them is always weaker)? For each of the definitions, can you give an example of a protocol (probably absurd) meeting the definition, which is 'clearly' not sensible to be claimed to be PFS? Any other issue?

- (From Wikipedia [484]). An encryption system has the property of forward secrecy if plain-text (decrypted) inspection of the data exchange that occurs during key agreement phase of session initiation does not reveal the key that was used to encrypt the remainder of the session.
- A protocol has PFS if the compromise of long-term keys does not allow an attacker to obtain past session keys.

Chapter 6

Public Key Cryptography

As we discussed in Section 1.6.1, cryptography has been applied for over two millennia. However, until relatively recently, cryptography was always based on the use of *symmetric keys*. In particular, in Chapter 2, we studied symmetric cryptosystems, also called shared-key cryptosystems, which use the same key k for encryption ($c \leftarrow E_k(m)$) and for decryption ($m \leftarrow D_k(c)$); see in Figure 1.4. Similarly, in Chapter 4, we focused on shared-key (symmetric) message authentication code (MAC) schemes, which also used only one key k to compute the authenticator (tag) that we will send with a message to prove its authenticity, and later to compute the authenticator for a message received and confirm it is identical to the one received with the message, proving its authenticity.

This was changed quite dramatically by the publication, in 1976, of a seminal paper by Diffie and Hellman introducing *public key cryptography* Ref. [155]. Public key cryptography, also called *asymmetric cryptography*, is built on the idea that we may use *different yet related keys* for different functions of the same scheme, e.g., for encryption and for decryption. Of course, this means that we cannot choose the two keys randomly since they should be *related*; for example, if we use a key e to encrypt, and a key d to decrypt, the pair (e, d) should be related to properly retrieve the plaintext: $m = D_d(E_e(m))$.

The advantage of asymmetric cryptography is that, for many applications, *one key can be public* and only the other kept private. For example, Alice can publish her encryption key $A.e$, allowing everyone to encrypt messages to her by computing $c = E_{A.e}(m)$, with only Alice knowing the corresponding private decryption key

Photo Credit: Chuck Painter / Stanford News Service

Figure 6.1. The discovery of Public Key Cryptography by Whitfield Diffie and Martin Hellman, as imagined by the author.

$A.d$ such that $m = D_{A.d}(c)$. We refer to such asymmetric cryptosystems as *public key cryptosystem* (PKC); see illustration in Figure 1.5.

In Ref. [155], Diffie and Hellman identified three types of public-key schemes: *public key cryptosystem*, *signature schemes* and *key agreement*. They also presented a design but only for *key agreement*. This discovery of the revolutionary concept of asymmetric cryptography is recreated in Figure 6.1.[1]

In this chapter, we introduce public key cryptography and discuss four types of public key schemes, including the three identified in Ref. [155]:

Public key cryptosystems: In Chapter 2, we defined public key cryptosystems and their correctness and indistinguishability requirements (Sections 2.1.3 and 2.9.6). In this chapter, we discuss the RSA public key cryptosystem as well as the El-Gamal public key cryptosystem and two variants of the Diffie–Hellman (DH) public key cryptosystems.

Signature schemes: In Chapter 1, we defined signature schemes and their correctness and unforgeability requirements (Sections 1.5.1 and 1.5.8). In this chapter, we discuss the RSA signature scheme, which is based on the same hard problem which underlies the RSA public key cryptosystem.

[1]Thanks to Whit and Marty for approving my use of this imaginary dialog.

Key agreement protocols: We introduce key agreement protocols and discuss the Diffie–Hellman (DH) key agreement protocol and its PFS.

Key encapsulation mechanisms: We introduce key encapsulation mechanisms and discuss their use for *hybrid encryption*, which are public key cryptosystem constructions which internally combine a 'regular' public key cryptosystem with a symmetric key cryptosystem, to allow reasonably efficient encryption of long messages.

We also discuss applications of public key schemes, different variations and extensions, and attacks, most notably, the Bleichenbacher attack.

6.1 Introduction to PKC

The basic observation leading to asymmetric cryptography is quite simple in hindsight: *security requirements are asymmetric*, and therefore, we may be able to give the adversary *public keys* to certain functions, which are not required to be infeasible for the attacker.

For example, to protect confidentiality, an encryption scheme should prevent an attacker from *decrypting ciphertext*, requiring the key used for *decryption* to be secret (*private*), but not necessarily the key used for *encryption*, which some schemes may allow to be *public*. Similarly, an authentication scheme should prevent an attacker from *forging documents which appear authentic*, requiring the authentication (or *signing*) key to be secret (*private*), but not necessarily the key used to verify authenticity, which some schemes may allow to be *public*.

Let us begin this chapter by discussing the three basic types of public key schemes introduced in Ref. [155], which are still the most important types of public key schemes: *public key cryptosystem (PKC)*, *signature schemes* and *key agreement* protocols.

6.1.1 Public key cryptosystems

PKCs are encryption schemes consisting of three algorithms, (KG, E, D). The (randomized) key generation algorithm KG generates a pair of correlated keys: a *public encryption key* e used by the (randomized) encryption algorithm E and a ***private (secret) decryption key*** d used by the decryption algorithm D. The encryption key is not secret; it should only facilitate encryption of plaintexts and should not facilitate decryption of ciphertexts into the original plaintexts; therefore, an adversary should not be able to learn information about the plaintext when given the corresponding ciphertext, even if the attacker is also given the public key used for encryption.

In Chapter 2, we already discussed public key cryptosystems. See the illustration of their operation in Figure 1.5, their correctness requirement in Section 2.1.3 and their IND-CCA security requirement in Section 2.9.6. In this chapter, we present few *designs* of public key cryptosystems. Specifically, we present the El-Gamal PKC in Section 6.4.2, the Diffie–Hellman (DH) PKC in Section 6.4.1 and the most well-known PKC, RSA, in Section 6.5. We also briefly discuss homomorphic public key cryptosystems and their applications, in Sections 6.4.3 and 6.4.4, respectively.

6.1.2 Signature schemes

Signature schemes, also called *digital signature schemes*, are authentication schemes which ensure non-repudiation, i.e., when properly used, allow validation that a particular party has authenticated (signed) a given message.

Signature schemes consist of three algorithms, (KG, S, V), for Key Generation, Signing and Verifying, respectively. The (randomized) key generation algorithm KG generates a pair of correlated keys: a ***private (secret) signing key*** s used by the signing algorithm S to authenticate (sign) messages, and a ***public verification key*** v used by the verification algorithm V to verify a given message and a purported signature over the message. The verification key is not secret; it should only allow validation of authenticity and should not facilitate signing; therefore, an adversary should be unable to forge signatures even if given the verification key.

In Chapter 1, we already discussed signature schemes, whose operation is illustrated in Figures 1.8 and 1.9. In Section 1.5, we define signature schemes and their correctness and unforgeability requirements (Definitions 1.1, 1.2 and 1.6, respectively). In Section 6.6.1, we present and discuss the RSA signature scheme.

Both signature schemes and message authentication code (MAC, see Chapter 4) functions are used for *authentication* of messages, which is based on the *unforgeability* requirement (Definition 1.6). The difference is that MAC functions use a *single secret key* k for authenticating and for validating messages, while signature schemes use a distinct private signing key s for signing (authenticating), and a distinct public verification key v for validating authenticity. This allows signature schemes to ensure non-repudiation.

We presented constructions for one-time signature schemes in Section 3.4.2. In Section 6.6, we discuss several variants of the RSA signature scheme, which may be used to sign an unbounded number of messages.

6.1.3 Key agreement protocols

A *key agreement protocol* establishes a shared secret key among two[2] parties, by exchanging public information, which we refer to as *public keys*. Since the exchanged information is public, the protocol should ensure the secrecy of the shared key against an eavesdropping adversary. Furthermore, the protocol should ensure secrecy of the shared key even if the adversary not only has eavesdropping capabilities but, furthermore, is also given the entire contents of the memory of both parties before the protocol starts, including any key kept by the parties. This makes key agreement protocols different from symmetric-key key exchange protocols, which assume a secret shared key not known to the attacker, an assumption avoided by key agreement protocols.

Later in this chapter, we discuss several key agreement protocols. The most important is the *Diffie–Hellman (DH) key agreement protocol.* The Diffie–Hellman (DH) key agreement protocol was proposed in Ref. [155], a seminal paper of Diffie and Hellman. We study both unauthenticated and authenticated variants of the Diffie–Hellman (DH) key agreement protocol, in Sections 6.2.4 and 6.3, respectively. Note that key agreement protocols are also key exchange protocols;

[2]There are also protocols for key agreement involving more than two parties; we focus on the two-party case.

in particular, we may also refer to Diffie–Hellman (DH) key agreement by the name DH key exchange.

We focus on the (typical) case of a protocol involving only two flows: the first from Alice (the *initiator*) to Bob (the *responder*) and the second from Bob to Alice. To motivate the unauthenticated scenario, think that Alice and Bob meet in public and want to establish secure communication between them; however, it being a public place, their discussion may be overheard, e.g., by Eavesdropping Eve. The key agreement protocol would allow them to establish a shared secret key, known only to the two of them, in spite of the possible eavesdropping by Eve.

A two-flows key agreement protocol $\mathcal{KE}$ consists of three algorithms, $\mathcal{KE} = (KA, KB, KC)$; its operation is illustrated in Figure 6.2. During the run of the protocol, we allow the adversary (eavesdropping Eve) only to *eavesdrop* to the communication between the parties; this is in contrast to a man-in-the-middle (MitM) adversary, who can also modify or inject messages between the parties.

Key agreement protocols are more computationally demanding than the shared-key key exchange protocols, which we discussed in Chapter 5. Therefore, key agreement protocols are typically used

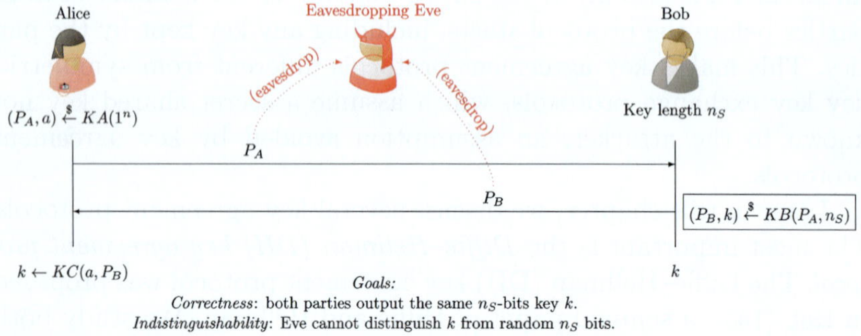

Figure 6.2. Operation of a two-flows key agreement protocol $\mathcal{KE} = (KA, KB, KC)$, such as the Diffie–Hellman (DH) key agreement protocol (presented later). A two-flow key agreement protocol is defined by three efficient probabilistic algorithms: KA, generating Alice's keypair, KB, generating Bob's keys, and KC, which Alice uses to derive the shared symmetric key, whose length we denote by n_S (and provide as input to KB and KC). The protocol should be secure against an *eavesdropping adversary Eve* but may be vulnerable to a *man-in-the-middle* (MitM) adversary.

only periodically. The shared-key produced by key agreement protocols is usually referred to as a *master key* since rather than using it directly to encrypt and/or authenticate the traffic between the peers, it is used to derive shared *session keys*, which are used to protect (encrypt and/or authenticate) the traffic. The derivation of the session keys from the master key may use (more computationally efficient) shared-key key exchange protocols, as discussed in Chapter 5. Alternatively, a combined protocol may share the master key and also share session-keys based on the master key; in particular, this is done by the widely used TLS protocol, which we study in Chapter 7.

Defining two-flows unauthenticated key agreement protocols: Let us now define an unauthenticated key agreement protocol; for simplicity, let's focus on protocols using two flows, as in Figure 6.2. A *two-flows key agreement* protocol can be defined by three efficient probabilistic functions:

KA: *Alice's key generation*, which Alice (the initiator) uses to generate her public key P_A and her private key a. Receives as input a *security parameter*[3] 1^n, in unary.

KB: *Bob's key generation*, which Bob (the responder) uses to generate his public key P_B and the shared symmetric key k. KB accepts as input Alice's public key P_A and the desired length n_S of the symmetric key k, which should be polynomial in the security parameter 1^n. We omit n_S when it is clear from context or irrelevant.

KC: *key combining*, which Alice uses to generate the shared symmetric key k, by combining Alice's private key a and Bob's public key P_B.

An unauthenticated key agreement protocol should ensure two requirements: *correctness* and *indistinguishability*. The *correctness* requirement is that the keys derived by Alice and Bob should be

[3]The security parameter can be the same or related to the effective key length of the protocol. Note that the public and private keys are often longer than the effective key length, see Section 6.1.5.

the same, i.e.,

$$(P_A, a) \overset{\$}{\leftarrow} KA(1^n), (P_B, k) \overset{\$}{\leftarrow} KB(P_A, n_S) \Rightarrow k = KC(a, P_B) \tag{6.1}$$

In addition, correctness requires that the shared key would be of the specified length, i.e., $|k| = n_S$.

Indistinguishability requires, intuitively, that an eavesdropping adversary, who 'sees' P_A and P_B, cannot learn anything about the shared key k; equivalently, it requires that the adversary cannot *distinguish* between the shared symmetric key k and a randomly generated bit string of length n_S.

Note that, often, key agreement protocols are vulnerable to a man-in-the-middle attacker; see Exercise 6.8. We use the term *authenticated key agreement protocols* for key agreement protocols that are secure against a MitM attacker, assuming that the attacker is *not* given access to one or more secret and/or private keys. Authenticated key agreement protocols *authenticate* the flows, using shared secret key(s) or using (known) public key for one or both parties. We present authenticated variants of the Diffie–Hellman (DH) key agreement protocol in this chapter. Some of the variants of the TLS protocol, which we discuss in Chapter 7, are also authenticated key agreement protocols.

6.1.4 Advantages of Public Key Cryptography (PKC)

PKC is not just a cool concept; it is very useful, allowing solutions to problems which symmetric cryptography fails to solve, and making it easier to solve other problems.

We first identify three important challenges which *require* the use of asymmetric cryptography (PKC):

Security without assuming shared key: Using public key cryptography, we can establish secure communication between parties, without requiring them to previously share a secret key between them, or to share a secret key *and* communicate with a trusted third party (such as a *Key Distribution Center* (KDC), see Section 5.5). One method to do so is to use a *key agreement* protocol; this is secure if the attacker has only eavesdropping capabilities during the exchange (i.e., not secure against a MitM attacker). Another alternative is to use the public key of one of the two parties, or of both parties, to secure the connection, usually by securely exchanging a shared key; using the public key of the peer, we can authenticate a run of a key agreement protocol, or encrypt a shared key using the public key of the peer and send to the peer. To allow a party, e.g., the client (Alice), to validate the public key of the other party, e.g., the server *Bob.com*, we usually use a *public key certificate*; public key certificates are a very important aspect of applied cryptography, and we discuss them extensively in Chapter 8.

Signatures provide *evidence*, i.e., ensure *non-repudiation*: Only the owner of the private key can digitally sign a message, but everyone can validate this signature. This allows recipients of a signed message to know that once they validated the signature, they have the ability to convince other parties that the message was signed by the sender (non-repudiation). This is impossible using (shared-key) MAC schemes. Non-repudiation is crucial for important applications such as signing an agreement, payment order or recommendation/review. Non-repudiation is also essential to hold a *certificate authority* (CA) accountable for certificates that it issued, which is essential to establish a secure Public Key Infrastructure (PKI); see Chapter 8.

Stronger resiliency to exposure: In Section 5.6, we discussed the goal of resiliency to exposure of secret information, in particular, exposure of the 'master key' of shared-key key exchange protocols, and presented the *forward secrecy* and *recover security key exchange handshake*. In Section 5.6.3, we also briefly discussed some stronger resiliency properties, including *perfect forward secrecy* (PFS) and *perfect recover security* (PRS). Designs for achieving such stronger resiliency notions are all based on public key cryptography; we discuss these in Section 6.3.

Public key cryptography also makes it *easier* to design and deploy secure systems. Specifically:

Easier key distribution: Public keys are easier *to distribute* since they can be given in a public forum (such as directory) or in an incoming message; note that the public keys still need to be authenticated, to be sure we are receiving the correct public keys, but there is no need to protect their secrecy. Distribution is also easier since each party only needs to distribute one (public) key to all its peers, rather than setting up different secret keys, one per each peer.

Easier key management: Public keys are easier to maintain and use since they may be kept in non-secure storage, as long as they are validated before being used.

Less keys: Only one public key is required for each party, compared to a total of $\frac{n\cdot(n-1)}{2} = O(n^2)$ shared keys required for each pair of n entities. Namely, we need to maintain — and refresh — less keys.

Considering all these advantages, one may wonder why not *always* use public key cryptography. The reason is that there is also a price to the use of PKC. Let us discuss this price.

6.1.5 The price of public key cryptography: assumptions, computations and length

With all the advantages listed above, it may seem that we should *always* use PKC. However, public key cryptography has three significant drawbacks: assumptions (and therefore, risk of vulnerability if these prove incorrect), computation time and the length of the keys, signatures and ciphertexts.

All of these drawbacks are due to the fact that when attacking a public key cryptography scheme, the attacker has the *public key* which corresponds to the private key. The private key is closely related to the public key — for example, the private decryption key 'reverses' encryption using the public key; yet, the public key should not expose (information about) the private key, or otherwise assist the attacker in performing the 'private operation' (e.g., decryption). It is challenging to come up with a scheme that allows this relationship between the encryption and decryption keys, and yet where the public key does not expose the private key.

Considering the challenge of designing asymmetric cryptosystems, it should not be surprising that all known public-key schemes have considerable drawbacks compared to the corresponding shared-key (symmetric) schemes. There are two types of drawbacks: *overhead* and *required assumptions*.

Public key cryptography assumptions and quantum cryptanalysis: Applied public key schemes, such as RSA, DH, El-Gamal and elliptic curves public key cryptosystems, all rely on specific computational assumptions. Mostly, these assumptions are on the hardness of specific number-theoretic problems, mainly two: *factoring* and *discrete logarithm*.

These specific hardness assumptions, and several others, are usually considered *well founded*. This is due to the extensive efforts of mathematicians and other experts to find efficient algorithms for these problems. In particular, factoring and discrete logarithms have been studied for many years, long before their use for PKC was proposed; and efforts increased by far as PKC became known and important.

It is certainly conceivable that efficient factoring algorithms exists and would someday be found. Such a discovery may even occur suddenly, as sometimes happen in algorithmic and mathematical breakthroughs. For example, in [435], Schnorr presented a new factoring algorithm, claiming it is fast enough to 'destroy the RSA cryptosystem'. This claim appears incorrect with respect to that particular factoring algorithm; however, it is possible that an improved factoring algorithms will be discovered. Such discovery may require increase of RSA key length to ensure security, or possibly make RSA completely insecure.

Computers supporting *quantum cryptography*, i.e., *quantum computers*, are another concern. On a sufficiently powerful quantum computer, it would be possible to solve, efficiently, both the factoring and the discrete logarithm problems, using appropriate quantum cryptography algorithms. Sufficiently powerful quantum computers do not *yet* exist, but there is considerable progress, and they may become feasible in the future — possibly even during the next several years. NIST is leading an effort to evaluate and standardize *post-quantum public key cryptographic schemes*, including public key cryptosystems and signature schemes. Post-quantum public key cryptographic schemes would remain secure even when large-scale quantum computing becomes feasible. We discuss the impact of quantum computing on cryptography, including both the use of quantum cryptography for cryptanalysis and the development of post-quantum cryptography (PQC), in Section 10.1.

The overhead of public key cryptography — computation costs and length: Another drawback of public key (asymmetric) cryptography is that all of the proposed schemes — definitely, all proposed schemes which were not broken — have much higher overhead, compared to the corresponding shared-key schemes. There are two main types of overhead: *computation time* and *length* (of keys, signatures and ciphertexts).

The system designers choose the key-length of the cryptosystems they use, based on the *sufficient effective key length* principle (Principle 5). These decisions are based on the perceived resources and motivation of the attackers, on their estimation or bounds of the expected damages due to exposure, and on the constraints and overheads of the relevant system resources. Finally, a critical consideration is the estimates of the required key length for the cryptosystems in use, based on known and estimated future attacks. Such estimates and recommendations are usually provided by experts proposing new cryptosystems, and then revised and improved by experts and different standardization and security organizations, publishing key-length recommendations.

Longer keys have several drawbacks. The least significant drawback is the most obvious one: the extra storage required for the key and the increased overhead of transmitting the key. Two other drawbacks are much more significant. First, the processing time of cryptosystems is usually super-linear in the key length; a cubic relation of the processing time to the key length is typical, meaning that longer keys imply much slower processing. Second, longer keys normally translate to longer ciphertexts (for public key cryptosystems) and longer signatures (for signature schemes).

We present three well-known recommendations for key lengths in Table 6.1. These recommendations are marked in the table as *LV'01, NIST2014* and *BSI'17*, and were published, respectively, in a seminal 2001 paper by Lenstra and Verheul [327], by NIST in 2014 [32] and by the German BSI organization in 2017 [108]. See these and much more online at Ref. [207].

Recommendations are usually presented with respect to a particular *year* in which the ciphertexts are to remain confidential (the three

Table 6.1. Comparison of key length and computing time for asymmetric and symmetric cryptography. Table shows three recommendations for key-length, in bits, required for confidentiality against 'commercial' adversaries. The recommendations are given for widely deployed public-key (asymmetric) and shared-key (symmetric) cryptosystems; the rows refer to the year in which confidentiality is to be preserved (2020, 2030 and 2040). The recommendations are based on predictions of advances in both computing power and cryptanalysis. The LV recommendations are from a 2002 paper [327], the NIST recommendations are from a 2014 publication [32] and the BSI values are from a 2017 publication [108]. The bottom row compares the performance of the schemes for the Crypto++ implementation.

	Symmetric Cryptography			Factoring (RSA), Discrete-log (DH)			Elliptic curves (ECIES)		
Estimation Year	LV 2002	NIST 2014	BSI 2017	LV 2002	NIST 2014	BSI 2017	LV 2002	NIST 2014	BSI 2017
2020	86	112	128	1881	2048	2000	161	224	250
2030	93	112	128	2493	2048	3000	176	224	250
2040	101	128	128	3214	3072	3000	191	256	250
Crypto++ [142]	$4.5 \cdot 10^9$ bytes/s 128-bits AES			$3 \cdot 10^5$ bytes/s 2048-bits RSA/DH			$3 \cdot 10^4$ bytes/s 256-bits ECIES		

Source: Based on Ref. [142].

rows for 2020, 2030 and 2040 in Table 6.1). Experts estimate the expected improvements in the cryptanalysis capabilities of attackers over years, due to improved hardware speeds, reduced hardware costs, reduced energy costs (due to improved hardware), and, often more significantly but hardest to estimate, improvements in methods of cryptanalysis. Such predictions cannot be done precisely, and hence, recommendations differ, sometimes considerably.

Table 6.1 presents the recommendations for four typical, important cryptosystems (in columns two to four). Column two presents the recommendations for a *symmetric key cryptosystem*, such as AES. The recommendations for symmetric cryptosystems are not limited to AES; they apply to *any* symmetric (shared-key) cryptosystem. They only require that the best attacks against the system are generic attacks such as *exhaustive search* (Section 2.4.1) or *table lookup* (Section 2.4.2); symmetric cryptosystem against which there is a more effective attack are typically considered insecure and avoided.

Column three presents the recommendations for RSA and El-Gamal, the two oldest and of the most well-known public key cryptosystems; we discuss both cryptosystems, in Sections 6.4.2 and 6.5. This column also applies to the Diffie–Hellman (DH) key agreement protocol; in fact, the El-Gamal cryptosystem is essentially a variant of the DH protocol, as we explain in Section 6.4.2. RSA and El-Gamal/DH are based on two different number-theoretic problems: the factoring problem (for RSA) and the discrete-logarithm problem (for DH/El-Gamal), but the best-known attacks against both are related, with running time which is exponential in *half* the key length. We briefly discuss these problems in Section 6.1.8.

The fourth column of Table 6.1 presents the recommendations for elliptic curves-based public-key cryptographic schemes, such as the ECIES public key cryptosystem [348] and the ECDSA signature scheme [270]. As the table shows, the recommended key lengths for elliptic curves-based public-key cryptographic schemes are, quite consistently, significantly lower than the recommendations for RSA and El-Gamal/DH public key cryptosystems; this makes elliptic curves-based public key cryptosystems and signature schemes attractive in applications where longer keys are problematic, due to storage and/or communication overhead. We do not cover elliptic curves cryptosystems in this book; these are covered in other courses and books, e.g., Refs. [23, 235, 456].

Table 6.1 shows that the required key length is considerably higher for public-key schemes, compared to shared-key (symmetric) schemes. Symmetric cryptography requires only about half of the key length required, for the same level of security, by elliptic curves cryptosystems, and only about 5% of the key length required when using the RSA and DH public-key schemes. The lower key-length recommendations for elliptic curves cryptography makes these schemes attractive in the (many) applications where key length is critical, such as when communication bandwidth and/or storage are limited.

The bottom row of Table 6.1 compares the *running time* of implementations of AES with 128-bit key in counter (CTR) mode, RSA with 1024 and 2048-bit key and 256-bit ECIES elliptic curve cryptosystem. We see that symmetric cryptosystems such as AES are multiple orders of magnitude faster. It supports about $4.5 \cdot 10^9$ bytes/s, compared with about $3 \cdot 10^5$ bytes/s for the comparably secure 2048-bit RSA, and less than $3 \cdot 10^4$ bytes/s for ECEIS. We used the values reported for one of the popular cryptographic libraries, Crypto++ [142].

Minimize the use of public key cryptography: In this section, we have seen several serious concerns with the use of asymmetric (public key) cryptography. First, as Table 6.1 shows, asymmetric (public key) cryptography has much higher overhead compared to symmetric cryptography.

Second, applied public-key techniques may be vulnerable to further improvements in quantum computing.

Finally, there exists only a very few candidate public key cryptosystems whose security is proven based on generic, well-founded assumptions; this is not the case for practical public key cryptosystems, deployed in real systems, whose security has not been reduced to a generic, well-founded assumption. The security of most public key cryptosystems is often based simply on failures to break them or, less often, on provable reduction to a specific assumption, e.g., the hardness of the discrete log problem. Such specific assumptions may have held for many years but may yet be sometime broken, by new algorithms. This is in contrast to symmetric key cryptosystems, whose security is well established by reduction to a generic, well-founded problem (such as the security of the underlying block cipher).

These considerations, and especially the first one, motivate the following principle:

Principle 12 (Minimize the use of public key cryptography). *Designers should avoid, or at least minimize, the use of public-key cryptography.*

Consider that typical messages are much longer than the size of inputs to the public-key algorithms. If we ignored the high costs of asymmetric cryptography, we could split the input into 'blocks' whose size is the allowed input-size of the public-key algorithms and then use an appropriate mode of operation, like these presented for symmetric key cryptosystems and MAC schemes, for applying the public-key algorithms to multiple blocks. However, the resulting computation costs would have been absurd. Even *more* absurd, although theoretically possible, would be to modify the public-key operation to directly support longer inputs.

Luckily, there are simple, efficient and well-known solutions, to both encryption and signatures, which are used essentially universally, to apply these schemes to long, typically Variable Input Length (VIL), messages. Specifically, for signatures, use the *Hash-then-Sign* (HtS) paradigm, see Section 3.3.5, and for encryption, use the *hybrid encryption* paradigm, which we discuss in the following section (Section 6.1.6).

6.1.6 Hybrid encryption

The huge performance overhead of public key cryptosystems implies that they are typically not used when the parties share a symmetric key. Furthermore, even when the parties do *not* share a symmetric key, we usually do not use directly the widely used, 'classical' *asymmetric* cryptosystems (KG^A, E^A, D^A), e.g., RSA, to encrypt messages, for two reasons: First, public key schemes, and in particular public key cryptosystems, are much slower than shared key schemes, and their overhead grows usually super-linearly as a function of the input length. Second, 'classical' public key cryptosystems are often designed to only support short, fixed input length messages, e.g., messages shorter than the key length; this design is mostly motivated from the high overhead of encrypting longer messages.

So how do we (efficiently) encrypt messages, including long messages, using a public key? The solution is to construct and use a public key cryptosystem which can encrypt long messages with reasonable efficiency, by *combining* a symmetric (shared-key) cryptosystem or authenticated encryption scheme (E^S, D^S), e.g., AES, with an appropriate public key cryptosystems.

In this section, we discuss a simple design of a *hybrid encryption* scheme, which combines the symmetric key cryptosystem (E^S, D^S) with a *public key cryptosystem (PKC)* $\mathcal{PKC}^A \equiv (KG^A, E^A, D^A)$. The result is a *hybrid* asymmetric cryptosystem (PKC), which we denote $\mathcal{PKC}^H \equiv (KG^H, E^H, D^H)$, which is reasonably efficient for long messages. We present another construction of a hybrid encryption scheme in Section 6.1.7, which uses a key encapsulation mechanism instead of using a public key cryptosystem. For both constructions, the encryption and decryption of any message involves only a single invocation of the public key scheme, plus the efficient application of symmetric-key operations.

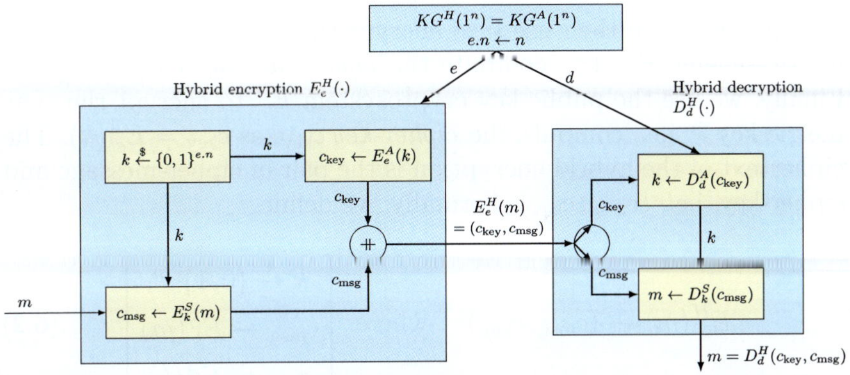

Figure 6.3. Hybrid encryption scheme $\mathcal{PKC}^H \equiv (KG^H, E^H, D^H)$, constructed by randomly selecting an n-bits shared key $k \xleftarrow{\$} \{0,1\}^n$, encrypting the message m using the key k with a symmetric (shared-key) cryptosystem or an Authenticated Encryption scheme (E^S, D^S), and encrypting the shared key k using a public key cryptosystem (asymmetric encryption) $\mathcal{PKC}^A \equiv (KG^A, E_e^A, D^A)$, with security parameter 1^n.

Note our use of mnemonic superscripts to distinguish between the three cryptosystems: A for the 'classical' asymmetric cryptosystem $\mathcal{PKC}^A \equiv (KG^A, E^A, D^A)$, S for the symmetric scheme (E^S, D^S) and H for the *hybrid encryption* scheme $\mathcal{PKC}^H \equiv (KG^H, E^H, D^H)$.

The construction is illustrated in Figure 6.3. The hybrid encryption scheme (KG^H, E^H, D^H) uses the same key-generation function as that of the underlying asymmetric encryption scheme, i.e., $KG^H(1^n) = KG^A(1^n)$. Formally, the public key e should also indicate the required length of the shared (symmetric) key. For simplicity, we assume that this length is simply the security parameter n and that it is included in the public key, specifically, that the public key e encodes n as a field[4] $e.n = n$.

To perform hybrid encryption, we are given a message m and a public key e. We first select a random (n-bits) symmetric key

[4]This simplification is an abuse of notation since we will still use e as the public key of the public key cryptosystem $\mathcal{PKC}^A \equiv (KG^A, E^A, D^A)$; while, strictly speaking, we should only use the public key generated by KG^A without the encoding of n as $e.n$. In practice, the length of the symmetric key is often a constant, removing the need to encode it in the public key e.

$k \xleftarrow{\$} \{0,1\}^{e.n}$. We then use k to encrypt the message using the symmetric scheme E^S, i.e., compute the *cipher-message* $c_{\text{msg}} = E^S_k(m)$. Finally, we use the public key cryptosystem E^A to encrypt the symmetric key k, i.e., compute the *cipher-key* c_{key}, as $c_{\text{key}} = E^A_e(k)$. The ciphertext of the hybrid encryption is the pair of cipher-message and cipher-key, i.e., $(c_{\text{msg}}, c_{\text{key}})$. Formally, we define

$$E^H_e(m) \leftarrow (c_{\text{msg}}, c_{\text{key}}) \quad \text{where} \begin{bmatrix} k \xleftarrow{\$} \{0,1\}^{e.n} \\ c_{\text{msg}} \leftarrow E^S_k(m) \\ c_{\text{key}} \leftarrow E^A_e(k) \end{bmatrix} \tag{6.2}$$

It remains to explain how we perform hybrid decryption $D^H_d(c_{\text{msg}}, c_{\text{key}})$, given the private key d and the ciphertext, where the ciphertext should be a pair consisting of a cipher-message c_{msg} and a cipher-key c_{key}. The hybrid decryption process is also illustrated in Figure 6.3. We first decrypt the symmetric key, by $k \leftarrow D^A_d(c_{\text{key}})$ and then use this key k to decrypt the message, using the symmetric function: $m \leftarrow D^S_k(c_{\text{msg}})$. Formally, we define the hybrid decryption process as

$$D^H_d(c_{\text{msg}}, c_{\text{key}}) \leftarrow D^S_k(c_{\text{msg}}), \quad \text{where } k \leftarrow D^A_d(c_{\text{key}}) \tag{6.3}$$

The security of the hybrid encryption scheme $\mathcal{PKC}^H$ follows from that of the underlying schemes, $\mathcal{PKC}^A \equiv (KG^A, E^A_e, D^A)$ and (E^S, D^S). Namely, if $\mathcal{PKC}^A$ and (E^S, D^S) are IND-CCA secure, then $\mathcal{PKC}^H$ is IND-CPA (respectively, IND-CCA) secure. The proof is beyond our scope. Correctness is much easier to show and we leave it as an exercise.

Exercise 6.1. Prove that if both the public key cryptosystem (KG^A, E^A, D^A) and the symmetric key cryptosystem (E^S, D^S) cryptosystems ensure correctness (per Definitions 2.1 and 2.3, respectively), then the hybrid cryptosystem (KG^H, E^H, D^H), defined as above, is also an asymmetric cryptosystem (PKC) that ensures correctness.

Note that the symmetric scheme we use, (E^S, D^S), can also be an *Authenticated Encryption (AE)* scheme, introduced in Section 4.5.1.

An Authenticated Encryption scheme ensures both authentication and confidentiality; in particular, it prevents an attacker from sending manipulated ciphertexts. When (E^S, D^S) is an Authenticated Encryption scheme, then an attacker cannot manipulate c_{msg} to perform chosen ciphertext attack since a change in c_{msg} is detected by the validation performed by D^S. Namely, if $\mathcal{PKC}^A$ is an IND-CCA secure public key cryptosystem and (E^S, D^S) is an IND-CPA Authenticated Encryption scheme, then $\mathcal{PKC}^H$ is an IND-CCA public key cryptosystem.

6.1.7 Key Encapsulation Mechanism (KEM) schemes

We now describe another design of a hybrid encryption scheme. This design, like the design of Section 6.1.6, constructs the hybrid encryption by combining a symmetric, shared-key authenticated encryption (E^S, D^S) with a public key scheme. However, the public key scheme which we use is *not* a public key cryptosystem (PKC); it is a different type of a public key scheme, which we call a *key encapsulation mechanism (KEM)* scheme. Hybrid encryption has been the motivation for introducing KEM schemes, in Ref. [442], and remains the main application of KEM schemes.

Given a secure public key cryptosystem, we can easily construct a key encapsulation mechanism, as we show in the following. However, we usually go in the reverse direction, since the design of a key encapsulation mechanism is less complex than the design of a public key cryptosystem, and their security may be easier to achieve. Let us explain what is a key encapsulation mechanism in more details, how we can build it from a public key cryptosystem and how we can use it for hybrid encryption.

Intuitively, a KEM allows one party, say Alice, using the public key e_B of another party, say Bob, to generate a shared key k and an *encapsulation* of k, denoted c_{key}. Alice can now safely send c_{key} to Bob. Bob should be able to *decapsulate* c_{key} and retrieve k, using its corresponding private key d_B. In contrast, an eavesdropper obtaining c_{key} should not be able to learn anything about k, i.e., k should be pseudo-random even given c_{key} and e (but not given d). Note that when talking about a KEM, we usually refer to e as the (public) *encapsulation key* and to d as the (private) *decapsulation key*.

We define a key encapsulation mechanism (KEM) as a public-key cryptographic scheme with three functions:

Key generation (KG): Given a security parameter 1^n, generates a pair of keys, a *public encapsulation key* e and a *private decapsulation key* d.

Encapsulate key ($Encaps_e(\cdot)$): Generate and output a n-bits shared key k, together with a *cipher-key* c_{key}, which is basically an encrypted/encapsulated version of k.

Decapsulate ($Decaps_d(c_{\textbf{key}})$): Returns the shared key k when given the cipher-key c_{key}, i.e., the encrypted/encapsulated version of k, and the corresponding decapsulation key d.

Indistinguishability requirements for key encapsulation mechanisms: The indistinguishability requirements for key encapsulation mechanism are similar to the indistinguishability notions we defined, in Section 2.9.6 for public key cryptosystems, i.e., IND-CPA and IND-CCA. The main difference is that KEM encapsulation does not have an input message; its only input is the encapsulation key e.

In Figure 6.4, we define the key encapsulation mechanism IND-CPA indistinguishability test, from which it should be easy to define an IND-CPA secure key encapsulation mechanism. The definitions of the key encapsulation mechanism IND-CCA indistinguishability test and of an IND-CCA secure key encapsulation mechanism follow similarly.

Hybrid encryption using a key encapsulation mechanism (KEM): The design shown in Figure 6.3 constructs a hybrid encryption scheme from an asymmetric (public key) cryptosystem

$$
\begin{array}{l}
T^{KEM-IND-CPA}_{\mathcal{A},\langle KG,E,D\rangle}(b,n) \\
\{ \\
\quad (e,d) \xleftarrow{\$} KG(1^n) \\
\quad (k[0], c_{\text{key}}) \leftarrow Encaps_e(\cdot) \\
\quad k[1] \xleftarrow{\$} \{0,1\}^n \\
\quad b^* \xleftarrow{\$} \mathcal{A}^{KG,E,D}(c_{\text{key}}, k[b], e, 1^n) \\
\quad \text{Return } b^* \\
\}
\end{array}
$$

Figure 6.4. The key encapsulation mechanism IND-CPA test.

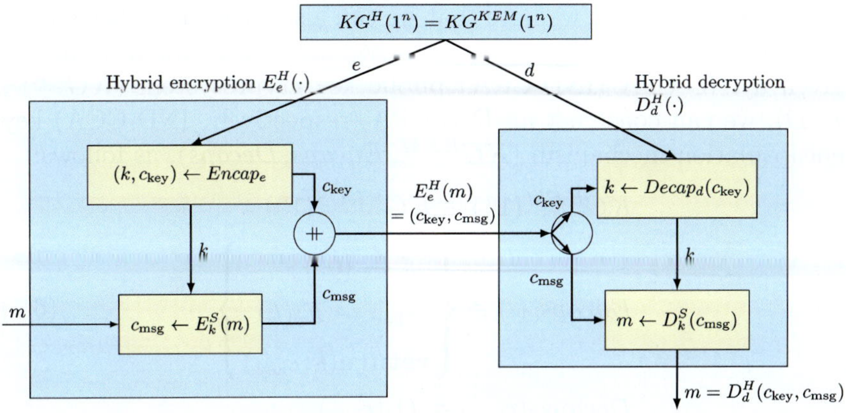

Figure 6.5. A hybrid public key cryptosystem (KG^H, E^H, D^H), constructed by applying an asymmetric key encapsulation mechanism (*KEM*) $(KG^{KEM}, Encaps, Decaps)$, with security parameter 1^n, to generate an n-bits shared key $k \xleftarrow{\$} \{0,1\}^n$, and then encoding and authenticating the message m using the key k with a symmetric (shared-key) authenticated encryption scheme (E^S, D^S).

(KG^A, E^A, D^A). This cryptosystem should ensure security when encrypting the n-bits shared key k. As we see later, in typical public key cryptosystems such as RSA, the encryption process requires the use of secure padding schemes to ensure security. The padding adds complexity to the design and analysis and makes it harder to ensure and prove security.

Figure 6.5 shows an alternative design for a hybrid public key cryptosystem (PKC) (KG^H, E^H, D^H); in this design, the PKC is constructed from a *key encapsulation mechanism* (*KEM*) $(KG^{KEM}, Encaps, Decaps)$ and a symmetric (shared-key) cryptosystem (E^S, D^S).

Constructing a key encapsulation mechanism: Key encapsulation mechanisms are usually designed directly from specific hardness assumptions, e.g., factoring. For example, in Section 10.2, we discuss key encapsulation mechanism constructions used for post-quantum cryptography (PQC). We can then build a hybrid encryption scheme from the key encapsulation mechanism, using the construction of Figure 6.5. In fact, this is the current design for post-quantum public key cryptosystems.

For completeness, we note that we can also construct a key encapsulation mechanism from a public key cryptosystem. Specifically, given a IND-CPA (IND-CCA) public key cryptosystem (KG^{PKC}, E, D), we can construct an IND-CPA (respectively, IND-CCA) key encapsulation mechanism ($KG^{KEM}, Encaps, Decaps$), as follows:

$$KG^{KEM}(1^n) \equiv KG^{PKCS}(1^n)$$

$$Encaps_e(\cdot) \equiv \left\{ \begin{array}{c} k \xleftarrow{\$} \{0,1\}^{e.n} \\ c_{\text{key}} \leftarrow E_e(k) \\ \textbf{return}(k, c_{\text{key}}) \end{array} \right\} \tag{6.4}$$

$$Decaps_d(c_{\text{key}}) \equiv D_d(c_{\text{key}})$$

As before, for simplicity, Equation (6.4) abuses notation and encodes the symmetric key length as $e.n$.

6.1.8 The factoring and discrete logarithm hard problems

Cryptography, and in particular public-key cryptography, is based on the theory of complexity, and specifically on (computationally) *hard problems*. Intuitively, a hard problem is a family of computational problems, with two properties:

Easy to verify: There is an efficient algorithm to verify solutions.
Hard to solve: There is no known efficient algorithm that solves the problem (with significant probability), in spite of considerable efforts to find such algorithm.

Note that the hardness property refers to *known* algorithms. The reader may wonder why we do not make a stronger requirement such as a *proof* that there is *no* efficient algorithm to solve the problem. Let us explain, intuitively, why we do not require such proof. The set of problems that can be *solved* in time polynomial in the input length is denote P, while the set of problems whose solutions can be *verified* in time polynomial in the input length is denote NP. We require that the solutions to the problem can be validated efficiently, i.e., the problem is in NP; therefore, a proof that there is no efficient algorithm to solve the problem, i.e., the problem is *not* in P, implies that $P \neq NP$. This may be true; in fact, it is fair to say that cryptographers mostly expect that $P \neq NP$, since if $P = NP$, then many definitions of the security of cryptographic schemes cannot be satisfied by any construction. However, a *proof* that $P \neq NP$ — or that $P = NP$ — would be a solution to the most well known and investigated problem in the theory of complexity of computation, which withstood extensive efforts to solve it by many excellent cryptographers and experts in complexity theory and in algorithms. See Section A.1 or relevant books, e.g., Ref. [211].

Intuitively, public key schemes use hard problems, by having the secret key provide the solution to the problem, and the public key provides the parameters to verify the solution. To make this more concrete, we briefly discuss *factoring* and *discrete logarithm*. These two hard problems are the basis for many public key schemes, including the oldest and most well known, *RSA, DH* and *El-Gamal*, which we discuss in this chapter. Note that the best known algorithms to solve factoring are about as efficient as the best known algorithms to solve the discrete logarithm problem (see Table 6.1).

Note: Both the factoring and the discrete logarithm problems are well-known problems from the domain of number theory. Properly understanding these problems, as well as the operation and security of the public key cryptosystems we present which are related to these problems, may require familiarity with some basic notions of number theory. These are summarized in Section A.2.

6.1.8.1 *The factoring problem*

The factoring problem is one of the oldest problems in algorithmic number theory and is the basis for RSA and other cryptographic schemes. Basically, the factoring problem involves finding two integer divisors p, q (factors) of a large composite integer n, i.e., $n = p \cdot q$, where the divisors are non-trivial, i.e., greater than one ($p, q > 1$). The divisors p and q should be either prime numbers, or, all of their divisors should be large prime numbers.

Note that most numbers have small divisors — half of the numbers divide by two, third divide by three and so on. This allows the efficient *number sieve* algorithms to factor most numbers. This is the reason that the factoring problem refers specifically to factoring of a number n which has only *large* prime factors.

For simplicity, in the following definition, we assume that the number n is chosen randomly by some algorithm Gen, ensuring that n has only large prime factors. Namely, Gen should avoid numbers whose factors include small integers that can be factored easily by a number sieve algorithm. One important type of generation algorithm Gen selects the large composite number n as the product of two large random primes: $n = p \cdot q$.

Intuitively, factoring numbers generated by Gen is a hard problem if given a randomly generated composite number $n \overset{\$}{\leftarrow} Gen(1^l)$, there is no efficient algorithm that outputs, with non-negligible probability, a pair of non-trivial factors p and q ($p, q > 1$) such that $n = p \cdot q$. Note that we use 1^l as the security parameter since usually the composite number is denoted as n.

Definition 6.1 (The factoring problem). Let Gen be an efficient algorithm that, on input 1^l, outputs a composite integer n. We say that *factoring* is *hard* for composites selected by Gen if for every efficient algorithm $\mathcal{A}$ holds:

$$\Pr\left[n \leftarrow Gen\left(1^l\right);\ (p,q) \overset{\$}{\leftarrow} \mathcal{A}(n) \text{ s.t. } n = p \cdot q \wedge p,q > 1\right] \in NEGL(l) \tag{6.5}$$

Note that, as required, *verification* of the solution is an efficient operation. In fact, verification consists simply of confirming that $n = p \cdot q$.

6.1.8.2 *Discrete logarithms, finite groups and safe primes*

The *discrete logarithm* problem is another important, well-known problem from algorithmic number theory — and the basis for the DH (Diffie–Hellman) key agreement protocol, the El-Gamal cryptosystem, elliptic curves cryptography and additional cryptographic schemes. Before we present the problem, let us briefly discuss finite groups and generators.

Finite groups and generators: Discrete logarithms are similar to the 'regular' logarithm function $\log_b(x)$ over the real numbers $\mathbb{R}$, which returns the number $y \in \mathbb{R}$ s.t. $x = b^y$. The difference is that discrete logarithms are computed over a *finite group* rather than over the real numbers. Readers not sufficiently familiar with group theory can read the short review of this area in Section A.2.4.

In this book, we mostly consider discrete logarithms computed over the finite group $\mathbb{Z}_p^*$, consisting of the set of numbers $\{1, \ldots, (p-1)\}$, where p is a prime, and whose group operation is multiplication $\pmod p$. The group $\mathbb{Z}_p^*$ has $p-1$ members; the number of members in a group is called its *order*, i.e., the group $\mathbb{Z}_p^*$ has *order* $p-1$.

The group $\mathbb{Z}_p^*$ has at least one *generator*; the generator is an element $g \in \mathbb{Z}_p^*$ such that for every element in the group $x \in \mathbb{Z}_p^*$, there is an integer y such $x \equiv g^y \bmod p$. We say that y is the *discrete logarithm* of x (with respect to g). 'A group which has a generator is called a *cyclic group*.'

To help readers understand the concepts of a cyclic group and a generator, let us present a simple fact concerning them; we will later also use this fact (in the proof of Fact 6.4).

Fact 6.1. *Let g be a generator of a cyclic group $\mathbb{G}$ which contains $p-1$ elements, e.g., $\mathbb{Z}_p^*$. Then, for every integer k s.t. $1 \leq k < p-1$ holds $g^k \not\equiv 1$.*

Proof. Suppose for some $k : 1 \leq k < p-1$ holds $g^k \equiv 1$. Then, $g^{k+1} \equiv g^k \cdot g \equiv g$, and, in general, $g^i \equiv g^{i \bmod k}$, i.e., there are only $k < p-1$ different values for g^i for all possible integers i. However, this contradicts the assumption that g is a generator of $\mathbb{G}$ since, by definition, if g is a generator of $\mathbb{G}$, then every element $x \in \mathbb{G}$ must satisfy $x \equiv g^i$ for some integer i, and $\mathbb{G}$ contains $p-1 > k$ elements. □

The discrete logarithm problem: Discrete logarithms can be defined for *any finite cyclic group* $\mathbb{G}$, e.g., the cyclic group $\mathbb{Z}_p^*$, for prime p.

Intuitively, we say that the discrete logarithm problem is *hard* for finite cyclic group $\mathbb{G}$ with generator g, if there is no efficient algorithm $\mathcal{A}$ that solves the discrete logarithm problem for $\mathbb{G}$, with significant probability of success, for a random element $x \neq 1$. This is in contrast to the logarithm function over the real numbers, which is efficiently computable.

We define the discrete logarithm problem in the following; the definition is for a general finite cyclic group $\mathbb{G}$, with the group $\mathbb{Z}_p^*$ being a special case. In this definition, we consider an efficient algorithm *Gen* which receives, as input, a security parameter 1^n, and *generates* (outputs) the generator g and the order q of $\mathbb{G}$, i.e., the number of elements in $\mathbb{G}$. The definition requires the attacker to have negligible probability of success for a generator g chosen by the generation algorithm *Gen*.

Definition 6.2 (The discrete logarithm problem). Let *Gen* be an efficient algorithm that, on input 1^n, outputs (g, q) such that $\{1, g, \ldots, g^q\}$ is a cyclic group (using a given group operation). We say that the *discrete logarithm problem* is *hard* for groups generated by *Gen*, if for every efficient algorithm $\mathcal{A}$ holds:

$$\Pr\left[(g,q) \leftarrow Gen\left(1^n\right)\ ;\ y \overset{\$}{\leftarrow} \{1,\ldots,q\} : y = \mathcal{A}(g^y)\right] \in NEGL(n) \tag{6.6}$$

Note that for any group $\mathbb{G}$, it only requires an exponentiation to *verify* that $x = g^y$, and exponentiation can be computed efficiently over finite cyclic groups.

Smooth numbers and safe primes: Note that there are some cyclic groups for which the discrete-logarithm problem is *easy*, and in particular, for some primes p, the discrete-logarithm problem for $\mathbb{Z}_p^*$ is *easy*. In particular, this holds when $p-1$ is *smooth*, i.e., $p-1$ has only 'small' prime factors. When $p-1$ is smooth, there are known algorithms that efficiently compute discrete logarithms $\pmod p$; the most well known of them is the *Pohlig–Hellman algorithm* [402]. Let us state this important fact:

Fact 6.2 (Computing discrete logarithms $\pmod p$ is easy if $p-1$ is smooth). *Let p be a prime such that $p-1$ is* smooth, *i.e., $p-1$ has only 'small' prime factors. Then, there are known algorithms that efficiently compute discrete logarithms* $\pmod p$.

Examples of primes p s.t. $p-1$ is smooth. Let us give two simple examples of primes p such that $p-1$ is smooth. The first example is of Fermat's primes, i.e., primes of the form $p = 2^x + 1$ for integer x. The second, possible better[5] example is of Pierpont's primes, which are prime numbers of the form $p = 2^x \cdot 3^y + 1$ for integers x, y.

Fact 6.2 motivates the use of a modulus p where $p - 1$ has large factors, i.e., is *not smooth.* In this book, we focus on the most well-known family of such primes, which are called *safe prime*, as we define in the following.

Definition 6.3 (A safe prime). A prime number $p \in \mathbb{N}$ is called a *safe prime*, if $p = 2q + 1$ for some prime $q \in \mathbb{N}$. If p is a safe prime, we say that the group $\mathbb{Z}_p^*$, containing the numbers from 1 to $p - 1$, with the modular multiplication operation, is a *safe prime group.*

Many efforts have failed to find an efficient algorithm to compute discrete-logarithms for *safe prime groups* efficiently. As a result, the discrete-logarithm problem is widely believed to be *hard* for $\mathbb{Z}_p^*$ when p is a safe prime.

For efficiency and/or security considerations, some cryptographic designs use other finite cyclic groups for which the discrete logarithm problem is considered hard, which are not safe prime groups. One important example are groups defined using elliptic curves.

6.1.8.3 *Quadratic residues and exposing some discrete-log bits*

Suppose that the discrete logarithm assumption for safe prime groups holds, i.e., it *is* computationally hard to find the discrete-log x, given $g^x \bmod p$, where g is a generator of the safe prime group and x is chosen randomly. Does this mean that the attacker cannot learn *any* information on x? In particular, can we use x as a key?

The answer is *no.* Furthermore, we show that the attacker can efficiently learn *some* information about x — specifically, its *least-significant bit (LSb)*, i.e., if a is even ($LSb(x) = 0$) or odd ($LSb(x) = 1$). As we see later, this has important implications on the design of some discrete logarithm-based cryptographic schemes, e.g., using the Diffie–Hellman protocol; see Claim 6.2.

[5]Pierpont's primes may be a better example since very large Pierpont's primes are known; in fact, the number of Pierpont's primes is conjectured to be infinite. In contrast, only five Fermat's primes are known, and the largest currently known is $65537 = 2^{16} + 1$.

Quadratic residue: Learning $LSb(x)$ is based on the notion of *quadratic residue modulo p*, which has many uses in the mathematics of cryptography.

Definition 6.4 (Quadratic residue). Let p be a prime number, and let y be a positive integer. We say that y is a *quadratic residue modulo p*, if there is some integer z s.t. $y \equiv z^2 \pmod{p}$.

As early as 1748, Euler proved that that if $p \neq 2$, i.e., p is an odd prime, and if y is not divisible by p, then $y^{\frac{p-1}{2}} \equiv 1 \pmod{p}$ if y is a quadratic residue modulo p, and $y^{\frac{p-1}{2}} \equiv -1 \pmod{p}$ if y is not a quadratic residue modulo p. This observation is called *Euler's criterion.* Since $y^{\frac{p-1}{2}} \bmod p$ can be computed efficiently (by repeated squaring), it follows that we can efficiently determine Euler's criterion, i.e., find out whether y is a quadratic residue modulo p.[6]

Fact 6.3. *Given a prime p, there is an efficient algorithm that can determine if a given positive integer y is a quadratic residue modulo p.*

Proof. Follows from Euler's criterion and the fact that it can be efficiently computed. For a proof of Euler's criterion, see, e.g., Ref. [253]. □

We next show that $y = g^x \bmod p$ is a quadratic residue modulo p *if and only if* $LSb(x) = 0$, i.e., the least significant bit of x is zero, or equivalently, x is even. Combined with Fact 6.3, this shows that we can efficiently find the least-significant bit of the exponent x.

Fact 6.4. *Let p be a prime, g be a generator for* $\mathbb{Z}_p^*$ *and x be a positive integer. Then,* $y \equiv g^x \bmod p$ *is a quadratic residue mod p, if and only if* $LSb(x) = 0$, *i.e., x is even.*

Proof. Let us first prove that if x is even, i.e., $LSb(x) = 0$, then $y = g^x \bmod p$ is a quadratic residue. Since x is even, then there is some integer z s.t. $x = 2z$. Hence, $y \equiv g^{2z} \equiv (g^z)^2 \pmod{p}$; i.e., y is, indeed, a quadratic residue.

We now prove the other direction. Let $y = g^x \bmod p$ be a quadratic residue modulo p, where x is an integer; we prove that

---

[6]The value $y^{\frac{p-1}{2}} = 1 \pmod{p}$ is called *Legendre symbol* of y modulo p and denoted $\left(\frac{y}{p}\right)$; when y is divisible by p, i.e., $y \equiv 0 \pmod{p}$, we obtain $\left(\frac{y}{p}\right) = 0$.

$LSb(x) = 0$, i.e., x is even. This proof uses Fermat's theorem, which we present in Section A.2.3.

For any odd number m, there exists an integer k such that $m = 2k+1$. Let us assume, to the contrary, that g^m is a quadratic residue mod p, for some odd integer m ($LSb(m) = 1$); namely, $g^m \equiv z^2$ mod p for some integer z. From Fermat's theorem (Theorem A.1) follows that

$$z^{p-1} \equiv 1 \pmod{p} \tag{6.7}$$

However, on the other hand,

$$\begin{aligned} z^{p-1} &\equiv z^{2\cdot\frac{p-1}{2}} \equiv (z^2)^{\frac{p-1}{2}} \equiv (g^m)^{\frac{p-1}{2}} \equiv g^{(2k+1)\cdot\frac{p-1}{2}} \\ &\equiv g^{k\cdot(p-1)} \cdot g^{\frac{p-1}{2}} \pmod{p} \end{aligned} \tag{6.8}$$

Now, again from Fermat's theorem, we have

$$g^{k\cdot(p-1)} \equiv (g^{p-1})^k \equiv 1^k \equiv 1 \pmod{p} \tag{6.9}$$

By combining Equations (6.7)–(6.9), we have

$$g^{\frac{p-1}{2}} \equiv 1 \cdot g^{\frac{p-1}{2}} \equiv g^{k\cdot(p-1)} \cdot g^{\frac{p-1}{2}} \equiv z^{p-1} \equiv 1 \pmod{p} \tag{6.10}$$

Namely, $g^{\frac{p-1}{2}} \equiv 1 \pmod{p}$.

However, g is a generator of $\mathbb{Z}_p^*$, i.e., $g^k \not\equiv 1$ for every integer k s.t. $1 \leq k < p-1$, and in particular for $k = \frac{p-1}{2}$ (Fact 6.1). This contradicts $g^{\frac{p-1}{2}} \equiv 1 \pmod{p}$, i.e., Equation (6.10). □

Finding the least significant bit of the discrete log: Fact 6.4 shows that by (efficiently) finding if $g^x \bmod p$ is a quadratic residue modulo p (Fact 6.3), *we can efficiently find the least-significant bit of* x, denoted $LSb(x)$. Note that this argument does not say anything about the confidentiality of other bits of x. In particular, computing the entire discrete logarithm x given $g^x \bmod p$ can still be a hard problem, even if finding the least-significant bit of x is easy.

6.2 The Diffie–Hellman (DH) key agreement protocol

A major motivation for public key cryptography is to secure communication between parties, without requiring the parties to previously agree on a shared secret key. In their seminal paper [155], Diffie and Hellman published, for the first time, the *concept* of public key cryptography, including public key cryptosystem (PKC), which indeed allows secure communication without a preshared secret key. However, this paper did not contain a proposal for *implementing* a PKC.

Instead, in Ref. [155], Diffie and Hellman introduced the *key agreement* problem and present the *Diffie–Hellman (DH) key agreement protocol*, often referred to simply as the DH protocol. Although a key agreement protocol is not a public key cryptosystem, yet it also allows secure communication — without requiring a previously shared secret key. In fact, the *goal* of a key agreement protocol is to *establish* a shared secret key.

In this section, we explain the DH protocol, by developing it in three steps — each in a section. In Section 6.2.1, we discuss a 'physical' variant of the DH protocol, which involves physical padlocks and exchanging a box (locked by one or two locks). In Section 6.2.2, we present several prototype key agreement protocols, and in Section 6.2.4, we finally present the Diffie–Hellman (DH) key agreement protocol.

6.2.1 The physical key agreement protocolt

To help understand the Diffie–Hellman (DH) key agreement protocol, we first describe a *physical* key agreement protocol, illustrated by the sequence diagram in Figure 6.6. In this protocol, Alice and Bob exchange a secret key, by using a *box* and two padlocks — one of Alice and one of Bob. Note that initially, Alice and Bob do not have a shared key — and, in particular, Bob cannot open Alice's padlock and vice versa; the protocol, nevertheless, allows them to securely share a key.

Alice initiates the protocol by placing the key to be shared in the box and locking the box with her padlock. When Bob receives the locked box, he cannot remove Alice's padlock and open the box. Instead, Bob *locks* the box with his own padlock, *in addition to Alice's padlock.* Bob now sends the box, locked by *both* padlocks, to Alice.

Upon receiving the box, locked by both padlocks, Alice removes her own padlock and sends back the box, now locked only by Bob's padlock, back to Bob. Finally, Bob removes his own padlock and is

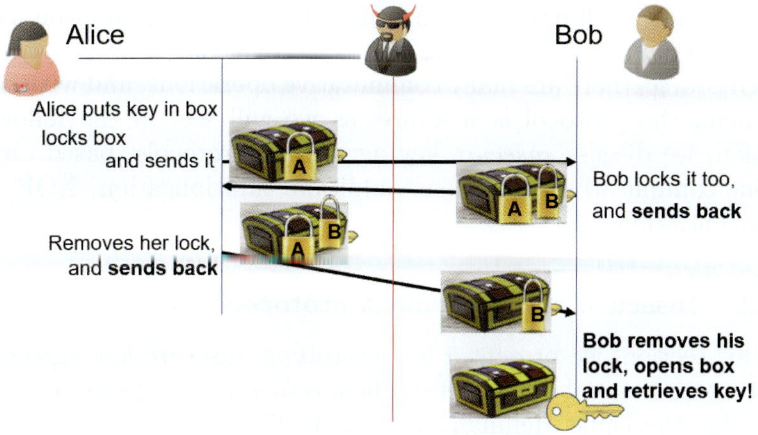

Figure 6.6. The physical key agreement protocol.

now able to open the box and find the key sent by Alice. We assume that the man-in-the-middle (MitM) adversary cannot remove Alice's or Bob's padlocks and, hence, cannot learn the secret in this way. The Diffie–Hellman protocol replaces this physical assumption, by appropriate cryptographic assumptions.

However, note that there is a further limitation on the adversary, which is crucial for the security of this physical key agreement protocol: the adversary should be unable to send a *fake padlock*. Note that in Figure 6.6, both padlocks are stamped by the initial of their owner — Alice or Bob. The protocol is not secure, if the adversary is able to put her own padlock on the box, but stamp her padlock with A or B, and thereby make it appear as if her padlock is Alice's or Bob's, respectively; the reader should work out how this ability would facilitate an attack, when the attacker can manipulate the box when in transit between Alice and Bob. This corresponds to the fact that the Diffie–Hellman protocol is only secure against an *eavesdropping adversary* but insecure against a *MitM* adversary.

The critical property that facilitated the physical key agreement protocol is that Alice can remove her padlock, even after Bob has added his own padlock. Namely, the 'padlock' operation is *commutative* — it does not matter if Alice placed her padlock first and Bob second, she can still remove her padlock as if it was applied last. In a sense, the key to cryptographic key agreement protocols, such as Diffie–Hellman, is to perform a mathematical operation which is also commutative.

Of course, there are many commutative operations, and with some of them, the protocol is insecure, as we will see. In the following section, we discuss *insecure* key agreement protocols, based on different commutative operations: addition, multiplication, XOR and exponentiation.

6.2.2 Insecure key agreement protocols

In this section, we present a few prototype, insecure key agreement protocols. Our goal in presenting them is to assist the reader in understanding the Diffie–Hellman protocol. Unlike the physical key agreement protocol of Section 6.2.1, these are 'real protocols', i.e., involve only the exchange of messages — no physical objects or assumptions. However, we show that these prototype key agreement protocols are insecure.

The XOR key agreement protocol: The sequence diagram in Figure 6.7 presents the first prototype: the *XOR key agreement protocol.* This prototype tries to use the XOR operator, to 'implement the padlocks' of Figure 6.6.

XOR is a natural candidate since we know that XOR can provide confidentiality when used 'correctly', e.g., in the one-time pad

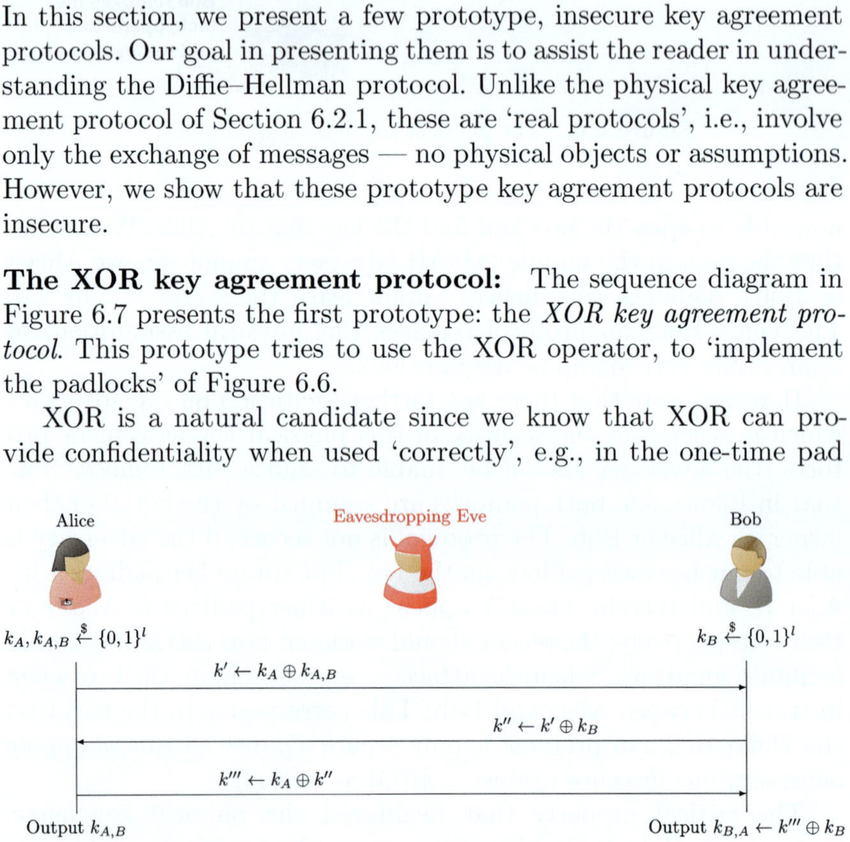

Figure 6.7. The (insecure) XOR key agreement protocol. This protocol ensures correctness $k_{A,B} = k_{B,A}$ but is insecure. Specifically, by eavesdropping to the three exchanged messages (k', k'' and k'''), Eve can find the key $k_{A,B}$. Can you find out how? See Exercise 6.2.

construction. Furthermore, XOR is commutative, and it is easy to see that this suffices to ensure the correctness of the XOR key agreement, i.e., the fact that $k_{A,B} = k_{B,A}$, as follows:

$$\begin{aligned} k_{B,A} &= k''' \oplus k_B \\ &= (k'' \oplus k_A) \oplus k_B \\ &= ((k' \oplus k_B) \oplus k_A) \oplus k_B \\ &= (((k_{A,B} \oplus k_A) \oplus k_A \\ &= k_{A,B} \end{aligned}$$

However, as the following exercise shows, the XOR key agreement protocol is insecure. In fact, not only does it not satisfy indistinguishability but worse: an eavesdropper can easily find the exchanged key.

Exercise 6.2 (XOR key agreement protocol is insecure). Show how an eavesdropping adversary may find the secret key exchanged by the XOR key agreement protocol, by (only) using the values sent between the two parties.

Solution: The attacker XORs all three messages (k', k'' and k'''), to obtain $k = (k \oplus k_A) \oplus (k \oplus k_A \oplus k_B) \oplus (k \oplus k_B)$. □

The addition and multiplication key agreement protocols: In Exercise 6.11, you are asked to define the addition and multiplication key agreement protocols and show that these are also insecure, much like the XOR key agreement protocol.

The exponentiation key agreement protocol: The attack on the XOR key agreement was due the fact that the attacker was able to 'remove' elements by applying the XOR again, due the combination of XOR's commutativity and the fact that for XOR, every element is its own inverse, i.e., $(\forall x \in \{0,1\}^l)\ x \oplus x = 0^l$. Similarly, in Exercise 6.11, you will show that the addition and multiplication key agreement protocols are insecure since the attacker can 'remove' elements by applying the 'inverse' operation (subtraction or division).

So, let us try to use a different mathematical operation that also ensures commutativity (for correctness), but where elements are (typically) not their own inverses, and not as easily inverted: *exponentiation*. In Figure 6.8, we show the resulting exponentiation key

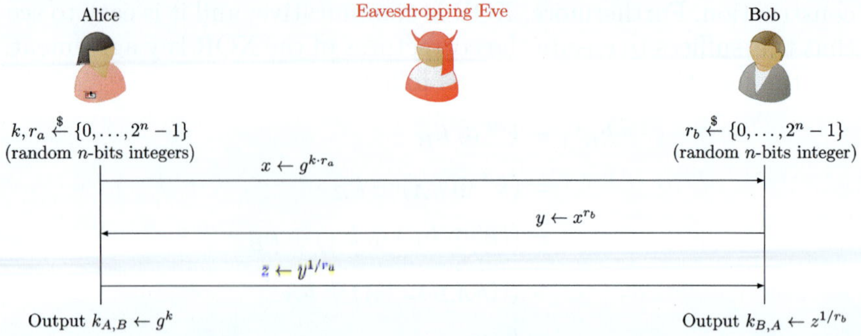

Figure 6.8. The (insecure and inefficient) exponentiation key agreement protocol, using some random integer $g > 1$. Alice outputs $k_{A,B} \leftarrow g^k$ while Bob outputs $k_{B,A} \leftarrow z^{1/r_b}$. In the text, we show that the protocol ensures correctness, namely, the two outputs will be identical ($k_{A,B} = k_{B,A}$). However, we also show that this protocol is insecure, i.e., the attacker can also find this value.

agreement protocol. As we see, the process is as follows, for some arbitrary random integer $g > 1$:

- Alice selects randomly k and r_a and Bob selects randomly r_b, all three as n-bits integers (integers between 0 and $2^n - 1$).
- Alice computes and sends to Bob $x \leftarrow g^{k\cdot r_a}$.
- Upon receiving x, Bob computes and sends to Alice $y \leftarrow x^{r_b}$.
- Upon receiving y, Alice computes and sends to Bob $z \leftarrow y^{1/r_a}$.
- Upon receiving z, Bob computes and outputs $k_{B,A} \leftarrow z^{1/r_b}$.
- Alice computes and outputs $k_{A,B} \leftarrow g^k$.

This protocol is quite inefficient, but let us ignore this inefficiency; we just present it to show its *correctness* and *vulnerability*, as a motivation and to build intuition to the *modular exponentiation key agreement* protocol that we show afterwards.

Let us first show that the exponentiation key agreement protocol ensures correctness, i.e., that $k_{B,A} = k_{A,B}$. Recall that $k_{A,B} = g^k$; now,

$$\begin{aligned} k_{B,A} = z^{1/r_b} &= \left(y^{1/r_a}\right)^{1/r_b} \\ &= y^{1/(r_b\cdot r_a)} = \left(x^{r_b}\right)^{1/(r_b\cdot r_a)} \\ &= x^{1/r_a} = \left(g^{k\cdot r_a}\right)^{1/r_a} \\ &= g^k = k_{A,B} \end{aligned}$$

Several steps in this argument rely on the commutativity of exponentiation, e.g., $(g^w)^u = (g^u)^w$. Can you identify which steps?

Let us now explain an attack recovering the key $k_{A,B}$ exchanged, similarly to the attack on the XOR key agreement. The attack uses the fact that the exponentiation operation may be *removed* to find the exponent, by computing the inverse operation, i.e., logarithm (base g). The logarithm function is less efficient than exponentiation, but, over the integers or real numbers, it is still considered an efficient operation since it can be computed in polynomial time.

Namely, an eavesdropper can compute the logarithm (base g) to remove the exponentiations from *all flows*, as follows. The attacker applies the logarithm operator, with basis g, to the three messages in Figure 6.8. This results in the values $x' = \log_g(x) = k \cdot r_a$, $y' = \log_g(y) = k \cdot r_a \cdot r_b$ and $z' = \log_g(z) = k \cdot r_b$. The attacker can now combine these three values to find k, by computing $\frac{x' \cdot z'}{y'} = \frac{(k \cdot r_a) \cdot (k \cdot r_b)}{(k \cdot r_a \cdot r_b)} = k$.

Of course, this attack used the value of g. This is justified since, in a key agreement protocol, the parties do not have any preshared secret input (see Figure 6.2); indeed, if g is secret, why don't the parties use g directly as a master shared key and only derive session keys as in the key exchange protocols of Chapter 5? Note that even if g is a preshared secret, the protocol is still vulnerable, with a modified attack (Exercise 6.12).

In spite of the insecurity of these prototype key agreement protocols, do not give up! In fact, we next show how we 'fix' the exponentiation key agreement protocol, and finally present a protocol which is believed to be *secure*. Note that we do not claim that this protocol *is* secure; indeed, like other designs based on supposedly computationally-hard problem, a *proof* that the design *is* secure is unlikely — it would imply a proof that $P \neq NP$; see Section A.1.

6.2.3 The modular exponentiation key agreement protocol, modular inverses and Fermat's theorem

The attack against the exponentiation key exchange protocol used the fact that the exponentiations are done over the field of the real numbers ($\mathbb{R}$), where there are efficient algorithms to compute logarithms (illustrated in Figure 6.8). This motivates changing this

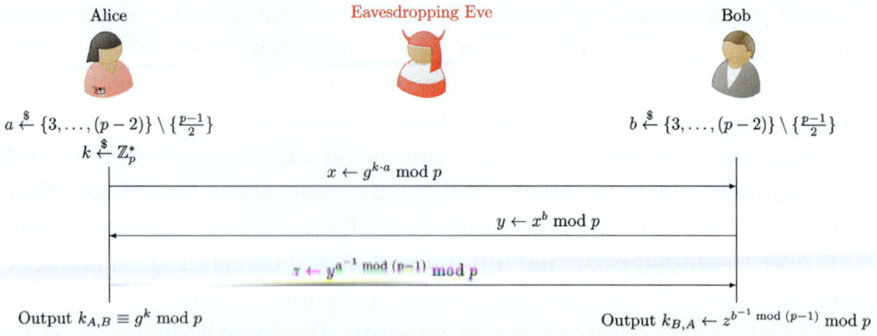

Figure 6.9. The modular exponentiation key agreement protocol, where p is a safe prime and g is a generator of $\mathbb{Z}_p^*$.

protocol, to use, instead, exponentiations over a group in which the (discrete) logarithm problem is considered hard.

In Figure 6.9, we present the *modular exponentiation key agreement protocol*. This protocol resembles the exponentiation key agreement protocol of Figure 6.8 but uses exponentiations over the finite cyclic group $\mathbb{Z}_{p-1}^* \equiv \{1,\ldots,p-2\}$, with a safe prime p. As we discussed in Section 6.1.8.2, for a safe prime p, the (discrete) logarithm problem over $\mathbb{Z}_{p-1}^*$ is considered a hard problem.

The parties in the protocol, Alice and Bob, each select randomly an integer, a and b, respectively, from the set $\{3,\ldots,(p-2)\} \setminus \{\frac{p-1}{2}\}$, namely, the numbers from 3 till $p-2$ except $\frac{p-1}{2}$. Then, the protocol uses the multiplicative inverses modulo $p-1$ of a and b, denoted a^{-1} $(\bmod\ p-1)$ and b^{-1} $(\bmod\ p-1)$, respectively.

Let us now define and discuss modular multiplicative inverses and also present Fermat's little theorem; this is essential to show the security and correctness of the modular exponentiation key agreement protocol.

6.2.3.1 *Modular multiplicative inverses and Fermat's little theorem*

Multiplicative inverses in modular arithmetic: Let us first explain what are multiplicative inverses modulo an arbitrary integer m and present conditions for an integer a to have a multiplicative inverse modulo m.

Definition 6.5 (Multiplicative inverses modulo m). Given two positive integers, m and a, we say that *a has a multiplicative inverse modulo m*, which we denote $a^{-1}(\text{mod } m)$, if $a \cdot a^{-1} \equiv 1 \pmod{m}$.

There is a simple condition for the existence of multiplicative inverses, as follows.

Fact 6.5. *An integer $a > 0$ has multiplicative inverse modulo integer $m > 0$, if and only if a and m are* coprime, *namely, they do not have a common divisor except the number* 1.

Proof. See, e.g., in Ref. [253]. □

The modulus p used in the modular exponentiation key agreement protocol is a safe prime. Namely, $p - 1$ has two divisors: 2 and the prime number $\frac{p-1}{2}$ (in addition to the trivial divisors of 1 and $p - 1$ itself). This is the reason that Alice and Bob select a and b, respectively, from the set $\{3, \ldots, (p-2)\} \setminus \{\frac{p-1}{2}\}$, i.e., excluding 2 and $\frac{p-1}{2}$, which are the only two non-trivial divisors of $p - 1$. Namely, for both a and b, their only common divisor with $p - 1$ is the number 1. Therefore, from Fact 6.5, both of them have multiplicative inverse modulo $p - 1$.

Fermat's little theorem: In order to show the correctness of the modular exponentiation key agreement protocol, we need first to present *Fermat's little theorem*, a well-known and important number-theory result.

Theorem 6.1 (Fermat's little theorem). *For any positive integer z and prime p holds:*

$$z^p \equiv z \pmod{p} \tag{6.11}$$

Proof. See, e.g., in Ref. [253]. □

By applying Fermat's little theorem we find that for any positive integers $w, q > 0$ and prime p holds:

$$w^{q+(p-1)} \equiv w^{q-1} \cdot w^p \equiv w^{q-1} \cdot w \equiv w^q \pmod{p} \tag{6.12}$$

By repeating this as necessary, we obtain the following:

Fact 6.6. *For any positive integers $w, q > 0$, where $q \not\equiv 0 \mod p$, and prime p holds:*

$$w^q \mod p = w^{q \mod (p-1)} \mod p \tag{6.13}$$

6.2.3.2 *Correctness and security of the modular exponentiation key agreement protocol*

Correctness: We can now prove the correctness of the modular exponentiation key agreement protocol, by using the commutativity of exponentiation, e.g., $(g^w)^u = (g^u)^w$, much like the correctness of the preceding key agreement protocols.

Claim 6.1. *The modular-exponentiation key agreement protocol ensures correctness, i.e., at the end of every run of the protocol in which messages are exchanged correctly, holds $k_{A,B} = k_{B,A}$.*

Proof. We show that correctness holds by repeatedly applying Fact 6.6 and the commutativity of exponentiation:

$$\begin{aligned}
k_{B,A} &= z^{b^{-1} \mod (p-1)} \mod p \\
&= \left(y^{a^{-1} \mod (p-1)}\right)^{b^{-1} \mod (p-1)} \mod p \\
&= \left(x^b\right)^{a^{-1} \cdot b^{-1} \mod (p-1)} \mod p \\
&= x^{b \cdot b^{-1} \cdot a^{-1} \mod (p-1)} \mod p \\
&= x^{a^{-1} \mod (p-1)} \mod p \\
&= \left(g^{k \cdot a}\right)^{a^{-1} \mod (p-1)} \mod p \\
&= g^{k \mod p-1} = g^k \mod p \\
&= k_{A,B}
\end{aligned} \tag{6.14}$$

□

Security: Is the modular exponentiation key agreement protocol secure, i.e., does it ensure indistinguishability?

An attacker may try to break the modular-exponentiation key agreement protocol of Figure 6.9 by computing the (discrete) logarithm of the three values exchanged by the protocol, like done in the attack above against the 'regular' exponentiation key agreement protocol (Figure 6.8). However, we specified that p should be a safe prime, and computing discrete logarithms is believed to be computationally hard when the modulus p is a large *safe prime*, i.e., $p = 2q+1$ for some large prime q; see Definitions 6.2 and 6.3.

There may be another way to break the protocol. Like for most cryptographic protocols and schemes, we do not have a complete, unconditional proof of security; such a proof would also prove that $P \neq NP$, and therefore is unlikely to be found (Section A.1).

Note that there is no advantage for the parties to select the a, b or k exponents from a larger set (not limited to $\{1, \ldots, p-1\}$); all the values sent by the protocol, as well as the key, will be exactly the same as when using the corresponding exponents $\bmod(p-1)$.

In the following section, we present the Diffie–Hellman protocol — which is essentially an improved and simplified variant of the modular-exponentiation key agreement protocol of Figure 6.9.

6.2.4 The Diffie–Hellman (DH) key agreement protocol

We now finally present the Diffie–Hellman (DH) key agreement protocol (Figure 6.10). The protocol uses the (safe) prime group $\mathbb{Z}_p^*$, i.e., using multiplications modulo p, where p is a safe prime, i.e., $p = 2q+1$ where q is a prime. The protocol assumes a given (public) choice of parameters: the safe prime p and the generator g.

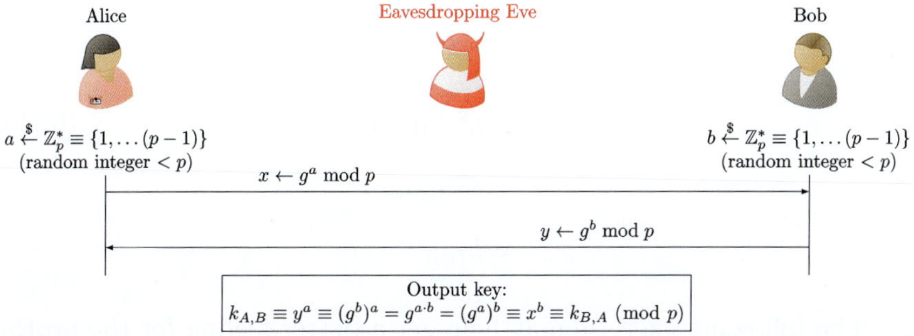

Figure 6.10. The Diffie–Hellman key agreement protocol. The protocol uses (mod p) computations, where p is a prime. It is believed to be hard to compute the resulting key $g^{ab} \bmod p$, when p is a safe prime ($p = 2q + 1$ where q is a prime).

The protocol consists of only two flows: in the first flow, Alice sends $g^a \bmod p$, where $a \in \{1, \ldots, p-1\}$ is a *private key* chosen randomly by Alice; and in the second flow, Bob responds with g^b mod p, where b is a private key chosen randomly by Bob. The result of the protocol is a shared secret value $g^{ab} \bmod p$, computed by Alice as $k_{A,B} = \left(g^b \bmod p\right)^a \bmod p = g^{ba} \bmod p$ and by Bob as $k_{B,A} = \left(g^a \bmod p\right)^b \bmod p = g^{ab} \bmod p$.

The Diffie–Hellman key agreement protocol is, essentially, a simplified, and slightly optimized, variant of the modular exponentiation key agreement protocol of Figure 6.9. In particular, the hopes for the security of both protocols rely on the difficulty of computing discrete logarithms and would fail if p is smooth, i.e., has only small factors. The choice of *safe primes* ($p = 2q + 1$ for prime q) is hoped to be 'safe', i.e., to ensure security.

The basic difference between the two protocols is that in the Diffie–Hellman protocol, the key output is not $g^k \bmod p$ for some random k, as happens for the exponentiation key agreement. Instead, the key being output (exchanged) is g^{ab}. This makes the protocol a bit simpler and more efficient: only two flows instead of three, no need to compute inverses ($a^{-1} \bmod (p-1)$ and $b^{-1} \bmod (p-1)$), and one less exponentiation.

The correctness of the Diffie–Hellman key agreement protocol, i.e., the fact that $k_{A,B} = k_{B,A}$, follows from the commutativity of exponentiation (and modular exponentiation), as follows:

$$\begin{aligned} k_{A,B} &\equiv y^a \bmod p \\ &\equiv (g^b)^a \bmod p \\ &\equiv g^{a \cdot b} \bmod p \\ &\equiv x^b \bmod p \\ &= k_{B,A} \end{aligned} \tag{6.15}$$

The following exercise may help get a better feeling for the protocol and how it works.

Exercise 6.3 (Diffie–Hellman (DH) key agreement). Let $p = 7$.

1. Is $p = 7$ a safe prime? Show.
2. Find a generator g for $\mathbb{Z}_7^*$; show that g is a generator and how you found it.
3. Alice and Bob run the DH protocol with the prime p and generator g. Alice selects $a = 3$, and Bob selects $b = 6$. Compute the values sent by Alice and Bob, and show the computation of the shared key by each of them, resulting in the same value.

DH is vulnerable to a MitM attacker: Both the Diffie–Hellman (DH) and the modular-exponentiation key agreement protocols are vulnerable to a MitM attacker; they are designed only against an *eavesdropping adversary.* In fact, as shown in Figure 6.11, all a MitM attacker needs to do is to fake the message from a party, allowing it to impersonate that party (establishing a shared key with the other party). Indeed, in practice, most practical designs, systems and standards use one of the *authenticated* variants of the DH protocol, which we discuss in Section 6.3.1.

6.2.5 The Computational Diffie–Hellman (CDH) assumption

Figure 6.11 shows that the DH key agreement protocol is vulnerable against a MitM adversary. Well, not all key agreement protocols

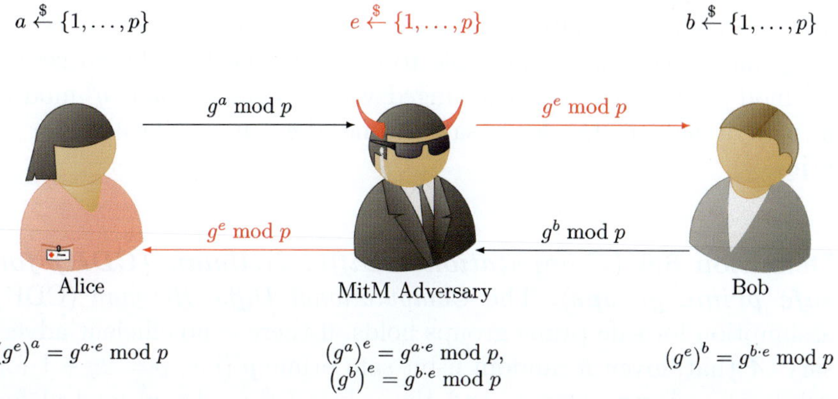

Figure 6.11. MitM attack on the DH key agreement protocol. The DH key agreement protocol is believed to be secure against an eavesdropping adversary. An authenticated variant of the protocol should be secure against a man-in-the-middle (MitM) adversary.

are required to be secure against a MitM adversary. However, definitely, key agreement protocols *are* hoped to be secure against an *eavesdropper*. Does the DH key agreement protocol ensure security against an eavesdropper? Namely, can we assume that the key output by the DH protocol cannot be computed by an eavesdropping adversary?

We already discussed that the DH key agreement protocol is vulnerable to an eavesdropper, when deployed using a group in which the computation of discrete logarithms is easy, e.g., if $p-1$ is a *smooth number*. Therefore, let us focus on the case where the DH key agreement protocol uses a group in which discrete logarithm is assumed to be a computationally hard problem, e.g., the 'mod p' group where p is a safe prime. Would this be secure against an eavesdropper?

So far, this has not been *proven*; there is no proof that if DH is computed (using a safe prime p), then the resulting key cannot be efficiently computed by an adversary. There isn't even a general proof showing that such attack against DH would imply an efficient method to compute discrete logarithms (modulo a safe prime p), although this was shown in some specific cases.

Instead, the common approach is to *assume* that when the DH protocol is run using a safe prime p, then an eavesdropping adversary cannot guess the resulting shared key. This assumption, which is stronger than the assumption of hardness of discrete-log, is called the CDH assumption. The CDH assumption essentially means that it is infeasible to compute the DH shared secret $g^{ab} \bmod p$, given the two exchanged values $g^a \bmod p$ and $g^b \bmod p$, if p is a sufficiently long safe prime (i.e., $p = 2q+1$ for a prime q).

Definition 6.6 (*Computational Diffie–Hellman (CDH) for safe prime groups*). The *Computational Diffie–Hellman* (CDH) assumption for safe prime groups holds, if there is no efficient adversary $\mathcal{A}$ that, given a random n-bit safe prime p (i.e., $p = 2q+1$ for prime q) and generator g, and the values $(g^a \bmod p, g^b \bmod p)$ for random $a, b \xleftarrow{\$} \{1, \ldots, p-1\}$, returns, with non-negligible probability, $g^{ab} \bmod p$.

Namely, for every efficient algorithm $\mathcal{A}$ and random n-bit safe prime p and generator g holds:

$$\Pr_{a,b \xleftarrow{\$} \mathbb{Z}_p^*} \left[\mathcal{A}(g^a \bmod p, g^b \bmod p) = g^{ab} \bmod p\right] \in NEGL(n) \quad (6.16)$$

Note that the definition allows the random choice of $a = 1$ (or $b = 1$), although for $a = 1$ holds $g^{ab} = g^b$. However, the number of possible values in $\mathbb{Z}_p^*$ is exponential in n, i.e., the probability of such 'bad choice' is negligible. Can you find another 'bad choice' for a or b?

At least one bit of $g^{ab} \bmod p$ is exposed! Even assuming that the CDH assumption holds for safe prime groups, an eavesdropper is still be able to learn (at least) one bit about $g^{ab} \bmod p$. Specifically, an attacker, observing $g^a \bmod p$ and $g^b \bmod p$ from a run of the DH protocol, can efficiently find whether $g^{ab} \bmod p$ is a *quadratic residue* modulo p, i.e., if there exists some $z \in \mathbb{Z}_p^*$ such that $g^{ab} \equiv z^2 \bmod p$ (Definition 6.4). Let us show how.

Claim 6.2. *Let p be a prime, g be a generator for $\mathbb{Z}_p^*$ and a, b be integers. Given $g^a \bmod p$ and $g^b \bmod p$, we can efficiently deduce if $g^{ab} \bmod p$ is a quadratic residue modulo p.*

Proof. From Fact 6.3, we can efficiently find if $g^a \bmod p$ and $g^b \bmod p$ are quadratic residues modulo p. From Fact 6.4, this gives the least significant bit (parity) of a and of b; obviously, ab is even if either a or b is even. Again from Fact 6.4, the least significant bit of ab indicates the quadratic residuosity of $g^{ab} \bmod p$. □

6.2.6 Secure derivation of keys from the DH protocol

An eavesdropper to the DH key agreement can observe $g^a \bmod p$ and $g^b \bmod p$; hence, from Claim 6.2, the attacker can know if $y \equiv g^{ab} \bmod p$ is a quadratic residue modulo p. Therefore, using $y \equiv g^{ab} \bmod p$ directly as a key may not be advisable, as even assuming that the CDH assumption is true, still an eavesdropper can learn partial information about y (i.e., if it is a quadratic residue). Note that while we show only exposure of this specific information — the quadratic residuosity of $g^{ab} \bmod p$ — there *could* be ways to expose more[7] information without violating the CDH assumption.

So, how can we use the DH key agreement protocol to securely exchange a key? One option is to simply ignore this concern. However, let us discuss two more prudent options.

First option — use the *generalized* Diffie–Hellman (DH) key agreement protocol with a DDH group: A generalization of the DH key agreement protocol, which we simply call the *generalized DH key agreement protocol*, uses an arbitrary cyclic group $\mathbb{G}$ instead of the specific group $\mathbb{Z}_p^*$; see Figure 6.12. In some such groups $\mathbb{G} \neq \mathbb{Z}_p^*$, the (stronger) *Decisional Diffie–Hellman (DDH) assumption* (Definition 6.7) is believed to hold; we refer to such groups as *DDH groups*. Therefore, when using the generalized DH key agreement protocol with a DDH group, the value of the derived key k_{AB} is assumed to be secret, *without any leakage*. Let us define the DDH assumption (a bit informally).

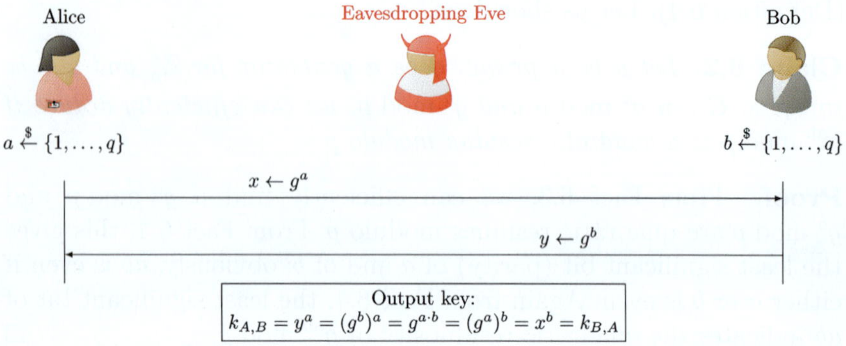

Figure 6.12. The generalized Diffie–Hellman key agreement protocol, for an arbitrary cyclic group $\mathbb{G}$ with order q. All operations are group operations, denoted like the usual multiplication notation. This protocol is believed to be secure when the group $\mathbb{G}$ is a DDH group, i.e., a cyclic group where it is believed that the DDH assumption holds, i.e., it is infeasible to *distinguish* between g^{ab} and a random group element. Note that the DDH assumption does *not* hold for $\mathbb{Z}_p^*$.

[7]It may possible to expose even 80% of the bits! See Ref. [91].

Definition 6.7 (The Decisional Diffie–Hellman (DDH) Assumption and DDH groups). Group $\mathbb{G}$, with order q and generator g, satisfies the *DDH assumption* if there is no efficient algorithm $\mathcal{A}$ that can distinguish, with significant advantage compared to guessing, between $\left[g^a, g^b, g^{ab}\right]$ and $\left[g^a, g^b, g^c\right]$, for a, b and c selected randomly from $\{1, \ldots, q\}$. A group for which the DDH assumption is believed to hold is called a *DDH group.*

In Figure 6.12, we present the generalized DH protocol, using an arbitrary cyclic group $\mathbb{G}$ rather than the specific group $\mathbb{Z}_p^*$ used in the original DH protocol. We denote the group operation of $\mathbb{G}$ as multiplication, *in lieu* of the mod-p multiplication used by $\mathbb{Z}_p^*$. The protocol ensures key secrecy if the DDH problem is computationally infeasible (i.e., hard) for $\mathbb{G}$.

The generalized DH protocol assumes an agreed-upon DDH group $\mathbb{G}$ and generator g, with a known order q. Like the original DH protocol (Figure 6.10), the protocol has only two flows. In the first flow, Alice sends g^a, where $a \in \{1, \ldots, q\}$ is a secret chosen randomly by Alice, and in the second flow, Bob responds with g^b, where $b \in \{1, \ldots, q\}$ is a secret chosen randomly by Bob. Both 'exponentiations' (g^a and g^b) are done by repeatedly applying the group operation.

The result of the protocol is a shared secret value g^{ab}, computed by Alice as $k_{A,B} = \left(g^b\right)^a = g^{ba}$ and by Bob as $k_{B,A} = \left(g^a\right)^b = g^{ab}$.

Note that the secret value exchanged, g^{ab}, is an element of the group $\mathbb{G}$, i.e., it is not a uniformly random string. For many applications, this requires mapping of g^{ab} into a random string.

One group where DDH assumption is assumed to hold is $\mathbb{Q}_p$, the subgroup of $\mathbb{Z}_p^*$ consisting of only the *quadratic residues* in $\mathbb{Z}_p^*$, for a safe prime p (i.e., $p = 2q+1$, for prime q). Certain elliptic curves are also believed to be DDH groups, i.e., to satisfy the DDH assumption. See more examples in Ref. [91].

Second option — extract a secret, random key from the partially random g^{ab} mod p: The second option is to use the DH protocol as described, i.e., with a safe prime group $\mathbb{Z}_p^*$, but to securely *extract* (derive) a shared key k from g^{ab} mod p. Section 3.5 discusses the two common ways to extract a shared key from a mostly random shared secret data: using either a *randomness extractor hash* *function* or a Key Derivation Function (KDF). In either case, this approach requires, basically, that the $g^{ab} \bmod p$ contains 'sufficient' randomness, to ensure that the output of the extractor or KDF is pseudorandom — basically, a variant of DDH with respect to the specific extractor or KDF used.

6.3 Using DH for Resiliency to exposures: the Auth-h-DH and DH-ratchet protocols

As discussed above, and demonstrated in Figure 6.11, the DH protocol is vulnerable to a MitM attacker; its security is only against a passive, eavesdropping-only attacker. In most practical scenarios, attackers who are able to eavesdrop have some or complete ability to also perform active attacks such as message injection; it may seem that DH is only applicable to the relatively few scenarios of eavesdropping-only attackers.

However, while the 'basic' DH protocol is indeed not widely used, *extensions* of it, which ensure security against MitM attackers, are used extensively in practice. We discuss several such extensions. In this section, we discuss two extensions: the *authenticated-h-DH (Auth-h-DH) protocol* (Section 6.3.1) and the *DH-ratchet* protocol (Section 6.3.2). The Auth-h-DH protocol provides secure key exchange but does not ensure authentication (of either entity). The *DH-ratchet* protocol provides both key exchange and authentication and ensures *both* perfect forward secrecy (PFS) *and* perfect recover security (PRS); however, it has the significant disadvantage that it requires preservation of state by both parties. Both protocols do not require public key operations beyond these required by the DH protocol. (The different notions of resiliency to key exposures are compared in Table 5.3.)

Other protocols extend the DH protocol to provide stateless key agreement with perfect forward secrecy, without requiring preservation of state by the entities; these protocols can also provide authentication of one or both parties. In Chapter 7, we present the TLS protocol, which supports several variants of DH-based key agreement, ensuring key agreement with server authentication, and potentially client authentication, and ensuing PFS and recover security, without requiring preservation of state (as required by the ratchet protocol). The DH protocol is also the basis to Krawczyk's *SIGMA* ('SIGn and MAc') protocol [304], which has multiple variants, several of them deployed in several systems, in particular, in the *Internet Key Exchange* (IKE) protocol [114, 285], which is the standard key exchange protocol of the IP security (IPsec standard) [291]. All of these protocols require public-key signatures in addition to the DH computations (this is reflected in the name SIGMA).

6.3.1 The authenticated-*h*-DH (Auth-*h*-DH) protocol: ensuring perfect forward secrecy (PFS)

Assuming that the parties share a secret master key MK, it is quite easy to extend the DH protocol in order to protect against MitM attackers. All that is required is to use a message authentication code (MAC) scheme to authenticate the DH flows. To ensure security without requiring the use of DDH group (i.e., the DDH assumption), we

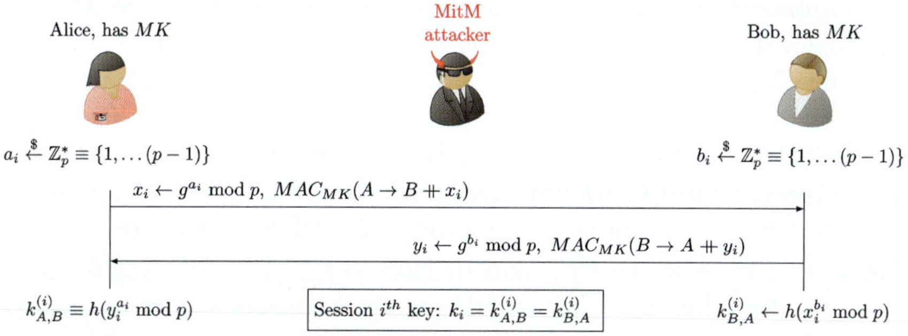

Figure 6.13. The Auth-*h*-DH key agreement protocol, showing the *i*th exchange. This protocol ensures secure key agreement — but *not* authentication — against MitM attackers, with *perfect forward secrecy (PFS)*, but no recovery of security after exposure. The protocol uses a MAC function (MAC) and a keyless randomness extractor hash function h, and requires Alice and Bob to share a secret *master key* MK.

may extract the key using an extractor hash function h (or a KDF). See Figure 6.13, showing the Auth-h-DH, the resulting *authenticated* variant of the DH protocol using hash h to extract the key.

Correctness follows similarly to the argument for 'regular' DH protocol:

$$\begin{aligned} k^{(i)}_{A,B} &\equiv h\left(y_i^{a_i} \bmod p\right) = h\left(\left(g^{b_i}\right)^{a_i} \bmod p\right) = h\left(g^{b_i \cdot a_i} \bmod p\right) \\ &= h\left(\left(g^{a_i}\right)^{b_i} \bmod p\right) = h\left(x_i^{b_i} \bmod p\right) \\ &= k^{(i)}_{B,A} \end{aligned} \tag{6.17}$$

The following informal lemma presents the security properties which are ensured by Auth-h-DH. We only give an informal argument for the validity of the lemma.

Lemma 6.1. *Assuming the extended CDH assumption, the Auth-h-DH protocol (Figure* 6.13*) ensures* secure key agreement (indistinguishability) *with* perfect forward secrecy *(PFS), provided that MAC is a secure MAC function and that h is a secure randomness extractor hash function.*

Argument: Let us first consider a run where the key MK is unknown to the attacker, i.e., was not exposed. Hence, since MAC is a secure MAC, then the protocol outputs a key only if the message it receives was sent by the peer; hence, the exponent used (a_i or b_i) was selected randomly by Alice or Bob and unknown to the attacker. From the *extended CDH* assumption (Section 6.2.6), and the assumption that h is a randomness extractor hash, it follows that the session key k_i (set by Alice to $k^{(i)}_{A,B}$ and by Bob to $k^{(i)}_{B,A}$) is indistinguishable from random, i.e., the Auth-h-DH protocol ensures secure key agreement. Note that the protocol cannot ensure that both parties will generate the same k_i since a MitM attacker may change messages or simply drop one of the messages (causing the key to be output by only one party).

The PFS property also follows, since it requires that the key k_i is secure, even if MK is exposed, as long as the exposure occurs *after* session i was completed; and our analysis did not exclude such exposure *after* the session was over. □

Note, however, the limitations and security weaknesses of the Auth-h-DH protocol. First, the protocol provides key agreement, but it does *not ensure* authentication of either entity. Second, the protocol does not provide *any* recovery from exposure of the master key MK. Furthermore, if a MitM attacker learns one of the two 'private keys' of some exchange i, i.e., learns either a_i or b_i, then this allows the attacker to successfully impersonate, from now on, as *either* entity *and* to know the key exchanged with the peer. Namely, security is not recovered even after exposure of only a_i or b_i, without exposure of the master key MK See Exercise 6.19.

KDF-based variants of the Auth-h-DH protocol: As mentioned in Section 3.5, keyless generic randomness extractor hash functions do not exist. Therefore, it may be better to use, instead, a KDF, which can also output as many pseudorandom bits as needed. Let us discuss briefly two variants of the Auth-h-DH protocol, which use a KDF instead of a (keyless) randomness extractor hash function.

Variant 1 — a two-keyed KDF-based variant of Auth-h-DH: The first variant simply replaces the keyless randomness extractor hash h of Figure 6.13, with the KDF-extract function, i.e., the key is derived as KDF_{salt}, where *salt* is a random and non-secret (known) key, which does not expose the master key MK used by the MAC function.

Variant 2 — a secure variant of Auth-h-DH, using a combined KDF/MAC: Another variant of Auth-h-DH uses the same function f and the same master key MK to replace both the MAC function and the KDF function. This variant requires f to satisfy both the MAC and the KDF functionalities. This is a stronger assumption, but it makes the design simpler and more efficient; therefore, it is often preferred.

See Exercise 6.18 for questions related to these and other variants of the Auth-h-DH protocol. And here is a more basic exercise about the Auth-h-DH protocol.

Exercise 6.4. Alice and Bob share master key MK and perform the Auth-h-DH protocol daily, at the beginning of every day i, to set up a 'daily key' k_i for day i. Assume that Mal can eavesdrop on communication between Alice and Bob every day but perform MitM attacks only every even day (i s.t. $i \equiv 0 \pmod 2$). Assume further that Mal is given the master key MK on the fifth day. Could Mal decipher messages sent during day i, for $i = 1, \ldots, 10$?

Note that the results of Exercise 6.4 show that the Auth-h-DH protocol does *not* ensure the *recover security* property (Section 5.6.2). We next show extensions that improve resiliency to key exposures, and specifically recover security after exposure, provided that the attacker does not deploy the MitM ability for one handshake.

6.3.2 The DH-ratchet protocol: perfect forward secrecy (PFS) *and* perfect recover security (PRS)

The Auth-h-DH protocol ensures perfect forward secrecy (PFS), but does *not* ensure recover security, and definitely not perfect recover security (PRS), both presented in Section 5.6. In fact, a single exposure of the master key, at some point in time, suffices to make all future handshakes vulnerable to a MitM attacker — even if there has been some intermediate handshakes without (any) attacks, i.e., during which the attacker had neither MitM nor eavesdropper capabilities. To see that the Auth-h-DH protocol does not ensure recover security, see Exercise 6.4.

Note that the (shared key) RS-ratchet protocol presented in Section 5.6.2 (Figure 5.21) achieved recovery of security — albeit, not perfect recover security (PRS). Namely, the Auth-h-DH protocol does not even strictly improve resiliency compared to the RS-ratchet protocol (Section 5.6.2); see Table 6.2.

In this section, we show how to achieve *both* PFS *and* PRS. Specifically, we present the *DH-ratchet* protocol, illustrated in Figure 6.14, which ensures *both* PFS *and* PRS. This protocol uses a function f, which is assumed to be *both* a PRF and a KDF.

Like the Auth-h-DH protocol presented above, the DH-ratchet protocol also authenticates the DH exchange; hence, as long as the authentication key is unknown to the attacker *at the time when the protocol is run*, then the key exchanged by the protocol is secret. The improvement, compared to the Auth-h-DH protocol, is in the key used to authenticate the DH exchange; instead of using a fixed MK as done by the Auth-h-DH protocol (Figure 6.13), the DH-ratchet

Table 6.2. Resiliency to key exposures of key exchange protocols. Note: The TLS and SIGMA protocols (Chapter 7 and Ref. [304], respectively) have the same properties as marked for the Auth-h-DH protocol but also support entity authentication (for TLS, client authentication is optional).

Protocol	Section	Secure Key Setup	Forward Secrecy (FS)	Perfect Forward Secrecy (PFS)	Recover Security	Perfect Recover Security (PRS)	Stateless?
2PP-key exchange	5.4.1	✓	✗	✗	✗	✗	✓
FS-ratchet	5.6.1	✓	✓	✗	✗	✗	✓
RS-ratchet	5.6.2	✓	✓	✗	✓	✗	✗
DH-ratchet	6.3.2	✓	✓	✓	✓	✓	✗
Auth-h-DH	6.3.1	✓	✓	✓	✗	✗	✓

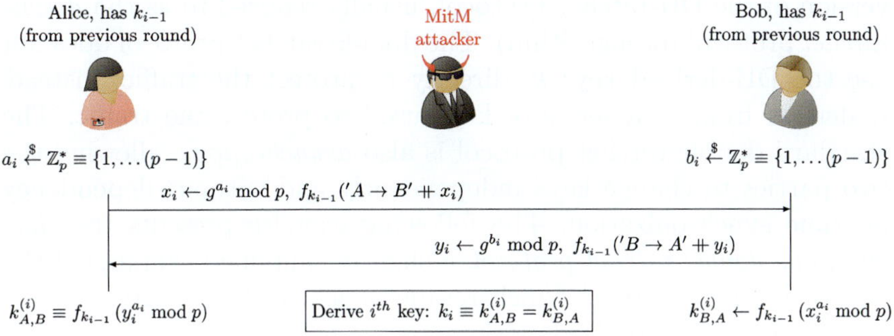

Figure 6.14. Round i of the DH-ratchet key agreement protocol, ensuring PFS and PRS against MitM attacker, assuming that f is both a PRF and KDF.

protocol authenticates the ith DH exchange using the *session key* exchanged in the *previous* round (exchange), i.e., k_{i-1}. An initial shared secret key k_0 is used to authenticate the first round, i.e., $i = 1$.

Lemma 6.2 (DH-ratchet ensures PFS and PRS). *The DH-ratchet protocol (Figure* 6.14*) ensures secure key agreement with PFS and PRS, assuming that f is both a PRF and KDF.*

Sketch of proof: The PFS property follows, like in Lemma 6.1, from the fact that k_i, the session key exchanged during session i, depends on the result of the DH protocol, i.e., is secure against an eavesdropping-only adversary. The protocol also ensures secure key setup since a MitM adversary cannot learn k_{i-1} and hence cannot forge the DH messages.

The PRS property follows from the fact that if at some session i' there is only an eavesdropping adversary, then the resulting key $k_{i'}$ is secure, i.e., unknown to the attacker, since this is assured when running DH against an eavesdropping only adversary. It follows that in the following session $(i'+1)$, the key used for authentication is unknown to the attacker; hence, the execution is again secure — and results in a new key $k_{i'+1}$ which is again secure (unknown to attacker). This continues, by induction, as long as the attacker is not (somehow) given the key k_i to some session i, before the parties receive the messages of the following session $i+1$. □

Many instant messaging applications use a slightly *more* advanced version of the DH-ratchet protocol, usually referred to as the *double ratchet* protocol (or algorithm). The double ratchet protocol does not use the DH-derived keys k_i directly to protect the traffic; instead, it derives from k_i a series of keys used to protect the traffic. The standard double ratchet protocol is also *asynchronous*, allowing the two parties to change keys independently and without dependency on time synchronization. The following exercise presents the *Synchronous double ratchet protocol*, a slightly simplified example of the double ratchet protocol which retains much of its security benefits but assumes synchronized clocks.

Exercise 6.5 (The synchronous double ratchet protocol). Alice and Bob use low-energy devices to communicate. To ensure secrecy, they run, daily, the DH-ratchet protocol (Figure 6.14), but want to further improve security, by changing keys every *hour*. However, to save energy and time, the hourly process should use only very efficient computations — and no exponentiations. Let k_i^j denote the key they share after the jth hour of the ith day, where $k_i^0 = k_i$ (the key exchanged in the 'daily exchange' of Figure 6.14):

1. Show how Alice and Bob should set their hourly shared secret key k_i^j.

2. Identify the security benefits of your solution, compared to the 'regular' DH ratchet protocol

Solution:

1. $k_i^j = f_{k_i^{j-1}}(42)$ (the value 42 is arbitrary[8]).
2. The protocol uses k_i^j as the 'session key', i.e., the key used to protect the traffic in the jth hour of the ith day. Assume the first hour of the day is numbered $j = 1$. The advantage is that exposure of k_i^j, for any hour $j > 0$, does not expose the 'ratchet master key' of that day $k_i = k_i^0$. Hence, such exposure only exposes traffic sent during this hour but not traffic sent in any other hour (or day). This is in contrast with the DH-ratchet protocol, where exposure of the session key k_i, used throughout day i, exposes all the traffic of day i and, furthermore, exposes future traffic until the key is recovered (in a day in which the attacker does not eavesdrop).

6.4 The DH and El-Gamal public key cryptosystems

In this section, we discuss two related public-key cryptosystems, both based on the discrete-logarithm problem: the (well-known) El-Gamal PKCS and the DH PKCS, which is basically a transformation of the DH key agreement protocol into a public key cryptosystem. In the next section (Section 6.5), we present a third system, the (well-known) RSA public key cryptosystem.

6.4.1 The DH PKC and the Hashed Diffie–Hellman cryptosystem

In their seminal paper [155], Diffie and Hellman presented the concept of public-key cryptosystems — but did not present an implementation. On the other hand, they did present the DH key agreement protocol (Figure 6.10). We next show that a minor tweak allows us to turn the DH key agreement protocol into a PKC; we accordingly

[8]Actually, the value 42 is a homage to a great book.

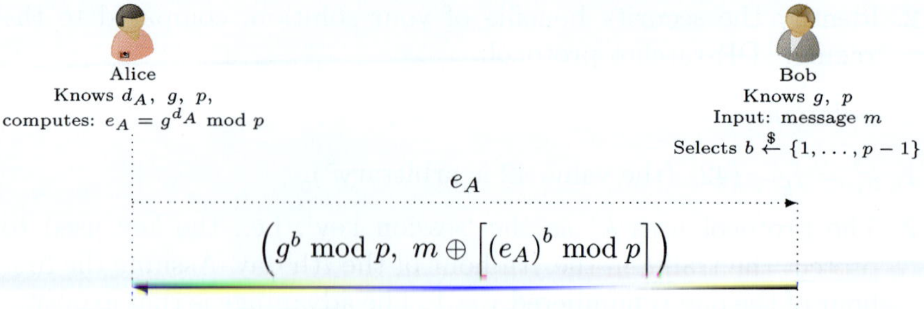

Figure 6.15. The DH public key cryptosystem (DH PKC). Bob encrypts plaintext message m, using Alice's public key e_A and the public parameters: a safe prime p and generator g of the group $\mathbb{Z}_p^*$. The ciphertext consists of the *pair of strings* $\left(g^b \bmod p,\ m \oplus \left[(e_A)^b \bmod p\right]\right)$. The value b is selected randomly and known only to Bob; Bob should randomly select a new value b for each encryption.

refer to this PKC as the DH PKC, and a variant of it that also uses a hash function h as the DH-h PKC.

The DH PKC: Let us first present the *DH public key cryptosystem*, illustrated in Figure 6.15. As can be seen, this public key cryptosystem is essentially an adaptation of the DH key agreement protocol (Figure 6.10), using a safe prime p. Essentially, instead of Alice selecting a random secret a and sending $g^a \bmod p$ to Bob in the first flow of the DH protocol, Alice selects *a fixed private key* d_A, exactly in the same way, i.e., $d_A \xleftarrow{\$} \{1,\ldots,p-1\}$. Next, Alice computes her *public key* e_A, as $e_A \equiv g^{d_A} \bmod p$.

Bob encrypts a message m using Alice's public key e_A by selecting a random value $b \in \{1,\ldots,p-1\}$ and then computing two values: $g^b \bmod p$ and $m \oplus e_A^b \bmod p$. Bob sends these two values to Alice; note that this is essentially Bob's role in the DH protocol. Namely, Bob computes the ciphertext according to Equation (6.18):

$$E_{e_A}(m) = \left\{\begin{matrix} b \xleftarrow{\$} \{1,\ldots,p-1\} \\ \text{Return } \left(g^b \bmod p\ ,\ m \oplus (e_A)^b \bmod p\right) \end{matrix}\right\} \tag{6.18}$$

Note that *the ciphertext is the pair* $\left(g^b \bmod p\ ,\ m \oplus (e_A)^b \bmod p\right)$.

Upon receiving such a ciphertext, which we denote (c_b, c_m), Alice can decrypt it by computing the following:

$$D_{d_A}(c_b, c_m) = c_m \oplus \left[(c_b)^{d_A} \bmod p\right] \tag{6.19}$$

To see that the DH PKC ensures correctness, i.e., that decryption recovers the plaintext, we observe that:

$$\begin{aligned}
&D_{d_A}(E_{e_A}(m)) \\
&\quad = D_{d_A}\left(g^b \bmod p,\ m \oplus (e_A)^b \bmod p\right) \\
&\quad = D_{d_A}\left(g^b \bmod p,\ m \oplus \left(g^{d_A} \bmod p\right)^b \bmod p\right) \\
&\quad = \left(m \oplus \left(g^{d_A} \bmod p\right)^b \bmod p\right) \oplus \left[\left(g^b \bmod p\right)^{d_A} \bmod p\right] \\
&\quad = m \oplus \left(g^{d_A \cdot b} \bmod p\right) \oplus \left(g^{b \cdot d_A} \bmod p\right) \\
&\quad = m
\end{aligned}$$

The security of DH PKC and the Hashed DH PKC: Intuitively, the security of DH PKC seems to follow from the *CDH* assumption (Definition 6.6). Let us present a *wrong reduction argument* which seems to support this (misleading) intuition. Assume an attacker $\mathcal{A}^{DHPKC}$ is able to learn a random message m from e_A and $E_{e_A}(m)$. Then we can design an attacker $\mathcal{A}^{CDH}$ that will be able to compute $g^{ab} \bmod p$, given $g^a \bmod p$ and $g^b \bmod p$, as follows. Given $g^a \bmod p$ and $g^b \bmod p$, the attacker $\mathcal{A}^{CDH}$ will define $e_A = g^a \bmod p$ and $c_b = g^b \bmod p$ and select a random ciphertext c_m. When $\mathcal{A}^{DHPKC}$ returns m, then $\mathcal{A}^{CDH}$ uses it to find the shared secret $g^{ab} \bmod p$, by computing $g^{ab} \bmod p = m \oplus c_m \bmod p$.

However, this argument has a flaw. Specifically, the argument was based on the assumption that the attacker $\mathcal{A}^{DHPKC}$ is able to learn the exact, complete message m. However, a secure encryption scheme should also prevent *disclosure of partial information* about the plaintext, as formalized by the *indistinguishability test for public key cryptosystems*, as defined in Definition 2.9. Hence, even if the CDH assumption holds, the DH PKC may not be a secure encryption.

In fact, Claim 6.2 shows that an attacker *can* learn partial information about $g^{ab} \bmod p$ from the public values $g^a \bmod p$ and $g^b \bmod p$ — even if the CDH assumption holds. This may, therefore, expose partial information about m when using the Diffie–Hellman public key cryptosystem (DH-PKC) as presented in Figure 6.15.

One solution to this is to modify the design. Recall that DH-PKC uses the (mod p) group (with a safe prime p). We could, instead, use a *DDH group* (Definition 6.7), i.e., a cyclic group $\mathbb{G}$ that is believed to *hide all partial information*, as in Section 6.2.6.

Figure 6.16 presents a different solution: the *hashed DH PKC*. In the hashed DH PKC, we apply a cryptographic hash function h to e_A^b, before XORing it with the message. Namely, we compute $c_m = m \oplus h(e_A^b \bmod p)$. Specifically, this should be a *randomness-extractor hash* function. The output of a randomness-extractor hash h should be indistinguishable from random; hence, it should hide all partial information about the key. The ciphertext is, therefore, the pair:

$$E_{e_A}(m) \equiv \left(g^b \bmod p, m \oplus h\left((e_A)^b \bmod p\right)\right)$$

Yet another variant of the DH PKC uses a keyed key-derivation function $KDF_s(g^{d_A \cdot b} \bmod p)$, with a uniformly random key/salt s. See discussion of randomness extractor hash functions and Key Derivation Functions (KDF) in Section 3.5.3.

Exercise 6.6. Show the correctness of the DH-h PKC.

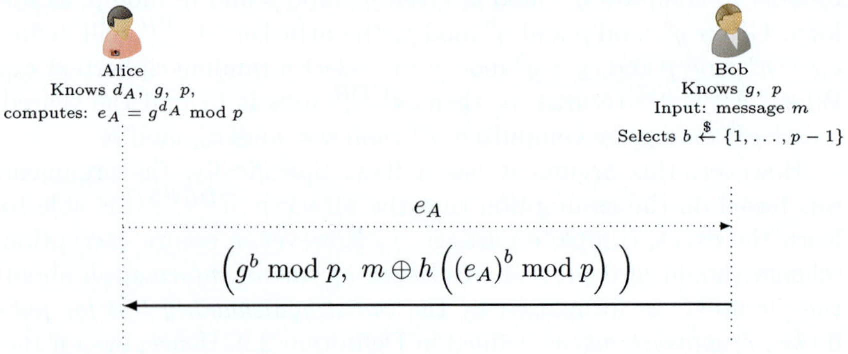

Figure 6.16. The hashed Diffie–Hellman cryptosystem: same as the DH PKC (Figure 6.15, except for hashing the 'one-time key' $e_A^b \bmod p$.

6.4.2 The El-Gamal PKC

The El-Gamal PKC is another encryption scheme based on the *DH key agreement* protocol, which is closely related to the DH PKC. As for the DH PKC, we discuss three variants of the El-Gamal PKC: (1) using the (mod p) group (for a safe prime p), (2) using DDH group and (3) the *Hashed El-Gamal cryptosystem.*

The original design of the El-Gamal PKC, in Ref. [196], uses multiplications (mod p) where p is a safe prime, like the DH PKC. Key generation is also done as in DH PKC, i.e., Alice's selects her private key randomly as $d_A \xleftarrow{\$} \{2, \ldots, p-1\}$ and computes her *public key* e_A as: $e_A \equiv g^{d_A} \bmod p$. Even the encryption process is similar to DH PKC: Bob selects a random value $b \in [2, p-1]$, and computes and sends to Alice a pair of values (c_b, c_m), where $c_b \equiv g^b \bmod p$ and $c_m \equiv m \cdot e_A^b \bmod p$, as in Equation (6.20):

$$E_{e_A}(m) = (c_b, c_m) \equiv \left(g^b \bmod p \ , \ m \cdot e_A^b \bmod p\right) \qquad (6.20)$$

The difference between the original El-Gamal PKC and the DH PKC is in how Bob *uses* the e_A^b value to encrypt the message m. In the original El-Gamal PKC, Bob *multiples* m, i.e., computes $c_m \leftarrow m \cdot e_A^b \bmod p$, while in DH PKC, Bob uses exclusive-or, i.e., computes $c_m \leftarrow m \oplus e_A^b$. Decryption is also modified accordingly, by multiplying c_m by the multiplicative-inverse of $c_b^{d_A}$, denoted $c_b^{-d_A}$, namely, using (modular) division instead of exclusive-or, i.e.,

$$D_{d_A}(c_b, c_m) = c_m \cdot c_b^{-d_A} \bmod p \qquad (6.21)$$

Correctness follows similarly to DH PKC.

Unfortunately, similarly to DH PKC, the original El-Gamal PKC may expose partial information about the plaintext message m. And, like for DH PKC, there are two solutions, both similar to the corresponding DH-PKC solution: *Hashed El-Gamal cryptosystem* or using El-Gamal with a *DDH* group (Definition 6.7).

The first solution, the Hashed El-Gamal cryptosystem, is similar to Hashed Diffie–Hellman cryptosystem. Namely, in the encryption process, we hash the 'one-time pad' e_A^b before using it to hide the message m. Namely, encryption is, as usual, a pair (c_b, c_m), except that c_m is computed as $c_m \leftarrow m \cdot h(e_A^b)$. We also compute the hash for decryption:

$$D_{d_A}(c_b, c_m) = c_m \cdot \left(h\left(c_b^{d_A}\right)\right)^{-1} \bmod p \tag{6.22}$$

The second solution, using El-Gamal with a *DDH* group, is similar to the use of a DDH group with the DH PKC. Namely, computations are done over a cyclic group $\mathbb{G}$ believed to ensure the *DDH assumption* (Definition 6.7). Using the usual convention where we denote the operation of group $\mathbb{G}$ like we normally denote multiplication, the encrypt and decrypt operations of El-Gamal become even a bit simpler (compared to Equations (6.20) and (6.21)):

$$E_{e_A}(m) = \left(g^b, e_A^b \cdot m\right); \quad D_{d_A}(c_b, c_m) = c_m \cdot c_b^{-d_A} \tag{6.23}$$

The El-Gamal public key cryptosystem using a *DDH* group is believed to be secure, i.e., to prevent disclosure of any partial information about the plaintext. In addition, the DDH El-Gamal PKC is *multiplicative homomorphic*; we explain this property and some of its important applications in the following section.

Let us describe the DDH El-Gamal PKC in more details; we also illustrate it in Figure 6.17. We use g to denote a generator of $\mathbb{G}$ and q to denote the *order* of $\mathbb{G}$, i.e., the number of elements in $\mathbb{G}$; in other words, $\mathbb{G} = \{g^1, \ldots, g^q\}$, where the group operation is denoted

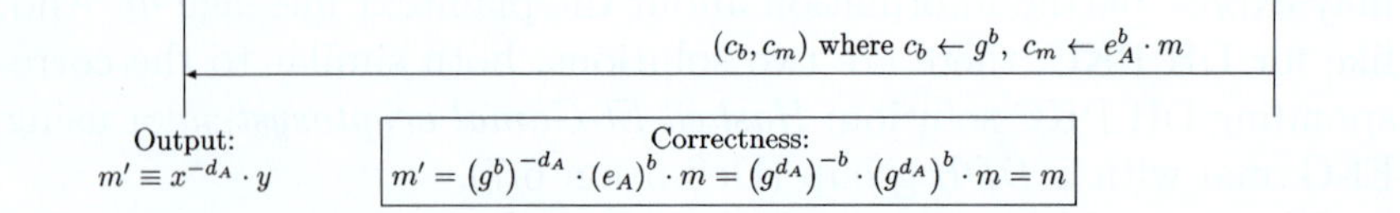

Figure 6.17. The El-Gamal public key cryptosystem using a DDH cyclic group $\mathbb{G}$, whose order we denote by q; exponentiations and multiplications are done using the corresponding operations of $\mathbb{G}$. The private key of Alice, denoted d_A, and the value b used by Bob, are both selected randomly from the set $\{1, \ldots, q\}$. Alice computes her public key as $e_A = g^{d_A}$.

by multiplication. Alice selects her private key d_A to be a random element in the group, i.e., $d_A \xleftarrow{\$} \{g^1, \ldots, g^q\}$, and her public key is simply $e_A = g^{d_A}$. Note the use of the standard notations of multiplication and exponentiation for the corresponding group operations of $\mathbb{G}$. As shown in Figure 6.17, the El-Gamal encryption of plaintext $m \in \mathbb{G}$, denoted $E_{e_A}(m)$, is computed as follows:

$$E_{e_A}(m) \leftarrow \begin{Bmatrix} b \xleftarrow{\$} [1, q] \\ \text{Return } \left(g^b \ , \ m \cdot e_A^b\right) \end{Bmatrix} \tag{6.24}$$

El-Gamal decryption is defined as:

$$D_{d_A}(c_b, c_m) = c_b^{-d_A} \cdot c_m \tag{6.25}$$

The correctness property holds since for every message $m \in \mathbb{G}$ holds:

$$\begin{aligned} D_{d_A}(g^b \ , m \cdot e_A^b) &= \left[\left(g^b\right)^{-d_A} \cdot \left(m \cdot \left(g^{d_A}\right)^b\right)\right] \\ &= \left[g^{-b \cdot d_A} \cdot m \cdot g^{b \cdot d_A}\right] \\ &= m \end{aligned} \tag{6.26}$$

6.4.3 Homomorphic encryption and the El-Gamal cryptosystem

Consider a public key cryptosystem (KG, E, D) where the plaintext messages are elements from some group $\mathbb{G}$, whose group operation we denote by $\cdot$; for example, if the inputs are messages in $\mathbb{Z}_p^*$, then $\cdot$ is multiplication modulo p. We say that (KG, E, D) is a *homomorphic encryption* public key cryptosystem, if there is an operation, which we call the *ciphertext operation* and denote $\times$, defined over all pairs of ciphertext messages, such that for every public–private key pair (e, d) and every pair of plaintext message m_1, m_2 holds that $E_e(m_1) \times E_e(m_2)$ is an encryption of $m_1 \cdot m_2$, namely,

$$m_1 \cdot m_2 = D_d\left(E_e(m_1) \times E_e(m_2)\right) \tag{6.27}$$

When the group operation is (modular) multiplication, as when the plaintexts are messages in $\mathbb{Z}_p^*$, then $m_1 \cdot m_2$ is the multiplication of the two messages, and we say that (KG, E, D) is *multiplicative homomorphic*. Similarly, if the group operation is (modular) addition, then we say that (KG, E, D) is *additive homomorphic*; however, it may be easier to focus on multiplicative homomorphic.

For multiplicative homomorphic, it is convenient to think of $\times$ as a 'multiplication of ciphertexts' operation. Following this, the homomorphic property basically means that the multiplication of two ciphertexts, $E_e(m_1) \times E_e(m_2)$, is equivalent to the encryption of the multiplication of the two messages, $E_e(m_1 \cdot m_2)$.

In this section, we focus on a specific multiplicative homomorphic scheme: the El-Gamal public key cryptosystem using a DDH group $\mathbb{G}$, i.e., a cyclic group which is believed to satisfy the DDH assumption (Definition 6.7).

In the El-Gamal PKC defined over DDH group $\mathbb{G}$, plaintexts are elements of $\mathbb{G}$ and ciphertexts are pairs (c_b, c_m) of elements from the group $\mathbb{G}$. The El-Gamal $\times$ operation is applied to a pair of ciphertexts, e.g., (c_b, c_m) and $(c_{b'}, c_{m'})$, and is defined as:

$$(c_b, c_m) \times (c_{b'}, c_{m'}) \equiv (c_b \cdot c_{b'}, c_m \cdot c_{m'}) \tag{6.28}$$

Note that the 'multiplication operations' $\cdot$ are the operations of the group $\mathbb{G}$ rather than modular-multiplication operations — indeed, the modular-multiplication group $\mathbb{Z}_p^*$ is not a DDH group.

The following lemma shows that the $\times$ operator correctly computes the encryption of the multiplication of the two plaintext messages m and m' whose El-Gamal encryptions are (c_b, c_m) and $(c_{b'}, c_{m'})$, respectively.

Lemma 6.3. *Let* $d_A \xleftarrow{\$} [1, p-1]$ *and* $e_A = g^{d_A}$. *Then, for any two messages* $m, m' \in \mathbb{G}$ *holds and any El-Gamal encryption of them* $E_{e_A}(m)$, $E_{e_A}(m')$ *holds:*

$$m \cdot m' = D_{d_A}\left(E_{e_A}(m) \times E_{e_A}(m')\right) \tag{6.29}$$

Proof. Let b be the random exponent used to compute $E_{e_A}(m)$ and b' be the random exponent used to compute $E_{e_A}(m')$. Then:

$$E_{e_A}(m) = (g^b, m \cdot e_A^b)$$
$$E_{e_A}(m') = (g^{b'}, m' \cdot e_A^{b'})$$

Hence,

$$E_{e_A}(m) \times E_{e_A}(m') = (g^{b+b'}, m \cdot m' \cdot e_A^{b+b'})$$

And

$$D_{d_A}\left(E_{e_A}(m) \times E_{e_A}(m')\right) = \left(g^{b+b'}\right)^{-d_A} \cdot m \cdot m' \cdot \left(g^{d_A}\right)^{b+b'}$$
$$= m \cdot m'$$

□

6.4.3.1 *Homomorphic encryption cannot be IND-CCA secure*

In Section 6.4.4, we show some of the cool applications of homomorphic encryption for privacy, e.g., to ensure privacy in voting. However, there is a caveat: *homomorphic encryption schemes cannot be IND-CCA secure.* Let us explain now why this is the case.

To see that homomorphic encryption cannot be IND-CCA secure, we use the fact that in every group $\mathbb{G}$, there is a unique *identity element* which we denote by 1, and for every element $x \in \mathbb{G}$, there is a unique *inverse*, denoted x^{-1}, such that $x \cdot x^{-1} = x^{-1} \cdot x = 1$, where $\cdot$ denotes that group (multiplication) operation. See Section A.2.4.

Consider an arbitrary homomorphic encryption public key cryptosystem (KG, E, D), where the plaintext messages are taken from some group $\mathbb{G}$, the group operation is denoted by the multiplication operand $(\cdot)$ and the *ciphertext operation* is denote $\times$. Let $x \in \mathbb{G}$ be a plaintext message which differs from the group's identity element, i.e., $x \neq 1$, and let x^{-1} denote the (unique) inverse of x over group $\mathbb{G}$.

To show that (KG, E, D) is not IND-CCA-secure, we show that, given the public key e, we can distinguish between the encryption, using e, of x and the encryption of 1. Suppose we receive the challenge ciphertext c^*, which is the encryption of either x or of 1; we denote this 'challenge plaintext' by $m^* \in \{x, 1\}$. To find out m^*, we compute $c_1 = E_e(1)$.

We next compute $c_M \leftarrow c_1 \times c^*$. If $c_M = c^*$, then c^* must be the encryption of 1 (we leave to the reader to prove this, as part of Exercise 6.31). If $c_M \neq c^*$, then the adversary can invoke the decryption oracle and receive $D_d(c_M)$. This value would be the same as m^* (as the reader should also prove as part of Exercise 6.31).

We conclude that a homomorphic encryption scheme cannot be IND-CCA-secure. In spite of that, there are applications where the value of homomorphic encryption is sufficient to motivate using it, in spite of the loss of the IND-CCA-security. Of course, this should only be done when needed and requires extra care and expertise. For example, in Section 6.5, we present the *textbook RSA* PKC and show that it is a multiplicative homomorphic public key cryptosystem but also vulnerable to attacks which motivate the use of RSA with secure padding mechanisms, making these secure versions of RSA non-homomorphic.

6.4.4 Applications of homomorphic encryption

In this section, we give a glimpse of the important applications of homomorphic encryption. We focus on the El-Gamal multiplicative homomorphic encryption and demonstrate how it can be used for applications requiring *anonymity*, and specifically, for *anonymous voting*. This is a tiny taste from the extensive research on the use of multiplicative homomorphic encryption, fully homomorphic encryption, *Private Information Retrieval* and other cryptographic schemes to ensure *privacy* and *anonymity*, and, in particular, *private and secure voting*.

Private and secure voting: Secure voting is essential for democracy. One of the main requirements is, usually, *voting privacy*, i.e., preserving the confidentiality of the vote of each individual and only exposing the tally of entire populations. This may be achieved by use of physical designs such as a ballot box or trusted voting machines. However, these designs can raise concerns about whether the votes are counted correctly.

There is extensive research on the use of cryptography to ensure *secure electronic voting*. We focus on *voter privacy*, i.e., ensuring the secrecy of the vote of specific individuals. We assume that each voter is able to securely encrypt their vote; this allows us to present a cryptographic protocol, without considering the challenges involving human voters.

First, let us consider a trivial design for an e-voting system: voters encrypt their votes with the public key of a trusted server, to which they then send their votes; the server *decrypts* and then *tallies* the votes. This system requires complete trust in the server; in particular, the server can trivially know the vote of each voter.

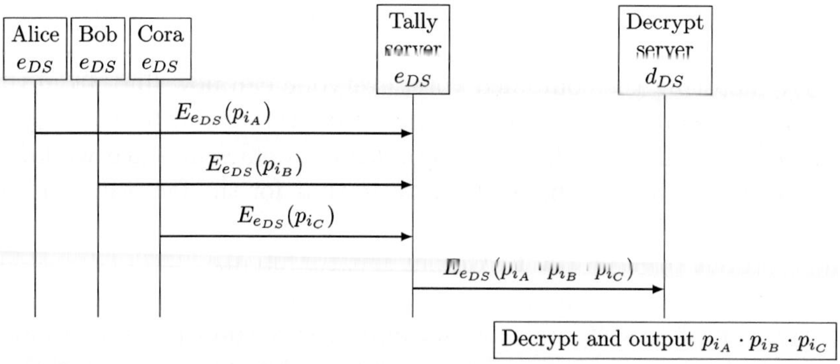

Figure 6.18. Example of privacy-preserving voting using two servers and multiplicative-homomorphic encryption, e.g., El-Gamal PKC; $p_i > 1$ is a small prime number assigned to candidate i. Voter i sends $E_{e_{DS}}(p_i)$, their vote (p_i) encrypted using the public key e_{DS} of the Decrypt server (DS), to the tally server. The tally server sends $e_{DS}(p_{i_A} \cdot p_{i_B} \cdot p_{i_C})$ to the decrypt server, who outputs the combined vote $p_{i_A} \cdot p_{i_B} \cdot p_{i_C}$. By factoring this, we find how many votes were given to each candidate i.

To ensure voter privacy, we separate the two functions of the server and use *two* servers: a *tally server* and a *decrypt server*. We also switch the order of operations: the encrypted votes are sent first to the tally server, who aggregates all of them into a single (encrypted) tally value and then sends the encrypted tally value to the decrypt server, who decrypts to produce the final outcome. This privacy-preserving voting process is shown in Figure 6.18.

For simplicity, we present the design assuming the 'naïve' El-Gamal PKC, i.e., with operations over the modular prime group $\mathbb{Z}_p^*$ and without hashing, although this scheme may leak some information about the plaintext. However, it helps to present a simple example.

As shown, each candidate i is assigned a unique small prime number: $p_i > 1$. Each voter, e.g., Alice, selects one candidate, say i_A (with identifier p_{i_A}), and sends to the tally server $E_{e_{DS}}(p_{i_A})$. We assume that the encryption is done using the El-Gamal cryptosystem, with some prime modulus p.

The homomorphic multiplication operation $\times$ allows the tally server to combine the encrypted votes by computing $x \equiv E_{e_{DS}}(p_{i_A}) \times E_{e_{DS}}(p_{i_B}) \times E_{e_{DS}}(p_{i_C})$ and sending x to the decrypt server. Specifically, from Equation (6.27), $x = E_{e_{DS}}(p_{i_A}) \times E_{e_{DS}}(p_{i_B}) \times E_{e_{DS}}(p_{i_C}) = E_{e_{DS}}(p_{i_A} \cdot p_{i_B} \cdot p_{i_C})$, i.e., x is the encryption of $p_{i_A} \cdot p_{i_B} \cdot p_{i_C}$. Hence, the decrypt server outputs $p_{i_A} \cdot p_{i_B} \cdot p_{i_C}$, i.e., the combined plaintext vote.

By factoring the combined vote, everyone can now find, from the combined plaintext vote, how many votes were given to each candidate i. Note that this factoring operation is efficient since we know exactly all of the possible factors. Note that for the factoring to provide correct result, the combined vote must always be less than p, the modulus used by the El-Gamal cryptosystem.

Obviously, this is not a complete description of a secure voting system. A complete system would not only ensure voter privacy but also prevent *cheating* by users and by the servers. Furthermore, recall that, for simplicity, the design uses the insecure variant of the El-Gamal public key cryptosystem, where computations are over the $\mathbb{Z}_p^*$ group, without hashing. Finally, communication to the tally server should be encrypted.

Another application — Re-encryption: Let us point out another application of multiplicative homomorphic encryption, such as the El-Gamal PKC: *re-encryption*. Namely, consider encryption $(c_m, c_b) = E_{e_A}(m)$ of plaintext m using public key e_A. Let $(c_1, c_{b,1}) \leftarrow E_{e_A}(1)$ be an encryption of 1 using e_A, and let $(c'_m, c'_b) \leftarrow (c_m, c_b) \times (c_1, c_{b,1})$. From the homomorphic property (Equation (6.27)), (c'_m, c'_b) is an encryption of $m \cdot 1 = m$, i.e., it is also an encryption of m. A further property of re-encryption is that an adversary cannot distinguish between the re-encryption of (c_m, c_b) and an encryption of a different message $\hat{m} \neq m$. Re-encryption is used in different protocols, often for *anonymous communication*; there are other solutions to ensure anonymity, including *Tor* and *anonymous remailer* [145, 156], all based on cryptography.

Re-encryption preserves the same decryption key. El-Gamal also allows a similar, but different, mechanism, called *proxy re-encryption*, where another entity called *proxy* is given a special key, denoted $e_{A \to B}$ and computed by Alice, that allows the proxy to transform a ciphertext message encrypted with the key of Alice, $c = E_{e_A}(m)$, into an encryption of the same message but with Bob's key, $c' = E_{e_B}(m)$. Proxy re-encryption has been proposed for different applications, such as monitoring of encrypted traffic. For more details on this mechanism and its applications, see Ref. [85].

Re-encryption (and proxy re-encryption) require the use or awareness of the public key e_A with which the message was encrypted.

In some applications, it is desirable to allow re-encryption without specifying the public key, e.g., for *recipient anonymity*. In such case, one can use an elegant extension called *universal re-encryption*, which allows re-encryption without knowledge of the encryption key e_A. This is done by appending the encryption $E_{e_A}(1)$ to each ciphertext; see details in Ref. [215].

6.4.5 Fully homomorphic encryption (FHE)

Fully homomorphic encryption schemes are schemes which are homomorphic with respect to *both* multiplication *and* addition. Namely, fully homomorphic encryption support *both* operations over the ciphertexts. The first FHE scheme was presented by Gentry in 2009, followed by several additional designs, many of them with improved efficiency; see, e.g., Refs. [101, 201, 463].

FHE schemes are powerful tools, allowing computation, given only the ciphertexts, of the encryption of *arbitrary functions* of the plaintext. Namely, FHE allows *arbitrary computations over encrypted data.*

Using fully homomorphic encryption, a client can encrypt some secret inputs, e.g., x_1, x_2, and send the ciphertexts $c_1 = E_e(x_1), c_2 = E_e(x_2)$ to an untrusted computation server; the server will use the multiplication and addition operations over the ciphertexts to compute some function f over the encrypted data, obtaining $E_e(f(x_1, x_2))$, the encryption of the result of the function applied to the inputs, and send it to the client, who will decrypt to obtain $f(x_1, x_2)$. Note that some of the encrypted inputs may be provided by other parties since encryption only requires the public key.

Such schemes have different applications, e.g., in *cloud computing*, where an untrusted cloud service is performing some computation on encrypted values. For example, FHE is one of the ways to implement *Private Information Retrieval (PIR)* schemes, allowing a client to retrieve a value from a table kept by a server without exposing the index of the entry retrieved to the server; e.g., see Ref. [202].

The challenge, however, is performance. There have been impressive improvements in the performance of fully homomorphic encryption schemes, e.g., from Gentry's pioneering work [201] to the much more efficient design of [101]. However, known FHE schemes still have significant overheads, in terms of computation time and/or the length of the keys and the ciphertext. This is in comparison to schemes that are homomorphic with respect to only one operation, mainly, multiplication or addition, which are also much simpler. We have seen one such scheme, the El-Gamal scheme; in the following section, and in particular in Section 6.5, we discuss another example, the *textbook RSA* public key cryptosystem.

6.5 The RSA public key cryptosystem

In 1978, Rivest, Shamir and Adelman presented the first proposal for a public key cryptosystem, as well as a digital signature scheme [418]. This beautiful scheme is usually referred to by the initials of the inventors, i.e., RSA; it was awarded the Turing award in 2002 and is still widely used. We cover here only some basic details of RSA; a more in-depth study is recommended, by taking a course in cryptography and/or reading one of the many books on cryptography covering RSA in depth, e.g., Ref. [253].

6.5.1 RSA key generation

Key generation in RSA is more complex than for DH and El-Gamal. We first list the steps and then explain them:

- Select a pair of large prime numbers p, q, specifically, both p and q would have $\lceil \frac{N}{2} \rceil$ bits. Let $n = p \cdot q$. As a result, n would have at least N bits.
- Select a value e which is co-prime to $\phi(n)$, i.e., $gcd(e, \phi(n)) = 1$. The $\phi(n)$ function is called *Euler's totient function*; we discuss it in Section A.2.3. For the specific choice of $n = p \cdot q$, for p, q being prime, the value of Euler's totient function would be $\phi(n) = (p-1) \cdot (q-1)$.
- Compute d to be the multiplicative inverse of e modulo $\phi(n)$, i.e., $d = e^{-1} \bmod \phi(n)$ and $e \cdot d \equiv 1 \pmod{\phi(n)}$.
- The public key is (e, n) and the private key is (d, n).

Selecting e to be co-prime to $\phi(n)$ is necessary — and sufficient — to ensure that e has a multiplicative inverse modulo $\phi(n)$ which we denote d, i.e., that $d = e^{-1} \bmod \phi(n)$ is defined (Fact 6.5). To find the inverse d, we can use the extended Euclidean algorithm (see, e.g., Ref. [253]). Given two integers a, b, the extended Euclidean algorithm finds a pair of integers c and d such that $a \cdot c + b \cdot d = gcd(a, b)$. We use $a \leftarrow \phi(n)$ and $b \leftarrow e$ and obtain c and d such that $\phi(n)\cdot c+e\cdot d = gcd(\phi(n),e)$. Since we picked e to be co-prime to $\phi(n)$, it follows that $gcd(\phi(n),e) = 1$; therefore, as required, $d = e^{-1} \bmod \phi(n)$, or:

$$e \cdot d \equiv 1 \pmod{\phi(n)} \tag{6.30}$$

As noted above, the public key of RSA is (e, n) and the private key is (d, n). The modulus n should be part of the keys since it is required for both encryption and decryption. However, we — and others — often abuse notation and refer to the keys simply as e and d.

6.5.2 Encryption using textbook RSA and using padded RSA

The RSA cryptosystem is based on the *RSA-encrypt* function $E_e^{RSA}(m)$, applied to plaintext m using public key e, and the RSA decryption function $D_d^{RSA}(c)$, applied to ciphertext c and using the private key d. These functions are computed as follows:

$$E_e^{RSA}(m) = m^e \bmod n \tag{6.31}$$

$$D_d^{RSA}(c) = c^d \bmod n \tag{6.32}$$

Here, the message m is encoded as a positive integer and limited to $m < n$, ensuring that $m = m \bmod n$. In Section 6.5.3, we show that this ensures *correctness*, i.e., correct decryption. Namely, for every message $m < n$ holds:

$$c \leftarrow E_e^{RSA}(m) = m^e \bmod n \;\Rightarrow\; m = D_d^{RSA}(c) = c^d \bmod n \tag{6.33}$$

In practice, the plaintexts would be further limited to contain less bits than n, i.e., $|m| < |n|$.

We use the term *textbook RSA* encryption, for RSA encryption performed by directly applying the RSA-encrypt function to the plaintext, i.e., using E^{RSA} as defined above.

As we explain in Section 6.5.5, textbook RSA encryption has significant vulnerabilities. Therefore, in practice, RSA cryptosystems always use a *padding scheme* together with the RSA functions (Equations (6.31) and (6.32)). The padding addresses the known vulnerabilities and allows us to establish the security of RSA encryption based on the *RSA assumption*, which we present in Section 6.5.5.

Padding is defined by a pair of functions $(pad, unpad)$. The input to *pad* and the output of *unpad* are plaintext messages. We say that the padding scheme $(pad, unpad)$ *ensures correctness* if unpadding of a padded message always recovers the message as it was before padding. Namely, for every message allowed message m, i.e., m in $\text{dom}(pad)$ (the domain of *pad*), the *pad* and *unpad* functions should ensure that:

$$(\forall m \in \text{dom}(pad))\ m = unpad(pad(m)) \tag{6.34}$$

In addition, while padded messages would normally be longer than the corresponding unpadded messages, this length increase should be bounded. We say that a padding function *pad* has l_{pad}−bits pad if for every message m holds $|pad(m)| \leq |m| + l_{pad}$.

Consider an arbitrary public key cryptosystem $(\mathcal{KG}, \mathcal{E}, \mathcal{D})$ that ensures correctness and allows messages up to l bits, and let $(pad, unpad)$ be a padding scheme that ensures correctness with l_{pad}−bits pad, where $l > l_{pad}$, and whose domain includes l−bit messages ($\{0,1\}^l \subseteq \text{dom}(pad)$). Then, the corresponding *padded public key cryptosystem* $(\mathcal{KG}, \hat{\mathcal{E}}, \hat{\mathcal{D}})$, where $\hat{E}_e(m) = E_e(pad(m))$ and $\hat{D}_d(c) = unpad(D_d(c))$, also ensures correctness, namely,

$$(\forall m \text{ s.t. } |m| + l_{pad} < |n|,\ (e, d) \leftarrow (1^n))$$

$$m = unpad(\mathcal{D}_d(\mathcal{E}_e(pad(m)))) = \hat{D}_d(\hat{E}_e(m)) \tag{6.35}$$

Let us now consider the specific case of (padded) RSA encryption and show that from the correctness of RSA (Equation (6.33)) follows the *correctness of padded RSA*. Namely, for every message m and $c \leftarrow E_e^{RSA}(pad(m))$ holds $m = unpad(D_d^{RSA}(c))$. Or:

$$(\forall m \text{ s.t. } |m| + l_{pad} < |n|)$$

$$m = unpad\left(\left([pad(m)]^e \bmod n\right)^d \bmod n\right) \tag{6.36}$$

Note that the plaintexts messages have to be at least l_{pad} bits shorter than the modulus n, ensuring that the padded messages would be shorter than n.

We illustrate textbook-RSA vs. padded-RSA in Figure 6.19 and discuss standard RSA padding in Section 6.5.6.

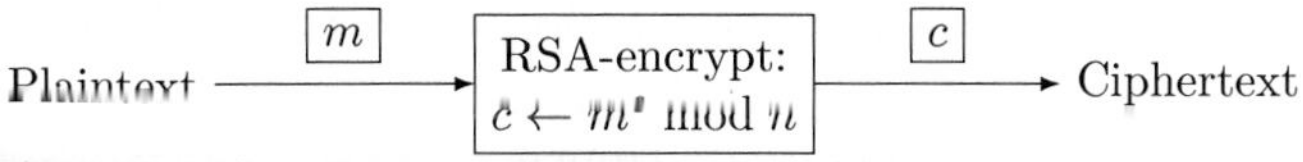

(a) Textbook-RSA, presented in Section 6.5.2 and shown to be vulnerable in Section 6.5.5.

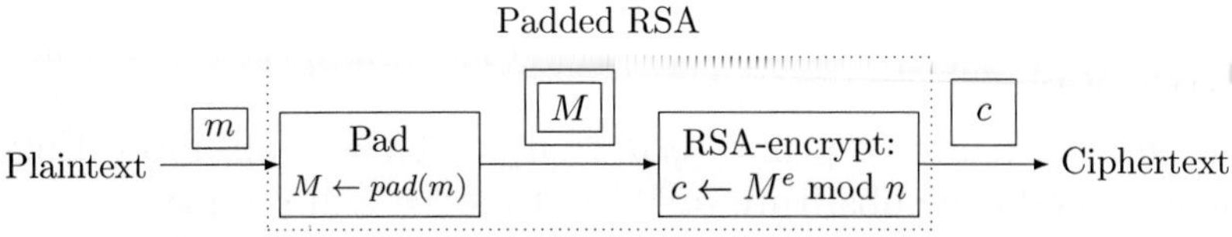

(b) Padded RSA following the PKCS #1 standard; see Section 6.5.6. Version 1.5 of PKCS #1 is vulnerable (see Section 6.5.7); version 2.2 of PKCS #1, also referred to as OAEP, is considered secure (see Section 6.5.8). We use M for the padded plaintext ($M = Pad(m)$).

Figure 6.19. RSA encryption: (a) textbook RSA (vulnerable) vs. (b) padded RSA (could be secure or vulnerable, depending on the padding used).

In the following sections, we discuss RSA's *correctness, efficiency* and *security* (Sections 6.5.3, 6.5.4 and 6.5.5, respectively).

6.5.3 Correctness of RSA

In this section, we show that textbook RSA ensures correctness, i.e., decryption always recovers correctly the encrypted plaintext. As we discussed above, correctness of padded RSA follows, as long as we use a padding scheme which ensures correctness.

Namely, we show that:

$$(\forall m < n)\, [m^e \bmod n]^d \equiv m \pmod n \tag{6.37}$$

Textbook RSA's correctness is based on *Euler's theorem* (Theorem A.3), which says that for any co-prime integers m, n, holds $m^{\phi(n)} = 1 \bmod n$, where $\phi(n)$ is *Euler's totient function*, defined as the number of positive integers which are less than n and co-prime to n. We use the theorem, to explain RSA's correctness (Equation (6.37)).

Note that for any primes p, q holds $\phi(p) = p-1$, $\phi(q) = q-1$, and $\phi(p \cdot q) = (p-1)(q-1)$ (Lemma A.1). You may note that this means that Euler's theorem is a generalization of Fermat's little theorem (Theorem A.1). Recall that $e \cdot d = 1 \pmod{\phi(n)}$, i.e., for some integer i it holds that $e \cdot d = 1 + i \cdot \phi(n)$. Hence,

$$\begin{aligned} m^{e \cdot d} \bmod n &= m^{1+i\cdot\phi(n)} \bmod n \\ &= m \cdot \left(m^{\phi(n)}\right)^i \bmod n \end{aligned}$$

Recall Equation (A.5) : $a^b \bmod n = (a \bmod n)^b \bmod n$. Assuming that m and n are co-prime ($gcd(m, n) = 1$), we can apply Euler's theorem and can substitute $m^{\phi(n)} = 1 \bmod n$ and receive:

$$m^{e \cdot d} \bmod n = m \cdot \left(m^{\phi(n)} \bmod n\right)^i \bmod n \tag{6.38}$$

$$= m \cdot 1^i \bmod n = m \bmod n \tag{6.39}$$

It follows that for some integer i:

$$\begin{aligned} D_d^{RSA}(E_e^{RSA}(m)) &= D_d^{RSA}(m^e \bmod n) \\ &= (m^e \bmod n)^d \bmod n \\ &= m^{e \cdot d} \bmod n \\ &= m \cdot \left(m^{\phi(n)} \bmod n\right)^i \bmod n \\ &= m \cdot 1^i \bmod n \\ &= m \bmod n = m \end{aligned} \tag{6.40}$$

Note that $m \bmod n = m$ since we restricted plaintext messages m so that $m < n$. Namely, under the assumption (above) that m and n are co-primes, we have shown the correctness of textbook RSA.

What about the assumption that m and n are co-primes? This assumption does not always hold. Recall that the message — m may be any positive integer s.t. $1 < m < n$. Most, but not all, of these possible messages — i.e., integers smaller than n — are co-prime to n. In fact, the number of integers smaller than n and co-prime to n is exactly the definition of $\phi(n)$, which we know to be $\phi(n) = \phi(p \cdot q) = (p - 1) \cdot (q - 1) = n - q - p + 1$.

So, *most* possible messages m are indeed co-prime to n. Still, $p+q-2$ messages are *not* co-prime to n; this number is much smaller than n but is still polynomial in n (roughly $n^{\frac{1}{2}}$), and our explanation does not hold for these values. We assure the reader, however, that correctness holds also for these values; it 'just' requires a slightly more elaborate argument. Such arguments, usually using the Chinese remainder theorem, can be found in many textbooks on cryptography and number theory, e.g., Ref. [250].

6.5.4 RSA's efficiency

The RSA algorithms are conceptually simple; however, their computation requires considerable resources. The basic reason for that is that RSA security completely breaks down if an attacker is able to factor n and find its factors (p and q); this allows computation of $\phi(n) = (p-1)\cdot(q-1)$. This allows the attacker to efficiently compute the private key d from the public key e since $d \equiv e^{-1} \pmod{\phi(n)}$. After all, that's how we computed d to begin with!

Factoring is a well-studied problem, and while no *polynomial* factoring algorithm is known, there are algorithms that improve efficiency considerably compared to naïve factoring. As a result, RSA keys should be quite long, as shown in Table 6.1; note that the key length should be chosen based on the maximal time at which the encryption should remain secret and not based on the current time. For example, for information whose confidentiality should be preserved until 2040, the modulus n should be about 3000 bits, i.e., p and q should be random prime with about 1500 bits.

Computations, especially exponentiation, with such extremely long numbers, require significant computational resources. The computations are modulo n, which keeps the results from becoming even longer, but this requires computation of the modulus of the result (and optionally of intermediate values), and the computation of the modulus also requires significant computational resources.

Therefore, efficiency is a major consideration for implementations of RSA. In this section, we discuss only one of the most basic optimizations: *choosing e to improve efficiency.*

The public exponent e is not secret, and, so far, we only required it to be co-prime to $\phi(n)$. This motivates choosing e that will improve efficiency — usually, to make encryption faster. In particular, choosing $e = 3$ implies that encryption — i.e., computing $m^e \bmod n$ — requires only *two* multiplications, i.e., is significantly more efficient than exponentiation by larger number.

However, there are several concerns with such extremely small e; in particular, if m is also small, specifically, if $m^e < n$, then $c = m^e \bmod n = m^e$, i.e., c is the result of raising m to the power of e *over the integers* — the modulus operation has no impact since the result is still less than n. In this case, we can perform the reverse operation — decryption — by computing the eth root of c, i.e., $m = c^{1/e}$, again performing the computation over the integers (rather than (mod n)). Computing $c^{1/e}$ is not trivial, but it is computationally efficient.

There are additional attacks on RSA with very-low exponent e, e.g., Ref. [133]. Some of these attacks are for the case where a party may encrypt and send the same message, or 'highly related' messages, to multiple recipients.

These attacks motivate (1) the use of padding to break any possible relationships between messages, as well as (2) the choice of larger value for e.

Common choices for a larger value of e are the Fermat primes 17, $257 = 2^8 + 1$ and $65537 = 2^{16} + 1$. The reason to choose these specific primes is again *efficiency*; using these values, the exponentiation operation $m^e \bmod n$ requires only a small number of multiplications, respectively. For example, to compute m^5, we only need three multiplications: first compute $m^2 = m \cdot m$, then compute $m^4 = m^2 \cdot m^2$, and finally compute $m^5 = m^4 \cdot m$. Similarly, we can compute m^8 as $m^4 \cdot m^4$. In Exercise 6.37, you are asked show how to compute efficiently exponentiations by the Fermat primes $17, 257$ and 65537.

Encrypting plaintexts longer than the modulus — hybrid encryption: To complete our discussion of RSA efficiency, let us mention that, in practice, plaintexts are typically longer than the RSA modulus n. Therefore, usually, RSA encryption, like other public-key cryptosystems, is applied using *hybrid encryption* (Section 6.1.6), i.e., it is only used to encrypt a shared key, which is then used to encrypt the plaintext. This is important, since the (padded) input m to the RSA-encrypt function must be less than the modulus n, or decryption will output $m \bmod n$ instead of m. Using a modulus n which is longer than expected (padded) messages will result in unacceptable overhead. See Section 6.1.6 and Figure 6.3.

6.5.5 The RSA assumption and the vulnerability of textbook RSA

Now that we have seen that RSA ensures correctness, it is time to discuss its security. We first discuss the underlying security assumption and then discuss several vulnerabilities of textbook RSA, which are the reason that in practice, we always use padded RSA; we discuss standard padding schemes used for RSA encryption in the following sections, beginning with Section 6.5.6.

The security of RSA encryption is based on the *RSA assumption.* Intuitively, the RSA assumption is that there is only negligible probability that an efficient adversary $\mathcal{A}$ correctly recovers the plaintext m, given the ciphertext $m^e \bmod n$ and the public key (e, n). Let us restate the RSA assumption a bit more formally.

Definition 6.8 (RSA assumption). Choose n, e as explained above, i.e., $n = pq$ for p, q chosen as random l-bit prime numbers, and e is co-prime to $\phi(n)$. The *RSA assumption* is that for any efficient algorithm $\mathcal{A}$ and constant c, and for sufficiently large l, holds:

$$\Pr\left[\mathcal{A}((e,n), m^e \bmod n) = m\right] \in NEGL(l) \tag{6.41}$$

where m is chosen randomly $m \xleftarrow{\$} [2, n-2]$.

The RSA assumption is also referred to sometimes as the *RSA trapdoor one-way permutation assumption.* The 'trapdoor' refers to the fact that d is a 'trapdoor' that allows inversion of RSA; the 'one-way' refers to the fact that computing RSA (given public key (e, n)) is easy, but inverting is 'hard'; and the 'permutation' is due to RSA being a permutation (and in particular, invertible).

One obvious question is the relation between the RSA assumption and the assumption that factoring is hard. One relation is simple: if the RSA assumption is correct, then factoring must be hard. Assume that some adversary A_F can efficiently factor large numbers, specifically, the modulus n (which is part of the RSA public key). Hence, A_F can factor n, find q and p, compute $\phi(n)$ and proceed to compute the decryption key d, given the public key $< e, n >$, just like done in RSA key generation. We therefore conclude that if factoring is easy, i.e., if there exists such adversary A, then the RSA assumption cannot hold (and RSA is insecure).

We do *not* have a proof that the reverse is necessarily true. Namely, as far as we currently know, it is *possible* that factoring is hard, yet the RSA assumption is false, and there is an efficient attack that can invert RSA encryption with non-negligible probability. However, there are several results which do provide some support to the hope that breaking RSA may imply the ability to factor. In particular, Maurer and Aggarwal show that breaking RSA *does imply factoring* if we consider only adversaries whose computational abilities are limited to certain 'group operations', in what is called the *generic group model* [9].

Assume now that we are willing to accept the RSA assumption. What, then, about the security of RSA, when used as a public key cryptosystem (PKC)? In this section, we discuss textbook RSA and argue that it is vulnerable; this motivates the PKCS #1 specifications for 'padded RSA encryption', which we discuss in the following section.

Textbook RSA is multiplicative homomorphic encryption: Before we discuss the vulnerabilities of textbook RSA, let us point out an important property of it: *textbook RSA is multiplicative homomorphic.* Indeed, this follows quite simply:

$$\begin{aligned} E_e^{RSA}(m_1 \cdot m_2) &= (m_1 \cdot m_2)^e \bmod n \\ &= m_1^e \cdot m_2^e \bmod n \\ &= E_e^{RSA}(m_1) \cdot E_e^{RSA}(m_2) \bmod n \end{aligned}$$

Vulnerabilities of textbook RSA: As we discussed in Section 6.4.3, a homomorphic encryption scheme cannot be IND-CCA secure. This is a drawback, requiring extra care in design of secure applications using a homomorphic encryption scheme. However, in the case of textbook RSA, there are additional vulnerabilities, which makes the use of textbook RSA inadvisable. A partial list includes the following:

1. The textbook RSA PKC is *deterministic*, unlike the El-Gamal PKC. Namely, using textbook RSA, encryption of the same plaintext m will always result in the same ciphertext $c = m^e \bmod n$. Suppose that the attacker guesses (or knows) a set of likely (or possible) plaintexts, say m_1, m_2 and m_3. The attacker can easily compute, say, $c_1 = m_1^e \bmod n$; if the plaintext message m was the same as m_1, then $c = c_1$. Textbook RSA encryption resembles, in this sense, the insecure ECB mode of operation (Section 2.10), which has the same vulnerability. In general, secure encryption — shared key or public key — should be randomized and/or stateful.
2. Textbook RSA is vulnerable to *low-exponent attacks*, especially when sending short, low-value messages m. We already mentioned the trivial attack when $m^e < n$. See more elaborate low-exponent attacks in Refs. [133, 374]; these exploit scenarios where we send identical or related messages to multiple recipients.
3. The RSA assumption does not rule out a potential *exposure of partial information* about the plaintext, e.g., a particular bit. There are some positive results, in particular, $log(n)$ least-significant bits were shown to be as secure as the entire preimage [12, 182]. However, these results still leave that possibility of exposing other bits, like the one bit of the discrete logarithm (see Section 6.1.8.3).
4. Finally, while every homomorphic encryption scheme is vulnerable to chosen-ciphertext attack (CCA), textbook RSA is also vulnerable to *much weakened* version of CCA attacks, where the attacker only needs to receive very limited information about the ciphertext. In Section 6.5.7, we present Bleichenbacher's attack, which can effectively 'break' textbook RSA given only a one-bit error indicator, specifically, indication if the result of textbook RSA decryption is a 'properly padded plaintext'. Furthermore, this attack breaks not only textbook RSA but also some versions of *padded RSA*, in particular, when using the (widely used and very simple) RSA PKCS #1 version 1.5, which we discuss in the following section.

6.5.6 Padded RSA encryption with PKCS #1 v1.5

In the previous section, we saw that textbook RSA has significant vulnerabilities, making it inadvisable to use it. Therefore, to improve security, practical deployments always use *padded RSA*, i.e., apply a *pad* function to the message before applying the encryption operation, and a corresponding *unpad* function to recover the plaintext after decryption. The *unpad* function should recover the message before padding, which ensures the *correctness of padded RSA*, i.e., for every message m we always have $m = unpad(D_d^{RSA}(E_e^{RSA}(pad(m)))$ (Equation (6.36)).

Practical deployments of RSA encryption often use one of the padding schemes specified in different versions of the PKCS #1 specifications[9] [475].

Before version 2.0, PKCS #1 defined only one padding, which we refer to as the *PKCS #1 v1.5 padding*; version 2.0 added the *Optimal Asymmetric Encryption Padding* (OAEP), based on the design from Ref. [49]. In this section, we discuss the v1.5 padding; in Section 6.5.7, we discuss Bleichenbacher's attacks against RSA using PKCS #1 v1.5 padding, and, finally, in Section 6.5.8, we discuss the OAEP padding.

PKCS #1 version 1.5 was designed mainly to address two of the vulnerabilities of textbook RSA: deterministic output and low-exponent attacks. Another goal was to prevent chosen-ciphertext attacks (CCA). These goals motivated the following aspects of the padding:

- To prevent an attacker from identifying multiple encryptions of the same plaintext, possibly by the attacker encrypting some guesses of possible plaintexts, PKCS #1 version 1.5 includes a significant number of random bits.
- To prevent the low-exponent attacks (vulnerability 2), the padding prepends random bits to the message bytes. To further ensure a sufficiently large value for the padded-plaintext, PKCS #1 version 1.5 prepends the random bits with a non-zero byte.
- To prevent chosen-ciphertext attacks, PKCS #1 version 1.5 adds redundancy. Most significantly, the two most significant bytes of the padded plaintext would always have the same value, $0x0002$, which is validated during the *unpad* operation.

---

[9]PKCS stands for *Public Key Cryptography Standards* for standard padding. The PKCS specifications were published by RSA Security LLC; versions 1.5, 2.0, 2.1 and 2.2 were defined by the IETF, in RFCs Refs. [272,280,282,475], respectively.

Based on these guidelines, the PKCS #1 version 1.5 algorithm, $Pad_{v1.5}(\cdot)$, is defined as follows. Given an input (pre-padding) plaintext message m, and a random string r of at least eight non-zero random bytes, we compute the padded message $M = Pad_{v1.5}(m)$ as:

$$Pad_{v1.5}(m) = 0x00 +\!\!+ 0x02 +\!\!+ r +\!\!+ 0x00 +\!\!+ m \qquad (6.42)$$

To ensure that the binary value of M is less than n, as required for correct decryption, the (pre-padding) message m must contain less than $l - 11$ bytes, where l is the length of the modulus n (in bytes). The value of the second byte ($0x02$) prevents low-exponent attacks (by being non-zero). In addition, the fact that the second byte is $0x02$ identifies that the operation applied to the input was RSA encryption and not, say, RSA signing.

In the decryption process, we first obtain the padded message M, from which we can easily extract and return only the plaintext m. The message should be returned only if the padding is correct, i.e., begins with $0x0002$, followed by at least eight non-zero bytes, and finally followed by a zero byte. If M deviates from this in any way, an error indicator is returned.

As the readers hopefully agree, the PKCS #1 version 1.5, defined in Equation (6.42), is simple to understand and easy to implement. These properties are part of the reason that this padding was quickly adopted by many systems and is still quite widely deployed. However, the *PKCS #1 version 1.5* turns out to be vulnerable to some attacks. The first and most important of these is *Bleichenbacher's padding side channel attack*, which we discuss in the following section and illustrate in Figure 6.20.

6.5.7 Bleichenbacher's padding side-channel attack on PKCS #1 v1.5

In 1998, Daniel Bleichenbacher presented possibly the first and most important attack against the RSA public key cryptosystem [88]. Bleichenbacher's attack is effective against the use of the *PKCS #1 version 1.5.*

Bleichenbacher's attack is a *padding-error oracle attack*, introduced in Section 2.11 (and illustrated in Figure 2.37). Namely, the attacker can provide ciphertexts $c_1, c_2, \ldots$ and receive indication of

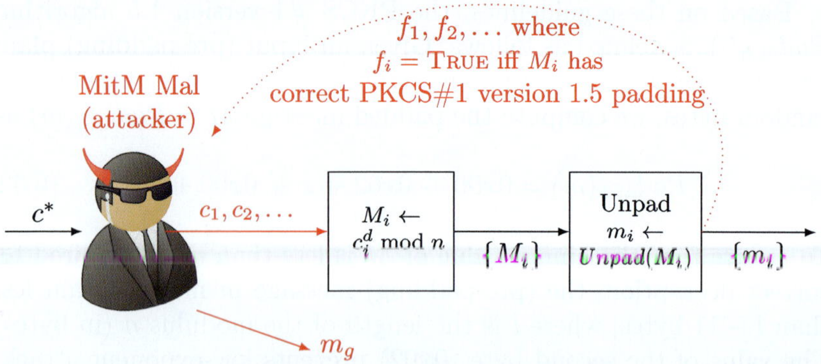

Figure 6.20. Bleichenbacher's attack on RSA PKCS #1 version 1.5. The attacker is given ciphertext c^* and outputs a *guess plaintext* m_g. The attacker's goal is to compute the 'correct' plaintext, $m_g = m^*$, where $m^* = (c^*)^d \bmod n$. To compute m_g, the attacker sends ciphertexts $c_i = c^* \cdot s_i^e \bmod n$, where s_i are different integers. The attacker receives only the one-bit-feedback side channel indications $\{f_i\}$, where f_i is true if M_i, the ith output of the textbook RSA decryption function, has correct PKCS #1 version 1.5 padding. We use m_i to denote the outcome of the PKCS #1 decryption of c_i, i.e., the result of unpadding M_i.

which of these ciphertexts corresponds to a properly padded plaintext. Note that this attack model is much weaker than the 'regular' chosen-ciphertext attack model, where the attacker receives the *decryptions* of the chosen ciphertexts.

Bleichenbacher's attack against the PKCS #1 version 1.5 padding: We discuss Bleichenbacher's attack against RSA encryption using the *PKCS #1 version 1.5*; this padding is very popular and used by numerous systems and standards, including several variants of the important SSL and TLS protocols (Chapter 7). Bleichenbacher's attack, and variants of it, apply to many systems and standards. In particular, Manger [345] showed a variant that can attack even a variant of OAEP standardized as version 2.0 of PKCS #1. As shown in Ref. [423], this attack can also be applied against many implementations of PKCS #1 v1.5, with greater efficiency than the original Bleichenbacher attack, facilitating attacks even against TLS 1.3. We note that Manger's attack exploits a seemingly minor detail of PKCS #1 version 2.0, which differs from the original Optimal Asymmetric Encryption Padding (OAEP) design; this detail was fixed in version 2.2 of PKCS #1 [364].

The setup of Bleichenbacher's attack is illustrated in Figure 6.20. The attacker's goal is to compute a string M which is the same size as the modulus n, which we denote l bytes, and such that $M = (c^*)^d \bmod n$, for a given 'challenge ciphertext' c^*. Basically, M would be the padded version of the original plaintext m encoded by PKCS #1 version 1.5, as in Equation (6.42); it would then be trivial for the attacker to unpad M and find the original plaintext m.

Bleichenbacher's attack works for arbitrary c^*, i.e., c^* *is not necessarily the result of PKCS #1 v1.5 encryption.* This can be very useful in some scenarios and is exploited in some attacks based on Bleichenbacher's attack, including attacks we discuss in Chapter 7. We focus on the simpler and common case where c^* *is* the result of RSA PKCS #1 v1.5 padded encryption of some plaintext m^*, which simplifies the attack a bit.

Often, the attacker obtains c^* by eavesdropping to a transmission from a benign sender, which obtained c^* by encrypting some secret ('challenge') message m^* using RSA with PKCS #1 v1.5 padding. In this case, if the attacker succeeds to compute $(c^*)^d \bmod n$, this gives the padded challenge message $M^* = Pad(m^*)$, which easily provides m^* itself, since $m^* = UnPad(Pad(m^*)) = UnPad(M^*)$.

Since c^* is the result of RSA encryption using PKCS #1 v1.5, we have $M^* = Pad_{v1.5}(m^*)$. From the definition of the pad in Equation (6.42), we know that a properly padded message such as M^* must begin with $0x0002$. Hence,

$$2B \leq M^* < 3B, \text{ where } B \equiv 2^{8(l-2)} \tag{6.43}$$

where l is the length, in bytes, of n (and hence of M). Note that Equation (6.43) does not reflect any knowledge about the plaintext m^* or the private key, only about the padded-plaintext $M^* \leftarrow Pad_{v1.5}(m^*)$ and the public key (n, e).

The attack generates a sequence of sets $\{\mathcal{M}_i\}_{i \geq 0}$, each containing one or more intervals of integers, where the correct solution, M^*, is in one of these intervals. The initial set, $\mathcal{M}_0$, simply contains one interval containing all the l-bytes strings beginning with $0x0002$, i.e.,

$$\mathcal{M}_0 \equiv \{\ [2B, 3B - 1\ ]\} \tag{6.44}$$

All padded strings, and therefore also M^*, are contained in $[2B, 3B-1]$, i.e., in $\mathcal{M}_0$. The attacks proceed to iteratively produce additional sets of intervals, $\{\mathcal{M}_i\}$, such that for every $i > 0$, the set of values contained in (the intervals in) $\mathcal{M}_i$ is a strict subset of the set of values in $\mathcal{M}_{i-1}$, but always includes the correct solution M^*. The attack completes when $\mathcal{M}_i$ contains only one value — which must, therefore, be the correct solution, M^*.

Note that when the number of elements in $\mathcal{M}_i$ is sufficiently small, the attacker could also exhaustively look for the solution, i.e., the value $M_g \in \mathcal{M}_i$ such that $c^* = M_g^e \bmod n$. This is often more efficient than continuing the attack until $\mathcal{M}_i$ contains only a single element. In particular, we can use the fact that every correctly padded message, with PKCS #1 v1.5, would contain at least one byte of only zero bits between the random string and the actual (unpadded) plaintext, which should rule out roughly 255/256 of the values in $\mathcal{M}_i$. Similarly, we can use any additional information we may have about the plaintext, such as a specific format or known contents of part of the plaintext.

The attack computes, for every $i > 0$, two values: first, an integer s_i, and then, the set of intervals $\mathcal{M}_i$. The attack terminates when $\mathcal{M}_i$ contains only a single value (which would be the solution M^*). The computation is done iteratively over i, beginning with $i = 1$.

Computation of s_1: Let us first describe the special case of computing s_1. We compute s_1 as the smallest integer such that the textbook RSA decryption of $c^* \cdot (s_1)^e \bmod n$ has correct padding, as we learn from the one-bit-feedback upon sending $c^* \cdot (s_1)^e \bmod n$ to the decryption device. Namely, $m^* \cdot s_1 \bmod n$ is well padded and, in particular, begins with $0x0002$. Note: It suffices to begin searching for s_1 from the minimal value of $\frac{n}{3B}$ since for smaller values of s_1, $m^* \cdot s_1 \bmod n$ cannot begin with $0x0002$ (i.e., is not well padded).

Computation of s_i *for* $i > 1$*, if* $\mathcal{M}_{i-1}$ *contains more than one interval*: In this case, s_i is the smallest integer such that $s_i > s_{i-1}$ and the decryption of $c^* \cdot (s_i)^e \bmod n$ has correct padding, and, in particular, the resulting plaintext, $m^* \cdot s_i \bmod n$, begins with $0x0002$.

Computation of s_i *for* $i > 1$*, if* $\mathcal{M}_{i-1}$ *contains exactly one interval,* $\mathcal{M}_{i-1} = \{[a, b]\}$: In this last case, choose small integers r_i, s_i such that the decryption of $c^* \cdot (s_i)^e \bmod n$ has correct padding and that the following two conditions hold:

$$r_i \geq 2\frac{b \cdot s_{i-1} - 2B}{n}$$
$$\frac{2B + r_i \cdot n}{b} \leq s_i < \frac{3b + r_i \cdot n}{a} \tag{6.45}$$

Computation of $\mathcal{M}_i$: After s_i has been found, we compute the new set $\mathcal{M}_i$ as:

$$\mathcal{M}_i \leftarrow \bigcup_{(a,b,r)} \left\{ \left[\max\left(a, \left\lceil \frac{2B + rn}{s_i} \right\rceil\right), \min\left(b, \left\lfloor \frac{3B - 1 + rn}{s_i} \right\rfloor\right) \right] \right\}$$
$$\text{for all } [a, b] \in \mathcal{M}_{i-1} \text{ and for } \frac{a \cdot s_i - 3B + 1}{n} \leq r \leq \frac{b \cdot s_i - 2B}{n} \tag{6.46}$$

The size of the intervals in the $\mathcal{M}_i$ sets decreases in each iteration. Analysis of the rate of decrease, and of the required number of padding-correctness feedback queries, is beyond our scope. See Ref. [88], where Bleichenbacher estimates that the attack will require about 2^{20} (about a million) queries.

Finally, we prove that the attack finds M^*.

Lemma 6.4. *For every $\mathcal{M}_i$ produced by the Bleichenbacher attack as describe above, holds $M^* \in \mathcal{M}_i$.*

Proof. We already mentioned that $M^* \in \mathcal{M}_0$. Assume that $M^* \in \mathcal{M}_{i-1}$, and we prove that $M^* \in \mathcal{M}_i$.

Whenever we choose s_i, we confirm, using the padding-correctness feedback, that $m^* \cdot s_i \bmod n$ is well padded and, in particular, begins with $0x0002$. Namely, for some integer r holds:

$$2B \leq M^* \cdot s_i - r \cdot n \leq 3B - 1 \tag{6.47}$$

Namely,

$$\frac{2B + r \cdot n}{s_i} \leq M^* \leq \frac{3B - 1 + r \cdot n}{s_i} \tag{6.48}$$

Now, since $M^* \in \mathcal{M}_{i-1}$, then there exists an interval $[a, b] \in \mathcal{M}_{i-1}$ which contains M^*, i.e., $a \leq M^* \leq b$. Substituting M^* in Equation (6.47), we have:

$$\frac{a \cdot s_i - (3B - 1)}{n} \leq r \leq \frac{b \cdot s_i - 2B}{n} \tag{6.49}$$

The combination of Equations (6.48) and (6.49) implies that M^* must be in one of the intervals in $\mathcal{M}_i$, as defined in Equation (6.46).

□

6.5.8 Optimal Asymmetric Encryption Padding (OAEP)

To improve the security of RSA encryption, it is usually used with more secure padding schemes, which are designed to prevent chosen-ciphertext attack attacks, including Bleichenbacher's attack. The *Optimal Asymmetric Encryption Padding* (OAEP) scheme was proposed by Bellare and Rogaway [49]. From version 2.0 of the PKCS #1 standard until the version 2.2 [475], the current version, the standard includes both OAEP as well as the PKCS #1v1.5 padding. OAEP is more secure than PKCS #1v1.5 padding and does not have significantly higher overhead, so there is rarely any reason to use the legacy PKCS #1v1.5 padding, except backwards compatibility with systems not supporting OAEP. The OAEP design can be seen as a variant of the Feistel construction (Section 2.8.3).

OAEP further improves the security of RSA, mainly by the following two mechanisms:

Mixing plaintext bits: To deal with the concern that RSA may expose partial information, OAEP mixes up all the bits of the plaintext before applying textbook-RSA encryption. The mixing makes it necessary to expose many or all bits of the input to the textbook RSA encrypt function, in order to expose any information about the plaintext.

Plaintext-awareness against chosen-ciphertext attacks: To foil chosen-ciphertext attacks (CCA), OAEP adds *known redundancy* to the plaintext before applying encryption to it. The OAEP decryption process returns the decrypted plaintext, only if it contains the same redundancy. This should make it infeasible for the attacker to learn sensitive information by CCA, i.e., sending manipulated ciphertext messages, since, almost always, their decryption would not have the correct redundancy (and be rejected). Bellare and Rogaway coined the term *plaintext-aware encryption* for encryption with such validation function as part of the decryption process, where an attacker must know ('be aware of') a plaintext m in order to create a ciphertext c which will be decrypted into m. If the attacker produces ciphertext c' without knowing a corresponding plaintext m', then the decryption of c' is bound to result in an error indication rather than in a decrypted plaintext m'.

Following Ref. [49], we first present simplified versions of the OAEP padding, which only implements the 'mix all bits' mechanism, to *prevent exposure of partial information*, but does not add redundancy to defend against chosen-ciphertext attack (CCA). Later, we describe the (non-simplified) OAEP padding, which extends the simplified padding schemes and also *adds redundancy to defend against CCA attacks.*

Three simplified OAEP padding schemes: Pad_0, Pad_1 and Pad_2. Before we describe the 'complete' OAEP scheme, we discuss a simplified version of it, $Pad_2(\cdot)$, illustrated in Figure 6.21. In fact, $Pad_2(\cdot)$ is already quite complex, and therefore, we first discuss two simpler functions, Pad_0 and Pad_1, and only then Pad_2.

Let us first discuss Pad_0. Consider an attacker who can only *expose a single bit* in the preimage of the RSA encryption; we don't know *which bit.* To prevent such attacker from exposing any bit of the input to Pad_0, we select a random string r of the same length as the input as a 'one time mask' for the input. More precisely, let DB ('data block') denote[10] the input to the simplified padding functions; then $Pad_0(\cdot)$ is defined as:

$$Pad_0(DB) \stackrel{\$}{\leftarrow} r + DB \oplus r \text{ where } r \stackrel{\$}{\leftarrow} \{0,1\}^{|DB|\cdot 8} \tag{6.50}$$

[10]The notation DB follows RFC 8071 [475], a standard defining OAEP and other mapping functions.

Namely, the simplified padding function Pad_0 selects a random one-time pad r to 'encrypt' DB; the padded output $Pad_0(DB)$ consists of the random pad r, concatenated to the 'masked' plaintext $DB \oplus r$. Note that the length of r is $|DB|$ bytes, i.e., $|DB| \cdot 8$ bits.

Since we assumed that the attacker can expose only *one* bit from the preimage of the RSA function, then the attacker can only learn either one bit of r or one bit of $DB \oplus r$. In either case, the exposed bit provides *no* information on the input data block DB.

The $Pad_0(\cdot)$ mapping is rather naïve; it uses a long pad random r — as long as DB — and yet it protects only against exposure of a single bit. What if the attacker can expose *two* bits of the preimage, e.g., the first bit of $DB \oplus r$ *and* the (corresponding) first bit of r? And, do we really need to send such a long pad — as long as the input DB? We improve on both aspects with the next version of the simplified padding, Pad_1.

Improving upon Pad_0 — the Pad_1 simplified OAEP padding scheme: The Pad_1 function uses a shorter random string r; the string r would now only contain l_h bytes ($l_h \cdot 8$ bits), where l_h is the number of bytes in the output of a keyless cryptographic hash function h (which is used later in the construction). In particular, typically, $|r| = l_h << |DB|$. Obviously, now we cannot directly XOR DB with r. Instead, we XOR DB with $g(r)$, where g is modeled as a randomly selected function, whose input is a string of l_h bytes and whose output is a string as long as DB. Intuitively, g *expands* r into a longer pseudorandom string $g(r)$. The fact that $|g(r)| = |DB|$ allows us to use $g(r)$ as a 'pseudo-one-time-pad' to mask DB. Namely, $Pad_1(\cdot)$ is defined as:

$$Pad_1(DB) \xleftarrow{\$} r + (DB \oplus g(r)) \text{ where } r \xleftarrow{\$} \{0,1\}^{l_h \cdot 8} \tag{6.51}$$

Clearly, Pad_1 has lower overhead than Pad_0 since r is shorter. Furthermore, if we view g as a 'random oracle', then security also improved since even if the attacker exposes several — but not most — of the bits of the random string r, then the bits of $g(r)$ would still be unknown (pseudorandom).

However, suppose that the attacker can expose *all* (or most) of r directly from the ciphertext (output of RSA encryption), allowing the attacker to compute $g(r)$. Furthermore, assume that the attacker can also expose one or more bits of $g(r) \oplus DB$. Since the attacker has already $g(r)$, knowing bits of $g(r) \oplus DB$ allows the attacker to expose the corresponding bits of DB. Note that exposure of r plus one or few bits of $g(r) \oplus DB$ doesn't mean that the RSA encryption function is invertible since r only contains l_h bytes, which is surely much less than the length of DB (which is why Pad_1 is more efficient than Pad_0). Of course, such exposure *would* imply that the RSA encryption function is *weaker than we hoped* since r contains l_h bytes, and the hope is that given an RSA-encrypted message, it is either infeasible to expose any bit of the message, or it is only possible to expose very few bits, not l_h bytes.

Further improving — the *Pad*₂ simplified OAEP padding scheme: The final simplified OAEP padding, $Pad_2(\cdot)$, improves security further; it provides efficient and effective protection even if the attacker can expose a large part of the input to the textbook RSA encryption. We illustrate $Pad_2(\cdot)$ in Figure 6.21.

The Pad_2 padding function applies the same *hash then one-time pad* method used by Pad_1, but Pad_2 uses this method *twice:* first, to protect the 'data block' DB, like done by Pad_1, but then again, to protect the random pad r itself. Specifically, given an input data block DB, the Pad_2 algorithm first selects a random l_h string $r \overset{\$}{\leftarrow} \{0,1\}^{l_h \cdot 8}$ and then computes the 'pseudorandom pad' $g(r)$ which it uses to 'one-time-pad encrypt' the input, DB. The result is the value $x \leftarrow DB \oplus g(r)$; since $g(r)$ should be pseudorandom, then x should also be pseudorandom. Next, Pad_2 applies another cryptographic function f to this pseudorandom value x and uses the output, $f(x)$, as another 'pseudo-random-pad' to mask r.

Like g, the goal of f is also to produce a 'pseudorandom pad' to be used to mask a value (this time, r); note, however, that unlike g, the output of f is only l_h bytes long since this is the length of r. Namely, f is a hash (compressing) function, unlike g which is expanding rather than compressing.

To simplify the unpadding process, in Pad_2, we require that the input data block DB has a fixed number of bytes, specifically, $l_{RSA} - l_h - 1$ bytes, where l_{RSA} is the length in bytes of the RSA modulus n

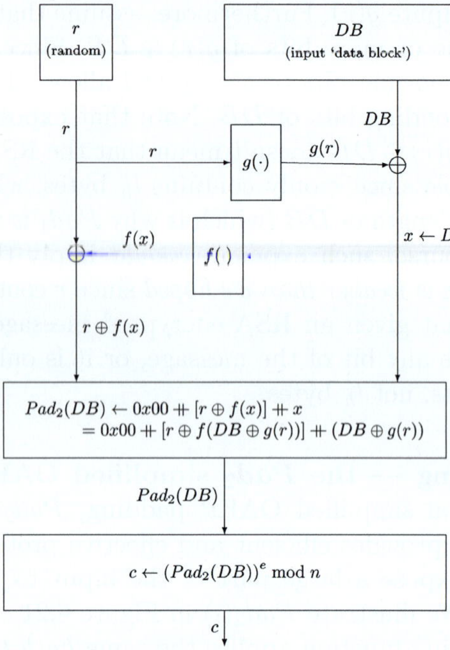

Figure 6.21. Simplified-OAEP ($Pad_2(\cdot)$) padded RSA encryption. The goal of the $Pad_2(\cdot)$ padding function is to protect against partial exposure of RSA preimage. Note that the unpadding function corresponding to Pad_2 cannot validate that the ciphertext is the result of applying encryption to a correctly padded plaintext; hence, $Pad_2(\cdot)$ does not ensure plaintext-awareness (and does not prevent CCA attacks).

and l_h is the length in bytes of the output of the hash function $h(\cdot)$. This mean that the output of Pad_2 contains one more byte, on top of the (masked) random bits r and the (masked) input DB. This extra byte is simply set to be the all-zeros byte; namely, Pad_2 outputs the padded message $0x00 + [r \oplus f(x)] + x$.

The reason we prepend the all-zeroes byte is somewhat 'technical', as follows. The output of the padding is to be used as input to the textbook RSA encryption function and, therefore, has to be smaller than the RSA modulus n, and a simple way to ensure that it is smaller than n is to have some leading zero bits. We don't really need a whole byte, but it is more convenient to use a whole byte so that r contains exactly $l_h \cdot 8$ random bits.

Considering that the $l_h + 1$ most significant bytes of the output of Pad_2 consist of an all-zeroes byte followed by l_h random bytes, this ensures that the output of Pad_2 is less than the modulus n, as required for inputs to the RSA encryption.

To sum up, the Pad_2 function and the corresponding $UnPad_2$ function are

$$Pad_2(DB) \equiv \left\{ \begin{array}{l} 0x00 +\!\!+ [r \oplus f\,(DB \oplus g(r))] +\!\!+ (DB \oplus g(r))\,, \\ \text{where } r \xleftarrow{\$} \{0,1\}^{l_h \cdot 8} \end{array} \right\}$$

$$UnPad_2(\pi) \equiv \left\{ \begin{array}{l} \text{If } |\pi| \geq l_{RSA} \text{ bytes, then return } \perp \\ \text{Prepend zeros so that } |\pi| = l_{RSA} \text{ bytes} \\ x \leftarrow \pi[l_h + 1 :] \text{ (the } l_{RSA} - (l_h + 1) \\ \qquad \text{least significant bytes of } \pi) \\ r \leftarrow f(x) \oplus \pi[1 : l_h]; \\ \text{Return } x \oplus g(r) \end{array} \right\}$$

The reader can confirm that the Pad_2 padding ensures correctness, i.e., $m = UnPad_2(Pad_2(m))$.

OAEP padding: We now, finally, describe the 'complete' Optimal Asymmetric Encryption Padding (OAEP), as presented in Ref. [49], and later standardized by the IETF, with minor improvements, as RFC 8071 [475]. Our description mostly follows that of RFC 8071 [475]. See Figure 6.22.

The design of OAEP is parameterized by the length l_h, in bytes, of the output of the hash function h, which is also the length of the output of the mixing function $f(\cdot)$, and the length l_{RSA}, in bytes, of the RSA modulus n. The length l_m of the input plaintext m must be an integral number of bytes, and must be at most $l_{RSA} - 2 \cdot l_h - 2$ bytes.

Let us compare OAEP, as illustrated in Figure 6.22, to the simplified Pad_2 padding function, illustrated in Figure 6.21. We see that OAEP applies the Pad_2 function to the data block DB, which it computes as $DB \leftarrow h(Label) +\!\!+ pad +\!\!+ 0x01 +\!\!+ m$. The *pad* is a string consisting of $l_{RSA} - l_m - 2 \cdot l_h - 2$ zero ($0x00$) bytes; note that if $l_m = l_{RSA} - 2 \cdot l_h - 2$, then *pad* is the empty string.

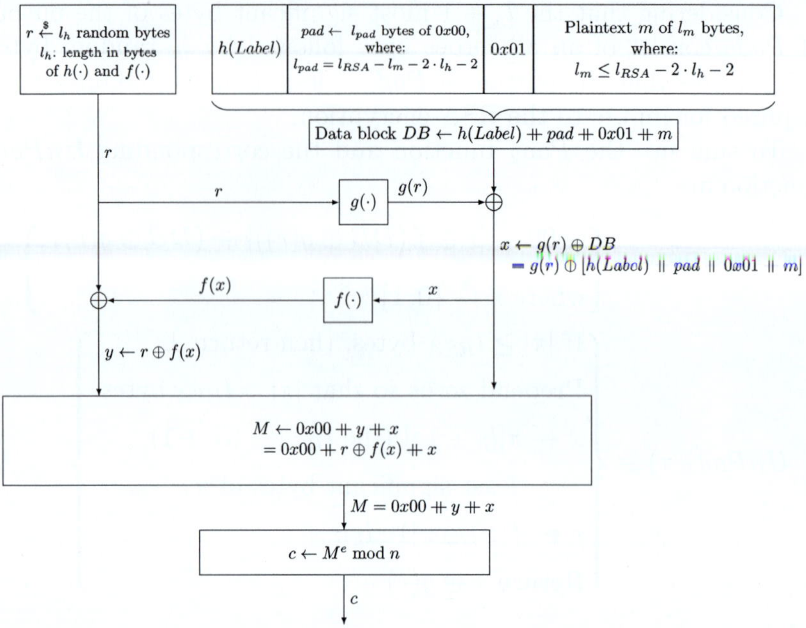

Figure 6.22. OAEP padding [49,364], where l_h denotes the length of the output of the functions h and f, and l_{RSA} denotes the length of the RSA modulus n. The length l_m of the input plaintext m must be at most $l_{RSA} - 2 \cdot l_h - 2$.

For clarify, let us restate the OAEP padding function, $Pad_{OAEP}^{Label}(m)$:

$$Pad_{OAEP}^{Label}(m) = Pad_2(h(Label) \mathbin{+\!\!+} pad \mathbin{+\!\!+} 0x01 \mathbin{+\!\!+} m)$$
$$= \left\{\begin{array}{l} 0x00 \mathbin{+\!\!+} [r \oplus f\left(DB \oplus g(r)\right)] \mathbin{+\!\!+} \left(DB \oplus g(r)\right), \\ \text{where } DB = h(Label) \mathbin{+\!\!+} pad \mathbin{+\!\!+} 0x01 \mathbin{+\!\!+} m, \\ pad = (0x00)^{l_{RSA} - l_m - 2 \cdot l_h - 2}. \\ \text{and } r \xleftarrow{\$} \{0,1\}^{l_h \cdot 8}. \end{array}\right\} \tag{6.52}$$

Exercise 6.7. Write the OAEP unpad function, $UnPad_{OAEP}^{Label}(\pi)$, and prove that OAEP ensures correctness.

Let us explain the roles of the three fields prepended to m in DB.

Hash of label $h(Label)$: The *Label* is a string determined by the designers of the particular application; by default, *Label* would be the empty string, resulting in the fixed value which is the output of the hash function when given an empty string. Upon decryption of a well-formed ciphertext, the decryption algorithm verifies that it recovers the correct value of $h(Label)$ which is prepended by the encryption algorithm. This prevents an attacker from sending chosen-ciphertext which is not an output received from the encryption algorithm. This defense against CCA attacks is referred to in Ref. [49] by the term *plaintext-awareness.*

Zero-bytes pad *pad*: The *pad* string ensures that the data block DB will be of the maximal possible number of bytes. This helps ensure that even if m is very short, the input to the RSA function would not be much smaller than the modulus n. This may foil attacks exploiting vulnerabilities of RSA encryption of short messages, such as mentioned in Sections 6.5.4 and 6.5.5.

Separating $0x01$ byte: This byte allows the unpadding process to recover any leading zero bytes of m rather than considering them a part of the zero-bytes pad *pad*.

There are (minor) differences between the details of the OAEP design between Ref. [49] and the RFC 8071 [475]. Readers interested can read Ref. [475] and the security analysis in Ref. [49] and in follow-up works.

6.6 Signature schemes

We now briefly discuss the third types of public-key cryptographic schemes: *signature schemes.* We already introduced signature schemes and their security notions in Section 1.5.1. Signature schemes consist of three efficient algorithms (KG, S, V), illustrated in Figure 1.8:

Key-generation KG: A randomized algorithm, whose input is the key length l, and which outputs the private signing key s and the public validation key v, each of length l bits.

Signing S: A (deterministic or randomized) algorithm, whose inputs are the signing key s and a message m, and whose output is a signature σ.

Validation V: A deterministic algorithm, whose inputs are the validation key v, the purported signature σ and a message m. The output of the validation function is binary; it should be *true* if σ is a valid signature for the message m, and *false* otherwise.

Figure 1.9 illustrates the process of signing a message (by Alice) and validation of the signature (by Bob). We denote Alice's keys by $A.s$ (for the private signing key) and $A.v$ (for the public validation key).

Signature schemes have two unique properties, each of which is essential for critical applications: *non-repudiation* and *public-key based authentication*.

Non-repudiation: Non-repudiation is a guarantee that once a party, say Alice, establishes the authenticity of a particular message m, i.e., validates that m was issued (signed) using the private key s corresponding to a given public validation key v, then any third party performing the same validation process will be convinced that m was signed using this (unknown) private key s. Non-repudiation is crucial for many applications, such as contract signing; the recipient of a signed message/contract m knows that it can convince a third party that the message is 'authentic'.

Non-repudiation does not hold for symmetric-key message authentication code (MAC) schemes, which are the main topic of Chapter 4. A recipient can validate an incoming message has the correct MAC code but cannot prove this to another party — in particular, since the recipient is able to compute herself the MAC code for arbitrary messages.

Public-key based authentication: The other unique property of signatures i that signature schemes facilitate authentication of information using only the *public key* of the originator. This may appear less exciting and special than non-repudiation, but the ability to authenticate information based only on a known, trusted public key, has completely revolutionized cybersecurity and electronic commerce. In the following paragraphs, and in Figures 6.23 and 6.24, we present two of the most important application of public-key-based authentication: *certificates* and *secure boot*, and both are based mostly on the ability to authenticate information using only a public key.

Certificates — using a known public key to authenticate other public keys: Public key cryptosystems and key agreement protocols facilitate establishing of private communication and shared symmetric secret keys between two remote parties, using only public information (keys). However, this still leaves the question of authenticity of the public information (keys).

In some scenarios, it is reasonable to assume attack models where ensuring authenticity is trivial or quite easy, and does not require cryptography. The simplest case is when the adversary is completely passive and cannot interfere with the communication in any way, e.g., an eavesdropper. In this case, it suffices to simply send the public key or other public value, as done in the Diffie Hellman (DH) key agreement protocol.

It is also easy to setup authentic public keys assuming the *trust on first use (TOFU) attack model*, where the adversary is inactive or passive during the *initial* exchange. The parties can then exchange authentic keys and use them throughout the execution. The trust on first use (TOFU) attack model is also referred to as *leap of faith* authentication [477].

Another attack model where ensuring authenticity is quite easy, and does not require cryptography, is the *off-path attack model* [205]. In the off-path attack model, the attacker may *inject* fake messages, but cannot eavesdrop on messages sent between the parties, intercept messages sent to other entities or interfere with the transmission of messages sent between other parties. In this case, Alice can send a random challenge (nonce) to Bob, and Bob can authenticate a message to Alice by including the random challenge that Bob received from Alice. Internet security is often analyzed assuming the off-path attack model, since spoofing is often easy, but eavesdropping on traffic or modifying traffic requires stronger attack capabilities.

However, in applied cryptography, we mostly consider the stronger *man-in-the-middle (MitM) attack model*, where the adversary can modify, block and inject (spoof) messages, as well as eavesdrop on messages.

To ensure security against a MitM attacker, the parties should either share a secret key — or, one party must have or obtain the authentic key of its peer. Signature schemes provide a solution to this challenge. Namely, a party receiving signed information from a remote peer can validate that information, using only the public signature-validation key of the signer.

Furthermore, signatures also allow a party, say Alice, to validate the public key of a peer, say Bob, using a signature on Bob's key, where the signature is by a *trusted third party*, which Alice trusts to

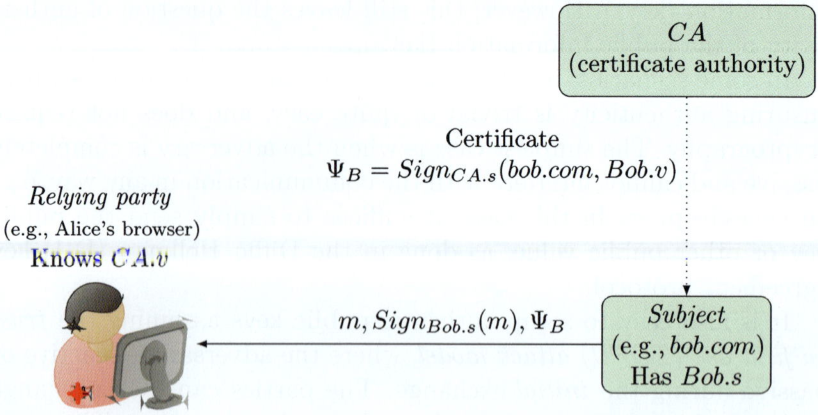

Figure 6.23. Certificate issuing (dotted arrow) and usage (solid arrow) flows, simplified. A certificate authority (CA) issues a certificate to the public signature-validation key *Bob.v* of the website *bob.com*. See Chapters 7 and 8.

validate Bob's public key. This solution is called a *public key certificate*, and the trusted third party is called a *certificate authority* (CA). See Figure 6.23.

As illustrated in Figure 6.23, a public key certificate is a signature by an entity called the *issuer* or *certificate authority* (CA), over the public key of the *subject*, e.g., the website *Bob.com*. In addition to the public key of the subject, e.g., *Bob.v*, the signed information in the certificate contains attributes such as the validity period, and, usually, an identifier and/or a name for the subject (Bob.com).

Once Bob.com receives the signed certificate $Cert_B$, they can deliver $Cert_B$ to a *relying party* (e.g., Alice), possibly via insecure channels such as the Internet. This allows the relying party (Alice) to use the public key of Bob.com, i.e., rely on it, e.g., to validate Bob's signature over a message m, as shown in Figure 6.23. Note that this requires Alice to trust this CA and to have its validation key, $CA.v$.

This discussion of certificates is very basic; details are provided in Chapter 7, which discusses the important Transport Layer Security (TLS) and Secure Socket Layer (SSL) protocols, which use certificates, and additional details are in Chapter 8, which discusses Public Key Infrastructure (PKI), which provides and manages certificates for SSL/TLS and other applications.

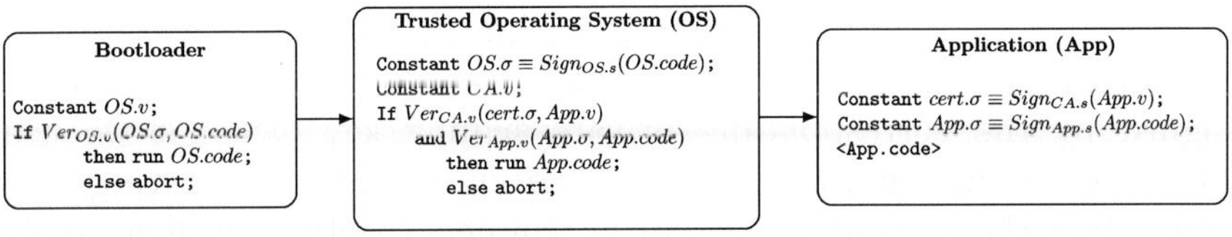

Figure 6.24. Simplified illustration of a secure boot process.

Using signatures and certificates for secure boot: In Figure 6.24, we discuss a very important application of signatures and certificates: the *secure boot process.*

To explain the secure boot process, let us first quickly describe the basic operation of the boot process (ignoring security), and then we explain how to secure the boot process. Computers are general-purpose computing devices, which means that they can run arbitrary different programs rather than being limited to one fixed program or to a limited set of programs which are pre-installed.

The secure boot process allows the computer, using a small, fixed and very limited *bootloader* program, to load and execute arbitrary different *applications.* Furthermore, these applications are supported by a powerful *operating system,* and while the same operating system can support many applications, the same computer (and therefore the same bootloader) can support different operating systems, most of which developed long after producing the computer, with its built-in, fixed bootloader. In fact, the bootloader may be provided[11] in a special type of memory chip which can only be read but cannot be modified, and therefore called *read only memory* (ROM).

Malware is one of the most common and harmful cybersecurity threats. One approach to prevent malware is to only run authenticated code; for example, in Lab 1, we have seen how to use hash functions and signatures to validate downloads. We now discuss a more extreme design against malware: the *secure boot process.*

A simplified secure boot process is illustrated in Figure 6.24. The process only allows the computer to run a *trusted operating system,* and the trusted operating system only allows execution of *authenticated, certified applications.*

[11]In modern computers, the bootloader is often provided on other types of chips, which *can* be modified.

Specifically, the bootloader has, within it, a public *operating system validation key* $OS.v$. Every trusted operating system must be signed by the corresponding private signing key $OS.s$; if we use $OS.code$ to denote the code of a specific trusted operating system, then the operating system is shipped together with a signature $OS.\sigma \equiv Sign_{OS.s}(OS.code)$. The bootloader code validates this signature and runs the operating system only if the validation is successful.

Similarly, the trusted operating system only allows execution of authorized applications. Typically, multiple entities can authenticate authorize applications, e.g., trusted software vendors may be certified to authenticate their own authorized applications. To facilitate this, the trusted operating system would maintain the public validation key of a *certificate authority* (CA) (or the keys of multiple CAs); in Figure 6.24, we show the case of a single CA, whose public validation key is denoted $CA.v$.

As can be seen in the simplified code shown, applications may come with a certificate, denoted $App.cert$, signed by the key $CA.s$ which corresponds to the known public key $CA.v$ of the certificate authority (CA). The certificate identifies another public validation key, $App.v$, which the operating system uses to validate a signature $App.\sigma$ over the application itself, $App.code$. Note that in reality, certificates typically contain much more information, such as the signing entity, e.g., the vendor of the software, the validity period for the certificate and much more; see Chapter 8.

6.6.1 RSA-based signatures

RSA signatures were proposed in the seminal RSA paper [418] and are based on the RSA assumption, with the same key-generation process as for the RSA public key cryptosystem. The only difference in key generation is that in a signature scheme, the public key is used for signature *verification*, and therefore denoted v, while the private key is used for *signing* (signature computation), and therefore denoted s. Actually, this is imprecise since both signing and signature verification operations also make use of the modulus n; therefore, the complete public (verification) key is (v, n) and the complete private (signing) key is (s, n).

There are two main variants of RSA signatures: signature with message recovery (Section 6.6.1.1) and signature with appendix (Section 6.6.1.2). In practice, almost all applications of RSA signatures use signature with appendix.

6.6.1.1 *RSA signatures with message recovery*

RSA signatures with message recovery, also referred to as *textbook RSA signatures*, is a naive signature scheme based on RSA. This scheme is similar to RSA textbook encryption. To sign a message m, compute the RSA function over the message using the private signing key s, as in:

$$Sign_s^{RSA}(m) = m^s \bmod n \tag{6.53}$$

To verify that a given string σ is the correct signature over message m, we verify that the RSA function applied to the signature, using the public verification key (v, n), returns m, i.e.,

$$Verify_v^{RSA}(m, \sigma) = \begin{cases} \text{TRUE if } m = \sigma^v \bmod n, \\ \text{FALSE otherwise} \end{cases} \tag{6.54}$$

Note that, as for RSA encryption, we usually do not explicitly write the modulus n as part of the public and private keys. This is a common abuse of notation; formally, n is a part of both keys, as it is used in the computation.

As can be seen from Equation (6.54), textbook RSA signatures have the nice property that the signature suffices to recover the signed message, provided that the plaintext message can be identified as valid plaintext[12]; there is no need to send both message and signature. This property is referred to as message recovery and is the reason that textbook RSA signatures are often referred to as RSA signatures with message recovery.

Textbook RSA signatures are almost *never used* in practice. One reason is that textbook RSA signatures can be applied only if the message m is less than n, which is rarely, if ever, the case. Therefore, in

[12]If there is no efficient mechanism to identify valid plaintext messages, then an attacker could send a random string and it would be 'recovered' into some 'random' message; such a scheme would fail to ensure existential unforgeability.

practice, RSA signatures always involve some additional processing, typically using the *Hash-then-Sign* Section (3.3.5) construction, i.e., computing $Sign_s^{RSA}(h(m))$; in this case, it is obviously impossible to take advantage of the 'message recovery feature'. But even for the rare case of signing messages which are shorter than the modulus n, and hence do not require hashing, the use of textbook RSA signatures may result in vulnerabilities, e.g., vulnerabilities similar to these outlined for textbook RSA encryption in Section 6.5.5. Therefore, in practice, we use ***signatures with appendix***, as described in Section 6.6.1.2.

Encrypting with the private key? The textbook RSA signing equation (6.53) is exactly the same as the textbook RSA encryption equation (6.31), except for the use of the private signing key s instead of the public encryption key e. Therefore, you may find reference to textbook RSA signatures as 'encryption with the private key'. This term is incorrect with respect to secure RSA signatures and encryption, which both use (different) padding schemes, and, for signatures, also hashing.

6.6.1.2 *RSA signature with appendix*

In practice, as discussed in Section 3.3.5, input messages are of variable length — and rarely shorter than modulus. Hence, real signatures apply the *Hash-then-Sign* (HtS) paradigm, using some cryptographic hash function h, whose range is contained in $[1, \ldots, n-1]$, i.e., allowable input to the RSA function. This gives the *HtS RSA signature scheme* $(S^{RSA,h}, V^{RSA,h})$, defined as:

$$S_s^{RSA,h}(m) = ([h(m)]^s \bmod n,\ m)$$
$$V_v^{RSA,h}(\sigma, m) = \{m \text{ if } h(m) = \sigma^v \bmod n, \text{ error otherwise}\}$$

The resulting HtS RSA signature scheme is secure, if RSA is secure and h is a CRHF, or, if we adopt the random oracle model (ROM), and consider h as a random function; see Chapter 3.

This type of signature scheme is called *signature with appendix* since it requires transmission of both original message and its signature.

In practice, RSA signatures usually do not use exactly HtS signature design above. Instead, signatures usually use an encoding of the message called the *PSS encoding*, which involves randomization and other defenses. The Probabilistic Signature Scheme (PSS) and PSS encoding were proposed in Ref. [50] and standardized in RFC 8017 [364].

6.7 Lab: breaking textbook and weakly-padded RSA

Lab 4 (Breaking textbook RSA and weakly padded RSA). In this lab, you will learn how to decrypt, using only the public key, messages encrypted using textbook RSA encryption, as well as padded RSA encryption, using weakened versions of PKCS #1 padding.

The labs and installation instructions are available from https://github.com/CyberSec-labs/labs; see more details in the preface.

1. The files you will need to complete parts 1 through 5 of the lab will all be found within the *lab/lab-input* directory. The file *d1* contains the private key, the file *e1* contains the public key and the file *n1* contains the modulus of the RSA key. The file *TextbookRSA.py* contains functions for textbook RSA encryption and decryption.

   In this part, you will perform decryption using three padding methods: textbook RSA (no padding), PKCS #1 v1.5 and OAEP; all decryptions will use the private key given in the file *d1*. The ciphertexts to be decrypted are given in the *lab/lab-input* directory, as the files *cx1a, cy1a, cx1b, cy1b, cx1c* and *cy1c*. As shown in Table 6.3, use textbook RSA (no padding) to decrypt the files whose names end in *a* use PKCS #1 version 1.5 padding to decrypt the files whose names end in *b* and use OAEP to decrypt the files whose names end in *c*. Save and submit the results in the corresponding files *mx1a, my1a, mx1b, my1b, mx1c* and *my1c*.

   To allow you to check if your decryptions are correct, the *lab/lab-input* directory contains also two files, *m1* and *m2*,

Table 6.3. Ciphertexts and corresponding padding for part 1 of Lab 4.

file	*cx1a* and *cy1a*	*cx1b* and *cy1b*	*cx1c* and *cy1c*
padding	None (textbook RSA)	PKCS #1 v1.5	OAEP

containing plaintext messages. For each pair of *a*, *b* or *c* files, one of the two files should match either *m1* or *m2*. If one of a pair matches, then the other decryption should be correct as well.

2. In this part of the lab, you will write code to encrypt the *m1* and *m2* plaintext files, using the three padding methods (textbook RSA, PKCS #1 version 1.5 and OAEP), and the same RSA keys as in part 1. You can test your code by checking that performing the corresponding decryption, which you wrote in part 1, on the encrypted message will yield the original message. You will not submit anything for this part of the lab.

   Do you obtain the same ciphertexts as given in part 1? Explain.
3. In the *lab/lab-input* directory, you will find the files *e2* and *n2*, which make up the public RSA key and the modulus used for encryption in the this part and the following two parts. You will also find there the directory *ciphertexts*, containing eavesdropped ciphertexts, the directory *plaintexts*, containing likely plaintexts, and the file *pair0-1.csv*, which identifies one plaintext and its corresponding ciphertext.

   Your goal is to find two plaintexts and their corresponding ciphertexts from these two directories. You will use textbook RSA for decryption, and one of the pairs you identify should be the same as the one identified by *pair0-1.csv* file; this will help you in testing your code. You will then submit, in the file *pair0-2.csv*, the second identified pair, using the same format as of *pair0-1.csv*. Measure the runtime.
4. In this and the following part, you will 'break' RSA when used with a naïve padding function denoted NP_l. The NP_l padding uses l random bits and is defined as:

$$NP_l(m) \stackrel{\$}{\leftarrow} 0x02 + \{0,1\}^l + 0^{8-(l \mod 8)} + m \tag{6.55}$$

   Namely, $NP_l(m)$ consists of the fixed byte $0x02$, followed by l random bits, concatenated with $8-(l \mod 8)$ zero bits, and finally followed by the message m. Note that $8-(l \mod 8)$ is the number of additional (zero) bits required to make sure that the complete string will be an integer number of bytes.

   In this part, we use $l = 4$, i.e., the NP_4 padding; in the following part, we use $l \in \{8, 12, 16, 20\}$.

   Reusing the ciphertexts and plaintexts directories from the previous part, identify two pairs of corresponding plaintexts and ciphertexts that employ NP_4 padding, i.e., NP_l with $l = 4$ (padding with 4 random bits). One of the pairs you identify should match the pair identified in *pair4-1.csv*; the number 4 in the file name reflects the number of random bits, $l = 4$. You will then submit the other pair in *pair4-2.csv*. Once again, measure the runtime.

5. In this part of the lab, you will, again, identify pairs of corresponding plaintexts and ciphertexts, from the respective sub-directories within *lab/lab-input*. The pairs correspond to encryption using the same $NP_l(m)$ function (Equation (6.55)), for $l \in \{8, 12, 16, 20\}$. Similarly to the previous part, for each of the methods for choosing r, one of the pairs you find will match the pair in the given *csv* file, and you will submit the other pair in a new *csv* file. Similarly to the convention used in the previous part, the *csv* files with a given plaintext-ciphertext pairs will be named *pair8-1.csv*, *pair12-1.csv*, *pair16-1.csv* and *pair20-1.csv*, and the csv files you will submit, with the other pair, will be named *pair8-2.csv*, *pair12-2.csv*, *pair16-2.csv* and *pair20-2.csv*.
6. Create a graph showing the runtime of finding the plaintext-ciphertext pair in parts 3, 4, and 5, as a function of l, the number of random bits used in the padding. Note that part 3 corresponds to $l = 0$. Estimate the time required, using this approach, to find the match for $l = 64$, i.e., eight bytes of randomness.

Challenge: In the previous parts of this lab, you identified plaintext corresponding to a given ciphertext and have seen how the randomized padding can make that task more difficult. To do so, you made use of a list of possible plaintexts that may correspond to the ciphertext. In practice, the number of possible plaintexts may be too large, and the padding used is usually too long, making this type of attack impractical. However, with a weak padding scheme, it may still be possible for an attacker to decrypt ciphertexts in some practical scenarios. In particular, the Bleichenbacher attack, which we discussed in Section 6.5.7, allows the attacker to decrypt ciphertexts encrypted using RSA with the PKCS #1 version 1.5 padding scheme.

In this part, you will implement a variant of the Bleichenbacher attack, designed against the naïve padding function $NP_l(m)$, for $l = 64$ and $l = 96$, i.e., 8 and 12 bytes of randomness. This part uses the RSA public key and modulus from the files *e2* and *n2*.

You will find the file *Padding_Check.pyc* which will serve as the oracle that tells you whether or not a ciphertext is properly padded according to $NP_l(m)$. The files *c64-1* and *c64-2* will be the ciphertexts for padding using $l = 64$ random bits (8 bytes), and the files *c96-1* and *c96-2* are the ciphertexts for $l = 96$ random bits (12 bytes). The files p64-1 and p96-1 are the original (unpadded) plaintexts for their corresponding ciphertexts, given to help you test your code. When you are able to find *p64-1* by running the attack on *c64-1*, run the attack on *c64-2* and submit the recovered plaintext in *p64-2*. Repeat similarly for *c96-1* and *c96-2* and submit *p64-2*.

Hint: Use *big-endian* byte ordering to ensure correct processing.

Note: The *Padding_Check.pyc* program contains the private decryption key d. Therefore, you could try to find d by reverse-engineering this program. We used simple *obfuscation* to make this a bit harder. We recommend to solve this challenge by using the Bleichenbacher attack rather than by reverse-engineering the program and finding the private key. Or, do both of the attacks and compare!

To lecturers: You can provide the decryption oracle as a web service, instead of providing it as a program. This will prevent students from solving the challenge by finding d via reverse-engineering.

Discussion: Explain why it is significantly easier to attack the NP_l padding, compared to the Bleichenbacher attack against the PKCS #1 v1.5 padding.

6.8 Additional exercises

Exercise 6.8. Show that every key agreement protocol (KA, KB, KC), as defined in Section 6.1.3, is vulnerable to a man-in-the-middle (MitM) attack. Namely, show, using a sequence diagram, how for any protocol (KA, KB, KC), a MitM attacker can perform the following:

1. Find the key output by the initiator (Alice).
2. Find the key output by the responder (Bob).
3. Find the keys output by both initiator and responder. *Hint*: The initiator and responder may generate different keys.

Exercise 6.9. Present a design for a hybrid PKCS, using a key encapsulation mechanism (KEM) and (a) a pseudorandom generator (PRG) or (b) a hash function, using the random oracle model (ROM).

Exercise 6.10. Design a key agreement protocol, using (only) a *key encapsulation mechanism* (*KEM*).

Exercise 6.11 (The addition and multiplication key agreement protocols). 1. Present a sequence diagrams similar to Figures 6.7 and 6.8, but using addition instead of XOR or exponentiation, respectively.
2. Show that the resulting protocol is vulnerable to an eavesdropping attacker.
3. Repeat the previous items using multiplication (instead of XOR, exponentiation or addition).

Exercise 6.12. Show that the exponential key agreement protocol (Figure 6.8) is insecure against an eavesdropper, even if the base g used by the protocol is a secret shared between Alice and Bob.

Exercise 6.13 (Justification for limitations on possible random inputs for key agreement protocols). Show that in both the Diffie–Hellman (DH) key agreement protocol and the modular exponentiation key agreement protocol, there will be no gain in security if the parties choose their random inputs a and b from a larger set, say $\{1, \ldots, 8 \cdot p\}$. Show that the same holds for the selection of g.

Exercise 6.14. 1. Present the Diffie–Hellman (DH) key agreement protocol, i.e., define the corresponding (KA, KB, KC) functions.
2. We presented two assumptions regarding the security of the DH protocol: the Computational Diffie–Hellman (CDH) assumption and the Decisional Diffie–Hellman (DDH) assumption. Show that *one* of these assumptions does not suffice to ensure key-indistinguishability.

Exercise 6.15. It is proposed that to protect the Diffie–Hellman (DH) key agreement protocol against impersonation by a MitM attacker, we add an additional 'confirmation' exchange after the protocol terminated with a shared key $k = h(g^{ab} \mod p)$. In this confirmation, Alice will send to Bob $MAC_k(g^b)$ and Bob will respond with $MAC_k(g^a)$. Show a sequence diagram illustrating an attack, showing how a MitM attacker can impersonate as Alice (or Bob).

Exercise 6.16. Suppose that an efficient algorithm to find discrete log is found so that the Diffie–Hellman (DH) key agreement protocol becomes insecure; however, some public-key cryptosystem $(\mathcal{KG}, \mathcal{E}, \mathcal{D})$ is still considered secure, consisting of algorithms for, respectively, key-generation, encryption and decryption:

1. Design a key-agreement protocol which is secure against an eavesdropping adversary, assuming that $(\mathcal{KG}, \mathcal{E}, \mathcal{D})$ is secure (as a replacement to DH).
2. Explain which benefits the use of your protocol may provide, compared with using the cryptosystem $(\mathcal{KG}, \mathcal{E}, \mathcal{D})$ to protect the confidentiality of messages sent between Alice and Bob against a powerful MitM adversary, by encrypting each message. Assume Alice and Bob have known public keys (which can be used for encryption or signature validation).

Exercise 6.17. Let **G** be a group in which the Decisional Diffie–Hellman (DDH) assumption is believed to hold, and whose members are binary strings. Assume that there is an efficient attacker $\mathcal{A}$ who can find a specific bit in g^{ab}, given only g^a and g^b. Show that the DDH assumption does not hold for $\mathbb{G}$, i.e., that there is an efficient (PPT) attacker $\mathcal{A}'$ that can distinguish, with significant advantage over random guess, between g^{ab} and between g^x for x taken randomly from $\mathbb{G}$.

Exercise 6.18. It is sometimes proposed to use a pseudorandom function (PRF) as a Key Derivation Function (KDF), e.g., to extract a pseudo-random key $k' = PRF_k(g^{ab} \mod p)$ from the DH exchanged value $g^{ab} \mod p$, where k is a uniform random key (known to attacker). In particular, Section 6.3.1 illustrates a variant of the Auth-h-DH protocol that uses a function f assumed to fulfill both the PRF requirements *and* the KDF requirements. In this exercise, we explore alternatives:

1. Let f be a secure PRF; note that f may be a KDF or not. Show a function f' which is (1) also a PRF and (2) not a secure KDF.
2. Let g be a secure KDF; note that g may be a PRF or not. Show a function g' which is (1) also a KDF and (2) not a secure PRF.
3. Present a variant of the Auth-h-DH protocol, as a modification of Figure 6.13, which uses only a PRF, instead of both the MAC and the KDF. Explain why this variant is secure.

4. Show that using the same key for the MAC and for the KDF in Figure 6.13 can cause a vulnerability, even if the MAC and the PRF are both secure. Note: This is an example of the *principle of key separation* (Section 2.7.4).

Exercise 6.19 (Exploiting weaknesses of the Auth-*h*-DH protocol). The Auth-h-DH protocol (Figure 6.13) provides key agreement, but it does *not ensure* authentication or recovery from key exposure. Present sequence diagrams which shows the following possible exploits by a MitM attacker:

1. Attacker can mislead Alice into thinking she completed the protocol successfully with Bob, even when Bob is not participating at all, i.e., entity-authentication of Bob fails. Note: The attack is not required to expose the key that Alice will receive for the session (supposedly) with Bob, i.e., this is only an attack on entity authentication, not on key agreement.
2. Repeat, for misleading Bob into thinking he completed the protocol successfully with Alice, where, as in Figure 6.13, Bob is the entity responding (the server, in client-server scenario).
3. Suppose that the attacker, Eve, is given the private exponent a_i chosen by Alice in the ith exchange of the protocol. Show that this suffices for Eve to complete any number of future exchanges with Bob, say exchange $j > i$, so that Bob will think that it completed the protocol successfully with Alice, *and* that the attacker will share the secret key $k_j = k^{(j)}_{A,B} = k^{(j)}_{B,A}$.
4. Repeat, for similarly misleading Alice, but still for the case that Eve is given a_i.

Exercise 6.20 (How *not* to ensure resilient key agreement). Figure 6.25 illustrates a slightly different protocol for authenticating the DH protocol, using a changing key k_i (the goal is to ensure resilient key agreement). Present a sequence diagram showing that this protocol is not secure.

Exercise 6.21. The protocol in Figure 6.26 is an (incorrect) attempt at a robust-combiner authenticated DH protocol:

1. Show a sequence diagram for an attack showing that this variant does not ensure entity authentication.

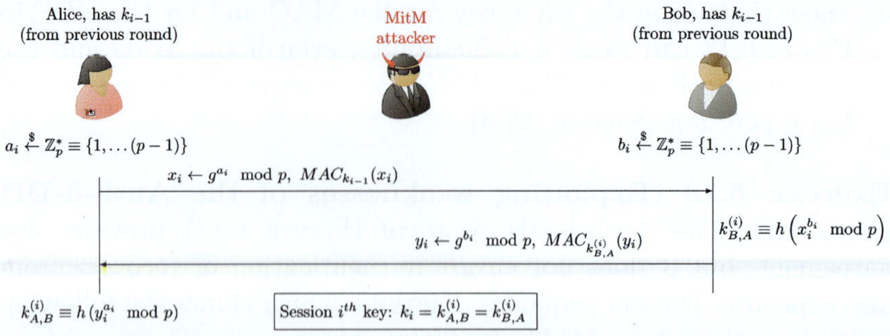

Figure 6.25. How *not* to ensure resilient key agreement: illustration for Exercise 6.20.

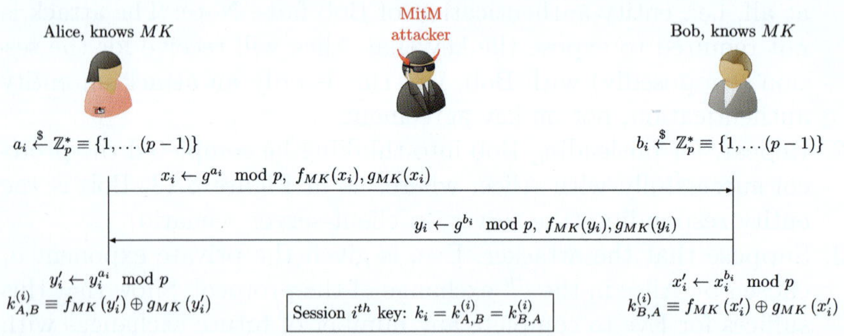

Figure 6.26. Insecure 'robust-combiner' authenticated DH protocol, studied in Exercise 6.21.

2. Show a simple fix that achieves the goal (robust combiner authenticated DH protocol).

Exercise 6.22. Assume it takes 10 seconds for any message to pass between Alice and Bob:

1. Assume that both Alice and Bob initiate the ratchet protocol (Figure 6.14) every 30 seconds. Draw a sequence diagram showing the exchange of messages between time 0 and time 60 seconds; mark the keys used by each of the two parties to authenticate messages sent and to verify messages received.
2. Repeat, if Bob's clock is 5 seconds late.

Exercise 6.23. In the DH ratchet protocol, as described (Figure 6.14), the parties derive symmetric keys k_i and use them to authenticate data (application) messages they exchange between them, as well as the first message of the next handshake:

1. Assume a chosen-message attacker model, i.e., the attacker may define arbitrary data (application) messages to be sent from Alice to Bob and vice verse at any given time, and 'wins' if a party accepts a message never sent by its peer (i.e., that message passes validation successfully). Show that, as described, the protocol is insecure in this model.
2. Propose a simple, efficient and secure way to avoid this vulnerability, by only changing *how the protocol is used* — without changing the protocol itself.

Exercise 6.24. The DH protocol, as well as the ratchet protocol (as described in Figure 6.14), are designed for communication between only two parties.

1. Extend DH to support key agreement among three parties.
2. Similarly extend the ratchet protocol.

Exercise 6.25 (DH-Ratchet). Figure 6.14 shows the DH-Ratchet key agreement protocol, where the key used to authenticate the DH exchange as well as the data messages are changing periodically (as indicated), and where f is a PRF (pseudorandom function).

Assume that this protocol is run daily, from day $i = 1$, and where k_0 is a randomly chosen secret initial master key, shared between Alice and Bob; messages on day i are encrypted and authenticated using session key k_i, by selecting a random string r and sending r and $f(r||f_{k_i}(r) \oplus m)$. An attacker can eavesdrops on the communication between the parties on all days, and on days $3, 6, 9, \ldots$ it can also spoof messages (send messages impersonating as either Alice or Bob) and act as man-in-the-middle (MitM). On the fifth day ($i = 5$), the attacker is also given the initial master key Mk_0:

- Explain why sending r and $f(r||f_{k_i}(r) \oplus m)$ ensures authenticity and confidentiality, provided that k_i is secret.

- What are the days whose messages the attacker will be able to decrypt (find out) upon day ten?
- Show a sequence diagram of the attack, and list calculations done by the attacker.

Exercise 6.26 (Insecure variant of DH-Ratchet). Figure 6.27 shows a variant of the DH-Ratchet protocol, using a (secure) pseudorandom function f to derive the session key.

1. Does this protocol ensure forward secrecy? If so, explain; if not, present sequence diagram of attack.
2. Repeat, for perfect forward secrecy (PFS).
3. Repeat, for recover security.
4. Repeat, for perfect recover security (PRS).

Exercise 6.27 (GSM). Design a more secure variant of the GSM handshake protocol, which foils the downgrade attack to $A5/1$ (Section 5.5.5.1). The mobile and visited network can identify support of this variant by referring to it as a new cipher, say $A5/Ni$. The actual data encryption can use a secure stream cipher which we denote $A5/i$.

The change may involve one or few new handshake messages between mobile and visited network, but no change to the rest of the GSM network, in particular, no change to the home network. Your solution may require the mobile and/or visited network to use additional cryptographic mechanisms, including public key mechanisms, but only during the handshake.

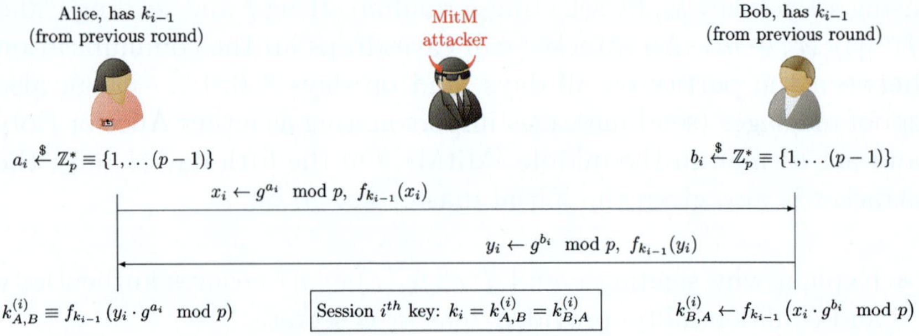

Figure 6.27. Insecure variant of the DH-ratchet protocol, for Exercise 6.26.

Hint: Your solution should use public key cryptography to set the key to be used by $A5/i$.

Exercise 6.28 (El-Gamal encryption). In this exercise, use the $\mathbb{Z}_p^*$ group (where p is a prime) to compute (the original) El-Gamal encryption. Let $p = 5$.

1. Find a generator g for $\mathbb{Z}_p^*$.
2. Let's select the private key of Alice as $d_A = 2$. Compute Alice's public key, $e_A = g^{d_A} \mod p$.
3. Compute El-Gamal encryption of 4 and 3: $c_4 \equiv E_{e_A}(4)$, $c_3 \equiv E_{e_A}(3)$. Comment: This is a randomized encryption, so another encryption may result in a different output!
4. Compute the decryptions of c_4 and of c_3.
5. Explain why El-Gamal encryption using $\mathbb{Z}_p^*$ group — even for a large safe prime p — does not satisfy the requirements of secure encryption.

Exercise 6.29. Use the values of p, g from Exercise 6.28, and perform all multiplications $\pmod p$:

1. Compute $c_{3\cdot4} \equiv c_3 \times c_4$, using the definition of $\times$ from Equation (6.28).
2. Compute the decryption of $c_{3\cdot4}$. Explain why the result is as expected from Lemma 6.3.

Exercise 6.30. Show that the hash-based version of the El-Gamal public key cryptosystem is *not* multiplicative homomorphic.

Exercise 6.31. In Section 6.4.3.1, we show that homomorphic encryption cannot be IND-CCA-secure:

1. The argument claims that 'if $c_M = c^*$, then c^* must be the encryption of 1'. Prove it.
2. The argument also claims that $D_d(c_M) = m^*$. Prove this too.
3. Present an alternative proof, by presenting the code of an efficient (PPT) adversary that 'wins' in the IND-CCA game, but without computing the encryption of the identity element 1.

Exercise 6.32. Consider El-Gamal encryption with $p = 5$ and the same g and public key as used in Exercise 6.29. Use this as the public key of the e_{DS} *decrypt server* for the privacy-preserving voting scheme of Figure 6.18. Let there be two candidates: 2 and 3 (actually, we can't have more with $p = 5$ — why?):

1. Alice and Bob vote 2 and Cora votes 3; compute the encrypted votes.
2. Compute the encrypted combined vote (output of Tally).
3. Decrypt the combined vote.
4. The output may not be correct; explain why.
5. Show at least one way in which *each* corrupt party (voter, tally server or decrypt server), by itself (no collaboration), can manipulate the results.

Exercise 6.33. We saw that El-Gamal encryption (Equation (6.24)) may be re-randomized, using the recipient's public key, and mentioned that this may be extended into an encryption scheme which is *universally re-randomizable*, i.e. where re-randomization does not require the recipient's public key. Design such an encryption scheme.

Hint: Begin with El-Gamal encryption, and use the encrypting of the number 1 as part of the ciphertext. Or see [215].

Exercise 6.34. A public key cryptosystem is *IND-rCCA* secure, if it passes the IND-CCA test, when the attacker is restricted to avoid any ciphertext queries whose output is the challenge message m^* [115]. Show the following:

1. The El-Gamal PKC is not IND-rCCA secure.
2. Textbook RSA is not IND-rCCA secure.
3. Every IND-CCA-secure public key cryptosystem is also IND-rCCA secure.

Exercise 6.35. The RSA key generation algorithm requires the selection of two large primes p, q:

1. Present an attack showing it is not secure to save time by using $p = q$.
2. Present an attack showing it is not secure to first choose p, then let q be the next-largest prime.
3. Present an attack showing it is not secure to first choose p, then let q be the smallest prime larger than $2p$.

Exercise 6.36. You are given textbook-RSA ciphertext $c = 281$, with public key $e = 3$ and modulus $n = 3111$. Compute the private key d and the message $m = c^d \mod n$.

Hint: It is probably best to begin by computing the factorization of n. □

Exercise 6.37. Given an integer m, show how to compute m^e using a small number of multiplications, for e being one of the following three Fermat primes: 17, 257 and 65537.

Exercise 6.38 (Tiny-message attack on textbook RSA). We discussed that RSA should always be used with appropriate padding and that textbook RSA (no padding) is insecure, in particular, is not randomized so definitely does not ensure indistinguishability:

1. Show that textbook RSA may be completely decipherable, if the message length is less than $|n|/e$. (This is mostly relevant for $e = 3$.)
2. Show that textbook RSA may be completely decipherable, if there is only a limited, known set of possible messages.
3. Show that textbook RSA may be completely decipherable, if the message length is less than $|n|/e$, except for a limited, known set of additional (longer) possible messages.

Exercise 6.39. Consider the use of textbook RSA for encryption (no padding). Show that it is insecure against a chosen-ciphertext attack.

Exercise 6.40. Consider a variation of RSA which uses the same modulus N for multiple users, where each user, say Alice, is given its key pair $(A.e, A.d)$ by a trusted authority (who knows the factoring of N); note the use of the dot notation to identify the key owners. Show that one user, say Mal, given his keys $(M.e, M.d)$ and the public key of another user, say $A.e$, can compute $A.d$.

Hint: Recall that each user's private key is the inverse of the public key (mod $\phi(n)$), e.g., $M.e = M.d^{-1} \mod \phi(n)$.

Exercise 6.41 (Curveball-like public key validation vulnerability). Public key cryptosystems often use the term 'public key' to refer to only one component of the public key. For example, with

RSA, people often refer to e as the public key, although the actual RSA public key consists of the pair (e, n), i.e., also includes the modulus n.

Consider an application which validates an RSA signature of Alice using the given public key (e_A, n), but only validates that e_A is as specified in the certificate of Alice, and fails to validate that n in any way. Show how this allows an attacker to trick the recipient into believing — incorrectly — that an incoming message (generated and sent by the attacker) was signed by Alice.

Note: A similar situation exists with other public key algorithms, e.g., elliptic curves, where the public key consists of a specification of a curve and of a particular 'public point' on the curve, and people sometimes refer only to the point as if it is the (entire) public key. In particular, this led to the *Curveball vulnerability* in the Windows certificate-validation mechanism [446], which was due to validation of only the 'public point' and use of the curve selected by the attacker.

Exercise 6.42. Consider the use of textbook RSA for encryption as well as for signing (using hash-then-sign), with the same public key e used for encryption and for signature-verification, and the same private key d used for decryption and for signing. Show this is insecure against chosen-ciphertext attacks, i.e., allows either forged signatures or decryption.

Exercise 6.43. The following design is proposed to send email while preserving sender-authentication and confidentiality, using known public encryption and verification keys for all users. Namely, assume all users know the public encryption and verification keys of all other users. Assume also that all users agree on public key encryption and signature algorithms, denoted E and S, respectively.

When one user, say Alice, wants to send message m to another user, say Bob, she computes and sends: $c = E_{B.e}(m + \text{'Alice'} + S_{A.s}(m))$, where $B.e$ is Bob's public encryption key, $A.s$ is Alice's private signature key and 'Alice' is Alice's (unique, well-known) name, allowing Bob to identify her as the sender. When Bob receives this ciphertext c, he first decrypts it, which implies it was sent to him. To validate that the message was sent by Alice, he looks up Alice's public verification key $A.v$ and verifies the signature:

1. Explain how a malicious user Mal can cause Bob to believe he received a message m from Alice, although Alice never sent that message to Bob. (Alice may have sent a different message, or sent that message to somebody else.)
2. Propose a simple, efficient and secure fix.

Exercise 6.44 (Combining public key signatures and encryption). Many applications require both confidentiality, using recipient's public encryption key, say $B.e$, and non-repudiation (signature), using sender's verification key, say $A.v$. Namely, to send a message to Bob, Alice uses both her private signature key $A.s$ and Bob's public encryption key $B.e$, and to receive a message from Alice, Bob uses his private decryption key $B.d$ and Alice's public verification key $A.v$:

1. It is proposed that Alice will select a random key k and send to Bob the triplet: $(c^K, c^M, \sigma) = (E_{B.e}(k), k \oplus m, Sign_{A.s}(\text{'}Bob\text{'} + k \oplus m))$. Show this design is insecure, i.e., a MitM attacker may either learn the message m or cause Bob to receive a message that Alice never sent yet believe that the message came from Alice.
2. Propose a simple, efficient and secure fix. Define the sending and receiving process precisely.
3. Does your solution prevent replay (receiving multiple times a message sent only once)? If not, can you improve it to prevent replays?

Chapter 7

The Transport Layer Security (TLS) Protocol

In this chapter, we discuss the *Transport Layer Security (TLS)* protocol, which is the main protocol used to secure connections over the Internet — and, in particular, web-communication.

7.1 Introduction to TLS

The TLS protocol is possibly the most widely used security protocol; it is definitely used in many applications including some of the most important applications, in particular, to secure the communication between web clients and web servers. One reason for this wide use is that TLS is easy to deploy; it can be implemented as a user application on top of the standard *Transmission Control Protocol* TCP transport-layer protocol, which is supported by practically all operating systems. TLS has multiple implementations, including well-supported open-source implementations, and supports many extensions and diverse requirements and scenarios. Some of these extensions and changes were adopted as an inherent part of a new revision of the protocol, and many others can be deployed using the built-in extensions mechanism of TLS (Section 7.4.3), which became a standard part of TLS beginning with version TLS 1.1.

TLS has been studied and improved extensively. In fact, we believe that TLS is the most widely studied, analyzed and improved practical cryptographic protocol. The extensive efforts to analyze TLS, including discovery of many vulnerabilities and the introduction of countermeasures to address vulnerabilities and to improve security, give us considerable confidence in the security of the (later versions of) TLS.

From a security point of view, the popularity of TLS is a double-edged sword. On the one hand, this wide popularity motivates extensive efforts by the 'white-hat' security community, including researchers from academia and industry, to identify vulnerabilities and improve the security of the protocols and their implementations. This research, whose goal is to improve security and result in publications and improved standards, resulted in significant improvements to the security of TLS; many attacks and corresponding countermeasures were published by researchers, and new versions of the protocols were gradually more and more secure, culminating with TLS 1.3, which has significant design changes whose goal is to improve security.

On the other hand, this wide popularity also implies that 'black-hat crackers' have a strong motivation to find vulnerabilities in the TLS protocols and in their popular implementations. In fact, the desire to 'break' secure connections may even motivate powerful organizations to invest extensive efforts in 'injecting' intentional, hidden vulnerabilities (*cryptographic backdoors*) into the specifications and implementations of TLS and of other popular cryptographic systems, libraries, protocols and standards.

One example of what may be a cryptographic backdoor is the *Dual Elliptic Curve Deterministic Random Bit Generator* (*Dual_EC_DRBG*), which was found vulnerable in Ref. [124]. Support for the Dual_EC_DRBG was included in NIST, ANSI and ISO/IEC standards, and it was implemented in the widely used BSAFE cryptographic toolkit from RSA and used by implementations of TLS. There are claims that the NSA created and promoted the Dual_EC_DRBG as a cryptographic backdoor, and allegedly even paid RSA to make it the default pseudorandom generator in BSAFE. One evidence for NSA's involvement came from the NSA memos exposed by *Snowden* in 2013. These memos further indicated that the NSA spent $250 million per year to insert backdoors into software, hardware and standards; see Refs. [66, 486].

Some of this purported effort to insert trapdoors into standards seems to have been directed at TLS. In particular, consider Ref. [415], a proposal for a TLS extension by Eric Rescorla,[1] working as a consultant to the US government, and Margaret Salter, an NSA employee. The purported goal of this extension was to increase the number of random bits exchanged during the TLS handshake. However, these additional random bits seem to significantly improve the efficiency of the Dual_EC_DRBG attack. This was taken as an indication that this was another attempt to insert a cryptographic trapdoor — in this case, to the TLS specifications; see Ref. [66].

This widespread use of TLS also has important implications for learning and teaching TLS. Obviously, the importance of TLS motivates studying it; furthermore, the evolution of TLS and the different attacks and countermeasures are a valuable, interesting lesson, which can help identify and avoid vulnerabilities in different protocols and systems. On the other hand, this also means that there is an excessive wealth of important and interesting information — indeed, entire books were dedicated to cover TLS, e.g., Refs. [390, 411], and even they do not cover all aspects and attacks. We have tried to maintain a reasonable balance; however, there were many hard choices and surely there is much that could be improved.

In the following section (Section 7.1.1), we present a brief history of TLS and SSL, and the three main phases of the development of the TLS/SSL protocols: (1) the *proprietary SSLv2* design, (2) *the evolution* from *SSLv3* to *TLS version 1.2* and finally (3) the *TLS 1.3 re-design*. Later in this chapter, we dedicate a section to each of these three phases.

Why discuss older versions? One motivation to describe the older TLS and SSL versions is to learn about protocol vulnerabilities and attacks, which can help us to develop the intuition to identify vulnerabilities in different protocols and to design secure protocols.

Another motivation is that these attacks are often still relevant, for two reasons: First, many clients and servers still support outdated

[1]The author wishes to note that he respects Eric as an individual and as a major contributor to TLS and other security efforts, and does not believe that Eric had intentionally assisted in creating cryptographic trapdoors.

versions. Second, several downgrade attacks (Section 5.5.5) break implementations of newer versions of TLS, by exploiting their support for older, vulnerable versions.

7.1.1 A brief history of SSL and TLS

The TLS standards are defined by the Internet Engineering Task Force (IETF), as an evolution of the *Secure Socket Layer (SSL)* protocols.

The SSL protocols were developed by the Netscape corporation (rather than by the IETF); SSLv3 benefited from some feedback from researchers and the Internet security community, while earlier versions were developed within Netscape. Version 3 of SSL (SSLv3) is similar to version 1.0 of TLS.

Netscape corporation, established in 1994, was one of the very first companies to focus on the commercial potential of the web. At the time, a major concern was the ability to perform online purchases securely. Credit cards were quickly recognized as an appropriate payment method since they were already used widely for phone purchases and mail orders; such remotely authorized transactions were referred to as *card-not-present*, to identify the risk due to reliance on card details without visual confirmation of the physical card and handwritten signature, which were required for the more common (at the time) *card-present* transactions. However, the transmission of credit card information over the Internet was considered less secure, than the somewhat-protected transmission of credit card information in a phone call or by mail. In both phone and physical mail, there is some level of authentication of the merchant since the customer initiated the phone call or addressed the physical mail, but Internet communication may be viewed by different providers and, depending on technology, even other users. A secure solution was considered essential for the commercial use of the Web.

Netscape came out with the first protocol to protect credit card transactions over the Web — the SSL protocol. SSL initial goal was, basically, to provide security for credit card transactions, which will be comparable to the security of credit card transactions performed remotely, over phone or mail. Such remote transactions, where the customer's signature cannot be verified, are referred to as *card-not-present* transactions, in contrast to *card-present* transactions, where merchants are expected to verify the customer's handwritten signature over the transaction slip.[2] SSL-protected web transactions became, basically, a new way to perform card-not-present transactions. Indeed, very quickly, the use of SSL to protect web credit card transactions became widely adopted and expected by customers.

Importantly, the use of SSL was not limited to credit card transactions, and it did not take very long for SSL to be widely used to protect other webpages as well. SSL, as its name (*Secure Socket Layer*) implies, provides *general-purpose secure communication* interface, extending TCP's widely used socket API [455]. To secure web communication, Netscape defined the HTTPS protocol, which is basically the same as the web *HTTP* protocol, except that HTTP runs over TCP, without security, while HTTPS runs over a secure transport layer protocol (initially SSL and later TLS), providing security.

The design of SSL as a secure variant of the socket API gave it important advantages over alternative protocols proposed around the same years. The closest contender was *Secure HTTP (SHTTP)* [416], a general-purpose security extension for the *HTTP* protocol, but SHTTP was significantly more complex to understand, implement and deploy and was not widely adopted.

Another complex proposal was the *Secure Electronic Transactions (SET)* protocol, developed by a consortium including Visa, Mastercard, GTE, IBM, Microsoft and others. Before SET, there were two similar proposed protocols by competing groups: the *Secure Transaction Technology (STT)* from Visa and Microsoft, and the *iKP* protocol, developed by IBM [40, 41], which later became the *Secure Electronic Payment Protocol (SEPP)*, published by IBM together with Mastercard, Netscape, Cybercash and GTE (now Verizon).

SET, STT, SEPP and iKP were all designed for the specific task of securing credit card transactions, with the goal of providing security comparable to that of *card-present* transactions. To achieve this, clients were expected to use a private signing key and a certificate for the corresponding public validation key, where the certificate was

[2]These years, most credit card transactions do not involve validation of handwritten signatures, even when the consumer is present in the point of sale, but at the time, this was unconceivable.

to be obtained from their credit card issuer, and digitally sign each purchase. This signature was to be a secure digital alternative to the handwritten signature on a credit card slip. To securely achieve these goals, these protocols were significantly more complex to understand, implement and deploy, compared to SSL. The complex development process by multiple competing entities, with several competing early proposals, surely did not help.

Three main advantages helped SSL to quickly become a success. First, SSL was quickly implemented and deployed by Netscape, whose browser was, by far, the most popular at the time, with a large lead over all other browsers combined. Second, while SET, STT and iKP provided better security for credit card transactions, they were limited to this credit card application; in contrast, SSL could be used for other applications requiring secure client to server communication, not only for credit card purchases. In particular, although the original motivation for deploying SSL was to encrypt the credit card number in transit, protecting against an eavesdropper, it soon become apparent that *server authentication*, followed by key exchange and use of the shared key to encrypt and authenticate the communication, provide security functions critical to many websites.

The third advantage of SSL is its simplicity. SSL is simple in its concept, simple to implement, simple to integrate in browsers and other applications and, most significantly, simple and easy to adopt. Specifically, SET and iKP required adoption by credit card processors as well as merchants and customers, with private keys and certificates for each party, while SSL required only adoption by the browsers used by customers and by the web servers used by websites, including — but not limited to — merchant websites.

Furthermore, while SSL and TLS always perform *server authentication*, they make *client authentication optional*. In practice, TLS is usually deployed using only server authentication, which requires only the servers (merchants) to obtain public key certificates and use a corresponding private key. Client authentication is rarely used since it requires *clients* to obtain public key certificates and to use corresponding private keys installed in every device that the client uses to for web browsing.

Once the customer uses an SSL-enabled browser and the merchant's website supports SSL or TLS, the three parties to the credit card transaction (merchant, customer and credit card processor) can operate basically in the same way as they would operate in pre-web card-not-present scenarios; no additional change to their systems or processes is required.

The importance of such simplicity and ease of deployment and use for applied security mechanisms cannot be overstated, and we return to it when we introduce, later in this chapter, the *Keep It Simple and Secure (KISS)* principle (Principle 14).

The first publication of SSL was in June 1995, when Netscape published SSLv2 (SSLv2) [248]. Later in 1995, Microsoft published and implemented a similar protocol for protecting communication between client and server, the *Private Communication Technology (PCT)* [57]. PCT was similar to SSLv2, and basically unrelated to the SET design, although both were from Microsoft (and both abandoned).

SSLv2 had significant design vulnerabilities, and its publication allowed the web security community to expose these vulnerabilities. In November 1996, Netscape published the much-improved SSLv3 [192] (which was later, in August 2011, published as RFC 6101 [191]). The specification published was quite complete, allowing independent interoperable implementations.

Also in 1996, the IETF established a working group to develop an agreed standard protocol to replace the proprietary-developed SSL and PCT protocols. To avoid arguments on which of the two names should be used, a new name was chosen: the TLS (Transport Layer Security) protocol. In January 1999, the IETF published RFC 2246 [152], which defined TLS 1.0, the first standard version of TLS, produced by the TLS working group and closely based on SSLv3.

Although SSLv3 and TLS 1.0 addressed some of SSLv2's vulnerabilities, they still had serious additional vulnerabilities. In April 2006, the TLS working group of the IETF published TLS 1.1 as RFC4346 [153] to fix the issues discovered in TLS 1.0. However, additional vulnerabilities and concerns were discovered, motivating another release: TLS 1.2 [154] (published as RFC5246 in August 2008). These three TLS versions (1.0–1.2) were all quite similar to SSLv3, only fixing clearly exploitable vulnerabilities and adding features. The most important features were the *TLS extensions* mechanism, defined already for TLS 1.0 [83], and in particular the Server Name Indication (SNI) extension. See Section 7.4.3 for discussion of TLS extensions, including of the SNI extension.

After vulnerabilities were discovered also in TLS 1.2, the working group decided to do a major redesign. This took about 10 years; the IETF published TLS 1.3 [412], as RFC8446, only in August 2018. TLS 1.3 is still the latest version of TLS.

In contrast to previous designs, the TLS 1.3 designers gave preference to mechanisms with proven security properties; ideally, we would like the complete TLS protocol to be provably secure. While a complete proof of security was not yet published for TLS 1.3, there are encouraging and important partial results, e.g., Refs. [69,195,366]. As a result on this stronger emphasis on security, as well as due to significant changes to improve performance (mainly, reduce latency), TLS 1.3 is a major deviation from the previous versions.

7.1.2 High-level overview

The TLS and SSL protocols were originally designed to secure the communication between a web browser and a web server, and, while they are now widely deployed for additional applications, web security remains their main application.

In Figure 7.1, we present a highly simplified overview of this typical use-case. The figure shows how Alice, a web user, surfs to the TLS protected website *HTTPS://B.com*; we focus on the simpler variants of TLS, which are based on RSA encryption, and denote *B.com*'s public RSA encryption key by $S.e$. Note that the addresses (URL) of TLS protected websites begin with the protocol name *HTTPS* rather than the protocol name *HTTP*, used for unprotected websites. The process consists of the following steps:

Step 0 (in advance) — Web server obtains certificate: Before the web server *B.com* can provide TLS service, it needs to obtain a *certificate* Ψ_S for its public key $S.e$ and domain name *B.com*. The certificate should be signed by a *certificate authority (CA)*, which can either be a *root CA* or another CA which was certified by a root CA; a *root CA* is one of a list of CAs that are trusted 'directly' by the client (i.e., in this case, the browser). To obtain the certificate, the administrator of the web server sends to the CA, in flow $0.a$, the domain name, *B.com*, the web server's public encryption key, $S.e$, and optionally additional inputs, such as identifiers

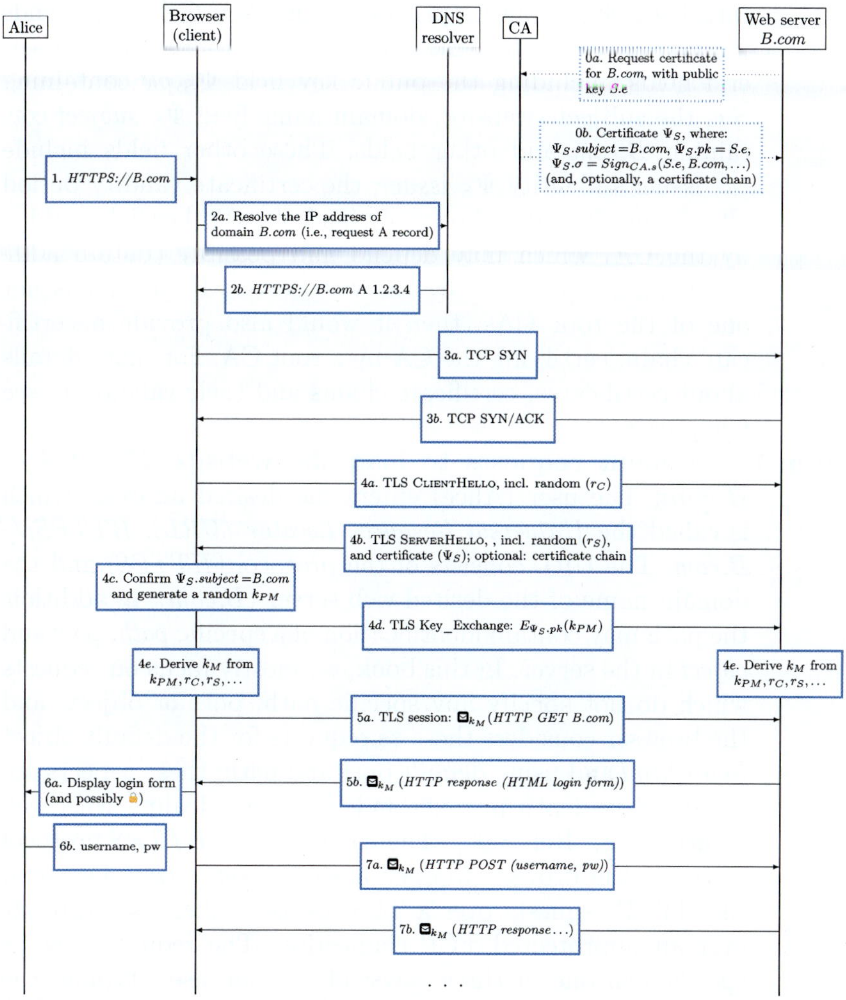

Figure 7.1. A simplified overview of the operation of TLS, to secure the login between the browser and the web server, using RSA for key exchange. In this chapter, we simplify by considering a single certificate; in practice, the server usually sends, in step 4*b*, a certificate chain, as we discuss in Chapter 8.

and parameters (omitted). The CA should validate that the request indeed comes from the owner of the specified domain name (*B.com*); the CA should also validate any additional inputs (if provided). We discuss the different validation processes in Section 8.2.3. If validation passes, the CA signs the certificate Ψ_S using its private signing key $CA.s$ and sends Ψ_S to the server (flow $0.b$). The certificate Ψ_S contains several fields, including the public key field $\Psi_S.pk$ containing $S.e$, the subject (website) domain name field $\Psi_S.subject$ containing $B.com$ and other fields. These other fields include the issuer's identity $\Psi_S.issuer$, the certificate validity period ($\Psi_S.from$, $\Psi_S.to$) and possibly (and often) other fields added by the CA, which may depend and possibly contain additional inputs provided by the web server. If the CA is not one of the root CAs, then it would also provide a certificate chain, certifying the CA by a root CA. For more details about certificates, certificate chains and their validation, see Chapter 8.

Step 1 — client requests to load the website *HTTPS:// B.com*: The user (Alice) enters the desired address, which is called the *Universal Resource Locator (URL)*, *HTTPS:// B.com*. The URL consists of the protocol (*HTTPS*) and the domain name of the desired web server (*B.com*); in addition, the path may contain identification of a specific *path, port* and *object* in the server. In this book, we mostly focus on requests which do not specify any specific path, port or object, and the browser considers these as requests for the default object *index.html* and using default port and path; these aspects are discussed in-depth in texts and standards dealing with web security, e.g., Ref. [500]. The choice of the *HTTPS* protocol instructs the browser to open a *secure connection*, i.e., send the HTTP requests over a TLS session rather than directly over an unprotected TCP connection. The request may be specified in one of three ways: (1) by the user 'typing' the URL into the address bar of the browser, i.e., 'manually', (2) 'semi-automatically', by the user clicking on an *hyperlink* or bookmark which specified this URL, or (3) 'automatically' by the browser, which it does for *embedded* hyperlinks, such as an embedded image, script or frame (another webpage displayed as part of the current page), as well as for a *redirect* hyperlink, instructing the browser to load a webpage from a different URL instead of the current one.

Step 2 — resolving the domain name into an IP address: To communicate with the *B.com* web server, the browser needs the IP address of the server, as communication over the Internet is done using the *Internet Protocol (IP)*, where source and destination are specified by their IP addresses. The *Domain Name System (DNS)* provides resolution (mapping) from domain names to IP addresses, which can be either 32-bit IP version 4 addresses or 128-bit IP version 6 addresses, using records of type A and of type AAAA, respectively. We illustrate a request for an IPv4 address (A record) from the browser to the DNS resolver (flow $2a$) and a response from the DNS resolver to the browser specifying the requested IPv4 address (flow $2b$). The step is skipped if the IP address is already known, typically, cached from a previous connection. Note that a corrupted or poisoned DNS resolver may return an incorrect IP for the website, e.g., the IP of the attacker; the TLS connection will prevent the attacker from impersonating as the requested website ($B.com$). See Figure 9.1 for an attack by a rogue or corrupted DNS resolver, which is effective if the user requests the (unprotected) URL *HTTP://login.b.com*; this attack shows that TLS should be used to protect the login page itself rather than using unprotected login page and only using TLS to protect the password when it is submitted by the user.

Step 3 — TCP handshake: The TLS protocol runs over the *Transmission Control Protocol (TCP)*, which provides important services such as reliability, congestion control and flow control. The first two flows of a TCP connections are called the *TCP handshake* and contain only control signals, no data. The first flow is referred to as *TCP SYN* (flow $3a$), and the second flow is referred to as *TCP SYN/ACK* (flow $3b$).

Step 4 — TLS handshake: The TLS protocol also begins with a *handshake*, i.e., few control flows, which establish the secure connection. In the following sections, we describe few versions of the handshake used by different versions of SSL and TLS; in Figure 7.1, we illustrate a simplification of the variant of the handshake of TLS 1.0-1.2 and of SSLv3, using RSA encryption for key exchange.

Step $4a$ — ClientHello: All TLS and SSL handshakes begin with the client (often, the browser) sending the ClientHello message, which contains the *client random* r_C, and other inputs, including a few mandatory fields and often also optional fields; we discuss these in the following sections.

Step 4*b* — ServerHello: In all TLS and SSL handshakes, the server responds by sending the ServerHello message, which contains the *server random* r_S. Usually, the ServerHello message is sent together with the server's certificate Ψ_S, and, if necessary, the certificate chain. Some additional fields may also be included.

Step 4*c* — Validate certificate and generate premaster key: The browser (client) validates the certificate Ψ_S (using the certificate chain if needed); in particular, it verifies whether the domain name in the certificate is the same as the domain name in the URL provided by Alice, i.e., that $\Psi_S.subject = B.com$. Then, the browser selects a random shared key k_{PM} called the *premaster key*.[3]

Step 4*d* — *Key_Exchange*: The client encrypts the premaster key k_{PM} using the server's public key $\Psi_S.pk = S.e$ and sends the ciphertext (encryption of k_{PM}) to the server in the *Key_Exchange* message.

Step 4*e*: In this step, applied locally by the server and by the client, they both derive the *master key* k_M from the premaster key k_{PM}, and the exchanged client and server random (r_C and r_S). We later discuss the derivation of the master key from the premaster key in different versions of TLS (and in SSLv3).

Step 5 — the TLS session (record protocol), initial webpage: At this point, the browser and server can communicate securely, with the confidentiality, integrity and authenticity of the communication protected using the TLS *record protocol*

[3]In version 2 of SSL, the client generates here a key called the *master key* and denoted k_M, which in SSLv3 and in TLS is derived from the premaster key k_{PM} in Step 4*e*. Step 4*e* is not done in version 2 of SSL.

and the shared master key k_M.[4] We use the envelope symbol to denote the protection provided by the record protocol (of TLS or SSL), with the key as subscript, i.e., $\boxtimes_{k_M}(\cdot)$. When visiting a webpage requested by the user, as in the given example, the browser first sends an HTTP GET request, requesting the webpage (flow $5a$); the server responds by sending back the page, written in *HTML (Hypertext Markup Language (HTML))*, e.g., a login form (flow $5b$). Note that the protocol specified in the URL of this HTTP request is *HTTPS* since the HTTP request and response are protected by the TLS (or SSL) record protocol.

Step 6 — page displayed to user: Flow $6a$ represents the browser displaying the webpage to the user (Alice), possibly with one or more *security indicators*, e.g., a padlock 🔒. Flow $6b$ represents the user entering user name and password. Chapter 9 discusses security aspects involving the human user.

Step 7 — additional HTTPS requests and response: Flows $7a$ and $7b$ are examples of additional HTTPS requests and responses, i.e., HTTP requests and responses protected by the TLS (or SSL) record protocol. In flow $7a$, the browser sends the username and password; the interaction typically continues with the server response (flow $7b$) and additional requests and responses (not shown). Again, the protocol specified in the URL of these HTTP requests is *HTTPS*, which instructs the browser to send these HTTP requests and responses over the TLS (or SSL) record protocol. As long as these requests are sent over the same TCP connection, they are part of the same TLS/SSL *session*, i.e., use the key exchanged by the same handshake. Once this TCP connection is closed, future HTTPS requests will result in a new TLS/SSL session, including a new handshake. To reduce overhead, a new

---

[4]This is a simplification; all versions of TLS and SSL derive *multiple* shared symmetric keys from the master keys k_M; the details, which we discuss later, differ between different versions of TLS and SSL.

TLS/SSL session may reuse a shared key exchanged in a previous session if kept by client and server, using the *session resumption* handshake in SSL and TLS versions before 1.3 (Figures 7.8, 7.12), or the Pre-Shared Key (PSK) handshake in TLS 1.3 (Figure 7.21).

7.1.3 Security goals

TLS and SSL are designed to ensure security between two computers, usually referred to as a *client* and a *server*, in spite of attacks by a man-in-the-middle (MitM) attacker. The goals include the following:

Key exchange: Securely setup a secret shared key, preventing exposure of this key to a MitM attacker.

Server authentication: Authenticate the identity of the server, i.e., assure the client that it is communicating with the right server.

Connection Integrity: Validate that the communication received by one party is exactly identical to the communication sent by the peer, in spite of a MitM attacker. If the protocol cannot ensure that the communication received is identical to the communication sent by the peer, then TLS aborts the connection, with an error message, rather than deliver information without integrity. Note that TLS is run over the TCP protocol, which ensures integrity against benign errors; therefore, any communication failure must be due to an attack, and aborting the connection is a sensible response. TLS detects and prevents not just corruption of an individual message but also *message re-ordering*, *message duplication* and truncation attacks, where the MitM attacker drops the last message(s) sent by the peer.

Connection confidentiality: TLS ensures that a MitM attacker cannot learn anything about the information sent between the two parties, except for the 'traffic pattern' — amount of information sent/received at any given time in the connection.

Client authentication: Authenticate the identity of the client. TLS supports a built-in client authentication mechanism, but its use is optional; in fact, TLS is usually used without client authentication, allowing an anonymous, unidentified client to connect to the server. The common way for servers to authenticate clients — when desired — is by an authentication mechanism which is not part of TLS, except that it may reply on the protection offered by exchanging messages protected by the TLS record protocol; in particular, client authentication may be performed by the client sending a *secret credential* within the TLS secure connection, such as a password or cookie.

Perfect forward secrecy (PFS): Version 3 of SSL and all versions of the TLS handshakes support the (optional) use of authenticated Diffie–Hellman (DH) key agreement, which ensures perfect forward secrecy (PFS), as discussed in Section 6.3.1. PFS is defined in Definition 5.3.

Crypto-agility: A cryptographic protocol supports *crypto-agility* if it allows the parties to select the specific cryptographic algorithms they use for a given function (e.g., block cipher, hash function or signatures). We introduced and discussed the importance of crypto-agility in Section 5.5.4; in particular, crypto-agility is essential, when a vulnerability is found or suspected in a particular algorithm. TLS supports crypto-agility; it allows the cryptographic algorithms to be negotiated in each session, through *cipher suite negotiation.* However, several versions of TLS are still vulnerable to downgrade attacks; see Section 7.5.

All versions of TLS, as well as SSLv3, were designed to meet these goals; for SSLv2, PFS was not a goal. Of course, the goals were not always ensured *securely*, due to different vulnerabilities; we present some of the important vulnerabilities in this chapter, and in particular, see Table 7.2.

7.1.4 Engineering goals

In addition to the security goals, the success of TLS and SSL is largely due to their focus — from the very first versions, SSLv2 — on important, generic 'engineering goals', applicable to any system, mainly, *efficiency, ease of deployment and use, extensibility* and *versatility.* By addressing these goals, TLS and SSL became widely used and applied in a very wide range of applications and scenarios. Let us briefly discuss these *engineering goals*.

Efficiency: Efficiency is always a desirable goal. In the case of TLS, there are two main efficiency considerations: *computational overhead* and *latency*.

In terms of *computational overhead*, the main consideration is minimizing the computationally intensive public-key operations. To minimize public-key operations, once the handshake establishes a shared key (using public key operations), the parties may reuse this key to establish future connections without requiring additional public-key operations. We refer to the set of connections based on the same public-key exchange as a *session* and a handshake that reuses the pre-exchanged shared key as a *session resumption* handshake. SSL already supported session resumption, and TLS has further enhanced and improved the session resumption mechanisms.

In terms of minimizing *latency*, the main consideration is to minimize the number of *round trip exchanges* since the Round Trip Times are often the dominant element impacting the overall delay/latency of the communication (Fact 5.1). End-to-end delays, including both queuing and propagation delays, are typically on the order of dozens to even hundreds milliseconds and are usually much higher than the transmission delays, especially for the limited amount of information sent in TLS handshake exchange. Reducing the number of round trips became even more important as transmission speeds increased over the years. This is reflected by the fact that until TLS 1.3, all designs had a fixed number of (two) round-trips to complete the handshake, and the client could send application messages over the TLS connection only after these two round-trip were done and the handshake completed. In contrast, a TLS 1.3 handshake requires only a single round-trip before sending a protected message, and TLS 1.3 even allows the clients to send a request already in the first exchange, albeit with some limitations and reduced security properties, see Section 7.6.

A more minor efficiency consideration is minimization of bandwidth; this is mainly significant in scenarios where bandwidth is limited, such as very noisy wireless connections.

Ease of deployment and use: The success and wide use of the (SSL and) TLS protocols are largely due to their ease of deployment

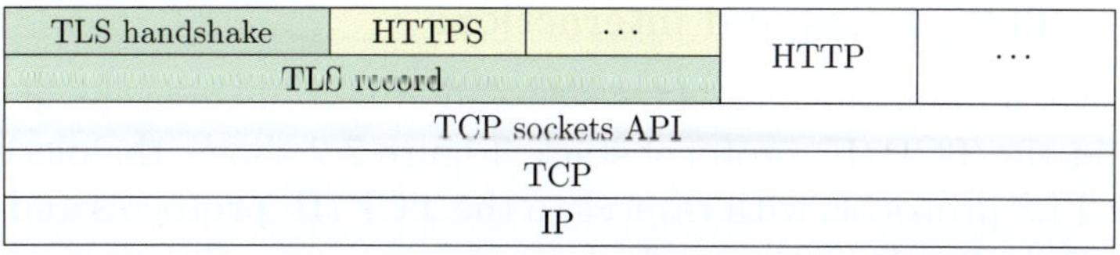

Figure 7.2. Placement of TLS in the TCP/IP protocol stack.

and usage. As shown in Figure 7.2, the TLS protocol is typically implemented 'on top' of the popular *TCP sockets API* and then used by applications, directly or via the *HTTPS* or other protocols. This architecture makes it easy to install and use TLS, without requiring changes to the operating system and kernel. This is in contrast to some of the other communication-security mechanisms, in particular the *IP security (IPsec)* protocol [158, 189], which, like TLS, is an IETF standard for securing communication against eavesdropping and MitM attackers. The ease of deployment and use of TLS is probably the reason that TLS has become an almost-universal security substrate for many systems, even where other protocols may have advantages. For example, IPsec provides some security advantages over TLS, for the application of protecting a *Virtual Private Network (VPN)*, in particular, IPsec can protect the integrity and the confidentiality of the Internet Protocol headers; in spite of this, it is more common to use TLS to protect VPNs, rather than to use IPsec, since TLS is easier to deploy and use.

Extensibility and versatility: Extensibility is always important — definitely for a widely deployed security protocol such as TLS, which is used in diverse scenarios and environments. Indeed, part of the success of TLS derives from its extensibility and versatility; the protocol supports many optional mechanisms, e.g., client authentication and flexibility such as crypto-agility (Principle 11). Furthermore, from TLS version 1.1 (and even earlier for some implementations), the TLS protocol supports a built-in *extensions* mechanism, providing even greater flexibility (Section 7.4.3). Some TLS extensions have proved extremely important and popular, and often been published as standards, while others are deployed only by specific clients and servers, e.g., to address unique requirements or experiment with new mechanisms.

7.1.5 TLS phases and interactions

The ease of deployment of TLS is largely due to its convenient placement in the TCP/IP protocol stack. Figure 7.2 shows the placement of the TLS protocols with respect to the TCP/IP protocols and other relevant protocols in the stack.

As can be seen in Figure 7.2, the TLS handshake protocol (first box in top line, in green) establishes keys for, and also uses, the TLS record layer protocol (first box in second line, also in green). The HTTPS[5] protocol and other application protocols that use the TLS record protocol are in two middle boxes of the top line (in yellow). Application protocols that do *not* use TLS for security, including the HyperText Transfer Protocol (HTTP), are in the two last boxes in the two top lines. These protocols, as well as TLS itself, all use the TCP protocol, via the sockets library layer. TCP ensures reliable (but insecure) communication using the (unreliable and insecure) Internet Protocol (IP).

Phases of TLS connections: The placement of TLS in the TCP/IP stack is also reflected in the *phases* of TLS connections, which we illustrate in Figure 7.3.

TLS connections are done over the TCP transport protocol; therefore, to establish a TLS connection, we first set up the TCP connection over which TLS will interact. The TCP connection setup process is usually referred to as the *TCP three-way handshake* since it involves three flows, usually referred to as the *Syn* packet, the *Syn/Ack* packet and the *Ack* packet. The TCP three way handshake establishes parameters which allow TCP to ensure reliable communication, without loss, duplication or reordering of information, and to perform congestion control and flow control; see, e.g., Refs. [129,308].

The first two flows of the TCP three-way handshake, i.e., the Syn and Syn/Ack TCP packets, contain only TCP information, i.e., do not include any TLS data. In Figure 7.3, we use dashed arrows for these flows, and for the other flows involving only TCP information and no TLS data. We refer to these two flows as the *TCP handshake* phase of the TLS connection.

[5]HTTPS stands for 'HyperText Transfer Protocol Secure'.

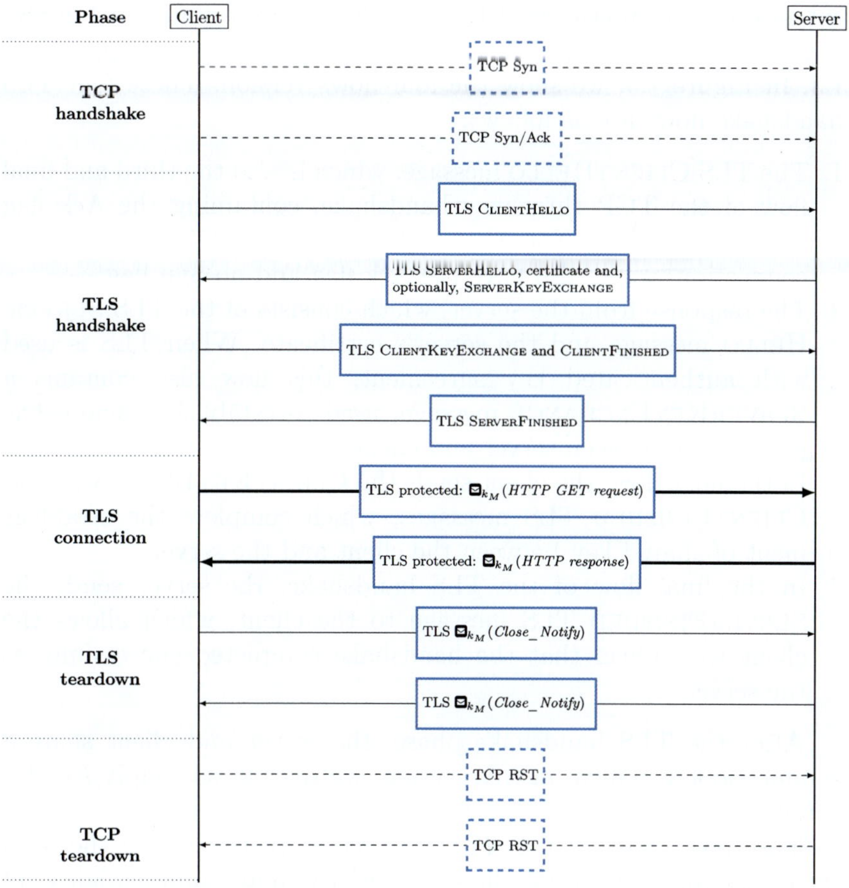

Figure 7.3. Overview of the phases of a TLS connection. TCP-only flows are dashed; TLS session flows, containing application messages, are emphasized by using thick lines. We show only a single pair of application messages, HTTP GET request and HTTP response, but there could be multiple application message exchanges during the same TLS connection. SSL connections have similar phases.

The next phase is the TLS handshake, where the parties run the TLS (or SSL) *handshake protocol*; we discuss different versions of the handshake protocol in Sections 7.3–7.6.

The TLS handshake phase is used to authenticate the server, agree on a shared secret key and optionally authenticate the client. The handshake also provides additional functions such as negotiation of cryptographic algorithms and other options, and transmission of TLS extensions. This phase consists of four flows (two round trips) in SSL and in TLS versions 1.0–1.2, and of two flows (one round trip) in TLS 1.3. In Figure 7.3, we show the four-flows version. These four TLS handshake flows are as follows:

1. The TLS ClientHello message, which is also the third and final flow of the TCP three-way handshake, containing the Ack flag (but not Syn flag). Note that all the following TCP packets in the connection would also have the Ack flag and no Syn flag.
2. The response from the server, which consists of the TLS ServerHello message and the server's certificate. When TLS is used with authenticated key agreement, this flow also contains a ServerKeyExchange message, used to establish a symmetric key shared between server and client.
3. In the next flow, the client sends the ClientKeyExchange and ClientFinished TLS messages, which complete the establishment of shared key between the client and the server.
4. In the final flow of the TLS handshake, the server sends the ServerFinished TLS message to the client, which allows the client to confirm that the handshake completed successfully at the server.

After the TLS handshake phase, the server and client share a symmetric key, which, in this section, we refer to as simply k_M, for simplicity.

The next phase is the *TLS connection* phase, where the *TLS record protocol* protects the authenticity and confidentiality of packets containing application data exchanged between client and server, using the shared key k_M; we discuss the record protocol in Section 7.2. In Figure 7.3, we include in the connection phase flows the keyed envelope icon 🖂$_{k_M}$, to clarify that these messages are protected by the record protocol using the master key k_M (or, more precisely, using keys derived from k_M). This phase may include exchange of multiple application messages between the client and server, although in Figure 7.3, only one message is sent in each direction.

When the application signals to the TLS layer that the connection should be terminated, TLS moves to the *TLS teardown* phase, in which the parties exchange the TLS *Close_Notify* messages. Typically and in Figure 7.3, the client initiates the teardown. Like the application messages, the TLS teardown messages are protected using the master key k_M shared between the client and the server; as in the TLS connection phase, we denote this using the keyed envelope icon ✉$_{k_M}$. A TLS connection could also be terminated by directly closing the TCP connection, and this is actually done by many implementations, to reduce overhead. However, the TCP connection could be also closed by an attacker since TCP messages are not authenticated, while the TLS teardown messages, if sent after the handshake is complete, are authenticated, ensuring that the peer is ready to close the connection. If the TCP connection is closed with the TCP teardown, then TLS may issue an alert since it is possible that some information sent was not yet received due to such attack, which we call a *truncation attack*.

Finally, in the *TCP teardown phase*, TLS tears down the TCP connection. This is usually done by having the parties exchange TCP RST (reset) packets, i.e., packets where the RST bit is turned on, causing the peer to immediately abort the connection and send a RST packet back. There is also a more 'graceful' TCP connection-closure process, using TCP FIN packets, which ensures that both parties have sent all of their pending traffic, but it involves a bit more overhead and is not required by TLS since the TLS teardown phase already guarantees that there is no pending traffic. Since these flows contain only TCP data, without TLS data, they are illustrated using dashed arrows.

7.2 The TLS record protocol

In this section, we begin our in-depth discussion of the TLS protocols, by discussing the *TLS record protocol*, which is the most widely deployed record protocol. We discussed the basic principles underlying record protocols and simple record protocols in Chapters 4 and 5. The TLS record protocol is more complex, with some unique aspects and instructive vulnerabilities.

Like other record protocols, the TLS record protocol protects the confidentiality, integrity and authenticity of the communication, using symmetric cryptography. The symmetric key used by the record protocol would be previously setup, securely, by the *handshake protocol*, which we discuss in the following sections.

We discuss the record protocol before we move to the more complex TLS handshake protocol since the record protocol is simpler and similar to the shared key protocols of Chapter 5; understanding the record protocol can help understand the more complex handshake protocol. In particular, by presenting attacks on vulnerable record protocol options, we motivate some of the mechanisms of the handshake protocol.

We focus on the common case, where the TLS record protocol is applied 'on-top' of an underlying reliable communication protocol — typically, TCP.[6] Hence, without an attack, messages sent are received reliably, without losses, duplications or re-ordering; any deviation must indicate an attack and justifies closing the connection.

Both TCP and the TLS record protocol treat the data from the application as one long stream of bytes, regardless of the sequence of (usually multiple) calls in which the protocol receives the data from the application. Namely, the application in the receiver should parse the stream of bytes which the record protocol outputs, into the different application-level units (typically called messages).

The record protocol involves authentication, encryption and a few other functions applied to the data. We already discussed such combinations in Section 4.5; in this section, we focus on the TLS-specific aspects and designs.

Derivation of record-protocol shared keys: The record protocol uses shared (symmetric) keys derived from the shared master key (k_M) established by the handshake protocol. Different designs of the TLS handshake protocol derive the keys for the record protocol in different ways, although all versions derive from k_M separate shared keys for the traffic from client to server, vs. for traffic from server to client.

There are significant differences in the number of keys and their derivation between different versions of the record protocol, as follows:

- SSLv2 derives one key for the traffic from client to server, denoted k_C, and one key for the traffic from server to client, denoted k_S.

[6]We do not cover *DTLS* [413], a variant of TLS, designed to work over the UDP protocol, i.e., over an unreliable datagram service.

Derivation is done using the (specific, insecure) hash function MD5. See Section 7.3.2.

- SSLv3 and versions 1.0–1.2 of TLS use separate shared keys for encryption and for authentication, in addition to the separation between keys from client to server and keys from server to client; the resulting four keys are derived from k_M (and values exchanged during the handshake). The message authentication code (MAC) keys are denoted k_C^A and k_S^A, used for authentication of messages sent from client to server and for authentication of messages sent from server to client, respectively. Similarly, the shared, symmetric encryption keys are denoted k_C^E and k_S^E, used for encryption of messages sent from client to server and for authentication of messages sent from server to client, respectively. See Section 7.4.1.
- TLS version 1.3, like SSLv2, derives one key for the traffic from client to server, denoted k_C, and another key for the traffic from server to client, denoted k_S. However, unlike SSLv2, derivation can use arbitrary functions which satisfy well-defined specification, and, if these assumptions hold, derivation is secure. See Section 7.6.5.

Crypto-agility and cipher suite negotiation: TLS supports *crypto-agility*, i.e., implementations can use different cryptographic algorithms. The cipher suite defines cryptographic algorithms used by both record protocol and handshake protocol. For the AtE record protocol, the cipher suite defines the symmetric key cryptosystem, the MAC algorithm and the (optional) compression algorithm. For the AEAD record protocol, the record protocol has less options: it is defined by a single AEAD algorithm.

Obviously, in each TLS connection, the client and the server must agree on and use the same algorithms; the set of cryptographic algorithms negotiated by the parties is called the *cipher suite*, and the process for agreeing on the cipher suite to be used is called *cipher suite negotiation.* We discuss the TLS negotiation mechanisms, and associated vulnerabilities and attacks, in Section 7.5.

Organization of this section: In Section 7.2.1, we discuss the TLS *Authenticate-then-Encrypt (AtE)* record protocol, used in SSL and in versions of TLS until TLS 1.2. In Section 7.2.2, we present the *TLS error oracle attack model*, which defines the capabilities we assume are available to attackers of the TLS record and handshake protocols. In Sections 7.2.3–7.2.6, we present attacks exploiting vulnerabilities in the AtE record protocol. These vulnerabilities and exploits motivate the adoption of a more secure design: the *AEAD record protocol*, which we discuss in Section 7.2.7 (see also discussion of AEAD schemes in Section 4.5.1). TLS 1.3 supports *only* the AEAD record protocol, while TLS 1.2 supports both versions of the record protocol (the AtE record protocol and the AEAD record protocol).

7.2.1 The Authenticate-then-Encrypt (AtE) record protocol

We begin our discussion of the TLS record protocol, by focusing on the AtE design. The AtE record protocol was the only record protocol supported by (both versions of) SSL; it was also the only record protocol of TLS until version 1.2. Version 1.2 of TLS supports both the AtE record protocol and the AEAD record protocol, and TLS 1.3 only supports the AEAD record protocol.

Figure 7.4 illustrates the sequence of processing steps applied by the sender, running the TLS AtE record protocol. These steps are applied to an input message m that the sender receives, typically, from the application.[7] Let us discuss each of the steps in the order they are applied by the sender of the data:

Fragment: Break the message m sent over TCP, i.e., sent by the application in one TCP *send*(m) event. Then, m will be broken by the record protocol into a set $F(m)$ containing a number $\varphi(m) \equiv \lceil \frac{m}{16 \cdot 1024} \rceil \geq 1$ of fragments. We denote the fragments by $f_i(m)$, i.e., $F(m) \equiv \{f_i(m)\}_{i=1}^{\varphi(m)}$. The concatenation of these fragments is the original message m, i.e., $m = f_1(m) + \cdots + f_{\varphi(m)}(m)$. Each fragment $f_i(m)$ is of size exactly 16 KB, i.e., 16384 $(= 16 \cdot 1024)$

[7]TLS also uses the record protocol to protect some of its own control messages, specifically, its control messages sent after a TLS has established a shared key (allowing it to apply the record protocol). For example, see the *Close_Notify* messages in Figure 7.3.

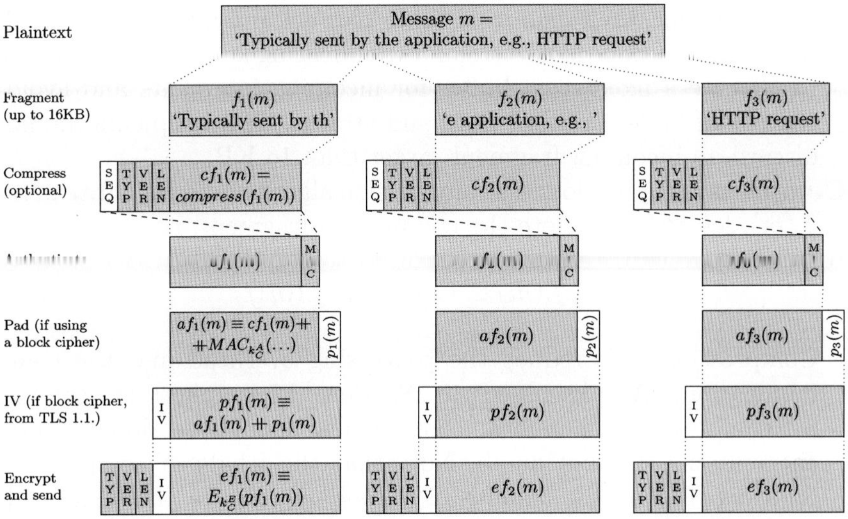

Figure 7.4. The Authenticate-then-Encrypt (AtE) design of the record protocol of SSL and TLS. Note that the *pad* and *IV* fields are only used for block ciphers; furthermore, the IV field was added only from TLS 1.1. The MAC is computed over the sequence number (SEQ), type (TYP), version (VER), length (LEN) and compressed fragment. The type, version and length fields are sent, as plaintext, together with the corresponding encrypted fragments. See text for details. The record protocol used (only) the AtE design until TLS 1.1; TLS 1.2 supports the use of either the AtE design or the AEAD design (Section 7.2.7).

bytes, except the last fragment $f_{\varphi(m)}(m)$, whose length is *at most* 16KB. Namely,

$$f_i(m) \equiv \begin{cases} \text{If } i < \varphi(m) & m\left[(i-1)\cdot\varphi(m) : i\cdot\varphi(m)-1\right] \\ \text{else:} & m\left[(i-1)\cdot\varphi(m) : |m|-1\right] \\ \text{Where:} & \varphi(m) \equiv \lceil \frac{m}{16\cdot 1024} \rceil \end{cases} \tag{7.1}$$

The fragmentation process is illustrated in the top two lines of Figure 7.4. Note that the record protocol may also aggregate multiple (short) 'messages', sent in consecutive 'send' event, into one fragment; this is less common and not shown in the figure.

One motivation for fragmentation is to allow *pipeline* operation, reducing the latency. For example, the sender may process the first fragment, then send it while, in parallel, processing the second fragment. Another motivation for fragmenting is to allow recipients to allocate a fixed-sized buffer for incoming fragments and avoid the risk of buffer overflow bugs and attacks. TLS recipients should discard an incoming fragment larger than 16 KB.

Compress: Apply a lossless compression algorithm to each fragment $f_i(m)$; let $cf_i(m)$ denote the compressed fragment, i.e.,

$$cf_i(m) \equiv \text{Compress}(f_i(m)) \tag{7.2}$$

Compression may reduce the processing overhead and the communication. As discussed in Section 4.5, ciphertext cannot be compressed. Therefore, compression should be done before encryption — or not at all. Note that the *length* of compressed data depends on the amount of redundancy in the plaintext, and encryption usually does not hide the *length* of the (compressed) plaintext; hence, there is a risk of exposure of the (approximate) amount of redundancy in the plaintext, when applying compress-then-encrypt. The *CRIME, BREACH* and *TIME compression attacks* [36, 355, 419, 438] all exploited, in different ways, the fact that TLS applies compression before encryption. These attacks motivated *disabling of TLS compression*, and currently TLS compression is rarely used (and not even supported in TLS 1.3). However, compression attacks may still be possible, in the (common) use of application-level compression; this is exploited in the BREACH attack [208]. We discuss these attacks in Section 7.2.6.

Authenticate: The AtE record protocol authenticates the plaintext by applying a MAC function, before encryption. The input to the MAC function consists of the concatenation of a *Sequence number (SEQ)* field, indicating the sequence number of the record, the *type (TYP), version (VER)* and *length (LEN)* fields, and the *Compressed Fragment* itself. The type, version and length fields are defined as follows:

Type (TYP): One byte indicating the type of data in this record. The most common type is 'application data', which is encoded by 0x17, e.g., in Figure 7.4, we have TYP='0x17'. Other types are used for TLS control messages, e.g., the *Close_Notify* and the *Change_Cipher_Spec (CCS)*[8] messages; note that TLS control messages can only be protected by the record protocol after the TLS handshake establishes a shared key between client and server.

***Version (VER)*:** A one byte identifier of the version of TLS.

***Length (LEN)*:** A two-byte field whose value is the number of bytes in the (optionally compressed) fragment. We use $LEN_i(m)$ to denote the value of LEN in the ith fragment of m, i.e., $LEN_i(m) \equiv |cf_i(m)|$.

In SSLv3 and in TLS versions 1.0–1.2, we use k_C^A (k_S^A) to denote the shared key for authenticating traffic from client to server (respectively, from server to client); we discuss the derivation of these keys in Section 7.4.1. Therefore, the *authenticated fragment* $af_i(m)$, i.e., the MAC of the ith fragment of a message m sent by the client, is calculated by:

$$af_i(m) = cf_i(m) + \text{MAC}_{k_C^A}\begin{pmatrix}\text{SEQ} + \text{TYP} + \text{VER}+ \\ +\text{LEN}_i(m) + cf_i(m)\end{pmatrix} \quad (7.3)$$

Note that to avoid clutter, we abuse notation and simply write $af_i(m)$ for the ith authenticated fragment, although, of course, it is actually also a function of the authentication key k_C^A.

A similar equation, identical except for using k_S^A instead of k_C^A, is used for the authenticated fragments of messages sent from the server to the client.

Padding: When using a block cipher, the TLS AtE record protocol appends a *padding* string, ensuring that the total length of the input to the encryption is an integral number of blocks, as shown in Figure 7.5.

Both SSL and TLS use their own padding schemes (SSL padding and TLS padding, respectively). When using a block cipher whose blocks are of length of l bytes, the *padded fragments* $\{pf_i(m)\}$ of

[8]The Change_Cipher_Spec (CCS) is used to signal that the record protocol begins using the newly negotiated keys and cipher suite; it was deprecated in TLS 1.3.

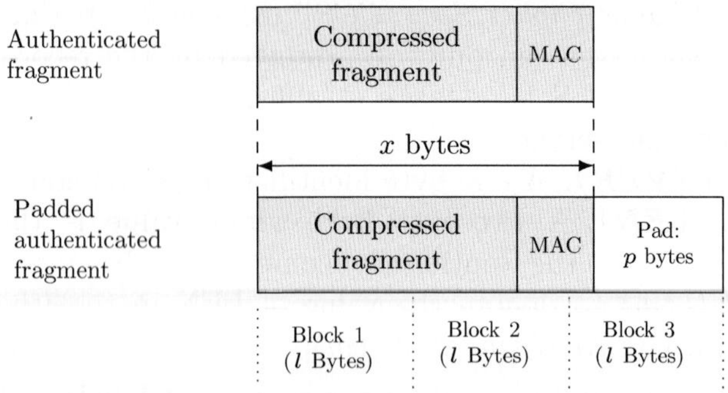

Figure 7.5. Padding in the AtE record protocol of SSL and TLS, when using a block cipher with block of l bytes; $l = 8$ for DES and $l = 16$ for AES. The pad contains $p = l - (x \mod l)$ bytes, where x is the length of the authenticated fragment (compressed fragment plus MAC); e.g., if $l = 16$ and $x = 35$, then $p = 13$, and the padded authenticated fragment fits in three blocks (as in the figure). In TLS, all p pad bytes must contain $p - 1$. In the SSL record protocol, only the last pad byte must contains $p - 1$; the other $p - 1$ pad bytes may have any value. Stream-cipher encryption does not require padding.

message m are calculated as follows:

$$pf_i(m) = af_i(m) + pad(l - (|af_i(m)| \mod l)$$

where:

$$\text{pad}(j) = \begin{cases} \text{TLS padding:} & j \geq 1 \text{ bytes containing } j-1 \\ \text{SSL padding:} & \begin{array}{c}(j-1 \text{ arbitrary bytes}) + \\ +(\text{one byte containing } j-1)\end{array} \end{cases} \quad (7.4)$$

For a pad of j bytes, in SSL padding, the last byte contains $j - 1$ and the other bytes can contain any value, while in TLS padding, all bytes contain $j - 1$. This seemingly minor difference is actually significant. For example, this will be evident when we discuss the *Poodle padding attack* in Section 7.2.3, which exploits this property of SSL padding.

Both schemes, like other padding schemes, allow validation of the correctness of the pad after decryption and then removal of the pad. See the discussion of padding schemes, including additional attacks exploiting padding, in Section 2.11.

TLS 1.2 allows the pad to add additional blocks to the padded fragment, which can help obfuscate the exact length of the fragment, which makes it harder to distinguish between two (encrypted) plaintext messages by detecting the different lengths of the padded fragments of the two messages.

Prepend IV: Some of the block cipher encryption modes of operation, e.g., CBC, require an *initialization vector* (*IV*), which is usually selected randomly; see Section 2.10. In TLS 1.1 and 1.2, the IV is sent by the record protocol, prepended to the ciphertext, as shown in Figure 7.4. SSL and TLS 1.0 try to save the (very limited) resources required to select and send the IV, by deriving the IV from the previous record sent. This flawed design was exploited by the devastating BEAST attack (Section 7.2.4 and [165]); its publication was a main driver for adoption of TLS 1.1. See Section 7.2.4.

Encrypt: Finally, the record protocol encrypts the concatenation of the *compressed plaintext fragment*, the *MAC* and, if used, the *padding*. In SSLv3 and TLS versions 1.0–1.2, traffic from client to server is encrypted using the shared key k_C^E and traffic from server to client is encrypted using the key k_S^E; for the derivation of these keys, see Section 7.4.1.

AtE and security: The record protocols for SSLv3 and TLS versions 1.0–1.2 use the *AtE* design. Recall, from Section 4.5.3 (or Ref. [303]), that AtE can be insecure for some choices of MAC and symmetric key cryptosystem schemes but that, on the other hand, AtE *is* secure for some of the standard modes of operation, in particular CBC, if the underlying block cipher is secure. Both TLS and SSL use the CBC mode when encrypting with a block cipher; so, it may appear that their use of AtE is ensures security; e.g., see Ref. [303].

However, as can be seen in Figure 7.4, when using a block cipher, TLS uses *padded encryption*, e.g., padded CBC, for which AtE is vulnerable. The padding allows attacks exploiting the use of EtA; we discuss some of these in Sections 7.2.3–7.2.5. Before that, in Section 7.2.2, we discuss the relevant *adversary model*, which we call the TLS error oracle attack model.

Note that TLS can support also variants of the record protocol that *are* secure when using any secure symmetric key cryptosystem and MAC scheme. These secure variants use *Encrypt-then-Authenticate (EtA)* or secure *Authenticated Encryption*. The

EtA design has been standardized, as a TLS extension (Section 7.4.3), to improve the security of TLS 1.0–1.2 [224]. The record protocol of TLS 1.3 does not have this issue since it always uses Authenticated Encryption with Associated Data (AEAD) (Section 7.2.7).

7.2.2 The TLS error oracle attack model

Following the *attack model principle* (Principle 1), we now discuss what are the capabilities that may be available to an attacker trying to 'break' the EtA record protocol; we refer to these capabilities as the *TLS error oracle attack model*. Intuitively, this attacker model combines the capabilities of a MitM attacker with the padding-error oracle attack model and the *cross-site attack model*. Let us discuss the padding-error oracle attack and cross-site attacks.

Padding-error oracle attacks: An attacker against TLS can often know if the decryption of a given ciphertext message results in valid or invalid plaintext, i.e., if the decrypted plaintext has valid padding and MAC field. This is basically the padding-error oracle attack model, which we discussed in Section 2.11 (in particular, see Figure 2.37); the padding-error oracle attack model is also used in the Bleichenbacher padding attack against RSA (Section 6.5.7). The TLS padding error oracle attack model further assumes that the attacker can *distinguish* between a padding error and a MAC-validation error. The distinction between these two types of errors turns out to be quite helpful for attackers. In version 2 of SSL, distinguishing between the errors was easy for a MitM attacker since each of these two errors resulted in a different error message (sent in the clear). In SSLv3 and all TLS versions, the error messages are encrypted; nevertheless, different attacks, against different versions and implementations, were able to detect the whether a failure is due to invalid padding or to invalid MAC, based on differences in the timing of the response, i.e., a *timing side channel*. For example, see the Poodle padding attack Section 7.2.3.

Cross-site attacks: Cross-site attacks are attacks launched by a *rogue (attacker) website* visited by a victim client. This happens often; one of the features that made the web so successful is that browsers have defense mechanisms designed to allow them to load and use content, including webpages, media and even scripts, from untrusted websites; these untrusted websites are, in turn, often loaded by another website visited by the client, and most of this loading and usage of untrusted content is done automatically by the browser, without user involvement. In particular, a rogue website can send automatically executed hyperlinks to the browser and thereby cause the browser to send a request to an attacker-chosen benign (victim) website, e.g., embedding an image or a script in the rogue webpage. Such attacks are referred to as *cross-site attacks*. Cross-site attacks are of the most common attacks on web security.

Authenticating cookies and other secrets: Often, the goal of cross-site attackers is to expose information about a secret string x, taken from some (possibly known) distribution, which is sent by the browser to the benign (victim) website, as part of the request induced by the rogue website; the request also contains contents chosen by the attacker, i.e., this reflects *partial chosen-plaintext attack (CPA) capabilities.*

These could be different secret strings sent in this way by the browser, including a password and a secret token (often, a *CSRF token*, used to prevent cross-site request forgery (CSRF) attacks). However, the most common secret string x is an *authenticating cookie* that the browser automatically includes with every request that it sends to the benign website *B.com.*

Cookies are strings of one or more characters (bytes), received from a webpage, say of domain name *foo.bar*, and sent by the browser, automatically, with requests sent to webpages with the same domain name (*foo.bar*). *Authenticating cookies* are cookies used as a means of user authentication, i.e., to authenticate requests coming from authorized clients; they very convenient to use and therefore used by many websites.

Browsers implement several security mechanisms on cookies, including restrictions on cookie storage, access to cookies and transmission of cookies. The restrictions may depend on attributes sent with the cookie, e.g., the *secure, HttpOnly* and *SameSite* attributes. These restrictions — some of which enforced only in more recent browsers — may make it harder or infeasible for cross-site attackers to expose authenticating cookies, in particular using cryptographic attacks on the TLS record protocol, such as these described in this chapter. For example, a cookie which was set with the SameSite attribute set to *Strict* is never sent in cross-site requests, and a cookie set with the default SameSite attribute of *Lax* is sent in cross-site requests only if they are considered 'safe navigations'. See the discussion of cookies and security in Section 9.6.3.1 and details in Ref. [75].

For simplicity, we ignore these restrictions on cross-site transmission of cookies. We further simplify by allowing the attacker to cause the user's browser to generate requests of the form $p + x + s$, where p and s are attacker-chosen prefix and suffix strings, respectively, and x is the secret string that the attacker tries to learn, e.g., an authenticating cookie. We further assume that the attacker knows the length $|x|$ of the secret string.

Non-cryptographic cross-site attacks: The most common — and most widely known — cross-site attacks are actually attacks circumventing non-cryptographic web defense mechanisms, most significantly, the *Same Origin Policy (SOP)*. Possibly the most well known of these are the *cross-site scripting (XSS) attacks*, which, among other abuses, often expose authenticating cookies, and the *CSRF attacks*, which *abuse* (unknown) authenticating cookies to perform unauthorized operations. We discuss the use of authenticating cookies and other topics related to web security in Section 9.6.3.1.

TLS error handling: Since TLS runs over TCP, the ciphertexts received by the TLS server and client should be exactly as sent by the peer (client and server, respectively). Therefore, any invalid ciphertext must be due to an attack; and, accordingly, the TLS record protocol aborts a connection upon receiving an invalid ciphertext. TLS negotiates a new pseudorandom master key for each connection, even when re-using the same premaster key k_{PM}, i.e., the same public-key-based key exchange.

7.2.3 Padding attacks: Poodle and Lucky13

The use of *AtE* by SSL and by versions 1.0, 1.1 and (optionally) 1.2 of TLS may result in vulnerabilities to *padding-error oracle attacks.* We earlier discussed padding-error oracle attacks against padded encryption (for symmetric key cryptosystem in Section 2.11 and for RSA in Section 6.5.7), where encryption was done to a padded plaintext message, without authentication or integrity checks on the plaintext. In contrast, the AtE record protocol encrypts fragments after they were authenticated and only then padded, as illustrated in Figure 7.5; hence, the protocol validates the MAC on the plaintext only *after removing* the padding. The padding of the authenticated fragment is illustrated in Figure 7.5.

TLS uses *TLS padding*, where each of the p pad bytes contain the binary value $p-1$, and SSL uses SSL padding, where the last byte of the pad contains $p-1$ and the other bytes can contain any value. In both cases, we assume that an attacker may be able to distinguish between a padding error (wrong padding in the decryption of the ciphertext) and authentication error (padding is correct but, after removing it, MAC is invalid).

In SSLv2, error messages were sent in the clear, making it trivial for an attacker to distinguish between padding errors and authentication errors. However, in SSLv3 and all versions of TLS, error messages of both kinds are sent encrypted (protected by the record protocol), with the hope of making padding attacks infeasible or at least harder. Note also that upon detecting any error, including padding and authentication errors, the connection is aborted. Indeed, early padding attacks such as these presented by Vaudenay [467] resulted in only limited information leakage from the encrypted messages.

However, these early attacks were followed by more realistic, although still hard to exploit, attacks, such as the password interception attacks of Ref. [116]. These attacks used a *timing side channel* to distinguish between padding errors and MAC errors, based on differences in the processing time of the two. Effective attacks, based on measurable timing differences, are known for both SSLv3 and TLS 1.0.

Although these attacks seemed very hard to exploit, we think that they *should* have sufficed to motivate the TLS 1.1 and 1.2 designers to change from the (insecure) *AtE* of TLS to the (secure) *Encrypt-then-Authenticate* paradigm, or to an *AEAD*-based record protocol, following the conservative design principle (Principle 3). Unfortunately, this did not happen.

Instead, the TLS 1.1 and 1.2 specifications include additional countermeasures that attempt to prevent distinguishing between pad errors and MAC errors, such as computing the MAC even if the pad is invalid. Such countermeasures are ingenious but unreliable. Furthermore, these countermeasures cannot prevent a possible padding attack that works without distinguishing between MAC and pad failures.

We discuss two of the most important padding oracle attacks: the *Lucky13* attack against TLS and the *Poodle* attack against SSLv3. Lucky13 requires the ability to distinguish between MAC and pad failures, while Poodle works even if the two errors are indistinguishable, making Poodle easier to exploit. Both of these attacks are against the use of a block cipher with the CBC mode of operation.

The Poodle padding attack (against SSLv3): SSLv3 can use either the RC4 stream cipher or a block cipher such as DES or AES with the CBC mode of operation. We discuss RC4 vulnerabilities in Section 7.2.5; here, we show that SSLv3 is also vulnerable when using a block cipher (with CBC), due to the *Poodle padding attack*.

The Poodle padding attack was introduced in Ref. [362], based on previous ideas and observations made already, years earlier, in Refs. [359, 467]. In Ref. [362], the authors also showed the *Poodle downgrade attack*, allowing downgrade from many implementations of TLS (versions 1.0–1.2) to SSLv3 and then deploying the Poodle padding attack. We discuss the Poodle downgrade attack in Section 7.5.

The main observation underlying the Poodle attack is a property of the SSL padding (see Section 2.11). Namely, when using a block cipher with l-bytes blocks, a ciphertext c is properly SSL-padded if it contains an integral number of l-bytes blocks, i.e., $|c| \equiv 0 \pmod{l}$, and its last byte contains a number $l' < l$. The unpadded ciphertext is $D_{k_M}(c)$ with the last $l' + 1$ bytes removed. Note that SSL padding does not require the non-last bytes of the pad to have a specific value, which is an important difference from TLS padding, where *all* padding bytes should contain the same value (the pad length minus one).

A simplified Poodle attack: Before we explain the Poodle attack against SSL, we begin with a simplified, weaker attack. In this weaker attack, the attacker captures some ciphertext message c, consisting of some number n of (l-bytes) blocks, which we denote $c = \langle c_1, \ldots, c_n \rangle$.

Let $p \equiv \langle p_1, \ldots, p_n \rangle$ denote the pre-encrypted (padded plaintext) input to the SSL CBC encryption, which is the result of fragmenting the plaintext message given to the record protocol, appending the MAC and pad and prepending the *type (TYP), version (VER)* and *length (LEN)* fields (see Figure 7.4 and Section 7.2). Note that $|p| = |c|$ since SSL (and TLS 1.0) uses the last ciphertext block of the previously sent message as the initialization vector (IV), i.e., does not prepend an IV block to the ciphertext c. (This aspect isn't actually critical to the Poodle attack, though.)

In this simplified, weak attack, the attacker only learns, with the small probability of $\frac{1}{256}$, the value of the last pre-encrypted byte in one of the blocks, say block i, where $i < n$; namely, the attacker learns byte $p_i[l-1]$. Depending on i, this byte would either be part of the (optionally compressed) fragment input or part of the appended MAC.

Furthermore, this weak attack requires that the pad is of a whole block, i.e., p_n consists of l pad bytes; therefore, unpad(p) consists of the rest of the blocks, namely,

$$\text{unpad}(p) = \langle p_1, \ldots, p_{n-1} \rangle \tag{7.5}$$

Note also that in this case, the last byte of the pad would have the value $l - 1$, i.e., $p_n[l - 1] = l - 1$; SSL padding does not restrict the other bytes.

The reader may wonder why we even bother with such a weak attack, with all of its assumptions and restrictions. The answer is that we later show how to improve on all of these aspects, creating an effective, realistic and efficient attack; indeed, often effective attacks are improvements of attacks which appear impractical and too weak (motivating the conservative design principle, Principle 3). Let us therefore explain how the weak attack works. Before reading our explanation, we recommend that readers first try to work out this weak attack themselves, though.

We present the attack assuming that the attacker intercepts ciphertext c sent from the client to the server; handling the case where c was sent from the server to the client follows in the same way (just changing the notation for the keys). Instead of sending c to the server, the attacker sends to the server $c' \leftarrow \langle c_1, \ldots, c_{n-1}, c_i \rangle$.

Namely, the only change in c' compared to c is in the last block, which contains a copy of the c_i block, instead of the original c_n block.

Let $p' = \langle p'_1, \ldots, p'_n \rangle$ denote the result of applying the corresponding CBC decryption by the recipient to c'. Since SSL does not prepend an IV to the ciphertext, we have $|p'| = |c'| = |c| = |p|$.

Assume that SSL uses the same IV to decrypt c' as it would have used to decrypt c, and let us denote it by c_0. From the design of CBC Section (2.10.9), for $j < n$, we have:

$$\begin{aligned} p'_j =& D_{k_C^E}(c'_j) \oplus c'_{j-1} \\ =& D_{k_C^E}(c_j) \oplus c_{j-1} = p_j \end{aligned} \tag{7.6}$$

Recall that we assumed that the padding length is a complete block (l bytes) and therefore the last byte, containing the pad-length minus one, has the value $p_n[l-1] = l-1$. But what about $p'_n[l-1]$?

Let us first consider the case where $p'_n[l-1] = p_n[l-1] = l-1$. This is a legitimate SSL padding; therefore, unpad$(p') = \langle p'_1, \ldots, p'_{n-1} \rangle$. From Equation 7.6, we have unpad(p') = unpad(p). Therefore, in this case, the server would receive the correct unpadded message, i.e., the same one as sent by the client (and was encoded into the intercepted ciphertext c), and therefore, containing the correct MAC; therefore, the manipulated ciphertext c', just like the original ciphertext c, would be considered as valid.

We next show that if $p'_n[l-1] \neq l-1$, then c' would be invalid. We first recall that with SSL padding, the pad should never be longer than the block size. Therefore, if $p'_n[l-1] > l-1$, then unpad(p') returns a padding error.

It remain to consider the case that $p'_n[l-1] < l-1$. In this case, unpad(p') = unpad$(p) + \hat{p}$, where $\hat{p}$ is some non-empty string, in fact, a string containing $l-1-p'_n[l-1] > 0$ bytes. Assume that SSL uses a MAC of length l' bytes, and therefore, upon receiving c', the server parses unpad(p') as a concatenation of a message part m' and a MAC part a', i.e., unpad$(p') = m' + a'$, where $l' = |a'|$ (and m' is simply the rest of unpad(p')).

The server will now perform the MAC validation, using the shared authentication (MAC) key denoted k_C^A, i.e., check if $a' = MAC_{k_C^A}(m')$. Obviously, m' is not the message sent by the client and encoded into the intercepted ciphertext c; therefore, it is reasonable to expect that m' was never sent by the client. If the MAC is secure, then it should be infeasible to obtain a message m' which was never sent by the client, together with the correct authenticator $a' = MAC_{k_C^A}(m')$; therefore, we assume that the check fails, i.e., $a' \neq MAC_{k_C^A}(m')$. Namely, in this case, upon receiving c', the server will indicate an authentication failure.

In summary, if $p'_n[l-1] = l-1$, then the server will consider c' as valid, otherwise, i.e., if $p'_n[l-1] \neq l-1$, then the server will consider c' as invalid (a padding error or an authentication failure). Therefore, the attacker may be able to learn $p'_n[l-1]$. More precisely, the attacker can know if $p'_n[l-1] = l-1$.

What can the attacker learn about the original plaintext p from knowing whether $p'_n[l-1] = l-1$? We show that this allows the attacker to learn the value of $p_i[l-1]$, i.e., to expose one byte of the plaintext encoded into the intercepted message c. Note that while $c'_n = c_i$, this does *not* meant that $p'_n = p_i$ since SSL uses CBC encryption, not ECB.

Let us consider the design of the CBC decryption function (Figure 2.36), when using the shared key k_C^E. We have:

$$\begin{aligned} p'_n &= D_{k_C^E}(c'_n) \oplus c'_{n-1} = D_{k_C^E}(c_i) \oplus c_{n-1} \\ p_i &= D_{k_C^E}(c_i) \oplus c_{i-1} \end{aligned} \tag{7.7}$$

By combining the two equations, we have $p_i = p'_n \oplus c_{n-1} \oplus c_{i-1}$. In particular, if the attacker knows that $p'_n[l-1] = l-1$, then the attacker can recover $p_i[l-1]$, the last byte of the ith block of the original plaintext, as follows:

$$\begin{aligned} p_i[l-1] &= p'_n[l-1] \oplus c_{n-1}[l-1] \oplus c_{i-1}[l-1] \\ &= (l-1) \oplus c_{n-1}[l-1] \oplus c_{i-1}[l-1] \end{aligned} \tag{7.8}$$

This completes the simplified Poodle attack; in the special case where the ciphertext c contains a padding of a whole block, the attacker can learn if $p_i[l-1]$, the last block of some block i (where i is chosen by the attacker), has the value $(l-1) \oplus c_{n-1}[l-1] \oplus c_{i-1}[l-1]$. By itself, this may not seem like a very serious vulnerability. However, we now explain how to turn this simplified attack into the complete Poodle padding attack.

The complete Poodle padding attack: The complete Poodle attack is a cross-site attack, i.e., exploits the fact that the client's browser 'visits' the attacker's webpage, i.e., loads an attacker-controlled webpage. This allows the attacker to cause the browser to send requests to arbitrary websites. The browser often includes a *secret* x in the request, often, an *authenticating cookie*. The attacker can also control parts of the request string, both before the cookie (mainly, the location, i.e., URL) and after the cookie (e.g., the contents of the request). Note that this design allows the attacker to send many requests, to different locations (URLs), with arbitrary contents for each request. These abilities of the attacker are reflected by the fact that the TLS error oracle attack model allows the attacker to prepend chosen prefix p to the to the secret x and to append chosen suffix s to x, although the attack actually does not require such complete control, as we explain.

We explain how each of the simplifications and assumptions are replaced by appropriate improvements to the attack.

Finding the desired byte(s): The simplified attack can only find the last byte of the ith pre-encrypted block, i.e., $p_i[l-1]$. To find a byte in an arbitrary location, e.g., a specific byte of the cookie sent in a request from browser to website, the attacker uses the fact that they can control the length of the location (URL) in the request, using a longer or shorter URL as required to make sure that the desired byte of the cookie, which appears after the URL, would be the last byte in a known (ith) pre-encrypted block, i.e., would be byte $p_i[l-1]$. The attacker can repeat the attack with longer or shorter URL strings to find additional bytes as necessary.

Making sure that the pad would consist of the entire last block, p_n: The simplified attack *assumed/required* that the pad would consist of the entire last block, p_n (and therefore, also that $p_n[l-1] = l-1$). The complete Poodle attack *ensures* that this will hold rather than assume it, by using the fact that the attacker can include arbitrary number of content bytes after the secret byte(s) that the attacker tries to find; therefore, the attacker can control the length of the plaintext before padding — and the length of the pad.

Finding the byte: The simplified attack only finds if $p_i[l-1]$, the last block of some block i, has the value $(l-1) \oplus c_{n-1}[l-1] \oplus c_{i-1}[l-1]$. This basically finds the byte $p_i[l-1]$ with probability $\frac{1}{256}$ since the values of c_{n-1} and of c_{i-1} are, basically, pseudorandom. To actually find $p_i[l-1]$, the attacker can repeat the attack with different content bytes, generating as many pseudorandom values of c_{n-1} and c_{i-1} each time, until finding the correct one, which will give $p_i[l-1]$.

Finally, we note that the attack as described so far, exposed a specific byte $p_i[l-1]$ from the pre-encryption string; how does this allow the attacker to learn bytes of the plaintext? By inspecting the TLS padding process (Figure 7.4), we see that, unless compression is used, all bytes of the plaintext message become part of the bytes of the pre-encryption string. In many implementation, compression is not actually used as part of the record layer, but even if compression is used, the attacker can use the above attack carefully to find all or most bytes of the compressed fragments of the message, from which the attacker can retrieve the plaintext. Relying on compression to improve the protection of encryption is not a good idea!

The Lucky13 attack: We only briefly discuss the *Lucky13* padding-error oracle attack [10] against TLS. Lucky13 extends the padding oracle attacks from Section 2.11, specifically the attack against PKCS #7 padding in Exercise 2.17. Lucky13 uses careful timing side channel analysis, to *distinguish between pad errors and MAC errors*; this requires circumventing the countermeasures designed to prevent the distinction between padding errors and authentication failures which are implemented in 'serious' implementations of TLS (and some implementations of SSLv3). If the attacker can distinguish between the two types of failures, then the attack continues similarly to the attack in Exercise 2.17, or, even more closely to the attack described in Ref. [116].

Like in the Poodle attack, and in more details in Exercise 2.17, Lucky13 uses carefully constructed plaintexts, allowing it to extract the secret x one byte at a time. The attack cleverly uses the fact that in the (rare) cases that the pad is *valid*, the padding bytes are removed. It designs the plaintext carefully to cause a difference in the number of invocations of the compression function used iteratively by the MAC algorithm; see Section 3.8, providing a timing side channel. The details are elegant; while we do not cover them, the reader is encouraged to read the clearly written description by Al Fardan and Paterson in Ref. [10].

7.2.4 The BEAST attack: Exploiting CBC with predictable-IV

The high-level design of the TLS record layer is defined for an arbitrary encryption algorithm; however, the specifications define a limited number of standard cipher suites. The use of a limited set of standard options is sensible since the server and the client should use the same cipher suite. In particular, TLS 1.0 and 1.1 support only *one* block cipher mode of operation, the Cipher Block Chaining (CBC) mode (Section 2.10.9). In fact, in TLS 1.0 and 1.1, the only other symmetric key cryptosystem is the RC4 stream cipher (which has known vulnerabilities).

In this section, we briefly discuss the BEAST[9] attack, which exploits a vulnerability due to *incorrect* use of CBC mode in TLS 1.0 and SSL, which was corrected in later versions of TLS. Specifically, the vulnerability is due to the fact that TLS 1.0 and SSL use a *predictable Initialization Vector (IV).*

As presented in Section 2.10.9, the correct use of the CBC mode of operation requires the use of a *random* IV for each message. The value of the IV does *not need to be secret*, and in most implementations — including TLS 1.1 and 1.2 — the IV is sent 'in the clear', visible to an eavesdropper. However, the SSL design — adopted also by TLS 1.0 — used the handshake protocol to derive the IV for the first fragment in a connection, similarly to the derivation of the shared keys used by the record protocol. This means that both sender and recipient have a shared, pseudorandom IV for the first fragment; therefore, the protocol *does not send the IV* along with the rest of the ciphertext. Furthermore, SSL and TLS 1.0 also do not send an IV when applying CBC encryption to the following fragments. Instead, for the non-first fragment in the connection, the SSL and TLS 1.0 design use as an

[9]BEAST stands for Browser Exploit Against TLS.

IV the last ciphertext block of the previous fragment sent over the connection. Namely, for non-first fragments, we use the value of the last ciphertext block sent as the IV.

The motivation for using this non-standard design is not clear to the author. Maybe the designers felt that this is a better design since it makes it (a bit) harder for the attacker to know the IV, or maybe they simply wanted to save the (minimal) bandwidth used required to send the IV block.

Using a pseudorandom IV is fine, as long as the attacker cannot know it in advance. So, there may be no problem with using the IV derived securely from the handshake protocol for the *first* fragment in a connection. However, *what about the use of the last ciphertext block in one fragment, as the IV for the first block in the following fragment?*

Since the ciphertext is produced by a block cipher, the value of a ciphertext block is chosen randomly (or, more precisely, pseudorandomly); therefore, it may appear to be secure to use the last ciphertext block as the IV. However, this intuition is misleading; it is an example of the risk of trusting intuition instead of carefully validating the security of a design and of not relying on the exact cryptographic properties of the underlying mechanisms. Specifically, the security of CBC requires the IV to be *unpredictable*. However, in TLS 1.0, an eavesdropper can observe the ciphertext, including the last ciphertext block of a fragment; since this ciphertext block would then be used as the IV for encrypting and decrypting the first block of the next fragment, this allows the adversary to know the IV *before* the block is encrypted or decrypted, and the requirement of a pseudorandom IV is not maintained. Note also that the two fragments could belong to different messages, e.g., two different HTTP requests or responses, since browsers typically use the same TLS connection to send multiple requests/responses (between the browser and a fixed server).

We next show how this use of predictable IV is exploited by the *BEAST attack* [165], allowing exposure of a secret string x sent using SSL or TLS 1.0. A typical scenario is where x is an *authenticating cookie*; see Section 9.6.3.1.

The cryptographic aspects of the BEAST attack are all based on an attack published already in 2004 by Bard [30], and even earlier, in 2002 and 1995, for the *Secure Shell (SSH)* and *IP security (IPsec)* protocols, in Refs. [44, 420]. Hence, following the *conservative design* principle (Principle 3), the TLS designers *should* have avoided the use of observable IV, i.e., the value of the last-sent ciphertext block, preventing this vulnerability; however, this was done only beginning with TLS 1.1. Until then, the designers ignored these well-known warnings, and continued to use the last-sent ciphertext block as the IV for the next fragment. We can only speculate that Bard's attack [30] seemed to be too challenging and impractical.

One challenge is that Bard's attack requires to control the *very first block* of the new fragment, but in the classical use of TLS to secure HTTP communication between browser and website, every HTTP request begins with a fixed header. So, it seems that the attacker cannot control the first block — and the attack is prevented. Bard's paper [30] showed this problem may be overcome, but the solution wasn't very practical.

In Ref. [165], Duong and Rizzo presented the BEAST attack, along with practical methods allowing the deployment of the attack in realistic scenarios. In particular, they exploited the common case of a *cross-site attacker*, i.e., an attacker controlling a website, e.g., www.666.org visited by the client; this allows the attacker to run scripts using different mechanisms supported by the browser, including JavaScript and the WebSocket API [229, 499]. Many cross-site attacks against web security mechanisms have been exploited in practice and reported by researchers, but most of them are non-cryptographic, e.g., cross-site scripting (XSS) and CSRF (see Section 9.6.3.1); however, the author believes that the BEAST attack was the first cross-site attack against TLS (or other cryptographic protocols). The cross-site attack model was later used by several attacks against TLS, including the Poodle, CRIME, TIME and CAT attacks.

The BEAST attack assumes three capabilities of the attacker:

Eavesdropping: The attacker should be able to eavesdrop on communication between the client and the server. This is the standard attacker model assumed for protecting confidentiality since if the attacker cannot eavesdrop, encryption may not even be necessary.

Secret at attacker-controlled location: Attacker can cause client to send a request containing the secret authenticating cookie (or other secret), denoted x, with attacker-controlled offset from the beginning of the request, over a new connection or a new fragment of a connection. We discuss authenticating cookies and related defenses and attacks in Section 9.6.3.1; for more details on cookies, see Ref. [75].

Chosen-prefix plaintext in a follow-up fragment: Attacker can cause the client to transmit attacker-chosen plaintext content in (the beginning of) a new fragment of an existing connection; as a result, when using SSL and TLS 1.0, the client will use as IV the last ciphertext block sent over this connection. In Ref. [165], Duong and Rizzo showed how the attacker can obtain this capability, in the common case where website (*B.com*) uses the *WebSocket* mechanism [180].

In addition, the BEAST attack assumes that the record protocol does not deploy compression. While the SSL and TLS record protocols allow compression, compression is indeed often not used.

Let us now explain how the BEAST attack works. Our description is simplified by assuming the *chosen-prefix attack model*, which combines the two last capabilities above. Namely, we assume that the attacker can view the IV of a block of plaintext and then select an arbitrary string r and receive the CBC encryption of $r +\!\!+ x$, where x is the secret that the attacker tries to find, using the given IV value. In reality, the attacker would have more restricted capabilities, e.g., it would not be able to control the entire prefix; for the complete details of the BEAST attack, assuming only the weaker capabilities above (and explaining how these capabilities can be obtained in realistic scenarios), see Ref. [165]. We also present the attack for the specific case of using a block cipher with 8 bytes blocks, such as DES; the reader should be able to adjust the attack for other block sizes, e.g., 16 bytes as used by AES.

BEAST — finding the most significant byte ($x[1]$) of the secret x: The attack exposes the secret/cookie x byte by byte. We first explain how the attacker can find the first (most-significant) byte of the secret/cookie x, which we denote $x[1]$; later, we explain how to extend the attack and expose the other bytes of x.

The attacker first provides a prefix r^* containing arbitrary 15 bytes, i.e., 120 bits; to illustrate the attack, we use the prefix r^* = '123456789ABCDEF'. This ensures that the plaintext to the record protocol encrypted would be $P^* = r^* + x$ and consist of $15 + |x|$ bytes, where $|x|$ is the number of bytes in the cookie/secret x. We denote the ith block of P^* by P_i^*; in particular, $P_1^* =$ '12345678' and $P_2^* =$ '9ABCDEF' $+ x[1]$.

Recall that in SSLv3 and TLS 1.0–1.2, the parties derive four separate shared keys from the master shared key k_M. These four shared keys derived from k_M are denoted k_C^E, k_S^E, k_C^A and k_S^A. The subscript determines the direction of the traffic to which the key is applied; k_C^E and k_C^A are used for traffic from client to server, while k_S^E and k_S^A are used for traffic from server to client. The superscripts denote the use of the key: the two keys with superscript A are used for authentication (using a MAC function), and the two keys with superscript E are used for encryption keys (using the CBC mode of operation). See details of the key derivation in Section 7.4.1. The attack is focused on breaking the encryption of traffic from client to server, i.e., on the encryption using the k_C^E shared key.

We use C^* to denote the ciphertext, i.e., the result of encrypting P^* using CBC and the block cipher (E, D) with the encryption key k_C^E. Namely, $C^* = CBC.E^E_{k_C^E}(P^*)$. We denote the two first blocks of the ciphertext by C_1^* and C_2^*. Let us focus on C_2^*. From the definition of CBC encryption (Section 2.10.9), we have that:

$$C_2^* = E_{k_C^E}(C_1^* \oplus P_2^*) = E_{k_C^E}\left(C_1^* \oplus (\text{'9ABCDEF'} + x[1])\right) \quad (7.9)$$

It is convenient to define $y \equiv C_1^* \oplus (\text{'9ABCDEF'} + x[1])$; using this notation, Equation 7.9 simplifies to:

$$C_2^* = E_{k_C^E}(y) \quad (7.10)$$

Now, the attacker can find $x[1]$, by repeating the following process for every possible value of $x[1]$, i.e., for all the values $x' \in \{0,1\}^8$:

1. Eavesdrop to learn the last block of the ciphertext of the previous fragment; this will be used as the IV of the next fragment.
2. Cause the client to encrypt the block $P'(x')$ as the next fragment, where $P'(x') \equiv IV \oplus C_1^* \oplus (\text{'9ABCDEF'} + x')$. Since we use CBC encryption, the input to the block cipher $E_{k_C^E}(\cdot)$ would be $IV \oplus P'(x')$, which is $C_1^* \oplus (\text{'9ABCDEF'} + x')$.

3. Eavesdrop to learn the resulting block of ciphertext. If this block is exactly C_2^*, then $x[1] = x'$, i.e., the attacker found $x[1]$.

To see why this algorithm returns the correct value for $x[1]$, recall that $E_{k_C^E}(\cdot)$ is a permutation, i.e., if the ciphertext block is C_2^* then the input to $E_{k_C^E}(\cdot)$ must be $C_1^* \oplus (\text{'9ABCDEF'} + x[1])$ (Equation 7.9). Namely, for the given x', it holds that:

$$P'(x') = C_1^* \oplus (\text{'9ABCDEF'} + x[1]) \tag{7.11}$$

Since $P'(x') \equiv IV \oplus C_1^* \oplus (\text{'9ABCDEF'} + x')$, it follows that $x[1] = x'$.

Finding other bytes: To find $x[2]$ after we found $x[1]$, we repeat the same process as for finding $x[1]$, except that now we use a prefix r^* which is one byte shorter, e.g., $r^* =$ '123456789ABCDE'. This ensures that the plaintext to the record protocol encrypted would be $P^* = r^* + x$ and consist of $14 + |x|$ bytes, where $|x|$ is the number of bytes in the cookie/secret x. Note that we already know the 15th byte of this plaintext, i.e., $x[1]$. Therefore, we can now find the next byte, $x[2]$, using exactly the same process as above, as $x[1]$ is simply the 15th byte of r^*.

To find additional bytes, we again repeat the same process, each time using a prefix which is one byte shorter. This seems to be limited to finding up to the 15th first bytes of the secret/cookie x, but the readers would find it quite easy to extend the process and find all bytes of x, even if x contains more than 15 bytes.

7.2.5 Exploiting RC4 biases to recover plaintext

BEAST, Lucky13 and Poodle are all critical attacks against the use of CBC encryption as specified by SSL and TLS (1.0–1.2). Several countermeasures were proposed to these attacks. One popular countermeasure is to use stream-cipher encryption, using the RC4 stream cipher, instead of using a block cipher, such as DES or AES.

However, RC4 was known, for years, to have some vulnerabilities, such as the bias of the second byte, observed and exploited in Ref. [346]. Therefore, following the conservative design principle (Principle 3), it should have been *avoided*, and definitely not used as a 'more secure' alternative to CBC-mode.

This choice to use RC4 as a supposedly more secure alternative to CBC was another example of underestimating the risk due to what appeared as 'impractical vulnerabilities' — this time, supposedly impractical vulnerabilities of the RC4 stream cipher.

In the common use of TLS to protect HTTP communication, the beginning of the information sent by the client is normally the HTTP header — which begins with well-known bytes. Therefore, we cannot exploit the known (and significant) bias of the second RC4 byte [346].

However, in Ref. [13], it was shown that RC4 has additional biases, which may allow exposure of confidential, sensitive communication, such as the cookie. This included two types of biases:

Single byte biases: Biases were detected for some output bytes of RC4, not just the second byte — although the second byte does have the largest bias found. In Ref. [13], additional biases were found in the first 256 bytes of RC4. By careful analysis of the results of a large number of encryptions of the same secret x, the attack can recover the secret with significant probability, which depends on the number of encryptions and on the positions of the secret (earlier positions usually had more bias). For example, after 2^{25} encryptions, the first 50 bytes were recovered with probability of more than 50% per byte. A common defense against this bias is to use the output of RC4 only from a rather high byte number, e.g., ignoring (dropping) the first thousand bytes.

Double-byte biases: RC4 also has biases of *pairs* of bytes in different (adjacent) positions, as reported already in 2000 [183]. By carefully analyzing such pairs, using the known biases, the attacker can recover the plaintext *from arbitrary positions.*

The combination of the attacks on CBC and RC4 was an important motivation to the development and adoption of other cipher suites and of improved record protocols, mainly, the AEAD record protocols (Section 7.2.7).

7.2.6 Exploiting Compress-then-Encrypt: The CRIME, TIME and BREACH attacks

We conclude our discussion of attacks against the TLS record protocol, by discussing attacks which focus on the *compression* of the plaintext before encryption. As we discussed in Section 4.5.5, when we apply compression to plaintext and then encrypt, there is a risk of exposure of partial information about the plaintext. In particular, an attacker would able be to distinguish between the compressed-then-encrypted ciphertexts of two equal-length plaintexts p_1, p_2, if p_1 has high redundancy (compresses to a much shorter string) while p_2 has low redundancy (compression does not reduce its length).

However, the potential exposure due to plaintext compression may not appear to be a serious threat — and this threat, identified already in 2002 [289], was mostly ignored for many years. In particular, as shown in Figure 7.4, the AtE TLS record protocol includes an (optional) compression process, and applications using TLS often apply their own processing to the messages, before sending them via TLS.

As you find in Exercise 7.4, under the TLS error oracle attack model, it can be quite easy to deploy this attack and expose part or all of a secret, e.g., an authenticating cookie. Deploying such an attack in practice involves several challenges. First, the attacker may not be able to completely control the entire plaintext (except for the secret). Second, when using a block cipher, small changes in the length of the plaintext may not cause corresponding changes in the length of the ciphertext. Third, the deployed compression schemes are considerably more complex than the scheme in Exercise 7.4, and, as the exercise shows, details of the compression scheme are very relevant to the feasibility of the attack.

The CRIME attack [419], presented by Duong and Rizzo, demonstrated how these and other challenges can be overcome, allowing efficient exposure of a *cookie* or other secrets repeatedly sent in HTTP requests or responses. Specifically, the demonstration focused on the exposure of cookies when the communication uses TLS compression. We do not describe the attack here since the principle is quite simple (as is evident from Exercise 7.4), and the attack necessarily involves details of the compression mechanisms in use, which are beyond our scope; see a good description in Ref. [36].

In their presentation, Duong and Rizzo also discussed potential variants of the CRIME attack that can extract secrets sent in HTTP responses, such as a *CSRF token*, as well as the potential abuse of other compression mechanisms, such as the widely deployed HTTP compression. We discuss CSRF and CSRF tokens in Section 9.6.3.1.

Contrary to the conservative design principle (Principle 3), the main response to CRIME was disabling of only TLS compression — although Duong and Rizzo already discussed attacks which do not depend on TLS compression. Ignoring Principle 3 was obviously a CRIME, and the punishment followed, in the form of two additional effective, convincing attacks that exploited HTTP compression mechanisms: TIME [36] and BREACH [208].

The BREACH attack showed how HTTP compression allows the application of CRIME to expose secrets in HTTP responses, most notably the above-mentioned CSRF tokens.

TIME, like BREACH, also assumes only HTTP compression (not TLS compression). But TIME also extends CRIME in a more profound way: it shows how to expose secrets in HTTP requests, such as cookies, *without requiring eavesdrop capabilities.* Namely, the attacker does not have the entire capabilities in the TLS error oracle attack model; it only controls a website visited by the user. This is the *cross-site attack* model, which is the most commonly deployed model in studies of non-cryptographic web security. Luckily, TIME seems significantly harder to deploy, namely, it may require an extensive amount of queries and time.

For details of the TIME and BREACH attacks, see Refs. [36] and [208].

Preventing Compress-then-Encrypt Exposure: There are several possible countermeasures to the Compress-then-Encrypt exposure. We mention three of them.

The most certain way to avoid exposure of confidentiality due to the use of Compress-then-Encrypt is simple: *do not compress.* While the use of compression for *data* can be critical for performance, it may be acceptable to avoid compression of the sensitive information. For example, cookies are sent in the HTTP headers, which are usually much shorter than the payload; in most scenarios, the overhead due to not compressing the headers would not be significant.

Another possible countermeasure is to perform special encoding to sensitive data that will prevent compress-then-encrypt exposure of (only) that data — while allowing compression of non-sensitive data. For example, we can apply a 'randomizing transform' to sensitive data s, such as authenticating cookies and CSRF tokens, before applying compression. One simple randomizing transform would exclusive or the sensitive data s, with a random or pseudorandom string r, which is appended to the data separately. A standard transform may even be embedded into TLS, requiring the application only to mark the sensitive data s. This could be a nice programming project for the interested reader and may be a useful extension to TLS.

One unavoidable challenge, however, of this approach, is the need to *identify* the sensitive data s. Some kinds of sensitive data may be amenable to automated identification (e.g., cookies), but other types may require the programmer to annotate the data. This is a serious disadvantage, as the countermeasure is prone to be done incorrectly.

Finally, TLS 1.3 supports the *zeros pad* field, which can contain an arbitrary number of bytes containing zero. The number of zero bytes can be selected randomly, to provide limited obfuscation of the exact impact of compression.

7.2.7 The TLS 1.3 AEAD-based record protocol

Most of the vulnerabilities identified for the TLS AtE record protocol can be avoided by adopting one of the two secure designs discussed in Section 4.5: the *EtA* design, which uses first an encryption scheme and then an authentication scheme, or the *AEAD* design, which combines encryption (for confidentiality) and authentication.

RFC 7366 [224] applies the 'classical' *EtA* paradigm. The specifications use TLS extensions to signal the use of EtA rather than AtE. It could be deployed in versions 1.0–1.2 of TLS.

The TLS 1.3 record protocol *always* uses the *AEAD* design, which ensures both confidentiality *and* authenticity; see Section 4.5.1. AEAD schemes accept two types of data: *plaintext*, which is encrypted and authenticated, and *associated data*, which is only authenticated, not encrypted.

The design of the AEAD record protocol is illustrated in Figure 7.6. Without going into all of the 'small print fields' used by the protocol, which we discuss in the following, this design is simpler than that of the AtE record protocol (Figure 7.4). First, instead of a

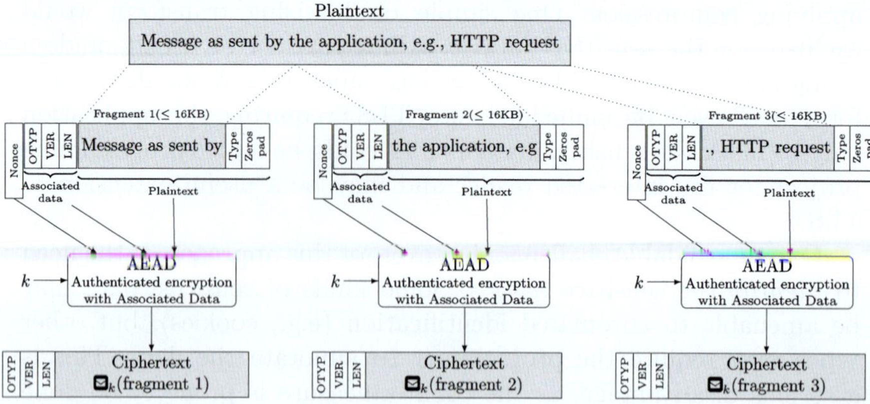

Figure 7.6. The AEAD Record Protocol (used always in TLS 1.3, and optionally in TLS 1.2). The ciphertext produced by the *Authenticated Encryption with Associated Data (AEAD)* function provides encryption of the plaintext input as well as authentication of both the plaintext and the associated data, using a nonce which should be unique in each invocation. The design contains several 'small print fields', e.g., SEQ and OTYP, which are explained in the text, and can be mostly ignored for intuitive understanding.

separate encryption scheme and authentication scheme, we use just the AEAD scheme; we also need only one key to achieve both confidentiality and authenticity. Second, the AEAD function provides all the functions of the classical block cipher modes of operation and more; it does not require a separate padding operation or a random initialization vector, although it does require a unique input called *nonce* to ensure security [90]. This makes the AEAD design simpler to use and, in particular, avoids the need for variants (for stream cipher and for block cipher).

The AEAD record protocol does not support a TLS compression function. Note that by not supporting TLS compression, the AEAD record protocol trivially does not suffer from the Compress-then-Encrypt vulnerabilities deployed by the CRIME attack (Section 7.2.6).

The simplicity of the TLS AEAD-based record protocol follows the KISS principle (Principle 14) and helps avoid implementation vulnerabilities. This simplicity can also facilitates verification of the security of the TLS 1.3 record layer specifications and of appropriately developed implementations, e.g., see Ref. [147].

The seven small print fields: The TLS 1.3 record protocol comes with seven fields whose meaning and use can be a bit obscure. Readers may mostly ignore these 'seven small print fields', but let us explain them anyway. We present these 'small print' fields by their positioning, from left to right, in Figure 7.6.

Nonce: The AEAD function requires provision of a field called nonce, whose value should be unique in every invocation; the same nonce value should be used in the Encrypt-and-Authenticate operation and in the corresponding Decrypt-and-Verify operation. The nonce can be seen as a substitute to the random or unique IV required by most modes of operation, and to the counter used by the CTR mode of operation. The nonce input is 32 bits, and as the value should only be used once in the TLS connection, it imposes a (very high) limit on the number of fragments in a connection. TLS 1.3 uses, for the nonce, a counter of the fragment from the beginning of the connection. To separate between the nonce used to send fragments and the nonce used to receive fragments, we add to the counter value one of two fixed, different 32 bits strings, one string for encrypting fragments sent and the other for decrypting fragments received. This ensures a unique nonce for each fragment.

OTYP: This field is referred to in the TLS 1.3 specifications [412] as the *opaque type*; it is included only for backward compatibility with the TYP field of earlier versions of TLS and should always contain the fixed type of 23, indicating application data — even if, in reality, the fragment contains a different type of record, such as of the alert or handshake protocols. The 'real type' of the record is included in the plaintext, with the fragment data, and therefore its value is hidden from an eavesdropper.

VER: The *legacy version* field. This field is (also) only included for backward compatibility with earlier versions of TLS and should always contain the value 0x0303. The protocol learns the 'real' version of TLS from the handshake protocol since, in TLS 1.3, the record layer is invoked only after negotiation by the handshake protocol, which authenticate the protocol version.

LEN: The *length* of the ciphertext fragment, i.e., of the *output* of the AEAD. The length is provided as part of the associated data input to the AEAD; therefore, it should be computed *before* applying the OAEP, taking into account the length of the plaintext input and the expansion performed by the OAEP.

Type: This is the 'real' type of the fragment. It is a one-byte identifier of the protocol to handle the data sent by this fragment; the TLS 1.3 RFC [412] defines several types including application data (23), the handshake protocol (22), and alert messages (21) and the heartbeat extension [436]; there's also a type defined for the Change_Cipher_Spec (CCS) messages (24), although TLS 1.3 does not use CCS.

Zeros pad: This is an optional field, which can have arbitrary number of bytes whose value is 0x00 (zero). A random or otherwise selected number of zero pad bytes may be used to hide the size of the fragment from an attacker which can observe the TLS ciphertexts. The motivation to hide the length of the fragment is mainly due to the Compress-then-Encrypt vulnerabilities and attacks (CRIME, TIME and BREACH), see Section 7.2.6.

7.3 The SSLv2 handshake protocol

In this section, we discuss the *SSL version 2 (SSLv2)* handshake protocol, its features and some of its main vulnerabilities. SSLv2 (SSLv2) is the earliest officially published version of the SSL protocol [248], and its handshake protocol is interesting — beyond its historical importance. One motivation to study SSLv2 is that it already introduces much of the basic concepts and designs used in later versions — and, since it is a bit simpler, it is a good way for us to introduce these basic TLS concepts and designs. Another motivation is that the SSLv2 handshake has some serious vulnerabilities; understanding these vulnerabilities is instructive, to develop the ability to detect flaws in cryptographic protocols and to understand and motivate the design of later versions of the TLS handshake protocol. Finally, surprisingly, there are still some implementations that *support* SSLv2, even if they mostly prefer later versions, which may make them vulnerable to ***downgrade attacks***; we discuss a specific cipher suite downgrade attack against SSLv2 in Section 7.5.1, and later delve more into downgrade attacks in Section 7.5.

The SSLv2 handshake is a non-trivial cryptographic protocol, with support for multiple options and mechanisms — mostly supported also by later versions (of TLS and SSL) as well, often with extensions and improvements, and removal of insecure mechanisms. We describe the protocol in the following sections. In Section 7.3.1, we present the 'basic' SSLv2 handshake protocol. In Section 7.3.2, we explain the *key-derivation* process used by SSLv2. In Section 7.3.3, we present the SSLv2 *session resumption* handshake, which allows us to reuse the shared key exchanged in a previous handshake between the same client and server, to open a new connection without additional public key operations. In Section 7.3.4, we discuss how SSLv2 supports the (optional) client-authentication feature. Finally, in Section 7.5.1, we discuss how SSLv2 handles cipher suite negotiation and explain how an attacker may exploit the (insecure) SSLv2 cipher suite negotiation mechanism, to launch the simple yet effective *cipher suite downgrade attack*.

Terms and notations: SSLv2, as described in the original publications, e.g., in Ref. [248], uses several terms and notations which were modified in later versions. For consistency with the rest of this chapter, we use the terms used by the later versions, also when describing SSLv2; these terms are often also more intuitive. For example, we use the terms *client random* r_C and *server random* r_S, as in SSLv3 and TLS, although the SSLv2 documentation refers to these fields as the *challenge* and the *connection-ID*, respectively.

7.3.1 SSLv2: The 'basic' handshake

In this section, we discuss the 'basic' SSLv2 handshake, illustrated in Figure 7.7, which is a simplification of the SSLv2 handshake protocol. This simplified version does not include cipher suite negotiation, session resumption and client authentication. We discuss these additional aspects of SSLv2 in the following sections.

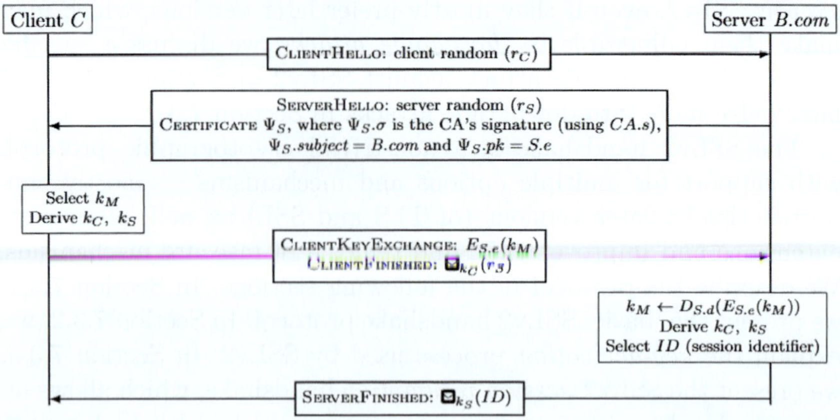

Figure 7.7. Basic SSLv2 handshake: new session, no client authentication and ignoring cipher suite negotiation. The client and server select random strings (r_C, r_S, respectively) and exchange them in the ClientHello and ServerHello messages. The server *B.com* sends its certificate Ψ_S (earlier received from a CA). The client verifies that the certificate is valid and properly signed (by a trusted CA) and that the subject's domain name in the certificate matches the desired server domain. If so, the client selects randomly a shared *master key* k_M, encrypts it using RSA encryption with the server's public key $S.e$ and sends to the server. The client to server key k_C and the server to client key k_S are derived from the master key k_M and the random r_C and r_S values, using the $MD5$ cryptographic hash, as in Equation 7.12. We protect the ClientFinished and ServerFinished messages using the SSL record protocol with the key of the corresponding direction (k_C for ClientFinished and k_S for ServerFinished); we denote this by $\boxdot_{k_C}$ and $\boxdot_{k_S}$, respectively. The ClientFinished contains the server's random r_S, preventing replay, and the ServerFinished contains an identifier ID, allowing efficient *session resumption* (Figure 7.8).

The Hello messages: The SSLv2 handshake begins with the client sending a ClientHello message to the server, specifying the client's protocol version and the *client random*, r_c, a random bit-string used to randomize the key derivation. The server responds with the ServerHello message, which contains the server random, r_S, and the server's public-key certificate. The certificate contains the server's public key, the server's RSA public encryption key $S.e$, the domain name of the server, e.g., B.com, and additional fields. The certificate is signed by an authorized *certificate authority (CA)*, using the CA's private signing key $CA.s$.

The client verifies the certificate. This includes several checks: does the client trust the signing CA? Is the certificate properly signed? Is the domain that the client tries to connect to, e.g., *B.com*, the same as the subject domain name in the certificate (or one of the domains allowed by the certificate)? Has the certificate expired or revoked? There are a few more checks; we discuss certificates and their validation in Chapter 8.

The CLIENTHELLO and SERVERHELLO messages retain these basic functions and fields in later versions of TLS and SSL; the most significant changes are in TLS 1.3.

7.3.2 SSLv2 key-derivation

The SSLv2 handshake protocol establishes a shared *master key*, which we denote k_M. In SSLv2, the master key k_M is selected by the client, and sent encrypted, using RSA, to the server, in the CLIENTKEYEXCHANGE message. Namely, the client sends $E_{S.e}(k_M)$.

The public key encryption of k_M by the client and the corresponding decryption of k_M by the server are the most computationally intensive operations of SSL; therefore, it is desirable for the protocol to be secure even if the client reuses the same master key k_M in multiple connections, assuming that the master key was not exposed. To ensure this, we use the *client random* (r_C) and *server random* (r_S) fields from the CLIENTHELLO and SERVERHELLO messages, respectively. Namely, we combine r_C and r_S with the master key k_M, and use the combination to derive session-specific cryptographic keys for the session. The derived cryptographic keys are used to protect communication in the connection, using shared key encryption and decryption, and using shared key authentication and verification of messages (using a MAC function).

In SSLv2, the parties derive and use *(only) two* keys from k_M and the random nonces r_C, r_S: the *client-to-server key* k_C and the *server-to-client key* k_S. The client uses k_C to encrypt and authenticate messages it sends, and k_S to decrypt and validate messages it receives from the server. These keys are derived by both parties from the master key k_M, using the MD5 hash function, as follows:

$$
\begin{aligned}
k_C &\leftarrow MD5(k_M + \text{“1”} + r_C + r_S) \\
k_S &\leftarrow MD5(k_M + \text{“0”} + r_C + r_S)
\end{aligned}
\tag{7.12}
$$

Intuitively, the design expects the MD5 function to extract pseudorandom output keys, provided that its input contain sufficient randomization, in particular, assuming that k_M is pseudorandom; namely, MD5 here is used as a randomness extractor hash function (Section 3.5).

However, assuming that MD5 is a randomness extractor hash function would not suffice for other aspects of the design, such as the fact that k_C and k_S should be *independently pseudorandom*, i.e., each of them should remain pseudorandom even if the other is exposed. An even stronger assumption is required. One option is to assume that $MD5(k_M + x)$ is a pseudorandom function (PRF), when we consider k_M as the key of the PRF and x as the input to the PRF. Or, we can adopt the random oracle model (ROM) (Section 3.6), i.e., analyze the protocol as if MD5 was selected randomly, i.e., is a random function. See Exercise 7.7.

The use of the random numbers r_C and r_S in the derivation of k_C and k_S ensures that different, independently pseudorandom client and server keys are used in different connections, even if, to reduce the overhead due to public-key computations, we use the same master key k_M in these connections.

Using separate independently pseudorandom keys in different connections has three motivations. First, to prevent *replay* of messages — from either client or server; see Exercise 7.11. Second, to reduce the total amount of known and chosen plaintext that can be available for cryptanalysis of a key, and the amount of plaintext that is exposed by successful cryptanalysis. Finally, to avoid the possibility that known or chosen plaintext from one connection, e.g., from the public login page of a website, may help attack against data sent in another connection, which may not have the same amount of known or chosen plaintext. The last two motivations follow the *key separation principle* (Section 2.7.4).

The key separation principle also motivates the use of two separate keys: k_C, to protect messages from client to server, and k_S, to protect messages from server to client. In particular, many websites are public and send exactly the same information to all users; however, we may want to protect the confidentiality of the contents, e.g., queries, sent by the users. By separating between k_C and k_S, the confidentiality of the traffic from client to server, protected by k_C, can be preserved, even if the attacker was able to find out k_S, e.g., by exploiting the large amount of known plaintext sent from server to client (a known-plaintext attack (KPA)). Note further that using a stream cipher with the same key in both directions could result in insecure reuse of the same keypad for encryption of two different messages.

On the other hand, the fact that SSLv2 uses the same secret key for both encryption and authentication *violates* the key separation principle. This can cause vulnerability even if both encryption and MAC are independently secure; see Exercise 4.6. Indeed, this was fixed in later versions of SSL and TLS. SSLv3 and TLS 1.0–1.2 derive separate keys for encryption and for authentication; e.g., the two keys k_C^E and k_C^A to protect client traffic. TLS 1.3 only needs one key in each direction (like SSLv2), but this is since TLS 1.3 uses an AEAD scheme, which ensures both authentication and encryption using a single key.

7.3.3 SSLv2: *ID*-based session resumption

The main overhead of the TLS protocol is due to the computationally-intensive public key operations. Often, there are multiple connections between the same (client, server) pair, over a short period of time; in such cases, the server and client may reuse the master key exchanged previously, thereby avoiding additional public key operations. To facilitate reuse of the master key, the server includes an identifier ID at the end of the handshake; to reuse the same master key in another connection, the client sends this ID with its ClientHello, and if the server has the corresponding key, the session is *resumed* efficiently, avoiding additional public key operations. We illustrate this *ID-based session resumption* process in Figure 7.8.

The impact of session resumption can be quite dramatic. The savings are mostly on the computation (CPU) time; instead of computing public-key encryption of the master key k_M (for client) and decryption (for server) for every TCP connection, we now need only require these operations for the first TCP connection in a session. The ratio of the computation time with and without session resumption is typically on the orders of 100 for typical usage, such as for protecting web communication using the *HTTPS* protocol, i.e., running *HTTP* over *TLS*.

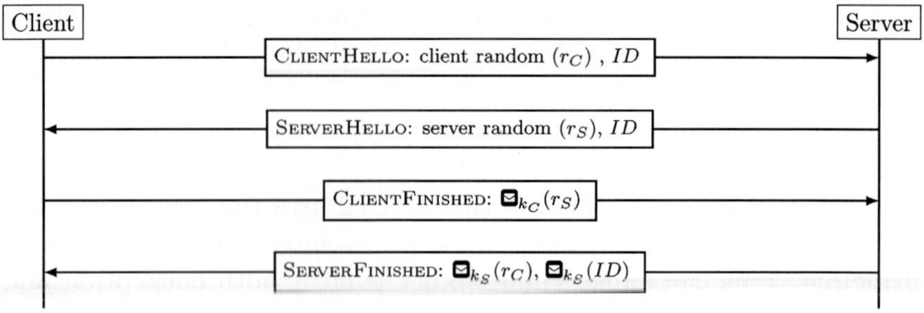

Figure 7.8. SSLv2 handshake, with ID-based session resumption. The client can initiate this handshake by including the ID field in the 'ClientHello' message. If the server has the corresponding (ID, k_M) in its cache, then it indicates this by sending the same ID value with its ServerHello response; this is called an *ID-hit*. As shown, in this case, the parties *resume the session* using the previously exchanged master key k_M. To resume the session, the parties derive a new pair of shared keys from k_M, using Equation (7.12). This avoids the computational overhead of the public key operations (encryption by client and decryption by server of master key k_M), as well as the overhead of transmitting and validating the certificate $S_{CA.s}(S.e, \text{B.com})$. If the server does not have the (ID, k_M) pair in cache, then the handshake continues as in Figure 7.7, i.e., without resumption; to allow future resumption, the server includes with the ServerHello message a *different* identifier, $ID' \neq ID$.

Session resumption in SSLv2 is always based on the use of the ID. This ID-based session resumption mechanism has a significant drawback: it requires the server to be *stateful*, specifically, to maintain state for each session (for the session-ID and the master key). In the typical case where the same web server is running over multiple machines, this requires that this storage be shared between all of these servers, or to ensure that a client will contact the same machine each time — a difficult, sometimes infeasible, requirement. These drawbacks motivate the adoption of alternative methods for session resumption, most notably, the TLS *session ticket resumption mechanism* (Section 7.4.4).

Note that the session resumption protocol is one reason for requiring the use of client and server random numbers; see Exercise 7.8.

7.3.4 SSLv2 client authentication

All versions of TLS and SSL support an (optional) *client authentication* mechanism, where the client proves its identity by sending a certificate for a public key and then 'proves' its possession of the corresponding private key. In SSLv2, the 'proof' is done by performing RSA encryption using PKCS #1 version 1.5 padding, which is vulnerable to the Bleichenbacher attack, Section 6.5.7, although the specifications refers to this operation as 'signing'; SSLv3 and all TLS versions use a signature for client authentication.

The client certificate should identify a client allowed to communicate with the server and be signed (issued) by a CA trusted by the server, just like server certificates should be signed by a CA trusted by the client.

In SSLv2, the information 'signed' by the client is the MD5 hash of several fields, including a challenge sent by the server with the request for client authentication and the server's certificate.

This design is vulnerable to a simple MitM attack; this is beyond its use of the vulnerable PKCS #1 version 1.5 padding. Furthermore, it has often been implemented insecurely, e.g., not properly validating the certificate or relying only on the certificate when the server does not receive the client's 'signature' or that 'signature' is invalid. The design is very different than the client authentication mechanism in SSLv3 and in TLS, and the attack is so simple that we leave it as an exercise (Exercise 7.9) and do not discuss this subject any further.

7.4 The handshake protocol: From SSLv3 to TLS 1.2

We now discuss the evolution of the handshake protocol, beginning with version 3 of SSL (SSLv3, [191]) and including versions 1.0, 1.1 and 1.2 of TLS (TLS 1.0–1.2, [152, 154, 468]). These four handshake protocols are quite similar; we mention the more important of the few differences. Later, in Section 7.6, we present version 1.3 of TLS (TLS 1.3), which is the latest version of TLS and involves significant changes from these earlier versions.

These versions of the handshake protocol have multiple mechanisms and options; we do not cover *all* of them. One important mechanism we will not cover is for handshake *renegotiation*. Renegotiation allows clients and servers to change negotiated aspects of the session. One important use for renegotiation is when a server decides to ask for client authentication, after the session began without client authentication (i.e., with an anonymous client). Renegotiation

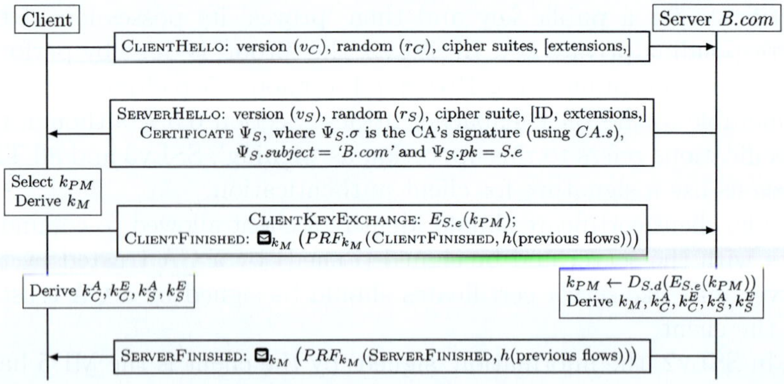

Figure 7.9. The basic RSA-based handshake, in TLS 1.0, 1.1 and 1.2; the SSLv3 handshake is similar. In TLS 1.2, the cipher-suite defines the hash h used in the *Finished* flows (with default *SHA-256*); in TLS 1.0 and 1.1, the hash is the concatenation of *MD5* and *SHA-1*. In all versions, the hashes are applied to the concatenation of the previous flows. The ClientFinished and ServerFinished are used as the *label* input for the *PRF* algorithm used by TLS (defined in the RFCs). The master key k_M is computed, as in Eq. (7.13), from the pre-master key k_{PM}.

is a rather complex mechanism and subject to few attacks, see Refs. [70, 414]; it is not supported by TLS 1.3.

Figure 7.9 illustrates the basic variant of the handshake protocol used by the SSLv3 protocol and by versions 1.0–1.2 of the TLS protocol. Like in SSLv2, this variant uses RSA encryption for key exchange, using the server's public encryption key which we denote here by $S.e$; the key is provided by the *pk* field of the server's public key certificate Ψ_S, which the server sends to the client in the second flow. The client uses the server's public key $S.e$ to encrypt and share with the server a symmetric key denoted k_{PM}, referred to as the *premaster key*.

In the following sections, we discuss the main improvements introduced in these versions of TLS, including the following:

Improved key derivation and handshake integrity (Section 7.4.1): The key derivation process was significantly overhauled with SSLv3. In particular, the ClientKeyExchange message of the basic exchange includes the *premaster key* k_{PM}, from which the protocol derives the master key k_M. As before, the master key k_M is used to derive the keys for the record protocol, used to encrypt and authenticate data on the connection. In addition to the separation between the premaster key k_{PM} and the master key k_M, these versions of the handshake protocol, unlike SSLv2, correctly separate between the encryption keys and the authentication keys.

DH key exchange and PFS (Section 7.4.2): From SSLv3, the TLS protocols support authenticated DH key agreement, as an alternative to the use of RSA-based key exchange (which is the only key exchange method in SSLv2). DH key agreement has the advantage of ensuring *PFS*.

The TLS extensions mechanism (Section 7.4.3): The TLS handshake protocol, from version 1.1, has a built-in *extensions mechanism* that allows clients and servers to support mechanisms which are beyond the standard mechanisms in the specifications. Some of these extensions are very important, e.g., the Server Name Indication (SNI) extension.

Session ticket resumption (Section 7.4.4): All versions of TLS support both the 'traditional' ID-based session resumption mechanism and an alternative session resumption mechanism, based on *session tickets* and defined in RFC 5077 [427]. Session resumption based on session tickets allows the server to resume sessions *without requiring any server-side state* per session, in contrast to ID-based session resumption which requires the servers to maintain state for each session.

Improved client authentication (Section 7.4.5): TLS supports an improved design for client authentication.

Two of these changes — improved key derivation and improved handshake integrity — have impact already on the 'basic' handshake. To see this impact, compare the 'basic' handshake of SSLv3 to TLS 1.2 (Figure 7.9) to Figure 7.7 (the corresponding for SSLv2). We therefore begin our discussion with these two changes.

7.4.1 SSLv3 to TLS 1.2: keys, derivation and handshake integrity

Deriving master key from premaster key: From SSLv3, the handshake protocol exchanges a *pre-master key* k_{PM}, instead of the master key k_M exchanged in SSLv2. The parties derive the master key k_M from the pre-master key k_{PM}, using a PRF, as in Equation (7.13):

$$k_M = \text{PRF}_{k_{PM}}(\text{“master secret”} + r_C + r_S) \tag{7.13}$$

The main motivation for the additional step of deriving the master key k_M from the pre-master key k_{PM} is that k_{PM} may not be a perfectly uniform secret binary string, as required for a cryptographic key. When exchanging the shared premaster key k_{PM} using the basic, RSA-based handshake, this may happen only if the client does not select a random k_{PM}, e.g., when the client does not have a sufficiently good source of randomization. However, TLS also supports establishing the shared key using the DH key agreement protocol and using mod p groups ($\mathbb{Z}_p^*$) with a safe prime p; as we explain in Section 6.2.4, this relies on the Computational Diffie–Hellman (CDH) assumption, and, in fact, we know that the attacker may be able to learn at least one bit of information about the exchanged key. By deriving the master key from the premaster key, the designers apparently hoped to ensure that the entire master key k_M would be pseudorandom, even if the premaster key is not fully pseudorandom, e.g., the attacker can know one bit or few bits of k_{PM}. TLS 1.3 improved on this heuristic design.

Deriving connection keys: Another important improvement of the handshake protocols of SSLv3 to TLS 1.2, compared to the SSLv2 handshake, is in the derivation of the connection keys which are used for encryption and authentication by the record protocol.

Specifically, recall that in SSLv2, we derived from the master key k_M two keys, k_S for protecting traffic sent by the server S and k_C for protecting traffic sent by the client C, as in Equation (7.12). In SSLv3 and TLS, we use k_M to derive *six* independently pseudorandom values: two authentication (MAC) keys, (k_C^A, k_S^A), two encryption keys, (k_C^E, k_S^E), and two initialization vectors, (IV_C, IV_S). As before, the subscripts designate the direction of the traffic to which the key (or IV) is applied, C for traffic from client to server and S for traffic from server to client; and the superscripts designate the use of the key, A for authentication (MAC) and E for encryption. The IV values are used, if necessary, to initialize the CBC (or other) mode of operation (Section 2.10).

To derive these six pseudorandom values, the protocol generates from k_M a long string which is referred to as *key block*, which is sufficiently long to be partitioned into the six values. The exact details of the derivation differ between these different versions of the handshake protocol, and arguably, *none* of the derivations is fully justified by standard cryptographic definitions and reductions. We present the following simplification, leaving the exact details for exercises; the interested reader can find the full details in the corresponding RFC specifications.

Our simplification is defined using a generic pseudorandom function PRF, whose input is an arbitrary-length string, and whose output is a 'sufficiently long' pseudo-random binary string called *key-block*, as follows:

$$\textit{key-block} = \text{PRF}_{k_M}(\text{`key expansion'} + r_C + r_S) \tag{7.14}$$

The key block is then partitioned into the *six* keys/values, as illustrated in Table 7.1.

7.4.2 SSLv3 to TLS 1.2: DH-based key agreement

From SSLv3, the TLS handshake supports DH key agreement. Three types of DH key agreement are supported: the *Diffie–Hellman ephemeral (DHE)*, the *static DH key agreement* and the *anonymous (unauthenticated) DH key agreement*. The DHE handshake is the most popular TLS handshake method, due to its significant security benefits, mainly, support for PFS. The static (certified) DH method is not often used, as it does not offer increased security (or other benefits). We discuss both of these methods (DHE and static DH key agreement), mainly to avoid confusion between them.

We do not discuss at all the third alternative, the anonymous DH key agreement, since it does not provide server authentication and,

Table 7.1. Derivation of connection keys and IVs, in SSLv3 to TLS 1.2.

key-block = $\text{PRF}_{k_M}(\text{`key expansion'} + r_C + r_S)$					
k_C^A	k_S^A	k_C^E	k_S^E	IV_C	IV_S

therefore, rarely used. It may be used in special circumstances, to provide anonymity of the *server.* It is possible to authenticate the server after the handshake is complete, but this is not trivial. Furthermore, the server may usually be identified anyway from its IP address, unless communication is done over an anonymous connection, such as using Tor.

When using any of the DH key agreement methods, the parties derive a shared key k_{PM}, referred to as the *pre-master key*, using the DH protocol with modular group $\mathbb{Z}_p^*$, where p is an agreed upon safe prime p, and using an agreed-upon generator g. Each party uses a randomly generated private key: $S.x$ for the server and $C.y$ for the client. The parties compute and exchange their 'public keys', $g^{S.x}$ (for the server) and $g^{C.y}$ (for the client). The parties then derive the pre-master key k_{PM}, as in 'plain' DH key agreement, namely,

$$k_{PM} = g^{C.y \cdot S.x} \bmod p \tag{7.15}$$

Recall that when using a modular group, the value exchanged by the DH protocol is not pseudorandom; namely, security may rely only on the *CDH (Computational Diffie–Hellman)* assumption; the stronger *DDH (Decisional Diffie–Hellman)* assumption does not hold for modular groups (Definition 6.7). This is one motivation for not using k_{PM} directly as a key to cryptographic functions. Instead, we derive from the pre-master key k_{PM} another key, the *master key* k_M, which should be pseudorandom; we discussed this in Section 7.4.1.

DH static (certified) handshake: In the static (certified) DH key exchange, the server's DH public key is signed as part of the signing process of a *public key certificate.* Namely, the signing entity is a *CA* which is trusted by the browser, and the certificate contains the domain name (e.g., B.com) and other parameters, such as expiration date: $S_{CA.s}((g, p, g^{S.x} \bmod p), \text{B.com}, \ldots)$. See Figure 7.10.

In practice, the use of a certificate implies that the server's DH public key, $g^{S.x}$, is fixed for long periods, similarly to the typical use of RSA or other public key methods. Hence, the static (certified) DH key exchange is similar in its properties to the RSA key exchange; the difference is simply that instead of using RSA encryption to exchange the key, and relying on the RSA (and factoring) assumptions, the

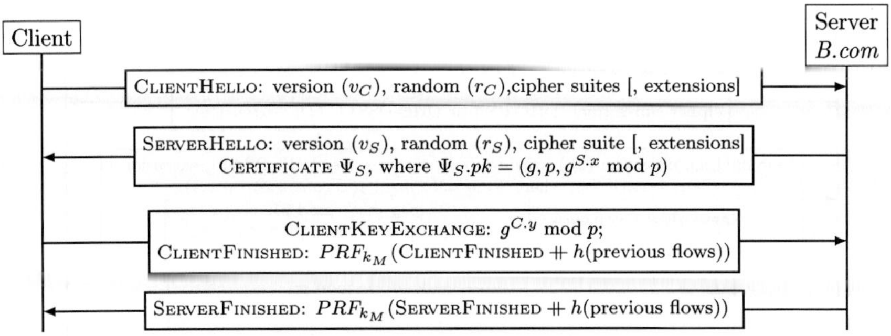

Figure 7.10. SSLv3 to TLS 1.2: the static DH handshake, using static DH public key and parameters for the server, $(g, p, g^{S.x} \bmod p)$, certified by a CA. The pre-master key k_{PM} is computed as in Equation (7.15), and master key k_M is computed — from k_{PM} — as in Equation (7.13).

static (certified) DH key exchange relies on the DH (and discrete-logarithm) assumptions.

Diffie–Hellman ephemeral (DHE) handshake — ensuring Perfect Forward Secrecy (PFS): The *DHE* key exchange uses a different, randomly chosen private key for each exchange; for DH, this means that each party selects a new private exponent ($S.x$ for the server, $C.y$ for the client) in each handshake. This is illustrated in Figure 7.11.

The DH exchange is 'server-authenticated', i.e., the server *signs* its 'public' DH value ($g^{S.x} \bmod p$) and links it with the particular handshake by including in the signed data also the server and client random numbers (r_S and r_C). To allow the client to validate this signature, the server (e.g., *B.com*) should send a public key certificate Ψ_S that specifies its public *signature-verification key S.v*.

Once the TLS session terminates, the private exponents are erased — as well as any keys derived from them, including the pre-master key k_{PM}, the master key k_M, the derived key block (Equation (7.14)) and the keys derived from it (k_S^A, k_S^E, k_C^A, k_C^E). This ensures perfect forward secrecy (PFS) (see *Definition* 5.3), i.e., the ith session between client and server is secure against a powerful MitM attacker, even if the attacker is given all the keys and other contents of the memory of both client and server before and after the

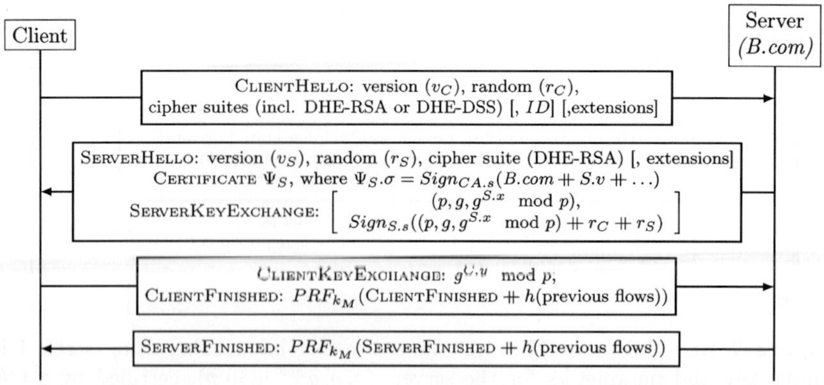

Figure 7.11. SSLv3 to TLSv1.2: the DH Ephemeral (DHE) handshake. The DH exponents $S.x$ and $C.y$ are chosen randomly for this handshake. The server signs its DH parameters (p, g and public key $g^{S.x} \bmod p$), together with the client and server random (r_C and r_S). The signature uses the server's (private) signing key $S.s$; the client verifies it using the corresponding server's verification public key $S.v$, which is sent in the certificate Ψ_S signed by a trusted certificate authority (CA). The client then selects a random exponent $C.y$ and sends its DH key agreement public key $g^{C.y} \bmod p$ in the ClientKeyExchange message, together with the ClientFinished message authenticating the handshake. The pre-master key k_{PM} is computed as in Equation (7.15), and the master key k_M is computed as in Equation (7.13).

ith session, as long as the keys are given only *after* the ith handshake is completed.

See Exercises 7.17 and 7.18.

7.4.3 The TLS extension mechanism

One of the most important improvements of TLS over SSL is that TLS supports a flexible and secure *extensions mechanism*. This mechanism allows clients to specify additional fields, not defined in the protocol but supported (and 'understood') by some — often most — of the servers. Servers should ignore unknown extensions.

TLS extensions are defined in RFC 4366 [84].[10] Support for extensions became a (mandatory) part of the TLS specifications from TLS 1.1. In fact, extensions are also supported by many TLS 1.0

[10]Based on an earlier specification in RFC 3546 [83].

implementations since the TLS extensions mechanism has been carefully designed to maintain backwards compatibility with TLS 1.0 implementations (that did not adopt it), by sending, together with the regular ClientHello and ServerHello messages, also extended versions of these two messages, which are ignored by versions of TLS 1.0 that do not support extensions.

Some standard extensions facilitate important functionality, including functionality needed to improve security. Developers of clients and servers may define additional, non-standard extensions.

We discuss two important extensions: one in this section (the SNI extension) and another in the following section (the session ticket extension, in Section 7.4.4).

The Server Name Indication (SNI) extension: The *SNI* is one of the most important and widely used extensions. The main use of SNI is to allow a single web server to serve webpages belonging to multiple different domain names, i.e., multiple websites, e.g., *a.com* and *b.org*. Each domain name may require a different certificate; the SNI extension allows the client to indicate the desired server domain name early on in the protocol, before the web server has to send a certificate to the client — allowing the server to send the desired certificate based on the webpage that is being requested. Before the SNI extension, the common way for a web server to support multiple websites, with different domain names, was by having each site use a dedicated port — an inconvenient and inefficient solution.

The SNI extension is valuable even for servers which host only a single domain. This is since the SNI extension allows the server to verify that the domain that the client wants to connect with is the same as the hosted domain, before the server spends the considerable computational resources to complete the TLS handshake. This avoids spending server resources due to incorrect client requests sent to the server.

By requiring the SNI extension, a web server can also prevent a potential *Denial of Service* (*DoS*) attack, exhausting server's resources. Without SNI, a rogue website could abuse visits by benign users, to attack other sites; this kind of DoS attack is called a *cross-site DoS attack*.

There is another, more subtle, security advantage for a server to require the client to send the SNI extension. Attackers often scan the IP address space to find web servers and then try to attack them, i.e., open an TCP connection and send ClientHello to a random IP address, without knowing which server is hosted at that IP (if at all). If the web server requires the SNI extension, it will not respond with its certificate, which contains its domain name, before the client sends the ClientHello with the SNI extension including that domain name. This defeats this specific type of scanning attack.

Support of SNI was one of the main factors motivating websites and clients to adopt TLS rather than continue using SSL. Many servers refuse handshakes where the client does not include the SNI extension in ClientHello.

7.4.4 SSLv3 to TLS 1.2: Session resumption

Already from SSLv2, the SSL and TLS handshake protocols support the ID-based *session resumption* mechanism. In session resumption, the handshake of a new connection between a client C and a server S reuses the master key k_M established during a previous connection between C and S; we say that the two connections belong to the same *session*. Session resumption allows a considerable reduction in the computational overhead of SSL and TLS, which is mainly due to the public key operations, required only once per session. Session resumption also avoids unnecessary retransmission of the server's public key certificate.

Webpages often involve opening a very large number of TCP connections to the same server, to download different objects. The reduction in CPU time can easily be a ratio of dozens or even hundreds.

However, ID-based session resumption requires the server to maintain state, specifically, the mapping from each session-ID to the corresponding master key k_M (and possibly other details). The amount of state is not very large, but this requirement is still challenging, especially for large websites which are supported by multiple servers, often in different locations.

From TLS 1.1, there is an alternative mechanism for session resumption which is *stateless*: the *session ticket extension*. In this section, we discuss both session resumption mechanisms.

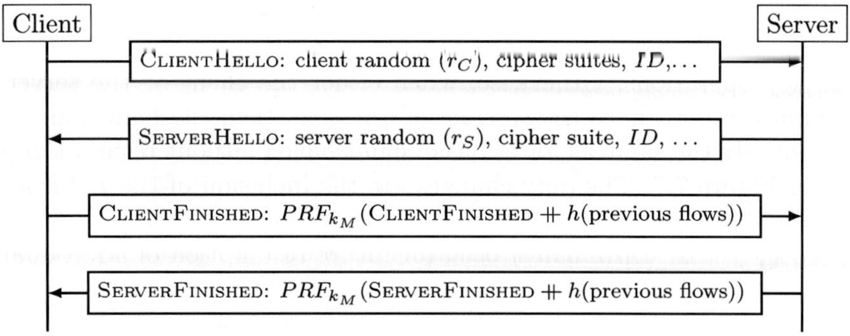

Figure 7.12. SSLv3 to TLS 1.2 handshake, with ID-based session resumption.

***ID*-based session resumption in SSLv3 and TLS 1.0-1.2:** We begin with the (stateful) ID-based session resumption mechanism. This mechanisms did not change much from its implementation in SSLv2.

Figure 7.12 illustrates the handling of ID-based session resumption, in the SSLv3 handshake protocol, and in versions 1.0–1.2 of the TLS protocol. In the figure, the ClientHello message contains the session-ID (identifier), denoted simply ID, which was received from server in a previous connection.

ID-based session resumption is possible when the server has the entry (ID, k_{PM}, γ), with the same ID as of the client, saved from a previous connection, where k_{PM} is the session's premaster key and γ contains 'related information' such as the cipher suite used in the session. The resumption process proceeds as follows:

1. The client includes the session ID in its ClientHello message.
2. The server identifies that it has the corresponding (ID, k_{PM}, γ) entry. To signal that resumption succeeded, it send the same ID to the client. If the client does not send an ID or the server does not have the corresponding (ID, k_{PM}, γ) entry, then the server selects an unallocated ID and sends it to the client. If the server finds the (ID, k_{PM}, γ) entry, then it continues the TLS session using k_{PM} as the premaster key and using the cipher suite specified in γ.
3. If the client receives the same ID as it sent, then it uses the stored premaster key k_{PM} for the session and immediately proceeds to send the ClientFinished message.

When the session information was available to both client and server, the protocol avoids the use of computationally expensive public key operations. Otherwise, when either the client or the server, or both, do not have the session information, then the handshake is essentially the same as for a 'basic' handshake (without resumption), as in Figure 7.7. The only changes are the inclusion of the ID from client (if it has it) and the inclusion of an ID in the ServerFinished message, to be (optionally) used for future resumption of additional connections (in the same session).

Session-ID resumption — challenges and concerns: The basic challenge of ID-based session resumption is the need to maintain state and lookup the state using the ID. This is a signficant challenge since web servers are usually replicated; replication is important, for load-balancing and scalability, and to reduce latency by providing service from a server closer to the clients, e.g., in a content distribution network (CDN).

Also, to minimize the storage and lookup time overhead, the cache of saved session information cannot be too large; on the other hand, if the cached is too small, then the resumption mechanism is less effective.

Another challenge is that the exposure of the premaster key k_{PM} exposes the entire communication to an eavesdropper; namely, the storage of the key may foil the perfect forward secrecy (PFS) mechanism. To ensure PFS, we must ensure that all copies of the key k_{PM} are discarded, which can be a non-trivial challenge due to the use of multiple servers.

The session ticket extension and its use for session resumption: The TLS extension mechanism provides an alternative, *stateless* session resumption mechanism. The idea is simple: together with the *finish* message of a successful handshake, the server attaches a *session ticket extension*, containing a *session ticket*. Later, when the client re-connects to the same server, it attaches the previously received session ticket, again using the session ticket extension. See Figure 7.13.

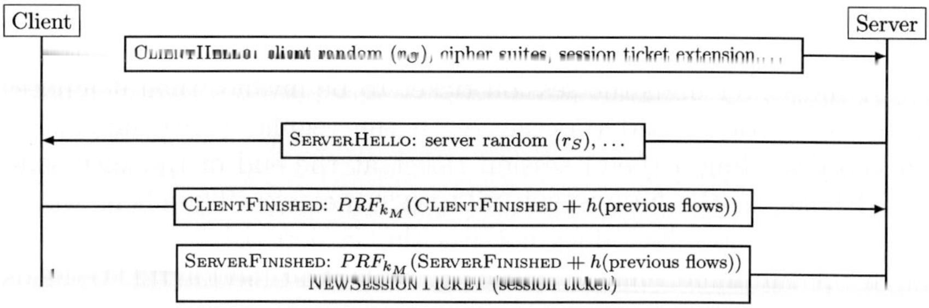

Figure 7.13. Session resumption using a *session ticket*. If the client has a valid session ticket, then it sends to the server the session ticket in the session ticket extension as part of the ClientHello message. The server should be able to validate the session ticket as one that the server issued previously, and not too long ago, and to retrieve the shared premaster-key k_{PM} encrypted within the ticket. After the handshake is completed successfully, the server may send a new session ticket, by sending to the client the NewSessionTicket message containing the new session ticket.

The session ticket allows any of the servers running the website to recover the value of the premaster key k_{PM} of the session with the client. On the other hand, the session ticket design should prevent attackers, eavesdropping on the ticket as sent by the client, from finding k_{PM}. This is achieved by having k_{PM}, and other values sent in the session ticket, encrypted using a secret, symmetric *session ticket encryption key*, which we denote k_{STEK}, known (only) to all authorized servers. Note that k_{STEK} is not shared with clients or derived by TLS; the method of generating it and sharing it between the servers is implementation-specific. Since k_{STEK} is a shared symmetric key, it is usually simply selected randomly.

Clients cannot decrypt the session tickets; hence, they must store both the session ticket, like a cookie, as well as the session's premaster key k_{PM}. Together, they allow the client to perform its part of the handshake.

The contents of the session ticket are only used by the servers and are opaque to the clients, i.e., not 'understood' or used by the clients; hence, different implementations may use different tickets. RFC 5077 [427] recommends a structure which uses the EtA construction, with the encrypted contents including the protocol version, cipher suite, compression method, master secret key, client identity and a timestamp.

If the server finds the session ticket to be invalid, then it ignores the session ticket and proceeds with the regular (full) handshake, possibly sending a (new) session ticket at the end of the successful handshake, in the NEWSESSIONTICKET message. The client would detect that the server does not use the session ticket but proceeds with the full handshake by noticing, with the SERVERHELLO, fields or messages sent only for the full handshake, e.g., the CERTIFICATE.

The *timestamp* allows the server to limit the validity period of a ticket (and the keys contained within); if the server receives a ticket which already expired, or is invalid for any other reason, it simply ignores it and proceeds with the 'regular' handshake, establishing a new pre-master key (and potentially sending a new ticket to the client).

The limited validity period for the ticket is important, to limit the risk from exposure of the keys in a particular ticket — via cryptanalysis or in other ways, such as abuse of a vulnerability of the browser. Limiting the validity of tickets is clearly also necessary to ensure *PFS*; however, this is not *sufficient*. Specifically, to ensure PFS, we should also limit the ability of an attacker to decipher messages from past recorded ciphertexts of long-terminated connections, using an exposed *session ticket encryption key* k_{STEK}. Let us discuss this challenge.

PFS with session ticket encryption keys: To preserve PFS, e.g., on a daily basis, we need to make sure that each *session ticket encryption key* k_{STEK} is kept for only the allowed duration — e.g., up to 24 hours ('daily'). We can maintain this key only in memory and never write it to disk or other non-volatile storage, making it easier to ensure it is not kept beyond the desired period (e.g., daily). This rule may require us to maintain several ticket-keys concurrently, e.g., generate a new key once an hour, allowing it to 'live' for up to 24 hours.

In the typical case of replicated servers, the ticket keys k_{STEK} should be distributed securely to all replicates. Changing the key becomes even more important, with it being used by so many machines.

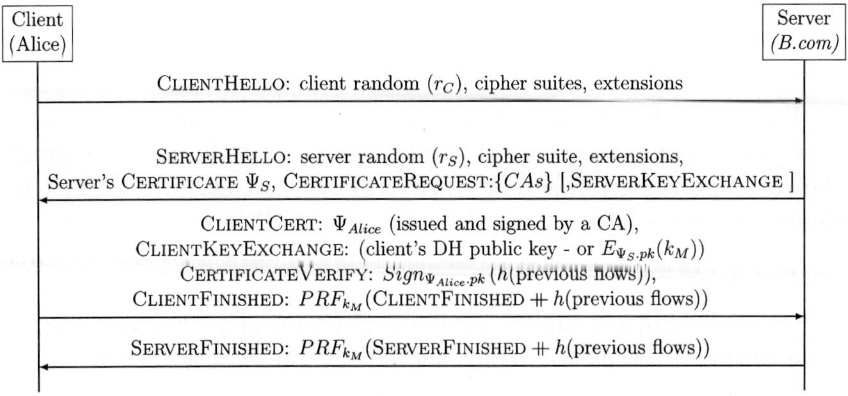

Figure 7.14. Client authentication in SSLv3 and versions 1.0–1.2 of TLS.

7.4.5 SSLv3 to TLS 1.2: Client authentication

Already from SSLv2, the TLS and SSL protocols support a mechanism for authenticating clients, as an optional service of the handshake. In this section, we describe how this optional *client authentication* mechanism works, in SSLv3 and in TLS 1.0–1.2.

The TLS client authentication mechanism is illustrated in Figure 7.14. The mechanism consists of three additions to the versions of the handshake not supporting client authentication. First, the server signals the need for client authentication, by including the CertificateRequest field together with the ServerHello message. The CertificateRequest field identifies the certificate-authorities (issuers) which are accepted by this server; namely, client authentication is possible only if the client has a certificate from one of these entities.

Next, the client attaches, to its ClientKeyExchange message, two fields. The first is the certificate itself; the second, called CertificateVerify, is a *digital signature* over the handshake messages. The ability to produce this signature serves as proof of the identity of the client. The signature in the CertificateVerify message includes also the messages sent by the client just before it, i.e., the ClientKeyExchange message and the ClientCert (see Exercise 7.19).

The client authentication mechanism is quite simple and efficient; however, it is not widely deployed. In reality, TLS is typically deployed using only the public key (and certificate) of the server, i.e., only allowing the client to authenticate the server but without client authentication.

The reason for the limited use of TLS client authentication is that it requires clients to use a private key and to obtain a certificate on the corresponding public key; furthermore, that certificate must be signed by an authority trusted by the server. This raises two serious challenges: First, clients often use multiple devices, and this requires them to have access to their private keys on these multiple devices, which raises both usability and security concerns. Second, clients must obtain a certificate, which should be issued by a CA trusted by the server.

As a result, most websites prefer to avoid the use of TLS client authentication. Instead, websites use more convenient mechanisms for client authentication, performed over the established TLS connection. The common mechanisms include passwords, authenticating cookies, FIDO and multi-factor authentication (MFA); see Chapter 9.

Note also that the client authentication mechanism requires the client to send their certificate 'in the clear'. This may be a privacy concern since the certificate may allow identification of the client; see Exercise 7.19.

7.5 Negotiations and downgrade attacks

The evolution of TLS saw an increasingly complex set of different options and choices: different usage modes, different protocol versions, different cipher suites (from SSLv2) and different extensions (from TLS 1.1). To allow this flexibility, and following the *crypto-agility principle* (Principle 11), the SSL and TLS specifications and implementations use different *negotiation* mechanisms whose goal is for client and server to agree on the set of options to be used. This set of options *should* be supported by both parties, and this set of options *should* be the one preferred by at least one of the two parties, among all sets of options supported by both parties.

However, some negotiation mechanisms are vulnerable to *downgrade attacks*, where an attacker causes the parties to use a vulnerable set of options, although both parties *support and prefer* a different, secure set of options. As we have seen for GSM (Section 5.5.5), downgrade attacks can be simple to understand and deploy yet break down security. Furthermore, downgrade attacks could persist for years, or, as we say, *old versions die slowly*. The situation with TLS is quite similar.

In this section, we discuss the pre-TLS-1.3 negotiation mechanisms, and several effective, and quite simple, downgrade attacks. We exclude discussion of TLS 1.3 since its negotiation mechanisms are quite different, mostly due to insights from these downgrade attacks.

Let us begin with SSLv2, which is completely vulnerable to downgrade attacks.

7.5.1 SSLv2 cipher suite negotiation and downgrade attack

We illustrate how SSLv2 supports crypto-agility, i.e., the SSLv2 *cipher suite negotiation* mechanism, in Figures 7.15 (with abstract cipher suites) and 7.16 (with specific cipher suites).

The negotiation mechanism is quite simple: the client sends the entire set of cipher suites that it supports with the ClientHello message, and the server responds, in the ServerHello message, with the cipher suites supported by the server. Finally, the client

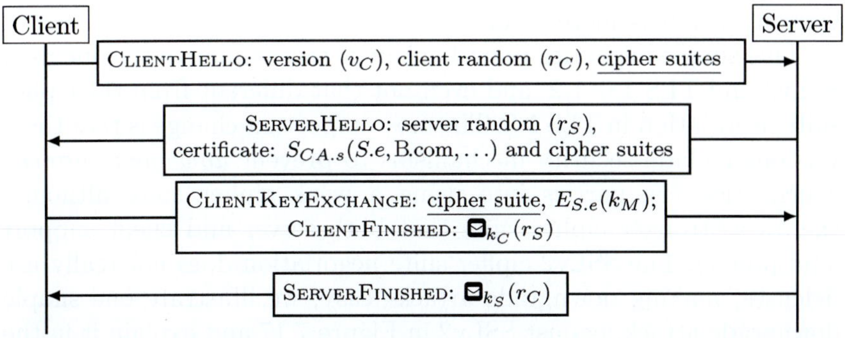

Figure 7.15. SSLv2 handshake, with details of cipher suite negotiation (underlined). The ClientHello message indicates the options supported by the client; the ServerHello message contains the subset of these, which are also supported by the server. The client chooses one of these and indicates the choice in the ClientKeyExchange message.
Note: The negotiation was modified in later versions.

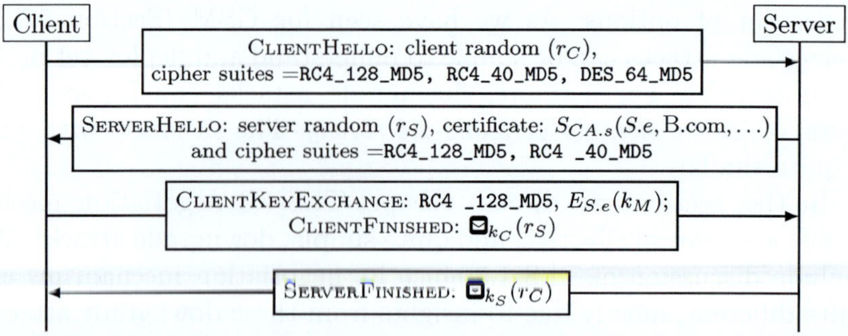

Figure 7.16. Example of SSLv2 cipher suite negotiation. In this example, the client offers three cipher suites, and the server supports two of these. The negotiation was changed from SSLv3.

selects a cipher suite supported by both itself and the server and identifies it in the ClientKeyExchange message.

In the specific scenario shown in Figure 7.16, the client supports three cipher suites, all using the MD5 hashing algorithm but with three different ciphers and key lengths (128-bits keys or 40-bits keys for RC4, and 56-bits keys with DES). The server supports only RC4, with either 128-bits keys or 40-bits keys. The 40-bit keys are well known to be insecure; the reason that they are supported by some clients and server is that until about 2000, these were the only keys allowed for products sold or distributed outside of the USA, due to USA export controls. However, the client chooses to use the 128-bits version since it is more secure.

This simple negotiation mechanism is very similar to the one used SSLv3 and TLS 1.0–1.2, and even not that different from the cipher suite negotiation in TLS 1.3. The most important change is that these versions include security mechanisms to prevent *downgrade attacks*, which trick the parties into using a weak cipher suite although there's a stronger cipher suite that both server and client support (and prefer). The SSLv2 cipher suite negotiation does not really use defenses, making downgrade attacks easy; we illustrate one simple downgrade attack against SSLv2 in Figure 7.17 and explain it in the following.

Downgrade attack against SSLv2: In SSLv2, the finish messages only confirm that the parties share the same server and client keys (K_S and K_C, respectively) but not the integrity of the rest of

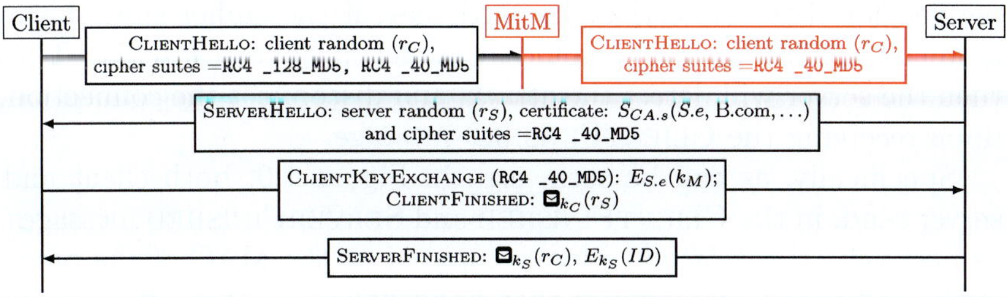

Figure 7.17. Cipher suite downgrade attack on SSLv2, by a MitM attacker. Server and client end up using master key k_M with only 40 secret bits, which the attacker can find by exhaustive search. Attacker does not need to find the key during the handshake; parties use the 40-bit key for entire connection, attacker may even just record ciphertexts and decrypt later.

the hello messages — in particular, there is no authentication of the cipher suites sent by server and client. This allows simple downgrade attacks, removing 'strong' ciphers from the list of ciphers supported by client and/or server.

Figure 7.17 illustrates how a MitM attacker may perform this downgrade attack against SSLv2; in the example illustrated, the attacker removes the 'regular-version' 128-bit RC4 encryption from the list of ciphers supported by the client, leaving only the weaker 'export-version' 40-bit RC4 encryption.

7.5.2 Defenses against downgrade attacks in SSL and TLS 1.0–1.2

From SSLv3, the security of the cipher suite negotiation mechanism was improved. The most important change is defense to ensure *handshake integrity*; this prevents the *cipher suite downgrade attack* of Figure 7.17. Two other changes are (1) extended cipher suites that specify also the key-exchange mechanism (SSLv2 cipher suites specified only the symmetric cryptography) and (2) the server chooses the cipher suite (in the SERVERHELLO message, i.e., second flow), instead of the client (in third flow).

Handshake integrity foils cipher suite downgrade: Beginning with SSLv3, the handshake protocol includes a simple mechanism for validating the integrity of *all* handshake messages. The client and server authenticate the entire handshake, using the master key derived for that connection. In particular, if the cipher suite downgrade attack of Figure 7.17 would be launched against SSLv3 or TLS, then the server will detect the attack, and disconnect the connection, upon receiving the CLIENTFINISHED message.

Specifically, as can be seen, e.g., in Figure 7.9, both client and server send, in the CLIENTFINISHED and SERVERFINISHED messages, respectively, a *validation value*, computed as the MAC of the previously exchanged messages of that handshake and thereby ensuring the integrity of the handshake. Upon receiving the finished message from the peer (server or client, respectively), the value is checked; if it is not properly authenticated then the handshake is aborted.

Similarly to the keys-derivation process (Section 7.4.1), the details slightly differ among the different versions, and we present a slight simplification, consistent with the one we used in Section 7.4.1. Both validation values are computed following the 'hash-then-authenticate' paradigm, using a hash function h, assumed to be collision resistant, and a PRF. The validation value sent with the CLIENTFINISHED message, which we denote v_C, is computed as:

$$v_C = PRF_{k_M}(\text{CLIENTFINISHED} + h(\text{handshake-messages})) \quad (7.16)$$

Similarly, the validation value sent with the SERVERFINISHED message, which we denote v_S, is computed as:

$$v_S = PRF_{k_M}(\text{SERVERFINISHED} + h(\text{handshake-messages})) \quad (7.17)$$

Note the similarity to the derivation of the key block (Equation 7.14).

Security analysis of the finished messages validation: Let us give an intuitive explanation to the security provided by Finished messages validation mechanism, focusing on the prevention of cipher suite downgrade attacks.

For simplicity, assume that the client and server both support *two* cipher suites: a *secure cipher suite* X, which they prefer over a *vulnerable cipher suite* V. Also, focus on the (typical) handshake, with server authentication but without client authentication. In this case, the protocol should ensure that if the handshake completes successfully at a client, then it also completed successfully at the server, and the two parties use cipher suite X, the preferred and more secure cipher suite.

Consider an execution in which the client completes the handshake successfully. In such execution, the client must have received a valid ServerFinished message, i.e., the client's value of v_S, computed as in Equation 7.17 using the handshake messages received by the client, is the same as the value received from the server, which we denote v'_S, and which is also computed as in Equation 7.17, but using the handshake messages received by the server.

The security follows from the use of 'hash-then-authenticate'. Let us elaborate a bit, mainly to highlight the assumptions involved. The first assumption is that *the master key k_M cannot be exposed* by an attacker sending a (manipulated or fabricated) ServerFinished message. Namely, k_M is *pseudorandom* and known during the handshake, only to the client and to the intended server.

Note that this assumption, and other assumptions identified in the following, *should* hold for *all supported cipher suites.* Also, recall that, from SSLv3, the cipher suite specifies both the symmetric-encryption mechanisms and the key exchange mechanisms. Hence, *all* key exchange mechanisms supported by the client must be secure, to the limited extent of preventing exposure of k_M during a successful handshake.

The basic argument for security is that when the client receives a valid ServerFinished message, with $v_S = v'_S$, then the server must have previously sent that message, and client and server must have seen identical handshake messages. This argument is based on the assumption that k_M is pseudorandom and on the use of *hash-then-authenticate* in the computation of both Finished messages.

Furthermore, we rely on the assumption that the PRF is secure and that the hash function h is a collision-resistant hash function. The observant reader will note that the second 'assumption' is not really an assumption as much as a *simplification* since h is a keyless hash and *there are no keyless collision-resistant hash functions* (Section 3.3.2); we can say the argument is made under the random oracle model (ROM).

The rest of the security argument follows. A PRF provides message authentication (Section 4.4.2), when used with a pseudorandom key (in this case, k_M). Hence, when the client receives v'_S, this implies that the server, previously, computed $v'_S = PRF_{k_M}$ (ServerFinished $+\!\!+$ h(handshake-messages)), providing as input (ServerFinished $+\!\!+$ h(handshake-messages)), and then sent v'_S to the client. Since the client computed the same value ($v_S = v'_S$), it follows that the inputs to the PRF provided by client and server were the same. From the collision-resistance of h, the inputs to the hash were also the same. It follows that both parties have seen identical handshake messages. In particular, they must have seen the same cipher suite negotiation messages and hence, cipher suite downgrade attacks are impossible from SSLv3.

7.5.3 Finished fails: The Logjam and FREAK cipher suite attacks

In spite of the above security analysis of Finished message validation, two ciphertext downgrade attacks have circumvented the defense: *FREAK* and *Logjam*. Both attacks exploit the fact that, due to USA export regulations until around 2000, SSLv3 and TLS 1.0 support several cipher suites which use short, vulnerable keys; the attacker can find the keys quickly enough, to allow the attacker to complete the TLS handshake (without causing a timeout). These very weak cipher suites were supposed to be used (only) for exported versions of TLS, i.e., versions distributed outside the USA. These two downgrade attacks trick the client and/or server into using these weak, exportable versions, even when communicating with a party that supports the stronger, non-exportable versions.

In both of these attacks, the attacker impersonates as the server by finding the master key k_M and then abusing it to send a fake — but valid — SERVERFINISHED message. A client would *time-out* and abort a handshake which does not successfully complete within a reasonable maximal delay (timeout) which we denote τ; typical values for τ are from few seconds to 30 seconds or even more.

The FREAK attack: The FREAK[11] attack [67] downgrades the handshake to use the RSA_EXPORT cipher suite, which uses a weak, 512-bit modulus N, which can be factored in hours or even

[11] *FREAK* stands for *Factoring RSA Export Keys*, combined with the words *weak* and *freak*, which seem to describe the attack well.

minutes by available powerful computers such as available in computing clouds; it is assumed that adversaries may be able to perform such factoring significantly faster, at least, with significant probability. The attack exploited a subtle bug in several implementations of TLS, which caused the client to receive the weak (512-bit) key although the client was using the strong (non-export) RSA cipher suite. For details, see [67].

The Logjam attack: The Logjam attack [7] is also a downgrade attack exploiting an exportable version of TLS. Specifically, the Logjam attack exploits a vulnerability of the exportable version of the DHE key exchange (Figure 7.11). For exportability, this version uses only 512-bits groups. The computation of discrete log in such groups is feasible but still requires considerable computational resources. The time required to compute discrete log over the (relatively short) 512-bits groups, using available hardware, is assumed to be significantly longer than the typical or even high value for the handshake timeout bound τ (e.g., 30 seconds). Therefore, the use of 512-bits groups would have been considered reasonably secure for use in the DHE key exchange, if the attacker would have had to perform the discrete-log operation *during* the handshake.

However, the Logjam attack circumvents this challenge, by using a *precomputation mechanism*, which the attacker applies *before* the handshake, allowing the attacker to complete the discrete-log operation *during* the handshake in time which is in the order of 30 seconds, i.e., often without abort due to the timeout τ.

The Logjam attack also uses a downgrade attack, allowing Logjam to trick a client into using the exportable DHE key exchange, although both client and server support both non-exportable and exportable DHE, allowing Logjam to succeed. The complete Logjam attack is illustrated in Figure 7.18; we next explain the two mechanisms.

Precomputation mechanism: Logjam relies on the fact that, for a given prime p and generator g, it is possible to precompute *a hint* allowing reasonably-efficient computation of discrete logarithms. The precomputation function $Hint \leftarrow \text{precompute}(p, g)$ requires as inputs only the prime p and the generator g; later, given $g^b \bmod p$ and the precomputed $Hint$, the attacker can efficiently compute the discrete logarithm using the hint, as $b \leftarrow DiscLog(g^b \bmod p, Hint)$.

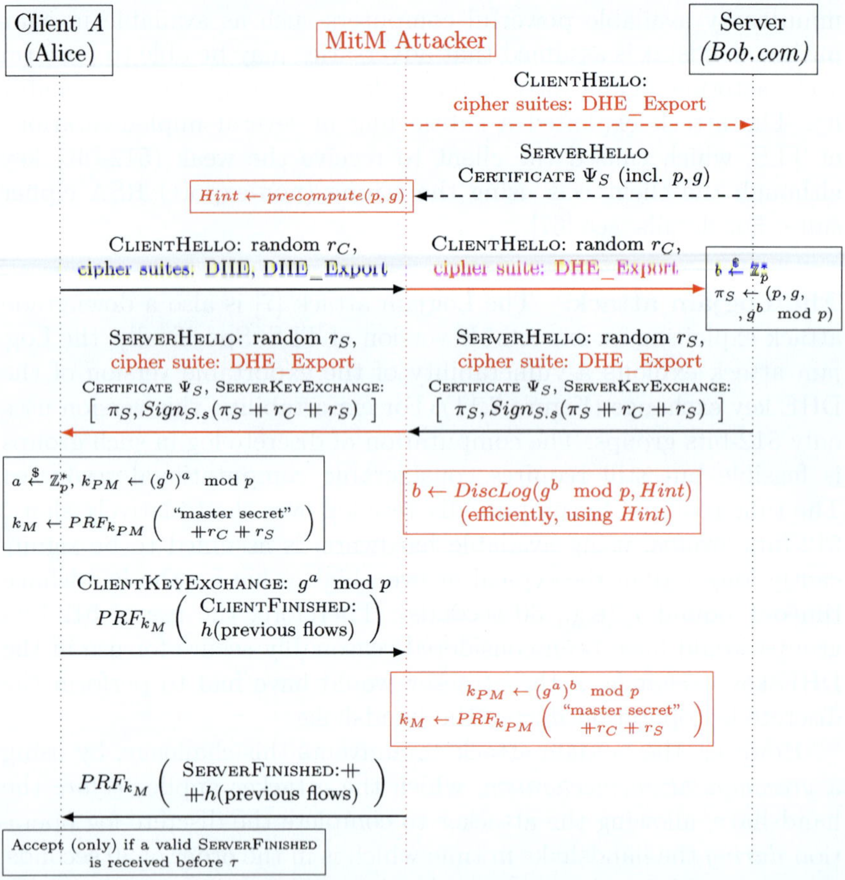

Figure 7.18. The Logjam MitM cipher suite downgrade attack against servers supporting the exportable (weak keys) version of the DH Ephemeral (DHE) key exchange. The attack works for the case of known DH group (p, g), allowing the attacker to precompute the most computationally challenging part of the discrete log computation and use it for the different exponents and handshakes. The MitM attack illustrated begins once this precomputation is done. Note that the client aborts the handshake if it does not complete successfully within τ time. Details in text.

The precompute(p, g) operation is *feasible for 512-bits groups*, although it would surely take more than the client's timeout τ (of typically 30 seconds or less). If the server is reusing the same prime p and generator g for multiple or all handshakes, then the attacker can compute $Hint \leftarrow$ precompute(p, g) *in advance*, allowing the attacker to later compute $b \leftarrow DiscLog(g^b \bmod p, Hint)$ efficiently, during the handshake with the client. See the flows from the server (e.g., *B.com*) to the client in Figure 7.18; the server chooses b randomly in each handshake but uses the same group $(p,\ g)$.

The researchers found that many web servers indeed reuse the same p and g for many handshakes, only choosing randomly, in each handshake, the server's secret exponent (b), facilitating the Logjam attack; see Ref. [7].

Downgrade to exportable DHE handshake: As shown in Figure 7.18, the Logjam attack succeeds even when the client supports (also) the use of the strong, *non-exportable* DHE variant of TLS, which we denote in the figure by specifying the value of DHE as a cipher suite. The server achieves this by modifying the cipher suite value to *DHE_Export* when forwarding the CLIENTHELLO message to the server, thereby causing the server to use the weak, exportable DH group. As a result, the client continues the handshake as when interacting with a server that only supports the *DHE_Export* cipher suite.

Note that due to this downgrade attack, the server receives a modified CLIENTHELLO message, where the cipher suites field was modified by the attacker. If the client and server would have exchanged the CLIENTFINISHED and SERVERFINISHED messages between them at this time, then they would have detected the attack since each of them would compute the hash over different flows. However, in the Logjam attack, the client only sees the SERVERFINISHED as sent by the attacker, not by the server, and the server does not receive any CLIENTFINISHED message at all.

7.5.4 Backward compatibility and protocol version negotiation

SSL was an immediate success; it was widely deployed soon after it was released (as SSLv2). Hence, when introducing SSLv3, designers had to seriously consider *backward compatibility*, namely, allowing a client/server running SSLv3, to interact with a server/client, respectively, running SSLv2. With the definition of (different versions of) TLS, backward compatibility became critical; basically, a new version has almost no chance of adoption without backward compatibility with earlier versions.

TLS protocol version negotiation: The ClientHello messages of TLS 1.0–1.2 and SSLv3 are very similar, and the ClientHello and ServerHello messages include protocol-version identification. This allows a simple and efficient *version negotiation mechanism* for implementations of TLS 1.0–1.2, allowing the implementations to use the most updated version of the protocol supported by both the client and the server.

This *TLS version negotiation mechanism* works as follows. When a TLS server receives a ClientHello indicating an older version, it simply continues the negotiation using this older version of the protocol. Similarly, when a TLS server receives a ClientHello indicating a protocol version newer than the one supported by the server, then the server continues the negotiation using its own (older) version of the protocol. Namely, if the server runs version v_S, and receives ClientHello indicating version v_C, then the server responds with ServerHello using version $\min(v_S, v_C)$.

This version negotiation mechanism allows TLS servers running any version of TLS, or running SSLv3, to interact with clients running any version of TLS or SSLv3; only SSLv2 is incompatible. In all cases, the clients detect the lowest-common version which is to be used from the ServerHello message, and continue the protocol using that version. Importantly, the *same handshake continues*; the hope here is that the integrity mechanism of the Finished messages validates that the downgrade was, indeed, selected by the server. As we explain, this is not necessarily true.

Vulnerability of TLS version negotiation: The TLS version negotiation mechanism relies on the ClientFinished and ServerFinished messages to detect downgrade attacks. However, as we saw for the Logjam attack, these messages can fail to protect the integrity of the handshake, if the attacker can expose the master key computed by the benign participant during the handshake, i.e., before the participant aborts the handshake due to time-out. Therefore, this mechanism can be vulnerable, allowing the attacker to downgrade the handshake to a vulnerable version of TLS. In particular, this was exploited in the CAT attack [423], which is an optimized version of the Bleichenbacher attack which succeed in decrypting the premaster key against many TLS implementations; by exploiting the vulnerability of the TLS version-negotiation mechanism, the CAT attacks was successfully applied even to implementations supporting TLS 1.3.

The SSL version negotiation mechanism and SSLv3 version downgrade attack: The above TLS protocol version negotiation mechanism does not support SSLv2 since SSLv2 uses a different ClientHello format. The SSLv3 specification [191] specified a different version negotiation mechanism, which allows SSLv3 clients to interact with SSLv2 servers.

The SSL version negotiation mechanism works by the following simple *downgrade dance*: an SSLv3 client first sends the SSLv3 ClientHello message; but if a valid ServerHello is not received, it sends the SSLv2 ClientHello. This allows interoperability of an SSLv3 client with an SSLv2 server. The other case, of SSLv2 client and SSLv3 server, is handled like the TLS mechanism, i.e., the SSLv3 server detects receipt of SSLv2 ClientHello and continues the handshake using SSLv2.

The SSL version negotiation (downgrade dance) mechanism is vulnerable to a simple downgrade attack. Basically, a MitM attacker drops the SSLv3 ClientHello message, thereby causing the client to connect using SSLv2. See the following exercise. The designers were aware of this risk, and the SSLv3 standard notes that this method for backward compatibility will be 'phased out with all due haste'; however, it took more than a decade for the support for SSLv2 to be phased out of the standards (in Ref. [462]) and implementations.

Exercise 7.1 (The SSLv3 version downgrade attack). Show message sequence diagram for a MitM version downgrade attack, tricking an SSLv3 server and an SSLv3 client who sends SSLv2-format ClientHello (for backward compatibility), into completing the handshake using SSLv2 and using a weak (40-bit) cipher.

Hint: See this attack (referred to as 'version rollback attack') in Ref. [471]. □

Kocher's *ad hoc* defense against downgrade to SSLv2: In practice, interactions between most TLS and SSLv3 servers and clients are protected from the protocol downgrade attack of Exercise 7.1, by an ingenious *ad hoc* defense, designed by Paul Kocher.

These clients signal their support of SSLv3, by encoding a 'signal' of that in the *padding* used in the RSA encryption. For details on this and other issues related to this downgrade attack (also referred to as version rollback), see Ref. [471] and appendix E.2 of the TLS 1.0 specifications, RFC2246 [152].

7.5.5 The TLS downgrade dance and the Poodle version downgrade attack

The TLS backward compatibility mechanism (Section 7.5.4) requires support by the server. Namely, when the server receives a CLIENTHELLO using version not yet supported by the server, then the server should respond by indicating to the client the version supported by the server. This is not trivial. While CLIENTHELLO messages of different TLS versions use basically the same design, there are several additions from SSLv3 onward, including the important TLS extensions mechanism (from TLS 1.1, but also supported by many TLS 1.0 implementations). While the additions to CLIENTHELLO have been carefully designed to be ignored by implementations following correctly and precisely the specifications of the previous versions, some lower-version implementations may fail to process them correctly or, for some other reason, do not continue with the protocol using their (lower-version) protocol.

Many clients try to work with such servers anyway, by the following alternative version-negotiation process, which we call the *TLS downgrade dance*: (a) first, try to connect using the latest version; (b) if receiving an error or no response, try to connect using an older version (and repeat, using older-yet versions, as necessary). The reader will note that this downgrade dance is basically an extension of the SSL downgrade dance described earlier. Therefore, not surprisingly, it is also vulnerable to a downgrade attack. An attacker can simply block connection attempts (or send back a fake error message), causing the client to use an older, vulnerable version of the protocol. This was exploited in Ref. [362] to apply the Poodle attack to clients which support TLS 1.1 or 1.2, and therefore we refer to it as the *Poodle version downgrade attack*.

Exercise 7.2 (The Poodle version downgrade attack). Consider client that supports the TLS downgrade dance described above.

Namely, the client first tries to connect using TLS 1.2; if that fails, it tries to connect using TLS 1.1; and if that also fails, it tries to connect using TLS 1.0. Present a message sequence diagram for deploying the Poodle attack against such client, even when the server supports TLS 1.2.

The obvious way to foil the version downgrade attack is to only use the TLS version negotiation mechanism, i.e., not to perform the downgrade dance. However, evidently, this may cause loss of backward compatibility with many servers, a price that client developers were often not willing to pay. We next present the *SCSV* signaling mechanism, which allows *secure* use of the TLS downgrade dance.

7.5.6 Securing the TLS downgrade dance: The SCSV cipher suite and beyond

Exercise 7.2 shows a potential vulnerability for a common case, where clients use the downgrade dance to ensure backward compatibility with servers supporting older (lower) versions of the TLS protocol. How can we mitigate this risk, while still allowing clients to use the TLS downgrade dance, in order to to interact with servers running older versions, that do not properly implement the TLS negotiation mechanism?

A standard solution is the *TLS fallback Signaling Cipher Suite Value (SCSV)* cipher suite, specified in RFC 7507 [360]. Clients that support SCSV, first try to connect to the server using their current TLS version — no change from clients not supporting SCSV. The difference is only when this initial connection fails, and the client decides to try the downgrade dance, to support connections with servers supporting (only) older versions of TLS.

In these downgrade dance handshakes, the client adds a special cipher suite to its list of supported *cipher suites*, sent as part of the ClientHello message. The special cipher suite is called *TLS_FALLBACK_SCSV* and is encoded by a specific string. Unlike the original (and main) goal of the *cipher suites* field, the SCSV is not an indication of cryptographic algorithms supported by the client. Instead, the existence of SCSV indicates to the server that this handshake message is sent as part of a downgrade dance by the client, i.e., that the client supports a *higher* version than the one specified in the current handshake. If the server receives such handshake, and supports a higher version of the protocol itself, this would indicate an error or attack, as this client and server should use the higher version. Therefore, in this case, the server responds with an appropriate indication to the client.

Note that if the attacker is able to expose the master key *during the handshake*, as done in the Logjam attack, then the SCSV defense is ineffective.

7.5.7 DROWN and other Cross-Protocol attacks

Modern protocols, such as (newer versions of) TLS, support secure extensions and backward compatible versions. However, there is yet an important element of secure extensibility that is sometimes neglected: *version-based key separation* (Section 2.7.4). Namely, suppose the same key — in particular, public-private key pair — is used by both a vulnerable protocol and a secure protocol. Then, it may be possible to expose the key by running the vulnerable protocol, and exploit this to attack the system also when using the secure protocol. This kind of attack is called a cross-protocol attack.

In Section 5.5.5, we have seen cross-protocol attacks against GSM. We now briefly mention the DROWN attack [24], a cross-protocol attack against TLS implementations, which is due to the lack of version-based key separation. A significant number of web servers were found to support SSLv2 *using the same public–private key pairs* as they use for improved-security TLS handshakes. This makes these servers vulnerable to an improved Bleichenbacher attack presented in Ref. [24], which allows to perform operations using the RSA private key.

7.5.8 The SSL-stripping attack and HSTS

To complete our discussion of downgrade attacks, we discuss what is probably the most extreme downgrade attack attack against TLS and SSL: Marlinspike's [347] *SSL-stripping* attack. In the SSL-stripping attack, the attacker tricks the client into using an *insecure (HTTP) connection*, i.e., not to use HTTPS (i.e., HTTP over TLS or SSL) at all. This is done although both server and client support HTTPS,

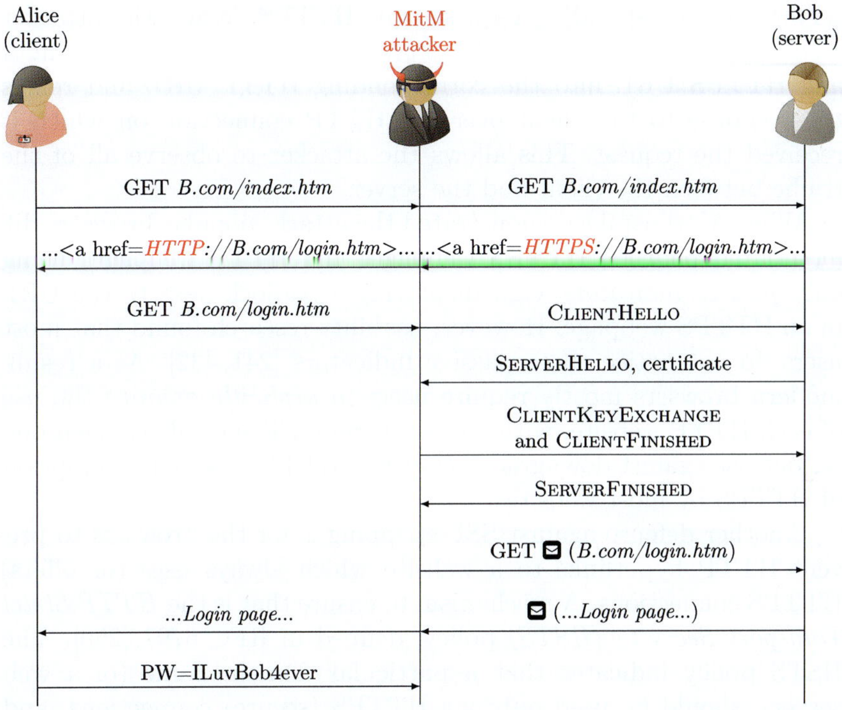

Figure 7.19. The *SSL-stripping* MitM Attack on an HTTPS website. For simplicity, we present the attack against a website *B.com* whose *index.htm* homepage is unprotected, but contains a link to a protected login page. Namely, the first flow from Alice is sent over an unprotected (HTTP) connection.

using compatible versions of SSL and TLS. We note that this attack is mostly of historical interest; it is not likely to succeed with updated browsers and using more modern websites, as we explain.

SSL-stripping is a MitM attack against a web server and may work even when the web server provides only HTTPS service (does not support unprotected HTTP connections). The attack assumes, however, that the browser (client) receives the website address (URL) over an unprotected (HTTP) connection.

The attacker modifies HTTPS URL sent to the client in responses over the unprotected (HTTP) connection, into the corresponding HTTP links. When the client follows these unprotected links and sends a request using HTTP, the attacker sends to the legitimate server the corresponding request over HTTPS. When the attacker receives the response from the server, the attacker again modifies any HTTPS URL into the corresponding HTTP URL and relays the response to the client over the HTTP connection on which it received the request. This allows the attacker to observe all of the traffic between the client and the server.

When Marlinspike demonstrated the attack, popular browsers differentiated between HTTPS webpages and HTTP webpages using only *passive indicators*, e.g., displaying a padlock next to the URL in an HTTPS webpage. However, usability research found that most users do not notice these passive indicators [241, 432]. As a result, modern browsers mostly require users to *explicitly approve* the use of each HTTP website, with a clear warning. The result is much better defense against downgrade attacks to HTTP – as well as adoption of HTTPS by most websites.

Another defense against SSL-stripping is for the browsers to prevent HTTP hyperlinks to a website which always uses (or offers) HTTPS connections. A mechanism to ensure that is the *HTTP Strict Transport Security (HSTS)* policy, defined in RFC 6797 [250]. The HSTS policy indicates that a particular domain name (of a web server), should be used only via HTTPS (secure) connections, and not via unprotected (HTTP) connections. HSTS is sent as an HTTP header field (Strict-Transport-Security), in an HTTP response sent by the web server to the client. The use of HSTS also instructs the browser to reject *invalid certificates*,[12] rather than prompt the user to decide on whether to use the invalid certificate or not.

The HSTS policy must be known to the browser *before* it connects to the server. This may be achieved in two ways:

Caching — *max-age*: The HSTS header field has a parameter called *max-age*, which defines a period of time during which the browser should 'remember' the HSTS directive, i.e., keep it in cache. Any connection within this time would be protected by

[12]Invalid certificates include certificates which do not have a valid certificate chain to a root certificate (including self-signed certificates), expired/revoked certificates, certificates with incorrect domain and certificates using weak or unsupported algorithms. See Chapter 8.

HSTS. Namely, suppose that at time T, a browser receives an HTTP response containing the HSTS header with *max-age* $= m$ from site *example.com*, over a secure connection (i.e., using TLS). Assume that later, but before time $T + m$, the browser again is directed to request an object from *example.com*; then the browser will open the link to *example.com* only over a secure connection, i.e., using TLS. This motivates the use of a large value for *max-age*, however, note that if a domain must move back to HTTP for some reason, or there are failures in the secure connection attempts for some reason, e.g., expired certificate, then the site may be unreachable for *max-age* seconds.

Pre-loaded HSTS policy: The browser maintains a list of HSTS domains which are *preloaded*, i.e., do not require a previous visit to the site by this browser. This avoids the risk of a browser accessing an HSTS-using website but without a cached HSTS policy. However, this requires the browser to be preloaded with the HSTS policy — a burden on the site and on the browser, and some overhead for this communication. An optional parameter of the HSTS header instructs web crawlers run by browser vendors to add the site to the HSTS preload list.

HSTS supports a reporting mechanism using which the browsers can report attempts to connect to a website for which HSTS is defined, but without using HTTPS, or using an invalid certificate. Reporting is done in addition to blocking of the website.

7.5.9 Three principles: Secure extensibility, KISS and minimize attack surface

The different downgrade attacks show the importance and the challenge of *secure backward compatible* upgrades. Backward compatibility is essential, to motivate adoption of a new versions of protocols. For example, without backward compatibility, a web server using SSLv2 is unlikely to upgrade to SSLv3, until most clients would upgrade to SSLv3; and clients would not upgrade to SSLv3, until there are many web servers they can interact with using SSLv3. We conclude that backward compatibility is essential for successful upgrade. On the other hand, we see that the backward compatibility mechanisms may allow vulnerabilities that can be exploited by downgrade attacks. It is therefore necessary to ensure a *secure extension mechanism allowing backward compatibility*. In particular, every practical security protocol should support a *secure version negotiation* mechanism.

We conclude the principle of *secure extensibility by design*, which requires built-in secure mechanisms for extensions and backward compatibility. This is another important design principle for secure systems and protocols, cryptographic or otherwise.

Principle 13 (Secure extensibility by design). *When designing security systems or protocols, one goal must be to build-in secure mechanisms for extensions, downward compatible versions, and negotiation of options and cryptographic algorithms (cipher suite negotiation).*

However, backward compatibility, like other options and extensions, increases the *attack surface* and makes the system *more complex*, both of which imply greater risk of vulnerabilities. Let us discuss these two issues.

First, *flexibility brings complexity, and vulnerabilities lurk in complexity*: the simpler the system, the easier it is to protect. This is the important *KISS principle.*[13]

Principle 14 (The Keep It Simple and Secure (KISS) Principle). *The simpler a system is, the easier it is to protect; for better security, minimize complexity, options, flexibility and extensibility.*

The KISS principle is closely related to the *minimize attack surface* principle. Let us first explain the concepts of *attack surface* and *attack vector*. An attack vector is an element of the system, which may have a flaw which can be exploited by an attacker to 'break' the system; attack vectors may be defined in different ways, e.g., functions, classes, lines of code, cryptographic functions, API calls, software/hardware modules or protocol variants. The *attack surface* is a rough measure of the number or extent of the attack vectors in a given system. In a simplified case, let n denote the attack surface,

[13]The KISS principle originates from the US navy, where it meant 'Keep It Simple, Stupid'. We changed it a bit, to *Keep It Simple and Secure (KISS)*.

corresponding to n attack vectors, each with probability p_v of a (discovered) vulnerability. The probability that the overall system will be secure, i.e., not have any discovered vulnerability, is only $(1 - p_v)^n$. Hence, we need to minimize 'attack surface', n, as well as to minimize the probability of vulnerability, p_v.

Principle 15 (Minimize the attack surface). *Systems should be designed to minimize their* attack surface, *i.e., minimize the number of their* attack vectors. *Roughly, the probability of vulnerability of a system, is exponential in the number of attack vectors.*

7.6 The TLS 1.3 handshake: Improved security and performance

In this section, we (finally) discuss the handshake protocol of the current version of TLS, which is TLS 1.3 [412]. Both the TLS 1.3 handshake protocol and the TLS 1.3 (AEAD) record protocol (Figure 7.6) are major re-designs, whose main goal was improved performance and security compared to earlier versions. Another goal was to *simplify*, a goal on its own right, but also helping to improve security by reducing the risk of vulnerabilities, following the KISS principle (Principle 14).

Note that while TLS 1.3 indeed benefits from significant simplifications, it also introduces new complexities; arguably, these complexities can be justified by the security benefits they provide to different scenarios.

In our description of TLS 1.3, we make some additional simplifications, to focus on the main aspects and innovations and avoid technical details.

While TLS 1.3 supports backwards compatibility, it is not always consistent with previous versions; consistency with previous versions was *not* a main goal for TLS 1.3. Indeed, the TLS 1.3 handshake protocol, and especially the key derivation mechanisms, differ considerably from previous versions, even in the terminology used. For example, the term *premaster key* is not used. This, unfortunately, adds another challenge to the reader familiar with the previous versions.

TLS 1.3 security improvements: The security improvements of the TLS 1.3 handshake include the following:

- TLS 1.3 has significantly improved defenses against downgrade attacks, including *version downgrade attacks*; see Section 7.6.1.
- TLS 1.3 does not support the (previously widely used) RSA-based key exchange. This avoids many attacks on RSA implementations, mainly variants of *Bleichenbacher's attack*, such as DROWN (Section 7.5.7 and Ref. [24]) and ROBOT [89]. Note, however, that TLS 1.3 still allows the use of RSA signatures for authentication of the handshake flows, including of the public DH values. The signature can be vulnerable to a cross-protocol attack, if (incorrectly) using the same RSA private key for TLS 1.3 CertificateVerify signature, as the key used by insecure protocols such as earlier TLS versions; see Section 7.6.6.
- TLS 1.3 handshake always uses DHE key exchange to provide a fresh secret shared key in every exchange, using either finite fields or elliptic curves. This ensures *perfect forward secrecy* (*PFS*; Definition 5.3). Note, however, that TLS 1.3 does not ensure *perfect recover security (PRS)* since it relies on the secrecy of the server's private key for signing the exchange; see Exercise 7.20. The reliance on a fixed private key was exploited by the few known attacks against the TLS 1.3 handshake protocol, which motivates periodic key updates. The use of this single key-exchange mechanism helps simplify the handshake.
- TLS 1.3 disallows the use of other cipher suites with known weaknesses, most notably, these using 'export-grade' cryptography. This foils cipher suite downgrade attacks which exploits the use of weak, 'export-grade' cryptography, such as the Logjam attack [7], exploiting support for 512 bit DH groups, and the FREAK attack [67], exploiting the use of ephemeral 512 bit RSA private keys. We discuss both of these attacks in Section 7.5.3.
- Previous versions of TLS allowed the server to specify an arbitrary DH group, by sending the modulus p and generator g. This allows different servers to select different groups, which may help foil discrete-logarithm precomputation attacks such as in the Logjam attack (Section 7.5.3). However, as in many cases, *flexibility resulted in vulnerability*; in particular, many servers ended up using *weak groups* (and often, the same weak groups). TLS 1.3 uses

standard finite groups or elliptic curves; these should correspond to carefully chosen groups and curves, properly defined, e.g., in Refs. [206, 316]. This use of specific, studied groups/curves follows the cryptographic building blocks principle (Principle 8).

- In the TLS 1.3 Server_Key_Exchange message, the server signs the *entire* handshake, not just the DHE parameters and the client and server random numbers (r_C and r_S) as in previous versions. In particular, when the client receives and validates this signed Server_Key_Exchange, it confirms that the server received correctly the supported-versions, cipher suites and supported-groups information sent in ClientHello. This defends against downgrade attacks (Section 7.5).
- For signatures and hashing, TLS 1.3 forbids the use of the vulnerable RSA PKCS #1 v1.5 and SHA-1 algorithms. Secure alternatives are specified instead: PSS padding for signatures and for hashing, SHA-256, SHA-384 or SHA-512. See PKCS #1 v2.2 (RFC 8017), RFC 5756 and RFC4055 [364, 430, 461].
- TLS 1.3 removed support for handshake *renegotiation*. Renegotiation added complexity, vulnerabilities (e.g., Refs. [70, 414]) and attack surface. TLS 1.3 provides an alternative mechanism to support the main use case for renegotiation, which is, invoking client authentication only 'as-needed', after the handshake completes.
- TLS 1.3 design prefers cryptographic designs which are amenable to proofs of security, and hence their security is more well established, even at the cost of (reasonable) extra complexity. This is done *without* requiring an explicit attack exploiting the previous, intuitive or less-established design. In particular, the TLS 1.3 key derivation process, which we discuss in Section 7.6.5, is based on provably secure cryptographic constructions — but is arguably more complex than key derivation in previous versions of TLS.
- TLS 1.3 specifies the use of *PSK*. This single mechanism replaces multiple mechanisms in previous versions: different PSK-based cipher suites, with and without DH [26, 27, 175], as well as session resumption, both ID-based and session ticket based (Section 7.4.4).
- TLS 1.3 protects fields and messages as soon as the necessary keys are established. In particular, it protects the extensions sent in the ServerHello and later messages, and it protects the Certificate (sent after ServerHello). One benefit from

protecting the certificate is improved *privacy*. Namely, consider an eavesdropper on the communication between Alice's browser and a TLS-protected server; the eavesdropper cannot decipher the application-layer communication (since it's done over TLS); however, when using versions prior to TLS 1.3, the eavesdropper may be able to identify the server used by Alice, by viewing the server's certificate. In TLS 1.3, the certificate is sent encrypted, which may prevent this identification — assuming that the server cannot be identified using other means such as its IP address or timing of responses.

TLS 1.3 Performance Improvement — reduced latency overhead (less round trips): The main *performance improvement* of TLS 1.3 handshake is due to *reduced handshake latency*, which results mainly from the reduction in the number of round trips. Most applications use the *request-response* communication pattern, where the client sends a request to the server who sends back a response. The *handshake latency* is the time since the client application initiated the connection (and transferred the request to the client's TLS module), and until it receives the response from the server.

Modern networks use fast transmission rates; hence the latency is mostly due to propagation and queuing delays. Namely, as explained in Fact 5.1 and illustrated in Table 5.2, the dominant factors in determining the delay are the number of round trips and the Round Trip Time (RTT); we can mostly ignore the transmission time of the packets. This means that it doesn't matter that much if we send somewhat longer messages or multiple messages consecutively, without waiting for a response. The latency is mostly determined by the delay due to *waiting* for a response before sending the next message, i.e., by the number of *round trips*.

Clearly, request-response interaction requires at least one *round trip*: sending the request to the server and receiving the response. In addition, any protocol running over TCP, including HTTP, requires another round trip for the TCP handshake. Previous versions of TLS require *two more round trips*: one for the CLIENTHELLO and SERVERHELLO interaction, and another for the CLIENTFINISHED and SERVERFINISHED interaction (including the CLIENTKEYEXCHANGE message). See Figures 7.3 and 7.7.

In contrast, the typical TLS 1.3 handshake requires only *one round trip* (on top of the TCP round trip and the request-response round trip). Furthermore, TLS 1.3 supports a *zero round trips* handshake,[14] where *one* client request, containing *some* application data, can be sent as part of the initial flow from the client; see Section 7.6.4.

Our presentation of the TLS 1.3 handshake protocol: In the following sections, we present a simplified overview of the TLS 1.3 handshake protocol, covering the most important aspects of the protocol. In Section 7.6.1, we discuss the TLS 1.3 negotiation and backward compatibility mechanisms. In Section 7.6.2, we discuss the TLS 1.3 1-RTT ('full') DH handshake. In Section 7.6.3, we discuss the PSK handshake, used to support both off-band shared keys and session resumption. In Section 7.6.4, we discuss the *zero-TTL handshake*, which avoids entirely the delay-overhead of earlier versions of TLS and even of the 'full' TLS 1.3 handshake. In Section 7.6.5, we discuss the *key derivation* process of the TLS 1.3 handshake protocol. Finally, in Section 7.6.6, we discuss *cross-protocol attacks*, which are the only attacks known to the author that exploit a vulnerability in the TLS 1.3 specifications.

Overall, we tried to cover the most important aspects of the TLS 1.3 handshake mechanism. However, we had to make some simplifications and omissions. As one important example, see Exercise 7.23, which discusses the risk of *DoS* on TLS servers, and two defenses against it, including using the *Cookie* extension. The Cookie extension can also be used to off-load state from the TLS server to the client, see Ref. [412].

7.6.1 TLS 1.3 negotiation and backward compatibility

In Section 7.5, we discussed the cipher suite and version negotiation mechanisms of previous versions of TLS. The redesign of TLS 1.3

[14]The number of one and zero round trips refers only to the round trips required by TLS, on top of round trips necessary even without TLS. In reality, any request-response requires a round trip; if done over TCP, then the TCP handshake required an additional round trip.

includes a significant change in these negotiation mechanisms. However, this redesign was done carefully to ensure backward compatibility with earlier versions of TLS.

7.6.1.1 *Cipher suite negotiation*

In previous versions of TLS, as well as SSLv3, the cipher suites defined three separate aspects: (1) the record protocol ciphers, e.g., AES, (2) the key exchange mechanism (RSA, DH or PSK), and (3) the signature algorithm. This resulted in an exponential explosion in the number of cipher suites, with unnecessary complexity (and room for error).

TLS 1.3 separates the cipher suite negotiations info *four* distinct aspects:

Record protocol cipher suite: The AEAD algorithm and the hash function used for key derivation.

DH group: The DH group (or elliptic curve).

Signature algorithm: The signature algorithm used for server authentication, i.e., to sign the SERVERFINISHED message.

Pre-Shared Key: Identifies pre-shared keys and specifies whether such keys are to be used to authenticate a DH key exchange, providing *PFS*, or to be used directly as the shared secret between the parties. See Section 7.6.3.

7.6.1.2 *TLS 1.3 version negotiation: The Supported_Versions extension and server-random signaling*

TLS included a version negotiation mechanism from early on; however, as we discussed in Section 7.6.1, many TLS servers did not implement it correctly, leading clients to adopt the insecure downgrade dance and exposing them to the Poodle version downgrade attack.

Upon early, experimental deployment of TLS 1.3, it was discovered that many TLS servers *still* do not implement this version negotiation mechanism. At first, it appeared that clients should be able to use downgrade dance securely, by using the *SCSV* extension (Section 7.5.6), designed to prevent a MitM attacker from causing unnecessary downgrades. No such luck; it was soon realized that there are also many TLS 1.2 servers that do not support SCSV, which would have allowed a Poodle-like downgrade attack against TLS 1.3.

The TLS 1.3 designers decided to *change the version negotiation mechanism*, in a way which is *backward compatible with TLS 1.2 and TLS 1.1 servers.* Specifically:

1. TLS 1.3 clients list the versions they support, in order of preference, in the *Supported_Versions* extension. Supported_Versions is a new *mandatory* extension, which should be supported by all new TLS servers and clients (running version 1.3 or future versions). If this extension is absent, the server should continue the handshake using TLS 1.2. If the extension is present, the server uses the 'best' version supported both by the client and by itself and indicates it in the Supported_Versions extension sent back (with SERVERHELLO).
2. Clients running TLS 1.3 can support interoperability with servers running TLS 1.2 or older versions by sending a CLIENTHELLO message which is compatible with TLS 1.2, *including the version identifier of TLS 1.2*, rather than that of TLS 1.3. TLS servers running version 1.2 or an earlier version should handle this correctly, if they implement version negotiation correctly. TLS 1.3 servers will manage since they use the *Supported_Versions* extension, which provides a *new version negotiation mechanism.*
3. A TLS 1.3 server can support interoperability with clients running older versions of TLS as well as clients running SSLv3 using one of the following two options:

   Supported_Versions: The first option is when the client uses the *Supported_Versions* extension; in this case, version negotiation can proceed just like with clients supporting TLS 1.3 (or future versions).

   Server-random signaling: The second option is used upon receiving a CLIENTHELLO indicating an older version and without the *Supported_Versions* extension. To support such clients, the server can respond with a SERVERHELLO formatted like in TLS 1.2 (or even TLS 1.1). However, to allow TLS 1.3 clients to detect a possible downgrade attack, the server signals this by encoding a fixed special value in the 8 least-significant bytes of the server random string r_S. TLS 1.3 clients abort the handshake if they detect the special value in the server random they receive in the SERVERHELLO message. A different value is used for downgrade to TLS 1.1 vs. downgrade to TLS 1.2, allowing TLS 1.2 clients to detect downgrades to TLS 1.1.

For more details on the TLS 1.3 version negotiation and its defenses against downgrade attacks, see the specifications (RFC 8446 [412]) and the analysis in Ref. [68]. See also Ref. [324] for a downgrade attack attack exploiting vulnerabilities in some implementations of TLS 1.3.

7.6.2 TLS 1.3 full (1-RTT) DH handshake

We next present the TLS 1.3 1-RTT DH handshake, illustrated in Figure 7.20. This is the typical initial TLS 1.3 handshake, always

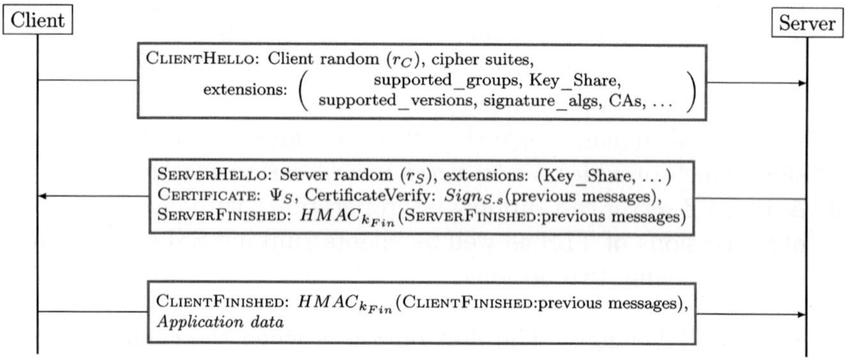

Figure 7.20. TLS 1.3 1-RTT full Diffie–Hellman handshake. To ensure the integrity of the handshake, the CertificateVerify message contains a signature over the entire *handshake* until it, i.e., including all of the messages; similarly, the CLIENTFINISHED and SERVERFINISHED messages contain a MAC (specifically, HMAC) over all of the messages sent and received before them (including CertificateVerify and, for CLIENTFINISHED, also including SERVERFINISHED). All of the messages in the handshake protocol, and application messages sent after the handshake is completed, are protected by the record protocol, using different derived keys, as described in Section 7.6.5; e.g., when a PSK is available, it is used to protect the CLIENTHELLO message. The k_{Fin} key, used for the HMAC computed in the CLIENTFINISHED and SERVERFINISHED messages, is also similarly derived.

used by a client and server on their first connection, and optionally used in subsequent connections.

In contrast to the previous sections (and previous versions of TLS), the TLS 1.3 full handshake *always* uses the DH key agreement protocol for key exchange; therefore, it *always* ensures PFS.

The handshake ensures server authentication using the server's signature over the initial handshake messages, sent in a message called CERTIFICATEVERIFY. This signature authenticates the server's DH component ($g_i^{b_i} \bmod p_i$). By including the initial handshake messages in the signed content, the signature also protects against downgrade attacks.

The TLS 1.3 full (1-RTT) handshake allows the client to send the request after a *single* round-trip; that's why it is called a *1-RTT* handshake. Namely, the server (single) flow contains both the SERVERHELLO message (with the server's DH exponent, extensions, certificate and signature) *and* the SERVERFINISHED message, which ensures the integrity of the exchange.

In order to allow the server to send the *finished:* message in its (single) flow, it has to receive all the necessary keying information from the client earlier — i.e., already in the CLIENTHELLO message. Since TLS 1.3 always uses DH key exchange, this means that the client must send sufficient information for the server to determine the group (for finite field DH) or curve (for Elliptic Curves DH) to be used; furthermore, the client needs to even provide its DH public key share (e.g., $g^a \bmod p$). TLS 1.3 can provide all this information efficiently in the CLIENTHELLO, by supporting only a limited number of *standard DH finite groups and elliptic curves.*

The client indicates the DH groups (including elliptic curves) that it supports, in the SUPPORTED_GROUPS extension, and its DH public key share, in the KEY_SHARE extension. Both extensions *must* be sent as part of the TLS 1.3 CLIENTHELLO message. There is a cost here in overhead of computing and sending these values — but the savings in RTT are usually much more significant. The client may provide the public key share only for some of the groups; if there is no public key share for the group preferred by the server, the server can send a special message, HELLORETRYREQUEST, and the client will send a 'corrected' CLIENTHELLO. (In this case, the handshake will require two RTTs.)

Three other mandatory extensions in the TLS 1.3 CLIENT HELLO identify: (1) the SUPPORTED_VERSIONS, (2) the SIGNATURE_ALGORITHMS supported and (3) the CERTIFICATE_AUTHORITIES (CAs) trusted by the client. By requiring the supported versions extension, TLS 1.3 protects against version downgrades. The goal of the two other mandatory extensions is, apparently, to avoid incompatibilities, i.e., a situation where the server may use a signing algorithm not supported by the client, or a certificate from a CA not supported by the client.

The SERVERHELLO message is quite similar to the SERVERHELLO of previous versions, except that it also provides the server's public key share for the DH exchange, in an aptly named extension. It is followed by the server's certificate and the TLS 1.3 CERTIFICATE-VERIFY message, which authenticates the server *and* ensures the handshake integrity, by including a signature over the entire handshake (to this point). Finally, the server sends its (authenticated) SERVERFINISHED message, again much like in previous versions (just earlier!).

The final flow of the handshake contains the CLIENTFINISHED message, authenticating the entire handshake (until this point), much like in earlier versions.

The TLS 1.3 record protocol and using it to protect the handshake: Both client and SERVERFINISHED messages may be followed immediately by application data sent by the respective parties, protected by the TLS 1.3 record protocol, using the shared key. As described in Section 7.2.7, the TLS 1.3 record protocol uses AEAD to protect both the confidentiality and the authenticity of the messages, requiring only one (shared) key in each direction. As for SSLv2, we use k_C to denote the key used to protect application messages from client to server and k_S to denote the key used to protect application messages from server to client. Note that TLS 1.3 also uses the record protocol (and AEAD) to protect the messages of the handshake but with different keys: $\hat{k}_C$ for handshake messages from client to server and $\hat{k}_S$ for handshake messages from server to client.

7.6.3 TLS 1.3 full (1-RTT) Pre-Shared Key (PSK) handshake

The TLS 1.3 PSK mechanism can be used for *session resumption*, using a key shared in an earlier session, or with out-of-band PSKs, as previously supported by several special cipher suites [26, 27, 175]. The mechanism is based on *session tickets* and does not require the server to maintain state for each client or session ticket, much like the session ticket extension mechanism used with earlier versions of TLS. See Figure 7.21, which shows how the client sends a session ticket in the ClientHello message, to complete the TLS 1.3 handshake using a PSK. The figure is for the 'full', 1-RTT handshake.

For both session resumption and out-of-band pre-shared keys, TLS 1.3 supports two *PSK modes*, which offer different costs and benefits:

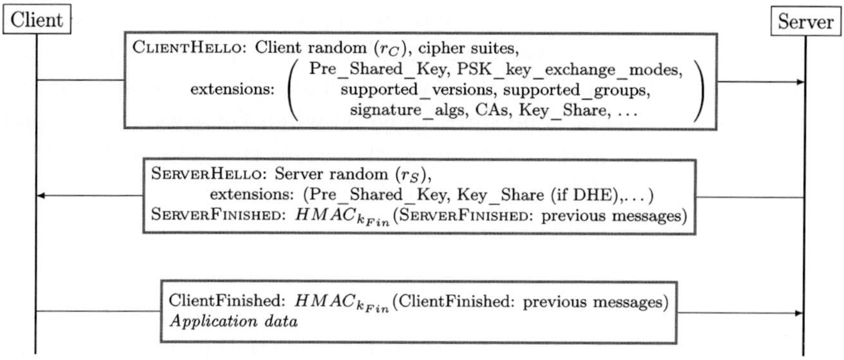

Figure 7.21. TLS 1.3 full (1-RTT) Pre-Shared Key (PSK) handshake; the ClientHello message includes a session ticket from a *Pre_Shared_Key* extension received from the server in a previous handshake. The PSK_key_exchange_modes extension can be used to indicate if the PSK can be used to authenticate a DHE (providing PFS) and/or to provide shared-key only handshake (without PFS). All of the messages in the handshake protocol, and application messages sent after the handshake is completed, are protected by the record protocol, using different derived keys, as described in Section 7.6.5; e.g., when a PSK is available, it is used to protect the ClientHello message. The k_{Fin} key, used for the HMAC computed in the ClientFinished and ServerFinished messages, is also similarly derived.

The PSK key exchange (PSK_KE) mode: The PSK is used to secure the session without the use of DH key exchange, or any other public key operation. The advantage is reduced computational costs and associated delay and energy costs; as shown in Table 6.1, symmetric cryptography requires a tiny fraction of the computational resources required by public-key cryptography. There is also a reduction in the amount of data sent, which is meaningful in some unusual situations; usually, this reduction is insignificant. The disadvantage of the a PSK key exchange (PSK_KE) mode is that it does not ensure *PFS*.

The PSK and DHE (PSK_DHE_KE) mode: The pre-shared key is used to authenticate the DH key exchange, instead of using the server's certificate and signature (with the CertificateVerify message). This mode has three uses. The first is simply to reduce the overhead of the transmission and verification of the certificate and the signature, while retaining the added security provided by PFS. The second is to use is for scenarios where the server does not have a certificate and cannot perform the certificate-based verification (CertificateVerify message), and the security of the DH key exchange is based on the shared-key authentication. The third usage is when the server does send both certificate and signature; in this case, the goal is the added security provided by the shared key, e.g., in case of exposure of the server's private key.

In Figure 7.21, we focus on the session resumption case, by presenting a handshake which *uses* the PSK from the previously sent ticket, to *resume the session*, i.e., performing a pre-shared key handshake.

The PSK_key_exchange_modes extension specifies which Pre-Shared Key mode(s) the client wants to use: the PSK key exchange (PSK_KE) mode and/or the PSK and DHE key exchange (PSK_DHE_KE) mode. This extension is relevant for the use of the PSK in the current handshake (if it uses a PSK) and for any new pre-shared keys which the server may share using the NewSessionTicket message.

The NewSessionTicket message provides the client with one or more 'tickets'. The ticket(s) sent after a successful handshake, refer to a PSK, derived from a dedicated shared secret called the RESUMPTION_MASTER_SECRET (rms). The RESUMPTION_MASTER_SECRET is one of the secrets and keys derived for the session; the derivation uses a keyed function, which we denote h^{Expand}. As a simplification, consider rms to be a secret key, and h^{Expand} to be a PRF; for more precise details, see Section 7.6.5.

The PSK associated with the ticket is derived from the *ticket_nonce*, which is one of the fields sent in the NEWSESSIONTICKET, and the RESUMPTION_MASTER_SECRET (rms), as follows:

$$PSK(ticket\_nonce) = h^{\text{Expand}}_{\text{rms}}(\text{`resumption'}, ticket\_nonce) \quad (7.18)$$

The CLIENTHELLO message of the handshake using the PSK includes two PSK-related extensions: the *PSK_key_exchange_modes* extension, discussed above, and the *Pre_Shared_Key extension.* The Pre_Shared_Key extension identifies one or more pre-shared keys known to the client, allowing the server to use any of these that the server may have cached to establish the new connection. For session resumption, the PSK identifier is the *ticket*, provided in a previous NEWSESSIONTICKET message. The server also uses the Pre_Shared_Key extension to signal that it uses a specific pre-shared key (from the list provided by the client).

In Figure 7.21, the handshake contains the Key_Share extension. This extension includes the server's DH public key share and, therefore, is used if, and only if, using the DH key exchange (with finite field or elliptic curve). We conclude, therefore, that the client's PSK_key_exchange_modes extension allowed the use of PSK_KE, which was then chosen by the server.

7.6.4 TLS 1.3 zero-RTT Pre-Shared Key (PSK) handshake

In Figure 7.22, we present the *TLS 1.3 zero-RTT PSK handshake.* This is a special form of a PSK handshake, in which we use the PSK to *secure some data sent in the* CLIENTHELLO message. Specifically, this data is contained in records which sent in the first flow, sent from the client to the server, rather than with the third flow, after the handshake is complete, as in the full (1-RTT) TLS handshake.

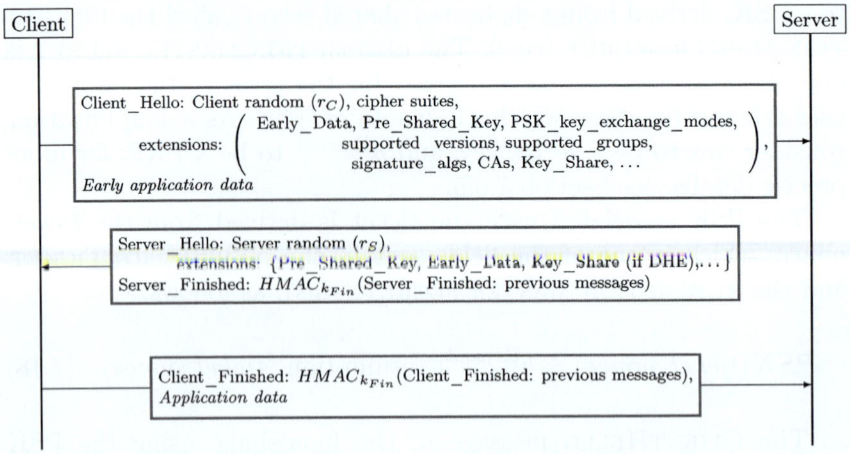

Figure 7.22. TLS 1.3 Zero-RTT Pre-Shared Key (PSK) Handshake (simplified). The client provides some 'early application data' to the server immediately after the Client_Hello message, without waiting for the server's response. All of the messages in the handshake protocol, and application messages including the early-data records, are protected by the record protocol, using different derived keys, as described in Section 7.6.5; when a PSK is available, it is used to protect the ClientHello message. The k_{Fin} key, used for the HMAC computed in the ClientFinished and ServerFinished messages, is also similarly derived. Note that the server responses — even to the early data — are sent only after the handshake successfully completes.

Since *Early_Data* is sent as part of the very first flow of the connection, the delay until it arrive includes only the time since the client sends this message and until the server receives it. Namely, there is no need to wait for any round trip of handshake messages, before the client can send this 'early' application data to the server. In other words, the *Early_Data* is sent without waiting for any round trips to complete, i.e., with *zero RTT latency.* The only delay is, therefore, the unavoidable time for the data itself to transfer from client to server, and for the TCP handshake. Note that it is also possible to avoid the round-trip time of the TCP handshake, by using protocols which do not require a handshake for the (secure) delivery of data, typically by running over the connectionless UDP transport protocol rather than over the connection-based TCP transport protocol. This includes DTLS [413, 417], which is essentially TLS over UDP, and QUIC [162, 264], which integrates the functions of TCP and of TLS. These protocols, however, are beyond our scope.

The Early_Data does not benefit from all the protections offered by TLS. In particular, it is only protected by the PSK; therefore, it does not benefit from PFS. Furthermore, an attacker can replay the CLIENTHELLO message; this may cause the server to re-process the Early_Data records, unless appropriate countermeasures prevent this (see the following). Therefore, *Early_Data* should only be used for client requests which do not require PFS, and either where re-processing is allowed, or with appropriate countermeasures to prevent re-processing. A typical example for a legitimate, common use of Early_Data (and zero-RTT handshake), where both the lack of PFS and the possibility for re-processing are not a concern, is when the client sends a query to the server, authenticated by a password or cookie sent with the request, and receives back a (protected) response. Note that this refers to a query, such as inquiring about the balance, but not a transaction, such as making a payment.

Two alternative countermeasures against re-processing of Early_Data are possible. The first possible countermeasure is to allow each ticket to be used only once; this requires the server to maintain track of already-used tickets, similarly to the use of session-ID for session resumption in earlier versions. An alternative countermeasure is to limit the lifetime of the ticket, using the *ticket_lifetime* field of the NEWSESSIONTICKET message.

7.6.5 TLS 1.3 key derivation

TLS 1.3 makes extensive use of key derivation, using a pair of keyed functions: a *key expansion* function h^{Expand} and a *key extraction* function $h^{Extract}$. Both functions are defined in Ref. [306], based on the *HMAC* construction and a given hash function h. The hash function h is defined as part of the TLS 1.3 cipher suite.

The key expansion function h^{Expand} is similar to a PRF; like a PRF, it should receive a pseudorandom key, and outputs a pseudorandom string. The length of its output pseudorandom string is specified as one of its inputs. It receives one more input, which is basically the input information to the PRF. The TLS specifications defines different inputs for each derivation.

The key extraction function $h^{Extract}$ is similar to a keyed *Key Derivation Function (KDF)*. Namely, the output of $h_x(y)$ is a (short) pseudorandom string, provided the *either* (a) x is pseudorandom (secret) and y is a unique value, *or* (b) x is a 'salt' (randomly chosen but known to attacker), and y is a high-entropy string, i.e., intuitively, contains 'sufficient secret random bits'.

The TLS 1.3 handshake protocol applies $h^{Extract}$ and h^{Expand} to derive multiple pseudorandom, independent keys for different purposes. Simplifying:

1. When using a PSK, we use it (or actually, a key derived from it) as a key to h^{Expand}, to generate several pseudorandom 'early secrets/keys'. We use one key to protect the Early_Data (if sent), and another key, which we denote k_1, as the key for the next derivation step.
2. We next derive $k_{handshake} = h^{Extract}_{k_1}(\text{shared\_secret})$, where shared_secret is the (mostly) secret output of the DH key exchange. We use $k_{handshake}$ as the key to h^{Expand}, to generate several pseudorandom keys, including a key to protect client-to-server handshake messages, a key to protect server-to-client handshake messages and a key k_2 which we use for the next derivation step.
3. We next derive $k_{\text{Master}} = h^{Extract}_{k_2}(0)$. We use k_{Master} as the key to h^{Expand}, to generate pseudorandom keys, including a key to protect client-to-server application messages and a key to protect server-to-client application messages.

7.6.6 Cross-protocol attacks on TLS 1.3

We complete out discussion of TLS 1.3 by briefly discussing *cross-protocol attacks*, a type of attacks which *can* be effective against standard-complying implementations of TLS 1.3; arguably, the standard could have specified certain countermeasures which would have prevented this, as we discuss in the following.

First, recall that cross-protocol attacks are attacks which exploit a vulnerability in one ('weak') protocol P_W, to attack another, 'strong' protocol, P_S. The attacks exploit *two* flaws: the vulnerability of P_W, and the fact that P_S and P_W use the same private/secret key, in violation of the *key separation principle* (Section 2.7.4).

In particular, while TLS 1.3 does not use RSA encryption, *TLS 1.3 does use signatures* — often RSA signatures — for CERTIFICATEVERIFY. In many implementations, the same private key is used for these TLS 1.3 RSA signatures, and for vulnerable RSA decryption, typically, using version 1.5 or 2.0 of PKCS #1. In particular, many TLS 1.3 implementations were found to use the same private key (to sign CERTIFICATEVERIFY) as used for RSA decryption by older TLS implementations (of the same organization). This allows use of the Bleichenbacher attack and variants of it, e.g., Manger's attack, to allows the attacker to 'perform the private-key RSA operation', potentially allowing the attacker to sign the CERTIFICATEVERIFY message.

One variant of this attack was published in Ref. [265]; however, it required quite extensive computational abilities from the attacker. The DROWN attack (Section 7.5.7, [24]), published a year later, is a much more efficient and practical attack, but it is only applicable if the same private RSA key was also used in an implementation of SSLv2; we find it surprising that the researchers found that even in 2016, there was a very significant number of web servers which supported SSLv2 *and* reused the same private key for TLS 1.3 signing and SSLv2 decryption. *Old versions die slowly.*

These cross-protocol attacks are not necessarily a major concern for the use of TLS 1.3, for two reasons. The first reason is a technical challenge: the attacker must complete the attack, and in particular abuse the lower-version TLS version to sign the CERTIFICATEVERIFY message, before the client aborts the connection (due to not receiving CERTIFICATEVERIFY in time). This challenge makes deployment of the attack challenging — but it may still be possible in some scenarios.

The second reason for cross-protocol attacks to be of limited concern, is that the attacks only works when the TLS 1.3 implementation *uses the same private key* (for signatures) as used by lower versions of TLS (for encryption). Such reuse of the same key for two different purposes (decryption and signing) and by two different versions of TLS should be avoided; indeed, it is a 'double violation' of the key separation principle (Section 2.7.4). Implementations of TLS 1.3 should avoid this, and use a different private (signing) key then the private (decryption) key used by lower versions.

Furthermore, typically, the same private key is used for two different purposes and protocol, only when using also the same *certificate*. Specifically, TLS 1.3 could require that the certificate contains a KEY USAGE extension, that explicitly *forbids* its use for decryption. While this would not absolutely prevent cross-protocol attacks, it would probably make them extremely unlikely, as certificates of keys currently used (for encryption) by older versions of TLS are unlikely to contain a KEY USAGE extension forbiddings the use of the private key for decryption. For details about the KEY USAGE and other certificate extensions, see Section 8.2.2.

7.7 TLS: Final words and further reading

The TLS protocols are the most widely used, and definitely the most studied, applied cryptographic protocol. Extensive efforts by many cryptographers and security experts were invested in validating and improving the security of TLS. It is instructive to observe that these efforts resulted in the discovery of a large number of serious vulnerabilities. We discussed several of these, focusing on specification vulnerabilities. We summarize some of the most important TLS specifications vulnerabilities in Table 7.2.

We did not cover many of the *implementation vulnerabilities*, although some of them, in particular the Heartbleed bug [118, 501], had comparable and even greater impact.

We can learn some important lessons from this history of attacks and improvements, including:

A crack today, a break tomorrow: Many devastating attacks, e.g., BEAST and Poodle, can be traced to vulnerabilities reported years earlier, but ignored since they appeared impractical. Or as stated in Ref. [10], *attacks only get better*.

Vulnerabilities die hard: Even after a vulnerability has been discovered and countermeasures adopted, attackers are often able to continue taking advantage of the vulnerability, in different ways. First, attackers are often able to adjust the attack and circumvent the countermeasures. Second, attacker are often able to *downgrade* the system to use an outdated, vulnerable version, possibly using downgrade attacks. Third, attackers are sometimes able to use

Table 7.2. Important TLS/SSL attacks due to specifications vulnerabilities.

Name	Year	References	Versions	Ciphers	Type
BEAST	2011	§7.2.4, [165]	SSL, TLS 1.0	CBC	Cryptanalysis
CRIME	2012	§7.2.6, [419]	TLS 1.0-1.1	n/a	Compression
Lucky13	2013	§7.2.3, [10]	SSL, TLS 1.0-1.2	CBC	Padding, timing
RC4-biases	2013	§7.2.5, [13]	SSL, TLS 1.0-1.2	RC4	Cryptanalysis
BREACH	2013	§7.2.6, [208]	TLS 1.0-1.2	n/a	Compression
TIME	2013	§7.2.6, [36]	TLS 1.0-1.2	n/a	Compression
Poodle-padding	2014	§7.2.3, [362]	SSLv3	CBC	Padding
Poodle-downgrade	2014	§7.5.5, [362]	TLS 1.0-1.2	n/a	Version downgrade
FREAK	2015	§7.5.3, [67]	TLS 1.0-1.2	RSA	Cipher suite downgrade
Cross-Bleichenbacher	2015	§7.6.6, [265]	TLS 1.3	RSA	Cross-protocol and Bleichenbacher
DROWN	2016	§7.6.6, [24]	TLS 1.0-1.3	RSA	Cross protocol and Bleichenbacher
Logjam	2018	§7.5.3, [7]	TLS 1.0-1.2	DHE	Cipher suite downgrade
ROBOT	2018	[89]	TLS 1.0-1.2	RSA	Bleichenbacher
Bleichenbacher's CAT	2019	§7.5.4, [423]	TLS 1.0-1.3	RSA	Bleichenbacher and downgrade

cross-protocol attacks, where they exploit a vulnerable system to circumvent the (strong) defenses of *another* system which uses the same keys. It is much better to design systems securely from early on; of course, an advice easier given than followed. At least, use a conservative design (Principle 3).

Separate keys: Cross-protocol attacks such as DROWN [24] remind us of the importance of *key separation* (Section 2.7.4). The use of TLS 1.3, or of any secure protocol, may not help, if we reuse the same private key in an insecure way, allowing key exposure.

Test, test, test: While we focused on specification flaws, many attacks on TLS, exploit *implementation flaws*, e.g., the Heartbleed bug. Testing for security is difficult, however, vital for the security of the system, since vulnerabilities will not be detected by normal use of the system. Of course, testing is harder for larger and more complex systems; which brings us to the next and final item.

KISS! Finally, we see again and again the importance of the Keep It Simple and Secure (KISS) principle (Principle 14): keep specifications, design and code small and simple, minimize complexity and attack surface and avoid unnecessary options and flexibility. The KISS principle is important against both specification and implementation vulnerabilities. The design of TLS 1.3 began with an extensive effort to follow this principle and eliminate unnecessary options. However, with features creeping in, there are reasons to be concerned that vulnerabilities may be found, in implementations and/or in the specifications themselves.

7.8 Additional exercises

Exercise 7.3 (Fragmentation and compression).

1. The TLS and SSL record protocols uses fragments of size up to 16 KB. Explain potential disadvantage of using much longer fragments (or no fragments).
2. Explain potential disadvantage of using much shorter fragments.
3. Identify both pros and cons for the fact that TLS applies fragmentation before compression (for the AtE protocol).

4. Suppose compression is not used. Why would we apply fragmentation before authentication and encryption?
5. The record protocols of TLS 1.0 to 1.2 apply compression, then authentication. Is it possible to reverse the order, i.e., apply authentication and then compression? Can you identify advantages to either order?

Exercise 7.4 (Vulnerability of Compress-then-Encrypt). One of the important goals of TLS is to hide the value of authenticating cookies sent by a browser, as part of an HTTPS connection. Consider a *cross-site attacker*, i.e., the attacker controls a rogue website visited by the victim user; further, assume that the attacker can eavesdrop on the (protected) communication, following the TLS error oracle attack model. This allows the attacker to control the contents of the request sent by the browser, except for the *Cookie HTTP header*, which is added by the browser and which consists of the string 'Cookie:' followed by the value of the (unknown) cookie:

1. Assume that the length of the cookie is known, that it contains only alphanumeric characters, and the use of the following compression scheme. The compression scheme identifies the longest string α which appears at least twice in the uncompressed data; it then replaces the occurrences of α by a special character, say '!', and concatenate to the data the same special character (e.g., '!'), followed by α. Present an efficient attack which has a good chance to expose the first character of the cookie.
2. Extend the attack, to find the entire cookie.
3. What is the maximal number of requests required by the attack, for a cookie of l characters?
4. What is the expected number of requests required by the attack, for cookie of l alphabetic characters selected randomly (with uniform distribution)?

Note: Compression is supported by all versions of the SSL and TLS record protocols except TLS 1.3, but often not deployed.

Exercise 7.5 (BEAST attack). We discussed the BEAST attack in Section 7.2.4:

1. Present a sequence diagram for the attack finding the first byte $x[1]$ of the secret/cookie.

2. Explain and present pseudo-code for an attack finding the entire string x, even if x consists of more than 8 bytes.

Exercise 7.6 (SSLv2 ServerFinished replay). The SSLv2 handshake includes r_S in the ClientFinished message to prevent replay, but does not include r_C in the ServerFinished message:

1. Show a replay attack for a variant of the protocol which does not include r_S in ClientFinished.
2. Explain why the attacker cannot replay the ServerFinished message (from a previous handshake), although it does not contain r_C.

Exercise 7.7 (SSLv2 key derivation). SSL uses MD5 for key derivation (Equation 7.12). In this question, we explore the required properties from MD5 for the key derivation to be secure:

1. Show that it is *not* sufficient to assume that MD5 is collision-resistant, for the key derivation to be secure.
2. Repeat, for the one-way function property.
3. Repeat, for the randomness-extraction property.
4. Assume that $MD5(k_M + x)$ is a PRF, when we consider k_M as the key of the PRF and x as the input to the PRF. Show that this implies that k_C and k_M would indeed be independently pseudorandom, i.e., each of them should remain pseudorandom even if the other is exposed.
5. Show that if we model MD5 as a truly random function, i.e., analyze the protocol using the ROM, then the assumption in the previous item is true.

Exercise 7.8. Consider implementations of the SSLv2 protocol, where the (1) client random or (2) server random fields are omitted (or always sent as a fixed string). Show a message sequence diagram for two corresponding attacks, one allowing replay of messages to the client, and one allowing replay of messages to the server.

Hint: Perform replay of messages from one connection to a different connection (both using the same master key, i.e., same session). □

Exercise 7.9 (SSLv2 client authentication). The SSLv2 client authentication mechanism requires clients to perform RSA encryption of the MD5 hash of several fields, including a random challenge sent by the server and the server's certificate:

1. Show a MitM attack allowing an attacker to impersonate as a client.
2. Propose a simple improvement that will prevent the attack (without significant overhead).
3. Suppose that the input to the signature did not contain the server's certificate. Show a sequence diagram showing an attack on your improved version (with this modification).

Exercise 7.10 (TLS handshake: resiliency to key exposure). Figure 7.9 presents the RSA-based TLS handshake. This variant of the handshake protocol was popular in early versions, but later 'phased out' and completely removed in TLS 1.3. The main reason was the fact that this variant allows an attacker that obtains the server's private key, to decrypt all communication with the server using this key — before and after the exposure:

1. Show, in a sequence diagram, how a MitM attacker who is given the private key of the server at time T_1, can decrypt communication done by the server at past time $T_0 < T_1$.
2. Show, in a sequence diagram, how TLS 1.3 avoids this impact of exposure of the private key.
3. Show, in a sequence diagram, how a MitM attacker who is given the private key of the server at time T_1, can decrypt communication done by the server at future time $T_2 > T_1$.
4. Explain which feature of TLS 1.3 can reduce the exposure of future communication and how.
5. Which other versions of TLS could prevent either attacks (of items 1 and 3)? Using which mechanisms (cipher suites, extensions, other)?

Exercise 7.11 (Non-random client/server). Some devices may not have a source of random bits; in this exercise, we explore possible resulting vulnerabilities, and a possible work-around:

1. Consider a IoT-lock, which receives the lock/unlock requests over TLS, as a web server — but without access to a source of randomness. Show a replay attack allowing an attacker to open the lock by replaying messages of a legitimate user.

2. Consider a monitoring station displaying images from security cameras, by initiating TLS connections to the cameras and receiving the current images. Show a replay attack allowing an attacker to replay old images (while cracking the safe).
3. Assume that the devices have non-volatile memory. Show how it can be used to ensure secure interactions, even though the devices still do not have a source of random bits.

Your answer should present a sequence diagram and the relevant equations. Present the attack for the most updated version of SSL or TLS that you can, and explain why you think the attack may fail for later versions (if applicable).

Exercise 7.12 (TLS Hosting). Often, the same web server is used to host multiple websites, with different domain names. The web server can serve the correct web pages/resources for each domain name by inspecting the *HTTP host* header, which indicate the domain name. However, when using TLS, the server needs to send the certificate *before* it receives the *host* header. Explain how that can be dealt with in the best way:

1. Using SSL.
2. Using TLS 1.1 or a later version.

Hint: The web server can select the certificate based on different fields of the SSL/TLS handshake, including ports as well as extensions included in the ClientHello message.

Exercise 7.13 (Protocol version downgrade dance attack). Implementations of TLS and SSL specify the version of the protocol in the ClientHello and ServerHello messages. If the server does not support the client's version, then it replies with an error message. When the client receives this error message ('version not supported'), it re-tries the handshake using the best-next version of TLS supported by the client. This method of ensuring backward compatibility with older versions of TLS is referred to as downgrade dance:

1. Present a sequence diagram showing how a MitM attacker can exploit the downgrade dance mechanism, to cause the server and client to use an outdated version of the protocol, allowing the attacker to exploit vulnerabilities of that version.

2. The TLS fallback Signaling Cipher Suite Value (SCSV) [360], discussed in Section 7.5.6, is designed to mitigate this risk. Let v_C denote the TLS version run by the client and v_S denote the TLS version run by the server. Present a sequence diagrams showing TLS connections where (1) client and server support SCSV and $v_c > v_s$, (2) same, $v_c = v_s$, (3) same, $v_c < v_s$, (4) any of these, with a MitM attacker who tries to cause use of version $v_m < \min(v_c, v_s)$.

Exercise 7.14 (Logjam downgrade attack). Consider the Logjam downgrade attack, illustrated in Figure 7.18:

1. Show exactly how the attacker computes the premaster key k_{PM} from the DH values sent by the client ($g^a \bmod p$) and the server ($g^b \bmod p$). In particular, explain exactly how the computation is done, considering that the client does not directly intercept a, b, g^a or g^b, only $g^a \bmod p$ and $g^b \bmod p$.
2. Explain why the attack fails if the server computes a randomly chosen group (g, p) in each handshake.

Exercise 7.15 (Client-chosen cipher suite downgrade attack). In many variants of the TLS handshake, e.g., the RSA-based handshake in Figure 7.9, the authentication of the (previous) handshake messages in the Finish flows is relied upon to prevent a MitM attacker from performing a downgrade attack and causing the client and server to use a less-preferred (and possibly less secure) cipher suite. In this process, the server can choose which of the client's cipher suites would be used. To ensure the use of the cipher suite most preferred by the *client*, even if less preferred by the server, some client implementations send only the most-preferred cipher suites. If none of these is acceptable to the server, then the server responds with an error message. In this case, the client tries to perform the handshake again, specifying now only the next-preferred cipher suite (s), and so on.

1. Show how a MitM attacker can exploit this mechanism to cause the server and client to use a cipher suite that *both* consider inferior.

2. Suggest a fix to the implementation of the client which achieves the same goal, yet is not vulnerable to this attack. Your fix should not require any change in the server.

Exercise 7.16 (TLS server without randomness). An IoT device provides *HTTP* interface to clients, i.e., acts as a tiny web server. For authentication, clients send their commands together with a secret password, e.g., *on, <password>* and *off, <password>*. Communication is over TLS for security, with the RSA-based TLS handshake, as in Figure 7.9.

The IoT device does not have a source of randomness, hence, it computes the server-random r_S from the client-random, using a fixed symmetric key k_S (kept only by the device), as: $r_S = AES_{k_S}(r_C)$:

1. Present a message sequence diagram showing how an attacker, which can eavesdrop on a connection in which the client turned the device 'on', can later turn the device 'on' again, without the client being involved.
2. Would your answer change (and how), if the device supports ID-based session resumption? Ticket-based session resumption?
3. Show a secure method for the server to compute the server-random method, which will not require a source of randomness. The IoT device may use and update a state variable s; you solution consists of the computation of the server-random: $r_S =$______________ and of the update to the state variable performed at the end of every handshake: $s =$______________.

Exercise 7.17 (Diffie–Hellman ephemeral (DHE) without signing random). Consider a variant of the DHE handshake (Figure 7.11), where the server does not sign the client and server random values (r_C and r_S, respectively). Explain, with a sequence diagram, how an attacker can exploit this.

Exercise 7.18 (Diffie–Hellman ephemeral (DHE)). Consider a client and server that use TLS 1.2 with DHE public keys, as in Figure 7.11. Assume that the client and server run this protocol daily, at the beginning of every day i. (Within each day, they may use session resumption to avoid additional public key operations, but this is not relevant to the question.) Assume that Mal can (1) eavesdrop on communication every day, (2) perform MitM attacks (only) every

Table 7.3. Table for Exercise 7.18.

Day	Eavesdrop?	MitM?	Given keys?	Exposed on...	Justify
1	Yes	No	No		
2	Yes	Yes	No		
3	Yes	No	No		
4	Yes	Yes	Yes		
5	Yes	No	No		
6	Yes	Yes	No		
7	Yes	No	No		
8	Yes	Yes	No		

even day (i s.t. $i \equiv 0 \pmod 2$), (3) is given all the keys known to the server on the fourth day.

Note: The server erases any key once it is not longer in use (i.e., on fourth day, attacker is not given the 'session keys' established n previous days).

Fill the 'Exposed on' column of day i in in Table 7.3, indicating the first day $j \geq i$ in which the adversary should be able to decrypt (expose) the traffic sent on day i between client and server. Write 'never' if the adversary should never be able to decrypt the traffic of day i. Justify your answers.

Exercise 7.19 (Client authentication). In Figure 7.14, we present a simplified sequence diagram of the client authentication handshake in SSLv3 and TLS versions 1.0–1.2:

1. In the figure, the CertificateVerify message contains a signature over the (hash of) the entire exchange until this message, including the ClientCert (e.g., Ψ_{Alice}) and the ClientKeyExchange message. Explain, using a sequence diagram, an attack against a variant of this handshake where the ClientCert is not included in the input to the signature in the CertificateVerify message. Or, if you think there is no such attack, present your argument, with sequence diagrams for attacks you considered and failed. Assume RSA key exchange.
2. Repeat, for the case where the ClientKeyExchange is not included in the input to the signature in the CertificateVerify message.
3. Repeat previous items, when using the DHE handshake.

4. Explain, with a sequence diagram, a modified design for client authentication which also authenticates the client using a certificate, but hides the certificate from an eavesdropping adversary.

   Note: There are few possible solutions, including solutions which follow similar ideas used to hide the client's identity in other protocols, including the *Tor* anonymous network [156] and by the *IPsec* protocol [189].

Exercise 7.20 (TLS with perfect recover security (PRS)). Consider a client that has three consecutive TLS connections to a server. An attacker has different capabilities in each of these connections as follows:

- In the first connection, attacker obtains all the information kept by the server (including all keys).
- In the second connection, attacker is disabled.
- In the third connection, attacker has MitM capabilities.

In this question, we investigate how to protect the communication between client and server during the third connection from exposure:

1. Show a sequence diagram showing that with TLS 1.2, even when using the strongest standard options (e.g., use of DH key agreement for PFS), communication during third connection is exposed to a MitM attacker.
2. Repeat, for TLS 1.3.
3. Present an improvement to TLS 1.3 that will protect communication during third connection against a MitM attacker. Simplify your solution by assuming *no attack during the second connection.*
4. Extend to provide same protection, even if the attacker can *eavesdrop — but not act as a MitM— during the second connection.*
5. How can your improvement be implemented using TLS 1.3, allowing backward compatibility, i.e., a 'normal' TLS 1.3 interaction when one of the two parties (client or server) does not support your improvement?

Exercise 7.21. A Pierpont's prime is a prime number of the form $2^u \cdot 3^v + 1$, where u, v are non-negative integers; Pierpont's primes are a generalization of Fermat's primes (see Section 6.1.8.2). Assume that Alice's browser sends, in the ClientHello message of TLS 1.3, the set of exponentiations $\{g_i^{a_i} \bmod \mathrm{p_i}\}$, where for some i, say $i = 3$, the prime p_3 is a Pierpont prime:

1. Assume that the server B.COM selects to use $g_3^{a_3} \bmod p_3$, i.e., sends back $g_3^{b_3} \bmod p_3$ as part of the SERVERHELLO message. Present a sequence diagram showing how a MitM attacker would be able to eavesdrop and modify messages sent between Alice and Bob.
2. Assume that the server prefers p_2, such that there is some prime q_2 such that $p_2 = 2 \cdot q_2 + 1$. Explain why the MitM attack of the previous item fails.
3. Present a sequence diagram showing that the attacker is still able to impersonate as the website, by a modification of the previous attack.
4. Extend the impersonation attack to a complete MitM attack against Alice and B.COM, assuming typical user authentication by sending an authenticating cookie or a username and password over the established TLS connection.
5. Suppose that the client holds a PSK (and ticket); would this prevent the attack? Explain.

Exercise 7.22. This exercise continues Exercise 2.33, see the ANSI X9.31 design presented there.

Some TLS implementations use ANSI X9.31 as a PRG, to generate keys, nonces and IVs for encryption. Assume fixed key k (known to attacker), and that the values T_i are the current time, in seconds. Explain a possible vulnerability; you may make reasonable assumptions, e.g., on the use of different outputs of the PRG and on clock synchronization. Demonstrate how an attacker may exploit the vulnerability, using a sequence diagram.

Present the attack for the most updated version of TLS that you can; if it is not TLS 1.3, explain why you believe versions more updated than the one you used are not vulnerable to this attack.

Exercise 7.23 (Protecting TLS 1.3 servers from computational DoS). TLS servers can be subject to a DoS attack, in which the attacker overload the server with CLIENTHELLO messages, each time causing the server to perform computationally intensive operations. In TLS 1.3, the attacker can cause the server to perform two or three computationally intensive operations: signing the CERTIFICATEVERIFY message and computing the server's DH key share, and possibly also computing the DH shared key. All this requires minimal computational costs to the attacker:

1. Explain the attack, using sequence diagram.
2. Explain how the Cookie extension of TLS 1.3 can help against this attack, following the details in RFC 8446 [412]. Identify assumptions/limitations of this defense.
3. An alternative way to defend against such DoS attacks is to use the PSK to *authenticate the* CLIENTHELLO message. This defense can allows the server to establish connections with clients which have a PSK, even when, due to the attack, other clients cannot establish a connection. Show a sequence diagram illustrating such a defense and explaining how it foils the attack. The solution should not require any change in the TLS 1.3 handshake protocol.

Exercise 7.24 (TLS 1.3 early-response attack). TLS 1.3 supports sending queries from the client in the Early_Data, sent in the first flow (zero-RTT); however, the server can send responses only after the handshake completes successfully. Show why, by showing an attack against a modified protocol where the server sends, already with the SERVERHELLO message, a response to the query in the Early_Data. Explain the attack using a sequence diagram.

Hint: Consider an application such as a web-mail service, where the length of the response can leak sensitive information. For example, the response would be very short if the server did not receive any email messages for the user that corresponds to the query, and quite long if the server received such emails (e.g., when the response contains these emails). See Ref. [199] for the related *cross-site search attacks*, which exploit vulnerabilities of some web services.

Chapter 8

Public Key Infrastructure (PKI)

A big advantage of public key cryptography is that public keys are easier to distribute, as they are not secret; we only need to ensure their *authenticity*. The main mechanism for authenticating public keys are *public key certificates*, which provide a public key signed by a trusted entity called a *certificate authority (CA)*. In this chapter, we discuss *Public Key Infrastructure (PKI)*, i.e., the mechanisms for issuing, validating, revoking and otherwise managing (public key) certificates, expanding upon the high-level discussion of certificates in the context of the TLS protocol in Chapter 7.

The basic concept of public key certificates was proposed already in 1978, soon after the first publications of public key cryptography [300]. PKI was also deployed and standardized early on, with a first standard, *X.509v1* [119], published in 1988. Additional X.509 standards were published later, with the most important being version 3 of X.509 (*X.509v3*), published in 1997. Other important PKI standard include (different versions of) *PKIX*, the IETF's profile of X.509, published beginning with 1999 [131, 256, 257], and the *Certificate Transparency (CT)* specifications [319, 320]. In this chapter, we discuss some of the important aspects related to these standards (X.509, PKIX and CT).

For many years, PKI was basically identified with X.509, especially X.509v3. Even now, most significant PKI deployments and mechanisms follow X.509v3, with few extensions and exceptions. One exception is the handling of *revocations*, i.e., signaling that a certificate should not be trusted, e.g, due to key exposure. The original revocation mechanism of X.509v3 was the *Certificate revocation list (CRL)*, but it was found too inefficient, and other mechanisms have been deployed and proposed; see Section 8.3.

With the growing importance and use of the Web, there were growing concerns about vulnerabilities of the PKI system, mainly due to repeated, high profile *certificate authority failures* and *rogue certificates* (see Sections 8.1.5 and 8.4). Several proposals were made to improve PKI security, and one of them, CT [319, 320], is now in wide use, and required by most browsers; we discuss CT in Section 8.5.

Topics: We introduce PKI schemes in Section 8.1. In Section 8.2, we discuss *certificate extensions*, not to be confused with TLS extensions (Section 7.4.3); we cover the X.509v3 extensions mechanism, as well as specific important extensions. Section 8.3 discusses *certificate revocation*. In Section 8.4, we discuss the challenge of *rogue certificate authorities* and countermeasures. Finally, Section 8.5 discusses the CT mechanism, whose main goal is detection of rogue certificates and their issuers.

8.1 Introduction to PKI

8.1.1 Certificates, issuers and subjects

PKI schemes define how to issue, manage and use *certificates*. A certificate Ψ is a string, which encodes several *fields*; we use the dot notation to identify a specific field. In particular, one of these fields, which we denote $\Psi.\sigma$, is a signature over the other fields. The set of the certificate fields which are signed, i.e., the certificate fields except the signature field, are referred to as the *to be signed (TBS)* fields. The entity which signs (issues) the certificate, using its private signing key, is called the *issuer*; an identifier for the issuer is often included in the certificate, as the field $\Psi.issuer$. Often, one of the fields certified is a certified public key $\Psi.pk$; such certificates are properly called *public key certificates*, but when the discussion is only of public key certificates, e.g., in this chapter, we simply use the term *certificate*.

We also use dot notation to refer to the keys of entities, e.g., we use $\Psi.issuer.s$ to denote the issuer's (private) signing key, and $\Psi.issuer.v$ to denote the corresponding public verification key. The issuer's keys

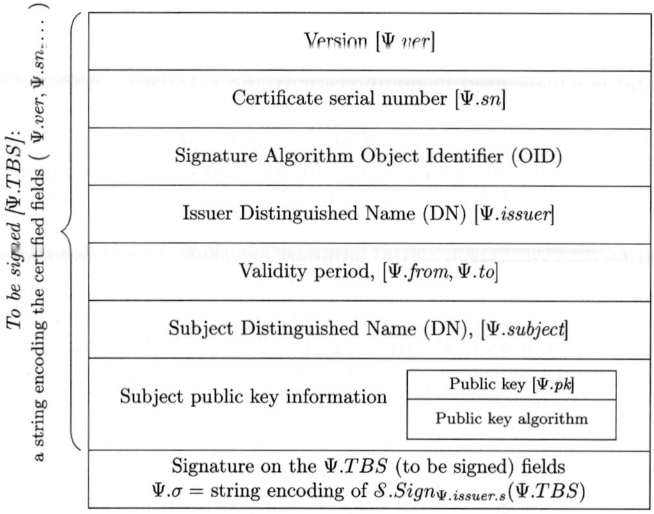

Figure 8.1. X.509 version 1 (X.509v1) certificate fields; in square bracket, the dot notations we use for important certificate fields. Additional fields were added in later versions of X.509.

are typically *not* included in the certificate and should not be confused with $\Psi.pk$, the *certified* (signed) public key in a public key certificate, which normally differs from the issuer's public key used to verify the certificate.

The first standard certificate format is X.509v1, published in 1988 [119] by the International Telecommunication Union (ITU). X.509v1 was published as a part of the X.500 global directory standard [122], designed to facilitate global interoperability between the directory services provided by telecommunication operators of different countries.

Figure 8.1 shows the fields of the X.509v1 certificate, which are as follows:

Version ($\Psi.ver$): The version of X.509 to which this certificate complies, i.e., for X.509v1 certificates, simply the number 1.

Certificate serial number ($\Psi.sn$): A serial number of the certificate, unique among all of the certificates issued by this CA. The best practice is to select the serial number *randomly*, not sequentially. This foils *chosen-prefix collision* attacks, which were shown to produce fake certificates against

Note 8.1: Object Identifier (OID).

The ASN.1 standard [120, 160] was defined jointly by the ITU and ISO organizations and is widely used in many systems and standards. ASN.1 defines the concept of an *object identifier (OID)*; an OID is a unique identifier for arbitrary objects. OIDs allow identification of objects and their types, which helps interoperability between different implementations, and are therefore used by many standards, including X.509. Object identifiers are usually written using dotted decimal notation, i.e., as a sequence of decimal numbers, e.g., 2.23.140.1.1, separated by dots (as shown). OID numbers are assigned hierarchically to organizations, categories and individual (specific) objects, with the assigned OIDs concatenated (from the right), i.e., the leftmost component identifies the top-level OID. The top-level OIDs are zero (0), allocated to ITU, one (1), allocated to ISO, or two (2), allocated jointly to ISO and ITU. When an organization is assigned an OID, it may use it as a prefix to new OIDs which it can assign to organizations, categories or specific objects, by concatenating one or multiple numbers (from the right). For example, the CA/Browser forum is assigned OID 2.23.140 and has assigned the OID 2.23.140.1.1 to identify certificates which were validated using Extended Validation (EV) (Section 8.2.3). There is also a more verbose, readable notation for OIDs, called the "named OID" notation; named OIDs includes symbolic names for each component of the OID. For example, the named OID notation for the 2.23.140.1.1 OID is

{ JOINT-ISO-ITU-T(2) INTERNATIONAL-ORGANIZATIONS(23) CABROWSERFORUM(140) CERTIFICATEPOLICIES(1) EXTENDEDVALIDATION(1) }

The X.509 standards use OIDs to identify different types of objects, including extensions, policies and algorithms. For example, RFC 3279 [34] defines OIDs for many cryptographic algorithms and processes used in Internet protocols, e.g., the RSA signature algorithm.

CAs using sequential serial numbers and a vulnerable hash function, including MD1 and SHA-1; see Section 8.2.5 and Refs. [326, 452, 454].

Signature algorithm OID: An object identifier (OID) for the signature algorithm used to sign the certificate; see Note 8.1.

Issuer DN (Ψ.*issuer*): The *Distinguished Name (DN)* of the *issuer* of the certificate, i.e., the entity that produced and signed the certificate. We discuss Distinguished Names (DNs) in Section 8.1.2.

Validity period (Ψ.*from*, Ψ.*to*): The period during which the certificate is expected to be valid; certificates may be revoked before the end of their validity period.

Subject Distinguished Name ($\Psi.subject$): The *Distinguished Name (DN)* of the *subject* of the certificate, i.e., the entity to whom the certificate was issued. The subject is expected to know the private key corresponding to $\Psi.pk$, the certified public key. We discuss DNs in Section 8.1.2.

Subject public key information: This field includes two parts, one containing the certified public key $\Psi.pk$, and the other identifying, using an OID, the public key algorithm with which $\Psi.pk$ is to be used, including key length, e.g., RSA/2048. The same OID is used for RSA encryption and for RSA signatures; a padding scheme is not specified.

Signature $\Psi.\sigma$: A signature over $\Psi.TBS$, which is a string encoding of the above fields (the *TBS fields*).

The X.509v1 fields are required in every X.509 certificate, although there are X.509 certificates where some fields are left empty. In particular, some certificates do not specify a subject identifier; we use the term *identity certificate* for a certificate that contains an identifier for the subject ($\Psi.subject$). Also, some certificates do not contain a certified public key ($\Psi.pk$). We use the term *public key certificate* when we want to emphasize that a certificate contains a certified public key ($\Psi.pk$).

Other certificate formats may include a different set of fields. In particular, we next describe the certificate fields in X.509v2 and X.509v3.

Certificates in X.509v2 and X.509v3: X.509v2 and X.509v3 added two (X.509v2) or three (X.509v3) fields to these defined by X.509v1; see Figure 8.2.

The two fields added by X.509v2 are for unique identifiers — one for the subject and one for the issuer (CA). These fields were defined to ensure uniqueness, in situations where the DN may fail to ensure uniqueness, as discussed in Section 8.1.2. However, these unique identifier fields are not in wide use, as they are entirely unrelated to the meaningful identifiers used in typical applications.

Version 3 of X.509 (X.509v3) dramatically increased the expressiveness of X.509 certificates, by adding the *extensions* field, which facilitates many applications and use cases. Usually, the extensions field of a certificates is longer than all of the other fields combined.

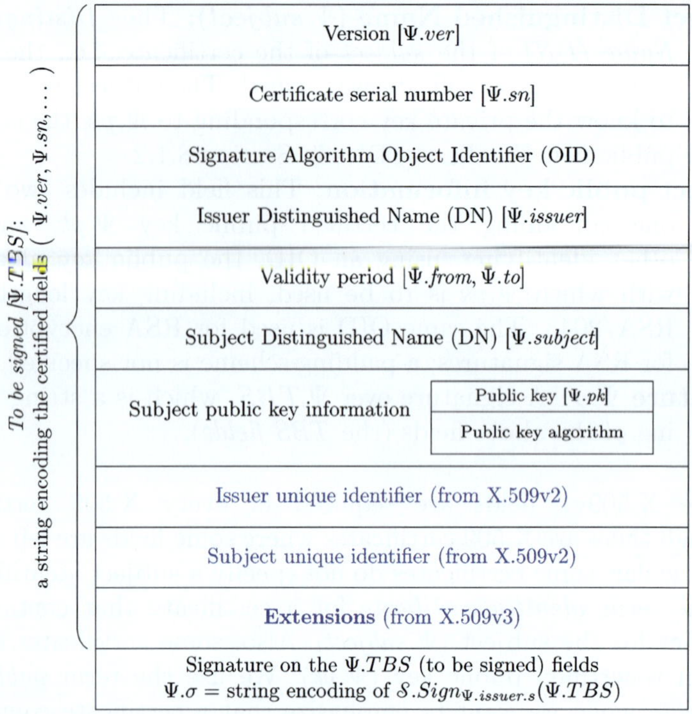

Figure 8.2. X.509 certificate fields in X.509v2 and in X.509v3. X.509v2 added two fields to X.509v1: the issuer unique identifier field and the subject unique identifier field. X.509v3 added one more field, the (very important) *extensions* field. The extension field is usually much longer than all other fields.

Issuing a certificate and certificate encoding: To request a CA to issue an X.509 certificate, the subject typically generates a (public, private) key pair and sends the public key to the CA, with specific requested attributes, such as the the subject distinguished name or, for the common case of a website certificate, the domain name. The CA should *validate* that the public key was received from an entity which is entitled to the requested attributes, e.g., an entity with the specified name or domain name. We discuss the main validation methods for domain names in Section 8.2.3; they include: the easy-but-insecure *Domain Validation (DV)*, the harder-but-more-secure *Organization Validation (OV)* and the hardest-but-most-secure *Extended Validation (EV)*.

If the validation passes, the CA constructs the certificate Ψ, including the validated attributes from the relying party, as well as other attributes determined by the CA, such as serial number and validity period, and then signs it, using the CA's private signing key, which we denote $issuer.s$. More precisely, the CA signs $\Psi.TBS$, which denotes a string encoding of the TBS fields, i.e., computes the signature $\Psi.\sigma$ over $Cert.TBS$ using the private signing key $issuer.s$. Namely,

$$\Psi.\sigma \leftarrow \mathcal{S}.Sign_{CA.s}(\Psi.TBS) \tag{8.1}$$

Certificate encoding, the dot notation and certificate schemes: Certificates involve two encoding operations, which, for simplicity, we mostly ignore in our discussion, e.g., in Equation 8.1.

First, we need to encode the different fields of the certificate into the string $\Psi.TBS$ to be the input to the signature operation. Second, we need to encode the resulting signature $\Psi.\sigma$, together with the other fields of the certificate, into a string that can be sent, received and parsed back into the individual fields. Depending on the transmission mechanism, there may be some restrictions on this encoding, e.g., to send a signature in email headers, it must consist only of printable characters.

PKI standards define multiple, non-trivial *encoding schemes* to perform these encoding operation, e.g., BER, DER, PEM, and SPKI [131, 174, 251, 273].

To refer to the value of a field in a certificate, we use *dot notation*; e.g., we use $\Psi.issuer$ to refer to the issuer field of an X.509 certificate Ψ.

See Ref. [493] for a definition of a *certificate scheme*, which abstracts of the details of the encodings used in certificates, providing a more precise way of defining the issuing process of a certificate $\Psi.\sigma$, the validation process and the process for accessing the value of a specific field in the certificate Ψ.

On our use of the term 'field': Different PKI schemes define different fields. However, some of the most important values in certificates, including in X.509 certificates, are not mapped to one of the X.509 fields. Typically, these values should be placed in a specific *part* of an X.509 field. For example, as shown in Figure 8.2, in X.509 certificates, the public key $\Psi.pk$ should be placed in the *SubjectPublicKey* part of the *SubjectPublicKeyInfo* field. Similarly, several important values are specified within certain *X.509 extensions*, which should all be included in the extensions field added in X.509v3 (Section 8.2).

However, we find it convenient to use the term *certificate field* to refer to specific, important items included in certificates, regardless of whether these are defined as an X.509 field or as a part of a field.

To refer to a specific field within the certificate Ψ, we use the dot notation; we list the most important fields in Table 8.1. We also show the relevant fields, using dot notations, in square brackets in Figures 8.1 and 8.2. Only one certificate field, $\Psi.serial$, maps directly to an X.509 field. Other fields are mapped to specific parts of X.509 fields, e.g., $\Psi.to$, which, in X.509, is a part of the *Validity* field. Several important fields are included only in X.509v3 certificates, and located as a component of one of the certificate extensions, i.e., within the X.509v3 *extensions* field. For example, the $\Psi.cA$ flag, which defines that the subject of the certificate is a CA (i.e., may issue certificates), is a component of the BASIC CONSTRAINTS extension, described in Section 8.2.4.1.

We list the basic certificate fields in Table 8.1.

Table 8.1. Basic fields of certificate Ψ.

Field	Description	Term(s) in X.509
$\Psi.issuer$	An identifier for the issuer of certificate Ψ.	Issuer *Distinguished Name* (*DN*) and/or issuer alternative name (*IAN*), e.g., DNS name or email.
$\Psi.from$	Date and time when certificate Ψ becomes valid.	The *notBefore* entry of the *Validity* certificate field.
$\Psi.to$	Date and time when Ψ expires (become invalid).	The *notAfter* entry of the *Validity* certificate field.
$\Psi.serial$	Certificate serial number.	The *serialNumber* certificate field.
$\Psi.subject$	An identifier for the subject of the certificate Ψ.	Subject *DN* and/or *subject alternative name* (*SAN*), e.g., DNS name or email.
$\Psi.pk$	The public key certified.	The *SubjectPublicKey* part of the *SubjectPublicKeyInfo* field.
$\Psi.cA$	A flag signaling that the $\Psi.subject$ is a CA, i.e, is allowed to issue certificates.	The *CA* part of the basic constraints extension; see Section (8.2.4.1).

The X.509 standards requires all certificates to contain a subject identity, i.e., to be identity certificates. Typical X.500 certificates also define a public key, i.e., are identify public key certificates. However:

- X.509v3 also defines a different type of certificates called *attribute certificates*, which do not contain a public key. X.509v3 considers attribute certificates as separate from public key certificates, and their main use is for access control rather than for authentication. There are also semantic differences, for example, the entity identified in them is called the *holder* rather than the *subject.*
- It is possible to use the X.509 format for public key certificates, but without including a value in the identity fields and/or without specifying a public key. In fact, many TLS server certificates do not specify the server's identity in the X.509 *subject DN* field; usually, these certificates do specify the website's domain in the dNSName component of the SAN extension.

8.1.2 X.500 Distinguished Names (DNs)

In this section, we discuss DNs, a basic concept in X.509 certificates. X.509 was developed by the ITU as part of the X.500 global directory standard [122], which was based on the phone directories which, at the time, were a service provided by the telecommunication companies. The phone directory services used a person's common name as an identifier; the goal of Distinguished Names was to provide a better identifier for the X.500 directory.

Common names are *meaningful identifiers.* However, obviously; common names are not unique — in fact, some common names are quite common. In classical phone directories, this is addressed by returning a set of results containing all relevant entries, along with relevant attributes, e.g., location, that may assist in using the results.

The goal was for DNs to be meaningful, similarly to common names, but also unique. The DN consists of *several* keyword-value pairs, one of which is the common name. By including additional keyword-value pairs, DN can be made unique. Typical, standard keywords are shown in Table 8.2; however, a directory is free to use any keyword it desires.

X.500 DN keyword-value pairs are specified as a sequence, i.e., as an *ordered* list. This allows the DNs to be organized as a hierarchy,

Table 8.2. Common X.500 Distinguished Name keywords and their meanings.

Keyword	Meaning
`CN` (Common Name)	The common name of the entity (person's name, server's domain name)
`O` (Organization)	The name of the organization (e.g., company)
`OU` (Organization Unit)	The name of a unit within the organization
`C` (Country)	The two-letter ISO country code (e.g., US)
`L` (Locality)	The name of the locality or city

using the sequence of keywords as the nodes. However, the order of different keywords and their specific values can differ between different DNs, especially when issued by different issuers.

One of the goals of DNs was to allow interoperability among multiple issuing organizations while maintaining the uniqueness of DNs. This uniqueness could have been implemented by separating between the DNs spaces of different issuers by using a convention such as using a fixed keyword to identify the issuer; however, this was not mandated, maybe since the ITU assumed that different issuers will anyway issue distinct DNs, e,g., since each issuer will only use their specific organization name, country name, or combination of country and organization or locality names. This is in contrast to a strictly hierarchical name space such as of the Internet's Domain Name System (DNS), where each domain is managed by a single organization, who can only define sub-domains within this domain. The OID mechanism (Note 8.1) is another example of a hierarchical name space.

It is also possible that the same issuer will need to assign Distinguished Names to two (or more) persons with the same common name, which have the same set of keywords used by the issuer (e.g., organization). As a result, administrators may have to enforce uniqueness by 'modifying' the common name or adding another keyword to ensure uniqueness. For example, if there are multiple IBM UK employees with the name Julian Jones, the second to join may be assigned the Distinguished Name *CN=Julian Jones2, O=IBM, C=GB*. This results in *less meaningful DNs*, which can be especially problematic since systems and users are likely to expect DNs to be unique. For example, a messaging system may automatically complete the *Distinguished Name* incorrectly, and the user may not notice it, ending up by sending a message to the wrong Julian Jones.[1]

In practice, many certificates use alternative identifiers for the subject and issuer, such as the *SAN* and the IssuerAltName (*IAN*). See Section 8.2.1.

8.1.3 Relying parties, CAs and certificate chains

In public key cryptography, a public key is usually used by parties who do not know the corresponding *private* key. The main use of public key certificates is to provide a public key to a party and allow that party to *validate* the public key, and then to use it, i.e., to *rely* on it. We use the term *relying party* to refer to a party which receives a certificate Ψ, validates it and then *relies* on it, i.e., uses the certified public key $\Psi.pk$.

In the typical case of TLS for web server authentication, the relying party is the browser and the subject is the website. TLS uses X.509v3 certificates, and usually identify the subject using the domain name of the website, e.g., *Bob.com.* This typical use-case is illustrated in Figure 8.3.

The certificate validation process is a critical, non-trivial part of the design of a PKI scheme; we discuss it in the following subsection. One basic requirement from a valid certificate is that it would include a valid signature $\Psi.\sigma$, which the relying party validates using a public key that the relying party trusts, i.e., *relies on*, for certificate validation; such public keys which are used to establish trust in certificates are called *trust anchors.* Typically, a trust anchor public keys is provided in a *self-signed certificate* Ψ, i.e., Ψ is signed by the same public key $\Psi.pk$ which is certified by Ψ. Relying parties maintain a set of root certificates, called the *root certificates store.* Browsers typically have dozens or even hundreds of root certificates in their root certificates store.

[1]The author wishes to use this opportunity to apologize to both Julian Jones.

Most PKIs allow root CAs to issue public key certificates either to end-entities or to other CAs, called *intermediary CAs* and *leaf CAs*. Intermediary CAs may also issue certificates either to end-entities or to other intermediary CAs as well as to leaf CAs, while leaf CAs should only issue certificates to end-entities (non-CAs). When a certificate Ψ is issued by a non-root CA, i.e., $\Psi.issuer$ is not a root CA, then validation requires at least one sequence of certificates establishing the trust in $\Psi.issuer$, beginning with a certificate issued by a root CA. Such a sequence of certificates is called a *certificate chain* or, equivalently, a *certificate path*.

Figure 8.3 illustrates the certificate issuing process for a certificate Ψ_B issued to the website *Bob.com*. Certificate Ψ_B is issued by a leaf CA (LCA), which was certified by an intermediary CA (ICA), which was certified by the root CA *Root*; we therefore say that Ψ_B had a *certificate path* of length three. The figure also illustrates the transmission of the certificate chain, which in this case consists of a sequence of only two certificates: Ψ_{ICA}, issued by the root CA *Root* to the ICA INT, and Ψ_{LCA}, issued by the intermediary CA INT to

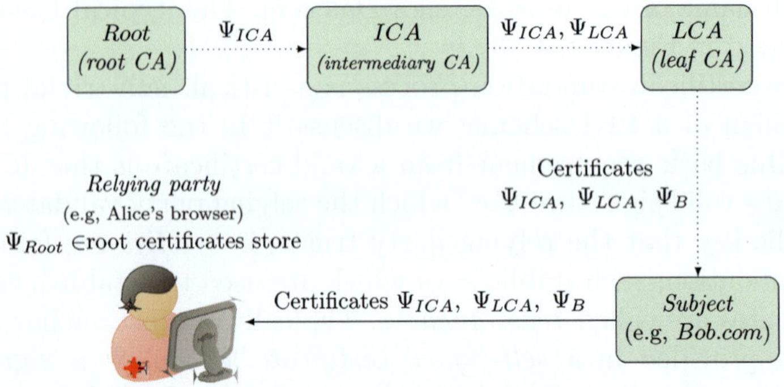

Figure 8.3. Certificate issuing (dotted arrows) and usage (solid arrow) flows. Let Ψ_{Root} denote the self-signed root certificate of the root CA *Root*; we assume that Ψ_{Root} is in the root store of Alice's browser. The root CA issues certificate Ψ_{ICA} to the *ICA*, the *ICA* issues certificate Ψ_{LCA} to the leaf CA and the leaf CA issues certificate Ψ_B to the subject, e.g., website *Bob.com*. Every certificate is signed using the private signing key of the issuer and identifies the public key of its subject. For example, $\Psi_{\text{ICA}}.pk$ is the public key of the ICA, which validates Ψ_{LCA}. X.509v3 requires (only) the CA certificates Ψ_{ICA} and Ψ_{LCA} to have the *cA* flag turned on; the end certificate Ψ_B should not have *cA* turned on. For certificate path validation, see Section 8.1.4.

the LCA. In TLS, the server (e.g., *Bob.com*) sends to the client (e.g., browser) its certificate Ψ_B, received from the LCA, together with the certificate chain. The client uses these certificates, and additional inputs, to validate Ψ_B, as we describe in the next subsection.

After issuing a certificate Ψ, the CA sends Ψ to the subject $\Psi.subject$. Usually, the subject provides Ψ to the relying party, e.g., web servers send their certificate to the client with the SERVERHELLO message, during the TLS handshake. In the typical case where the issuer is not a root CA, the certificate Ψ is usually sent together with its certificate chain, i.e., a sequence of certificates from a root CA which establishes trust in Ψ.

8.1.4 Certificate validation

Before using (relying on) a certificate Ψ, the relying party should *validate* Ψ. The certificate validation process is an important part of the PKI; in practical PKIs such as X.509, it is typically a non-trivial process.

In most of this section, we focus on validation in X.509v3 and PKIX. Toward the end of this section, in Section 8.1.4.1, we briefly discuss other certificate validation processes, mainly the *web of trust*.

X.509v3 validation of certificates issued by a root CA: In X.509v3, certificate validation always begins with a certificate issued by a root CA; a certificate which was not issued by a root CA can only be valid if it comes with a certificate chain, beginning with a certificate issued by a root CA. Let us therefore first focus on the special case of validation of a certificate Ψ issued by a root CA, i.e., $\Psi.issuer$ is a root CA, with a known, trusted public validation key $\Psi.issuer.v$.

Validation of certificates issued by a root CA requires a *subset* of the checks necessary when validating certificates issued by non-root CAs (i.e., by intermediary CAs or leaf CAs). We refer to this set of checks as *basic certificate validation*, and it consists of the following checks:

Validity period: The relying party checks the validity period specified in the certificate Ψ, i.e., the period between $\Psi.from$ and $\Psi.to$. If the public key is used for encryption or to validate signatures on responses to challenges sent by the relying party, then the certificate should be valid at the relevant times, including at the current time. However, we may also consider a signature to be valid for some time t in the past, if t is within the validity period of the certificate, and we have evidence showing that the signature was already existing at time t, e.g., the signature is in a secure, time-stamped log, or its existence at time t is attested by a trustworthy *time-stamping* service.

No revocation: Most PKIs support a mechanisms to *revoke* certificates; a revoked certificate is invalid. Therefore, part of the certification validation process includes validation that the certificate was not revoked, typically by presenting a signature from a trusted entity attesting that the certificate was not revoked. We discuss revocations in Section 8.3.

Signature algorithms: The relying party confirms that it can apply and trusts the validation algorithm of the signature scheme identified in the *signature algorithm OID* field of the certificate. If the certificate is signed using an unsupported algorithm, or an algorithm known or suspected to be insecure, validation fails.

Validate signature: The relying party next uses the trusted public validation key of the issuer, $\Psi.issuer.v$, and the signature-validation process as specified in the certificate, to validate the signature over all the 'to be signed' fields in the certificate, i.e., all fields except the signature itself.

Additional validations: PKI schemes may involve additional, PKI-specific validations. Many of these validations are related to different X.509v3 extensions; see Section 8.2. In particular, CT requires additional validations to ensure *transparency*, i.e., allow subjects to be aware of certificates issued to their identities (typically, to their domain name); see Section 8.5.

X.509v3 validation of certificate path: More often, a certificate Ψ is issued by an *ICA* or an *LCA*, i.e., rather than directly being issued by a root CA. In this case, validation of the certificate requires a *valid certificate chain (certificate path)* from a root CA. For example, consider the scenario in Figure 8.3, i.e., validation of the certificate Ψ_B using the certificate chain $(\Psi_{\text{ICA}}, \Psi_{\text{LCA}})$ and the root certificate Ψ_{Root}.

In general, consider a chain of certificates $\Psi_0, \Psi_1, \ldots, \Psi_{r-1}, \Psi_r$, where Ψ_r is a root certificate. The validation of this chain involves the following checks.

Issuer: For every certificate Ψ_i in the chain, where $i < r$, verify correct issuer identification, i.e., verify that $\Psi_i.issuer = \Psi_{i+1}.subject$.

Basic certificate validation: Perform the *basic certificate validation process*, as described above, for each certificate in the chain. In particular, we verify the signature on the certificate, using the public signature-validation key of the issuer $\Psi_i.issuer.v$; the public key should be obtained from a root certificate (if the issuer is a root CA), or from the earlier certificate on the chain (which was already validated).

Constraints: X.509v3 specifies three standard extensions that restrict valid certificate chains: BASIC CONSTRAINTS, NAME CONSTRAINTS and POLICY CONSTRAINTS; we describe them in Section 8.2.4. For example, the BASIC CONSTRAINTS extension includes the optional *cA* flag, which should be true for every certificate issued to a CA, including to *LCA*. Only the last certificate in the chain, Ψ_0, may not have this flag turned on, signaling that it is an end-entity certificate.

Other validations: Relying parties may perform additional validations on the path, as directed by other extensions and/or based on the policy of the relying party. For example, a relying party may restrict some root CA to only issue end-entity certificates, i.e., ignore an *cA* flag included in certificates issued by this CA.

8.1.4.1 *Web of trust (PGP) and trust establishment*

Not all PKIs follow the X.509v3 certification validation process described above. For example, in the *PGP Web-of-Trust* PKI [197], every party, e.g., Abe and Al, decides on a level of trust for each of their peers, say Alice, e.g., 'full' or 'marginal' trust. Suppose that Alice communicates for the first time with another party, Bob, who trusts Abe and Al (e.g., either 'full' or 'marginal' trust). Alice provides Bob with her certificates from Al and from Abe, and Bob will decide whether to trust Alice, based on Bob's trust level in Al and in Abe, and based on the trust level indicated in the certificates that Alice has from Al and from Abe. More generally, a party Bob decides whether to trust a peer Alice and to what level, based on the number of valid certificates of a given trust level that Bob receives for Alice.

Namely, in the web of trust, each entity, e.g., Abe and Al, issues certificates to other parties, i.e., acts as an X.509 CA; note that no *cA* flag is required in the issuer's certificate.

Other designs allow *negative ratings*, i.e., one party recommending *not* to trust another party. The determination of whether to trust an entity based on a set of certificates — and/or other credentials and inputs — is referred to as the *trust establishment* or *trust management* problem. This problem was studied extensively, e.g., see Refs. [86, 87, 244, 245, 332].

8.1.5 Rogue certificates

Relying parties *rely* on the root CAs to only certify trustworthy intermediary CAs and leaf CAs. Therefore, the relying party may trust the information in valid, properly signed certificates, in particular, the identification of the subject of the certificate and their public key. This trust is not always justified; some (valid, signed) certificates contain *wrong or misleading information*, i.e., should not be relied upon. We refer to such certificates as *rogue certificates*.

There are two basic categories of rogue certificates: *fake-PK rogue certificates*, i.e., a certificate Ψ containing an attacker-chosen public key $\Psi.pk$ for a benign subject identity (e.g., benign domain name), and *misleading-identity rogue certificates*, i.e., certificates issued to an attacker-chosen identity, which are likely to mislead users and cause them to mistake for a benign identity. Let us consider separately these two kinds of rogue certificates.

8.1.5.1 *Rogue certificates with a fake public key*

A CA should carefully validate that certificate requests are properly authorized, to avoid certifying a certificate Ψ whose public key $\Psi.pk$ was chosen by the attacker, although the subject identifier $\Psi.subject$ is not owned by the attacker, e.g., the benign $\Psi.subject = www.Bob.com$.

A valid rogue certificate Ψ containing attacker's public key $\Psi.pk$ for a benign subject $\Psi.subject$ are typically due to one of the following causes:

Corrupt CA: A corrupt CA $\Psi.issuer$, knowingly certifying wrong information.

CA break-in: An attacker exploiting an exposed private signing key of $\Psi.issuer$, exposed by breaking into the CA. Such break-ins are usually done remotely or by a rogue employee of the CA (an *insider attack*).

CA validation failure: A benign CA $\Psi.issuer$ unintentionally certifying the attacker's public key $\Psi.pk$ after incorrectly concluding that the request is valid, using the validation mechanisms deployed by $\Psi.issuer$.

Bypassing of CA validation: An attacker exploiting a vulnerability of a benign $\Psi.issuer$ to trick it into certifying a public key provided by the attacker $\Psi.pk$ for a benign identifier, e.g., the domain $\Psi.subject =$ *www.Bob.com*, without properly deploying the validation mechanisms which are normally used by $\Psi.issuer$.

Forgery of CA's signature: A cryptanalytical signature forgery attack allowing an attacker to produce signatures which appear valid using the CA's signature-validation key, without the use of the corresponding private signing key kept by the CA.

Several of these causes reflect a failure of the issuing CA ($\Psi.issuer$), i.e., we can say that $\Psi.issuer$ is *accountable* for these rogue certificates. This surely holds for the cases of corrupt CA, CA break-in and bypassing of CA validation. If the accountable CA is not a root CA, i.e., it is a *LCA* or an *ICA*, then the CAs certifying it are also partially accountable; root CAs and intermediary CAs should carefully check before certifying another CA.

In the cases of signature forgery and validation failure, the relying party itself may also be responsible to some extent. The relying party is aware of the signature scheme being used and of the type of certificate validation (which is indicated in the certificate); therefore, the relying party should not trust certificates signed using a vulnerable signature scheme or validation method.

In particular, with some exceptions, (updated) browsers do not accept certificates signed using the MD5 and SHA-1 hash functions since both functions are known to have collisions [451,452]; if fact, it was shown that for both hash functions, the collisions can be abused for certificate forgery (see Section 8.2.5 and Refs. [326,328,454]). Note that in these cases, where the vulnerability is in the hash function, the CA is also partially responsible, since the CA used an insecure hash function. For example, the CA/Browser forum has determined that SHA-1 should not be used, with few exceptions, after January first, 2016 [109]; the use of MD5 was aborted much earlier.

The situation is more complex for rogue certificates obtained by circumventing a weak validation process. In particular, Domain Validation (DV) can be circumvented by MitM attackers or by exploiting different vulnerabilities of Internet routing or of the Domain Name System (DNS), see Section 8.2.3. However, the use of DV is very common; in fact, the vast majority of website certificates have been validated using DV. This motivates the use of additional defenses; see Sections 8.4.1 and 8.5.

8.1.5.2 *Rogue certificates with misleading subject identity*

Rogue certificates with misleading subject identity contain *correct but misleading subject identifiers*, such as a domain name, e.g., *bankofamerlca.com*, which is different-from-but-similar-to the domain name of a victim benign website, e.g., *bankofamerica.com.* Such misleading certificates are used in *phishing* and other attacks exploiting vulnerabilities of human users. We discuss *human-centered security* in Chapter 9; however, let us discuss already here rogue certificates with misleading information, since this is one of the main problems with the current PKI.

Attackers often use misleading certificates to create a *spoofed website* which impersonate as a trusted website. The goal of the impersonating may be to manipulate the user into disclosing sensitive information, e.g., passwords, or to trick the user into installing malware. Misleading certificates may also be sent with malware, to trick the user into install the malware, by causing the user to consider the malware as produced and signed by a trusted software producer. A final example is abuse of such certificate to send an impersonated (spoofed) message, e.g., when using email or other messaging platform that supports user identification by certificates.[2]

[2]This applies only to properly signed email, e.g., using S/MIME [408]. More common methods of email sender authentication, including DKIM [139] which uses signatures, can be circumvented even without a misleading certificate; see Ref. [239].

The main categories of rogue certificates with misleading subject identity include the following:

Homographic (visually misleading) domain names: The attacker uses domain names which appear *visually* to be the exact domain names of a legitimate, trusted entity, although, they actually just exploit visual similarities between different characters. One way to create visually misleading domain names is by abusing support for *International Domain Names (IDN)*, using a domain name where some letters are replaced by lookalike letters from another language. For example, one of the following two domain names, `Paypal.com` and `Paypal.com`, contains a Cyrillic character; can you identify which? Most users cannot. To prevent such abuse of IDN, most browsers display mixed-font domain names using *Punycode* [136], which would present a clearly different string (e.g., the second domain name above would be displayed as `xn-aypal-9pf.com`). Attackers now use other homographic attacks, such as replacing letters by similarly looking digits or (different) lower/upper case letters, e.g., Paypal.com and paypal.com. See an example of a homographic domain name one not using IDN in Figure 8.4, and the corresponding 'solution' in Figure 8.5.[3]

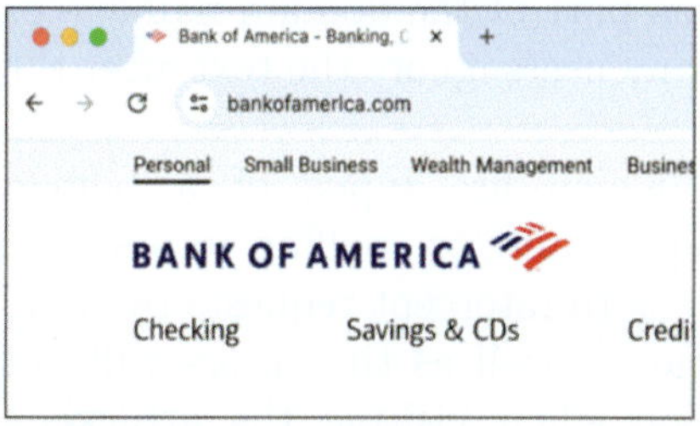

Figure 8.4. Example of a homographic attack, using a rogue certificate with a misleading domain name (in the dNSName component of the SubjectAltName extension). This example is (intentionally) relatively easy to identify; can you identify which of the two URLs is correct, which phishing? See the solution in Figure 8.5.

[3]As of July 2024, the website used here as an example, *BankofAmerica.com* does not seem to be in use; it is owned by *Domains By Proxy, LLC*, which does not expose the identity of the 'real' owner of the domain. The original *BankofAmerica.com* domain is owned by the *Bank of America corporation.*

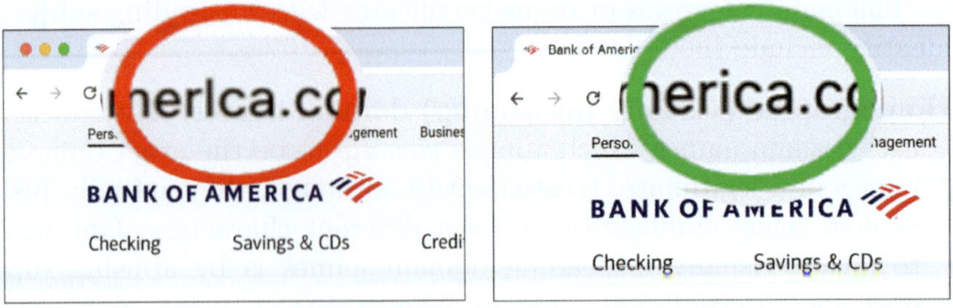

Figure 8.5. Example of homographic attack: the solution to the challenge of Figure 8.4.

Domain-name hacking: The attacker registers and uses a domain name which is visibly different from the domain name of the impersonated website; however, the difference is such that users may mistake the attacking domain for a part of the benign website. These attacks rely on the fact that most users are not aware of the details of the syntax of domain names and of URLs and the hierarchical allocation of domain names, as described in Note 8.2; we refer to this problem, where users fail to understand security-relevant indicators since the indicators involve non-trivial technical details, as the *cryptography is in Greek* problem. For example, Domain-name hacking often uses a dash as part of the domain name, e.g., *https://usps.com-vit.xyz*, since many users ignore the text after the dash.

Typosquatting: Domain names which are typos of a benign domain name, such as due to typing and/or spelling errors, e.g., *bankofamrica.com*. The hope here is to intercept requests by users which mistyped the domain name, as well as that users will not notice the different domain name when visiting the attacker's domain.

One technique to defend against misleading domain names is to buy them in advance; e.g., while the bank called Banc of California uses the domain *bancofcal.com*, the bank also bought the potential typo *bankofcal.com*, which redirects to *bancofcal.com*.

The concerns about misleading certificates and domain names are some of the many challenges which a designer faces, when trying to protect systems involving human users. For further discussion of designing systems to protect human users, see Chapter 9.

Note 8.2: IP addresses, Domain names and Universal Resource Locators (URLs).

Communication on the Internet is done over the Internet Protocol (IP), by sending packets to a destination specified by an IP address located in the packet. IP addresses are binary strings consisting of either 32 bits (in version 4 of the IP protocol, IPv4) or 128 bits (in version 6 of the IP protocol, IPv6); IPv4 and IPv6 are the only versions of IP in use. Both types of IP address has standard printable representations. IPv4 addresses are represented as four integers between 0 and 255 separated by dots, e.g., 1.2.3.4 [403]. IPv6 addresses are represented as eights groups of four hexadecimal digits each separated by colons, e.g., 1234:5678:ABCD:EF01:0000:0000:0000:0001, which can be abbreviated to 1234:5678:ABCD:EF01::1 (by removing leading zeros in a group and the longest sequence of all-zeroes groups) [286].

For convenience and other reasons, users and applications mostly use higher-level identifiers called *domain names*, which can be mapped to IP addresses using the *Domain Name System (DNS)*. Domain names consist of one or more parts, called *labels*, separated by dots, e.g., *www.Bob.com*. Each label is a string of up to 63 characters, where the allowed characters are letters, digits and the hyphen symbol.

Domain names are assigned hierarchically. *Domain name registrars* allow applicants to register unregistered domain names; the registration is for a limited period and must be periodically renewed. We refer to the individual or organization who registered the domain name as its *owner*. The owner of a domain, e.g., *Bob.com*, controls registration of *subdomains*, e.g., *www.Bob.com*. Domains consisting of only one part, e.g., *com*, are called *top-level domains (TLDs)*. Note that the most-significant part of the domain name is on the right, in contrast to the usual convention for writing both numbers and IP addresses. For more information on DNS and its security mechanisms, see Section 8.4.2.

The web uses richer identifiers called *Universal Resource Locators (URLs)*, which include and extend the domain names. A URL identifies a specific *web-resource* as well as the *protocol* to be used to request the resource (mainly, HTTP or HTTPS). There are many types of web resources, e.g., *HTML files*, which define the contents of a webpage using the *Hypertext Markup Language (HTML)*, scripts (typically written in JavaScript [499]), images and fonts.

Most URLs are of the form `protocol://domain/path` or `protocol://domain/path?query`, where `protocol` is the protocol (mostly, HTTP or HTTPS), `domain` is the domain name identifying the host running the web server, `path` is a location (path) identifying the specific resource within the server, e.g., *index.html* or *scripts/a.js*, and the optional *query* contains query parameters, typically passed to a server-side script handling the request. The `domain` can contain, beyond the domain name of the host, also the optional `port` and/or `userinfo` values, using the syntax `userinfo@host:port`, where `port` is an integer indicating a specific server software to be used, and `userinfo` provides username and password information. Sometimes, a URL may end with an additional component `#fragment`, appended at the end, that identifies a specific location within an HTML document. For more details on URLs, see RFC 3986 [62].

8.2 Certificate extensions

As shown in Figure 8.2, X.509v3 certificates include an *extensions* field. We discuss some specific, important extensions in the following subsections. But first, let us discuss the extensions mechanism itself, since this is a clever mechanism that balances between the need to allow extendibility and the concern of using a certificate incorrectly, due to ignoring or incorrectly handling an important extension.

Each extension has the following three components:

Extension identifier: This specifies the type of the extension. The extension identifier is specified using an OID, to facilitate interoperability.

Extension value: This is an arbitrary string which provides the value of the extension. For example, a possible value for the key-usage extension would indicate that the certified key is to be used as a public encryption key, while a possible value for the NAME CONSTRAINTS extension may be *Permit C=GB*, allowing the subject of the certificate to issue its own certificates, but only with the value 'GB' (Great Britain) to their 'C' (country) keyword.

Criticality indicator: This is a binary flag, i.e., an extension can be marked as critical or as non-critical. The value of the criticality indicator flag in an extension instructs relying parties how to handle the certificate if the relying party is not familiar with this type of extension, as indicated by the extension identifier. A relying party *should not use* a certificate which includes an extension marked as critical, if the relying party is not familiar with this type of extension. In contrast, relying parties may use certificates containing a non-critical extension, even if they are not familiar with it, by simply ignoring that non-critical extension.

We next discuss few examples of *standard extensions*, i.e., certificate extensions defined in standards. X.509v3 and PKIX each include several standard extensions, with many of them appearing in both X.509v3 and PKIX; other extensions are defined in other standards (e.g., the TLS-feature extension, see Example 8.3). Some standard extensions should always be marked critical, others should always be marked non-critical, and others may be marked as either critical or non-critical depending on needs. We present three examples of standard extensions, one of each of these types.

Example 8.1. The **KEY USAGE** extension, which indicates the allowed usages of the certified public key of the subject. In X.509v3, the KEY USAGE extension can be marked either critical or not; in PKIX, it must be marked as critical. The standards require this extension to be supported by both clients and servers.

Details: The KEY USAGE extension defines applications for which the certified public key may be used, including signature validation, encryption of keys, encryption of data, key agreement, validating the signature over a certificate or over a Certificate revocation list (CRL) and more. A CA certificate, where the key may be used to validate a certificate, must include the KEY USAGE extension, with the bit allowing to use the key for validating signatures over certificates. Otherwise, the usage of the extension is not mandatory and also not necessary when the public key algorithm can only be used for a specific, e.g., a key which can only be used for validating signatures.

Let us give an example of an attack on a TLS 1.3 client, if the KEY USAGE extension is not used in a certificate, or if a client does not support it and the extension is not marked as critical (and therefore the client relies on the certificate, ignoring the extension). Assume that a TLS server runs an older version of TLS that is vulnerable to some variant of the Bleichenbacher attack Section (6.5.7). This may allow the attacker to forge an RSA signature using the private (decryption) key. Without enforcement of the KEY USAGE extension, the attacker can now abuse the signature in different applications which rely on signatures, e.g., the TLS 1.3 handshake. This cross-protocol attack succeeds even if the server has correctly separated between the TLS 1.3 signature-verification public key and the public encryption key used by the old, vulnerable version. □

Example 8.2. The **EXTENDED KEY USAGE** extension, which allows the issuer to further define allowed specific applications for which the public key certified can be used, beyond the categories specified in the KEY USAGE extension. The EXTENDED KEY USAGE extension may be marked either critical or non-critical.

Details: The EXTENDED KEY USAGE extension allows us to restrict the use of the certified key to any (subset) of the following specific applications: *TLS server, TLS client, code signing, email protection, timestamping* and *OCSP signing.* The extension may also indicate the special value *anyExtendedKeyUsage*; this is useful when one relying party application *requires* the certificate to include the EXTENDED KEY USAGE extension and another application should use the key for a purpose not supported by the extension. Note that when using the anyExtendedKeyUsage value, it is sensible to mark the extension as *non-critical*, allowing some relying party applications to use the certificate without even parsing this extension. In contrast, the extension should be marked as *critical* if the goal is to restrict the use of the certified key to one of the applications supported by the extension. □

Example 8.3. The ***TLS-feature*** extension, defined in RFC 7633 [231],[4] used in TLS server certificates to indicate that the server supports one or more specific *TLS extensions* (see Section 7.4.3). The *TLS-feature* extension should always be marked as a non-critical extension, allowing use of the certificate by TLS clients that do not support the extension.

Details: The term *TLS-feature* actually refers to TLS extensions, but since both TLS and PKIX use the term 'extension' for these different purposes, the decision was to use, instead, the different term *feature*. Unfortunately, this refers to TLS extensions as 'features', which is also confusing, since the TLS specifications refer to them as 'extensions'. This extension should be marked non-critical since some TLS clients may not support it; if the TLS-feature X.509 extension would be marked critical, these clients would reject the certificate, and the connection would fail. □

The flexibility offered by the 'criticality indicator' makes the X.509 extensions mechanism very versatile; this idea could be used by other standards and design, to allow flexible extensions. For example, TLS client and servers simply ignore unknown TLS extensions, i.e., always treat them as non-critical, as discussed in Chapter 7. The following exercise shows how this flexibility could be added for TLS extensions, e.g., allowing a client to use a critical TLS extension,

[4]The TLS-feature extension isn't one of the standard extensions defined in either X.509v3 [261] or PKIX [131]; it was developed later, specifically, to allow a certificate to mark that the server always uses the *must-staple* TLS extension, see Section 8.3.3.

requiring the server to indicate an error if the server does not support that TLS extension.

Exercise 8.1. Design a TLS extension allowing TLS clients to mark (other) TLS extensions as critical or non-critical.

In the following sections, we discuss several important standard certificate extensions and their validation.

8.2.1 The SubjectAltName (SAN) and the IssuerAltName (IAN) extensions

Both X.509v3 and PKIX define the standard *SAN* and *IAN* extensions, providing alternative identification mechanisms (names) to complement or replace the *Distinguished Name* mechanism, providing identification for identifying, respectively, the subject and the issuer.

The SAN and IAN extensions allow the use of different types of names, identifiers and addresses for the subject and issuer, as alternatives to identifying the subject and issuer in the *subject* and *issuer* fields in X.509 certificates, respectively. A certificate may contain multiple SANs and IANs.

One important alternative name is a DNS name, referred to as *dNSName*, e.g., *www.Bob.com.* These forms of dNSName are used by most Internet protocols and are familiar to most users. Other alternative names include *email addresses, IP addresses* and *URLs/URIs*, and a single certificate may contain multiple alternative names, even of the same type, e.g., multiple dNSName entries.

The use of alternate names is very common; in many PKIX certificates, the subject and the issuer *Distinguished Name* fields are left empty. In this case, the identification can done by the corresponding extension.

Indeed, PKIX [131] specifies that when the CA can only validate one (or more) of the alternative name forms, then the subject *Distinguished Name* field must be empty; this is often the case in practice, in particular, when the CA can only validate the domain name of the subject, i.e., using Domain Validation (DV) (Section 8.2.3). PKIX specifies that in such cases, where the SAN extension is the only identification and the subject *Distinguished Name* field is empty, then the SAN extension should be marked as *critical.* Otherwise, when there is a (properly validated) subject *Distinguished Name*, then the SAN extension should be marked as non-critical.

In contrast, PKIX does allow certificates where the *issuer* Distinguished Name is empty and yet there is no IAN extension; furthermore, if included, PKIX requires that the IAN extension be marked as non-critical. The reason for that is that the standard PKIX certificate path validation algorithm (Section 8.1.4) does not validate the alternative names in the IAN extensions. The situation is different for the SAN extension, which provides, in most applications, a crucial identification of the owner (subject) of the certificate; for example, in TLS, it identifies the website. Note, however, that the X.509 standard does allow the IAN extension — as well as the SAN extension — to be marked as either *critical* or *non-critical*.

TLS implementations usually allow certificates to include *wildcard domain names* for the subject (in a dNSName entry of the SAN). Instead of identifying a specific, single subject domain name, wildcard domain names use the *wildcard notation* to specify a set of subject domain names. For TLS, this support is defined in RFC 6125 [425]. Wildcard domain names are domain names where some of the labels (strings containing alphanumeric characters and possibly hyphens) are replaced with the *wildcard character* '*'; there are often restrictions on the location of the wildcard character, e.g., it may be allowed only in the complete left-most label of a DNS domain name, as in `*.example.com`. Wildcard domain names are not addressed in PKIX [131] or in X.509v3 [261]; RFC 6125 [425] mentions several security concerns regarding their use.

8.2.2 Authority and subject key identifier extensions

The *subject key identifier extension* provides an identifier for the certified subject's public key. This allows the relying party to identify that key when necessary, e.g., when validating a signature signed by one of multiple signature keys of the subject, if the relying party is provided with the key identifier together with the signature.

An important special case is when the subject is itself a CA which may use different private signing keys, e.g., $\{s_1, s_2\}$, with corresponding certificates Ψ_1, Ψ_2 for the corresponding public verification keys $\{v_1, v_2\}$. Suppose a relying party receives a certificate Ψ which was certified by this CA, i.e., $\Psi.issuer = \Psi_1.subject = \Psi_1.subject$. It is convenient if the relying party would know the identifier, say i, of the public verification key v_i that the relying party should use to validate Ψ; otherwise, the relying party may need to try every public key known to it, and, if it does not know a matching verification key, to fetch all the certificates for the verification keys of the CA (in this example, only two, Ψ_1, Ψ_2).

The *authority key identifier extension* provides a way for a certificate to indicate the authority's certificate to be used to validate the certificate, by containing the same identifier as indicated in the subject key identifier extension of the corresponding certificate of the issuer. Note that the term 'authority' here simply refers to the issuing CA.

The main use of the key identifier extensions is for convenience and efficiency. A more unusual application is the use of client certificates Ψ which do not explicitly identify their issuer.

Both X.509v3 and PKIX specify that authority and subject key identifier extensions should be marked as non-critical. Which makes sense; not using these mechanisms can only result in wasting resources, but not in using a certificate incorrectly.

8.2.3 The certificate policy extensions and Domain/Organization/Extended Validation

A *certificate policy (CP)* is a set of rules that indicate the applicability of the certificate to a particular use, such as indicating a particular community of relying parties that may rely on the certificate, and/or a class of relying party applications or security requirements, which may rely on the certificate. Certificate policies (CPs) inform relying parties of the level of confidence they may have in the validity of the bindings between the certified public key and the information in the certificates regarding the subject, including the subject identifiers. Namely, the CP provides information which may assist the relying party to decide whether or not to trust a certificate for a particular purpose.

The CP may also be viewed as a legally-meaningful document, which may define, and often limit, the liability and obligations of the issuer (CA) for potential inaccuracies in the certificate, and define statutes to which the CA, subject, and relying parties should conform. Certificates may be governed by laws and regulations; however, these legal and regulatory aspects are beyond our scope.

Standard certificate policies and types of validations — DV, OV, EV and QWAC-valid: The certificate policies extension is often used to identify a *standard policy*; the policy is specified by the *policy OID* field. In Table 8.3, we show some of the most important and widely used standard policies for different types of certificates.

Most of the policies in Table 8.3 were defined by the *CA-Brower Forum (CABF)*, in Ref. [187], and focus on the process used by the CA to validate certificate-issuing requests, for either TLS or code-signing certificates. The CABF defined three standard validation processes: *DV*, *OV* and *EV*, given in order of increasingly secure validation.

We explain these three CABF validation processes in the following, but first let us mention one additional policy which appears

Table 8.3. Standard certificate policies. OIDs are from the CA/Browser Forum object registry https://cabforum.org/resources/object-registry/, whose OID is 2.23.140; the policies are identified by OIDs as marked, following the prefix 2.23.140. The prices cited are examples of yearly certificate costs taken from https://www.sslshopper.com/ on February 2025, with the addition of the zero cost (free) option for TLS-DV certificates from https://letsencrypt.org. EV code signing certificates prices obtained directly from the websites of the CAs. QWAC information is from Sectigo's website. We did not include (higher-priced) certificates bundled with additional services.

Application	Validation	Domains	Price range	OID
TLS	DV	Single	Free to $249	2.23.140.1.2.1
TLS	DV	Multiple	Free to $249	2.23.140.1.2.1
TLS	DV	Wildcard	Free to $849	2.23.140.1.2.1
TLS	OV	Single	$39 to $390	2.23.140.1.2.2
TLS	OV	Multiple	$32 to $1275	2.23.140.1.2.2
TLS	OV	Wildcard	$249 to $1860	2.23.140.1.2.2
TLS	EV	Single	$100 to $973	2.23.140..2.2
TLS	EV	Multiple	$181 to $2728	2.23.140.1.2.2
TLS	QWAC	Single	$299 (Sectigo)	1.3.6.1.4.1.6449.1.2.1.7.5
Code-signing	OV	n/a	$129 to $434	2.23.140.1.3
Code-signing	EV	n/a	$349 to $816	2.23.140.1.3

in Table 8.3. This is the *Qualified Website Authentication Certificate (QWAC) validation* policy, which was defined by the European Union, in the *European Digital Identity Regulation (Regulation 2024/1183, also known as eIDAS2)*. EIDAS2 defines requirements from certificate issuers, websites and relying parties, and the improved validation of website certificates [137, 378].

The CABF validation processes — OV, EV and DV: The 'classical' CABF validation process is Organization Validation (OV), defined (for TLS certificates) in Ref. [185]. To issue an OV certificate, the CA should confirm that the requesting entity can manage the specified domain name and that the domain is registered to an organization which is a legal entity (whose name may be specified in the subject field of the certificate).

The Extended Validation (EV) process, defined (for TLS certificates) in Ref. [186], extends the OV process by additional verifications before issuing the certificate. These include verifying the physical address of the organization, verifying that the organization is active and verifying a reliable means of communication with the organization.

The Domain Validation (DV) process only validates that the requesting entity has control over the requested domain name. DV is a fully automated process for the issuing CA. The validation process often uses the Automated Certificate Management Environment (ACME) protocol [181]; if the requesting entity also uses ACME, then the validation process is also automated for it. Therefore, DV verification is a quick and easy process. This allows DV certificates to be offered for free — mainly, by the *Let's Encrypt* CA — or for a low fee.[5]

However, DV is not a very secure validation process. It involves a process where the domain owner demonstrates their ability to control the domain, typically, by adding a CA-specified DNS record or HTTP resource (webpage), or responding to email. This process can be circumvented easily by the MitM attacker; see Exercise 8.7.

[5]Although, as can be seen in Table 8.3, some CAs charge significant fees for DV certificates: $249 for a single or multiple domain certificate and even $849 for a wildcard certificate.

Details of the DV verification process: A typical DV verification process is illustrated in Figure 8.6. The specific validation we show in Figure 8.6 uses a DNS record to validate the client's public validation key $B.v$ for the domain name *Bob.com* and then issues a certificate Ψ_B where $\Psi_B.pk = B.v$ and $\Psi_B.dNSName =$ *'Bob.com'*.

Let us explain this typical DV verification process. The subject first contacts the CA to requests a DV-certificate for the domain they own, say Bob.com. The CA responds with a challenge, consisting of a specific, randomly-chosen sub-domain of Bob.com, say ch_1.Bob.com (where ch_1 is a random string), and with another randomly chosen challenge, ch_2. The subject has to set the DNS record of type TXT of the sub-domain ch_1.Bob.com to a string encoding the pair of values $B.v$ (the subject's public key) and $Sign_{B.s}(ch_2)$, i.e., the signature

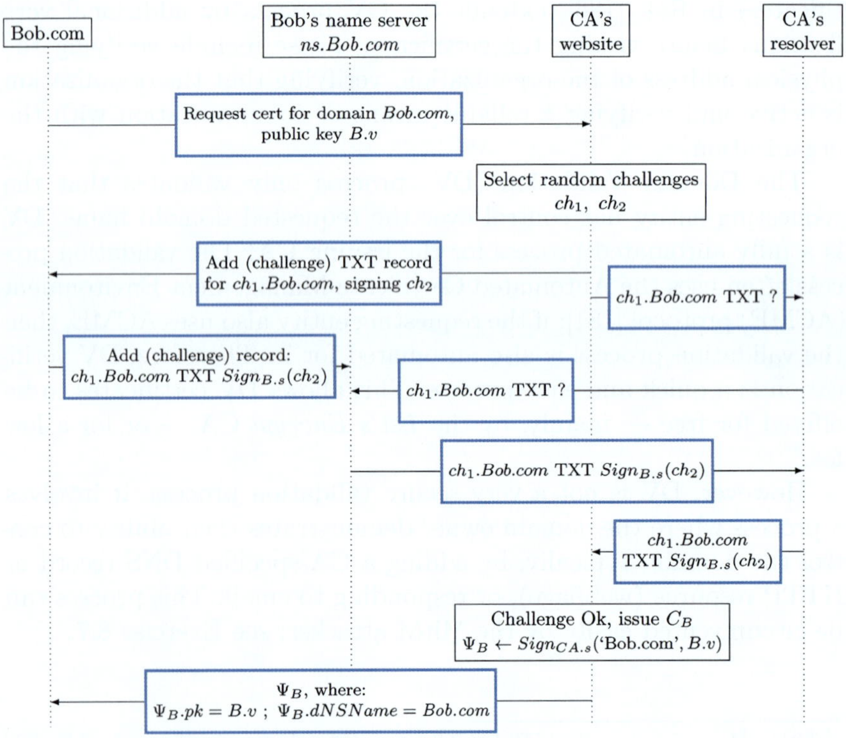

Figure 8.6. Domain validation; in practice, often automated using the ACME protocol [181].

using the corresponding private signing key $B.s$ over the second challenge ch_2 randomly selected by the CA.

After the subject has set properly the TXT DNS record for ch_1.Bob.com, they inform the CA that they are ready for the CA to complete the validation process. The CA then makes a DNS query for the domain ch_1.Bob.com, and receives back the value, which is the string encoding of $Sign_{B.s}(ch_2)$. The CA uses the given public validation key $B.v$ to validate the signature on ch_2; if validation succeeds, the CA certifies $B.v$ as the public validation key for the domain *Bob.com*. Namely, the certificate contains the SubjectAltName (*SAN*) extension, with the dNSName entry set to *Bob.com*.

DV is vulnerable to network attacks, including *MitM* attacks and off-path attacks, exploiting weaknesses of the *DNS* or of the *routing* infrastructure; e.g., see Refs. [77, 102, 141] and Exercise 8.7.

To increase the security of DV, the CA may send multiple challenges from different servers, in different network locations. The CA may also use multiple different validation techniques, e.g., requiring the subject to set up a web resource in the domain Bob.com (e.g., http://Bob.com/ch_3.txt) or in a subdomain (e.g., http//ch_4.Bob.com/ch_5.txt), or sending an email to an email address in a subdomain, possibly the email listed in the WhoIs record of the domain. However, the security of all of these methods ultimately depend on the security of the DNS query process and, therefore, is vulnerable to the network attacks, which may exploit the weaknesses of routing system and/or of the DNS.

The impact of validation-type on the use of the certificate: In principle, the type of validation applied by the issuing CA *could* be used by relying parties to determine their use of the certificate; it is conceivable that fraudsters would be less likely to obtain EV or OV certificates, mainly due to their stronger validation requirements.[6] Namely, the risk of a rogue certificate may be a bit lower for OV and EV certificates than for DV certificates.

However, web browsers, probably the most significant class of relying parties, do accept DV certificates. Until around 2019, most major

[6]DV certificates are also free, but the financial cost would rarely deter an attacker from obtaining an OV or EV, if the attack would be more likely to succeed using them.

browsers reflected the difference in the type of validation quite clearly in their user interface. In particular, for sites using EV certificates, some versions of browsers display, near the URL, the organization name, and the name of the CA that identified the site; this was originally proposed in Ref. [241], who found that displaying the name of the organization and the name of the CA helped users identify spoofed websites. However, more recent browsers use the same user interface indicators for all types of certificates. In principle, the validation type can be identified by users interacting with the user interface to look up the details of the certificate, but experiments conducted by the author show that very few, if any, users do this, even expert users and even for highly sensitive sites. Some justifications given for this change, in Ref. [218], are that these indications were found ineffective and that the additional indicator interferes with the browser approach of presenting a warning against sites which are *not* protected by TLS.

Exercise 8.2. Use your browser to visit you bank, a newspaper and a government websites, and the browser's user interface to see the details of the certificate and compare the certificate validation methods.

8.2.4 The certificate path constraints extensions

In this section, we present the three *certificate path constraints* extensions that are defined in X.509 and PKIX: BASIC CONSTRAINTS, NAME CONSTRAINTS and POLICY CONSTRAINTS. These constraints are relevant only for a certificate Ψ issued to a subject, e.g., Ψ.*subject*=*Bob.com*, by a CA (Ψ.issuer) who is not a root CA, i.e., Ψ.*issuer* is a *LCA* or an *ICA*; it is *not* one of the root CAs, directly trusted by the relying party (say Alice). Alice uses the certificate path constraints extensions in its decision of whether it should trust the certificate Ψ or not.

For example, in Figure 8.3, the relying party (Alice) receives three certificates: (1) a certificate for the subject, e.g., the website *Bob.com*, signed by some *LCA*, (2) a certificate for *LCA* signed by an *ICA* and (3) a certificate for *ICA* signed by a root CA *Root*. In this case, we will say that the subject, *Bob.com*, has a *two-hop certificate path* from *Root* since *LCA* is certified by *ICA* which is certified by the root CA *Root*.

In more complex scenarios, e.g., the one in Figure 8.7, there are additional intermediary CAs in the certificate path from the trust anchor to the subject. In Figure 8.7, the subject, website *Bob.com*, is certified via an indirect certification path with four hops, i.e., including a root CA *Root*, two intermediary CAs, *ICA* and *ICA2*, and *LCA*. The subject *Bob.com* is certified by *LCA*, which is certified by *ICA2*, which is certified by *ICA*, and only *ICA* is certified by the root CA *Root*. Hence, in this example, the certification path consists of *four* certificates: (1) Ψ_{ICA}, the certificate issued by the root CA *Root* to

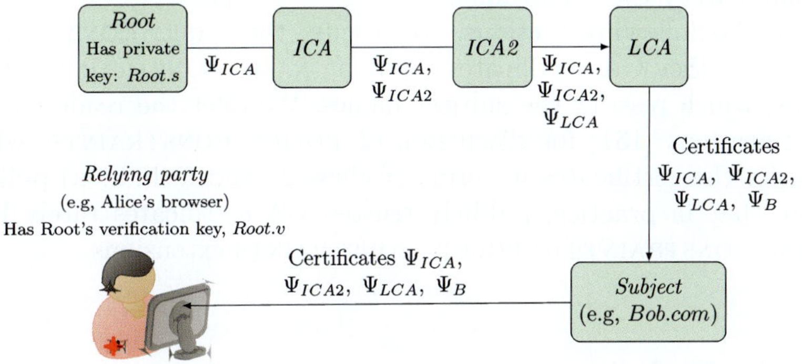

	Constraints extensions: Ψ_{ICA}				Ψ_{ICA2}, Ψ_{LCA}	Ψ_B valid?
	Basic		Name		Basic	
	cA	pathLen	Permit	Exclude	cA	
1	TRUE	none	*Bob.com*	none	TRUE	Yes
2	TRUE	2	*Bob.com*	*x.Bob.com*	TRUE	Yes
3	TRUE	3	*com*	*C.com*	TRUE	Yes
4	TRUE	5	Not included		TRUE	Yes
5	(any)	1 or 0	(any)	(any)	(any)	No
6	(any)	(any)	*cat.com*	(any)	(any)	No
7	(any)	(any)	(none)	*Bob.com*	(any)	No
8	(any)	(any)	(any)	(any)	FALSE	No

Figure 8.7. A certificate path containing a subject (e.g., website *Bob.com*) and four CAs: a root CA *Root*, two intermediary CAs ($ICA, ICA2$) and a LCA. The table shows the impact of different values of the BASIC CONSTRAINTS and NAME CONSTRAINTS extensions. In rows 1–3, assume that Ψ_{ICA2} does not have a pathLen parameter in the BASIC CONSTRAINTS extension (or $pathLen \geq 1$). In all rows, assume that none of the certificate has POLICY CONSTRAINTS (or that they are satisfied). In row 4 assume that the intermediate certificates Ψ_{ICA}, Ψ_{ICA2}, Ψ_{LCA} all have the *cA* flag set in the BASIC CONSTRAINTS extension and that the certificates Ψ_{ICA2}, Ψ_{LCA} do not have any constraints extensions.

the intermediary CA *ICA*, (2) and (3), the two certificates Ψ_{ICA2} and Ψ_{LCA}, issued by the intermediary CAs *ICA* and *ICA2*, respectively, to the *ICA ICA2* and the *LCA*, respectively, and finally (4) Ψ_B, the certificate issued by the *LCA* to the subject (*Bob.com*).

Note that, somewhat contrary to their name, the certification path constraints extensions in a certificate Ψ cannot *prevent* $\Psi.subject$, or other CAs certified by $\Psi.subject$, from issuing certificates which do not comply with these constraints. The constraints only limit the accountability of the issuing CA, $\Psi.issuer$, to only certificates which satisfy the constraints. Effectively, this is an indication to the relying party that $\Psi.issuer$ does not recommend relying on certificates which do not satisfy the constraints.

In the following sections, we discuss the BASIC CONSTRAINTS, which restrict CA certificates, and the NAME CONSTRAINTS extensions, which restrict the subject names. We refer the reader to the specifications [131] for discussion of POLICY CONSTRAINTS, which restrict the certificates in terms of allowed (and forbidden) policies. Note that in practice, publicly trusted CA certificates rarely have NAME CONSTRAINTS or POLICY CONSTRAINTS extensions.

8.2.4.1 *The basic constraints extension*

The BASIC CONSTRAINTS extension of a certificate Ψ defines a boolean flag denoted $\Psi.cA$ and, optionally, an integer denoted[7] $\Psi.pathLen$, both with the (non-standard) capitalization used here. Let us explain how these are used.

The *cA* flag indicates whether the Ψ is a CA certificate, i.e., if $\Psi.pk$ can be used (as a signature validation key) to validate certificates. More precisely, if Ψ has no BASIC CONSTRAINTS extension or if $\Psi.cA$ = FALSE, then relying parties should not rely on $\Psi.pk$ to validate certificates, i.e., Ψ is not a CA certificate. For example, in both Figures 8.3 and 8.7, the root CA (*Root*) signs certificate Ψ_{ICA}. The root CA should specify that *ICA* is a trusted (intermediate) CA,

---

[7] We use *pathLen* as a shorthand; the specification actually uses the longer term *pathLenConstraint*.

by setting the cA flag in the BASIC CONSTRAINTS extension of Ψ_{ICA} to *TRUE*.

Note that there are additional conditions for using $\Psi.pk$ to validate certificates. In particular, Ψ should contain the KEY USAGE extension and the extension should allow the use of $\Psi.pk$ for validating certificates. On the other hand, even if Ψ is not a CA certificate, e.g., with $\Psi.cA = $ FALSE, the key $\Psi.pk$ *could* be used to validate certificates if it is authorized by another certificate Ψ', with $\Psi'.pk = \Psi.pk$ and $\Psi'.cA = $ TRUE.

The other parameter of the BASIC CONSTRAINTS extension is the (optional) integer value *pathLen*. This is a limit on the length of the certificate path. Namely, consider a certificate path $\Psi_0, \Psi_1, \ldots, \Psi_l$ and assume that each certificate in the path has a signature which validates successfully using the public key of the next certificate in the chain, i.e., $(i \geq 0) Verify_{\Psi_{i+1}.pk}(\Psi_i.TBS, \Psi_i.\sigma) = $ TRUE. One condition for Ψ_0 to be validated successfully using this certificate path is that for every i, either Ψ_i does not define *pathLen*, or $\Psi_i.pathLen \geq i - 1$. For example, in Figure 8.7, for Ψ_B to be valid, we must have either $\Psi_{\text{ICA}}.pathLen \geq 2$ or no *pathLen* in Ψ_{ICA}.

8.2.4.2 *The* NAME CONSTRAINTS *extension*

The NAME CONSTRAINTS extension is used in certificates issued to a subject CA, such as the intermediary CAs in Figures 8.3 and 8.7. The NAME CONSTRAINTS extension restricts the set of subject names to be certified by the subject CA, as well as by any subsequent CA. For example, in Figure 8.7, the NAME CONSTRAINTS extensions, which is included in the certificate Ψ_{ICA} issued by a root CA (*Root*) to *ICA*, would restrict certificates issued by *ICA, ICA2* and *LCA*; this is not relevant to the subject, i.e., the website *Bob.com*, since it is not a CA (and cannot issue certificates).

The NAME CONSTRAINTS extension has two possible parameters, which we denote by the terms[8] *permit* (to define permitted name spaces) and *exclude* (to forbid name spaces, typically within the permitted name space). Focusing on the PKIX profile, both parameters are identifiers for names, usually a domain name; we focus on this case. When a domain name is specified, this is taken to include

[8]The specification uses the longer terms *permittedSubtrees* and *excludedSubtrees*.

sub-domains, e.g., if a NAME CONSTRAINTS contain parameter *permit* (only) for domain name com, then this allows subdomains such as *google.com*, but not names in other top-level domains such as *x.org*. The *exclude* parameter takes precedence; i.e., if a certificate contains both *permit* for domain name, say *edu*, and *exclude* for subdomain, *uconn.edu*, then this allows subsequent certificates only for domains in the *edu* top-level domain and excludes domains in the subdomain *uconn.edu*. See examples in the table in Figure 8.7.

Figure 8.8 presents an example of a typical application of the NAME CONSTRAINTS extension, using X.509 DNs. In this example, the NTT Japan CA issues a certificate to IBM Japan, allowing the IBM Japan CA to certify any certificates with the value 'IBM' for the organization (O) keyword — implying that IBM Japan cannot certify other organizations. Also, see IBM Japan certifying the 'main', corporate IBM CA, but excluding sites where the value of the country (C) keyword is Japan, i.e., not allowing corporate IBM CA to certify sites

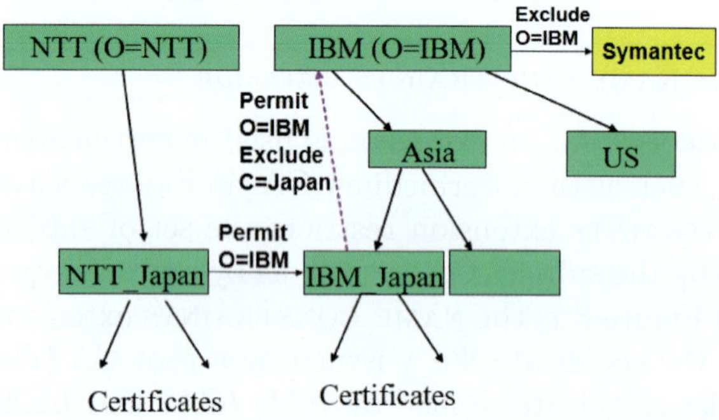

Figure 8.8. Example of the use of the NAME CONSTRAINTS extension, where constraints are over distinguished name keywords. NTT Japan issues a certificate to IBM Japan, with the NAME CONSTRAINTS *Permit O=IBM*, i.e., allowing it to certify only DNs with the value 'IBM' to the 'O' (organization) keyword, since NTT Japan does not trust IBM Japan to certify other organizations. IBM Japan certifies the global IBM, only for names in the IBM organization (*Permit O=IBM*), and excluding names in Japan (*Exclude C=Japan*). As a result, NTT trusts certificates issued by IBM to different parts of IBM, e.g., IBM US, but would not trust certificates issued by IBM to IBM Japan or to other companies, e.g., Symantec. Similarly, IBM certifies Symantec for all names, except names in the IBM organization.

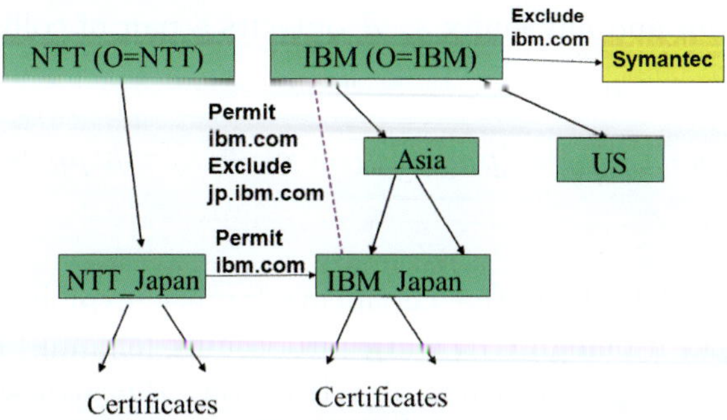

Figure 8.9. Example of the use of the NAME CONSTRAINTS extension with distinguished names (*dNSName*).

in Japan, even IBM sites. Note that such certificate issued by corporate IBM would also be trusted by relying parties using only NTT Japan as a trust anchor, provided that other relevant constraints such as certificate path length are satisfied (or not specified).

Figure 8.9 presents a similar example but using DNS domain names instead of X.500 DNs.

8.2.5 Exploiting chosen-prefix collisions to issue a rogue CA certificate

Suppose that the hash function h used by a benign certificate authority, CA_B, is vulnerable to chosen-prefix collision attacks; namely, CA_B uses h to sign (issue) certificates, following the Hash-then-Sign paradigm (Section 3.3.5). In this section, we show that an attacker $\mathcal{A}$ can exploit this vulnerability of h, to trick CA_B into signing a seemingly legitimate certificate Ψ_L, producing the signature $\sigma_L = Sign_{CA_B.s}(\Psi_L)$, such that σ_L also a valid signature for a rogue CA certificate Ψ_R.

The attack exploits the fact that chosen-prefix collision attacks are known against both MD5 and SHA-1, standard keyless hash functions which were often used in signing certificates (see Refs. [328, 451–453] and Section 3.3.6). Specifically, for both hash functions ($h \in \{$MD5,SHA-1$\}$), there is an efficient algorithm $\mathcal{A}$ that finds a chosen-prefix collision for h. Namely, given any pair of same-length prefixes p_L, p_R and any suffix s, $\mathcal{A}$ outputs a pair of collision strings $c_L \neq c_R$ such that

$$(\forall p_L, p_R, s \text{ s.t. } |p_L| = |p_R|)\ h(p_L + c_L + s) = h(p_R + c_R + s) \tag{8.2}$$

Let us explain how the certificate-forgery exploit works. The attacker tricks a benign CA, CA_B into issuing (signing) a seemingly legitimate website certificate, Ψ_L. However, the attacker carefully engineers the customer-provided fields of the certificate, most significantly, the subject (website) domain name and the public key fields, so that the hash of Ψ_L would be identical to the hash of the *rogue CA certificate* Ψ_R. Figure 8.10 illustrates the two certificates; note our use of the subscript L for the legitimate certificate, on the left, and of the subscript R for the rogue certificate, on the right.

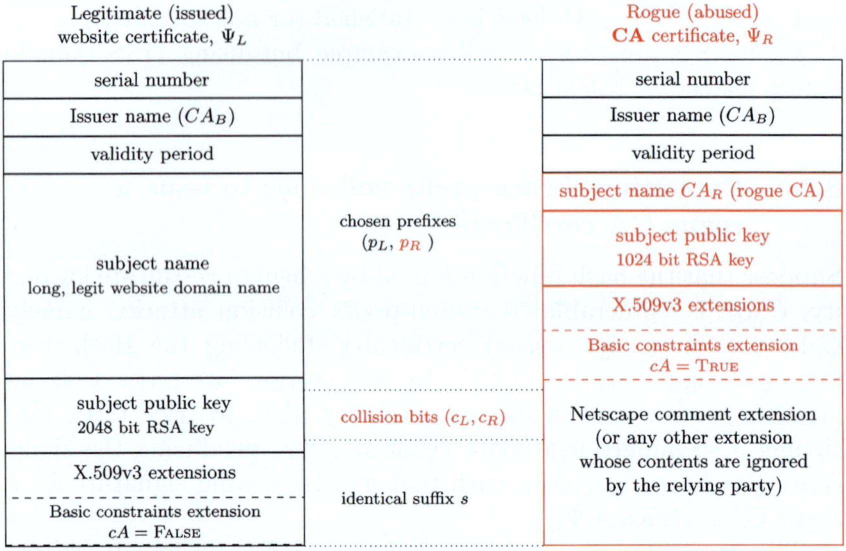

Figure 8.10. Attacker exploiting chosen-prefix collision of hash function h, used in signing, to trick a benign-yet-vulnerable issuing certificate authority, CA_B, into signing a 'legitimate' certificate Ψ_L, engineered such that the $h(\Psi_L) = h(\Psi_R)$, where Ψ_R is a rogue (fake yet valid) CA certificate supposedly issued by CA_B to another (rogue) certificate authority CA_R. The (simplified) illustration is based on Ref. [454], where this exploit was first presented for MD5.

Since $h(\Psi_L) = h(\Psi_R)$, the signature that CA_B provided for Ψ_L is also a valid signature for the Ψ_R. Namely, certificate-forgery the attacker can present Ψ_R, with that signature, and it would be deemed valid to (benign) relying parties, e.g., browsers.

Let us explain the mapping of the relevant fields of the two certificates.

The serial number, issuer (CA) name and validity period fields: The two certificates begin with those three fields. In the rogue certificate Ψ_R, the attacker can use arbitrary serial number and validity period, but will be sure to use the correct issuer name CA_B since the certificate should be validated using the public key of the issuing CA.

In the legitimate certificate Ψ_L, the attacker has no control over the values of these fields. However, the CA name is (typically) known to the attacker. Furthermore, the attacker *may* be able to *predict* the values of the validity period and serial number fields, with reasonable probability of success; for details, see Ref. [454]. Note that predictable serial numbers *were* used by some CAs at the time of Ref. [454], but after the attack was presented, CAs are required to use randomized serial numbers, which would make this attack fail.

The subject name field: The certificate-forgery attacker can select this field for both the rogue certificate and the legitimate certificate. The CA will validate that the request comes from the owner of the domain name, which means that the domain name requested should be owned by the attacker, but this does not interfere with the attack; note that the attacker is at complete freedom in choosing the subject name of the rogue certificate. Therefore, even if CA_B prevented the rogue certificate from being a CA certificate, using the *pathLen* parameter of the BASIC CONSTRAINTS extension, the attacker could still use the attack, to obtain rogue certificates to arbitrary domains chosen by the attacker.

The subject names that the attacker uses for the two certificates have very different lengths. In the rogue certificate, the attacker will use a rather short subject name (i.e., name for the rogue CA), while in the legitimate certificate, the attacker will request the CA to issue a certificate to a legitimate-but-long domain name. The reason is that the domain name is the last field in the prefix p_L of the legitimate certificate, to be followed by the collision bits (c_L), and while the two prefixes (p_L and p_R) can differ, they should have the same length; and the rogue prefix p_R should contain additional fields that the attacker needs to control, which we discuss next.

The subject public key field: In the legitimate certificate Ψ_L, this field is taken from the client's certificate request, i.e., it would be controlled by the attacker. In the certificate-forgery attack, the attacker abuses this field to contain the random collision bits, i.e., c_L. The attack uses the longest public key available at the time (2048 bits) since that makes it easier to find a collision.

In contrast, in the rogue certificate Ψ_R, the attacker needs to place a public key that the attacker generated; this is necessary since the attacker needs to know the corresponding private key. Therefore, the subject public key field has to be part of the prefix p_R chosen by the attacker. Since the length of p_R and p_L must be identical, this motivates the use of the shortest-allowed CA public key (at the time when Ref. [454] was published, 1024 bits).

The X.509v3 extensions field: Both certificates end with the extensions field, which includes mandatory and optional extensions, as determined by the issuing CA and as requested by the customer. As described earlier, the (mandatory) BASIC CONSTRAINTS extension includes a boolean attribute called *cA*, whose value is TRUE for CA certificates and FALSE for non-CA certificates. Namely, this attribute would be FALSE in Ψ_L. However, in Ψ_R, the attacker will place the extension with the *cA* attribute set as TRUE, indicating that the subject of the certificate is also a CA.[9]

The two certificates must have the same length in order to have colliding hash values. To ensure this, the rogue certificate Ψ_R contains an additional extension that fills up the space, ensuring that the two certificates will match in length. This extension would also contain the collision bits (c_R). Therefore, this should be an extension that will not foil the validity of Ψ_R, even when part of it is a sequence of meaningless bits (in particular, c_R). In Ref. [454] (and Figure 8.10), this is achieved by the *Netscape comment* extension, which is ignored by relying parties (e.g., browsers), but one could also

[9]The benign CA issuing the certificate *could* have prevented the attack if its own certificate would have prevented issuing of certificates to other CAs by using the *pathLen* parameter of the BASIC CONSTRAINTS extension. See Section 8.2.4.1.

use some meaningless non-critical extension. Note that the attacker can also add any other extension to either certificates.

8.3 Certificate revocation

Usually, certificates are used until they expire, i.e., throughout their validity period, which, for non root CAs, is typically between a few months to a year. Around the expiration date, certificates are often *re-issued.*

However, sometimes, a certificate should be *revoked*, i.e., invalidated before its planned and specified expiration time. In X.509, revocation is done by the CA, usually upon appropriate (and authenticated) request from the subject. A simple revocation mechanism called *CRL* has been part of X.509 from its earliest versions [119]; however, efficient certification turned out to be quite a challenge, and multiple designs were proposed.

Different reasons for revoking a certificate are listed in the PKIX [131] and X.509 [262] standard; we roughly categorize them as follows:

Subject key exposure: Private keys should be well protected from exposure; however, exposures do happen. Normally, exposures are quite rare and sporadic. However, a discovery of a software vulnerability may cause exposure of many private keys, as happened due to the *Heartbleed bug* [118,501].

CA failures: Usually, certificate authorities operate in a secure, trustworthy manner, and issue correct certificates to the rightful subjects — as required and expected. However, there have also been incidents where CAs have failed in different ways, including *vulnerable subject identification*, e.g., insecure email validation, *issuing intermediate-CA certificates to untrusted entities*, e.g., to all customers, and even *CA compromise and issuing of rogue certificates* or what appears to be *intentional issuing of rogue certificates.* See Section 8.4 and Table 8.4.

Subject misbehavior: Certificates may be revoked upon discovery that the certificate was requested without authorization, discovery that the certificate was misused or could be misleading or discovery that the subject violated its obligations or terms of use.

Cryptanalytical certificate forgery: Certificate-based PKIs all use and depend on the Hash-then-Sign (HtS) mechanism, and therefore become vulnerable if the signature scheme, or the hash function, is vulnerable. Certificate forgery was demonstrated when using hash functions vulnerable to *chosen-prefix collision* attacks, specifically, using MD5 [452], and later also using SHA-1 [328,452]; see Chapter 3 and Section 8.2.5.

Revocation due to change: These revocations are due to a change which invalidates the information in the certificate. This can be a change to the certified name or to other certified attributes, e.g., removal of some (certified) privilege. Other reasons for change are when the certified entity ceases to operate, or just stops using the certified public–private key pair, for a benign reason (such as change of business or change to a more secure key or algorithm).

Other revocations: Some revocations may be for other reasons, such as a request by the subject, a legal obligation of the CA, or some mistake or failure of the CA.

Typically, revocations occur in a low rate, e.g., a few dozens of revocations daily. However, software and CA vulnerabilities can result in exceptional 'waves' of revocations. One example is the *Heartbleed bug*, published in April 2014, which resulted in several days with many revocations, including one day with more than 10,000 revocations [118, 501]. An even larger revocation event occurred in March 2020, when the Let's Encrypt CA had to revoke 1.7M certificates due to a bug in their *Certificate Authority Authorization (CAA)* validation code [1, 302]. Read about CAA in Section 8.4.1 and Ref. [232].

Revocation mechanisms — CRLs, OCSP, short-lived certificates and others: Revocation mechanisms are methods to inform the relying parties that a certificate was revoked. This turns out to be a significant challenge — definitely much larger than originally anticipated.

The early X.509 design [119] only offered one method for revocation, the *CRL*. A CRL is, essentially, a list of the revoked certificates, typically signed by the issuing CA. CRLs are still widely *implemented* and supported by CAs; however, most relying parties prefer to use other mechanisms to check for revocations, since CRLs often have excessive overhead, mainly in terms of peak bandwidth. We discuss CRLs in Section 8.3.1

Another revocation mechanism which was standardized is *OCSP*, the *Online Certificate Status Protocol (OCSP)* [429]. We discuss OCSP in Section 8.3.2, and the *OCSP stapling* variant in Section 8.3.3. In Section 8.3.4, we discuss a few non-standardized revocation mechanisms.

Finally, we mention that another approach is to avoid revocation altogether, by using *short-lived certificates.* After all, the revocation process itself always takes some time. Suppose that a certificate Ψ is revoked at time t_R; with any revocation mechanisms, there is some delay Δ_R such that the certificate may still be considered valid until time $t_R + \Delta_R$. Therefore, there is never a need to revoke certificates with validity periods not longer than Δ_R. Let us explain further this issue of validation and freshness of the revocation information.

Validation and freshness of revocation information: When using any revocation mechanism to validate a certificate, say Ψ_B, relying parties must validate that Ψ_B was not revoked. Different revocation mechanisms use different types of *revocation information* to prove that a certificate was not yet revoked, e.g., a CRL is a list identifying all of the certificates which were revoked, and therefore, if a certificate Ψ_B is not included in the CRL, then Ψ_B was not revoked by the time at which the CRL was issued. Other revocation mechanisms use different types of revocation information, but the revocation information is always *signed and time-stamped*, allowing any party to validate its *authenticity and freshness.*

For example, suppose Alice's browser connects to *Bob.com* and receives a certificate Ψ_B, i.e., Ψ_B.*subject='Bob.com'*. As part of its validation of Ψ_B, the browser should validate that Ψ_B was not revoked. Usually, this amounts to validating a CRL or some other *revocation information* indicates that Ψ_B was not revoked. The revocation information, which we denote RI, should be authenticated and *time-stamped.* The time stamp may indicates an 'issuing time' $RI.t_I$ and/or an 'expiration time' $RI.t_E$, after which the revocation information RI is not considered fresh any more; if the expiration time is not included, then it may be computed from the issuing time as we explain in the following. The browser should only trust the revocation information RI until time $RI.t_E$; after that, the website should provide fresh revocation information.

Note that it is possible that a certificate Ψ_B is revoked at time t_R yet still be considered valid for some time after t_R; this may happen when there is some valid revocation information RI such that $RI.t_I < t_R \leq RI.t_E$. Such a period when a certificate was revoked (at t_R) but still considered valid (until $RI.t_E$) is unavoidable, due to *network delays, clock drift* and, most significantly, *efficiency*. Efficiency requires us to issue and distribute the revocation information RI only once in a period of some length, which we denote Δ_{RI}; this is necessary to limit the overhead due to signing and distributing the revocation information. Namely, if it may take up to Δ_{com} seconds to distribute the revocation information, the clock of the issuer of the revocation information and of the relying party may Δ_{clk} seconds before or after the real time, and the CA issues new revocation information once every Δ_{RI} seconds, then revocation information RI issued at with the issuer clock value $RI.t_I$ should contain expiration time computed as

$$RI.t_E = RE.t_I + (\Delta_{com} + 2 \cdot \Delta_{clk} + \Delta_{RI}) \tag{8.3}$$

If the revocation information RI includes the issuing time $RI.t_I$ but not the expiration time $RI.t_E$, then the relying party would rely on it until some bounded time after $RI.t_I$, basically estimating the outcome of Equation 8.3.

We leave it to the reader to figure out why Equation 8.3 doubles the maximal clock drift Δ_{clk}.

Distribution of revocation information: Often, the relying party receives the revocation information directly from the CA. However, since, usually, the revocation information is signed and time-stamped, then it could also be relayed by third parties. This fact is utilized by *OCSP stapling*, where the revocation information is provided by the *subject*, 'stapled' to the certificate. OCSP stapling is specified for the common case where the certificate is provided by a TLS Server, and in this case, it is provided in the ServerHello message; see Section 8.3.3.

Retrieving revocation information: periodically or as-needed (online)? There are two main options for the retrieving revocation information: *periodically*, e.g., daily, or *as-needed*, i.e., when the relying party needs the revocation information to validate a specific certificate. Online (as-needed) retrieval may reduce the bandwidth overhead since it avoids downloading unnecessary revocation information; on the other hand, the relying party must wait for the revocation information to arrive, introducing delay (waiting for the response) and the risk of communication failures. Online retrieval may also allow an attacker to perform a *DoS* attack against the CA or other Online Certificate Status Protocol (OCSP) server, by a 'flood' of revocation queries. There are also *privacy* concerns, due to the exposure of the identity of the certificates used by the relying party.

The OCSP protocol retrieves revocation information *as-needed*, i.e., as the name implies, it provides an online service to validate certificate status. Most other revocation mechanisms, including CRLs, usually retrieve revocation information periodically.

8.3.1 Certificate Revocation List (CRL)

The X.509 designers may have expected revocation to be very rare, with a small number of certificates which were revoked (but not yet expired) at any given time. In this case, a simple solution is for the CA to periodically sign and distribute a time-stamped list of all revoked certificates. Such a list is called a *CRL*. The CA may also authorize another entity to issue CRLs; the term *CRL issuer* can be used, to refer to the entity issuing the CRLs — the CA or an entity authorized by the CA. However, for simplicity, we mostly refer to the typical case where the CA is also the CRL issuer.

CRLs are defined as part of the X.509 standard, already from X.509v1 [119]. The contents of the CRL enhanced with later versions. Figure 8.11 shows the contents of the widely used CRL defined in X.509v3 [261]. As can be seen, this CRL shares quite a lot with the X.509v3 certificate (Figure 8.2); in particular, it has similar version,[10] signature algorithm OID, issuer *Distinguished Name*, subject *Distinguished Name* and extensions fields.

[10]Confusingly, the CRL specification support extensions from CRL version 2, not 3 (as might be expected for X.509v3 certificate). Furthermore, in CRLs, the version field is optional; when the version field is absent, this indicates version 1, which does not support extensions. In practice (and this book), CRLs are always version 2, i.e., contain both version and extension fields.

CRLs also contain the following additional fields, which are not used in certificates:

thisUpdate: The time at which the CRL was issued (signed), according to the CRL issuer's clock; this is essentially the time $RI.t_I$ in Equation 8.3.

nextUpdate: If specified, the *nextUpdate* time, denoted $t_{nextUpdate}$, bounds the time when an updated CRL will be issued, which provides a bound for the 'expiration date' for the CRL. The relying party can surely consider the CRL as fresh up to $t_{nextUpdate}$ — or even add a bit of time to account for the network delay (Δ_{com}) and the possible drift of clock values from real time (Δ_{clk}). To make sure that it has an updated CRL, a relying party may send a request for a new CRL prior to the nextUpdate time, e.g., at $t_{nextUpdate} - 2 \cdot \Delta_{com}$ (why?).

revokedCertificates: This field lists one or more CRL Entries. The contents of CRL Entries are shown in Figure 8.11(b). Each CRL Entry contains (1) the certificate serial number of a revoked certificate, (2) the revocation date (and time) and (3) optional extensions, defined similarly to the X.509v3 certificate extensions. Note that there is also a similar extensions field to the entire CRL (crlExtensions), which we describe in the following.

crlExtensions: An optional field, that may contain extensions to the CRL, much like the X.509 certificate extensions (and the extensions field of a particular CRL entry, discussed above).

As we discuss in the following, an issuer (CA) may use the same CRL for all of the certificates that it issues, or issue separate CRLs for different sets of certificates, defined using a CRL extension.

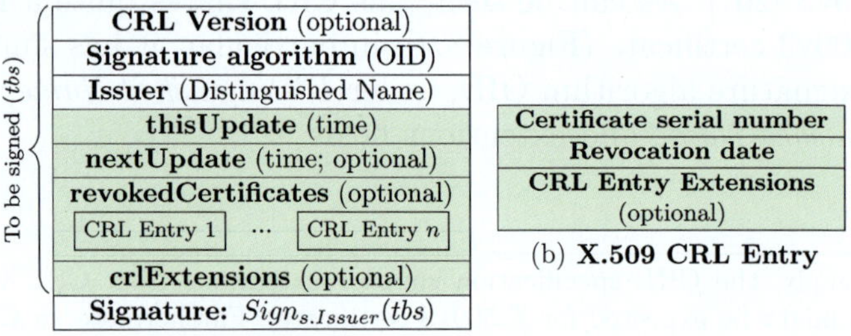

(a) **X.509 CRL** (b) **X.509 CRL Entry**

Figure 8.11. Certificate revocation list (CRL): CRL fields (a) and CRL entry fields (b). Fields with white background correspond to X.509v3 certificate fields.

A relying party should use a valid, non-expired CRL to check if a certificate issued by the CA was revoked. The CRL is usually cached until it expires or is replaced by a more recently issued CRL (from the same issuer, and if relevant, for the same set of certificates). The relying party may request the CRL when needed, or when the current CRL is about to expire (to avoid waiting for the new CRL to arrive).

The *CRL Distribution Point (cRLDistributionPoints)* certificate extension: To retrieve the CRL, the relying party may use the *cRLDistributionPoints* certificate extension, defined in Refs. [131, 261]; this extension defines how (using what protocol) to retrieve the CRL, what address to use, and the CRL issuer (if it differs from the issuer of the certificate). Multiple distribution points may be defined.

CRL optimization extensions: *Bandwidth overhead* is a major concern with CRLs since CRLs can often be quite large. Measurements of CRL overhead were reported in Ref. [501], who found median CRL of 51KB, and Ref. [449], who found average CRL of 173KB; note that these measurements were of actual CRLs in use, which often use the extensions as we explain below to reduce CRL length. Since every relying party needs to download the CRL from every CA, this becomes significant overhead. Note also that CRLs expiration times are the same for all clients; therefore, there is a peak period when many clients download new CRLs.

Furthermore, special events can cause a burst of many revocations, resulting in much larger CRLs. Almost 9% of the certificates (36,781 certificates), from different CAs, were revoked during April 2014 due to Heartbleed bug [118], resulting in a CRL of 76MB [501], and 1.7 million certificates were revoked by Let's revoke during March 2020 due to a CAA-rechecking bug [302]. Even in periods without such events, about 1% of the non-expired certificates are revoked at a given moment — which can still result in excessively long CRLs.

Three standard X.509 CRL extensions may reduce the bandwidth overhead of CRLs:

The Delta CRL extension lists only new revocations, which occurred since last 'regular' CRL (called base-CRL). When a relying party has a sufficiently recent base-CRL, it only retrieves the Delta CRL; the base-CRL is retrieved only as needed. To validate that a given certificate is not revoked, check if it is contained either in the Delta-CRL or in a base-CRL, issued not earlier than the time specified in the Delta-CRL. For this method to be effective, relying parties should cache, and periodically download, the base-CRL. Therefore, the storage requirements are the same as when using 'regular' CRLs.

The *Issuing Distribution Point* CRL extension: A CRL, available from the location defined in the certificate's CRL Distribution Point (cRLDistributionPoints) extension, should contain all revoked certificates which were issued by the CA and not yet expired. By default, all certificates issued by the CA are available from the same distribution point. However, often, CAs prefer to use multiple smaller CRLs, by splitting the set of certificates into separate sets, called *scopes*, e.g., based on issuing time. X.509v3 [261] specifies that in this case, the CRL must contain the standard, critical CRL extension called *Issuing Distribution Point*, which defines the relevant scope. The main motivation for a CA to use multiple CRLs, each with distinct scope (defined using the Issuing Distribution Point CRL extension), and using different corresponding locations in the cRLDistributionPoints extension in the certificates, is to reduce the bandwidth overhead. The use of multiple distribution points (and scope) reduces the length of each CRL, at the cost of requiring the CA to sign and distribute multiple CRLs. When relying parties download CRLs only as-needed, this may reduce the required bandwidth, but at the cost of reduced likelihood that the required CRL is cached, i.e., more cases where the relying party must download the CRL to validate a certificate, which can cause significant delay and availability concerns.

The Authorities Revocation List (ARL) extension lists only revocations of CA certificates. This is essentially equivalent to placing CA certificates in a dedicated distribution point and becomes meaningful mainly when relying parties download only the ARL, and use other mechanisms, such as OCSP, for non-CA certificates.

Even with such optimizations, CRLs may still introduce significant bandwidth overhead.

When to download CRLs: Periodically (in advance) or as-needed? The original X.509 CRL design, was to download all CRLs *in advance*, in a periodical process, e.g., daily [119]. This periodical process should be done with sufficient frequency, to make sure that the revocation information is reasonably updated (fresh). Since CRLs can be quite long, and many CRLs are not required in any given day, this results in considerable overhead; furthermore, many relying parties are likely to request the CRL concurrently, creating very high peak load.

Therefore, implementations often fetch the CRLs only *as-needed (online)*. However, this may cause increased delay (waiting for information to arrive), reduced reliability (what to do if revocation information is unavailable) and privacy concerns (e.g., exposing the website being visited). As a result, the use of CRLs has become less common.

When adopting the approach of fetching the revocation information only as-needed, it becomes unclear why to fetch information for all certificates (in the given distribution point) and not just for the specific certificates required. This is basically the approach of the standardized alternative to CRLs called the *OCSP* standard, which we discuss in the following Section 8.3.2.

8.3.2 The Online Certificate Status Protocol (OCSP)

OCSP is defined in RFC6960 [429]. As shown in Figure 8.12, OCSP is a request-response protocol, providing a signed indication to the relying party, showing the 'current' status of certificates (details below). The protocol involves two entities: the OCSP client, who sends an *OCSP request* to request the status of one or more certificates, and the OCSP responder (server), who responds with a (signed) OCSP response, indicating the status of the certificate(s).

The OCSP responder, i.e., the entity that processes OCSP requests and sends responses, is an entity trusted by the relying party; for simplicity, we will assume this is the CA itself, although it could also be another entity, delegated by the CA. Each OCSP response message is signed by the OCSP responder (which we assume to be the CA). This allows the relying party to validate the response, even

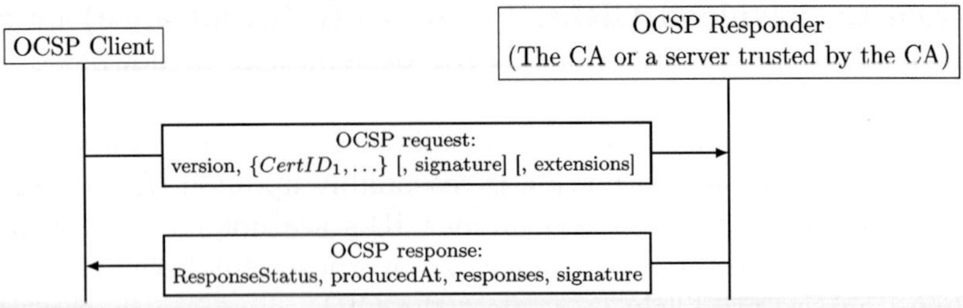

Figure 8.12. The *Online Certificate Status Protocol* (*OCSP*). The request includes one or more certificate identifiers $\{CertID_1, \ldots\}$; requests are optionally signed. The OCSP response is signed by the responder and includes response for each $CertID$ in the request. Each of these 'individual responses' includes the $CertID$, cert-status, time of this update, time of the next update and optional extensions. Certificate status is either *revoked, good* or *unknown.*

if the relying party receives the response via an untrusted intermediary, e.g., the subject (website).

In this section, we focus on the *relying party initiated* OCSP deployment, where OCSP client, i.e., the entity that sends the OCSP request, is the relying party, e.g., browser, as shown in Figure 8.13. Later, in Section 8.3.3, we discuss *OCSP stapling*, where the subject, e.g., the TLS server, sends the OCSP request, i.e., acts as the OCSP client.

The OCSP request identifies one or multiple certificates whose status is requested, each identified by a field called a *CertID*. The CertID identifies a certificate as well as the issuing CA, by specifying the certificate serial number and (the hash of) the DN of the CA and its public key. A request identifying multiple certificates is sometimes referred to as a *multi-certificate OCSP request.*[11] The support for multi-certificate OCSP requests and responses is important for efficiency, especially to handle the common case where an OCSP client needs a response validating the status of a certificate chain.

OCSP allows, but does not require, requests to be signed. However, an *OCSP response is always signed* by the OCSP responder (often, the CA). The response contains the time at which is was produced by the OCSP responder, as well as the time when

[11]Not to be confused with the similarly named TLS extension defined in RFC 6961 [400], which often uses this OCSP functionality.

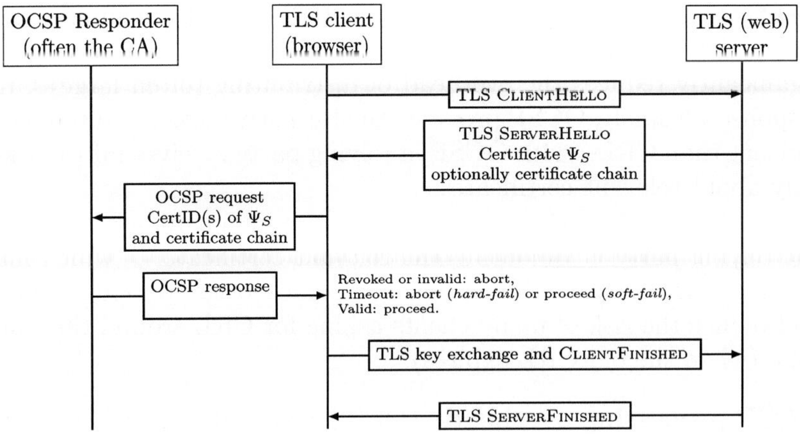

Figure 8.13. TLS handshake with OCSP initiated by the relying party. There are several concerns with this form of using OCSP, including privacy exposure, overhead on CA, and handling of delayed/missing OCSP response by the client/browser (see Figure 8.14). The concerns motivated updated browsers to support and prefer *OCSP stapling*, where the TLS/web server makes the OCSP request, instead of the client/browser (see Figure 8.15).

the responder was last updated on the certificate status, and the time planned for the next update; if the certificate was revoked, the response includes the revocation time. Note that OCSP normally ensures freshness only using these timestamps; requests do not include a nonce to be signed in the response. This allows the same response to be used for multiple requests, as long as they can all share the same response-production time.

The OCSP response includes a status for each certificate identified (by CertID) in the request. The status has three possible values: *revoked*, *good* and *unknown*. The 'unknown' response is typically sent when the OCSP responder does not serve OCSP requests for the issuer of the certificate in question or cannot resolve their status at the time (e.g., due to lack of response from the CA). These *unknown* responses are *ambiguous*; relying parties are left to decide how to interpret and respond to them.

Motivations to use OCSP rather than CRLs: The length of an OCSP response is linear in the number of certificates validated in this response, i.e., the number of *CertID*s in the corresponding OCSP request. This is usually much less than the number of revoked certificates of this CA, as sent in a CRL. In the common case where the total number of revoked certificates may be large, this significantly reduces the overhead of distributing (often large) CRL responses. Namely, OCSP provides an alternative which is often more efficient than CRLs; with OCSP, a relying party receives information only about relevant certificates.

In addition, OCSP responses are sent on a timely fashion, when the relying party is validating the relevant certificate — which may provide a more 'fresh' indication compared to the periodical CRL and reduce the risk of many clients asking for CRL around the same time (when the old CRL expires).

OCSP processing overhead: OCSP would often have higher processing overhead than CRLs since every OCSP response is *signed* by the OCSP responder, while the CA only needs to sign a complete CRL. This can become a significant computational burden on the OCSP responder. In addition to signing, there is the overhead of processing each of the (many) OCSP requests.

Consider the typical case, of a CA providing OCSP responder service. Normally, CAs cannot charge for the overhead of handling OCSP requests, and to provide reliable service, they should be ready to respond to a large number of clients making OCSP queries during a short period; this may occur due to external events which may cause many clients to access the same or different resources about the same time, which we refer to as *flash crowd*[12] events. A flood of many requests can also result from an intentional *Denial of Service (DoS)* attack. The DoS attack may even not be directed against the CA; one popular method of a DoS attack against a website is to cause many browsers to establish TLS connections with this server and send requests to it, which can result in many OCSP requests to the CA.

Due to the overhead concerns, an OCSP responder may limit its services to authorized OCSP clients. To support this, OCSP requests may be signed or otherwise authenticated. However, we are not aware of this being deployed.

[12]The term Flash Crowd is the name of a sci-fi novella by Larry Niven, describing 'physical flash crowd' due to the use of a transfer booth.

Relying-party initiated OCSP challenges — privacy, delay and failures: OCSP, and specifically relying party initiated OCSP, has its own set of challenges. One challenge is *privacy*; the contents of the OCSP requests identifies the certificate. In particular, this identifies the website when OCSP is initiated by the browser. Furthermore, since different webpages contain different resources, it would often be possible to identify a particular webpage, not just the website. Some OCSP clients and responders may run OCSP over TLS or otherwise encrypt the request and response, but even in these cases, there is privacy exposure to the OCSP responder. Furthermore, even with encryption of OCSP requests and responses, the *timing patterns* create a *side channel* that may allow an eavesdropper to identify visited websites.

Another challenge is *delay*; since OCSP is an online, request-response protocol, its deployment at the beginning of a connection often results in considerable delay. A relying party, e.g., a browser, may need to wait considerable time until it receives the OCSP response or times-out.

Finally, possibly the largest challenge are OCSP *failures*, which we discuss in the following.

Handling failures in relying party initiated OCSP: An OCSP request may fail in multiple ways, including, when the response is 'unknown', which does not provide information on the status of the certificate. OCSP also fails when the OCSP client fails to establish communication or receive response from the OCSP server. Another reason is when the OCSP responder sends back an *OCSP failure return code*, indicating a reason for failure. These reasons include the following:

- Lack of signature on OCSP request (when required by OCSP responder).
- Request not properly authorized/authenticated, e.g., not from known IP address, or missing/incorrect authentication information, when required by OCSP responder. Authentication information should be provided by the client in an appropriate OCSP extension.
- Technical reasons, such as overload or internal error.

Any of these failures creates a dilemma for the relying party (typically, browser) that made the corresponding OCSP request: how should the relying party respond? The following are the main options — and why each of them seems unsatisfactory:

Wait: The most common problem is timeout, and one possible response is for the relying party to continue waiting for the OCSP response, possibly resending the request periodically, and not 'give up'. However, OCSP servers could fail or become inaccessible forever, or for extremely long, leaving the relying party in this state.

Hard-fail: Abort the connection (and inform the user). That is clearly a 'safe' alternative, i.e., prevent use of a revoked certificate. However, the OCSP interaction may often fail or return ambiguous response due to benign reasons, such as network connectivity issues or overload of the OCSP responder. In particular, OCSP responders often do not have sufficient resources to handle high load of OCSP requests. Therefore, this approach is not widely adopted.

Ask user: The relying party may, after some timeout, invoke a user-interface dialog and ask the user to decide if to continue with the connection or abort it. For example, a browser may invoke a dialog, informing the user that the certificate-validation process is taking longer than usually, and ask the user what action it should take. While this option may seem to empower the user, in reality, users are rarely able to understand the situation and make an informed decision, and are very likely to continue with the connection; see the discussion of usability in Chapter 9. Hence, except for 'shifting the responsibility' to the user, this option is inferior to direct soft-fail, discussed in the following.

Soft-fail: Finally, the relying party may simply continue as if it received a valid OCSP response. By far, this is the most widely-adopted option. In the typical case of a benign failure to receive the OCSP response, this option is reasonable. However, this choice leaves the user vulnerable to an impersonation attack using a revoked certificate, when the attacker can block the OCSP response; see Figure 8.14. Since our need for cryptography is mainly due to concerns about a MitM attacker, who can surely block communication, this option results in a vulnerability.

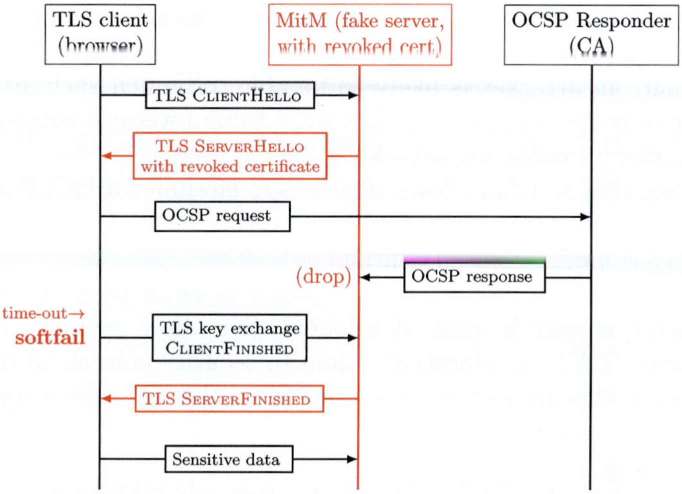

Figure 8.14. The MitM soft-fail Attack on a TLS connection using OCSP. The attack assumes relying party initiated OCSP deployment, where the TLS-client (browser) sends the OCSP request (acts as OCSP client), and (vulnerable) soft-fail handling of timeouts and ambiguous OCSP responses. The attacker is impersonating as a website, to which the attacker has the private key; the corresponding certificate is already revoked, but the attack allows the attacker to trick the browser into accepting it anyway, allowing the impersonation attack to succeed. The browser queries the CA (or other OCSP server) to receive a fresh certificate status. However, the attacker 'kills' the OCSP request, or the OCSP response (figure illustrates dropping of the response). After waiting for some time, the browser times out and accepts the revoked certificate sent by the impersonating website, although no OCSP response was received. This soft-fail behavior is used by most supporting OCSP browsers since the alternatives (very long timeout, asking the user, or hard-fail) are not well received by users.

The MitM attack on soft-fail relying party initiated OCSP: As Figure 8.14 shows, the soft-fail approach essentially nullifies the value of OCSP validation — against an attacker that can block or sufficiently delay the OCSP request/response, if the attacker has exposed the private key of the TLS (web) server, or has obtained a fake certificate for the server's domain (that was later revoked). Both exposing of the private key and obtaining a fake certificate are challenging attacks. However, such attacks do occur, which is one reason we need revocations. The other condition, of being able to block the OCSP response, may be feasible, e.g., by sending an excessive number of OCSP requests to the OCSP responder (e.g., the CA) at the same time as the OCSP request from the relying party. In particular, an attacker is likely to be able to launch such attack by intentionally invoking appropriate links from a website controlled by the attacker (a cross-site attack).

We see that soft-fail allows attackers to circumvent OCSP and use revoked certificates, by intentionally causing a failure to the OCSP challenge-response communication.

In spite of this vulnerability, *soft-fail is often used by browsers.* The main reason is that developers give more weight to *user-experience (UX)* considerations, than to security considerations. We summarize this important observation in the *UX>Security* precedence rule (Note 8.3).

Note 8.3: The UX>Security Precedence Rule Principle.

Loss of usability, availability, performance, reliability and functionality harm the *user-experience (UX)*. User experience has a direct, immediate impact on the success of a product. In contrast, security and privacy considerations are rarely visible to the users. As a result, even when vendors and developers care about security and privacy, they usually prefer to compromise on these goals, if the only available alternative would be harming the *user-experience (UX)* aspects: *availability, functionality, performance, usability* and *reliability.* We refer to this as the *UX>Security precedence rule.*

Principle 16 (The UX>Security Precedence Rule). Vendors and developers usually give precedence to the *user-experience (UX)* considerations (*availability, functionality, performance, usability* and *reliability*) over *security* and *privacy* considerations.

The challenge for designers and researchers is to find solutions which will ensure sufficient security but avoid or minimize harm to the user-experience (UX). For further discussion of human-centered aspects of security and cryptography, see Chapter 9.

We next describe *OCSP stapling*, where the OCSP client is the *subject* of the certificate rather than the relying party. The goal of OCSP stapling is to mitigate these security, privacy and efficiency concerns.

8.3.3 OCSP stapling and the must-staple mechanism

In the previous section, we have seen several disadvantages of the relying party initiated OCSP deployment, where the relying party sends the OCSP requests (i.e., acts as the OCSP client). In this section, we discuss an alternative approach, *OCSP stapling*, where the OCSP request is sent by the *subject*, typically the website. Namely, OCSP stapling moves the responsibility to obtain 'fresh' OCSP signed responses to the *subject* (e.g., web server), rather than placing this responsibility (and burden) on every client (e.g., browser). This addresses the privacy exposure and reduces the overhead on the OCSP responder (typically, the CA) since it now needs only to send a single signed OCSP response to each subject (website) — much less overhead than sending to every relying party (browser). Furthermore, since now only the subject is supposed to make OCSP requests, the CA may limit the service to its customers, which are the subjects of the certificates.

Therefore, of all the concerns discussed for the relying-party-based OCSP, the main concern that remains is handling of OCSP failures, and in particular, the *MitM soft-fail* attack (Figure 8.14).

Note that OCSP stapling can only be deployed for TLS and other applications which involve online communication between the relying party and the subject (typically, browser and webserver, respectively). For example, it is not applicable to validation of signatures over emails.

Let us focus on the typical scenario, where the relying party is a browser running TLS, who receives a certificate Ψ_B from the web (and TLS) server, e.g., *Bob.com*, who is the *subject* of the certificate Ψ_B. In *OCSP stapling*, the subject (web server) sends OCSP requests to the OCSP responder (CA), requesting the status for Ψ_B. The webserver could send the requests as-needed, but more often, it would send requests periodically, *without waiting* for the TLS ClientHello message from the client. The CA (or other OCSP responder) sends back the OCSP response (status of Ψ_B). The response is signed, including the current time. This response should satisfy browsers (as relying parties), at least until *Bob.com* will 'refresh' it by again sending a fresh OCSP request for Ψ_B and receiving a response. The webserver, e.g., *Bob.com* provides the same OCSP response σ in the ServerHello TLS message, to all ServerHello requests indicating that the client supports OCSP stapling. Toward the expiration time of the OCSP response σ, the server sends a new OCSP request and obtains a fresh OCSP response σ'.

When an OCSP stapling-supporting browser connects to *Bob.com*, it indicates its support for OCSP stapling by including, in

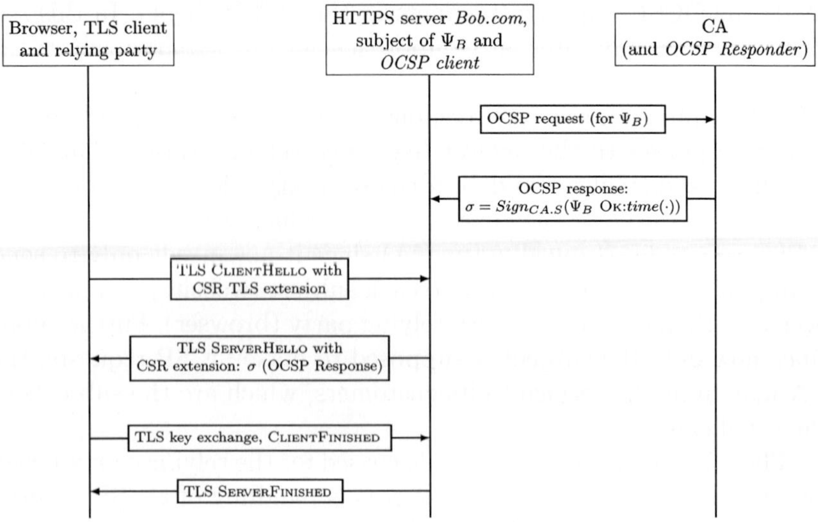

Figure 8.15. *OCSP stapling* in the TLS protocol, using the *Certificate Status Response (CSR)* TLS extension, for a typical TLS connection between browser and web server *Bob.com*, the subject of certificate Ψ_B. *Bob.com* received Ψ_B from the CA (not shown); the CA is also the OCSP responder. The web (and TLS) server *Bob.com* periodically sends OCSP requests to the CA (also OCSP responder), requesting the status of its own certificate Ψ_B. The CA sends back the OCSP response, $\sigma = Sign_{CA.S}(\Psi_B \text{ OK}:time(\cdot))$, signaling that Ψ_B was not revoked up to time $time(\cdot)$. The browser sends the TLS CSR extension to *Bob.com* with TLS CLIENTHELLO, to request OCSP stapling. The server sends back σ, the OCSP response, also in the CSR extension. The TLS handshake now completes as usual.

CLIENTHELLO, the *Certificate Status Response (CSR) TLS extension.* If the server supports stapling and has a valid OCSP response σ, then the server *staples* (includes) the OCSP response σ, which it places in the CSR TLS-extension, sent in the server's response. See this scenario in Figure 8.15.

Once the browser receives the OCSP response (in the CSR TLS-extension), it validates the response, i.e., validates the signature of the CA (using the CA's public validation key $CA.v$), and then validates that the response indicates non-revocation and that the *time* indicated is 'recent enough'. When all is Ok, the browser completes the TLS handshake with *Bob.com* and then continues with the TLS connection.

Multi-certificate stapling? Figure 8.15 illustrates the OCSP stapling process for a TLS connection between a browser and a webserver, where there is no certificate chain. The only case where there is no certificate chain is where the certificate was issued by a root CA. In fact, the original OCSP stapling specification, RFC 6066 [172], does not support stapling of multiple certificates. This is addressed in RFC 6961 [400], the *multiple certificate status* extension, and later also in TLS 1.3, RFC 8446 [412].

The MitM soft-fail attack on OCSP stapling: Let us now return to discuss the handling of ambiguous OCSP responses, and in particular, handling of the case where no OCSP response is received. For OCSP stapling, such failure may happen either between subject of the certificate, typically the webserver, who acts as the OCSP client, and the CA (OCSP responder); or between the relying party, typically the browser, and the subject (webserver). In particular, this will happen if the webserver does not support OCSP stapling.

In any case, the bottom line is that the browser does not receive a OCSP stapling response from the webserver. In the 'optional' OCSP stapling design, this simply directs the browser to attempt to resolve the revocation situation by itself. The browser would now perform an OCSP query directly with the OCSP responder (typically, the CA).

However, now we are basically back in the case where OCSP is deployed by the relying party. So, let us consider again the browser's response if it fails to receive a response to its OCSP request. This places the browser in similar dilemma to the one discussed earlier — and most implementations would adopt, again, the *soft-fail* approach, i.e., use the certificate *assuming* that it was not revoked. Namely, again, this design is vulnerable to an *MitM soft-fail* attack, similar to the one presented earlier (Figure 8.14). The attack is only slightly modified due to the failed effort for OCSP stapling and probably should be quite clear from Figure 8.16.

One way to defend against the *MitM soft-fail* attack (Figure 8.16) is using the *must-staple* extension to the server's X.509 certificate, which we discuss next.

OCSP must-staple — using the *TLS-feature* X.509 extension to enforce OCSP stapled response: The attacks of Figures 8.14

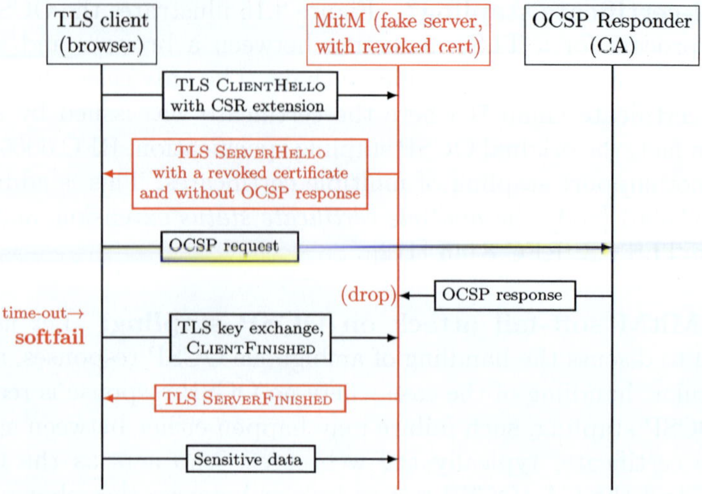

Figure 8.16. *MitM soft-fail* attack on OCSP stapling TLS client (browser), using a revoked TLS server (website) certificate; assume that the attacker has the certified (and revoked) private key. The browser sends the CSR TLS extension; however, the website's certificate does not have the must-staple mechanism (using the TLS-feature extension), or the client does not respect this extension. The attacker impersonates as the webserver and sends the TLS server-hello and certificate messages; the attacker does not send the OCSP response, which would have indicated revocation. The client is misled into thinking that the server does not support OCSP stapling. The client may now send an OCSP request to the appropriate OCSP responder, e.g., the relevant CA, but the MitM attacker would 'kill' the OCSP request or response (the figure shows killing of the response). After time-out, the client 'gives up' on the OCSP response, and 'soft-fails', i.e., accepts the certificate and establishes the connection with the impersonated website.

and 8.16 show the risk of adopting the *soft-fail* approach. The soft-fail mechanism is the equivalent of deciding to allow bypassing of airport security screening, whenever the line becomes too long. A likely outcome of such policy would be that an attacker will find ways to cause the line to be congested, and then use the bypass to avoid screening and perform an attack. We sum this up with the following principle.

Principle 17 (Soft-fail security is failed security). Defenses should not be bypassed due to failures or high load: *if defenses are bypassed upon failure or high load, attacker may cause failures*

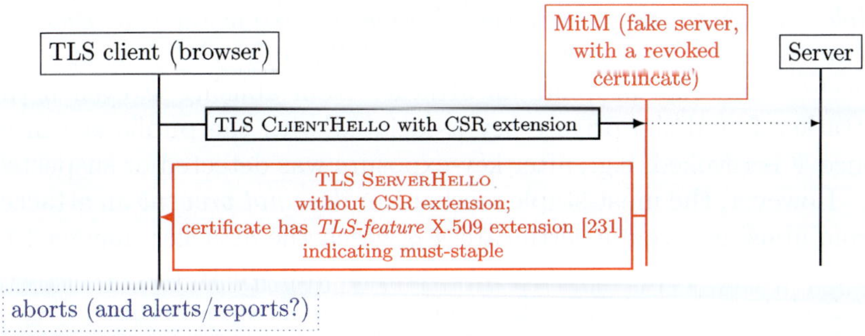

Figure 8.17. The use of the *TLS-feature* X.509 extension [231], to indicate *must-staple*, defends against the *MitM soft-fail* attack on OCSP stapling TLS client of Figure 8.16. As in Figure 8.16, the attacker tries to impersonate a website, to which the attacker has the private key and the corresponding certificate, which was already revoked. As in Figure 8.16, the client sends Client-Hello request, with the CSR TLS extension, i.e., asking the server to staple OCSP response. As in Figure 8.16, the attacker responds without the CSR extension, i.e., trying to mislead the client into falling back to sending an OCSP request (and then soft-failing). However, the *OCSP must-staple* mechanism, indicated in the TLS-feature X.509v3 extension, instructs the client to refuse to continue without a valid OCSP response from the server.

(or high load) to bypass defenses. Namely, *soft-fail security is failed security.*

This motivates adoption of the harsher, *hard-fail* approach. However, if the browser refuses to connect to any website that does not staple an OCSP response, then it would fail to connect to many legitimate websites that simply do not support OCSP stapling. This would not be sensible — not to mention that it would 'violate' the *UX>Security* precedence rule (Principle 16).

The solution is called *OCSP must-staple.* It is implemented using an X.509v3 extension called *TLS-feature* [231], which indicates specific TLS extensions and features supported by the website, including an indication for OCSP must-staple. The OCSP must-staple indication implies that the website *always* performs OCSP stapling, i.e., *always staples* OCSP responses. As shown in Figure 8.17, this foils the *MitM soft-fail* attack on OCSP stapling TLS client of Figure 8.16.

Must-staple may fail to prevent abuse of rogue certificate: Suppose that a relying party supports the must-staple mechanism (using the TLS-feature extension). Consider a certificate Ψ for the site

Bob.com, which specifies, in the TLS-feature extension, that *Bob.com* always uses OCSP stapling, i.e., that it follows the *OCSP must-staple* mechanism. This prevents an attacker from abusing Ψ even if the attacker found the private key associated with the public key in Ψ, once Ψ is revoked, e.g., after key-exposure was detected or suspected.

However, the must-staple mechanism *does not prevent* an attacker from abusing a rogue certificate Ψ_R which the attacker managed to manipulate a legitimate CA into signing, and where the private key of Ψ_R is known to the attacker, until this certificate is revoked. Worse; if Ψ_R does not include the TLS-feature extension with indication of the use of the *OCSP must-staple* mechanism, then the attacker will be able to continue abusing Ψ_R even after $\Psi_R.issuer$ revokes it, by simply blocking the corresponding OCSP response from reaching the client. The attack would succeed in spite of the fact that the original certificate uses must-staple. Note that it seems that currently, *none* of the root CAs trusted by the browsers includes must-staple in all of its certificates, therefore, it is very likely that a CA that will agree to issue the rogue certificate Ψ_R without the must-staple extension.

Must-staple adoption challenges: Unfortunately, measurements of must-staple adoption and support by CAs, webservers and browsers were, so far, not very encouraging [125]. In particular, CAs may be reluctant to support must-staple, due to the added complexity or due to concerns about false-positives due to incorrect implementations (by browser or server); indeed, it is not clear that CAs have a strong incentive in such a change. The concerns about false positives also exists for both relying parties (browsers) and servers.

We still hope that some must-staple mechanism will be adopted, as it offers significant security advantages, with high efficiency to relying parties and subjects. There does not appear to be any technical reason for either the incorrect processing or for failures of the webservers to receive OCSP responses (and then provide them to the browsers).

Indeed, this is an example of the significant *adoption challenge* facing designers of new Internet and web security mechanisms. Adoption considerations should be an important part of the design process. In the following exercise, we discuss some issues which may help — or hinder — the adoption of the OCSP or similar *must-staple* mechanism.

Exercise 8.3. For each of the following variants of the OCSP *must-staple* mechanism, explain possible impacts on adoption, security and performance:

1. Always mark the TLS-feature extension as a critical X.509 extension.
2. Always mark the TLS-feature extension as a non-critical X.509 extension.
3. When a browser receives from a website a certificate with TLS-feature extension indicating *must-staple*, but without the OCSP stapling response, then the browser would not abort the connection, but make the OCSP request itself, and abort the connection only if this request also fails.

8.3.4 Other revocation designs: OneCRL, CRLsets and CRVs

The disadvantages of CRLs and of OCSP motivate the design of alternative revocation mechanisms. Currently, alternative revocation mechanisms are deployed by several major browsers, albeit in proprietary manner. This includes Google Chrome's *CRLsets* [312] and Mozilla's *OneCRL* [216]. Both CRLsets and OneCRL prefetch CRLs but only for a subset of the most popular/important certificates, mostly CA certificates; in 2015, Liu *et al.* reported in Ref. [501] that only 0.35% of the revoked certificates were reported in CRLsets. The revocation information is collected by the vendor of these browsers, and retrieved by the browser from the vendor, typically daily, e.g., as part of the daily software update process.

Several recent papers investigated other designs of revocation mechanisms; these designs, including CRLite [317] and CRV [449], facilitate reasonably-efficient prefetching of the revocation status of large collections of certificates. Let us briefly describe the Certificate Revocation Vector (CRV) design [449].

Certificate Revocation Vector (CRV): The Certificate Revocation Vector (CRV) is a bit vector which contains '1' for revoked certificates and '0' for non-revoked certificates. Most bits in the CRV would normally be '0' (not revoked). Specifically, if we use n to denote the total number of certificates and r to denote the number of revoked certificates, then we expect $r << n$. For example, if at most 10% of the certificates are revoked, then $r \leq 0.1 \cdot n$. By transmitting the CRV vector in compressed form, the overhead is further reduced, especially for typical, low revocation percentages.

Furthermore, CRVs can be updated even more efficiently. Let CRV(d) denote the value of the CRV of period (often, day) d. To update from CRV($d-1$) to CRV(d), we can distribute the *Delta CRV* ΔCRV(d), which is the bit-vector which contains '1' only for certificates which were revoked *during period (day) d*. Therefore,

$$\text{CRV}(d) = \text{CRV}(d-1) \vee \Delta\text{CRV}(d) \tag{8.4}$$

The ΔCRV vector is usually *very* sparse, therefore compresses *very* well, as the number of revocation in day d, denoted r_d, is usually not more than few dozens, resulting in very short ΔCRVs (of $r_d \cdot \log n$ or less bits).

Unfortunately, in practice, certificates are usually not identified by sequential numbers; in fact, the best practice is that certificate serial numbers are random 20-bytes (159 bits) positive integers (Section 8.2). This introduces an adoption challenge to this design. For more details on the CRV mechanism, including this challenge, see Ref. [449].

8.4 Certificate authority failures and countermeasures

The CA is the keystone of the public key infrastructure. The naïve view of PKI security is that certificate authorities are fully trusted, honest and well-protected entities that are never corrupted. Ideally, CAs should carefully validate certificate requests, and attackers would never be able to obtain a rogue certificate.

In practice, a CA could be *rogue*, *negligent* or *vulnerable*, allowing an attacker to obtain rogue certificates. Another way for attackers to obtain rogue certificates is by circumventing the certificate validation process (Section 8.2.3). In particular, the Domain Validation (DV) process is not very secure; it can be foiled by MitM attackers, even when attackers have only MitM capabilities for only parts of the network, e.g., see Ref. [141]. A rogue certificate may be issued either directly by a root CA, directly trusted by the relying party, or by an *ICA* or a *LCA* which are themselves certified by a trusted root CA.

CAs should follow the best practices to ensure their security, avoid exposure and abuse of their signing keys, and use secure processes for certificate validation. In particular, CAs should limit validity periods of certificates, especially for domain validated certificates. In addition, CAs should try to minimize risks due to rogue certificates, including efficient, reliable mechanisms for detecting and revoking rogue certificates.

To minimize the risk of rogue certificates, a CA should use the appropriate PKIX extensions to prevent and limit abuse of certificates that the CA issues, including the following:

- In all certificates, include the BASIC CONSTRAINTS extension and specify it as critical.
- In a non-CA certificate Ψ, make sure to set in the BASIC CONSTRAINTS extension the values $\Psi.cA = \text{FALSE}$ and $\Psi.pathLen = 0$. In addition, include in Ψ the KEY USAGE extension, marked critical, with the KEYCERTSIGN flag set to FALSE.
- In a CA certificate Ψ where $\Psi.subject$ is a LCA, use $\Psi.pathLen = 0$. Note that in all CA certificates we should have $cA = \text{TRUE}$.
- In a CA certificate Ψ where $\Psi.subject$ is an ICA, use the minimal sufficient value for $\Psi.pathLen = 0$. Specifically, use $\Psi.pathLen = 1$, unless it is absolutely necessary for $\Psi.subject$ to be able to certify ICAs (in which case, a larger value is necessary). If possible, Ψ should also contain the NAME CONSTRAINTS extension, with the maximal restrictions. For example, set PERMITTEDSUBTREES to *uconn.edu* to only allow certification of UConn's domains, including *uconn.edu* itself and subdomains such as *www.uconn.edu*.

In multiple incidents, certificate authorities, mostly validated by a certificate path beginning with a one of the root CAs of popular browsers, issued multiple rogue or invalid certificates, or had their keys exposed and abused to issue rogue certificates; see Table 8.4. Such rogue certificates were abused for eavesdropping, MitM and other attacks, some of which attributed to nation-state actors; e.g., the 2011 attacks on the Comodo and DigiNotar CAs were attributed to hackers [322].

Arguably, current browsers trust too many root CAs and do not sufficiently restrict CAs. For example, Ref. [166] found 1832 browser-trusted signing certificates, each representing a trusted CA

Table 8.4. Notable certificate authority (CA) failures. Several of the CAs mentioned, and others, were removed from the root CA programs; e.g., see Mozilla's list of removed root CAs [368].

CA, year(s)	Description and Reference
Verisign, 2001	Verisign issues Microsoft code-signing certificates to attacker [184].
Thawte, 2008	Validation failures of Thawte and StartSSL [504].
Comodo, 2008	CertStar, a reseller of Comodo, issued certificates without validation [331].
Comodo, 2011	Rogue certificates for major sites (e.g., Gmail) [288, 322, 382].
DigiNotar, 2011	DigiNotar CA compromised, 531 rogue certificates found, including for **.google.com*, used for MitM against Iranian users [322, 485].
TurkTrust, 2011–2012	TurkTrust issued intermediary CAs certificates to end entities; abused to issue certificate for **.google.com* (detected on Dec. 2012) [313].
Trustwave, 2012	Trustwave issued intermediary CA certificate for eavesdropping [409].
ANSSI, 2013	ANSSI (French CA) issued intermediary CA certificate for MitM [491].
NICCA, 2014	Intermediary CA NICCA (India) issued rogue certs for Google domains [315].
CNNIC, 2015	Rogue certificates issued by MCS (Egypt), certified by CNNIC (China) [170, 369].
WoSign, 2015	WoSign and StartCom (owned by WoSign) removed from revoked as CAs after validation and other failures.
Symantec, 2015–2017	Symantec issued unauthorized certs for over 176 domains [391].
Qaznet, 2019	Kazakhstan forces users to install Qaznet root CA, use it for MitM [407].
DarkMatter, 2019	Mozilla, Google revoke intermediary CA of surveillance firm DarkMatter [74], refuse to make it a root CA.
Let's Encrypt, 2020	Let's Encrypt detected a bug in their CAA-validation code, affecting 3 million certificates [1].
TrustCor, 2022	Root CA TrustCor exposed as related to Spyware [352].

(mostly, ICAs and LCAs). Out of these, about 40% were academic institutions, and about 20% were commercial CAs.

A relying party should enforce the restrictions on certificates defined by standard extensions, in particular, KEY USAGE, BASIC

CONSTRAINTS and NAME CONSTRAINTS. On top of that, relying parties should only use trustworthy root CAs. We say that a CA is non-trustworthy if the CA issues rogue certificates themselves, or issues CA certificates to non-trustworthy intermediary CAs or leaf CAs. Note that, by design, for any PKIX-valid certificate Ψ, we can identify an ***accountable root CA***, i.e., a root CA which either issued Ψ or issued a CA certificate to a CA who is accountable for Ψ; see Ref. [493]. The ability to identify accountable CAs and remove root CAs which are found non-trustworthy is important and motivates root CAs to improve their security and to carefully vet the trustworthiness of intermediary CAs.

In the following section, we discuss several basic defenses against rogue certificates. In Section 8.5, we present CT, an important extension of PKIX, which provides transparent, publicly available information about issued certificates; the main motivation for the development and use of CT is the need to detect and revoke rogue certificates and rogue/negligent CA.

8.4.1 Mitigating CA failures: Key Pinning, HPKP and other defenses

Several mechanisms can help mitigate the risk of rogue certificates obtained due to certificate authorities failures. PKIX and X.509 already include some defenses against certificate authorities failures, most notable, the certificate path constraints extensions, and especially the NAME CONSTRAINTS and BASIC CONSTRAINTS, discussed in Section 8.2.4.2. Of course, these restrictions should be defined by the root CA or ICA certifying the faulty CA; and, unfortunately, their use appears to be limited and insufficient to mitigate certificate authorities failures. In particular, Ref. [166] found that most CA certificates did not have a *pathLen* restriction, and only *seven* included the NAME CONSTRAINTS extension. Admittedly, NAME CONSTRAINTS can only be applied when the certified CA has a restricted name spaces, and this has limited applicability, since most domain names are in one of the generic top level domains (gTLD) such as *com, net* and *edu.*

In the rest of this section, we discuss mitigation of CA failures using *key pinning*, i.e., identifying the specific public key(s) used by a subject, and in particular the HPKP specifications. In the following section, we discuss *DNS-based PKI mechanisms* and their use to mitigate certificate authorities failures and rogue certificates. In Section 8.5, we discuss *CT*, which provides a public, auditable log of certificates, allowing *detection* of rogue certificates, and, thereby, of CA failures.

Static public key pinning: Fraudulent certificates can be foiled and/or detected by the relying party, typically the browser, when the browser is aware of the correct public key or certificate. Such 'burned-in' public keys are usually referred to as *static pinning* (or static public key pinning). The fact that the keys must be known in advance and cannot change is a major disadvantage, limiting the use of this technique to very special cases, e.g., Google pinning its own public key in Chrome.

Dynamic key pinning and HPKP: Static pinning is problematic since keys do change *sometimes*, e.g., due to unexpected revocations. Furthermore, static pinning is based on decisions of the browser's vendor, which may not be relevant to the usage of a particular user. This motivates the use of *dynamic pinning*, where the *website* specifies the pinning of one or multiple public keys, for limited time. *Dynamic pinning* of public keys or certificates allows secure sites to direct the browser to 'pin' the given public key to the domain, for a specified period; see specifications for *HTTP Public Key Pinning (HPKP)* [176]. HPKP foils the use of fraudulent public keys, even if attacker obtains a rogue certificate for the fraudulent key, properly signed by a CA trusted by the relying party. With dynamic pinning, the server essentially declares *I will use only this PK for the specified period.* The client remembers this indication and refuses the use of other public keys for the specified period.

In addition to, or instead of, *refusing* 'other' keys, the site may request clients to report cases where they receive a key or certificate which differs from the pinned one, i.e., use this mechanism for *detection.*

Based on these arguments, key pinning with HPKP may sound like a great defense. However, key pinning has significant *availability* drawbacks. Therefore, providing (another) example of the *UX>Security* principle (Principle 16), the HPKP specification is not supported by *any* of the major browsers (beginning in 2018). These availability drawbacks include the following:

1. If the private key of the pinned public key is lost, then the domain/website becomes unreachable until the pinning expires. The same problem occurs if the certificate is revoked and a new key should be used, e.g., due to concerns about exposure of the private key, if there is no backup, then the domain/website becomes unreachable upon revocation. To reduce this risk, the HPKP specification requires pinning of at least two keys.
2. Suppose that an attacker exposes the private key of a website and that the attacker can modify the website. Then the attacker can include a (new) HPKP header in the modified site, which will *not include any key known to the site owner.* The result would be that the site becomes unreachable using the keys known to the site owner; this would happen even if the website did not use HPKP at all.

8.4.2 The DNS and DNS-based security mechanisms

Internet *domain names* are strings containing one or more parts, called *labels*, separated by dots. Each label consists of alphanumeric characters and the hyphen ('-') symbol, e.g., *www-1.foo.bar.* Domain names can use either upper case or lower case characters, but these are considered equivalent, e.g., the *fee.bar, Fee.Bar* and *FEE.bar* are different ways of writing the same domain name.

The *Domain Name System (DNS)* provides the mapping from *domain names* to different types of data, in records called *resource records (RRs)*; the system distributes the information efficiently, with multi-layer caching, in the client machines (by *DNS stub resolver* modules) and in middleboxes, mainly, *DNS resolvers.* The most well-known types of RRs map the domain name to the corresponding IP address used to communicate with the domain (typically, server); resource record (RR) of type *A* map the domain name to the (32-bits) addresses used by IPv4, and RRs of type *AAAA* map the domain name to the (128-bits) addresses used by IPv6. See discussion of domain names and IP addresses in Note 8.2. DNS supports many other types of RRs, e.g., the widely used *CNAME* (canonical name) resource record, which defines an alias name for the domain, and many others. We discuss a few types of RRs in the following, e.g., the *NS* RR, which identifies the *name server* of the domain.

The DNS organizes domain names hierarchically, with each domain name is owned and managed by an organization assigned (registered) to it, usually for a limited time that may be extended. The manager of a domain name, e.g., *foo.bar*, can define *sub-domains*, which are domain names ending in that domain name and with one or more additional labels to the left, e.g., *www.foo.bar* and *www1.fee-fie.foo.bar*; note that the most-significant part of the domain name is on the right, in contrast to the usual convention for writing both numbers and IP addresses.

The manager of a domain name, e.g., *foo.bar*, operates the *name servers* of the domain, which are servers that run the DNS protocol and provides RRs for domain names included in the domain. The manager defines the domain names of the name servers of the domain (in NS RRs) and their mappings to IP addresses (in A and/or AAAA RRs). For example, the manager of domain *foo.bar* defines the names of its name servers, e.g., *ns.foo.bar* and *ns.cdn.net*; note that the name servers of a domain may be in other domains.

At the top of the hierarchy is the *root (empty) domain*, managed by the Internet Corporation for Assigned Names and Numbers (ICANN). The ICANN assigns the domain names right below the root, called the *top-level domains (TLDs)*, and consists of only one label. The TLDs include *country code top-level domains (ccTLDs)*, allocated to each country (*us, uk, in, ru*...), and *generic top-level domains (ccTLD)* (*com, net, edu*, ...). The TLDs define the *second-level domains*, e.g., the name server of *com* can provide the name and the IP address of the name server of *fie.com*, by providing the corresponding *NS* and *A* (or *AAAA*) RRs (upon request). Since domain names are assigned hierarchically, a higher-level domain name can define mappings for lower-level domain names which end in that higher-level domain name, e.g., the manager of *foo.bar* can define mappings for *www.foo.bar* and of *ns1.fee-fie.foo.bar*.

The hierarchical organization and management of the DNS, as well as its support for efficient distribution and caching, make it widely used to distribute per-domain security information, including several mappings identifying ***security policies***, ***blacklists***, and different *security relevant properties* of the domain name. However, the use of DNS to distribute security information should take into account that an attacker may try to trick the system to provide fake DNS RRs. In fact, the DNS protocol has only minimal defenses against a network attacker, who may be able to send fake DNS responses, typically to the DNS resolver; these attacks are called *DNS poisoning*. DNS poisoning can be done by a MitM attacker, and even by weaker, off-path attackers, who can only send spoofed (fake) packets, albeit using more complex attacks (e.g., Refs. [205, 246, 247, 333, 343]). However, the integrity of DNS responses can be ensured by using appropriate DNS RRs, as per the *DNSSEC* specifications, and then used to safely protect security-sensitive data, in particular, to improve the security of PKI systems, by defending against rogue certificates and CA failures.

We next briefly discuss DNSSEC, as well as the two main applications of DNS to improve PKI security: DANE and CAA.

DNS can be protected using the *DNSSEC* standard extension to the DNS standards (RFC 4033 [20]), which uses signatures to ensure authenticity of DNS responses. Both DANE and CAA can be protected from MitM attackers using DNSSEC; however, note that the deployment of DNSSEC still faces significant challenges and is quite limited. DNSSEC is, basically, a special type of a PKI system, although it was not presented as such (and lacks some of the PKI mechanisms, e.g., revocations).

In particular, two types of RRs provide a PKI function: protection against the risk of certificate authorities issuing rogue, misleading certificates, either due to a failure of the validation process, or when the certificate is signed by the private signing key of a rogue or vulnerable CA. These two records are the *DNS-Based Authentication of Named Entities (DANE)* [252] and the *Certificate Authority Authorization (CAA)* [232]. Let us briefly describe these standards:

DNSSEC: The *DNS security (DNSSEC)* specifications (RFCs 4033-4035 [20–22], RFC 5155 [321] and other RFCs) define different DNS RRs and procedures for authentication of DNS information. To ensure authenticity, DNSSEC uses signature schemes and collision-resistant hash functions, provided in the *RRSIG* and *DS* RRs, and authenticates public keys in *DNSKEY* records. Therefore, DNSSEC is, basically, a special type of PKI, which hierarchically defines public signature keys for domain names and their validation. There are some major PKI functions which are not supported by DNSSEC, most significantly, it does not support revocation (or transparency, as discussed in the next section). On the other hand, using the *NSEC* or *NSEC3* RRs, DNSSEC provides a *Proof of Non-Existence* of a RR, which is a function not existing in PKIX and X.509.

DANE: *DANE* specifications (RFC 6698 [252]) provides an additional mechanism for relying parties to validate public keys, certificate and certificate chains. Specifically, the *TLSA* DNS RR provides an additional security mechanism for TLS server authentication, beyond the use of PKIX certificates and certificate chains, namely, to protect against impersonation of the TLS servers of a domain, using a rogue certificate issued to the same domain name (due to a CA or validation failure). The record have multiple options, but the goal of all of them is to protect against a rogue certificate. Specifically, the TLSA record can include a public key, a certificate, or the hash of a public key or a certificate. The TLSA record also defined the requirements from the key or certificate which is included in the record (or whose hash is included in the records). The options are as follows: (1) the key or certificate should be the one used by the TLS server, indicating whether the TLSA record provides the complete validation of that key/certificate or whether a standard certificate path from a trusted root CA is required too, (2) the key or certificate must be of one of the certificate authorities in the certificate path provided by the TLS server, and (3) the key/certificate must be of the root CA in the certificate path provided by the TLS server.

CAA: CAA specifications (RFC 8659 [232]) provides mechanisms which certificate authorities should follow, to improve their validation of certificate requests, in particular, improving the security of DV. Specifically, the CAA RR defines restrictions on the certificates to the issued for the domain, and possibly, for subdomains. CAA requires certificate authorities to check for a CAA record for the domain, and issue the certificates only if it satisfies the specified restrictions; if the domain has no CAA record, the CA should check for restrictions of the higher-level domain, e.g., if a certificate is requested for *www.foo.com* and there is no CAA for this domain, the CA should look for a CAA record for *foo.com*. The record can specify one or more restrictions. Restrictions include the following: (1) restriction of the CA(s) which may issue certificates for the domain, (2) ditto, but for *wildcard* certificates, (3) requirement for reporting certificate requests (e.g., by email) and (4) additional restrictions, not defined in the standard, which may be mandatory (critical) or non-mandatory (non-critical). Relying parties *may* also consider the value of the CAA record when evaluating a certificate, although its main role is to restrict the issuing of new certificates.

Note that TLSA, CAA and other security-related DNS resource records should be protected by DNSSEC, to provide security against MitM and even merely off-path attackers.

8.5 Certificate Transparency (CT)

CT [222, 318] is an extension of PKIX which significantly improves the transparency and security of PKI. In fact, CT is currently the main tool to defend against rogue certificates and CAs. CT is backward-compatible with PKIX, i.e., a CT-certificate is compatible (acceptable) by relying parties using PKIX. There is an extensive standardization, implementation and deployment effort for CT [318–320], and CT is enforced by all popular browsers and supported by most websites and CAs. Our description mostly follows the CT 2.0 specifications (RFC9162 [320]).

Motivation for CT: what is missing in PKIX? PKIX and X.509 ensure *accountability*, i.e., the ability to identify a root CAs which is accountable for any (rogue) certificate. This allows distrusting a negligent, vulnerable or rogue root CA, by detecting their accountability to (possibly multiple) rogue certificates. In particular, the major browsers have policies for managing their root stores (list of root CAs), and would remove CAs suspected to be negligent, vulnerable or rogue; e.g., see Refs. [18, 367, 404]. This is in addition to the support for revocation of the specific certificates detected or suspected of being rogue.

However, X.509 and PKIX do not provide mechanisms for *detecting* rogue certificates; this makes it harder to ensure timely revocation of certificates, as well as to detect rogue, vulnerable or negligent CAs. Of course, a relying party that receives a rogue certificate could publish it, but this certainly is not a viable method of detection.

For example, Google included in the Google Chrome browser a check for the public key it received for Google websites. This check allowed Google to detect the 2011 MitM attack on Iranian users and few other attacks (Table 8.4). Note that although, in this incident, over 300,000 users were attacked, still, *not a single user* detected and reported the attack. The attack was only detected by Google Chrome; it was not detected by other browsers since other browsers did not perform this non-standard check. This incident may have motivated Google to develop CT.

8.5.1 Certificate Transparency (CT) concepts and entities

In this section, we present the concepts and entities of CT. Let us begin with the main new goal: *transparency.*

The transparency goal: A *PKI ensures transparency* if it allows entities to learn about every certificate *before* the certificate becomes valid. Therefore, *transparency facilitates effective detection of rogue certificates, and, thereby, accountability.* In more details, transparency allows to:

Detect equivocating certificates by monitoring domain names: CT allows detection of certificates issued for a given domain name (or, in general, identifier). This allows the 'owner' of the domain to detect unauthorized certificates issued to its domain name, which we call *equivocating certificates.*

Detect other suspect certificates: CT also allows monitoring of *all* certificates issued — by a particular logger, multiple loggers or all loggers. This allows to detect different types of suspect certificates, such as the misleading certificates discussed in Section 8.1.5, as well as certificates not conforming with the specifications that should be enforced by CAs, e.g., certificates using a vulnerable signature scheme or missing the basic constraints extension.

Detect suspect CAs: By monitoring all of the certificates issued by a CA, it becomes possible to detect a rogue or abused CA, e.g., a CA that issues certificates without sufficient validation.

The original CT documents [222, 314, 318] further stated the intuitive, ambitious goal of *No Trusted Third Party (NTTP)*. We interpret the NTTP goal to mean that transparency should be guaranteed even if several 'trusted entities', such as CAs, are corrupt. As we explain in the following, under this interpretation, the NTTP goal is not fully ensured by the CT specifications [319, 320] published so far; more details see Ref. [493]. However, CT definitely ensures transparency even if the CA is rogue (assuming other entities are benign, though).

CT logs and loggers: The main idea allowing CT to achieve transparency is simple: *every certificate issued is made available in a public log.* One way to implement this idea would have been for each CA to maintain a publicly available log of the certificates issued by that CA. However, this would fail to ensure transparency of certificates issued by a corrupt CA, or a CA whose key was exposed and used to issue rogue certificates.

Therefore, the CT designers separated the log functionality from the CA and moved it to a new entity called a *logger*. A CA should send each certificate it issues to at least one logger. The logger would add the certificate to a publicly available log that the logger maintains. The logger then provides the CA with a signed attestation that the logger logged the certificate at the stated time; we call this attestation a *Signed Certificate Timestamp (SCT)*. The SCT should be attached to or become part of the certificate, when delivered from the CA to the subject of the certificate (typically, the owner of the domain or website), and when the certificate is provided to the relying parties. CT-compliant relying parties consider a certificate to be valid only if it comes with a valid SCT, or with a valid set of SCTs; relying parties may require SCTs from multiple loggers. In particular, when the certificate is used in TLS, the certificate and the SCT (or SCTs) are sent from the web server to the client as part of the TLS handshake (together with the SERVERHELLO message). The SCT allows the relying parties to know that the certificate was logged (by that logger); the logger becomes *accountable* for the public availability (transparency) of this certificate.

CT loggers provide several services whose goals are to (1) ensure that the log is public, (2) prove that the log is managed correctly and (3) allow validation that a specific certificate, attested to by an SCT, was logged. We describe these services and their usage in Section 8.5.3.

Monitors: To ensure transparency, logs should be *monitored* to detect suspect certificates. In principle, loggers could make the logs available to every interested entity; this would allow, e.g., the owner of a domain, e.g., *BobBank.com*, to inspect all logged certificates and thereby detect any equivocating certificates issued to *BobBank.com*, or certificates to possibly misleading domain names, including homographic domain names (e.g., *BoBank.com*, *Bob-Bank.com*) and other misleading domain names (e.g., *BobBank.com-accounts.top*); see Section 8.1.5. However, this would require every interested party to inspect all logs, which may not be economically viable.

For better efficiency and flexibility, CT introduces another type of entities called *monitors*. A monitor queries multiple (or all) loggers to obtain copies of their logs, and inspects the certificates logged. Monitors can perform some checks on the responses from the logger, allowing them to identify some logger failures.

Typically, monitors are contracted by a domain owner, to alert the domain owner of equivocating and suspect certificates, i.e., certificates which may mislead people trying to access the owner's service (usually, website). The domain owner typically requests the monitor for alerts upon new certificates with the same domain name (equivocating certificates). A monitor may also offer alerts for domain names meeting other criteria, e.g., homographic or other misleading domain names; for example, see Ref. [117], where you can also find many examples of misleading domain names found in CT logs.

Ideally, a monitor would inspect all logs. If a monitor inspects only some logs, then the domain owner may need to request alerts from multiple monitors, to be sure that it learns of relevant certificates from all logs.

The current CT specifications [319, 320] do not cover the interactions between the monitor and its customers, whereby the monitor alerts or informs its customers, such as domain owners, of suspect certificates. Indeed, as specified, CT only strives to ensure that all certificates are logged and made available to monitors.

Audit: Auditing is an optional process that validates the SCTs and other attestations provided by a logger. Some (early) CT documents [222, 318] mention another new PKI entity to perform the audit function, the *auditors*; however, the auditor functionality was not fully specified, and Ref. [222] says most auditors will likely be built into browsers, i.e., are a function of CT relying parties.

The current CT specification, CT 2.0 [320], provides limited auditing functionality. This auditing mechanism protects against some logger misbehaviors, but additional mechanisms are required against other misbehaviors; see Section 8.5.3.

In the current implementations of CT, the main defense against corrupt loggers is not auditing but *redundancy*; for a certificate to be valid, it must come with SCTs from two (and sometimes more) different loggers. This solution has significant overhead — and could arguably be insufficient since the attacker can intentionally select a CA which uses vulnerable or corrupt loggers (if such exists).

8.5.2 Certificate Transparency: high level design

Issuing and using CT certificates: Figure 8.18 illustrates the processes of issuing and using CT certificates. For simplicity, we show and discuss logging of the certificate with a single logger, although, in practice, certificates are typically logged with two (or more) loggers; we also simplify by considering the case where the certificate (Ψ_B) is issued by a root CA, which we denote simply as CA.

The process begins with the subject, e.g., the website *Bob.com*, requesting a certificate, by sending to the CA its public key, domain name and other details to be included in the certificate. The CA should establish the identity of the subject, using the appropriate

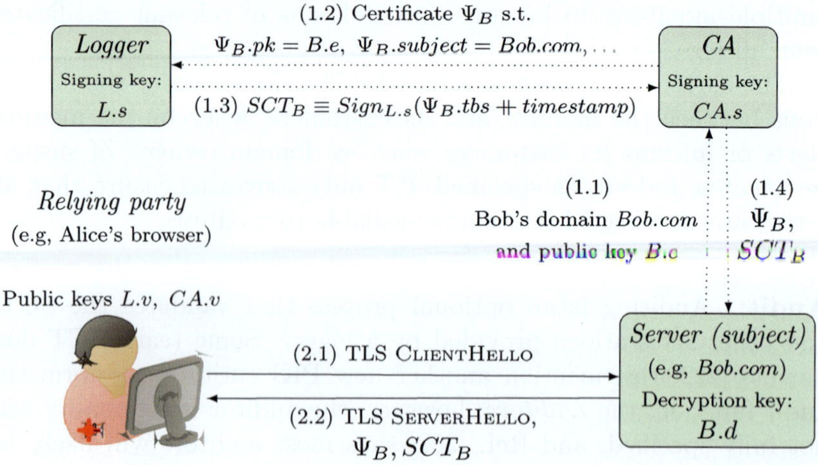

Figure 8.18. The CT certificate issuing (dotted arrows) and usage for TLS handshake (solid arrows). The issuing process begins with flow 1.1, in which the subject, e.g., website, sends their domain (e.g., *Bob.com*) and public key $B.e$ to the certificate authority (CA). The certificate authority should validate the domain *Bob.com*. The validation process is not shown here and depends on the type of validation; e.g., see Figure 8.6 for Domain Validation (DV). In flow 1.2, the CA sends the newly issued certificate Ψ_B to the logger L. The logger validates that Ψ_B conforms with required standards, and then adds Ψ_B to the log and generates a Signed Certificate Timestamp (SCT). In flow 1.3, L sends to the CA the SCT, SCT_B, which is a signature over the to-be-signed fields of the certificate, $\Psi_B.tbs$, and a timestamp. The CA provides Ψ_B and SCT_B to the subject *Bob.com* (flow 1.4). In flow 2.1, the websites receives the TLS ClientHello from a relying party. In flow 2.2, the website responds to the relying party with ServerHello, the certificate Ψ_B and the SCT SCT_B. The relying party validates Ψ_B as in PKIX, and, in addition, validates that it has sufficient set of valid SCTs, in particular, validates the signature on SCT_B.

validation process (Section 8.2.3). If all is well, the CA issues the certificate Ψ_B and sends it to the logger.

The logger first validates the certificate Ψ_B. Validation includes checking that the certificate is correctly formatted and signed by a CA supported by the logger, follows correctly the PKIX and CT standards [131,320], has a valid certificate chain from a root CA and has an acceptable validity period.

If the logger finds Ψ_B to be valid, then it adds Ψ_B to the log and produces the SCT, which we denote by SCT_B. The SCT SCT_B is a signature over $\Psi_B.tbs$, the set of *to-be-signed (tbs)* fields certified (signed) in Ψ_B, and a timestamp indicating the logging time. Namely, $SCT_B \leftarrow Sign_{L.s}(\Psi_B.tbs + date)$, where $L.s$ is the logger's private signing key. The logger then sends SCT_B back to the CA.

The CA bundles the certificate Ψ_B together with SCT_B and sends the bundle to the subject *Bob.com.* This 'bundling' can be done using an X.509v3 extension, using a TLS extension, or using an OCSP extension. Bundling the SCT in an X.509v3 extension is most common, since it allows interoperability with unmodified web servers. In this case, we refer to the certificate Ψ_B sent to the logger as a *precertificate*; the CA now signs the 'real' certificate, Ψ'_B, which contains the same fields as the original certificate — and, in addition, SCT_B, which is placed in an X.509v3 extension called the *transparency information extension.* Each of these bundling methods can support multiple SCTs for the certificate SCTs (from different loggers).

A relying party uses the certificate Ψ_B together with the SCT SCT_B (or multiple SCTs) to validate the fields in the certificate. Often, the relying party is a TLS client, such as a web browser, communicating with a TLS server, such as a web server. In such cases, the web server sends the SCT (or SCTs) bundled with the certificate, namely, together with the *Server_Hello* message, in response to the ClientHello message from the client.

In addition to the validation of the X.509v3 certificate and certificate chain, as done by any PKIX-compliant relying party, a CT-compliant relying party should also validate the SCT (or SCTs). An SCT should be signed by a logger trusted by the relying party. The set of SCTs should satisfy the policy of the relying party (most browsers require two SCTs signed by different loggers). To validate the signature on an SCT which is bundled within the certificate, the relying party should first reconstruct the input to the logger's SCT computation, namely, the *precertificate.* This is done by removing the transparency information extension.

The CT Merkle tree ($\mathcal{MT}$), STHs and MMD: CT loggers maintain the log of certificates as a *Merkle tree ($\mathcal{MT}$)*; see Section 3.7.2. CT relies on the properties of the Merkle tree to detect misbehaving loggers, as described in Section 8.5.3.

Each leaf of the Merkle tree is a hash of the to be signed (TBS) contents of a logged certificate. We use $\mathcal{MT}.\Delta(\{\Psi_1, \ldots, \Psi_n\})$ to denote the *digest* of the $\mathcal{MT}$ whose leaves are the sequence of the hashes of the TBS fields of the certificates $\{\Psi_1, \ldots, \Psi_n\}$.

The CT specifications uses the term *tree head* to refer to the combination of (1) the digest of the log's Merkle tree at a given time, (2) the timestamp at which the digest is computed and (3) the number of certificates in the log at that time. Periodically, the logger *signs* the tree head of the current log; the combination of the signature, the tree head fields, and the timestamp is called a *Signed Tree Head (STH)*. The STH is a key element of the CT design; therefore, let us define it and its components.

Definition 8.1 (A Signed Tree Head (STH)). A STH is a tuple of the following components:

- STH.Δ, the digest of the log, i.e., of the sequence of (hashes of the TBS fields of) the logged certificates.
- STH.*timestamp*, the time of computing the STH.
- STH.n, the number of certificates in the log at that time.
- STH.*logger*, the logger issuing (and signing) the STH.
- STH.*log_id*, the identifier of the log. (Each logger may maintain multiple logs.)
- STH.σ, the loggers' signature over the STH.

Since a Merkle tree ensures collision-resistance, it is safe to assume, given a set of leaves corresponding to a given STH digest, that this is the set that was signed by the logger. It is convenient to abuse notation and write $\Psi \in$ STH when Ψ corresponds to an entry of the Merkle tree whose digest is STH.Δ, i.e., Ψ was included in the log corresponding to the STH.

The logger commits to a *maximal delay* between one STH of the log and the next STH; this maximal delay between STHs is called the *Maximal Merge Delay (MMD)*. The MMD is also the maximal time allowed between issuing an SCT and including the corresponding certificate in the log (and in the input to the STH). A logger also commits to a *maximal* number of STHs that the logger would produce within an interval of time of length MMD.

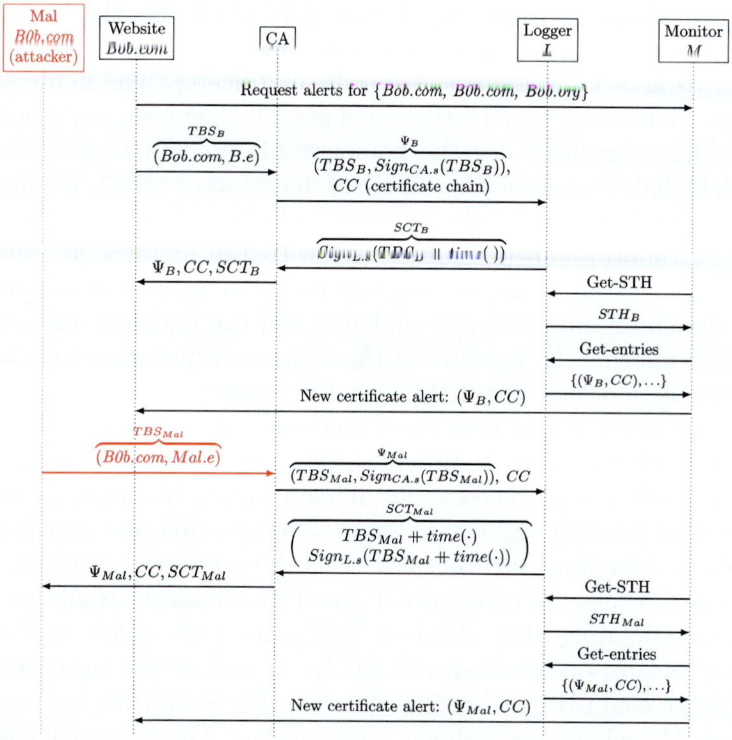

Figure 8.19. Monitoring process in CT, with a benign logger L. Website *Bob.com* requests the monitor M to monitor the domains *Bob.com, B0b.com* and *Bob.org*. Then, the website requests a certificate Ψ_B binding its domain *Bob.com* with its public key $B.e$. The CA submits Ψ_B and its certificate chain, denoted CC for brevity, to (benign) logger L. The logger sends back the (signed) SCT_B, which the certificate authority sends to *Bob.com* together with Ψ_B and the certificate chain (CC).

The monitor periodically queries the logger for newly issued certificates. This is done by first asking for the current STH, and, upon finding from the STH that new certificates were logged, requesting their entries. Once the monitor receives (Ψ_B, CC) from the logger, it alerts *Bob.com* as requested.

We then show an attacker *Mal* who receives from the certificate authority a certificate, Ψ_{Mal}, binding domain *B0b.com* to *Mal*'s public key, *Mal.e*. Monitor M alerts *Bob.com* about Ψ_{Mal} after learning about it from L.

The loggers provide a service, *get-sth*, which provides the latest STH of the log. This service is key to the *monitoring process*, which is illustrated in Figure 8.19.

The monitoring process: Figure 8.19 illustrates the Certificate Transparency (CT) monitoring process, and how it allows a domain owner to detect the issuing of specific certificates. The figure shows certification of the 'real' certificate of domain *Bob.com*, and of a rogue misleading certificate for the homographic domain name *B0b.com*, which includes the public key *Mal.e* of the attacker (*Mal*). We simplify the interaction between the monitor and the website and show how the (legitimate) website 'subscribes' with the monitor for updates on certificates issues for the domain *Bob.com*, as well as for the suspect domain names *B0b.com* and *Bob.org*; the figure shows how the monitor informs the websites of these two certificates as soon as the monitor is informed about them by the logger.

The process begins with the domain owner, the website *Bob.com*, requesting the monitor to provide alerts to the domain owner, whenever a certificate is issued to its domain name, *Bob.com*, as well as to the two possibly misleading domain names *B0b.com* and *Bob.org*. We then show how *Bob.com* ask the CA to issue a certificate, and how the CA logs the certificate Ψ_B and its certificate chain, receives the corresponding SCT, denoted SCT_B, from the logger, and sends the certificate Ψ_B bundled with SCT_B, as well as the corresponding certificate chain (if needed), to *Bob.com*. For simplicity, we focus on a single CA which uses a single, benign logger. Only nominal changes are required for the case where the attacker uses a different CA from the one used by the benign domain owner and where they use different loggers; it is only required that the monitor will monitor a logger used by each CA. The case of misbehaving loggers is a bit more complicated, and we discuss it in Section 8.5.3.

We then show how the monitor learns about Ψ_B and informs the website. This process consists of two requests that the monitor sends to the logger. In the first request, the monitor asks for the latest STH produced by the logger, using the *get*-STH logger endpoint; we denote the returned STH by STH_B. From STH_B, the monitor M learns that how many new certificates were logged since M received the previous STH (and how many). The monitor then requests the entries corresponding to these new certificates, using the *get-entries* logger endpoint.

Next, we show how Mal requests and receives a certificate Ψ_{Mal} for *B0b.com*, following a similar process. In the illustrated example, Mal is using the same CA, although, of course, Mal could use a different

CA. Note that a different certificate authority may use a different logger, and would surely use a different certificate chain, unless both CAs are root CAs, which do not need a certificate chain at all. The reader should be able to modify the diagram to handle such issues, resulting in a bit more cluttered diagram.

Finally, we see how the monitor M learns about this new certificate Ψ_{Mal}. This begins with M asking L again for an updated STH, this time receiving $\text{STH}_{\text{Mal}} \neq \text{STH}_B$; the two STHs differ since the corresponding Merkle tree contains new entries (at least one — the hash of $\Psi_{\text{Mal}}.TBS$). The monitor requests these new entries; among them, it detects Ψ_{Mal} (and the corresponding certificate chain, CC), and therefore alerts *Bob.com*. The monitor sends the alert since *Bob.com* requested alerts upon issuing of a certificate for the domain *B0b.com*.

8.5.3 Misbehaving loggers: attacks and defenses

In this section, we extend our discussion of the CT design, to consider attacks by misbehaving loggers, and defenses against these attacks in the CT specifications [319, 320].

8.5.3.1 *The certificate omission attack*

We first consider a simple logger misbehavior called a *certificate omission* attack. In a certificate omission attack, a corrupt logger fails to inform the monitor, by time $t + MMD$, about a certificate Ψ_{Mal} submitted to the log by a CA, although the logger sent to the CA an SCT for Ψ_{Mal} at time t or earlier. The certificate omission attack is illustrated in flows 1–8 of Figure 8.20.

Figure 8.20 begins, in flow 1, with the website *Bob.com* requesting the monitor M for alerts upon detecting new certificates to its domain, *Bob.com*, and to the homographic domain *B0b.com*. In flows 2–5, the attacker, Mal receives a CT certificate for *B0b.com* from the CA. The CA validates ownership of *B0b.com* (not shown) and then signs Ψ_{Mal} and sends it to the (rogue) logger L (flow 3). The logger sends back the corresponding SCT, which we denote SCT_{Mal} (flow 4). In flow 5, the certificate authority sends to Mal the certificate Ψ_{Mal}, the certificate chain (denoted again CC), and the SCT (SCT_{Mal}).

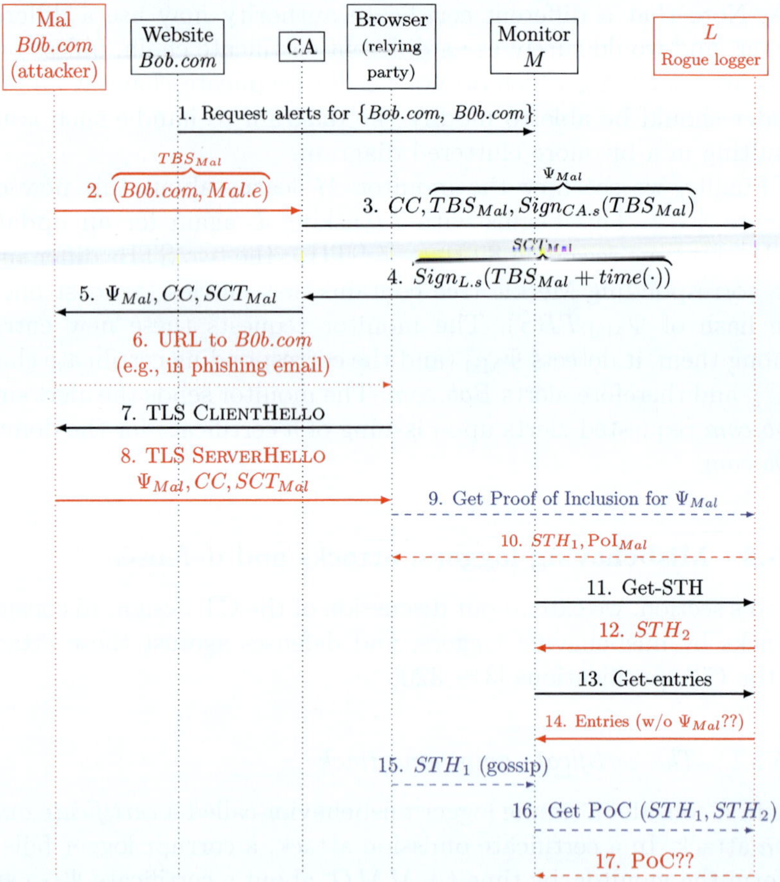

Figure 8.20. Rogue logger attacks (certificate omission in flows 1–8 [Section 8.5.3.1] and split-world attack in flows 10–14 [Section 8.5.3.4]) and CT defenses (SCT-auditing in flows 9–10 [Section 8.5.3.2] and STH-gossiping, together with Proof of Consistency, in flows 15–17 [Section 8.5.3.5]).

Flow 6 illustrates how Mal manipulates the user into entering the misleading website *B0b.com*. We used dotted arrow since the manipulation can be in different ways; one method is a *phishing* email/message, containing a hyperlink (URL) to *B0b.com*. In phishing attacks, attackers use different aspects of human behavior to manipulate users, often into entering misleading websites; see Section 9.1.1.

Flows 7 and 8 show the beginning of the TLS handshake between the user's browser and the misleading website *B0b.com*. In flow 8, the website sends the TLS SERVERHELLO message and provides the browser with website's certificate Ψ_{Mal}, for the domain *B0b.com*, the certificate chain CC and the SCT (SCT_{Mal}).

At this point, we see that the attacker abused the certificate for the misleading domain name *B0b.com*, abusing the certificate Ψ_{Mal} and SCT_{Mal}. Ideally, we would like to ensure that before this occurs, Ψ_{Mal} would already be known to M, allowing the monitor M to alert the legitimate domain owner (of *Bob.com*), who may take corrective action, such as requesting the CA to revoke Ψ_{Mal}. However, what prevents a misbehaving logger from omitting Ψ_{Mal} from the certificates it reports to M in flow 14, and from the leaves of the Merkle tree whose tree head is signed in STH_2?

We next discuss *SCT auditing*, an optional CT mechanism designed to defend against certificate omission logger attacks.

8.5.3.2 *SCT auditing*

We now explain *SCT auditing*, an optional CT mechanism whose goal is to defend against certificate omission logger attacks, as well as the reasons that this defense is not widely deployed.

The *SCT auditing* mechanism is illustrated in flows 9 and 10 of Figure 8.20. In flow 9, the relying party requests the logger to provide a *Merkle tree Proof of Inclusion (*POI*)* for a certificate, in this example Ψ_{Mal}. The logger endpoint that provides the POI is called *get-proof-by-hash*, probably since when using this endpoint, the client provides the hash of the certificate.

The response is shown in flow 10: an STH in which the certificate is included, and the POI allowing the relying party to validate that the certificate is included in (the Merkle tree whose digest is signed in) the STH. For example, the Proof of Inclusion PoI_{Mal} returned together with STH_1 in flow 10 allows the browser to confirm that $\Psi_{\text{Mal}} \in \text{STH}_1$, i.e., the certificate Ψ_{Mal} is included in the Merkle tree whose digest is signed in the (valid-signed) STH_1.

SCT auditing is defined in the CT specifications [319, 320], but it is not mandatory to use. In practice, it is not deployed by current CT-adopting browsers, for two main reasons: *privacy exposure* and *limited effectiveness*, which we discuss in Sections 8.5.3.3 and 8.5.3.4, respectively.

8.5.3.3 *Privacy exposure due to SCT auditing*

Privacy is a major concern with SCT auditing. The SCT auditing process exposes the certificate being validated by the relying party to the logger. This, in turn, often allows the logger to identify the website visited by the browser. The logger is often able to identify the precise webpage visited, not just the domain, since many webpages contain resources, e.g., images, from other domains, and the browser will open a separate TLS connection to retrieve such resources, which may result in corresponding additional SCT auditing requests. This is, therefore, a *significant privacy exposure.*

To reduce this privacy exposure, the browser may send the request over an anonymous network, such as Tor [156]. However, the use of Tor may not completely prevent the exposure, and has significant overhead; it also makes it impossible to know if a lack of response is due to a failure of a Tor relay or a failure of the logger.

Another way to reduce the privacy exposure is for relying parties to send their SCTs to a semi-trusted entity called an *auditor.* The auditor can ask the logger for the PoI and corresponding STH, and warn users against trusting a logger found to be corrupt or non-responsive. The use of an auditor by many relying parties will significantly reduce the privacy exposure of the relying parties to the logger; however, it creates a similar privacy exposure towards the auditor. The use of an auditor may also help reduce the overhead of this defense, in particular, the load on the logger, and make it less likely for loggers to ignore PoI requests.

Google Chrome browser supports a different, centralized auditing service, with some mechanisms to reduce privacy exposure. Basically, this service maintains a set of *validated certificates* (more precisely, hashed certificates, i.e., leaves of the Merkle tree) and allows relying parties to check if a given certificate is in this set without exposing the certificate, using a *Private Information Retrieval* (PIR) protocol. If the certificate is in the set, then the relying party considers this as a confirmation from the service that the certificate was logged. If the certificate is not in the set, then the relying party *may* submit the certificate to the auditing service. See details in Refs. [269, 493].

8.5.3.4 *Foiling SCT auditing: the split-world attack*

The SCT auditing process has limited effectiveness, since there are two ways in which a corrupt logger may foil it: the *split-world attack* in which the logger replies to the audit with a different STH than the one it sends to the monitors, and the naïve approach of simply *not responding*. Let us discuss this naïve attack.

Foiling SCT-auditing by not responding: One simple method to defeat SCT-auditing is when the corrupt logger does *not* send the response to the request for STH and PoI (the response shown in flow 10 in Figure 8.20).

The requesting entity (often browser) can time out; however, should it then consider the logger L as faulty? The specifications do not state this. In fact, it seems likely that a benign logger L may also, sometimes, be unable to provide a timely, valid response, e.g., due to concurrent requests from many clients (possibly caused intentionally by an attacker). Furthermore, in the natural case where the PoI request is sent by a relying party (browser, typically), as shown in Figure 8.20, then a corrupt logger L may not care much if that particular browser considers the logger as suspect.

Foiling SCT auditing by inconsistent STHs — the split-world attack: The split-world attack is a more subtle attack, which is illustrated in flows 10–14 of Figure 8.20. In a split-world attack, a corrupt logger responds to the request for PoI with an STH (STH_1) computed over a log which does contain Ψ_{Mal}, allowing the logger to provide the corresponding PoI for Ψ_{Mal}. However, the corrupt logger provides to monitors other STHs, which reflect a log without Ψ_{Mal}. For example, in Figure 8.20, the logger sends STH_1 in flow 10, and STH_2 in flow 12, where $\Psi_{Mal} \in STH_1$ but $\Psi_{Mal} \notin STH_2$.

The CT specifications mention the split-world attack and the possible use of gossip and Proof of Consistency (PoC) to detect such attacks; let us discuss these defenses.

8.5.3.5 *Using gossip and Proof of Consistency against the split-world attack*

The CT design discusses two mechanisms, *gossip* and PoC, which, together, may detect the split-world attack.

Gossip protocols allow entities to share information. CT monitors, relying parties and other entities can use a gossip protocol to share between them different STHs. This is illustrated in flow 15 of Figure 8.20, where the browser sends STH_1 to monitor M, who previously received the inconsistent STH STH_2.

The monitor now has a pair of STHs, e.g., STH_1 and STH_2. The monitor requests the logger to provide a PoC, using the *get-sth-consistency* endpoint of the logger. This is illustrated in flow 16 of Figure 8.20, where M requests the PoC showing consistency of STH_1 and STH_2. The CT specifications [320] shows an algorithm to construct a concise PoC and an efficient algorithms to verify the PoC. The PoC allows validation that the set of leafs (certificates) whose digest (tree head) is signed in STH_2 is a superset of the set of leafs (certificates) whose digest is signed in STH_1.

Recall that STH_2 was sent (in flow 12) after STH_1 (in flow 10); assume, therefore, that $STH_2.timestamp > STH_1.timestamp$. In this case, the PoC needs to show that STH_2 is a consistent continuation from STH_1. However, the design ensures that it is infeasible to find a valid PoC, if STH_2 is *inconsistent* with STH_1, i.e, if there is a certificate Ψ_{Mal} s.t. $\Psi_{Mal} \in STH_1$ yet $\Psi_{Mal} \notin STH_2$. In this way, the combination of the gossip and the PoC mechanisms could detect a logger that tries to foil SCT auditing or otherwise produces inconsistent STHs.

Unfortunately, so far, a gossip protocol for CT was not specified, standardized or analyzed, although there have been some efforts to define such a protocol. Note also that a logger could also fail to send a response to the PoC requests, similarly to the attack above where the logger does not respond to PoI requests.

8.6 Lab: TLS and PKI

Lab 5 (TLS and PKI). In this lab, you will learn how to connect a TLS client to a TLS server, and experiment with different issues related to certificates and their validation.

The labs and installation instructions are available from https://github.com/CyberSec-labs/labs; for more details, see the preface.

The lab requires a Linux machine with OpenSSL installed. To perform the lab using a Windows machine, you may install, if necessary, and use WSL (Windows Subsystem for Linux).

In the *lab/question* directory, you will find the files *server.py* and *client.py*. Most of the server code has been given to you, and you can run it as is, using the command: *python3 server.py*.

You will also find several sub-directories containing certificates in the *lab/certs* directory, including nine sub-directories whose name is a single letter. Each of these nine single-letter sub-directories contains a client certificate, and each of these client certificates has a distinguishing feature which will allow you to identify it. We map each feature to a number from 1 to 9, as follows:

1. A valid certificate.
2. An expired certificate.
3. An invalid self-signed CA certificate.
4. A certificate with an invalid Common Name (CN) attribute.
5. A certificate which uses MD5, known to be an insecure hash function.
6. A certificate with an unknown critical extension.
7. A certificate whose usage for TLS client authentication contradicts its KEY USAGE extension.
8. A certificate which has an invalid.
9. A certificate provided an invalid certificate chain, i.e., an unknown CA authority.

The mapping between the certificates and the directories is randomized; in the lab, you find the mapping by identifying the distinguishing feature of each certificate. When you complete identifying the mapping of these nine certificates, submit your answer in the form *<directory>_<directory>_<directory>*. . . , For example, if the mapping is in alphabetical order of the directories, then you should submit: *A_B_C_D_E_F_G_H_I*.

First, implement the missing login in *client.py* so that it would successfully connect to the server, when using a valid client certificate. Run the client in a separate terminal using the command: *python3 client.py*. Connect to the server using each of the certificates and key given to you in the *lab/certs* directory. You should find that three certificates passed while six failed. You should be able to identify four of the certificates that failed: an expired certificate (number 2), an MD5 certificate (number 5), a certificate with unknown critical extension (number 6) and a certificate with incorrect KEY USAGE (number 7).

Two of the certificates failed due to an unknown CA; one of them failed due to invalid certificate chain (number 9) and then other failed since it is a self signed certificate (number 3). To determine which is which, view the error messages on the terminal where you are running the server. One error message distinctly shows that a certificate is self-signed, and the other shows that it was unable to get the local issuer certificate for the certificate chain.

We next investigate the three certificates which passed the current validation currently implemented in *server.py*. One of them is simply a valid certificate (number 1), one has an invalid common name (number 4) and the third has an invalid SAN. To determine which is which, modify the code in *server.py*. Specifically, in *server.py*, there is a function where you must return False to reject certificates that have an invalid common name, e.g., for blacklisted clients, or an invalid SAN. Complete this function and reject all connections from a client with a common name of *invalid_client*, or from a client with a SAN of *DNS:invalid_san.com*. Run the modified server with the client, to learn which certificate is which.

In your submission folder, submit your solution in *solutions.txt* in the aforementioned form and order.

8.7 Additional exercises

Exercise 8.4. Provide a security motivation for the fact that the signature process is specified as one of the (signed) fields within the certificate. Do this by constructing two 'artificial' CRHFs, h^A and h^B; to construct h^A and h^B, you may use a given CRHF h. Your constructions should allow you to show that it could be insecure to use certificates where the signature process (including hashing) is not clearly identified as part of the signed fields. Specifically, design h^A, h^B to show how an attacker may ask a CA to sign a certificate for one name, say *Attacker*, and then use the resulting signature over the certificate to forge a certificate for a different name, say *Victim*.

Exercise 8.5. Some X.509v3 extensions are quite elaborate and may contain many elements of different types; for example, the *SAN* extension. A relying party may receive a certificate with a known extension, but containing an element of unknown type, or incorrectly formatted. X.509 does not specify the correct behavior in such case, and implementations may consider the entire extension as unrecognized; if the extension is marked critical, this results in rejecting the entire certificate, i.e., considering it invalid.

Specify a format for an extension which will allow defining *critical* and *non-critical* element types. *Critical* elements must be recognized by the relying party or the entire extension is deemed unrecognized, and *non-critical* elements may be safely ignored by the relying party if not recognized, while still handling the other elements in this extension.

Is this mechanism of potential use within an X.509v3 critical extension? Within a non-critical extension?

Exercise 8.6. Locate the certificate information in your browser, and do the following:

1. Count, or estimate, the number of root CAs.
2. Count, or estimate, the number of intermediary CAs.
3. Can you give two examples of root CAs that you believe belong to organizations or companies that you know and trust? Explain.
4. Can you give two examples of root CAs that you believe belong to organizations or companies that you do not know or do not trust? Explain.
5. Can you give two examples of intermediary CAs that you believe belong to organizations or companies that you know and trust? Explain.
6. Can you give two examples of intermediary CAs that you believe belong to organizations or companies that you do not know or do not trust? Explain.
7. For one of the root CAs, view its details, and identify the extensions. For extensions covered in this chapter, explain their fields. For other extensions, identify what they are used for.
8. For one of the intermediary CAs, view its details, and identify the extensions. For extensions covered in this chapter, explain their fields. For other extensions, identify what they are used for.

Use screen shots to document your results.

Exercise 8.7. Present a sequence diagram showing how a MitM attacker can circumvent the DV process, as described in Figure 8.6.

Exercise 8.8. A website *eve.com* receives a TLS certificate from a CA *CA.org*. Present a mistake that *CA.org* could make in the certificate, which would allow *eve.com* to impersonate as the website for domain *Bob.com*. Present the fields in a certificate Ψ_{Eve} allowing the impersonation attack, and the fields in a 'corrected' certificate Ψ'_{Eve} (that does not allow such impersonation attack).

Exercise 8.9. The examples in Figure 8.7 considered, for Ψ_{ICA2} and Ψ_{LCA}, only the cA flag:

1. Present a similar table where you assume that Ψ_{ICA} is as in line 1 of the original table, and present similar scenarios to what is in the original table, but for Ψ_{ICA2}.
2. Repeat, for Ψ_{LCA}.

Exercise 8.10. It is sometimes desirable for certificates to provide evidence of sensitive information, such as gender, age or address. Such information may be crucial to some services, e.g., to limit access to a certain chat room only to individuals of specific gender. It is proposed to include such information in a special extension and to protect the privacy of the information by hashing it; for example, the extension may contain $h(DoB)$ where DoB stands for date of birth. When the subject wishes to prove her age, she provides the certificate together with the value DoB, allowing relying party to validate the age:

1. Should such extensions be marked critical? Why?
2. Show that the design above fails to preserve privacy, by describing the algorithm an attacker would use to find out the sensitive information (e.g., DoB), without it being sent by the subject (e.g., Client). Use pseudo-code or flow-chart. Explain why your algorithm is reasonably efficient.
3. Present an improved design which would protect privacy properly. Your design should consist of the contents of the extension (instead of the insecure $h(DoB)$), and any additional information which should be sent inside or outside the certificate to provide evidence of age.

4. Prove, or present clear argument, for security of your construction, under the random oracle model.
5. Present a counterexample showing that it is not sufficient to assume that h is a collision-resistant hash function, for the construction to be secure.

For a real-life example of such leakage, in the Verisign CZAG extension, see Ref. [410]

Exercise 8.11 (Comparison of periodical revocation mechanisms). Assume a set of up to 64 million certificates, and certificates identified by serial numbers from 1 to 64 million, encoded, where necessary, by the minimal number of bits sufficient for these 64-million distinct serial numbers:

1. What will be the size (in bytes) of the CRL, assuming 1% of the certificates were revoked? Ignore the size of elements of the CRL except the list of serial numbers of revoked certificates, and assume (typical although sub-optimal) 96-bit representation for each serial number. Repeat, if 10% of the certificates were revoked.
2. Repeat, for delta-CRL, assuming 1000 certificates revoked during the last day.
3. Repeat both items, assuming efficient representation for serial numbers.
4. Repeat first item, for CRV instead of CRL, without compression.
5. Repeat second item, for ΔCRV instead of Delta-CRLs, without compression.
6. Create random CRVs and ΔCRVs, and then compress them using standard compression utility, and compare the length of the compressed versions.

Exercise 8.12 (SCSV certificate extension and the downgrade dance attack). The TLS fallback Signaling Cipher Suite Value (SCSV) TLS extension [360], discussed in Section 7.5.6, is designed to mitigate the protocol version downgrade dance attack; see also Exercise 7.13:

1. Consider a MitM attacker who impersonates as webserver *victim.com*, to cause the client to downgrade to an insecure version of TLS; in this version, the attacker is able to find out the master key during the handshake. To foil SCSV, the attacker ignores

it, i.e., behaves as if *victim.com* does not support SCSV. Show a sequence diagram showing how this attacker is able to establish the connection with the client in spite of SCSV.
2. Present an alternative defense to SCSV, which also prevents protocol downgrade attacks using a signaling mechanism, but a different signaling mechanism which uses an X.509v3 certificate extension.
3. Should your X.509v3 extension be always marked critical? Always non-critical? Sometimes (when?)? Justify.
4. Suppose a domain adopts your design, and upgrades its certificate accordingly. Is it required to revoke the previous certificate? Justify; if it is required — present an attack if this isn't done (with sequence diagram).
5. This X.509v3 extension signaling mechanism has the disadvantage that it requires a new certificate; it may take many domains considerable time to upgrade their certificates; even the CA may take time to support this extension. Explain how the new extension may co-exist with the current SCSV signaling mechanism, providing the current level of SCSV defense to domains which did not yet adopt the new X.509 extension. Explain this using sequence diagram for the interaction of a client with such 'legacy-SCSV' website.

Exercise 8.13 (Preventing cross-protocol attacks). The website *Bob.com* uses TLS 1.3, but attackers are able to impersonate as this server, by exploiting the fact that another website of the same organization, *vuln.Bob.com*, used SSLv2, with the same certificate as that of *Bob.com*:

1. Explain the attack using a sequence diagram.
2. Show how and which standard certificate extension(s) could have been used to prevent the use of the same certificate for these two purposes, by ensuring key separation (Section 2.7.4).

Exercise 8.14. As shown in Ref. [166], a large number of browser-trusted CAs are operated by organizations such as universities, non-CA companies or other organizations, e.g., religious organizations. For example, assume that one of these is *nu.ne*, a university, which obtained this signing certificate as an ICA of a trusted root CA, say *root.ca*. Note that *nu.ne* would be a (non-existent) Nigerian university, as indicated by its use of the Nigerian country code TLD (ccTLD) *ne*. The *nu.ne* university obtained this CA certificate so it may certify its different departments and project websites. Assume that the private key of *nu.ne* is compromised by an attacker, which also has MitM capabilities:

1. Would this allow the attacker to intercept the traffic between the user and (1) the university, (2) other Nigerian sites, (3) other universities, (4) additional sites (which)? Assume standard use of X.509v3.
2. What would be a typical process for detection of the exposure of the private key of *nu.ne*? Can you bound the time or number of fake certificates issued until exposure?
3. Describe and explain any changes in your answers to the previous items, due to adoption of CT by relevant entities.
4. What should be the mitigation, once the exposure is detected?

Exercise 8.15 (Web-of-Trust). In this exercise we consider *Web-of-Trust* PKI, first proposed and often associated with the *PGP* [197] e-mail and file encryption/signing software. In a web of trust, each user can certify the (public key, name) mappings for people she knows, acting as a CA. To establish secure communication, two users exchange certificates they obtained for their keys, and possibly also certificates of the signers. Each user u maintains a directed graph (V_u, E_u) whose nodes V_u are (*public key, name*) pairs from the set of all certificates known to u, and where there is an edge from one node, say (pk_A, Alice) to another, say (pk_B,Bob), if u has a certificate over (pk_B,Bob) using key pk_A; the graph has a special 'trust anchor' entry for user u herself, denoted (pk_u, u). Each user u decides on a maximal *certificate path length* $L(u)$; we say that u *trusts* (pk_B,Bob) if there is a path of length at most $L(u)$ from (pk_u, u) to (pk_B,Bob) in (V_u, E_u).

Specify an efficient algorithm allowing u to determine if she should *trust* (pk_B,Bob). What is the complexity of this algorithm? Note: You may use well-known algorithm(s), in which case, just specify their names and reference, there is no need to copy them in your answer.

Exercise 8.16 (Attacks against OCSP and OCSP stapling). Consider the following powerful attacker model — the attacker has MitM capabilities:

1. An attacker gets hold of the private key of a bank, say *Bank.com*, whose corresponding public key is certified in Ψ_B. The bank detects the exposure, generates a new public-private keypair, receives a certificate Ψ'_B for the new public key and revokes the certificate Ψ_B for the exposed key. Show, with a sequence diagram, how the attacker can continue to impersonate as the bank and even act as a MitM to traffic between the customer and the bank, in spite of the fact that the bank's website uses OCSP stapling. You may assume that the *must-staple* certificate extension [231] is not used.
2. Explain, again using a sequence diagram, how use of the *must-staple* certificate extension may prevent this attack.
3. Assume that the attacker now manages to trick another CA into issuing a fake certificate for *Bank.com*, which we denote Ψ''_B. Show, with a sequence diagram, how the attacker can continue to impersonate as the bank.
4. Repeat, when the attacker obtains a certificate for an impersonating domain name of your choice — select what you think will be domain name likely to succeed to trick users.
5. For each of the following defenses, could they help against the attacks in the previous two items? How or why not? Assume that the defenses are supported by the browser. The defenses to consider: HPKP, HSTS, DANE, CAA and CT.

Exercise 8.17 (Keyed hash and certificates). Many cryptographic protocols and standards, e.g., X.509, PKIX and CT, rely on the use of the 'Hash-then-Sign' paradigm, based on the assumption that the hash function in use, $h(\cdot)$, is a (keyless) CRHF:

1. Explain why this assumption is only a simplification, namely, why no keyless hash function can be collision-resistant.
2. One way to 'fix' such protocols is by using, instead, a *keyed* CRHF. Explain why your argument for non-existence of a keyless CRHF does not also imply non-existence of keyed-CRHF.
3. Design how to issue X.509 certificates using a keyed-CRHF, such the certificates can be properly validated by both (1) relying parties that support the keyed-CRHF mechanism *and* (2) 'legacy' relying parties that are not modified and still support only the existing certificate-validation mechanism.

4. If your design in the previous item makes use of any new or existing X.509 extension(s), explain and justify whether the extension(s) should be marked as critical, as non-critical, or if for some applications an extension should be marked critical and for others marked non-critical.

Exercise 8.18 (OCSP Hash-chain Variant). To avoid computational burden on the OCSP responder, it is proposed to use an alternative mechanism to OCSP, which will usually avoid the use of signatures as long as the certificate isn't revoked, yet ensure secure revocation information. Specifically, add an extension, say called 'OCSP-chain', to the X.509 public-key certificate. The OCSP-chain extension will contain an n-bit binary string $x_0 \in \{0,1\}^n$. A simple, efficient algorithm uses x_0 to validate a 'daily validation token' (i, x_i) to be sent by the CA; the CA sends the token (i, x_i) only if the certificate was not revoked i days after it was issued. Your solution may use a cryptographic hash function h, and 'security under the random oracle model' suffices, i.e., modeling as if h is a random function:

1. Validation of token (i, x_i) is done by checking that $x_0 =$ ________________.
2. Assume that the certificate's maximal validity period is 1000 days. The CA computes/selects x_i, for $0 \leq i < 1000$, by $x_i \leftarrow$ ________________, and selects x_{1000} by $x_{1000} \leftarrow$ ______________________.
3. Should the OCSP-chain extension be always marked critical? Always non-critical? Sometimes critical and sometimes not? Justify.
4. Assume that the probability of a random certificate to be revoked on a particular day is less than 10^{-5}. A further optimization reduces the number of hash-chain computations by the CA, by 'grouping' 100 certificates in a common 'hash-chain group'. As long as none of these certificates is revoked, they all use the same 'hash-chain group token'; only when one of them is revoked, a per-certificate token will be sent. This extension requires an extended version of the OCSP-chain extension, i.e., the extension should not simply contain an n-bit binary string $x_0 \in \{0,1\}^n$ as before. Instead, the extension should contain ________________, and the 'daily validation token' will change from (i, x_i) to ________________ (before any of the certificates in the group is

revoked) and to ______________ (after one or more of the certificates in the group is revoked).

Exercise 8.19. Modify Figure 8.19 to handle the case where the attacker uses a different CA from the one used by the benign domain-owner, and that each of the CAs use a different logger.

Exercise 8.20 (Malicious CA). Let MalCA be a malicious CA, trusted (e.g., as a root CA) by browsers.

1. Assume *Bob.com* generates a signing public-private key pair $(B.s, B.v)$ and has $B.v$ certified by MalCA. Present sequence diagram showing how MalCA can eavesdrop on communication between the site *https://Bob.com* and a client, Alice, in spite of their use of TLS 1.3. Your solution should be a very simple attack. Assume the use of only the defenses explicitly mentioned.
2. Assume that Alice uses CT and does not communicate with websites that do not provide a properly signed *SCT*. Assume a single, trustworthy logger, L, and a single, trustworthy monitor, M. Present a sequence diagram showing how this setup may prevent or deter MalCA from performing the attack.
3. Assume that the private key of *Bob.com* is exposed by MalCA; however, the exposure is detected, and Bob revokes its certificate. Furthermore, both Alice and *Bob.com* deploy OCSP stapling, and Bob's public key certificate includes the *must-staple* extension. Show, with sequence diagram, how MalCA may still eavesdrop to communication between Alice and *Bob.com*.

Exercise 8.21 (CT Revocation and the 'Zombie Certificate Attack'). The (legitimate) website *Bob.com* receives a CT certificate for its public key $B.e$ from the CA A, with SCT signed by logger L. After a year, *Bob.com* detects that its private key was exposed and abused by attackers; it immediately requests A to revoke Ψ_B and issue a certificate using the newly-generated public key $B'.e$, and receives the corresponding certificate $C'_B = Sign_{A.s}(Bob.com, B'.e)$. Assume that Alice's browser is using OCSP, applying soft-fail, except for certificates with the OCSP must-staple indication (Section 8.3.3), where the browser applies the hard-fail policy. In the following items, your answers should include a message sequence diagram for each scenario, indicating TLS and OCSP messages, certificates and SCTs. For the first few items of this question, assume the use of HL-CT:

1. Alice instructs her browser to visit *Bob.com*; however, an attacker, Mal, is able to interfere with the address resolution process, directing the browser to the IP address of Mal, say 6.6.6.6, instead of the IP address of the legitimate *Bob.com* website, say 1.2.3.4. The attacker does not have other traffic-manipulation capabilities, in particular, is not a MitM. Show what happens when Alice's browser tries to establish TLS 1.2 connection with *Bob.com*, assuming that the browser uses OCSP. Denote Mal's public key by $M.e$.
2. Repeat, when the attacker has MitM capabilities (between all parties).
3. Repeat, assuming now (but not before!) that Ψ_B and C'_B include the must-staple mechanism.
4. Repeat, when the attacker controls also A.
5. What, if any, would change in your answer when using CT?

1. Alice instructs her browser to visit *Bob.com*; however, an attacker that is able to interfere with the address resolution process, directs [illegible] instead of the IP address of the legitimate *Bob.com* website, say 1.2.3.4. The attacker does not have other malicious capabilities; in particular, is not a MitM. Show what happens when Alice's browser tries to establish TLS 1.2 connection with *Bob.com*. [illegible] Alice [illegible] *Bob.com*.
2. Repeat, when the attacker has MitM capabilities (between all parties).
3. Repeat, assuming now (but not before!) that Φ_B and C_B include the most simple mechanism.
4. Repeat, when the attacker controls also *A*.
5. What, if any, would change in your answer when using CT?

Chapter 9

Human-Centered Security and Cryptography

In the previous chapters, we often referred to the communicating entities by common names — most commonly, we used the 'classical' names Alice and Bob. In a few places, we mentioned the distinction between the human users and their computing and communicating devices — the most important example being in Section 8.1.5, where we discussed *misleading certificates and domain names*, i.e., certificates for domain names which mislead human users in different ways, to gain unwarranted trust. This is just one aspect of the large and very important area of *human aspects of cybersecurity* — probably the most important and least understood part of cybersecurity. Kevin Mitnick, one of the most famous hackers and the author of several books about hacking, most notably his memoir [357], put it eloquently in his testimony to the U.S. Senate [356]:

> The human side of computer security is easily exploited and constantly overlooked. Companies spend millions of dollars on firewalls, encryption, and secure access devices and it's money wasted because none of these measures address the weakest link in the security chain: the people who use, administer, operate and account for computer systems.

In this chapter, we discuss *social engineering* attacks, which are attacks that exploit human psychology and cognitive biases to deceive and manipulate users, and *human-centered security*, which is the important and insufficiently studied area of designing systems to ensure security, taking into account the same human psychology and cognitive biases.

Contents of this chapter: In Section 9.1, we introduce *human-centered security.* In Section 9.2, we discuss the important specific problem of *login ceremonies*, in which we focus in the rest of this chapter; the term *ceremony* refers to a process or protocol involving interactions between computers and humans [283]. In Section 9.3, we discuss *password-based login ceremonies*, which are (still?) the most common factor of authentication, attacks on password-based login mechanisms, and *password managers*, which can improve the security and convenience of password-based login. In Section 9.4, we focus on attacks on password systems due to exposure of the password file, and designs to reduce the risks due to such exposure, including *hashed, salted and peppered password files*. In Section 9.5, we discuss *Password-Authenticated Key Exchange* (PAKE) protocols, which use of passwords to establish secure communication without relying on public key certificates. Finally, in Section 9.6, we discuss login ceremonies beyond passwords, including the *FIDO2* standards (Section 9.6.4) for authenticator devices (*something you have* login ceremonies).

9.1 Introducing human-centered security and cryptography

The challenge of *human-centered security* is to ensure security for systems which are used, administered and operated by humans. Ensuring security for systems used by humans is challenging, sometimes in surprising ways. Some challenges are obvious: we cannot expect a user to remember an 128-bit key or to make complex calculations as used by typical cryptographic functions. However, other challenges may be less obvious, and are often overlooked by designers. For example, as we discussed in Section 8.1.5, users are often *misled* by rogue certificates since they do not note the use of a visually similar domain name, or the significance of some variations in the domain name. An even more disturbing reality is that users often fail to notice the lack of security indicators, such as the display of a padlock icon and similar indicators for the use of HTTPS vs. HTTP (Section 9.3.1).

Furthermore, when prompted, users often allow the use of websites with revoked or invalid certificates, and install unsigned software or software signed by unknown entities. When faced with such actions by users, systems designers may despair, saying, *how can we protect users who do not follow the security guidelines?*

However, most security experts disagree. We cannot protect *all* users *all* of the time, but you can *protect most users most of the time.* Or, to quote the well known security expert Steve Bellovin:

> When most people don't use security tools correctly, the problem is with the tools, not with the people.

The area of *secure usability* or *human-centered security* deals with the security of systems as used by 'normal people'. This includes the study of security of systems when used by people with disabilities, older people, very young people, and other special populations.

One of the early and most well-known works in this area is the paper *Why Johnny Can't Encrypt* by Whitten and Tygar [478]. The name *Johnny* represents, in Ref. [478] and many follow-up papers, the typical users, with their human weaknesses, traits and biases. Let us define this as the basic principle of human-centered security, which we call the *Johnny's principle.*

Principle 18 (Johnny's principle: 'secure' is 'secure as used by Johnny'). *Systems should be designed and evaluated for security when used by Johnny (i.e., 'normal users').*

Human-centered security focuses on the design of *secure ceremonies*, i.e., secure interactions between the human user and computer systems and devices, to ensure security. We use the term *ceremony* to emphasize the involvement of humans in the interaction, in contrast to the term *protocol*, which, in cybersecurity, is used for interactions between different automated systems.

9.1.1 Biases and other challenges of protecting humans

The basic challenge of human-centered security is that human behavior is not optimized to ensure secure use of automated mechanisms. In fact, human behavior is the complex result of eons of evolution under dramatically different conditions, and against different threats, than these experienced by users of computer systems and automated devices. Human abilities, behavior and cognition have been optimized to respond efficiently to the risks and predators occurring in a natural environment; cybersecurity has completely different risks and predators, to which we humans were not designed. Detection of attacks is critical for security both in the jungle and in the web, but the skills and behaviors that help detect an attacking predator in the jungle, are very different from these required to detect an impersonating website or a phishing email. Many human traits which served humanity well during evolution, may result in vulnerability to attacks when using computer systems, especially when the designers did not take human-centered security in mind.

In particular, humans have several biases and other behavioral traits that make it challenging to ensure security of a system used or operated by a human. Let us list some of these challenges.

The principle of least effort: The *principle of least effort* is a basic behavioral hypothesis, saying that a person will choose a course of action that appears to require the smallest amount of effort or expenditure of energy [464]; in practice, this usually means to choose the *quickest* response or minimal action, such as using default values.

Inattentional blindness: When humans focus on a specific task or activity, they often unintentionally ignore and do not notice unrelated events [225, 340]. This phenomena is called *inattentional blindness* and has been used, for ages, by magicians and confidence artists; it is only natural that it is also serving cybersecurity attackers.

Subconscious error correction: Humans apply, subconsciously, *error correction* to information obtained by the senses, mainly seeing and hearing. As a result, humans tend to ignore seemingly minor errors, such as a typo. This can be abused by attackers when the same information is presented to the user but also processed by a computer, e.g., facilitating rogue certificates with misleading domain names, see Section 8.1.5.2.

Click-whirr responses: When a person is stimulated frequently in a certain way that requires the person to respond in the the same way, the person often responds to the stimulus 'automatically', without careful evaluation of the specifics of the stimulus. This phenomena, referred to as *click-whirr* response or a *fixed-action pattern*, can be abused by attackers, e.g., when users click 'Ok' on a dialogue without reading and considering the message, or enter their password into a login prompt without considering if the prompt is presented at the correct time. The term click-whirr response was coined in Ref. [126] by Cialdini; originally, the term referred to the activation of a tape recorder by pressing a button ('click'), which is automatically followed by a movement ('whirr') and playing of the recorded message. The application of this principle to the responses of human users to specific stimuli was proposed in Ref. [283]. Notice how this behavior can be explained by the principle of least effort combined with subconscious error correction.

Truth bias: People tend to assume that communication is honest (correct), without considering (sufficiently or at all) the possibility of deceit [329]. The truth bias has merit, as it helps cooperation in a team, but it makes persons vulnerable to cyber-predators.

Cryptography is in Greek: Cryptography and security are complex, technical subjects, and most users do not know much about them. For example, many users are unaware of the fact that *domain names* are organized in a hierarchical ownership structure (see Section 8.4.2). Even more users do not know how the domain-name syntax reflects the hierarchy, e.g., understand the critical distinction in trust between *s666.bank.com*, *s666-bank.com* and *bank.s666.com.*

Default bias: Users often use the default values offered by the system. One reason for that is the that it is easier to use the default values rather than to consider alternatives and choose the best one, i.e., following the principle of least effort. Another reason is that users assume that the designers know to pick safe default values. Users are often less confident in their own understanding of the alternatives — especially when the question involves security and cryptography (i.e., the question is 'in Greek').

The curse of knowledge: Developers, cryptographers and other cybersecurity experts are well versed in information technology, cybersecurity and cryptography. This can make it difficult for them to realize the challenges of understanding cybersecurity risks by typical users. This *curse of knowledge* makes it harder to develop designs which are secure and convenient when used by typical users.

Usability beats security: Usable-security design impacts the user-experience (UX) — and may often result in conflicts with (non-security) usability and even marketing considerations. In such conflicts, the (non-security) UX considerations usually have precedence; see Note 8.3. Indeed, human-centered security is often a neglected part of the education and training of developers, security experts and cryptographers.

An R&D challenge — secure-usability is hard to measure: A related challenge to researchers and developers is that *secure-usability is hard to measure.* Programmers and engineers mostly focus on well-defined specifications and measurable metrics of success. Both of these rarely exist for usable-security design. In fact, it is quite challenging to correctly measure the impact of different designs on the security of a system when used by typical users. Some of the difficulties are due to the fact that human behavior is often modified over time and scenarios. In particular, humans may behave differently in their normal work compared to their behavior during an experiment. The awareness of being evaluated for their vulnerability to an attack may make users more careful than normal, while their awareness that the attacks are not 'real' and will not impact their real system and data can make them careless. Ideally, a reliable measure of the effectiveness of different attacks and defenses should be done over long-term experiments in an environment which is as realistic as possible, using the user's real data and system. It is challenging to perform such experiments ethically.

9.1.2 Principles of human-centered security

In this section, we offer a few important principles of human-centered security. We begin with the oldest one: the *fail-safe defaults* principle, rephrased and slightly extended in Ref. [241] as *Security Should be Default, and Defaults Should be Secure*; this principle is also sometimes referred to as *secure by default* or *deny by default.* The fail-safe defaults principle was published as early as 1975, in a seminal paper on computer and information security by Saltzer and Schroeder [428]. It follows from the *default bias* and the *principle of least effort.*

Principle 19 (Fail-safe defaults). *Whenever possible, the default choices of a system should be secure (fail-safe). Namely, if a less-secure option exists, it should not be the default. Default settings should provide adequate security; only clearly trustworthy parties may be trusted by default. Namely, Security Should be Default, and Defaults Should be Secure.*

The fail-safe defaults principle was stated already in 1975, when changing a default value required editing of a configuration file, and was therefore done mostly by expert users. We offer an extension of it for the current reality, where systems often offer users dialogues with multiple options, with one of them being the default. In this case, we believe that *only secure options should be offered.* Namely, systems should *refrain*, as much as possible, from even *offering* options which may make the user vulnerable to attacks.

Principle 20 (Defend, don't ask). *Systems should not offer users insecure options or allow users to expose security. When insecure options are essential, make their use harder, prevent click-whirr approval and present clear warnings.*

In other words, users expect the system to protect them, even if they make the wrong choice; they don't expect their judgments to be critical to the security of the system. If a dialog offers multiple options, users often assume that all options are acceptable. If it is absolutely necessary to support less secure, potentially vulnerable options, then these should be offered in clearly marked dialogues, such as under an 'advanced' tab, and come with appropriate warnings.

Whenever possible, developers should avoid relying on warnings. The fact that users ignore warnings was validated in multiple experiments, including realistic experiments where users used their own personal devices, which was hoped to guarantee that they will not ignore the risks [173, 307]. In hindsight, the failures of warnings are not surprising; users are so used to see warnings, that they ignore them as a click-whirr response.

In fact, when possible, systems should be designed to *take advantage of click-whirr responses to improve security.* For example, a browser can require users to click on a specific browser button whenever they enter their bank website; as a result, if the user clicks on this button when entering a different website, this may indicate an impersonating website which impersonates the bank (see Section 9.3.2).

Principle 21 (Use click-whirr responses to improve security). *Designers should, where possible, incorporate click-whirr responses in their user-interface design, in such ways that will provide useful security indications, such as an indication that the user considers the current website as one of its trusted websites (e.g., website of the user's bank).*

Finally, we consider the challenge of security warnings, which are all too often ignored by users. Here, we adopt a principle from research by the author [241].

Principle 22 (Alerts should wake up). *Indicate security alerts, that is, potential security exposures, using a clear, hard-to-ignore, interruptive audio/visual signal, and in such way that would be clear and understandable to all, or at least most, users.*

9.2 Login ceremonies

A basic cybersecurity challenge is *authenticating the user* to a computing system or service, e.g., a website. Typically, this involves interaction with the users mostly when the user begins its interaction with the system, a process we refer to as the *login ceremony.*

Login ceremonies are based on an authenticating capability which is available to the authorized user but not to an imposer. This is similar to the entity-authentication mechanisms of Chapter 5, which are based on a secret key shared between the parties but unknown to the attacker.

The most familiar login ceremony is where the user provides an identifier (username, user-id) and a *password.* However, passwords have serious drawbacks, both for usability and for security, which motivates the use of other login ceremonies, to be used instead of or together with passwords.

We categorize login ceremonies based on the type of capability used by the user to authenticate — and assumed to be unavailable to the attacker. A common term to these capabilities is *factors of (user) authentication*; they include the following:

Something you know: This are login ceremonies based on information known to the user but unlikely to be known to an attacker or to be successfully guessed by an attacker. The most well-known and widely used login ceremonies are of this type, mostly based on a *password*. We discuss password-based login ceremonies in Section 9.3, and password-exposure attacks and countermeasures in Section 9.4. In Section 9.5, we discuss PAKE protocols, which ensure password-based secure login and establish a secure connection, with security against eavesdropper and MitM attacker, and without relying on PKI (and TLS). In Section 9.6.1, we discuss two other *something you know* login ceremonies: *personal knowledge questions* (PKQs) and *graphical passwords*, respectively.

Something you have: In this factor of authentication, the authentication is provided by the combination of the user and of a trusted device or object, called an *authenticator*. There is a wide range of devices and objects which could be used as authenticators, ranging form a piece of paper containing *one-time passwords* (OTPws) (Section 9.6.2) to a smartphone or a dedicated hardware token (Section 9.6.3). One especially important type of authenticator is a device which supports the *FIDO2* design (Section 9.6.4).

Something you are, aka biometric authentication: *Biometrics* are measurable properties which differ among individuals, and hence may be used to identify a particular user. Diverse properties are used for biometric authentication, including fingerprints, facial recognition, voice recognition, gait and more. Biometric authentication is highly appropriate for direct authentication of the user by a device in proximity, which can measure and validate the biometric data. Direct biometric authentication is often used to control access to the computer embedding the biometric measurement device but can also be used for authentication by a trusted device which is adjacent to the user, communicating securely with a remote server. This includes user authentication by a trusted device that receives the user's biometric data from a remote server to which the user wants to login, performs the biometric measurement, verifies it and sends the results to the server; or a trusted device that makes the measurement and sends the results securely to the server. Biometric data is sometimes viewed as a secret identifier carried by the user; however, this is risky, since an attacker may be able to collect the same biometric data from the user independently or obtain it from some insufficiently protected repository.

Somebody you know: This type of authentication ceremony authenticates a user, typically as a fall back authenticator when more convenient authenticators fail, using a predefined set of semi-trusted *friends/helpers* of the user. This is based on the assumption that these 'friends' can authenticate the user, using some human authentication mechanism such as direct recognition. This authentication factor was proposed in Refs. [100, 433]. We will not elaborate on this factor.

Somewhere you are: A weak level of authentication may be obtained from the *location* of the user, possibly approximated by the IP address of the device used by the user (for remote login). This is mostly relevant in controlled-access environments, such as offices, and connection to a local area network is sometimes used as such indicator. This authentication factor is usually used only to provide additional confirmation of authentication, to strengthen a more secure form of authentication. We will not elaborate on this factor.

Continuous user authentication ceremonies: Ideally, we should authenticate the user during the entire work-session and not only during the login ceremony. To protect the communication from the user's device, e.g., laptop, to a remote machine (server), we can use TLS (Chapter 7) or a similar protocol. A *continuous user authentication ceremony* address the complementing goal of authenticating the users to their device.

Usability is the major challenge of continuous user authentication ceremonies. A ceremony should be acceptable to the users, and users would hate a ceremony which requires their constant awareness or involvement. Some systems perform semi-continuous user authentication by automatically logging-out the user after a period of inactivity; users are very sensitive to the length of this period and are likely to be unhappy if a short period is used.

More advanced continuous user authentication mechanisms may monitor the presence of the user, possibly verifying a biometric characteristic of the user, which provides an additional level of authentication. Such continuous authentication biometrics include interaction patterns, e.g., typing characteristics, or movement patterns, e.g., *gait-based authentication* [194].

9.3 Password-based login ceremonies

Passwords are a natural, widely-used *something you know* factor of authentication. Passwords are ancient; they have been used for person-to-person authentication already in the second century BC by the Roman army [490]. Passwords were used for user-authentication already from the first general purpose time-sharing operating system, the Compatible Time-Sharing System (CTSS), developed in MIT in 1961; this password system was also the first to be hacked, in 1965 [323].

What are passwords? Passwords have important advantages: passwords are simple and easy to use, implement and deploy; do not require any hardware; and are versatile. Passwords are also convenient, as long as a person uses passwords only for a few systems, and uses each of these systems quite frequently. This usually is not the case any more; most people use passwords for many systems, some of which they use rarely. This motivates unsafe habits such as the use of weak password, password reuse and password sharing, leading to vulnerabilities. The wide use of passwords for many websites and applications motivates the use of *password managers* (Section 9.3.6), as well as of other factors of authentication, to improve the convenience and security of login to many websites and applications. Typically, passwords are strings of characters, which are allowed or even required to be quite long. For example, passwords are often required to contain at least eight characters. The number of potential passwords of sufficient length can be large; for example, there are $64^{12} = 2^{72}$ passwords composed of 12 characters from a set of 64 possible characters, e.g., the 52 (lowercase and uppercase) alphabetic characters, the ten digits and two special symbols. Therefore, if a password is chosen *uniformly at random* from this set, then is equivalent to a 72-bits key, which can make brute-force and exhaustive search attacks impractical.

In reality, however, users do not choose passwords uniformly at random from the set of all allowed passwords. Indeed, users choice of passwords is extremely non-uniform and roughly follows *Zipf's law*, i.e., the frequency of a password is roughly proportional to its rank among all possible passwords [342]. For example, when users are allowed to choose, about half of the passwords were found to consist only of lower-case letters [148]. Using 12 random lower-case letters is equivalent to about 56-bits keys, which are much less secure than 72-bits keys, but may still be acceptable for many applications; however, in reality, passwords are usually shorter — and, more significantly, *not* chosen uniformly. Therefore, while brute-force guessing of passwords is impractical, strategical password guessing is often feasible.

To make guessing of passwords less likely, there are few well-known recommendations or rules for the choice and usage of passwords. These recommendations, with some variations, are given to users by many sources, including services and websites that they use, and include the following:

- Use long, hard-to-guess passwords, avoiding personally associated data and with multiple types of characters (lower and upper case, numerals and special characters).
- Do not use the same password to login into different systems, i.e., avoid *password reuse*.
- Do not maintain written (or other) records of the password.
- Change the passwords frequently.
- Do not share the password with anyone.

In practice, users often do not follow these rules; e.g., see Refs. [357, 506]. The main reason is *convenience*. Users often prefer passwords which are easily memorable and easy to enter, i.e., short passwords, password related to relevant terms or personally associated data, and/or passwords using convenient key locations, all of which violate the first 'password rule' above and imply the *distribution of passwords is extremely non-uniform*. Similarly, for convenience, users often violate the other rules: they use the same password in multiple systems (password reuse), write passwords down, change them rarely and share them (with family, friends and colleagues). This common violation of the 'password security rules' should not surprise us since it follows from the *UX>Security precedence rule* (Note 8.3).

These user behaviors have major implications on the design and evaluation of both attacks and defense of password-based login ceremonies, and motivate attackers to discover and abuse passwords. Attackers use a variety of *attack vectors* to expose passwords:

Impersonating website attacks: Attackers often manipulate users into exposing their own passwords to the attacker. Most commonly, users are tricked into entering their password into a *spoofed login form* placed in an impersonating (spoofed) website, which the users mistake to be the login form of the website of a service in which they have an account; see Section 9.3.2.

Dictionary attacks are based on the attacker constructing and using a list of candidate-passwords, called a (password) *dictionary*, and then try to login using the candidate-passwords in the dictionary. The dictionary is only a tiny fraction of the set of all possible passwords, which may make it feasible for the attacker to try a significant fraction of the entries in the dictionary, or even all of them. Dictionary attacks are often effective, since users choice of passwords is highly non-uniform, and often the guesses of passwords from the dictionary are successful. We discuss dictionary attacks and the construction of the dictionary in Section 9.3.4.

Compromised password files and personal data: Attackers abuse exposed files containing sensitive customer data, including password files. The passwords in the files are often protected, usually by encryption or hashing, but attackers are often able to find them out in spite of this; see Section 9.4.2. Once a password is found, the attacker can use it to login to the site/service whose password file was exposed. Furthermore, in spite of the guidance to use each password only in one site/service, users often use the same password in multiple sites/services; this allows attackers to use a password file exposed from one service/site, to break into accounts of the same users in other services and sites. This is referred to as the *credential stuffing* attack. Credential stuffing can be quite effective. For even higher success rates, attackers may also try to login using tweaked passwords, i.e., heuristically derived 'tweaks' of the leaked passwords; this attack is called *credential tweaking*, see Section 9.4.5.1 and Refs. [394, 395]. These heuristics may use *personal user data*, obtained from public data (e.g., social networks), from compromised files, or from social engineering. As an example of using social engineering to obtain user data, attackers may trick users into registering into a website and then abuse the user-provided personal information and password to login into other websites where the user may have an account.

Eavesdropping: Passwords may be exposed by eavesdropping to communication where the password is transmitted in plaintext. Eavesdropping may also expose a string which is a known function of the password — such as a hash of the password, or encryption using the password as a key — which may then be used for a variant of offline dictionary attacks (Section 9.4). The eavesdropping threat motivate the use of password-based remote login over a secure connection, typically using TLS (Chapter 7); see Section 9.3.1.

Shoulder surfing and password-entry side channels: *Shoulder surfing* refers to observation of the typing of the password by the user, by looking at the keys pressed by the user or looking on the screen displaying the password as it is typed. The basic countermeasure is not to display the password as it is typed; this was already done in the 'ancient' CTSS system, at least from 1965 [138]. An attacker in close proximity to the user may still be able to observe some information. For example, attackers may learn some information about the password, e.g., its length, by the sound produced upon typing each character [61] or by observing the special symbol such as asterisk which many systems display upon typing a character of the password. This unintentional (often partial) exposure of password is a special form of a *side channel*, similar to the timing side channel and other side channels exploited in cryptanalysis, e.g., see Section 6.5.7.

Exposure of written passwords: Passwords are supposed to be only remembered, and not written down, since a written password may be exposed. However, many users do write passwords down [357,506], often due to concerns about recalling the password when required to login.

Man-in-the-Browser and key-loggers: Another common way to steal passwords is directly from the user's browser or computing device. This is mostly done by 'hacking' the browser into collecting the passwords or by running a *key-logger malware* that collects information typed by the user.

Many of these attacks exploit the failure of users to follow the password security rules above. However, recall Johnny's principle (Principle 18); when most users fail to use the system securely, the problem is with the system and not with the users. Indeed, the password security rules ignore basic human behaviors and challenges. Users need to remember passwords, and a long random string is hard to remember. Therefore, users prefer to choose easy-to-remember passwords, to write the passwords down, and to reuse the same passwords, or minor tweaks of them, in different systems.

Some designs try to address these user behaviors by requiring passwords to satisfy some requirements (minimal length, use of different types of characters, etc.), evaluating password 'strength' heuristically and presenting it to the user and/or requiring new passwords to meet a 'minimal strength', or selecting strong passwords for the users and requiring them to memorize them. However, several works show that such designs, which ignore user convenience, are not advisable. In fact, not only such designs cause user annoyance, they can also harm security, by motivating users to write down passwords or use other ways to circumvent the policy enforcement mechanisms, e.g., see Refs. [6, 260]. Indeed, as the title of Ref. [6] says, we should remember that *users are not the enemy*, and design systems to be secure *and* convenient for their users.

9.3.1 Password-based web-form login ceremonies

The most common login ceremony is the password-based web-form login ceremony, where the user enters username and password into a fields in the login webpage. Most login webpages use the HTTPS protocol, i.e., run the HTTP protocol over the TLS protocol, as illustrated in Figure 7.1. The TLS protocol first performs *server authentication*, i.e., authenticates that the server has a public key certificate to the domain name requested by the browser. Then, TLS protects the confidentiality and the integrity of the communication, using shared-keys established using the server's public key certificate. Considering this, what are the possible attacks against password-based web-form login? Let us list the main concerns.

Login page via unprotected websites: In the past, many web-form login pages were not properly protected using HTTPS, allowing password exposure by an eavesdropper, a *MitM* attacker or a *DNS-poisoning* attacker [238]. The vulnerability to DNS poisoning attacker is especially critical, since multiple DNS poisoning attacks, by weak off-path attackers have been shown, e.g., Refs. [246, 247]. This vulnerability also exists when the login form is received over an insecure connection, yet the form submits the password over a secure connection. We demonstrate an attack against this design in Figure 9.1. The reader may want to compare Figure 9.1 with Figure 7.1, which shows the basic flows of a TLS connection. This

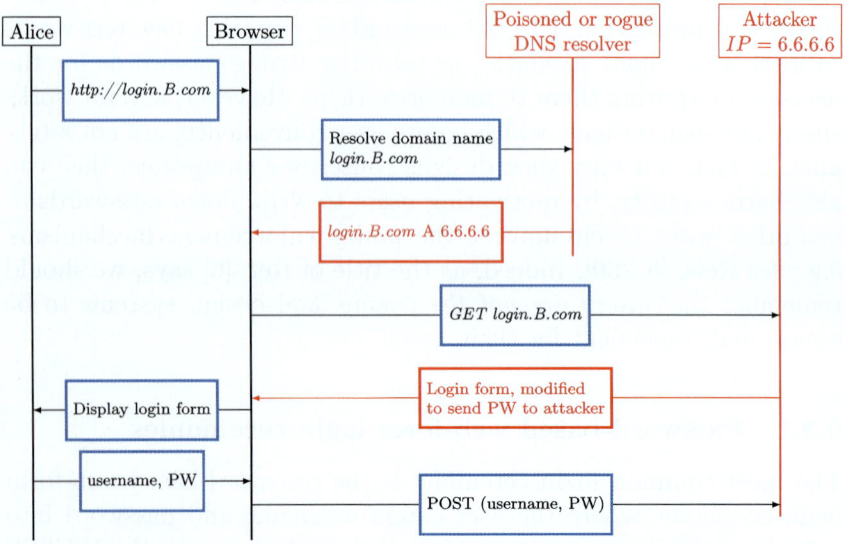

Figure 9.1. Attack exposing the user's password, exploiting DNS poisoning (or rogue DNS resolver). The attack exploits the fact that the client requests the insecure URL *http://login.B.com*, i.e., the login webpage is sent over an insecure (HTTPS) connection. The attack is effective even if the benign login page sends the submitted password over a secure (TLS) connection since no request is sent to the benign website!

attack became less relevant in the recent years since most popular and/or important websites are protected, i.e., use HTTPS (HTTP over TLS), and browsers warn users against the use of unprotected webpages.

Impersonating websites: In this (widely used) attack for exposing passwords, users enter their passwords into the login form of an *impersonating website*, usually using a *rogue certificate* (Section 8.1.5). Usually, the domain name of the impersonating website differ from the domain name of the legitimate website whose password is exposed. We discuss this common attack in Section 9.3.2, and defenses in Section 9.3.3.

TLS failures: While TLS is indeed a well-known security protocols, there have also been multiple vulnerabilities found in versions and implementations of TLS; we describe several of these vulnerabilities in Chapter 7. Users often use outdated versions of browsers, which may use vulnerable versions of TLS; and, of course, new vulnerabilities of TLS, as used by browsers, may yet be discovered.

9.3.2 Impersonating website and phishing attacks

The most common attack on password login ceremonies is the *impersonating website* (also called *spoofed website*) attack. The impersonating website uses an attacker-controlled domain name but impersonates a website in a different domain (the *impersonated website*). The goal of the attacker is to cause users to visit the impersonating website yet believe that they visit impersonated website and, therefore, to enter into the impersonating login form their username an password for the impersonated website.

Impersonating website attacks are common since they are *easy to launch* yet *highly effective*. These attacks are easy to launch due to the following reasons:

- There are only few restrictions on purchasing an attacker-chosen domain name; the process is quick, fully online, inexpensive, and can be done in a way which can hardly be traced back to the attacker, e.g., using the stolen credit card credentials. The main restriction on domain names is that it is impossible to purchase an already allocated domain name. In addition, some domain registrars limit domain names which are flagged as suspicious, and there are some restrictions on specific top-level domain names (e.g., the *edu* top level domain). However, impersonating website attacks are often successful using domain names which pass these restrictions.

- Once the attacker has purchased a domain name, the attacker can map it to a server controlled by the attacker and obtain a valid public key certificate for the server from a benign certificate authority (CA), by using Domain Validation (DV) (Section 8.2.3).
- Attackers are often able to cause victim users to reach the impersonating website, with minimal investment of time or expense, and in ways which are hard to trace to the attacker. This is most commonly done by *phishing* attacks, where the attacker sends to the victim a phishing message (*bait*). The bait is impersonated to appear to come from the impersonated website, and urges the user to follow a link, which purportedly is to the impersonated website, but actually leads to the impersonating website.

Figure 9.2 illustrates the typical process of a phishing attack culminating with the exposure of the user's credentials (username and password) to the impersonating website. The *bait* (phishing message) can be sent via email or other messaging systems, such as SMS (*Smishing*), instant-messaging applications and social networks. The process consists of the following steps:

Buy domain: The attacker buys a misleading (impersonating) domain name, to be used by the impersonating website. The most relevant types of misleading domain names are *homographic* (visually impersonating) domain names, *domain-name hacking* and *combosquatting* domain names. See the discussion of rogue certificates in Section 8.1.5. It is often not hard to find candidate domain names that will not fall under the limited restrictions on domain names imposed by DNS registrars and CAs. Registering such a (non-restricted) domain name is a quick, easy process which can be automated and done anonymously and inexpensively; payment is often done using stolen payment mechanisms (e.g., credit card).

Setup server: Once the domain name is obtained, the attacker can easily setup an email server and a web server for the domain. The domain's DNS records are configured to point to the correct address for the servers.

Obtain certificate: Using the email and web servers, the attacker can pass the DV process and obtain a (domain validated)

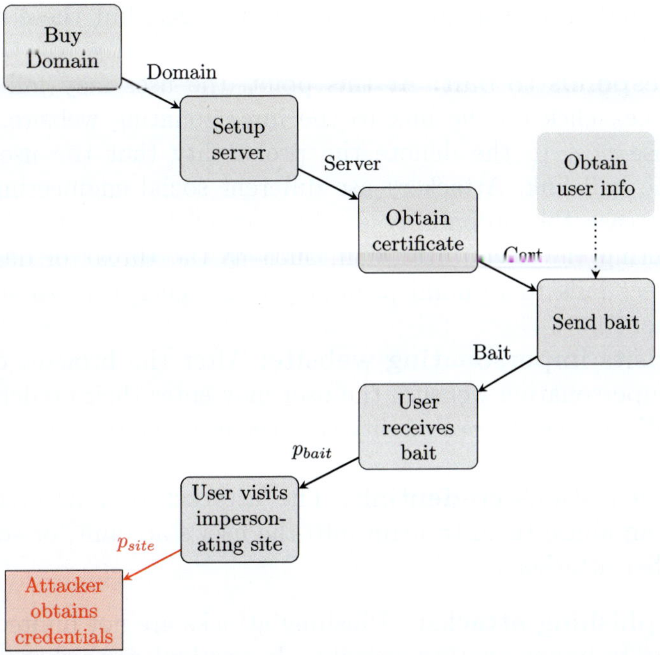

Figure 9.2. Typical phishing attack, using a bait to lure a victim user to an impersonating website. The bait (phishing message) may be sent using email, SMS, messaging applications or social networks. We use p_{bait} and p_{site} to denote the probability of attacker succeeding in the last two steps (other steps are almost sure to succeed).

certificate for the domain (Section 8.2.3). Many certificate authorities support DV and place limited restrictions, if any, on the certified domain names beyond these imposed by the domain registrars. Similarly to registering (non-restricted) domain name, certification is also a quick, easy process which can be automated and done anonymously and inexpensively, often using a stolen payment mechanism (e.g., credit card).

Send bait: The attacker sends bait messages to users, using one or multiple messaging systems, such as email, SMS (*Smishing*), instant-messaging applications and social networks. In many phishing attacks, the same bait message is sent to many users; more advanced *spear phishing* attacks use user-specific information to create customized baits, which can be more effective. Messaging systems may try to detect and block bait messages, as well as other undesirable spam an phishing messages, but these defenses often fail.

User responds to bait: At this point, the user may fall for the bait, i.e., click on the link to the impersonating website, or not. We use p_{bait} to the denote the probability that the user clicks on the bait-link. Attackers use different social engineering tricks to increase the probability of the user clicking on the link and attracting the user's attention, such as the threat of damage if the user fails to respond promptly (e.g., 'click here to stop this payment').

User visits impersonating website: After the browser displays the impersonating website, the user may enter their credentials or not. We denote the probability that the user enters their credential by p_{site}.

Attacker obtains credentials: The attacker obtains credentials and can abuse them to login into the user's account, or sell them to other attackers.

Other phishing attacks: Phishing attacks are not limited to luring users to impersonating websites. In particular, phishing attacks may lure users to install malware, contact the attacker and provide their private or sensitive information, or do other operations that degrade the user's security.

Other social engineering tricks to lure users to impersonating websites: There are also other ways, besides phishing, in which attackers lure victims to impersonating websites. These include *viral* or *social baits*, designed to trick users into propagating them (as well as to connect themselves to the impersonating site), *search engine poisoning*, where attackers trick search engines into returning impersonating websites, and *typosquatting* domains, which users reach when mistyping a (benign) domain name.

9.3.3 Defenses against impersonating websites

Both industry and academia are well aware of the threat of impersonating websites and performed efforts in different types of defenses. These efforts resulted in some improvement, but none have been sufficiently effective; there is still a strong need to improve the defenses against impersonating websites, and readers are encouraged to devise better defenses. In this section, we briefly discuss some of the proposed and deployed defenses.

Identification and security indicators: Consider an impersonation attack against a TLS-protected benign site, with certificate Ψ, public key $\Psi.pk$ and domain name $\Psi.subject$. Due to TLS server authentication, there are four options of impersonating websites: (1) use Ψ after exposing the corresponding private key, (2) use another certificate Ψ', with the same domain name but a public key chosen by the attacker, (3) use a certificate Ψ'' with a misleading domain name chosen by the attacker or (4) use an unprotected (HTTP, not HTTPS) website, with either a misleading domain name or the same domain name as of Ψ.

The first two options require the attacker to break security mechanisms, i.e., to expose the server's private key (option 1) or to cause a CA to issue an equivocating certificate (chosen by the attacker). Let us focus on options 3 and 4, where the attacking website uses a domain name different than $\Psi.subject$ (option 3) or uses HTTP rather than HTTPS (option 4); both of these changes *should* be visible to the user; therefore, these are social engineering attacks.

Impersonating webpages by using HTTP rather than HTTPS: Let us consider first the use of HTTP (option 4). Until 2017, browsers indicated a TLS-protected (HTTPS) webpage, by displaying an indicator such as a padlock icon next to the address bar, and displaying HTTPS in the beginning of the URL. The only indicators for an unprotected (HTTP) webpage was the *lack* of the padlock icon, and displaying HTTP, rather than HTTPS, in the beginning of the URL. This facilitated the SSL-stripping attack (Section 7.5.8).

During 2017 and 2018, the Chrome browser led a transition into warning users of unprotected (HTTP) webpages. This began by displaying a 'Not secure' warning before the URL for webpages considered 'sensitive', then (from 2018) to display it for all unprotected webpages.

This was followed by *removing* the padlock indicator for HTTPS, with the goal of making clear that pages *should* all use HTTPS (making HTTP the exception), and also avoiding user confusion, since it was realized that users interpreted the padlock to indicate that the page is trustworthy — allowing attackers to gain trust merely by using HTTPS webpages.

Finally, around 2021–2022, most browsers adopted an optional or default mode where users are warned by a prominent dialog upon accessing an HTTP webpage and must explicitly instruct the browser to proceed and display the page. This makes it significantly more likely that users will avoid HTTP webpages or be extra cautious when using them.

Impersonating webpages by using a different, misleading domain name: Browsers indicate the domain name as part of the URL in the location bar and indicate the use of HTTPS (TLS) vs. the use of (unprotected) HTTP, e.g., by displaying a padlock for HTTPS sites or a warning for HTTP-only sites. If users would validate correctly these indicators, this would prevent impersonation attack (assuming TLS security). Researchers evaluated different improvements to the indicators, e.g., indications of the website's identity, e.g., using the company's logo, and of identifying CA; and user-specified, personalized textual or graphic identifier for each site [241]. Experiments found that improvement in detection rates by the use of such improved indicators are insufficient; the rates of successful spoofing attacks remained higher than desired [241, 432]. Indeed, relying on users to observe indicators go contrary to the click-whirr response trait, i.e., users typically focus on their goals (opening a specific site) and get used to skip the 'unnecessary' step of observing the indicators. As a result, impersonation of login (and other) webpages using a different but misleading domain name, remains a viable, commonly abused attack.

Blacklists as defense against impersonating and other malicious websites: In this approach, the system uses a *blacklist*, which is a set of detected impersonating and other malicious websites. The browser (or another mechanism) warns the user against using these sites or prevents their use. Such blacklists services include Google's Safe Browsing [217], Microsoft's Defender Smartscreen [396] and others, and are widely used.

Maintaining an accurate blacklist, with good coverage of impersonating and other malicious sites, is a challenge; and the blacklist can never be fully updated, since some delay is inherently involved in detecting such websites and reporting them. The blacklists can also never be complete — an attacker may expose the impersonating website only to specific victims in *spear phishing* attacks.

Another concern with blacklists is *privacy* exposure. In the naïve blacklist implementation, the browser queries the blacklist service to check if the current website is blacklisted; this exposes the visited website to the blacklist. Different cryptographic mechanism can be used to reduce this privacy exposure, including a *Private Information Retrieval* (PIR). The PIR allows the client to know if the domain is blacklisted, without exposing the domain to the operator of the blacklist; e.g., see Refs. [149, 202, 502]

Automated detection of impersonating websites: Multiple works investigate *automated tools* for the detection of impersonating websites rather than relying on the user to detect them (using the browser's indicators). Many of these tools use machine learning and/or heuristics to compare the visual content and/or the organization of visited sites to the impersonated website, which may be a website in which the user maintains an account [19, 494, 495]. With the improvements in artificial intelligence, it seems possible, or even likely, that such techniques would improve and be adopted by browsers.

9.3.4 Password dictionaries

Password dictionaries are lists whose entries are *candidate passwords*, often sorted in the order of their estimated usage frequency. Password dictionaries are of the main tools used by attackers to break into user accounts, using *online dictionary attacks* (Section 9.3.5) and offline dictionary attack (Section 9.4).

In this section, we explain how attackers can build the dictionary.

Building password dictionaries: Password dictionaries can be constructed in different ways, including the following:

Regular dictionaries: Users may use words in a natural language such as English as their passwords; therefore, one way to build a password dictionary is by using all or certain subset of the words in a regular dictionary, e.g., an English dictionary. However, this type of dictionary was found to be ineffective, e.g., see Ref. [148].

Known passwords: The underlying assumption of password dictionaries is that some passwords are popular. The attacker can use known passwords, from exposed password files or from a server controlled by the attacker, to construct the password dictionary. This allows to sort the entries by the frequency of their usage as passwords.

Dictionaries built using patterns and grammars: In Ref. [476] and following works, researchers found that effective dictionaries can built by learning password patterns and common grammars; in particular, Ref. [476] found that *Probabilistic Context-Free Grammars* (PCFG) are especially effective.

Personalized dictionaries: Attackers can use known personal information to create a *personalized password dictionary*, used to attack a specific user; as we explain in the following, this was found to allow significant improvement in the effectiveness of the dictionary (see also Ref. [334]). Attackers use different methods to obtain personal information, including using publicly available information such as from social networks, using impersonating websites and other social engineering attacks, and using files exposed from breached services. Different types of personal information may be available to the attacker and found useful, including the user's name and address, their date of birth, their interests and gender and similar information for the friends and family of the user.

AI-generated dictionaries: The attacker can use generative machine learning system to generate the dictionary, by learning patterns from exposed dictionaries and from corresponding personal information of the users and site-specific information. See Figure 9.3.

Attacker: *given an example of hundred passwords that a user named Alice, whose boyfriend name is Bob, is likely to use.*

ChatGPT: `While it's not advisable to use personally related information like names or relationships in passwords, I can provide you with hundred example passwords... :`

AliceLovesBob1	BobAndAlice42	AliceBobForever!
SweetAliceAndBob%	ILoveBob567	BobHeartsAlice
AliceAndBobForever	BobAliceTogether	AliceAndBob4Life
BobLovesAlice123	AliceBobHappiness	BobAliceAlways
AliceBob2023#	BobAndAlice2022	LoveAliceBob
Bob123Alice	AliceLovesBob!	BobAliceForever21
AliceNBobLove!	ForeverAliceAndBob	...

Figure 9.3. Using AI (ChatGPT) to generate a personalized password dictionary.

Password dictionaries are effective. In multiple measurements, it was found that password dictionaries can be very effective, i.e., many passwords used by users are found in dictionaries. Let us give some of the results from three studies:

- In Ref. [342], about 40% of the passwords in multiple exposed password files were found have also been used in another exposed password file exposed (the one from the *RockYou* website, containing 32,603,043 users using 14,344,386 different passwords), significantly lower percentages were found when using smaller password files.
- In Ref. [259], 86% of the passwords in a newly exposed password file were found to have already appeared in a collection of about 500 million passwords, collected from multiple exposed password files.
- Li *et al.* [334] found almost 50% of the passwords in a personalized dictionary and about 27% of the password in a grammar-based dictionary (without personalization), both using a dictionary of only 2 million passwords. Both dictionaries were built following the Probabilistic Context-Free Grammars (PCFG) approach proposed in Ref. [476].

Importantly, in Ref. [342], the study compared both highly sensitive sites (such as *hotmail*) and sites which appear to be significantly less sensitive (such as *computerbits*). One may have expected users to be much more careful about the passwords they use for highly sensitive sites; however, the results in Ref. [342] show a rather weak dependency on the site or service whose passwords are being attacked.

9.3.5 Online dictionary attacks

Dictionary attacks find the password PW_u of a user u by exploiting the fact that often, PW_u is in a dictionary used by the adversary; this may be a general dictionary D or a user-customized dictionary $D(u)$ which the adversary using some information that the attacker obtains about user u.

Password dictionaries can be used by the attacker with or without an exposed password file. Without a password file, the attacker can launch what we call an *online dictionary attack*, where the attacker attempts the login ceremony with different passwords from the dictionary, in the hope of finding the correct password; we discuss these attacks in this subsection. In contrast, in an *offline dictionary attacks*, the attacker checks different passwords from the dictionary against a file obtained by the attacker (hashed/encrypted) passwords files; we discuss these attack in Section 9.4.

Defenses against online dictionary attacks: The main defense against online dictionary attacks is to limit the rate of login attempts. When the rate is exceeded, the server may impose delays, require the user to solve a *CAPTCHA*, require the user's device to perform a proof of work (PoW) or require the use of an additional factor of authentication.

The rate of login attempts may be limited for each specific user; however, when attacking many users in a set U, attackers can circumvent this by trying to login into the accounts of different users. Therefore, systems often impose additional limitations on the rate of login requests typically per each (IP) address of the client device. This IP-address-rate-limiting is effective in the typical case of an attacker using a specific client address. A MitM attacker can use different addresses, and thereby circumvent this defense; however, most attackers are off-path, i.e., do not have MitM capabilities. An off-path attacker may be able to send traffic using a fake (spoofed) IP address, but this would usually not allow them to circumvent the per-address rate limit, since login connections are typically performed using an transport protocol such as *TCP* or *QUIC* [308], and often even over TLS, and an off-path attackers would be unable to perform the interaction required by these protocols.

Note that often multiple client devices may use the same IP address concurrently, by communicating via a Network Address Translation (NAT) router, such as most home routers. However, the total number of devices communicating via the same NAT router with the same server is quite small. Therefore, this defense is usually an effective method to handle online dictionary attacks.

9.3.6 Password managers

Users use services from many different organizations, and therefore often reuse the same password to login to different sites and services.

Password managers consist of software and/or services, whose goal is to help users use separate, different passwords for different sites, thereby improving convenience and/or security. Password managers may be integrated with the browser, and automatically fill in the passwords; this has to be done carefully to avoid exposing the password to a maliciously crafted webpage, see Ref. [424].

Most password managers use a file to store the passwords for different sites; we refer to this file as a *password vault*. Other password managers do not rely on any long-term storage of passwords, allowing them to avoid risks due to attacker obtaining the password vault, but resulting in some limitations on their operation. We first discuss password managers using a vault, which are also referred to as *stateful password managers* (Section 9.3.6.1). We then discuss 'stateless' password managers, or, more precisely, password managers which do not require maintaining a secure password vault; see Section 9.3.6.2.

9.3.6.1 *Stateful password managers*

Stateful password managers store user passwords in a file, called *password vault*. As long as the vault is protected from access by an attacker, stateful password managers provide a convenient and secure mechanism for users to store and retrieve passwords for different passwords for different sites and services, without requiring the user to remember all of these passwords.

Stateful password managers allow users to choose their passwords, making it easier for users to use different passwords in different sites, and provide some or all of the following functions:

Assisted password selection: Password managers can suggest strong passwords and/or warn users against the use of weak passwords and against password reuse.

Password autofill: Automatically fill the password upon login, making it easier for users to use separate, and also longer and more complex, passwords.

Automatically generated strong passwords: Password managers often offer automatically generated strong passwords, which are significantly more secure than typical user-provided passwords.

Alerts: Password managers may *alert* users against using weak or exposed passwords. This includes alerting the user if the user chooses a weak password, but also, more significantly, alerting the user if one of their passwords becomes compromised, such as following an exposure of a service used by the user. Password managers may also alert the user when a password used by the user is included in *any* password-file exposed. To detect that the same password is contained in an exposed password file, the password manager may use a Compromised credential checking (C3) service, see Section 9.4.5.

Automated updates: Password managers may automatically update the password when the site requires a new password.

Availability across devices: Some password managers are provided as a network service, allowing access to the user's passwords without requiring the user to use a specific device on which the passwords are stored.

Considering their convenience and security advantages, it may appear strange that stateful password managers are not more widely used. However, there are some concerns and risks to the use of stateful password managers, mainly due to the fact that they are a *single point of failure*. Specifically, the concerns include the following:

Compromise: A breach of the password manager, or of the user's password and/or other means that the users use to authenticate themselves to the password manager, can expose all of the passwords.

Vulnerabilities: Several works identified vulnerabilities of password managers, e.g., Refs. [335, 385, 444]. Most of the vulnerabilities found in the earlier works were already fixed [385], but few new vulnerabilities were found, too.

Availability: The user cannot login without access to the password manager.

A critical aspect of stateful password managers is the protection and availability of the *password vault*, i.e., the file containing the passwords. Password vaults can be stored locally in the user's machine, remotely on a server, or both. An obvious disadvantage of storing the vault in a remote server is that the server will have access to the vault; also, an exposure of the server will lead to exposure of the vault. The contents of the password vault may be encrypted using a 'master password', but if the file is exposed, an attacker may be able to find the master key using an offline dictionary attack. Some designs use cryptographic mechanisms to detect or prevent these attacks, see Refs. [276, 277, 130]. Another alternative is to use a stateless password manager, as we discuss in the following.

9.3.6.2 *Stateless password managers*

Stateless password managers are more limited than stateful password managers, but arguably more secure, since they do not store the user's passwords. Instead, a stateless password manager receives from the user a *master password* PW_M, and uses PW_M to *derive* a different, strong password for each site or service s. In this way, a stateless password manager helps to ensure that the user authenticates to different sites using different passwords, as well as to avoid the use of weak passwords which can be guessed by a dictionary attack.

An attacker may try to abuse the password derived for one site s_A, possibly a site owned by the attacker, to expose the password derived for another (benign) site s_B, or to expose the master password PW_M (and thereby expose the passwords for all sites). Indeed, since stateless password managers do not use any long-term secret information (such as a password vault/file), the attacker can simply perform a dictionary attack on the master password PW_M by deriving the password for s_A using each password pw in the dictionary, and comparing to the value sent by the browser when the user connects to s_A (which is known to the attacker). If the derivation of the site-password from PW_M is efficient, then this dictionary attack would succeed whenever PW_M appears in the dictionary. To make such attacks less feasible, stateless password managers derive the site's password using an intentionally-slow operation, e.g., using many iterations of a cryptographic hash function h.

Halderman *et al.* proposed to further protect against such dictionary attacks, by having the stateless password manager derive, for each user, a 'cached password' PW_C from the master key [228]. In Ref. [228], the derivation uses cryptographic hash function h, basically using the computation:

$$PW_C = h^{k_1}(PW_M) \tag{9.1}$$

The password manager will cache the cached password PW_C for a significant period (e.g., until the user disconnects). Whenever the browser needs to login to a specific site, e.g., s_A or s_B, the stateless password manager uses the cached password PW_C, together with the master password PW_M, to derive the site-specific passwords. For example, for a site whose name is s, the derivation in Ref. [228] is basically as follows:

$$PW_s = h^{k_2}(s + PW_M + PW_C) \tag{9.2}$$

where k_1, k_2 are integers, with $k_2 \ll k_1$, e.g., in Ref. [228], $k_1 \approx 1000 \cdot k_2$.

To see the advantage of deriving first the cached password PW_C and then using it to derive for each site s the site's password PW_s, consider an attacker that tries to find the password for the benign site s_B, using an offline dictionary attack on the master password PW_M. Assume that the master password is in the dictionary D used by the attacker, and that the attacker controls a site s_A to which the user logins, thereby, obtaining $PW_{s_A} = h^{k_2}(s_A + PW_M + PW_C)$, as per Equation (9.2).

Under this assumptions, the attacker can find PW_M and PW_C as follows. For every possible master password $p_M \in D$, the attacker first computes $p_C = h^{k_1}(p_M)$ (Equation (9.1)) and then computes $p_{s_A} = h^{k_2}(s_A + p_M + p_C)$. The attacker now compares p_{s_A} to the password it receives from the client, which should be $PW_{s_A} = h^{k_2}(s_A + PW_M + PW_C)$. If the two match, then, with very high probability, $p_M = PW_M$ and $p_C = PW_C$, and the attacker can easily compute also PW_{s_B} for any other site s_B.

To test one possible value from D, this attack requires the attacker to compute h a total of $k_1 + k_2$ times. In contrast, the benign clients needs to compute h only k_1 times to compute PW_C, and then only k_2 times to compute the site's password for each specific site s_B. Since the client computes PW_C initially, probably before visiting any site, and then uses the result to login into many sites, say n sites, the per-site number of hashes would be only $k_2 + \frac{k_1}{n} \ll k_1$.

Note that this argument does not *prove* that the attacker cannot find in some more efficient way the master password PW_M, or the password for some benign site s_B. In fact, this seems non-trivial to prove even under the random oracle model (ROM) (and the author is not aware of such proof being published).

The description above glosses over several subtle points; let us discuss a few of these; see also Ref. [424].

Site-specific policies on allowed passwords: The derived, site-specific passwords generated according to Ref. [228], i.e., PW_s for site s, would be arbitrary n-bits strings, where n is the length of the output of h. Therefore, they may not match the password policies of site s, such as regarding allowed password length and the allowed and required characters. Therefore, stateless password managers map the site-specific passwords (PW_s) into passwords conforming with the password policy P_s of site s.

Same-password sites: Sometimes, multiple servers, with different domain names, use the same passwords for the same users (i.e., with the same usernames). Most commonly, these would be sites which use subdomains of the organization's domain, or different domains belonging to the same organization, e.g., *foo.com*, *foo.co.uk* and *foo.net*.

Periodical password change policies: Many sites impose limit on the maximal time allowed for use of a password, after which the password may be changed. It seems possible for a stateless password manager to support periodical password changes, at least assuming that the user logs-on at least once each period; however, this requires careful design. The author is not aware of such designs being proposed or implemented, e.g., periodical password change is not supported by the design in Ref. [228]. See Exercise 9.3.

9.4 Password-file exposures and offline dictionary attacks

Password files are an obvious target for attacking password systems, and should be stored securely, preventing their exposure to an attacker. This is well understood, yet, we know of the exposure of many password files over the years, often with the password files exposed by the hackers in the Internet; and presumably more password files were exposed without the exposure being publicly known. In fact, the first multiuser system, the CTSS, was also the first to be attacked by exposure of its password file, only a few years after it was deployed [323]. Therefore, an important aspect of password security is the design of mechanisms to *prevent abuse of exposed password files* and to *detect the exposure of password files.*

Abuse-resistant password file and offline dictionary attacks: Password files should be designed to provide significant resistant to abuse, even when a password file is obtained by the attacker. The basic way to ensure this is for the password file to contain, for each user, a value allowing *validation* of the purported-password received from the user, instead of containing the actual password. This is typically achieved by using *encryption* or *hashing* of the password. These defenses may be sufficient against exposure of hard-to-guess passwords, but could be vulnerable to *offline dictionary attacks* when the password appears in a dictionary used by the attacker.

We discuss *encrypted* password files in Section 9.4.1. In Section 9.4.2, we introduce *hashed password files* and offline dictionary attacks against exposed hashed password files. We then discuss improved-security designs for password files, designed to protect against offline dictionary attacks, by adding to the hashed password a (non-secret) *salt* (Section 9.4.3), and possibly also a (secret) *pepper* (Section 9.4.4).

Detecting exposure of password files: Another important defense is to *detect* the exposure of the password file. Detection is relevant to the specific user, whose password was exposed (from any password file), as well as the administrator of a system whose password file was exposed. We discuss this subject in Section 9.4.5.

9.4.1 Encrypted password files

One obvious way to protect against password file exposures is to maintain an *encrypted password file* EPW, containing an entry EPW(u) for each user-id u.

Using encrypted passwords is of limited help if the key is kept together with the encrypted passwords. Instead, encrypted-password systems will usually consist of a *server* maintaining the encrypted password file EPW and a *cryptographic co-processor* module containing a symmetric encryption key k. The cryptographic co-processor will (1) compute the encrypted password entry EPW[u] for user u, when given the password PW_u for user u, (2) verify submitted password p for user u against the corresponding entry EPW[u] and (3) allow update of the entry EPW[u] when given the pair of the (correct) current password p and the new password p' for user u.

To defend against dictionary attacks, the module would limit the rate of verification queries, with a strict restriction, say at least T_U seconds between successive queries for the same user, and a rather loose restriction on the total rate of queries for all users, say at least $T_{All} \ll T_U$ seconds between any two successive queries. The system should also ensure the integrity of the password file.

Let us show an implementation of the password encryption and password verification functions, using a symmetric key cryptosystem (E, D) and a MAC scheme MAC. For simplicity, we assume that the key k actually consists of two keys, one for each scheme: $k = (k_E, k_{\text{MAC}})$. Then, we have the following:

To encrypt password: Upon input password PW_u and user-id u, return the pair (c, a), where $c \leftarrow E_{k_E}(PW_u)$ and $a = \text{MAC}_{k_{\text{MAC}}}(c + u)$. The server saves the pair (c, a) as the entry $\text{EPW}[u]$.

To verify password: Upon input password p, user u and password file entry $\text{EPW}[u]$, parse $\text{EPW}[u]$ into the pair (c, a). Then, return FALSE if (1) $a \neq \text{MAC}_{k_{\text{MAC}}}(c + u)$, (2) $p \neq D_{k_E}(c)$, (3) less than T_U seconds passed since the last verify query for user u or (4) less than T_{All} seconds passed since the last verify query. Otherwise, return TRUE.

The above implementation follows the generic *Encrypt-then-Authenticate construction*. The reader can modify the scheme to use, instead, an arbitrary Authenticated Encryption or AEAD (Authenticated Encryption with Associated Data) scheme; see Section 4.5.1, instead of using a symmetric key cryptosystem and a MAC scheme as above. See Exercise 9.7.

An obvious challenge of this approach is the requirement for using secure hardware, as well as the concern for complete failure if this hardware device fails. Most systems and designs do not depend on such secure hardware module, and instead, use *hashed password files*, which we discuss in the following sections.

9.4.2 Hashed password files and attacks

To reduce the exposure from a leaked passwords file, password files often contain, for each user u with password PW_u, an entry computed from PW_u using a cryptographic hash function h (or a keyed hash function h_k, but we focus on keyless hash, to reduce clutter and since most implementations use keyless hash).

We consider two natural designs for the entries:

Uniform hashing: The entry for user u simply contains $h(PW_u)$.

Per-user hashing: The entry for user u contains the hashing of the username and password, e.g., $h(u + PW_u)$.

If the hash function h is a one-way function, and the password PW_u is chosen randomly from a sufficiently large space, e.g., a sufficiently long random string, then it should be infeasible for an attacker given the entry ($h(PW_u)$ or $h(u + PW_u)$) to find PW_u, or any other password PW' which will have the same hash, i.e., for universal hashing, $h(PW') = h(PW_u)$, and for per-user hashing, $h(u + PW') = h(u + PW_u)$.

However, users do not choose passwords randomly. In reality, many of the passwords are taken from a not-very-large list of 'common passwords' called a *dictionary* D. The attacker can use the dictionary in an offline dictionary attack to find matching passwords. We discuss two variants: the *linear* and the *rainbow table* offline dictionary attacks.

9.4.2.1 *Linear offline dictionary attack on hashed password files*

In this attack, the attacker computes, for each password x in the dictionary D, the corresponding entry: $h(x)$ for uniform hashing and $h(u + x)$ for per-user hashing. If the entry in the password file for user u matches the computed value for password x, then the attacker concludes that x is a valid password for user u. (There is a small probability that user u uses actually a different password which hashes to the same value; this would be an extremely rare event, but, even if it happens, the attacker can still use x as the password.)

Note that in the common case, where the attacker is looking for the password for any user with an entry in the file (or for one of a set of users), then the attack would be much more efficient against the uniform-hashing design. If the attack is against the per-user hashing design, then the attacker will have to repeat it for every user name.

If the attackers have sufficient storage capability, then they can precompute the hashed values even before having access to the password file (*pre-exposure*); later, when the password file is exposed (*post-exposure*), they can lookup the hashed values and identify any matches. In the uniform hashing design, this requires precomputing and storing $|D|$ entries; in the per-user hashing design, the number should be multiplied by the number of user names (which should also be predictable).

The total amount of computation — and of storage, if using pre-computations — can be large. If using uniform hashing, or if the attacker only tries to expose the password of a single user, then we need one hash computation for each dictionary entry, i.e., $|D|$ computations; if using pre-computation of the hash value, we need to maintain $|D|$ hash values. If using per-user hashing, and the attacker wants to find passwords for any of a large set of U users, then the number of hash computations, and storage for hash values if pre-computing, is $|D| \cdot |U|$. These numbers can be excessive, when the attacker wants to find passwords in a large dictionary, which may be necessary, in particular, due to system-imposed requirements on passwords. In this common case, the attacker may prefer to use the *rainbow table* variant of the attack, which we present in the following, and which offers a tradeoff between the storage size required and the amount of hashing computations required after the password file is exposed.

9.4.2.2 *The rainbow table offline dictionary attack on hashed password files*

The *rainbow table* is an optimization of the offline dictionary attack, designed where the total number of possible hashed-password values, which we denote by N, is very large, making it inefficient to compute all N hashes after password-file exposure, as well as to pre-compute and store all N hashes.When using universal-hashing or when the attacker is interested in the password of a particular user u, the number of hashed-password values is $N = |D|$; when the attacker wants to find passwords for users in a large set U and the password file uses per-user hashing, the number of hashed-password values is $N = |U| \cdot |D|$. In both cases, the number may be very large, and the rainbow table attack becomes attractive.

The rainbow table offers a tradeoff between the size of a precomputed list of hashed values kept by the attacker and the number of hash-computations required after password-file exposure. The attack consists of two phases: a *pre-exposure phase*, which the attacker performs before the password file is exposed, and a *post-exposure phase*, which the attacker performs using the exposed password file.

For simplicity, we describe the attack for the case where the password file uses uniform hashing, i.e., contains, for each user u, the value $h(PW_u)$, i.e., the hash of the password PW_u of user u, without involving the user-name u in the input to the hash function. The adaptation for the case where u is used as part of the input is straightforward and results in the obvious higher overhead and complexity.

Pre-exposure phase: In the pre-exposure phase, the attacker computes the *rainbow table*; let us explain what this is, referring to Figure 9.4, which illustrates a tiny rainbow table containing four *chains* each including three hashed-passwords, for a total of 12 hashed-password values.

The attack is parameterized by the number of chains, which we denote c, and the length of each chain, which we denote l. The attacker also uses a set of l functions, $\{r_1, \ldots, r_l\}$, which we refer to as the *rainbow functions*. Each of the functions r_i should be thought of as a random mapping from the outputs of the hash function h, to candidate passwords from the dictionary D.

The attacker first selects c random passwords, denoted $p_{1,1}$ to $p_{c,1}$, each taken from D. For each of these, we compute their hash, i.e., $h(p_{i,1})$ for $i = 1, \ldots, c$.

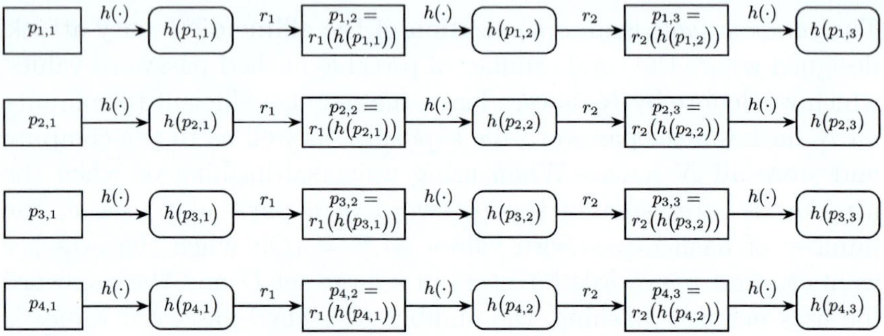

Figure 9.4. Rainbow table containing four chains, each with three hashed-password values, for a total of 12 hashed-password values. The attack uses the same hash function h as used in the computation of the hashed passwords in the file, and a set of l *rainbow functions* $\{r_1, \ldots, r_l\}$.

The attacker now computes the rest of the c chains. Namely, for $i = 1, \ldots, c$, the attacker computes the remaining $l-1$ hashed passwords on the chain, $p_{i,j}$ for $j = 2, \ldots, l$, by iteratively computing $p_{i,j} = r_{j-1}(h(p_{i,j-1}))$. See Figure 9.4.

To complete the pre-exposure phase, the attacker retain the initial and final values of each chain, i.e., the values $p_{i,1}$ and $h(p_{i,l})$ for $i = 1, \ldots, c$. This requires $2 \cdot c$ storage locations (each sufficient for one password from D and for one hash value) and a total of $c \cdot l$ computations of the hash function h and of the rainbow functions r_j.

Post-exposure phase: In this phase, the attacker uses the $p_{i,1}$ and $h(p_{i,l})$ values which were produced by the pre-exposure phase, for the c chains ($i = 1, \ldots, c$), to find the passwords from the dictionary D whose hash appear in the file.

This is done by repeating the following process for j going down from l to 1, i.e., going 'backwards' from the ends of the chain toward their beginning, possibly aborting the process upon finding the desired password(s). For simplicity, we describe the process for finding one specific password PW, whose hash $h(PW)$ is given. We abort the process upon finding PW (or failing, typically when $PW \notin D$).

It is convenient to denote $h(PW)$ by h_1 and perform the following computation. We first check if h_1 is one of the end-points of the c chains, i.e., if for some $i \in \{1, \ldots, c\}$ holds $h(p_{i,l}) = h_1$. Suppose this holds for some i; then we use the corresponding beginning of the chain, $p_{i,1}$, to efficiently compute $p_{i,l}$, by re-computing the chain, i.e., $\{p_{i,j}\}_{j=2}^{l}$. Once we find $p_{i,l}$, we have that $h(p_{i,l}) = h_1$, i.e., $p_{i,l}$ is a valid password resulting in the hashed password $h_1 \equiv h(PW)$, as required. (Usually, $p_{i,l}$ is the same as the original password PW, although in principle we could also have reached another password with the same hash; this is very unlikely, but even if it happens, this other password is anyway just as good for the attacker.)

Assume, therefore, that $h_1 = h(PW)$ is *not* one of the end-points of the c chains. In this case, we compute $h_2 \equiv h\big(r_{l-1}(h_1)\big)$, and check if h_2 is one of the c end-points of the c chains.

Suppose that for some chain i holds $h_2 = h(p_{i,l})$; then, we compute chain i, as explained above, stopping when we obtain $p_{i,l-1}$, since we have $h_1 = h(p_{i,l-1})$, i.e., $h(p_{i,l-1}) = h(PW)$, as required.

What if there is no chain i such that $h_2 = h(p_{i,l})$? In this case, we compute $h_3 = r_{l-2}(h_2)$ and check if h_3 is one of the c end-points of the c chains. We repeat until finding the password — or exhausting all of our chains.

The total number of passwords in the c chains is $l \cdot c$. Several of them may be identical, but most will be distinct, i.e., with $l \cdot c = |D|$, most of the passwords in the dictionary D will be in one of the chains, and found by the attacker. The attacker may use $l \cdot c > |D|$ to capture even more, or all, of the passwords in D.

Storage: The rainbow table requires the attacker to store, for each of the c chains, its beginning ($p_{i,1}$) and its end ($h(p_{i,l})$); the number of bits required is at most $2 \cdot c \cdot n$ where n is the length of the output of the hash function h.

Computations: The pre-exposure phase requires $c \cdot l$ computations of the hash h and of the rainbow functions r_j. The post-exposure phase requires up to l computations of a chain, each requiring up to l computations of the hash function h and of one of the the rainbow functions r_j. Therefore, the total number of post-exposure computations is bounded by $2 \cdot l^2$ computations (of either hash or rainbow functions).

The attacker can use longer chains (larger l) to reduce the storage size, at the cost of increasing the number of post-exposure computations, or shorter chains, to reduce the number of post-exposure computations, at the cost of more storage.

9.4.2.3 *Slow-hashing defense against offline dictionary attacks*

To defend against offline dictionary attacks, the hashing of passwords is often done using a hash function intentionally designed to be slower than regular hash functions, or by iterating a hash function many times. Both approaches were adopted, from 1980s, in the Unix operating system [179,365]; in particular, Unix used an intentionally slow hash function (*crypt*). Of course, this method increases the computational costs of validating passwords, in the same ratio that it increases the costs for the attacker.

This method of slowing down offline dictionary attacks by using a slow hash function has proven more tricky than expected. In particular, researchers found ways to compute *crypt* more efficiently, allowing efficient cracking of passwords, e.g., using special co-processors such as using graphic processing unit (GPUs) rather than general-purpose CPUs, allowing efficient password cracking for hash functions which use multiple iterations [287].

Even such non-standard hardware solutions are, however, limited in their memory capabilities. This motivated the design of hash functions dedicated to password-hashing, such as *scrypt* [15, 399] and *Argon2* [78, 79]. These hash functions are designed to be *memory-hard*, i.e., their evaluation requires a large amount of memory; evaluation with less memory is inefficient.

We next present a different, complementary defense against offline dictionary attacks: the use of a *salted passwords* file. The impact of this is to make the pre-exposure of hashed passwords impractical. The hash of the salted passwords is also different for different users, like per-user hashing; therefore, an online attack must be done against each user entry separately.

9.4.3 Hashing of passwords with salt

Once a password file is exposed, attackers can exploit it for offline dictionary attacks against a specific user or against all (or multiple) users. As we saw above, the *rainbow table* attacks facilitates efficient password cracking, allowing a tradeoff between post-exposure computations and storage.

However, we now show that by adding a random, non-secret value called *salt* to the input of the hash function, together with the password, we can prevent the use of the pre-exposure phase to optimize the post-exposure computations. As a side effect, the salt also makes it unnecessary to include the user identifier in the input to the hash function in order to ensure per-user hashing since anyway the password of each user would be hashed with a different random hash value.

This improved defense is called *salted passwords.* Salted passwords were used already in the early Unix design [179, 365]. The design works as follows:

Computing salted password file: For every user u with password PW_u, select a random l-bit salt ($salt_u \xleftarrow{\$} \{0,1\}^l$) and compute the *salted password* $SPW_u \leftarrow h(salt_u + PW_u)$. Note that we use l to denote the number of salt bits. The entry for user u in the (salted) password file consists of the pair $(salt_u, SPW_u)$.

Validating passwords upon login: Let (u', PW') be a username-password pair provided by a user upon login. To validate the pair, validate that $SPW_{u'} = h(salt_{u'} + PW')$, where $(salt_{u'}, SPW_{u'})$ is the entry of u' in SPW.

The salt values are stored in the salted password file since they are used for validation. Since the salt values are random l-bits strings, they would normally be different for different users; therefore, even if two users select the same password (often, from the dictionary D), their entries in the password files will be different since each would have a different salt and therefore also a different hash of the salted password.

Salt values should be *unpredictable* until the password file is exposed; this forces the attacker to compute the candidate values in the dictionary only after the password file is exposed, i.e., prevents preprocessing of the dictionary D. As a result, the attack requires $O(|D|)$ hash operations for each entry in the password file.

The salt values should be sufficiently long to make it unlikely that multiple (or many) users will have the same salt values, which would allow a variant of the efficient attack to be used against sets of users with the same salt value. This would also prevent the attacker from precomputing a 'salted dictionary' for every possible salt value.

Offline dictionary attacks on salted passwords: The use of salted password files significantly improves the protection, compared to plaintext, encrypted or even hashed password files. However, *offline dictionary attacks* remains feasible, especially when attacking only one or few users, using their (exposed) salt value, if their password is contained in a reasonably sized dictionary. For example, recall that Li *et al.* [334] found that using a dictionary of two million entries allows us to find half of the passwords (if the dictionary is personalized) or 27% of the passwords (with a non-personalized dictionary). Performing two million hash operations is feasible even for memory-hard hash functions like *Argon2*, and even when the attacker is using only standard, general-purpose computers rather than dedicated hardware.

These limitations mean that it is still important to protect the password file; and, they motivate the use of further security enhancements, as we discuss in the following sections.

9.4.4 Hashed passwords with pepper

As we discussed in Section 9.4.3, using salted password files foils multi target and pre-exposure offline dictionary attacks. However, once a salted password file is exposed, attackers can use an offline dictionary attack to find passwords.

This motivated researchers to design variants whose goal is to further improve the security following the exposure of the (hashed and salted) password file. The most well-known approach, proposed in Refs. [287, 344], involves concatenating (another) string of random bits to the password before hashing it; unlike the salt, these bits, often referred to as *pepper*, are kept secret, i.e., are not included in the entry together with the hashed password; some authors refer to the pepper bits as a *secret salt.* Most designs use different random pepper bits for each user, similarly to the use of salt bits, to prevent an adversary from finding the pepper bits once and reusing them for all users.

To validate the password, the server needs to obtain the pepper bits of the user; we discuss in the following different ways for the server to obtain the pepper bits. All of these designs ensure that the pepper bits are kept secret from the attacker; therefore, to test a guess for the password against the hashed value in the password file, the attacker must try all the combinations of the pepper bits, which multiplies the number of hash operations required by $2^{|\text{pepper}|}$.

The different ways in which the server obtain the pepper bits include the following:

The server guesses the pepper bits [344]: In this design, the server has to try all possible values of the pepper bits, just like the attacker — except that the attacker does not know the password, while the server receives the passport from the user. The impact of this design is similar to that of an iterated hash function: password validation takes more time — for both password cracking and legitimate password validation (during the login process).

Encrypted pepper bits: In this design, the server, or a separate cryptographic co-processor, decrypts the pepper bits. The risk of this design is disclosure of the decryption key used to encrypt the pepper bits, or direct disclosure of the pepper bits. A cryptographic co-processor module can reduce this concern; however, the use of a cryptographic co-processor module allows an even more efficient solution described next.

PoWdered pepper: In this design, the pepper bits are hidden by a *proof of work* (PoW); the client device finds the popper bits, by solving the PoW. Let us explain. For simplicity, we present a design which uses only pepper bits and no salt bits; it is easy to extend this design to support both pepper and salt bits. For user u with password PW_u, select a random l-bit pepper and compute the *peppered hashed password* $PH_u \leftarrow h(pepper_u + PW_u)$. Then, we create a PoW that allows exposure of the pepper $pepper_u$; for simplicity, we present the design using a simple PoW mechanism based on a PoW hash function h, following the ROM, and similar to the Bitcoin design (Section 3.9.2). Namely, we compute the value $PoW_u \leftarrow h(pepper_u + O^n)$, where n is a security parameter. The server then discards $pepper_u$ but retains both PH_u and PoW_u in the entry for user u in the passwords file. Upon login of user u, the server send PoW_u to the user's machine. The user machine solves the PoW, i.e., finds the value of $pepper_u$. The client can now complete the login by sending to the server both password and PoW. Now that the server and client share both pepper and password, they can also derive another secret value to be used as a key to authenticate their communication, e.g., $h(pepper_u + PW_u +$ *'session key'*$)$. Note that this design requires support by the client, i.e., cannot be used with existing clients.

9.4.5 Detecting exposure of passwords and password files

Attack *detection* is a central part of the defenses of most systems, e.g., plays a critical role in network security. Therefore, to complete our discussion of security mechanisms for dealing with password-file exposures, we discuss defenses focusing on *detection*. We discuss two types of detection mechanisms. In Section 9.4.5.1, we discuss *compromised credential checking (C3)* services, which detect the exposure of the password PW_u of a particular user u, when a password file containing PW_u is exposed. In Section 9.4.5.2, we then discuss *honeywords*, also known as *decoy passwords*, which are used for a very different type of detection, namely, the detection of the exposure of the password file of a specific organization (which deploys this defense).

9.4.5.1 *Detecting password exposure using compromised credential checking (C3) services*

Compromised credential checking (C3) services detect and warn users against using compromised passwords, i.e., passwords which appeared in exposed password files, or passwords which may have been compromised by other exposures. A typical C3 service provides an API that is used to detect the use of compromised password, by users (using web services or client software) and by organizations (to identify users whose passwords are in exposed password files). The alerts may be limited to exposure of the password in conjunction with a given user name or identifier, which addresses password reuse and can foil credential stuffing attacks, i.e., attacks exploiting the reuse of the same password across multiple sites. Alternatively, the service may alert upon any appearance of the password in an exposed password file, which would provide more alerts, including alerting for the use of common passwords.

The first C3 service is *Have I Been Pwned* (HIBP) [259]. An improved service, called *Might I Get Pwned* (MIGP) [395], also alerts users for tweaked passwords, i.e., passwords which are a minor, guessable variant of the user's password, such as appending/ prepending a number or changing an appended/prepended number. If heeded, MIGP would also protect the user against *credential tweaking* attacks (see Lab 6, item 5).

The false-positives vs. false negatives tradeoff for C3 services: Alerts due to appearance of the user's password in password files, for accounts not related to the user, and alerts due to tweaked passwords may annoy some of the users. On the other hand, if heeded, such alerts could provide better protection against dictionary attacks. There are two competing goals here: the desire to detect as many of the attacks as possible, i.e., minimize *false negatives* (undetected attacks), and the critical need to minimize 'false alerts', i.e., *false positives* (alerts raised incorrectly, without an attack). Selecting the best tradeoff between minimizing false negatives and minimizing false positive is a critical aspect of the design of all types of detection systems.

Client privacy for C3 services: The protocol between the client and the compromised credential checking (C3) service should not disclose the password to the C3 service. To achieve this, both HIBP [259] and MIGP [395] use an advanced cryptographic protocol called *Private Set Intersection* (PSI) protocol [190], which allows the identification of passwords which appear both in the set of compromised credentials (hosted by the C3 service) and in the collection of passwords used by the user or by multiple users using the same password manager. The details of PSI protocols are beyond our scope.

There are other privacy-preserving mechanisms that could be used to check if passwords used by a user are compromised (and kept by the C3 service). All of these mechanisms, like PSI, are based on cryptography. These mechanisms include the use of *anonymous communication*, e.g., using *Tor* [156] and using *authenticated Private Information Retrieval* (PIR) [128].

9.4.5.2 *Detecting password file exposure with honeywords (decoy passwords)*

A different detection goal, which is very important for organizations, is to detect when the password file of the organization is exposed. One way to detect password file exposure is by using *honeywords*, also known as *decoy passwords*. This is done by detecting attempts to login using information from the exposed password file. The idea is to add to the password file a number of *decoy passwords*, also called *honeywords*, i.e., entries which do not correspond to a real password. Instead, the system monitors any login attempt using the decoy passwords; such attempts signals that the system is under attack — and, probably, the password file was compromised. Since being proposed in 2013 [278], there have been significant study of honeywords, some of it pointing out and/or addressing the concern that attackers may be able to distinguish between a honeyword and a 'real' password. See Ref. [472] for a discussion of this concern and an improved design, the *Bernoulli honeywords*, which addresses it and prevents such distinguishing.

Honeywords (decoy passwords) are a special type of a *honeypots*, which are 'decoy resources', used to detect an attack by detecting access to the 'decoy resource'; these 'decoy resources' are not used except for detection.

Let us give another simple example of a honeypot: a *decoy email account.* A user lists one or more decoy email accounts in their file of contacts; attackers who obtain unauthorized access to a user's contact file, often abuse it to send spam and/or phishing messages to the contacts therein. Once the user receives an email to one of their decoy accounts, they know that their file of contacts was exposed.

9.5 Password-Authenticated Key Exchange (PAKE)

A typical web-based login ceremony is based on first establishing a secure connection, using TLS, and then authenticating the user, using passwords and/or other user authentication mechanisms. When, as in most websites, the login ceremony uses only passwords for user authentication, then it is vulnerable to an online dictionary attack, where the attacker tried to login using different entries in the dictionary until finding the correct password. The server should defend against online dictionary attacks by blocking the user after several failures.

TLS-protected login ceremony should also be secure from an eavesdropping or MitM adversary. In particular, attackers should be unable to perform an offline dictionary attack, even after eavesdropping on the TLS-protected login of the legitimate user, and after a (limited) number of interactions with the server and with the user, where the user interacts via a non-modified (benign) browser.

However, the security of the TLS-protected login relies on the server's certificate, which should be validated correctly by the browser. As we discussed in Chapter 8, browsers trust a large number of certificate authorities, and there have been multiple PKI failures and abuses. This raises the question: can we establish secure communication, secure against a MitM attacker, using only a password, i.e., *without relying on a server certificate?*

In this section, we introduce PAKE login protocols, designed to address this goal. PAKE protocols allow two parties, Alice and Bob, to *exchange a shared secret key* using only a password.

We focus on the common case where one party, Alice, is a user, and the other party, Bob, is a server, and on authentication of the user by the server. PAKE protocols only rely on the user's password PW, i.e., do not require the user to have any trusted public key (of a certificate authority or of the server). The protocol should be secure against MitM attackers, assuming only a *weak password*, i.e., a password PW chosen (randomly) from a limited-size dictionary D known to the attacker.

The concept of PAKE protocols, i.e., password-based login secure against an offline dictionary attacks, was first proposed by Bellovin and Merritt in 1992 [54], where they presented the Encrypted Key Exchange (EKE) protocol. Since then, there has been extensive research on PAKE protocols, e.g., see Refs. [2, 4, 47, 98, 267]. This includes standardization efforts by the IETF, including the *OPAQUE* [97] and *CPace* [3] protocols, and others, e.g., Refs. [3, 97, 236, 310, 434].

There are two main categories of PAKE protocols: *Balanced PAKE*, also called *symmetric PAKE*, which includes CPace [97]; and *Augmented PAKE*, also called *asymmetric PAKE*, which includes OPAQUE [97].

In *Balanced PAKE* protocols, both parties maintain copy of the password (in plaintext). Balanced PAKE protocols ensure the basic PAKE security goal of preventing password exposure based on MitM attacks. However, in the typical client-server scenario, the use of Balanced PAKE is not ideal since it means that the server knows the password of each user, i.e., exposure of the password file leads immediately to exposure of the passwords of the users. To provide some security even if the password file is exposed, one should use an *Augmented PAKE* protocol.

Augmented PAKE protocols, also called *asymmetric PAKE* protocols, provide additional security guarantees beyond these provided by Balanced PAKE protocols. Namely, Augmented PAKE protocols provide a limited defense even if the server's password file is exposed. Namely, to find the password (without online dictionary attack), the attacker must *both* expose the password file *and* perform an offline dictionary attack. This is in addition to preventing, like Balanced PAKE protocols, an offline dictionary attack using information eavesdropped or obtained by a MitM attack

There is also a stronger category of Augmented PAKE protocols, called *Strong Augmented PAKE*, where the attacker can only perform the offline dictionary attack *after* disclosure of the hashed-passwords file; one such protocol is the *OPAQUE* [97, 267] protocol which is currently developed by the IRTF. This is in contrast to 'regular-strength' Augmented PAKE protocols, where an attacker is often able to perform (most or all) of the offline dictionary attack even before the attacker obtains the (hashed) password file. Therefore, the improvement of Strong Augmented PAKE protocols, such as OPAQUE compared to other Augmented PAKE protocols, is similar to the improvement obtained by 'salting' a hashed-passwords file (see Section 9.4.3).

Advanced PAKE protocols such as CPace and OPAQUE are relatively complex and therefore outside our scope. Instead, in the rest of this section, we first discuss two naïve but insecure Balanced PAKE protocols (in Section 9.5.1), and then we discuss the EKE2 protocol (Section 9.5.2) [47], a provably secure variant of the original EKE Balanced PAKE protocol [54].

To simplify, throughout this section we adopt the *random oracle model* (ROM; see Section 3.6). Namely, the protocols we present will use a hash function $h : \{0,1\}^* \rightarrow \{0,1\}^n$, which, for analysis purposes, we assume to be a random function (from arbitrary-length strings to n-bits strings, where n is a 'sufficiently large' security parameter).

9.5.1 Two naïve, insecure PAKE protocols

To motivate the design of the EKE2 protocol, and to understand the challenges of PAKE protocols, we now present two simple, insecure Balanced PAKE protocols: naïve-PAKE and naïve-DH-PAKE.

Naïve-PAKE: Figure 9.5 illustrates the *naïve-PAKE protocol.* Like all PAKE protocols, naïve-PAKE does not require the user to know the public key of the server, or to receive and validate a certificate. Yet, the protocol authenticates the client and establishes a shared key, without sending the password in the clear. The goal is to provide security against a MitM attacker, even when the user's password PW is *weak*, i.e., chosen from a limited-size *dictionary* D.

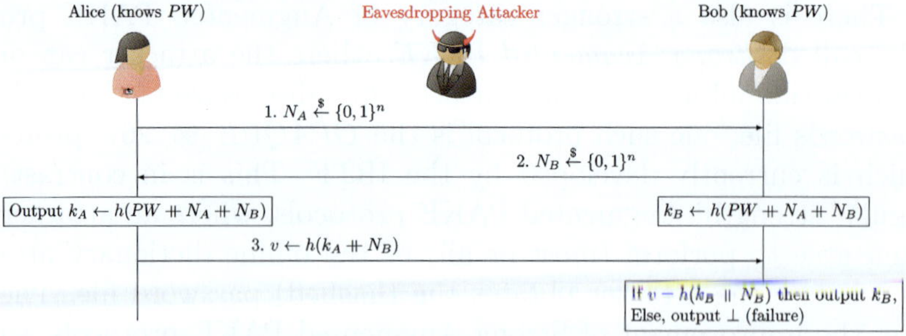

Figure 9.5. The naïve-PAKE protocol between Alice (user) and Bob (server). Flows 1 and 2 perform the key exchange. Flow 3 completes the login by authenticating the client, and validating that the parties share the same key ($k_A = k_B$). This protocol is insecure since, as we show in the text, an eavesdropper can use flow 3 to launch an offline dictionary attack.

However, we show that the naïve-PAKE protocol does *not* achieve this goal; it is vulnerable to an *offline dictionary attack* by an eavesdropper.

The naïve-PAKE protocol requires the server to know the user's password PW, i.e., it is a *Balanced PAKE* protocol. The protocol has three flows (flows 1–3). In flows 1 and 2, the user (Alice) and the server (Bob) exchange random challenges (nonces), $N_A, N_B \xleftarrow{\$} \{0,1\}^n$. The nonces are strings of n random bits, where n is sufficiently large. After flow 2, both parties compute a *session key*. We use k_A and k_B to denote the session key computed by Alice (the user) and by Bob (the server), respectively; in runs where there is no active attacks, the session keys would be identical, i.e., $k_A = k_B$. If Alice sends N_A and receives N_B, then she computes $k_A = h(PW + N_A + N_B)$; similarly, if Bob sends N_B and received N_A, then he computes $k_B = h(PW + N_A + N_B)$. Namely, if both receive the nonce sent by the correct peer, then the two keys would be the same.

The third flow (flow 3) allows Bob to authenticate Alice (perform the login) and validate that they share the same key. We show one simple implementation for this flow, where Alice sends the *validator* $v \leftarrow h(k_A + N_B)$. Bob authenticates Alice by confirming that it receives the same value as v when computing $h(k_B + N_B)$. If the parties received the correct flows, $k_A = k_B$ and this validation will be successful.

This simple protocol suffices to ensure user-authentication if the password is 'strong', e.g., chosen as an n-bits string (for sufficiently large n). However, the goal of PAKE protocols is to ensure security even for weak passwords, i.e., when $PW \in D$ for a limited-size dictionary D. Let us show that this goal is not achieved, i.e., show an efficient offline dictionary attack against this protocol. The attack requires only an eavesdropping adversary.

The attack is launched by eavesdropping on the flows during the login of a benign user (Alice) to the benign server (Bob). Let N_B and N_A be the nonces, obtained in flows 1 and 2, and v denote the value of the third flow, i.e., $v = h(k + N_B)$ and $k_A = k_B = h(PW + N_A + N_B)$.

To find the password $PW \in D$, the attacker computes, for every $p \in D$, the values $k_p \leftarrow h(p + N_A + N_B)$ and $x_p \leftarrow h(k_p + N_B)$. Let $D' \equiv \{p|v = x_p\}$; clearly, $PW \in D'$. Since h is a random function, then usually $|D'| = 1$, and rarely would D' be significantly larger. If $|D'| = 1$ then $D' = \{PW\}$, i.e., the password is found; if $|D'|$ is sufficiently small (but greater than one), the attacker can simply try to login using the different passwords in D', by impersonating as Alice and running the protocol to see which password is correct (online dictionary attack using the small dictionary D'). In the very unlikely case that D' is a large set, the attacker can eavesdrop to another exchange, with a different N_B, reducing the size of the set of candidate password strings D'.

We conclude that naïve-PAKE is vulnerable to an offline dictionary attack by an eavesdropping adversary.

Naïve-DH-PAKE: We next present the naïve-DH-PAKE protocol, which protects against an offline dictionary attack by an eavesdropping adversary, by incorporating the DH protocol (Section 6.2.4). The idea is to first exchange a key using the DH key exchange, which is secure against an eavesdropper, and then to use the password to validate the authenticity of the flows of the DH key exchange, in the hope of preventing a MitM attack on the key exchange. We illustrate the naïve-DH-PAKE protocol in Figure 9.6.

The naïve-DH-PAKE indeed prevents the attack by an eavesdropping attacker. However, as we illustrate in Figure 9.7, a MitM attacker, impersonating as Bob, can still find the password PW by

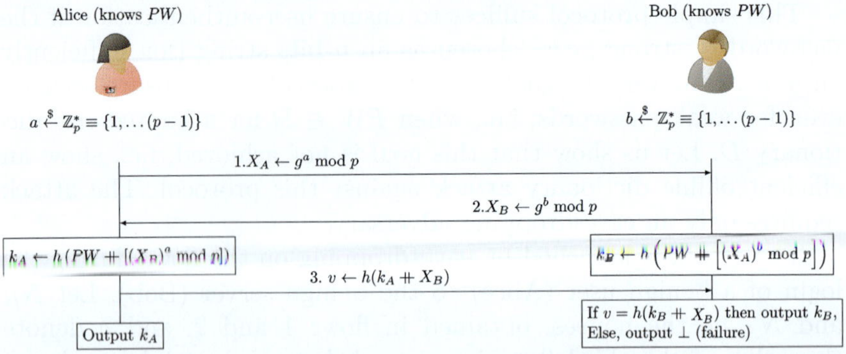

Figure 9.6. The naïve-DH-PAKE protocol between Alice (user) and Bob (server). Flows 1 and 2 are the DH key exchange. Flow 3 authenticates flows 1 and 2, as well as the user, by sending the hash of the shared key k_A concatenated to the second flow X_B. Figure 9.7 shows that this protocol is vulnerable to an offline dictionary attack by a *MitM* attacker.

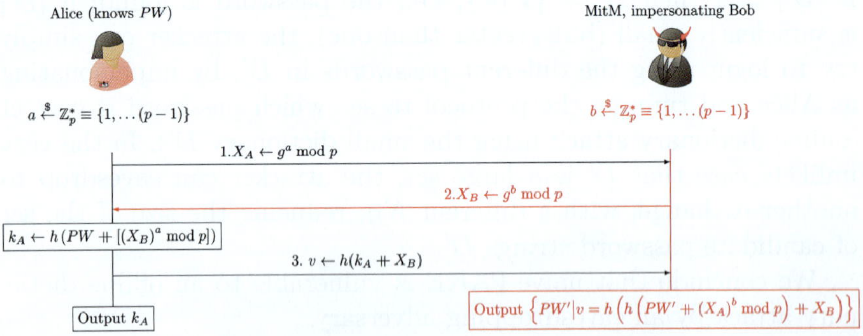

Figure 9.7. A MitM offline dictionary attack against the naïve-DH-PAKE protocol. The attacker impersonates as Bob. When it receives the validator v in flow 3, the attack can use v to launch an offline dictionary attack and find the password PW, as explained in the text.

performing an offline dictionary attack. Obviously, after the attacker found the password PW, they can also complete the protocols with the benign Bob.

The attack is quite similar to the eavesdropper offline dictionary attack, shown above, against naïve-PAKE. The attacker simply impersonates as Bob during the DH exchange; as a result, it obtains from Alice the value of $X_A \equiv g^a \bmod p$, which Alice sends in flow 1. The attacker computes and sends X_B just like Bob would have done (flow 2). Then, in flow 3, the attacker receives the validator $v \leftarrow h(k_A + X_B)$ from Alice. Let us show how the attacker can use v to find the password PW, by an offline dictionary attack.

The attacker finds the password $PW \in D$ as follows. First, the attacker computes, following the DH protocol, the value $K_B \leftarrow (X_A)^b \bmod p$, just like Bob would have done. Then, the attacker finds the value(s) $PW' \in D$ such that $v = h\left(h\left(PW' + (X_A)^b\right) + X_B\right)$; one of these PW' values will be the correct password PW. Usually, there will be only one value PW', i.e., $PW' = PW$; if there are few values, the attack can simply try all of them (a small online dictionary attack), as in the attack against the naïve-PAKE protocol.

9.5.2 The EKE2 PAKE protocol

We finally present EKE2, a provably-secure PAKE protocol. EKE2 was presented, and proven secure, in Ref. [47]. We will not present the proof since it is non-trivial; note that it relies not only on the ROM, but also on another simplifying model, called the *ideal cipher model*, which we do not cover in this text. Specifically, the protocol uses a hash function h, which we model as a random oracle (random function from the set of all binary strings, to strings of n bits), and a block cipher (E, D), which is modeled as a perfect cipher. The EKE2 protocol is a variant of the original EKE protocol, presented by Bellovin and Merritt in Ref. [54]. The main change is that EKE2 uses a cyclic group $\mathbb{G}$ where the *DDH* assumption is believed to hold, while EKE uses the (mod p) group.[1] The order q and a generator g of $\mathbb{G}$ are assumed to be public parameters, i.e., known to the parties and to the attacker.

EKE2 is a *Balanced PAKE* protocols, namely, it uses a (weak) password PW shared between Alice (typically, a client) and Bob (typically, a server), to establish secure communication between them. Figure 9.8 illustrates the protocol.

[1]In fact, see in Ref. [54] a subtle vulnerability of the EKE protocol due to its use of the $(\bmod\, p)$ group and a partial countermeasure.

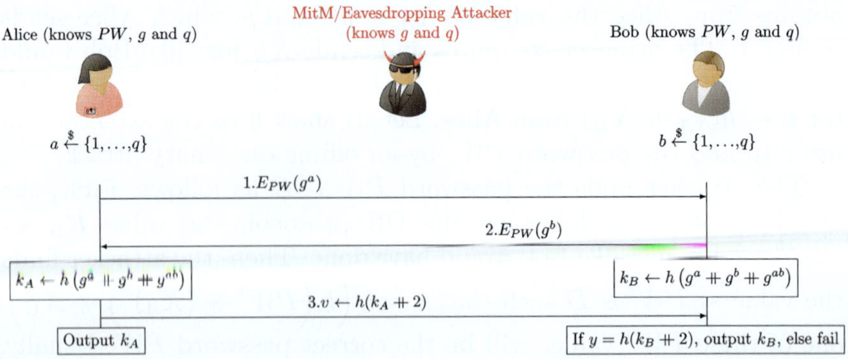

Figure 9.8. The EKE2 PAKE Protocol between Alice (user) and Bob (server). Flows 1 and 2 are encryptions of the DH key exchange. Flow 3 authenticates the user and the key exchanged by the DH flows. The protocol uses a hash function h (modeled as a random oracle), a block cipher (E, D) (modeled as a perfect cipher) and a group q where DFG hods.

The EKE2 protocol has the following steps:

1. Alice selects a random value in $a \xleftarrow{\$} \{1, \ldots, q\}$. She computes $E_{PW}(g^a)$ and sends it to Bob.
2. Bob also selects a random value in $b \xleftarrow{\$} \{1, \ldots, q\}$ and computes $E_{PW}(g^b)$ and sends it to Alice.
3. Alice decrypts the incoming message to retrieve g^b and uses it to compute $\left(g^b\right)^a = g^{ab}$. She then computes and outputs the key $k_A \leftarrow h(g^a \mathbin{+\!\!+} g^b \mathbin{+\!\!+} g^{ab})$.
4. Bob decrypts the incoming message to retrieve g^a, and uses it to compute $(g^a)^b = g^{ab}$. He then computes the key $k_B \leftarrow h(g^a \mathbin{+\!\!+} g^b \mathbin{+\!\!+} g^{ab})$.
5. Alice computes the validator $v \leftarrow h(k_A \mathbin{+\!\!+} 2)$ and sends it to Bob.
6. Upon receipt of v, Bob confirms that $v = h(k_B \mathbin{+\!\!+} 2)$. If so, it outputs 'success' and k_B.

When the flows are exchanged correctly between Alice and Bob, then $k_A = k_B = h(g^a \mathbin{+\!\!+} g^b \mathbin{+\!\!+} g^{ab})$ and the protocol completes successfully.

Note that the fact that the validator v is computed as $v \leftarrow h(k_A \mathbin{+\!\!+} 2)$ is rather arbitrary. The important thing is to make sure that the validator v would not expose the shared key $k_A = k_B$ since it is sent 'in the clear', i.e., exposed to the attacker; on the other hand, the computation of v by Alice should convince Bob that Alice has received the correct shared key ($k_A = k_B$).

9.6 Login ceremonies beyond passwords

In this section, we discuss several login ceremonies which do not involve (textual) passwords. Passwords are easy to deploy and well known to users; however, they also have significant disadvantages, in terms of both security and usability, which motivates the use of other, non-password login ceremonies, to be used to *complement* passwords or *instead of* passwords.

Improving security: Some non-password login ceremonies may have security advantages compared to passwords. For example, consider a device which identifies the user securely, e.g., using *biometrics*, and then securely authenticates the login to a server, using cryptography — a classical, high-security *something you have* factor of authentication.

Another way to improve security is to use non-password login ceremonies *together* with passwords, namely, use two (or more) authentication factors. We refer to login ceremonies which require users to authenticate successfully in multiple ways, often, by providing their password *and also* authenticate using another mechanism, as *two-factor authentication* (2FA) (or *multi-factor authentication* (MFA)). For example, many systems require users to provide a password and also to authenticate by providing a code sent to their mobile phone.

Improving usability: Passwords are easy to use, but they also have two significant usability disadvantages.

The first usability drawback of passwords is that users need to type the passwords, which can be annoying, especially if done frequently. Some other login ceremonies allow *automated authentication*, without the interaction required for password login ceremonies. A basic example is the use of *authenticating cookies*, sent automatically by the browser. Another example are are user authentication mechanisms such as facial recognition, which are often done automatically by the computer. Both of these mechanisms are often used in conjunction with passwords; cookies usually expire after a period, often quite short, and sometimes only persist until the browser is closed; and facial recognition sometimes fails to identify the benign user, in which case the user needs a 'backup' authentication mechanism, and passwords are often used for this purpose.

An even larger usability drawback of passwords is that users often forget their passwords. Many systems combine the use of passwords with an alternative authentication mechanism, which can be used when users forget their passwords. Such mechanisms are often less convenient and used only in such scenarios (where the user forgot the password); in this case, we use the term *fallback authentication.*

In this section: In this section, we discuss some of the more important non-password login ceremonies. In Section 9.6.1, we discuss *something you know* login mechanisms beyond passwords, mainly, PKQs and *graphical password* schemes. Both of these are used *mainly* for *fallback authentication*, probably since practitioners consider these ceremonies as less convenient than passwords for normal use, but likely to be usable by users who forgot their passwords.

In Section 9.6.2, we discuss *one-time password* (OTPw) schemes, where the user authenticates using a list of OTPWs, using each OTPw in the list only once (for one login). OTPw authentication is a very special form of a *something you have* factor of authentication, where the 'something' is this list of one-time passwords.

In Section 9.6.3, we discuss the more general case of authenticator devices, specifically, *something you have* authentication using a computing device.

Finally, in Section 9.6.4, we discuss the *FIDO2* technology, which is a set of standards for *something you have* login ceremonies, ensuring interoperability between different authenticator devices, client devices and servers.

9.6.1 Something *else* you know: beyond passwords

Something you know authentication mechanisms have the advantage of avoiding dependency on dedicated devices (as for *something you have* mechanisms) or measuring biometric (as for *something you are* mechanisms).

In this section, we briefly discuss two non-password *something you know* authentication mechanisms: PKQs and *graphical passwords*. Both mechanisms are mostly used for *fallback authentication*, i.e., as an alternative user authentication mechanism when the regular login mechanism cannot be used, typically, for users that forgot their password.

Personal knowledge questions (PKQs): In the *PKQs* login process, the user has to provide the correct answers to a set of PKQs, also referred to as *security questions*. Several studies have shown that users have high success rate in recalling most answers correctly, even after long period during which they did not authenticate using PKQs [226,505]. Studies also compared different types of PKQs, ranging from 'classical' questions like *mother maiden name*, user-chosen questions and other questions.

Ideally, the questions would be such that users will know the correct answers based on the question rather than relying on users to *remember* the answers; namely, ideally, the answer should be a fixed fact which is expected to be known to the user (but not to an imposer). In reality, there often may be some element of memorization involved. Therefore, in some implementations, questions may come with a *cue* to aid the user to answer correctly, relying on the fact that human memory is much better in cue-based recall than in recalling information without a corresponding cue. For example, Ref. [266] proposed the use of questions focusing on user personal preferences, with multiple-choice answers, and had encouraging results for memorability.

Results were less encouraging regarding security, i.e., the ability of an attacker to guess or find the correct answers. Looking again in Ref. [266], we see that their limited experiment found that 24 or more questions may be required to make guessing impractical. Furthermore, more recent studies, often using real-world experience, found more disappointing results. In particular, these works found that attackers are often able to successfully guess the correct answers [92,405,431]; furthermore, it was found that users often fail to recall the correct answers, often due to the fact that users intentionally give incorrect answers, due to the belief that this improves security (see Ref. [92]). Due to these disappointing results, PKQs are not as widely used anymore.

Graphical passwords: Graphical passwords are another family of *something you know* authentication mechanisms; the idea is to use the user's visual memory, which may be better than user's ability to recall textual answers or to answer consistently to textual ques. There are multiple proposals and studies of graphical password schemes; Ref. [71] surveys many of these proposals, and categorizes them into three types, based on the memory task involved in remembering and entering the password: *recall*, *cued recall* and *recognition*.

Recall-based graphical password schemes require the user to reproduce a secret drawing. To use a recall-based graphical password scheme, the user first selects the secret drawing, usually, by drawing it freely. The most widely used scheme of this type is the *pattern screen lock*, supported by many versions of Android devices; this variant uses a three-by-three grid displayed on the device. Each user is assigned an identifying, secret pattern, which is a sequence of up to nine dots on the grid. The sequence should be connected in one continuous movement of a finger between pairs of adjacent points (vertically, horizontally or in diagonal), which makes it easier for users to authenticate by reproducing the pattern they selected. To set up the pattern, the user draws it by connecting the points using one continuous finger movement ('swipe'); the user has to repeat the drawing few times, to ensure that the pattern is memorized, and then the pattern is saved by the device and used for future unlocking of the device. Since users often need to unlock their phones, they end up doing the pattern frequently, and therefore it is not common that users are 'locked out' due to forgetting their pattern, although this obviously does occur.

Other designs of recall-based graphical passwords were proposed for applications such as login to a website. However, in some of these designs and applications, users had difficulties recalling recall-based graphical passwords.

An even larger concern is the *security* of recall-based graphical passwords, mainly due to the existence of some side channels. In particular, Ref. [25] and later works have shown that attackers are often able to find the Android screen-lock pattern by exploiting *traces* left by the user's finger movement ('smudge'). Recall-based graphical passwords can also be vulnerable to *shoulder surfing*; the distribution of the secret drawing (or patterns) is also biased, which may allow attackers to guess the correct pattern/drawing.

Cued-recall graphical password schemes try to improve the users ability to recall the identifying secret information, by providing a *cue* to help the recall process. In most such designs, in particular the PassPoints [480] system, the authentication is done by having the user select a specific sequence of points on a given image; the image provides the cue that helps the users recall the identifying sequence of points.

Recognition based graphical password schemes follow a different approach; they require the user to *recognize* a set or a sequence of images, which were chosen by the user, or assigned randomly to the user during system setup. Using user-chosen images may improve the ability of users to recognize their chosen images, however, it may also make it easier for the attacker to guess the correct images.

Recognition-based graphical password schemes take advantage of the fact that *humans are better at recognition than at recall* [227]. Different types of images were proposed, including random art [151], portrait photos of persons, user-provided images and more. To ensure secure identification, the user should correctly identify the correct set or sequence of images from a large set displayed to the user. Such authentication process is time-consuming, and therefore these type of schemes are acceptable as a fallback authentication mechanism, but not for regular login. On the other hand, since fallback authentication occurs infrequently, there is a concern that users may forget their sequence or set of images and fail to authenticate.

Recognition-based graphical password schemes can also provide additional benefits, including a defense that detects *impersonating websites* and improves the reliability of the fallback authentication, as proposed in Ref. [243]. In this design, the user u selects, initially, a set of images I_u. In normal login, the user u is presented with few images, where *one* of the images is from I_u and the others are random images. As part of the login process, the user should select the image from I_u; this has three advantages. First, this mechanism provides a slight additional defense against online dictionary attacks, since the user must give the correct password as well as select, from the images presented, the one taken from I_u. Second, this helps uses detect an *impersonating website*, since impersonating websites are unlikely to display any of the user's images. Finally, this design trains each user u to remember and identify the set I_u of images they selected. If the user forgets their password, then the system allows them to authenticate by identifying multiple images from I_u, displayed together with many other images. See details in Ref. [243].

Note that this mechanism should be well designed to avoid exposing the set I_u of user-identifying images to an attacker.

9.6.2 OTPw and hash chain login ceremonies

A OTPWs list [93,488] is a 'low-end' *something you have* login ceremony, where the user only need to maintain a list of *one-time passwords*; the list can be kept on paper and/or as a file (on phone, computer and/or cloud).

To protect against exposure of the of the OTPw when used, each OTPw can be used only once. To protect against exposure of the OTPw due to exposure of the server's password file, the server only keeps the result $h(OTPw)$ of a hash function h applied to the OTPw. This allows the server to *verify* the OTPw upon login but prevents exposure of the OTPWs, even if the server's password file is exposed. The design is described in Section 3.4.1.

We denote the list of OTPWs by $x_1, x_2, \ldots, x_m$. The length m of the list is a tradeoff between *convenience* (using the same list for many logins), *security* (the risk of losing list with many passwords) and *efficiency*.

Let us explain the basic operation of OTPw-lists and then discuss two variants. In every login, the user sends the ith OTPw, x_i, to the server. The server would already have the corresponding hashed OTPw, i.e., $h(x_i)$, allowing the server to validate the purported OTPw. (The two variants we discuss in the following have different methods for the server to have the hashed OTPw $h(x_i)$.) The server allows the login, i.e., the login is successful, if the hash of the purported OTPw equals the stored $h(x_i)$. Note that each one-time password x_i is only used once.

Like regular passwords, OTPWs list authentication is vulnerable to *server impersonation attacks.* Such attacker may obtain the OTPw from the client and then use it to login to the server. However, the attacker can use this OTPw only for one login, and the attack may be detected when the user fails to login using the same OTPw.

Let us now explain the two variants of the OTPw-list login ceremonies: the *basic* and the *hash chain* OTPWs list ceremonies.

The basic one-time passwords list login ceremony: In the basic OTPws list design, each OTPw x_i is an independently chosen random n-bits string, i.e., $(\forall i \in \{1, \ldots, m\}) x_i \xleftarrow{\$} \{0,1\}^n$. The server maintains the set of hashes of the OTPws, i.e., $\{h(x_i)\}_{i=1}^{m}$, allowing the server to verify each OTPw. This design was implemented by the *OTPw* application [93, 488].

This design has two drawbacks. First, the server needs to maintain all the hashed-OTPw values used for validation $\{h(x_i)\}_{i=1}^{m}$, although we only use one of them in each login. Second, if an attacker can observe the OTPw-list, then they can use one or more high-numbered entries to login into the user's account; it would probably take the user a long time to reach that entry and possibly detect the attack.

The hash chain login ceremony: To improve on the two drawbacks of the basic OTPWs list design, Lamport proposed, as early as 1981 [311], the use of a *hash chain* for OTPWs list authentication. The hash chain design was later implemented and standardized as *S/Key* [233, 234, 284].

In the hash chain OTPWs list login ceremony, each user is assigned randomly *one* random preimage for the hash function h, which we use as the 'last' OTPw, i.e., x_m. We then derive the rest of the user's OTPWs $\{x_i\}_{i=1}^{m-1}$ by recursive hashing, as follows (see Figure 9.9):

$$x_{m-1} = h(x_m), \ldots, x_2 = h(x_3) = h^{m-2}(x_m),$$
$$x_1 = h(x_2) = h^{m-1}(x_m) \tag{9.3}$$

We initialize the server with the value $x_0 = h(x_1) = h^m(x_m)$, requiring one more hash operation.

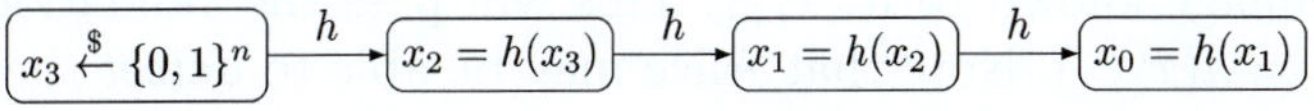

Figure 9.9. The hash chain design, illustrated for $m = 3$, i.e., allowing three logins.

The client uses x_m for up to m login ceremonies. In the ith login ceremony, the client computes and sends to the server the value $x_i = h^{m-i}(x_m)$. The server should already have the corresponding validator value $x_{i-1} = h(x_i) = h^{m-i+1}(x_m)$. Therefore, once the client provides the correct OTPw (preimage) $x_i = h^{m-i}(x_i)$ value, the server can validate it (by confirming that $x_{i-1} = h(x_i)$). The server then retains x_i to authenticate the next $((i+1)^{st})$ login, where the client would send x_{i+1}, and so on.

The server needs to store, after $i \geq 0$ login ceremonies, only the single *hashed OTPw* value x_i.

For usability, *S/Key* encodes each OTPw as a sequence of six short words, each containing up to four characters. The words are taken from a known 2048-word dictionary, i.e., each word encodes eleven bits.

9.6.2.1 *Hash chain: birthday attack and the Leighton–Micali design*

The hash chain construction may be vulnerable to the following *birthday attack*. Consider the use of a chain resulting from m hash applications; let x_m be the randomly selected leftmost OTPw in the chain, and let $x_i = h(x_{i+1})$ as in Equation (9.3). The attacker computes the hash of another hash chain of the same length (m), denoted $x'_{m-1} = h(x'_m), \ldots, x'_0 = h(x'_1)$, with a random initial value x'_m. Following the ROM, assume that h is a random function from arbitrary binary strings to $\{0,1\}^n$. As discussed in Section 3.3.4, when the length of the chains, m, grows to $2^{n/2}$ and more, there will be, with high probability, a collision between a pair of digest in some positions in the two chains, i.e., $x'_i = x_j$ for some $i, j \in [1, \ldots, m]$.

Assume that when the user logins for the jth time, by sending the OTPw x_j to the server, the OTPw x_j is intercepted by the attacker, allowing the attacker to detect the collision $x'_i = x_j$. Then, the attacker can forge the next authentication by sending the preimage known to it, x'_{i+1}. This will pass the validation, since $x_j = x'_i = h(x'_{i+1})$. Note that Alice may be able to *detect* the attack, since the attack is likely to prevent Alice from authenticating, as after the attack Bob expects to receive the preimage of x'_{i+1}, which Alice would not send.

A naïve solution to this concern is to ensure that $m \ll n/2$, which makes the birthday attack ineffective. To do this, we can use relatively long digests, i.e., make n sufficiently long, and/or use relatively short hash chains, i.e., make m sufficiently small. However, both options — increasing n or decreasing m — would result in noticeable overhead.

The *Leighton–Micali hash chain* is a small modification to the design of the hash chain, proposed by Leighton and Micali [325],[2] that foils this birthday attack without significant overhead. The modified design *hashes each OTPw* x_i *using a different hash function* h_i, *i.e.,* $x_i = h_i(x_{i+1})$. We can derive these different hash functions h_i from a single hash function, which we denote H, by including the index i as part of the input to H, e.g.,

$$x_i = h_i(x_{i+1}) = H(x_{i+1} +\!\!+\, i) \tag{9.4}$$

Under the ROM (see Section 3.6), we consider H as a random function. The reader should be able to show that in this case, each h_i would also be an (independently) random function, and that the birthday attack fails.

The reader may note the similarity to the rainbow table technique of Ref. [384].

Note that it seems quite challenging to prove the security of the hash chain design without the ROM, or even to modify the design to allow provable security without the ROM. See Exercise 9.8.

9.6.3 Login ceremonies using authenticator devices

Authenticator ceremonies use a module called an *authenticator*, to authenticate a user to a website or other service; for simplicity, let us focus on the case of a user connecting to a website. We use the term *platform* to refer to the device which the user uses to communicate to the website; typically, the platform is the user's phone, tablet or computer. Often, the authenticator is a software module running on the platform device. In other cases, the authenticator is a separate

[2]This design is a small part of Ref. [325]; it appears toward the end of column 13.

device from the platform; a separate device may offer better security and/or convenience.

Authenticators are used to improve security, improve convenience, or for fallback authentication. The improvement in security may be due to the authenticator being more secure than other factors of authentication, e.g., an authenticator may perform secure user identification using biometrics, and then run a secure authentication and key exchange protocol against the server. Another way for an authenticator to improve security is by requiring authentication using the device *in addition* to other factors of authentication, i.e., as a part of *two-factor authentication* (2FA) or MFA.

Authenticator ceremonies may differ in multiple aspects, including the *type* of authenticator, *user identification and presence* mechanisms and *vulnerability to exposure* of platform and server files. Let us briefly discuss each of these aspects; then, we discuss a few important authenticators and ceremonies. These include *cookies* (Section 9.6.3.1), *SMS* messages (Section 9.6.3.3), *HOTP* and *TOTP* (Section 9.6.3.4), *T/Key* (Section 9.6.3.5) and *FIDO2* (Section 9.6.4).

Types of authenticators: built-in, app or hardware token: Some authenticators use *built-in* function of general-purpose device such as a phone or a computer. The most well known examples of such authenticators are *authenticating cookies* kept by the browser (Section 9.6.3.1), *authenticating SMS* messages sent to the user's phone number, and *authenticating emails* sent to the user's email account (Section 9.6.3.3). The device providing the authenticator function may also be the platform, e.g., this is always the case when using cookies; or, it may be a separate device, such as an authenticating SMS or email, that can be used to authenticate access from another device, usually, by providing a code or a URL used to validate login (from the same or another device).

Built-in authenticators are easy to deploy, with no costs associated with a dedicated authenticator module. They are also easy to use, especially considering their wide, universal use. Another advantage is that each of these authenticator mechanisms is used by many different services, without requiring any coordination or trust between them.

However, built-in authenticators often have weak security. For example, an attacker may be able to access the user's email in different ways, such as by temporary access to the user's account, or by intercepting the email, which may sometimes[3] be done using DNS poisoning or attacks on Internet routing. Furthermore, built-in authenticators depend on the user-identification mechanism of the user's device, which may be weak.

Dedicated, separate authenticator modules may offer better security. Such separate authenticator modules may be implemented as applications (or 'apps') or as a separate hardware device, often referred to as a *hardware token*. Hardware tokens may be used to provide some defense against user impersonation even when the platform is insecure. However, hardware tokens involve additional costs, and are arguably less convenient, since users need to carry the token with them.

Authenticators of all kinds may require user involvement in the authentication ceremony, such as entering a challenge to the authenticator and/or copying a OTPw from the authenticator to the service's user interface, e.g., to a website that the user is logging into.

User authentication and presence validation — possession, biometrics, and others: Authenticators use different methods to authenticate (identify) the user. Authenticators implemented in a device carried by the user provide some level of user-authentication simply from the fact that the user has the authenticator in their possession. On top of that, many authenticators enforce some additional means for user authentication/identification. These means include a password or a PIN, using biometric identification, and using a built-in user authentication mechanisms which exist in general-purpose device, e.g., the locking mechanism used by users to control access to their mobile phones.

Some authenticator ceremonies, in particular FIDO2 (Section 9.6.4), allow the server to ask the authenticator to validate the *presence* of the user, i.e., make sure that the user is present at the time of the authentication. This minimizes the risk that the authenticator

---

[3]Email communication is often protected from interception attacks, mainly by using TLS between mail servers.

identifies the user at some time t, and later, at some later time $t' > t$, the authenticator automatically authenticates the user to a service, while the user is actually away from the authenticator. The validation of presence may require some interaction with the user, ranging from a simple button click to biometric authentication, or rely on mechanisms to ensure *continuous authentication.*

Vulnerability to the exposure of platform and server files: Some authenticator ceremonies are vulnerable to the exposure of files of the server and/or of the platform. For example, cookies ceremonies (Section 9.6.3.1) are vulnerable to exposure of the file containing the cookie of either server or client. Authenticator ceremonies which use a shared key to authenticate the user to the server in the login process, in particular, the HOTP and TOTP ceremonies (Section 9.6.3.4), are similarly vulnerable to exposure of the server's file containing the shared keys.

Other authenticator ceremonies are not vulnerable to exposures of the server or platform files. In particular, this holds for ceremonies where the server authenticates the user using a *public key*, where the corresponding private key is kept by the authenticator, such as FIDO2 (Section 9.6.4), and also for ceremonies based on one-time passwords, e.g., S/Key (Section 9.6.2) and T/Key (Section 9.6.3.5).

9.6.3.1 *Web security and cookies as authenticators*

A cookie is a string sent to the browser by a website, and then kept by the browser (for a period defined by a cookie parameter). Whenever the browser sends a request to some website, it attaches cookies it has from that website; see Figure 9.10. Cookies are used for many purposes, including the authentication of requests sent by the user's browser to the website. The use of cookies for user authentication is convenient to users, since cookies do not require user involvement at all.

In Figure 9.10, we illustrate the use of a cookie, whose name is SecAuth, to authenticate the requests from the client to the server. Note that the cookie sent by the server (using the 'set-cookie:' HTTP header) has the 'Secure' attribute, instructing the browser to send it only over TLS-protected connections (i.e., with HTTPS requests, but not with HTTP requests). In this figure, all requests were sent

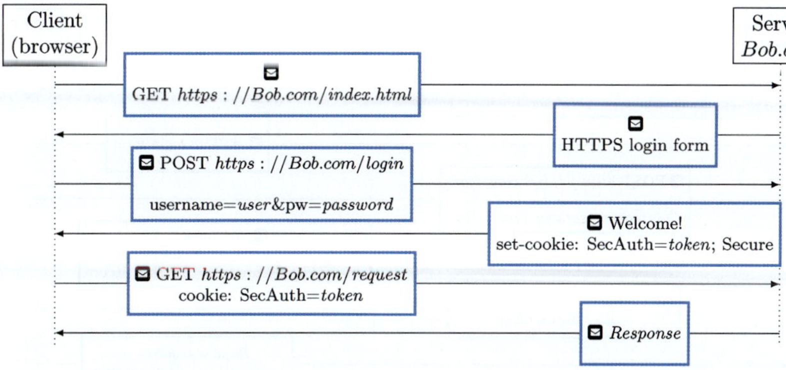

Figure 9.10. Cookie-based user authentication by website. The server sets the cookie after the user logins successfully; the *Secure* attribute instructs the browser to send the cookie only over secure connections, i.e., connections using HTTPS (over TLS), which we identify by including the 🔒 symbol in the flows. As long as a cookie received from a website remains cached, the client attaches it automatically to requests it sends to the same website, allowing the server to authenticate the client without requesting the password again.

using the HTTPS protocol, i.e., HTTP requests sent securely over a TLS connection. To emphasize this, we include the 🔒 symbol in the requests and responses.

Due to their convenience, cookies are widely used; however, many websites restrict the lifetime of cookies, thereby requiring users to periodically login, i.e., authenticate themselves, using a different mechanism, often, a password. The reason for that is that cookies may be accessible and abused by attackers in different ways, depending on the attacker's capabilities and on the *cookie parameters*.

An *eavesdropping attacker* may observe the cookie as it is sent between browser and website, unless it is properly encrypted. This is usually prevented by sending sensitive contents, including cookies, only over TLS-protected connections, i.e., using the HTTPS protocol where the traffic is protected using TLS, as shown in Figure 7.2. The *Secure* cookie parameter instructs the client (browser) that this cookie should be sent to the server only in requests sent over secure (HTTPS) connections, i.e., only over TLS. Figure 9.11 shows the different behavior of the *auth* cookie, set without the 'Secure' attribute, and of the *SecAuth* cookie, set with the 'Secure' attribute.

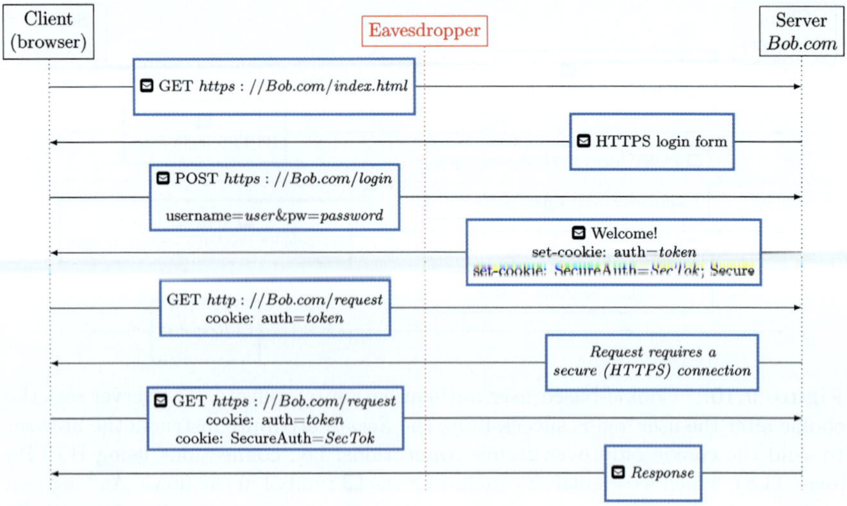

Figure 9.11. Eavesdropper attack on cookies. The eavesdropper can learn the value of cookies sent over an insecure connection (HTTP rather than HTTPS, i.e., not using TLS). The SecureAuth cookie has the *Secure* parameter; therefore, it is only sent over the secure (HTTPS) connection.

An eavesdropping attacker could learn the value of the *auth* cookie, but not of the *SecAuth* cookie; see Figure 9.11.

9.6.3.2 *Web security basics: sandbox, SOP and cross-site attacks*

We now briefly touch on the large and important topic of web security, focusing on attacks that expose or exploit authenticating cookies.

Most of these attacks are launched by *rogue (malicious) websites*, exploiting the fact that the web facilitates interactions with many websites. Users often visit rogue websites, without being aware of it; furthermore, webpages can — and often do — include resources from other (benign and rogue) websites. *Browsers should be secure against attacks by rogue websites.*

The most common type of attack by rogue websites, involve the rogue website, when visited by a (benign) user, cause the user's browser to send maliciously crafted requests to a benign website, often, exploiting and/or exposing the authenticating cookies that the browser sends automatically with the requests to the benign website. Such attacks are called *cross-site attacks*.

Many of the cross-site attacks, and other attacks by rogue websites, take advantage of the fact that browsers (usually[4]) execute scripts received with the webpage, mostly written in *JavaScript*. Browsers allow scripts access to webpage contents, cookies and other resources. These scripting capabilities are a key component of the web. Therefore, it is critical for browsers to maintain security even while accessing rogue sites and running scripts.

Browsers restrict the capabilities of scripts in different ways to ensure security against cross-site attacks and other rogue-website attacks. The two most basic restrictions are the *sandbox* mechanism and the *Same Origin Policy* (SOP).

Browser's sandbox: Browsers restricts scripts so that the scripts would only be able to interact with the browser; scripts should not be able to interact directly with the operating system of the host, without explicit user approval. These restrictions are referred to as the browser's *sandbox*; the goal is to prevent a script from performing attacks beyond what the contents presented to the user of the rogue webpage.

The Same Origin Policy (SOP): Browsers should prevent a script received from a rogue website, from accessing contents and resources, including cookies, which the browser receives from other websites. This defense is called the SOP.

Let us briefly describe two of the most important cross-site attacks: *cross-site scripting* (XSS) and *cross-site request forgery* (CSRF).

Cross-site scripting (XSS): XSS is a way to circumvent the SOP, by causing the browser to execute a rogue script received from a rogue website (*666.org*), but with the browser considering that script as coming from a benign website (*bob.com*). A successful XSS attack will trick the browser into allowing the script to access resources from the benign website (*bob.com*). Most XSS attacks exploit vulnerabilities in the benign website, which cause the website to send the rogue script as part of a response sent to a request from the browser, without

[4]Users can instruct their browsers to disable scripts, but few do, as this 'breaks' the functionality of many websites.

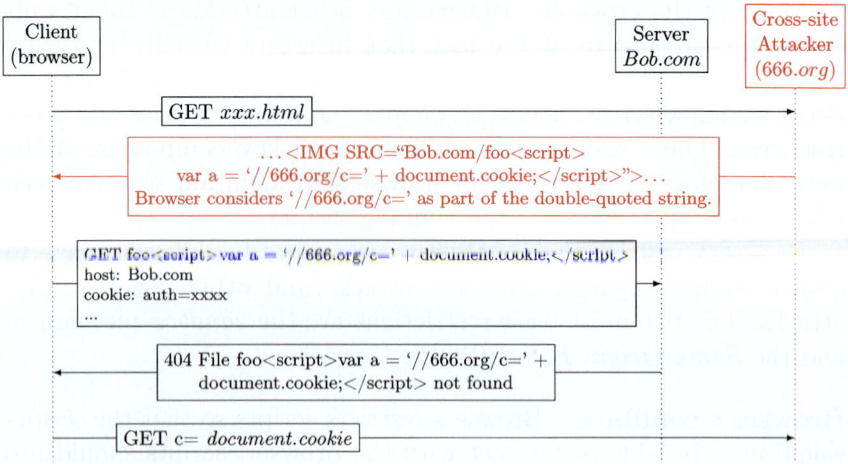

Figure 9.12. XSS cookie-stealing reflection attack. When *Bob.com* does not find the requested file, it sends back a webpage containing the text 404 File *filename* not found, where *filename* is the name of the requested-but-not-found file, without any filtering (sanitation). The attacker creates a link with the *filename* containing a script. The browser executes the script with origin of *Bob.com*; and the script sends the cookie to the attacker, supposedly to initialize a variable, i.e., steals the cookie.

being aware that this part of the response would be parsed as script by the browser.

In particular, in a *reflection XSS* attack, as illustrated in Figure 9.12, the attack is launched by the cross-site attacker (666.*org*), i.e., a website controlled by the attacker which is visited by the user, and which attacks the benign site *Bob.com* where the user has an account (and a cookie).

The attack is launched when the user visits *666.org*, by the response from *666.org* instructing the browser to send a specific request to the benign site *Bob.com*. The request is to a resource (file) which does not exist on *Bob.com*, and therefore *Bob.com* responds with an error webpage, with the error message indicating *file <filename> not found* (error code 404). In the <*filename*> field, the server puts the non-existing file name, received from the browser (after the browser received it as part of the webpage from *666.org*).

This filename actually contains a *script*, typically written in JavaScript. The benign server 'reflects' the script as part of its error message; however, from the point of view of the browser, the script is now received from *Bob.com*. Therefore, the browser allows the script to access *document.cookie*, which embeds the cookie for domain *Bob.com*. This allows the script to expose the cookie to the attacker. The example shows one of multiple ways for the attacker to expose the cookie.

Cross-site request forgery (CSRF): CSRF is an attack which *abuses* the cookie authentication mechanism used by a benign website, *without* necessarily exposing the cookie (as done by many XSS attacks, e.g., in Figure 9.12). Instead, in a CSRF attack, the attacker exploits the fact that cookies are automatically attached to requests sent to the corresponding website. Therefore, by causing the browser to send a request to the benign server, to which the browser automatically attaches the authenticating cookie, the attacker tricks the benign site into executing an operation which was not authorized by the user.

Figure 9.13 illustrates a CSRF attack launched by the cross-site attacker (666.*org*) when the user visits it. The attack consists of including in the webpage a request for an embedded object, specifically an image (*¡IMG¿* tag), from domain *Bob.com*. The browser automatically includes the cookie of domain *Bob.com*. If the request is interpreted by *Bob.com* as asking for a particular operation, e.g., payment to *666.org*, and *Bob.com* validates the request only using the cookie mechanism, then the operation would probably succeed.

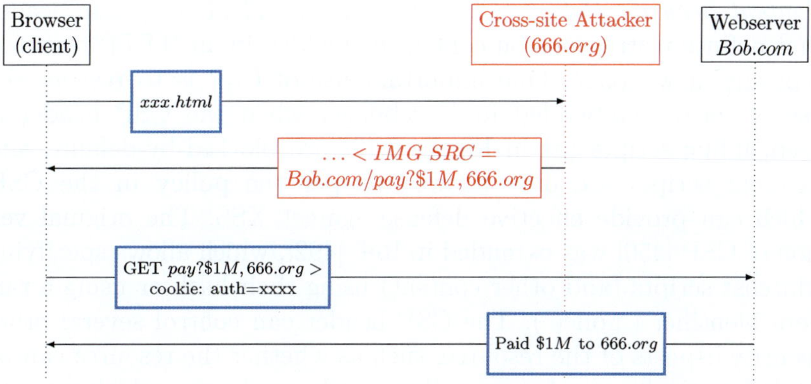

Figure 9.13. Cross-Site Request Forgery (CSRF) attack.

Defenses: There are multiple defenses against XSS, CSRF and other cross-site attacks. In particular, many of the attacks exposing and/or abusing authenticating cookies can be foiled by proper use of *cookie parameters*; see Ref. [75]. Several standard HTTP headers can further protect against cross-site and other rogue-website attacks.

The HttpOnly cookie parameter: There is often no need for scripts to access cookies used for authentication; if the server includes the *HttpOnly* parameter when it sets-up the cookie, then this cookie will be inaccessible by scripts, including scripts whose origin is considered to be the same website as the cookie. This mechanism prevents most XSS attacks from stealing the cookies, e.g, as illustrated in Figure 9.12.

The SameSite cookie parameter: The simple CSRF attack illustrated in Figure 9.13 would *fail against most modern browsers*, due to a defense implemented by most versions of browsers from around 2017. The attack still works, if the cookie is setup with the *SameSite* parameter, configured with value *none*, which basically opt-outs of this defense. The defense instructs modern browsers to not attach cookies in cross-site requests for embedded objects. The attack can be modified to be an external link, i.e., a link that opens a new webpage in *Bob.com*, but this is a less-appealing attack since the user may detect this unsolicited page opening. Note that the *SameSite* cookie parameter can also be set as *SameSite=Strict*, which instructs the browser not to attach the cookies to *any* cross-site request; this completely prevents the abuse of that cookie in CSRF attacks.

Content Security Policy (CSP): CSP is an HTTP response header that defines restrictions on content embedded in an HTTP resource, typically, a webpage. One important use of CSP is to restrict the use of scripts embedded in a webpage; when the CSP header is used, inline scripts (as in Figure 9.12) are blocked-by-default, and external scripts are only allowed as per the policy in the CSP, which can provide effective defense against XSS. The original version of CSP [450] was extended in Ref. [492], which allows specifying whitelist scripts (and other content) using their hash or using a random identifier ('nonce'). The CSP header can control several other security aspects of the resource, such as whether the resource can be loaded, typically as a frame, within another webpage, which can protect against *clickjacking*, an attack which uses the browser's support for multiple layers, to trick users into clicking on buttons without being aware of it.

Bottom line: Authenticating cookies are convenient but provide only weak security. Cookies may be exposed by sites failing to set cookie parameters correctly, which is surprisingly common [375], due to TLS vulnerabilities (Chapter 7), or due to vulnerabilities in the use of TLS by the browsers [70].

Sites using authenticating cookies, should set up cookie parameters to limit the lifetime of the cookies, using them to authenticate requests from the user only for limited time after the user completes a secure login ceremony. Furthermore, sites relying on cookies for normal use, often require additional authentication for sensitive transactions.

9.6.3.3 *SMS, email and other communication-based authenticators*

Many websites authenticate users by sending a OTPw to the user via a 'secure channel', mainly, email, SMS or a phone call. Usually, the user should type the OTPw in an appropriate field in the site's login page. This type of authentication requires a bit more user involvement than regular passwords; therefore, it is used mostly to complement another authentication mechanisms, either as a second factor of authentication, e.g., in addition to passwords, or for fallback authentication, i.e., recovery from the loss of the main method of authentication, often, users forgetting their password. On the other hand, the process is quite convenient for users; only few simple, familiar and easy operations are required.

The security of these ceremonies depends on it being infeasible for an attacker to obtain the OTPw. Attackers may obtain the OTPw using different attacks, as follows.

Network attacks: The assumption that the OTPw is sent over a secure channel is not always justified. Email communication may be subject to eavesdropping attacks as well as interception using DNS poisoning. Cellular networks can also be vulnerable. The early cellular networks were very vulnerable, e..g, see GSM vulnerabilities in Sections 5.5.3 and 5.5.5. Vulnerabilities have also been found in more modern cellular networks, e.g., see Refs. [254, 275, 373].

Obtaining access to the user's account or device: Email accounts are not always well protected, allowing exposure of OTPw sent by email. SMS messages can also be intercepted by obtaining access to the user's phone, physically or using malware on the phone; see such attacks and a proposed defense for Android phones in Ref. [293]. Attackers can also obtain SMS messages sent to the user using the *SIM-swap* social engineering attack, where the attacker tricks the operator of the cellular provider to change the association of the user's phone number so that it will reach the attacker's mobile phone (with the attacker's SIM) [275, 373].

Cross-site social engineering attacks: Another type of social-engineering attack is directed at the end user rather than on the the cellular provider; the attack is mostly effective against SMS-based authentication. This attack, presented in Ref. [200], targets the account of a benign user (Alice) visiting the rogue website *666.org*. The rogue website presents a form where Alice she should enter an authentication code that *666.org* sent to Alice by an SMS message. In reality, the attacker performs the login ceremony against a benign website, e.g., *Bob.com*, in which the attacker believes that Alice may have an account, where *Bob.com* uses SMS-based authentication. Typically, *Bob.com* supports fallback authentication using SMS, and the attacker claims to be Alice and to have forgotten the password. Therefore, *Bob.com* sends a OTPw to Alice over SMS. Alice may not note that the message came from *Bob.com* and enter the OTPw into the form displayed by *666.org*. Websites using SMS-based authentication using a OTPw should phrase the SMS message to try to prevent this kind of attacks, but users may still fall for the attack due to human traits such as *click-whirr response* and *inattentional blindness* (Section 9.1.1). The attack is harder to prevent when the rogue website is impersonating as the victim website *Bob.com*, with an impersonating, misleading domain name (and certificate), e.g., *Bob.com-666.org*; see Section 8.1.5.2.

9.6.3.4 *Shared-key one-time password authenticator ceremonies: HOTP, TOTP and OCRA*

We now briefly discuss three OTPw designs published by the IETF as informational RFCs: *HMAC-based One-Time Password*

(HOTP) [370], *Time-based One-Time Password (TOTP)* [371] and *OATH Challenge-Response Algorithm (OCRA)* [372].

The three specifications (HOTP, TOTP and OCRA) are closely related. They involve only two parties: the *relying party*, typically a website, and the *authenticator*. The three designs are based on a symmetric key cryptography, using a key k shared between the authenticator and the relying party. Authentication is based on a OTPw, which is computed by truncating the output of the HMAC function (Section 4.4.5), using the shared key k; the truncation is done to some number d of decimal digits. Typically, the user copies the d-digits OTPw from the display of the authenticator to an input field of website, motivating the truncation to a small number of digits (d); the value $d = 6$ is typical. The difference between the schemes is in the input to the HMAC function.

HMAC-based One-Time Password (HOTP) [370]): In HOTP, the input to the HMAC function is a counter c. The value of c is the number of invocations of the authenticator so far, which the authenticator maintains in non-volatile storage. Namely, for the cth authentication, the authenticator computes the cth OTPw, denoted $pw_{k,d}^{\text{HOTP}}(c)$, using shared key k and truncating to d digits, as

$$pw_{k,d}^{\text{HOTP}}(c) = HMAC_k(c) \bmod 10^d \tag{9.5}$$

The server maintains the last (highest) counter c' that was used in a successful authentication by the authenticator. To validate a purported OTPw p received from the client, the server first checks if $p = hmac_k(c' + 1)$, i.e., is it the next expected HOTP OTPw. If it is, then authentication succeeded. If it isn't, this may be caused by the loss of one or more OTPw values generated by the authenticator, requiring the server to *resynchronize*. HOTP servers allow for some small number s of lost OTPWs; authentication succeeds as long as for some s' s.t. $1 \leq s' \leq s$ holds $p = HMAC_k(c' + s')$. See Exercise 9.11.

Note that if an attacker obtains the shared key k, then they can *clone* the authenticator and successfully login using the cloned authenticator, just like the benign user. However, interleaving login sessions of the cloned authenticator and of the original authenticator will cause loss of synchronization. Login may still be possible if the gap between the counter of the original authenticator and the counter of the clone is not too large. HOTP systems should try to detect such repeated loss of synchronization and warn of the possible cloning of the authenticator.

Time-based One-Time Password (TOTP) [371]): In TOTP, the input to the HMAC function is a slowly changing function of the time. Specifically, the TOTP OTPw changes once every *time step* X, where X is given in seconds; a typical value is $X = 30$ (for time step of 30 seconds).

We compute the TOTP OTPw at Unix time[5] t (given in seconds), by applying the truncated-HMAC of HOTP (Equation (9.5)) to the number of X time-step periods in t. The computation uses the shared key k, the time step X (in seconds) and the number of digits d, as follows:

$$pw_{k,d,X}^{\text{TOTP}}(t) = pw_{k,d}^{\text{HOTP}}\left(\left\lfloor \frac{t}{X} \right\rfloor\right) = HMAC_k\left(\left\lfloor \frac{t}{X} \right\rfloor\right) \bmod 10^d \tag{9.6}$$

TOTP requires weak-synchronization of the clocks of the authenticator and of the server, and thereby avoids the risk of loss of synchronization, or the need to allow for s lost OTPWs. On the other hand, this implies that TOTP does not facilitate detection of a cloned authenticator.

OATH Challenge-Response Algorithm (OCRA) [372]: OCRA is a shared-key OTPw design developed as part of the Open Authentication (OATH) initiative [220]. As its name implies, OCRA is based on *challenge-response authentication*; specifically, the server sends a challenge (nonce) to the authenticator, who applies a cryptographic function to it, e.g., HMAC, to create the response. The OCRA design is quite similar to the shared-key *request-response* (RR) authentication protocols of Section 5.3.

In the typical case, the cryptographic function *is* HMAC, or, more precisely, the truncated-HMAC of HOTP (Equation (9.5)), using the shared key k; the difference of OCRA from HOTP and TOTP is in the input value. For OCRA, the input is the concatenation of several

[5]Unix time is the number of non-leap seconds since midnight UTC on January first, 1970.

fields, including the OCRA cipher suite, which we denote *OCRA-Suite*, and challenge 'questions' Q (usually, one or more nonces). The input may contain several additional fields, including a counter C (similar to HOTP), the number T of time steps (similar to TOTP), the hash of a password P, and a string S containing information about the current session. The computation also uses the shared key k and the number of digits d, as follows:

$$\begin{aligned} pw^{\text{OCRA}}_{k,d}(\textit{OCRASuite}, Q, C, T, P, S) \quad (9.7) \\ = pw^{\text{HOTP}}_{k,d}\left(\textit{OCRASuite} \mathbin{+\!\!+} C \mathbin{+\!\!+} Q \mathbin{+\!\!+} P \mathbin{+\!\!+} S \mathbin{+\!\!+} T\right) \\ = HMAC_k\left(\textit{OCRASuite} \mathbin{+\!\!+} C \mathbin{+\!\!+} Q \mathbin{+\!\!+} P \mathbin{+\!\!+} S \mathbin{+\!\!+} T\right) \bmod 10^d \end{aligned}$$

OCRA allows mutual authentication, namely, in addition to having the server send the challenge to the authenticator and the authenticator computing and sending the result, we can also have the client send the challenge to the server and the server returning the result.

Disadvantages of using shared key authentication: The security of the three designs depends on the secrecy of the shared key. In particular, if the server's file containing the shared-keys of different users is exposed, then all of the shared keys are exposed. Of course, the file containing the shared-keys should not be exposed, but this kind of exposures does happen; indeed, this was the motivation for using hashing and salt to provide some defense to passwords even after password file exposure. This motivate the use of designs which do not require sharing of secrets between authenticator and server, including *T/Key* and *FIDO2*, both discussed in the following.

Another disadvantage of the shared-key design is that it can be difficult to use the same authenticator belonging to a user, to authenticate the user to multiple services. This drawback is addressed by FIDO2 but not by T/Key.

9.6.3.5 *T/Key: a time based hash chain authentication ceremony*

T/Key [299] is an interesting design that provides time-based authentication, like TOTP (Section 9.6.3.4), but avoids the reliance on a shared secret key. Instead, T/Key authenticates the user using a *hash chain*, like S/Key (Section 9.6.2). By using time-based authentication, T/Key avoids the need to maintain synchronized state between the server and the authenticator, as required both by HOTP and by the hash chain design (used by S/Key).

The T/Key design is quite similar to that of the Leighton–Micali hash chain design of Section 9.6.2.1. However, let us first present a simplified version of it, which we denote *sT/Key* (for 'simplified T/Key). The sT/Key design follows the 'classical' hash chain design (as in S/Key).

The (simplified) sT/Key design: In both S/Key and sT/Key, we select a chain-length m, and the client selects a random n-bits string $x_m \xleftarrow{\$} \{0,1\}^n$ to be used as the 'last OTPw'. We then compute and initialize the server with the value $x_0 = h^m(x_m)$. The difference is in the computation of the OTPw that the client sends to the server in order to login, and in how the server validates this incoming OTPw.

Using the 'classical hash chain design', e.g., in S/Key, the OTPw is a function of the number of login ceremonies. As in Equation (9.3), the client computes and sends $x_i = h^{m-i}(x_m)$ during the $i \geq 1$ successful login ceremony. The server validates x_i using the value $x_{i-1} = h^{m-(i-1)}(x_m)$, which the server receives in the $i-1$ successful login.

In sT/Key, the client computes the OTPw very similarly, for login events during the period $[t_0 + (i-1) \cdot X, t_0 + i \cdot X]$, there t_0 denotes the time at which the server was initialized with x_0, and X denotes the lifetime of a given OTPw (as in TOTP).

The server validation is also quite similar, with the main difference being that when validating the OTPw x_i, the server may not have the value of x_{i-1}, since x_{i-1} is sent only if there is a login during the previous period, i.e., during $[t_0 + (i-2) \cdot X, t_0 + (i-1) \cdot X]$. However, as long as the server has *any* previous OTPw, say x_j, where $j < i$, the server can use x_j to validate x_i, by confirming that $x_j = h^{i-j}(x_i)$.

Note that this implies that sT/Key uses much longer chains than S/Key. In S/Key, a chain of length m suffices for m login ceremonies; in sT/Key, a chain of the same length m suffices only for login ceremonies during a period of length $X \cdot m$ seconds. As we discussed in Section 9.6.2.1, this makes the sT/Key design vulnerable to birthday attack on h. The (complete) T/Key design uses chains of the same length as sT/Key, but instead of using the 'classical' hash chain design with a single hash function h, it uses the Leighton–Micali hash chain, which uses multiple hash functions h_i, all derived from a single hash function H.

The (complete) T/Key design: The T/Key design is very similar to the (simplified) sT/Key design; the difference is that instead of using the same hash function h for every 'link in the chain', we use different hash functions h_i, thereby avoiding the vulnerability to the birthday attack.

In T/Key, like in the other schemes, we first choose the chain-length m and the random n-bits string $x_m \xleftarrow{\$} \{0,1\}^n$, and then compute and initialize the server with the value x_0. However, in T/Key, we compute x_0 recursively as follows:

$$x_{m-1} = h_m(x_m); \; \ldots \; ; x_{i-1} = h_i(x_i); \; \ldots \; ; x_0 = h_1(x_1) \qquad (9.8)$$

The client also uses Equation (9.8) to compute the OTPw x_i for login events during the period $[t_0 + (i-1) \cdot X, t_0 + i \cdot X]$, which is very similar to the operation of sT/Key, except for using a different hash function for each step. Similarly, the server uses Equation (9.8) to validate the OTPWs it receives.

When adopting the ROM, the functions h_i can be derived from a fixed hash function H as in Equation (9.4), i.e., $h_i(x_i) = H(x_i + i)$.

For details, see Ref. [299].

9.6.4 The FIDO2 registration and authentication ceremonies

The last authenticator ceremony we discuss is FIDO2. *FIDO2* is a set of technology standards defined by the *Fast IDentity Online (FIDO) Alliance consortium.* The goal of FIDO2 is to provide convenient ways of user authentication that improves security compared to the use of (only) passwords; when used *in lieu* of passwords, FIDO2 may also offer greater convenience. FIDO2 has significant adoption and may become a popular method for user authentication, either by itself, for a *device you have* authentication, or as a part of a two-factor or MFA solution. FIDO2 is based on public-key cryptography and

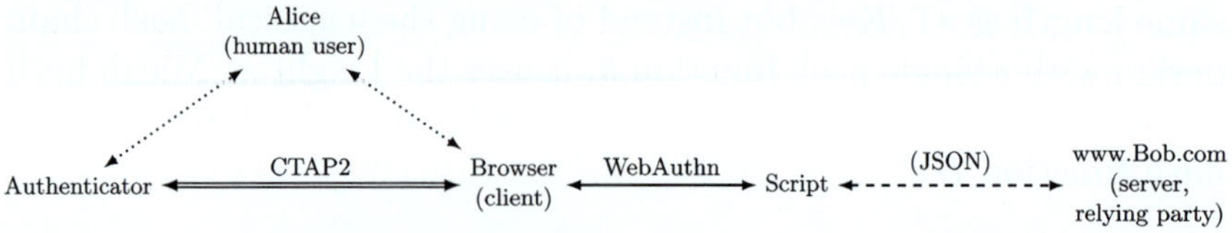

Figure 9.14. FIDO communication channels.

allows a user to use the same authenticator for multiple relying parties (servers); this is a significant advantage over the HOTP, TOTP and OCRA standards, discussed above.

The FIDO2 standards facilitate *device you have* or *two-factor authentication* (2FA) with interoperability between three independent agents: an *authenticator* token, a *client* agent (typically, browser) and a *relying party* or *server* agent, which is usually a website requiring user authentication. Both the browser (client) and the authenticator also interact with a human user (being authenticated). Another component is a *script*, embedded in the webpage which the browser receives from the server. The interactions between all of these components (human user, authenticator, browser, script and server) are illustrated in Figure 9.14.

Figure 9.14 also indicates the two FIDO2 protocols: the *Client To Authenticator Protocol* (CTAP2, [14]), which defines the interactions between the authenticator and the client (browser), and the *WebAuthn* [271] API, which defines the interactions between the client and the script received from the relying party (server). The interactions between the script and the server are not standardized; different servers can send scripts supporting different protocols, therefore, this does not need to be standardized; often, the interaction uses the JSON (JavaScript Object Notation) data-interchange format [104].

Let us briefly describe the FIDO2 registration and authentication processes, illustrated in Figures 9.15 and 9.16, respectively. For simplicity, our description treats the script and the server as one entity, the relying party, which we name *Bob.com* to be concrete.

The *FIDO2 registration* process (Figure 9.15) allows a user to establish support by a specific website for login ceremonies using a (new) FIDO2 authenticator. The process begins with the user logging to the website (e.g., *Bob.com*), and requesting registration of a

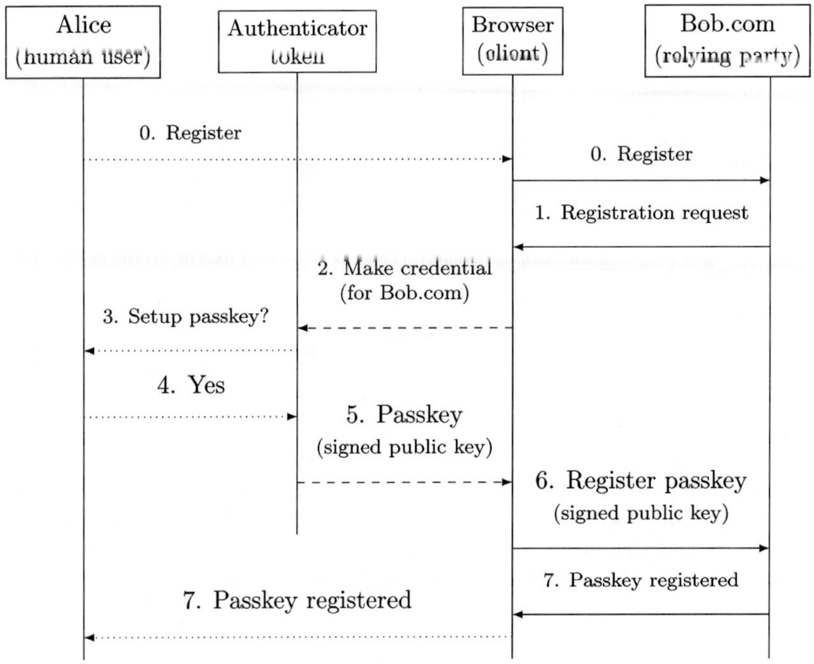

Figure 9.15. FIDO2 authenticator registration ceremony. The ceremony allows a user, *who is already logged in* to the webserver (e.g., Bob.com), to establish a *passkey* generated by a FIDO2 authenticator. The passkey contains a public key and an identifier; the server will use the public key to secure the communication with the authenticator. Dotted lines are user interface interactions and dashed lines are CTAP2 interactions.

new credential; FIDO2 often uses the term *passkey* for the credential. The process where the user logs-in and requests to register a new passkey is indicated by flow 0, from Alice to browser and then from browser to website, in Figure 9.16. Note that the login process registering a new FIDO2 authenticator could use an already-registered FIDO2 authenticator; this would allow users to have redundancy so that they will not lose access if they lose their authenticator, or if an authenticator has a failure.

In flow 1, the website replies with the *WebAuthn registration request* message, which includes parameters including a random challenge value (*nonce*) and identifications, both of the relying party (website) and of the user account. The client (browser) send these

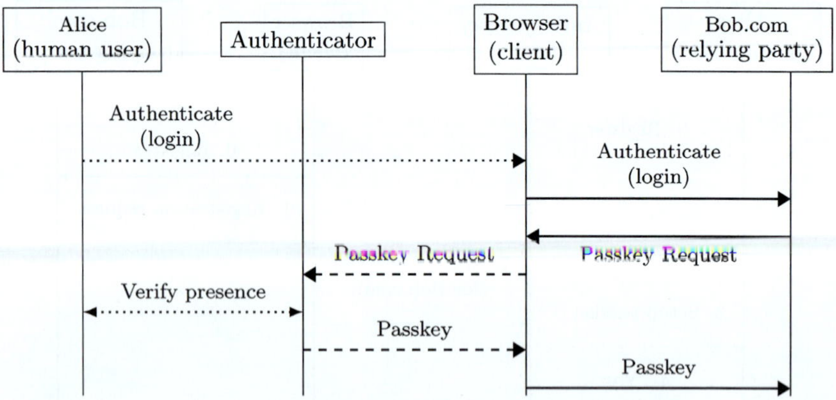

Figure 9.16. FIDO2 authentication (simplified). Alice (the human user) initiates the authentication process, typically, by pressing a 'login' button on Bob.com. The dotted lines are flows between Alice and the authenticator or browser; the dashed lines are the CTAP2 (client to authenticator protocol) flows, between the browser and the authenticator, and the solid lines are the WebAuthn flows, between browser (client) and Bob.com (relying party, web server).

parameters to the authenticator in the *authenticatorMakeCredential* CTAP2 message (flow 2), which requests the authenticator to create a new passkey.

The authenticator should confirm the request with the user (Alice); this is usually referred to as *presence validation*. Some authenticators perform only *basic presence validation*, e.g., where the user clicks a button, while others require *strong presence validation*, e.g., validating the user's fingerprint. The validation process is indicated in Figure 9.15 by flows 3 and 4. Some authenticators do not support any interaction with the user and provide presence validation by detection of proximity between the authenticator and the client device (platform), typically, using NFC (Near Field Communication) [135].

After the presence validation completed successfully, the authenticator generates the *passkey*, as a keypair (sk_{AU}, pk_{AU}), where sk_{AU} (pk_{AU}) is called the *authentication private (respectively, public) key*. The authenticator now creates the *credential*, which is a signature, called an *attestation*, over the passkey's public key pk_{AU}, the nonce and other parameters. The signature is computed using a dedicated private key sk_{AT} called the *attestation private key*, which is pre-loaded to the authenticator in its production ('burnt-in'). The corresponding attestation public key, pk_{AT}, is provided to all relying parties.

After creating the credential, the authenticator sends the credential to the client (browser), in flow 5. The client forwards the credential to the website (relying party), using an WebAuthn call called *navigator.credentials.create* (flow 6 in Figure 9.15; we use there the shorter term 'credentials create').

Recall that the credential contains the attestation signature, which the relying party (website) validates using the *attestation public key* pk_{AT}, obtained securely from the producer of the authenticator; this allows the website to require the use of authenticators from producers it trusts. The website also validates that the credentials contains the correct challenge value (*nonce*) and identifications. Once validation completes successfully, the relying party saves the authentication public key pk_{AU} which it uses for future authentications of the user (Alice). The website will inform the user, via the client (browser), of the successful completion of the passkey registration (flow 7).

Once registration has completed successfully, the user can authenticate themselves, multiple times, using the authenticator. This is done with the *FIDO2 authentication* process. The FIDO2 authentication process is shown in Figure 9.16, with simplification of some technical details.

9.7 Lab: Password security

Lab 6 (Password security). This lab we investigates different ways for attackers to crack passwords.

Some of the defense mechanisms in this lab use cryptographic hash functions. We use the SHA-256 hash function, which has multiple implementations you can use (e.g., in the *hashlib, PyCryptodome* and *cryptography* Python libraries).

In each question you should expose one password. Measure the time required to solve each item; this may help you appreciate the value of different attacks and defenses. Note that part of the challenge of this lab is to implement your programs efficiently; an inefficient implementation to some of these questions may require many hours of running time. For example, you may want to take advantage of the fact that we provide the Python code of the different functions, allowing you to call them from your code. Also, you may use an optimized implementation of Python such as from www.pypy.org.

The labs and installation instructions are available from https://githuB.com/CyberSec-labs/labs; see more details in the preface:

1. Many users select weak passwords; for example, in 2020, the password *123456* was used by over 2 million users. The file *MostCommonPWs* lists a few of the most common passwords. You are asked, say by George Washington, to help find the password of *Benedict Arnold*, who is suspected of treason (see Note 9.1). The username is simply his first name, *Benedict*. Try different passwords from *MostCommonPWs* against the login program of the server, *Login.pyc*, to find out Benedict's password. You can do this manually; however, find the password using a Python script, *Break1.py*, that should also print the runtime (which should be very short).

   Submit in your submissions folder the password in file *Login_1.csv*.

   Note: The file *LoginTemplate.py* may help you understand how *Login.pyc* works; we created *Login.pyc* from *LoginTemplate.py* by replacing the string *##passwrd* with a random password from *MostCommonPWs*.
2. After breaking into Benedict's account, you found there a file called *gang*, that contains the usernames of other traitors in his 'gang'. Surely another gang member also uses one of the common passwords in the file *MostCommonPWs*. Modify *Break1.py* into *Break2.py*, which will find another gang member who uses one of the passwords in *MostCommonPWs*, by using the login program *Login.pyc*.

   Submit in your submissions folder the name of the gang member and their password in file *Login_2.csv* in *csv* format, i.e., *username,password*.
3. Even when users do not use one of the obviously weak passwords such as these in *MostCommonPWs*, they still often use commonly used passwords. Find the password of an additional gang member, whose password is from the 'dictionary' of 100,000 common passwords, which you will find in the file *PwnedPWs100K*. This file is from *https://haveibeenPwned.com*, which is a useful, recommended resource on passwords.

Modify *Break2.py* so that the modified program, *Break3.py*, will try out all of the passwords in *PwnedPWs100K*, for the gang members whose password was not found yet. Try to make *Break3.py* efficient! Run *Break3.py*, see how long it takes to find the password for another gang member.
Note: While in reality the passwords in the file are sorted by popularity, we pick them uniformly, i.e., each password is equally likely. Confirm the exposure using *Login.pyc*.

Submit in your submissions folder (only) the name and password of another gang member exposed (only) in this question, as file *Login_3.csv*.

4. Often, attackers get hold of a leaked file of passwords and use it to break into accounts of the same users at other services, where the users reused the same passwords. This attack is called *credential stuffing*. There were billions of passwords exposed in the recent years, and the numbers seem to even grow over time. Attackers often use a password file exposed from one service/site, to break into accounts of the same users in another service/site — since many users use the same password in multiple sites.

   In this question, you will use credential stuffing to find the passwords of additional gang members. These will be quite random passwords. You receive an exposed passwords file, *PwnedPWfile*, and will write a program, *Break4.py* to find accounts (and passwords) for gang members that appear in the file. For any gang member whose passwords is listed, *Break4* will check if the password 'works' against the login program *Login.py*.

   Submit in your submissions folder (only) the name and password of the gang member exposed (only) in this question, as file *Login_4.csv*.

5. To reduce the exposure from a leaked passwords file, password files are usually kept in a form which makes it easy to check if a given string is the correct password (of a given user) but harder to find the passwords given only the file. In this question, we discuss a basic form of this defense, described in Section 9.4.2, where the file contains the hash of the passwords, instead of containing the actual passwords. You are given another exposed passwords file, *HashedPWs*, which contains, for each user x, the results

of applying a cryptographic hash function $h(\cdot)$ to the password PW_x of user x, i.e., $h(PW_x)$. (In the following question, we see an improved defense.)

Write a new program, *Break5.py*, that uses the file *HashedPWs* to find, as quickly as possible, the name and password of an additional gang member. It will be infeasible to test all random passwords (why?); instead, focus on gang members who pick a random password from *PwnedPWs100K*, and concatenate to it two random digits. Many users do such minor tweaks to their passwords, such as concatenating one or two digits, to bypass password-choice requirements, or in the incorrect hope that this suffices to prevent password guessing; attacks that try passwords from a dictionary, and apply common tweaks, are called *password tweaking*. For gang members whose passwords you recover using *HashedPWs*, use *Login.pyc* to check if the gang member used the same password also in the target server.

Submit in your submissions folder (only) the name and password of one gang member exposed (only) in this question, as file *Login_5.csv*.

Hint: Think carefully about how to do this efficiently, or it may be quite slow.

6. To further improve security, password files usually do *not* contain the hash of the password PW_x of user x, i.e., $h(PW_x)$. Instead, the password file contains *two* values for each user x: a random value $salt_x$ chosen for user x, called the *salt* of x, and the result of hashing a combination of the user's password PW_x and of their salt $salt_x$. In this question, you are given a file *SaltedPWs* which contains, for each user x, the pair $(salt_x, h(salt_x + PW_x))$.

   Write a new program, *Break6.py*, that uses the file *SaltedPWs* to find the passwords of as many additional gang members as possible that use passwords from *PwnedPWs100K* concatenated with *one* random digit, as quickly as possible. Use *Login.pyc* to check if the gang member used the same password also in the target server.

   Submit in your submissions folder (only) the name and password of one gang member exposed (only) in this question, as file *Login_6.csv*.

Note 9.1. Historical background: Benedict Arnold.

Benedict Arnold, once a celebrated American leader from Connecticut, achieved early military victories in the Revolutionary War. However, feeling slighted, he switched sides in 1780. He attempted to secretly hand over the crucial fort West Point to the British, using a *book cipher*, where each word was encoded as a series of three numbers separated by periods. These numbers represented a page number of the agreed book, a line number on that page and a word number in that line. The plot was foiled, branding Arnold a traitor. He fled to England, forever remembered for his betrayal. See Ref. [180]

Obviously, Benedict Arnold did not actually use a computer; we use his name in the lab just as character, and to introduce readers to this small bit of Connecticut history.

9.8 Additional exercises

Exercise 9.1 (Password dictionary attacks). An attacker has a collection of 100,000 usernames, each associated with a password, from exposed password files. The attacker tries to find credentials of (username, password) pairs for another site, *vic.com*. Assume that 50,000 users of *vic.com* appear in the collection, 10,000 using a (username, password) pair which appears in the collection, 10,000 using a username from the collection but with the password of a different user from the collection, 10,000 using a username which is known but does not appear in the collection, but use a password from the collection, and the rest using both username and password not in the collection:

1. Assume that the attacker only has online access to *vic.org* and that the site allows only up to three unsuccessful consecutive login attempts in any minute. What is the expected time for the attacker to find one (username, password) pair?
2. Estimate the time required to find the 10,000 (username, password) pairs which appear in the collection.
3. Assume that the attacker found all the 10,000 (username, password) pairs which appear in the collection. What would be the expected additional time to find one more (username, password) pair (from these using other passwords in the collection)?
4. Under the same assumption, estimate the additional time required to find additional 20,000 (username, password) pairs such that

the password appears in the collection (on top of the 10,000 pairs already found).

5. Repeat items 1–4, if the attacker has access to the *hashed* password file of *vic.com*, and assuming that each hash operation takes 10^{-6} seconds. Separate between precomputation time (for work that can be done before the hashed password file is exposed) and the rest of the attack time; both times should be minimized but especially the time after the exposure.
6. Repeat items 1–4, if the attacker has access to the *salted* password file of *vic.com*, assuming again that each hash operation takes 10^{-6} seconds, and assuming a salt of eight bits. As in the previous item, separate between the attack precomputation time and the rest of the attack time.
7. Repeat the previous item, for a salt of 20 bits.

Exercise 9.2. Many websites invoke third-party payment services, such as PayPal. These services reduce the risk of exposure of client's credentials such as credit card number, by having the seller's site open a new 'pop-up' window, at the payment provider's site, say PayPal, and then having the users enter their credentials at PayPal's site:

1. Assume that a user is purchasing at the attacker's site, *666.org*. Explain how *666.org* may be able to trick the user into providing their credentials to the attacker. Assume typical user, and exploit typical human vulnerabilities. Present, using a sequence diagram, the most effective attack you can.
2. Identify the human vulnerabilities exploited by your construction.
3. Propose up to three things that may help to reduce the chance of such attack.

Exercise 9.3. In this exercise, you will design a stateless password manager, for websites where keys must be changed once every period of length T_C, e.g., 100 days, or sooner. Assume that the user visits each of the websites at least once every period of length $T_V \ll T_C$, e.g., T_V may be 10 days. Assume also that the password manager can detect when a login attempt fails; for simplicity, you may assume that the password manager can detect if the failure is due to wrong password or expired password (and ignore other causes for failure).

Furthermore, assume that the password manager can, upon failure, perform a new login with a different password:

1. Denote the master password by PW_M. Propose how to derive from PW_M a password $PW_s(t)$ for site s at time t, using only a hash function h (which you may analyze using the random oracle model). Assume that the adversary can perform up to n_A hash operations in an attack; your solution should attempt to use the minimal number of hash computations necessary to ensure security.
2. Assume that the login fails with a 'password expired' message. Propose how to derive a new password $PW'_s(t)$, to be used to reset the password.
3. Assume that the login fails with a 'incorrect password' message. Propose another password $PW''_s(t)$ that should be used for login. Explain why PW'' should be the correct password.

Exercise 9.4 (Anti-impersonating website browser). A bank wants to design a special browser for its employees, which will reduce the risk of them falling to impersonating website attacks. It considers the following changes from regular browsers. For each, specify if it would have significant, small, negligible or no positive impact on security, and evaluate, based on secure usability principles:

1. Do not open websites as results of clicking on URLs received in emails.
2. If user clicks on URL in email, browser displays warning and asks user to confirm that the URL is correct before requesting that page.
3. On the first time, per day, that the user surfs to a protected site, popup a window with the certificate details and ask the user to confirm the details, before requesting and displaying the site.

Exercise 9.5. In some operating systems, whenever the user installs new software, a pop-up screen displays details and asks the user to approve installation — or to abort. Many programs are signed by a vendor, with a certificate for that vendor from a trusted CA; in this case, the pop-up screen displays the (certified) name of the vendor and the (signed) name of the program. Other programs are not signed, or the vendor is not certified; in these cases the pop-up screen displays the names given by the program for itself and for the vendor, but with a statement that this was not validated:

1. Identify secure usability principles violated by this design, and explain how an attacker can exploit human vulnerabilities to get malicious programs installed.
2. An organization wishes to prevent installation of malware, so it publishes to its employees a list of permitted software vendors so that employees would verify their names before installing. Present criticism.
3. Propose an alternative method that an operating system could offer that would allow organizations a more secure way to ensure that only programs from permitted vendors would be run.

Exercise 9.6. Some browsers display the location bar using only Latin characters, typically, by converting URL that contain both Latin characters and non-Latin Unicode characters using *Punycode* encoding [136], which encodes every Unicode character as one or more ASCII characters:

1. Which abuse this defense is designed to prevent? Identify, with example.
2. Is there a risk of abuse of such browsers for domain-name hacking? (See Section 8.1.5.2.) Explain with examples.

Exercise 9.7. Consider an encrypted password file design using a cryptographic co-processor as in Section 9.4.1:

1. Consider a design where the entries in the encrypted password file EPW(u) are the encryption $E_{k_E}(PW_u)$ of user u's password PW_u, using the symmetric encryption key k_E. Suppose that the co-processor does not limit the rate of password verifications and produces output for the verification of a given purported password PW_u against the encrypted entry EPW$[u]$ in 1 microsecond. Suppose that half of the passwords in the file are included in a dictionary of one million passwords. Explain how the password of any user u can be found in 1 second or less with probability half or more.
2. How long would it take to find the password any user u with probability half, if the rate of verifications was limited to one

operation per T_{AU} seconds, e.g., with $T_{AU} = 0.1s$, i.e., allowing up to 10 verifications per second (for all users)?

3. The design in Section 9.4.1 is a bit different, in particular, password operations requires input of the user identify u, and the rate of verifications for each specific user u is limited to one in every T_U seconds, e.g., with $T_U = 10$. How long would it now take to find the password of a any user u with probability half? — Assume 10,000 users.
4. Explain why the limitation is placed only on the verification operations and not on the encryption operation.

Exercise 9.8 (A vulnerable hash chain using a OWF). Given an n-bits string x, let $pl(x)$ be the maximal number such that the $pl(x)$ most significant bits of x are all 1; i.e., $x = x \vee (1^{pl(x)} + 0^{n-pl(x)})$ and for every j s.t. $pl(x) < j \leq n$ holds $x \neq x \vee (1^j + 0^{n-j})$. Let $h' : \{0,1\}^* \to \{0,1\}^n$, and define $h : \{0,1\}^* \to \{0,1\}^n$ as follows:

$$h(x) \equiv h'(x) \vee (1^{pl(x)+1} + 0^{n-(pl(x)+1)}) \tag{9.9}$$

- Show that if h' is a OWF, then h is also a OWF.
- Show that a hash chain using h as the hash function would be insecure.
- Show that the same also holds for a hash chain using h as the hash function, when using the Leighton–Micali design (Section 9.6.2.1). **(Harder)**

Hint: exploit the fact that even when the input to a hash function is distributed randomly, the output may not be uniformly random.

Exercise 9.9 (Hash chain). In Exercise 9.8 we presented a hash function h which is a OWF (assuming an underlying function h' is a OWF), yet, a hash chain using h would be vulnerable.

1. Assume that h' is *also* known to be a SPR hash function. Would h, constructed from h' as in Equation (9.9) be a SPR hash function too?
2. Extend the solution to Exercise 9.8 to show a that the hash chain construction may be vulnerable, even when using a hash function which is *both a one-way function and a second-preimage-resistant hash function.*

3. Recall the improved hash chain design proposed by Micali and Leighton (Section 9.6.2.1), i.e., to compute x_i as: $x_i = h(x_{i-1}||i)$. Obviously, h cannot be a permutation over its inputs; present an alternative assumption which suffices to make this design secure.
4. *Challenge:* Is it true that the hash chain construction may be vulnerable, even when using a hash function which is *both a* OWF *and a CRHF*? Prove it or present a counterexample.

Exercise 9.10 (Improved hash chain). Recall the improved hash chain design proposed by Micali and Leighton (Section 9.6.2.1), i.e., to compute x_i as $x_i = h(x_{i-1}||i)$. Obviously, h cannot be a permutation over its inputs; present an alternative assumption which suffices to make this design secure.

Exercise 9.11 (HOTP resynchronization and clone-detection). Recall that in the HOTP design, the server checks received purported OTPw values against s allowed values, to allow for a potential loss of synchronization (Section 9.6.3.4). Assume we use $d = 6$, $s = 10$ and that the system locks the user's account for 24 hours after five consecutive events in which an incorrect OTPw is received:

1. What is the probability of the attacker succeeding in a login attempt by sending one guess of the OTPw?
2. What is the probability of the attacker succeeding in a login attempt by sending up to five guesses of the OTPw?
3. What is the attacker strategy that succeeds to login most quickly, and how long would this take, on average?

Exercise 9.12 (FIDO). Define the contents of the FIDO2 authentication flows (Figure 9.16), based on your understanding of cryptographic protocols, and/or by consulting the FIDO2 documentation, in particular, the specifications of CTAP2 and of WebAuthn [14,271].

Chapter 10

Conclusions and Quantum Computing

Cybersecurity and cryptography are large and rapidly changing areas. Our goal was to introduce these areas, hopefully giving readers a solid foundation for understanding these challenging areas, and the ability to follow up and learn more. There are many important sub-areas that we did not cover at all and others that we have only touched briefly.

We introduced applied cryptography and discussed shared and public key cryptosystems, authentication schemes including digital signatures and message authentication code schemes, hash functions and their applications and variants, Merkle trees, blockchains, and protocols using them, including TLS.

We discussed several aspects of network security, web security and human-centered security, focusing on aspects related to cryptography, including Public Key Infrastructure (PKI), malware, login ceremonies and resiliency to exposure. We covered many attacks and defenses.

There are many important topics that we left for advanced texts and courses. Some of the important areas we did not cover (or only mentioned in few words). In cryptography, some of the topics we did not (sufficiently) cover include *concrete security, secret sharing, zero-knowledge proofs and arguments, multiparty computation, elliptic curves, lattice-based cryptography, multivariate cryptography, fully homomorphic encryption, privacy*, and *identity-based encryption.* In cybersecurity, some of these topics include the security of machine learning systems, access control, operating systems security, database security, disinformation, social networks security, risk management, security for cyber-physical systems and more.

We certainly did not cover the important *non-technical aspects of cybersecurity*, such as cybersecurity policy, law, regulations, national strategies, international relations, economics, social, mental health, ethics, insurance and more.

In the rest of this chapter, we briefly touch on three additional important areas of applied cryptography, which are all related to the important and fascinating subject of *quantum computing.*

In Section 10.1, we introduce quantum computing and discuss algorithms for quantum computers that may allow efficient solutions to problems which are believed to be computationally hard on non-quantum computers, including factoring and discrete logarithms. In Section 10.2, we discuss *post-quantum cryptography* (*PQC*), i.e., cryptographic schemes which are believed to be secure even if the attacker can use a powerful quantum computer. Finally, in Section 10.3, we discuss how quantum computing may be *used to facilitate security*; specifically, we discuss *quantum key distribution* (QKD), whose goal is to ensure *unconditionally secure key distribution.*

These three sections are mostly based on text kindly provided by my friend and colleague Walter Krawec, a leading expert in the area of quantum cryptography. I apologize for any mistakes I have introduced while editing and slightly extending Walter's text.

10.1 Quantum computers and their use in cryptanalysis

Quantum computers utilize *quantum bits* (*qubits*) to process information. Qubits are the basic unit of quantum information; a qubit is a probabilistic superposition of two basis states, which are usually denoted as $|0\rangle$ and $|1\rangle$, and represent the corresponding classical bits (0 and 1). However, a qubit can also take a *superposition* value, combining $|0\rangle$ and $|1\rangle$. We represent a qubit, say $|\psi\rangle$, as a linear combination of the two basis states, i.e., $|\psi\rangle = \alpha_0 |0\rangle + \alpha_1 |1\rangle$, where α_0 and α_1 are complex numbers called *probability amplitudes.*

Qubits have interesting properties. In particular, *we cannot measure the value of a qubit.* Namely, when we try to measure a qubit, we receive a bit, whose value is distributed based on the probability amplitudes of the qubit. For example, if you were to measure the qubit $\alpha_0 |0\rangle + \alpha_1 |1\rangle$, you would "see" (or *observe*) the basis qubit $|0\rangle$, i.e., the bit 0, with probability $|\alpha_0|^2$, and the basis qubit $|1\rangle$, i.e., the bit 1, with probability $|\alpha_1|^2$. Since the outcome must be either 0 or 1, it follows that the probability amplitudes α_0 and α_1 should satisfy $\alpha_0^2 + \alpha_1^2 = 1$.

In other words, we can only *sample* a qubit, i.e., obtain a regular bit whose value is randomly chosen based on the value of the qubit. It may seem that we can *estimate* the probability amplitudes α_0 and α_1 of the qubit $|\psi> = \alpha_0 |0\rangle + \alpha_1 |1\rangle$ by statistically sampling the distribution of the bit resulting from multiple measurements. However, this would fail: *upon measurement, the value of the qubit changes to the measured bit value.* Namely, the qubit *collapses* to the observed bit value. So, if the original qubit was in the state $\alpha |0\rangle + \alpha_1 |1\rangle$, and if someone measures it and observes $|0\rangle$, the state collapses to $|0\rangle$, that is, the qubit becomes $|0\rangle$ and the original state is destroyed.

It is also impossible to *clone* a qubit, i.e., turn a single qubit $|\psi\rangle$ into two qubits with the same value as $|\psi\rangle$; this property is called the *no-cloning* theorem of quantum mechanics. If cloning was possible, then we could have estimated the amplitudes of a qubit by cloning it and statistically sampling it.

These qubit properties, i.e., no-cloning and state collapse upon measurement, are important for cryptography and security. In particular, an attacker cannot copy quantum data (in qubits) to attack offline at a later point in time. These are some of the properties of quantum devices which facilitate QKD, whose goal is to ensure *unconditionally secure key distribution*, and other designs using quantum computing to improve security; we discuss some of these in Section 10.3.

While measuring a qubit causes it to collapse, and we can't clone a qubit, *some* operations on qubits are possible; we refer to these by the term *quantum gates*. In this section, we discuss quantum computing, i.e., computing using quantum gates, including quantum gates operating on *quantum registers*. As we discuss, quantum computing can be a powerful computational tool, which may allow efficient solutions to hard computation problems including efficient cryptanalysis attacks on classical public key cryptosystems such as RSA and DH.

Quantum gates, registers, and algorithms: *Quantum gates* are operations on qubits and on *qubits registers*, which are ordered sets of qubits. The probability distribution of the different qubits in a quantum register may be dependent; i.e., a register containing n qubits, represents a probability distribution over 2^n basis states. We denote the 2^n basis states of the qubits in an n-qubits register by $\{|0^n\rangle, |0^{n-1}1\rangle, \ldots, |1^n\rangle\}$. Therefore, a quantum gate is an operation over distributions of an exponential number of states.

We denote a register $|R\rangle$ of n qubits as a linear combination of the 2^n basis states, i.e., as $|R\rangle = \sum_{\rho=0^n}^{1^n} \alpha_\rho |\rho\rangle$. When a qubits register $|R\rangle$ is measured, the result is the basis state ρ with probability α_ρ^2. Hence, for any valid state $|R\rangle = \sum_{\rho=0^n}^{1^n} \alpha_\rho |\rho\rangle$, the probability amplitudes α_ρ should satisfy

$$\sum_{\rho=0^n}^{1^n} \alpha_\rho^2 = 1 \tag{10.1}$$

Quantum computers apply quantum operations (gates) and then measure the final outcome; quantum algorithms are algorithms that use quantum operations, i.e., algorithms that are designed to be used on a quantum computer. The fact that quantum registers represent a probability distribution over 2^n basis states allows some quantum algorithms to have considerably lower time-complexity compared to known non-quantum algorithms, or even compared to proven lower bounds on the time complexity of non-quantum algorithms. Let us discuss a few of the most well known quantum algorithms, mainly, *Grover's algorithm* [221], published by Grover in 1996, and *Shor's algorithms* [440], published by Shor in 1994.

Grover's algorithm: Grover's algorithm, also known as the *quantum search algorithm*, allows us to search a table of n arbitrary (unsorted) entries for a particular value, finding the result in expected time $O(\sqrt{n})$. This is a *quadratic speed-up* compared to the best-possible search using non-quantum operations, whose expected time to find the correct value is $n/2$, since it needs to check the value of half of the entries until it finds the correct value.

From the cryptographic point of view, we can think of Grover's algorithm as a *quantum exhaustive search algorithm*. This is since

Grover's algorithm allows to invert an arbitrary function f, i.e., given an image y, find x such that $y = f(x)$; this allows to invert any n-bit one-way function in time $O(\sqrt{2^n}) = O(2^{n/2})$, instead of time $O(2^n)$ required by exhaustive search. Similarly, given a pair of ciphertext c and corresponding plaintext $p = D_k(c)$, where k is an n-bits shared or private key, Grover's algorithm allows us to find the key k such that $p = D_k(c)$ in time $O(2^{n/2})$.

In other words, suppose that n bits suffice to make exhaustive search impractical against an attacker using a non-quantum computer. To provide comparable security against an attacker performing the search using Grover's algorithm and using a computer with the same speed but supporting also quantum operations, we need $2n$ bits.

The quadratic improvement provided by Grover's algorithm is very significant, and can be applied to many problems. However, while many cryptographic problems can be solved by exhaustive search, there are often more efficient attacks, and, usually, it is not trivial to obtain further quadratic speedup by applying Grover's algorithm.

In particular, consider finding collisions for an n-bits hash function h. Collisions can be found by the birthday attack in time $O(2^{n/2})$, using constant storage, using a classical computer (Section 3.3.4). Grover's algorithm cannot be directly applied to provide an additional quadratic speed-up. However, other quantum algorithms can find collisions with a speedup: $O(2^{n/3})$ operations requiring $O(2^{n/3})$ storage using the BHT algorithm [103], or $O(2^{2n/5})$ operations, $O(n)$ qubits and $O(2n/5)$ storage using the algorithm of Ref. [123].

Both algorithms seem to require excessive storage requirements, and their speedup over the birthday attack is less than quadratic. Therefore, it appears that using hash functions with digest length of $n = 256$ bits, e.g., SHA-256, is still sufficiently secure, even if quantum computers become available. That is, unless, or until, significant stronger quantum cryptanalysis attacks will be found.

Other quantum algorithms may provide even higher speedup for specific problems. For example, Kuwakado and Morii show in Ref. [309] a quantum algorithm that distinguishes in polynomial time between a random permutation and the three-rounds Feistel construction cipher (Section 2.8.3). This is an *exponential* speedup compared to classical attacks. However, the practical implications of this result are limited, first, since it is only distinguishing and not exposing keys, and second, since it only applies to the (three rounds) Feistel construction cipher. DES uses more rounds, and AES does not use the Feistel construction design at all.

Grover's algorithm remains, so far, the most significant quantum algorithm for attacking block ciphers such as AES, providing 'only' a quadratic speedup over exhaustive search. Therefore, if AES with keys of 128 bits provides sufficient security against classical (non-quantum) attacks for a particular application, then keys of 256 bits should suffice also against attacks using quantum computers (with the same speed for each operation).

We next discuss Shor's algorithms, which, similarly to Ref. [309], provide an exponential speedup; however, Shor's algorithms are applicable to very practical problems such as factoring and discrete logarithm.

Shor's algorithms: In 1994, Shor presented several related quantum algorithms [440], which allow efficient, polynomial time solutions to several problems which are considered hard (on classical computers), including *factoring* and computing *discrete logarithms.* Shor's algorithms involves non-quantum pre-processing and post-processing steps, which reduce several problems to a specific problem, which Shor shows how to solve efficiently using quantum operations.

The hardness of the *factoring* and *discrete logarithms* problems is essential to the security of classical public key algorithms such as RSA, DH and cryptographic schemes based on elliptic curves such as the ECIES public key cryptosystem [348] and the ECDSA signature scheme [270]. Given a quantum computer supporting operations on a sufficient number of qubits, it would thus become possible to break these, and several other, public key cryptographic schemes [440]. Such schemes should, therefore, be replaced by alternative, post-quantum cryptographic (PQC) schemes; see Section 10.2.

Practical impact of quantum computing on cryptography: Quantum computers have not yet developed to allow operations on sufficiently-large qubit registers, to allow their use to efficiently break real-world systems, such as RSA (using currently deployed key lengths, see Table 6.1). For instance, the number of qubits needed to successfully factor an RSA composite $n = pq$ is several times the number of bits of n; the number may even be measured in the millions, depending on how "noisy" or imperfect those qubits are. Existing quantum computing platforms suffer from high noise.

However, once such systems are available, it is estimated, in Ref. [204], that the time required to break an RSA key would only be a number of hours. This estimate is using plausible assumptions on quantum hardware.

There have been considerable, rapid progress in the development of quantum computers, and it seems possible that within several years or few decades, quantum computers may be able to efficiently run Shor's algorithm, for significant problem sizes, possibly breaking RSA, DH and more. It is therefore important to design and study systems that will remain secure, even against adversaries which can use such a quantum computer.

We hope that this abbreviated discussion gives the reader some feeling for the differences between quantum computing and classical computing. For a proper introduction to quantum computing, see, e.g., Refs. [381, 496].

Two directions of research, *quantum cryptography* and *post-quantum cryptography*, aim to build systems secure against quantum-enabled adversaries, i.e., adversaries who are able to execute quantum algorithms in addition to classical algorithms. Both directions have advantages and disadvantages:

Post-quantum cryptography (PQC): PQC [65, 379] are cryptographic schemes using computational hardness assumptions which are assumed to be hard even for quantum computers to solve. PQC schemes use classical information processing, i.e., they are compatible with the existing Internet and computing technologies, and do not require new communication infrastructure or hardware. However, their security depends on unproven computational assumptions. We discuss PQC in Section 10.2.

Quantum cryptography: Quantum cryptography [107, 401] uses properties of quantum physics to design devices which ensure security, without requiring unproven computational assumptions. Section 10.3 discusses quantum cryptography, and specifically QKD, whose goal is to ensure *unconditionally secure key distribution.*

Both fields hold many fascinating open research problems; they can also be combined into hybrid systems. We first discuss PQC, which addresses the concern we just discussed, namely, the possibility that improved quantum computing devices may allow efficient cryptanalysis of public key schemes.

10.2 Post-Quantum Cryptography (PQC)

PQC uses classical information processing to achieve security against adversaries with quantum (and classical) computing capabilities.

As we discussed above, Grover's algorithm can significantly reduce the time required for exhaustive search, which is an effective attack against strong block ciphers, such as AES. However, the speedup is 'only' quadratic; therefore, we can defend against it by doubling the key length, compared to the key length sufficient against exhaustive search with a non-quantum computer. There are no known quantum algorithms that provide better speedup against AES; therefore, AES, with keys of 256 bits, is considered a post-quantum secure scheme. Similarly, cryptographic hash functions such as SHA-256 are also considered post-quantum secure.

However, important public key cryptosystems and digital signatures, including designs based on factoring (e.g., RSA) and on discrete-log (e.g., DH, El-Gamal and elliptic curves schemes) are vulnerable to attacks using quantum computers, with Shor's algorithms. This motivates extensive efforts to identify and standardize public key cryptosystems and signature schemes that will be secure against attackers with quantum computing capabilities.

One particularly interesting approach to the development of cryptographic schemes robust to advances in algorithms for specific problems is the design of PKC schemes based on *lattice* problems. Lattice problems seem resilient to quantum-computing; furthermore, some of the results in this area have proofs of security based on the general and well-founded complexity assumption of NP-completeness. Details are beyond our scope; see, e.g., Refs. [23, 398].

NIST [11, 363, 389] is leading an effort to evaluate and standardize *post-quantum public key cryptographic schemes*, i.e., schemes which would remain secure even when large-scale quantum computing becomes feasible. The stated goal is for this to be an open process, reaching community consensus on multiple post-quantum public key schemes. The scope include post-quantum schemes for signatures, public key encryption, mainly using a key encapsulation mechanism (KEM), and public key key agreement protocols.

There are two motivations to identify *multiple* post-quantum public key schemes (for the same goal, e.g., signatures or KEM). The first reason is *redundancy:* if a newly discovered vulnerability is found in one scheme, making attacks easier, then another scheme could be used. For especially sensitive applications, one can use a robust combiner to combine two schemes into a single scheme which will remain secure even if one of the two is broken, at the cost of suffering the performance overhead of both schemes. See Appendix A of FIPS 204 [386].

The second reason to identify multiple schemes is that *different schemes offer different tradeoffs* between security categories, public and private key sizes, block/signature size, computational complexity and other measures.

To allow designers to choose a PQC scheme which is sufficiently secure for a given application, NIST classifies PQC schemes, with different parameter values, to one of five categories, defined based on estimated security strength (with 1 being the weakest and 5 being the strongest). The categories provide a rough estimate of the security of the PQC public key scheme, with the specified values for its parameters, by comparing it to the security of symmetric cryptographic schemes to an attacker with comparable capabilities, including the use of quantum computers. Categories 1, 3 and 5 are compared to the security of breaking a secure block cipher, e.g., AES, with key length of 128, 192 and 256 bits, respectively. Similarly, categories 2 and 4 are compared to the security of finding a collision for a collision-resistant hash, e.g., SHA-3, with digest length of 256 and 384 bits, respectively.

So far, the effort resulted in three draft standards (*FIPS*); two additional algorithms have been selected to be standardized:

FIPS 203 (ML-KEM) [387]: The *Module-Lattice based key encapsulation mechanism* (ML-KEM), based on the CRYSTALS-Kyber design [95].

FIPS 204 (ML-DSA) [388]: The *Module-Lattice based Digital Signature Algorithm* (ML-DSA), based on the CRYSTALS-Dilithium design [161].

FIPS 205 (SLH-DSA) [388]: The *stateless hash based Digital Signature Algorithm* (SLH-DSA), based on the SPHINCS+ algorithm [64]. SPHINCS+ is an improvement of the previously published SPHINCS algorithm [63]. SLH-DSA uses extensively Merkle trees (Section 3.7.2), improving dramatically upon the simpler-and-weaker hash-based signatures discussed in Section 3.4.2. SLH-DSA can be implemented with different hash functions; the standard supports the SHAKE [33] and the SHA-2 hash functions.

FALCON (FN-DSA): The FALCON [188, 457] signature scheme was selected by NIST but not yet published as a FIPS. It is expected to be published soon, probably as FIPS 206.

HQC: The HQC [193] (Hamming Quasi-Cyclic) key encapsulation mechanism was also selected by NIST but not yet published as a FIPS. HQC is based on the hardness of decoding random linear codes; since this is a different problem than the one used by ML-KEM (Kyber), HQC may provide an alternative, in case that a vulnerability is discovered in ML-KEM.

Two specifications for *stateful hash-based signature schemes* were also published, as NIST recommendation SP 800-208 [132]. The first is the *eXtended Merkle Signature Scheme* (XMSS), defined in RFC8391 [258], and the second is the *Leighton–Micali signature scheme* (LMS), defined in RFC8554 [351].

Table 10.1 compares the size, in bytes, of the public keys and of signatures using the different variants of several of these post-quantum signature schemes.

The first important observation is that all of these schemes have significantly longer signatures than the comparable classic (non-quantum) signatures. FALCON has the shortest signatures, but even

Table 10.1. Security and performance tradeoffs for post-quantum signature schemes.

Scheme	Identifier	Security Category	Pub. Key (bytes)	Signature (bytes)	Sign (cycles)	Verify (cycles)
ML-DSA (FIPS 204)	44	2(≈SHA3-128)	1312	2420	**333,013**	118,412
	65	3 (≈AES-192)	1952	3309	529,106	179,424
	87	5 (≈AES-156)	2592	4627	642,192	279,936
SLH-DSA-SHAKE (FIPS 205)	128s	1 (≈AES-128)	**32**	7856	4,682,570,992	4,764,084
	128f	1 (≈AES-128)	**32**	17088	239,793,806	12,909,924
	192s	3 (≈AES-192)	48	16224	8,091,419,556	6,465,506
	192f	3 (≈AES-192)	48	35664	386,861,992	19,876,926
	256s	5 (≈AES-256)	64	29792	7,085,272,10[illegible]	10,216,560
	256f	5 (≈AES-256)	64	49856	763,942,25[illegible]	19,886,032
FALCON (FIPS 206?)	512	1 (≈AES-128)	897	**666**	1,009,764	**81,036**
	1024	5 (≈AES-256)	1793	1280	2,053,08[illegible]	160,596

Note: The smallest values are marked using **bold** font.
Source: Data is from Ref. [482].

FALCON-512, which is the weakest (category 1, i.e., roughly as strong as AES-128), has signatures of 666 bytes, about twice than 2048-bits RSA signatures, and *much* longer than the widely used elliptic curves signatures, e.g., ECDSA.

Both ML-DSA and FALCON also have much longer public keys; however, SLH-DSA has short public keys — only 32 bytes for the two 128 bit versions.

On the other hand, SLH-DSA is much slower in both signature and verification times, *and* has significantly longer signatures than the two other schemes (and hence, much longer than signatures of classical schemes). In contrast, both ML-DSA and FALCON have relatively low computational times. In fact, their computation times appear to be comparable to non-quantum ('classical') signatures (e.g., ECDSA). ML-DSA has faster signatures, and FALCON has faster verification times.

As expected, for the three schemes, the public key and signature sizes, as well as the computational time required, increase for the higher security categories.

10.3 Quantum cryptography

The underlying theme of quantum cryptography is to utilize quantum states (e.g., qubits) to perform security tasks, in a way which would be secure (even) against quantum computers. Quantum cryptography was, for a while, synonymous with QKD though, today, it encompasses additional cryptographic primitives. Still, QKD is the most celebrated result, and so we focus on it here.

With QKD, the goal is to permit two users, Alice and Bob, to establish a shared secret key. Here, security will be against a *computationally unbounded adversary* — in particular, the only assumption one needs to make on the power of the adversary is that they obey the same laws of physics that Alice and Bob do (and, of course, that these laws are as science currently believes). Note that secure key distribution against computationally unbounded adversaries is an impossible task using classical communication alone.

Multiple QKD protocols are known, each with various advantages and disadvantages. The first QKD protocol published is the *BB84 QKD protocol*, named after its two creators, Bennett and Brassard, who published it in 1984 [60]. Other protocols include B92 [59], SARG04 [5], LM05 [339] and Extended-B92 [338] just to list a few.

All of these QKD protocols take advantage of the fact that qubits, unlike classical bits, can be prepared and sent in a multitude of manners. Furthermore, due to the no-cloning theorem of quantum mechanics, any attempt to attack quantum information must be *active* as an adversary is not capable of copying the transmitted quantum information — unless there is a fundamental flaw in the theory of quantum physics.

By encoding a classical bit string (the key that Alice wants to send to Bob), in a variety of randomly chosen manners, any attempt at eavesdropping will necessarily disturb the information; the disturbance can be detected by Bob. Not only this, but for a correctly designed QKD protocol, there is a direct correlation between the amount of disturbance in the quantum channel and the maximal amount of information an adversary may hold on the transmitted information. The more bits the adversary learns, the more disturbance, and hence the more likely is the recipient (Bob) to detect the attack. This is in stark contrast to classical information, where eavesdropping can be wholly passive, and involves no disturbance to the channel.

Let us explain the basic idea of the *BB84 QKD protocol*, which is based on the *Hadamard* gate, one of the well-known quantum logic gates, the building blocks of quantum computing. The Hadamard gate takes a qubit $|i\rangle$ (for $i = 0$ or 1) and changes it to the qubit $\frac{1}{\sqrt{2}}|0\rangle + (-1)^i \frac{1}{\sqrt{2}}|1\rangle$. By applying the Hadamard gate again, to the qubit $\frac{1}{\sqrt{2}}|0\rangle + (-1)^i \frac{1}{\sqrt{2}}|1\rangle$, we receive the original qubit $|i\rangle$, i.e., the Hadamard gate reverses itself.

From this, BB84 works essentially as follows. Alice chooses a random bit; we denote this bit by k, or as the qubit $|k\rangle$. The protocol will share the bit k with Bob, and then k will become one bit in the key to be shared between Alice and Bob. Alice then randomly chooses whether or not to apply the Hadamard gate to this qubit $|k\rangle$. She keeps secret both choices (her key bit k and her choice whether to use the Hadamard gate) and sends the resulting qubit to Bob. Now, when Bob receives the qubit, he alerts Alice to this fact using a classical authenticated channel. At this point Alice reveals to Bob whether she applied the Hadamard gate to $|k\rangle$ or not. If she did, then Bob also applies the Hadamard gate to the qubit he received; otherwise,

Bob uses the qubit as received. At this point, the qubit that Bob has received should be of the form $|k\rangle$ and so Bob will measure and learn the key bit k.

But what happens if there is a MitM adversary, say Mal? Let's assume that Mal captures the qubit when it travels from Alice to Bob. Mal cannot make a copy due to the no cloning theorem. Also, if Mal tries to extract information by measuring the qubit, then Mal may destroy the state since Mal does not know if Alice used the Hadamard gate or not. If Mal measures right away and Alice did use the Hadamard gate, then Mal will get a random outcome and the original state collapses. Similarly, if Mal applies the Hadamard gate (guessing that Alice did so), but Alice did not use the Hadamard gate, then, again, the measurement afterwards would be random. In other words, any attack has a chance of destroying the qubit and, furthermore, potentially gives random information. Due to state collapse, this interference can be detected by Bob.

Security proofs for QKD protocols generally involve the following process: first determine what observations users can make on the quantum channel (for instance what is the probability of an error in the quantum signal). Second, use this information to upper-bound an adversary's information on the raw key transmission. From this, classical error correction and a cryptographic process of *privacy amplification* are performed to derive a final secret key.

One important property of a QKD protocol is its *key rate*, denoted r, which is the ratio of secret key bits to number of qubits sent. Another important property is the *noise tolerance* of the protocol — that is the noise threshold for which the key-rate becomes zero as an adversary has potentially too much information. We use Q to denote the probability of an error in the quantum signal.

For BB84, when $Q = 0$ (there is no noise), the key-rate is $r = 1$, meaning that the users get one secret key bit for every qubit sent. When $Q = 11\%$, the rate r drops to zero; thus, BB84's noise tolerance is 11%. Between these two extremes, the rate is strictly positive but decreasing as Q increases.

QKD, and quantum communication in general, can be achieved in a variety of ways. Typically photons are used to encode and transmit quantum information but even here there are several degrees of freedom within the photon that may be used by Alice and Bob to encode their key information. Typically, polarization, phase and timing are considered. These photons may be transmitted over fiber channels or through free space (including the use of satellites for QKD) [401].

While QKD security in the ideal setting is information theoretic and does not require any computational assumptions on the adversary, one weakness of current QKD progress is in the numerous opportunities for side channel attacks on the actual devices due to the imprecision of current-day devices. This can include attacks involving Alice's source (which may not create one qubit each time but perhaps multiple copies by accident) and attacks involving Bob's measurement device. However, there are technological countermeasures to these attacks. There are also alternative protocols which can be proven secure using an even stronger security model such as *measurement device independence* [72, 441], where the adversary is assumed to fully control the measurement devices thus mitigating any side channel attack against them.

considered, these photons may be transmitted over fiber channels or through free space, including the use of satellites for QKD [40].

[illegible]

and does not require any computational assumptions on the adversary. One weakness of the current QKD progress is the numerous opportunities for side-channel attacks on the optical devices due to the imperfection of current-day devices. This can include attacks involving [illegible] perhaps multiple copies by accident) and attacks involving the measurement device. However, there are technological countermeasures to these attacks. There are also alternative protocols which can be proven secure using an even stronger security model such as measurement device independence [42, 44], where the adversary is assumed to fully control the measurement devices, thus mitigating any side-channel attack against them.

Appendix A

Background

A.1 Background: computational complexity

Most cryptographic schemes assume restrictions on the computational abilities of the adversary, although there are also definitions and constructions of *unconditionally secure* cryptographic schemes (e.g., one-time pad (OTP), see Section 2.5). Restrictions on the computational ability of the adversary rules out attacks which are usually infeasible in practice, such as *exhaustive search* — trying out all possible keys (Section 2.4.1).

How, however, can we give a well-defined meaning to a restriction on the adversary's computational abilities? This can be quite tricky. However, the theory of *computational complexity* provides an elegant solution. In this introductory book, we only use a few basic notions and properties from the theory of complexity, which we summarize in this subsection. Hopefully, this will suffice to allow readers who are not familiar with computational complexity to follow this textbook. It may also motivate some readers to take a course or read one of the many excellent textbooks on computational complexity, e.g., Refs. [134, 211], which will provide a more complete and precise coverage. Our discussion uses a few notations from Table 1.1.

Comparing the run-time of algorithms: The main measure we use for computational resources required by a given algorithm, is the maximal run-time of the algorithm, when run over a specific computer (machine); note that this is also a bound on their space (memory) requirements. The theory of complexity defines precise, simplified *computation models*, which corresponds to the capabilities of the machine (computer) on which the algorithm will be run. The run-time is the number of operations (steps) required by the algorithm when using the specified computation model.

The number of operations of an algorithm depends on its inputs. It is useful to bound the run-time of the algorithm as a function of a value which characterizes the 'difficulty' of the inputs. One simple measure is the *length*, in bits, of the inputs to the algorithm. In this book, we focus on this measure. Namely, we say that the run-time of an algorithm $\mathcal{A}$ is bounded by function $T_{\mathcal{A}}$, if the number of steps of the algorithm for any input x can never exceed $T_{\mathcal{A}}(|x|)$.

Time and space complexities, and the big-O notation: We usually compare algorithms in terms of their *time and space complexities*, which are simplified bounds on the runtime and on their storage (memory) requirements, respectively.

We often use the big-O notation to compare the (time and space/memory) complexities of an algorithm. The big-O notation bounds the *asymptotic* value of the function, ignoring any multiplicative factors. Given two functions f and g, defined over the integers, we say that f is in $O(g)$, which we denote by denote this by $f(n) = O(g(n))$, if

$$(\exists c > 0) \lim_{n \to \infty} \frac{f(n)}{g(n)} < c \tag{A.1}$$

Or, equivalently, there are some constants $c, n_0 > 0$ such that for all $n > n_0$, holds $\frac{f(n)}{g(n)} < c$. In particular, $g(n) = O(g(n))$ (which follows easily for $c = 1$).

A function f can have multiple big-O notations; we use the most compact and tight, e.g., $3 \cdot n^2 + 5 \cdot n = O(n^2)$. More generally, if $f(n)$ is a polynomial, $f(n) = c_0 + c_1 \cdot n + \cdots + c_l \cdot n^l$ where $c_l \neq 0$, then we would use $f(n) = O(n^l)$ as the natural, and simple, big-O notation. By doing this, it becomes easier to compare the asymptotic behavior of functions.

Note that the big-O notation is closed under addition and multiplication by a constant. Namely, consider two functions which are $O(g(n))$, say $f(n) = O(g(n))$ and $f'(n) = O(f(n))$. Then, for any constants $c, c' > 0$ holds that $f''(n) = O(g(n))$, where $f''(n) = c \cdot f(n) + c' \cdot f'(n)$. For example, $O(3 \cdot n^2 + 5 \cdot n) = O(n^2)$.

The big-O notation is convenient to compare the runtime and the space (i.e., storage/memory) requirements of algorithms. Let $T_{\mathcal{A}}(n)$ denote an upper bound on the run time of algorithm $\mathcal{A}$, where n is the number of bits in the input to $\mathcal{A}$. We say that $\mathcal{A}$ has *time-complexity* $O(f(n))$ if $T_{\mathcal{A}}(n) = O(f(n))$, i.e., if the run-time of $\mathcal{A}$ is in $O(f(n))$. For example, we say that the time complexity of algorithm $\mathcal{A}$ is at most *linear*, if $T_{\mathcal{A}}(n) = O(n)$. Similarly, we say that the time complexity is *polynomial* if $T_{\mathcal{A}}(n) = O(n^c)$ and that it is *exponential* if $T_{\mathcal{A}}(n) = O(c^n)$, both for any constant c.

Efficient probabilistic polynomial time (PPT) algorithms and functions: We refer to algorithms whose time complexity is polynomial as *efficient algorithms*. Other terms you may see include *polynomial-time* or *polytime* algorithms, or the term probabilistic polynomial time (PPT), which emphasizes the fact that the algorithm can be randomized.

Security mechanisms, and in particular cryptographic schemes, should be efficient yet ensure security against adversaries with reasonable capabilities, in particular, computational capabilities. To properly study security, we need a precise definition for these terms ('efficient' and 'reasonable computational capabilities').

Definition A.1 (Efficient PPT algorithms and efficiently computable functions). Let A be a deterministic or probabilistic algorithm. We say that A is a *efficient (or PPT)*, if the time complexity of A is polynomial, i.e., $O(n^c)$ for some constant c. Namely, there is some polynomial p such that when A is given any input x, then A terminates after performing at most $p(|x|)$ operations, i.e., after running time which is bounded by a polynomial p applied to the length of the input x to the algorithm A. We use PPT to denote the set of all efficient (PPT) algorithms; namely, $\mathcal{A}$ is efficient if $\mathcal{A} \in PPT$.

We say that f is an *efficiently computable function*, and write $f \in PPT$, if there is an efficient algorithm A that computes f.

A problem is said to be *hard* if there is no efficient algorithm that solves it (with significant probability of success).

Note that efficient algorithms *could* have *impractical* runtime (or space complexity), i.e., 'efficient' algorithms can still be impractical. For example, for $n = 1024$, we have $2^n = 2^{1024} \ll n^{103} = 2^{10\cdot 103} = 2^{1030}$, i.e., an algorithm whose time complexity is bounded by the (polynomial) n^{103} would still be impractical for most applications where the input size can be $n = 1024$. However, the time complexity of polynomial-time algorithms rarely has a degree as high as 103, in fact, only very, if any, proposed PPT algorithms have degree larger than 10 (usually much less). Furthermore, exponential functions grow very quickly. Therefore, it is relatively uncommon for algorithms with exponential time-complexity to be still usable for practical purposes.

The computational model: Definition A.1 does not specify the *computation model*, i.e., what operations can the algorithm perform in a single time unit. In other words, we did not specify the computer on which the program runs: can the algorithm multiply numbers as a single operation, or only add numbers? What is the size of the registers (basic storage units), e.g., can the algorithm add two 32 bit numbers as a single operation, or maybe two 64 bit numbers? Surely, such aspects can influence the number of operations required to perform a given computation (algorithm).

Considering a specific computational model will make it much more difficult to evaluate the efficiency of algorithms, since their performance will depend on the specific machine (computer) on which they run; indeed, this is the reason that computer benchmarks consider a mix of different applications and algorithms.

Luckily, however, the asymptotic computational complexity of algorithms changes only by a constant, when changing between different typical computational models. Namely, the big-O notation for the computational complexity does not depend on the specific computational model or the specific computer running the algorithm. In particular, if an algorithm is efficient in one typical computational model or computer, then it is also efficient in other typical computational models and computers. This includes computers with arbitrary (yet fixed) register size and with a wide variety of operations (essentially, every operation that can be computed efficiently). For details, see, e.g., Refs. [134, 211]. The main exception to this rule are quantum computers (Chapter 10), which support quantum operations, which may require exponential time on 'classical' (non-quantum) computers.

Note, also, that the size of the output of an efficient algorithm is necessarily bounded by a polynomial in the input length since each output operation can only produce a limited number of output bits. Therefore, we can combine two (or more) efficient algorithms, and their combination is also an efficient algorithms. This fact is important enough for us to state it properly

Fact A.1. *If $A(x)$ and $B(y)$ are efficient algorithms, then $B(A(x))$ is also an efficient algorithm.*

The $P \stackrel{?}{=} NP$ question: Let us now introduce the most famous open question in the theory of computer science: $P \stackrel{?}{=} NP$. The question refers to two classes of algorithms — P and NP. Let us first introduce these two important *complexity classes*:

- The class P is similar to PPT; it contains all *deterministic* polynomial time algorithms. Since every deterministic algorithm is also a randomized algorithm (simply never flipping coins), then $P \subseteq PPT$.
- The class NP contains functions whose solutions can be *verified* in polynomial time. Namely, if $f \in NP$, then there is a predicate[1] $v \in P$ such that $v(x, y) = \text{TRUE}$ if and only if $y = f(x)$. Note that every function in P is also in NP, i.e., $P \subseteq NP$.

The name NP stands for *non-deterministic polynomial-time*; see Refs. [134, 211] for discussion of the concept of *non-deterministic computation*. As explained there, every algorithm $\mathcal{A}$ in NP can be emulated by a deterministic algorithm $\mathcal{B}$. However, this generic emulation is inefficient: the run-time of $\mathcal{B}$ may be *exponential* in the inputs. Of course, there are many problems for which we can find a non-deterministic polynomial-time algorithm $\mathcal{A}$ but to which we can also find an efficient (deterministic or randomized polynomial-time algorithm) $\mathcal{B}$. But is this always possible? That is *the* question, at least in the theory of computer science. This question is often referred to as $P \stackrel{?}{=} NP$.

The $P \stackrel{?}{=} NP$ question asks, if the two sets, P and NP, are identical. Since $P \subseteq NP$, the only question is whether also the reverse holds, i.e., $NP \subseteq P$; if this holds then $P = NP$. This problem has been thoroughly studied, and a solution, either showing that $P = NP$ or showing that $P \neq NP$ (hence $P \subsetneq NP$), would have

[1]A predicate is simply a function whose output is always one of the two values TRUE and FALSE.

dramatic implications on several areas. In particular, many cryptographic schemes, including RSA, would be deemed insecure if it is found that $P = NP$.

The factoring problem: The factoring problem is one of the oldest problems in algorithmic number theory and is the basis for RSA and other cryptographic schemes. Basically, the factoring problem involves finding the prime divisors (factors) of a large integer. However, most numbers have small divisors — half of the numbers divide by two, third divide by three and so on. This allows efficient *number sieve* algorithms to factor most numbers. Therefore, the factoring hard problem refers specifically to factoring of numbers which have only *large* prime factors.

For the RSA cryptosystem, in particular, we consider factoring of a number n computed as the product of two large random primes: $n = pq$. It is not *known* whether factoring is in P, i.e., is efficiently computable; if it is, then there is an efficient algorithm that finds the RSA private key and allows decryption of messages. However, factoring definitely is in NP; hence, if $P = NP$, factoring is also in P, which would imply that RSA is insecure.

To see that factoring is in NP, we observe that there is an efficient algorithm to *verify* the factors of a large composite number such as $n = pq$. Namely, given p and q, there is an efficient algorithm that finds if $n = pq$. In fact, in this case, verification consists simply of multiplying p by q and comparing the result to n.

The security parameter 1^n: The running time of efficient algorithms is bounded by a polynomial in the *length of the input.* For many algorithms, this is natural since the computation required depends on the size of their inputs; for example, a B-tree allows search in time $O(\log(n))$, where n is the number of items in the tree (which is the input to the algorithm) [134].

This raises some issues when we consider cryptographic schemes and their security against an adversary. Consider, for example, a public key cryptosystem (KG, E, D). The only input required to the key generation algorithm KG is the desired key length n; consider the case where n is the length of both private and public key. If we provide the length n in binary, as typical, then this would be input of only $\log(n)$ bits to KG.

However, key generation may require computations which are polynomial in the length of the keys n, not in $\log(n)$. In fact, just outputting the generated a key containing n bits, clearly requires at least n bit-output operations. In practice, key generation requires much more work. For example, in RSA, key generation requires multiplication of primes p, q whose length is $O(n)$, as well as checking for primality and computation of the multiplicative inverse (see Section 6.5); each of these computations is polynomial in the key length n, i.e., exponential in $\log(n)$.

The solution is to provide the required key length in *unary* rather than binary (or decimal). Namely, to request generation of n output bits, we provide as input n encoded in unary, i.e., the string 1^n. We refer to this input string as the *security parameter.* We also provide the security parameter as input to the adversary since surely the adversary should be able to perform computations comparable to these of the scheme.

A.2 Background: number theory and group theory

Number theory is often used in the design and analysis of cryptographic schemes. In this section, we introduce a small part of number theory that is necessary for our study of applied cryptography, mostly focusing on *modular arithmetic.*

A.2.1 The modulo operation and modular arithmetic

Modular arithmetic is based on the *modulo* operation. The modulo operation has two inputs: an integer, say a, and a positive integer m, which is called the *modulus.* The modulo operation is denoted $a \bmod m$ and returns the *remainder* of division of the integer a by the modulus m, i.e., the number r s.t. $0 \leq r < m$ and $a = r + i \cdot m$ for some integer i. For example, $13 \bmod 4 = 1$ since $13 = 1 + 3 \cdot 4$. Note that for any given $a, m \in \mathbb{Z}$ such that $m > 0$, there is exactly one remainder of a modulo m, as the reader should be able to confirm.

We say that a and b are *congruent modulo* m, or that a is a *residue* of b modulo m, if they have the same remainder when divided by n. The remainder of a modulo m is always a residue of a. The following definition tries to make these basic concepts more clear and introduces the congruence notation.

Definition A.2 (Residue, congruence, and the modulo operation, $\mathbb{Z}_m$). Let $m > 0$ be an integer. We say that integers a and b are *congruent modulo* m, or, equivalently, that a is a *residue* of b modulo m, if $a - b$ is divisible by m, i.e., there is some integer i such that $a - b = i \cdot m$. We denote the fact that a is congruent modulo m with b by the notation:

$$a \equiv b \pmod{m}$$

We use $\mathbb{Z}_m$ to denote the set of integers from zero to $m - 1$, i.e., $\{0, \ldots, m - 1\}$. Every integer b is congruent to an integer $r \in \mathbb{Z}_m$, i.e., $0 \leq r < m$; we say that $r \geq 0$ is the *remainder* of b modulo m. For any given integer b and positive integer m, there is exactly one such remainder of b modulo m; we denote this remainder by $b \bmod m$. We refer to mod as the modulo operation and to m as the *modulus*.

The reader should be able to show that *congruence modulo* m is an *equivalence relation*, namely, that it satisfies the following properties:

Reflexivity: $a \equiv a \pmod{m}$.
Symmetry: $a \equiv b \pmod{m}$ if $b \equiv a \pmod{m}$.
Transitivity: if $a \equiv b \pmod{m}$ and $b \equiv c \pmod{m}$ then $a \equiv c \pmod{m}$.

Modular arithmetic is the computation of expressions involving arithmetic operations over integers, where the operations include modulo operations. The mod operation is applied after all 'regular' arithmetic operations, such as addition and multiplication; i.e., $(a + b \bmod m) = [(a + b) \bmod m]$.

The reader should be able to confirm the following useful, basic properties of the modular operation, which hold for every integers $a, b, m \in \mathbb{Z}$ where $m > 0$:

$$(a + b) \bmod m = [(a \bmod m) + (b \bmod m)] \bmod m \tag{A.2}$$

$$(a - b) \bmod m = [(a \bmod m) - (b \bmod m)] \bmod m \tag{A.3}$$

$$a \cdot b \bmod m = [(a \bmod m) \cdot (b \bmod m)] \bmod m \tag{A.4}$$

$$a^b \bmod m = (a \bmod m)^b \bmod m \tag{A.5}$$

Example A.1. Let $A = a_n a_{n-1} \ldots a_2 a_1 a_0$ be an $n+1$-digits number. Let us use Equations (A.2) and (A.4) to prove that A is divisible by 3 if and only if the sum of its digits $\sum_{i=0}^{n} a_i$ is divisible by 3:

$$\begin{aligned}\sum_{i=0}^{i}(10^i a_i) \bmod 3 &= \sum_{i=0}^{i}(10^i a_i \bmod 3) \bmod 3 \\ &= \sum_{i=0}^{i}[(10^i \bmod 3)(a_i \bmod 3)] \bmod 3 \\ &= \sum_{i=0}^{i}[(1)(a_i \bmod 3)] \bmod 3 \\ &= \sum_{i=0}^{i}(a_i \bmod 3) \bmod 3 \\ &= \sum_{i=0}^{i} a_i \bmod 3\end{aligned}$$

The reader can prove the similar rule for division by 9.

Exercise A.1. Use Equation (A.5) to show that for any integers a, b holds: $a^b \bmod (a-1) = 1$.

Similar properties hold for any polynomial $p(x)$ with integer coefficients and input ($x \in \mathbb{Z}$), as well as for a polynomial $p(x_1, x_2, \ldots)$ with integer coefficients and multiple integer parameters ($x_1, x_2, \ldots \in \mathbb{Z}$):

$$[p(x)] \bmod m = [p(x \bmod m)] \bmod m \tag{A.6}$$

$$[p(x_1,\ x_2, \ldots)] \bmod m = p(x_1 \bmod m, x_2 \bmod m, \ldots) \bmod m \tag{A.7}$$

These properties often make it much easier to compute the residue of a complex expression or calculation, as the following exercise shows.

Exercise A.2. Compute the following values:

1. $9 \bmod 7$
2. $45 \bmod 7$
3. $445 \cdot \left(81 \cdot 34^{13} + 83 \cdot 33^{345}\right) \bmod 4$

Solutions:

1. $9 \bmod 7 = 2$ since $9 = 2 + 1 \cdot 7$
2. $45 \bmod 7 = 3$ since $45 = 3 + 6 \cdot 7$
3. Denote $445 \cdot \left(81 \cdot 34^{13} + 83 \cdot 33^{345}\right) \bmod 4$ by x. Then we find x as follows:

$$\begin{aligned}
x &= 445 \cdot \left(81 \cdot 34^{13} + 83 \cdot 33^{345}\right) \bmod 4 \\
&= (445 \bmod 4) \cdot \big((81 \bmod 4) \cdot (34 \bmod 4)^{13} \\
&\quad +(83 \bmod 4) \cdot (33 \bmod 4)^{345}\big) \bmod 4 \\
&= 1 \cdot \left(1 \cdot 2^{13} + 3 \cdot 1^{345}\right) \bmod 4 \\
&= \left(2 \cdot 4^{6} + 3\right) \bmod 4 \\
&= 3 \bmod 4 = 3
\end{aligned}$$

□

A.2.2 Multiplicative inverses

Note that *division was not* included in Equations (A.2)–(A.7); in fact, division of two integers, $\frac{a}{b}$, is not always an integer — hence, $\left(\frac{a}{b}\right) \bmod m$ may not even be defined.

Of course, in 'regular' algebra, we often use division to solve equations; what can we do in modular arithmetic? The answer is that often — but not always — we can *multiply by the multiplicative inverse* instead of dividing. This is also true for 'regular' algebra, i.e., over the reals: every non-zero real number $x \in \mathbb{R}/0$, i.e., $x \neq 0$, has a multiplicative inverse which we denote by x^{-1} or $\frac{1}{x}$, and for any y holds $\frac{y}{x} = y \cdot x^{-1}$.

Given two positive integers, m and a, we say that *a has a multiplicative inverse modulo m*, which we denote $a^{-1} \pmod{m}$, if $a \cdot a^{-1} \equiv 1 \pmod{m}$. Without loss of generality, the multiplicative inverse is always between 1 and $m - 1$ (which makes it unique).

We briefly introduced multiplicative inverses modulo m in Section 6.2.3. In particular, we mentioned (Fact 6.5) that an integer a has multiplicative inverse modulo integer $m > 0$, if and only if a and m are *coprime*, namely, they do not have a common divisor (except 1).

If d and n are co-primes, then for every y, x holds:

$$y \cdot d \equiv x \pmod{n} \Leftrightarrow y \equiv x \cdot d^{-1} \pmod{n} \tag{A.8}$$

For example, see the following exercise.

Exercise A.3. Compute:

1. $12^{-1} \bmod 5$.
2. Find x such that $x \cdot 144 \bmod 5 = 2$.

Solution:

1. $12^{-1} \bmod 5 = (12 \bmod 5)^{-1} \bmod 5 = 2^{-1} \bmod 5$, so let's find the inverse of 2 modulo 5, which is probably a bit easier. Namely, we need to find integers a, b so that $a \cdot 2 + b \cdot 5 = 1$. One simple solution is $a = 3, b = -1$, since: $3 \cdot 2 + (-1) \cdot 5 = 1$. Hence, $12^{-1} \bmod 5 = 2^{-1} \bmod 5 = 3$. To check that we were not wrong, let us perform the modular multiplication, i.e., $(12 \cdot 12^{-1}) \bmod 5 = (12 \cdot 3) \bmod 5 = 36 \bmod 5 = 1$, as required.
2. To find this value x, we need to multiply by the multiplicative inverse of 144 modulu 5, denoted $144^{-1} \bmod 5$. As explained in proof of Fact 6.5, it is sufficient to find $(144 \bmod 5)^{-1} \bmod 5 = 4^{-1} \bmod 5$. Actually, in the previous item we already found that $2^{-1} \bmod 5 = 3$, so we can use this to know that $4^{-1} \bmod 5 = 2^{-1} \cdot 2^{-1} \bmod 5 = 9 \bmod 5 = 4$. Hence, we need to solve $x \cdot 144 \cdot 144^{-1} \bmod 5 = 2 \cdot 144^{-1} \bmod 5$, i.e., $x = 2 \cdot 4 \bmod 5$, i.e., $x = 3$. Let us check the solution: $3 \cdot 144 \bmod 5 = 12 \bmod 5 = 2$, as required.

□

The computation of multiplicative inverses allows us to compute modular division efficiently. To compute $\frac{x}{d} \bmod n$ efficiently, we multiply $x \pmod{n}$ by the multiplicative inverse $d^{-1} \pmod{n}$ (Equation (A.8)) and then reduce the result modulo n.

Can we similarly compute *exponentiation* efficiently? Equation (A.5) shows that we may reduce the *base* in the exponentiation, i.e., $a^b \bmod m = (a \bmod m)^b \bmod m$. But what about reducing the exponent b? That seems to be often even more important than reducing the base!

In the next two subsections, we present Fermat's little theorem and Euler's theorem; these theorems allow reductions in the exponent, to improve the efficiency of exponentiations.

Fermat's little theorem and Euler's theorem also provide an efficient method to compute multiplicative inverses modulo a prime (Fermat) or a composite whose factorization is known (Euler). However, recall that the factoring problem is considered hard (Section A.1); when the factors are hard to compute, computing multiplicative inverses is also hard. In fact, this is crucial to the security of the well-known and important RSA public key cryptosystem, which we discuss in Chapter 6. Specifically, in RSA, the private key is the multiplicative inverse of the public key, which means that if it is possible to efficiently compute multiplicative inverses, then RSA is insecure.

A.2.3 Fermat's little theorem and Euler's theorem

Fermat's little theorem[2] allows us to efficiently compute multiplicative inverses modulo a prime p and to simplify computation of exponentiation modulo a prime, by reducing the exponent modulo $p-1$. We already presented it briefly in Section 6.2.3, but let us repeat this important result, since we later present Euler's theorem, which generalizes Fermat's little theorem to the case of a composite modulus, allowing efficient computation of multiplicative inverses and reducing the exponent, when the factoring of the modulus is known.

Theorem A.1 (Fermat's little theorem). *For any positive integer a and prime p holds:*

$$a^p \equiv a \pmod{p} \tag{A.9}$$

Proof. See, e.g., Ref. [253]. □

When $a \not\equiv 0 \pmod{p}$, i.e., a is not a multiple of p, then a has an inverse $a^{-1} \bmod p$ (Fact 6.5), and the following follows.

Fact A.2. *For any prime p and any positive integer a such that $a \not\equiv 0 \pmod{p}$, holds $a^{p-1} = 1 \pmod{p}$. Also, the multiplicative inverse modulo p of a, i.e., $a^{-1} \pmod{p}$, is $a^{p-2} \pmod{p}$.*

[2]The name Fermat's *little* theorem helps us to distinguish this theorem from the famous *Fermat's last theorem.*

The following exercise makes another useful observation which follows (easily) from Fermat's little theorem.

Exercise A.4. Show that for any positive integer a, q, where $q \not\equiv 0 \pmod{p}$, holds:

$$\begin{aligned} a^q \bmod p &= a^{q \bmod (p-1)} \bmod p \\ &= (a \bmod p)^{q \bmod (p-1)} \bmod p \end{aligned} \tag{A.10}$$

The following exercise uses Fermat's little theorem and Fact A.2.

Exercise A.5. Compute the following, without a calculator, using Fermat's little theorem (Theorem A.1):

1. $13^{31} \bmod 31$
2. $17^{734} \bmod 4$
3. $19^{26} \bmod 17$
4. $3^{-1} \bmod 11$. Show how you confirmed your answer.

Euler's totient function and theorem: Fermat's little theorem allows us to reduce the exponent when computing modulo a prime p. We can often reduce the exponent even when computing modulo a composite number n, using *Euler's theorem* (Theorem A.3). Euler's theorem is a fundamental result from number theory, which is a generalization of Fermat's little theorem.

In order to present Euler's theorem, we must first introduce *Euler's totient function* $\phi(n)$, also referred to as *Euler's totient function.*[3]

The Euler's totient function ϕ: For every integer $n > 1$, we define $\phi(n)$ as the number of positive integers which are less than n and *co-prime* to n. Two integers i, n are *co-prime* if they do not have any common divisor (except 1, of course, which divides all integers), and the number 1 itself is considered co-prime to all (larger) integers. Namely,

$$\phi(n) \equiv |\{i \in \mathbb{N} | i < n \wedge \gcd(i, n) = 1\}| \tag{A.11}$$

where $\gcd(i, n)$ is the *greatest common divisor* of i and n, i.e., the largest integer j s.t. $0 = i \bmod j$ and $0 = n \bmod j$.

[3]The word 'totient' comes from 'how many' in Latin.

Table A.1. Euler's totient function $\phi(n)$, computed for small integers; see Equation (A.11).

n	1	2	3	4	5	6	7	8	9	10
$\phi(n)$	1	1	2	2	4	2	6	4	6	4
Factors?	None	None	None	$2 \cdot 2$	None	$2 \cdot 3$	None	2^3	$3 \cdot 3$	$2 \cdot 5$

In addition, we define $\phi(1)$ to be 1.

Euler's totient function $\phi(n)$, computed for small integers, is shown in Table A.1.

The following lemma shows that if $p > 1$ is a prime, then $\phi(p) = p-1$; see four examples in Table A.2. Furthermore, for a multiplication of two different primes p, q holds $\phi(p \cdot q) = (p-1) \cdot (q-1)$. See the two examples in Table A.1 $\phi(6) = 2$ and $\phi(10) = 4$.

Lemma A.1. *For any prime $p > 1$ holds $\phi(p) = p - 1$. For prime $q > 1$, if $q \neq p$, then $\phi(p \cdot q) = (p - 1)(q - 1)$.*

Proof. A prime p is clearly co-prime to any positive integer smaller than it, hence $\phi(p) = p - 1$.

For primes p, q, the number of positive integers smaller than $p \cdot q$ is again $p \cdot q - 1$, but some of them are divided by either p or by q. Let $A_p \equiv \{p, 2p, \cdot (q-1)p\}$ denote the set of positive integers smaller than $p \cdot q$ divided by p, and $A_q \equiv \{q, 2q, \cdot (p-1)q\}$ denote the set of positive integers smaller than $p \cdot q$ divided by q. Then,

$$\phi(p \cdot q) = (p \cdot q - 1) - |A_p \cup A_q| \tag{A.12}$$

Let us compute the size of $|A_p \cup A_q|$. First note that no positive integer smaller than $p \cdot q$ can be divided by *both* p and q, since they are (different) primes. Hence, $|A_p \cup A_q| = |A_p| + |A_q|$. Directly from the definition of each of these sets, we see that $|A_p| = q - 1$ and $|A_q| = p - 1$.

By substituting in Equation (A.12), we have

$$\phi(p \cdot q) = (p \cdot q - 1) - (p - 1) - (q - 1) = p \cdot q - p - q + 1 = (p - 1)(q - 1)$$

□

The following lemma generalizes Lemma A.1 and states that Euler's totient function is *multiplicative* for co-prime inputs, as follows.

Lemma A.2 (Euler's totient function multiplicative property). *If a and b are co-prime positive integers, then $\phi(a \cdot b) = \phi(a) \cdot \phi(b)$.*

Proof. Omitted. □

Note that if a is co-prime to both b and c, than a is co-prime to bc. Hence, Lemma A.2 generalizes to a multiplication of multiple co-primes, e.g., if each pair among a, b and c is co-prime, then $\phi(a \cdot b \cdot c) = \phi(a) \cdot \phi(b) \cdot \phi(c)$.

We are getting close to being able to compute Euler's totient function for any integer, given its factors. However, the lemmas so far do not allow us to compute Euler's totient function of an integer which is a *power of a prime*, i.e., p^i where p is a prime and i is a positive integer, or for an integer which has such factor. For example, $9 = 3^2$ and $\phi(3) = 2$, but $\phi(9) = 6$. Let us now compute Euler's totient function for p^i.

Lemma A.3. *For any prime p and integer $l > 0$ holds $\phi(p^l) = p^l - p^{l-1}$.*

Proof hint: Use the same idea as in proof of Lemma A.1. □

Given a number n and a set of pairs $\{(p_i, l_i)\}$ such that $n = \Pi_{i=i}^{n}\left(p_i^{l_i}\right)$, where $\{p_i\}$ is a set of distinct primes (all different), and l_i is a set of positive integers (exponents of the different primes), we say that $\{(p_i, l_i)\}$ is a *factorization* of n. We next observe that using the above lemmas, we can compute Euler's totient function $\phi(n)$, given the factorization of n; this generalizes the previous lemmas.

Lemma A.4. *Let $n = \Pi_{i=i}^{n}\left(p_i^{l_i}\right)$, where $\{p_i\}$ is a set of distinct primes (all different), and l_i is a set of positive integers (exponents of the different primes). Then,*

$$\phi(n) = \phi\left(\Pi_{i=i}^{n}\left(p_i^{l_i}\right)\right) = \Pi_{i=1}^{n}\left(p_i^{l_i} - p_i^{l_i-1}\right) \qquad \text{(A.13)}$$

Proof. Every pair of powers of distinct primes $(p_i^{l_i}, p_j^{l_j})$ are co-primes; hence from Lemma A.2, generalized to a multiplication of multiple co-primes, it follows that $\phi(n) = \Pi_{i=1}^{n}\phi(p_i^{l_i})$. The claim follows from Lemma A.3. □

Table A.2. Table for Exercise A.6.

n	31	93	49	81	1024	60		
Factors								
$\phi(n)$							60	108

We next present *the fundamental theorem of arithmetic*, also referred to as the *unique factorization theorem*, which says that *every* integer $n > 1$ has a *unique* factorization; hence, for every $n > 1$, we can apply Lemma A.4 to compute its Euler's totient function $\phi(n)$. The first presentation and proof of this theorem are due to Euclid; we only present the theorem, not the proof.

Theorem A.2 (The fundamental theorem of arithmetic). *Every number $n > 1$ has a unique representation as a product of powers of distinct primes.*

Proof. Omitted; see textbook in number theory or archaeology. □

Note that the number 1 is not considered as a prime (although it is considered to be co-prime with larger integers). If it was, then the theorem would have been incorrect, or should have been rephrased to exclude 1 factors.

The following exercise may improve your understanding of Euler's totient function and the different ways to compute it.

Exercise A.6. Fill in the missing values for n, factors of n and $\phi(n)$ in Table A.2.

Euler's theorem. Finally, we can now present Euler's theorem:

Theorem A.3 (Euler's theorem). *For any co-prime integers m, n holds $m^{\phi(n)} = 1 \bmod n$. Furthermore, for any integer l holds:*

$$m^l \bmod n = m^{l \bmod \phi(n)} \bmod n \tag{A.14}$$

With Euler's theorem, we now have several modular arithmetic tools. First, we have the 'basic' modular-reduction rules (Equations (A.2)–(A.7)). Second, we have Fermat's little theorem and Euler's theorem. Finally, to apply Euler's theorem, we can use Lemmas A.1–A.4 to compute the Euler's totient function $\phi(m)$ for an integer m, if we have the factorization of m.

The following exercise requires the use of these tools to compute several modular computations. The challenge, of course, is to identify and use the 'right tool' for each exercise.

Exercise A.7. Prove the following, using the appropriate 'tools' among these we learned. There may be more than one way to prove:

1. $13^{31} \bmod 31 = 13$.
2. $17^{734} \bmod 4 = 1$.
3. $27^{26} \bmod 10 = 9$.
4. $35^{841} \bmod 12 = 11$.

A.2.4 Group theory, cyclic groups and generators

In this section, we introduce a few basic notions from the domain of group theory, which are used widely in applied cryptography, and also a bit in this book.

Let us first define a *group*. A group is a pair $(G, \cdot)$ consisting of a set G of elements and an *operation* denoted $\cdot$. The operation $\cdot$ should be defined on *all pairs* of elements from G, and its outcome is always also in G, i.e., G is closed under the operation $\cdot$. In this book (and in many texts), we usually use the symbol $\cdot$ for the operation of the group, like the typical notation for multiplication, i.e., $a \cdot b \in G$ for every $a, b \in G$; we may sometimes omit the dot and simply write ab, with the same meaning, or use the standard notation for exponentiation, e.g., $a^2 \equiv a \cdot a$. Other texts may use other symbols for the group operation, e.g., $*$ or $+$; in particular, different symbols may be used to define multiple operations.

The requirements from the group operation are simple, and familiar from both regular arithmetic and modular arithmetic. Let us now define a group, including these requirements from the group operation.

Definition A.3. A group is a set G of elements and an operation, denoted $\cdot$, satisfying the following requirements:

Associativity: For every $a, b, c \in G$ holds $(a \cdot b) \cdot c = a \cdot (b \cdot c)$.
Identity element: There exists a (unique) element in G, which we call the identity element and denote by $1 \in G$, such that for every element $a \in G$ holds $a = a \cdot 1 = 1 \cdot a$.

Inverse: For each element $a \in G$, there is exactly one element $a^{-1} \in G$ such that $a \cdot a^{-1} = a^{-1} \cdot a = 1$, where 1 is the identity element. We say that a^{-1} is the *inverse* of a. (From the identity element property, it follows that the identity element is always its own inverse.)

A *commutative group*[4] is a group that also satisfies the following:

Commutativity: For every $a, b \in G$ holds $a \cdot b = b \cdot a$.

A group can be *finite* or *infinite*, i.e., contain a finite or infinite number of elements. The *order* of a finite group is the number of elements in the group. We focus on *finite commutative groups*, mainly, the prime-order multiplicative group $\mathbb{Z}_p^*$.

The *prime-order multiplicative group* $\mathbb{Z}_p^*$ is a finite group whose order is a prime number p, whose set of elements is $\mathbb{Z}_p^* = \{1, \ldots, (p-1)\}$, with the group operation, denoted $\cdot$, being multiplication modulo p.

The associativity, identity element and commutativity properties follow directly from these properties of modular multiplication.

To show the inverse property, consider any element $a \in \mathbb{Z}_p^*$, except the identity element 1 (one). From Fact A.2, a has a (unique) inverse ($a^{-1} = a^{p-2} \bmod p$). Hence, the inverse property also holds.

We use the *exponentiation notation* to denote repeated application of the group operation $\cdot$ with the same operand, i.e., $a^1 = a$ and $a^i = a^{i-1} \cdot a$ for every positive integer i. Exponentiation generalizes naturally to zero or negative exponents, with a^0 defined to be the unit element of the group, denoted simply 1, and a^{-i} defined as the multiplicative inverse of a^i.

The additive group Z_n: Another commutative group is the finite *additive group* denoted Z_n (or $\mathbb{Z}_n$), which consists of the set $\mathbb{Z}_n = \{0, 1, \ldots, (n-1)\}$, for integer $n > 1$, and where the group operation is addition modulo n. For this group, it is more natural to denote the group operation by $+$. The fact that Z_n is a group follows directly from the corresponding properties of modular addition. In particular, for any element $i \in \{0, 1, \ldots, n\}$, the inverse element is $(n - i) \bmod n$. Note that zero is the inverse of itself.

---

[4]Commutative groups are also called *Abelian groups*.

Cyclic groups and generators: We now define the important concepts of a *(finite) cyclic group* and a *generator*.

Definition A.4 (Cyclic group and generator). A group G is *cyclic*, if there is an element $g \in G$ such that for every element $a \in G$, there is an integer i such that $a = g^i$. Such an element g is called a *generator* of G.

By definition, if G is a cyclic group with generator g, then there is an integer $q > 0$ such that $g^q = 1$. Therefore, $g^{q+1} = g^p \cdot g = 1 \cdot g = g$, and, in general, $g^i = g^{i \bmod q}$. Namely, the group G contains q elements, or in other words, G is of order q.

The reader should find it easy to show the following simple observation: for every element $a \in G$, there are some positive integers, e.g. $i > 0$, s.t. $a^i = 1$. We define the *order* of an *element* $a \in G$ as the *smallest* such integer, i.e., the smallest possible integer $q > 0$ such that $a^q = 1$. The reader can also show another simple observation: a is a generator of G if and only if the order of a is the same as the order of G.

In Section 6.1.8.2 we define the discrete logarithm problem, which is another important number-theoretic problem considered computationally hard. The discrete logarithm problem is used as the basis for several public key schemes, including the El-Gamal public key cryptosystem, the Diffie–Hellman (DH) key agreement protocol, elliptic curves cryptosystems and more.

A.3 Background: probability

Probabilistic analysis and algorithms are very important for computer science in general and for cryptography in particular. However, only the very basics are required for our study of applied cryptography. For more in-depth coverage, take a course and/or read one of the many excellent textbooks, e.g., Refs. [134, 219, 358].

Probability deals with events which result in a value from some predefined set. For simplicity, we only consider a *finite* set of possible outcomes. The classical example is a coin-flip, which has two possible outcomes: Head or Tail. With a fair coin, either outcome is equally likely, and, even for a biased coin, we expect each coin-flip to be independent of other coin flips.

Let $\{x_1, x_2, \ldots, x_n\}$ denote the set of n outcomes of coin-flips, i.e., $(\forall i \leq n)\ x_i \in \{\text{Head,Tail}\}$; each of the x_i values is called a *random variable*, i.e., it is a variable whose value is set by a *random experiment*. Since we expect each coin flip to be independent of the others, it makes sense to compute the *average* number of outcomes with a given value, e.g., Head. We refer to the average fraction of Head outcomes as the *probability* (likelihood) that the random outcome of a coin flip would be Head. Let $\Pr(x = \text{Head})$ denote the probability that an outcome x of a random coin toss is Head, and denote $\Pr(\text{Tail})$ similarly. Then,

$$\begin{aligned} \Pr(x = \text{Head}) &= \lim_{n\to\infty} \frac{\sum_{i=1}^{n}\{1 \textbf{ if } x_i = \text{Head}, 0 \textbf{ else}\}}{n} \\ \Pr(x = \text{Tail}) &= \lim_{n\to\infty} \frac{\sum_{i=1}^{n}\{1 \textbf{ if } x_i = \text{Tail}, 0 \textbf{ else}\}}{n} \end{aligned} \tag{A.15}$$

Clearly, $0 \leq \Pr(x = \text{Head}) \leq 1$, $0 \leq \Pr(x = \text{Tail}) \leq 1$ and $\Pr(x = \text{Head}) + \Pr(x = \text{Tail}) = 1$. If x is the random outcome of a *fair* coin flip, then $\Pr(x = \text{Head}) = \Pr(x = \text{Tail}) = \frac{1}{2}$.

These concepts extend naturally to the any random experiment with a finite set of possible outcomes $Y = \{y_1, \ldots, y_m\}$. Again, we use x to denote the outcome of a random experiment and $\{x_1, x_2, \ldots, x_n\}$ to denote the outcomes of n experiments:

$$\begin{aligned} (\forall j : 1 \leq j \leq m) \qquad \Pr(x = y_j) &= \lim_{n\to\infty} \frac{\sum_{i=1}^{n}\{1 \textbf{ if } x_i = y_j, \ \textbf{ else } 0\}}{n} \\ \sum_{j=1}^{m} \Pr(x = y_j) = 1 \end{aligned} \tag{A.16}$$

Note that probabilities are always between zero and one. It is often convenient to refer to probability as a percentage, which is between 0 and 100. In speaking language, we often omit the word 'probability' and only refer to the percentage, as in 'I'm 100% sure I will break this system'.

We mostly deal with *uniform probabilities*, i.e., every value in $Y = \{y_1, \ldots, y_m\}$ is equally likely. We use the notation $x \stackrel{\$}{\leftarrow} Y$ to denote that x is a random value chosen *uniformly* from the finite set Y.

For any predicate $\pi : Y \to \{\text{TRUE}, \text{FALSE}\}$, let $\Pr_{x \xleftarrow{\$} Y}(\pi(x))$ denote the probability that $\pi(x) = \text{TRUE}$ when x is chosen randomly from Y. For example, for the simple predicate $\pi_{y_j}(x) \equiv \{\text{TRUE } \textbf{if } x = y_j, \text{ FALSE } \textbf{otherwise}\}$, and assuming values from Y are chosen with uniform probability, we have

$$(\forall j : 1 \leq j \leq m) \Pr_{x \xleftarrow{\$} Y} \pi_{y_j}(x) = \Pr_{x \xleftarrow{\$} Y} (x = y_j) = \frac{1}{m} = \frac{1}{|Y|} \tag{A.17}$$

Note: *We cannot choose uniformly from an infinite set.* Lucky for us, in this book we only deal with finite sets. For example, we can't pick a random string, with uniform probability, from the set of all strings (of arbitrary length).

Example A.2. Here are some simple probabilities, mostly calculated already. Try to understand the calculations, and then find the missing values:

- Let Die $= \{1, \ldots, 6\}$ be the set of possible outcomes of a die roll. Then $\Pr_{x \xleftarrow{\$} \text{Die}}(x = 5) = \frac{1}{6}$, $\Pr_{x \xleftarrow{\$} \text{Die}}(x > 3) = \frac{1}{2}$, $\Pr_{x \xleftarrow{\$} \text{Die}}$ $(x \geq 3) =$________
- $\Pr_{x \xleftarrow{\$} \{00,01,10,11\}}(x = 00) = \frac{1}{4}$, $\Pr_{x,x' \xleftarrow{\$} \{00,01,10,11\}}(x = x') =$________

Note that in the second item, we refer to the probability of a predicate π which depends on two random variables, x' and x'', chosen uniformly (and hence independently) from sets X' and X'', i.e., $\Pr_{x' \xleftarrow{\$} X', x'' \xleftarrow{\$} X''}(\pi(x', x''))$. An important special case is when $\pi(x', x'') = \pi'(x') \wedge \pi''(x'')$, i.e., the predicate π is the conjunction of two predicates π' and π'', which each depend only on one of the two inputs (x' and x'', respectively). In this case, we have

$$\Pr_{x' \xleftarrow{\$} X', x'' \xleftarrow{\$} X''}(\pi(x', x'')) = \Pr_{x' \xleftarrow{\$} X'}(\pi'(x')) \cdot \Pr_{x'' \xleftarrow{\$} X''}(\pi''(x''))$$

Namely,

$$\Pr_{x' \xleftarrow{\$} X', x'' \xleftarrow{\$} X''}(\pi'(x') \wedge \pi''(x'')) = \Pr_{x' \xleftarrow{\$} X'}(\pi'(x')) \cdot \Pr_{x'' \xleftarrow{\$} X''}(\pi''(x'')) \tag{A.18}$$

Equation (A.18) is often useful. In particular, often the same predicate π is applied to both variables x', x'', and often x' and x'' are chosen (uniformly) from the same set. This gives the following special cases:

$$\Pr_{x',x'' \xleftarrow{\$} X} (\pi'(x') \wedge \pi''(x'')) = \Pr_{x' \xleftarrow{\$} X} (\pi'(x')) \cdot \Pr_{x'' \xleftarrow{\$} X} (\pi''(x'')) \tag{A.19}$$

$$\Pr_{x',x'' \xleftarrow{\$} X} (\pi(x') \wedge \pi(x'')) = \Pr_{x' \xleftarrow{\$} X} (\pi(x')) \cdot \Pr_{x'' \xleftarrow{\$} X} (\pi(x'')) \tag{A.20}$$

Note that Equation (A.20) can be simplified, since $\Pr_{x' \xleftarrow{\$} X}(\pi(x')) = \Pr_{x'' \xleftarrow{\$} X}(\pi(x''))$, as we just use a different variable name in the two expressions (x'' and x'). Hence, we have

$$\Pr_{x',x'' \xleftarrow{\$} X} (\pi(x') \wedge \pi(x'')) = \left(\Pr_{x \xleftarrow{\$} X} (\pi(x)) \right)^2 \tag{A.21}$$

Bibliography

[1] Josh Aas. 2020.02.29 CAA rechecking bug, March 2020. https://community.letsencrypt.org/t/caa-check-incident-december-7-2015/9633. Let's Encrypt.

[2] M. Abdalla, F. Benhamouda, and P. MacKenzie. Security of the J-PAKE password-authenticated key exchange protocol. In *2015 IEEE Symposium on Security and Privacy*, pp. 571–587. IEEE, 2015.

[3] M. Abdalla, B. Haase, and J. Hesse. CPace, a balanced composable PAKE. Internet-Draft draft-irtf-cfrg-cpace-10, Internet Engineering Task Force, September 2023 Work in Progress.

[4] M. Abdalla and D. Pointcheval. Simple password-based encrypted key exchange protocols. In *Topics in Cryptology–CT-RSA 2005: The Cryptographers' Track at the RSA Conference.*, pp. 191–208. Springer, 2005.

[5] A. Acin, N. Gisin, and V. Scarani. Coherent-pulse implementations of quantum cryptography protocols resistant to photon-number-splitting attacks. *Physical Review A*, 69:012309, January 2004.

[6] A. Adams and M. A. Sasse. Users are not the enemy. *Communications of the ACM*, 42(12):40–46, 1999.

[7] D. Adrian, K. Bhargavan, Z. Durumeric, P. Gaudry, M. Green, J. A. Halderman, N. Heninger, D. Springall, E. Thomé, L. Valenta, *et al.* Imperfect forward secrecy: How Diffie-Hellman fails in practice. *Communications of the ACM*, 62(1):106–114, 2018.

[8] Association for Financial Professionals (AFP). Afp payments fraud and control survey. Survey Report, Association for Financial Professionals, 2024. Available at: https://www.afponline.org/training-resources/resources/survey-research-economic-data/Details/payments-fraud.

[9] D. Aggarwal and U. Maurer. Breaking RSA generically is equivalent to factoring. *IEEE Transactions on Information Theory*, 62(11):6251–6259, 2016.

[10] N. J. Al Fardan and K. G. Paterson. Lucky thirteen: Breaking the TLS and DTLS record protocols. In *2013 IEEE Symposium on Security and Privacy*, pp. 526–540. IEEE, 2013.

[11] G. Alagic, G. Alagic, D. Apon, D. Cooper, Q. Dang, T. Dang, J. Kelsey, J. Lichtinger, Y.-K. Liu, C. Miller, *et al.* Status Report on the Third Round of the NIST Post-Quantum Cryptography Standardization Process, 2022.

[12] W. Alexi, B. Chor, O. Goldreich, and C. P. Schnorr. RSA and Rabin functions: Certain parts are as hard as the whole. *SIAM Journal on Computing*, 17(2):194–209, 1988.

[13] N. AlFardan, D. J. Bernstein, K. G. Paterson, B. Poettering, and J. C. Schuldt. On the security of RC4 in TLS. In *22nd USENIX Security Symposium (USENIX Security 13)*, pp. 305–320, 2013.

[14] F. Alliance. Client to authenticator protocol (CTAP) — Version 2.1. Technical Report, FIDO Alliance, October 2020.

[15] J. Alwen, B. Chen, K. Pietrzak, L. Reyzin, and S. Tessaro. Scrypt is maximally memory-hard. In *Annual International Conference on the Theory and Applications of Cryptographic Techniques*, pp. 33–62. Springer, 2017.

[16] J. H. An, Y. Dodis, and T. Rabin. On the security of joint signature and encryption. In *Advances in Cryptology — Eurocrypt 2002*. Lecture Notes in Computer Science, Vol. 2332, pp. 83–107. Springer-Verlag, 2002.

[17] American National Standards Institute (ANSI). ANSI X9.23 Financial Institution Encryption of Wholesale Financial Messages, 1998.

[18] Apple. Apple Root Store Policy. Other. https://www.apple.com/certificateauthority/ca_program.html.

[19] C. Ardi and J. Heidemann. Auntietuna: Personalized content-based phishing detection. In *NDSS Usable Security Workshop (USEC)*, 2016.

[20] R. Arends, R. Austein, M. Larson, D. Massey, and S. Rose. DNS Security Introduction and Requirements. RFC 4033 (Proposed Standard), March 2005. Updated by RFCs 6014, 6840.

[21] R. Arends, R. Austein, M. Larson, D. Massey, and S. Rose. Protocol Modifications for the DNS Security Extensions. RFC 4035 (Proposed Standard), March 2005. Updated by RFCs 4470, 6014, 6840, 8198, 9077, 9520.

[22] R. Arends, R. Austein, M. Larson, D. Massey, and S. Rose. Resource Records for the DNS Security Extensions. RFC 4034 (Proposed

Standard), March 2005. Updated by RFCs 4470, 6014, 6840, 6944, 9077

[23] J. P. Aumasson. *Serious Cryptography: A Practical Introduction to Modern Encryption.* No Stratch Press, San Francisco, CA, 2017.

[24] N. Aviram, S. Schinzel, J. Somorovsky, N. Heninger, M. Dankel, J. Steube, L. Valenta, D. Adrian, J. A. Halderman, V. Dukhovni, *et al.* DROWN: Breaking TLS using SSLV2. In *25th USENIX Security Symposium (USENIX Security 16)*, pp. 689–706, 2016.

[25] A. J. Aviv, K. Gibson, E. Mossop, M. Blaze, and J. M. Smith. Smudge attacks on smartphone touch screens. In *4th USENIX Workshop on Offensive Technologies (WOOT 10)*, 2010.

[26] M. Badra. Pre-Shared Key Cipher Suites for TLS with SHA-256/384 and AES Galois Counter Mode. RFC 5487 (Proposed Standard), March 2009.

[27] M. Badra and I. Hajjeh. ECDHE_PSK Cipher Suites for Transport Layer Security (TLS). RFC 5489 (Informational), March 2009.

[28] J. Baek, R. Steinfeld, and Y. Zheng. Formal proofs for the security of signcryption. *Journal of Cryptology*, 20:203–235, 2007.

[29] M. Barbosa, G. Barthe, K. Bhargavan, B. Blanchet, C. Cremers, K. Liao, and B. Parno. SoK: Computer-aided cryptography. In *IEEE Symposium on Security and Privacy*, 2021.

[30] G. V. Bard. A challenging but feasible blockwise-adaptive chosen-plaintext attack on SSL. In M. Malek, E. Fernández-Medina, and J. Hernando, editors. *Proceedings of SECRYPT*, pp. 99–109. INSTICC Press, 2006.

[31] E. Barkan, E. Biham, and N. Keller. Instant ciphertext-only cryptanalysis of GSM encrypted communication. *Journal of Cryptology*, 21(3):392–429, 2008.

[32] E. Barker. NIST Special Publication 800-57 Part 1 Revision 4 — Recommendation for Key Management (Part 1: General), 2016.

[33] P. Barsocchi, G. Oligeri, and C. Soriente. Shake: Single hash key establishment for resource constrained devices. *Ad Hoc Networks*, 11(1):288–297, 2013.

[34] L. Bassham, W. Polk, and R. Housley. Algorithms and Identifiers for the Internet X.509 Public Key Infrastructure Certificate and Certificate Revocation List (CRL) Profile. RFC 3279 (Proposed Standard), April 2002. Updated by RFCs 4055, 4491, 5480, 5758, 8692.

[35] M. Becker and A. Desoky. A study of the DVD content scrambling system (CSS) algorithm. In *Proceedings of the Fourth IEEE International Symposium on Signal Processing and Information Technology, 2004*, pp. 353–356. IEEE, 2004.

[36] T. Be'ery and A. Shulman. A Perfect CRIME? Only TIME Will Only Tell. In *Blackhat Europe*, March 2013.

[37] M. Bellare, A. Boldyreva, and A. O'Neill. Deterministic and efficiently searchable encryption. In *Advances in Cryptology-CRYPTO 2007: 27th Annual International Cryptology Conference, Santa Barbara, CA, USA, August 19–23, 2007. Proceedings 27*, pp. 535–552. Springer, 2007.

[38] M. Bellare, R. Canetti, and H. Krawczyk. Keying hash functions for message authentication. In N. Koblitz, editor, *Advances in Cryptology — CRYPTO'96*. Lecture Notes in Computer Science, Vol. 1109, pp. 1–15. Springer-Verlag, 18–22 August 1996.

[39] M. Bellare, R. Canetti, and H. Krawczyk. HMAC: Keyed-hashing for message authentication. Internet Request for Comment RFC 2104, Internet Engineering Task Force, February 1997.

[40] M. Bellare, J. A. Garay, R. Hauser, A. Herzberg, H. Krawczyk, M. Steiner, G. Tsudik, E. V. Herreweghen, and M. Waidner. Design, implementation, and deployment of the iKP secure electronic payment system. *IEEE Journal of Selected Area in Communications*, 18(4):611–627, 4 2000.

[41] M. Bellare, J. A. Garay, R. Hauser, A. Herzberg, H. Krawczyk, M. Steiner, G. Tsudik, and M. Waidner. iKP: A family of secure electronic payment protocols. In *Proceedings of the First USENIX Workshop of Electronic Commerce*, pp. 89–106, Berkeley, July 1995. USENIX Association.

[42] M. Bellare, R. Guérin, and P. Rogaway. XOR MACs: New methods for message authentication using finite pseudorandom functions. In *Annual International Cryptology Conference*, pp. 15–28. Springer, 1995.

[43] M. Bellare, J. Kilian, and P. Rogaway. The security of the cipher block chaining message authentication code. *Journal of Computer and System Sciences*, 61(3):362–399, 2000.

[44] M. Bellare, T. Kohno, and C. Namprempre. Breaking and provably repairing the SSH authenticated encryption scheme: A case study of the encode-then-encrypt-and-MAC paradigm. *ACM Transactions on Information and System Security (TISSEC)*, 7(2):206–241, 2004. Full version of the paper 'Authenticated encryption in SSH: Provably fixing the SSH binary packet protocol' presented in ACM CCS 2002 (by the same authors).

[45] M. Bellare, T. Krovetz, and P. Rogaway. Luby-Rackoff backwards: Increasing security by making block ciphers non-invertible. In *Advances in Cryptology–Eurocrypt*, 1998.

[46] M. Bellare and C. Namprempre. Authenticated encryption: Relations among notions and analysis of the generic composition paradigm. *Journal of Cryptology: The Journal of the International Association for Cryptologic Research*, 21(4):469–491, October 2008.
[47] M. Bellare, D. Pointcheval, and P. Rogaway. Authenticated key exchange secure against dictionary attacks. In *International Conference on the Theory and Applications of Cryptographic Techniques*, pp. 139–155. Springer, 2000.
[48] M. Bellare and P. Rogaway. Random oracles are practical. A paradigm for designing efficient protocols. In *Proceedings of the 1st ACM Conference on Computer and Communications Security*, pp. 62–73, 1993.
[49] M. Bellare and P. Rogaway. Optimal asymmetric encryption. In *Workshop on the Theory and Application of of Cryptographic Techniques*, pp. 92–111. Springer, 1994.
[50] M. Bellare and P. Rogaway. The exact security of digital signatures—how to sign with RSA and Rabin. In U. Maurer, editor, *Advances in Cryptology—EUROCRYPT 96*. Lecture Notes in Computer Science, Vol. 1070, pp. 399–416. Springer-Verlag, 12–16 May 1996.
[51] M. Bellare and P. Rogaway. Collision-resistant hashing: Towards making UOWHFs practical. In *Annual International Cryptology Conference*, pp. 470–484. Springer, 1997.
[52] M. Bellare and P. Rogaway. The security of triple encryption and a framework for code-based game-playing proofs. In *Annual International Conference on the Theory and Applications of Cryptographic Techniques*, pp. 409–426. Springer, 2006.
[53] M. Bellare and A. Sahai. Non-malleable encryption: Equivalence between two notions, and an indistinguishability-based characterization. In *Advances in Cryptology-CRYPTO'99*, pp. 78–78. Springer, 1999.
[54] S. Bellovin and M. Merritt. Encrypted key exchange: Password-based protocols secure against dictionary attacks. In *Proceedings 1992 IEEE Computer Society Symposium on Research in Security and Privacy*, pp. 72–84. IEEE, 1992.
[55] S. M. Bellovin. Frank Miller: Inventor of the one-time pad. *Cryptologia*, 35(3):203–222, 2011.
[56] S. M. Bellovin. Vernam, Mauborgne, and Friedman: The one-time pad and the index of coincidence. In P. Y. A. Ryan, D. Naccache, and J.-J. Quisquater, editors. *The New Codebreakers*. Lecture Notes in Computer Science, Vol. 9100, pp. 40–66. Springer, 2016.
[57] J. Benaloh, D. S. Butler Lampson, T. Spies, and B. Yee. The private communication technology (PCT) protocol. Internet Draft,

Microsoft Corporation, October 1995. Available at: https://datatracker.ietf.org/doc/html/draft-benaloh-pct-00.

[58] J. C. Benaloh and M. de Mare. One-way accumulators: A decentralized alternative to digital signatures (extended abstract). In T. Helleseth, editor, *Advances in Cryptology — EUROCRYPT'93, Workshop on the Theory and Application of of Cryptographic Techniques, Lofthus, Norway, May 23–27, 1993, Proceedings.* Lecture Notes in Computer Science, Vol. 765, pp. 274–285. Springer, 1993.

[59] C. H. Bennett. Quantum cryptography using any two nonorthogonal states. *Physical Review Letters*, 68:3121–3124, May 1992.

[60] C. H. Bennett and G. Brassard. Quantum cryptography: Public key distribution and coin tossing. In *Proceedings of IEEE International Conference on Computers, Systems and Signal Processing*, Vol. 175. New York, 1984.

[61] Y. Berger, A. Wool, and A. Yeredor. Dictionary attacks using keyboard acoustic emanations. In *Proceedings of the 13th ACM Conference on Computer and Communications Security*, pp. 245–254, 2006.

[62] T. Berners-Lee, R. Fielding, and L. Masinter. Uniform Resource Identifier (URI): Generic Syntax. RFC 3986 (Internet Standard), January 2005. Updated by RFCs 6874, 7320, 8820.

[63] D. J. Bernstein, D. Hopwood, A. Hülsing, T. Lange, R. Niederhagen, L. Papachristodoulou, M. Schneider, P. Schwabe, and Z. Wilcox-O'Hearn. SPHINCS: Practical stateless hash-based signatures. In E. Oswald and M. Fischlin, editors, *Advances in Cryptology — EUROCRYPT*. Lecture Notes in Computer Science, Vol. 9056, pp. 368–397. Springer, 2015.

[64] D. J. Bernstein, A. Hülsing, S. Kölbl, R. Niederhagen, J. Rijneveld, and P. Schwabe. The SPHINCS+ signature framework. In *Proceedings of the 2019 ACM SIGSAC Conference on Computer and Communications Security*, pp. 2129–2146, 2019.

[65] D. J. Bernstein and T. Lange. Post-quantum cryptography. *Nature*, 549(7671):188–194, 2017.

[66] D. J. Bernstein, T. Lange, and R. Niederhagen. Dual EC: A standardized back door. In *The New Codebreakers*, pp. 256–281. Springer, Berlin, Germany, 2016.

[67] B. Beurdouche, K. Bhargavan, A. Delignat-Lavaud, C. Fournet, M. Kohlweiss, A. Pironti, P.-Y. Strub, and J. K. Zinzindohoue. A messy state of the union: Taming the composite state machines of TLS. In *2015 IEEE Symposium on Security and Privacy*, pp. 535–552. IEEE, 2015.

[68] K. Bhargavan, C. Brzuska, C. Fournet, M. Green, M. Kohlweiss, and S. Zanella-Béguelin. Downgrade resilience in key-exchange protocols. In *2016 IEEE Symposium on Security and Privacy (SP)*, pp. 506–525. IEEE, 2016.

[69] K. Bhargavan, C. Fournet, M. Kohlweiss, A. Pironti, P.-Y. Strub, and S. Zanella-Béguelin. Proving the TLS handshake secure (as it is). In *Advances in Cryptology–CRYPTO 2014: 34th Annual Cryptology Conference, Santa Barbara, CA, USA, August 17–21, 2014, Proceedings, Part II 34*, pp. 235–255. Springer, 2014.

[70] K. Bhargavan, A. D. Lavaud, C. Fournet, A. Pironti, and P. Y. Strub. Triple handshakes and cookie cutters: Breaking and fixing authentication over TLS. In *2014 IEEE Symposium on Security and Privacy*, pp. 98–113. IEEE, 2014.

[71] R. Biddle, S. Chiasson, and P. C. Van Oorschot. Graphical passwords: Learning from the first twelve years. *ACM Computing Surveys (CSUR)*, 44(4):1–41, 2012.

[72] E. Biham, B. Huttner, and T. Mor. Quantum cryptographic network based on quantum memories. *Physical Review A*, 54(4):2651, 1996.

[73] E. Biham and A. Shamir. *Differential Cryptanalysis of the Data Encryption Standard*. Springer-Verlag, Berlin, 1993.

[74] C. Bing and J. SCHECTMAN. Inside the UAE's secret hacking team of american mercenaries. Technical Report, *Reuters*, January 2019.

[75] S. Bingler, M. West, and J. Wilander. Cookies: HTTP State Management Mechanism. Internet-Draft draft-ietf-httpbis-rfc6265bis-19, Internet Engineering Task Force, February 2025. (Work in Progress; will probably be published as an RFC).

[76] R. Bird, I. Gopal, A. Herzberg, P. A. Janson, S. Kutten, R. Molva, and M. Yung. Systematic design of a family of attack-resistant authentication protocols. *IEEE Journal on Selected Areas in Communications*, 11(5):679–693, 1993.

[77] H. Birge-Lee, Y. Sun, A. Edmundson, J. Rexford, and P. Mittal. Bamboozling certificate authorities with BGP. In *27th USENIX Security Symposium*, pp. 833–849, 2018.

[78] A. Biryukov, D. Dinu, and D. Khovratovich. Argon2: New generation of memory-hard functions for password hashing and other applications. In *2016 IEEE European Symposium on Security and Privacy (EuroS&P)*, pp. 292–302. IEEE, 2016.

[79] A. Biryukov, D. Dinu, D. Khovratovich, and S. Josefsson. Argon2 Memory-Hard Function for Password Hashing and Proof-of-Work Applications. RFC 9106 (Informational), September 2021.

[80] A. Biryukov and A. Shamir. Cryptanalytic time/memory/data tradeoffs for stream ciphers. In *International Conference on the Theory and Application of Cryptology and Information Security*, pp. 1–13. Springer, 2000.

[81] A. Biryukov, A. Shamir, and D. Wagner. Real time cryptanalysis of A5/1 on a PC. In *Fast Software Encryption: 7th International Workshop, FSE 2000 New York, NY, USA, April 10–12, 2000 Proceedings 7*, pp. 1–18. Springer, 2001.

[82] J. Black, P. Rogaway, and T. Shrimpton. Encryption-scheme security in the presence of key-dependent messages. In K. Nyberg and H. M. Heys, editors, *Selected Areas in Cryptography*. Lecture Notes in Computer Science, Vol. 2595, pp. 62–75. Springer, 2002.

[83] S. Blake-Wilson, M. Nystrom, D. Hopwood, J. Mikkelsen, and T. Wright. Transport Layer Security (TLS) Extensions. RFC 3546 (Proposed Standard), June 2003. Obsoleted by RFC 4366.

[84] S. Blake-Wilson, M. Nystrom, D. Hopwood, J. Mikkelsen, and T. Wright. Transport Layer Security (TLS) Extensions. RFC 4366 (Proposed Standard), April 2006. Obsoleted by RFCs 5246, 6066, updated by RFC 5746.

[85] M. Blaze, G. Bleumer, and M. Strauss. Divertible protocols and atomic proxy cryptography. In K. Nyberg, editor, *Advances in Cryptology — EUROCRYPT'98, International Conference on the Theory and Application of Cryptographic Techniques, Espoo, Finland, May 31–June 4, 1998, Proceeding*. Lecture Notes in Computer Science, Vol. 1403, pp. 127–144. Springer, 1998.

[86] M. Blaze, J. Feigenbaum, and A. D. Keromytis. Keynote: Trust management for public-key infrastructures. In *International Workshop on Security Protocols*, pp. 59–63. Springer, 1998.

[87] M. Blaze, J. Feigenbaum, and J. Lacy. Decentralized trust management. In *Proceedings 1996 IEEE Symposium on Security and Privacy*, pp. 164–173. IEEE, 1996.

[88] D. Bleichenbacher. Chosen ciphertext attacks against protocols based on the RSA encryption standard PKCS# 1. In *Advances in Cryptology — Crypto 1998*. Lecture Notes in Computer Science, Vol. 1462, pp. 1–12. Springer, 1998.

[89] H. Böck, J. Somorovsky, and C. Young. Return of Bleichenbacher's oracle threat (ROBOT). In *27th USENIX Security Symposium (USENIX Security 18)*, pp. 817–849, 2018.

[90] H. Böck, A. Zauner, S. Devlin, J. Somorovsky, and P. Jovanovic. Nonce-disrespecting adversaries: Practical forgery attacks on GCM

in TLS. In *10th USENIX Workshop on Offensive Technologies (WOOT 16)*, 2016.

[91] D. Boneh. The decision Diffie-Hellman problem. In *International Algorithmic Number Theory Symposium*, pp. 48–63. Springer, 1998.

[92] J. Bonneau, E. Bursztein, I. Caron, R. Jackson, and M. Williamson. Secrets, lies, and account recovery: Lessons from the use of personal knowledge questions at Google. In *Proceedings of the 24th International Conference on World Wide Web*, pp. 141–150, 2015.

[93] J. Bonneau, C. Herley, P. C. Van Oorschot, and F. Stajano. The quest to replace passwords: A framework for comparative evaluation of web authentication schemes. In *2012 IEEE Symposium on Security and Privacy*, pp. 553–567. IEEE, 2012.

[94] N. Borisov, I. Goldberg, and D. Wagner. Intercepting mobile communications: The insecurity of 802.11. In *Proceedings of the Seventh Annual International Conference on Mobile Computing and Networking (MOBICOM-01), New York, July 16–21 2001*, pp. 180–188. ACM Press, 2001.

[95] J. Bos, L. Ducas, E. Kiltz, T. Lepoint, V. Lyubashevsky, J. M. Schanck, P. Schwabe, G. Seiler, and D. Stehlé. Crystals-kyber: A CCA-secure module-lattice-based KEM. In *2018 IEEE European Symposium on Security and Privacy (EuroS&P)*, pp. 353–367. IEEE, 2018.

[96] C. Bösch, P. H. Hartel, W. Jonker, and A. Peter. A survey of provably secure searchable encryption. *ACM Computing Surveys*, 47(2):18, 2014.

[97] D. Bourdrez, D. H. Krawczyk, K. Lewi, and C. A. Wood. The OPAQUE Asymmetric PAKE Protocol. Internet-Draft draft-irtf-cfrg-opaque-13, Internet Engineering Task Force, December 2023. Work in Progress.

[98] V. Boyko, P. MacKenzie, and S. Patel. Provably secure password-authenticated key exchange using Diffie-Hellman. In *Advances in Cryptology—EUROCRYPT 2000: International Conference on the Theory and Application of Cryptographic Techniques Bruges, Belgium, May 14–18, 2000 Proceedings 19*, pp. 156–171. Springer, 2000.

[99] R. Braden, D. Borman, and C. Partridge. Computing the Internet checksum. RFC 1071 (Informational), September 1988. Updated by RFC 1141.

[100] J. Brainard, A. Juels, R. L. Rivest, M. Szydlo, and M. Yung. Fourth-factor authentication: Somebody you know. In *Proceedings of the*

13th ACM Conference on Computer and Communications Security, pp. 168–178, 2006.

[101] Z. Brakerski and V. Vaikuntanathan. Efficient fully homomorphic encryption from (standard) LWE. *SIAM Journal on Computing*, 43(2):831–871, 2014.

[102] M. Brandt, T. Dai, A. Klein, H. Shulman, and M. Waidner. Domain validation++ for MitM-resilient PKI. In *Proceedings of the 2018 ACM SIGSAC Conference on Computer and Communications Security*, pp. 2060–2076, 2018.

[103] G. Brassard, P. Høyer, and A. Tapp. Quantum cryptanalysis of hash and claw-free functions. In C. L. Lucchesi and A. V. Moura, editors, *LATIN'98: Theoretical Informatics, Third Latin American Symposium, Campinas, Brazil, April 20–24, 1998, Proceedings.* Lecture Notes in Computer Science, Vol. 1380, pp. 163–169. Springer, 1998.

[104] T. Bray, editor, The JavaScript Object Notation (JSON) Data Interchange Format. RFC 8259 (Internet Standard), December 2017.

[105] B. Brewster. Portfolio: Theory and practice. *The Yale Literary Magazine*, 47(5), February 1882.

[106] M. Briceno, I. Goldberg, and D. Wagner. A pedagogical implementation of A5/1 and A5/2, 1999. Archived at: https://cryptome.org/jya/a51-pi.htm. Accessed on January 2025.

[107] A. Broadbent and C. Schaffner. Quantum cryptography beyond quantum key distribution. *Designs, Codes and Cryptography*, 78(1):351–382, 2016.

[108] Bundesamt für Sicherheit in der Informationstechnik (BSI). Kryptographische verfahren: Empfehlungen und schlussell, February 2017.

[109] CA/Browser Forum. Ballot 118 — SHA-1 sunset (passed). CA/Browser Forum Ballot, October 2014. See at: https://cabforum.org/2014/10/16/ballot-118-sha-1-sunset-passed/.

[110] P. Camacho, A. Hevia, M. Kiwi, and R. Opazo. Strong accumulators from collision-resistant hashing. In *Information Security: 11th International Conference, ISC 2008, Taipei, Taiwan, September 15–18, 2008. Proceedings 11*, pp. 471–486. Springer, 2008.

[111] J. Camenisch and A. Lysyanskaya. Dynamic accumulators and application to efficient revocation of anonymous credentials. In *Advances in Cryptology—CRYPTO 2002: 22nd Annual International Cryptology Conference Santa Barbara, California, USA, August 18–22, 2002 Proceedings 22*, pp. 61–76. Springer, 2002.

[112] R. Canetti. Universally composable security. *Journal of the ACM (JACM)*, 67(5):1–94, 2020.

[113] R. Canetti, R. Gennaro, A. Herzberg, and D. Naor. Proactive security: Long term protection against break-ins. *RSA Laboratories' CryptoBytes*, 3(1):1–8, 1997.

[114] R. Canetti and H. Krawczyk. Security analysis of IKE's signature-based key-exchange protocol. In M. Yung, editor, *Advances in Cryptology — CRYPTO 2002, 22nd Annual International Cryptology Conference, Santa Barbara, California, USA, August 18–22, 2002, Proceedings*. Lecture Notes in Computer Science, Vol. 2442, pp. 143–161. Springer, 2002.

[115] R. Canetti, H. Krawczyk, and J. Nielsen. Relaxing chosen-ciphertext security. In *Advances in Cryptology — Crypto 2003*, Vol. 2729, pp. 565–582. Springer, 2003.

[116] B. Canvel, A. Hiltgen, S. Vaudenay, and M. Vuagnoux. Password interception in a SSL/TLS channel. In *CRYPTO — Annual International Cryptology Conference*. LNCS, Vol. 2729, pp. 583–599. Springer, 2003.

[117] M. Cardwell. Detecting phishing sites using certificate transparency monitoring, January 2019. Blog post.

[118] M. M. Carvalho, J. DeMott, R. Ford, and D. A. Wheeler. Heartbleed 101. *IEEE Security & Privacy*, 12(4):63–67, 2014.

[119] Consultative Committee for International Telephony and Telegraphy (CCITT) (Blue Book). Recommendations X.509 and ISO 9594-8. Information Processing Systems-OSI-The Directory Authentication Framework (Geneva: CCITT), 1988.

[120] Consultative Committee for International Telephony and Telegraphy (CCITT) (Melbourne). Specification of Abstract Syntax Notation One (ASN.1). Open Systems Interconnection-Basic Reference Model, 1988.

[121] V. Cerf. ASCII Format for Network Interchange. RFC 20 (Internet Standard), October 1969.

[122] D. Chadwick. *Understanding X. 500: The Directory*. Chapman & Hall, Ltd., Boca Raton, FL, 1994.

[123] A. Chailloux, M. Naya-Plasencia, and A. Schrottenloher. An efficient quantum collision search algorithm and implications on symmetric cryptography. In *Advances in Cryptology–ASIACRYPT 2017: 23rd International Conference on the Theory and Applications of Cryptology and Information Security, Hong Kong, China*, pp. 211–240. Springer, December 2017.

[124] S. Checkoway, M. Fredrikson, R. Niederhagen, A. Everspaugh, M. Green, T. Lange, T. Ristenpart, D. J. Bernstein, J. Maskiewicz, and H. Shacham. On the practical exploitability of dual EC in TLS

implementations. In *Proceedings of the 23rd USENIX Conference on Security Symposium*, pp. 319–335. USENIX Association, 2014.

[125] T. Chung, J. Lok, B. C. 0002, D. R. Choffnes, D. Levin, B. M. Maggs, A. Mislove, J. P. Rula, N. Sullivan, and C. Wilson. Is the web ready for OCSP must-staple? In *Internet Measurement Conference*, pp. 105–118. ACM, 2018.

[126] R. Cialdini. *Influence: Science and Practice*, 5th edn. Allyn and Bacon, 2008.

[127] S. Cohney, M. D. Green, and N. Heninger. Practical State Recovery Attacks against Legacy RNG Implementations, 10 2017. Available at: https://duhkattack.com/paper.pdf.

[128] S. Colombo, K. Nikitin, H. Corrigan-Gibbs, D. J. Wu, and B. Ford. Authenticated private information retrieval. In *32nd USENIX Security Symposium (USENIX Security 23)*, pp. 3835–3851, 2023.

[129] D. E. Comer. *Internetworking with TCP/IP*. Addison-Wesley Professional, Boston, 2013.

[130] IEEE Computer Society and LAN/MAN Standards Committee. IEEE 802.11: Wireless LAN Medium Access Control and Physical Layer Specifications, August 1999.

[131] D. Cooper, S. Santesson, S. Farrell, S. Boeyen, R. Housley, and W. Polk. Internet X.509 Public Key Infrastructure Certificate and Certificate Revocation List (CRL) Profile. RFC 5280 (Proposed Standard), May 2008. Updated by RFCs 6818, 8398, 8399.

[132] D. A. Cooper, D. C. Apon, Q. H. Dang, M. S. Davidson, M. J. Dworkin, C. A. Miller, *et al.* Recommendation for stateful hash-based signature schemes. *NIST Special Publication*, 800(208): 2020.

[133] D. Coppersmith. Small solutions to polynomial equations, and low exponent RSA vulnerabilities. *Journal of Cryptology*, 10(4):233–260, 1997.

[134] T. H. Cormen, C. E. Leiserson, R. L. Rivest, and C. Stein. *Introduction to Algorithms*. MIT Press, Cambridge, MA, 2009.

[135] V. Coskun, K. Ok, and B. Ozdenizci. *Near Field Communication (NFC): From Theory to Practice*. John Wiley & Sons, Hoboken, NJ, 2011.

[136] A. Costello. Punycode: A Bootstring encoding of Unicode for Internationalized Domain Names in Applications (IDNA). RFC 3492 (Proposed Standard), March 2003. Updated by RFC 5891.

[137] Council of European Union. Com/2021/281, Revision of the eIDAS Regulation — European Digital Identity (EUid), 2021.

[138] P. Crisman. *The Compatible Time-Sharing System: A Programmer's Guide*, 2nd edn. MIT Press, Cambridge, MA, 1965. Available at: https://archive.org/details/ctss-programmers-guide-2e.

[139] D. Crocker, T. Hansen, and M. Kucherawy, editors. DomainKeys Identified Mail (DKIM) Signatures. RFC 6376 (Internet Standard), September 2011. Updated by RFCs 8301, 8463, 8553, 8616.

[140] J. Daemen and V. Rijmen. *The Design of Rijndael: AES-the Advanced Encryption Standard.* Springer Science & Business Media, Heidelberg, Germany, 2013.

[141] T. Dai, H. Shulman, and M. Waidner. Let's downgrade let's encrypt. In *Proceedings of the 2021 ACM SIGSAC Conference on Computer and Communications Security*, pp. 1421–1440, 2021.

[142] W. Dai. Crypto++ 6.0.0 benchmarks, 2018. version of 01-23-2018.

[143] I. B. Damgård. Collision free hash functions and public key signature schemes. In *Workshop on the Theory and Application of of Cryptographic Techniques*, pp. 203–216. Springer, 1987.

[144] I. B. Damgård. A design principle for hash functions. In G. Brassard, editor, *Advances in Cryptology—CRYPTO'89.* Lecture Notes in Computer Science, Vol. 435, pp. 416–427. Springer-Verlag, 1990, 1989.

[145] G. Danezis, R. Dingledine, and N. Mathewson. Mixminion: Design of a type iii anonymous remailer protocol. In *Proceedings of 2003 Symposium on Security and Privacy, 2003*, pp. 2–15. IEEE, 2003.

[146] Q. Dang. Secure hash standard, NIST FIPS, 180–4, August 2015.

[147] A. Delignat-Lavaud, C. Fournet, M. Kohlweiss, J. Protzenko, A. Rastogi, N. Swamy, S. Zanella-Béguelin, K. Bhargavan, J. Pan, and J. K. Zinzindohoue. Implementing and proving the TLS 1.3 record layer. In *2017 IEEE Symposium on Security and Privacy (SP)*, pp. 463–482. IEEE, 2017.

[148] M. Dell'Amico, P. Michiardi, and Y. Roudier. Password strength: An empirical analysis. In *2010 Proceedings IEEE INFOCOM*, pp. 1–9. IEEE, 2010.

[149] D. Demmler, A. Herzberg, and T. Schneider. Raid-PIR: Practical multi-server PIR. In *Proceedings of the 6th Edition of the ACM Workshop on Cloud Computing Security*, pp. 45–56. ACM, 2014.

[150] Y. Desmedt. Threshold cryptosystems. In *International Workshop on the Theory and Application of Cryptographic Techniques*, pp. 1–14. Springer, 1992.

[151] R. Dhamija and A. Perrig. Deja Vu–A user study: Using images for authentication. In *9th USENIX Security Symposium (USENIX Security 00)*, 2000.

[152] T. Dierks and C. Allen. The TLS Protocol Version 1.0. RFC 2246 (Historic), January 1999. Obsoleted by RFC 4346, updated by RFCs 3546, 5746, 6176, 7465, 7507, 7919.

[153] T. Dierks and E. Rescorla. The Transport Layer Security (TLS) Protocol Version 1.1. RFC 4346 (Historic), April 2006. Obsoleted by RFC 5246, updated by RFCs 4366, 4680, 4681, 5746, 6176, 7465, 7507, 7919.

[154] T. Dierks and E. Rescorla. The Transport Layer Security (TLS) Protocol Version 1.2. RFC 5246 (Proposed Standard), August 2008. Obsoleted by RFC 8446, updated by RFCs 5746, 5878, 6176, 7465, 7507, 7568, 7627, 7685, 7905, 7919, 8447, 9155.

[155] W. Diffie and M. E. Hellman. New Directions in Cryptography. *IEEE Transactions on Information Theory*, IT-22(6):644–654, November 1976.

[156] R. Dingledine, N. Mathewson, and P. F. Syverson. Tor: The second-generation onion router. In M. Blaze, editor, *Proceedings of the 13th USENIX Security Symposium, August 9–13, 2004, San Diego, CA, USA*, pp. 303–320. USENIX, 2004.

[157] D. Dolev, C. Dwork, and M. Naor. Nonmalleable cryptography. *SIAM Review*, 45(4):727–784, 2003.

[158] N. Doraswamy and D. Harkins. *IPSec: The New Security Standard for the Internet, Intranets, and Virtual Private Networks.* Prentice Hall Professional, Hoboken, NJ, 2003.

[159] B. Dowling, F. Günther, U. Herath, and D. Stebila. Secure logging schemes and certificate transparency. In *European Symposium on Research in Computer Security*, pp. 140–158. Springer, 2016.

[160] O. Dubuisson. *ASN. 1 Communication between Heterogeneous Systems.* Morgan Kaufmann, Cambridge, MA, 2000.

[161] L. Ducas, E. Kiltz, T. Lepoint, V. Lyubashevsky, P. Schwabe, G. Seiler, and D. Stehlé. Crystals-dilithium: A lattice-based digital signature scheme. *IACR Transactions on Cryptographic Hardware and Embedded Systems*, pp. 238–268, 2018.

[162] M. Duke. QUIC Version 2. RFC 9369 (Proposed Standard), May 2023.

[163] V. Dukhovni. Opportunistic Security: Some Protection Most of the Time. RFC 7435 (Informational), December 2014.

[164] O. Dunkelman. Techniques for cryptanalysis of block ciphers. Thesis (ph.D.), Faculty of Computer Science, Technion — Israel Institute of Technology, Haifa, Israel, 2006.

[165] T. Duong and J. Rizzo. Here come the XOR ninjas. Presented at Ecoparty, 2011. Available at: http://www.hpcc.ecs.soton.ac.uk/~dan/talks/bullrun/Beast.pdf.

[166] Z. Durumeric, J. Kasten, M. Bailey, and J. A. Halderman. Analysis of the HTTPS certificate ecosystem. In K. Papagiannaki, P. K. Gummadi, and C. Partridge, editors. *Proceedings of the 2013*

Internet Measurement Conference, IMC 2013, Barcelona, Spain, October 23–25, 2013, pp. 291–304. ACM, 2013.

[167] M. Dworkin. Recommendation for block cipher modes of operation: Methods and techniques. Technical Report, NIST SP 800-38A (National Inst of Standards and Technology), 2001.

[168] M. Dworkin. Recommendation for block cipher modes of operation: Galois/Counter Mode (GCM) and GMAC. Technical Report, NIST SP 800-38D (U.S. National Inst of Standards and Technology), November 2007. Available at: http://csrc.nist.gov/publications/nistpubs/800-38D/SP-800-38D.pdf.

[169] M. J. Dworkin. Recommendation for Block Cipher Modes of Operation: The CMAC mode for authentication. Special Publication (NIST SP)-800-38B, 2016.

[170] J. Dyer. China accused of doling out counterfeit digital certificates in 'serious' web security breach. *VICE News*, April 2015.

[171] S. Dziembowski and K. Pietrzak. Leakage-resilient cryptography. In *IEEE 49th Annual IEEE Symposium on Foundations of Computer Science 2008. FOCS '08*, pp. 293–302. IEEE, 2008.

[172] D. Eastlake 3rd. Transport Layer Security (TLS) Extensions: Extension Definitions. RFC 6066 (Proposed Standard), January 2011. Updated by RFCs 8446, 8449, 9325.

[173] S. Egelman, L. F. Cranor, and J. Hong. You've been warned: An empirical study of the effectiveness of web browser phishing warnings. In *Proceeding of the Twenty-Sixth Annual SIGCHI Conference on Human Factors in Computing Systems*, CHI'08, pp. 1065–1074, ACM, New York, NY, USA, 2008.

[174] C. Ellison, B. Frantz, B. Lampson, R. Rivest, B. Thomas, and T. Ylonen. SPKI Certificate Theory. RFC 2693 (Experimental), September 1999.

[175] P. Eronen and H. Tschofenig, editors. Pre-Shared Key Ciphersuites for Transport Layer Security (TLS). RFC 4279 (Proposed Standard), December 2005. Updated by RFC 8996.

[176] C. Evans, C. Palmer, and R. Sleevi. Public Key Pinning Extension for HTTP. RFC 7469 (Proposed Standard), April 2015.

[177] A. Evans Jr, W. Kantrowitz, and E. Weiss. A user authentication scheme not requiring secrecy in the computer. *Communications of the ACM*, 17(8):437–442, 1974.

[178] L. Ewing. Linux 2.0 penguins. Example of using the GIMP graphics software. Accessed on 1 September 2017.

[179] D. C. Feldmeier and P. R. Karn. Unix password security-ten years later. In *Conference on the Theory and Application of Cryptology*, pp. 44–63. Springer, 1989.

[180] I. Fette and A. Melnikov. The WebSocket Protocol. RFC 6455 (Proposed Standard), December 2011. Updated by RFCs 7936, 8307, 8441.

[181] C. Filsfils, S. Previdi, editors, B. Decraene, and R. Shakir. Resiliency Use Cases in Source Packet Routing in Networking (SPRING) Networks. RFC 8355 (Informational), March 2018.

[182] R. Fischlin and C.-P. Schnorr. Stronger security proofs for RSA and Rabin bits. In *Advances in Cryptology — EUROCRYPT'97: International Conference on the Theory and Application of Cryptographic Techniques Konstanz, Germany, May 11–15, 1997 Proceedings 16*, pp. 267–279. Springer, 1997.

[183] S. R. Fluhrer and D. A. McGrew. Statistical analysis of the alleged RC4 keystream generator. In *International Workshop on Fast Software Encryption*, pp. 19–30. Springer, 2000.

[184] R. Forno and W. Feinbloom. Inside risks: PKI: A question of trust and value. *Communications of the ACM*, 44(6):120, 2001.

[185] CA/Browser Forum. Baseline requirements for the issuance and management of publicly-trusted certificates. Technical Report 2.0.1, CABF, May 2024. Available at: https://cabforum.org/baseline-requirements-documents/.

[186] CA/Browser Forum. Guidelines for the issuance and management of extended validation certificates. Technical Report 2.0.1, CABF, May 2024. Available at: https://cabforum.org/extended-validation/.

[187] CA/Browser Forum. Object registry of the CA/browser forum, Viewed June 2021. Available at: https://cabforum.org/object-registry/.

[188] P.-A. Fouque, J. Hoffstein, P. Kirchner, V. Lyubashevsky, T. Pornin, T. Prest, T. Ricosset, G. Seiler, W. Whyte, Z. Zhang, *et al.* Falcon: Fast-Fourier Lattice-based Compact Signatures over NRTU. Submission to the NIST's Post-Quantum Cryptography Standardization Process, 2018.

[189] S. Frankel and S. Krishnan. IP Security (IPsec) and Internet Key Exchange (IKE) Document Roadmap. RFC 6071 (Informational), February 2011.

[190] M. J. Freedman, K. Nissim, and B. Pinkas. Efficient private matching and set intersection. In *Advances in Cryptology-EUROCRYPT 2004: International Conference on the Theory and Applications of Cryptographic Techniques, Interlaken, Switzerland, May 2–6, 2004. Proceedings*, Vol. 3027, pp. 1–19. Springer, 2004.

[191] A. Freier, P. Karlton, and P. Kocher. The Secure Sockets Layer (SSL) Protocol Version 3.0. RFC 6101 (Historic), August 2011.

[192] A. O. Frier, P. Karlton, and P. C. Kocher. The SSL protocol version 3.0, November 1996. Available at: https://datatracker.ietf.org/doc/html/draft-ietf-tls-ssl-version3-00. Published as Internet Draft draft-ietf-tls-ssl-version3-00.

[193] P. Gaborit, O. Ruatta, G. Zémor, A. Hauteville, T. Pöppelmann, F.-X. Standaert, J. V. Herrewege, and N. Negru. HQC: Hamming quasi-cyclic, 2024. Fourth round version; Accessed on 25 June 2024.

[194] D. Gafurov, E. Snekkenes, and P. Bours. Spoof attacks on gait authentication system. *IEEE Transactions on Information Forensics and Security*, 2(3–2):491–502, 2007.

[195] S. Gajek, M. Manulis, O. Pereira, A.-R. Sadeghi, and J. Schwenk. Universally composable security analysis of TLS. In *International Conference on Provable Security*, pp. 313–327. Springer, 2008.

[196] T. E. Gamal. A public key cryptosystem and a signature scheme based on discrete logarithms. *IEEE Transactions on Information Theory*, 31(4):469–472, 1985.

[197] S. Garfinkel and N. Makarevitch. *PGP: Pretty Good Privacy.* O'Reilly International Thomson, Paris, France, 1995.

[198] M. Gebhardt, G. Illies, and W. Schindler. A note on the practical value of single hash collisions for special file formats. In *Sicherheit*, Vol. 77, pp. 333–344. Citeseer, 2006.

[199] N. Gelernter and A. Herzberg. Cross-Site Search Attacks. In I. Ray, N. Li, and C. Kruegel, editors, *Proceedings of the 22nd ACM SIGSAC Conference on Computer and Communications Security (CCS)*, pp. 1394–1405. ACM, 10 2015.

[200] N. Gelernter, S. Kalma, B. Magnezi, and H. Porcilan. The password reset MitM attack. In *IEEE Symposium on Security and Privacy.* IEEE Computer Society, 2017.

[201] C. Gentry. Fully homomorphic encryption using ideal lattices. In *Proceedings of the Forty-First Annual ACM Symposium on Theory of Computing*, pp. 169–178, 2009.

[202] C. Gentry and S. Halevi. Compressible FHE with applications to PIR. In *Theory of Cryptography Conference*, pp. 438–464. Springer, 2019.

[203] E. Ghosh, O. Ohrimenko, D. Papadopoulos, R. Tamassia, and N. Triandopoulos. Zero-knowledge accumulators and set algebra. In *Advances in Cryptology–ASIACRYPT 2016: 22nd International Conference on the Theory and Application of Cryptology and Information Security, Hanoi, Vietnam, December 4–8, 2016, Proceedings, Part II 22*, pp. 67–100. Springer, 2016.

[204] C. Gidney and M. Ekerå. How to factor 2048 bit RSA integers in 8 hours using 20 million noisy qubits, 2019. *arXiv preprint arXiv:1905.09749.*

[205] Y. Gilad, A. Herzberg, and H. Shulman. Off-path hacking: The illusion of challenge-response authentication. *IEEE Security & Privacy*, 12(5):68–77, 2014.

[206] D. Gillmor. Negotiated Finite Field Diffie-Hellman Ephemeral Parameters for Transport Layer Security (TLS). RFC 7919 (Proposed Standard), August 2016.

[207] D. Giry. Cryptographic key length recommendation. Version 32.3, May 24, 2020. https://keylength.com.

[208] Y. Gluck, N. Harris, and A. Prado. Breach: Reviving the crime attack. *Black Hat USA*, 2013.

[209] O. Goldreich. *Foundations of Cryptography, Volume 1: Basic Tools.* Cambridge University Press, Shaftesbury Rd., Cambridge, UK, 2001.

[210] O. Goldreich. *Foundations of Cryptography: Volume 2, Basic Applications.* Cambridge University Press, Shaftesbury Rd., Cambridge, UK, 2009.

[211] O. Goldreich. *P, NP, and NP-Completeness: The Basics of Complexity Theory.* Cambridge University Press, Shaftesbury Rd., Cambridge, UK, 2010.

[212] O. Goldreich, S. Goldwasser, and S. Micali. How to construct random functions. *Journal of the ACM*, 33(4):792–807, 1986.

[213] S. Goldwasser and S. Micali. Probabilistic encryption. *Journal of Computer and System Sciences*, 28(2):270–299, April 1984.

[214] S. Goldwasser, S. Micali, and R. L. Rivest. A digital signature scheme secure against adaptive chosen-message attacks. *SIAM Journal on Computing*, 17(2):281–308, 1988.

[215] P. Golle, M. Jakobsson, A. Juels, and P. Syverson. Universal re-encryption for mixnets. In *Cryptographers' Track at the RSA Conference*, pp. 163–178. Springer, 2004.

[216] M. Goodwin. Revoking intermediate certificates: Introducing OneCRL. Mozilla Security Blog, March 2015. https://blog.mozilla.org/security/2015/03/03/revoking-intermediate-certificates-introducing-onecrl/.

[217] Google. Google Safe Browsing. https://transparencyreport.google.com/safe-browsing/overview. Accessed on 20 January 2024.

[218] Google. EV UI moving to page info, 2019. Available at: https://chromium.googlesource.com/chromium/src/+/HEAD/docs/security/ev-to-page-info.md.

[219] C. M. Grinstead and J. L. Snell. *Introduction to Probability.* American Mathematical Society, 201 Charles St., Providence, RI, 2012.

[220] OATH Authentication, LLC. OATH reference architecture, release 2.0, 2007.

[221] L. K. Grover. A fast quantum mechanical algorithm for database search. In *Proceedings of the Twenty-Eighth annual ACM Symposium on Theory of Computing*, pp. 212–219, 1996.

[222] B. Gruber. How certificate transparency works, August 2013. Available at: https://www.certificate-transparency.org/how-ct-works.

[223] C. G. Günther. An identity-based key-exchange protocol. In *Workshop on the Theory and Application of Cryptographic Techniques*, pp. 29–37. Springer, 1989.

[224] P. Gutmann. Encrypt-then-MAC for Transport Layer Security (TLS) and Datagram Transport Layer Security (DTLS). RFC 7366 (Proposed Standard), September 2014.

[225] P. Gutmann. Engineering security, 2014. https://www.cs.auckland.ac.nz/~pgut001/pubs/book.pdf.

[226] W. J. Haga and M. Zviran. Question-and-answer passwords: An empirical evaluation. *Information Systems*, 16(3):335–343, 1991.

[227] F. Haist, A. P. Shimamura, and L. R. Squire. On the relationship between recall and recognition memory. *Journal of Experimental Psychology: Learning, Memory, and Cognition*, 18(4):691, 1992.

[228] J. A. Halderman, B. Waters, and E. W. Felten. A convenient method for securely managing passwords. In *Proceedings of the 14th International Conference on World Wide Web*, pp. 471–479, 2005.

[229] W. Hales. *HTML5 and JavaScript Web Apps.* O'Reilly Media, Inc., Santa Rosa, CA, 2012.

[230] C. Hall, D. Wagner, J. Kelsey, and B. Schneier. Building PRFs from PRPs. In *Annual International Cryptology Conference*, pp. 370–389. Springer, 1998.

[231] P. Hallam-Baker. X.509v3 Transport Layer Security (TLS) Feature Extension. RFC 7633 (Proposed Standard), October 2015.

[232] P. Hallam-Baker, R. Stradling, and J. Hoffman-Andrews. DNS Certification Authority Authorization (CAA) Resource Record. RFC 8659 (Proposed Standard), November 2019.

[233] N. Haller. The S/KEY One-Time Password System. RFC 1760 (Informational), February 1995.

[234] N. Haller, C. Metz, P. Nesser, and M. Straw. A One-Time Password System. RFC 2289 (Internet Standard), February 1998.

[235] D. Hankerson, A. J. Menezes, and S. Vanstone. *Guide to Elliptic Curve Cryptography.* Springer Science & Business Media, Heidelberg, Germany, 2006.

[236] F. Hao, editor. J-PAKE: Password-Authenticated Key Exchange by Juggling. RFC 8236 (Informational), September 2017.

[237] M. E. Hellman. A cryptanalytic time-memory trade-off. *IEEE Transactions on Information Theory*, 26(4):401–406, 1980.

[238] A. Herzberg. Why Johnny can't surf (safely)? Attacks and defenses for web users. *Computers & Security*, 28(1–2):63–71, 2008.

[239] A. Herzberg. DNS-based email sender authentication mechanisms: A critical review. *Computers & Security*, 28(8):731–742, 2009.

[240] A. Herzberg. Folklore, practice and theory of robust combiners. *Journal of Computer Security*, 17(2):159–189, 2009.

[241] A. Herzberg and A. Jbara. Security and identification indicators for browsers against spoofing and phishing attacks. *ACM Transactions on Internet Technology (TOIT)*, 8(4):16, 2008.

[242] A. Herzberg, H. Leibowitz, E. Syta, and S. Wrótniak. MoSS: Modular security specifications framework. In T. Malkin and C. Peikert, editors, *Advances in Cryptology — CRYPTO 2021*, pp. 33–63. Springer International Publishing, Cham, 2021. Full version at: https://eprint.iacr.org/2020/1040.

[243] A. Herzberg and R. Margulies. Training Johnny to authenticate (safely). *IEEE Security & Privacy*, 10(1):37–45, 2012. Special issue on 'Developments in Authentication Technologies'.

[244] A. Herzberg and Y. Mass. Relying party credentials framework. *Electronic Commerce Research*, 4(1–2):23–39, 2004.

[245] A. Herzberg, Y. Mass, J. Mihaeli, D. Naor, and Y. Ravid. Access control meets public key infrastructure, or: Assigning roles to strangers. In *Proceeding 2000 IEEE Symposium on Security and Privacy. S&P 2000*, pp. 2–14. IEEE, 2000.

[246] A. Herzberg and H. Shulman. Security of patched DNS. In *Computer Security — ESORICS 2012 — 17th European Symposium on Research in Computer Security, Pisa, Italy, September 10–12, 2012. Proceedings*, pp. 271–288, 2012.

[247] A. Herzberg and H. Shulman. Fragmentation Considered Poisonous: Or one-domain-to-rule-them-all.org. In *IEEE CNS 2013. The Conference on Communications and Network Security, Washington, D.C., U.S.* IEEE, October 2013.

[248] K. E. Hickman and T. Elgamal. The SSL protocol (version 2), June 1995. Archived copy at: http://drive.google.com/file/d/1vOT0WazE667Y-vwfGws0GMow98DX3i7B/view?usp=sharing, Published as Internet Draft draft-hickman-netscape-ssl-01.txt.

[249] F. Hillebrand. *GSM and UMTS: The Creation of Global Mobile Communication.* John Wiley & Sons, Inc., Hoboken, NJ, USA, 2002.

[250] J. Hodges, C. Jackson, and A. Barth. HTTP Strict Transport Security (HSTS). RFC 6797 (Proposed Standard), November 2012.

[251] P. Hoffman, M. Blanchet, E. Lafon, Y. Galand, C. Elphick, and M. Moeller. International organization for standardization, information technology — ASN.1 — Basic encoding rules (BER). In ITU-T Recommendation X.690 | ISO/IEC 8825-1:2002, pp. 1–105, 2002. Also covers DER.

[252] P. Hoffman and J. Schlyter. The DNS-Based Authentication of Named Entities (DANE) Transport Layer Security (TLS) Protocol: TLSA. RFC 6698 (Proposed Standard), August 2012. Updated by RFCs 7218, 7671, 8749.

[253] J. Hoffstein, J. Pipher, J. H. Silverman, and J. H. Silverman. *An Introduction to Mathematical Cryptography.* Springer, New York City, 2008.

[254] S. Holtmanns and I. Oliver. SMS and one-time-password interception in LTE networks. In *2017 IEEE International Conference on Communications (ICC)*, pp. 1–6. IEEE, 2017.

[255] R. Housley. Cryptographic Message Syntax (CMS). RFC 5652 (Internet Standard), September 2009. Updated by RFC 8933.

[256] R. Housley, W. Ford, W. Polk, and D. Solo. Internet X.509 Public Key Infrastructure Certificate and CRL Profile. RFC 2459 (Proposed Standard), January 1999. Obsoleted by RFC 3280.

[257] R. Housley, W. Polk, W. Ford, and D. Solo. Internet X.509 Public Key Infrastructure Certificate and Certificate Revocation List (CRL) Profile. RFC 3280 (Proposed Standard), April 2002. Obsoleted by RFC 5280, updated by RFCs 4325, 4630.

[258] A. Huelsing, D. Butin, S. Gazdag, J. Rijneveld, and A. Mohaisen. XMSS: eXtended Merkle Signature Scheme. RFC 8391 (Informational), May 2018.

[259] T. Hunt. Troy hunt: 86% of passwords are terrible (and other statistics), 2018. https://www.troyhunt.com/86-of-passwords-are-terrible-and-other-statistics/.

[260] P. Inglesant and M. A. Sasse. The true cost of unusable password policies: Password use in the wild. In E. D. Mynatt, D. Schoner, G. Fitzpatrick, S. E. Hudson, W. K. Edwards, and T. Rodden, editors, *Proceedings of the 28th International Conference on Human Factors in Computing Systems, CHI 2010, Atlanta, Georgia, USA, April 10–15, 2010*, pp. 383–392. ACM, 2010.

[261] International Telecommunication Union. ITU-T X.509 Recommendation Version 3: Information Technology — Open Systems Interconnection — The Directory: Authentication Framework, June 1997.

[262] International Telecommunication Union. Recommendation ITU-T X.509, OSI — The Directory: Public-Key and Attribute Certificate Frameworks, 2016.

[263] International Organization for Standardization (ISO). Data Cryptographic Techniques: Data Integrity Mechanism Using a Cryptographic Check Function Employing a Block Cipher Algorithm. ISO/IEC 9797, 1989.

[264] J. Iyengar and M. Thomson, editors. QUIC: A UDP-Based Multiplexed and Secure Transport. RFC 9000 (Proposed Standard), May 2021.

[265] T. Jager, J. Schwenk, and J. Somorovsky. On the security of TLS 1.3 and QUIC against weaknesses in PKCS# 1 v1. 5 encryption. In *Proceedings of the 22nd ACM SIGSAC Conference on Computer and Communications Security*, pp. 1185–1196, 2015.

[266] M. Jakobsson, E. Stolterman, S. Wetzel, and L. Yang. Love and authentication. In *CHI'08: Proceeding of the Twenty-Sixth Annual SIGCHI Conference on Human Factors in Computing Systems, New York, NY, USA, 2008*, pp. 197–200. ACM, 2008.

[267] S. Jarecki, H. Krawczyk, and J. Xu. OPAQUE: An asymmetric PAKE protocol secure against pre-computation attacks. In *Advances in Cryptology–EUROCRYPT 2018: 37th Annual International Conference on the Theory and Applications of Cryptographic Techniques, Tel Aviv, Israel, April 29-May 3, 2018 Proceedings, Part III 37*, pp. 456–486. Springer, 2018.

[268] J. Jean. TikZ for Cryptographers, 2016. https://www.iacr.org/authors/tikz/. CBC figures by Diana Maimut.

[269] G. L. Joe DeBlasio. Opt-out SCT Auditing in Chrome. Other. https://docs.google.com/document/d/16G-Q7iN3kB46GSW5b-sfH5MO3nKSYyEb77YsM7TMZGE/.

[270] D. Johnson, A. Menezes, and S. Vanstone. The elliptic curve digital signature algorithm (ECDSA). *International Journal of Information Security*, 1:36–63, 2001.

[271] M. B. Jones, A. Kumar, and E. Lundberg. Web authentication: An API for accessing public key credentials (level 3), September 2023. https://www.w3.org/TR/webauthn-3/. World Wide Web Consortium (W3C) Recommendation.

[272] J. Jonsson and B. Kaliski. Public-Key Cryptography Standards (PKCS) #1: RSA Cryptography Specifications Version 2.1. RFC 3447 (Informational), February 2003. Obsoleted by RFC 8017.

[273] S. Josefsson and S. Leonard. Textual Encodings of PKIX, PKCS, and CMS Structures. RFC 7468 (Proposed Standard), April 2015.

[274] A. Joux. *Algorithmic Cryptanalysis.* CRC Press, Boca Raton, FL, 2009.

[275] R. P. Jover. Security analysis of sms as a second factor of authentication. *Communications of the ACM*, 63(12):46–52, 2020.

[276] A. Juels and T. Ristenpart. Honey encryption: Encryption beyond the brute-force barrier. *IEEE Security & Privacy*, 12(4):59–62, 2014.

[277] A. Juels and T. Ristenpart. Honey encryption: Security beyond the brute-force bound. In *Advances in Cryptology–EUROCRYPT 2014: 33rd Annual International Conference on the Theory and Applications of Cryptographic Techniques, Copenhagen, Denmark, May 11–15, 2014. Proceedings 33*, pp. 293–310. Springer, 2014.

[278] A. Juels and R. L. Rivest. Honeywords: Making password-cracking detectable. In *Proceedings of the 2013 ACM SIGSAC Conference on Computer & Communications Security*, pp. 145–160, 2013.

[279] D. Kahn. *The Codebreakers: The Comprehensive History of Secret Communication from Ancient Times to the Internet.* Simon and Schuster, New York City, 1996.

[280] B. Kaliski. PKCS #1: RSA Encryption Version 1.5. RFC 2313 (Informational), March 1998. Obsoleted by RFC 2437.

[281] B. Kaliski. PKCS #7: Cryptographic Message Syntax Version 1.5. RFC 2315 (Informational), March 1998.

[282] B. Kaliski and J. Staddon. PKCS #1: RSA Cryptography Specifications Version 2.0. RFC 2437 (Informational), October 1998. Obsoleted by RFC 3447.

[283] C. Karlof, J. D. Tygar, and D. A. Wagner. Conditioned-safe ceremonies and a user study of an application to web authentication. In *Proceedings of the Network and Distributed System Security Symposium, NDSS.* The Internet Society, 2009.

[284] P. Karn. The S/key one-time password system. In *Proceedings of the ISOC Symposium on Network and Distributed System Security, San Diego, CA, February 1994.* ISOC (Internet Society), 1994.

[285] C. Kaufman, P. Hoffman, Y. Nir, and P. Eronen. Internet Key Exchange Protocol Version 2 (IKEv2). RFC 5996 (Proposed Standard), September 2010. Obsoleted by RFC 7296, updated by RFCs 5998, 6989.

[286] S. Kawamura and M. Kawashima. A Recommendation for IPv6 Address Text Representation. RFC 5952 (Proposed Standard), August 2010.

[287] G. Kedem and Y. Ishihara. Brute force attack on UNIX passwords with SIMD computer. In *8th USENIX Security Symposium (USENIX Security 99)*, 1999.

[288] G. Keizer. Solo Iranian hacker takes credit for Comodo certificate attack. *Computer World*, 2011.

[289] J. Kelsey. Compression and information leakage of plaintext. In *International Workshop on Fast Software Encryption*, pp. 263–276. Springer, 2002.

[290] J. Kelsey, B. Schneier, D. Wagner, and C. Hall. Cryptanalytic attacks on pseudorandom number generators. In S. Vaudenay, editor, *Fast Software Encryption: 5th International Workshop*, Lecture Notes in Computer Science, Vol. 1372, pp. 168–188, Paris, France, 23–25 March 1998. Springer-Verlag.

[291] S. Kent and K. Seo. Security Architecture for the Internet Protocol. RFC 4301 (Proposed Standard), December 2005. Updated by RFCs 6040, 7619.

[292] A. Kerckhoffs. La cryptographie militaire. *Journal des Sciences Militaires*, IX, 1883.

[293] D. Kim and J. Ryou. Securesms: Prevention of SMS interception on android platform. In *Proceedings of the 8th International Conference on Ubiquitous Information Management and Communication*, pp. 1–6, 2014.

[294] C. A. Kirtchev. A cyberpunk manifesto, Cyberpunk Review, 1997. Disponible en: http://www.cyberpunkreview.com/wiki/index.php.

[295] A. Klein. Attacks on the RC4 stream cipher. *Designs, Codes and Cryptography*, 48(3):269–286, 2008.

[296] A. Klein. Cross layer attacks and how to use them (for DNS cache poisoning, device tracking and more). In *2021 IEEE Symposium on Security and Privacy (SP)*, pp. 1179–1196. IEEE, 2021.

[297] L. R. Knudsen and M. Robshaw. *The Block Cipher Companion*. Information Security and Cryptography. Springer, Berlin, 2011.

[298] N. Koblitz and A. Menezes. Critical perspectives on provable security: Fifteen years of "another look" papers. *Advances in Mathematics of Communications*, 13(4):517–558, 2019.

[299] D. Kogan, N. Manohar, and D. Boneh. T/key: Second-factor authentication from secure hash chains. In *Proceedings of the 2017 ACM SIGSAC Conference on Computer and Communications Security*, pp. 983–999, 2017.

[300] L. M. Kohnfelder. Towards a practical public-key cryptosystem. Bachelor's thesis, Massachusetts Institute of Technology, 1978.

[301] P. Koopman. 32-bit cyclic redundancy codes for internet applications. In *Proceedings 2002 International Conference on Dependable Systems and Networks (DSN 2002), Bethesda, MD, Washington, DC, USA, June 2002*, pp. 459–472. IEEE Computer Society, 2002.

[302] N. Korzhitskii and N. Carlsson. Revocation statuses on the internet. In *Passive and Active Measurement: 22nd International Conference, PAM 2021, Virtual Event, March 29–April 1, 2021, Proceedings 22*, pp. 175–191. Springer, 2021.

[303] H. Krawczyk. The order of encryption and authentication for protecting communications (or: How secure is SSL?). In J. Kilian, editor, *Advances in Cryptology — CRYPTO' 2001*. Lecture Notes in Computer Science, Vol. 2139, pp. 310–331. International Association for Cryptologic Research, Springer-Verlag, Berlin, Germany, 2001.

[304] H. Krawczyk. Sigma: The 'SIGn-and-MAc' approach to authenticated Diffie-Hellman and its use in the ike protocols. In *Annual International Cryptology Conference*, pp. 400–425. Springer, 2003.

[305] H. Krawczyk. Cryptographic extraction and key derivation: The HKDF scheme. In T. Rabin, editor, *Advances in Cryptology — Proceedings of CRYPTO*. Lecture Notes in Computer Science, Vol. 6223, pp. 631–648. Springer, 8 2010. Available at: https://ia.cr/2010/264.

[306] H. Krawczyk and P. Eronen. HMAC-based Extract-and-Expand Key Derivation Function (HKDF). RFC 5869 (Informational), May 2010.

[307] K. Krol, M. Moroz, and M. A. Sasse. Don't work. Can't work? Why it's time to rethink security warnings. In *2012 7th International Conference on Risks and Security of Internet and Systems (CRiSIS)*, pp. 1–8. IEEE, 2012.

[308] J. F. Kurose and K. W. Ross. *Computer Networking: A Top-Down Approach*, 4th edn. Addison-Wesley, Reading, MA, 2009.

[309] H. Kuwakado and M. Morii. Quantum distinguisher between the 3-round Feistel cipher and the random permutation. In *2010 IEEE International Symposium on Information Theory*, pp. 2682–2685. IEEE, 2010.

[310] W. Ladd. SPAKE2, a Password-Authenticated Key Exchange. RFC 9382 (Informational), September 2023.

[311] L. Lamport. Password authentication with insecure communication. *Communications of the ACM*, 24(11):770–772, 1981.

[312] A. Langley. Revocation checking and Chrome's CRL, February 2012. https://www.imperialviolet.org/2012/02/05/crlsets.html. Accessed on 23 February 2025.

[313] A. Langley. Enhancing digital certificate security. *Google Security Blog*, January 2013.

[314] A. Langley. Certificate transparency: Comparison with other technologies, July 2014. Available at: http://http://www.certificate-transparency.org/comparison.

[315] A. Langley. Maintaining digital certificate security. *Google Security Blog*, January 2014.

[316] A. Langley, M. Hamburg, and S. Turner. Elliptic Curves for Security. RFC 7748 (Informational), January 2016.

[317] J. Larisch, D. R. Choffnes, D. Levin, B. M. Maggs, A. Mislove, and C. Wilson. CRLite: A scalable system for pushing all TLS revocations to all browsers. In *IEEE Symposium on Security and Privacy*, pp. 539–556. IEEE Computer Society, 2017.

[318] B. Laurie. Certificate transparency. *Communications of the ACM*, 57(10):40–46, 2014.

[319] B. Laurie, A. Langley, and E. Kasper. Certificate Transparency. RFC 6962 (Experimental), June 2013. Obsoleted by RFC 9162.

[320] B. Laurie, E. Messeri, and R. Stradling. Certificate Transparency Version 2.0. RFC 9162 (Experimental), December 2021.

[321] B. Laurie, G. Sisson, R. Arends, and D. Blacka. DNS Security (DNSSEC) Hashed Authenticated Denial of Existence. RFC 5155 (Proposed Standard), March 2008. Updated by RFCs 6840, 6944, 9077, 9157, 9276.

[322] N. Leavitt. Internet security under attack: The undermining of digital certificates. *Computer*, 44(12):17–20, 2011.

[323] J. Lee and R. Rosin. The project MAC interviews. *IEEE Annals of the History of Computing*, 14(2):14–35, 1992.

[324] S. Lee, Y. Shin, and J. Hur. Return of version downgrade attack in the era of TLS 1.3. In *Proceedings of the 16th International Conference on emerging Networking Experiments and Technologies*, pp. 157–168, 2020.

[325] F. T. Leighton and S. Micali. Large provably fast and secure digital signature schemes based on secure hash functions, July 1995. US Patent 5,432,852.

[326] A. Lenstra and B. De Weger. On the possibility of constructing meaningful hash collisions for public keys. In *Information Security and Privacy: 10th Australasian Conference, ACISP 2005, Brisbane, Australia, July 4–6, 2005. Proceedings 10*, pp. 267–279. Springer, 2005.

[327] A. K. Lenstra and E. R. Verheul. Selecting cryptographic key sizes. *Journal of Cryptology*, 14(4):255–293, 2001.

[328] G. Leurent and T. Peyrin. SHA-1 is a shambles: First chosen-prefix collision on SHA-1 and application to the PGP web of trust. In *29th USENIX Security Symposium (USENIX Security 20)*, pp. 1839–1856, 2020. https://www.usenix.org/conference/usenixsecurity20/presentation/leurent.

[329] T. R. Levine. Truth-default theory (TDT) a theory of human deception and deception detection. *Journal of Language and Social Psychology*, 33(4):378–392, 2014.

[330] S. Levy. *Crypto: How the Code Rebels Beat the Government, Saving Privacy in the Digital Age*. Viking, New York City, 2001.

[331] J. Leyden. CA issues no-questions asked Mozilla cert. *The Register*, December 2008.

[332] N. Li, J. C. Mitchell, and W. H. Winsborough. Design of a role-based trust-management framework. In *Proceedings 2002 IEEE Symposium on Security and Privacy*, pp. 114–130. IEEE, 2002.

[333] X. Li, C. Lu, B. Liu, Q. Zhang, Z. Li, H. Duan, and Q. Li. The Maginot line: Attacking the boundary of DNS caching protection. In *32nd USENIX Security Symposium (USENIX Security 23)*, pp. 3153–3170, 2023.

[334] Y. Li, H. Wang, and K. Sun. Personal information in passwords and its security implications. *IEEE Transactions on Information Forensics and Security*, 12(10):2320–2333, 2017.

[335] Z. Li, W. He, D. Akhawe, and D. Song. The Emperor's new password manager: Security analysis of web-based password managers. In *23rd USENIX Security Symposium (USENIX Security 14)*, pp. 465–479, 2014.

[336] H.-J. Liao, C.-H. R. Lin, Y.-C. Lin, and K.-Y. Tung. Intrusion detection system: A comprehensive review. *Journal of Network and Computer Applications*, 36(1):16–24, 2013.

[337] M. Luby and C. Rackoff. How to construct pseudorandom permutations from pseudorandom functions. *SIAM Journal on Computing*, 17(2):373–386, April 1988.

[338] M. Lucamarini, G. Di Giuseppe, and K. Tamaki. Robust unconditionally secure quantum key distribution with two nonorthogonal and uninformative states. *Physical Review A*, 80(3):032327, 2009.

[339] M. Lucamarini and S. Mancini. Secure deterministic communication without entanglement. *Physical Review Letters*, 94(14):140501, 2005.

[340] A. Mack. Inattentional blindness: Looking without seeing. *Current Directions in Psychological Science*, 12(5):180–184, 2003.

[341] A. Mairh, D. Barik, K. Verma, and D. Jena. Honeypot in network security: A survey. In *Proceedings of the 2011 International Conference on Communication, Computing & Security*, pp. 600–605, 2011.

[342] D. Malone and K. Maher. Investigating the distribution of password choices. In *Proceedings of the 21st International Conference on World Wide Web*, pp. 301–310, 2012.

[343] K. Man, X. Zhou, and Z. Qian. DNS cache poisoning attack: Resurrections with side channels. In *Proceedings of the 2021 ACM SIGSAC Conference on Computer and Communications Security*, pp. 3400–3414, 2021.

[344] U. Manber. A simple scheme to make passwords based on one-way functions much harder to crack. *Computers & Security*, 15(2):171–176, 1996.

[345] J. Manger. A chosen ciphertext attack on RSA optimal asymmetric encryption padding (OAEP) as standardized in PKCS# 1 v2. 0. In *Annual International Cryptology Conference*, pp. 230–238. Springer, 2001.

[346] I. Mantin and A. Shamir. A practical attack on broadcast RC4. In *International Workshop on Fast Software Encryption*, pp. 152–164. Springer, 2001.

[347] M. Marlinspike. More tricks for defeating SSL in practice. *Black Hat USA*, 2009.

[348] V. G. Martínez, L. H. Encinas, *et al.* A comparison of the standardized versions of ECIES. In *2010 Sixth International Conference on Information Assurance and Security*, pp. 1–4. IEEE, 2010.

[349] M. Matsui. Linear cryptanalysis method for DES cipher. In *Workshop on the Theory and Application of of Cryptographic Techniques*, pp. 386–397. Springer, 1993.

[350] D. McGrew. An Interface and Algorithms for Authenticated Encryption. RFC 5116 (Proposed Standard), January 2008.

[351] D. McGrew, M. Curcio, and S. Fluhrer. Leighton-Micali Hash-Based Signatures. RFC 8554 (Informational), April 2019.

[352] J. Menn. Mysterious company with government ties plays key internet role. *The Washington Post*, 11 2022.

[353] R. C. Merkle. A certified digital signature. In G. Brassard, editor, *Advances in Cryptology — CRYPTO'89*. Lecture Notes in Computer Science, Vol. 435, pp. 218–238. Springer-Verlag, 1990, August 1989.

[354] R. C. Merkle. One way hash functions and DES. In *Advances in Cryptology — CRYPTO'89*, pp. 428–446. Springer, Berlin, August 1990.

[355] C. Meyer and J. Schwenk. Lessons learned from previous SSL/TLS attacks — A brief chronology of attacks and weaknesses. *IACR Cryptology ePrint Archive*, 2013:49, 2013.

[356] K. Mitnick. The testimony of an ex-hacker, March 2000. Appeared in Fronline. Available at: https://www.pbs.org/wgbh/pages/ frontline/shows/hackers/whoare/testimony.html. Testimony to the U.S. Senate Committee on Governmental Affairs.

[357] K. Mitnick and W. Simon. *Ghost in the Wires: My Adventures as the World's Most Wanted Hacker.* Back Bay Books, New York City, 2012.

[358] M. Mitzenmacher and E. Upfal. *Probability and Computing: Randomized Algorithms and Probabilistic Analysis.* Cambridge University Press, Cambridge, UK, 2005.

[359] B. Moeller. Security of CBC ciphersuites in SSL/TLS: Problems and countermeasures, May 2004.

[360] B. Moeller and A. Langley. TLS Fallback Signaling Cipher Suite Value (SCSV) for Preventing Protocol Downgrade Attacks. RFC 7507 (Proposed Standard), April 2015. Obsoleted by RFC 8996.

[361] S. A. Mohammed, S. Shirmohammadi, *et al.* A multimodal deep learning-based distributed network latency measurement system. *IEEE Transactions on Instrumentation and Measurement*, 69(5):2487–2494, 2020.

[362] B. Möller, T. Duong, and K. Kotowicz. This POODLE bites: Exploiting the SSL 3.0 fallback, September 2014. Security Advisory.

[363] D. Moody, G. Alagic, D. C. Apon, D. A. Cooper, Q. H. Dang, J. M. Kelsey, Y.-K. Liu, C. A. Miller, R. C. Peralta, R. A. Perlner, *et al.* Status report on the second round of the NIST post-quantum cryptography standardization process. Technical Report NISTIR 8309, NIST, 2020.

[364] K. Moriarty editor, B. Kaliski, J. Jonsson, and A. Rusch. PKCS #1: RSA Cryptography Specifications Version 2.2. RFC 8017 (Informational), November 2016.

[365] R. Morris and K. Thompson. Password security: A case history. *Communications of the ACM*, 22(11):594–597, 1979.

[366] P. Morrissey, N. Smart, and B. Warinschi. The TLS handshake protocol: A modular analysis. *Journal of Cryptology*, 23:187–223, April 2010.

[367] Mozilla. Mozilla Root Store Policy, Version 2.8. Other. https://github.com/mozilla/pkipolicy/blob/2.8/rootstore/policy.md.

[368] Mozilla. Removed CA certificate list. https://ccadb-public.secure.force.com/mozilla/RemovedCACertificateReport.

[369] Mozilla. The MCS incident and its consequences for CNNIC, April 2015. https://blog.mozilla.org/security/files/2015/04/CNNIC-MCS.pdf.

[370] D. M'Raihi, M. Bellare, F. Hoornaert, D. Naccache, and O. Ranen. HOTP: An HMAC-Based One-Time Password Algorithm. RFC 4226 (Informational), December 2005.

[371] D. M'Raihi, S. Machani, M. Pei, and J. Rydell. TOTP: Time-Based One-Time Password Algorithm. RFC 6238 (Informational), May 2011.

[372] D. M'Raihi, J. Rydell, S. Bajaj, S. Machani, and D. Naccache. OCRA: OATH Challenge-Response Algorithm. RFC 6287 (Informational), June 2011.

[373] C. Mulliner, R. Borgaonkar, P. Stewin, and J.-P. Seifert. SMS-based one-time passwords: Attacks and defense. In *Detection of Intrusions and Malware, and Vulnerability Assessment: 10th International Conference, DIMVA 2013, Berlin, Germany, July 18–19, 2013. Proceedings 10*, pp. 150–159. Springer, 2013. Short paper; extended version available as TU Berlin Technical Report 2014-02. Online at: https://depositonce.tu-berlin.de/bitstreams/2b74f199-ddd7-464e-a65a-70d10fc5a305/download.

[374] M. Mumtaz and L. Ping. Forty years of attacks on the RSA cryptosystem: A brief survey. *Journal of Discrete Mathematical Sciences and Cryptography*, 22(1):9–29, 2019.

[375] Y. Mundada, N. Feamster, and B. Krishnamurthy. Half-baked cookies: Hardening cookie-based authentication for the modern web. In *Proceedings of the 11th ACM on Asia Conference on Computer and Communications Security*, pp. 675–685, 2016.

[376] M. Naor and M. Yung. Universal one-way hash functions and their cryptographic applications. In *Proceedings of the Twenty-First Annual ACM Symposium on Theory of Computing*, pp. 33–43, 1989.

[377] National Bureau of Standards. *Data Encryption Standard.* U.S. Department of Commerce, Washington, DC, USA, January 1977.

[378] M. Negreiro and M. Niestadt. Updating the European digital identity framework. Briefing: EU Legislation in Progress. European Parliamentary Research Service, Luxembourg, 2021.

[379] H. Nejatollahi, N. Dutt, S. Ray, F. Regazzoni, I. Banerjee, and R. Cammarota. Post-quantum lattice-based cryptography implementations: A survey. *ACM Computing Surveys (CSUR)*, 51(6): 1–41, 2019.

[380] B. C. Neuman and T. Ts'o. Kerberos: An authentication service for computer networks. *IEEE Communications Magazine*, 32(9):33–38, 1994.

[381] M. A. Nielsen and I. L. Chuang. *Quantum Computation and Quantum Information.* Cambridge University Press, Cambridge, UK, 2010.

[382] J. Nightingale. Comodo certificate issue — Follow up. *Mozilla Security Blog*, March 2011.

[383] P. Norvig. English letter frequency counts: Mayzner revisited, 2013. Available at: https://norvig.com/Mayzner.html.

[384] P. Oechslin. Making a faster cryptanalytic time-memory trade-off. In *Annual International Cryptology Conference*, pp. 617–630. Springer, 2003.

[385] S. Oesch and S. Ruoti. That was then, this is now: A security evaluation of password generation, storage, and autofill in browser-based password managers. In *Proceedings of the 29th USENIX Conference on Security Symposium*, pp. 2165–2182, 2020.

[386] National Institute of Standards and Technology (NIST). Module-lattice-based Digital Signature Standard (Draft), August 2023.

[387] National Institute of Standards and Technology (NIST). Module-lattice-based Key-encapsulation Mechanism Standard (Draft), August 2023. Based on the CRYSTALS — Kyber proposal.

[388] National Institute of Standards and Technology (NIST). Stateless Hash-based Digital Signature Standard (FIPS 205), August 2023. Based on the SPHINCS+ proposal.

[389] National Institute of Standards and Technology (NIST). Post-quantum Cryptography, 2024.

[390] R. Oppliger. *SSL and TLS: Theory and Practice.* Artech House, Norwood, MA, 2016.

[391] D. O'Brien, R. Sleevi, and A. Whalley. Chrome's plan to distrust symantec certificates. *Google Security Blog*, September 2017.

[392] C. Paar and J. Pelzl. *Understanding Cryptography — A Textbook for Students and Practitioners.* Springer, Berlin, 2010.

[393] D. Paez. How 'PWNED' went from hacker slang to the internet's favorite taunt, March 2020.

[394] B. Pal, T. Daniel, R. Chatterjee, and T. Ristenpart. Beyond credential stuffing: Password similarity models using neural networks. In *2019 IEEE Symposium on Security and Privacy (SP)*, pp. 417–434. IEEE, 2019.

[395] B. Pal, M. Islam, M. S. Bohuk, N. Sullivan, L. Valenta, T. Whalen, C. Wood, T. Ristenpart, and R. Chatterjee. Might I get PWNED: A second generation compromised credential checking service. In *31st USENIX Security Symposium (USENIX Security 22), Boston, MA, August 2022*, pp. 1831–1848. USENIX Association, 2022.

[396] V. Pamnani and P. Matarazzo. Microsoft Defender SmartScreen, August 2023, https://learn.microsoft.com/en-us/windows/security/operating-system-security/virus-and-threat-protection/microsoft-defender-smartscreen/, Accessed on 20 January 2024.

[397] S. Pasini and S. Vaudenay. Hash-and-sign with weak hashing made secure. In *Australasian Conference on Information Security and Privacy*, pp. 338–354. Springer, 2007.

[398] C. Peikert. A decade of lattice cryptography. *Foundations and Trends in Theoretical Computer Science*, 10(4):283–424, 2016.

[399] C. Percival and S. Josefsson. The scrypt Password-Based Key Derivation Function. RFC 7914 (Informational), August 2016.

[400] Y. Pettersen. The Transport Layer Security (TLS) Multiple Certificate Status Request Extension. RFC 6961 (Proposed Standard), June 2013. Obsoleted by RFC 8446.

[401] S. Pirandola, U. L. Andersen, L. Banchi, M. Berta, D. Bunandar, R. Colbeck, D. Englund, T. Gehring, C. Lupo, C. Ottaviani, *et al.* Advances in quantum cryptography. *Advances in Optics and Photonics*, 12(4):1012–1236, 2020.

[402] S. Pohlig and M. Hellman. An improved algorithm for computing logarithms over GF (p) and its cryptographic significance (corresp.). *IEEE Transactions on Information Theory*, 24(1):106–110, 1978.

[403] J. Postel. Internet Protocol. RFC 791 (Internet Standard), September 1981. Updated by RFCs 1349, 2474, 6864.

[404] Chrome Root Program Policy, Version 1.5. https://www.chromium.org/Home/chromium-security/root-ca-policy/.

[405] A. Rabkin. Personal knowledge questions for fallback authentication: Security questions in the era of facebook. In *Proceedings of the 4th Symposium on Usable Privacy and Security*, pp. 13–23, 2008.

[406] S. Radack. Secure hash standard: Updated specifications approved and issued as federal information processing standard (FIPS) 180-4. Technical Report, National Institute of Standards and Technology, 2012.

[407] R. S. Raman, L. Evdokimov, E. Wurstrow, J. A. Halderman, and R. Ensafi. Investigating large scale https interception in kazakhstan. In *Proceedings of the ACM Internet Measurement Conference*, pp. 125–132, 2020.

[408] B. Ramsdell and S. Turner. Secure/Multipurpose Internet Mail Extensions (S/MIME) Version 3.2 Message Specification. RFC 5751 (Proposed Standard), January 2010. Obsoleted by RFC 8551.

[409] F. Y. Rashid. Mozilla asked to revoke Trustwave CA for allowing SSL eavesdropping. *eWeek*, February 2012.

[410] S. G. Renfro. Verisign CZAG: Privacy leak in X.509 certificates. In *11th USENIX Security Symposium (USENIX Security 02), San Francisco, CA, August 2002*. USENIX Association, 2002.

[411] E. Rescorla. *SSL and TLS: Designing and Building Secure Systems*, Vol. 1. Addison-Wesley, Reading, MA, 2001.

[412] E. Rescorla. The Transport Layer Security (TLS) Protocol Version 1.3. RFC 8446 (Proposed Standard), August 2018.

[413] E. Rescorla and N. Modadugu. Datagram Transport Layer Security Version 1.2. RFC 6347 (Proposed Standard), January 2012. Obsoleted by RFC 9147, updated by RFCs 7507, 7905, 8996, 9146.

[414] E. Rescorla, M. Ray, S. Dispensa, and N. Oskov. Transport Layer Security (TLS) Renegotiation Indication Extension. RFC 5746 (Proposed Standard), February 2010.

[415] E. Rescorla and M. Salter. Extended Random Values for TLS. Internet-Draft draft-rescorla-tls-extended-random-02, Internet Engineering Task Force, March 2009. Work in Progress.

[416] E. Rescorla and A. Schiffman. The Secure HyperText Transfer Protocol. RFC 2660 (Historic), August 1999.

[417] E. Rescorla, H. Tschofenig, and N. Modadugu. The Datagram Transport Layer Security (DTLS) Protocol Version 1.3. RFC 9147 (Proposed Standard), April 2022.

[418] R. L. Rivest, A. Shamir, and L. Adleman. A method for obtaining digital signatures and public-key cryptosystems. *Communications of the ACM*, 21(2):120–126, 1978.

[419] J. Rizzo and T. Duong. Crime: Compression ratio info-leak made easy. In *Ekoparty Security Conference*, 2012.

[420] P. Rogaway. Problems with proposed IP cryptography, 1995. Unpublished Manuscript. Available at: https://cs.ucdavis.edu/~rogaway/papers/draft-rogaway-ipsec-comments-00.txt.

[421] P. Rogaway. Authenticated-encryption with associated-data. In V. Atluri, editor, *ACM Conference on Computer and Communications Security*, pp. 98–107. ACM, November 2002. Full version available at: http://www.cs.ucdavis.edu/~rogaway/papers/ad.html.

[422] P. Rogaway, M. Bellare, and J. Black. OCB: A block-cipher mode of operation for efficient authenticated encryption. *ACM Transactions on Information and System Security (TISSEC)*, 6(3):365–403, 2003. Extending the version published in CCS'02.

[423] E. Ronen, R. Gillham, D. Genkin, A. Shamir, D. Wong, and Y. Yarom. The 9 lives of Bleichenbacher's CAT: New cache attacks on TLS implementations. In *2019 IEEE Symposium on Security and Privacy (SP)*, pp. 435–452. IEEE, 2019.

[424] B. Ross, C. Jackson, N. Miyake, D. Boneh, and J. C. Mitchell. Stronger password authentication using browser extensions. In *SSYM'05: Proceedings of the 14th Conference on USENIX Security Symposium*, pp. 17–31. USENIX Association, Berkeley, CA, USA, 2005.

[425] P. Saint-Andre and J. Hodges. Representation and Verification of Domain-Based Application Service Identity within Internet Public Key Infrastructure Using X.509 (PKIX) Certificates in the Context

of Transport Layer Security (TLS). RFC 6125 (Proposed Standard), March 2011. Obsoleted by RFC 9525.

[426] J. Salowey, A. Choudhury, and D. McGrew. AES Galois Counter Mode (GCM) Cipher Suites for TLS. RFC 5288 (Proposed Standard), August 2008. Updated by RFC 9325.

[427] J. Salowey, H. Zhou, P. Eronen, and H. Tschofenig. Transport Layer Security (TLS) Session Resumption without Server-Side State. RFC 5077 (Proposed Standard), January 2008. Obsoleted by RFC 8446, updated by RFC 8447.

[428] J. H. Saltzer and M. D. Schroeder. The protection of information in computer systems. *Proceedings of the IEEE*, 63(9):1278–1308, 1975.

[429] S. Santesson, M. Myers, R. Ankney, A. Malpani, S. Galperin, and C. Adams. X.509 Internet Public Key Infrastructure Online Certificate Status Protocol — OCSP. RFC 6960 (Proposed Standard), June 2013. Updated by RFC 8954.

[430] J. Schaad, B. Kaliski, and R. Housley. Additional Algorithms and Identifiers for RSA Cryptography for use in the Internet X.509 Public Key Infrastructure Certificate and Certificate Revocation List (CRL) Profile. RFC 4055 (Proposed Standard), June 2005. Updated by RFC 5756.

[431] S. Schechter, A. B. Brush, and S. Egelman. It's no secret. measuring the security and reliability of authentication via "secret" questions. In *2009 30th IEEE Symposium on Security and Privacy*, pp. 375–390. IEEE, 2009.

[432] S. Schechter, R. Dhamija, A. Ozment, and I. Fischer. The emperor's new security indicators. In *SP'07: Proceedings of the 2007 IEEE Symposium on Security and Privacy*, pp. 51–65. IEEE Computer Society, Washington, DC, USA, 2007.

[433] S. Schechter, S. Egelman, and R. W. Reeder. It's not what you know, but who you know: A social approach to last-resort authentication. In *CHI'09: Proceedings of the 27th International Conference on Human Factors in Computing Systems*, pp. 1983–1992. ACM, New York, NY, USA, 2009.

[434] J. Schmidt. Requirements for Password-Authenticated Key Agreement (PAKE) Schemes. RFC 8125 (Informational), April 2017.

[435] C. P. Schnorr. Fast factoring integers by SVP algorithms. Cryptology ePrint Archive, Report 2021/232, 2021. https://eprint.iacr.org/2021/232.

[436] R. Seggelmann, M. Tuexen, and M. Williams. Transport Layer Security (TLS) and Datagram Transport Layer Security (DTLS) Heartbeat Extension. RFC 6520 (Proposed Standard), February 2012. Updated by RFC 8447.

[437] C. E. Shannon. Communication theory of secrecy systems. *Bell System Technical Journal*, 28:656–715, October 1949.

[438] Y. Sheffer, R. Holz, and P. Saint-Andre. Summarizing Known Attacks on Transport Layer Security (TLS) and Datagram TLS (DTLS). RFC 7457 (Informational), February 2015.

[439] M. Shirvanian, N. Saxena, S. Jarecki, and H. Krawczyk. Building and studying a password store that perfectly hides passwords from itself. *IEEE Transactions on Dependable and Secure Computing*, 16(5):770–782, 2019.

[440] P. W. Shor. Algorithms for quantum computation: Discrete logarithms and factoring. In *Proceedings 35th Annual Symposium on Foundations of Computer Science*, pp. 124–134. IEEE, 1994.

[441] P. W. Shor and J. Preskill. Simple proof of security of the BB84 quantum key distribution protocol. *Physical Review Letters*, 85(2):441, 2000.

[442] V. Shoup. Using hash functions as a hedge against chosen ciphertext attack. In *Advances in Cryptology — Eurocrypt 2000*, pp. 275–288, 2000.

[443] V. Shoup. Sequences of games: A tool for taming complexity in security proofs. Cryptology ePrint Archive, Report 2004/332, 2004. https://eprint.iacr.org/2004/332.

[444] D. Silver, S. Jana, D. Boneh, E. Chen, and C. Jackson. Password managers: Attacks and defenses. In *23rd USENIX Security Symposium (USENIX Security 14)*, pp. 449–464, 2014.

[445] E. Simion. Entropy and randomness: From analogic to quantum world. *IEEE Access*, 8:74553–74561, 2020.

[446] J. Simpson. An in-depth technical analysis of CurveBall (CVE-2020-0601). Published in Trend Micro Security Intelligence Blog, February 2020. Available at: https://blog.trendmicro.com/trendlabs-security-intelligence/an-in-depth-technical-analysis-of-curveball-cve-2020-0601/.

[447] S. Singh. *The Science of Secrecy: The Secret History of Codes and Codebreaking*. Fourth Estate, London, UK, 2001.

[448] N. P. Smart. *Cryptography Made Simple*. Information Security and Cryptography. Springer, Berlin, 2016.

[449] T. Smith, L. Dickenson, and K. E. Seamons. Let's revoke: Scalable global certificate revocation. In *NDSS*. The Internet Society, 2020.

[450] S. Stamm, B. Sterne, and G. Markham. Reining in the web with content security policy. In *Proceedings of the 19th International Conference on World Wide Web*, pp. 921–930, 2010.

[451] M. Stevens, E. Bursztein, P. Karpman, A. Albertini, and Y. Markov. The first collision for full SHA-1. In *Advances in Cryptology–CRYPTO 2017: 37th Annual International Cryptology Conference, Santa Barbara, CA, USA, August 20–24, 2017, Proceedings, Part I 37*, pp. 570–596. Springer, 2017. Available at: https://eprint.iacr.org/2017/190.pdf. Presents the SHAttered attack; see PDF collision demo at: https://shattered.io.

[452] M. Stevens, A. K. Lenstra, and B. de Weger. Chosen-prefix collisions for MD5 and colliding X.509 certificates for different identities. In M. Naor, editor, *Advances in Cryptology — EUROCRYPT 2007, 26th Annual International Conference on the Theory and Applications of Cryptographic Techniques, Barcelona, Spain, May 20–24, 2007, Proceedings*. Lecture Notes in Computer Science, Vol. 4515, pp. 1–22. Springer, 2007.

[453] M. Stevens, A. K. Lenstra, and B. De Weger. Chosen-prefix collisions for md5 and applications. *International Journal of Applied Cryptography*, 2(4):322–359, 2012.

[454] M. Stevens, A. Sotirov, J. Appelbaum, A. K. Lenstra, D. Molnar, D. A. Osvik, and B. de Weger. Short chosen-prefix collisions for MD5 and the creation of a rogue CA certificate. In S. Halevi, editor, *Advances in Cryptology — CRYPTO 2009*. Lecture Notes in Computer Science, Vol. 5677, pp. 55–69. Springer, 2009.

[455] W. R. Stevens, A. M. Rudoff, and B. Fenner. *Unix Network Programming Volume 1: The Sockets Networking API*, 3rd edn. Addison-Wesley Professional, Boston, 2003.

[456] D. R. Stinson. *Cryptography: Theory and Practice*. CRC Press, Boca Raton, FL, 2005.

[457] J.-P. Tillich, P.-A. Fouque, J. Hoffstein, P. Kirchner, V. Lyubashevsky, T. Pornin, T. Prest, Z. Ricosset, W. Seiler, and M. Treger. Falcon: Fast fourier lattice-based compact signatures. *Journal of Mathematical Cryptology*, 12(1):1–37, 2018.

[458] G. Tsudik. Message authentication with one-way hash functions. *ACM SIGCOMM Computer Communication Review*, 22(5):29–38, 1992.

[459] A. M. Turing. On computable numbers, with an application to the entscheidungsproblem. *Proceedings of the London Mathematical Society*, 42(2):230–265, 1936.

[460] A. M. Turing. Computing machinery and intelligence. *Mind*, 59(236):433–460, October 1950.

[461] S. Turner, D. Brown, K. Yiu, R. Housley, and T. Polk. Updates for RSAES-OAEP and RSASSA-PSS Algorithm Parameters. RFC 5756 (Proposed Standard), January 2010.

[462] S. Turner and T. Polk. Prohibiting Secure Sockets Layer (SSL) Version 2.0. RFC 6176 (Proposed Standard), March 2011. Updated by RFC 8996.

[463] M. Van Dijk, C. Gentry, S. Halevi, and V. Vaikuntanathan. Fully homomorphic encryption over the integers. In *Annual International Conference on the Theory and Applications of Cryptographic Techniques*, pp. 24–43. Springer, 2010.

[464] G. R. VandenBos. *APA Dictionary of Psychology*. American Psychological Association, 2007. Available at: https://dictionary.apa.org/.

[465] M. Vanhoef. Fragment and forge: Breaking Wi-Fi through frame aggregation and fragmentation. In *30th USENIX Security Symposium (USENIX Security 21)*, pp. 161–178, 2021.

[466] M. Vanhoef and F. Piessens. Key reinstallation attacks: Forcing nonce reuse in WPA2. In B. M. Thuraisingham, D. Evans, T. Malkin, and D. Xu, editors. *Proceedings of the 2017 ACM SIGSAC Conference on Computer and Communications Security, CCS 2017, Dallas, TX, USA*, pp. 1313–1328. ACM, 2017.

[467] S. Vaudenay. Security flaws induced by CBC padding — Applications to SSL, IPSec, WTLS ... In L. R. Knudsen, editor, *Advances in Cryptology — EUROCRYPT 2002*. Lecture Notes in Computer Science, Vol. 2332, pp. 534–546. Springer, 2002.

[468] S. Venkata, S. Harwani, C. Pignataro, and D. McPherson. Dynamic Hostname Exchange Mechanism for OSPF. RFC 5642 (Proposed Standard), August 2009.

[469] G. S. Vernam. Secret signaling system, July 22, 1919. US Patent 1,310,719.

[470] J. Von Neumann. Various techniques used in connection with random digits. *Applied Math Series*, 12(36–38):1, 1951.

[471] D. Wagner, B. Schneier, *et al.* Analysis of the SSL 3.0 protocol. In *The Second USENIX Workshop on Electronic Commerce Proceedings*, pp. 29–40, 1996.

[472] K. C. Wang and M. K. Reiter. Bernoulli honeywords. In *Proceedings of the Network and Distributed System Security (NDSS) Symposium*. Internet Society (ISOC), 2024.

[473] X. Wang, X. Lai, D. Feng, H. Chen, and X. Yu. Cryptanalysis of the hash functions MD4 and RIPEMD. In *Advances in Cryptology–EUROCRYPT 2005: 24th Annual International Conference on the Theory and Applications of Cryptographic Techniques, Aarhus, Denmark, May 22–26, 2005. Proceedings 24*, pp. 1–18. Springer, 2005.

[474] X. Wang and H. Yu. How to break MD5 and other hash functions. In *Annual International Conference on the Theory and Applications of Cryptographic Techniques*, pp. 19–35. Springer, 2005.

[475] K. Watsen. NETCONF Call Home and RESTCONF Call Home. RFC 8071 (Proposed Standard), February 2017.

[476] M. Weir, S. Aggarwal, B. De Medeiros, and B. Glodek. Password cracking using probabilistic context-free grammars. In *2009 30th IEEE Symposium on Security and Privacy*, pp. 391–405. IEEE, 2009.

[477] D. Wendlandt, D. G. Andersen, and A. Perrig. Perspectives: Improving SSH-style host authentication with multi-path probing. In *USENIX Annual Technical Conference*, Vol. 8, pp. 321–334, 2008.

[478] A. Whitten and J. D. Tygar. Why Johnny can't encrypt; A usability evaluation of PGP 5.0. In *Proceedings of the 8th USENIX Security Symposium (SECURITY-99), Berkeley, CA, August 23–26 1999*, pp. 169–184. Usenix Association, 1999.

[479] S. B. Wicker and V. K. Bhargava. *Reed-Solomon Codes and Their Applications*. John Wiley & Sons, Hoboken, NJ, 1999.

[480] S. Wiedenbeck, J. Waters, J.-C. Birget, A. Brodskiy, and N. Memon. Passpoints: Design and longitudinal evaluation of a graphical password system. *International Journal of Human-Computer Studies*, 63(1–2):102–127, 2005.

[481] N. Wiener. *Cybernetics, or Control and Communication in the Animal and the Machine*. John Wiley, New York, 1948.

[482] T. Wiggers. Post-quantum Signature Schemes Zoo, 2025. A Collection of Post-quantum Digital Signature Schemes, visited March 2025.

[483] Wikipedia. Block cipher mode of operation, 2017. Accessed on 1 September 2017.

[484] Wikipedia Contributors. Forward secrecy — Wikipedia, The Free Encyclopedia, 2020. https://en.wikipedia.org/w/index.php?title=Forward_secrecy&oldid=973196673. Accessed on 16 August 2020.

[485] Wikipedia Contributors. Diginotar — Wikipedia, The Free Encyclopedia, 2021. https://en.wikipedia.org/w/index.php?title=DigiNotar&oldid=1036090956. Accessed on 7 August 2021.

[486] Wikipedia Contributors. Dual EC DRBG — Wikipedia, The Free Encyclopedia, 2021. Accessed on 14 August 2021.

[487] Wikipedia Contributors. RC4 — Wikipedia, The Free Encyclopedia, 2021. https://en.wikipedia.org/w/index.php?title=RC4&oldid=1058328794. Accessed on 3 January 2022.

[488] Wikipedia Contributors. OTPW — Wikipedia, The Free Encyclopedia, 2023. Accessed on 25 May 2024.

[489] Wikipedia Contributors. Arnold cipher — Wikipedia, The Free Encyclopedia, 2024. Accessed on 24 March 2024.

[490] Wikipedia Contributors. Password — Wikipedia, The Free Encyclopedia, 2024. https://en.wikipedia.org/w/index.php?title=Password&oldid=1261110770.

[491] K. Wilson. Revoking trust in one ANSSI certificate. *Mozilla Security Blog*, December 2013.

[492] World Wide Web Consortium (W3C). Content Security Policy Level 2, December 2016. W3C Recommendation.

[493] S. Wrótniak, H. Leibowitz, E. Syta, and A. Herzberg. Provable security for PKI schemes. In *Proceedings of the 2024 ACM SIGSAC Conference on Computer and Communications Security, CCS*, 2024.

[494] G. Xiang, J. Hong, C. P. Rose, and L. Cranor. Cantina+ a feature-rich machine learning framework for detecting phishing web sites. *ACM Transactions on Information and System Security (TISSEC)*, 14(2):1–28, 2011.

[495] P. Yang, G. Zhao, and P. Zeng. Phishing website detection based on multidimensional features driven by deep learning. *IEEE Access*, 7:15196–15209, 2019.

[496] N. S. Yanofsky and M. A. Mannucci. *Quantum Computing for Computer Scientists*. Cambridge University Press, Cambridge, UK, 2008.

[497] T. Ylonen and C. Lonvick, editors. The Secure Shell (SSH) Protocol Architecture. RFC 4251 (Proposed Standard), January 2006. Updated by RFCs 8308, 9141.

[498] T. Ylonen and C. Lonvick, editor, The Secure Shell (SSH) Transport Layer Protocol. RFC 4253 (Proposed Standard), January 2006. Updated by RFCs 6668, 8268, 8308, 8332, 8709, 8758, 9142.

[499] N. C. Zakas. *Understanding ECMAScript 6: The Definitive Guide for JavaScript Developers*. No Starch Press, San Francisco, CA, 2016.

[500] M. Zalewski. *The Tangled Web: A Guide to Securing Modern Web Applications*, 1st edn. No Starch Press, San Francisco, CA, USA, 2011.

[501] L. Zhang, D. R. Choffnes, T. Dumitras, D. Levin, A. Mislove, A. Schulman, and C. Wilson. Analysis of SSL certificate reissues and revocations in the wake of Heartbleed. *Communications of the ACM*, 61(3):109–116, 2018.

[502] M. Zhou, A. Park, W. Zheng, and E. Shi. Piano: Extremely simple, single-server PIR with sublinear server computation. In *2024 IEEE Symposium on Security and Privacy (SP)*, pp. 4296–4314. IEEE, 2024.

[503] K. Zuse. Method for automatic execution of calculations with the aid of computers (1936). In B. Randell, editor, *The Origins of Digital Computers: Selected Papers*, 3rd edn, Texts and Monographs in Computer Science, pp. 163–170. Springer-Verlag, Heidelberg, Germany, 1982.

[504] M. Zusman. Criminal charges are not pursued: Hacking PKI. *DEFCON 17*, 2009.

[505] M. Zviran and W. J. Haga. Cognitive passwords: The key to easy access control. *Computers & Security*, 9(8):723–736, 1990.

[506] M. Zviran and W. J. Haga. Password security: An empirical study. *Journal of Management Information Systems*, 15(4):161–185, 1999.

Index

B

C

N

O

Q

R

S

T